**CLYMER**®

# MERCRUISER
## STERN DRIVE SHOP MANUAL
### 1998-2004 • Alpha, Bravo One, Bravo Two and Bravo Three

*The world's finest publisher of mechanical how-to manuals*

**CLYMER**®

P.O. Box 12901, Overland Park, KS 66282-2901

FIRST EDITION
First Printing September, 2004

SECOND EDITION
First Printing August, 2004
Second Printing November, 2006

Printed in U.S.A.

CLYMER and colophon are registered trademarks of Prism Business Media Inc.

ISBN-10: 0-89287-914-9

ISBN-13: 978-0-89287-914-4

Library of Congress: 2004094981

AUTHOR: Mark Rolling.

TECHNICAL PHOTOGRAPHY: Mark Rolling.

COVER: Photo courtesy of Cobaltboats.com.

PRODUCTION: Holly Messinger.

# CLYMER®

**Publisher** Shawn Etheridge

## EDITORIAL

*Managing Editor*
James Grooms

*Associate Editors*
Rick Arens
Steven Thomas

*Authors*
Jay Bogart
Michael Morlan
George Parise
Mark Rolling
Ed Scott
Ron Wright

*Technical Illustrators*
Steve Amos
Errol McCarthy
Mitzi McCarthy
Bob Meyer

*Group Production Manager*
Dylan Goodwin

*Senior Production Editors*
Greg Araujo
Darin Watson

*Production Editors*
Justin Marciniak
Holly Messinger

## MARKETING/SALES AND ADMINISTRATION

*Sales Channel & Brand Marketing Coordinator*
Melissa Abbott Mudd

*Sales Managers*
Justin Henton
Dutch Sadler
Matt Tusken

*Business Manager*
Ron Rogers

*Customer Service Manager*
Terri Cannon

*Customer Service Account Specialist*
Courtney Hollars

*Customer Service Representatives*
Dinah Bunnell
Felicia Dickerson
April LeBlond

*Warehouse & Inventory Manager*
Leah Hicks

## PRiSM
BUSINESS MEDIA™
P.O. Box 12901, Overland Park, KS 66282-2901 • 800-262-1954 • 913-967-1719

*The following books and guides are published by Prism Business Media*

**More information available at *clymer.com***

# Contents

# QUICK REFERENCE DATA

## VEHICLE DATA

MODEL:_____ YEAR:_____

VIN NUMBER:_____

ENGINE SERIAL NUMBER:_____

CARBURETOR SERIAL NUMBER OR I.D. MARK:_____

Record the numbers here for your reference.

## ENGINE IDENTIFICATION CODES

| Model | Code |
|---|---|
| 3.0 | |
|   Serial No. 0L096999-Prior | RX |
|   Serial No. 0L097000-On | RP |
| 4.3L | |
|   Two-barrel carburetor | LJ |
|   Four-barrel carburetor | LK |
|   Electronic fuel injection | LK |
| 5.0L | ZA |
| 5.7L, 350 Mag | MH |
| MX 6.2 | OM |
| 7.4 liter MPI | XW |
| 454 Mag MPI | UA |
| 502 Mag MPI | HJ |
| 496 Mag | * |
| 496 Mag HO | * |

*Engine model code was not available at the time of printing.

## MAINTENANCE SCHEDULE

| | |
|---|---|
| Before each use (saltwater or freshwater use) | Check engine oil level<br>Check the drive lubricant level<br>Check the power steering fluid level[1]<br>Check the trim system fluid level<br>Check the propeller<br>Check the fuel system<br>Check the steering system<br>Check the cooling system<br>Check the lanyard or stop switch |
| After each use (saltwater use) | Flush the seawater section |
| | (continued) |

| | |
|---|---|
| Weekly (saltwater or freshwater use) | Check engine oil level |
| | Check coolant level |
| | Check power steering fluid[1] |
| | Check drive unit fluid |
| | Check battery level |
| | Check trim pump fluid |
| | Inspect anodes |
| | Inspect the water inlets |
| 30 days or 25 hours of operation (saltwater use) | Inspect alternator wiring |
| | Clean alternator air openings |
| | Inspect alternator drive belt |
| | Adjust alternator drive belt tension |
| 100 days or 100 hours of operation (saltwater or freshwater use) | Check drive belt condition |
| | Check drive belt tension |
| 60 days or 50 hours of operation (saltwater use) | |
| | Lubricate the propeller shaft |
| | Apply corrosion preventative spray |
| 120 days or 100 hours of operation (saltwater or freshwater use) | |
| | Lubricate the propeller shaft |
| | Apply corrosion preventative spray[5] |
| | Inspect the serpentine drive belt [1] |
| End of the first boating season (saltwater or freshwater use) | |
| | Check engine alignment |
| | Change engine oil and filter |
| | Clean the flame arrestor and breather hoses |
| | Change PVC valve[1] |
| | Change drive unit lubricant |
| | Torque gimbal ring bolts |
| | Torque engine mounting bolts |
| | Lubricate the gimbal bearing |
| | Inspect the universal joints |
| | Lubricate the universal joints[4] |
| | Lubricate and inspect steering system components |
| | Inspect wiring |
| | Test the pressure cap[1] |
| | Inspect hoses |
| | Tighten hose clamps |
| | Inspect and test the drive unit grounding wires |
| | Lubricate and inspect the control cables |
| | Inspect the exhaust system |
| | Adjust the ignition timing |
| End of the first boating season (saltwater or freshwater use) | |
| | Inspect the steering head |
| | Lubricate and inspect the remote control |
| | Inspect the carburetor |
| | Adjust the carburetor[1] |
| | Inspect the throttle body[1] |
| Once a year or 100 hours of operation (saltwater or freshwater use) | |
| | Change engine oil and filter |
| | Clean the flame arrestor and breather hoses |
| | Change PVC valve[1] |
| | Change drive unit lubricant |
| | Torque gimbal ring bolts |
| | Clean and inspect the spark plugs |
| | Torque engine mounting bolts |

(continued)

## MAINTENANCE SCHEDULE (continued)

| | |
|---|---|
| Once a year or 100 hours of operation (continued) | Lubricate the gimbal bearing<br>Lubricate and inspect steering system components<br>Inspect wiring<br>Test the pressure cap[1]<br>Inspect hoses and clamps<br>Inspect and test the drive unit grounding wires<br>Lubricate and inspect the control cables<br>Inspect the exhaust system<br>Adjust the ignition timing<br>Inspect the steering head<br>Lubricate and inspect the remote control<br>Inspect the carburetor[1]<br>Adjust the carburetor[1]<br>Inspect the throttle body[1] |
| Once a year (saltwater or freshwater use) | Clean and paint exposed surfaces<br>Replace the fuel filter(s)<br>Test the corrosion control system[1]<br>Test the coolant[1]<br>Clean the heat exchanger[1]<br>Inspect drive unit bellows and clamps |
| Every two years or 300 hours of operation (freshwater use) | Check engine alignment<br>Lubricate engine coupling<br>Inspect the universal joints and coupling splines<br>Lubricate the universal joints[4] |
| Once a year or 300 hours of operation (saltwater or freshwater use) | Check engine alignment[5]<br>Lubricate engine coupling[5]<br>Inspect the universal joints and coupling splines[5]<br>Lubricate the universal joints[4,5] |
| Every two years or 400 hours of operation (saltwater or freshwater use) | Change the engine coolant[2] |
| Every five years or 1000 hours or operation (saltwater or freshwater use) | Change the engine coolant[3] |

1. This maintenance item may not apply to all models.
2. Closed cooling system models using standard ethylene glycol coolant (not 5/100 extended life).
3. Closed cooling system models using 5/100 extended life coolant.
4. Applies only to models equipped with a bravo drive unit.
5. This maintenance interval applies if the engine is operated in saltwater or polluted water.
6. If equipped with standard spark plugs. Every 3 years or 300 hours if equipped with platinum tip plugs.

## SPARK PLUG SPECIFICATIONS

| Model | Spark plug No. | Gap specification |
|---|---|---|
| 3.0L | | |
|   AC plug | MR43LTS | |
|   Champion plug | RS12YC | |
|   NGK plug | BPR6EFS | |
|   Spark plug gap | – | 0.035 in. (0.9 mm) |
| 4.3L, 5.0L, 5.7L, 350 Mag and MX6.2L | | |
|   1998-2004 carburetor-equipped models | | |
|     AC plug | MR43LTS | |
|     Champion plug | RS12YC | |
|     NGK plug | BPR6EFS | |
|     Plug gap | – | 0.045 in. (1.1 mm) |

(continued)

## SPARK PLUG SPECIFICATIONS (continued)

| Model | Spark plug No. | Gap specification |
|---|---|---|
| 4.3L, 5.0L, 5.7L, 350 Mag and MX6.2L (continued) | | |
| 1998-2001 fuel injection (TBI and MPI) models | | |
|   AC plug | MR43LTS | |
|   Champion plug | RS12YC | |
|   NGK plug | BPR6EFS | |
|   Plug gap | – | 0.045 in. (1.1 mm) |
| 2002-2004 multi-port fuel injection (MPI) models | | |
|   AC plug | 41-932 | 0.060 (1.5 mm) |
| 7.4L MPI | | |
|   AC plug | MR43LTS | |
|   Champion plug | RV12YC | |
|   NGK plug | BPR6EFS | |
|   Plug gap | – | 0.045 in. (1.1 mm) |
| 454 Mag, 502 Mag | | |
|   AC plug | MR43T | |
|   Champion plug | RV15YC4 | |
|   NGK plug | BR6FS | |
|   Plug gap | – | 0.040 in. (1 mm) |
| 496 Mag, 496 Mag HO | | |
|   Nippon Denso | TJ14R-P15 | |
|   Plug gap | – | 0.060 in. (1.5 mm) |

## ENGINE OIL CAPACITY

| Model | qt. | L |
|---|---|---|
| 3.0L | 4 | 3.8 |
| 4.3L | 4.5 | 4.3 |
| 5.0L, 5.7L, 350 Mag, MX 6.2 | 5.5 | 5.25 |
| 7.4 MPI, 454 Mag, 502 Mag | 7 | 6.6 |
| 496 Mag, 496 Mag HO | 9 | 8.5 |

## CLOSED COOLING SYSTEM CAPACITY

| Model | qt. | L |
|---|---|---|
| 3.0L | 9 | 8.5 |
| 4.3L | 18 | 17 |
| 5.0L, 5.7L and 350 Mag, MX 6.2 | 20 | 19 |
| 7.4 MPI, 454 Mag, 502 Mag | 18 | 17 |
| 496 Mag, 496 Mag HO | 19 | 18 |

## GEARCASE LUBRICANT CAPACITY

| Drive unit type | oz. | L |
|---|---|---|
| Alpha | 40 | 1.2 |
| Bravo I | 88 | 2.6 |
| Bravo II | 104 | 3.1 |
| Bravo III | 96 | 2.8 |

## IGNITION TIMING SPECIFICATIONS

| Model | Timing at idle speed |
|---|---|
| 3.0L | |
|   Serial No. 0L096999-Prior | 1° BTDC |
|   Serial No. 0L097000-0L340999 | 1° ATDC |
|   Serial No. 0L341000-On | 2° ATDC |
| 4.3L, 5.0L, 5.7L and 350 Mag | |
|   Carburetor models | 10° BTDC |
|   All EFI models | 8° BTDC |
| 7.4 MPI, 454 Mag, 502 Mag | 8° BTDC |

## IDLE SPEED SPECIFICATIONS

| Model | Idle speed (rpm) |
|---|---|
| 3.0L | 700 |
| 4.3L, 5.0L, 5.7L, 350 Mag | |
|   Carburetor models | 650 |
|   EFI models | 600 |
| 7.4 MPI, 454 Mag, 502 Mag | 600 |

## ENGINE FIRING ORDER

| Model | |
|---|---|
| 3.0L models | 1-3-4-2 |
| 4.3L models | 1-6-5-4-3-2 |
| 5.0L, 5.7L, 350 Mag, MX 6.2 | 1-8-4-3-6-5-7-2 |
| MX 6.2 | 1-8-4-3-6-5-7-2 |
| 7.4L MPI, 454 Mag, 502 Mag | 1-8-4-3-6-5-7-2 |
| 496 Mag, 496 Mag HO | 1-8-7-2-6-5-4-3 |

## BATTERY REQUIREMENTS

| Model | cca rating | mca rating | Ah rating |
|---|---|---|---|
| 3.0L | 375 | 475 | 90 |
| 4.3L, 5.0L and 5.7L | | | |
|   Carburetor models | 375 | 475 | 90 |
|   EFI models | 750 | 950 | 180 |
| MX 6.2, 7.4 MPI, 454 Mag, 502 Mag | 750 | 950 | 180 |
| 496 Mag, 496 Mag HO | 750 | 950 | 180 |

# Chapter One

# General Information

This detailed, comprehensive manual contains complete information on maintenance and overhaul. Hundreds of photos and drawings guide the reader through every procedure, step by step.

Troubleshooting, tune-up, maintenance and repair are not difficult if the right equipment and knowledge are available. Most of the procedures in this manual can be performed by a person with average intelligence and mechanical ability. See Chapter Two for information on some specific tools and techniques.

A shop manual is a reference, and all Clymer books are designed for ease of use. All chapters are thumb tabbed and important topics are indexed at the end of the manual. All procedures, tables, photos and instructions in this manual assume the reader may be working on the machine or using the manual for the first time.

Keep the manual with other tools in the workshop or boat. It will help you to better understand how your boat runs, lower repair and maintenance costs and generally increase your enjoyment of your boat.

## MANUAL ORGANIZATION

Chapter One provides general information useful to marine owners and mechanics.

Chapter Two discusses the tools and techniques for preventative maintenance, troubleshooting and repair.

Chapter Three provides troubleshooting procedures for all engine systems and individual components.

Chapter Four provides maintenance, lubrication and tune-up instructions.

Additional chapters cover storage, adjustment and specific repair. All disassembly, inspection and assembly instructions are in step-by-step form. Specifications are included at the end of each chapter.

## WARNINGS, CAUTIONS AND NOTES

The terms WARNING, CAUTION and NOTE have specific meanings in this manual.

A WARNING emphasizes areas where injury or even death could result from negligence. Mechanical damage may also occur. WARNINGS *are to be taken seriously.*

A CAUTION emphasizes areas where equipment damage could result. Disregarding a CAUTION could cause permanent mechanical damage, though injury is unlikely.

A NOTE provides additional information to make a step or procedure easier or clearer. Disregarding a NOTE could cause inconvenience, but would not cause equipment damage or injury.

## ENGINE OPERATION

All MerCruiser engines are of a four-stroke design. **Figure 1** shows gasoline four-stroke engine operation.

## TORQUE SPECIFICATIONS

The materials used in the manufacture of the engine may be subjected to uneven stresses if the fasteners of the various subassemblies are not installed and tightened cor-

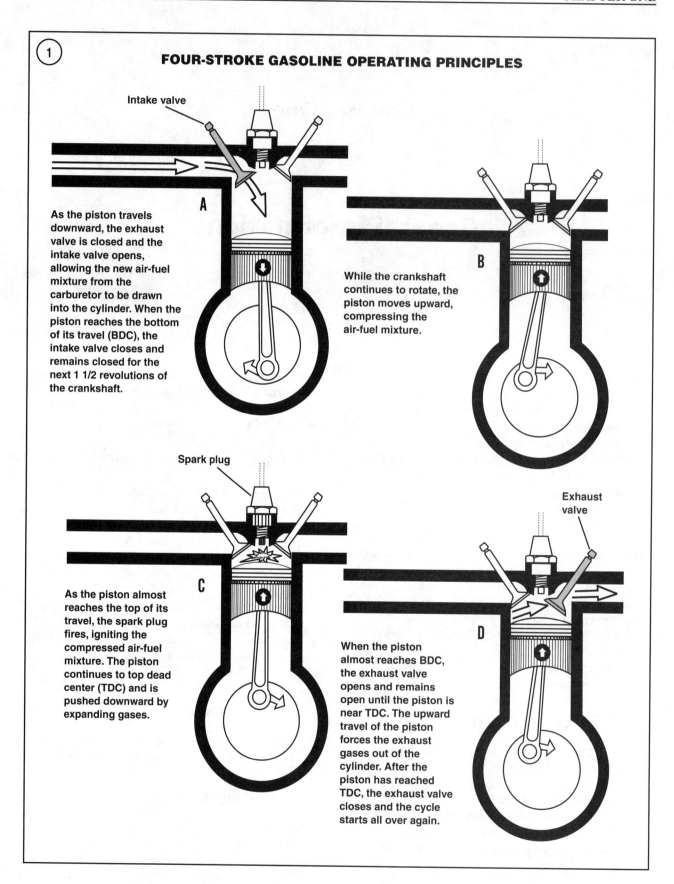

**FOUR-STROKE GASOLINE OPERATING PRINCIPLES**

Intake valve

A

As the piston travels downward, the exhaust valve is closed and the intake valve opens, allowing the new air-fuel mixture from the carburetor to be drawn into the cylinder. When the piston reaches the bottom of its travel (BDC), the intake valve closes and remains closed for the next 1 1/2 revolutions of the crankshaft.

B

While the crankshaft continues to rotate, the piston moves upward, compressing the air-fuel mixture.

Spark plug

C

As the piston almost reaches the top of its travel, the spark plug fires, igniting the compressed air-fuel mixture. The piston continues to top dead center (TDC) and is pushed downward by expanding gases.

Exhaust valve

D

When the piston almost reaches BDC, the exhaust valve opens and remains open until the piston is near TDC. The upward travel of the piston forces the exhaust gases out of the cylinder. After the piston has reached TDC, the exhaust valve closes and the cycle starts all over again.

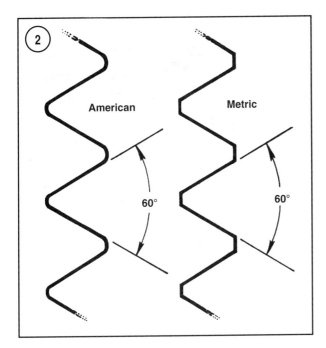

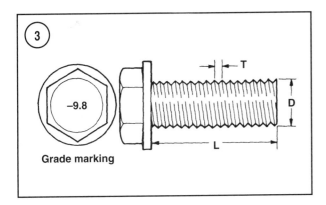

Grade marking

rectly. Fasteners that are improperly installed or work loose can cause extensive damage. It is essential to use an accurate torque wrench, described in Chapter Two, with the torque specifications in this manual.

Specifications for torque are provided in Newton-meters (N·m), foot-pounds (ft.-lb.) and inch-pounds (in.-lb.). Torque specifications for specific components are at the end of the appropriate chapters.

## FASTENERS

The materials and design of the various fasteners used on marine equipment are specifically chosen for performance and safety. Fastener design determines the type of tool required to work with the fastener. Fastener material is carefully selected to decrease the possibility of physical failure or corrosion. See *Galvanic Corrosion* in this chapter for information on marine materials.

### Threads

Threaded fasteners secure most components. They are usually secured by turning them clockwise (right-hand threads). However, if the normal rotation of the component would possibly loosen the fastener, it may have left-hand threads. Left-hand threaded fasteners, if used, are noted in the text.

Two dimensions are required to match the size of the fastener: the number of threads in a given distance and the outside diameter of the threads.

Two systems are currently used to specify threaded fastener dimensions: the U.S. Standard system and the metric system. Although fasteners may appear similar, close inspection shows that the thread designs are not the same (**Figure 2**). Pay particular attention when working with unidentified fasteners; mismatching thread types can damage threads.

*NOTE*
*To ensure the fastener threads are not mismatched or cross-threaded, start all fasteners by hand. If a fastener is hard to start or turn, determine the cause before tightening with a wrench.*

The length (L, **Figure 3**), diameter (D) and distance between thread crests (pitch) (T) classify metric screws and bolts. The numbers 8—1.25 × 130, may identify a typical bolt. This indicates the bolt has diameter of 8 mm. The distance between thread crests is 1.25 mm and the length is 130 mm. Always measure bolt length as shown in **Figure 3** to avoid purchasing replacements of the wrong length.

The numbers located on the top of the fastener indicate the strength of metric screws and bolts. The higher the number, the stronger the fastener is. Unnumbered fasteners are the weakest.

Many screws, bolts and studs are combined with nuts to secure particular components. To indicate the size of a nut, manufacturers specify the internal diameter and the thread pitch.

The measurement across two flats on a nut or bolt indicates the wrench size.

*WARNING*
*Do not install fasteners with a strength classification lower than what was originally installed by the manufacturer. Doing so may cause equipment failure and/or damage.*

### Self-Locking Fasteners

Several types of bolts, screws and nuts incorporate a system that creates interference between the two fasteners. Interference is achieved in various ways. The most common type is the nylon insert nut and a dry adhesive coating on the threads of a bolt.

Self-locking fasteners offer greater holding strength than standard fasteners, which improves their resistance to vibration. Most self-locking fasteners cannot be reused. The materials used to form the lock become distorted after the initial installation and removal. It is a good practice to discard and replace self-locking fasteners after their removal. Do not replace self-locking fasteners with standard fasteners.

### Washers

There are two basic types of washers: flat washers and lockwashers. Flat washers are simple discs with a hole to fit a screw or bolt. Lockwashers prevent a fastener from working loose. Washers can be used as spacers and seals, or to help distribute fastener load and to prevent the fastener from damaging the component.

As with fasteners, when replacing washers make sure the replacement washers are of the same design and quality.

### Cotter Pins

A cotter pin is a split metal pin inserted into a hole or slot to prevent a fastener from loosening. In certain applications, the fastener must be secured in this way. For these applications, a cotter pin and castellated (slotted) nut is used.

To use a cotter pin, first make sure the diameter is correct for the hole in the fastener. After correctly tightening the fastener and aligning the holes, insert the cotter pin through the hole and bend the ends over the fastener (**Figure 4**). Unless instructed to do so, never loosen a torqued fastener to align the holes. If the holes do not align, tighten the fastener just enough to achieve alignment.

Cotter pins are available in various diameters and lengths. Measure length from the bottom of the head to the tip of the shortest pin.

### Snap Rings

Snap rings (**Figure 5**) are circular-shaped metal retaining clips. They help secure parts and gears in place such as shafts, pins or rods. External type snap rings retain items

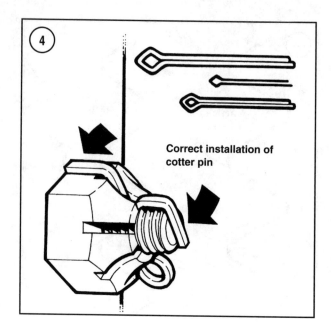

Correct installation of cotter pin

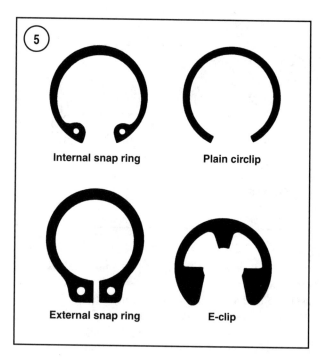

Internal snap ring          Plain circlip

External snap ring          E-clip

on shafts. Internal type snap rings secure parts within housing bores. In some applications, in addition to securing the component(s), snap rings of varying thickness also determine endplay. These are usually called selective snap rings.

Two basic types of snap rings are used: machined and stamped. Machined types (**Figure 6**) can be installed in either direction, since both faces have sharp edges. Stamped types (**Figure 7**) have a sharp edge and a round

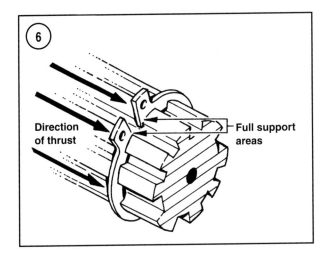

Direction of thrust — Full support areas

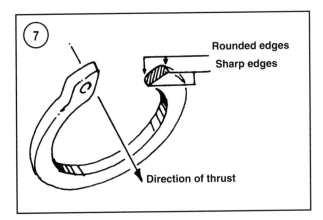

Rounded edges
Sharp edges
Direction of thrust

edge. When installing a stamped snap ring in a thrust application, install the sharp edge facing away from the part producing the thrust.

Observe the following when installing snap rings:

1. Remove and install snap rings with snap ring pliers. See *Snap Ring Pliers* in Chapter Two.

2. In some applications, it may be necessary to replace snap rings after removing them.

3. Compress or expand snap rings only enough to install them. If overly expanded, they lose their retaining ability.

4. After installing a snap ring, make sure it seats completely.

5. Wear eye protection when removing and installing a snap ring.

## LUBRICANTS

Periodic lubrication helps ensure a long service life for any type of equipment. It is especially important with marine equipment. Using the correct type of lubricant is as important as performing the lubrication service, although in an emergency the wrong type is better than none. The following section describes the types of lubricants most often required. Make sure to follow the manufacturer's recommendations for lubricant types.

### Four-Stroke Engine Oil

The American Petroleum Institute (API) and the Society of Automotive Engineers (SAE) classify four-stroke (cycle) engine oil in several categories. Oil containers display these classifications on the label. The API classification is not an indication of oil quality.

API oil classification is indicated by letters; oils for gasoline engines are identified by an S, such as SF, SG, SH or SJ. Diesel applications are identified by the letter C. Using the type recommended by the manufacturer is important, but some earlier classifications of oil may be difficult to find.

Viscosity is an indication of the oil's thickness or ability to flow at a specific temperature. The SAE uses numbers to indicate viscosity; thin oils have low numbers while thick oils have high numbers. A *W* after the number indicates that the viscosity testing was done at low temperature to simulate cold-weather operation. Engine oils fall into the 5 to 50 range.

Multigrade oils (for example 5W-20) include additives that modify the oil to be less viscous (thinner) at low temperatures and more viscous (thicker) at high temperatures. This allows the oil to perform efficiently across a wide range of engine operating conditions. The lower the number, the easier the engine will start in cold climates. Higher numbers are usually recommended for engines running in hot weather conditions.

### Gearcase Oil

Gearcase lubricants are assigned SAE viscosity numbers under the same system as four-stroke engine oil. Gearcase lubricant falls into the SAE 72-250 range. Some gearcase lubricants are multi-grade; for example, SAE 85-90.

Three types of marine gearcase lubricant are generally available; SAE 90 hypoid gearcase lubricant is designed for older manual-shift units; Type C gearcase lubricant contains additives designed for the electric shift mechanisms; High viscosity gearcase lubricant is a heavier oil designed to withstand the shock loading of high performance engines or units subjected to severe duty use. Always use a gearcase lubricant of the type specified by the units' manufacturer.

## Grease

Grease is lubricating oil with thickening agents added to it. The National Lubricating Grease Institute (NLGI) grades grease. Grades range from No. 000 to No. 6, with No. 6 being the thickest. Typical multipurpose grease is NLGI No. 2. For specific applications, manufacturers may recommend water-resistant type grease or one with an additive such as molybdenum disulfide ($MoS2$).

## GASKET SEALANT

Sealants are used in combination with a gasket or seal and are occasionally alone. Follow the manufacturer's recommendation when using sealants. Use extreme care when choosing a sealant different from the type originally recommended. Choose sealants based on their resistance to heat, various fluids and their sealing capabilities.

One of the most common sealants is RTV, or room temperature vulcanizing sealant. This sealant cures at room temperature over a specific time period. This allows the repositioning of components without damaging gaskets.

Moisture in the air causes the RTV sealant to cure. Always install the tube cap as soon as possible after applying RTV sealant. RTV sealant has a limited shelf life and will not cure properly if the shelf life has expired. Keep partial tubes sealed and discard them if they have surpassed the expiration date.

Non-hardening gasket sealing compounds are generally used in combination with a gasket to fill in small imperfections in the gasket or sealing surface. Do not use gasket sealing compound that is old, has begun to solidify or is darkened in color.

Anaerobic sealants cure only in the absence of air. These types of sealant are capable of filling gaps up to 0.030 in. (0.8 mm). Do not use anaerobic sealant if one of the surfaces is flexible.

## Applying Sealant

Clean all old gasket residue from the mating surfaces. If a scraper is used, work carefully to avoid damaging the sealing surfaces. An aerosol gasket remover can speed up the removal process and prevent damage to the mating surface that may be caused by using a scraping tool. Most of these types of products are very caustic. Read and follow the manufacturer's instructions when using gasket removal products.

Remove all gasket material from blind threaded holes; it can cause inaccurate bolt torque. Spray the mating surfaces with aerosol parts cleaner and then wipe with a lint-free cloth. The area must be clean for the sealant to adhere.

Apply RTV sealant in a continuous bead 2-3 mm (0.08-0.12 in.) thick. Circle all the fastener or alignment pin holes unless otherwise specified. Do not allow any sealant to enter these holes. Do not apply excess amounts of sealant, as it may be squeezed into other components. Assemble and tighten the fasteners to the specified torque within the time frame recommended by the RTV sealant manufacturer.

Apply anaerobic sealants in the same manner as RTV types, but reduce the bead thickness to 1 mm (0.04 in.).

## GALVANIC CORROSION

A chemical reaction occurs whenever two different types of metal are joined by an electrical conductor and immersed in an electrolyte. Electrons transfer from one metal to the other through the electrolyte and return through the conductor.

The hardware on a boat is made of many different types of metal. The boat hull acts as a conductor between the metals. Even if the hull is wood or fiberglass, the slightest film of water (electrolyte) within the hull provides conductivity, creating a good environment for electron flow (**Figure 8**). Unfortunately, this electron flow results in galvanic corrosion, causing one of the metals involved to corrode. The amount of electron flow (and, therefore the amount of corrosion) depends on the following factors:

1. The types of metal involved.
2. The efficiency of the conductor.
3. The strength of the electrolyte.

## Metals

The chemical composition of the metals used in marine equipment has a significant effect on the extent and speed of galvanic corrosion. Certain metals are more resistant to corrosion than others. These electrically negative metals are commonly called *noble* and include titanium, 18-8 stainless steel and nickel. Noble metals act as the cathode in any reaction. Metals that are more subject to corrosion are electrically positive; they act as the anode in a reaction. These include zinc, aluminum and magnesium.

In some cases, galvanic corrosion can occur within a single piece of metal. Common brass is a mixture of zinc and copper, and, when immersed in an electrolyte, the zinc portion of the mixture corrodes away as reaction occurs between the zinc and copper particles.

Marine equipment, including the hull and drive unit, can act as conductors. Large metal objects, when firmly attached together, provide a more efficient conductor than

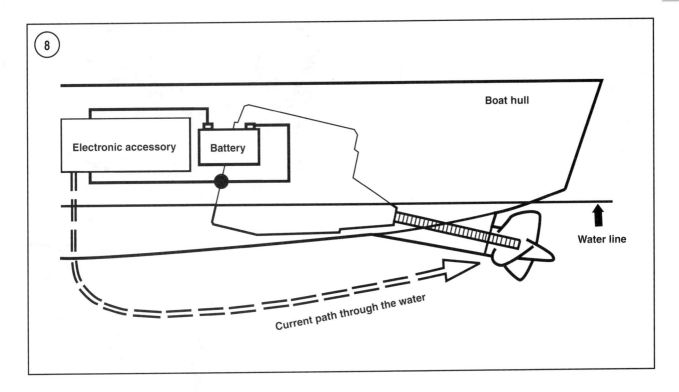

(8)

Electronic accessory   Battery   Boat hull

Water line

Current path through the water

water. Rubber attachments and vinyl-based paint act as insulators between metal components.

The water in which a boat operates acts as the electrolyte for the corrosion process. Cold, clean freshwater is the poorest electrolyte. Pollutants increase conductivity; brackish or saltwater is an efficient electrolyte. Operating the boat in highly conductive conditions causes more severe and rapid corrosion. This is one of the reasons that most manufactures recommend a freshwater flush after operating in polluted, brackish or saltwater.

Because of the environment in which marine equipment must operate, it is practically impossible to totally prevent galvanic corrosion. There are several precautions that will slow the process. It is also possible to isolate corrosion to specific areas with sacrificial anodes and Mercathode impressed current systems.

Simple precautions will reduce the amount of corrosion taking place outside the hull. These are *not* substitutes for the corrosion protection methods discussed under *Sacrificial Anodes* and *Mercathode Impressed Current Systems* in this chapter, but they can help these methods reduce corrosion.

Use fasteners of a metal more noble than the parts they secure. If corrosion occurs, the parts they secure may suffer but the fasteners are protected. The larger secured parts are more able to withstand the loss of material, but major problems could arise if the fasteners corrode to the point of failure.

Keep all painted surfaces in good condition. If paint is scraped off and bare metal exposed, corrosion rapidly increases. Use a vinyl- or plastic-based paint, which acts as an electrical insulator.

Do not apply metal-based anti-fouling paint to any metal parts of the boat or the drive unit. This type of paint reacts with the metal and results in corrosion between the metal and the layer of paint. Maintain a minimum 1 in. (25 mm) border between the painted surface and any metal parts. Organic-based paints are available for use on metal surfaces.

Where a corrosion protection device is used, remember that it must be immersed in the electrolyte along with the boat to provide any protection. If the drive unit is out of the water while the boat is docked, any anodes on the drive unit may be removed from the corrosion process, rendering them ineffective. Never paint or apply any coating onto anodes or other protection devices. Paint or other coatings insulate them from the corrosion process.

Any change in the boat's equipment, such as the installation of a new stainless steel propeller, changes the electrical potential and may cause increased corrosion. Keep this in mind if adding any equipment or changing exposed materials. Add additional anodes or other protection equipment as required to ensure the corrosion protection system is up to the task. The expense to repair corrosion damage usually far exceeds that of additional corrosion protection.

### Sacrificial Anodes

Sacrificial anodes are designed to do nothing but corrode. Properly fastening such pieces onto the boat causes them to act as the anode in *any* galvanic reaction that occurs; any other metal in the reaction acts as the cathode and is not damaged.

Anodes are usually made of zinc. Later model Quicksilver anodes are manufactured of an aluminum and indium alloy. This alloy is less noble than the aluminum alloy in drive system components, and provides the desired sacrificial properties. The aluminum and indium alloy is more resistant to oxide coating than zinc anodes. Oxide coating occurs as the anode material reacts with oxygen in the water. The oxide coating acts as an insulator, dramatically reducing corrosion protection.

Proper anode selection is critical to providing adequate protection. First determine how much surface area requires protection and use the Military Specification MIL-A-818001 as a general rule. The specification states that one square inch of new anode protects either:

1. 800 square in. (5161 cm$^2$) of freshly painted steel.
2. 250 square in. (1613 cm$^2$) of bare steel or bare aluminum alloy.
3. 100 square in. (645 cm$^2$) of copper or copper alloy.

This rule is for a boat at rest. If underway, additional anode area is required to protect the same surface area.

The anode must make good electrical contact with the metal it protects. If possible, attach an anode onto all metal surfaces requiring protection. If this is not possible, all metal components must be electrically bonded. All MerCruiser drive systems are equipped with continuity wires (**Figure 9**); providing electrical bonding for the drive system components.

Good quality anodes have inserts made of a more noble material around the anode fastener holes. Otherwise, the anode could erode away around the fastener hole, allowing the anode to loosen or possibly fall off, thereby loosing needed protection.

### Mercathode Impressed Current System

All MerCruiser engines using a Bravo drive unit are equipped with a Mercathode impressed current system. An Alpha drive unit can be retrofitted with this system. The Mercathode impressed system consists of the anode (A, **Figure 10**), control module (**Figure 11**) and sensor (B, **Figure 10**). The anode is coated with a highly noble metal, such as platinum, which is almost corrosion-free and can last indefinitely. The sensors, under the boat's waterline, allow the control module to monitor the potential for corrosion. If electrical current flow reaches the point

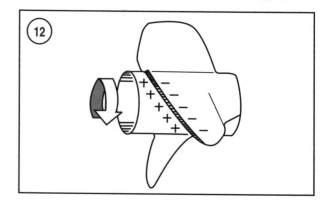

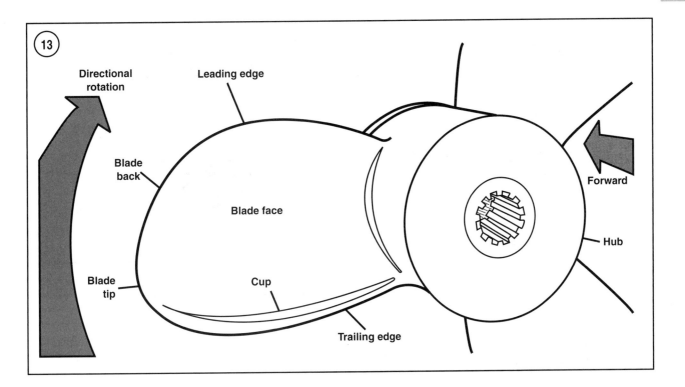

indicating galvanic corrosion, the control module applies positive battery voltage to the anode. Current then flows from the anode to all other metal component, regardless of how noble or non-noble these components may be. Essentially, the electrical current from the battery counteracts the galvanic reaction to dramatically reduce corrosion damage.

Only a small amount of current is needed to counteract corrosion. Using input from the sensor, the control module provides only the amount of current needed to suppress galvanic corrosion. Most systems consume a maximum of 0.2 Ah at full demand. Under normal conditions, these systems can provide protection for 8-12 weeks without recharging the battery. Keep in mind that this system must have constant connection to the battery.

An impressed current system is more expensive to install than sacrificial anodes but, considering its low maintenance requirements and the superior protection it provides, the long-term cost may be lower.

## PROPELLERS

The propeller is the final link between the boat's drive system and the water. A perfectly maintained engine and hull are useless if the propeller is the wrong type or has deteriorated. Although propeller selection for a specific application is beyond the scope of this manual, the following provides the basic information needed to make an in-

formed decision. A professional at a marine dealership is the best source for a propeller recommendation.

### Propeller Operation

As the curved blades of a propeller rotate through the water, a high-pressure area forms on one side of the blade and a low-pressure area forms on the other side of the blade (**Figure 12**). The propeller moves toward the low-pressure area, carrying the boat with it.

### Propeller Parts

Although a propeller is usually a one-piece unit, it is made of several different parts (**Figure 13**). Variations in the design of these parts make different propellers suitable for different applications.

The blade tip is the point on the blade furthest from the center of the propeller hub or propeller shaft bore. The blade tip separates the leading edge from the trailing edge.

The leading edge is the edge of the blade nearest the boat. During forward gear operation, this is the area of the blade that first cuts through the water.

The trailing edge is the surface of the blade furthest from the boat. During reverse gear operation, this is the area of the blade that first cuts through the water.

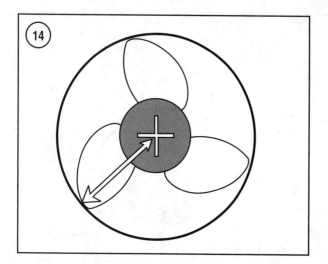

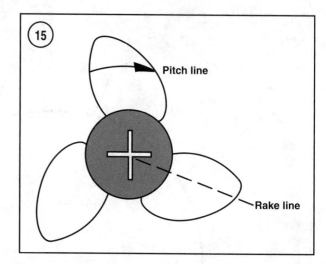

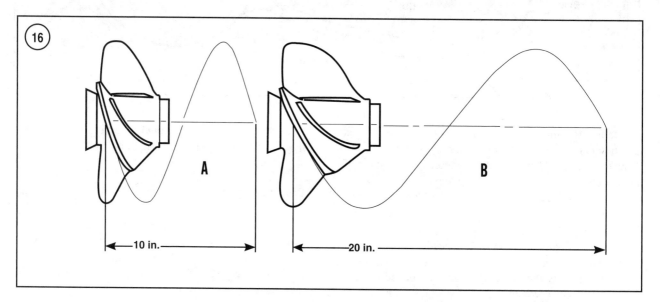

The blade face is the surface of the blade that faces away from the boat. During forward gear operation, high-pressure forms on this side of the blade.

The blade back is the surface of the blade that faces toward the boat. During forward gear operation, low-pressure forms on this side of the blade.

The cup is a small curve or lip on the trailing edge of the blade. Cupped propeller blades generally perform better than non-cupped propeller blades.

The hub is the central portion of the propeller. It connects the blades to the propeller shaft (part of the boat's drive system). On most drive systems, engine exhaust is routed through the hub; in this case, the hub consists of an outer and inner portion, connected by ribs.

The diffuser ring is used on through-hub exhaust models to prevent exhaust gasses from entering the blade area.

**Propeller Design**

Changes in length, angle, thickness and material of propeller parts make different propellers suitable for different applications.

*Diameter*

Propeller diameter is the distance from the center of the hub to the blade tip, multiplied by two. Essentially it is the diameter of the circle formed by the blade tips during propeller rotation (**Figure 14**).

*Pitch and rake*

Propeller pitch and rake describe the placement of the blades in relation to the hub (**Figure 15**).

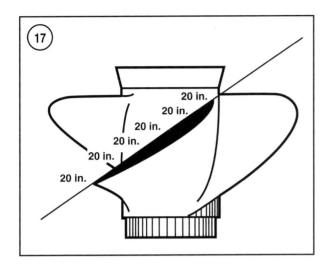

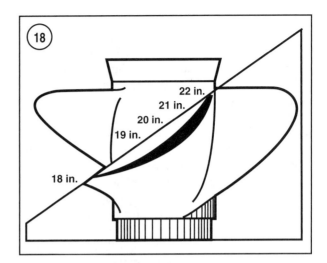

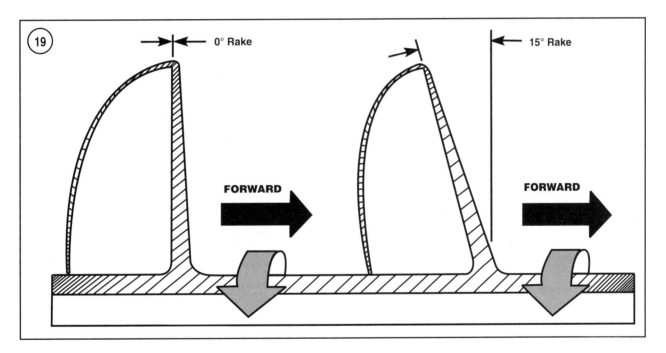

Pitch describes the theoretical distance the propeller would travel in one revolution. In A, **Figure 16**, the propeller would travel 10 in. (25.4 cm) in one revolution. In B, **Figure 16**, the propeller would travel 20 in. (50.8 cm) in one revolution. This distance is only theoretical; during operation, the propeller achieves only 75-85% of its pitch. Slip rate describes the difference in actual travel relative to the pitch. Lighter, faster boats typically achieve a lower slip rate than heavier, slower boats.

Propeller blades can be constructed with constant pitch (**Figure 17**) or progressive pitch (**Figure 18**). Progressive pitch starts low at the leading edge and increases toward the trailing edge. The propeller pitch specification is the average of the pitch across the entire blade. Propellers with progressive pitch usually provide better overall performance than constant pitch propellers.

Blade rake is specified in degrees and is measured along a line from the center of the hub to the blade tip. A blade that is perpendicular to the hub (**Figure 19**) has 0° rake. A blade that is angled from perpendicular (**Figure 19**) has a rake expressed by its difference from perpendicular. Most propellers have rakes ranging from 0-20°. Lighter, faster boats generally perform better using a propeller with a greater amount of rake. Heavier, slower boats generally perform better using a propeller with less rake.

### Blade thickness

Blade thickness is not uniform at all points along the blade. For efficiency, blades are as thin as possible at all points while retaining enough strength to move the boat. Blades are thicker where they meet the hub and thinner at the blade tips (**Figure 20**). This is necessary to support the heavier loads at the hub section of the blade. Overall blade thickness is dependent on the strength of the material used.

When cut along a line from the leading edge to the trailing edge in the central portion of the blade (**Figure 21**), the propeller blade resembles an airplane wing. The blade face, where high pressure exists during forward gear rotation, is almost flat. The blade back, where low pressure exists during forward gear rotation, is curved, with the thinnest portions at the edges and the thickest portion at the center.

Propellers that run only partially submerged, as in racing applications, may have a wedge shaped cross-section (**Figure 22**). The leading edge is very thin; the blade thickness increases toward the trailing edge, where it is thickest. If this type of propeller is run totally submerged, it is very inefficient.

### Number of blades

The number of blades used on a propeller is a compromise between efficiency and vibration. A one-bladed propeller would the most efficient, but it would create an unacceptable amount of vibration. As blades are added, efficiency decreases, but so does vibration. Most propellers have three or four blades, representing the most practical trade-off between efficiency and vibration.

### Material

Propeller materials are chosen for strength, corrosion resistance and economy. Stainless steel, aluminum, plastic and bronze are the most commonly used materials. Bronze is quite strong but rather expensive. Stainless steel is more common than bronze because of its combination of strength and lower cost. Aluminum alloy and plastic materials are the least expensive but usually lack the strength of stainless steel. Plastic propellers are more suited for lower horsepower applications.

### Direction of rotation

Propellers are made for both right-hand and left hand rotations although right-hand is the most common. As viewed from the rear of the boat while in forward gear, a right-hand propeller turns clockwise and a left-hand pro-

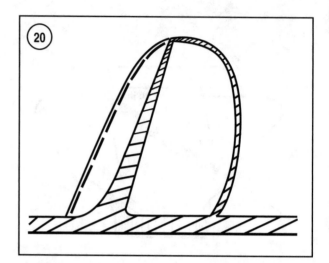

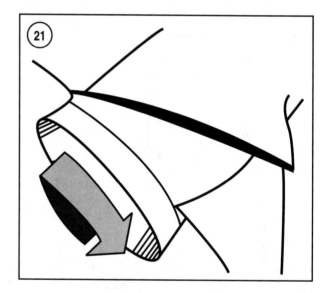

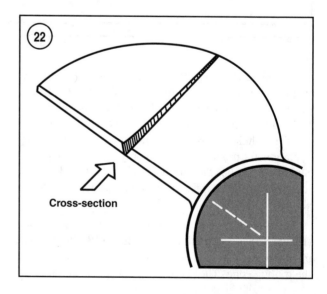

**Cross-section**

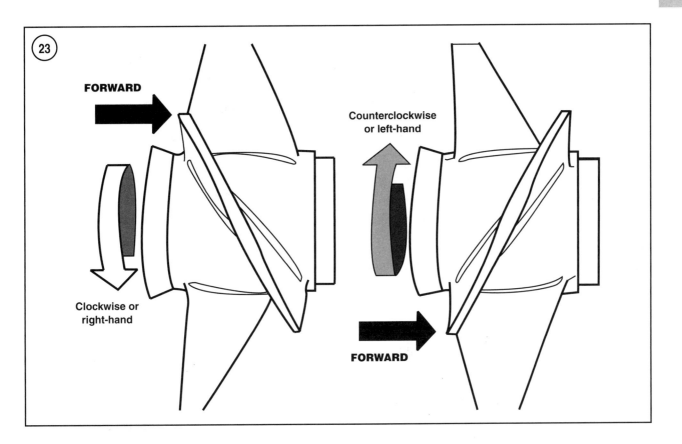

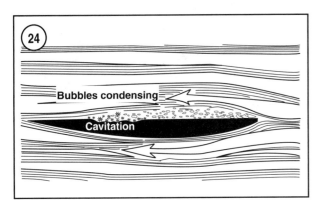

peller turns counterclockwise. Off the boat, the direction of rotation is determined by observing the angle of the blades (**Figure 23**). A right-hand propeller's blades slant from the upper left to the lower right; a left-hand propeller's blades are opposite.

## Cavitation and Ventilation

Cavitation and ventilation are *not* interchangeable terms; they refer to two distinct problems encountered during propeller operation.

To understand cavitation, consider the relationship between pressure and the boiling point of water. At sea level, water boils at 212° F (100° C). As pressure increases, such as within an engine cooling system, the boiling point of the water increases—it boils at a temperature higher than 212° F (100° C). The opposite is also true. As pressure decreases, water boils at a temperature lower than 212° F (100° C). If the pressure drops low enough, water boils at normal room temperature.

During normal propeller operation, low pressure forms on the blade back. Normally the pressure does not drop low enough for boiling to occur. However, poor propeller design, damaged blades or using the wrong propeller can cause unusually low pressure on the blade surface (**Figure 24**). If the pressure drops low enough, boiling occurs and bubbles form on the blade surfaces. As the boiling water moves to a higher pressure area on the blade, the boiling ceases and the bubbles collapse. The collapsing bubbles release energy that erodes the surface of the propeller blade.

Corroded surfaces, physical damage or even marine growth combined with high speed operation can cause low pressure and cavitation on gearcase surfaces. In such cases, low pressure forms as water flows over a protrusion or rough surface. Boiling of the water causes bubbles to form and collapse as they move to a higher pressure area toward the rear of the surface imperfection.

This entire process of pressure drop, boiling and bubble collapse is called *cavitation*. The ensuing damage is called *cavitation burn*. Cavitation is caused by a decrease in pressure, *not* an increase in temperature.

Ventilation is a less complex process than cavitation. Ventilation refers to air entering the blade area, either from above the surface of the water or from a through-hub exhaust system. As the blades meet the air, the propeller momentarily looses it bite to the water subsequently losing most of its thrust. An added complication is that the propeller and engine over-rev, causing very low pressure on the blade back and massive cavitation.

All MerCruiser stern drive engines have a plate (**Figure 25**) above the propeller area designed to prevent surface air from entering the blade area. This plate is correctly called an *anti-ventilation plate*, although it is often incorrectly called an *anti-cavitation plate*.

Most propellers have an extended and flared hub section at the rear of the propeller (A, **Figure 26**); it is often called a diffuser ring. This feature forms a barrier, and extends the exhaust passage far enough aft to prevent the exhaust gasses from ventilating the propeller.

A close fit of the propeller to the gearcase (B, **Figure 26**) is necessary to keep exhaust gasses from exiting and subsequently ventilating the propeller. Using the wrong propeller attaching hardware can position the propeller too far aft, preventing a close fit. The wrong hardware can also allow the propeller to rub heavily against the gearcase, causing rapid and permanent wear to both components. Wear or damage to these surfaces allows the propeller to ventilate.

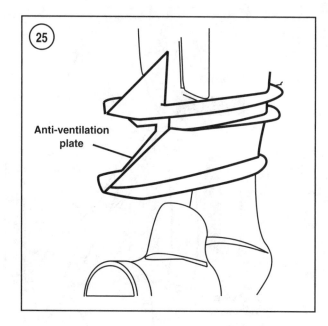

Anti-ventilation plate

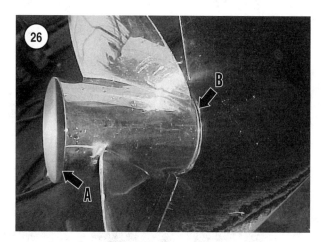

# Chapter Two

# Tools and Techniques

This chapter describes the common tools required for marine equipment repair and troubleshooting. Techniques that make the work easier and more effective are also described. Some of the procedures in this book require special skills or expertise; in some cases it is better to entrust the job to a MerCruiser dealership or qualified specialist.

## SAFETY

Professional mechanics can work for years and never sustain a serious injury or mishap. Follow these guidelines and practice common sense to safely service the vessel.

1. Do not operate the engine in an enclosed area. The exhaust gasses contain carbon monoxide, an odorless, colorless, and tasteless poisonous gas. Carbon monoxide levels build quickly in enclosed areas and can cause unconsciousness and death in a short time. Make sure the work area is properly ventilated, or operate the engine outside.

2. *Never* use gasoline or any extremely flammable liquid to clean parts. Refer to *Cleaning Parts* and *Handling Gasoline Safely* in this chapter.

3. *Never* smoke or use a torch in the vicinity of flammable liquids such as gasoline or cleaning solvent.

4. If welding or brazing, make sure that any fuel source is at least 50 ft. (15 m) away.

5. Use the correct type and size of tools to avoid damaging fasteners.

6. Keep tools clean and in good condition. Replace or repair worn or damaged equipment.

7. When loosening a tight fastener, be aware of what would happen if the tool slipped.

8. When replacing fasteners, make sure the new fasteners are of the same size and strength as the original ones.

9. Keep the work area clean and organized.

10. Wear eye protection *every* time the safety of your eyes is in question. This includes procedures involving drilling, grinding, hammering, compressed air and chemicals.

11. Wear the correct clothing for the job. Tie up or cover long hair so it cannot get caught in moving equipment.

12. Do not carry sharp tools in clothing pockets.

13. Always have a Coast Guard-approved fire extinguisher available. Make sure it is rated for gasoline (Class B) and electrical (Class C) fires.

14. Do not use compressed air to clean clothes, the engine or the work area. Debris may be blown into your eyes or skin. *Never* direct compressed air at yourself or someone else. Do not allow children to use or play with any compressed air equipment.

15. When using compressed air to dry rotating parts, hold the part so it cannot rotate. Do not allow the force of the air to spin the part. The air jet is capable of rotating parts at extreme speed. The part may be damaged or fly apart, causing serious injury.

16. Do not inhale the dust or particles created when removing gaskets. In most cases these particles contain asbestos. Inhaling asbestos particles is hazardous to health.

17. Never work on the machine while someone is working under it.

18. If placing the machine on a stand or securing it with a lift, make sure it is secure before walking away.

### Handling Gasoline Safely

Gasoline is a volatile, flammable liquid and is one of the most dangerous items in the shop. However, because gasoline is used so often, many people forget that it is hazardous. Only use gasoline as fuel for gasoline internal combustion engines. Keep in mind, when working on the engine, gasoline is always present in the fuel tank, fuel line and carburetor. To avoid a disastrous accident when working around the fuel system, carefully observe the following precautions:

1. *Never* use gasoline to clean parts. See *Cleaning Parts* in this chapter.
2. When working on the fuel system, work outside or in a well-ventilated area.
3. Do not add fuel to the fuel tank or service the fuel system while the machine is near open flames, sparks or where someone is smoking. Gasoline vapor is heavier than air; it collects in low areas and is more easily ignited than liquid gasoline. Always turn the engine off before refueling.
4. Allow the engine to cool completely before working on any fuel system component.
5. When draining the carburetor, catch the fuel in a plastic container and then pour it into an approved gasoline storage device.
6. Do not store gasoline in glass containers. If the glass breaks, a serious explosion or fire may occur.
7. Immediately wipe up spilled gasoline with rags. Store the rags in a metal container with a lid until they can be properly disposed of, or place them outside in a safe place for the fuel to evaporate.
8. Do not pour water onto a gasoline fire. Water spreads the fire and makes it more difficult to put out. Use a class B, BC or ABC fire extinguisher to extinguish the fire.

### Cleaning Parts

Cleaning parts is one of the more tedious and difficult service jobs performed in the home garage. There are many types of chemical cleaners and solvents available for shop use. Most are poisonous and extremely flammable. To prevent chemical exposure, vapor buildup, fire and serious injury, observe each product warning label and note the following:

1. Read and observe the entire product label before using any chemical. Always know what type of chemical is being used and whether it is poisonous and/or flammable.

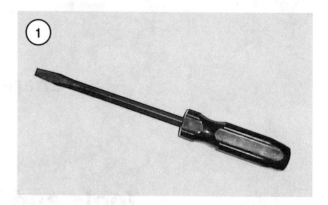

2. Do not use more than one type of cleaning solvent at a time. If mixing chemicals is called for, measure the proper amounts according to the manufacturer.
3. Work in a well-ventilated area.
4. Wear chemical-resistant gloves.
5. Wear safety glasses.
6. Wear a vapor respirator if the instructions call for it.
7. Wash hands and arms thoroughly after cleaning parts.
8. Keep chemical products away from children and pets.
9. Thoroughly clean all oil, grease and cleaner residue from any part that must be heated.

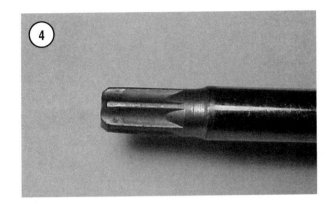

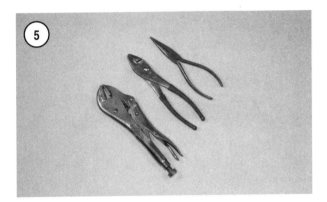

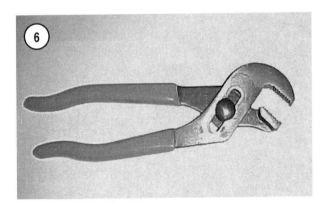

10. Use a nylon brush to clean parts. Metal brushes may cause a spark.

11. When using a parts washer, only use the solvent recommended by the manufacturer. Make sure the parts washer is equipped with a metal lid that will lower in case of fire.

## BASIC HAND TOOLS

A number of tools are required to maintain and repair a stern drive. Most of these tools are also used for home and automobile repairs. Some tools are made especially for working on a MerCruiser; these tools can be purchased from a MerCruiser dealership. Having the required tools always makes the job easier and more effective.

Keep the tools clean and in a suitable box. Keep them organized with related tools stored together. After using a tool, wipe off the dirt and grease with a shop towel.

The following tools are required to perform virtually any repair job. Each tool is described and the recommended size given for starting a tool collection. Additional tools and some duplication may be added as you become more familiar with the equipment. You may need all standard U.S. size tools, all metric size tools or a mixture of both.

### Screwdrivers

A screwdriver (**Figure 1**) is a very basic tool, but if used improperly can do more damage than good. The slot on a screw has a definite dimension and shape. Always use a screwdriver that comforms to the shape of the screw. Use a small screwdriver for small screws and a large one for large screws or the screw head will be damaged.

Three types of screwdrivers are commonly required: a slotted (flat-blade) screwdriver (**Figure 2**), Phillips screwdriver (**Figure 3**) and Torx screwdriver (**Figure 4**).

Use screwdrivers only for driving screws. Never use a screwdriver for prying or chiseling. Do not attempt to remove a Phillips, Torx or Allen head screw with a slotted screwdriver; this can damage the screw head to the point that even the proper tool cannot remove it.

Replace screwdrivers with worn or damaged tips.

### Pliers

Pliers come in a wide range of types and sizes. Pliers are useful for cutting, gripping, bending and crimping. Never use pliers to cut hardened objects or turn bolts or nuts. **Figure 5** shows several types of pliers.

Each type of pliers has a specialized function. General purpose pliers are mainly used for gripping and bending. Locking pliers are used for gripping objects very tightly, like a vise. Needlenose pliers are used to grip or bend small objects. Adjustable or slip-joint pliers (**Figure 6**) can be adjusted to grip various sized objects; the jaws remain parallel for gripping objects such as pipe or tubing. There are many more types of pliers. The ones described here are the most common.

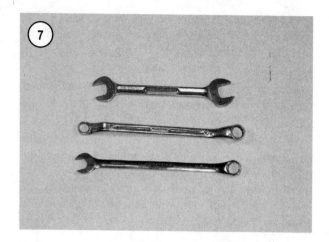

## Box-End and Open-End Wrenches

Box-end and open-end wrenches (**Figure 7**) are available in sets in a variety of sizes. The number stamped near the end of the wrench refers to the distance between two parallel flats on the hex head bolt or nut.

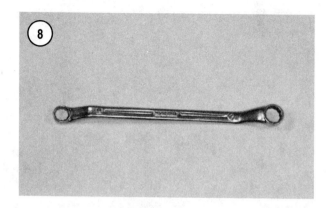

Box-end wrenches (**Figure 8**) provide a better grip to the nut and are stronger than open end wrenches. An open-end wrench (**Figure 9**) grips the nut on only two flats. Unless it fits well, it may slip and round off the points on the nut. A box end wrench grips all six flats. Box wrenches are available with 6-point or 12 point opening. The 6-point opening provides superior holding power; the 12-point allow a shorter swing if working in tight quarters.

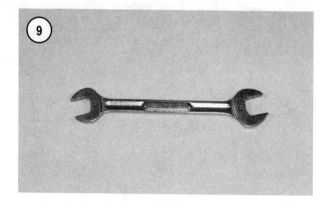

Use an open-end wrench if a box-end wrench cannot be positioned over the nut or bolt. To prevent damage to the fastener, avoid using an open-end wrench if a large amount of tightening or loosening force is required.

A combination wrench (**Figure 10**) has both a box end and an open end. Both ends are the same size.

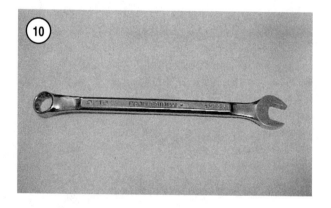

## Adjustable Wrenches

An adjustable wrench (**Figure 11**) can be adjusted to fit virtually any nut or bolt head. However, it can loosen and slip from the nut or bolt, causing damage to the nut and possibly physical injury. Use an adjustable wrench only if a proper size open- or box-end wrench in not available. Avoid using an adjustable wrench if a large amount of tightening or loosening force is required.

Adjustable wrenches come in sizes ranging from 4-18 in. overall length. A 6 or 8 in. size is recommended as an all purpose wrench.

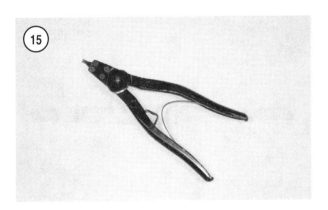

### Socket Wrenches

A socket wrench (**Figure 12**) is generally faster, safer and more convenient to use than a common wrench. Sockets, which attach to a suitable handle, are available with 6-point or 12-point openings and use 1/4, 3/8, and 1/2 in. drive sizes. The drive size corresponds to the square hole that mates with the ratchet or flex handle.

### Torque Wrench

A torque wrench (**Figure 13**) is used with a socket to measure how tight a nut or bolt is installed. They come in a wide price range and in 1/4, 3/8, and 1/2 in. drive sizes. The drive size corresponds to the square shaft that mates with the socket.

A typical 1/4 in. drive torque wrench measures in in.-lb. increments, and have a range of 20-150 in.-lb. (2.2-17 N•m). A typical 3/8 or 1/2 in. torque measures in ft.-lb. increments, and have a range of 10-150 ft.-lb. (14-203 N•m). Both of these ranges are used in the maintenance and repair or MerCruiser stern drives.

### Impact Driver

An impact driver (**Figure 14**) makes removal of tight fasteners easy and reduces damage to bolts and screws. Interchangeable bits allow use on a variety of fasteners.

### Snap Ring Pliers

Snap ring pliers are necessary to remove snap rings. Snap ring pliers (**Figure 15**) usually come with different size tips; many designs can be switched to handle internal or external type snap rings.

### Hammer

The correct hammer is necessary to prevent damage to other components. Use a plastic or rubber tip hammer (**Figure 16**) for most repairs. Soft-faced hammers filled with lead shot (**Figure 17**) produce more force than a rubber or plastic tip hammer, and are sometimes necessary to remove stubborn components.

*Never* use a metal-faced hammer as severe damage to engine components or tools will occur.

### Feeler Gauges

This tool has either flat or wire measuring gauges (**Figure 18**). Wire gauges are used to measure spark plug gap;

flat gauges are used for other measurements. A non-magnetinc (brass) gauge may be specified if working around magnetized components.

## Other Special Tools

Many of the maintenance and repair procedures require special tools (**Figure 19**). Most of the tools are available from a marine dealership; with the remainder available from tool suppliers. Instructions on use and manufacturer's part numbers are included in the appropriate chapters of this book.

Purchase the required tools from a local marine dealership or tool supplier. Some can be made locally by a qualified machinist, often at a lower price. Many marine dealerships and rental outlets will rent some of the required tools. Avoid using makeshift tools. Their use may result in damaged parts that cost far more than the recommended tool.

## TEST EQUIPMENT

This section describes equipment used to perform testing, adjustments and measurements on MerCruiser engines. Most of these tools are available from a local marine dealership or automotive parts store.

## Multimeter

This instrument is invaluable for electrical troubleshooting and service. It combines a voltmeter, ohmmeter and an ammeter in one unit. It is often called a VOM.

Two types of mutimeter are available, analog and digital. Analog meters (**Figure 20**) have a moving needle with marked bands on the meter face indicating the volt, ohm and amperage scales. An analog meter must be calibrated each time the battery or scale is changed.

A digital meter (**Figure 21**) is ideally suited for electrical troubleshooting because it is easy to read and more accurate than an analog meter. Most models are auto-ranging, have automatic polarity compensation and internal overload protection circuits.

Either type of meter is suitable for most electrical testing described in this manual. An analog meter is better suited for testing pulsing voltage signals such as those produced by the ignition system. A digital meter is better suited for testing involving a very low resistance or voltage reading (less than 1 volt or 1 ohm). The test instructions indicate if a specific type of meter is required.

Scale selection, meter specifications and test lead connection points vary by the manufacturer and model of the

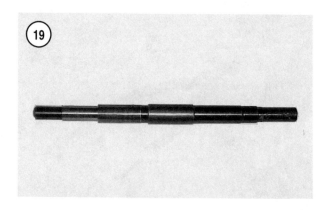

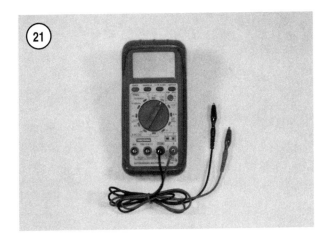

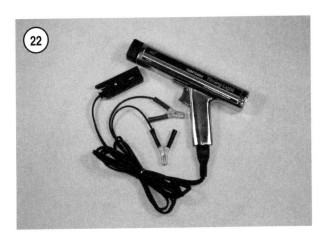

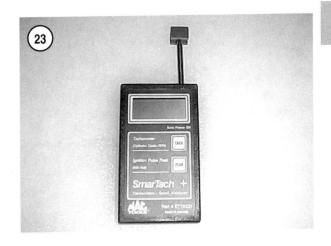

meter. Thoroughly read the instructions supplied with the meter before performing any test. The meter and certain electrical components on the engine can be damaged if tested incorrectly. Have the test performed by a qualified professional if you are unfamiliar with the testing or general meter usage. The expense to replace damaged equipment can far exceed the cost of having the test performed by a professional.

## Timing Light

This instrument is necessary to set the ignition timing while the engine is running. By flashing a light at the precise instant the spark plug fires, the position of the timing mark can be seen. The flashing light makes a moving mark appear to stand still next to a stationary timing mark.

Suitable timing lights (**Figure 22**) range from inexpensive models to expensive models with a built in tachometer and an adjustable timing advance compensator. A built-in tachometer is very useful as most ignition timing specifications refer to a specific engine speed.

A timing advance compensator delays the strobe enough to bring the timing mark to a certain place on the scale. This feature allows checking of the ignition timing at higher engine speeds where the amount of timing advance exceeds the marks on the scale. Although useful for troubleshooting purposes, this feature is not necessary to check or adjust the base ignition timing.

## Tachometer

A portable tachometer is needed for tuning and testing of marine engines. Ignition timing, carburetor adjustment, fuel pressure, and oil pressure tests must be performed at specific engine speeds. Tachometers are available with either an analog or digital display.

Carburetor adjustments are performed at idle speed. If using an analog type tachometer, choose one with a low range of 0-1000 rpm or 0-2000 rpm range and a high range of 0-6000 rpm. The high range setting is needed for testing purposes but lacks the accuracy needed at lower speeds. At lower speeds the meter must be capable of detecting changes of 25 rpm or less.

Digital tachometers (**Figure 23**) are generally easier to use than most analog type tachometers. They provide accurate measurement at all speeds without the need to

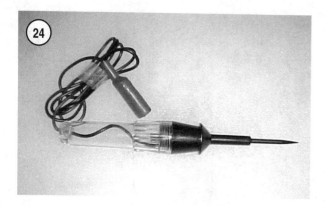

change the range or scale. Many of these use an inductive pickup to receive the signal from the ignition system.

### Test Lamp

Use a test lamp to test the electronic fuel injection and other electrical systems on the engine. Use only an unpowered test lamp (**Figure 24**). A battery powered test lamp can easily damage expensive ignition and fuel injection components. Verify the test lamp is suitable for testing ignition and other computerized components. The bulb in the test lamp must draw less than 300 mA @ 12 volts and provide a visible glow at 100 mA. Never improvise a test lamp using wire and a light bulb. Excessive amperage draw can easily damage expensive electrical components.

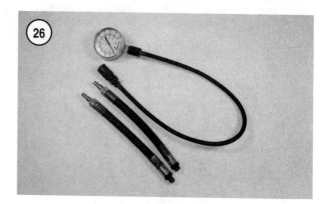

### Scan Tool

A scan tool (**Figure 25**) is used to retrieve data from the engine control module (ECM) on EFI models and the ignition system on carburetor equipped V6 and V8 models. Most problems can be correctly diagnosed without a scan tool, but this tool can save a great deal of time and reduces the chance of mis-diagnosis. Scan tools are offered by several different manufactures and vary in ease of use, feature and price.

Purchase this tool from a marine dealership or tool supplier. Ensure the tool is compatible with both MEFI 2 and MEFI3 MerCruiser EFI systems.

### Compression Gauge

This tool (**Figure 26**) measures the amount of pressure created in the combustion chamber during the compression stroke. Compression indicates the general engine

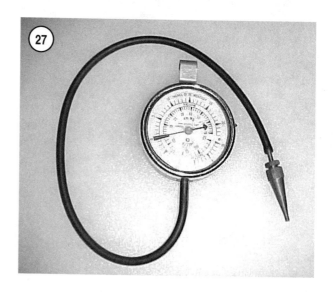

condition making it one of the most useful troubleshooting tools.

The easiest type to use has screw-in adapters that fit the spark plug holes. Press-in rubber tipped type gauges are also available. They are difficult to use on most MerCruiser engines due to limited access to the spark plug holes.

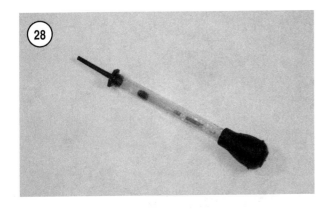

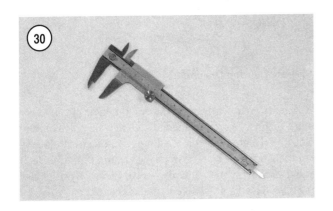

## Vacuum Gauge

The vacuum gauge (**Figure 27**) measures the intake manifold vacuum created during the engine intake stroke. Manifold air leakage, improper carburetor or timing adjustment and valve problems can be identified by interpreting the readings. If combined with compression gauge readings, other engine mechanical problems can be diagnosed.

Some vacuum gauges can also be used as fuel pressure gauges to help pinpoint fuel delivery problems.

## Hydrometer

Use a hydrometer to measure the specific gravity of the battery electrolyte. The specific gravity indicates the battery's state of charge by measuring the density of the electrolyte as compared to pure water. Choose a hydrometer (**Figure 28**) with automatic temperature compensation; otherwise the electrolyte temperature must be measured to determine the actual specific gravity.

## Precision Measuring Tools

Various tools are required to make precision measurements. A dial indicator (**Figure 29**), for example, is used to determine runout and end play of parts assemblies. It is also used to measure free movement between the gear teeth (backlash) in the drive unit.

Venier calipers (**Figure 30**), micrometers (**Figure 31**) and other precision tools are used to measure the size of parts (such as the piston).

Precision measuring equipment must be stored, handled and used carefully or it will not remain accurate.

## SERVICE HINTS

Most of the service procedures are straightforward and can be performed by anyone reasonably handy with tools. However, consider your skill level, available tools and equipment before attempting major disassembly of the engine or drive unit.

Some operations, for example, require the use of a press. Other operations require precision measurement. Have the procedure(s) or measurement(s) performed by a professional if the correct equipment or experience is lacking.

## Working With Electrical Components

All models covered in this manual have electronic ignition and/or fuel injection control systems. The control modules can withstand a rigorous marine environment, but they can be damaged under certain circumstances, such as improperly disconnecting the battery or a wire harness connection.

### *Battery precautions*

Disconnecting or connecting the battery can create a spike or surge of current throughout the electrical system. This spike or surge can damage certain circuits in the ignition module, engine control module or alternator. Always verify that the ignition switch is in the OFF position before connecting or disconnecting the battery, or changing the position of a battery switch (**Figure 32**).

Always remove the battery from the boat for charging. If the battery cables are connected, the charger may induce a damaging spike or surge of current into the electrical system. During charging, batteries produce explosive and corrosive gasses. These gasses can cause corrosion in the engine compartment and create an extremely hazardous condition.

Disconnect the cables from the battery prior to testing, adjusting or repairing many of the systems or components on the engine. This is necessary for safety, to prevent damage to test equipment and to ensure accurate testing or adjustment. Always disconnect or connect the battery cables as follows:

1. *Disconnecting the battery cables*—Disconnect the negative (–) then the positive (+) cable.

2. *Connecting the battery cables*—Connect the positive (+) then negative (–) cable.

### *Electrostatic discharge damage*

Sliding across the vinyl upholstery used in most boats can generate as much as 25,000 volts of static electricity in the human body. Electrostatic discharge occurs if an electrostatically charged individual (or object) contacts a non-charged surface. It takes a minimum of 4000 volts for the average person to even feel an electrostatic discharge. The engine control unit and many of the sensors can be damaged if subjected to an electrostatic discharge of as little as 100 volts.

Automotive technicians often use a special grounding strap, attached to the wrist, to prevent the buildup of an electrostatic charge. Grounding straps are available from automotive parts stores and most tool suppliers. If a ground strap is not available, first verify that no flamma-

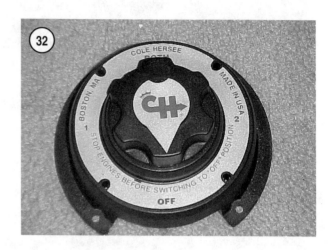

ble gas or liquid is present in the work area, then momentarily touch a known engine ground. Touch the ground prior to disconnecting, testing or connecting any wire harness or electrical component. Electrostatic discharge usually occurs only in very dry conditions. Electrostatic discharge seldom occurs under humid conditions.

> *WARNING*
> *Arcing produced by an electrostatic discharge can ignite flammable gas or liquids resulting in a fire or explosion. Never allow an electrostatic discharge near fuel or flammable material.*

## Preparation for Disassembly

Repairs go much faster if the equipment is clean before work begins. There are special cleaners such as Gunk or Bel-Ray Degreaser, for washing non-electrical engine components. Spray or brush on the cleaning solution, let it stand, then rinse with a garden hose. Clean oily or greasy parts with a cleaning solvent after removal.

Use pressurized water to remove marine growth and corrosion or mineral deposits from external components such as the drive unit or transom assembly. Avoid directing pressurized water at seals or gaskets; pressurized water can flow past seal and gasket surfaces and contaminate lubricating fluids.

> *WARNING*
> *Never use gasoline as a cleaning agent. It presents an extreme fire hazard. Always work in a well-ventilated area if using cleaning solvent. Keep a Coast Guard approved fire extinguisher, rated for gasoline fires, readily accessible in the work area.*

Much of the labor charged for dealership repairs is for removal and disassembly of other parts to access defective parts or assemblies. It is frequently possible to perform most of the disassembly at home, then take the defective part or assembly to the dealership for repair.

Before attempting any home repair, read the appropriate section in this manual in its entirety. Study the illustrations and text until all steps are fully understood. Make arrangements to purchase or rent all required special tools and equipment before starting the repair.

### Disassembly Precautions

During disassembly, keep a few general precautions in mind. Force is rarely needed to get things apart. If parts fit tightly, such as a bearing on a shaft, there is usually a tool designed to separate them. Never use a screwdriver to separate parts with a machined mating surface (such as cylinder heads and manifolds). The surfaces will be damaged and leak.

Make diagrams (or take photographs) wherever similar-appearing parts are found.

Cover all openings after removing parts to keep dirt, insects or other parts from entering.

Tag all similar internal parts for location and mounting direction. Reinstall all internal components in the same location and mounting direction as removed. Record the thickness and location of any shims as removed. Place small bolts and parts in plastic sandwich bags. Seal and label the bags with masking tape.

Tag all wires and hoses and make a sketch of the routing. Never rely on memory alone; it may be several days or longer before parts are reassembled.

Protect all painted surfaces from physical damage. Never allow gasoline or cleaning solvent on these surfaces.

### Assembly Precautions

No parts, except those assembled with a press fit, require unusual force during assembly. If a part is hard to install, determine why before proceeding.

When assembling parts, start all fasteners, then tighten them evenly in a crisscross pattern unless a specific tightening sequence or procedure is given.

When assembling parts, be sure all shims, spacers and washers are installed in the same position and location as removed.

Whenever a rotating part butts against a stationary part, look for a shim, spacer or washer. Use new gaskets, seals and O-rings if there is any doubt about the conditions of

the used ones. Unless otherwise specified, a thin coating of oil on gaskets may help them seal more effectively. Use heavy grease to hold small parts in place if they tend to fall out during assembly.

Use emery cloth and oil to remove high spots from piston surfaces. Use a dull scraper to remove carbon deposits from the cylinder head, ports and piston crown. *Do not* scratch or gouge these surfaces. Wipe the surfaces clean with a *clean* shop towel when finished.

If the carburetor must be repaired, completely disassemble it and soak all metal parts in a commercial carburetor cleaner. Never soak gaskets and rubber or plastic parts in these cleaners. Clean rubber or plastic parts with warm soapy water. Never use a wire to clean out jets and small passages; they are easily damaged. Use compressed air to blow debris from all passages in the carburetor body.

Work slowly and do the job right. The break-in procedure for a newly rebuilt engine or drive is the same as for a new one. Use the recommended break-in oil and follow the instructions provided in the appropriate chapter.

### SPECIAL TIPS

Because of the extreme demands placed on marine equipment, several points must be observed while performing service and repairs. The following are general suggestions that may improve the overall service life of the machine and help avoid costly failures.

1. Unless otherwise specified, apply a locking compound to all bolts and nuts, even if secured with a lockwasher. Use only the specified grade of threadlocking compound. A screw or bolt lost from an engine cover or bearing retainer could cause serious and expensive damage before the loss is noticed. When applying threadlocking compound, use only enough to lightly coat the threads. If too much is used, it can work its way down the threads and enter a bearing or seal.

2. Use caution when using air tools to remove stainless steel nuts or bolts; the threads of stainless steel fasteners are easily damaged by the heat generated if spun rapidly. To prevent thread damage, apply a penetrating oil as a cooling agent and loosen or tighten them slowly.

3. When straightening the tab of a fold-over type lockwasher, use a wide chisel, such as a dull wood chisel. Such a tool provides a better contact surface than a screwdriver or pry bar, making straightening easier. During installation, use a new fold-over type lockwasher. If a new washer is not available, fold over a tab on the washer that was not previously used. Reusing the same tab may cause the washer to break, resulting in a loss of locking ability and a loose piece of metal adrift in the engine. When folding the tab into position, carefully pry it toward the flat on

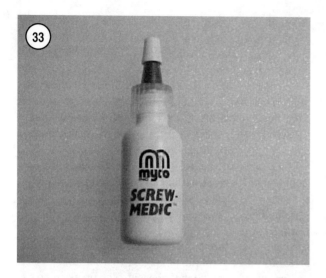

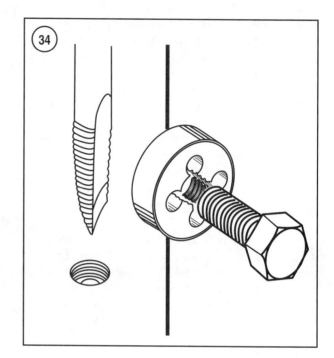

the bolt or nut. Use pliers to bend the tab against the fastener. Do not use a punch and hammer to drive the tab into position. The resulting fold may be too sharp, weakening the washer and increasing its chance of failure.

4. Use only authorized replacement parts if replacing missing or damaged bolt, screws or nuts. Many fasteners are specially hardened for the application. A wrong grade of bolt can cause serious and expensive damage.

5. Install only authorized gaskets. Unless specified otherwise, install them without sealant. Many gaskets are made with a material that swells when it contacts oil. Gasket sealer prevents them from swelling as intended and can result in oil leakage. Authorized gaskets are cut from material of a precise thickness. Installation of a too thick or too thin gasket in a critical area could cause expensive damage.

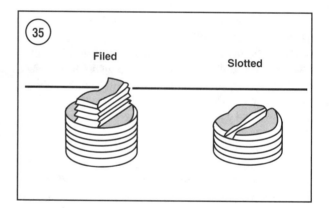

## MECHANIC'S TECHNIQUES

Marine engines are subjected to conditions very different from most engines. They are repeatedly subjected to a corrosive environment followed by periods of non-use for weeks or longer. Such use invites corrosion damage to fasteners, causing difficulty or breakage during removal. This section provides useful tips for removing stuck or broken fasteners and repairing damaged threads.

### Removing Stuck Fasteners

If a nut or bolt corrodes and cannot be removed, several methods may be used to loosen it. First, apply penetrating oil, such as Liquid Wrench or WD-40 (available at hardware or auto supply stores). Apply it liberally onto the threads and allow it to penetrate for 10-15 minutes. Tap

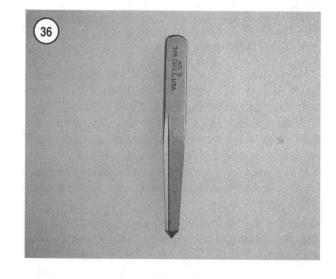

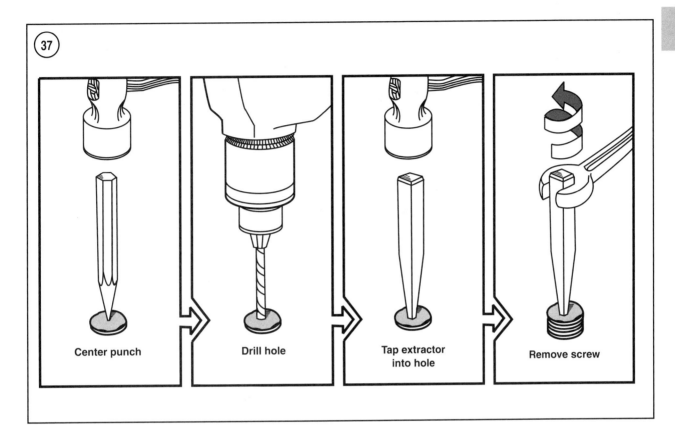

**Center punch**      **Drill hole**      **Tap extractor into hole**      **Remove screw**

the fastener several times with a small hammer; do not hit it hard enough to cause damage. Reapply the penetrating oil if necessary.

For stuck screws, apply penetrating oil as described, then insert a screwdriver in the slot. Tap the top of the screwdriver with a hammer. This loosens the corrosion in the threads allowing it to turn. If the screw head is too damaged to use a screwdriver, grip the head with locking pliers and twist the screw to loosen it.

A Phillips, Allen or Torx screwdriver may start to slip in the screw during removal. If slippage occurs, stop immediately and apply a dab of coarse valve lapping compound onto the tip of the screwdriver. Valve lapping compound or a special screw removal compound (**Figure 33**) is available from most hardware and automotive parts stores. Insert the driver into the screw and apply downward pressure while turning. The gritty material in the compound improves the grip to the screw, allowing more rotational force before slippage occurs. Keep the compound away from any other engine components. It is very abrasive and can cause rapid wear if applied to moving or sliding surfaces.

Avoid applying heat unless specifically instructed because it may melt, warp or remove the temper from parts.

### Repairing Stripped Threads

Occasionally, threads are stripped through carelessness or impact damage. Often the threads can be repaired with a tap (for internal threads on nuts) or die (for external threads on bolts) (**Figure 34**).

Damaged threads in a housing or component can often be repaired by installing a threaded insert.

### Removing Broken Bolts or Screws

The head of a bolt or screw may unexpectedly twist off during removal. Several methods are available for removing the remaining portion of the bolt or screw.

If a large portion of the bolt or screw projects out, try gripping it with locking pliers. If the projecting portion is too small, file it to fit a wrench or cut a slot in it to fit a screwdriver (**Figure 35**). If the head breaks off flush or cannot be turned with a screwdriver or wrench, use a screw extractor (**Figure 36**). To do this, center punch the remaining portion of the screw or bolt (**Figure 37**). Select the proper size extractor for the size of the fastener. Using the drill size specified for the extractor, drill a hole into the fastener. Do not drill deeper than the remaining fastener. Carefully tap the extractor into the hole (**Figure 37**). Back the remnant out with a wrench on the extractor.

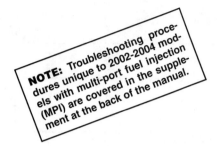

**NOTE:** Troubleshooting procedures unique to 2002-2004 models with multi-port fuel injection (MPI) are covered in the supplement at the back of the manual.

# Chapter Three

# Troubleshooting

This chapter describes troubleshooting and testing procedures for all engine systems. A MerCruiser engine package is comprised of three basic assemblies: the engine, the transom assembly and the drive unit. Other systems include the hydraulic trim and power steering. Troubleshooting is relatively simple matter if done logically. Taking a haphazard approach may eventually solve the problem, but it can be very costly in terms of wasted time and unnecessary parts replacement.

The first step is to determine which assembly is malfunctioning. Subsequent steps help determine which system of the assembly is malfunctioning. Further testing determines which component(s) of the system need adjustment or repair.

Most problems are very simple in nature and are easily corrected. Become familiar with the engine compartment, noting wire and hose connection points. Note the normal full throttle speed, idle speed, sound of the engine and any peculiarities. A rough idle, reduced power output, unusual sounds or strange odors usually indicate trouble. Perform a quick visual inspection at the first sign of trouble. Look for signs of fluid leakage and loose wires, hoses or belts. Refer to *Preliminary Inspection* for a list of items to check.

**Tables 1-3** list starting, ignition and fuel system troubleshooting items. **Tables 4-22** list test specifications and other useful information. **Tables 1-22** are located at the end of this chapter.

Proper lubrication, maintenance and periodic tune-ups will reduce the need to troubleshoot the engine. Lubrication, maintenance and tune-up are described in Chapter Four. Even with the best of care, however, problems can and eventually do occur.

## PRELIMINARY INSPECTION

Every internal combustion engine requires three things to run (**Figure 1**): an uninterrupted supply of fuel and air in the proper proportion, adequate compression and a source of ignition at the proper time. If any are inadequate the engine will not run properly. If any are missing the engine will not run.

Perform the following if the engine fails to start or runs improperly.

1. Check the position of the emergency stop (lanyard) switch.
2. Check for loose, dirty or damaged wire connections.
3. Check the fuses and circuit breaker.
4. Supply the engine with fresh fuel.
5. Fully charge the battery.
6. Clean the flame arrestor.
7. Check for spark at the plugs as described in this chapter.
8. Clean, inspect or replace the spark plugs.
9. Check for damaged or improperly adjusted throttle or shift cables.

If checking or correcting all of the previous items fails to correct the problem, refer to **Tables 1-3** for additional items to check. Refer to the causes listed next to the symp-

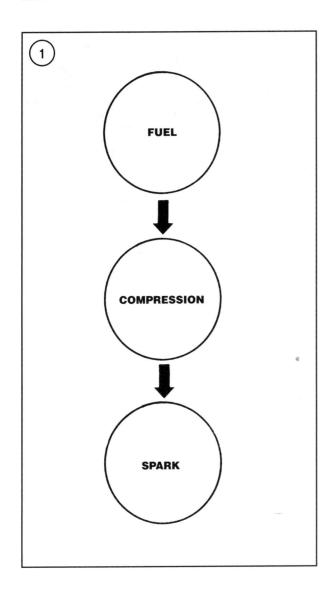

tom that best describes the problem. Perform the check, test or adjustment suggested under corrective action. Other useful information and tips are described with the specific test instructions.

Refer to the applicable table and other information provided in this chapter to troubleshoot all other engine systems.

## ENGINE AND DRIVE IDENTIFICATION

It is essential to identify the engine and drive model before ordering replacement parts or performing any testing or repairs. Some test and repair specifications vary by the engine model, serial number and the drive unit type used.

### Primary Serial Number Tag

The primary serial number tag is affixed to the flame arrestor cover (**Figure 2**) on all 3.0L, 4.3L, 5.0 L, 5.7L and 350 Mag models. The tag is affixed to the EFI component cover (**Figure 3**) on all remaining models. This tag includes the serial number for the engine, outdrive and transom assembly. A cellophane tag with the individual serial number is affixed to the decal by the engine installer. Compare the serial number on the tag with the actual number on the assembly. Boat builders and dealerships often change the drive unit or other assemblies without changing the original serial number

### Engine Serial Number

The engine serial number is stamped into a tag affixed to the starboard side of the cylinder block and near the flywheel housing mating surface (**Figure 4**).

### Drive Unit Serial Number

The drive unit serial number is stamped into a decal on the upper port side of the drive unit (A, **Figure 5**).

**Transom Assembly Serial Number**

The transom assembly serial number is stamped into a decal on the upper end of the transom assembly housing (**Figure 6**).

## DRIVE UNIT IDENTIFICATION

All 3.0 liter models use an Alpha drive unit (**Figure 7**). Models 4.3L, 5.0L and 5.7L and 350 Mag use either an Alpha or Bravo type drive unit. All other models use a Bravo drive unit.

Both Alpha and Bravo units are offered with several different overall drive ratios. The overall ratio indicates the number of rotations of the drive shaft needed to rotate the propeller shaft exactly one revolution. If the drive ratio stamping is 1.50, the drive shaft rotates one and one half turns to turn the propeller shaft one revolution.

Using other than the original ratio may cause poor performance, increased wear or failure of the engine or drive unit. If the boat is operated only at higher elevations, a drive with a higher ratio generally improves performance.

It is essential to identify the drive unit ratio before repairing or ordering parts for the drive unit. The overall drive unit ratio is stamped into the decal on the port side of the drive shaft housing (B, **Figure 5**). If the stamping is illegible, the drive unit ratio can be identified by inspecting certain internal components or marks on the unit. Refer to Chapter Eleven.

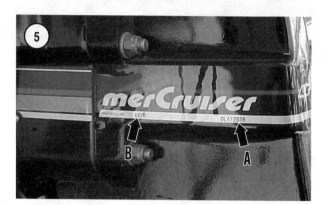

**Alpha Drive Unit**

Most lower horsepower models are equipped with an Alpha drive unit (**Figure 7**). Except for having a smaller dimension, this drive is very similar in appearance to a Bravo I drive unit. On an Alpha drive, the rear anchor pin is secured onto the trim cylinders with E-clips and a press-on plastic cover (**Figure 8**).

This type of drive unit is available in either right- or left-hand rotation. Drive unit rotation always refers to the direction the propeller rotates, as viewed from the rear, when in forward gear. Virtually all single engine boats use a right-hand drive; the right-hand drive is considered the standard rotation model. The left-hand drive is considered the counter-rotation model.

**Bravo I Drive Unit**

The Bravo I drive (**Figure 9**) is a heavy duty unit used primarily on high performance boats. The sleek contour of the gearcase allows efficient operation at speeds well in

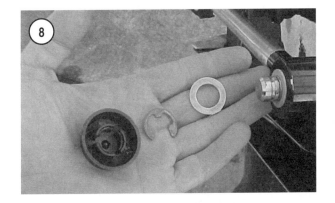

**3**

excess of 65 mph (104.6 km/h). Except for having a larger dimension, this drive is very similar in appearance to an Alpha drive. On a Bravo I drive, the rear anchor pin is attached to the trim cylinders with an elastic locknut and threaded on plastic cover (**Figure 10**).

This drive unit is bi-rotational; either a right-hand or left-hand propeller may be used. The direction the propeller shaft rotates is determined by the connection points of the shift cable in the remote control.

**Bravo II Drive Unit**

The Bravo II drive is a heavy-duty unit used generally on large displacement or work boats with a maximum speed of 45 mph (72.4 km/h) or less. Except for having a the larger gearcase, this drive is very similar in appearance to a Bravo I drive. The larger gearcase uses a much larger propeller (up to 20 in. [51cm] in diameter) than other Bravo or Alpha drive units. The large propeller and high drive ratio provides high thrust at lower engine speeds for enhanced acceleration. However, the large gearcase and propeller prevent efficient operation at speeds exceeding 45 mph (72.4 km/h).

This drive unit is bi-rotational; Either a right-hand or left-hand propeller can be used. The direction the propeller shaft rotates is determined by the connection points of the shift cable in the remote control.

**Bravo III Drive Unit**

The Bravo III type drive unit (**Figure 11**) is used on larger (over 20 ft. [6m]) single engine boats with a top speed exceeding 45 mph (72.4 km/h). The twin counter rotating propellers and higher drive ratio provide better handling and stronger acceleration than most single propeller drive units.

This drive is considered uni-rotational; A left-hand propeller is used for the front propeller and a right-hand propeller is used for the rear propeller.

**STARTING SYSTEM**

This section provided a brief description of how the electric starting system operates followed by testing instructions for the individual components.

The starting system consists of the battery, starter motor, slave solenoid, ignition switch, neutral-start switch and wiring.

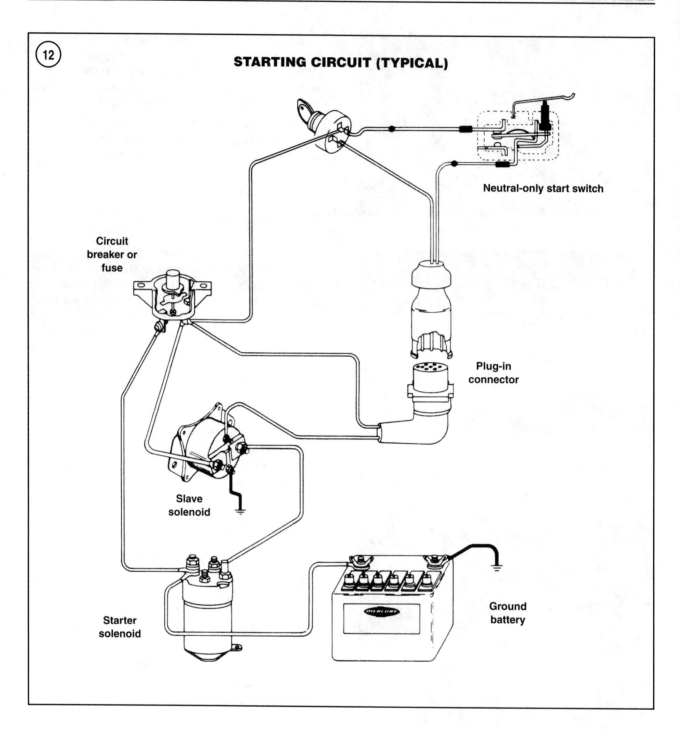

**(12)** **STARTING CIRCUIT (TYPICAL)**

Neutral-only start switch

Circuit
breaker or
fuse

Plug-in
connector

Slave
solenoid

Starter
solenoid

Ground
battery

## Starting System Operation

Refer to **Figure 12** for a typical starting circuit. Battery current is supplied to the ignition switch from a circuit breaker or fuse. When the ignition switch is turned to the START position, battery current flows to the neutral-start switch in the remote control. Current flows through the switch to charge the slave solenoid, provided the control is in the neutral position. When charged, the slave solenoid supplies current to the starter solenoid. This causes the starter solenoid to engage the starter motor with the flywheel teeth and supply current to operate the starter motor.

Once the engine is started and the ignition switch is released, the slave solenoid de-energizes, thereby de-energizing the starter solenoid. At this point the starter motor stops rotating and disengages the flywheel.

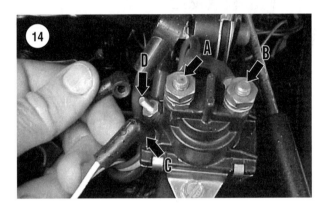

## Checking Voltage at the Slave Solenoid

Use a multimeter for this test. On carburetor equipped models, the solenoid mounts on a bracket behind or near the carburetor. On EFI models, the solenoid mounts near the engine control module. Open the electrical component box or remove the plastic engine covers to access the solenoid on EFI models. Refer to the wiring diagrams at the end of this manual and identify the wire colors connected to the relay. To prevent corrosion, apply a light coat of liquid neoprene to exposed terminals of the slave solenoid after testing. Liquid neoprene can be purchased at most automotive part stores.

1. Carefully pull the protective cover from the slave solenoid (**Figure 13**). Use an insulated screwdriver and carefully scrape the neoprene coating from the large wire terminals (A and B, **Figure 14**).
2. Test for proper voltage from the battery as follows:
    a. Touch the positive voltmeter lead to the red/purple wire terminal of the solenoid. The test lead must contact a clean area of the terminal.
    b. Observe the meter reading while touching the negative meter lead to an engine ground. The meter must read battery voltage. If not, test or check the circuit breaker or fuses, battery and wiring.

3. Test for proper voltage from the starter excitation circuit as follows:
    a. Shift the remote control to the neutral position. Disconnect the yellow/red and black wires (C and D, **Figure 14**) from the solenoid.
    b. Touch the positive voltmeter lead to the metal connector in the yellow/red wire boot. Touch the negative meter lead to the metal connector in the black wire boot.
    c. While an assistant rotates the ignition switch to the OFF, ON and START positions, observe the meter. The meter must indicate 12 VDC or greater with the switch in the START position and 0 volts with the switch in the OFF or RUN positions. Repeat this step with the negative meter lead connected to an engine ground.
    d. Repair the faulty ground wire if the voltage is correct only with the meter lead connected to an engine ground.
    e. Test the neutral-start switch, ignition switch, fuses and wiring if no battery voltage is present with the switch in the START position.
    f. Test the ignition switch and check for faulty wiring if the voltage is correct with the switch in the RUN and/or OFF positions.
4. Reconnect the yellow/red and black wires to the solenoid. Carefully snap the protective cover over the solenoid.

## Slave Solenoid Test

This test requires a fully charged battery, a multimeter and jumper wires.
1. Remove the slave solenoid as described in Chapter Ten. Calibrate a multimeter on the R × 1 scale.
2. Connect the positive ohmmeter lead to one of the large terminals on the solenoid as indicated in **Figure 15**. Connect the negative meter lead to the other large terminal. The meter reading must indicate no continuity. Otherwise replace the slave solenoid.
3. Connect a jumper wire from the battery positive terminal to one of the small terminals of the solenoid as indicated in **Figure 15**. Connect an additional jumper wire to the negative terminal of the battery.
4. Observe the meter while repeatedly touching the negative battery jumper to the remaining small terminal of the solenoid. The meter must indicate continuity and the solenoid must make a clicking noise each time the jumper lead makes connection. Otherwise replace the slave solenoid.
5. Remove all test leads and install the slave solenoid as described in Chapter Ten.

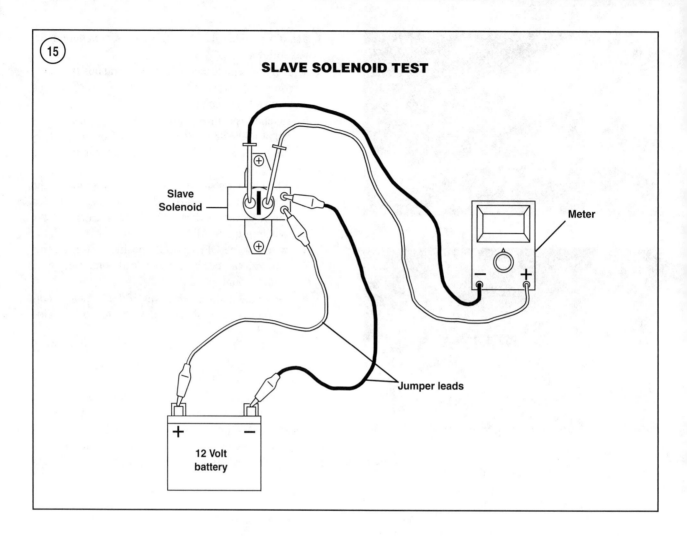

**SLAVE SOLENOID TEST**

Slave Solenoid

Meter

Jumper leads

12 Volt battery

**Starter Motor Voltage Test**

*WARNING*
*The engine may unexpectedly start or motor over during testing. Keep all persons, clothing, tools or loose objects away from the drive belts or other moving components on the engine.*

*CAUTION*
*Use a flush device to supply the engine with cooling water if testing the starter motor with the boat out of the water. Operation of the starter motor results in operation of seawater pump. The seawater pump is quickly damaged if operated without an adequate supply of water.*

This test requires a voltmeter and clear access to the starter solenoid terminals. The starter and solenoid are mounted onto the lower rear starboard side of the engine.

Correct test results are only possible if the test heads make good contact to the correct terminals.

The starter motor may operate during testing. Avoid entrapment in the belts or other moving components on the engine. The pressure switch bypass circuit test is included in this section. Although the terminals may be present on the starter, this circuit is used only on carburetor equipped V6 and V8 models.

1. Place the ignition switch in the OFF position and the remote control in the NEUTRAL position.

2. Check for battery voltage at the solenoid as follows:
   a. Carefully pull the protective boot away from the battery cable terminal.
   b. Touch the positive voltmeter lead to the battery cable terminal (A, **Figure 16**) on the starter solenoid.
   c. Touch the negative meter lead to an engine ground. The meter must indicate battery voltage. If not, test the battery and check for loose or dirty connections or a faulty battery switch.

3. Check for voltage from the excitation circuit as follows:

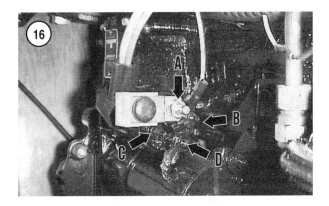

tive meter lead to an engine ground. Have an assistant repeatedly rotate the ignition key switch to the OFF and RUN positions. The meter must indicate 0 volts in either position. Otherwise test the starter solenoid.

b. Observe the meter while an assistant turns the ignition switch to the START position. The meter must indicate 12 volts or higher with the switch in the START position. Otherwise test the starter solenoid.

5. Check the starter cranking voltage as follows:

a. Disconnect the battery cables. Remove the tape and reconnect the large braided wire (D, **Figure 16**) to the starter solenoid. Reconnect the battery cables.

b. Activate the lanyard switch to prevent the engine from starting during this test. If the boat is not equipped with a lanyard switch, connect the coil secondary wire securely to an engine ground. Use a spark gap tester (**Figure 17**) or suitable jumper wire.

c. Connect the negative voltmeter lead to an engine ground. Touch the positive meter lead to the large braided wire terminal of the solenoid (D, **Figure 16**). The meter must read 0 volts. Otherwise test the starter solenoid.

d. Have an assistant turn the ignition switch to the START position. Observe the meter. The starter must activate and the meter reading must drop from 12.5 volts or higher to between 9.5 and 11.0 volts. Check for a loose or dirty terminal and test the battery if the voltage drops below 9.5 volts. Test the starter solenoid if the voltage reading exceeds 11 volts but the starter fails to activate.

6. Repair the starter motor if all voltage readings and the starter solenoid test correctly but the starter fails to operate. Starter repair instructions are provided in Chapter Ten.

7. Place the lanyard switch in the RUN position or reconnect the coil secondary wire onto the ignition coil.

**Neutral Start Test**

The neutral start switch is incorporated into the remote control on all MerCruiser stern drive models. Although controls are offered by many different manufacturers, switch operation and testing are very similar. The switch must open and interrupt the circuit connecting the ignition switch to the slave solenoid with the control in the FORWARD and REVERSE positions. The switch must close and complete the circuit with the control in the NEUTRAL position. A faulty switch can prevent the starter from operating in NEUTRAL or allow it to operate with the engine shifted into gear.

1. Disconnect the yellow/red neutral start switch wires (**Figure 18**) from the wiring harness.

a. Disconnect the battery cables. Remove the terminal nut and pull the large braided wire (D, **Figure 16**) from its starter solenoid terminal. Completely cover the wire terminal with a thick wrapping of electrical tape and position it away from all terminals and other components. Reconnect the battery cables.

b. Touch the positive voltmeter lead to the yellow/red terminals on the starter (B, **Figure 16**).

c. Touch the negative meter lead to an engine ground. Have an assistant turn the ignition switch to the OFF and RUN positions. The meter must indicate 0 VDC with the switch in either position. Otherwise test the ignition switch, slave solenoid and related wiring.

d. Have an assistant repeatedly turn the ignition switch from the RUN to START positions. The solenoid must make a clicking noise and the meter must read 12 volts or greater as the switch reaches the START position. Test the ignition key switch, slave solenoid and related wiring if low voltage occurs. Test the starter solenoid if 12 volts or greater is indicated yet the solenoid fails to make a clicking noise.

4. Check for proper operation of the bypass circuit as follows:

a. Touch the positive voltmeter lead to the purple/yellow wire terminal (C, **Figure 16**). Touch the nega-

2. Place the remote control in the NEUTRAL position. Calibrate an ohmmeter to the R×1 scale.

3. Connect the meter test leads to each of the yellow/red wires leading into the remote control. The meter must read continuity with the control in NEUTRAL.

4. Observe the meter while shifting the remote control into FORWARD and REVERSE gears. The meter must read no continuity with the control in FORWARD and REVERSE.

5. Repeat Steps 4 and 5 several times as the switch may fail intermittently. Replace the switch if it fails to perform as described.

6. Reconnect the yellow/red wires.

7. Check for proper operation of the neutral start switch before returning the engine to service. The starter must operate only with the remote control in NEUTRAL.

### Starter Solenoid Test

This test requires a fully charged battery, a multimeter, and jumper wires.

1. Remove the starter solenoid from the starter motor as described in Chapter Ten. Calibrate the ohmmeter to the R×1 scale.

2. Connect the positive ohmmeter lead to one of the large terminals on the solenoid (C, **Figure 19**). Connect the negative lead to the other large terminal. The meter reading must be no continuity. Otherwise replace the starter solenoid.

3. Connect a jumper wire from the positive battery terminal to the *S* terminal of the solenoid (A, **Figure 19**). Do not connect the jumper to the *R* terminal. Connect an additional jumper wire to the negative terminal of the battery.

4. Observe the meter while repeatedly touching the negative battery jumper to an unpainted location on the metal solenoid housing. The meter must indicate continuity and the solenoid must make a clicking noise each time the jumper lead makes connection. Otherwise replace the solenoid. Remove the jumper wires from the battery and solenoid.

5. On carbureted V6 and V8 models, connect the ohmmeter between the solenoid R terminal (B, **Figure 19**) and an unpainted metal area on the solenoid housing. The ohmmeter must indicate no continuity. Next, connect the ohmmeter between the solenoid R terminal (B, **Figure 19**) and either of the large solenoid terminals.

   a. Attach a jumper wire to the battery positive terminal and solenoid S terminal (A, **Figure 19**).

   b. Connect another jumper wire to the negative battery terminal. Observe the ohmmeter while repeatedly touching the jumper wire to an unpainted metal area of the solenoid housing. When the jumper is attached, the solenoid should click and the meter

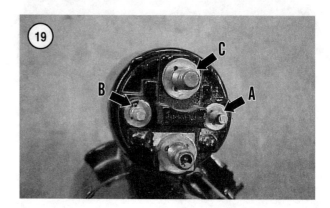

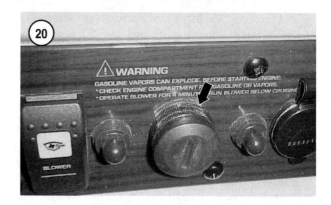

should indicate continuity. Also, the meter should indicate no continuity each time the connection is broken.

6. Replace the solenoid if it fails to operate as described.

### Ignition Switch Test

On most switches, the wires are connected to the terminals with small screws and wire identification marks are located next to each terminal. This test covers the standard three-terminal switch. Some switches have a fourth termi-

nal for use on many brands of outboard motors. If the switch has more than three terminals, perform the test using only the three indicated terminals.

1. Disconnect the cables from the battery. Remove the ignition key from the switch. Unthread the retaining nut (**Figure 20**) from the key side of the switch and carefully pull the switch from the back side of the dash. Remove the lockwasher (if so equipped) from the switch. Note the connections then disconnect all wires from the switch.

2. Insert the ignition key into the switch and place it in the OFF position. Calibrate the multimeter on the R × 1 scale.

3. Connect the positive ohmmeter lead to the B, BATT or red wire terminal (A, **Figure 21**) on the switch. Connect the negative meter lead to the I, IGN or purple wire terminal of the switch (B, **Figure 21**). The meter reading must indicate no continuity. Otherwise replace the ignition switch.

4. Place the ignition switch in the RUN or ON position. Connect the positive multimeter lead to the B, BATT or red wire terminal (A, **Figure 21**) on the switch. Connect the negative lead to the I, IGN or purple wire terminal of the switch. Observe the meter reading while turning the ignition switch to the START position. The meter must indicate continuity (0 resistance) with the switch in the ON and START positions. Otherwise replace the ignition switch.

5. Place the ignition switch in the OFF position. Connect the positive ohmmeter lead to the B, BATT or red wire terminal (A, **Figure 21**) of the switch. Connect the negative lead to the S or yellow/red wire terminal of the switch (C, **Figure 21**). Note the meter reading. Place the ignition switch in the ON position and again observe the meter reading. The meter must read no continuity with the switch in the OFF and ON positions. Otherwise replace the ignition key switch.

6. With all test leads connected as described in step 5, observe the meter while turning the ignition switch to the START position. The meter must indicate continuity. Otherwise replace the ignition key switch.

7A. *Screw type terminals*—Connect the wires to the switch as follows:

    a. Connect the red and/or orange instrument harness wire to the B or BATT terminal of the switch.

    b. Connect the purple instrument harness wires to the I or IGN terminal of the switch.

    c. Connect the yellow/red wire leading to the remote control to the S or START terminal of the switch.

7B. *Colored wires leading to the switch*—Connect each wire to its corresponding instrument harness or remote control wire.

8. Place the lockwasher (if so equipped) onto the threaded shaft of the switch. Place the ignition switch into the dash with the drain hole(s) (**Figure 22**) facing down. Securely tighten the retaining nut (**Figure 20**).

## IGNITION SYSTEM

### EST Ignition System

EST ignition is a battery powered, transistorized system and is used on all 3.0, 7.4 and 8.2 L models.

EST ignition also used on earlier 4.3, 5.0 and 5.7 liter models (serial No. 0L339999-prior) with electronic fuel injection. All EST systems use an epoxy coated coil (**Figure 23**) with plug type wire connectors.

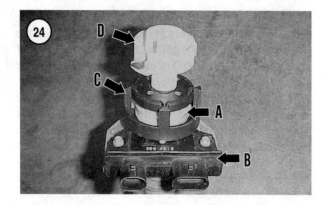

The EST distributor houses the pickup coil (A, **Figure 24**), ignition module (B), poles (C), rotor (D) and shaft. The number of poles on the rotor shaft match the number of cylinders in the engine.

The major components of this system (**Figure 25**) include the distributor, ignition coil, spark plugs and wires.

### Operation

When the ignition switch is ON, battery voltage is applied to the red wire attached to the ignition coil (**Figure 23**). A circuit inside the ignition coil provides battery voltage to the pink wire leading to the ignition module. The pink wire provides the current to operate the ignition module.

The camshaft driven rotor in the distributor rotates at one-half crankshaft speed. As it rotates, magnetic poles on the rotor shaft and pickup coil (C, **Figure 24**) align and misalign. When they are aligned, a magnetic field passes through the pickup coil and creates an electric pulse. This pulse is directed to the timing circuit inside the module.

The timing circuit modifies the pulse and directs it to a transistor in the module. The transistor functions as a switch to control current flow through the primary winding of the ignition coil.

The transistor switches ON when the pulse flows from the timing circuits and switches OFF when the pulse ceases. When switched on, the transistor provides a connection to ground for the ignition coil; this allows battery current to flow through the primary winding and create a magnetic field.

When switched off, the transistor interrupts the ground, which prevents battery current from flowing and causes the magnetic field to collapse. The collapsing magnetic field passes through the secondary winding of the coil inducing very high voltage current in this winding. This current flows through the high tension coil wire to the distributor rotor (D, **Figure 24**). The rotor directs the cur-

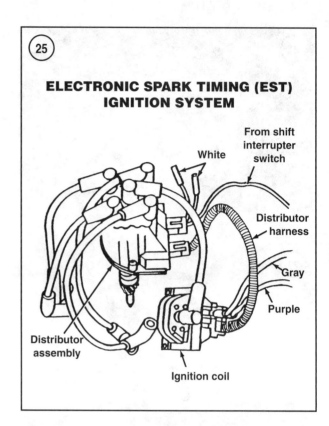

rent to the distributor cap terminal for the individual spark plug. High tension wires connect the cap terminals to the spark plugs. The voltage is high enough to jump the spark plug gap under normal operating conditions.

The shift interrupt switch used on 3.0L models connects to the white/green wire leading to the distributor. The switch activates only when shifting out of forward or reverse gears. When activated the switch directs battery current (using this wire) to the module. The module momentarily interrupts the ignition system, reducing the load on the gears for easier shifting into neutral. Under normal circumstances, the switch deactivates before the engine stalls.

**3**

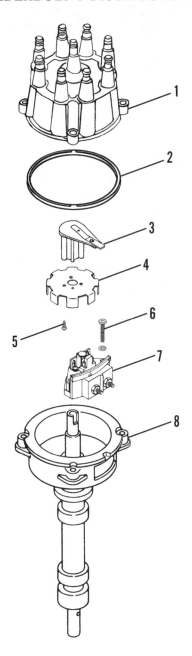

**THUNDERBOLT V DISTRIBUTOR**

1. Distributor cap
2. Gasket
3. Rotor
4. Sensor wheel
5. Screw (3)
6. Screw and washer (2)
7. Sensor
8. Distributor body

On Alpha One models equipped with electronic fuel injection (EFI), the shift interrupt switch connects in series with the white wire between the electronic control module (ECM) and ignition module. When shifting out of gear, the switch activates and opens the circuit and momentarily interrupts the ignition. When deactivated, the switch closes and the ECM resumes control of the ignition system.

The fuel air mixture in the cylinder must ignite and burn at a precise time to push the piston down during the power stroke. Since fuel burns at a relatively constant rate, spark must occur earlier with increased engine speed. Ideally, the pressure from the burning fuel should peak as the piston starts moving downward. This provides the maximum push on the piston and the maximum power output. If the spark is not advanced, the pressure peaks after the piston starts moving downward and power output decreases.

The timing advance circuit in the module automatically advances the ignition timing in proportion to the engine speed. This ignition system does not provide engine overspeed protection. However, the engine control module (used on EFI models) limits engine speed by shutting off the fuel injectors at a pre-determined engine speed. Refer to **Table 4** for maximum engine speed and overspeed activation specifications.

On EFI engines, the ECM computes the optimum amount of spark advance for the given operating conditions and adjusts the timing accordingly. The ECM timing circuit essentially overrides the timing circuit in the ignition module. The timing control circuit in the ignition module assumes control of the ignition timing should a fault occur in the ECM or the connecting wiring.

**Thunderbolt V Ignition System**

Thunderbolt V is a battery-powered, transistorized ignition system. Thunderbolt V is used on 1998-2004 carburetor-equipped 4.3L, 5.0L, 5.7L models and 1999-2001 4.3L, 5.0L and 5.7L models with electronic fuel injection. The system consists of the distributor, ignition module (carbureted engines) or ECM (EFI engines), ignition coil, spark plugs, spark plug wires and related circuitry. The ignition coil on Thunderbolt V ignition uses ring-type connectors and resembles a typical automotive ignition coil (**Figure 26**). The distributor (**Figure 27**) includes the sensor, sensor wheel and rotor. The number of openings in the sensor wheel matches the number of cylinders in the engine.

*Operation (carburetor models)*

When the ignition key switch is turned ON, battery voltage is applied to the purple wire connected to the ignition coil (**Figure 26**) and the ignition module (A, **Figure 28**). A circuit within the ignition coil provides battery voltage to a distributor sensor via the white/red wire. Current flowing through a coil winding in the sensor creates a magnetic field on one side of the sensor. A second coil is positioned on the other side of the sensor. The magnetic field produced from the first coil induces current in the second. The teeth of the sensor wheel pass between the coils with engine rotation to repeatedly block and open the field. This creates the signal to trigger the ignition system.

The rotor in the distributor rotates at one-half crankshaft speed. As the sensor wheel opens the field, the current generated in the second coil is directed via the white/green wire to the ignition module. The module completes the circuit to ground for the ignition coil via the gray wire. A strong magnetic field forms in the primary winding of the coil. As the sensor wheel closes the field, the current in the second sensor coil ceases. The ignition module in turn opens the ground circuit for the ignition coil. This causes the magnetic field in the ignition coil to collapse. The collapsing field passes through the secondary coil winding, creating high voltage electrical current. This current is directed via the coil wire to the center post on the distributor and to the rotor. The rotor directs the current to the distributor cap terminal for the individual spark plugs. High tension wires connect the cap terminals to the spark plugs. The voltage is high enough to jump the spark plug gap under normal operating conditions.

The shift interrupt switch on Alpha models connects to the white/green wire leading to the distributor. The switch activates only when shifting out of forward or reverse gears. When activated, this switch connects the lead to engine ground. When the white/green wire is grounded the ignition module switches off the ignition system. This reduces the load on the gears for easier shifting into neutral gear. Under normal circumstances, the switch deactivates before the engine stalls.

The fuel air mixture in the cylinder must ignite and burn at a precise time to push the piston down during the power stroke. Since fuel burns at a relatively constant rate, spark must occur earlier with increased engine speed. Ideally, the pressure formed from the burning fuel peaks as the piston starts moving downward. This provides the maximum push on the piston and the maximum power output. If the spark is not advanced, the pressure peaks after the piston starts moving downward and power output decreases.

The timing circuit in the module automatically advances the ignition timing with increased engine speed. If operated at a relatively constant speed for more than a few seconds, the timing circuit automatically advances the timing a few more degrees. The additional timing advance can enhance cruising speed fuel economy. The additional

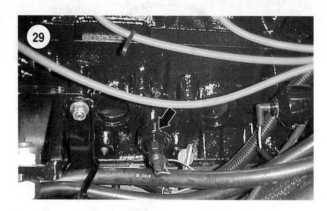

timing advance is removed if the engine speed drops, exceeds 4000 rpm or if the engine overheats.

In addition, an idle stabilizer circuit helps to prevent stalling and improve idle smoothness. The idle stabilizer advances or retards the ignition timing to help maintain the desired idle speed. For this reason, the idle stabilizer must be disabled before adjusting the carburetor or ignition timing (Chapter Six).

This system uses an overspeed protection system. The module interrupts the ignition if the engine exceeds the limit. Ignition resumes when the engine speed drops below the limit. Refer to **Table 4** for maximum engine speed and overspeed activation specifications.

A knock control system is used on 5.7L models. The knock sensor (**Figure 29**) mounts to the starboard side of the cylinder block. Engine noise (vibration) traveling through the cooling water is directed to the sensor where it creates a small electrical pulse. This pulse is directed via the blue wire to the knock sensor module (B, **Figure 28**). The module mounts next to and is connected to the ignition module (A, **Figure 28**). The module interprets the electrical pulses from the sensor to determine if detonation is present. If detonation is detected, the module retards the ignition timing until the detonation stops.

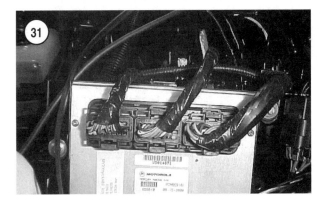

### Operation (EFI models)

When the ignition key switch is turned ON, battery voltage is applied to the purple and pink wires leading to the system relay. The relay switches on and delivers battery current to the ignition coil (**Figure 26**), sensor (7, **Figure 27**) and the ECM (**Figure 30**).

Current flowing through a coil winding in the sensor creates a magnetic field on one side of the sensor. A second coil is positioned on the other side of the sensor. The magnetic field produced by the first coil induces current in the other. As the engine rotates, the teeth of the sensor wheel pass between the coils to repeatedly block and open the field. This creates the signal to trigger the ignition system.

The camshaft-driven rotor in the distributor rotates at one-half crankshaft speed. As the sensor wheel opens the field, the current generated in the second coil is directed via the white/green and purple/white wires to the ECM (**Figure 30**). The module completes the circuit to ground for the ignition coil via the white wire. A strong magnetic field forms in the primary winding of the coil. As the sensor wheel closes the field, the electrical current in the second sensor coil ceases. The ECM in turn opens the ground circuit in the ignition coil, causing the magnetic field in the ignition coil to collapse. The collapsing field passes

through the secondary coil winding, forming high voltage current. The voltage is high enough to jump the spark plug gap under normal operating conditions. This current is directed via the coil wire to the center post on the distributor and to the rotor. The rotor directs the current to the distributor cap terminal for the individual spark plug. High tension wires connect the cap terminals to the spark plugs.

The shift interrupt switch used on Alpha models connects to the white wire leading to the ECM. The switch activates only when shifting out of forward or reverse gears. When activated, this switch connects the lead to engine ground. When the white/green wire is grounded, the ECM switches off the ignition system. This reduces the load on the gears for easier shifting into neutral. Under normal circumstances, the switch deactivates before the engine stalls.

The knock sensor (**Figure 29**) is mounted to the starboard side of the cylinder block. Engine noise (vibration) traveling through the cooling water is directed to the sensor where it creates a small electrical pulse. This pulse is directed via the blue wire to the ECM. The ECM interprets the electrical pulses from the sensor to determine whether detonation is present. If so, the ECM slows the ignition timing until the detonation stops.

The fuel/air mixture in the cylinder must ignite and burn at a precise time to push the piston down during the power stroke. Since fuel burns at a relatively constant rate, spark must occur earlier with increased engine speed. Ideally, the pressure formed from the burning fuel peaks as the piston starts moving downward. This provides the maximum push on the piston and the maximum power output. If the spark is not advanced, the pressure peaks after the piston starts moving downward and power output decreases.

The timing circuit in the ECM automatically provides the optimum timing advance for the given load and operating conditions.

The idle stabilizer advances or retards the ignition timing to help maintain the desired idle speed. For this reason, the idle stabilizer must be disabled before adjusting the carburetor or ignition timing (Chapter Six).

This system incorporates an overspeed protection system. The module interrupts the fuel injector operation if the engine speed exceeds the limit. The injectors resume operation as the engine speed drops below the limit. Refer to **Table 4** for maximum engine speed and overspeed activation specifications.

### Distributorless Ignition System

A distributorless ignition system is used on 496 Mag and 496 Mag HO models. The system includes the ECM (**Figure 31**), camshaft position sensor (**Figure 32**), crankshaft position sensor and eight ignition coils (**Figure 33**).

This is a solid state system that requires no adjustment, and except for the spark plugs, requires no maintenance.

The camshaft position sensor mounts to the timing chain cover. An electrical pulse is generated as a raised section on the timing gear sprocket passes near the sensor. This pulse is directed to the ECM. The ECM uses this pulse to determine which cylinder is approaching its compression stroke.

The crankshaft position sensor mounts to the rear of the cylinder block. Electrical pulses are generated as multiple protrusions on the crankshaft pass near the sensor. These pulses are directed to the ECM. The ECM uses the pulses to determine the piston position relative to the firing position.

When the ignition switch is ON, battery voltage is applied to the purple and pink wires leading to the system relay. The relay switches on and delivers battery current to the ignition coils and the ECM. A magnetic field forms as electric current flows through the primary coil winding.

The ECM uses input from the camshaft and crankshaft position sensors to determine the exact piston position for each cylinder. As the piston moves up on the compression stroke, the ECM opens the ground circuit for the corresponding ignition coil, causing the magnetic field in the ignition coil to collapse. The collapsing field passes through the secondary coil winding, creating high voltage electrical current. The voltage is high enough to jump the spark plug gap under normal operating conditions. This current flows through the high tension wire to the corresponding spark plug.

The fuel/air mixture in the cylinder must ignite and burn at a precise time to push the piston down during the power stroke. Since fuel burns at a relatively constant rate, spark must occur earlier with increased engine speed. Ideally, the pressure formed from the burning fuel peaks as the piston starts moving downward. This provides the maximum push on the piston and the maximum power output. If the spark is not advanced, the pressure peaks after the piston starts moving downward and power output decreases.

The timing circuit in the ECM automatically provides the optimum timing advance for the given load and operating conditions.

The idle stabilizer circuit advances or retards the ignition timing to help maintain the desired idle speed.

This system incorporates an overspeed protection system. The module interrupts the fuel injector operation if the engine speed exceeds a predetermined limit. The injectors resume operation as the engine speed drops below the limit. Refer to **Table 4** for maximum engine speed and overspeed activation specifications

## SPARK TEST

This test checks for ignition system output at the ignition coil and the spark plug connectors. A spark tester (**Figure 34**) is required for this procedure.

1. Disconnect the high tension coil lead from the distributor cap. On 496 Mag and 496 Mag HO models, disconnect the high tension lead from one of the spark plugs.

2. Connect the ground lead of the spark tester to a suitable engine ground such as a cylinder head bolt.

3. Connect the high tension coil lead or spark plug wire to the appropriate terminal on the spark tester. On adjustable spark testers, adjust the gap to approximately 1/4 in. (6.35 mm).

4. Shift the engine into neutral. Place the tester away from the spark plug openings.

5. Observe the spark tester while cranking the engine. The presence of a strong blue spark at the spark tester while cranking indicates the ignition system is producing output at the coil. If the spark is weak or absent, test the ignition system as described in this chapter.

6. On 496 Mag and 496 Mag HO models, reconnect the spark plug lead. Repeat steps 1-5 for each of the remaining coils.

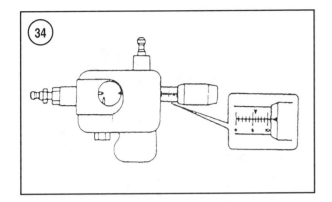

**3**

7. On all models except 496 Mag and 496 Mag HO, test for spark at the spark plug lead as follows:

   a. Reconnect the high tension coil lead to the distributor cap.

   b. Connect the ground lead of the spark tester to a suitable engine ground such as a cylinder head bolt.

   c. Connect one of the spark plug leads to the appropriate terminal on the spark tester. On adjustable spark testers adjust the gap to approximately 1/4 in. (6.35 mm).

   d. Observe the spark gap tester while cranking the engine. The presence of a strong blue spark at the spark gap tester while cranking indicates the ignition system is producing output to that cylinder.

   e. Reconnect the spark plug lead and repeat step 6 for the remaining cylinders.

   f. Check for a faulty rotor, distributor cap or spark plug lead if spark is present at the coil but missing or weak at any or all of the spark plug leads.

## Testing the Ignition System

Perform this test if a spark test reveals no spark at the ignition coil. This test requires a multimeter and a 12-volt test light. Use a scan tool, harness and test cartridge to test

Models 496 Mag and 496 Mag HO. Purchase the scan tool from a MerCruiser dealership.

Refer to the appropriate wire diagram at the end of the manual to locate the ignition system wires and connection points.

*WARNING*
*Use extreme caution when working around batteries. Batteries produce hydrogen gas that can explode and result in severe injury or death. Never make the final connection of a circuit to the battery as an arc may occur and lead to fire or explosion.*

### 3.0L models

1. Remove the distributor cap and ground the high tension coil wire. Observe the rotor while cranking the engine. The rotor must rotate. If it does not, the distributor gear is stripped and must be replaced *(see Chapter Ten)*. If the rotor operates as specified, install the cap and reconnect the high tension coil wire.

2. Place the lanyard switch in the RUN position. Turn the ignition switch to the RUN position. The dash gauges must turn on. Otherwise check for a blown fuse, tripped circuit breaker or loose wire connections. Correct the wiring and reset or replace the fuse to restore ignition system operation. Test the ignition switch as described in this chapter if the problem persists.

3. Observe the tachometer while cranking the engines. A 200 rpm or higher reading indicates the ignition module and pickup coil are operating correctly, and a faulty coil or wire is probably causing the no spark condition. Repair the wire or replace the coil as described in Chapter Ten.

4. Temporarily disconnect the white/green wire from the interrupt switch and repeat step 3. Replace the interrupt switch if the ignition system now operates. Reconnect the white/green wire.

5. Disconnect the wire harness connectors (A and B, **Figure 35**) from the ignition coil. Connect the ground lead of a test light to a suitable engine ground. Turn the ignition key switch to the RUN position. Touch the light probe to the purple wire terminal in the gray harness connector (A, **Figure 35**). The light must illuminate. Otherwise check for loose connections, damaged wiring, or a blown starter fuse.

6. Reconnect the gray harness connector to the coil. Do not connect the black harness connector (B, **Figure 35**). Turn the ignition switch to the RUN position. Touch the light probe to each of the two open terminals in the ignition coil. The light must illuminate when each terminal is

touched. Otherwise the coil is defective and must be replaced.

7. Reconnect the black and gray wire harness connectors onto the ignition coil. Turn the ignition switch to the RUN position. Disconnect the two-wire harness connector from the distributor. This harness contains a brown and pink wire. Touch the light probe to each of the two terminals in the distributor end of the harness. The light must illuminate as each terminal is touched. Otherwise replace the ignition coil-to-distributor harness as described in Chapter Ten.

8. Remove the distributor cap to access the pickup coil connector (**Figure 36**). Pull on the locking tab and carefully disconnect the coil leads from the ignition module. Calibrate the multimeter to the Rx1 scale. Touch one of the test leads to the metal distributor housing. Touch the other test lead to the white then green wire terminals. The meter must indicate no continuity when touching either wire terminal. Otherwise the pickup coil is shorted to ground and must be replaced ( Chapter Ten).

9. Calibrate the multimeter on the Rx100 scale. Connect one test lead to the white wire terminal and the other to the green wire terminal. The multimeter must indicate 500-1500 ohms. If not, the pickup coil is open or shorted internally and must be replaced. Reconnect the pickup coil connector and install the distributor cap.

10. Test for spark at the coil with the tachometer temporarily disconnected. Replace the tachometer if spark returns with the tachometer disconnected.

11. Replace the ignition module (Chapter Ten) if no spark is present at the coil but all over other components test as specified.

12. Replace the ignition coil if spark does not return after replacing the module.

### V6 and V8 EFI models (EST ignition)

1. Remove the distributor cap and ground the high tension coil wire. Observe the rotor while cranking the engine. The rotor must rotate. If not, the distributor gear is stripped and must be replaced as described in Chapter Ten. If the rotor turns, install the cap and reconnect the high tension coil wire.

2. Place the lanyard switch in the RUN position. Turn the ignition switch to the ON position. The dash gauges must turn on and the warning horn must sound for a few seconds. Otherwise check for a blown fuse, tripped circuit breaker or loose wire connections. Test the ignition switch as described in this chapter if the wiring and fuses test correctly. Test the system relay as described in this chapter if the gauges operate but the warning horn does not sound. Replace blown fuses, reset the circuit breaker or repair

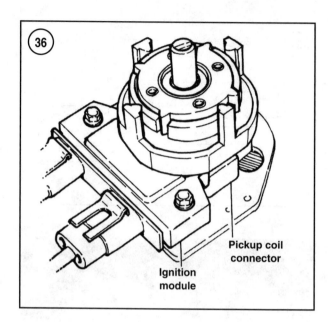

**Pickup coil connector**

**Ignition module**

faulty wiring until the gauges and horn perform as described.

3. Observe the tachometer while cranking the engines. A 200 rpm or higher reading indicates the ignition module and pickup coil are operating correctly. Inspect and repair the ignition coil wiring or replace the coil to restore ignition system operation.

4. Connect the ground lead of a test light to a suitable engine ground. Disconnect the gray and black harness connectors from the ignition coil. Turn the ignition switch to RUN. Touch the light probe to the purple wire terminal in the gray harness connector (A, **Figure 35**). The light must illuminate. Otherwise check for loose connections, damaged wiring or a faulty system relay. Test the relay as described in this chapter.

5. Reconnect the gray harness connector to the coil. Do not connect the black harness connector (B, **Figure 35**). Turn the ignition switch to the RUN position. Touch the light probe to each of the two open terminals in the ignition coil. The light must illuminate when either terminal is touched. Otherwise the coil is defective and must be replaced.

6. Reconnect the black and gray wire harness connectors to the ignition coil. Turn the ignition switch to the RUN position. Disconnect the two pin harness connector from the distributor. This harness contains a brown and pink wire. Connect the ground lead of a test light to a suitable engine ground. Touch the light probe to each of the two terminals in the distributor end of the harness. The light must illuminate as each terminal is touched. Otherwise replace the ignition coil-to-distributor harness to restore ignition system operation.

7. Turn the ignition key switch to RUN. Remove the distributor cap to access the pickup coil connector (**Figure 36**). Pull on the locking tab and carefully disconnect the coil leads from the ignition module. Calibrate the multimeter on the R×1 scale. Touch one of the test leads to the metal distributor housing. Touch the other test lead to the white, then the green wire terminals. The meter must indicate no continuity when touching either wire terminal. If continuity is noted, the pickup coil is shorted to ground and must be replaced, as described in Chapter Ten.

8. Calibrate the multimeter on the R×100 scale. Connect one test lead to the white wire terminal and the other to the green wire terminal. The multimeter must indicate 500-1500 ohms. If not, the pickup coil must be replaced. Reconnect the pickup coil connector and install the distributor cap.

9. Test for spark at the coil (as described in this chapter) with the tachometer temporarily disconnected. Replace the tachometer if spark returns.

10. Replace the ignition module (Chapter Ten) if no spark is present at the coil and all other components operate correctly.

11. Replace the ignition coil if spark does not return with a new module.

### V6 and V8 carbureted models

1. Remove the distributor cap and ground the high tension coil wire. Observe the rotor while cranking the engine. If the rotor does not turn, the distributor gear is stripped and must be replaced as described in Chapter Ten. If the rotor turns, install the cap and reconnect the high tension coil wire.

2. Place the lanyard switch in the RUN position. Turn the ignition switch to RUN. The dash gauges must turn on and the warning horn must sound for a few seconds. Otherwise check for a blown fuse, tripped circuit breaker or loose wire connection. Test the ignition switch as described in this chapter if the wiring and fuses check or test correctly. Test the system relay as described in this chapter if the gauges turn on but the warning horn does not sound. Replace faulty components or repair faulty wiring until the gauges and horn perform as described.

3. Observe the tachometer while cranking the engines. A 200 rpm or higher reading indicates the ignition module and pickup coils are operating correctly. Inspect and repair the ignition coil wiring or replace the coil to restore ignition system operation.

4. On Alpha models, disconnect the white/green wire from the interrupt switch and repeat Step 3. Replace the interrupt switch if the ignition system now operates. Reconnect the white/green wire.

5. Test for spark at the coil as described in this chapter with the tachometer temporarily disconnected. Replace the tachometer if spark returns.

6. Connect the ground lead of a test light to a suitable engine ground. Turn the ignition switch to the RUN position. Touch the light probe to the purple wire terminal on the ignition coil (**Figure 26**). The light must illuminate. Otherwise check the for loose connections, blown fuses or a tripped circuit breaker, damaged wiring or a faulty engine harness plug.

7. Disconnect the white/red and white/green wires from the distributor. Connect the negative voltmeter lead to a suitable engine ground. Connect the positive meter lead to the disconnected white/red wire. Do not connect the test lead to the sensor wire terminals. Turn the ignition key switch to the ON position. The meter must indicate battery voltage. Otherwise check for loose or corroded connections, or faulty wiring. Replace the ignition module if no faults are found in the wiring or terminals.

8. Turn the ignition switch to the OFF position. Calibrate a multimeter to the R×10 scale. Connect the positive ohmmeter lead to the red/white wire and the negative meter lead to the white/green distributor wire. The meter must read 100 ohms or higher. Otherwise replace the ignition sensor as described in Chapter Ten.

9. Reconnect the white/red wire to the distributor. Connect a spark tester to the ignition coil as described in this chapter. Connect a jumper lead onto a suitable engine ground. Turn the ignition switch to the ON position. Observe the spark gap tester while tapping the jumper against the white/green wire harness lead. Do not touch the jumper to the white/green distributor lead. The connection must be made and broken several times a second for accurate testing. Replace the ignition sensor as described in Chapter Ten if spark occurs during this test.

10. If a no spark condition persists, replace the ignition coil and repeat Step 9. Replace the ignition module if spark does not return after replacing the ignition coil. Reconnect the white/green wire to the distributor wiring.

### V6 and V8 EFI models (Thunderbolt V ignition)

1. Remove the distributor cap and ground the high tension coil wire. Observe the rotor while cranking the engine. If the rotor does not turn, the distributor gear is stripped and must be replaced (Chapter Ten). If the rotor turns, install the cap and reconnect the high tension coil wire.

2. Place the lanyard switch in the RUN position. Turn the ignition switch to the RUN position. The dash gauges must turn on and the warning horn must sound for a few seconds. Otherwise check for a blown fuse, tripped circuit

breaker or loose wire connections. Test the ignition switch as described in this chapter if the wiring and fuses check or test correctly. Test the system relay as described in this chapter if the gauges operate but the warning horn does not sound. Replace blown fuses, reset the circuit breaker or repair faulty wiring until the gauges and horn perform as described

3. Observe the tachometer while cranking the engines. A 200 rpm or higher reading indicates the ignition sensor, coil and ECM are operating correctly. Inspect and repair the ignition coil wiring or replace the coil to restore ignition system operation.

4. On Alpha models, disconnect the white wire from the interrupt switch and repeat step 3. Replace the interrupt switch if the ignition system now operates. Reconnect the white wire.

5. Test for spark at the coil as described in this chapter with the tachometer temporarily disconnected. Replace the tachometer if spark returns.

6. Connect the ground lead of a test light to a suitable engine ground. Turn the ignition switch to the RUN position. Touch the light probe to the red wire terminal on the ignition coil (**Figure 26**). The light must illuminate. Otherwise check the for loose connections, blown fuses or tripped circuit breakers, damaged wiring or a faulty engine harness plug. Test the system relay as described in this chapter if the wiring, fuse and harness plug test or check correctly.

7. Disconnect the purple/white and pink wires from the distributor. Connect the negative voltmeter lead to a suitable engine ground. Connect the positive meter lead to the disconnected pink wire. Turn the ignition key switch to the ON position. The meter must indicate battery voltage. If not, check for dirty wire terminals, a blown fuse or faulty wiring. Test the system relay as described in this chapter if the wiring, fuse and harness plug test correctly.

8. Turn the ignition key switch to the OFF position. Calibrate a multimeter to the R×10 scale. Connect the positive multimeter lead to the red/white wire and the negative meter lead to the white/green wire. The meter must read 100 ohms or higher. Otherwise replace the ignition sensor as described in Chapter Ten.

9. Reconnect the pink wire to the white/red distributor wire. Connect a spark tester to the ignition coil as described in this chapter under *Spark Test*. Connect a jumper lead to a suitable engine ground. Turn the ignition switch to the ON position. Observe the spark tester while lightly tapping the jumper against the purple/white wire harness lead. Do not touch the jumper to the white/green distributor lead. The connection must be made and broken several times a second for accurate testing. Replace the ignition sensor as described in Chapter Ten if spark occurs during

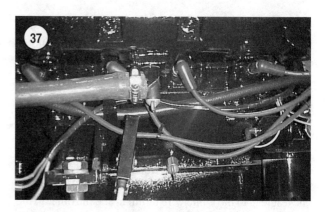

this test. Reconnect the purple/white wire to the green/white distributor wire.

10. If a no-spark condition persists, replace the ignition coil and repeat step 9.

11. If the spark does not return with the new coil, inspect all wires and terminals for defects. Replace the ECM to restore ignition operation only after inspecting and correcting all wiring and replacing all other ignition system components. Failure of the ECM is extremely rare and replacement rarely corrects the problem.

### *496 Mag and 496 Mag HO models*

Complete test instructions for this ignition system were not available at the time of printing. However, the following procedures will identify the cause of most ignition system malfunctions.

1. Place the lanyard switch in the RUN position. Turn the ignition key switch to the RUN position. The dash gauges must turn on and the warning horn must sound for a few seconds. Otherwise check for a blown fuse, tripped circuit breaker or loose wire connections. If the fuses and wire harness test correctly, test the ignition switch as described in this chapter. Test the system relay as described in this chapter if the gauges operate but the warning horn does not sound. Replace blown fuses, reset the circuit breaker or repair faulty wiring until the gauges and horn perform as described.

2. Observe the tachometer while cranking the engines. A 200 rpm or higher reading indicates the ECM is operating correctly and a faulty coil or ignition coil wiring is causing the no spark condition. Inspect and repair the ignition coil wiring or replace the coil.

3. Check for spark at the coil as described in this chapter.

4A. *No spark at any of the coils*—Connect a scan tool (Mercury part No. 91-823686A2) to the engine following the included instruction booklet. Following the instructions, scan the engine to determine if the camshaft or

crankshaft position sensor is operating correctly. Replace the faulty component as described in Chapter Eight.

4B. *Spark on some cylinders*—Switch the coil from a cylinder without spark with the coil from a cylinder with spark. If the malfunctioning cylinder now has spark, replace the defective coil. If the cylinder still does not have spark, check for loose or corroded connections or a defective wire or spark plug lead.

5. Replace the ECM to restore ignition operation only after inspecting and correcting all wiring and replacing all other ignition system components. Failure of the ECM is extremely rare and replacement rarely corrects the problem.

## KNOCK CONTROL TEST

This test must be performed under actual running conditions. The test requires an analog multimeter, timing light and a small metal hammer. A scan tool is required if testing EFI models.

### Carburetor Models

1. Connect the timing light pickup to the No. 1 cylinder spark plug lead (**Figure 37**). The No. 1 cylinder is located on the port side and closest to the front of the engine. Start the engine and allow it to reach normal operating temperature.

2. Select the 20 or 40 VDC scale on the multimeter.

3. Locate the purple/white wire between the carburetor and the starboard side rocker arm cover. Remove the plug from the wire (**Figure 38**). Connect the positive voltmeter lead to the purple/white wire terminal. Connect the negative meter lead to a suitable engine ground.

4. Direct the timing light to the timing pointer. The timing pointer is located on the port side of the timing chain cover.

5. Have an assistant operate the boat. Advance the throttle until the engine reaches approximately 3000 rpm. The meter must indicate 8-10 VDC. Otherwise check for faulty wiring, or loose or corroded terminals. Replace the knock sensor module (**Figure 28**) if the wiring and terminals are in good condition.

6. Observe the meter while lightly tapping the cylinder block near the knock sensor (**Figure 29**). You must tap the block several times per second for accurate testing. The voltage reading on the meter must drop while the block is being tapped.

7. Observe the ignition timing while tapping on the block as described in step 6. The timing must retard by several degrees while tapping on the block.

8. Replace the knock sensor if the voltage does not drop or the timing does not retard as described in step 6 and step 7. Knock sensor replacement procedure is described in Chapter Ten.

9. Repeat the test procedure with the replacement knock sensor. Replace the knock sensor module (Chapter Ten) if incorrect test results persist.

### EFI Models

This procedure requires a scan tool (Mercury part No. 91-823686A2) or equivalent and a small metal hammer. Refer to *Electronic Fuel Injection* in this chapter to identify the type of ECM used on the engine.

1. Start the engine and run until it reaches normal operating temperature.

2. Connect a scan tool to the engine following the included instruction booklet. Follow the instructions and scroll to the knock retard function on the tool.

3. Have an assistant operate the boat. Advance the throttle until the engine reaches approximately 3000 rpm.

4. Observe the scan tool while lightly tapping the cylinder block near the knock sensor (**Figure 29**). You must tap the block several times per second for accurate testing. The scan tool must indicate knock retard while the cylinder block is being tapped. On 7.4 MPI models, repeat the test while tapping next to each knock sensor. The scan tool must indicate knock retard when tapping next to each sensor.

5. Replace the knock sensor(s) if the timing fails to retard as described.

6. If the timing fails to retard with a replacement knock sensor, perform the following:

   a. *MEFI 2 ECM*—Replace the knock sensor module as described in Chapter Ten. Repeat the test procedure.

   b. *MEFI 3 ECM or PCM 555 ECM*—Thoroughly inspect the knock sensor wiring and terminals before

replacing the ECM. Failure of the ECM is extremely rare and replacement rarely corrects the problem.

## SHIFT INTERRUPT SWITCH TEST

A shift interrupt switch (A, **Figure 39**) is used only on engines equipped with an Alpha drive unit. Refer to *Electronic Fuel Injection* in this chapter to identify the type of ECM used on the engine.

All carburetor-equipped engines and EFI models with a MEFI 3 type ECM use a switch that electrically closes when activated. All EFI models with a MEFI 2 type ECM use a switch that electrically opens when activated.

> *WARNING*
> *Use extreme caution when working around batteries. Batteries produce hydrogen gas that can explode and result in severe injury or death. Never make the final connection of a circuit to the battery as an arc may occur and lead to fire or explosion.*

1. Disconnect the battery. Disconnect the shift interrupt switch leads from the engine wire harness.
2. Calibrate an ohmmeter on the R×1 scale. Connect the meter test leads to the interrupt switch leads. Note the meter reading.
   a. *Carburetor or MEFI 3 type ECM*—The meter must read no continuity.
   b. *MEFI 2 type ECM*—The meter must read continuity.
3. With the meter test lead connected as described in Step 2, push on the V-block (B, **Figure 39**) to activate the switch. Note the meter reading.
   a. *Carburetor or MEFI 3 type ECM*—The meter must read continuity.
   b. *MEFI 2 type ECM*—The meter must read no continuity.

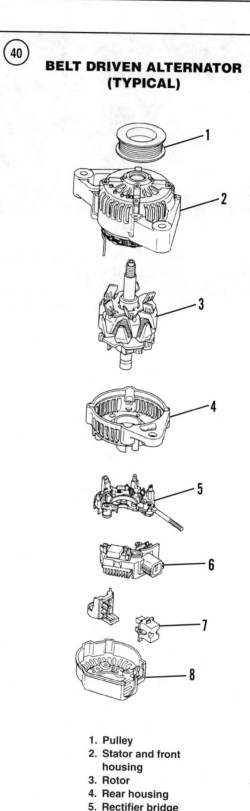

**BELT DRIVEN ALTERNATOR (TYPICAL)**

1. Pulley
2. Stator and front housing
3. Rotor
4. Rear housing
5. Rectifier bridge
6. Voltage regulator
7. Brushes
8. Shield

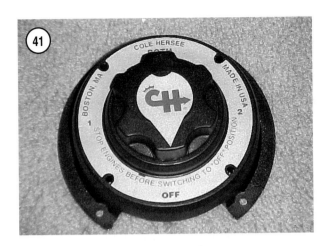

4. Connect the interrupt switch leads to the harness leads.

5. Replace the shift interrupt switch as described in Chapter Ten if it fails to perform as described. Connect the battery cables.

## BATTERY CHARGING SYSTEM

All models use an internally-regulated belt-driven alternator. The major components of the alternator (**Figure 40** typical) are the rotor, stator brushes, rectifier bridge and the regulator. All components of the charging system (except the wiring) are enclosed within the alternator housing.

The pulleys and drive belt spin the rotor (3, **Figure 40**) at approximately twice the engine speed. The brushes (7, **Figure 40**) maintain contact with the slip rings on the rotor.

When the ignition switch is turned ON, battery voltage is supplied to the alternator via the purple engine harness wire. This current passes through the voltage regulator to the positive brush lead. The current flows through the rotor winding and back to ground through the negative brush lead and the voltage regulator. Current flowing through the rotor winding creates a magnetic field.

Alternating current forms as the spinning magnetic field passes through the stator windings. The alternating current is directed to the rectifier bridge where diodes convert it to direct current. The direct current flows from the alternator output terminal to the battery.

The voltage regulator (6, **Figure 40**) controls the alternator output by controlling the amount of current flowing through the rotor winding. The regulator senses battery voltage via the red wire connecting the alternator to the engine wire harness. If the voltage drops below a predetermined value, the regulator allows additional current flow through the rotor. This increases the strength of the

magnetic field, thereby increasing alternator output. If the voltage exceeds a predetermined value, the regulator restricts current flow through the rotor. This decreases the strength of the magnetic field, thereby decreasing alternator output.

A series of diodes in the rectifier bridge directs some of the output current back to the rotor to sustain the magnetic field. This occurs when the engine speed exceeds approximately 1000 rpm. Once the alternator *energizes* it begins charging the battery and does not require current from the purple wire. The energized alternator produces output at all engine speeds. If not energized, the alternator essentially discharges the battery.

A charging system malfunction generally causes the battery to be undercharged. Modern boats are equipped with numerous electric accessories such as trolling motors, depth finders, radios and lighting. Frequently, the current required to operate these accessories exceeds the output of the charging system.

Monitor the voltmeter with accessories switched on and off. A voltage reading of 12.5 or less with only the accessories on indicates the electrical load exceeds the charging system output. Install an auxiliary battery and switch device (**Figure 41**) to prevent a discharged cranking battery. Wire the accessories to draw from the auxiliary battery.

> *WARNING*
> *Use extreme caution when working around batteries. Batteries produce hydrogen gas that can explode and result in severe injury or death. Never make the final connection of a circuit to the battery as an arc may occur and lead to fire or explosion.*

> *CAUTION*
> *Charging system damage will occur if the battery cables(s) or any charging system wires are disconnected while the engine is running. Make sure the battery-switching device is the type that does not break the circuit. Otherwise operate the switch only when the engine is not running.*

> *CAUTION*
> *Never run the engine without providing cooling water. Use either a test tank or flush/test device. Always remove the propeller before running the engine on a flush/test device.*

### Alternator Output Test

This procedure requires a digital multimeter.

1. Fully charge the battery as described in Chapter Ten.

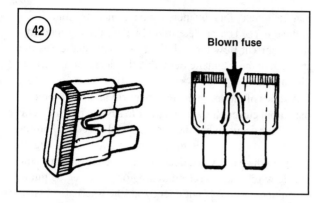

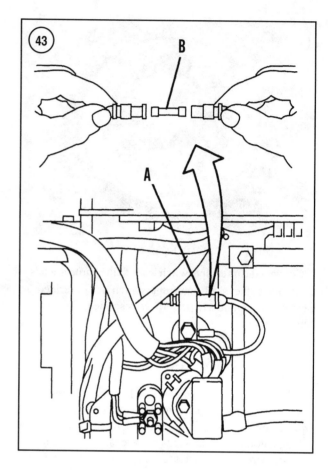

2. Check the external wiring as follows:
   a. Select the 20 VDC scale on the multimeter. Turn the ignition switch to the OFF position.
   b. Disconnect the red and purple engine harness leads from the alternator.
   c. Connect the negative voltmeter lead to an engine ground. Observe the meter while touching the positive lead to the red and purple harness terminals. The meter should indicate battery voltage on the red lead and 0 volt on the purple lead. Check for faulty wiring if voltage is not present at red wire. Check for a faulty ignition switch or wiring if voltage is present on the purple lead.
   d. Turn the ignition key switch to the ON position. Observe the meter while touching the positive lead to the purple wire terminal. The meter must indicate battery voltage. Otherwise test the ignition switch and inspect the wiring.
   e. Turn the ignition key switch to the OFF position. Reconnect the red and purple lead to the alternator.
3. Check for alternator output as follows:
   a. Select the 20 VDC scale on the multimeter.
   b. Connect the positive voltmeter lead to the positive battery terminal. Connect the negative lead to the negative battery terminal.
   c. Turn off all electrical accessories.
   d. Start the engine and raise the engine speed to approximately 1200 rpm. The meter must indicate 12.6-14.2 VDC.
   e. *Voltage reading exceeds 14.2 volt*—The voltage regulator is faulty or the alternator is shorted internally.
   f. *Voltage reading is less than 12.6*—The alternator is not charging the battery.
   g. Replace the alternator (Chapter Ten) if it fails to perform as described.
4. Test the rectifier bridge diodes as follows:
   a. Select the 2 VAC scale on the meter.

   b. Connect the positive lead to the positive battery terminal. Connect the negative lead to the negative battery terminal.
   c. Start the engine and raise the engine speed to approximately 1200 rpm. The meter must indicate 0.25 volts or less.
   d. Replace the alternator if the voltage reading exceeds specification.
5. Test the charging circuit wiring as follows:
   a. Turn the engine OFF. Active the lanyard switch to prevent the engine from starting. Operate the starter motor for 15 seconds.
   b. Select the 2 VDC scale on the meter. Connect the positive lead to the alternator output (orange wire) terminal. Do not disconnect the orange wire. Connect the negative lead to the positive battery terminal.
   c. Start the engine and raise the engine speed to approximately 1200 rpm. The meter must indicate 0.5 volt or less. Otherwise check for dirty or loose connections at the battery positive terminal and the starter fuse.

**3**

## Fuse Test

A blown fuse (**Figure 42**) can usually be identified visually. However, a fuse can appear to be in good condition, but still not have continuity. Therefore, it is good practice to check the continuity of all fuses using an ohmmeter any time an electrical problem is encountered.

Three different types of fuses are used. They include:

a. *The glass tube fuse (B,* **Figure 43**). This type of fuse is commonly mounted on the trim pump and protects the trim switch circuits. The fuse fits in a cylindrical holder (A, **Figure 43**). The trim switch fuse has a 10 amp rating.

b. *The square fuse (***Figure 44**). This type of fuse is mounted to the trim pump or the starter motor. It protects the trim system, charging system or other electrical components. These typically have a 55, 90 or 110 amp rating.

c. *The plug-in fuse (***Figure 42**). This type of fuse fits into the harness fuse holder (**Figure 45**) . This type of fuse is used on EFI models to protect the injectors, fuel pump and ECM circuits. The amperage rating is stamped on the end of the fuse.

Refer to the wiring diagrams at the back of this manual to determine the number and location of fuses. If an electric system or component fails to operate, always test the fuses before testing the rest of the system.

*WARNING*
*Use extreme caution when working around batteries. Never smoke or allow sparks to occur around a battery. Batteries produce explosive hydrogen gas that can explode and result in injury or death. Never make the final connection of a circuit to the battery terminal as an arc may occur leading to fire or explosion.*

1. Disconnect both cables from the battery.

2A. *Glass tube fuse*—Carefully pull the fuse (B, **Figure 43**) from its cylindrical holder (A).

2B. *Square fuse*—Remove the fuse from the starter or trim pump as described in Chapter Ten.

2C. *Plug-in fuse*—Carefully pull the cover from the fuse holder (**Figure 45**). Grasp the back of the fuse and pull it out of the holder.

3. Connect the ohmmeter to each fuse terminal and note the meter reading. If the fuse is good, the ohmmeter will indicate continuity.

4. No continuity means the fuse has failed and must be replaced. Remember that a fuse failure is usually the result of a shorted or overloaded circuit. Inspect all engine and instrument wires for damaged insulation, chafing, loose

d. Connect the negative lead to the alternator ground (black wire) terminal. Do not disconnect the black wire. Connect the negative lead to the positive battery terminal.

e. Place the lanyard switch in the RUN position. Start the engine and raise the engine speed to approximately 1200 rpm. The meter must indicate 0.5 volt or less. Otherwise check for dirty or loose connections at the battery positive terminal and all engine ground wires.

## FUSES, CIRCUIT BREAKER AND WIRE HARNESS

Fuses and circuit breakers protect the wiring harness and electric components from damage if a circuit overloads or shorts to ground. Refer to the wire diagrams located at the end of the manual to determine fuse and circuit breaker usage for all models.

*WARNING*
*Never replace a fuse without thoroughly checking the wire harness for defects. Never install a fuse with a capacity greater than the original fuse.*

or corroded connections or other damage. Repair damaged wiring or poor connections before replacing the fuse.

5. Install the fuse and connect the battery cables.

### Circuit Breaker Test

Depress the circuit breaker button (A, **Figure 46**) if the gauges fail to operate when the ignition switch is turned to the ON position. If the button pops back out, inspect all engine and instrument wires for damaged insulation, chafing, loose or corroded connections or other damage. Repair damaged wiring or poor connections prior to operating the engine. Test the circuit breaker if no fault is found in the wiring or if the gauges fail to operate with the button depressed. A multimeter is required for this test.

> *WARNING*
> *Use extreme caution when working around batteries. Never smoke or allow sparks around a battery. Batteries produce explosive hydrogen gas that can explode and result in injury or death. Never make the final connection of a circuit to the battery terminal as an arc may occur leading to fire or explosion.*

1. Remove the flame arrestor or plastic engine cover to access the circuit breaker. Disconnect the battery cables.

2. Pull the insulator boots away from the circuit breaker terminals (B, **Figure 46**). Disconnect the red/purple wire from the circuit breaker. Cover the disconnected wire terminal with electrical tape to prevent arcing if it contacts other components. Connect the battery cables.

3. Select the 20 or 40 VDC scale on the meter. Connect the negative voltmeter lead to a suitable engine ground. Observe the meter while touching the positive lead to the red wire terminal on the circuit breaker. The meter must indicate battery voltage. If not, check for a loose connection or faulty wiring at the starter solenoid.

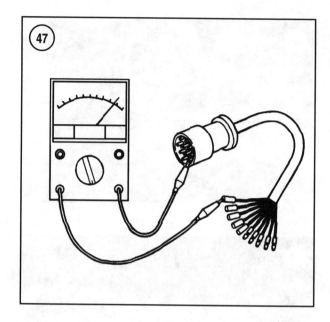

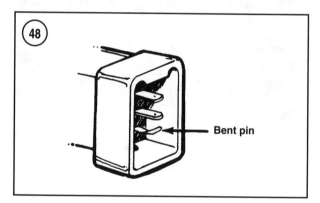

Bent pin

4. Touch the positive voltmeter lead to the open terminal on the circuit breaker. The meter must indicate battery voltage. If not, reset the circuit breaker and repeat the test. If the incorrect test results persist, the circuit breaker is defective and must be replaced (Chapter Ten).

5. Disconnect the battery cables. Remove the electrical tape and connect the red/purple wire to its terminal on the circuit breaker.

6. Connect the battery cables. Reset the circuit breaker and turn the ignition switch to the ON position. If the circuit breaker trips, replace it as described in Chapter Ten.

### Wire Harness Test

If an electrical malfunction occurs and testing indicates that all individual components are functioning properly, suspect the wiring harness. Disconnect all components

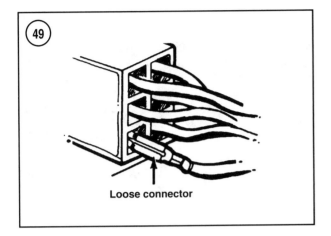

Loose connector

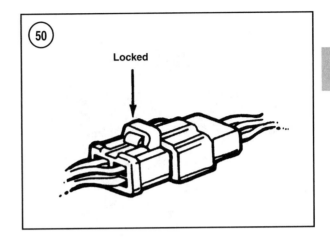

Locked

from the engine wire harness (**Figure 47**), then use an ohmmeter to test the harness for continuity.

Most wiring harness problems occur at the connectors and plugs. Inspect the connectors for bent pins (**Figure 48**) and loose connectors (**Figure 49**). Make sure the connectors lock together securely (**Figure 50**). Loose connectors are a major cause of intermittent electrical problems. To test the wiring harness, proceed as follows:

> *WARNING*
> *Use extreme caution when working around batteries. Never smoke or allow sparks to occur in or around a battery. Batteries produce explosive hydrogen gas that can explode and result in injury or death. Never make the final connection of a circuit to the battery terminal as an arc may occur leading to fire or explosion.*

1. Disconnect both cables from the battery.
2. Mark all wire terminals connected to the wire harness. Note the wire routing and disconnect all wires from the harness.
3. Refer to the wiring diagrams located at the end of the manual to identify the wire colors and corresponding connection to the engine. Connect the meter test leads to the harness connector pin and the other end of the selected wire (**Figure 47**).
4. Note the meter reading. The correct reading is continuity.
5. Note the meter reading while twisting, bending and pulling on the wire harness. A fault is indicated if the meter reading changes to no continuity. Often intermittent faults are found this way.
6. Repeat Steps 3-5 for the remaining wires in the harness.
7. Check for continuity between each pin and all other pins. The meter must indicate no continuity. If the meter

reads continuity, study the wire diagrams at the end of the manual and verify the suspect wires do not connect to a common circuit. If not, the suspect wires are shorted. Replace the harness.
8. Connect all components to the engine wire harness. Route all wires away from any moving components.
9. Clean the terminals, then connect the cables to the battery.

## FUEL SYSTEM

Fuel related problems are common with most stern drive engines. Gasoline has a relatively short shelf life and becomes stale within a few weeks under some conditions. Because marine engines may sit idle for several weeks at a time the gasoline often becomes stale.

As fuel evaporates, gummy deposits usually form in the carburetor or other fuel system components. These deposits may clog fuel filters, fuel lines, fuel pumps and small passages in the fuel system.

Fuel stored in the fuel tank tends to absorb water vapor from the air. Over time, this water separates from the fuel and settles to the bottom of the fuel tank, leading to the formation of rust If the engine refuses to start and the ignition system is not at fault, inspect the fuel in the tank. An unpleasant odor usually indicates the fuel has exceeded its shelf life and should be replaced. Refer to *Fuel Inspection* in this chapter.

> *WARNING*
> *Use extreme caution when working with the fuel system. Gasoline is extremely flammable and if ignited can cause injury or death. Never smoke or allow sparks to occur around fuel or fuel vapor. Wipe up any spilled fuel at once. Check all fuel hoses, connections and fittings for leakage after any fuel system repair.*

## Fuel Inspection

Check the condition of the fuel if the engine has been stored for some time and refuses to start. Use a suitable hand operated fuel pump to remove a sample of the fuel from the fuel tank. Pour the fuel sample into a clear container. Promptly clean up any spilled fuel.

Inspect and carefully smell the fuel. An unusual odor, debris, cloudy appearance or the presence of water indicates a problem with the fuel. If any of these conditions is noted, dispose of all the fuel in an environmentally responsible manner. Contact a local marine dealership or automotive repair facility for information on the proper disposal of the fuel.

## Choke Test

All carburetor equipped models use an automatic electric choke. This valve pivots on the shaft located at the front opening of the carburetor. When activated, it blocks the opening at the top of the carburetor (**Figure 51**). This causes a decrease in air and an increase in fuel delivered to the engine. A choke malfunction can cause hard starting, stalling or excessive exhaust smoke.

A thermal coil in the choke housing moves the shaft and choke valve with changing temperature. At ambient temperatures below approximately 70° F (21° C) the coil winds up This closes the choke valve (**Figure 51**), resulting in increased fuel delivery.

The ignition ON circuit supplies electric current to the choke heating coil via the purple or purple/yellow wire (**Figure 52**). A ground wire connected to the heater mounting screw completes the circuit. As the engine runs, the choke heating coil warms the thermal coil. This causes the coil to unwind and gradually open the choke valve (**Figure 53**). Under normal circumstances, the choke

valve reaches the full open position within a few minutes after starting the engine. Be aware that if key switch is inadvertently left in the ON position, the choke valve will open with the engine not running. This could cause hard starting on a cold engine. If this occurs, wait until the choke coil cools and closes the valve before starting the engine.

The engine must be completely cool before testing. This procedure requires a multimeter.

1. Verify that no fuel, vapor or other flammable substance is present in the engine compartment. Clean up any spilled fuel before proceeding.

2. Remove the flame arrestor as described in Chapter Eight. Move the throttle to wide open and back to idle. The choke valve must be closed (**Figure 51**). If not, remove the choke heater and check for proper assembly as described in Chapter Eight.

3. Start the engine and increase the speed to energize the alternator. Observe the choke valve. The valve must begin to open (**Figure 53**) as the engine runs. The choke valve must be fully open within a few minutes. Proceed with testing if the choke fails to open.

4. Touch the wire terminal side of the choke heating coil. The coil must feel warm.. Replace the choke heating coil

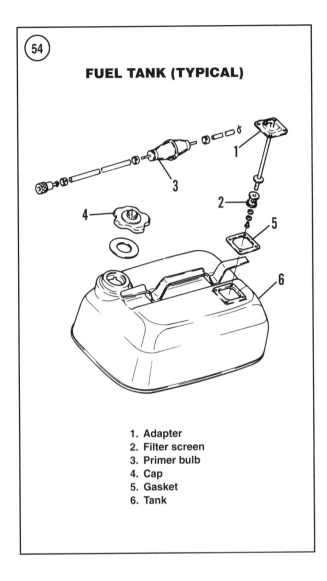

**FUEL TANK (TYPICAL)**

1. Adapter
2. Filter screen
3. Primer bulb
4. Cap
5. Gasket
6. Tank

## Fuel Tank and Fuel Hose Testing

A faulty fuel tank, fuel hose or related components can restrict fuel flow or allow air to enter the fuel flowing to the engine. In either case, the engine will misfire due to inadequate fuel delivery. In most instances the misfire occurs only at higher engine speeds because the fuel flow is adequate for low-speed operation.

The most effective method to determine whether the fuel tank is faulty is to temporarily run the engine on a known-good portable fuel tank (**Figure 54**). Ensure the tank used for testing has good fuel hoses, fresh fuel and secure fuel hose connections. Ensure the inside diameter of the fuel hose and fuel fitting of the test tank is 3/8 in. (9.5 mm) or larger. If the hose is too small the engine will continue to malfunction. This procedure must be performed under actual operating conditions.

> *WARNING*
> *Use extreme caution when working with the fuel system. Fuel is extremely flammable and if ignited can result in serious injury or death. Never smoke or allow sparks to occur around fuel or fuel vapor. Wipe up any spilled fuel at once. Check all fuel hoses, connections and fittings for leakage after any fuel system repair. Correct all fuel leakage before returning the engine to service.*

> *CAUTION*
> *Avoid using couplings or other patching methods to repair a damaged fuel hose. The coupling or patch may result in restricted fuel flow and lead to fuel starvation. A temporary repair usually fails and results in a fuel or air leak.*

> *NOTE*
> *The engine must be run at full throttle for several minutes to accurately check for a fuel tank related fault.*

1. Disconnect the fuel hose from the inlet fitting on the mechanical fuel pump (3.0L models) or the inlet fitting (3, **Figure 55**) on the water separating fuel filter.
2. Connect the portable fuel tank hose to the pump or filter inlet fitting. Securely tighten the clamps. Clean up any spilled fuel. Open the vent on the fuel tank cap.
3. Start the engine and check for fuel leakage. Correct leakage before proceeding.
4. Have an assistant operate the engine until the operational problem occurs. Vigorously pump the primer bulb. Test the fuel pressure as described in this chapter if the engine operates properly only while pumping the primer bulb.

if it is warm but the choke valve fails to open. Proceed with testing if the choke valve is cool.

5. Test the voltage supply to the choke heating coil as follows:

    a. Disconnect the purple or purple/yellow wire from the choke heating coil (**Figure 52**).

    b. Connect the positive voltmeter lead to the purple or purple yellow wire and the negative lead to the choke ground terminal. The meter must read 12.5 volt or higher with the engine running. Otherwise check for faulty engine harness wiring or terminal connections.

    c. Replace the choke heating coil (Chapter Eight) if the voltage supply is correct but the choke fails to open.

6. Reconnect the purple or purple/yellow wire. Install the flame arrestor as described in Chapter Eight.

**3**

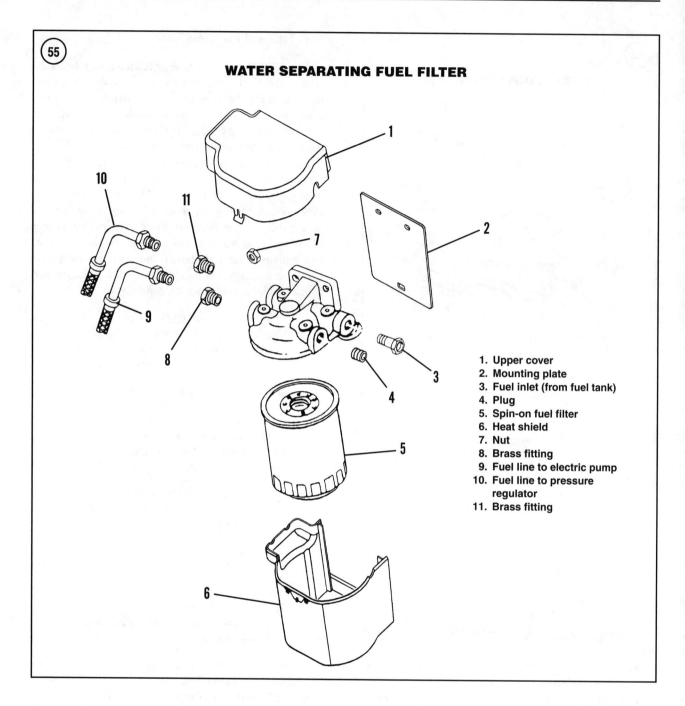

**WATER SEPARATING FUEL FILTER**

1. Upper cover
2. Mounting plate
3. Fuel inlet (from fuel tank)
4. Plug
5. Spin-on fuel filter
6. Heat shield
7. Nut
8. Brass fitting
9. Fuel line to electric pump
10. Fuel line to pressure regulator
11. Brass fitting

5. A problem with the fuel tank pickup, fuel, fuel hoses or antisiphon device is indicated if the engine performs properly while connected to the portable fuel tank.

6. A fault with other fuel system components, the ignition system, or other engine component is likely if the malfunction persists while using the portable fuel tank. Refer to **Table 2** and **Table 3** to determine which components to test, adjust or inspect.

7. Disconnect the portable fuel tank hose. Reconnect the fuel tank hose to the fuel pump filter inlet fitting. Clean up any spilled fuel. Check for and correct fuel leakage before operating the engine.

**Fuel Tank Vent**

Fuel tank venting is required for fuel to flow from the fuel tank to the engine. Inadequate venting allows a vacuum to form in the tank as fuel is drawn from the tank. With continued running the vacuum becomes strong

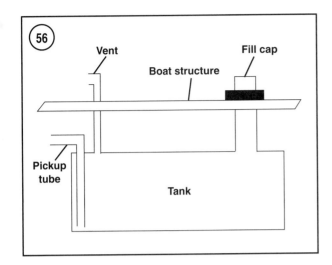

Figure 56

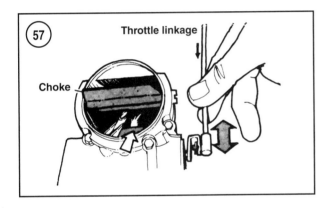

Figure 57

enough to prevent the fuel pump from drawing fuel from the tank. When the supply of fuel is less than the engine demands, fuel starvation occurs, resulting in decreased power or surging at higher engine speeds. Fuel starvation can also occur at lower speeds causing the engine to stall and not restart.

The vent system for an integral fuel tank includes a vent hose at the fuel tank, the vent hose and the hull vent fitting (**Figure 56**). This type of venting system is always open and may become blocked by insects or debris.

If inadequate fuel tank venting is suspected, loosen the fuel tank fill cap (**Figure 56**) to allow the tank to vent. Clean and inspect the fuel tank vent hose and all fittings if the fuel starvation symptoms disappear shortly after the cap is loosened.

## Antisiphon Devices

An antisiphon device prevents fuel from siphoning from the tank if a leak occurs in the fuel line between the tank and engine. The most common type is a spring

loaded check valve located at the fuel pickup hose fitting. Other types are the manual valve and solenoid activated valve. Antisiphon devices are an important safety feature and should not be bypassed.

Test for a faulty anti-siphon device by process of elimination. Run the engine using a portable fuel tank connected directly to the engine fuel pump. Perform this test under actual running conditions. If the engine performs properly while connected to the portable fuel tank, the fuel tank pickup, fuel hoses, primer bulb, fuel tank vent or antisiphon device may be faulty. If all fuel hose components are in good condition the malfunction is probably due to a blocked or faulty antisiphon device. Remove and replace the antisiphon device, following the instructions provided with the new component.

Replacement of the antisiphon device requires removal of the fuel hose and possibly the fuel tank pickup. Inspect the faulty valve prior to installing the new one. Clean the fuel tank if a significant amount of debris is found in the antisiphon device or fuel tank pickup. Debris in the fuel tank will usually cause a repeat failure. Inspect all fuel system hoses and filters for blockage if debris is in the fuel tank, fuel tank pickup or antisiphon device. Always correct any fuel system leakage prior to returning the engine to service.

*NOTE*
*Some antisiphon devices can be cleaned instead of replaced. Thoroughly inspect the device for wear, damage or corrosion. Replace the valve if in questionable condition.*

## Checking for Fuel in the Carburetor

Check for fuel at the carburetor if the engine refuses to start and the ignition system is operating properly.

1. Remove the flame arrestor as described in Chapter Eight.

2. Disconnect the battery cables.

3. Disconnect the throttle cable from the throttle lever. Manually open the check valve to allow a clear view of the accelerator pump discharge nozzles (**Figure 57**).

4. Observe the nozzles while rapidly opening and closing the throttle. Fuel must spray from the nozzles when the throttle opens. If little or no fuel sprays from the accelerator pump nozzles, test the fuel pressure as described in this chapter. If the fuel pressure is correct, replace the accelerator pump as described in Chapter Eight.

5. Install the flame arrestor as described in Chapter Eight. Install and adjust the throttle cables as described in Chapter Six.

**3**

6. Connect the battery cables. Check for fuel leakage before operating the engine.

### Fuel Pressure Test
### (Carburetor Equipped Models)

Refer to *Electronic Fuel Injection* in this chapter to pressure test EFI models.

This test requires a fuel pressure gauge, fuel inlet T-fitting (Mercury part No. 91-18078) or equivalent along with appropriate hoses and clamps.

For accurate testing, this procedure must be performed under actual running conditions.

> *WARNING*
> *Use extreme caution when working with the fuel system. Fuel is extremely flammable and if ignited can result in serious injury or death. Never smoke or allow sparks to occur around fuel or fuel vapor. Wipe up any spilled fuel at once. Check all fuel hoses, connections and fittings for leakage after any fuel system repair. Correct all fuel leakage before returning the engine to service.*

> *NOTE*
> *Always inspect all fuel filters before testing the fuel system.*

1. Disconnect the fuel inlet line as described in Chapter Eight under *Carburetor Removal*.
2. Thread the fuel inlet T-fitting into the carburetor fuel inlet fitting and tighten securely. Thread the fuel line into the T-fitting and tighten.
3. Connect the fuel gauge to the T-fitting as shown in **Figure 58**. Clean up any spilled fuel.
4. Observe the gauge while cranking or starting the engine. Compare the fuel pressure reading with the specification in **Table 5**.
5A. *3.0L models*—If the fuel pressure is low, connect a portable fuel tank to the engine as described under *Fuel Tank and Fuel Hose Test* in this chapter.
   a. Repeat Step 4.
   b. If the fuel pressure is now correct, inspect the fuel pickup and antisiphon valve for a restriction.
   c. If the fuel pressure is still insufficient, replace the fuel pump as described in Chapter Eight.
5B. *All other models*—If fuel pressure is low:
   a. Check fuel pump voltage as described under *Fuel Pump Voltage Test* in this chapter.
   b. Connect a portable fuel tank to the engine as described under *Fuel Tank and Fuel Hoses* in this chapter. Repeat Step 4.

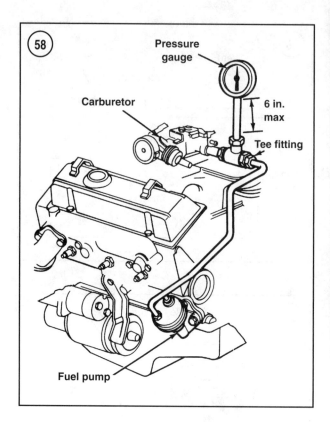

c. If the fuel pressure is now correct, inspect the fuel pickup in the tank and the antisiphon valve for a restriction.
d. If the fuel pressure is still low, replace the fuel pump. If fuel pressure is excessive, replace the fuel pump. See Chapter Eight.

6. Remove the fuel gauge and fitting. Connect the fuel line to the carburetor as described in Chapter Eight under *Carburetor Replacement*.

7. Check for and correct fuel leakage before operating the engine.

### Fuel Pump Voltage Test

This test requires a multimeter and a short jumper lead. Refer to the wire diagrams at the end of the manual for wire routing and connections.

The purple/yellow fuel pump wire connects to the oil pressure switch and the starter solenoid. The black fuel pump wire connects to engine ground. When the ignition switch is turned ON, battery voltage is applied to the purple wire of the oil pressure switch. When the ignition switch is turned to START, the starter solenoid applies battery voltage to the purple/yellow wire, causing the fuel pump to operate and supply fuel to the carburetor. When the oil pressure reaches approximately 4 psi. (27.6 kPa) or

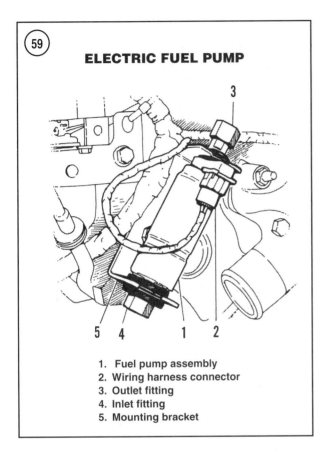

**ELECTRIC FUEL PUMP**

1. Fuel pump assembly
2. Wiring harness connector
3. Outlet fitting
4. Inlet fitting
5. Mounting bracket

higher, the oil pressure switch closes and applies battery voltage to the purple/yellow wire. This provides the current to operate the fuel pump when the ignition switch is in the RUN position.

If the oil pressure drops below approximately 4 psi. (27.6 kPa), the oil pressure switch opens and interrupts the current to the fuel pump. The engine stalls when the carburetor runs out of fuel. The engine will restart due to the current supplied to the pump by the starter solenoid. However, if low oil pressure persists, the engine will again

stall. The cycle repeats unless the oil pressure reaches the minimum specification.

The same symptoms will occur if the oil pressure switch fails in an open circuit condition, regardless of the engine's oil pressure.

1. Turn the ignition switch OFF. Carefully disconnect the wire harness (2, **Figure 59**) from the fuel pump (1).

2. Connect the positive voltmeter lead to the purple/yellow wire and the negative lead to the black wire terminal in the connector. The meter should read 0 volt. If the meter shows voltage is present, either the purple/yellow wire is shorted to a live wire, or the ignition switch is faulty. Check the wiring and ignition switch as described in this chapter.

3. With the test leads connected as described in Step 2, turn the ignition switch to the ON position. The meter must read 0 volt. If voltage is present, test the oil pressure switch as described in this chapter.

4. Ground the high tension coil lead to prevent the engine from starting.

5. With the test leads connected as described in Step 2, turn the ignition switch to the START position. The meter must read 9-12 volt. If the voltage is less than specified, perform the following:

    a. Repeat the test with the negative voltmeter lead connected to a suitable engine ground. If the voltage is now within specification, the black fuel pump ground wire is open. Repair the wire or terminal.

    b. Check for damage to the purple/yellow wire or a loose connection at the starter motor. If no faults are found with the wiring or connections, test the starter solenoid as described in this chapter.

6. Replace the fuel pump as described in Chapter Eight if the voltage is as specified but the fuel pump does not operate or the pump pressure is less than specified.

7. Clean the terminals and carefully connect the wire harness (2, **Figure 59**) to the electric fuel pump.

8. Reconnect the high tension coil lead.

### OIL PRESSURE SWITCH TEST

Perform this test to check the operation of the oil pressure switch (**Figure 60**) for the electric fuel pump. Refer to *Warning System* in this chapter to check the oil pressure switch used with the audio warning system.

This test requires a multimeter, a hand operated pressure/vacuum pump (**Figure 61**), and a suitable hose and clamps.

1. Remove the oil pressure switch as described in Chapter Eight.

2. Fit a hose over the fitting at the end of the switch and secure with a clamp. Connect the other end of the hose to the pressure port on the hand pump.

3. Calibrate a multimeter on the R×1 scale. Connect the test leads to each of the switch terminals. The meter must indicate no continuity.

4. Observe the meter while slowly applying air pressure to the switch. The meter reading must switch to continuity when the air pressure reaches approximately 4 psi. (27.6 kPa).

5. Replace the oil pressure switch if it fails to perform as specified. If the switch is satisfactory, reinstall it as described in Chapter Eight.

## CARBURETOR

The carburetor (**Figure 62**) meters air and fuel to the engine. Movement of the throttle plate in the carburetor controls the air flow into the engine. Air flowing through the carburetor causes fuel to flow from the carburetor into the engine. Calibrated openings in the carburetor control the rate of fuel flow at a given engine speed and throttle opening.

A carburetor problem can cause hard starting, rough idle or an inability to run at idle speed. Other symptoms are rough operation, hesitation during acceleration, poor performance at higher engine speeds and spark plug fouling.

*CAUTION*
*Always correct problems with the fuel, fuel tank and fuel pump before troubleshooting the carburetor.*

This section provides troubleshooting tips and instructions to help isolate the cause of most carburetor related problems.

1. If the engine is hard to start, idles roughly or stalls while idling, check for the following:
   a. Choke valve malfunction.
   b. Flooding carburetor.
   c. Improper carburetor adjustment or synchronization.
   d. Plugged carburetor passages.
2. If the engine runs roughly at various speeds, check the following:
   a. Improper carburetor adjustment or synchronization.
   b. Choke valve malfunction.
   c. Plugged carburetor passages.
   d. Improper float adjustment.
3. If the engine hesitates during acceleration, check the following:
   a. Faulty or improperly adjusted accelerator pump.
   b. Improper carburetor adjustment or synchronization.
   c. Plugged carburetor passages.
   d. Improper float adjustment.

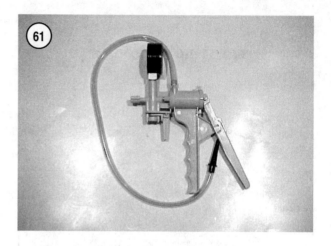

   e. Flooding carburetor.
   f. Choke valve malfunction.
   g. Incorrect propeller.
4. If spark plug fouling or excessive exhaust smoke occurs, check for the following:
   a. Choke valve malfunction.
   b. Improper carburetor adjustment or synchronization.
   c. Flooding carburetor.
   d. Plugged carburetor passages.
5. If poor performance at higher engine speeds occurs, check the following:
   a. Plugged carburetor passages.
   b. Choke valve malfunction.
   c. Low fuel pressure.
6. If the engine stalls when the throttle is returned to the idle position:
   a. Improper carburetor adjustment.
   b. Fuel saturated or improperly adjusted float.
   c. Flooding carburetor.
7. If the engine diesels (runs on after switching the ignition off) check the following:
   a. Improper idle speed adjustment.
   b. Improper throttle cable adjustment.
   c. Engine operating temperature.
   d. Grade or quality of fuel used.

### Flooding Carburetor

*WARNING*
*Use extreme caution when working with the fuel system. Fuel is extremely flammable and if ignited can cause injury or death. Never smoke or allow sparks to occur around fuel or fuel vapors. Wipe up any spilled fuel at once. Check all fuel hoses, connections and fittings for leaks after any fuel system repair. Correct all fuel system*

*leakage before returning the engine into service.*

A flooded carburetor is usually the result of debris in the needle valve or possibly a worn or damaged needle valve and seat. An improperly adjusted, damaged or fuel saturated float can also cause carburetor flooding. This allows too much fuel to enter the engine causing stalling or poor low speed operation. In many cases the engine will perform satisfactorily at higher engine speeds because the engine is able to burn the excess fuel.

Remove the flame arrestor and inspect the carburetor to verify carburetor flooding.

1. Make sure no fuel or vapor is present in the engine compartment.

2. Remove the flame arrestor as described in Chapter Eight. Connect the coil high-tension lead to an engine ground to prevent the engine from starting.

3. Have an assistant operate the starter. Inspect the bowl vent opening (**Figure 62**).

   a. If fuel flows from the vent, the carburetor is flooding. Immediately stop the engine. Repair the carburetor as described in Chapter Eight.

   b. If no fuel flows from the vent opening, the carburetor is not flooding at this time. Repair the carburetor if flooding symptoms persist.

4. Reconnect the coil high-tension lead.

## Carburetor Adjustment

Improper carburetor adjustment can result in stalling at idle speed, rough running at idle and/or mid range engine speeds, hesitation during acceleration and excessive exhaust smoke. In most cases the symptoms are present at lower engine speeds only.

Perform all applicable carburetor adjustments as described in Chapter Six. If the symptoms persist, refer to **Table 2** and **Table 3** for a list of additional items to check, test or adjust.

## Faulty or Improperly Adjusted Accelerator Pump

A faulty or improperly adjusted accelerator pump usually causes hesitation during rapid acceleration. Typically the engine performs properly during slow acceleration. Rapid acceleration causes an instantaneous pressure change within the intake manifold. This pressure change causes a momentary decrease in fuel delivery from the carburetor and a potential for hesitation or stalling. During rapid acceleration, the accelerator pump provides additional fuel to the engine to compensate for the decrease in fuel delivery.

Check for improper linkage installation if hesitation occurs during rapid acceleration. Refer to Chapter Eight.

Disassemble, clean and inspect the carburetor if the symptoms persist after adjustment.

## Plugged Carburetor Passages

Plugged jets, passages, orifices or vents in the carburetor can result in excessive fuel (rich condition) or inadequate fuel (lean condition) delivery. Typical symptoms of plugged carburetor passages include difficult starting, surging or misfiring at higher engine speeds or hesitation during acceleration. The symptoms can occur at any engine speed depending on the location and extent of the blockage. With plugged low-speed passages the engine may run roughly or stall at idle speed, but run well at higher engine speeds.

Remove, clean and inspect the carburetor only if all other fuel system components such as fuel, fuel tank and fuel pump are in good condition, but symptoms persist. Carburetor removal, cleaning, inspection and assembly are described in Chapter Eight.

> *CAUTION*
> *Continued operation with a lean fuel condition can lead to piston damage and engine failure.*

## Air Leakage at the Carburetor Mounting Surface

Air leakage at the carburetor mounting surface causes excessive air to be drawn into the engine, resulting in an excessively lean condition.

Typical symptoms of an air leak are:

1. A hissing or squealing noise emanating from the engine.

2. Rough idle characteristics.

3. Hesitation during acceleration.

4. Poor high speed performance.

5. Spark plug overheating.

A common method to locate the leakage is by using a spray type lubricant such as WD 40. With the engine running at idle speed, spray the lubricant onto the carburetor mating surface (**Figure 63**). If a leak is present the lubricant will be drawn into the engine at the point of leakage. Any change in the idle characteristic indicates leakage at the carburetor mounting surface.

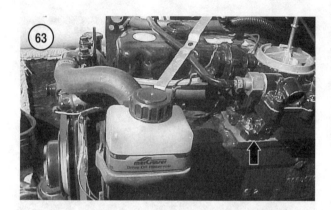

If leakage is detected, remove the carburetor, spacer if so equipped, and gaskets as described in Chapter Eight. Inspect the gasket surfaces. Replace the carburetor or intake manifold gaskets if they are disturbed. Even small tears or nicks will allow sufficient air leakage to cause an engine malfunction.

### Altitude Adjustments

> *CAUTION*
> *If the engine is later operated at a lower altitude, the carburetor and jets will need to be readjusted to their original settings. Internal engine damage can occur if the engine is run at lower altitudes with the higher altitude fuel system adjustments.*

When operating the outboard motor at high elevation, it is usually necessary to change the carburetor main jets and readjust the carburetor. Higher elevation decreases the amount of fuel required for proper operation. Contact a MerCruiser dealership in the area where the engine is operated for jet change or adjustment recommendations. Be aware that carburetor adjustments beyond the factory recommendation may cause damage to the engine.

### ELECTRONIC FUEL INJECTION

The major components of the fuel injection system are the engine control module (ECM), fuel delivery system and the various sensors, relays and actuators.

Three different types of engine control modules are used. The ECM must be identified before testing the electrical control system. Refer to the following to identify the engine control module.

1. A MEFI 2 type ECM is used on 1998-prior models. The MEFI 2 ECM is identified by the wire harness connection at the ends of module (**Figure 64**).

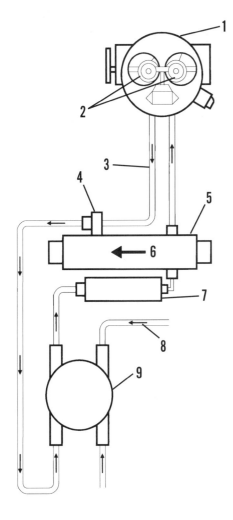

## THROTTLE BODY INJECTION SYSTEM (TBI)

1. Throttle body
2. Fuel injectors (2)
3. Hose (regulator to throttle body)
4. Fuel pressure regulator
5. Fuel cooler
6. Water flow
7. Electric fuel pump
8. Fuel inlet hose (from the fuel tank)
9. Water separating fuel filter

**3**

2. A MEFI 3 type ECM is used on 1999-on models (except 496 Mag and 496 Mag HO). The MEFI 3 ECM is identified by the harness connection on the side of the module (**Figure 65**).

3. A PCM 555 type ECM is used on 2002-2004 4.3L, 5.0L, 350 Mag, MX6.2L models with multi-port fuel injection (MPI) and all 496 Mag and 496 Mag HO models. The PCM 555 ECM is identified by the harness connections on the side of the ECM (**Figure 66**).

The fuel injection system used two different types of fuel delivery systems which vary in the number and location of the fuel injectors. 1998-2001 4.3L, 5.0L and 5.7L models use a throttle body injection (TBI) system. All other models use a multi-port fuel injection (MPI) system.

*NOTE*
*High-power electrical equipment such as stereos and communication radios may interfere with the electronic fuel injection system. Switch these devices off if trouble is detected with the engine. Avoid using these devices while the engine is running if normal engine operation resumes with these devices switched off.*

### Throttle Body Injection System (TBI)

The major components of the system are the water separating fuel filter, Cool Fuel System and the throttle body. The throttle body (1, **Figure 67**) mounts to the intake manifold in the same location as the carburetor on models so equipped. Two fuel injectors (2, **Figure 67**) mount in the throttle body assembly. The fuel injector discharge is directed into the air flowing toward the throttle plate.

The Cool Fuel System is comprised of the electric fuel pump (7, **Figure 67**), fuel cooler (5) and the fuel pressure regulator (4). The Cool Fuel System mounts on the port side of the engine between the engine mount and the oil pan.

The fuel pump draws fuel from the water separating filter (9, **Figure 67**) and pumps it through the fuel cooler where it is cooled by the water flowing through the cooler. The fuel cooler effectively prevents fuel boiling and the resultant vapor lock that can occur during hot weather operation.

The fuel pump is capable of delivering more fuel than the engine can consume. Also, the fuel pressure must be consistent for proper engine operation at all speeds and loads. Therefore, a fuel pressure regulator (4, **Figure 67**) is used to control fuel pressure and to provide a return path back to the vapor separator for unused fuel.

A sealed passage directs the pressurized fuel to the regulator. When the fuel pressure exceeds the regulator setting, the regulator opens and directs the excess fuel through the return

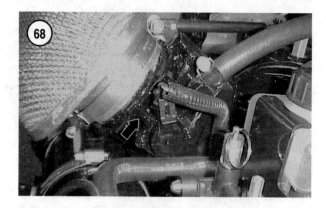

line, back to the water separating fuel filter. A hose (3, **Figure 67**) connects to a fitting on the regulator and the flame arrestor. Should the regulator develop an internal leak, fuel flows though this hose and into the throttle body. The engine will run very rich at lower engine speeds if this occurs.

### Multi port Injection System (MPI)

The major components of the system include the water separating fuel filter, Cool Fuel System, fuel rails and throttle body. The throttle body (**Figure 68**) contains the throttle valve, throttle position sensor and the idle air control motor (except 2002-2004 MPI models, 496 Mag and 496 Mag HO). On 2002-2004 4.3LMPI, 5.0 MPI and all 350 Mag and MX 6.2L models, the throttle body mounts to the intake manifold in the same location as the carburetor on models so equipped. On all other models the throttle body mounts on the front or side of the intake plenum.

The fuel rails (2, **Figure 69**) secure the eight fuel injectors (1) in the intake manifold. The fuel injectors discharge directly into each cylinder's intake port. The fuel rails also supply pressurized fuel to the injectors.

The Cool Fuel System consists of the electric fuel pump (11, **Figure 69**), fuel cooler (4) and fuel pressure regulator (7). The Cool Fuel System mounts to the port side of the engine between the engine mount and the oil pan.

The fuel pump draws fuel from the water separating filter (9, **Figure 69**) and pumps it through the fuel cooler where it is cooled by the water flowing through the cooler. The fuel cooler effectively prevents fuel boiling and the resultant vapor lock during hot weather operation. After the fuel cooler, the fuel flows through a line to the fuel rail and into the injectors. The engine control module (ECM) controls fuel injector operation.

The fuel pump is capable of delivering more fuel than the engine can consume. Also, the fuel pressure must be consistent for proper engine operation at all speeds and loads. Therefore, a fuel pressure regulator (7, **Figure 69**)

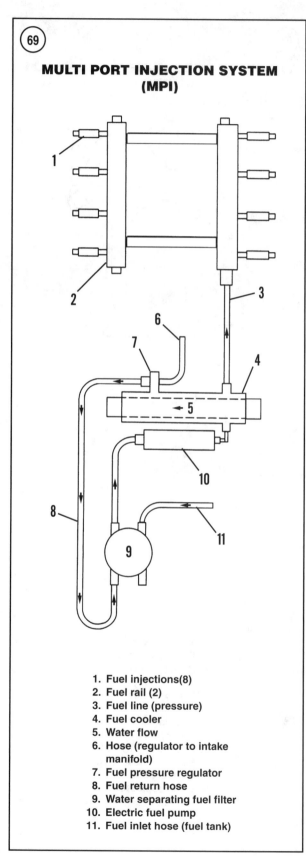

**MULTI PORT INJECTION SYSTEM (MPI)**

1. Fuel injections(8)
2. Fuel rail (2)
3. Fuel line (pressure)
4. Fuel cooler
5. Water flow
6. Hose (regulator to intake manifold)
7. Fuel pressure regulator
8. Fuel return hose
9. Water separating fuel filter
10. Electric fuel pump
11. Fuel inlet hose (fuel tank)

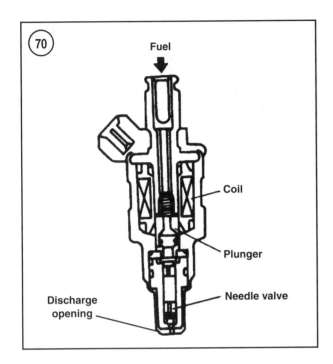

Fuel

Coil

Plunger

Needle valve

Discharge opening

is used to control fuel pressure and to provide a return path back to the vapor separator for unused fuel.

The air pressure in the intake manifold varies with engine load and throttle setting. For light loads or lower throttle settings, the air pressure is lower (higher vacuum). For higher loads or throttle settings, the air pressure is higher (lower vacuum). With an MPI system, the fuel pressure must be regulated to compensate for the varying intake manifold pressure. A hose (6, **Figure 69**) connecting the regulator and the intake manifold applies the actual vacuum to the diaphragm inside the regulator. This causes the regulator to open at a lower pressure with higher vacuum, or a higher pressure with low vacuum. If the regulator develops an internal leak, fuel will flow though this hose and into the intake manifold.

## Operation

When the ignition key switch is turned ON, battery voltage passes through the purple and pink wires to the system relay, energizing the relay. When energized, the relay applies battery voltage to the fuel injectors, ignition coil, fuel pump relay and engine control module (ECM). The ECM switches on when it receives the battery voltage from the relay. The ECM activates the horn for a few seconds and applies voltage to the fuel pump relay(s) for approximately two seconds via the dark green/white wire. This activates the fuel pump relay(s), which then supply battery voltage to the electric fuel pump(s). The fuel pump(s) pressurize the fuel delivery system in preparation for starting the engine. The ECM deactivates the fuel pump relay(s) after approximately two seconds.

When the ignition switch is turned to the START position, the ignition system operates and provides spark at the plugs. When the ECM receives input from the ignition system, it activates the fuel pump relays, causing the pumps to operate.

The fuel injectors (**Figure 70**) are solenoid activated fuel valves. When supplied with voltage, the injectors open and allow pressurized fuel to flow into the intake manifold. Battery voltage is supplied to the injectors by the system relay. The ECM controls injector operation by making and breaking the injector ground circuit.

The ECM determines the injector on-time based on input from the air pressure sensor, engine temperature sensor, air temperature sensor and throttle position sensor. The ECM controls the engine idle speed using the idle air control motor (IAC) (A, **Figure 71**). Electrical pulses from the ECM open or close the IAC to increase or decrease air flow into the intake manifold. The engine idles faster with increased air flow and slower with decreased air flow. The ECM determines if the throttle is at the idle setting using input from the throttle position sensor (B, **Figure 71**). Using input from the engine temperature sensor, the ECM increases the idle speed if the engine is cold, or decreases idle speed as the engine reaches normal operating temperatures. The ECM opens the IAC to compensate for additional load when the drive is shifted into gear. This allows for a consistent idle speed in or out of gear.

## Fuel Injection System Testing

The most basic test for any fuel injection system is the fuel pressure test. Perform this test if the engine will not start or performs improperly. Check or test other components only after verifying that the fuel pressure is correct.

If the fuel pressure is correct, check for trouble codes as described in this chapter. The following guidelines recommend testing or items to check by symptom. Perform the recommended test or inspection as described in this chapter.

1. If the engine refuses to start, perform the following:
   a. Place the throttle in the idle position.
   b. Place the lanyard switch in the RUN position.
   c. Check for a blown fuse.
   d. Check for spark at the coil.
   e. Inspect the fuel.
   f. Test the system relay.
   g. Test the fuel pressure.
   h. Check for injector operation.
   i. Check for trouble codes.
2. If the engine stalls at idle speed, perform the following:
   a. Inspect the fuel.
   b. Test the fuel pressure.
   c. Check the idle air control motor.
   d. Check for trouble codes.
3. If the engine idles roughly, perform the following:
   a. Inspect the fuel.
   b. Inspect or replace the spark plugs.
   c. Test the fuel pressure.
   d. Check the idle air control motor.
   e. Check for trouble codes.
4. If the engine stumbles during acceleration, perform the following:
   a. Inspect the fuel.
   b. Test the fuel pressure.
   c. Check for trouble codes.
5. If the engines misfires or runs rough at higher engine speeds, perform the following:
   a. Inspect the fuel.
   b. Test the fuel pressure.
   c. Inspect or replace the spark plugs.
   d. Check for trouble codes.
6. If the engine stalls during deceleration, perform the following:
   a. Check the idle air control motor.
   b. Check the fuel pressure.
   c. Inspect the fuel.

*NOTE*
*High-power electrical equipment such as stereos and communication radios may interfere with the electronic fuel injection system. Switch these devices off if the engine malfunctions.*

## System Relay Test

A faulty system relay or related wiring prevents operation of the ignition system, electric fuel pump and ECM.

*CAUTION*
*The system relay (A, **Figure 72**) and fuel pump relays (B and C) are identical and mount in the same general location. Refer to the wire diagrams at the end of the manual to identify the wires connected to the system relay.*

*CAUTION*
*The test light used to test the system relay must draw less than 300 mA with 12 volts applied. Otherwise the ECM or other components may sustain damage.*

1. Turn the ignition switch ON. The warning horn must sound for approximately two seconds. The system relay and related wiring is operating correctly if the horn sounds. If not, test the warning horn as described in the chapter. Proceed with testing if the warning horn operates correctly.

2. Check for blown fuses or dirty fuse contacts. Clean the terminals or replace the fuses as needed.

3. Turn the ignition switch OFF. Remove the system relay (A, **Figure 72**) as described in Chapter Eight.

4. Test the relay ground wire as follows:
   a. Connect the ground clip of the test light to the red wire on the slave solenoid or circuit breaker.
   b. Touch the test light probe to ground. The light must illuminate. Otherwise check for a discharged battery or faulty battery wire connections.
   c. Locate the terminal in the relay connector (harness side) for the black wire. Touch the test light probe to the terminal. The light must illuminate. Otherwise repair the fault in the black wire or its connection to ground.

5. Check the relay ON circuit as follows:
   a. Connect the wire clip of the test light to an engine ground. Touch the probe to a battery (+) terminal to verify the ground. The light must illuminate.

b. Touch the test light probe to the pink wire terminal in the harness side relay connector.

c. Turn the ignition switch to the ON position. The test light must illuminate. Otherwise check for a blown fuse, faulty ignition switch, loose or corroded wire connection or faulty wiring.

d. Turn the ignition switch OFF. The test light must not illuminate. If it does, check for faulty ignition key switch or shorted wiring.

6. Check the battery voltage supply to the relay as follows:

a. Connect the ground clip of the test light to an engine ground.

b. Touch the test light probe to the wire that corresponds to the relay terminal No. 30. The light must illuminate. If not, check for a blown fuse or poor connection in the circuit.

7. Replace the relay as described in Chapter Eight if all wiring checks correctly. Check for proper relay operation as described in step 1. Check for faulty wire connections to the ECM if the relay fails to perform as specified.

## Fuel Pressure Test

A fuel pressure test verifies that fuel is being supplied to the fuel injectors at the required pressure. This procedure requires a fuel pressure gauge (Mercury part No. 91-16850A5) capable of measuring up to 46 psi (3.2 kg/cm$^2$). The gauge must have a schrader valve adapter to measure pressure on models which use a throttle body injection (TBI) system. If using other than the Mercury gauge, an adapter is required to connect the gauge to the system. Use adapter (part No. 91-806901) on TBI models or adapter part No. 91-803135 on MPI models.

If the engine refuses to start, perform a static test as described in this chapter.

If fuel delivery problems are suspected, test the fuel pressure while running the engine under actual operating conditions. Refer to *Running Test* in this chapter. If a fuel restriction is present, the fuel pressure may be correct at slow engine speeds, but decline dramatically at higher throttle settings. If this symptom occurs, check the filters, antisiphon valve, and fuel tank pickup.

*WARNING*
*Use extreme caution when working with the fuel system. Fuel can spray out under high pressure. Never smoke or perform any test around an open flame or other source of ignition. Fuel and/or vapor can ignite or explode, resulting in damaged property, severe injury or death.*

### Static fuel pressure test

1. Turn the ignition switch to the ON position. The warning horn must sound and the fuel pump (both pumps on 496 Mag, 496 Mag HO and 2002-2004 MPI models with a Bravo drive) must run for approximately 2 seconds. Turn the ignition switch OFF.

a. If neither the horn nor fuel pump operates, test the system relay as described in this chapter.

b. If the horn sounds, but the fuel pump fails to operate, test fuel pump voltage as described in this chapter. Test the voltage for both fuel pumps on 496 Mag and 496 Mag HO models.

2A. *Throttle body injection (TBI)*—Disconnect the fuel line from the throttle body. See *Throttle Body* in Chapter Eight. Install the adapter (Mercury part No. 91-806901) into the throttle body then attach the fuel line to the adapter. Tighten the adapter and fuel line fitting securely. Attach the fuel pressure gauge to the adapter.

2B. *Multiport injection (MPI)*—Install the adapter (Mercury part No. 91-803135) to the fuel rail service port. See *Fuel Rail and Injectors* in Chapter Eight to locate the service port. Attach the fuel pressure gauge to the adapter.

3. Route the hoses away from belts, pulleys or other moving objects.

4. Turn the ignition switch to the ON position. Check for fuel leakage at the gauge fittings and adapter. Correct leakage before proceeding. Turn the ignition switch OFF.

5. Note the pressure on the gauge. The pressure must fall within the specification in **Table 5**. Otherwise proceed with testing.

6. If pressure exceeds the specification, replace the fuel pressure regulator as described in Chapter Eight. Repeat Step 5 and Step 6. Check for a fuel hose restriction if the pressure still exceeds the specification.

7. If the pressure is below the specification, perform the following:

a. Connect a portable fuel tank to the engine as described in this chapter.

b. Repeat step 4 several times to bleed air from the system. Wait 30 seconds or longer between each key ON/OFF cycle.

c. Check the fuel pressure as described in Step 4 and Step 5. If the fuel pressure is now correct, inspect the fuel tank, hoses, fuel pickup, clamps and fittings.

d. If the fuel pressure remains below specification, replace the fuel pressure regulator as described in Chapter Eight. Repeat Step 4 and Step 5. If the fuel pressure remains below specification, replace the electric fuel pump as described in Chapter Eight.

8. Remove the fuel pressure gauge and reattach the fuel line. Turn the ignition switch ON and check for leakage. Repair any leakage before returning the unit to service.

### *Running fuel pressure test*

1. Connect a fuel gauge to the system as described under Static Test in this chapter.

2. Start the engine and note the pressure reading. Operate the engine at multiple throttle settings, including wide open. Record the pressure reading at each throttle setting.

3. Compare the pressure readings with the specification in **Table 5**.

4. If the fuel pressure is less than the specification in **Table 5**, connect a portable fuel tank to the engine as described under *Fuel Tank and Fuel Hoses* in this chapter. Repeat Step 2 and Step 3.

   a. If the fuel pressure is now within the specification, inspect the fuel tank, hoses, pickup, and fittings for a restriction or air leak.

   b. If the fuel pressure is still low, replace the pressure regulator as described in Chapter Eight. Repeat this test. If the pressure is still less than the specification, replace the electric fuel pump. See Chapter Eight.

### Fuel Pump Voltage Test (EFI models)

Perform this test if the engine refuses to start and the electric fuel pump does not operate. Models 496 Mag and 496 Mag HO use a pair of electric fuel pumps. Refer to Auxiliary fuel pump voltage in this chapter for the test procedure. A multimeter is required for this test.

1. Verify proper operation of the ignition system as described under *Spark Test* in this chapter. Connect the high tension coil lead to an engine ground to prevent the engine from starting.

2. Disconnect the fuel pump harness from the rear of the Cool Fuel System (**Figure 73**).

3. Connect the positive voltmeter lead to the gray wire on the engine side of the harness. Connect the negative test lead to the black wire in the harness connector.

4. Observe the meter while turning the ignition switch to the ON position. The meter must indicate 12-14 volts for two seconds, then drop to 0 volt.

5. Observe the meter while turning the ignition switch to the START position. Do not operate the starter for more than 20 seconds. The meter must indicate 12-14 volts while the engine cranks and drop to 0 volts two seconds after the starter ceases.

6. Repeat Step 5 and Step 6 with the negative test lead connected to an engine ground.

   a. If the voltage is as specified in Step 5 and Step 6, the fuel pump voltage is correct. Replace the fuel pump as described in Chapter Eight.

   b. If the voltage is as specified in Step 5, but not Step 6, check for a poor connection or wire in the fuel pump circuit at the ECM or distributor.

   c. If the voltage is correct during Step 6, but not Step 5, repair the faulty fuel pump ground circuit.

   d. If the voltage is incorrect during Step 5 and Step 6, test the fuel pump relay as described in this chapter.

7. Reconnect the fuel pump. Reconnect the high tension spark plug lead.

### Auxiliary Fuel Pump Voltage

Perform this test if the engine refuses to start and the auxiliary fuel pump (**Figure 74**) does not operate. A multimeter is required for this test.

1. Verify proper operation of the ignition system as described under *Spark Test* in this chapter. To prevent the engine from starting, connect the high tension coil lead(s) to an engine ground.

2. Connect the positive voltmeter lead to the gray wire in the engine side of the fuel pump harness, and connect the negative lead to the black wire in the harness connector.

3. Observe the meter while turning the ignition switch to the ON position. The meter must indicate 12-14 volts for two seconds, then drop to 0 volts.

4. Observe the meter while turning the ignition key switch to the START position. Do not operate the starter for more than 20 seconds. The meter must indicate 12-14 volts while the engine cranks and drop to 0 volts two seconds after the starter ceases.

5. Repeat Step 4 and Step 5 with the negative test lead connected to an engine ground.

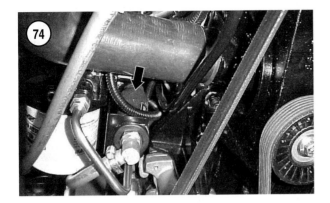

a. If the voltage is as specified in Step 5 and Step 6, the fuel pump voltage is correct. Replace the fuel pump as described in Chapter Eight.

b. If the voltage is as specified in Step 5, but not Step 6, check for a poor connection or wire in the fuel pump circuit at the ECM or distributor.

c. If the voltage is correct during Step 6, but not Step 5, repair the faulty fuel pump ground circuit.

d. If the voltage is incorrect during Step 5 and Step 6, test the fuel pump relay as described in this chapter.

6. Reconnect the engine harness to the fuel pump harness. Reconnect the high tension coil wires.

### Fuel Pump Relay Test

Failure of the fuel pump relay or its related wiring prevents operation of the ignition system, electric fuel pump and ECM.

*CAUTION*
*The system relay (A, **Figure 72**) and fuel pump relay(s) (B and C) are identical and mount in the same general location. Refer to the wire diagrams at the end of the manual and identify the wires connecting the fuel pump relay. Compare the wire colors to properly identify the relays.*

*CAUTION*
*The test light used to troubleshoot the fuel injection system must draw less than 300 mA with 12 volts applied. Otherwise the ECM or other components may sustain damage.*

*NOTE*
*Models 496 Mag and 496 Mag use two fuel pump relays. All other models use a single fuel pump relay. Test both relays on models so equipped.*

1. Turn the ignition switch to the ON position. The warning horn must sound for approximately two seconds. Otherwise test the system relay as described in this chapter.

2. Remove the fuel pump relay (B, **Figure 72**) as described in Chapter Eight. On 496 Mag and 496 Mag HO models, remove both fuel pump relays (B and C, **Figure 72**)

3. Test the relay ground wire as follows:

a. Connect the ground clip of the test light to the red wire on the slave solenoid or circuit breaker.

b. Touch the test light probe to ground. The light must illuminate. If not, check for a faulty test light, discharged battery or poor battery cable connections.

c. Touch the test light probe to the black wire in the harness side of the relay connector. The light should illuminate. If not, the black wire has an open circuit or a poor connection to ground.

4. On 496 Mag and 496 Mag HO models, repeat Step 3 on both relay connectors.

5. Next, test the relay ON circuit. Connect the ground clip of the test light to a good engine ground. Touch the test light probe to the No. 30 relay terminal and turn the ignition switch ON. The light should illuminate. If not, test the system relay as described in this chapter. Also check for blown fuses and poor connections.

6. Touch the test light probe to the green/white wire in the harness side of the relay connector. Note the test light and turn the ignition switch ON. The light should illuminate for two seconds then turn off. If not, check for a blow fuse or a poor connection of the green/white wire at the ECM.

7. If all test results are as specified, but the fuel pump relay fails to operate, replace it. Be sure to test both fuel pump relays on 496 Mag and 496 Mag HO models.

### Injector Operation Test

Perform this procedure if the engine fails to start or runs improperly. This procedure requires a mechanics stethoscope and a test light.

*CAUTION*
*The test light used to troubleshoot the fuel injection must draw less than 300 mA with 12 volt applied. Otherwise the ECM or other components may be damaged.*

1. Verify proper operation of the ignition system as described under *Spark Test* in this chapter. Connect the high tension coil leads to an engine ground to prevent the engine from starting. Place the throttle in the neutral position.

2A. *Throttle body injection system*—Remove the flame arrestor as described in Chapter Eight.

2B. *Multi port injection system*—Remove the plastic engine cover.

3. Disconnect one injector.

4. Check for proper switching of the injector drive circuit as follows:

    a. Connect the ground clip of the test light to an engine ground. Turn the ignition switch to the ON position. Touch the test light probe to the pink or red wire in the injector harness. The light must illuminate. Otherwise check for a blown fuse. Repair the faulty injector harness if the fuses are good.

    b. Connect the ground clip of the test light to the positive battery terminal. Touch the probe to an engine ground to verify the voltage source. The light must illuminate.

    c. Touch the probe to the blue or green injector harness terminal. On Models 496 Mag and 496 Mag HO, touch the probe to color opposite the pink wire terminal.

    d. Observe the test light while turning the ignition key switch to the ON position. Crank the engine for at least 20 seconds. The test light must flash ON and OFF with engine rotation. Otherwise check for a faulty wire or poor connection at the ECM.

    e. Reconnect the harness to the injector. Repeat the test for the remaining injectors.

5. Touch a mechanic's stethoscope to the injector body. Listen to the injector while cranking the engine. The injector must make a clicking noise. If not, replace the injector.

## TROUBLE CODES

The ECM continuously monitors the input voltage from the various sensors. The ECM stores a trouble code if the voltage from one or more of the sensors exceeds the pre-

determined limit. Unlike many other EFI systems, the code remains stored in the computer memory even if the battery is disconnected.

Two available types of tools for reading the stored trouble codes are the diagnostic code tool (**Figure 75**) and the scanning tool (**Figure 76** or **Figure 77**). The diagnostic code tool is relatively inexpensive whereas a scanning tool is quite costly. The diagnostic code tool can be used on all systems using the a MEFI 2 or MEFI 3 type ECM. The diagnostic code tool (**Figure 75**) cannot be used on engines using a PCM 555 type ECM.

The Rinda Scan Tool (**Figure 76**) can be used only on engines using a MEFI 2 or MEFI 3 type ECM. The Digital Diagnostic Terminal (**Figure 77**) can be used on MEFI 1, MEFI 2 MEFI 3 and PCM 555 type ECM.

**TROUBLE CODE 2-1**

On On   On          On On   On

Code 2   Code 1          Code 2   Code 1

Purchase the diagnostic code tool (part No. 94008) or Rinda Scan Tool (part No. 94050M) from Rinda Technologies, 4563 N. Elston Ave., Chicago, IL, 60630.

Purchase the Digital Diagnostics Tool (Mercury part No. 91-823686A2), harness (part No. 91-822560A2) and cartridge (part No. 91-803999) from a MerCruiser dealership.

*NOTE*
*On Models 496 Mag and 496 Mag HO, use only the Digital Diagnostic Terminal to troubleshoot the electronic control system. Follow the on screen instructions to determine if the sensors and actuators are functioning properly. The trouble codes described in this chapter do not apply to Models 496 Mag and 496 Mag HO.*

*NOTE*
*High-power electrical equipment such as stereos and communication radios may interfere with the electronic fuel injection system. Switch these devices off if trouble is detected with the engine.*

### Identifying Trouble Codes

#### *Diagnostic Code Tool*

Identify trouble codes by reading the flashing light sequence on the diagnostic code tool. Refer to the following example to understand how to identify codes.

A short duration light ON followed by a short duration light OFF then a short duration ON indicates a code 2 for the first digit of the trouble code (**Figure 78**). The second digit of the trouble code is displayed after a short light OFF period. In this example the second digit is a code 1. The code displayed in this example is 21. Each code flashes three times. A longer duration light OFF period separates the individual trouble codes. The flashing codes are displayed in repeating numerical order. **Figure 78** displays the flashing light sequence for a repeating code 21. To ensure that all codes are identified, always record them until they repeat.

1. Turn the key ignition switch to the ON position. Place the throttle in the idle position.

2. Remove the cover from the data link connector (**Figure 79**). Plug the diagnostic connector into the data link connector. Turn the switch on the code tool to the OFF position.

3. Turn the key ignition switch to the ON position. The light on the tool must illuminate steadily.

   a. If the light does not illuminate, check for a blown fuse or faulty wire terminal in the connector. Test the system relay if the wiring and fuses are in good condition.

   b. If the light is flashing, the black/white wire is shorted to ground.

4. Move the switch on the code tool to the ON position. The light on the code tool should display code 12. This code indicates the diagnostic system is functioning properly. If not, check for a faulty brown/white wire or terminal.

5. Read the flashing lights to determine the codes. Record all trouble codes. Move the switch on the code tool to the OFF position. Turn the ignition switch to the OFF position.

6. Refer to **Table 6** to match the code(s) to the sensor or system. Refer to the test procedure in this chapter for the stored trouble codes.

7. Perform the suggested repair. Clear the trouble codes as described in this chapter.

8. Remove the diagnostic code tool from the connector. Install the cover onto the data link connector (**Figure 79**).

#### *Scan Tool*

1. Turn the ignition switch to the OFF position. Place the throttle in the idle position.

2. Remove the cover from the data link connector (**Figure 79**). Connect the scan tool to the data link connector.

3. Turn the ignition switch to the ON position. Follow the instruction booklet and the on-screen instructions and retrieve the stored trouble codes.

4. Refer to **Table 6** to match the code to the sensor or system. Refer to the test procedure in this chapter for the stored trouble code.

5. Perform the suggested repair. Clear the trouble codes as described in this chapter.

6. Disconnect the scan tool from the data link connector. Install the cover onto the data link connector (**Figure 79**).

## Clearing Trouble Codes

Stored trouble codes can be cleared using either a diagnostic code tool (**Figure 75**) or a scan tool (**Figure 76** or **Figure 77**). The engine must be started to clear the codes.

> *WARNING*
> *Stay clear of the propeller shaft while running the engine on a flush/test device. Remove the propeller before running the engine to avoid injury. Disconnect all spark plug leads and the battery cables before removing or installing the propeller.*

> *CAUTION*
> *Never run the engine without providing cooling water. Use either a test tank or flush/test device. Remove the propeller before running the engine on a flush/test device. Use a test propeller to run the engine in a test tank.*

### *Diagnostic code tool*

1. Turn the ignition key switch to the OFF position. Place the throttle in the idle position.

2. Remove the cover from the data link connector (**Figure 79**). Plug the diagnostic connector to onto the data link connector.

3. Turn the switch on the code tool to the ON position. Turn the ignition switch ON.

4. Advance the throttle to wide open position then back to idle.

5. Turn the switch on the code tool to the OFF position. Do not turn the ignition switch off before starting the engine.

6. Start the engine and run if for approximately 15 seconds. Turn the ignition switch to the OFF position.

7. Check for stored trouble codes as described in this chapter. Check for a discharged battery if the code(s) did not clear.

8. Disconnect the diagnostic code tool from the data link connector. Install the cover onto the data link connector (**Figure 79**).

### *Scan tool*

The codes must be cleared with the engine running.

1. Turn the ignition switch to the OFF position. Place the throttle in the idle position.

2. Remove the cover from the data link connector (**Figure 79**). Connect the scan tool to the data link connector.

3. Start the engine and operate at idle speed. Follow the instruction booklet and the on-screen instructions to clear the stored trouble codes.

4. Stop the engine. Check for stored trouble codes as described in this chapter. Repeat the clearing codes procedure if the code(s) did not clear.

5. Disconnect the scan tool from the data link connector. Install the cover onto the data link connector (**Figure 79**).

## Scanning the Engine

Scan the engine if operational problems occur and no other faults or trouble codes are present. This procedure can identify faulty sensors or wiring where a trouble code may not set.

> *NOTE*
> *On 496 Mag, 496 Mag HO and all 2002-2004 models with multi-port fuel injection (MPI), use only the Digital Diagnostic Terminal to troubleshoot the electronic control system. Follow the on-screen instructions to determine if the sensors and actuators are functioning properly. The trouble codes described in this chapter do not apply to 496 Mag, 496 Mag HO and 2002-2004 models with MPI.*

1. Turn the ignition switch to the OFF position. Place the throttle in the idle position.

2. Remove the cover from the data link connector (**Figure 79**). Connect the scan tool to the data link connector.

3. Start the engine and operate at idle speed. Follow the instruction booklet and the on-screen instructions to monitor the data. Compare the sensor voltages and corresponding pressure or temperature readings with the normal ranges listed in **Table 7**. Pull or tug on wiring while observing data. Faulty wiring or connections are often located in this manner.

4. Check for faulty wiring or connections for any sensor or circuits that fall outside of the normal range. Replace

the suspect sensor if the wiring and connections are in good condition.

5. Stop the engine. Disconnect the scan tool from the data link connector. Install the cover onto the data link connector (**Figure 79**).

## IDLE AIR CONTROL MOTOR TEST

A faulty idle air control motor (A, **Figure 71**) can cause stalling at idle, excessive idle speed or stalling during deceleration. A faulty idle air control motor does not affect engine operation at higher engine speeds. A diagnostic code tool or scan tool is required to test the idle air control motor.

*NOTE*
*On Models 496 Mag and 496 Mag HO, use only the Digital Diagnostic Terminal to troubleshoot the electronic control system. Follow the on screen instructions to determine if the sensors and actuators are functioning properly. The trouble codes described in this chapter do not apply to Models 496 Mag and 496 Mag HO.*

1. Start the engine and run until it reaches normal operating temperature.

2. Turn the engine off. Remove the cover from the data link connector (**Figure 79**).

3. Connect the diagnostic code tool or scan tool to the data link connector.

4. Start the engine and place it in service mode. If using a diagnostic code tool, plate the switch on the code tool to in the ON position. If using a scanner, follow the on-screen instructions to enter service mode.

5. The engine must increase in speed while in the service mode. Otherwise perform the following:

a. Stop the engine. Disconnect the diagnostic code tool or the scan tool from the data link connector.

b. Remove the idle air control motor as described in Chapter Eight. Clean and inspect the wire terminals. Replace the idle air control motor if the wiring and terminals are good.

c. Install the idle air control motor as described in Chapter Eight.

d. Check the idle air control motor as described in this chapter. Check for faulty wiring or terminals at the ECM if the idle air control motor fails to perform as specified.

6. Install the cover onto the data link connector (**Figure 79**).

### Engine Temperature Sensor (Code 14 or 15)

An engine temperature sensor (**Figure 80**) is used on all EFI models and carburetor equipped V6 and V8 models. It provides a varying resistance value to the ECM or ignition module, to determine the approximate engine temperature.

On EFI models, the input allows the ECM to alter the ignition timing and fuel delivery for optimum performance at a given engine temperature. The input from the engine temperature sensor is also used by the ECM to determine when to activate the overheat warning system. A faulty engine temperature sensor can cause a fast idle, excessive exhaust smoke, decreased fuel economy, hard starting or a false overheat warning.

On carburetor equipped models, the input from the engine temperature sensor is used by the ignition module to determine engine temperature. If overheating occurs the module retards ignition timing.

Most faults are caused by corrosion on wire harness or sensor terminals. Always check for poor connections before testing or replacing the sensor.

This procedure requires a digital multimeter a liquid thermometer and a container of water that can be heated.

*CAUTION*
*Suspend the engine temperature sensor so only the overheat switch is below the surface of the water. An inaccurate reading will occur if the test leads contact the water.*

1. Remove the engine temperature sensor as described in Chapter Eight.

2. Connect the ohmmeter between the two sensor terminals.

3. Suspend the sensor in a container of water (**Figure 81**). Ensure the sensor does not touch the bottom or sides of the container and the tip of the sensor is completely below the water surface.

4. Add cold water or heat the container until the water temperature reaches the temperatures specified in **Table 8**. Do not freeze or boil the water. Record the resistance at each temperature.

5. Compare the resistance reading with the specification listed in **Table 8**. Replace the engine temperature sensor if incorrect resistance readings are noted.

6. Check for faulty wiring or corroded terminals if the resistance is as specified but trouble codes occur. Check the wire harness for open or short circuits as described in this chapter.

7. Install the engine temperature sensor as described in Chapter Eight.

### Throttle Position Sensor (Code 21 or 22)

A throttle position sensor (B, **Figure 71**) is used on all EFI models. It provides a varying voltage to the ECM the corresponds to throttle movement. This varying voltage allows the ECM to determine actual throttle opening and rate of opening. The ECM alters the ignition timing and fuel delivery for optimum engine performance for the given throttle opening.

A faulty throttle position sensor can cause a fast idle, stumble during acceleration, hard starting or stalling during deceleration.

Accurate testing of the throttle position sensor requires a scanning tool. If this tool is not available, replace the sensor as described in Chapter Eight. Clear the codes and operate the engine. Check for trouble codes. The wiring or connection is faulty if the code returns. Check the wire harness for open or short circuits as described in this chapter.

If a scan tool is available, connect the tool and scan the engine as described in this chapter. Perform the test with the ignition switch in the ON position with the engine not running. Scroll to the function that displays TP voltage. Monitor the voltage while slowly opening and closing the throttle. The voltage must increase or decrease linearly as the throttle moves. Otherwise replace the sensor as described in Chapter Eight. If the trouble code returns, check the wire harness for opens or shorts as described in this chapter.

*NOTE*
*On Models 496 Mag and 496 Mag HO, use only the Digital Diagnostic Terminal to troubleshoot the electronic control system. Follow the on screen instruction to determine if the sensors and actuators are functioning properly. The trouble codes described in this chapter do not apply to Models 496 Mag and 496 Mag HO.*

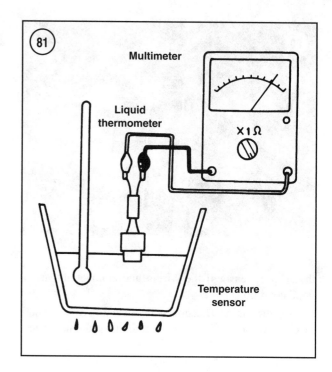

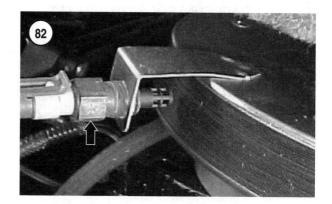

*NOTE*
*High-power electrical equipment such as stereos and communication radios may interfere with the electronic fuel injection system. Switch these devices off if trouble is detected with the engine*

### Air Temperature Sensor (Code 23 or 25)

An air temperature sensor (**Figure 82**) is used on all EFI models with a MEFI 3 or PCM 555 type ECM. This sensor is also used on engines using a multiport injection (MPI) system and a MEFI 2 type ECM. It provides a varying resistance value to the ECM. This varying resistance value allows the ECM to determine the temperature of the incoming air and alter the ignition timing and fuel deliv-

ery for optimum performance. A faulty air temperature sensor can cause excessive exhaust smoke, decreased fuel economy and lean operating conditions.

Most faults are caused by corrosion on the wire harness or sensor terminals. Always check for poor connections before testing or replacing the sensor.

This procedure requires a digital multimeter, an air thermometer, a supply of ice, and a common hair dryer.

1. Remove the air temperature sensor as described in Chapter Eight.

2. Connect the ohmmeter between the two sensor terminals. Measure the ambient temperature.

3. Compare the sensor resistance and ambient temperature measurements with the specifications in **Table 9**. The sensor resistance must fall within the range that includes the ambient temperature. Otherwise replace the sensor as described in Chapter Eight.

4. Observe the resistance measurement while surrounding the sensor tip with ice. The resistance must increase as the air surrounding the sensor cools. Otherwise replace the sensor as described in Chapter Eight.

5. Observe the resistance measurement while blowing hot air toward the sensor tip. Do not overheat the sensor. The resistance must decrease as the air surrounding the sensor warms. Otherwise replace the sensor as described in Chapter Eight.

6. Check for faulty wiring or corroded terminals if the temperature tests as specified yet trouble codes occur. Check the wire harness for opens or shorts as described in this chapter.

7. Install the air temperature sensor as described in Chapter Eight.

### Air Pressure Sensor (Code 33 or 34)

*NOTE*
*The elevation (above sea level) of the testing area must be determined for this procedure.*

*The elevation is listed on most topographical maps.*

An air pressure sensor (**Figure 83**) provides a varying voltage to the ECM relative to the air pressure in the intake manifold. This varying voltage allows the ECM to determine the pressure and alter the ignition timing and fuel delivery for optimum engine performance.

A faulty air pressure sensor can cause poor performance, excessive exhaust smoke, a rough or unstable idle, stumble during acceleration and decreased fuel economy.

Accurate testing of the throttle position sensor requires a scanning tool. If this tool is not available, replace the sensor as described in Chapter Eight. Clear the codes and operate the engine. Check for trouble codes. The wiring or connection is faulty if the code returns. Check the wire harness for open or short circuits as described in this chapter.

If a scan tool is available, connect the tool and scan the engine as described in this chapter. Perform the test with the ignition switch in the ON position and with the engine *not running*.

On the scanning tool, scroll to the function that displays the MAP voltage. Compare the voltage reading with the specification in **Table 10**. The voltage must match the voltage for the local elevation. Otherwise replace the sensor as described in Chapter Eight. If the trouble code returns, check the wire harness for opens or shorts as described in this chapter.

### Ignition Control Circuit (Code 41 or 42)

This code sets if a fault occurs in the circuit connecting the ECM to the distributor. On engines equipped with an MEFI 2 type ECM and Alpha drive unit, the shift interrupt switch is wired into this circuit. A faulty switch or an improperly adjusted shift cable can trigger this code. Check the shift cables and adjustment and test the shift interrupt switch before proceeding.

Refer to the wiring diagrams at the end of the manual to identify the wires connecting the ECM to the distributor. Disconnect the connectors and check for dirty or faulty terminals. Check the wire harness for open or short circuits as described in this chapter.

If no faults are found with the wiring, shift cables, or shift interrupt switch, replace the ignition module as described in Chapter Eight.

*NOTE*
*On Models 496 Mag and 496 Mag HO, use only the Digital Diagnostic Terminal to troubleshoot the electronic control system. Follow the on screen instruction to determine whether the sensors and actuators are*

*functioning properly. The trouble codes described in this chapter do not apply to Models 496 Mag and 496 Mag HO.*

*NOTE*
*High-power electrical equipment such as stereos and communication radios may interfere with the electronic fuel injection system. Switch these devices off if trouble is detected with the engine.*

## Knock Sensor and Knock Module Circuit (Code 43 or 44)

This code sets if the ECM detects continuous knock or fails to receive the signal from the knock sensor module (MEFI 2 ECM only). For either of these codes, test the knock control system as described in this chapter.

## Coil Driver Circuit (Code 45)

This code sets if the ECM detects excessive current draw from the ignition coil and connecting circuits. Excessive draw is generally caused by a shorted tachometer or related wiring, a faulty ignition coil or a short circuit in the wire connecting the ECM to the ignition coil.

Refer to the wiring diagrams at the end of the manual to identify the wires connecting the ECM to the ignition coil. Disconnect the connectors and check for dirty or faulty terminals. Check the wire harness for open or short circuits as described in this chapter under *Fuses, Circuit Breaker and Wire Harness*. Check the wire connecting the tachometer (gray wire) to the engine wire harness. Faulty connections at the back of the tachometer are common and may set this code.

If no faults are found with the wiring, clear the trouble codes as described in this chapter and run the engine. Check for trouble codes as described in this chapter. Replace the tachometer if the code returns.

## Memory Calibration Failure (Code 51 or 52)

This code sets if the ECM detects a fault in the internal memory circuits. If either of these codes are set, clear the codes as described in this chapter and run the engine. Check for trouble codes as described in this chapter. Replace the ECM if the code returns.

## Fuel Pressure Sensor (Code 61 or 62)

This sensor is used on all EFI models equipped with a MEFI 3 type ECM. It provides a varying resistance value

to the ECM, allowing the ECM to determine the fuel pressure and alter the ignition timing and fuel delivery for optimum performance. The input from the fuel pressure sensor is also used by the ECM to determine when to activate the low fuel pressure warning. A faulty fuel pressure sensor can cause excessive exhaust smoke, decreased fuel economy or a false low fuel pressure warning.

Be aware that these codes can set if the engine runs out of fuel, or during attempts to start the engine without sufficient fuel in the tank. If either of these codes is set, perform the following procedure:

1. Clear the trouble codes as described in this chapter. Run the engine and check for trouble codes. If the code returns, proceed with testing. Otherwise the fault was probably caused by running out of fuel or attempting to start the engine with insufficient fuel.
2. Test the fuel pressure as described in this chapter.
    a. If fuel pressure is low, correct the cause of low fuel pressure. Clear the trouble code as described in this chapter.
    b. If the fuel pressure is correct, replace the fuel pressure sensor as described in Chapter Eight.
3. Clear the trouble codes as described in this chapter. Run the engine and check for trouble codes. If the code returns, check for faulty sensor wiring and poor connections.

## WARNING SYSTEM

The warning system alerts the operator if a cooling or lubrication system failure occurs. Continued operation with the warning system activated can lead to serious and expensive engine damage. Refer to *Warning System Description* before testing any components. This section provides a brief description how the system operates and the components used. Refer to *Testing the Warning System* in this chapter for test procedures.

### Warning System Description

#### 3.0L models

This model is not factory equipped with a warning system. Monitor the dash mounted oil pressure gauge and engine temperature gauges frequently to detect problems before damage occurs. Check the oil level in the gearcase lubricant monitor (**Figure 84**) on a frequent basis. Check for lubricant leakage if the gearcase level drops below the add line.

An optional audio warning system kit is available for the model. The kit includes an oil pressure switch, overheat switch, warning horn and the wiring necessary to

connect these components to the engine and instrument harness. A purple wire connects the warning horn to the ignition ON terminal of the ignition switch, and supplies voltage to operate the horn. The tan/blue wire of the warning horn connects (via the instrument and engine wiring harnesses) to the gearcase lubricant monitor, oil pressure switch and overheat switch. Under normal operating conditions, all of these switches are electrically open.

The float switch in the reservoir closes if the lubricant level drops below a safe level. The oil pressure switch closes if the oil pressure drops below approximately 4 psi (28 kPa). The overheat switch closes if the engine overheats. Closing any of the switches completes the circuit to ground and the warning horn sounds a continuous tone.

The warning horn sounds as the ignition switch is turned to the ON position, because the engine has no oil pressure during startup. The horn should stop sounding a few seconds after the engine starts.

### Carbureted V6 and V8 engines

These models are factory equipped with an audio warning system. The system alerts the operator if the gearcase fluid level or oil pressure falls too low, or if the engine overheats.

The system includes the gearcase lubricant monitor (**Figure 84**), oil pressure switch, overheat switch, warning horn and related wiring.

A purple wire connects the warning horn to the ignition ON terminal of the ignition switch and supplies voltage to operate the warning horn. The tan/blue warning horn wire connects via the instrument and engine wiring harnesses to the gearcase lubricant monitor, oil pressure switch and overheat switch. Under normal operating conditions, all of these switches are electrically open.

The float switch in the reservoir closes if the lubricant level drops below a safe level. The oil pressure switch closes if the oil pressure drops below approximately 4 psi (28 kPs). The overheat switch closes if the engine overheats. Closing any of the switches completes the circuit to ground and the warning horn sounds a continuous tone.

The warning horn sounds as the ignition key switch is turned ON because the engine has no oil pressure during startup. The horn should stop sounding within a few seconds after starting the engine.

### EFI V6 and V8 engines

These models are factory equipped with an audio warning system. The system alerts the operator if the gearcase fluid level or oil pressure fall too low, or if the engine overheats. On models using a MEFI 3 type ECU, the warning system activates if the fuel pressure is low or if the input from one or more of the sensors exceeds the normal limits.

The system includes the gearcase lubricant monitor (**Figure 84**), oil pressure switch, warning horn, ECM and related wiring.

A purple wire connects the warning horn to the ON terminal of the ignition switch and supplies voltage to operate the horn. The tan/blue wire of the warning horn connects to the ECM via the instrument and engine wiring harnesses. Wires connect the gearcase lubricant monitor and oil pressure switch to the ECM. Under normal operating conditions these switches are electrically open.

The float switch in the reservoir closes if the lubricant drops below a safe level. The oil pressure switch closes if the oil pressure drops below approximately 4 psi (28 kPs). Closing either of the switches connects the ECM wire to ground. If the wire is grounded, the ECM completes the circuit to ground for the warning horn, causing it to sound.

On an MEFI 2 type ECM, the warning horn sounds a continuous tone until the fault is corrected.

On an MEFI 3 type ECM, the warning horn sounds in a repeating one second ON/ three seconds OFF pattern at engine speeds below 3000 rpm. The horn sounds continuously at engine speeds exceeding 3000 rpm.

The warning horn sounds for approximately two seconds as the ignition switch is turned to the ON position, as a test of the warning horn.

Check the oil level in the gearcase lubricant monitor (**Figure 84**) frequently. Check for lubricant leakage if the gearcase level drops below the add line. Monitor the oil pressure gauge and engine temperature gauges to detect problems before damage occurs.

**3**

**Warning System Test**

1. Test the warning horn as described in this chapter if the horn fails to sound when the ignition switch is turned ON.

2. Check the oil level in the gearcase lubricant monitor (**Figure 84**) before starting the engine. Check for lubricant leakage if the gearcase level drops below the add line.

3. Monitor the oil pressure gauge and engine temperature gauges frequently to detect problems before damage occurs. If either of the gauges fail to register, test them as described in this chapter.

4. If the warning horn sounds during engine operation, check the oil pressure and temperature gauges. Stop the engine as soon as possible to prevent serious damage to the engine or drive unit.

5A. Carbureted models:

   a. If low oil pressure is indicated, check the oil level as described in Chapter Four. Test the engine oil pressure as described in this chapter if the level is correct. Test the oil pressure switch if the oil pressure is correct but the warning horn sounds.

   b. If high oil pressure is indicated, test the oil pressure as described in this chapter. Test the gauge and sender if the oil pressure is correct.

   c. If engine temperature is excessive, test or inspect the cooling system components as described in this chapter. Test the gauge and temperature sender if the engine is not overheating.

   d. If the gauges show normal readings but the horn sounds, check the level in gearcase lubricant monitor (**Figure 84**). If the level is correct, test the lubricant monitor, engine temperature switch and oil pressure switch as described in this chapter.

5B. EFI models:

   a. If the gauge readings are normal but the horn sounds, scan the engine as described in this chapter.

   b. If the oil pressure is low, check the oil level as described in Chapter Four. Test the engine oil pressure as described in this chapter if the level is correct. Test the oil pressure switch if the oil pressure is correct yet the warning horn sounds.

   c. If the oil pressure is high, test the oil pressure as described in this chapter. Test the gauge and sender if the oil pressure is correct.

   d. If the engine temperature is excessive, test or inspect the cooling system components as described in this chapter. Test the gauge and temperature sensor if the engine is not overheating.

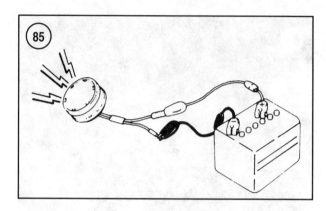

*Warning horn test*

> *WARNING*
> *Use extreme caution when working around batteries. Never smoke or allow sparks to occur in or around batteries. Batteries produce hydrogen gas that can explode and result in severe injury or death. Never make the final connection of a circuit at the battery, as an arc may occur and lead to fire or explosion.*

The warning horn is mounted behind the dashboard or near the remote control. Access to both wires is required to test the warning horn. Remove the horn as needed. Disconnect the horn from the instrument harness. Connect the horn leads to a battery using jumper leads (**Figure 85**). Replace the warning horn if it fails to emit a loud warning. Reconnect the horn leads.

**Engine Temperature Gauge Test**

1. Refer to the wire diagrams at the end of the manual to identify the temperature sender wires.

2. Disconnect the wire from the temperature sender (**Figure 86**). Do not remove the sender.

3. Turn the ignition switch to the ON position. Do not start the engine.

4. Connect one end of the jumper lead to the sender wire.

5. Observe the engine temperature gauge while repeatedly touching the free end of the jumper to an engine ground. The gauge must register full hot with the wire touching ground and full cold with the wire open. If not, check for faulty wiring or connections at the gauge. Replace the gauge if the wiring is in good condition.

6. Repeat Step 5 while touching the jumper to the body of the sender instead of an engine ground. The gauge must register as described. Otherwise remove the sender and clean the threads.

7. Turn the ignition key switch OFF.

8. Test the engine temperature sender if the gauge and wiring are in good condition but the gauge fails to register during engine operation.

### Engine Temperature Sender Test

This procedure requires a digital multimeter, a liquid thermometer and a container of water that can be heated.

*CAUTION*
*Suspend the engine temperature sender so only the overheat switch is below the surface of the water. An inaccurate reading will occur if the test leads contact the water.*

1. Remove the engine temperature sender as described in Chapter Eight.

2. Connect one ohmmeter lead to the switch terminal. Connect the other lead to the metal body of the sender.

3. Fill the container with cool tap water and suspend the tip of the sender in the water (**Figure 81**). Ensure the switch does not contact the bottom or sides of the container. Place a liquid thermometer in the container with the sender as shown in **Figure 81**.

4. Add cold water or heat the container until the water reaches the temperatures specified in **Table 11**. Record the resistance at each temperature.

5. Compare the resistance reading with the specification listed in **Table 11**. Replace the engine temperature if it fails to perform as described.

6. Install the engine temperature sender as described in Chapter Eight.

### Overheat Switch Testing

Identify the switch part number before testing. The test specifications vary by part number. A red plastic sleeve is installed on Part No. 48952. A black plastic sleeve is installed on Part No. 86080.

This test requires an ohmmeter, a liquid thermometer and a container of water that can be heated.

*CAUTION*
*Suspend the overheat switch so only the overheat switch is below the surface of the water. An inaccurate reading will occur if the test leads contact the water.*

1. Remove the overheat switch as described in Chapter Ten.

2. Connect one ohmmeter lead to the switch terminal. Connect the other lead to the metal body of the switch. The meter should indicate no continuity.

3. Fill the container with cool tap water and suspend the tip of the overheat switch in the water (**Figure 81**). Ensure the switch does not contact the bottom or sides of the container. Place a liquid thermometer in the container with the overheat switch as shown in **Figure 81**.

4. Begin heating and gently stirring the water while observing the ohmmeter. Record the temperature when the ohmmeter switches from no continuity to continuity.

5. The switching must occur within the temperature range specified in **Table 12**.

6. Allow the water to cool and record the temperature at which the ohmmeter switches from no continuity to continuity. The switching must occur at the range specified in **Table 12**.

7. Replace the overheat switch if it fails to perform as specified. Install the overheat switch as described in Chapter Ten.

### Oil Pressure Gauge Test

1. Refer to the wire diagrams at the end of the manual to identify the oil pressure sender wire.

2. Disconnect the wire from the oil pressure sender terminal (**Figure 87**). Do not remove the sender.

3. Turn the ignition switch to the ON position. Do not start the engine.

4. Connect one end of the jumper lead to the sender wire.

5. Observe oil pressure gauge while repeatedly touching the free end of the jumper to an engine ground. The gauge must register full pressure with the wire touching the ground and no pressure with the wire open. Otherwise check for faulty wiring or connections to the gauge. Replace the gauge if no faults are found with the wiring.

6. Repeat Step 5 while touching the jumper to the body of the sender instead of to an engine ground. The gauge must register as described above. Otherwise remove the sender and clean the threads.

7. Turn the ignition switch OFF position. Reconnect the wire to the sender. Verify proper gauge operation before operating the engine.

**Oil Pressure Sender Test**

> *WARNING*
> *Stay clear of the propeller shaft while running an outboard on a flush/test device. Remove the propeller before running the engine to avoid injury. Disconnect all spark plug leads and the battery cables before removing or installing the propeller.*

> *CAUTION*
> *Never run the engine without providing cooling water. Use either a test tank or flush/test device. Remove the propeller before running the engine on a flush/test device. Use a test propeller to run the engine in a test tank.*

> *NOTE*
> *A non-standard sender is used if the boat has dual control stations. **Table 13** lists the test specifications for the single and dual stations.*

1. Connect the oil pressure gauge to the engine as described under Oil Pressure Test in this chapter.

2. Disconnect the sender wire (**Figure 87**).

3. Connect one of the test leads to the terminal of the sender. Connect the other test lead to an unpainted surface on the sender body. The lead must contact bare metal for accurate testing.

4. Start the engine. Adjust the engine speed until the oil pressure reaches each specification listed in **Table 13**. Record the resistance reading at each oil pressure. Do not operate the engine with insufficient oil pressure.

5. Stop the engine. Record the resistance after the oil pressure drops to 0.

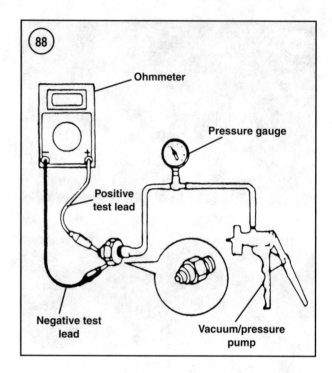

6. Compare the resistance readings with the specifications in **Table 13**. Replace the sender if any of the resistance readings are incorrect. Oil pressure sender replacement is described in Chapter Ten.

7. Repeat Step 4 and Step 5 with one test lead connected to an engine ground and one connected to the sender terminal. Remove the sender and clean the threads if the resistance readings differ from those taken in Step 4 and Step 5. Oil pressure sender replacement is described in Chapter Ten.

8. Remove the oil pressure gauge and related equipment as described in this chapter.

**Oil Pressure Switch Test**

This procedure requires a multimeter and a vacuum/pressure pump with a gauge, available from an automotive part or tool supply store.

1. Remove the oil pressure switch as described in Chapter Ten.

2. Carefully slide an appropriately sized hose over the fitting side of the oil pressure switch (**Figure 88**). Apply a clamp over the connection to ensure accurate test results.

3. Calibrate an ohmmeter on the R × 1 scale. Connect the positive ohmmeter lead to the wire terminal on the oil pressure switch (**Figure 88**) and the negative lead to the body of the switch.

4. Note the reading on the ohmmeter. The correct test result is no continuity.

5. Observe the ohmmeter and the pressure gauge while slowly applying pressure to the switch. The meter reading must change to continuity when the pressure reaches approximately 6 psi (41 kPa).

6. Relieve the pressure then repeat Step 5 several times to ensure an accurate result.

7. Replace the oil pressure switch if it fails to perform as specified.

8. Remove the test leads and pressure/vacuum pump from the oil pressure switch. Clean all hose material from the threaded section of the switch.

9. Install the oil pressure switch as described in Chapter Ten.

### Gearcase Lubricant Monitor Test

This test requires a multimeter and a soda straw.

1. Remove the monitor fill cap and correct the lubricant level as described in Chapter Four.

2. Disconnect the monitor leads (**Figure 84**) from the engine wire harness.

3. Calibrate the ohmmeter on the R×1 scale. Connect the ohmmeter test leads to the monitor leads. Do not inadvertently connect the ohmmeter leads to the engine wire harness.

4. The meter must indicate no continuity.

5. Use a soda straw to push the float to the bottom of the reservoir. Note the meter reading. The meter must indicate continuity.

6. Replace the lubricant monitor (Chapter Ten) if it fails to perform as specified.

7. Install the fill cap. Connect the monitor leads to the engine wire harness. The leads can connect to either harness connector.

## ENGINE MECHANICAL

This section provides instructions to determine if an engine malfunction is caused by mechanical failure. Engine compression and oil pressure testing are included in this section.

### Engine Noise

Some noise is generated during normal engine operation. A ticking noise or a heavy knocking noise that intensifies during acceleration is a reason for concern.

If a worn or damaged component is the suspected cause of engine noise, consider having a professional technician listen to the engine. In many cases only a trained ear can determine what component has failed.

Engine repair can be costly and time consuming. Investigate all noises thoroughly before disassembling the engine. A broken or loose bracket or fastener, loose engine mounts or faulty universal joint can cause a noise that is easily mistaken for internal engine failure.

*CAUTION*
*Running the engine with an abnormal noise may result in increased damage and greatly increase the cost of repairs.*

### *Ticking noise*

A ticking noise is common with valve train component failure or improperly adjusted valves.

A ticking noise can also result from a damaged piston. Inspect the spark plugs for damage or aluminum deposits (see preignition, **Figure 89**). Complete engine disassembly and repair is required if metal deposits are found on the spark plug. Perform a compression test as described in this chapter. Remove the cylinder head and inspect the valves, gaskets, pistons and cylinders if low compression is revealed. Cylinder head removal and installation is described in Chapter Seven.

If the spark plugs and compression are good, connect a timing light to one of the spark plug leads and start the engine. A valve train component failure is likely if the noise occurs in time with the flashing light. A connecting rod or crankshaft failure is likely if the noise occurs twice for every flash of the light.

Replace the lifters if a ticking noise persists and all other causes are ruled out.

### *Whirring or squealing noise*

A whirring or squealing noise is usually related to a problem with main or connecting rod bearings. Often the noise will become louder if the throttle is abruptly reduced to idle from a higher speed.

Sometimes the cylinder creating the noise can be identified using a mechanic's stethoscope (**Figure 90**). Touch the tip of the probe to the engine while listening. Compare the noise emanating from one area of the engine, cylinder head or crankcase, with the noise from the same area but different cylinder. A noise common to one cylinder only indicates a problem with its connecting rod bearing. A noise common to all cylinders indicates a problem with the crankshaft main bearings. Test the oil pressure as described in this chapter to determine if the noise is caused by insufficient lubrication. Be aware that belts, pulleys and the components they drive can generate a fair amount of noise. Use the stethoscope (**Figure 90**) to ensure the

## SPARK PLUG CONDITION

### NORMAL
- Identified by light tan or gray deposits on the firing tip.
- Can be cleaned.

### GAP BRIDGED
- Identified by deposit buildup closing gap between electrodes.

### OIL FOULED
- Identified by wet black deposits on the insulator shell bore and electrodes.
- Caused by excessive oil entering combustion chamber through worn rings and pistons, excessive clearance between valve guides and stems or worn or loose bearings. Can be cleaned. If engine is not repaired, use a hotter plug.

### CARBON FOULED
- Identified by black, dry fluffy carbon deposits on insulator tips, exposed shell surfaces and electrodes.
- Caused by too cold a plug, weak ignition, dirty air cleaner, too rich fuel mixture or excessive idling. Can be cleaned.

### LEAD FOULED
- Identified by dark gray, black, yellow or tan deposits or a fused glazed coating on the insulator tip.
- Caused by highly leaded gasoline. Can be cleaned.

### WORN
- Identified by severely eroded or worn electrodes.
- Caused by normal wear. Should be replaced.

### FUSED SPOT DEPOSIT
- Identified by melted or spotty deposits resembling bubbles or blisters.
- Caused by sudden acceleration. Can be cleaned.

### OVERHEATING
- Identified by a white or light gray insulator with small black or gray brown spots with bluish-burnt appearance of electrodes.
- Caused by engine overheating, wrong type of fuel, loose spark plugs, too hot a plug or incorrect ignition timing. Replace the plug.

### PREIGNITION
- Identified by melted electrodes and possibly blistered insulator. Metallic deposits on insulator indicate engine damage.
- Caused by wrong type of fuel, incorrect ignition timing or advance, too hot a plug, burned valves or engine overheating. Replace the plug.

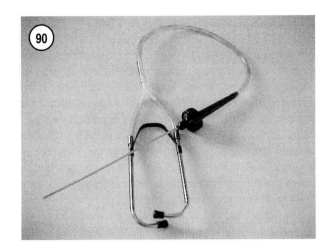

spark plug promptly to reduce the chance of damage to ignition system. Another method of isolating the cylinder is to remove one spark plug lead and attach it to an engine ground. Start the engine and listen to the noise. Install the spark lead and repeat the process for another cylinder. If the noise is less when one lead is grounded as compared with another, that cylinder is suspect. The stethoscope method of isolating cylinders is more effective for an amateur technician.

Always perform an oil pressure test if a knocking noise is detected. Knocking noise combined with low or unstable oil pressure generally indicates crankshaft main and/or connecting rod bearing damage. Refer to *Oil Pressure Test* in this chapter.

Bearing failure causes metal particles to accumulate in the oil pan. These particles are picked up by the oil pump where they are deposited in the oil filter. Inspect the oil filter if bearing failure is suspected. Remove the filter as described in Chapter Four. Cut open the filter and inspect the filter element. Bearing failure is likely if a significant amount of metal debris is found.

## Lubrication System Failure

Lubrication system failure can cause engine noise, increased wear and damage to the internal engine components (**Figure 91**), and eventual engine failure. Operating the engine with no or very little oil pressure will result in serious and expensive engine damage. Damage to some components can occur in a manner of seconds. To help prevent damage, stop the engine immediately if the warning horn sounds or the oil pressure gauge indicates low oil pressure.

Failure of the lubrication system results from the following common causes:
1. Incorrect oil level.
2. Oil leakage or high oil consumption.
3. Using contaminated, diluted or the wrong type of oil.
4. Failure of the oil pumping system.

> *CAUTION*
> *Damage can occur in a matter of seconds if the lubrication system fails. To help prevent serious engine damage, slow down and stop the engine at once if low oil pressure is indicated by the warning system.*

### *Incorrect oil level*

Incorrect oil level can result from improperly filling the engine or improperly checking the engine oil level.

noise is emanating from the engine before proceeding with an engine repair.

> *WARNING*
> *Use extreme caution when working on or around a running engine. Never wear loose fitting clothing. Take all necessary precautions to ensure no one gets near the flywheel or drive belts. Never allow anyone near the propeller or propeller shaft while the engine is running.*

### *Knocking noise*

Use a mechanic's stethoscope (**Figure 90**) to determine if the noise is emanating from the engine or elsewhere. The noise will be more pronounced in the crankcase area if a problem exists in the crankshaft and connecting rods.

Special insulated pliers are available that allow spark plug lead removal while the engine is running. The noise may lessen when the spark plug lead is removed on the suspected cylinder. This procedure is difficult to do and may result in damage to the electrical system. Ground the

If the oil level is too high, the crankshaft and other components will agitate the oil and cause bubbles to form. This foamy oil may cause a drop in oil pressure and lead to activation of the low oil pressure warning system. In some cases the oil pressure can remain above the low oil pressure activation point but the engine can still be damaged by inadequate lubrication.

Oil level check and oil filling instructions are provided in Chapter Four.

### Oil leakage or high oil consumption

A rapid drop in oil level can result from oil leakage or from high oil consumption. Common leakage points are at the rocker cover area, oil filter mounting surface, oil pan mating surfaces and fuel pump mounting surface (Model 3.0L). Finding the point of leakage can be difficult. Air flowing around the engine often distributes a thin film of oil on all external surfaces. To locate the point of leakage, carefully clean the engine using a shop towel and degreasing agent. Run the engine until it reaches operating temperature. Turn the engine off then wipe a white towel across all surfaces of the engine. Oil leakage is readily detected on the towel when the leakage point is contacted. Pinholes or casting flows may cause leakage to occur at other points on the engine. Many times simply tightening fasteners corrects oil leakage. Replace gaskets, seals or other effected components if the leakage continues.

All engines consume some oil while running. Some of the oil lubricating the cylinders and valves is drawn into the combustion chamber and subsequently burned. Oil consumption rates vary by model, condition of the engine and how the engine is used. Engines with high operating hours or engines with worn internal components generally burn much more oil than new or low hour engines. Damage to the piston and cylinders from detonation or preignition can cause increased oil consumption. New or recently rebuilt engines generally consume oil during the break-in period. After the break-in period the oil consumption should return to normal.

A typical symptom of excessive oil consumption is blue smoke coming from the exhaust during hard acceleration or high speed operation. Inspection of the spark plugs usually reveals fouling or an oily film on the spark plug (**Figure 89**).

Perform a compression test if the engine is smoking or an oil fouled plug is noted. Worn or damaged components will generally cause a low compression reading.

### Contaminated, diluted or wrong type of oil

Contaminants enter the engine oil during normal operation. Dirt or dust enters the engine along with the air used during normal operation. Dirt, dust and other particles are captured by the lubricating oil and circulated throughout the engine, although most of the larger particles are captured in the oil filter. Some smaller particles circulate through the engine with the lubricating oil. Frequent oil changes flush these particles from the engine before they reach high concentrations, which cause increased wear of internal engine components.

During normal operation, unburned fuel and water vapor accumulate in the lubricating oil. Oil also absorbs heat from the engine during operation. This heating causes the unburned fuel and water to evaporate from the oil and form crankcase vapor. The breather hose(s) or PVC valve and hose return the vapor to the combustion chamber where it burns or exits through the exhaust.

A faulty fuel system can dramatically increase the amount of unburned fuel in the oil. High levels of unburned fuel may not evaporate quickly enough to prevent oil dilution.

Failure to reach normal engine operating temperature prevents the fuel and water vapor from evaporating. This condition is generally caused by a faulty or improperly installed thermostat.

Wipe a sample of the oil from the dipstick between the thumb and forefinger. Compare the thickness of the oil with a sample of new oil. Smell the oil and look for a white or light colored residue.

A very thin feel, fuel smell in the oil or white residue indicates oil dilution. Test the cooling and fuel system, as described in this chapter, if oil dilution occurs.

Using the wrong grade, type or weight of oil can lead to increased engine wear or complete engine failure. Poor quality oil may not provide the level of protection required by the engine. Using the wrong type of oil usually leads to severe engine damage. Never use two-stroke outboard oil in a four-stroke engine. Using the improper weight of oil can prevent correct oil circulation during cold engine operation or allow excessive thinning of the oil at higher temperatures. Oil recommendations are provided in Chapter Four.

### Failure of the lubrication system

Failure of the lubrication system results in rapid wear of internal components and eventual engine seizure. Causes of oil pumping system failure include:
1. Worn, damaged or broken oil pump components.

2. Worn or damaged crankshaft or connecting rod bearings.
3. A blocked, damaged or loose oil pickup tube or screen.
4. A faulty or stuck oil pressure relief valve.

Failure of the lubrication system causes a loss of oil pressure and activation of the low oil pressure warning system. Continued operation results in rapid wear of internal components followed by eventual engine seizure. Check the oil pressure if the warning system activates after low oil level is ruled out as the cause. Refer to *Oil Pressure Testing* in this chapter.

### Detonation

Detonation damage is the result of the heat and pressure in the combustion chamber becoming too great for the fuel being used. Fuel burns at a controlled rate during normal combustion. If the heat and pressure become too high, the fuel explodes violently in the combustion chamber and can seriously damage internal engine components. The piston typically suffers most of the damage. Detonation usually occurs at higher engine speeds or during heavy acceleration. If the engine makes a pinging noise and loses power during acceleration, inspect the spark plugs for damage.

Aluminum deposits or a melted electrode (**Figure 89**) indicate detonation is occuring. . Perform a compression test to determine the extent of damage to the engine. Repair the engine if low compression is indicated. Correct the causes of detonation to prevent additional engine damage or repeat failures.

Conditions that promote detonation include:
1. Using a fuel with an insufficient octane rating.
2. Excessive carbon deposits in the combustion chamber.
3. Overheating of the engine.
4. Using an incorrect propeller or overloading the engine.
5. Lean fuel delivery.

6. Over-advanced ignition timing.

### Preignition

Preignition is caused by hot residue inside the combustion chamber which causes premature ignition. During preignition, the flame from the early ignition collides with the flame front initiated by the spark plug. A violent explosion occurs as these flame fronts collide. If preignition is allowed to continue, a hole will eventually burn through the piston crown (**Figure 92**). Inspect the spark plugs for aluminum deposits and perform a compression test if preignition is suspected. Preignition is commonly caused by:
1. Excessive carbon deposits in the combustion chamber.
2. Using the wrong heat range of spark plug.
3. Overheating of the engine.

### Engine Seizure

Engine seizure results from failure of internal engine components and can occur at any engine speed. Typically, an engine seizure is caused by failure of the crankshaft, connecting rod or piston, although the valve train components can also result in seizure.. Major repair is almost always required when engine seizure occurs.

Bear in mind that failure of the drive unit can also prevent flywheel rotation. Before suspecting the engine, remove the drive unit. Drive unit removal and installation is described in Chapter Eleven.

Engage the electric starter or manually rotate the engine with the drive unit removed. If the engine can be rotated, repair the drive unit as described in Chapter Eleven.

Water in the cylinders can hydraulically lock the cylinders and prevent flywheel rotation.

Refer to *Water Entering the Cylinder* in this chapter if the engine is seized while the drive unit is removed. Remove and repair the engine if the seizure is due to a reason other than water in the cylinders. Engine removal, repair and installation instructions are described in Chapter Seven.

### Water Entering the Cylinder

Water can enter the cylinder from a number of causes including:
1. Shutting the engine off at higher engine speeds.
2. Inadequate exhaust eloboww height.
3. Engine dieseling.
4. Water entering the throttle opening.
5. Water in the fuel.
6. Leaking exhaust manifold(s).
7. Leaking cylinder head gaskets.

8. Leaking water jackets in the cylinder block.
9. Leaking water jackets in the cylinder head.

The typical symptom is rough running, especially at idle. The engine may run correctly at higher speed as a small amount of water may not prevent normal combustion at higher speeds.

Water in the cylinder is almost always verified by inspection of the spark plugs. Water on the plug, a white deposit or a very clean appearance indicates water is entering the cylinder. If evidence of water is found, check all of the possible points of entry listed in this section.

### Shutting the engine off at higher engine speeds

Unless necessary to prevent and accident, never shut the engine off at speeds higher than idle. High vacuum forms in the intake manifold under this circumstance. This vacuum is applied to the exhaust passages due to camshaft overlap. High vacuum in the exhaust passages causes water to flow into the engine. Severe engine damage is likely in this event.

### Inadequate exhaust elbow height

The top of the exhaust elbow must extend a minimum of 15 in. (381 mm) above the water line. Otherwise water may siphon into the engine through the exhaust system. Measure the distance with the boat in the water and with normal loading and full fuel tank(s). Install exhaust riser kits if the water line-to-elbow distance is below the minimum specification.

### Engine dieseling

"Dieseling" describes a condition in which the engine runs after the ignition is switched off. Dieseling occurs if the fuel in the combustion chamber ignites from a source other than the spark plugs. It may be caused by excessive engine temperature, excessive combustion chamber deposits, poor quality fuel, and improper carburetor adjustment. The engine may run on for several seconds after switching it off and may actually run backward briefly at the end of the event. The backward engine rotation can draw water into the engine. If sufficient water enters the cylinders, the engine will hydraulically lock.

If the engine diesels, perform the following steps.
1. Remove the spark plugs and check for water. Ground the spark plug leads.
2. Rotate the engine to remove the water.
3. Install the spark plugs.
4. Change the engine oil.

5. Start the engine to remove residual water.
6. Correct the cause of dieseling before resuming operation.

### Water entering the throttle opening

The presence of water in the throttle opening indicates water is entering the engine. This condition results from submersion, a leaking engine cover or subjecting the engine to a considerable amount of water spray.

Water in the fuel allows water to enter the cylinders along with the incoming air. Inspect the fuel for the presence of water as described this chapter.

### Leaking exhaust manifold(s)

A leaking exhaust manifold allows water to enter the cylinders from the exhaust passages. High performance four stroke engines typically have an aggressive camshaft lift and duration creating a fair amount of valve overlap. Valve overlap allows reverse exhaust flow under certain conditions. Reverse exhaust flow may increase the chance of water entering the cylinders through the exhaust valves if water is present in the exhaust passages. Leaking exhaust elbow gaskets allow water into the exhaust passages. Correct leaking exhaust elbow gaskets if external leakage is detected or if water is found in a cylinder. Exhaust elbow removal, inspection and installation are provided in Chapter Nine.

### Leaking cylinder head gasket(s)

Exhaust, coolant, water or oil can leak from a failure of the gasket that seals the cylinder head to the cylinder block fails. Damage to the gasket often occurs when the engine has overheated. Symptoms of a leaking head gasket include:
1. Water in the oil.
2. Water entering the cylinder(s).
3. Overheating (particularly at higher engine speeds).
4. Rough running (particularly at lower engine speeds).
5. External water or exhaust leakage at the cylinder head-to-cylinder block mating surfaces.

Perform a compression test if any of these symptoms occur. Bear in mind that cylinder head gasket leakage is not always verified by a compression test. Often, two adjoining cylinders will show slightly lower compression than the rest. Removal and inspection of the gasket and mating surfaces verifies a gasket failure.

Remove the cylinder head and inspect the cylinders and piston domes if water is entering the cylinders and external causes are ruled out. Compare the appearance of the affected cylinder with other cylinders on the engine. Cylinders suffering from water intrusion usually have significantly less carbon buildup on the piston and combustion chamber. Rusting or corrosion of the valves, valve seats, cylinders and piston dome is also common when this condition is occurring. Complete engine repair is needed if the cylinders or piston domes are rusted or pitted. Refer to Chapter Seven for cylinder head removal and installation.

### *Leaking water jackets in the block or cylinder head(s)*

Leaking water jackets in the cylinder block or cylinder head can be difficult to find. Casting flaws, pinholes and cracks may or may not be visible. If water is entering the cylinder, but no visible defects in the gasket can be found, the cylinder block and/or cylinder block must be replaced. Continued operation with water intrusion will result in eventual engine failure.

### Water Entering the Oil

Normal condensation causes water to form in the oil. This is especially common if the engine is operated in cool and humid environments. Regular oil changes remove normal amounts of water before the engine suffers serious harm. Excessive amounts of water will dilute the oil and cause engine damage. Symptoms of excessive water include:
1. Water on the dipstick.
2. Water in oil drained from the crankcase.
3. A light color or milky oil appearance.

Excessive amounts of water in the crankcase are generally caused by water entering the cylinder, leaking water jackets in the cylinder block or head(s) or internal leakage in the oil cooler.

If the described symptoms occur, check for water entering the cylinder as described in this chapter. If water is not entering the cylinders, remove the oil cooler (if so equipped) as described in Chapter Nine. Have the cooler tested and repaired at a radiator repair shop.

### Timing Gear, Chain or Sprocket Failure

> *CAUTION*
> *Attempts to start the engine with improper valve timing or a broken timing chain can lead to damaged valves, pistons and other engine components.*

Excessive wear can allow the sprocket and chain to jump teeth, causing improper valve and ignition timing.

Typical symptoms include inability to start the engine, rough running or poor performance. This type of failure typically occurs on engines with very high operating hours. If these symptoms occur, check the ignition timing as described in Chapter Six. Suspect improper valve timing if the ignition timing is incorrect by several degrees or more.

Complete failure of these components impares valve and ignition system operation to the point that the engine will not start. Attempts to start the engine may cause a piston to contact a valve, resulting in serious engine damage.

### Sticking, Worn or Damaged Valves

Sticking, worn or damaged valves cause low compression, rough operation, poor performance and/or backfiring.

Corrosion or heavy carbon deposits can cause valves to stick in the open position. Valves can become bent or damaged from contacting the top of the piston or foreign objects in the combustion chamber.

Any of these conditions prevent the affected valve from closing completely, resulting in rough operation at lower engine speeds.

Backfiring occurs when a leaking valve allows the burning fuel to enter the intake manifold or exhaust passages. Backfiring or a popping noise from the intake is usually due to a stuck, worn or damaged intake valve. Backfiring or a popping noise coming from the exhaust is usually the result of a stuck, worn or damaged exhaust valve.

Perform a compression test if any the listed symptoms are noted.

Improper valve adjustment can cause the same symptoms as sticking, worn or damaged valves. Check the valve adjustment before disassembling the engine. Valve adjustment is described in Chapter Seven.

If backfiring is noted, run the engine with one spark plug lead at a time grounded. The backfire will stop when the spark plug lead is grounded on the affected cylinder. Remove the cylinder head and inspect the valves if backfiring and low compression are evident on the same cylinder and if improper valve adjustment has been ruled out.

Sticking valves are often the result of improper long term storage, water entering the cylinders or submersion of the engine. Using the wrong type of oil, improper fuel system operation or lugging the engine all contribute to increased deposits and wear of the valve and seat area.

Oil recommendations are provided in Chapter Four. Prevent lugging by selecting the correct propeller for the given engine and boat combination. Refer to Chapter One for propeller selection.

### Worn Valve Guides

Worn valve guides prevent consistent closing of the valves. A compression test usually will not verify an excessively worn valve guide because the valve tends to seat normally at cranking speed. Continued operation with worn valve guides will cause the valve seats to wear unevenly and the resultant low compression.

High oil consumption, fouled spark plugs and blue exhaust smoke during deceleration are typical symptoms of excessively worn valve guides and valve stem seals. Only cylinder head removal and inspection can confirm excessively worn valve guides. Refer to Chapter Seven.

### Camshaft Failure

Failure of any of the camshaft lobes can cause the same symptoms as a sticking or damaged valve. If the indicated symptoms occur, measure the camshaft lobe height as described in Chapter Seven.

Excessively worn camshaft lobes are generally the result of improper valve adjustment; using the incorrect type, grade or weight of oil; a high number or operating hours; or oil dilution. Valve adjustment is covered in Chapter Seven. Refer to *Lubrication System Failure* in this section for additional information on oil dilution.

### Rocker Arm Failure

Failure of a rocker arm results in loss of power and a ticking noise from the affected cylinder. Loss of compression results if the failure holds the corresponding valve open. Removal of the rocker arm cover allows visual inspection of the rocker arm and related components. Replace broken or worn rocker arms and components as described in Chapter Seven. Remove all remnants of the failed components from the cylinder head or oil pan before operating the engine. Engine failure can result if these remnants contact other moving components. Perform a compression test after assembly to check for potential damage to other components.

### Poor Performance

Poor performance can be caused by a fault in the ignition or fuel system, incorrect ignition timing, low compression, an exhaust restriction or using the wrong propeller. Check for and correct these items following the instructions described in this manual.

The basic MerCruiser engine is very similar in appearance to GM engines used in automobiles and light trucks.

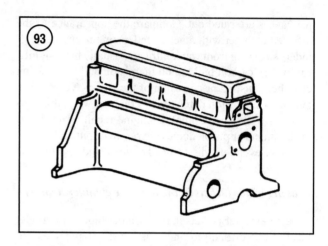

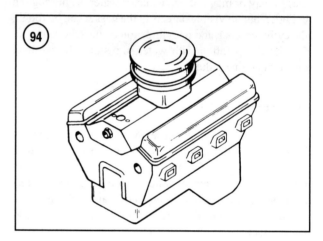

However, for a number of reasons, an automotive engine is simply not suited for a marine application. They are not as durable in this application and will not produce as much power. If you suspect that poor performance is due to using an automotive engine, check the engine identification code. On Model 3.0L, the code is stamped into the lower starboard side of the cylinder block (**Figure 93**). The identification code is stamped into the front of the cylinder block (**Figure 94**) on all other models. **Table 15** list the identification code for all models covered in this manual. Be aware that this code is not stamped in a replacement cylinder block.

### Oil Pressure Test

> *WARNING*
> *Stay clear of the propeller shaft while running an outboard on a flush/test device. Remove the propeller before running the engine to help avoid serious injury or death. Disconnect all spark plug leads and both*

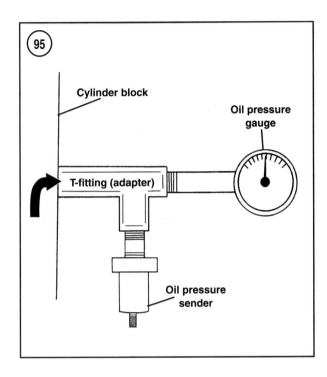

**Cylinder block**

**Oil pressure gauge**

**T-fitting (adapter)**

**Oil pressure sender**

battery cables before removing or installing the propeller.

*CAUTION*
*Never run the engine without first providing cooling water. Use either a test tank or flush/test device. Remove the propeller before running the engine on a flush/test device. Use a suitable test propeller to run the engine in a test tank.*

An oil pressure gauge, T-fitting and a shop tachometer are required to perform an oil pressure test. Perform the test while running the engine under actual operating conditions.

Test the oil pressure at the oil pressure sender port. Mounting locations, removal and installation for the oil pressure sender are described in Chapter Ten.

Use a fitting (**Figure 95**) with the same thread design as the oil pressure switch on the male and female ends. One of the female ends must have the same thread size and pitch as the oil pressure gauge. Oil pressure gauges and threaded adapters are available from most automotive parts stores. Tighten the fittings securely before running the engine.

Test the oil pressure as follows:
1. Run the engine until it reaches normal operating temperature.
2. Refer to Chapter Ten and remove the oil pressure sender.

3. Install the male end of the fitting into the oil pressure sender port (**Figure 95**). Securely tighten the fitting.
4. Install the oil pressure sender into one of the female openings of the fitting. Securely tighten the oil pressure sender.
5. Install the the oil pressure gauge (**Figure 95**) into the remaining female opening of the fitting. Securely tighten all fittings. Secure the oil pressure gauge hose to prevent it from contacting any moving components.
6. Following the manufacturer's directions, attach the shop tachometer to the engine.
7. Refer to **Table 14** to determine the correct speed to run the engine. Start the engine and immediately correct any oil leakage at the gauge and adapter fittings.
8. Shift the engine into forward gear. Observe the oil pressure gauge and advance the throttle to the specified engine speed (**Table 14**). Record the oil pressure. Return the engine to idle speed for a minute then switch it off.
9. Compare the oil pressure reading with the specification listed in **Table 14**. Oil pressure below the listed specification indicates a problem with the oil pumping system.
   a. Low oil pressure indicates low oil level, damaged or blocked pickup tube, worn or broken oil pump components, or worn crankshaft or connecting rod bearings. Inspect the oil pump and related components as described in Chapter Seven.
   b. Oil pressure exceeding 70 psi (482 kPa) when the engine is warm indicates a stuck or faulty oil pressure relief valve. Remove and inspect the valve as described under *Oil Pump* in Chapter Seven.
10. Remove the shop tachometer, oil pressure gauge and adapter. Install the oil pressure sender.

**Compression Test**

A good quality compression gauge and adapter are required for accurate compression testing. They are available at automotive parts stores and from tool suppliers. A small can of engine oil may also be required.
1. Remove the spark plugs and connect the spark plug leads onto a suitable engine ground, such as a clean cylinder head bolt.
2. Install the compression gauge into one of the spark plug holes (**Figure 96**). Securely tighten the hose adapter. Position the throttle in the wide-open position during testing.
3. Stand clear of the remaining spark plug openings during testing. Observe the compression gauge and operate the starter. Crank the engine a minimum of five revolutions at normal cranking speed. Record the compression reading.

4. Repeat Step 2 and Step 3 for the remaining cylinders. Record all compression readings.

5. All cylinders must have a minimum cranking pressure of 100 psi. (690 kPa). The compression on any cylinder must not be less than 70% of the highest compression reading.

6. If low compression is noted, pour approximately 1 teaspoon of clean engine oil into the suspect cylinder through the spark plug hole. Rotate the engine several revolutions to distribute the oil in the cylinder, then repeat Step 2 and Step 3.

    a. If the compression increases significantly, the piston rings and cylinder are excessively worn.

    b. If the compression does not increase, the compression leakage is the result of a worn valve face or seat.

7. Replace worn or defective engine components as described in Chapter Seven.

## COOLING SYSTEM

Inspect the cooling system if the gauge indicates overheating, the warning horn sounds, coolant overflows from the overflow reservoir, or if burnt paint or unusual odors occur. Overheating is caused by insufficient coolant flow through the engine or by a failure of the coolant to absorb engine heat as it flows through the engine..

MerCruiser engines use either a standard (**Figure 97**, typical) or closed cooling system (**Figure 98**, typical). A closed cooling system is standard factory equipment on Model 496 Mag and 496 Mag HO. Closed cooling is a factory or dealer installed option on all other models. Refer to the following for a description on how these systems operate.

### Standard Cooling System Operation

The seawater pump draws water through the water inlets in the drive unit and pumps it into the thermostat housing (**Figure 97**). A passage in the thermostat housing directs the water to the engine circulating pump. The circulating pump moves the water through the cylinder block and cylinder head(s). A small opening in the thermostat bleeds trapped air from the cylinder block and head(s). Once the block and heads fill completely, water passes through an opening in the thermostat and into the hose(s) leading to the exhaust manifold(s). The water passes through and cools the exhaust manifold(s). Finally the water mixes with the exhaust gasses and is discharged overboard.

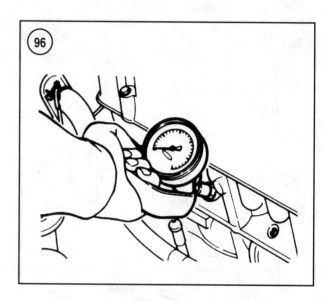

The thermostat remains closed when the engine temperature is less than the thermostat rating. When the thermostat is closed, the water essentially circulates through the cylinder block and head(s). This is necessary for quick warm up and to maintain a minimum operating temperature.

The thermostat opens when the engine reaches its normal operating temperature. The open thermostat allows water to exit the cylinder block and head. Cool water from the seawater pump flows into the cylinder block to replace the hot exiting water. The maximum engine temperature is determined by the amount of heat generated by the engine and the efficiency of the cooling system. Normal operating temperature is 143-175° F (62-79°C).

### Closed Cooling System Operation

The seawater pump draws water through the water inlets in the drive unit and pumps it to the heat exchanger (**Figure 98**). The water absorbs heat from the coolant as it flows through the heat exchanger. The water then passes through and cools the exhaust manifold(s). Finally the water mixes with exhaust gasses and is discharged overboard.

The circulating pump (**Figure 98**) draws coolant from the heat exchanger and moves it through the cylinder block and cylinder head(s).

The thermostat remains closed when the engine temperature is less than the thermostat rating. When the thermostat is closed, the coolant circulates through the cylinder block and heads to allow quick warm up and to maintain a minimum operating temperature.

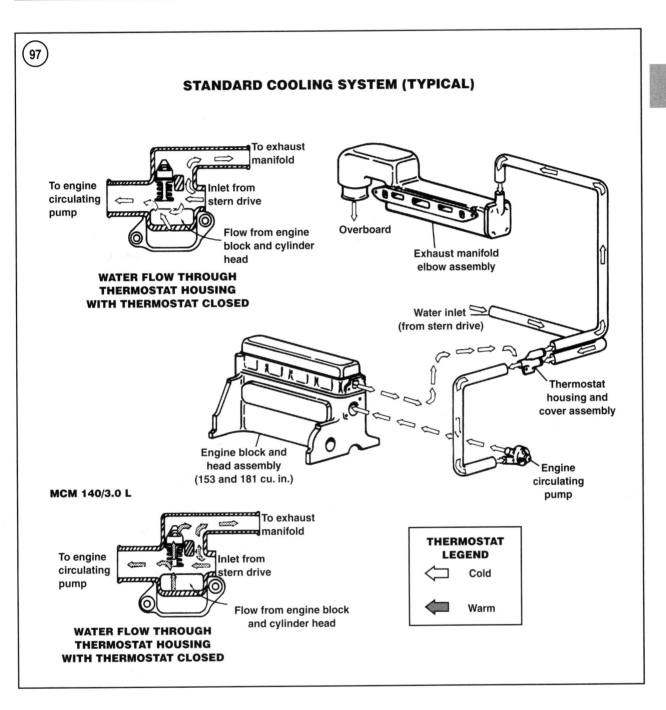

**STANDARD COOLING SYSTEM (TYPICAL)**

To exhaust manifold

To engine circulating pump

Inlet from stern drive

Flow from engine block and cylinder head

**WATER FLOW THROUGH THERMOSTAT HOUSING WITH THERMOSTAT CLOSED**

Overboard

Exhaust manifold elbow assembly

Water inlet (from stern drive)

Thermostat housing and cover assembly

Engine block and head assembly (153 and 181 cu. in.)

**MCM 140/3.0 L**

Engine circulating pump

To exhaust manifold

To engine circulating pump

Inlet from stern drive

Flow from engine block and cylinder head

**WATER FLOW THROUGH THERMOSTAT HOUSING WITH THERMOSTAT CLOSED**

| THERMOSTAT LEGEND | |
|---|---|
| ⇐ | Cold |
| ⬅ | Warm |

When the engine reaches its normal operating temperature, the thermostat opens, allowing coolant to flow through the heat exchanger. Maximum engine temperature is determined by the amount of heat generated by the engine and the efficiency of the cooling system. Normal operating temperature is 160-195° C (71-90° C).

Under certain conditions, a small amount of coolant can flow into the overflow reservoir. As the coolant and engine cool, the coolant contracts and is drawn back into the coolant reservoir. This is normal. However, check for engine overheating or a faulty reservoir pressure cap if the overflow reservoir fills with coolant.

### Cooling System Test

Most overheating problems are directly related to excessive wear or failure of water pump components. Inspect the water pump before inspecting any other cooling

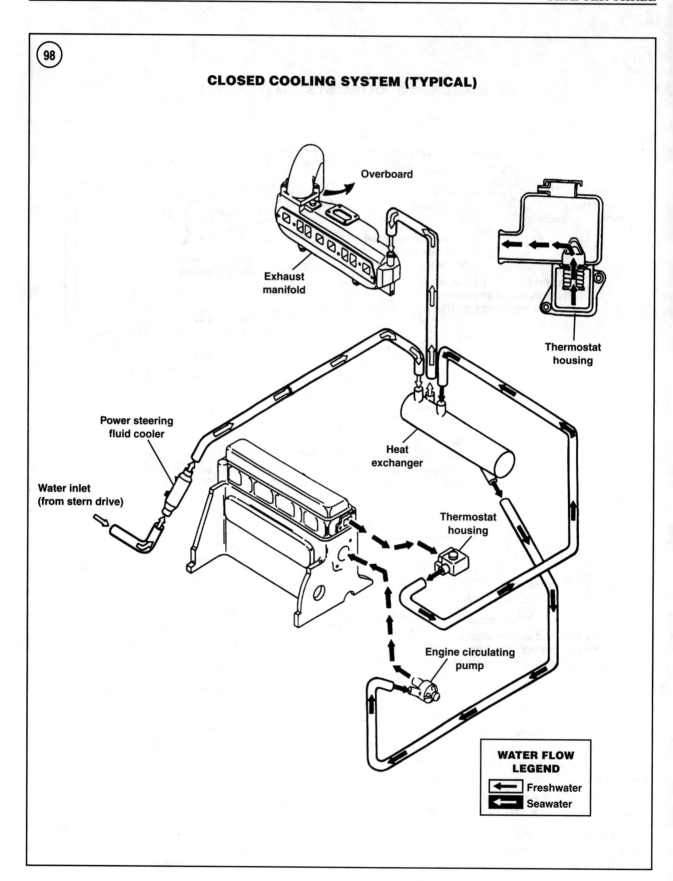

**(98)**

## CLOSED COOLING SYSTEM (TYPICAL)

Overboard

Exhaust manifold

Thermostat housing

Power steering fluid cooler

Heat exchanger

Water inlet (from stern drive)

Thermostat housing

Engine circulating pump

**WATER FLOW LEGEND**

← Freshwater

← Seawater

system components. Water pump inspection and repair instructions are described in Chapter Eleven for Alpha models and Chapter Nine for Bravo models.

Check for a worn or loose circulating pump drive belt. Replace the belt or correct the tension before proceeding.

Always verify the actual temperature of the engine using thermomelt sticks (**Figure 99**) before testing other cooling system components. Thermomelt sticks resemble crayons and are designed to melt at a specific temperature. The melting temperature is listed on the side of the stick.

Hold the sticks against the exhaust manifold(s), the cylinder head (near the spark plug) and the thermostat housing near the temperature sender or overheat switch.

Check the temperature during or immediately after the suspected overheat condition. Hold different temperature sticks to the power head to determine the temperature range the engine is reaching. Stop the engine if the temperature exceeds 195° F (90°C). Perform a cooling system inspection if excessive normal temperature is noted. Test the temperature sender or switch if an alarm or gauge indicates overheating but the thermomelt sticks indicate normal temperature. Troubleshooting an overheating problem with a flush/test attachment is extremely difficult because water supplied by the flushing adapter tends to mask problems with the cooling system. Perform this test with the engine in the water under actual operating conditions.

### *Standard cooling system*

1. If the cylinder heads and exhaust manifolds are overheating, test or inspect the following:
   a. Check for a restricted water inlet on the drive unit.
   b. Inspect the water pump as described in Chapter Eleven (Alpha drive) or Chapter Nine (Bravo drive).
   c. Remove the exhaust elbow and check for restricted water passages as described in Chapter Nine.

   d. Check for restrictions in the power steering and oil cooler.
   e. Check for leaking, restricted or collapsed cooling system hoses.
2. If the cylinder heads are overheating, but the exhaust manifold(s) is cool, test the thermostat as described in this chapter.
3. If the cylinder heads and exhaust manifolds are at normal temperature, test the overheat switch and temperature sender as described in this chapter.

### *Closed cooling system*

1. If coolant is flowing from the reservoir, test or inspect the following:
   a. Check the coolant level as described in Chapter Four. If the coolant level is low, pressure test the system as described in this chapter.
   b. Check for overheating with thermomelt sticks.
   c. Test the pressure cap as described in this chapter.
2. If the cylinder heads and exhaust manifolds are overheating, test or inspect the following:
   a. Check for a restricted water inlet on the drive unit.
   b. Inspect the water pump as described in Chapter Eleven (Alpha drive) or Chapter Nine (Bravo drive).
   c. Remove the exhaust elbow and check for restricted water passages as described in Chapter Nine.
   d. Check for restrictions in the power steering and oil cooler.
   e. Check for leaking, restricted or collapsed cooling system hoses.
3. If the cylinder heads are overheated, but the, exhaust manifold is cool, test or inspect the following:
   a. Check and correct the coolant level as described in Chapter Four.
   b. Test the thermostat as described in this chapter.
   c. Remove the heat exchanger cover and check for debris or deposits as described in Chapter Nine.
4. If the cylinder heads and exhaust manifold are at normal temperature, test the overheat switch and temperature sender as described in this chapter.

### **Thermostat Test**

If the engine is overheats or runs too cool, test the thermostat using a thermometer, a piece of string and a container of water that can be heated. The test specifications may vary depending on the material from which the thermostat is constructed. Brass thermostats are gold colored. They tend to turn green from exposure to corrosive water.

Stainless steel thermostats are silver colored. They tend to turn dark gray with exposure to corrosive water.

1. Remove the thermostat as described in Chapter Nine. Suspend the thermostat into the container of water with the string tied to the thermostat as shown in **Figure 100**.

2. Place the liquid thermometer in the container and begin heating the water. Observe the temperature of the water and the thermostat while heating the water.

3. Note the temperatures at which the thermostat begins to open and is fully opened. Replace the thermostat if the water begins to boil prior to the thermostat opening.

4. Remove the container from heat and observe the thermostat and the thermometer. Note the temperature at which the thermostat closes.

5. Compare the opening and closing temperatures with the specifications in **Table 16**. Replace the thermostat if it fails to perform as specified.

6. Install the thermostat as described in Chapter Nine.

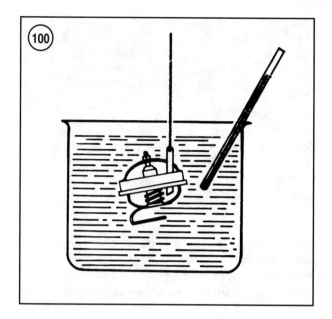

### Pressure Cap Test

This test requires a cooling system pressure tester, (**Figure 101**) available from an automotive part store or tool supplier. Take the pressure cap to the store when purchasing the tool to ensure it attaches properly to the cap.

1. Remove the pressure cap as described in Chapter Four.

2. Clean the rubber seal on the cap. Fit the pressure cap onto the tester (**Figure 101**) following the manufacturer's instructions.

3. Note the pressure reading while slowly applying pressure to the cap. Note the gauge reading when the cap reaches the relief pressure (air blows out of the tester).

4. Wait approximately two minutes and check the gauge reading to determine the cap holding pressure.

5. Compare the relief and cap holding pressure readings with the specifications in **Table 17**. Replace the pressure cap if it fails to perform as specified.

6. Install the pressure cap as described in Chapter Four under *Checking the Coolant Level*.

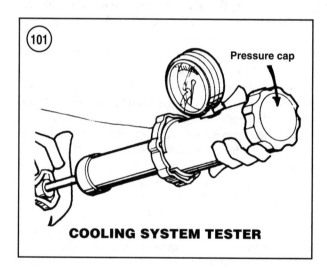

**COOLING SYSTEM TESTER**

### Pressure Test (Closed Cooling System)

Pressure test the closed cooling system if the system is losing coolant. This test requires a cooling system pressure tester (**Figure 101**), available from an automotive part store or tool supplier. Take the pressure cap to the store when purchasing the tool to ensure it matches the cap used on the engine. The engine must be completely cool before testing. Changes in engine temperature will affect the test results.

1. Remove the pressure cap as described under *Checking the Coolant Level* in Chapter Four.

2. Connect the tester to the pressure cap opening (**Figure 101**) according to the manufacturer's instructions.

3. Apply pressure until it reaches the test specification in **Table 17**. To check for leaks, spray a soap and water solution on the join where the tester connects to the system. Bubbles will form if air is leaking from the connections. Any air leakage will cause incorrect test results. Clean debris from the tester mating surface if it leaks.

4. Thoroughly inspect the external engine surfaces for coolant leakage. Correct leakage before proceeding.

5. The system must hold pressure for a minimum of two minutes.

   a. If no pressure drop is detected, check for leakage from the overflow reservoir or connecting hose. Otherwise the system is not leaking coolant.

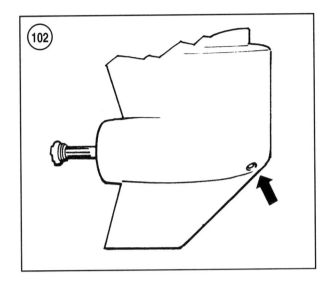

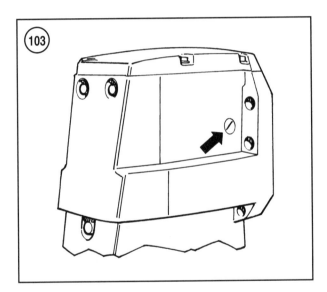

### Lubricant Inspection

Refer to Chapter Eleven to locate the drive unit drain/fill plug (**Figure 102**, typical). Position the drive unit in a vertical position. Do not remove the oil level plug (**Figure 103**, typical). Remove the drain plug and allow a teaspoon of lubricant to flow onto a small piece of cardboard. Quickly install the drain plug. Refer to Chapter Four to check and correct the lubricant level. Inspect the lubricant for water or other contaminants.

Pressure test the drive unit if the lubricant contains water. Refer to *Pressure Test* in this chapter. Failure to correct the leakage will lead to extensive internal component damage. Continued neglect will cause complete failure of the drive unit.

Fine metal particles form in the drive unit during normal usage. The lubricant may have a metallic flake appearance when inspected during routine maintenance. Fine metal particles tend to cling to the magnetic end of the drain plug. Rub a small amount of the meterial between the thumb and forefinger. If any of the material is large enough to feel, disassemble and repair the drive unit as described in Chapter Eleven.

### Drive Unit Pressure Testing

Pressure test the drive unit if external leakage is noted or if the lubricant contains water.

A suitable gearcase pressure tester is required to perform this test. Air pressure is applied to the drive unit and the pressure gauge indicates whether leakage is present. Apply a soap and water solution to the seals and other surfaces to identify location of the leak.

1. Thoroughly drain the drive unit as described in Chapter Four. Remove the drive unit as described in Chapter Eleven.

2. Install the pressure tester fitting into the level/vent or drain/fill plug opening. Securely tighten the pressure tester fitting.

3. Slowly apply pressure to the drive unit. Push, pull and turn all shafts while observing the pressure gauge as the pressure is slowly increased. Stop applying pressure when it reaches 100 kPa (14.5 psi).

4. Apply a soap and water solution to all seals and casting surfaces. Replace the seal or seal surface at any location where bubbles appear.

5. In most instances this procedure will locate the source of leakage. However, replace all seals and inspect all seal surfaces if the drive unit loses fluid but no visible leakage is detected. In some instances the leakage will only occur during operation.

b. If a drop in pressure is detected, remove the heat exchanger as described in Chapter Nine. Have the exchanger cleaned and checked at a radiator repair shop. Install the heat exchanger and retest. Check for leaking cylinder heads or intake manifold gaskets if the pressure drop persists.

6. Remove the pressure tester. Install the pressure cap as described in Chapter Four.

### DRIVE UNIT

If shifting difficulty, leakage or unusual noises occur, refer to **Table 18**. Test or inspect the items for the applicable symptom. Lubricant inspection and pressure test instructions are described in this section.

6. Slowly bleed the air from the drive unit. Install the drive unit as described in Chapter Eleven.

7. Fill the drive unit with the recommended lubricant as described in Chapter Four.

### Drive Unit Vibration or Noise

Normal drive unit noise is barely noticeable over normal engine noise. The presence of rough growling noises or a loud high-pitched whine is reason for concern. These noises usually are caused by failed or damaged internal components. Inspect the lubricant for metal contamination if abnormal noises are noted. In almost all cases, inspection of the lubricant will determine if drive unit components have failed.

#### Knocking or grinding noise

A knocking or grinding noise coming from the drive unit is likely caused by damaged gears or other components in the drive unit. Damaged gears typically create a substantial amount of larger metal particles. This type of failure usually results in damage to most internal components and complete repair is needed. Refer to Chapter Eleven for drive unit repair.

#### High pitch whine

If a high pitch whine is present it normally indicates a bearing problem or misaligned gears. The only way to verify a faulty gear or bearing is to disassemble the drive unit and inspect all components. Refer to Chapter Eleven for drive unit repair.

#### Vibration

In almost all cases an unusual vibration is due to a bent propeller shaft or damaged propeller. The propeller can appear to be in perfect condition but still be unbalanced. The best way to solve propeller vibration is to have the propeller checked at a propeller repair shop. Another option is to try a different propeller.

Always check for a bent propeller shaft if vibration is present. Check the propeller shaft as described in Chapter Eleven. A bent propeller shaft is usually caused by striking an underwater object while underway. In many cases other damage occurs to the drive unit.

Never operate the engine if severe vibration is present. Vibrating components place excessive stress to the gears, bearings and other engine components. Operating the en-

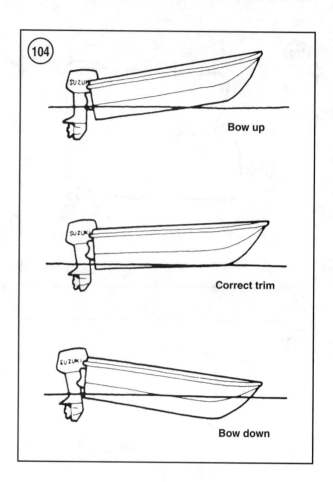

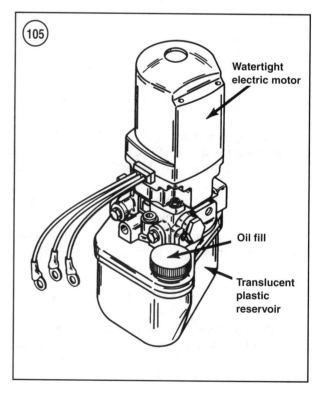

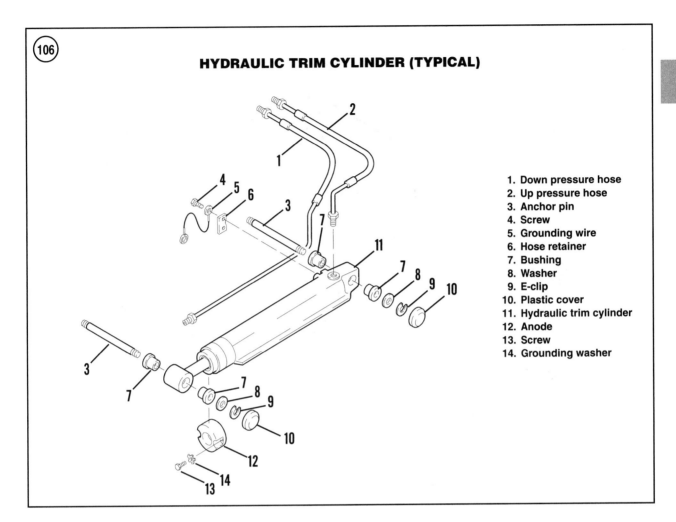

**HYDRAULIC TRIM CYLINDER (TYPICAL)**

1. Down pressure hose
2. Up pressure hose
3. Anchor pin
4. Screw
5. Grounding wire
6. Hose retainer
7. Bushing
8. Washer
9. E-clip
10. Plastic cover
11. Hydraulic trim cylinder
12. Anode
13. Screw
14. Grounding washer

**3**

gine with excessive vibration can seriously compromise the durability of the entire stern drive system.

> *WARNING*
> *Remove all spark plug leads and disconnect both battery cables before working around the propeller.*

### TRIM SYSTEM

Operating the boat with the drive tilted out raises the bow of the boat. This bow-up trim (**Figure 104**) may increase boat speed by reducing the amount of water contacting the hull. Tilting the drive out may also cause excessive bow lift and reduce visibility for the operator during acceleration. As the drive is tilted out, the propeller is positioned progressively closer to the water surface and may allow the propeller to draw in surface air (ventilate). Ventilation causes the propeller to lose its grip on the water and causes the engine speed to increase without increasing in thrust.

Operating the boat with the drive tilted in lowers the bow of the boat. This bow-down trim (**Figure 104**) improves rough water ride and reduces ventilation during acceleration. Be aware that tilting the drive in reduces boat speed and can contribute to a dangerous handling condition (bow steer) on some boats.

The correct trim angle is a compromise between the best acceleration and top speed. The angle chosen must not be high enough to cause a rough ride or low enough that handling suffers. Correct trim angle (**Figure 104**) positions the drive tilted out 3-5° from the water line on most applications.

### Trim System Operation

The trim system includes the trim pump (**Figure 105**), trim cylinders (**Figure 106**, typical), trim switches and related wiring (**Figure 107**).

Hydraulic pressure to operate the system is provided by the bi-directional hydraulic pump. The pump is driven by the bi-directional watertight electric motor (**Figure 105**).

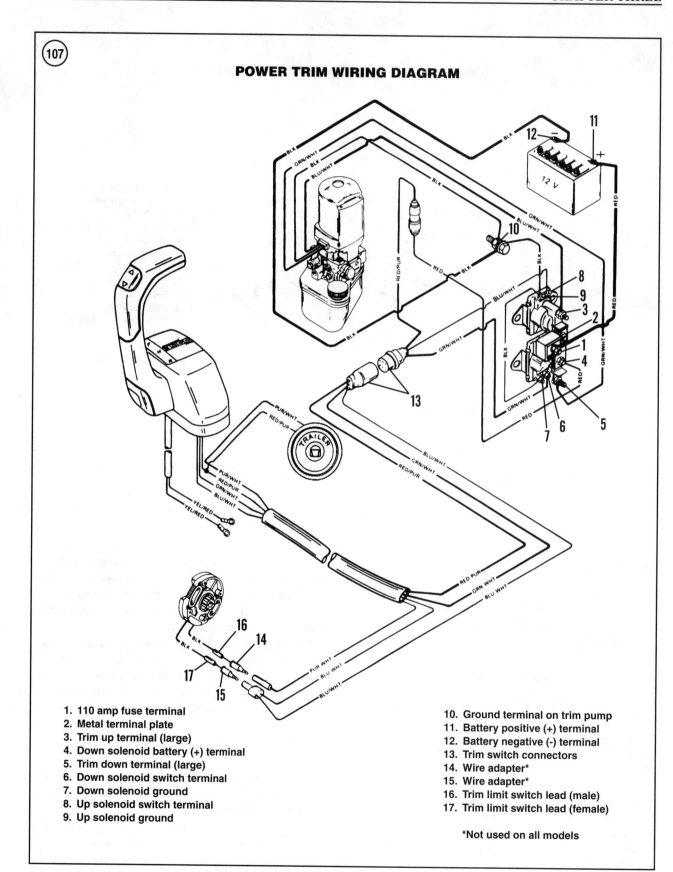

**POWER TRIM WIRING DIAGRAM**

1. 110 amp fuse terminal
2. Metal terminal plate
3. Trim up terminal (large)
4. Down solenoid battery (+) terminal
5. Trim down terminal (large)
6. Down solenoid switch terminal
7. Down solenoid ground
8. Up solenoid switch terminal
9. Up solenoid ground

10. Ground terminal on trim pump
11. Battery positive (+) terminal
12. Battery negative (-) terminal
13. Trim switch connectors
14. Wire adapter*
15. Wire adapter*
16. Trim limit switch lead (male)
17. Trim limit switch lead (female)

*Not used on all models

Current to operate the switches is provided by the red/purple wire and a 20 amp fuse (**Figure 107**). Current is supplied to the trim solenoids and the 20 amp fuse by dedicated battery cables and a 110 amp fuse (**Figure 107**).

When the up trim button is depressed, battery current is supplied to the UP solenoid terminal (8, **Figure 107**) by the blue/white wire. This energizes the up solenoid, supplying battery current to the up field windings in the trim motor. This makes the trim motor drive the hydraulic pump in the UP direction. Pressure is directed to the UP cavity in the trim cylinders. The trim rams extend when the pressure is high enough to offset the load of the propeller or weight of the drive unit. Fluid in the down cavity of the cylinders returns to the trim pump via the down hoses (1, **Figure 106**, typical). Releasing the switch de-energizes the UP trim solenoid, stopping the trim motor and pump. Valves in the trim pump close to prevent fluid from entering the pump from either the UP or DOWN hoses.

Upward movement of the drive moves the center portion of the trim limit switch. At a preset point, the trim limit switch opens the circuit connecting the trim switch to the UP solenoid terminal (8, **Figure 107**). This causes the up trim solenoid to de-energize, stopping the trim motor and pump. This feature prevents the drive unit from trimming up too far. Activating the trailer switch (**Figure 107**) bypasses the trim limit switch to allow the additional up trim range needed when trailering or beaching the boat.

When the DOWN trim button is depressed, battery current is supplied to the DOWN solenoid terminal (6, **Figure 107**) by the green/white wire. This energizes the DOWN solenoid, supplying battery current to the DOWN field windings in the trim motor. This causes the trim motor to drive the hydraulic pump in the DOWN direction. Pressure is directed via the DOWN hoses (1, **Figure 106**, typical) to the DOWN cavity in the trim cylinders. Fluid in the up cavity of the cylinders returns to the trim pump via the up hoses (2, **Figure 106**, typical). Releasing the switch de-energizes the DOWN trim solenoid stopping the trim motor and pump.

*NOTE*
*On 496 Mag, 496 Mag HO and all 2002-2004 models with multi-port fuel injection (MPI), the trim up circuit may be connected into the ECM circuitry. This arrangement prevents the trim up operation unless the ignition key switch is in the ON or RUN position. However, the trim down circuit will operate with the ignition key switch ON or OFF. On these models, turn the ignition key switch to the ON or RUN position before operating the trim system.*

### Electrical System Test

Test the electrical system if the trim motor does not operate or operates only in one direction. Perform the test or inspection for the applicable symptom listed in **Table 19**. Test instructions for the individual components are described in this section.

### *Fuse test*

Remove and test the 10 amp and 110 amp fuses as described under *Fuses, Circuit Breaker and Wire Harness* in this chapter.

### *Trim switches test*

This test requires a multimeter. Refer to **Figure 107** during testing.

1. Loosen the clamp and disconnect the trim switch connectors (13, **Figure 107**).

2. Place the drive in the full down position. Calibrate an ohmmeter to the R×1 scale.

3. Touch the positive multimeter lead to the red/purple wire in the trim switch connector (not the trim pump harness connector). Touch the negative meter lead to the green/white wire terminal.

4. Observe the meter while toggling the trim switch to the UP trim, DOWN trim and TRAILER positions. The meter must indicate continuity with the switch in the DOWN trim position and no continuity in the UP and TRAILER positions. Replace the trim switch or repair defective wiring if the trim switch fails to perform as specified.

5. Touch the positive meter lead to the red/purple wire in the trim switch connector (not the trim pump harness connector). Touch the negative meter lead to the blue/white wire terminal.

6. Observe the meter while toggling the trim switch to the UP trim, DOWN trim and TRAILER switch positions. The meter must indicate no continuity with the switch in the DOWN position and continuity in the UP or TRAILER positions.

a. If continuity is present with the switch in the DOWN position, replace the switch. If continuity is present with the switch in the TRAILER position only, inspect the switch wiring and connections. If the wiring and connections are in acceptable condition, replace the switch.

b. If continuity is present with the switch in the UP position only, test the trim limit switch as described in this chapter. If the trim limit switch operates correctly, repair the wiring or connections or replace the switch as appropriate.

  c. If there is no continuity in any switch position, re-
     pair the wiring or replace the switch as required.
7. Reconnect the trim switch harness connector (13, **Fig-ure 107**). Securely tighten the clamp.

### UP trim solenoid test

1. Remove the cover from the solenoids.
2. Touch the positive voltmeter lead to the fuse terminal (1, **Figure 107**). Touch the negative lead to the ground terminal (10, **Figure 107**). The meter must indicate battery voltage. Otherwise check for faulty battery connections or cables.
3. Touch the positive voltmeter lead to the metal terminal plate (2, **Figure 107**). Touch the negative lead to the ground terminal (10, **Figure 107**). The meter must indicate battery voltage. Otherwise test or replace the 110 amp fuse (**Figure 107**).
4. Touch the positive voltmeter lead to the fuse terminal (1, **Figure 107**). Touch the negative lead to solenoid ground terminal (9, **Figure 107**). The meter must indicate battery voltage. Otherwise repair the faulty ground (black) wire or terminal.
5. Touch the negative voltmeter lead to the ground terminal (10, **Figure 107**). Touch the positive lead to the blue/white wire (8, **Figure 107**). Observe the meter while operating the trim switch in the UP trim position. The meter must indicate battery voltage. Otherwise test the trim switche as described in this chapter.
6. Touch the negative voltmeter lead to the ground terminal (10, **Figure 107**). Touch the positive lead to the trim UP (blue/white) wire (3, **Figure 107**). Observe the meter while operating the trim switch in the UP and if necessary the TRAILER position. The solenoid must make a clicking noise and the meter must indicate battery voltage. Otherwise replace the up trim solenoid (Chapter Thirteen).
7. Repair or replace the trim motor if the trim solenoid operates correctly but the trim motor fails to operate. Install the terminal cover and secure with the screw

### DOWN trim solenoid test

1. Remove the cover from the solenoids.
2. Touch the positive voltmeter lead to the fuse terminal (1, **Figure 107**). Touch the negative lead to the ground terminal (10, **Figure 107**). The meter must indicate battery voltage. Otherwise check for faulty battery connections or cables.
3. Touch the positive voltmeter lead to the battery terminal (4, **Figure 107**) on the down solenoid. Touch the negative lead to the ground terminal (10, **Figure 107**). The meter must indicate battery voltage. If not, test the 110 amp fuse.
4. Touch the positive voltmeter lead to the fuse terminal (1, **Figure 107**). Touch the negative lead to solenoid ground terminal (7, **Figure 107**). The meter must indicate

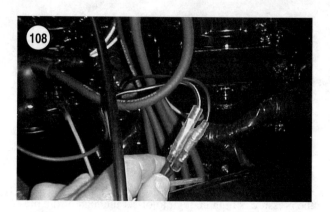

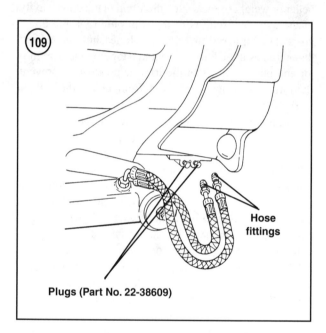

Plugs (Part No. 22-38609)

Hose fittings

battery voltage. Otherwise repair faulty ground (black) wire or terminal.
5. Touch the negative test lead to the ground terminal (10, **Figure 107**). Touch the positive lead to the green/white wire terminal (6, **Figure 107**). Observe the meter while operating the trim switch in the DOWN position. The meter must indicate battery voltage. Otherwise test the trim switche as described in this chapter.
6. Touch the negative test lead to the ground terminal (10, **Figure 107**). Touch the positive lead to the DOWN (green/white) wire (5, **Figure 107**). Observe the meter while operating the trim switch in the DOWN position. The solenoid must make a clicking sound and the meter must indicate battery voltage. Otherwise replace the down trim solenoid as described in Chapter Thirteen.
7. Repair or replace the trim motor if the trim solenoid operates correctly but the trim motor fails to operate. Install the terminal cover and secure with the screw.

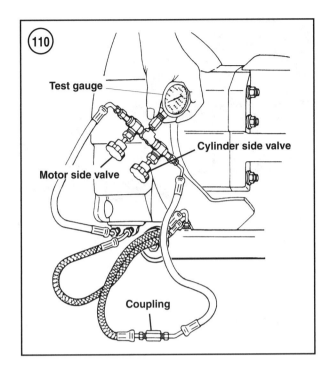

**Trim Limit Switch Test**

1. Place the drive unit in the full-down position. Disconnect the trim limit switch leads (16 and 17, **Figure 107**) from the trim switch harness.

2. Calibrate the ohmmeter on the R×1 scale. Connect the ohmmeter between the trim switch leads. Do not connect the meter to the trim switch harness.

3. With the drive unit fully down, the ohmmeter must indicate no continuity. If continuity is noted, time the trim limit switch as described under *Trim Limit Switch and Trim Sender Replacement* in Chapter Twelve. Replace the trim limit switch if continuity is still present after adjustment.

4. Observe the meter while operating the trim in the UP direction, then using the trailer switch. The meter must change from continuity to no continuity before the drive reaches the full-UP position. Otherwise replace the trim limit switch.

5. Connect the negative ohmmeter lead to an engine ground. Observe the meter while touching the positive lead to each of limit switch leads. The meter must indicate no continuity at each connection point. Otherwise the switch leads are shorted to ground and the switch must be replaced.

6. Connect the limit switch leads to the trim switch harness.

**Trim Gauge Test**

*WARNING*
*Arcing may occur during testing. Remove fuel, vapor or other combustible material from the engine compartment before proceeding.*

1. Disconnect the trim sender leads from the engine wire harness (**Figure 108**). Turn the ignition switch on.

2. Observe the trim gauge while touching a jumper to the disconnected leads (engine harness side). The meter needle must swing to the full- UP and DOWN position as the jumper is connected and disconnected. Otherwise check for faulty wiring at the gauge. Replace the trim gauge if the wiring is in good condition.

3. Turn the ignition switch OFF. Connect the trim sender leads to the engine harness leads.

**Trim Sender Test**

1. Disconnect the trim sender from the engine wire harness (**Figure 108**).

2. Calibrate an ohmmeter to the Rx10 scale. Connect the ohmmeter between the trim sender leads. Do not connect the meter to the engine harness.

3. Observe the ohmmeter while operating the system to the fully UP and DOWN positions. The resistance must change smoothly, in a linear amount as the drive moves. If the resistance change is erratic or jumpy, time the sender as described under *Trim Limit Switch and Trim Sender Replacement* in Chapter Twelve. Repeat this test and replace the trim sender if it still fails to operate as specified.

4. Reconnect the trim sender leads. Adjust the sender as described in Chapter Six.

**Hydraulic System Test**

Test the hydraulic system if the trim motor operates in both directions but the drive fails to move in one or both directions, leaks down from the trailering position, or trails out while in reverse gear or during deceleration.

This procedure requires a test gauge kit (Mercury part No. 91-52915a6 or equivalent). The battery must be fully charged for accurate test results.

1. Correct the trim fluid level as described in Chapter Thirteen. Place a suitable container under the outer transom housing to capture spilled fluid.

2. Place the drive unit in the full-DOWN position. Remove the aft trim cylinder anchor pin (Chapter Thirteen).

3. Place a block under the cylinders to prevent the trim rams from snagging on the drive unit or other objects as they extend and retract.

4. Disconnect the trim cylinder hoses (**Figure 109**) from the starboard side of the terminal block. Install plugs (Mercury part No. 22-38609 or equivalent) into each terminal block opening. Securely tighten the plugs.

5. Disconnect the UP pressure hose from the port side of the terminal block. Connect one of the pressure gauge hoses (**Figure 110**) to the terminal block opening. Securely tighten the hose fitting. Use the coupler (**Figure**

110) to connect the other pressure gauge hose to the disconnected trim cylinder hose.

6. Fully open both valves (**Figure 110**). Operate the trim pump in the UP and DOWN directions until one cylinder fully extends and contracts several times. Correct any leakage at the fittings before proceeding.

7. Observe the pressure gauge while operating the trim pump in the UP direction. Read the maximum pressure when the ram fully extends. The pressure must be 2200-2600 psi (15,169-17,927 kPa).

8. Stop the pump and observe the pressure gauge. The pressure must not drop below 1900 psi (13,100 kPa) for a period of two minutes. Refer to step 12 if the system tests as specified. Otherwise proceed with testing.

9. Operate the trim pump in the UP direction until the ram fully extends and the pressure reading peaks. Close the valve on the motor side of the gauge (**Figure 110**) and stop the pump. Observe the pressure gauge. The pressure must not drop below 1900 psi (13,100 kPa) for a period of two minutes. Otherwise replace or repair the port trim cylinder.

10. Fully open both trim gauge valves (**Figure 110**). Operate the trim pump in the UP direction until the ram fully extends. Close the valve on the cylinder side of the gauge (**Figure 110**). Operate the pump until the pressure reading peaks, then stop the pump. The pressure must be 2200-2600 psi (15,169-17,927 kPa). Otherwise replace the up pressure relief valve and thermal relief valve on the pump as described under *Pump Adapter Repair* in Chapter Thirteen.

11. Stop the pump and observe the pressure gauge. The pressure must not drop below 1900 psi (13,100 kPa) for a period of two minutes. If it does, repair the pump adapter as described in Chapter Thirteen.

12. Open both valves on the trim gauge (**Figure 110**). Operate the trim in the DOWN direction until the ram fully retracts. Disconnect the trim gauge from the terminal block and trim cylinder hose. Reconnect the UP pressure trim hose as described in Chapter Thirteen.

13. Disconnect the DOWN pressure hose from the port side of the terminal block. The down pressure hose connects to the fitting farthest from the boat transom, at the back end of the trim cylinder.

14. Connect one of the pressure gauge hoses to the terminal block opening. Securely tighten the hose fitting. Use the coupler to connect the other pressure gauge hose to the disconnected trim cylinder hose.

15. Observe the pressure gauge while operating the trim pump in the down trim direction. Read the maximum pressure when the ram fully retracts. The pressure must be 400-600 psi (2758-4137 kPa).

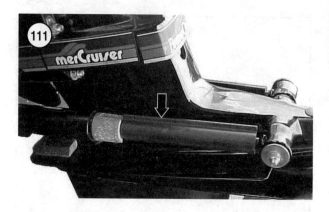

16. Stop the pump and observe the pressure gauge. The pressure must not drop below 400 psi (2738 kPa) for a period of two minutes.

   a. If the pressure is above or below specification, replace the down pressure relief valve as described under *Pump Adapter Repair* in Chapter Thirteen.

   b. If the pressure drops below specification after the pump stops, repair the pump adapter as described in Chapter Thirteen.

17. Disconnect the gauge hoses. Remove the plugs (**Figure 109**). Reconnect all hoses as described in Chapter Thirteen.

18. Disconnect the trim cylinder hose fittings (**Figure 109**) from the port side of the terminal block. Install plugs (Mercury part No. 22-38609 or equivalent) into each terminal block opening. Securely tighten the plugs.

19. Disconnect the UP pressure hose from the starboard side of the terminal block. Connect one of the pressure gauge hoses (**Figure 110**) to the terminal block opening. Securely tighten the hose fitting. Use the coupler (**Figure 110**) to connect the other pressure gauge hose to the disconnected trim cylinder hose.

20. Fully open both valves (**Figure 110**). Operate the trim pump in the UP and DOWN directions until one cylinder fully extends and contracts several times. Correct any leakage at the fittings before proceeding.

21. Observe the pressure gauge while operating the trim pump in the UP trim direction. Read the maximum pressure when the ram fully extends. The pressure must be 2200-2600 psi (15,169-17,927 kPa).

22. Stop the pump and observe the pressure gauge. The pressure must not drop below 1900 psi (13,100 kPa) for a period of two minutes. Refer to step 24 if the system tests as specified. Otherwise proceed with testing.

23. Operate the trim pump in the UP direction until the ram fully extends and the pressure reading peaks. Close the valve on the motor side of the gauge (**Figure 110**) and stop the pump. Observe the pressure gauge. The pressure

must not drop below 1900 psi (13,100 kPa) for two minutes. Otherwise replace or repair the starboard side trim cylinder. Fully open both valves (**Figure 110**).

24. Operate the trim system in the DOWN direction until the ram fully retracts. Disconnect the gauge hoses. Remove the plugs (**Figure 109**). Reconnect the trim hoses on both sides of the terminal block.

25. Install the aft trim cylinder anchor pin.

26. Fill and bleed the system as described in Chapter Thirteen.

27. Operate the trim system in the UP direction until the drive reaches the full tilt position. Support the drive with an overhead cable or support clips (**Figure 111**).

28. Disconnect the down pressure hose from the starboard side of the terminal block. Observe the hose and the terminal block opening while operating the trim system in the UP direction. Fluid must not flow from the terminal block opening or the disconnected trim hose. If it does, one of the trim cylinders is leaking internally.

 a. If fluid flows from the terminal block opening, repair or replace the port side cylinder.

 b. If fluid flows from the disconnected trim hose, repair or replace the starboard side cylinder.

29. Reconnect the hose to the terminal block. Remove the overhead cable or support clips. Operate the trim through several cycles to purge air from the hoses. Correct the fluid level as described in Chapter Thirteen.

## POWER STEERING

A power steering system malfunction is usually due to low fluid level or improper installation of the power steering cable. Check these items as described in Chapter Fourteen before testing the system. If no faults are found, test or inspect according to the symptoms listed in **Table 20**. Power steering pressure testing is described in this section.

### System Description

The power steering system includes the power steering pump, power steering actuator, power steering fluid cooler and the steering cable. The piston and control valve (**Figure 112**) are integrated into a single component referred to as the actuator. The pump is engine-driven by a belt and pulleys. The control valve and piston connect to the steering lever of the transom assembly. The steering cable moves the control valve with steering wheel movement.

During neutral operation (not moving the steering wheel) the pump moves fluid from the reservoir to the actuator. Passages in the actuator direct the fluid to the control valve. With no steering wheel movement, the fluid is directed to the cooler and back to the pump.

The steering wheel moves the steering cable, which moves the control valve. The control valve opens passages that direct pressurized fluid to the appropriate side of piston (**Figure 112**). Internal springs return the control valve to the neutral position when steering wheel movement stops.

A flow control valve mounted in the pump controls steering system pressure. The valve limits the pressure to 70-125 psi (483-862 kPa) when the steering wheel is not being moved. During steering movement, the system pressure can reach 1150-1250 psi (7929-8619 kPa).

### Stiff or Binding Cable or Helm

A binding steering cable or helm can lead the operator to believe the power steering system is not operating. The cable must move the control valve for steering assist to occur. Always check for a faulty steering cable or helm before pressure testing the system.

1. Temporarily disconnect the steering cable from the actuator and steering lever as described in Chapter Fourteen.

2. Rotate the steering wheel to the full port and starboard directions. The wheel must turn in both directions without excessive effort. Otherwise replace the steering cable or helm as described in Chapter Fourteen.

3. Reconnect the steering cable to the actuator and steering lever.

### Power Steering Pressure Test

> *WARNING*
> *Stay clear of the propeller shaft while running an outboard on a flush/test device. Remove the propeller before running the engine to help avoid serious injury or death. Disconnect all spark plug leads and both battery cables before removing or installing the propeller.*

> *CAUTION*
> *Never run the engine without first providing cooling water. Use either a test tank or flush/test device. Remove the propeller before running the engine on a flush/test device. Use a suitable test propeller to run the engine in a test tank.*

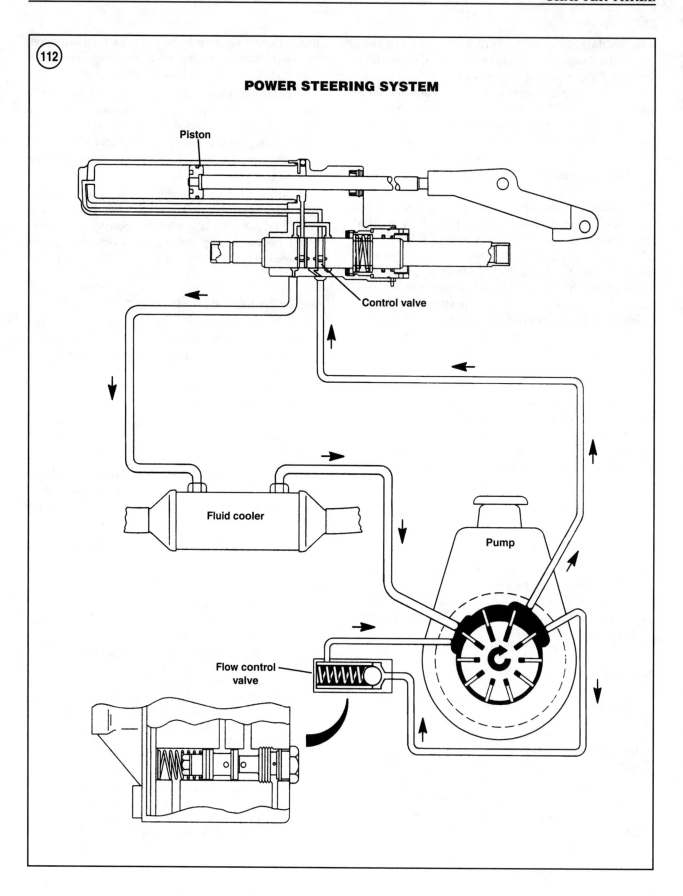

(112)

**POWER STEERING SYSTEM**

Piston

Control valve

Fluid cooler

Pump

Flow control
valve

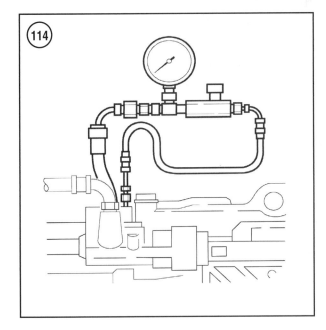

This procedure requires a pressure gage with a hose and shutoff valve (Mercury part No. 91-38053A4 or equivalent).

1. Check the fluid level and bleed air from the system as described in Chapter Fourteen.

2. Disconnect the pressure hose (**Figure 113**) from the power steering actuator.

3. Quickly connect the pressure gauge hoses to the disconnected hose and the actuator (**Figure 114**). The valve must be between the gauge and the actuator fitting (**Figure 114**). Fully open the valve.

4. Check the fluid level and bleed air from the system as described in Chapter Fourteen.

5. Start the engine and set the speed to 1000-1500 rpm. The pressure gauge must indicate 70-125 psi (483-862 kPa).

   a. If the pressure exceeds 125 psi (862 kPa), check for a restriction in the fluid cooler and return hose.

b. If the pressure is less than 70 psi (483 kPa), the pump or actuator is faulty. Proceed with testing.

6. Observe the pressure gauge while rapidly moving the steering wheel in the port and starboard directions. The gauge must indicate an immediate pressure increase when the wheel moves in either direction. Otherwise the pump or actuator is faulty.

7. Fully close the pressure gauge valve, read the pressure then quickly open the valve. Do not close the valve for more than 5 seconds at a time. Perform this step 3 times. Record each pressure reading. Each pressure reading must be 1150-1250 psi (7929-8619 kPa). The difference between the highest and lowest pressure reading must not exceed 50 psi (345 kPa). Stop the engine.

   a. If the pressure reading is less than 1150 psi (7929 kPa), disassemble and inspect or replace the pump as described in Chapter Fourteen.

   b. If the pressure reading exceeds 1250 psi (8619 kPa), remove clean and inspect the flow control valve as described in Chapter Fourteen.

   c. If the pressure difference exceeds 50 psi (345 kPa), remove, clean and inspect the flow control valve as described in Chapter Fourteen.

8. If the pressure is correct, replace the actuator to restore power steering operation.

9. Remove the pressure gauge. Reconnect the pressure hose to the actuator. Clean up spilled fluid.

10. Fill and bleed the system as described in Chapter Fourteen.

### Power Steering Fluid Cooler

A faulty power steering fluid cooler can allow water into the power steering fluid, leak power steering fluid into cooling water, restrict cooling water flow or restrict power steering fluid flow. If these symptoms occur, remove the power steering fluid cooler as described in Chapter Fourteen. Direct air through the passages to check for and remove restrictions. If suspected of leaking, have the cooler tested and repaired at a radiator repair shop.

## MERCATHODE SYSTEM

This section provides instructions used to determine if the Mercathode corrosion protection system is operating correctly. Test instructions for the anodes and grounding wires are also described.

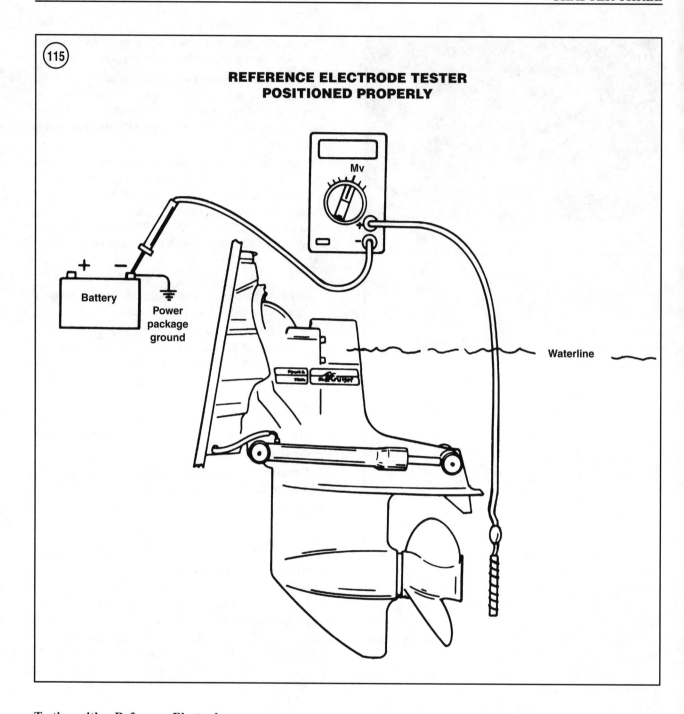

**REFERENCE ELECTRODE TESTER
POSITIONED PROPERLY**

### Testing with a Reference Electrode

This procedure checks for proper operation of the corrosion protection systems. A digital voltmeter and reference electrode (Mercury part No. 91-76675A 1) are required for this test. Perform this test after the boat has been moored in the water a minimum of eight hours. Test results vary with the mounting location of the electrode and the type of water where the boat is moored.

*NOTE*
*The battery must be fully charged to obtain accurate readings if the boat is equipped with a Mercathode system.*

1. Disconnect shore power if so equipped. Set a digital voltmeter to the 2000 mV or 2 VDC scale. Unplug the positive lead from the meter. Plug the reference electrode (Mercury part No. 91-76675A 1) into the positive lead port (**Figure 115**).

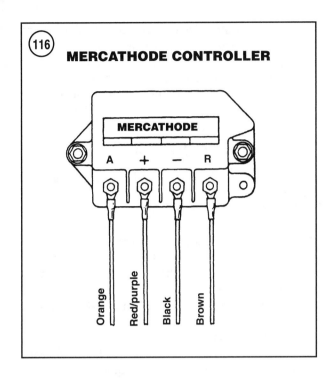

**(116)**

**MERCATHODE CONTROLLER**

MERCATHODE

A    +    —    R

Orange    Red/purple    Black    Brown

2. Connect the negative meter lead to the negative terminal of the battery or an engine ground.

3. Immerse the reference electrode into the water. Position the electrode within 6 in. (15 cm) of the back of the drive unit, but without making contact.

4. Wait a few minutes, then record the meter reading. The system is operating correctly if the voltage matches the following specifications:

    a. *Transom assembly mounted electrode in freshwater*—The voltage must be 620-1180 mV.

    b. *Transom assembly mounted electrode in salt, polluted or mineral laden water*—The voltage must be 750-1180 mV.

    c. *Hull-mounted electrode in freshwater*—The voltage must be 750-1050 mV.

    d. *Hull-mounted electrode in salt, polluted or mineral laden water*—The voltage must be 850-1050 mV.

5A. If voltage is high, refer to **Table 22**.

5B. If voltage is correct, corrosion is occurring. Refer to **Table 21**.

## Stray Current Test

Stray current occurs when a shorted or incorrectly connected wiring allows current to flow into the water. Stray current can originate from any electrical component that contacts water or a conductor that contacts water. A digital multimeter and reference electrode (Mercury part No.

91-76675A 1) is required for this test. Perform this test with the boat in the water.

1. Connect the reference electrode to the multimeter as described under *Testing with a Reference Electrode* in this chapter. Record the meter reading.

2. Disconnect all cables from the positive battery terminal. Record the meter reading. Stray current is indicated if the voltage in Step 2 is lower than the voltage in Step 1.

3. Identify the source of stray current as follows:

    a. Connect the positive battery cable.

    b. Disconnect the wiring or remove the fuse to electrically isolate a single accessory. Record the accessory and voltage meter reading. Reconnect the wiring or install the fuse. Repeat this step for each electrical accessory on the boat.

    c. Repair the wiring or accessory if the voltage lowers with that accessory isolated.

## Testing the Electrode Assembly Test

A digital voltmeter and reference electrode (Mercury part No. 91-76675A 1) are required for this test. Perform this test with the boat in the water.

1. Set a digital voltmeter on the 200 mV or 2 VDC scale. Disconnect the brown wire from the R terminal of the controller (**Figure 116**).

2. Connect the positive meter lead to the brown wire. Connect the negative lead to the battery negative terminal. Record the meter reading.

3. Remove the positive meter lead from the meter and the brown wire. Do not disconnect the negative lead from the battery.

4. Install a reference electrode (Mercury part no. 91-76675 A1) in place of the positive test lead. Place the reference electrode in the water as described under *Testing with a Reference Electrode* in this chapter. Record the meter reading.

5. The voltage reading in Step 2 must equal the voltage in Step 4. If not, replace the electrode assembly.

## Mercathode Controller Test

A digital voltmeter and jumper wire are required for this test. Perform the test with the boat in the water. Test results vary with the mounting location of the electrode and the type of water where the boat is moored. The electrode assembly is mounted on the hull or the bottom of the transom assembly (Chapter Fifteen).

1. Set a digital voltmeter on the 20 or 40 mV (DC) scale. Connect a jumper wire to the R terminal and ground terminal of the controller (**Figure 116**).

**3**

2. Connect the positive meter lead to the A terminal of the controller (**Figure 116**). Connect the negative meter lead to the ground terminal of the controller. Record the meter reading.

3. Compare the test results with the following specifications.

    a. *Transom assembly mounted electrode in freshwater*—Voltage must be 6.2-11.8 mV.

    b. *Transom assembly mounted electrode in saltwater*—Voltage must be 7.5-11.8 mV.

    c. *Hull mounted electrode in freshwater*—Voltage must be 7.5-10.5 mV.

    d. *Hull mounted electrode in saltwater*—Voltage must be 8.5-10.5 mV.

4. If the voltage reading is correct, the controller is operating properly. Otherwise replace the controller.

### Galvanic Isolator

Refer to Chapter Fifteen for a description of the galvanic isolator. The isolator is very reliable and most faults are the result of loose or faulty wiring. Test the operation of the corrosion control system as described under Testing with a reference electrode in this chapter. Perform the test and record the voltage reading with the shore power connected and disconnected. Have a qualified electrician replace the galvanic isolator if the voltage reading exceeds the specification only with the shore power connected.

### Anode and Grounding Wire Test

Refer to Chapter Fifteen to identify the locations for all anodes and grounding wires.

1. Calibrate an ohmmeter to the R×1 scale. Connect the negative lead to the negative battery cable.

2. Starting inside the engine compartment, touch the positive lead to each ground wire. The meter must read continuity at each test point. Otherwise repair or replace the faulty grounding wire.

3. Starting at the transom assembly, touch the test lead to the exposed surface of each anode on the transom and drive unit. The meter must read continuity at each test point. Check for loose or corroded drive fasteners, faulty ground wires or corroded anode mating surfaces if there is no continuity.

#### Table 1 ELECTRIC STARTING SYSTEM TROUBLESHOOTING

| Symptom | Cause | Corrective action |
|---|---|---|
| **Electric starter** | | |
|   **Does not operate** | Battery switched off | Switch the battery switch on |
| | Engine shifted in gear | Place the shift selector in neutral |
| | Loose or dirty battery terminals | Clean and inspect the battery terminals |
| | Discharged battery | Fully charge the battery |
| | Faulty battery | Test the battery (Chapter Seven) |
| | Faulty fuse | Test the fuse (on models so equipped) |
| | Tripped circuit breaker | Reset the circuit breaker |
| | Faulty circuit breaker | Test the circuit breaker |
| | Faulty neutral only start switch | Check for voltage at the slave solenoid |
| | | Test the neutral only start switch |
| | Faulty ignition switch | Check for voltage at the slave solenoid |
| | | Test the neutral only start switch |
| | Faulty slave solenoid | Check for voltage at the slave solenoid |
| | | Test the slave solenoid |
| | Faulty starter solenoid | Check for voltage at the starter solenoid |
| | | Test the starter solenoid |
| | Faulty starter motor | Check for voltage at the starter motor |
| **Electric starter (continued)** | | |
|   **Rotates slowly** | Loose or dirty battery terminal | Clean and inspect the battery terminals |
| | Discharged battery | Fully charge the battery |
| | Faulty battery | Test the battery (Chapter Seven) |
| | Faulty starter motor | Check for voltage at the starter motor |
| | Seized engine | Check for water in the cylinders |
| | – | Check for mechanical damage |
| | Seized drive unit | Check for an entangled propeller |
| | – | Inspect the lubricant drain plug |
| (continued) | | |

### Table 1 ELECTRIC STARTING SYSTEM TROUBLESHOOTING (continued)

| Symptom | Cause | Corrective Action |
| --- | --- | --- |
| Makes a grinding noise | Loose starter mounting bolts | Tighten the bolts |
| | Broken starter housing | Inspect the starter |
| | Damaged starter pinion | Inspect the starter pinion |
| | Damaged flywheel teeth | Inspect the flywheel teeth |
| | Wrong type of starter installed | Verify the starter part No. |
| | Starter too close to flywheel | Install thicker starter shim |
| | Starter too far from flywheel | Install thinner starter shim |
| | Faulty starter bendix | Inspect the starter bendix |
| Operates continuously | Faulty ignition switch | Check for voltage at the slave solenoid |
| | – | Test the ignition switch |
| | Faulty slave solenoid | Check for voltage at the slave solenoid |
| | – | Test the slave solenoid |
| | Faulty starter solenoid | Check for voltage at the starter solenoid |
| | Stuck starter solenoid | Test the starter solenoid |
| | Faulty wiring at the solenoid | Check for faulty wiring |
| | Stuck starter bendix | Check for voltage at the starter |
| | – | Inspect the starter bendix |
| Makes clicking noise (does not rotate) | Loose or dirty battery terminal | Clean and inspect the battery terminals |
| | Discharged battery | Fully charge the battery |
| | Faulty battery | Test the battery (Chapter Seven) |
| | Faulty starter solenoid | Check for voltage at the starter solenoid |
| | – | Test the starter solenoid |
| | Faulty starter motor | Check for voltage at the starter motor |
| | – | Repair the starter motor |
| | Seized engine | Check for water in the cylinders |
| | – | Check for mechanical damage |
| | Seized drive unit | Check for an entangled propeller |
| | – | Inspect the lubricant drain plugs |
| Operates while in gear | Faulty neutral only start switch | Test the neutral only start switch |

### Table 2 IGNITION SYSTEM TROUBLESHOOTING

| Symptom | Possible cause | Corrective action |
| --- | --- | --- |
| Engine will not start | Lanyard switch activated | Place the switch in the run position |
| | No current to the ignition system | Test the ignition system |
| | Faulty interrupt switch (Alpha) | Test the interrupt switch |
| | Faulty ignition key switch | Test the ignition key switch |
| | Blown fuse or circuit breaker | Check and test the fuses |
| | Faulty system relay (EFI) | Test the system relay |
| | Faulty tachometer | Temporarily disconnect the tachometer |
| | Faulty coil | Test the ignition system |
| | Faulty wire or connector | Test the wire harness. |
| | Faulty ignition sensor | Test the ignition system |
| | Faulty ignition coil | Test the ignition system |
| | Faulty ignition module | Test the ignition system |
| | Faulty rotor or cap | Replace the rotor and cap |
| | Faulty ECM (EFI models) | Test the ECM |
| | Faulty camshaft position sensor | Test the ignition system |
| | Faulty crankshaft position sensor | Test the ignition system |
| Poor performance (timing not advancing) | Engine left in base timing mode | Replace the ignition module |
| Ignition misfire | Engine reaching the rpm limit | Check the engine speed |
| | Faulty spark plug | Remove and inspect the spark plug |
| | Faulty spark plug wire | Inspect the spark plug wires |
| | Faulty rotor or cap | Replace the cap and rotor |
| | Faulty ignition coil | Replace the ignition coil |
| | Faulty ignition sensor | Test the ignition system |
| | Faulty tachometer | Temporarily disconnect the tachometer |

(continued)

Table 2 IGNITION SYSTEM TROUBLESHOOTING (continued)

| Symptom | Possible cause | Corrective action |
|---------|----------------|-------------------|
| Engine stalls | Faulty wire or connection | Inspect and test the wiring |
| | Faulty ignition sensor | Test the ignition system |
| | Faulty ignition coil | Replace the ignition coil |
| | Faulty tachometer | Temporarily disconnect the tachometer |

Table 3 FUEL SYSTEM TROUBLESHOOTING

| Symptom | Possible cause | Corrective action |
|---------|----------------|-------------------|
| Will not start | Contaminated fuel | Inspect the fuel |
| | Improper carburetor adjustment | Adjust the carburetor |
| | Choke valve not operating | Test the choke |
| | Plugged fuel filters | Check for fuel in the carburetor |
| | Faulty fuel pump | Check for fuel in the carburetor |
| | Fuel injectors not operating | Check for injector operation |
| | Faulty boat fuel tank | Test the fuel tank and hose |
| | Faulty fuel pump relay (EFI) | Test the fuel pump relay |
| | Loose by-pass wire | Test the fuel pump voltage |
| | Stuck inlet needle | Test the fuel pressure |
| | Plugged carburetor passages | Check for fuel at the carburetor |
| Engine stalls | Faulty oil pressure switch | Test the fuel pump voltage |
| | Contaminated fuel | Inspect the fuel |
| | Faulty fuel tank or hose | Test the fuel tank and hose |
| | Improper carburetor adjustment | Adjust the carburetor |
| | Plugged carburetor passages | Inspect the carburetor |
| | Faulty fuel pump relay (EFI) | Replace the fuel pump relay |
| | Faulty electric fuel pump | Test the fuel pump voltage |
| Poor performance | Plugged fuel filters | Inspect the fuel filters |
| | Faulty fuel pump | Test the fuel pressure |
| | Faulty boat fuel tank | Test the fuel tank and hose |
| | Faulty anti-siphon device | Test the fuel tank and hose |
| | Plugged carburetor passages | Inspect the carburetor |
| | Faulty fuel injectors | Clean the injectors |

Table 4 MAXIMUM ENGINE OPERATING SPEED

| Model | Speed (rpm) | Rev-limit activation |
|-------|-------------|----------------------|
| 3.0L models | 4400-4800* | |
| 4.3L models | | |
|   1998-2004 carburetor-equipped models | 4400-4800 | 4850-4900 |
|   1998-2004 fuel injection models (TBI and MPI) | 4400-4800 | 4900 |
| 5.0L and 5.7L models | | |
|   1998-2004 carburetor-equipped model | 4400-4800 | 4850-4900 |
|   1998-2001 fuel injection models (TBI and MPI) | 4400-4800 | 4900 |
|   2002-2004 multi-port fuel injection (MPI) models | 4600-5000 | 5100 |
| 350 Mag | | |
|   1998-2001 fuel injection models (TBI and MPI) | 4400-4800 | 4900 |
|   2002-2004 multi-port fuel injection (MPI) models | 4600-5000 | 5100 |
| MX6.2L | 4800-5200 | 5300 |
|   496 Mag | 4400-4800 | 4900 |
|   496 Mag HO | 4600-5000 | 5100 |

*This model does not have an overspeed protection system.

### Table 5 FUEL PUMP PRESSURE SPECIFICATIONS

| Model | Pressure |
| --- | --- |
| 3.0L | 5.25-6.25 psi (36-44 kPa)* |
| 4.3L | |
|   Carburetor models | 6-9 psi (41-62 kPa) |
|   1998-2001 (TBI models) | 30 psi (2.7 kPa) |
|   2002-2004 (MPI models) | 40-46 psi (276-317 kPa) |
| 5.0L and 5.7L models | |
|   Carburetor models | 3-8 psi (21-48 kPa) |
|    1998-2001 TBI models | 30 psi (2.7 kPa) |
|    2002-2004 MPI models | 40-46 psi (276-317 kPa) |
| 350 Mag and MX 6.2L models | |
|   1998-2001 (MPI models) | 34-38 psi (235-262 kPa) |
|   2002-2004 (MPI models) | 40-46 psi (276-317 kPa) |
| 7.4 MPI, 454 Mag, 502 Mag | 43 psi (296 kPa) |
| 496 Mag, 496 Mag HO | 43 psi (296 kPa) |

* With the engine speed adjusted to 1800 rpm.

### Table 6 EFI TROUBLE CODES

| Code | Fault |
| --- | --- |
| MEFI 1 or MEFI 2 systems | |
| 14 | Coolant temperature sensor |
| 21 | Throttle position sensor |
| 23 | Air temperature sensor |
| 33 | Air pressure sensor |
| 42 | Ignition control circuit |
| 43 | Knock control circuit |
| 51 | Calibration failure |
| MEFI 3 systems | |
| 14 | Coolant temperature sensor (low reading) |
| 15 | Coolant temperature sensor (high reading) |
| 21 | Throttle position sensor (high voltage reading) |
| 22 | Throttle position sensor (low voltage reading) |
| 23 | Air temperature sensor (low temperature reading) |
| 25 | Air temperature sensor (high temperature reading) |
| 33 | Air pressure sensor (high voltage reading) |
| 34 | Air pressure sensor (low voltage reading) |
| 41 | Open ignition control circuit |
| 42 | Grounded ignition control circuit, faulty bypass circuit |
| 43 | Faulty knock sensor circuit |
| 44 | Faulty knock sensor circuit |
| 45 | Coil driver failure |
| 51 | Calibration memory failure in engine control module |
| 52 | EEPROM failure in engine control module |
| 61 | Fuel pressure sensor (high pressure reading) |
| 62 | Fuel pressure sensor (low pressure reading) |

### Table 7 SCAN TOOL SPECIFICATIONS (MEFI 2 and MEFI 3)

| Selected data | Normal parameters |
| --- | --- |
| RPM | 600-700 |
| Desired rpm | 600 |
| Coolant temperature | 150-170° F (66-77° C) |
| Manifold air temperature | Varies with ambient air temperature[1] |
| Throttle position sensor | 0.4-0.8 volt |
| Throttle angle | 0-1% |
| Manifold air pressure | 13-16 in.Hg[2] |
| | (continued) |

**Table 7 SCAN TOOL SPECIFICATIONS (MEFI 2 and MEFI 3) (Continued)**

| Selected data | Normal parameters |
|---|---|
| Barometric voltage | 3-5 volts[2] |
| Battery voltage | 12-14.5 volts |
| Spark advance | 10° ATDC-30°BTDC[3] |
| Knock retard | 0° |
| IAC position | 0-40 |
| IAC base position | 0-40 |
| IAC follower | 0 |
| Injector on time | 2-3 ms |
| Injector on time cranking | 2.5-3.5 ms[4] |
| Gallons per hour | 1-2 |
| Run time | 00.00-1092.00[5] |
| Memcal checksum | Varies by model and software revision[6] |
| Oil pressure/IO lever | OK |
| Engine overtemp | OK |
| Lanyard stop | OFF |

1. Reading is normally slightly higher than the ambient air temperature.
2. Reading varies by altitude at the test site and weather conditions.
3. Spark advance readings normally fluctuate at idle speed.
4. Injector on time varies with air and coolant temperature.
5. Indicate the engine run time during the current scan session.
6. The alphanumeric characters must match those marked on the engine control module.

**Table 8 ENGINE TEMPERATURE SENSOR**

| Model | Temperature | Resistance (ohms) |
|---|---|---|
| All models | 210° F (100° C) | 185 |
| | 160° F (71° C) | 450 |
| | 100° F (38° C) | 1800 |
| | 70° F (21° C) | 3400 |
| | 40° F (4° C) | 7500 |

**Table 9 AIR TEMPERATURE SENSOR (ALL MODELS)**

| Temperature | Resistance (ohms) |
|---|---|
| 210° F (100° C) | 185 |
| 160° F (71° C) | 450 |
| 100° F (38° C) | 1800 |
| 70° F (21° C) | 3400 |
| 40° F (4° C) | 7500 |
| 20° F (-7° C) | 13,500 |

**Table 10 AIR PRESSURE SENSOR SPECIFICATIONS (ALL MODELS)**

| Elevation | Voltage |
|---|---|
| Less than 1000 ft. (305 m) | 3.8-5.5 |
| 1000-2000 ft. (305-610 m) | 3.6-5.3 |
| 2001-3000 ft (610-914 m) | 3.5-6.1 |
| 3001-4000 ft. (915-1219 m) | 3.3-5.0 |
| 4001-5000 ft. (1220-1524 m) | 3.2-4.8 |
| 5001-6000 ft. (1524-1829 m) | 3.0-4.6 |
| 6001-7000 ft. (1829-2134 m) | 2.9-4.5 |
| 7001-8000 ft. (2134-2438 m) | 2.8-4.3 |
| 8001-9000 ft. (2439-2743 m) | 2.6-4.2 |
| 9001-10,000 ft. (2744-3048 m) | 2.5-4.0 |

**Table 11 ENGINE TEMPERATURE SENDER SPECIFICATIONS**

| Temperature | Resistance (ohms) |
|---|---|
| 140° F (60° C) | 121-147 |
| 194° F (90° C) | 47-55 |
| 212° F (100° C) | 36-41 |

**Table 12 OVERHEAT SWITCH SPECIFICATIONS**

| Part No. | Temperature |
|---|---|
| 48952 (red sleeve) | |
|   Switches to continuity | 190-200° F (88-93° C) |
|   Switches back to no continuity | 150-170° F (66-77° C) |
| 87-86080 (black sleeve) | |
|   Switches to continuity | 215-225° F (102-107° C) |
|   Switches back to no continuity | 175-195° F (80-90° C) |

**Table 13 OIL PRESSURE SENDER SPECIFICATIONS**

| Actual oil pressure | Resistance (ohms) |
|---|---|
| Single station instrumentation | 0 psi (0 kPa) |
| 227-257 | |
| 20 psi (138 kPa) | 142-163 |
| 40 psi (276 kPa) | 92-114 |
| Dual station instrumentation | 0 psi (0 kPa) |
| 114-129 | |
| 20 psi (138 kPa) | 71-81 |
| 40 psi (276 kPa) | 46-57 |

**Table 14 OIL PRESSURE SPECIFICATIONS**

| @ idle speed | 4 psi (28 kPa)* |
|---|---|
| @ 2000 rpm | 30 psi (207 kPa)* |

*Minimum allowable oil pressure at the designated speed.

**Table 15 ENGINE IDENTIFICATION CODES**

| Model | Code |
|---|---|
| 3.0 | serial No. 0L096999-Prior |
| RX | |
| serial No. 0L097000-On | RP |
| 4.3L | Two-barrel carburetor |
| LJ | |
| Four-barrel carburetor | LK |
| Electronic fuel injection | LK |
| 5.0L | ZA |
| 5.7L, 350 Mag | MH |
| MX 6.2 | OM |
| 7.4 liter MPI | XW |
| 454 Mag MPI | UA |
| 502 Mag MPI | HJ |
| 496 Mag | * |
| 496 Mag HO | * |

*Engine model code was not available at the time of printing.

## Table 16 THERMOSTAT SPECIFICATIONS

| Model | Thermostat Position | Temperature |
|---|---|---|
| 3.0L | | |
| Standard cooling serial No. 0L340999-Prior (brass thermostat) | | |
| | Starts to open | 143° F (62° C) |
| | Fully opened | 168° F (76° C) |
| | Cool down closed | 133° F (56° C) |
| Standard cooling serial No. 0L341000-On (stainless steel thermostat) | | |
| | Starts to open | 160° F (71° C) |
| | Fully opened | 185° F (85° C) |
| | Cool down closed | 150° F (66° C) |
| Closed cooling | | |
| | Starts to open | 138-145° F (59-63° C) |
| | Fully opened | 170° F (77° C) |
| | Cool down closed | 128-135°F (53-57° C) |
| 4.3, 5.0,5.7 liter, 350 Mag | | |
| | Starts to open | 160° F (71°C) |
| | Fully opened | 185° F (85° C) |
| | Cool down closed | 150° F (66° C) |
| 7.4 MPI, 454 Mag, 502 Mag 496 Mag, 496 Mag HO | | |
| | Starts to open | 160° F (71°C) |
| | Fully opened | 185° F (85° C) |
| | Cool down closed | 150° F (66° C) |

## Table 17 CLOSED COOLING SYSTEM TEST SPECIFICATIONS

| Model | Pressure |
|---|---|
| 3.0L | |
| Pressure cap | |
| Relief pressure | 14 psi (97 kPa) |
| Minimum holding pressure | 11 psi (76 kPa) |
| System test pressure | 17 psi (117 kPa) |
| 496 Mag and 496 Mag HO | |
| Pressure cap | |
| Relief pressure | 14 psi (103 kPa) |
| Minimum holding pressure | 11 psi (76 kPa) |
| System test specification | 19 psi (131 kPa) |
| All other models | |
| Pressure cap | |
| Relief pressure | 16 psi (110 kPa) |
| Minimum holding pressure | 11 psi (76 kPa) |
| System test pressure | 20 psi (138 kPa) |

## Table 18 DRIVE SYSTEM TROUBLESHOOTING

| Symptom | Possible cause | Corrective action |
|---|---|---|
| Does not shift into gear | Slipping propeller drive hub | Inspect the drive hub |
| | Improperly adjusted shift cables | Adjust shift cables |
| | Faulty drive unit shift cable | Inspect drive unit cable |
| | Faulty remote control cable | Inspect remote control cable |
| | Drive unit installed improperly | Remove and reinstall drive unit |
| | Faulty remote control | Inspect the remote control |
| | Spun engine coupler | Inspect the coupler |
| | Broken or damaged clutch | Inspect clutch |
| | Broken or damaged shift shaft | Inspect shift shaft |
| | Broken shift linkage | Inspect shift linkage |
| (continued) | | |

**Table 18 DRIVE SYSTEM TROUBLESHOOTING (continued)**

| Symptom | Possible Cause | Corrective Action |
|---|---|---|
| Does not shift into gear (continued) | Broken gear teeth | Inspect the gears |
| | Broken drive shaft | Inspect the drive shaft |
| Does not shift out of gear | Improperly adjusted shift cables | Adjust shift cables |
| | Faulty drive unit shift cable | Inspect drive unit cable |
| | Faulty remote control cable | Inspect remote control cable |
| | Drive unit installed improperly | Remove and reinstall drive unit |
| | Faulty remote control | Inspect the remote control |
| | Broken or damaged clutch | Inspect clutch |
| | Broken or damaged shift shaft | Inspect shift shaft |
| | Broken shift linkage | Inspect shift linkage |
| | Worn or damaged shift spool | Inspect the shift spool |
| | Worn or damage shift yoke | Inspect the shift yoke |
| Hard to shift | Improperly adjusted shift cable | Adjust shift cables |
| | Engine is not running | Shift only with engine running |
| | Binding remote control cables | Check shift cables |
| | Improperly adjusted throttle cable | Remove excessive cable preload |
| | Incorrect shift cable length | Install correct length shift cable |
| | Shift cable bent too sharp | Eliminate sharp bends or loops |
| | Worn or damage remote control | Inspect remote control |
| | Faulty shift interrupt switch | Test the interrupt switch |
| | Improperly adjusted interrupt switch | Adjust the interrupt switch |
| | Tight or binding cable pivot points | Lubricate and/or loosen pivots |
| | Worn shift shaft bushing | Inspect the shift shaft bushing |
| | Corroded shift shaft bushing | Clean corrosion from the bushing |
| | Bent or binding shift shaft(s) | Inspect the shift shaft(s) |
| | Worn or binding shift linkages | Inspect the shift linkages |
| Jumps out of gear | Incorrectly adjusted shift cables | Adjust the shift cables |
| | Worn or damaged clutch | Inspect the clutch |
| | Bent or damaged shift shaft(s) | Inspect the shift shaft(s) |
| Slips under acceleration | Slipping propeller drive hub | Inspect the drive hub |
| | Improperly installed propeller | Check the propeller installation |
| | Drive trimmed out too far | Trim the drive unit down |
| | Propeller ventilation | See Chapter One |
| | Damaged propeller | Inspect the propeller |
| | Worn or damaged drive coupler | Inspect the engine drive coupler |
| | Worn engine coupling splines | Inspect the coupler and drive yoke |
| | Failed gears in drive unit | Check for metal in the lubricant |
| Vibration | Damaged propeller | Inspect the propeller |
| | Bent propeller shaft | Inspect the propeller shaft |
| | Improperly balanced propeller | Have the propeller balanced |
| | Engine out of alignment | Check engine alignment |
| | Improperly installed rear mounts | Check rear engine mounts |
| | Excessive gimbal ring end play | Measure gimbal ring end play |
| | Weak or damaged boat transom | Check the boat transom |
| Knocking noise at all steering and trim positions | Engine out of alignment | Check engine alignment |
| | Worn, damaged or missing O-ring(s) | Inspect O-rings on U-joint shaft |
| | Worn or damaged U-joint(s) | Inspect U-joints |
| | Improperly installed U-joint(s) | Inspect U-joints |
| | Wrong U-joints installed | Check part No. of the U-joints |
| | Improperly installed rear mounts | Check the rear engine mounts |
| | Worn or collapsed rear mounts | Inspect the rear engine mounts |
| | Worn or damaged gear(s) | Inspect the gears |
| | Exhaust pipe contacting the transom | Check installation of inner transom |
| | Worn engine coupling splines | Inspect the coupler and drive yoke |
| | Transom manufactured too thin | Correct transom thickness to 2-2 ¼ in. |
| | Transom manufactured too thick | Correct transom thickness to 2-2 ¼ in. |

(continued)

3

Table 18 DRIVE SYSTEM TROUBLESHOOTING (continued)

| Symptom | Possible Cause | Corrective Action |
|---|---|---|
| Knocking noise (continued) | Transom manufactured unevenly | Correct transom to within 1/8 in. variance |
| | Weak or damaged boat transom | Check the boat transom |
| Growling noise | Faulty gimbal bearing | Inspect the gimbal bearing |
| | Worn, damaged or missing O-ring(s) | inspect O-rings on U-joint shaft |
| | Worn engine coupling splines | Inspect the coupler and drive yoke |
| | Excessive gimbal ring end play | Measure gimbal ring end play |
| | Improperly installed gimbal bearing | Inspect the gimbal bearing installation |
| | Engine out of alignment | Check engine alignment |
| | Worn or collapsed rear mounts | Inspect the rear engine mounts |
| | Worn or damaged gear(s) | Inspect the gears |
| Knocking only when trimmed fully down | Faulty trim cylinder bushing | Replace worn, missing or damaged bushings |
| | Excessive gimbal ring end play | Measure gimbal ring end play |
| | Improperly installed gimbal bearing | Inspect the gimbal bearing installation |
| | Transom manufactured too thin | Correct transom thickness to 2-2 ¼ in. |
| | Transom manufactured uneven | Correct transom to within 1/8 in. variance |
| | Weak or damaged boat transom | Check the boat transom |
| Knocking noise only when turning | Worn or damaged U-joint(s) | Inspect U-joints |
| | Improperly installed U-joint cap(s) | Inspect U-joint caps |
| | Improperly installed gimbal bearing | Inspect gimbal bearing installation |
| | Faulty trim cylinder bushing | Replace worn, missing or damaged bushings |
| | Steering lever contacting the transom | Modify the transom opening |
| | Transom manufactured too thin | Correct transom thickness to 2-2 ¼ in. |
| | Transom manufactured uneven | Correct transom to within 1/8 in. variance |
| Gear whine at all speeds | Propeller installed improperly | Check propeller installation |
| | Damaged propeller | Inspect the propeller |
| | Bent propeller shaft | Inspect the propeller shaft |
| | Normal gear whine | Compare noise with another unit |
| | Improperly balanced propeller | Have the propeller balanced |
| | Worn or damaged gear(s) | Inspect the gears |
| | Worn or damaged bearing(s) | Inspect the bearings |
| | Improper gear shimming | Check the gear shimming |
| Gear whine at certain speeds | Normal gear whine | Compare noise with another unit |
| | Damaged propeller | Inspect the propeller |
| | Improperly balanced propeller | Have the propeller balanced |
| | Worn or damaged gear(s) | Inspect the gears |
| | Worn or damaged bearing(s) | Inspect the bearings |
| | Improper gear shimming | Check the gear shimming |

Table 19 HYDRAULIC TRIM TROUBLESHOOTING

| Symptom | Cause(s) | Corrective action |
|---|---|---|
| Trim motor does not operate up or down | Discharged battery | Fully charge and test the battery |
| | Loose or dirty wire connections | Clean and tighten the terminals |
| | Blown 20 A fuse | Test or replace the 20 A fuse |
| | Blown 110 A fuse | Test or replace the 110 A fuse |
| | Disconnected trim pump harness | Reconnect the harness |
| | Loose battery cable terminal | Securely tighten both terminals |
| | Dirty battery cable terminal | Clean both terminals |
| | Faulty trim switch | Test the trim switch |
| | Faulty switch wiring | Inspect the wiring |
| | Faulty trim solenoid ground wire | Repair the ground wire |
| | Faulty trim solenoids | Test both solenoids |
| | Open thermal switch | Repair the electric trim motor |

(continued)

**Table 19 HYDRAULIC TRIM TROUBLESHOOTING (continued)**

| Symptom | Cause(s) | Corrective Action |
|---|---|---|
| Trim motor does not operate up or down (continued) | Faulty trim motor | Repair the electric trim motor |
| | Binding hydraulic pump | Repair the hydraulic pump |
| Trim motor runs up only if activating the trailer switch | Faulty trim limit switch | Test the trim limit switch |
| | Loose or dirty wire connections | Clean and tighten the terminals |
| | Disconnected limit switch wires | Reconnect the wires |
| | Faulty limit switch wires | Inspect the wires |
| | Improperly adjusted limit switch | Adjust the trim limit switch |
| | Faulty trim switch | Test the trim switch |
| | Faulty switch wiring | Inspect the wiring |
| Trim motor runs up only if activating the UP trim switch | Faulty trim switch | Test the trim switch |
| | Faulty switch wiring | Inspect the wiring |
| Trim pump does not operate in the UP direction | Loose or dirty wire connections | Clean and tighten the terminals |
| | Disconnected limit switch wires | Reconnect the wires |
| | Faulty trim pump solenoid | Test the up solenoid |
| | Faulty trim solenoid ground wire | Repair the ground wire |
| | Faulty trim switch | Test the trim switch |
| | Faulty switch wiring | Inspect the wiring |
| | Faulty field winding in trim motor | Repair the trim motor |
| Trim motor does not operate in the DOWN direction | Faulty trim pump solenoid | Test the up solenoid |
| | Loose or dirty wire connections | Clean and tighten terminals |
| | Faulty trim solenoid ground wire | Repair the ground wire |
| | Faulty trim switch | Test the trim switch |
| | Faulty switch wiring | Inspect the wiring |
| | Faulty field winding in trim motor | Repair the trim motor |
| Trim motor runs slowly | Weak or discharged battery | Fully charge and test the battery |
| | Loose battery cable terminal | Securely tighten both terminals |
| | Dirty battery cable terminal | Clean both terminals |
| | Dirty thermal switch contact | Repair the electric trim motor |
| | Faulty trim motor | Repair the electric trim motor |
| | Faulty trim cylinder(s) | Check for binding cylinders |
| | Binding hydraulic pump | Repair the hydraulic pump |
| Blows the 20 A fuse | Faulty limit switch wires | Inspect the wires |
| | Faulty limit switch | Test the trim limit switch |
| | Faulty trim switch wiring | Inspect the trim switch wiring |
| Blows the 110 A fuse | Shorted battery (+) cable to pump | Repair the cable |
| | Shorted circuit in trim motor | Repair the trim motor |
| Trim motor runs continuously | Faulty trim switch wire | Inspect trim switch wiring |
| | Faulty trim switch | Test the trim switch |
| | Faulty trim solenoid | Test the trim solenoids |
| | Corroded harness terminals | Clean the harness terminals |
| Trim motor runs but the drive does not move up or down | Low trim fluid level | Correct the fluid level |
| | Air in the system | Bleed air from the system |
| | Incorrect cylinder hose connections | Correct hose connections |
| | Leaking trim pump hose | Inspect hoses |
| | Kinked trim pump hose(s) | Correct hose routing |
| | Faulty hydraulic pump | Test the trim system pressure |
| | Binding trim cylinder | Check trim cylinder(s) |
| | Binding drive unit | Check for free movement of drive |
| | Broken trim pump coupler | Inspect the coupler |
| Trim motor runs but the drive will not move down | Low trim fluid level | Correct the fluid level |
| | Air in the system | Bleed air from the system |
| | Plugged pickup screens | Remove reservoir and clean screen |

*(continued)*

3

**Table 19 HYDRAULIC TRIM TROUBLESHOOTING (continued)**

| Symptom | Cause(s) | Corrective Action |
|---|---|---|
| Trim motor runs but the drive will not move down (continued) | Incorrect cylinder hose connections | Correct hose connections |
| | Leaking gray trim hose | Inspect hoses |
| | Kinked trim pump hose | Correct the hose routing |
| | Faulty hydraulic pump | Test the trim system pressure |
| | Faulty trim cylinder | Test the trim system pressure |
| | Faulty down pressure relief valve | Replace the valve |
| | Faulty thermal relief valve | Replace the valve |
| | Binding trim cylinder | Check trim cylinder(s) |
| | Binding drive unit | Check for free movement of drive |
| Trim motor runs but the drive will not move up | Low trim fluid level | Correct the fluid level |
| | Air in the system | Bleed air from the system |
| | Plugged pickup screens | Remove reservoir and clean screen |
| | Incorrect cylinder hose connections | Correct hose connections |
| | Leaking black trim pump hose | Inspect hoses |
| | Kinked trim pump hose | Correct the hose routing |
| | Faulty hydraulic pump | Test the trim system pressure |
| | Faulty trim cylinder | Test the trim system pressure |
| | Faulty up pressure relief valve | Replace the valve |
| | Faulty thermal relief valve | Replace the valve |
| | Binding trim cylinder | Check trim cylinder(s) |
| | Binding drive unit | Check for free movement of drive |
| Trim motor runs but the drive moves slowly | Low trim fluid level | Correct the fluid level |
| | Air in the system | Bleed air from the system |
| | Wrong type of fluid in pump | Drain and refill trim system |
| | Operation in a very cold environment | Normal occurrence |
| | Plugged pickup screens | Remove reservoir and clean screen |
| | Incorrect cylinder hose connections | Correct hose connections |
| | Kinked or leaking trim pump hose | Correct the hose routing |
| | Faulty hydraulic pump | Test the trim system pressure |
| | Faulty trim cylinder | Test the trim system pressure |
| | Faulty up pressure relief valve | Replace the valve |
| | Faulty thermal relief valve | Replace the valve |
| | Binding trim cylinder | Check trim cylinder(s) |
| | Binding drive unit | Check for free movement of drive |
| Drive leaks down from the up position | Air in the system | Bleed the system |
| | Leaking hose fitting | Tighten fittings |
| | Leaking cylinder hose | Inspect the hoses |
| | Leaking black trim pump hose | Inspect hoses |
| | Faulty hydraulic pump | Test the trim system pressure |
| | Faulty trim cylinder | Test the trim system pressure |
| | Faulty thermal relief valve | Replace the valve |
| Drive comes up in reverse or when slowing down | Air in the system | Bleed the system |
| | Leaking hose fitting | Tighten fittings |
| | Leaking cylinder hose | Inspect the hoses |
| | Leaking gray trim pump hose | Inspect hoses |
| | Faulty hydraulic pump | Test the trim system pressure |
| | Faulty trim cylinder | Test the trim system pressure |
| Noisy pump operation | Low fluid level | Correct the fluid level |
| | Air in the system | Bleed the system |
| | Water in the system | Drain and refill the system |
| | Wrong fluid in the pump | Drain and refill the system |
| | Faulty trim motor | Repair the trim motor |
| | Faulty hydraulic pump | Pressure test the trim system |
| | Pump operation at end of travel | Normal occurrence |

**3**

## Table 20 STEERING SYSTEM TROUBLESHOOTING

| Symptom | Possible Cause | Corrective Action |
|---|---|---|
| Hard steering | Low fluid level in pump | Correct pump fluid level |
| | Wrong fluid in system | Drain and refill system |
| | Loose drive belt | Adjust the belt tension |
| | Broken drive belt | Replace the drive belt |
| | Broken drive belt pulley | Replace the pulley |
| | Faulty steering cable | Check steering cable for binding |
| | Steering cable too short | Install correct length cable |
| | Steering cable too long | Install correct length cable |
| | Steering helm not lubricated | Lubricate steering helm |
| | Faulty steering helm | Check for binding in helm |
| | Kinked power steering hose | Route hoses to avoid kinking |
| | Air in power steering system | Bleed air from the system |
| | Fluid leakage | Check for and correct fluid leakage |
| | Low power steering pressure | Test power steering pressure |
| Fluid leakage | Power steering pump overfilled | Correct the pump fluid level |
| | Loose hose clamp or fitting | Tighten the clamps or fittings |
| | Faulty hose | Inspect the hoses |
| | Air in the power steering system | Bleed air from the system |
| | Water in the fluid | Check power steering fluid cooler |
| | Leaking pump reservoir | Replace the power steering pump |
| | Leaking pump shaft seal | Replace the pump shaft seal |
| | Leaking O-ring in pump | Repair the pump |
| | Leaking fluid cooler | Have the cooler repaired |

## Table 21 CORROSION TROUBLESHOOTING

| Symptom | Possible Cause | Corrective Action |
|---|---|---|
| Entire drive corroding | Anodes out of the water | Lower the drive |
| | Missing or damaged grounding wire | Check wire between drive and engine |
| | Stray current corrosion | Perform test with reference electrode |
| | Large amount of stainless steel | Install an additional Mercathode system |
| | | Install additional anodes |
| | Moored in flowing water | Install additional protection |
| | Moored in warm water | Install additional protection |
| | Loose or dirty blown wire* | Clean and tighten terminal |
| | Loose or dirty orange wire* | Clean and tighten terminal |
| | Faulty electrode assembly* | Test the electrode assembly |
| | Faulty Mercathode controller* | Test the controller |
| | Painted electrode assembly* | Clean the electrode assembly |
| | Faulty wiring to Mercathode system* | Check the wiring |
| | Weak or discharged battery* | Fully charge and test the battery |
| Paint blistering | Battery charger connected improperly | Check connections and wiring |
| | Excessive exhaust gas deposits | Clean surfaces and apply wax |
| | Improper cleaning before painting | Sand surfaces and refinish |
| Stainless steel propeller corroding | Continuity washer missing | Install washer |
| | Debris on propeller shaft | Clean propeller shaft |
| | Improperly installed propeller | Check propeller installation |
| Corrosion on a single component | Missing or damaged grounding wire | Replace or repair wire |
| | Dirty grounding wire terminal | Clean and tighten wire terminal |
| Corrosion only on gimbal ring | Missing or damaged grounding wire | Replace or repair wire |
| | Dirty grounding wire terminal | Clean and tighten wire terminal |
| Corrosion in exhaust ports | Excessive exhaust gas deposits | Clean surfaces and apply wax |
| Corrosion after painting | Steel brush used to clean surfaces | Clean surfaces with a plastic brush |
| | Inadequate cleaning before painting | Sand surfaces and reapply paint |

(continued)

**Table 21 CORROSION TROUBLESHOOTING**

| Symptom | Possible Cause | Corrective Action |
|---|---|---|
| Corrodes after removing from water | Residual salt causing corrosion | Wash surfaces with fresh water |
| Crystals forming at mating surfaces | Salt crystal buildup | Clean surfaces and apply lubricant |
| Aluminum corroding only where lubricant is applied | Graphite in the lubricant | Clean surfaces and apply correct lubricant |
| Stainless steel components corroding | Foreign material on surfaces | Remove material and clean surfaces |
| | Component buried in sand | Remove from sand and clean surfaces |
| *Applies only to units equipped with Mercathode system. | | |

**Table 22 MERCATHODE SYSTEM TROUBLESHOOTING**

| Test results | Cause | Corrective Action |
|---|---|---|
| Low voltage | Drive is not grounded | Repair open grounding wire circuit |
| | Improper shore power connection | Install isolation unit |
| | Exposed metal components | Apply a finish to exposed metal components |
| | Painted anodes | Clean or replace anodes |
| | Anodes not grounded | Test for proper grounding |
| | Oxidation coating on anodes | Clean or replace anodes |
| | Anode(s) are depleted | Replace depleted anode(s) |
| | Improper type of bottom paint | Apply proper type of paint |
| | Foreign material on electrode | Clean or replace electrode assembly |
| | No power to electrode controller | Check power supply to the controller |
| | Faulty wire or connection | Check orange and brown wires |
| | Faulty electrode assembly | Test the electrode assembly |
| | Faulty Mercathode controller | Test the Mercathode controller |
| | Moored in flowing water | Install additional protection |
| | Moored in warm water | Install additional protection |
| High voltage | Stray current corrosion | Perform stray current test |
| | Open brown wire circuit | Repair wire or connection |
| | Faulty reference electrode | Test the electrode assembly |
| | Faulty Mercathode controller | Replace the Mercathode controller |

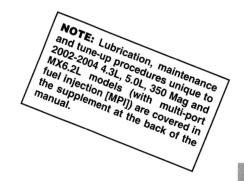

NOTE: Lubrication, maintenance and tune-up procedures unique to 2002-2004 4.3L, 5.0L, 350 Mag and MX6.2L models (with multi-port fuel injection [MPI]) are covered in the supplement at the back of the manual.

# Chapter Four

# Lubrication, Maintenance and Tune-Up

When operating properly, the MerCruiser stern drive engine provides smooth operation, reliable starting and excellent performance. This chapter describes the procedures necessary to keep the MerCruiser stern drive in peak condition.

**Table 1** lists torque specifications for fasteners and plugs. **Table 2** lists service intervals for all engine systems and components. Servie intervals are also provided in the Quick Reference Data at the front of the manual. **Tables 3-6** provide fluid capacities and spark plug recommendations. **Tables 1-6** are located at the end of this chapter.

If the engine becomes partially or completely submerged, refer to *Submersion* in this chapter. Service the engine as soon as possible to minimize the damage.

## BEFORE EACH USE

Certain items must be checked before each use to avoid engine damage or equipment failure. This section describes procedures for inspecting the following fluids and components:

1. Engine oil level.
2. Drive lubricant level.
3. Power steering fluid level.
4. Trim system fluid level.
5. Propeller.

6. Fuel system leakage.
7. Steering system looseness or binding.
8. Cooling system.
9. Lanyard (emergency stop) switch operation.

*CAUTION*
*Never run the engine with the oil level above the full line on the dipstick. Over filling can result in foaming of the oil and inadequate lubrication of internal components.*

### Engine Oil Level

To avoid overfilling the oil, wait until the engine has been switched off for 30 minutes or more. This allows the oil in the engine to drain into the oil pan.

On 3.0L models, the dipstick is located on the starboard side of the engine (**Figure 1**). On all other models, the dipstick is located at the front of the engine (**Figure 2**). The yellow handle makes it easy to identify.

The oil fill cap or tube attaches onto the rocker arm cover and passes through the electrical component cover on models 7.4 MPI, 496 Mag and 496 Mag HO. The cap has a yellow decal for easy identification. Refer to *Changing the Oil and Filter* in this chapter for oil recommendation.

Check the oil level as follows:

1. Pull the dipstick from the tube.

2. Wipe the dipstick with a clean shop towel.

3. Insert the dipstick fully into the tube.

4. Pull the dipstick from the engine and note the oil level. It should fall between the FULL and ADD marks (**Figure 3**).

5. Inspect the oil for the presence of water, a milky appearance, or significant fuel odor. Refer to *Engine* in Chapter Three if any of these conditions are noted.

6. If necessary, add oil until the level is even with the full mark. Do not overfill the engine. It is better for the oil level to be slightly low than overfilled. If the engine is overfilled, drain the excess oil as described under *Changing the Oil* in this chapter.

7. Insert the dipstick fully into the tube.

**Drive Lubricant Level**

The gearcase lubricant monitor (**Figure 4**) allows easy visual inspection of the lubricant level. The reservoir mounts at the top front of the engine. Refer to *Changing the Gearcase Lubricant* for lubricant recommendations.

> *NOTE*
> *To avoid overfilling, wait until the engine has been switched off for 30 minutes or more. Because the lubricant expands when it is hot, testing the lubricant level too soon after engine operation will give a false reading.*

Check and correct the level as follows:

1. Turn the engine off.

2. Note the lubricant level. With a cool engine, the lubricant level must be between the ADD and FULL (A, **Figure 4**) marks. If not, add lubricant as follows:

   a. Remove the fill cap (B, **Figure 4**).

   b. If the level is too high, use a syringe or other means to remove excess lubricant.

   c. If the monitor is empty, check for loose or damaged lubricant hoses and pressure test the gearcase as described in Chapter Three. Drain and refill the drive unit as described in this chapter.

   d. If the level is below the ADD line, add the necessary amount of gearcase lubricant.

   e. If the fluid has a milky appearance, pressure test the gearcase as described in Chapter Three.

   f. Replace the cap. Do not over tighten the cap, or the threads of the cap and reservoir will be damaged.

3. If a low lubricant level persists, check for loose or damaged lubricant hoses and pressure test the gearcase as described in Chapter Three.

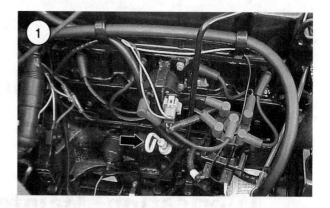

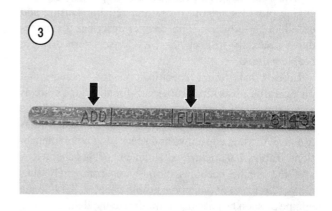

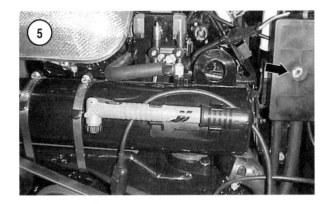

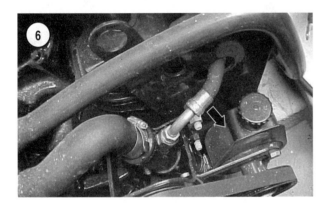

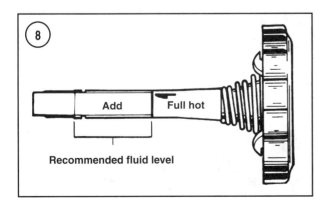

Add    Full hot

Recommended fluid level

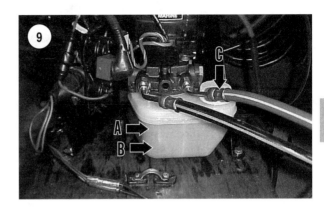

**4**

## Power Steering Fluid Level

Use only Dexron II automatic transmission fluid or Quicksilver Power Trim and Steering Fluid in the power steering system.

1. On 3.0L models, the pump and reservoir assembly mount on the upper starboard side of the engine. On 496 Mag and 496 Mag HO models, the plastic reservoir mounts on the front port side of the engine (**Figure 5**). The reservoir is separate from the pump. On all other models, the pump and reservoir assembly mount to the front port side of the engine (**Figure 6**).

2. Place the drive unit in the straight ahead position. Remove the fill cap (**Figure 7**).

3. Wipe the dipstick of the fill cap with a shop towel and reinstall it into the pump reservoir.

4. Remove the cap and note the fluid level on the dipstick (**Figure 8**). Correct the fluid level as follows:

    a. If the engine is warm, add fluid until the fluid level just reaches the upper end of the range (**Figure 8**).

    b. If the engine is cold, add fluid until the fluid level just reaches the groove below the ADD marking.

    c. If the reservoir is empty, fill and bleed the system as described in Chapter Fourteen.

5. Install the cap.

## Power Trim Fluid Level

The power trim pump (**Figure 9**) mounts in or near the engine compartment. Use only SAE 10W-30, 10W-40 engine oil or Quicksilver Power Trim and Steering Fluid in the power steering system. The transparent trim fluid reservoir allows visual inspection of the fluid level.

1. Place the drive in the full-down position.

2. Note the fluid level. With the drive down, the fluid level must be between the FULL (A, **Figure 9**) and ADD (B) marks.

3. If the reservoir is overfull, remove the fill cap (C, Figure 9) and remove excess fluid using a syringe.

4. If the reservoir is empty check for a leaking hose or fitting. Fill and bleed the system as described in Chapter Thirteen.

5. If the fluid has a milky appearance, check for a leaking external trim line or hose.

6. Install the cap. Do not overtighten the cap to prevent damage to the cap and reservoir.

### Propeller and Shaft Inspection

Inspect the propeller for cracked, damaged or missing blades (**Figure 10**). Operating the craft with a damaged propeller results in decreased performance, excessive vibration and increased wear of the drive unit components. Straighten small bent areas with locking pliers. Repair small nicks (**Figure 11**) with a metal file. To prevent an unbalanced condition, do not remove excessive amounts of material from the propeller. If significant damage is evident (**Figure 12**), have the propeller repaired at a propeller repair shop.

To check for a bent propeller shaft, disconnect the battery cables. Shift the engine to NEUTRAL. Spin the propeller while observing the propeller shaft. If the shaft wobbles noticeably, the propeller shaft is bent and must be replaced. See Chapter Eleven.

### Fuel System Inspection

Before starting the engine, open the engine cover and check for fuel leakage or fuel odor. If leakage or odor is noted, clean up spilled fuel and completely ventilate the engine compartment. Correct the source of the leakage before starting the engine.

After starting the engine, check for fuel odor and inspect all accessible fuel fittings, lines and hoses. The system is described in Chapter Eight.

### Steering System Inspection

Before starting the engine, rotate the steering wheel to the clockwise and counterclockwise limits. Note any binding or excessive slack as the wheel changes direction.

Inspect and repair worn or faulty components. Do not operate the boat if the steering is binding or loose.

### Coolant Level Inspection

Coolant level inspection applies only to models equipped with a closed cooling system. To avoid un-

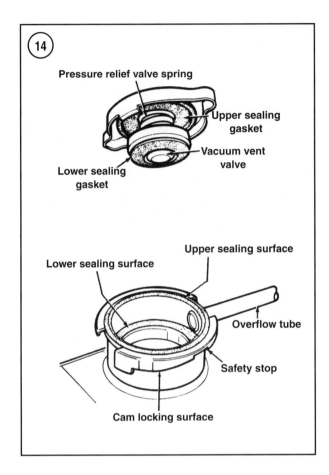

(14)

Pressure relief valve spring

Upper sealing gasket

Vacuum vent valve

Lower sealing gasket

Upper sealing surface

Lower sealing surface

Overflow tube

Safety stop

Cam locking surface

der-filling the cooling system, wait until the engine has been switched off for 30 minutes or more. The coolant level drops as the engine cools. Refer to *Coolant Change* in this chapter for coolant recommendations.

> *WARNING*
> *Do not remove the pressure cap from the closed cooling system if the engine is warm. Hot coolant may spray out of the reservoir and cause serious injury.*

> *WARNING*
> *Stay clear of the propeller shaft while running an engine on a flush/test adapter. Remove the propeller before running the engine. Disconnect the battery before removing or installing the propeller.*

> *CAUTION*
> *Never run the engine without first providing cooling water. Use either a test tank or a flush/test adapter. Remove the propeller before running the engine.*

1. Allow the engine to completely cool before removing the pressure cap.
2. To locate the pressure cap and reservoir:
   a. *Model 3.0L*—The reservoir and cap mounts onto the front of the cylinder head. The overflow reservoir mounts on the lower front starboard side of the engine.
   b. *Model 496 Mag and 496 Mag HO*—The reservoir and cap mount on the top and starboard side of the engine (**Figure 13**). These models do not use a separate overflow reservoir.
   c. *All other models*—The pressure cap and reservoir mount on the top of the heat exchanger.
3. Refer to *Heat Exchanger* in Chapter Nine to locate the heat exchanger. The overflow reservoir mounts on the lower front side of the engine.
4A. *Model 496 Mag and 496 Mag HO*—The coolant level must be even with the COLD FULL mark on the reservoir (B, **Figure 13**). Correct the coolant level as follows:
   a. Slowly loosen and remove the pressure cap (A, **Figure 13**).
   b. Wipe debris or crystallized coolant from the cap, cap seal and reservoir opening.
   c. Add the required amount of coolant to the reservoir.
   d. Install the pressure cap. Do not over tighten the cap, or the cap or reservoir threads will be damaged.
4B. *All other models*—Inspect the coolant level in the overflow reservoir. The level must be between the FULL and ADD marks. Remove the cap and add coolant as needed. Do not overfill the reservoir. Snap the cap fully onto the reservoir. If the overflow reservoir is low, correct the coolant level in the heat exchanger reservoir as follows:
   a. Cover the cap with a heavy shop towel. Using gloves, push down on the pressure cap. Rotate the cap until the tabs are clear of the cap locking surfaces (**Figure 14**). Lift the cap from the reservoir.
   b. Wipe debris and crystallized coolant from the cap and cap opening. Inspect the upper and lower gaskets (**Figure 14**) for cracked, missing or otherwise defective surfaces and replace if necessary.
   c. The coolant level must be even with the bottom of the reservoir filler neck. If the level is low, add the required amount of coolant to the reservoir.
   d. Align the locking tabs on the cap with the notches on the filler neck and install the cap. Push down and rotate the cap until it touches the safety stop.
5A. *Model 496 Mag and 496 Mag HO*—Start the engine. Allow the engine to reach normal operating temperature and check the coolant level. The level must be between the marks (B and C, **Figure 13**). Cool the engine and correct the level as needed.
5B. *All other models*—Start the engine. After the engine reaches operating temperature, check the fluid level in the

**4**

overflow reservoir. Cool the engine and correct the level as needed.

### Lanyard Switch (Emergency Stop Switch) Inspection

This switch is either incorporated into the remote control (**Figure 15**) or mounted on the dash board. Check the operation of the lanyard (emergency stop) switch before getting underway.
1. Start the engine. Do not shift into gear.
2. Pull the lanyard cord from the switch (**Figure 15**).
3. If the engine fails to stop, turn the ignition switch off. Repair or replace the switch before operating the engine.

### AFTER EACH USE

Certain maintenance procedures must be performed after each outing of the craft. Observing these requirements can dramatically reduce corrosion of engine components and extend the life of the engine.
1. Flush the cooling system.
2. Clean debris or contaminants from the engine surfaces.
3. Check the propeller and gearcase for damage.

> *WARNING*
> *Stay clear of the propeller shaft while running the engine on a flush/test adapter. Remove the propeller before running the engine to prevent injury or death. Disconnect the battery before removing or installing the propeller.*

> *CAUTION*
> *Never run the engine without first providing cooling water. Use either a test tank or a flush/test adapter. Remove the propeller before running the engine.*

### Flush the Cooling System

Flush the cooling system after each use to prevent deposit buildup and corrosion in the cooling passages. This is even more important if the engine was operated in salt, brackish or polluted water.

Engines equipped with a closed cooling system also benefit from regular flushing, because it reduces deposit buildup and corrosion in the heat exchanger, exhaust manifolds and fluid coolers.

Consider installing a freshwater flush kit if the boat is stored in the water. The kit includes hoses and fittings for connecting a garden hose onto the cooling system. This allows flushing of the cylinder block (standard cooling system only) and exhaust manifold(s) while in the water.

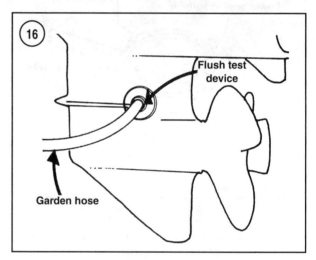

Flush test device

Garden hose

It does not flush the cooling passages in the drive unit. Follow the manufacturer's instructions for installation and use of the kit. Never start the engine while using a freshwater flush kit, because seawater pump will introduce contaminated water into the freshwater.

For engines stored on a trailer or boat lift, flush the engine using a flush/test adapter (**Figure 16** or **Figure 17**). Available from marine dealerships or marine supply stores, the adaptors flush the entire seawater side of the cooling system, including the water passage in the drive unit. The engine can also be flushed by operating it in a suitable test tank filled with clean water.

The two-piece flush/test adapter is easier to use than the slide-on type because it will not slip out of position during engine operation. Purchase a slide-on type flush/test adapter from a marine dealership automotive, hardware or sporting goods store. Purchase a two piece adapter (part number 44357A 2) from a MerCruiser dealership.

Flush the cooling system as follows:

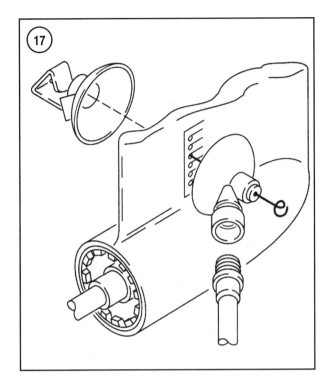

1. Remove the propeller as described in Chapter Eleven.

2A. *Slide-on type flush adapter* (**Figure 16**)—Connect the garden hose to the adapter. Beginning at the front edge of the gearcase, slide the cups onto each side of the gearcase. Position the cups over the water inlets.

2B. *Two-piece adapter* (**Figure 17**)—Connect the garden hose to the adapter. Squeeze the clamp plate on the connector opposite the hose, then pull the cup from the wire. Slide the wire with the cup attached through the water inlet openings. Squeeze the clamp plate enough to pass the wire through the cup and both sides of the clamp plate. Press both cups and the wire loop firmly against the gearcase then release the clamp plate.

3. Turn the water on. Make sure the flush adapter is positioned over the water screen. Start the engine and run at a fast idle (approximately 1500 rpm) in neutral until the engine reaches full operating temperature.

4. Continue to run the engine until the water exiting the engine is clear and the engine has run for a minimum of 5 minutes. Monitor the engine temperature. Stop the engine if it begins to overheat or water is not exiting with the exhaust.

5. Throttle back to idle and stop the engine. Remove the flush adapter. Install the propeller as described in Chapter Eleven. Allow the drive unit to remain in the vertical position for a few minutes to allow complete draining of the cooling system.

### Cleaning the Engine

Clean any dirt or vegetation from all external engine surfaces after each use. This step slows corrosion, reduces wear on gearcase and trim system seals, and makes worn or damaged components easier to see.

Never use strong cleaning solutions or solvents to clean the engine. Mild dish soap and pressurized water does an adequate job of cleaning most debris from the engine. To prevent water intrusion, never direct water into the exhaust openings. Avoid directing the high-pressure water spray at any openings, seals, plugs, wiring or wire grommets. The water may bypass seals and contaminate the trim fluid or enter the limit switch or sender.

Rinse all external surfaces with clean water to remove soap residue. Wipe the engine with a soft cloth to prevent water spots.

Use a dry cloth to wipe oil or debris from components inside the engine compartments. Never direct water onto any components within the engine. These components are not waterproof.

### Propeller and Gearcase Inspection

Inspect the gearcase after each outing. Smooth minor chips in the skeg with a file. Major damage to the skeg should be repaired at a propeller repair shop. Gearcase removal and installation are described in Chapter Eleven. Touch up chipped or abraded paint with Quicksilver Phantom Black Paint, available from a marine dealership. Inspect the propeller and shaft as described in this chapter.

### LUBRICATION

Proper lubrication is absolutely critical to engine operation. Lubricant helps prevent wear to the engine, gearcase and other areas, guards against corrosion, and provides smooth operation of moving parts.

Stern drives operate in a corrosive environment and often require special types of lubricants. Using the wrong type of lubricant can cause serious engine damage or substantially shorten the life of the engine.

Special lubricant pumps, available from most automotive parts stores, are required for some of the procedures described in this section. The lubricants described in these procedures are available from most marine suppliers or marine dealerships.

### Oil and Filter Change

Change the oil and filter at the end of the 20 hour break-in period, then at the intervals specified in **Table 2**. Always replace the filter when changing the oil, to prevent contaminants in the used filter from mixing with the fresh oil.

Use only the recommended oil filter available from a MerCruiser dealership. Oil filters designed for an automotive application may not meet the filtration requirement for the engine. Using the wrong filter can cause increased wear or serious engine damage.

Mercury marine recommends using Quicksilver 4-Cycle Marine Engine Oil in all gasoline models. This SAE 25-40 oil is suitable for use in all climates. If this oil is not available, use a good quality single viscosity oil that meets or exceeds API classification SE. The classification is usually printed on the container label or cap (**Figure 18**).

If using a single-viscosity oil, use SAE 20W if the expected maximum temperature will not exceed 32° F (0° C); SAE 30 if the expected temperature is 32-50° F (0-10° C) or SAE 40 if the temperature will exceed 50° F (10° C).

Use an oil filter wrench to loosen and tighten the oil filter.

Never overtighten the replacement filter, as this will make it difficult to remove later and may damage the filter. A damaged filter can rupture while underway, causing oil leakage and possible engine damage.

On 3.0L models, the filter mounts on the starboard side of the cylinder block (**Figure 19**).

On Bravo models, the filter mounts on a bracket on the top and port side of the engine (**Figure 20**).

On Alpha models the oil filter mounts on the rear port side of the cylinder block. An optional remote oil filter kit is available for these models. Consider installing this kit if the boat structure prevents reasonable access to the filter. Some EFI Alpha models are factory equipped with the remote mounted oil filter.

1. Place a container or shop towel under the filter to capture spilled oil.

2. Loosen the filter until the gasket just breaks contact with the mating surface. Allow a few minutes for the oil to drain from the filter. Turn the filter until free from the threaded adapter. Remove and quickly invert the filter.

3. Remove the gasket (**Figure 21**) from the cylinder block or adapter if it doesn't come off with the filter.

4. Empty the filter into a suitable container. Dispose of the filter in an environmentally responsible manner. Contact a marine dealership, auto repair shop or automotive parts store for information on the proper disposal of the oil filter.

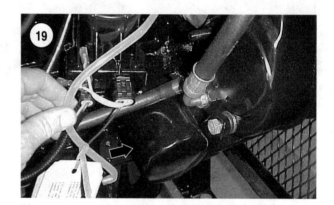

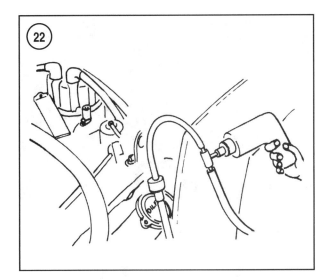

7. Change the engine oil as described in this chapter.

8. Start the engine and immediately check for oil leakage. Monitor the oil pressure gauge. The oil pressure must rise within a few seconds of starting the engine. Correct the oil leakage or low oil pressure before operating the engine.

### Engine oil change

If accessible, remove the drain plug from the oil pan and drain the oil into a suitable container. The most common method of removing the oil is to pump the oil from the pan using the dipstick tube. This requires some type of oil pumping device (**Figure 22**), available from automotive part stores and most marine supply businesses.

Some 2001-on models are equipped with an oil drain hose (**Figure 23**) and a quick connector that attaches the hose to the oil pan. The connector can be removed for draining the oil directly from the oil pan. The hose can be routed through the boat drain plug opening and into a suitable container outside of the boat. The hose can also be directed into a suitable container in the engine compartment.

> *WARNING*
> *Stay clear of the propeller shaft while running an engine on a flush/test adapter. Remove the propeller before running the engine. Disconnect the battery before removing or installing the propeller.*

> *CAUTION*
> *Never run the engine without first providing cooling water. Use either a test tank or a flush/test adapter.*

1. Replace the oil filter as described in this chapter. Remove the oil fill cap (**Figure 24**).

2A. To drain directly from the oil pan:
   a. Place a suitable container under the drain pan plug.
   b. If equipped with a quick connector and hose, push in on the tab (**Figure 25**) and carefully pull the con-

5. Thoroughly clean the filter mating surface on the cylinder block or remote adapter. Apply a light coat of engine oil to the gasket on the new filter.

6. Thread the filter onto the adapter until the sealing ring just contact the mating surface. Use a filter wrench and tighten the filter exactly one (1) turn. Do not over tighten the filter.

nector from the fitting and drain the oil. Clean all debris and oil from the fitting. Depress the tab and push the connector fully onto the fitting. Release the tab. Tug on the connector to verify a secure connection.

c. If equipped with a conventional drain plug, remove the plug and drain the oil. Clean the drain plug and the oil pan. Install and securely tighten the drain plug.

2B. To pump the oil from the dipstick tube:

a. Remove the dipstick.

b. Insert the oil pump hose into the dipstick tube.

c. Operate the pump to remove the oil.

d. Remove the pump hose and install the dipstick.

2C. To drain using the oil hose:

a. Disconnect the clamp and route the hose through the hull drain plug opening or into a suitable container. The container must be lower than the oil pan.

b. Remove the plug from the end of the hose and drain the oil.

c. Thread the plug into the end of the hose and securely tighten.

d. Route the hose end to a location on the engine higher than the rocker arm cover. Secure the hose with the clamp. The hose must not contact the drive belt(s) or other moving components.

3. Refer to **Table 4** to determine the engine oil capacity. Slowly pour 90% of this amount into the engine. Install the cap.

4. Start the engine and monitor the oil pressure gauge. The pressure must reach a normal range within 10 seconds of starting the engine. Otherwise check for an improperly installed oil filter.

5. Allow a few minutes for the oil to drain into the pan. Check and correct the oil level as described in this chapter.

**Gearcase Lubricant Change**

Change the gearcase lubricant at the intervals specified in **Table 2**. Use only Quicksilver Hi-Performance Gearcase Lubricant in the drive unit. This lubricant is available in quart and gallon containers. Refer to **Table 6** to determine the approximate gearcase capacity. A lubricant pump is required for this operation. Purchase the lubricant and pump from a MerCruiser dealership.

*CAUTION*
*Never use automotive gearcase or transmission lubricant in the gearcase. Automotive lubricants are usually not suitable for marine applications. The use of other than rec-*

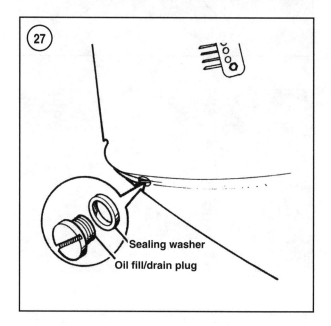

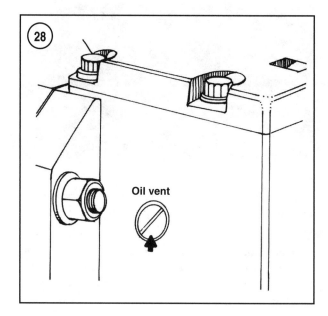

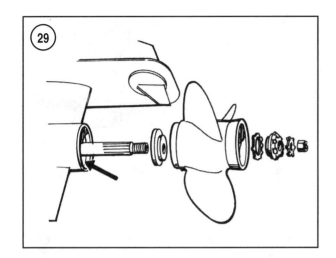

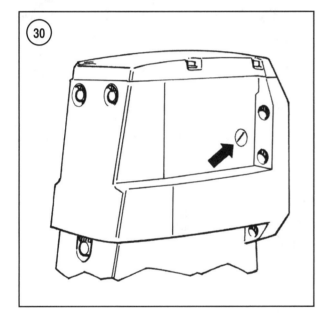

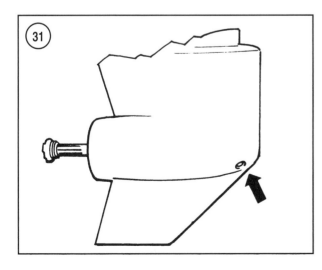

4

ommended lubricants can lead to increased wear, corrosion and drive unit failure.

*CAUTION*
*Inspect the sealing washers on all gearcase plugs. Replace missing or damaged sealing washers to prevent water or lubricant leakage.*

*NOTE*
*A small amount of very fine particles are usually present on the drain plug. These fine particles form during normal gearcase operation. Their presence does not necessarily indicate a problem. The presence of large particles, however, indicates a potential problem within the gearcase.*

1. Disconnect the battery cables. Place a suitable container under the gearcase. Remove the cap (**Figure 26**) from the lubricant monitor.

2. Refer to the following to locate the drain/fill and level/vent plugs.

   a. On Alpha drive models, the drain/fill plug is located on the lower port side of the gearcase (**Figure 27**). The level/vent plug is located on the port side of the drive shaft housing (**Figure 28**).

   b. On Bravo I models, the drain/fill plug is located on the bearing carrier (**Figure 29**). The level/vent plug is located on the starboard side of the drive shaft housing (**Figure 30**).

   c. On Bravo II models, the drain/fill plug is located on the lower starboard side of the gearcase (**Figure 31**). The level/vent plug is located on the starboard side of the drive shaft housing (**Figure 30**).

   d. On Bravo III models, the drain/fill plug is located on the starboard side on the gearcase and near the skeg (**Figure 32**). The level/vent plug is located on the starboard side of the drive shaft housing (**Figure 30**).

3. On Bravo I models, remove the propeller as described in Chapter Eleven. Remove the carrier anode as described in Chapter Fifteen.

4. Place the drive unit in the full-down position. Remove the drain/fill plug.

5. Rub a sample of gearcase lubricant between the thumb and forfinger. Fine metal particles normally appear in the lubricant. If the particles are large enough to feel, disassemble the drive and check for damaged components. Gearcase disassembly and reassembly are described in Chapter Eleven. If the lubricant is milky colored or water contaminated, pressure test the drive unit.

6. When the lubricant monitor is empty, remove the level/vent plug.

7. Allow the gearcase to drain completely. Tilt the drive and position the fill/drain opening at its lowest point to ensure the gearcase drains completely. After draining, return the drive to the upright position.

8. Remove the sealing washers from the plugs in the drive. Use a small pick to remove sealing washer remnants from the plug openings. Install new sealing washers onto each plug.

9. Thread the fitting of the lubricant pump into the drain/fill opening. *Slowly* pump lubricant into the drain/fill plug opening. Continue filling until lubricant flows from the level/vent plug opening. Without removing the pump, install the level/vent plug. Tighten the level/vent plug to the specification in **Table 1**.

10. Continue pumping until lubricant appears in the lubricant monitor (**Figure 26**). Remove the pump from the fill/drain opening and quickly install the drain/fill plug. Tighten the plug to the specification in **Table 1**.

11. On Bravo I models, install the carrier anode as described in Chapter Fifteen. Install the propeller as described in Chapter Eleven.

12. Check and correct the gearcase lubricant level as described in this chapter.

### Propeller Shaft Lubrication

Remove the propeller and lubricate the shaft at the intervals specified in **Table 2**. Remove the propeller and hardware (**Figure 29**) as described in Chapter Eleven. Apply a coat of Quicksilver 2-4-C Marine Lubricant (Mercury part No. 92-825407A12) or a good quality water-resistant grease onto the propeller shaft. Install the propeller and hardware as described in Chapter Eleven.

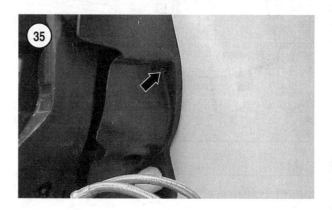

### Engine Coupler Lubrication

Lubricate the engine coupler at the intervals specified in **Table 2**. All models have a grease fitting (**Figure 33**) for the engine coupler. Pump spline grease (Mercury part No. 92-816391) into the fitting until resistance in felt. Do not apply excessive grease to the coupler.

If the grease fitting is inaccessible, remove the drive unit as described in Chapter Eleven. Use a long brush or stick and apply lubricant to the splines through the opening in the gimbal bearing (**Figure 34**).

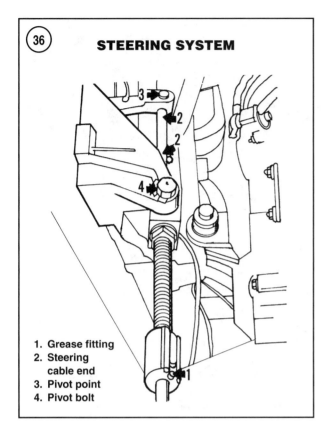

**STEERING SYSTEM**

1. Grease fitting
2. Steering cable end
3. Pivot point
4. Pivot bolt

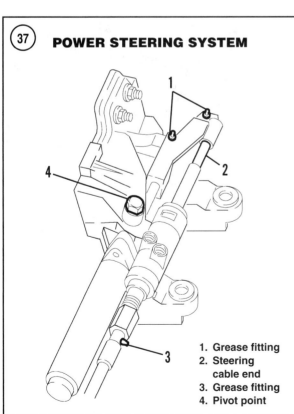

**POWER STEERING SYSTEM**

1. Grease fitting
2. Steering cable end
3. Grease fitting
4. Pivot point

### Gimbal Bearing Lubrication

Lubricate the gimbal bearing at the intervals specified in **Table 2**. Use only Quicksilver Universal Joint and Gimbal Bearing Grease (Mercury part No. 92-828052A2) in the gimbal bearing. Never use grease containing Teflon or other solids as it may pack around the bearing rollers causing them to slide instead of roll. The gimbal bearing will fail if the rollers slide.

1. Remove the drive unit as described in Chapter Eleven.

2. Pump grease into the grease fitting on the starboard side of the transom housing (**Figure 35**) until fresh grease exits the bearing (**Figure 34**). Wipe residual grease from the bellows.

3. Install the drive unit as described in Chapter Eleven.

### Universal Joint Lubrication and Inspection

Use only Quicksilver Universal Joint and Gimbal Bearing Lubricant (Mercury part No. 92-825052A2) in the universal joints. Other type of grease can cause rapid wear or failure of the universal joints.

Universal joint lubrication is required only on Bravo type drive units. Alpha drive units have sealed universal joints.

1. Remove the drive unit and inspect the universal joints as described in Chapter Eleven.

2. On Bravo drive, lubricate the universal joints as described in Chapter Eleven.

3. Reinstall the drive unit as described in Chapter Eleven.

### Steering System Lubrication

Lubricate the steering cable and all pivot points at the intervals listed in **Table 2**. Steering system lubrication is especially important if the engine is operated in saltwater, brackish or heavily polluted water.

1. Apply engine oil onto the steering system pivot points (3, **Figure 36** or 4, **Figure 37**).

2. Turn the steering wheel to full starboard. Apply a coating of Special Lube 101 (Mercury part No. 92-13872A1) onto the cable ends (2, **Figure 36** or 2, **Figure 37**). Turn the steering wheel several times, full port to full starboard, to distribute the lubricant.

*CAUTION*
*The steering cable must be in the retracted position before grease is injected into the fitting. The cable can become hydraulically locked when grease is injected with the cable extended.*

3. Some steering cables are provided with a grease fitting (1, **Figure 36** or 3, **Figure 37**). If so equipped, turn the steering wheel to the full port position. Pump water-resistant grease into the grease fitting until a slight resistance is felt. Avoid overfilling the steering cable with grease. Cycle the steering to full port and full starboard several times to distribute the lubricant.

4. On Alpha drives, pump Quicksilver 2-4-C Marine Lubricant (Mercury part No. 92-825407A12) into the hinge pin grease fittings (**Figure 38**) until grease exits the pivot points. Bravo drive units use bushings at this location and do not require regular lubrication.

## PERIODIC INSPECTION

### Bellows Inspection

Place the drive in the full-UP position and inspect all of the bellows (A, **Figure 39**) for tears, weathered or worn areas. Replacement procedures are described in Chapter Twelve.

### Engine Alignment

Check the engine alignment as described in Chapter Seven at the intervals specified in **Table 2**. A misaligned engine stresses the coupler, gimbal bearing and universal joint shaft, which can result in noisy drive operation, rapid wear and eventual failure of one or more of these components.

### Water Inlet Inspection

Remove vegetation, barnacles, salt crystals or other contaminants from the water inlets (**Figure 40**) at the intervals specified in **Table 2**. Blockage of the water inlets will eventually lead to insufficient water flow and the engine overheating. Use a bristle brush to remove vegetation and salt crystals. Scrape off barnacles or other marine life. If necessary, disassemble the gearcase to access the inner passages. Gearcase disassembly is described in Chapter Eleven.

Clean the inlets more frequently if the boat is stored in the water or used in saltwater.

### Gimbal Ring Fasteners

Tighten the gimbal ring fasteners (**Figure 41**) after the first 20 hours of use and at the intervals specified in **Table 2**. Tightening procedures are described in Chapter Twelve under *Gimbal ring installation*. Loose gimbal ring fasteners cause rapid wear of the upper swivel shaft and gimbal

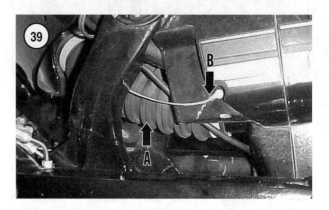

ring, which are expensive and time consuming to replace. Tighten the fasteners more frequently on high performance or work boat applications.

### Anode and Ground Wire Inspection

Inspect the ground wires and terminals (B, **Figure 39**) for loose terminals, frayed wiring or other damage. Inspect anodes (**Figure 42**) for deep pitting, excessive material loss or other defects as described in Chapter Fifteen.

Regular maintenance to these components is especially important if the boat is stored or operated in saltwater or

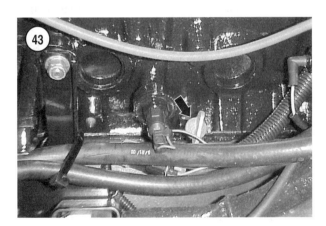

polluted water. Anode and ground wire mounting locations, together with replacement procedures, are described in Chapter Fifteen.

## Engine Coolant Change (Closed Cooling System)

To maintain cooling system efficiency, change the engine coolant at the intervals specified in **Table 2**. The coolant change intervals are determined by the type of coolant used.

Over time, certain chemicals in the coolant react with minerals in the water mixed with the coolant or metals in the cylinder block, forming crystaline deposits which coat the passages in the heat exchanger and cylinder block. These crystal deposits insulate the coolant from the component, preventing efficient heat transfer. As it builds, these deposits restrict the cooling flow, further compromising the cooling system, causing the engine to overheat.

Change the coolant on a regular basis to minimize these deposits. Heavy deposits can be removed using a commercially available cleaner. Always follow the manufacturer's instructions if using these products.

The manufacturer recommends using an ethylene glycol-based, extended-life 5/100 coolant in all closed cooling systems. Read the container label carefully and make sure the coolant meets these requirements.

If this type of coolant is not available, use a good quality ethylene glycol-based coolant. Do not use propylene glycol-type coolant in the closed cooling system.

Dilute the coolant with an equal amount of clear purified water. The cooling system must operate with a 50:50 mixture for efficient cooling and protection against freezing. Read the container label carefully. Some brands and types of coolant are premixed and do not require dilution with water.

Refer to **Table 5** to determine the cooling system capacity.

### Draining the coolant

1. Remove the pressure cap as described under *Checking the Coolant* in this chapter.
2. Refer to **Table 5** to determine the cooling system capacity. Have a suitable container on hand to hold the drained coolant.
3A. *Model 3.0*—Drain the system as follows:
   a. Remove the coolant drain plug from the bottom of the heat exchanger. The rear fitting drains seawater from the exchanger. The front fitting drains coolant from the exchanger.
   b. Remove the blue drain plug (**Figure 43**) from the port side of the cylinder block.
   c. Insert a wire into the openings to clear sediment.
   d. After draining is complete, install and securely tighten the plugs.
3B. *V6 and V8 models (except 496 Mag and 496 Mag HO)*—Drain the system as follows:
   a. Loosen the clamp and disconnect the circulating pump hose from the bottom of the heat exchanger. Refer to *Heat Exchanger* in Chapter Nine to identify the hose. Direct the disconnected hose into a suitable container.

b. Remove the blue drain plugs (**Figure 43**) from the port and starboard sides of the cylinder block. On 4.3-6.2L engines, the starboard cylinder block drain is located in the knock sensor fitting near the starter motor.

c. Insert a wire into the openings to clear sediment.

d. After draining is completed, install and securely tighten the drain plugs. Connect the hose onto the heat exchanger. Securely tighten the clamp.

3C. *Model 496 Mag and 496 Mag HO*—Drain the system as follows:

a. Remove the drain plugs (**Figure 44**) from each side of the cylinder block. Insert a wire into the openings to clear sediment.

b. After draining is completed, install and securely tighten the drain plugs.

3D. *All models (except 496 Mag and 496 Mag HO)*—Loosen the clamp and remove the hose from the bottom fitting of the overflow reservoir. After draining is completed, reconnect the hose. Securely tighten the clamp.

4. Properly dispose of the coolant. Contact an automotive repair shop or automotive parts store for disposal information.

### Filling the cooling system

Fill the cooling system slowly to prevent air from becoming trapped in the system. Refer to **Table 5** to determine the cooling system capacity. Suspect air entrapment if the amount of coolant added is significantly less than the capacity.

If the boat is in the water, add weight to the rear of the boat until the front of the engine is slightly higher than the rear. If the boat is on a trailer, use the trailer jack to correctly position the engine.

> *WARNING*
> *Stay clear of the propeller shaft while running an engine on a flush/test adapter. Remove the propeller before running the engine. Disconnect the battery before removing or installing the propeller.*

> *CAUTION*
> *Never run the engine without first providing cooling water. Use either a test tank or a flush/test adapter. Remove the propeller before running the engine.*

1A. *Model 3.0L*—Fill the system as follows:

a. *Slowly* pour the 50:50 mix of coolant and water into the reservoir until the level is approximately 1 in.

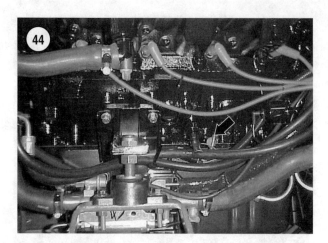

(25mm) below the reservoir neck. Do not install the cap at this time.

b. Start the engine. Advance the throttle to 1500 rpm. Continuously monitor the temperature gauge. Stop immediately if the engine starts to overheat.

c. Add coolant to maintain the level as necessary.

d. After the engine reaches normal operating temperature, add coolant to bring the level even with the bottom of the filler neck.

e. Install the pressure cap.

f. Add coolant into the overflow reservoir until it reaches the FULL mark.

g. Lift the reservoir from the bracket. Raise the bottle higher than the engine to purge air from the reservoir hose. Correct the coolant level as needed.

1B. *Model 496 Mag and 496 Mag HO*—Fill the system as follows:

a. *Slowly* pour the 50:50 mixture of coolant and water into the reservoir. Stop when the level reaches the full marking. Wait a few minutes for complete filling of the exchanger and block. Add additional coolant as needed.

b. Install the pressure cap. Start the engine. Operate the engine at idle speed only. Continuously monitor the temperature gauge. Immediately stop the engine if it starts to overheat.

c. Monitor the level in the reservoir. Stop the engine if the level drops below the ADD mark. Allow the engine to cool. Add coolant as described in this chapter.

1C. *All other models*—Fill the system as follows:

a. Loosen the air bleed fitting (**Figure 45**) on the thermostat housing.

b. *Slowly* pour the 50:50 mixture of coolant and water into the reservoir until coolant flows from the bleed fitting. Securely tighten the bleed fitting.

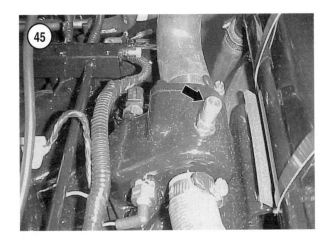

c. Add coolant until the level reaches the bottom of the filler neck.

d. Start the engine and advance the throttle to 1500 rpm. Continuously monitor the temperature gauge. Stop immediately if the engine starts to overheat.

e. Add coolant as needed to maintain a level even with the bottom of the filler neck.

f. After the engine reaches normal operating temperature, correct the coolant level and install the pressure cap.

g. Add coolant to the overflow reservoir until the level reaches the FULL mark.

h. Lift the reservoir from the bracket. Raise the bottle higher than the engine to purge air from the reservoir hose. Correct the coolant level as needed.

4. Allow the engine to completely cool. Check the coolant level as described in this chapter. Correct any leakage from the drain plugs.

## HEAT EXCHANGER CLEANING

Remove and clean the heat exchanger at the intervals specified in **Table 2**, as described in Chapter Nine.

## PRESSURE CAP TEST

Test the pressure cap at the intervals specified in **Table 2**, as described in Chapter Three.

## COOLANT TEST

Test the coolant at the intervals specified in **Table 2**. Pink litmus paper is required for this procedure. Purchase litmus paper from a pool supply or pet store.

1. Allow the engine to completely cool then remove the pressure cap.

2. Dip the litmus paper into the coolant and quickly remove it.

    a. If the paper changes from pink to blue, the coolant is alkaline. This is normal. Change the coolant at the intervals specified in **Table 2**.

    b. If the paper remains pink, the coolant is acidic and must be replaced. Check for a leaking cylinder head gasket as described under *Engine Compression Test* in Chapter Three.

3. Install the pressure cap.

## CLAMPS AND FITTINGS

Tighten all hose clamps and fittings at the intervals specified in **Table 2**. Refer to the appropriate chapter for clamp location and tightening instructions.

1. *Fuel system*—Refer to Chapter Eight.
2. *Exhaust and cooling system*—Refer to Chapter Nine.
3. *Transom assembly*—Refer to Chapter Twelve.
4. *Power steering system*—Refer to Chapter Fourteen.

## FUEL REQUIREMENTS

*CAUTION*
*Never run the engine on stale fuel. Varnish-like deposits form in the fuel system as the fuel deteriorates. These deposits block fuel passages and cause a lean condition in the combustion chamber. Damage to the pistons, valves and other power head components result from operating the engine with an excessively lean fuel mixture.*

Petroleum based fuels have a short shelf life. Some fuels begin to lose potency in as little as 14 days.

Purchase fuel from a busy fuel station. They usually have a higher turnover of fuel, ensuring that the fuel you buy there will be fresh. Always use the fuel well before it becomes stale. Refer to *Lay-up* in Chapter Five for information on fuel additives.

All models covered in this manual are designed to use regular unleaded fuel. Use fuel with an average octane rating of 87 or higher. Premium grade fuel offers little advantage over regular fuel under most operating conditions.

### Fuel Filter

Replace the fuel filters at the intervals specified in **Table 2**.

On models equipped with a two-barrel carburetor, the fuel filter is located in the fuel inlet fitting on the carbure-

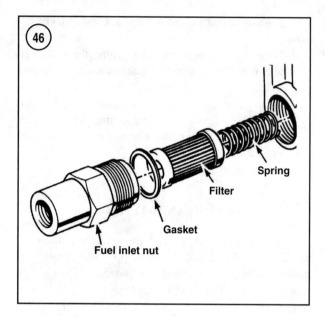

tor (**Figure 46**). An optional water separating fuel filter kit is available.

On models equipped with a four-barrel carburetor, a water separating fuel filter is used and mounts on the front and starboard side of the engine.

On all EFI engines, a water separating fuel filter is used. The filter (**Figure 47**) is located beneath the heat shield on the front starboard side of the engine.

> *WARNING*
> *Use extreme caution when working with or around fuel. Never smoke around fuel or fuel vapor. Make sure no flame or source of ignition is present in the work area. Flame or sparks can ignite the fuel or vapor resulting in fire or explosion.*

### *Replacement (carbureted models)*

1. Disconnect the fuel line from the carburetor as described in Chapter Eight.

2. Remove the fuel inlet fitting and filter as described under *Carburetor Disassembly* in Chapter Eight.

3. Inspect the filter for blockage or sediment. Inspect the fuel tank if rust or sediment is found in the filter.

4. Install the new fuel filter and connect the fuel line as described in Chapter Eight.

5. Start the engine and immediately check for fuel leakage. Do not operate the engine if it is leaking fuel.

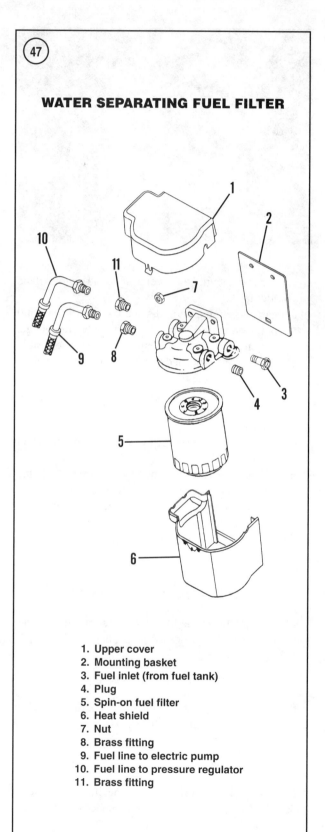

**WATER SEPARATING FUEL FILTER**

1. Upper cover
2. Mounting basket
3. Fuel inlet (from fuel tank)
4. Plug
5. Spin-on fuel filter
6. Heat shield
7. Nut
8. Brass fitting
9. Fuel line to electric pump
10. Fuel line to pressure regulator
11. Brass fitting

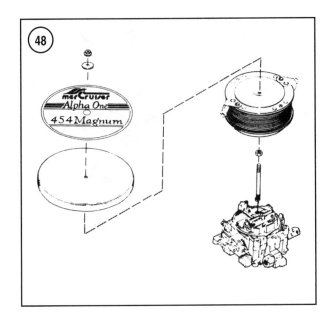

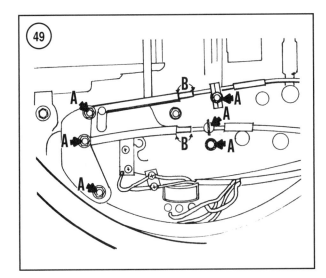

4. Empty the filter into a transparent container. Visually inspect the fuel. If a significant amount of water or sediment is present, drain and clean the fuel tank.

5. Apply a light coat of engine oil to the gasket on the filter. Fill the filter with clean fresh fuel.

6. Without spilling fuel, thread the filter onto the adapter. Use a filter wrench to tighten the filter. Be careful not to overtighten, or the threads on the filter and adapter will be damaged.

7. On EFI models, align the slot in the filter heat shield (6, **Figure 47**) with the bracket (2). Slide the shield over the filter. Align the upper cover (1, **Figure 47**) with the shield. Snap the tab of the cover over the boss on the shield.

8. Start the engine and immediately check for fuel leakage. Do not operate the engine if it is leaking fuel.

### FLAME ARRESTOR

Remove and clean the flame arrestor and cover (**Figure 48**, typical) at the intervals specified in **Table 2**. Removal, cleaning and installation are described in Chapter Eight.

Use solvent to clean the breather hoses. Dry the hoses with compressed air before installing them.

### PVC VALVE

Pull the valve from the grommet in the rocker arm cover. Spray carburetor and choke cleaner into the valve until the inner components are clean. Use compressed air to remove residual cleaner from the valve body. Shake the valve to check for a stuck internal valve. The valve should rattle in the body. If not, replace the PVC valve.

### CARBURETOR OR THROTTLE BODY

Clean the external surfaces of the carburetor or throttle with carburetor and choke cleaner.

Check for cracks, leaks or damage. Replace any damaged components before operating the engine.

### THROTTLE AND SHIFT CABLE

Inspect the pivot points (A, **Figure 49**) for loose, missing or overtightened fasteners. Apply engine oil to the throttle cable and shift cables pivot points (A, **Figure 49**). Apply a light coat of water-resistant grease to the slide portion of the cables (B, **Figure 49**). Operate the throttle and shift control to distribute the lubricant.

If binding or excessive play occurs, adjust the cables as described in Chapter Six.

*Replacement*
*(water separating fuel filter)*

Use an oil filter wrench to remove and install the filter.

1. On EFI models, pull up on the tab of the upper cover (1, **Figure 47**). Lift the cover from the bracket (2, **Figure 47**). Pull the heat shield (6, **Figure 47**) downward and remove it from the bracket.

2. Place a container or shop towels under the filter to capture spilled fuel.

3. Use an oil filter wrench to remove the filter. The gasket (**Figure 21**) should come off with the filter. If it sticks to the adapter, remove it and install it onto the used filter.

## Battery and Charging System Inspection

Unlike automobiles, boats may sit for weeks or more without running. Without proper maintenance the battery will lose its charge and deteriorate. Marine engines are exposed to a great deal of moisture, which causes heavy corrosion of the battery terminals. Clean the terminals and charge the battery at least every 30 days. Refer to Chapter Ten for complete battery testing, maintenance and charging instructions.

Wipe debris or salt crystals from the alternator. Inspect the drive belt for wear, damage or incorrect tension as described in this chapter. Check for loose alternator mounting fasteners and tighten as needed.

## Belt and Hose Inspection

Inspect the belts for wear, fraying, cracks, and oil-soaked surfaces. Replace the belt(s) if these or other defects occur. Small cracks commonly form in the small grooves of serpentine belts. This condition does not indicate a need for replacement unless the cracks extend lengthwise or into the body of the belt.

Push down on the belt at a point midway between two pulleys (**Figure 50**). The belt should depress approximately 1/4 in. (6 mm) with moderate pressure. Otherwise adjust the belt tension as described in Chapter Six.

Inspect all cooling and fuel system hoses for leakage, wear, weathered surface or other damage. Check the hoses for brittleness or excessive softness. Replace hoses with these or other defects.

## Corrosion Preventative Spray

Apply a light coating of corrosion preventative spray onto the exposed surfaces of the engine body. This maintenance step is especially important if the boat is stored or used in saltwater or polluted water.

Purchase this product from a marine dealership or marine supply facility. Always follow the label instruction. Avoid spraying into openings in the alternator or starter.

## TUNE-UP

A complete tune up is a series of adjustments, tests, inspections and parts replacements to return the engine to original factory specifications. Perform all operations listed in this section for a complete engine tune up.

## Compression Test

No tune up is complete without a compression test. An engine with low compression on one or more cylinders cannot be properly tuned. Perform a compression test before replacing any components or performing any adjustments. Correct the cause of low compression before proceeding with the tune up. The compression test procedure is described in Chapter Three.

## Spark Plugs

All 1992-On MerCruiser gasoline engine use a transistorized ignition system. These systems produce higher energy than conventional breaker point systems, providing longer spark plug life and less chance of spark plug fouling. Nevertheless, spark plugs operate in a harsh environment and eventually require replacement.

Maintenance intervals for the spark plugs vary by model.

Models 496 Mag, 496 Mag HO and 350 Mag MPI Horizon (2001-on) use platinum tipped spark plugs, which require service at 3 year or 300 operating hour intervals.

On all other models, clean and inspect or replace the spark plug at 1 year or 100 hour operating hour intervals.

Replacement spark plugs must be the correct size, reach and heat range to operate properly. Refer to the decal on the flame arrestor cover, electrical component cover or owner's manual for spark plug recommendation. Refer to the **Table 3** if the owner's manual is not available or the decal is illegible.

Spark plug condition can reveal much about the condition of the engine. Regular inspection allows problems to be indentified and corrected before expensive engine damage occurs. Remove the spark plugs and compare them to the ones shown in **Figure 51**.

Be sure to correct any engine problems before installing new spark plugs.

(51)

**4**

## SPARK PLUG CONDITION

### NORMAL
- Identified by light tan or gray deposits on the firing tip.
- Can be cleaned.

### GAP BRIDGED
- Identified by deposit buildup closing gap between electrodes.

### OIL FOULED
- Identified by wet black deposits on the insulator shell bore and electrodes.
- Caused by excessive oil entering combustion chamber through worn rings and pistons, excessive clearance between valve guides and stems or worn or loose bearings. Can be cleaned. If engine is not repaired, use a hotter plug.

### CARBON FOULED
- Identified by black, dry fluffy carbon deposits on insulator tips, exposed shell surfaces and electrodes.
- Caused by too cold a plug, weak ignition, dirty air cleaner, too rich fuel mixture or excessive idling. Can be cleaned.

### LEAD FOULED
- Identified by dark gray, black, yellow or tan deposits or a fused glazed coating on the insulator tip.
- Caused by highly leaded gasoline. Can be cleaned.

### WORN
- Identified by severely eroded or worn electrodes.
- Caused by normal ear. Should be replaced.

### FUSED SPOT DEPOSIT
- Identified by melted or spotty deposits resembling bubbles or blisters.
- Caused by sudden acceleration. Can be cleaned.

### OVERHEATING
- Identified by a white or light gray insulator with small black or gray brown spots with bluish-burnt appearance of electrodes.
- Caused by engine overheating, wrong type of fuel, loose spark plugs, too hot a plug or incorrect ignition timing. Replace the plug.

### PREIGNITION
- Identified by melted electrodes and possibly blistered insulator. Metallic deposits on insulator indicate engine damage.
- Caused by wrong type of fuel, incorrect ignition timing or advance, too hot a plug, burned valves or engine overheating. Replace the plug.

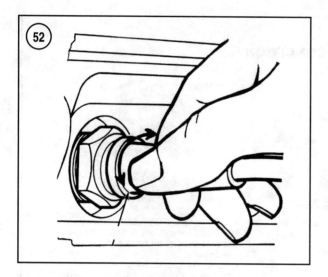

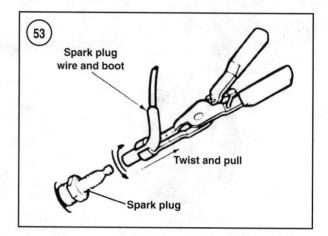

### Removal

1. Mark the cylinder number on the spark plug leads before removing them from the spark plugs. Disconnect the spark plug wires by twisting and pulling on the wire boot (**Figure 52**). If working on a hot engine in cramped quarters, grip the boot with spark plug boot pliers (**Figure 53**).
2. Use compressed air to blow debris from around the spark plugs before removing them. If the plug threads are corroded, apply a penetrating oil and allow it to soak in.
3. Sometimes the threads in the cylinder heads are damaged during spark plug removal. This condition can be repaired without removing the cylinder head by installing a special threaded insert.
4. Clean the spark plug holes in the cylinder head with a thread chaser (**Figure 54**). Thread the chaser by hand into each spark plug hole. Several passes may be required to remove all carbon or corrosion deposits from the threaded hole. Flush all debris from the holes with compressed air.

### Inspection

Compare the spark plugs to those shown in **Figure 51**. Spark plugs can give a clear indication of problems in the engine sometimes before the symptoms occur. Additional inspection and testing may be required if an abnormal spark plug condition is noted. Refer to Chapter Three for troubleshooting instructions.

### Installation

Use a gap adjusting tool (**Figure 55**) to adjust the spark plug gap (**Table 3**). Never tap the plug against a hard object to close the gap. The ceramic insulator can crack and

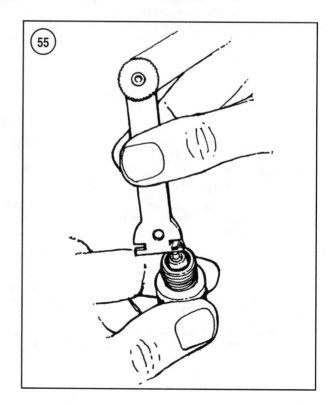

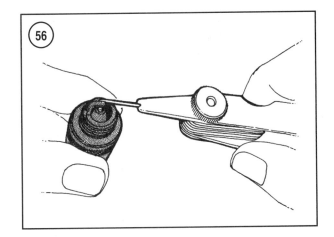

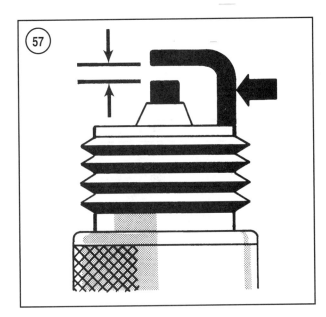

break away. Gapping tools are available at most auto parts stores.

1. Refer to **Table 3** to determine the correct spark plug gap.

2. Check the gap using a wire feeler gauge (**Figure 56**) of the same thickness as the recommended gap. The gauge should pass between the electrodes (**Figure 57**) with a slight drag.

3. Open or close the gap as necessary.

4. Inspect the spark plug for parallel electrode surfaces (**Figure 57**). Carefully bend the electrode until the surfaces are parallel and the gap is correct.

*NOTE*
*Some spark plug brands require the terminal end be installed prior to installation. Thread the terminal onto the spark plug as shown in **Figure 58**.*

5. Apply a very light coat of oil to the spark plug threads and thread them in by hand. Use a torque wrench to tighten the spark plugs to the specification in **Table 1**.

6. Apply a light coat of silicone lubricant to the inner surface of the spark plug caps. Carefully slide the cap over the correct spark plug. Snap the connector fully onto the spark plug.

**Valve Adjustment**

Excessive clearance causes valve system noise and may increase wear on some valve train components. Insufficient clearance can result in rapid wear of valve train components, reduced power and rough engine operation. Check the valve clearance at the intervals specified in **Table 2**. Valve adjustment is described in Chapter Seven.

**Carburetor Adjustment**

Proper carburetor adjustment is essential for smooth and efficient operation. Carburetor adjustment includes idle mixture and idle speed adjustment. Carburetor adjustment is described in Chapter Six.

**Ignition Timing**

The ignition timing is automatically set by the engine control unit (ECU) on Model 496 Mag and 496 Mag HO. The initial timing must be adjusted on all other models. Unlike most earlier MerCruiser engines, special procedures must be followed. Failure to follow these procedures can result in poor performance or serious engine damage. Ignition timing adjustment is described in Chap-

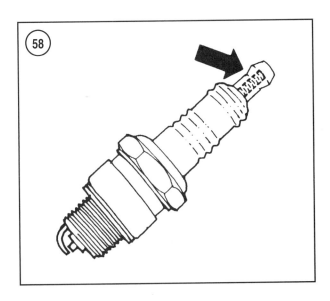

ter Six. Check the ignition timing at the intervals specified in **Table 2** and during the tune-up.

### Test Running the Engine

*NOTE*
*Perform this test with an average load in the boat and the drive unit trimmed to the correct angle for the best performance.*

1. Operate the engine using a flush/test device or in a test tank to ensure correct starting and idling before testing the boat on the water.
2. Connect a shop tachometer to the engine. Follow the manufacturer's instructions when attaching the tachometer onto the engine.

3. Note the idle speed while an assistant operates the boat. Refer to Chapter Six and adjust the idle speed.
4. Accelerate to wide-open throttle and note the engine speed. Refer to Chapter Three to determine the correct engine operating range. Check the propeller for damage or incorrect pitch if the engine speed is not within the recommended speed range. Refer to Chapter Three if the correct propeller is installed but the engine fails to reach the recommended speed range.
5. Check all fuel system, ignition system and timing adjustments.
6. Try a rapid acceleration and run the engine at various speed ranges. Refer to Chapter Three if rough operation is noted at any speed range or hesitation occurs during rapid acceleration.

### Table 1 TORQUE SPECIFICATIONS

| Fastener | ft.-lb. | in.-lb. | N•m |
|---|---|---|---|
| Spark plug | | | |
| 3.0L, 496 Mag and 496 Mag HO | | | |
| 1998-2004 | 22 | – | 30 |
| 4.3L, 5.0L, 5.7L and 350 Mag | | | |
| 1998-2001 | 15 | 180 | 20 |
| 2002-2004 | | | |
| New cylinder head | – | 18 | 24.4 |
| Used cylinder head | 132 | – | 15 |
| Drive unit drain/fill and level/vent plug | | | |
| Alpha | – | 30-50 | 3-6 |
| Bravo models | – | 40 | 5 |
| Oil pan drain plug | | | |
| 4.3L, 5.0L, 5.7L, 350 Mag | 15 | – | 20 |
| MX 6.2 | 18 | – | 25 |
| 7.4 MPI, 454 Mag, 502 Mag | 20 | – | 27 |
| 496 Mag, 396 Mag HO | 21 | – | 28 |

### Table 2 MAINTENANCE SCHEDULE

| Before each use (saltwater or freshwater use) | Check engine oil level |
|---|---|
| | Check the drive lubricant level |
| | Check the power steering fluid level[1] |
| | Check the trim system fluid level |
| | Check the propeller |
| | Check the fuel system |
| | Check the steering system |
| | Check the cooling system |
| | Check the lanyard or stop switch |
| After each use (saltwater use) | Flush the seawater section |
| | (continued) |

**Table 2 MAINTENANCE SCHEDULE (continued)**

| | |
|---|---|
| Weekly (saltwater or freshwater use) | Check engine oil level<br>Check coolant level<br>Check power steering fluid[1]<br>Check drive unit fluid<br>Check battery level<br>Check trim pump fluid<br>Inspect anodes<br>Inspect the water inlets |
| 30 days or 25 hours of operation (saltwater use) | Inspect alternator wiring<br>Clean alternator air openings<br>Inspect alternator drive belt<br>Adjust alternator drive belt tension |
| 100 days or 100 hours of operation (saltwater or freshwater use) | Check drive belt condition<br>Check drive belt tension |
| 60 days or 50 hours of operation (saltwater use) | Lubricate the propeller shaft<br>Apply corrosion preventative spray |
| 120 days or 100 hours of operation (saltwater or freshwater use) | Lubricate the propeller shaft<br>Apply corrosion preventative spray[5]<br>Inspect the serpentine drive belt [1] |
| End of the first boating season (saltwater or freshwater use) | Check engine alignment<br>Change engine oil and filter<br>Clean the flame arrestor and breather hoses<br>Change PVC valve[1]<br>Change drive unit lubricant<br>Torque gimbal ring bolts<br>Torque engine mounting bolts<br>Lubricate the gimbal bearing<br>Inspect the universal joints<br>Lubricate the universal joints[4]<br>Lubricate and inspect steering system components<br>Inspect wiring<br>Test the pressure cap[1]<br>Inspect hoses<br>Tighten hose clamps<br>Inspect and test the drive unit grounding wires<br>Lubricate and inspect the control cables<br>Inspect the exhaust system<br>Adjust the ignition timing<br>Inspect the steering head<br>Lubricate and inspect the remote control<br>Inspect the carburetor<br>Adjust the carburetor[1]<br>Inspect the throttle body[1]<br>Adjust the valves |
| Once a year or 100 hours of operation (saltwater or freshwater use) | Change engine oil and filter<br>Clean the flame arrestor and breather hoses<br>Change PVC valve[1]<br>Change drive unit lubricant<br>Torque gimbal ring bolts<br>Clean and inspect the spark plugs<br>Torque engine mounting bolts<br>(continued) |

4

## Table 2 MAINTENANCE SCHEDULE (continued)

| | |
|---|---|
| Once a year or 100 hours of operation (continued) | Lubricate the gimbal bearing<br>Lubricate and inspect steering system components<br>Inspect wiring<br>Test the pressure cap[1]<br>Inspect hoses and clamps<br>Inspect and test the drive unit grounding wires<br>Lubricate and inspect the control cables<br>Inspect the exhaust system<br>Adjust the ignition timing<br>Inspect the steering head<br>Lubricate and inspect the remote control<br>Inspect the carburetor[1]<br>Adjust the carburetor[1]<br>Inspect the throttle body[1] |
| Once a year (saltwater or freshwater use) | Clean and paint exposed surfaces<br>Replace the fuel filter(s)<br>Test the corrosion control system[1]<br>Test the coolant[1]<br>Clean the heat exchanger[1]<br>Inspect drive unit bellows and clamps |
| Every two years or 300 hours of operation (freshwater use) | Check engine alignment<br>Lubricate engine coupling<br>Inspect the universal joints and coupling splines<br>Lubricate the universal joints[4] |
| Once a year or 300 hours of operation (saltwater or freshwater use) | Check engine alignment[5]<br>Lubricate engine coupling[5]<br>Inspect the universal joints and coupling splines[5]<br>Lubricate the universal joints[4,5] |
| Every two years or 400 hours of operation (saltwater or freshwater use) | Change the engine coolant[2] |
| Every five years or 1000 hours or operation (saltwater or freshwater use) | Change the engine coolant[3] |

1. This maintenance item may not apply to all models.
2. Closed cooling system models using standard ethylene glycol coolant (not 5/100 extended life).
3. Closed cooling system models using 5/100 extended life coolant.
4. Applies only to models equipped with a bravo drive unit.
5. This maintenance interval applies if the engine is operated in saltwater or polluted water.

## Table 3 SPARK PLUG SPECIFICATIONS

| Model | Spark plug No. | Gap specification |
|---|---|---|
| **3.0L** | | |
| AC plug | MR43LTS | |
| Champion plug | RS12YC | |
| NGK plug | BPR6EFS | |
| Spark plug gap | – | 0.035 in. (0.9 mm) |
| **4.3L, 5.0L, 5.7L, 350 Mag and MX6.2L** | | |
| 1998-2004 carburetor-equipped models | | |
| AC plug | MR43LTS | |
| Champion plug | RS12YC | |
| NGK plug | BPR6EFS | |
| Plug gap | – | 0.045 in. (1.1 mm) |
| (continued) | | |

**4**

### Table 3 SPARK PLUG SPECIFICATIONS (continued)

| Model | Spark plug No. | Gap specification |
|---|---|---|
| 1998-2001 fuel injection (TBI and MPI) models | | |
|   AC plug | MR43LTS | |
|   Champion plug | RS12YC | |
|   NGK plug | BPR6EFS | |
|   Plug gap | – | 0.045 in. (1.1 mm) |
| 2002-2004 multi-port fuel injection (MPI) models | | |
|   AC plug | 41-932 | 0.060 (1.5 mm) |
| 7.4L MPI | | |
|   AC plug | MR43LTS | |
|   Champion plug | RV12YC | |
|   NGK plug | BPR6EFS | |
|   Plug gap | – | 0.045 in. (1.1 mm) |
| 454 Mag, 502 Mag | | |
|   AC plug | MR43T | |
|   Champion plug | RV8C | |
|   NGK plug | BR6FS | |
|   Plug gap | – | 0.040 in. (1 mm) |
| 496 Mag, 496 Mag HO | | |
|   Nippon Denso | TJ14R-P15 | |
|   Plug gap | – | 0.060 in. (1.5 mm) |

### Table 4 ENGINE OIL CAPACITY

| Model | qt. | L |
|---|---|---|
| 3.0L | 4 | 3.8 |
| 4.3L | 4.5 | 4.3 |
| 5.0L, 5.7L, 350 Mag, MX 6.2 | 5.5 | 5.25 |
| 7.4 MPI, 454 Mag, 502 Mag | 7 | 6.6 |
| 496 Mag, 496 Mag HO | 9 | 8.5 |

### Table 5 CLOSED COOLING SYSTEM CAPACITY

| Model | qt. | L |
|---|---|---|
| 3.0L | 9 | 8.5 |
| 4.3L | 18 | 17 |
| 5.0L, 5.7L and 350 Mag, MX 6.2 | 20 | 19 |
| 7.4 MPI, 454 Mag, 502 Mag | 18 | 17 |
| 496 Mag, 496 Mag HO | 19 | 18 |

### Table 6 GEARCASE LUBRICANT CAPACITY

| Drive unit type | oz. | L |
|---|---|---|
| Alpha | 40 | 1.2 |
| Bravo I | 88 | 2.6 |
| Bravo II | 104 | 3.1 |
| Bravo III | 96 | 2.8 |

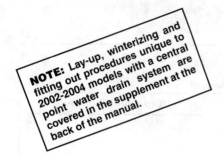

**NOTE:** Lay-up, winterizing and fitting out procedures unique to 2002-2004 models with a central point water drain system are covered in the supplement at the back of the manual.

# Chapter Five

# Lay-Up, Winterizing and Fitting Out

All major engine systems require some preparation before storage. Perform the procedures described in *Lay-Up* if the engine will not be operated for several weeks or longer,especially if the engine is used or stored in saltwater or heavily polluted water.

The engine must be winterized before being exposed to freezing temperatures. Water remaining in the cooling system can freeze and expand, causing serious damage to the cylinder block, manifolds, heat exchanger and other components. Always winterize the engine before transporting, storing or using the boat in high elevation areas which may experience freezing temperatures even during the summer months.

Fitting out prepares the engine for operation. Perform these procedures before returning the engine to service.

### LAY-UP

When preparing the engine for long term storage the objective is to prevent corrosion or deterioration during the storage period.

Perform any maintenance that will come due during the storage period. Maintenance requirements and procedures are described in Chapter Four. These requirements generally include the following:
1. Change the gearcase lubricant.
2. Check the fluid in the hydraulic trim system.
3. Lubricate the propeller shaft.

4. Remove and maintain the battery as described in Chapter Ten.

5. Check or change the coolant (closed cooling system).

6. Lubricate all steering, throttle and control linkage.

7. Lubricate the gimbal bearing, universal joints and hinge pins.

8. Change the engine oil and replace the oil filter.

9. Inspect and clean all sacrificial anodes.

10. Check all belts and hoses.

Besides the above maintenance items, the procedures described in this chapter will prepare the drive unit for storage. To reduce corrosion and prevent freeze damage, drain all of water from the cooling system as described in this chapter.

### Cleaning and Protecting External Surfaces

Clean vegetation, dirt or deposit buildup from the exterior of the drive unit and transom assembly. Wipe the engine components and apply a good corrosion preventative spray, available from most marine dealerships and marine supply stores. Flush the cooling system as described in Chapter Four.

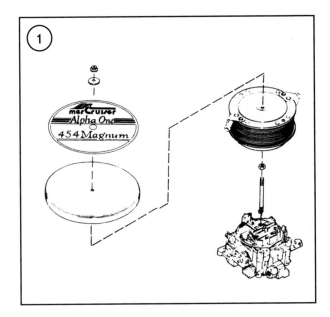

**Treating the Fuel**

Serious problems can be avoided if the fuel system is properly prepared for storage. Drain as much fuel from the fuel tank as possible. Clean or change all fuel filters.

Use a fuel stabilizer to help prevent the formation of gum or varnish in the fuel system during the storage period. Be aware that some additives may adversely affect some fuel system components if mixed incorrectly. Deterioration of hoses, check valves and other nonmetallic components may occur. Never mix these additives at a rate greater than specified on the label.

**Fogging the Engine**

Treat the cylinders with a fogging agent if the engine will not be used for several weeks or longer. This step can prevent corrosion inside the engine during the storage period. This is especially important if the engine is used or stored in saltwater or polluted water. The agent used and method for application depends on the type of fuel system used on the engine.

*WARNING*
*Stay clear of the propeller shaft while running an engine on a flush/test adapter. Remove the propeller before running the engine on a flush test device. Disconnect the battery before removing or installing the propeller.*

*CAUTION*
*Never run the engine without first providing cooling water. Use either a test tank or a flush/test adapter. Remove the propeller before running the engine on a flush test device.*

**5**

*Carbureted models*

1. Add the required amount of fuel stabilizer to the fuel tank. Run the engine for at least 10 minutes to distribute treated fuel throughout the fuel system.
2. Remove the cover and flame arrestor (**Figure 1**) as described in Chapter Eight.
3. Raise the engine speed to approximately 1500 rpm. Spray the fogging agent into the carburetor throat in 5-10 second intervals. Continue to spray the agent into the engine until heavy smoke comes out of the exhaust. This indicates the agent has passed through the engine. Stop the engine at this point.
4. Spray more of the fogging agent into the carburetor. Activate the lanyard switch. Operate the starter for a few seconds to distribute the agent over the cylinder walls. Reset the lanyard switch.

*EFI models*

Use a good quality TCW III outboard engine oil as a fogging agent.
1. Add the required amount of fuel stabilizer to the fuel tank. Run the engine for a minimum of 10 minutes to distribute treated fuel throughout the fuel system. Turn the engine off and disconnect the battery cables.
2. Pull up on the tab of the filter upper cover (1, **Figure 2**). Lift the cover from the bracket (2, **Figure 2**). Pull the heat shield (6, **Figure 2**) downward and remove it from the bracket.
3. Place a suitable container or shop towels under the filter to capture spilled fuel.
4. Use an oil filter wrench to remove the filter. The gasket should come off with the filter (**Figure 3**). If it doesn't, remove it from the adapter and install it onto the filter.
5. Empty the filter into a transparent container. Visually inspect the fuel. Drain and clean the fuel tank if a significant amount of water or sediment is present.
6. Pour 2 oz. (6mL) of two-cycle outboard engine oil into a small container. Fill the container with clean fresh fuel. Thoroughly mix the oil with the fuel.
7. Apply a light coat of engine oil to the filter gasket.
8. Pour the fuel/oil mixture into the filter. Add enough fresh fuel to completely fill the filter.

9. Taking care not to spill any fuel, thread the filter onto the adapter. Use a filter wrench to securely tighten the filter. Do not over tighten the filter, or the threads will be damaged, making removal difficult.

10. Remove the inlet fuel hose and fitting (3, **Figure 2**) from the filter adapter. To prevent fuel leakage, plug the disconnected hose and the fitting opening of the filter adapter.

11. Start the engine and allow it to run until it dies, then turn the key off..

12. Remove the plug from the filter adapter. Install and securely tighten the fitting (3, **Figure 2**). Remove the plug and connect the inlet fuel hose. Securely tighten the fuel hose clamp.

13. Remove and empty the filter as described in Step 3 and Step 4. Install a new fuel filter, but DO NOT fill with fuel, as described in Step 8.

14. Align the slot in the filter heat shield (6, **Figure 2**) with the bracket (2). Slide the shield over the filter. Align the upper cover (1, **Figure 2**) with the shield. Snap the tab of the cover over the boss on the shield.

### Drive Unit Storage

Always place the drive unit in the full-down and straight steering position (**Figure 4**) during storage. This prevents the rubber bellows from developing a set and helps prevent water from collecting in the cooling and exhaust passages. Water remaining in these passages can freeze and cause serious damage to the drive unit.

Insert a stiff wire into the gearcase speedometer opening (**Figure 5**) to remove sediment from the passage. This opening must be clear for the water to drain and accurate speed measurement.

Cover all exhaust openings to keep out insects or small mammals, which can enter the engine during the lay-up period.

Remove the gearcase drain plug and check for water or other contaminants as described in Chapter Three. Drain the lubricant if contaminated. Disassemble and inspect the drive unit as soon as possible to minimize damage caused by corrosion.

### WINTERIZING

Winterizing is a series of steps to drain all water from the cooling system. The exhaust manifolds must be drained on all models. The heat exchanger must be drained on all models equipped with a closed cooling system. The belt driven seawater pump must be drained on all models using a Bravo drive unit. Some V6 and V8 models using an Alpha drive are equipped with an optional

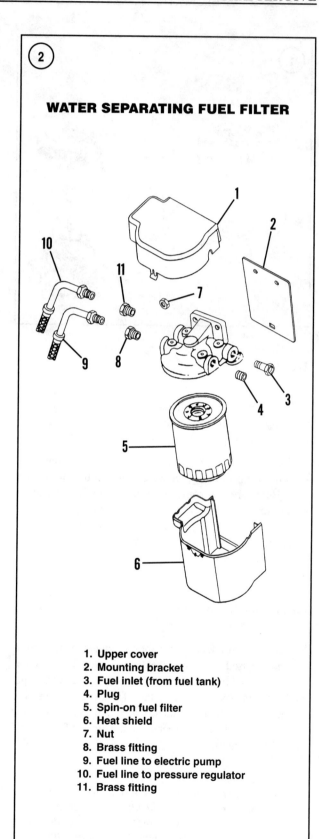

**WATER SEPARATING FUEL FILTER**

1. Upper cover
2. Mounting bracket
3. Fuel inlet (from fuel tank)
4. Plug
5. Spin-on fuel filter
6. Heat shield
7. Nut
8. Brass fitting
9. Fuel line to electric pump
10. Fuel line to pressure regulator
11. Brass fitting

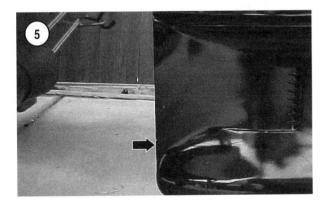

belt-driven seawater pump. If so equipped, this pump must be drained. Refer to Chapter Nine for hose routing and connection points.

Remove and recharge the battery at 30-day intervals as described in Chapter Ten. A discharged battery may freeze and rupture.

> *NOTE*
> *Manufacturers often make changes in production that affect hose routing, or water drain locations. Always refer to the owner's manual for specific drain locations.*

**3.0L Models**

All 2000-on models with standard cooling are equipped with water drain hoses (**Figure 6**). All other models use conventional drain plugs (**Figure 7**).

> *NOTE*
> *An O-ring must be installed onto the plastic drain plugs prior to installing them. The O-ring often clings to the fitting opening. Retrieve the O-ring if not found on the plug.*

1. Prepare the drive for storage as described in this chapter. Disconnect the battery cables.

2A. *Closed cooling system*—Drain water as follows:

   a. Remove the drain plug from the exhaust manifold (**Figure 7**). Do not remove the plug from the cylinder block or coolant will drain from the engine.

   b. Sediment may repeatedly block the plug opening during draining. Use a stiff wire to clear the opening until all water drains from the manifold.

   c. Remove the cover and gasket (**Figure 8**) to drain water from the cooler. This is easier than using the drain at the bottom of the exchanger, and allows inspection of the cooling passages.

   d. Inspect the water tubes in the exchanger for contaminants or corrosion. If necessary, remove and clean the heat exchanger as described in Chapter Nine. Have the exchanger repaired if coolant is leaking into the seawater passages.

   e. Test the coolant for adequate freeze protection as described in this chapter.

2B. *Standard cooling system (1998 and 1999)*—Drain water as follows:

   a. Remove the drain plugs from the exhaust manifold and cylinder block (**Figure 7**).

   b. Sediment may repeatedly clog the cylinder block and exhaust manifold drains. Use a stiff wire to clear the opening until all water drains from the manifold and cylinder block.

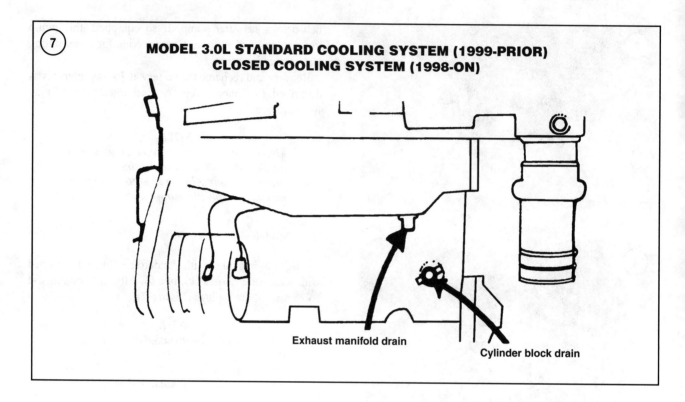

⑦ **MODEL 3.0L STANDARD COOLING SYSTEM (1999-PRIOR)**
**CLOSED COOLING SYSTEM (1998-ON)**

Exhaust manifold drain

Cylinder block drain

   c. Loosen the clamp and disconnect the large hose from the circulation pump (**Figure 9**).

**2C.** *Standard cooling system (2000-on)*—Drain water as follows:

   a. Push in on the tab (**Figure 6**) and pull both connectors from the drain hose bracket.

   b. Direct the hose ends to a location below the oil pan, using the drain hose rod (**Figure 10**) if necessary.

   c. Make sure water is draining from both hoses. If not, push in the tabs and disconnect the hoses from the manifold and cylinder block (**Figure 11**). If sediment is blocking the openings, use a stiff wire to clean it out.

**3A.** *Equipped with power steering*—Disconnect the hose that runs between the transom water fitting and the power steering fluid cooler (**Figure 12**). The cooler is located on the rear of the engine, directly above the flywheel. Drain all water from the hose and cooler.

**3B.** *Without power steering*—Disconnect the hose between the transom water fitting and the thermostat housing. Loosen the clamp and disconnect the hose from the thermostat housing.

4. If the boat is stored in the water, position the end of the disconnected cooling water hose well above the water line. Install a suitable plug into the hose and secure with the clamp. Do not reconnect the hose until ready to operate the engine. Otherwise seawater may siphon into the

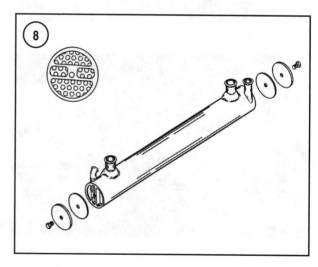

⑧

cooling system. Check for and correct water leakage before leaving the vessel.

**All V6 and V8 Models**
**(Except 496 Mag and 496 Mag HO)**

> *NOTE*
> *An O-ring must be installed onto the plastic drain plugs prior to installing them. The O-ring often clings to the fitting opening. Retrieve the O-ring if not found on the plug.*

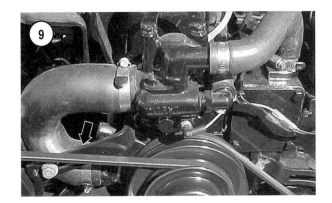

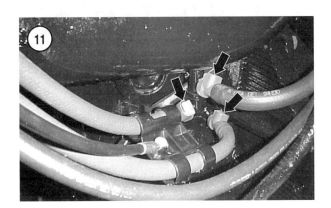

**5**

1. Prepare the drive for storage as described in this chapter. Disconnect the battery cables.

2A. *Closed cooling system*—Drain water as follows:

   a. Remove the drain plugs from the port and starboard exhaust manifolds (A, **Figure 13**). Do not remove the plug from the cylinder block (B, **Figure 13**), or coolant will drain from the engine.

   b. If sediment blocks the opening, use a stiff wire to clear the opening until all water drains from the manifold.

   c. Remove the cover and gasket (**Figure 8**) to drain water from the cooler. This is easier than using the drain at the bottom of the exchanger, and allows inspection of the cooling passages.

   d. Inspect the water tubes in the exchanger for contaminants or corrosion. If necessary, remove and clean the heat exchanger as described in Chapter Nine. Have the exchanger repaired if coolant is leaking into the seawater passages.

   e. Test the coolant for adequate freeze protection as described in this chapter.

2B. *Standard cooling system*—Drain water as follows:

   a. Remove the drain plugs from the exhaust manifold and cylinder block (A and B, **Figure 13**). On 4.3L-6.2L engines, the starboard cylinder block drain is located in the knock sensor fitting, near the starter motor. If a knock sensor is not used, the drain is located on the starboard side of the cylinder block.

   b. If sediment plugs the openings during draining, use a stiff wire to clear the cylinder block and exhaust manifold drains until all water is drained.

   c. On 1998 models, loosen the clamp and disconnect the large hose from the circulation pump (**Figure 9**). Drain water from the hose.

d. On 1999-on models, remove the fitting from the circulation pump hose (**Figure 14**). If sediment blocks the opening, use a stiff wire to keep the opening clear until all water is drained.

3A. *Bravo drive unit*—Loosen the clamps and remove the inlet and outlet hoses from the seawater pump (**Figure 15**). The pump is located on the lower front starboard side of the engine. Position the hoses as low as possible in the engine compartment to drain water from the power steering fluid and engine oil coolers.

3B. *Alpha drive unit*—Disconnect the hose that runs between the transom water fitting and the power steering fluid cooler (**Figure 12**). The cooler is located on the rear of the engine, directly above the flywheel. Drain all water from the hose and cooler.

4A. *EFI models*—Remove the fitting from the fuel cooler (C, **Figure 13**) and allow any water to drain. If sediment plugs the opening, use a stiff wire to clear the opening until all water has drained from the fuel cooler.

4B. *Carburetor equipped (1998) models*—Remove the drain plug from the composite tube.

4C. *Alpha drive equipped (1999-on)*—Loosen the clamp and disconnect the hose from the thermostat housing.

5. If the boat is stored in the water, secure the end of the disconnected cooling water hose (Step 4 or Step 5) well above the water line. Plug the hose and secure with the clamp. Do not reconnect the hose until ready to operate the engine, or seawater may siphon into the cooling system. Check for and correct water leakage before leaving the vessel.

**496 Mag and 496 Mag Ho Models**

These models are equipped with an air activated water drain system. Air lines connect the drain control mechanism (**Figure 16**) to the port and starboard water drain valves (**Figure 17**). Hoses connect the water drain valves

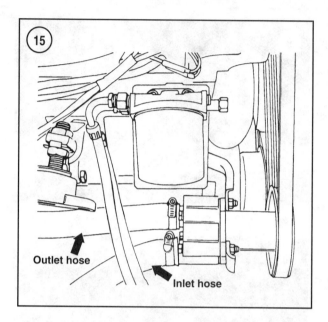

Outlet hose

Inlet hose

to passages in the exhaust manifold, seawater pump and heat exchanger. Use the pump (**Figure 18**) to activate the system. If the pump is missing or damaged, a bicycle tire pump or other air source can be used to activate the system.

*NOTE*
*An O-ring must be installed onto the plastic drain plugs prior to installing them. The O-ring often clings to the fitting opening. Retrieve the O-ring if not found on the plug.*

1. Prepare the drive for storage as described in this chapter.

2. Remove the cover (A, **Figure 16**) from the drain control mechanism. The Schrader valve is located under the cover. Remove the air pump (**Figure 18**) from its bracket.

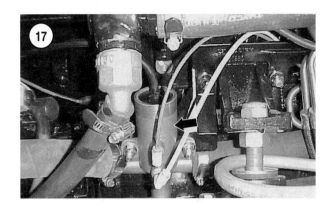

Fit the pump onto the Shrader valve on the drain control mechanism.

3. Pump air into the valve until both green indicator rods (B, **Figure 16**) fully extend from the mechanism. Remove the air pump. Install the cover over the Schrader valve.

4. Verify that water is draining into the bilge and both indicator rods remain extended. Otherwise the system must be manually drained.

5. To manually drain the system:

   a. Remove the two blue drain plugs from the fuel cooler. The fuel cooler is located on the lower port side of the engine between the engine mount and the oil pan.

   b. Disconnect both the inlet and outlet hoses (A and B, **Figure 19**) from the seawater pump. The seawater pump is located on the lower front starboard side of the engine. Remove the blue drain plug (C, **Figure 19**).

   c. If sediment blocks the fitting opening, use a stiff wire to clear the opening until all water is drained from the manifolds, seawater pump and fuel cooler.

   d. Remove the bolt, end cap and rubber seal from the heat exchanger (**Figure 20**).

   e. Inspect water tubes in the exchanger for contaminants or corrosion. If necessary, remove and clean the heat exchanger as described in Chapter Nine. Have the exchanger repaired if coolant is leaking into the seawater passages.

   f. Direct the disconnected hoses to the lowest possible position in the bilge. This is necessary to drain the power steering fluid and oil coolers.

6. Test the coolant for adequate freeze protection as described in this chapter.

7. Activate the lanyard switch to prevent the engine from starting. Crank the engine for a few seconds to remove residual water from the seawater pump. Do not start the engine.

### TESTING THE COOLANT

Use a coolant tester, available at an automotive parts store, for this operation.

1. Remove the pressure cap and check the coolant level as described in Chapter Four.

2. Draw a sample of the coolant into the tester. Read the tester to determine the freezing point of the coolant. The coolant must provide protection below the lowest temperature to which the engine will be exposed.

3. If necessary, change the coolant as described in Chapter Four. Before adding fresh coolant, test it to verify adequate protection at the lowest anticipated temperature.

**5**

4. Do not fill the system if the anticipated temperature is below the lowest temperature provided by the coolant. Never mix the coolant at a rate greater than 50:50. Install the pressure cap.

## FITTING OUT

Fitting out is a series of steps that prepare the engine for operation after storage or winterizing.

1. Perform all required maintenance as described in Chapter Four.

2. On Bravo models, service the water pump and replace the impeller as described in Chapter Nine.

3. Change or correct all lubricant levels as described in Chapter Four.

4. Supply the engine with fresh fuel.

5. Remove any covers from the exhaust openings.

6. Install and service the battery as described in Chapter Ten.

7. On closed cooling systems, install the rubber seal, cover and bolts as described in Chapter Nine.

8. Install the battery as described in Chapter Ten.

9. On 496 Mag and 496 Mag HO models, the air-activated water drains must be closed before operating the engine, or the cooling water will drain into the bilge and the engine will overheat. To close the valves, pull up on the ring (C, **Figure 16**) until the green indicator rods (B) fully retract.

10. On 3.0L models (2001), connect the drain hoses (**Figure 6**) to their fittings on the manifold, cylinder block and drain hose bracket.

11. Reconnect all hoses and install all removed drain plugs. Install O-rings onto the plastic drain plugs before installing them. Refer to Chapter Nine for hose routing and connection points.

12. Attach the hoses to the seawater pump (**Figure 15**) as described in Chapter Nine.

13. If the boat was stored in the water, remove the plugs from the cooling water hose. Connect the hose onto the seawater pump, power steering fluid cooler or thermostat housing. Securely tighten the hose clamp.

14. Supply cooling water and then start the engine. Immediately check for leaking water, coolant, oil or other fluids. Stop the engine and correct any leakage before operating the engine.

15. Run the engine at low speed until the engine reaches operating temperature. Check for proper operation of the cooling, electrical and warning systems and correct as required. Refer to Chapter Three for troubleshooting if a problem occurs.

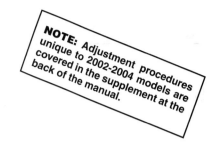
NOTE: Adjustment procedures unique to 2002-2004 models are covered in the supplement at the back of the manual.

# Chapter Six

# Adjustments

6

This chapter describes all required adjustments to MerCruiser gasoline engines, including the following:

1. Drive belt tension.
2. Trim sender.
3. Trim limit switch.
4. Shift cables.
5. Throttle cable.
6. Ignition timing.
7. Idle mixture.
8. Idle speed.
9. Trim tab.

**Tables 1-4** list torque and adjustment specifications. **Tables 1-4** are located at the end of this chapter.

## DRIVE BELTS

### Power Steering Belt (3.0L Models)

1. Loosen the power steering mounting and pivot bolts. Carefully swing the top of the power steering pump toward the cylinder head. Do not push on the reservoir or pry against the pump housing, which can damage the housing and cause leaks

2. If the belt is to be replaced, remove the belt from the power steering pump and circulation pump pulleys (**Figure 1**). Clean all grease or debris from the pulleys. Sand rust from the pulleys as needed. Install the new belt onto the pulleys.

3. Check the drive belt tension at a point on the belt midway between the power steering pump and circulation pump pulleys (**Figure 1**). Use a thumb to apply pressure on the belt (**Figure 2**).

4. Pivot the pump and adjust the belt tension until the belt depresses approximately 1/4 in. (6 mm) with moderate thumb pressure. Pivot the top of the pump away from the cylinder head to increase belt tension. Pivot the pump toward the head to decrease tension.

5. When the tension is corrected, securely tighten the pivot and mounting bolts. Torque specifications for the pump are listed in **Table 1**.

6. Start the engine and run for approximately 10 minutes. Stop the engine and check the belt tension.

### Alternator Belt (3.0L Models)

1. Loosen the alternator mounting and pivot bolts (**Figure 3**).

2. To replace the belt:

   a. Pivot the lower side of the alternator toward the engine.

   b. Remove the two bolts that secure the spacer to the mounting bracket and engine.

   c. Remove the spacer block. Remove the belt from the pulleys. Install the new belt onto the pulleys.

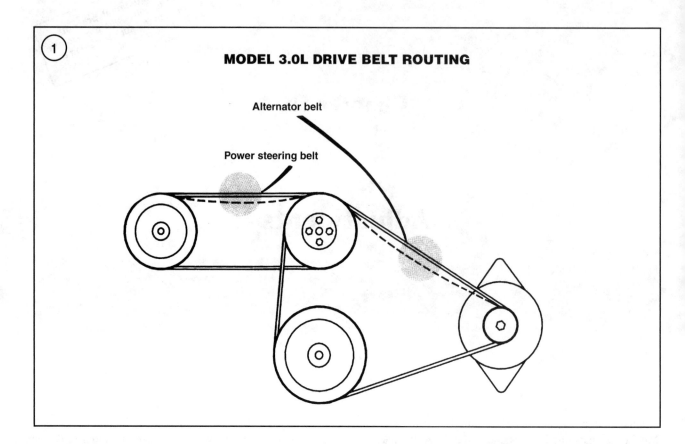

**① MODEL 3.0L DRIVE BELT ROUTING**

Alternator belt

Power steering belt

d. Install the spacer block between the mount and the engine. Install and securely tighten the bolts.

3. Check the drive belt tension at a point on the belt midway between the circulation pump and alternator pulleys (**Figure 1**). Use a thumb to apply pressure on the belt (**Figure 2**).

4. Pivot the alternator and adjust the belt tension until the belt depresses approximately 1/4 in. (6 mm) with moderate thumb pressure. Pivot the bottom of the alternator away from the cylinder block to increase the belt tension. Pivot the alternator toward the block to decrease the tension.

5. When the tension is corrected, securely tighten the pivot and mounting bolts (**Figure 3**). Torque specifications for the alternator are listed in **Table 1**.

6. Start the engine and run for approximately 10 minutes. Stop the engine and check the belt tension.

### V6 and V8 Models
### (Except 496 Mag and 496 Mag HO)

These models use an adjustable tensioner pulley (**Figure 4**), located on the upper front or upper starboard side of the engine.

1. Loosen locknut (A, **Figure 4**) until the pulley slides on the bracket. Do not remove the locknut.

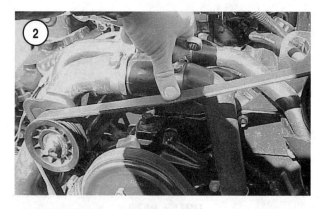

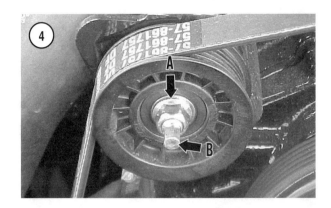

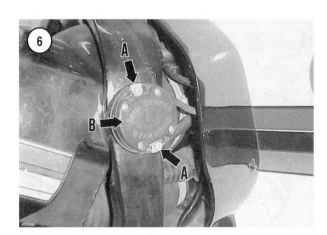

2. To replace the belt, move the pulley down to relieve all belt tension. Remove the belt from the pulleys and install the new belt onto the pulleys. Refer to Chapter Ten for belt routing.

3. Check the tension at a point on the belt midway between two pulleys . Choose two pulleys with the greatest span between them. Use a thumb to apply pressure to the belt (**Figure 2**).

4. Rotate the adjusting stud (B, **Figure 4**) until the belt depresses approximately 1/4 in. (6 mm) with moderate

thumb pressure. Hold the adjusting stud and securely tighten the locknut (A, **Figure 4**).

5. Connect the battery cable. Start the engine and run for approximately 10 minutes. Stop the engine and check the belt tension.

### 496 Mag and 496 Mag HO Models

The belt adjusting mechanism (**Figure 5**) is located on the lower port and front side of the engine.

1. Loosen the alternator pivot and attaching bolts.

2. Loosen the locknut (A, **Figure 5**).

3. To replace the belt, rotate the adjusting bolt (B, **Figure 5**) counterclockwise and pivot the alternator toward the cylinder block. Remove the belt from the pulleys and install the new belt. Refer to Chapter Ten for belt routing.

4. Check the tension at a point on the belt midway between the alternator and idle pulleys. Use a thumb to apply pressure on the belt (**Figure 2**).

5. Rotate the adjusting bolt (B, **Figure 5**) until the belt depresses approximately 1/4 in. (6 mm) with moderate thumb pressure. Hold the adjusting bolt and securely tighten the locknut (A, **Figure 5**).

6. Securely tighten the alternator pivot and attaching bolts.

7. Start the engine and run for approximately 10 minutes. Stop the engine and check the belt tension.

### TRIM POSITION SENDER ADJUSTMENT

*NOTE*
*On 496 Mag, 496 Mag HO and all 2002-2004 models with multi-port fuel injection (MPI), the trim up circuit may be connected into the ECM circuitry. This arrangement prevents the trim up operation unless the ignition key switch is in the ON or RUN position. However, the trim down circuit will operate with the ignition key switch ON or OFF. On these models, turn the ignition key switch to the ON or RUN position before operating the trim system.*

The trim position sender (**Figure 6**) is located on the starboard side of the gimbal ring.

1. Turn the steering wheel to full port. Place the drive unit in the full-down position.

2. Turn the ignition switch to the ON position. Do not start the engine.

3. Loosen but do not remove the screws (A, **Figure 6**).

4. Have an assistant observe the trim gauge. Rotate the trim sender body (B, **Figure 6**) counterclockwise until the trim gauge needle moves away from the full-down mark.

**6**

5. *Slowly* rotate the sender clockwise until the needle just aligns with the down mark. If the sender cannot be properly adjusted, check for improper sender timing as described in Chapter Twelve.

6. Tighten the screws (A, **Figure 6**). Operate the trim to the full-up and full-down positions while observing the gauge. The needle must align with the down mark just as the drive reaches the full-down position. Readjust the sender as needed. Several adjustments may be required.

7. The needle may or may not align with the up mark when the drive is fully tilted. Do not adjust the sender to correspond with the up mark on the gauge.

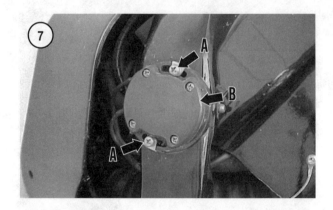

### Trim Limit Switch Adjustment

> *NOTE*
> *On 496 Mag, 496 Mag HO and all 2002-2004 models with multi-port fuel injection (MPI), the trim up circuit may be connected into the ECM circuitry. This arrangement prevents the trim up operation unless the ignition key switch is in the ON or RUN position. However, the trim down circuit will operate with the ignition key switch ON or OFF. On these models, turn the ignition key switch to the ON or RUN position before operating the trim system.*

The trim limit switch (**Figure 7**) is located on the port side of the gimbal ring. A yardstick or measuring tape is required for this procedure.

1. Turn the steering wheel to full starboard. Place the drive in the full-down position.

2. Trim the drive unit UP until the trim motor switches off. Do not operate the trailer switch. If the drive reaches the full tilt position before the motor switches off, check the switch timing as described in Chapter Twelve.

3. Measure the distance between the centers of the forward and aft anchor pins (**Figure 8**).

    a. *Alpha drive unit*— 20-3/4 in. (527 mm).

    b. *Bravo drive unit*— 21-3/4 in. (552 mm).

4. Adjust the switch as follows:

    a. Place the drive in the full-down position.

    b. Loosen the screws (A, **Figure 7**).

    c. If the center to center measurement exceeds the specification, rotate the switch body (B, **Figure 7**) slightly clockwise.

    d. If the center to center measurement is less than the specification, rotate the switch body (B, **Figure 7**) counterclockwise.

    e. Securely tighten the screws (A, **Figure 7**).

5. Place the drive unit in the full-down position. Operate the trim switch until the unit reaches the trim limit posi-

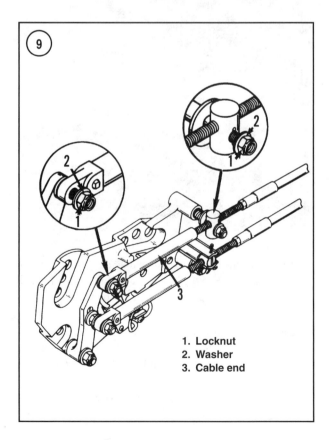

1. Locknut
2. Washer
3. Cable end

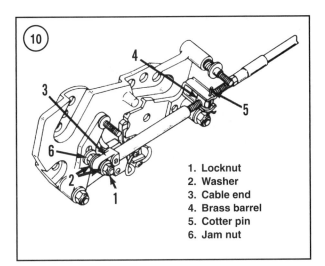

1. Locknut
2. Washer
3. Cable end
4. Brass barrel
5. Cotter pin
6. Jam nut

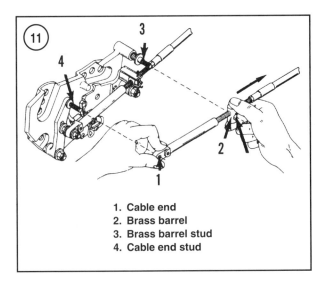

1. Cable end
2. Brass barrel
3. Brass barrel stud
4. Cable end stud

tion. Check the measurement as described in Step 3. Readjust as needed. Several adjustments may be required.

### SHIFT CABLE ADJUSTMENT

Adjust the shift cables after shift cable replacement or if the remote control or drive system is removed for any reason.

*CAUTION*
*Many engines using an Alpha drive unit are equipped with a shift spring. The spring fits onto the shift plate along with the remote control cable. The spring provides assistance when shifting the drive into neutral. Do not use the spring if the boat has a remote control with separate shift and throttle*

*handles. Otherwise the spring may unexpectedly shift the drive into neutral.*

### Alpha Drive

1. On V6 and V8 models, remove the flame arrestor cover as described in Chapter Eight. Remove the propeller as described in Chapter Eleven.
2A. *Standard rotation drive*—Place the remote control in the FORWARD gear full throttle position.
2B. *Counter-rotation drive*—Place the remote control in the REVERSE gear full throttle position.
3. Remove the cotter pin, cable pivot pin, nuts and washers (1 and 2, **Figure 9**). Remove the remote control shift cable (3, **Figure 9**) and shift spring from the plate.
4. Remove the cotter pin (5, **Figure 10**). Remove the locknut and outer washer (1 and 2, **Figure 10**). Remove the drive unit shift cable from the plate.
5. Loosen the jam nut (6, **Figure 10**). Push the shift arm stud to the bottom of the slot, closest to the pivot point. Securely tighten the jam nut.
6. Push the cable end toward the barrel while an assistant rotates the propeller shaft counterclockwise. The propeller shaft must stop as the clutch engages the gear. Do not rotate the propeller shaft clockwise or pull on the cable end.
7. Measure the distance from the center of the hole in the cable end to the center of the brass barrel. The measurement must be 6 in. (152 mm). Adjust the barrel to obtain this distance.
8. Without disturbing the cable distance, install the cable onto the plate as shown in **Figure 10**. Secure the cable with the cotter pin (1, **Figure 10**), washer (2) and nut (5). Do not over tighten the locknut (1, **Figure 10**). The outer washer (2, **Figure 10**) must spin freely.
9. Push the remote control cable end (1, **Figure 11**) toward the barrel (2) to remove slack from the cable.
10. Rotate the barrel (2, **Figure 11**) until the cable pivot aligns perfectly with the shift plate studs and cable pivot pin opening. Do not disturb the 6 in. (152 mm) shift drive cable distance. Do not install the remote control cable attaching hardware or shift spring at this time.
11. Remove the remote control cable from the plate. Rotate the barrel four complete turns away from the cable end. This lengthens the barrel-to-cable end distance.
12. Install the cable onto the shift plate and secure with the attaching hardware. Do not install the shift spring at this time.
13. Move the remote control to the NEUTRAL position. Check for complete disengagement of the shift clutch. The propeller shaft must spin freely in both directions.
14A. *Standard rotation*—Move the control to REVERSE gear while an assistant rotates the propeller shaft clockwise.

**6**

**14B.** *Counter-rotation drive*—Move the control to FORWARD gear while an assistant rotates the propeller shaft clockwise.

15. The clutch must engage and stop the propeller shaft rotation before the throttle begins to open. Otherwise reposition the shift arm stud as follows:

    a. Loosen the jam nut (6, **Figure 10**). Move the stud *slightly* away from the pivot bolt. Securely tighten the jam nut.

    b. Check for proper clutch engagement as described in Step 13 and Step 14. Loosen the jam nut and reposition the stud as necessary to achieve full clutch engagement. Several adjustments may be required.

    c. Do not move the stud too far, or the shift interrupt switch may activate during shifting.

    d. Securely tighten the jam nut.

**16A.** *Using a shift spring*—Move the remote control to the NEUTRAL gear position. Remove the nut, washer and cable pivot pin. Align the openings and install the shift spring onto the shift plate. The spring must align with the remote control shift cable attaching points. Otherwise readjust the cables. Secure the shift spring and cable with the washer, nut, cable pivot pin and cotter pin.

**16B.** *Without the shift spring*—Secure the remote control cable with the pivot pin, cotter pin, washer and nut.

17. Move the remote control to the NEUTRAL position. Check for complete disengagement of the shift clutch. The propeller shaft must spin freely in both directions.

18. Have an assistant rotate the propeller shaft while checking for full engagement of both forward and reverse gears. Both gears must engage before the throttle plate begins to open. Otherwise repeat the adjustment procedures. If unable to properly engage both gears, check for worn or damaged shift cables, shift shaft(s) or gearcase shift components.

19. Install the propeller as described in Chapter Eleven.

20. On V6 and V8 models, install the flame arrestor cover as described in Chapter Eight.

21. Start the engine and check for proper gear engagement and disengagement. Correct any shifting problems before operating the engine.

**Bravo I and Bravo II drives**

    This adjustment requires a small ruler and a cable adjusting tool (Mercury part No. 91-122427).

1. Place the remote control into NEUTRAL. Remove the propeller as described in Chapter Eleven.

**2A.** *Models 7.4 L MPI, 496 Mag and 496 Mag HO*—Remove the plastic engine cover.

**2B.** *All other models*—Remove the flame arrestor cover as described in Chapter Eight.

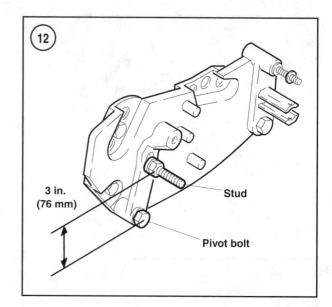

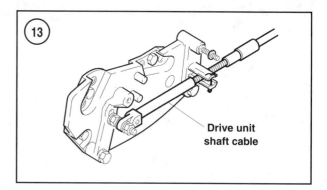

3. Remove the nut and washer, cotter pin and cable pivot pin. Remove the remote control shift cable from the shift plate.

4. Remove the remaining cotter pin, washer and nut. Remove the drive unit shift cable from the shift plate. Do not rotate the brass barrel on the cable, as this will upset the cable adjustment. If this happens, adjust the cable as described under *Shift Cable Installation* in Chapter Twelve.

5. Measure the distance from the center of the pivot bolt to the center of the shift arm stud (**Figure 12**). The distance should be 3 in. (76 mm). If necessary, loosen the jam nut and reposition the stud. Securely tighten the jam nut.

6. Install the drive unit shift cable onto the shift plate as shown in **Figure 13**. Secure the cable with the cotter pin, washer and nut. Do not over tighten the nut. The washer must spin freely.

7. Fit the cable adjusting tool onto the shift plate as shown in **Figure 14**. The rounded end must fit into the barrel slot and the opening must fit over the shift cable stud.

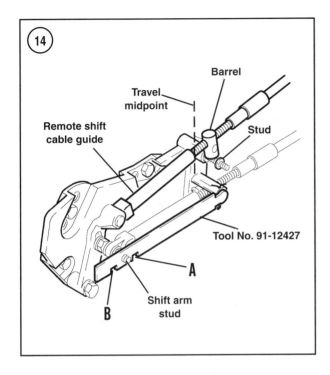

14

Travel midpoint

Barrel

Remote shift cable guide

Stud

Tool No. 91-12427

A

B

Shift arm stud

8. Rotate the propeller shaft to check for clutch disengagement. The shaft must rotate freely in both directions. Otherwise adjust the drive unit cable as described under *Shift Cable Installation* in Chapter Twelve.

9. Attach the remote control cable guide to the shift plate using the pivot pin and cotter pin. Push and pull on the cable to determine the midpoint of the slack in the cable. Mark the cable with the cable guide at the midpoint (**Figure 14**). Adjust the barrel to fit perfectly over the stud with the cable guide aligned with the midpoint mark.

10. Fit the adjusting barrel over the stud. Secure the barrel with a washer and nut.

11. Remove the cable adjusting tool. Fit the barrel over the stud and secure with a washer and nut.

12. Shift the remote control into forward gear. Align the rounded end of the cable adjusting tool with the barrel slot. The notch in the cable adjusting tool must align with the shift arm stud as follows:

    a. On a right-hand propeller, the stud must align with the slot closest to the rounded end of the tool (A, **Figure 14**).

    b. On a left-hand propeller, the stud must align with the slot farthest from the rounded end of the tool (B, **Figure 14**).

    c. If the slot does not align, loosen the jam nut on the shift arm stud. Reposition the stud to achieve the desired alignment. Securely tighten the jam nut.

13. Remove the cable adjusting tool. While an assistant rotates the propeller shaft, make sure both forward and re-

verse gears engage fully. Both gears must engage before the throttle plate begins to open. Otherwise repeat the adjustment procedures. If unable to properly engage both gears, check for worn or damaged shift cable, shift linkage or drive shaft housing components.

14. Install the propeller as described in Chapter Eleven.

15A. *Models 7.4 L MPI, 496 Mag and 496 Mag HO*—Install the plastic engine cover.

15B. *All other models*—Install the flame arrestor cover as described in Chapter Eight.

16. Start the engine and check for proper gear engagement and disengagement. Correct improper shifting before operating the engine.

**Bravo III Drive**

1. Place the remote control into NEUTRAL. Remove the propellers as described in Chapter Eleven.

2A. *Models 7.4 L MPI, 496 Mag and 496 Mag HO*—Remove the plastic engine cover.

2B. *All other models*—Remove the flame arrestor cover as described in Chapter Eight.

3. Remove the nut and washer, cotter pin and cable pivot pin, and remove the remote control shift cable from the shift plate.

4. Remove the remaining cotter pin, washer and nut. Remove the drive unit shift cable from the plate. Do not rotate the brass barrel on the cable, as this will upset the cable adjustment. If this happens, adjust the cable as described in Chapter Twelve.

5. Measure the distance from the center of the pivot bolt to the center of the shift arm stud (**Figure 12**). The distance should be 3 in. (76 mm). If necessary, loosen the jam nut and reposition the stud. Securely tighten the jam nut.

6. Install the drive unit shift cable onto the shift plate as shown in **Figure 13**. Secure the cable with the cotter pin, washer and nut. Do not over tighten the nut. The washer must spin freely.

7. Fit the cable adjusting tool onto the shift plate as shown in **Figure 14**. The rounded end must fit into the barrel slot and the opening must fit over the shift cable stud.

8. Rotate the inner propeller shaft to check for clutch disengagement. The shaft must rotate freely in both directions. Otherwise adjust the drive unit cable as described under *Shift Cable Installation* in Chapter Twelve.

9. Attach the remote control cable guide onto the shift plate using the pivot pin and cotter pin. Push and pull on the cable to determine the midpoint of the slack in the cable. Mark the cable with the cable guide at the midpoint (**Figure 14**). Adjust the barrel to fit perfectly over the stud with the cable guide aligned with the midpoint mark.

6

10. Fit the barrel over the stud. Secure the barrel with a washer and nut.

11. Remove the cable adjusting tool.

12. Shift the remote control into forward gear. Align the rounded end of the cable adjusting tool with the barrel slot. The shift arm stud must fit over the adjusting tool slot closest to the rounded end (A, **Figure 14**).

13. If the stud fits closer to the other slot (B, **Figure 14**), the remote control is set up for the wrong rotation. Correct by repositioning the cables to the correct pivot points in the remote control.

14. If the stud and slot do not align, correct as follows:
   a. Loosen the jam nut on the shift arm stud.
   b. Reposition the stud to achieve the desired alignment.
   c. Securely tighten the jam nut.

15. Remove the cable adjusting tool. While an assistant rotates the inner propeller shaft, make sure both forward and reverse gears engage fully. Both gears must engage before the throttle plate begins to open. Otherwise repeat the adjustment procedures. If both gears cannot be properly engaged, check for worn or damaged shift cables, shift linkage or drive shaft housing components.

16. Install the propellers as described in Chapter Eleven.

17A. *Models 7.4 L MPI, 496 Mag and 496 Mag HO*—Install the plastic engine cover.

17B. *All other models*—Install the flame arrestor cover as described in Chapter Eight.

18. Start the engine and check for proper gear engagement and disengagement. Correct improper shifting before operating the engine.

## THROTTLE CABLE

1A. *Models 7.4 L MPI, 496 Mag and 496 Mag HO*—Remove the plastic engine cover.

1B. *All other models*—Remove the flame arrestor cover as described in Chapter Eight.

2. If the engine is equipped with a carburetor, adjust the idle speed as described in this chapter.

3. Remove the pivot bolt or nut to free the adjusting barrel (**Figure 15** Typical).

4. Check for over tightening of the nut on the throttle lever. The washer on the pivot must spin freely.

5. Push the cable end until the throttle lever contacts the idle stop or idle speed screw. Hold the cable in this position.

6. Rotate the barrel until it aligns with the throttle stud or pivot bolt opening. Attach the cable with the pivot bolt or nut and washer. Do not over tighten the nut.

7. Start the engine and allow it to reach normal operating temperature.

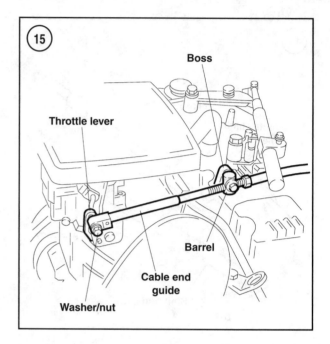

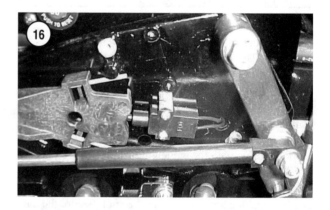

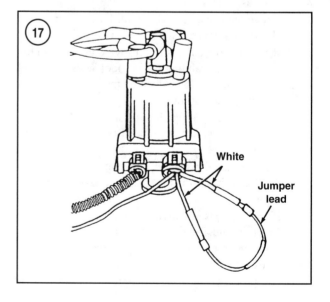

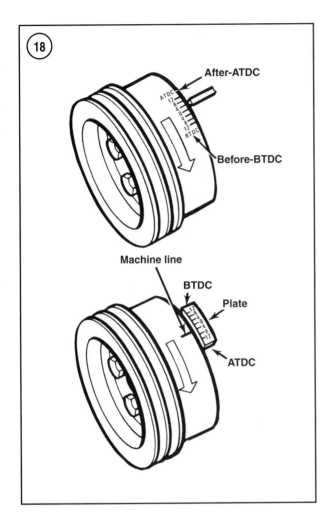

After-ATDC

Before-BTDC

Machine line

BTDC

Plate

ATDC

## IGNITION TIMING ADJUSTMENT

Check the timing at the required intervals (Chapter Four) and each time the distributor clamp screw is loosened. Timing adjustment is not required on 496 Mag, 496 Mag HO and 2002-2004 4.3L, 5.0L, 350 Mag and MX6.2L models with multi-port fuel injection (MPI).

Refer to *Electronic Fuel Injection* in Chapter Three to identify the ECU type.

Use an inductive timing light to read the ignition timing. Using a timing light with an adjustable timing advance compensator is not recommended.

The timing marks can become obscured with rust or debris, making them difficult to read. Clean the timing tab and harmonic balancer with a quick drying solvent. Apply white correction fluid to the pointer and the timing marks and wipe off the excess with a towel. The correction fluid fills in the slots and stamped timing markings for better visibility.

### 3.0L Models

This adjustment requires a 6 in. (152 mm) section of 16 gauge wire with male bullet connectors at each end.
1.  Start the engine and allow it to reach normal operating temperature. Stop the engine.
2.  Disconnect the shift interrupt switch (**Figure 16**) from the engine harness, then connect the engine harness wires together. Do not allow the shift interrupt switch wires to contact each other.
3.  Connect the jumper wire to each of the white leads extending from the distributor (**Figure 17**).
4.  Connect the timing light pickup to the No. 1 cylinder spark plug lead. The No. 1 cylinder is closest to the front of the engine.
5.  Start the engine, allow it to idle, and direct the timing light at the timing tab (**Figure 18**). The tab is located on port side of the timing gear cover. Refer to **Table 2** for the ignition timing specifications. If the ignition timing is correct, the specified timing mark on the tab will align with the mark on the harmonic balancer. The marks on the starboard side of the 0 mark are before top dead center (BTDC). The marks on the port side of the 0 mark are after top dead center (ATDC).
6.  If the timing marks are improperly aligned, loosen the distributor hold-down clamp (**Figure 19**). Use a distributor wrench if unable to access the clamp bolt with a conventional wrench.
7.  Rotate the distributor (**Figure 20**) until the specified mark on the timing tab (see **Table 2**) aligns with the harmonic balancer mark.
8.  Tighten the distributor clamp bolt to the specification in **Table 1**.

8.  Advance the throttle to 1300 rpm and quickly return to idle. Repeat this step several times. The engine must return to idle speed each time. If the engine does not return to idle each time, adjust the throttle cable as follows:

a.  Remove the pivot bolt or nut (**Figure 15**, typical) to free the adjusting barrel.

b.  Rotate the barrel one complete turn away from the cable end.

c.  Install the barrel and pivot bolt or nut.

d.  Check for consistent return to idle speed and readjust as needed. Several adjustments may be required. Do not excessively preload the cable, or the remote control may bind.

9A. *Models 7.4 L MPI, 496 Mag and 496 Mag HO*—Install the plastic engine cover.

9B. *All other models*—Install the flame arrestor cover as described in Chapter Eight.

9. Recheck the timing after tightening the distributor clamp and readjust if necessary.

10. Stop the engine. Remove the jumper wires from the distributor wires (**Figure 17**). Disconnect the engine harness wires (see Step 2). Connect the shift interrupt switch wires to the engine harness wires.

11. Start the engine and check the ignition timing. The ignition timing must be 10-14° BTDC at idle speed. Otherwise the timing is incorrectly adjusted or the ignition module is faulty.

12. Disconnect the timing light. Check for proper shift operation before operating the engine. The interrupt switch must momentarily interrupt the ignition when shifting out of FORWARD and REVERSE gears. Otherwise check for faulty connections or shift switch.

### V6 And V8 Models With a Carburetor

This adjustment requires a jumper wire with a male bullet connector at one end and an alligator clip on the other.

1. Remove the flame arrestor cover as described in Chapter Eight.

2. Connect the timing light pickup to the No. 1 cylinder spark plug lead (**Figure 21**). The No. 1 cylinder is located on the port side, closest to the front of the engine. Start the engine and allow it to reach normal operating temperature. The engine must be at idle speed during timing adjustment.

3. Remove the plug from the purple/white wire (**Figure 22**) located between the carburetor and starboard rocker arm cover. Connect a jumper lead to the wire and attach the jumper lead to a good engine ground.

4. Direct the timing light toward the timing pointer, which is located on the port side of the timing chain cover. Refer to **Table 2** for the ignition timing specification.

5. If the timing requires adjustment, loosen the distributor clamp (**Figure 19**). Use a distributor wrench if unable to access the clamp bolt with a conventional wrench.

6. Rotate the distributor (**Figure 20**) until the specified mark on the balancer (see **Table 2**) aligns with the pointer.

7. Tighten the clamp bolt to the specification in **Table 1**.

8. Recheck the timing after tightening the distributor clamp.

9. Stop the engine. Remove the jumper wire. Insert the plug into the purple/white wire connector (**Figure 22**).

10. Install the flame arrestor cover as described in Chapter Eight.

### V-6 and V-8 EFI Models (1998-2001 [Except 496 Mag and 496 Mag HO])

This adjustment requires a special timing plug (Mercury part No. 91-805474A1). A diagnostic code tool (see

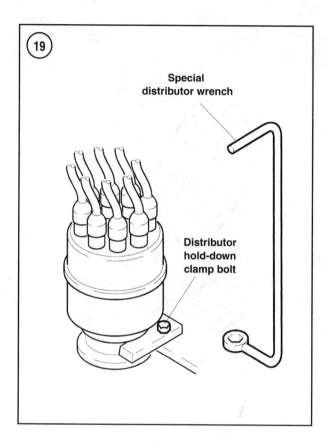

(19)

Special
distributor wrench

Distributor
hold-down
clamp bolt

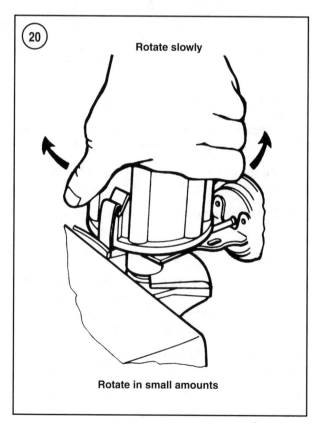

(20)

Rotate slowly

Rotate in small amounts

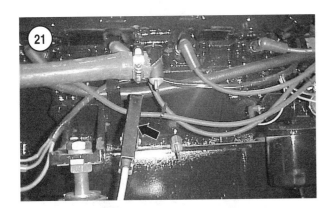

Electronic Fuel Injection in Chapter Three) can be used instead of a timing plug.

1A. *Model 7.4 MPI*—Remove oil fill cap and plastic engine cover from the top of the engine. Install the fill cap.

1B. *All other models*—Remove the flame arrestor cover as described in Chapter Eight.

2. Connect the timing light pickup to the No. 1 cylinder spark plug lead (**Figure 21**). The No. 1 cylinder is located on the port side closest to the front of the engine. Start the engine and allow it to reach normal operating temperature.

3. Remove the cover from the data link connector (**Figure 23**) located near the ECU.

4. Plug the tool onto the data link connector. If using a diagnostic code tool, turn the switch to the ON position.

5. The engine speed should automatically increase. If not, either the timing tool is not installed properly or the diagnostic code tool is not switched to the ON position.

6. Direct the timing light toward the timing pointer, which is located on the port side of the timing chain cover. Refer to **Table 2** for the ignition timing specification.

7. If the timing requires adjustment, loosen the distributor clamp (**Figure 19**). Use a distributor wrench if unable to access the clamp bolt with a conventional wrench.

8. Rotate the distributor (**Figure 20**) until the specified mark on the balancer (**Table 2**) aligns with the pointer.

9. Tighten the clamp bolt to the specification in **Table 1**. Recheck the timing after tightening the distributor clamp.

10. Remove the timing tool or diagnostic code tool from the data link connector and install the cover over the connector.

11. The engine must return to normal idle speed within a few minutes. If not, check the throttle cable adjustment.

12A. *Model 7.4 MPI*—Remove oil fill cap. Install the plastic engine cover onto the top of the engine. Install the fill cap.

12B. *All other models*—Install the flame arrestor cover as described in Chapter Eight.

## IDLE MIXTURE AND IDLE SPEED ADJUSTMENT

This adjustment requires an accurate shop tachometer. Idle speed and mixture adjustments are not required on EFI models.

> *NOTE*
> *On 2003 and 2004 models, refer to Chapter Sixteen at the back of the manual for idle mixture screws adjustment recommendations.*

### 3.0l Models

The carburetor on 3.0L models is equipped with a single idle mixture screw (**Figure 24**). The idle speed screw (**Figure 25**) is located on the side of the carburetor.

**6**

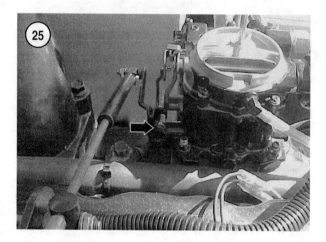

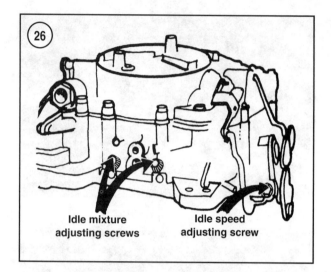

Idle mixture
adjusting screws

Idle speed
adjusting screw

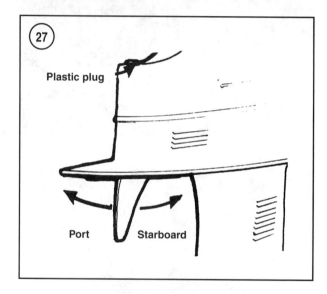

Plastic plug

Port          Starboard

1. Remove the flame arrestor cover as described in Chapter Eight. Disconnect the throttle cable from the carburetor.

2. Back out the idle speed screw until the screw tip does not contact the throttle cam. Tighten the screw until it just contacts the cam. Turn the screw clockwise two additional turns.

3. Turn the idle mixture screw in until lightly seated. Do not use excessive force, which may damage the screw tip or the carburetor. Back the screw out the number of turns specified in **Table 3**.

4. Reconnect the throttle cable. Follow the manufacturer's directions and connect the shop tachometer to the engine.

5. The boat must be in the water for the remaining adjustments. Have a qualified operater at the controls during the adjustment. Start the engine and run at 1500 rpm until it reaches normal operating temperature. Return to idle speed and disconnect the throttle cable.

6. Adjust the idle speed to obtain 550-600 rpm in neutral. Slowly turn the idle mixture screw clockwise until the engine starts to run roughly and the idle speed begins to drop. Note the screw position.

7. Observe the tachometer and count the number of turns while slowly turning the idle mixture screw counterclockwise. The engine should run smoother then start to run rough again with additional turning. Note the screw position when the engine starts to run roughly.

8. Turn the screw clockwise to the midway point between the two positions (Step 6 and Step 7). Fine tune the screw adjustment to achieve the smoothest and highest idle speed.

9. Adjust the idle speed screw to approximately 900 rpm. Have the assistant shift the engine into forward gear. Allow a few minutes for the idle speed to stabilize.

10. Hold the throttle lever firmly against the idle stop during adjustment. Slowly turn the idle speed screw until the engine reaches the idle speed specification in **Table 4**.

11. Adjust the remote control throttle cable as described in this chapter. Remove the shop tachometer. Install the flame arrestor cover as described in Chapter Eight.

**All Other Models**

Models 4.3LH and 4.3LXH are equipped with a four-barrel carburetor that uses two idle mixture screws (**Figure 26**). The idle speed screw (**Figure 26**) is located on the port side of the carburetor. All other models are equipped with a two-barrel carburetor that uses a single idle mixture screw (**Figure 24**). The idle speed screw (**Figure 25**) is located on the port side of the carburetor.

This adjustment requires a jumper wire with a male bullet connector at one end and an alligator clip on the other.

1. Remove the flame arrestor cover as described in Chapter Eight. Disconnect the throttle cable from the carburetor.

2. Rotate the idle speed screw until the screw tip breaks contact with the throttle cam or throttle stop (four-barrel carburetor). Turn the screw in until it just contacts the cam or stop. Turn the screw clockwise two additional turns.

3. Turn the idle mixture screw in until lightly seated. Do not use excessive force, which may damage the screw tip or carburetor. Back the screw out the number of turns specified in **Table 3**. If equipped with a four-barrel carburetor, adjust both screws as described.

4. Reconnect the throttle cable. Attach the shop tachometer onto the engine following the manufacture's instructions.

5. The boat must be in the water during the remaining adjustments. Have a qualified operater at the controls during the adjustment. Start the engine and run at 1500 rpm until it reaches normal operating temperature. Return to idle speed and disconnect the throttle cable.

6. Remove the plug from the purple/white wire (**Figure 22**) located between the carburetor and the starboard rocker arm cover. Attach the jumper lead to the purple/white wire and a good engine ground.

7. Adjust the idle speed screw to obtain 550-600 rpm in neutral. Slowly turn the idle mixture screw clockwise until the engine starts to run roughly and the idle speed begins to drop. Note the screw position.

8. Observe the tachometer and count the number of turns while slowly turning the idle mixture screw counterclockwise. With a four-barrel carburetor, adjust only one screw at this time. The engine should start to run smoother then start to run roughly with additional turning. Note the screw position when the engine just starts to run roughly.

9. Turn the screw clockwise to the midway point between the two positions (Step 7 and Step 8). Fine tune the screw adjustment to achieve the smoothest and highest idle speed.

10. If the engine is equipped with a four-barrel carburetor, repeat Steps 7-9 with the other mixture screw.

11. Adjust the idle speed to approximately 900 rpm. Have the assistant shift the engine into forward gear. Allow a few minutes for the idle speed to stabilize.

12. Hold the throttle lever firmly against the idle stop during adjustment. Slowly turn the idle speed screw until the engine reaches the idle speed specification in **Table 4**.

13. Disconnect the jumper lead from the purple/white wire. Install the plug into the purple/white wire connector.

14. Adjust the remote control throttle cable as described in this chapter. Remove the shop tachometer. Install the flame arrestor cover as described in Chapter Eight.

## TRIM TAB ADJUSTMENT

This adjustment is required on Model 3.0L and all other models equipped with a trim tab. Operate the boat at normal cruising speed and trim position to determine whether the trim tab needs adjustment. Perform adjustment if the steering wheel tends to pull or steer easier in one direction. Adjust the trim tab as follows:

1. Remove the plastic plug (**Figure 27**) from the access hole in the rear edge of the gearcase.

2. Insert a 1/2 in. socket and extension into the access hole and loosen the trim tab mounting bolt just enough to turn the trim tab.

3A. If the boat tends to pull toward the port side, pivot the trailing edge of the trim tab to the port side (**Figure 27**)

3B. If the boat tends to pull toward the starboard side, pivot the trailing edge of the trim tab to the starboard side.

4. Securely tighten the trim tab bolt. Test drive the boat. Readjust the trim tab if necessary; several adjustments may be required.

**6**

### Table 1 TORQUE SPECIFICATIONS

| Fastener | ft.-lb. | in.-lb. | N•m |
|---|---|---|---|
| **Alternator to bracket** | | | |
| Pivot bolt | 35 | – | 47 |
| Anchor bolt | 20 | – | 27 |
| **Distributor hold-down clamp** | | | |
| 3.0L | 20 | – | 27 |
| 4.3L, 5.0L, 5.7L and 350 Mag | 18 | – | 25 |
| 7.4 MPI, 454 Mag, 502 Mag | 24 | – | 33 |
| **Power steering** | | | |
| Pump bracket | 30 | – | 41 |
| Pump brace | 30 | – | 41 |

### Table 2 IGNITION TIMING SPECIFICATIONS

| Model | Timing at idle speed |
|---|---|
| 3.0L | |
|   Serial No. 0L096999-Prior | 1° BTDC |
|   Serial No. 0L097000-0L340999 | 1° ATDC |
|   Serial No. 0L341000-On | 2° ATDC |
| 4.3L, 5.0L, 5.7L and 350 Mag | |
|   Carburetor models | 10° BTDC |
|   All EFI models | 8° BTDC |
| 7.4 MPI, 454 Mag, 502 Mag | 8° BTDC |

### Table 3 IDLE MIXTURE SCREW (PRELIMINARY ADJUSTMENT)

| Model | Turn out |
|---|---|
| 3.0L | 1 1/4 |
| 4.3L | |
|   Two-barrel carburetor | 1 1/4 |
|   Four-barrel carburetor | 1 1/4 |
| 5.7L | 1 1/2 |

### Table 4 IDLE SPEED SPECIFICATIONS

| Model | Idle speed (rpm) |
|---|---|
| 3.0L | 700 |
| 4.3L, 5.0L, 5.7L, 350 Mag | |
|   Carburetor models | 650 |
|   EFI models | 600 |
| 7.4 MPI, 454 Mag, 502 Mag | 600 |

# Chapter Seven

# Engine

This chapter covers engine removal, disassembly, inspection, assembly and installation, as well as engine alignment and valve adjustment.

Much of the repair expense charged by a dealership is due to the labor to remove, disassemble and clean the engine components. Consider performing these operations yourself and allow a qualified technician to measure, inspect and assemble the engine. The service backlog at some dealerships can be several weeks or longer during the boating season. Performing this part of the job yourself may reduce down time and prevent the dealership from needing to store your boat. Be aware that some dealerships will not offer a warranty unless they perform the entire repair. Contact a local dealership and make the necessary arrangements before disassembling the engine.

Perform a proper engine break-in if any internal engine components are replaced. This allows the rough edges and surface imperfections on new components to lap in and conform to new contact surfaces. Break-in procedures are described at the end of this chapter.

## SPECIAL TOOLS

Where special tools are required or recommended, the tool part numbers are provided in the procedure. Some of the tools are offered by Mercury Marine with the remaining being offered by Kent-Moore. Purchase or rent the Mercury tools from a local MerCruiser dealership. Purchase Kent-Moore tools from Kent-Moore Special Tools, 29784 Little Mack, Roseville, MI 48066.

## REPLACEMENT PARTS

There are several differences between automotive engines and engines adapted for marine applications. For example, the cylinder head gasket must be corrosion-resistant. Marine engines use stainless steel or composite gaskets instead of the standard steel gasket used in automotive blocks. Brass core plugs must be used instead of the steel plugs used in automotive blocks. Since marine engines run at or near maximum speed most of the time, they use special lifters, valve springs, pistons, bearings, camshaft and other heavy duty components.

For these reasons, automotive parts should never be substituted for marine components.

## SERVICE PRECAUTIONS

When working on the engine, taking basic precautions will make your work easier, faster and more accurate:
1. Always make notes, drawings or photographs of all external engine components *before* beginning disassembly. An incorrectly routed hose or wire may interfere with linkage movement and result in a dangerous lack of throt-

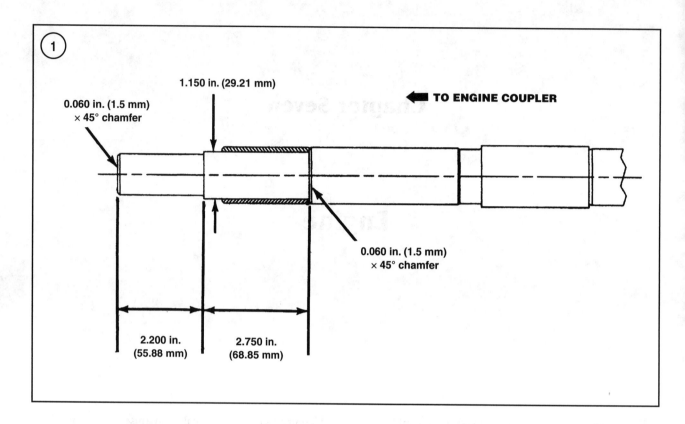

tle control. Hoses or wires may short or leak if allowed to contact sharp or moving parts. Check for components that can be installed in two or more positions and mark them accordingly.

2. Mark the up and forward direction of all components before removing them. If a cluster of components shares common wires or hoses, try to remove the entire assembly intact. This reduces the time required to disassemble and assemble the engine and reduces the chance of improper connections during assembly.

3. Mount the engine to an engine stand if the repair involves the pistons, rods or crankshaft. Support the engine with an overhead lift or blocks as needed for other repairs.

4. Use muffin tins or egg cartons to organize fasteners as they are removed. Mark all fasteners to ensure they are reinstalled in the correct location.

5. Use special tools where noted. In some cases, it may be possible to perform the procedure with makeshift tools, but this is not recommended. The use of makeshift tools can damage components or cause serious injury.

6. Use a vise with protective jaws to hold housings or components. If protective jaws are not available, insert wooden blocks on each side of the part before clamping them in a vise. Never clamp on thin castings, such as the piston skirt, which can be damaged by the clamping force.

7. Remove and install pressed-on parts with an appropriate mandrel, support and hydraulic press. Do not try to pry or hammer them from the component.

8. Refer to the appropriate table at the end of the chapter for torque specifications. Correct torque is vital to achieve the maximum clamping force without damaging the fastener.

9. Apply the recommended sealant or threadlocking compound onto the outer surfaces of seals. Lubricate seal lips during assembly.

10. Prior to installation, apply engine oil or other recommended lubricant to all internal components.

11. Work in a clean area and where there is good lighting and sufficient space for storing components. Keep small containers on hand for storing small parts. Cover parts with clean shop towels when you are not working with them.

12. Replace all seals, gaskets and O-rings if removed. These parts are inexpensive compared to the damage they will cause if they fail.

### ENGINE ALIGNMENT

This operation requires an alignment bar (Mercury part No. 91-805475A1) and spline grease (Mercury part No. 92-816391). If an alignment bar is not available, have the

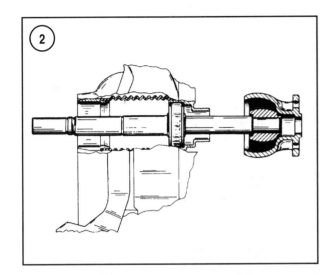

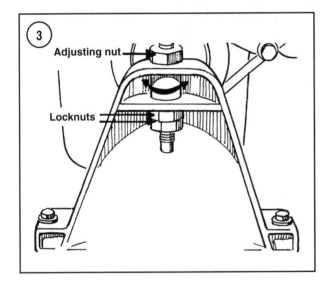

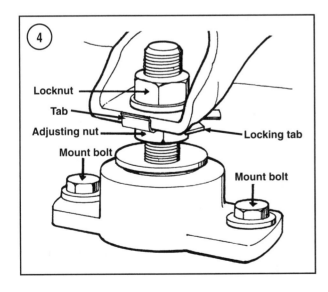

alignment performed by a qualified technician. Increased wear, noisy operation and eventual failure of the drive coupler will result from operating the engine with improper alignment.

*NOTE*
*The alignment bar (Mercury part No. 91-57797A3) used on earlier engines (1992-prior) can be used on 1993-on engines by machining the engine coupler end of the bar to the specifications shown in* **Figure 1**. *The modified bar and the bar specified for newer models (Mercury part No. 91-805475A1) can be used on earlier engines.*

1. Remove the drive unit as described in Chapter Eleven.

2. Apply spline grease to the engine coupler end of the shaft. Guide the bar through the gimbal bearing and into the engine coupler (**Figure 2**). Do not drive the bar into the engine coupler, or the coupler may be damaged. The bar must slide freely into and out of the engine coupler. If the bar slides freely, refer to Step 11.

3A. *3.0L models*—Fully loosen the locknuts (**Figure 3**).

3B. *V6 and V8 engines*—Fully loosen the locknut (**Figure 4**) on both the port and starboard side engine mounts. Carefully pry the locking tab (**Figure 4**) away from each adjusting nut.

4. Turn the adjusting nut 1/2 turn in the direction required to raise the engine. On V6 and V8 engines, the adjusting nuts must be raised and lowed the same distance on each side. Make sure the number of threads exposed on the mount studs are the same on both sides.

5. Attempt to insert the alignment bar. Push firmly on the end of the bar while moving the end in all four directions (**Figure 5**). This is necessary to align the gimbal bearing with the engine coupler.

6. Repeat Step 4 and Step 5 until the alignment bar slips into the engine coupler. If the adjusting nuts reach the upper limit and the bar cannot be inserted, turn the adjusting

7

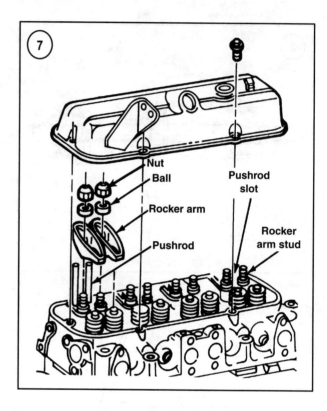

nuts to lower the engine. Lower the engine 1/2 turn at a time and repeat Step 5 until the bar slips into the engine coupler.

7. Pull the alignment bar from the engine coupler. Coat the engine coupler end of the bar with spline grease. Carefully insert the bar into the coupler. Do not rotate the bar.

8. Mark the top side of the bar. Carefully pull the bar from the engine coupler. Do not rotate the bar. Inspect the spline marks in the greased surface (**Figure 6**). The marks must be consistent around the entire surface. Otherwise perform additional adjustment as follows:

  a. If the marks are heavier on the top, the engine is too high in the front. Lower the engine 1/4 turn of the adjusting nut.

  b. If the marks are heavier on the bottom, the engine is too low in the front. Raise the engine 1/4 turn of the adjusting nut.

  c. Continue until the spline markings are consistent and the bar slides freely into and out of the engine coupler. Align the gimbal bearing (see Step 5) after turning the adjusting nuts.

9A. *3.0L models*—Securely tighten the upper locknut (**Figure 3**). Securely tighten the lower locknut against the upper locknut. Tighten the adjusting nut against the front engine mount.

9B. *V6 and V8 models*—Turn the adjusting nuts (**Figure 4**) just enough to align the locking tabs with a flat surface on the nuts. A tab must engage each engine mount bracket as shown in **Figure 4**. Use locking pliers to bend a tab against the flat surface of each adjusting nut. Securely tighten the locknuts.

10. Check for proper engine alignment as described in Step 2. Correct the alignment as needed.

11. Use a long stick, socket extension or brush and apply spline grease to the engine coupler splines. Apply enough grease to just coat the splines. Do not fill the opening with grease, or the drive shaft will hydraulically lock in the coupler and prevent installation of the drive unit.

12. Install the drive unit as described in Chapter Eleven.

## VALVE ADJUSTMENT

### 3.0, 5.0, 5.7 350 Mag and MX6.2 Models

Adjust the valves at the intervals specified in Chapter Four or if replacing the cylinder head, camshaft, lifters, pushrods or other valve train components.

Valve adjustment is required only on 3.0L, 5.0L, 5.7L, 350 Mag and MX6.2 models. Adjustment is not required on all other models. However, on such models the rocker arm fasteners must be tightened in the proper sequence as described under Cylinder Head Replacement in this chapter.

### 3.0L Models

1. Disconnect the battery cable. Place the No. 1 cylinder at TDC as described in this chapter. Remove the flame arrestor cover and the fuel pump-to-carburetor fuel line (Chapter Eight). Remove the spark plugs.

2. Disconnect the throttle cable. Disconnect or remove any components that may interfere with removal of the rocker arm cover.

3. Remove the fasteners and lift the rocker arm cover (**Figure 7**) from the cylinder head. Clean the rocker arm cover with solvent and dry with compressed air. Inspect the cover gasket for damage. Replace the gasket as needed.

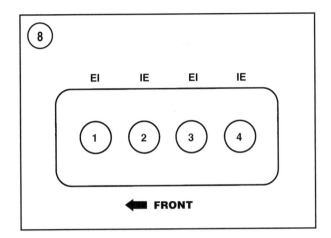

8

EI    IE    EI    IE

1    2    3    4

◀ **FRONT**

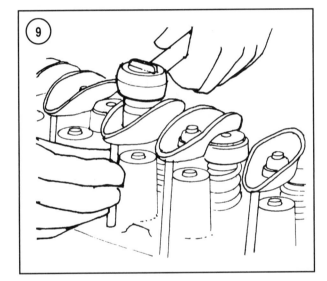

9

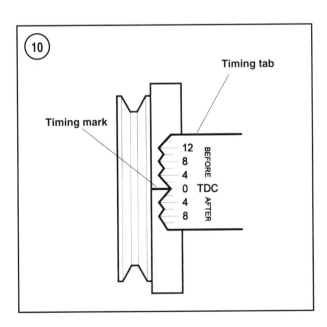

10

Timing tab

Timing mark

12
8
4   BEFORE
0  TDC
4   AFTER
8

4. With the No. 1 piston at TDC, adjust the following valves (**Figure 8**):
   a. No. 1 cylinder intake.
   b. No. 2 cylinder intake.
   c. No. 1 cylinder exhaust.
   d. No. 3 cylinder exhaust.
   e. No. 4 cylinder intake.

*NOTE*
*Turn the pushrod to determine if there is any lash between the rocker arm and pushrod. The pushrod will turn freely if lash is present.*

5. To adjust the valve lash loosen the adjusting nut until some lash is felt at the pushrod (**Figure 9**). While turning the pushrod, slowly tighten the nut until all lash is just removed. Then tighten the nut an additional ¾ turn.
6. Rotate the crankshaft clockwise exactly one turn and align the notch in the harmonic balancer with the 0 mark on the timing tab (**Figure 10**). The No. 4 piston is now at TDC.

*CAUTION*
*Do not turn the crankshaft counterclockwise or the water pump will be damaged.*

7. With the No. 4 piston at TDC, repeat Step 5 and adjust the following valves:
8. Install the rocker arm cover. Tighten the cover fasteners in several stages, following a crisscross pattern, to the specification in **Table 1**.
9. Install the flame arrestor and the fuel line. Connect the throttle cable and adjust it as described in Chapter Six.
10. Install the spark plugs.

**5.0L, 5.7L, 350 Mag and MX 6.2 Models**

1. Disconnect the battery cables. Position the No. 1 piston at TDC as described in this chapter.
2. Disconnect or remove any components that interfere with removal of the rocker arm covers.
3. Remove the fasteners and lift the rocker arm covers (**Figure 7**) from the cylinder heads. Clean the covers with solvent and dry them with compressed air. Inspect the cover gaskets for damage and replace them if needed.
4. With the No. 1 piston at TDC, adjust the following valves (**Figure 11**):
   a. No. 1 cylinder intake.
   b. No. 1 cylinder exhaust.
   c. No. 2 cylinder intake.
   d. No. 3 cylinder exhaust.
   e. No. 4 cylinder exhaust.

**7**

   f.  No. 5 cylinder intake.
   g.  No. 7 cylinder intake.
   h.  No. 8 cylinder exhaust.

*NOTE*
*Turn the pushrod to determine if there is any*
*lash between the rocker arm and pushrod.*
*The pushrod will turn freely if lash is present.*

5. To adjust the valve lash loosen the adjusting nut until
some lash is felt at the pushrod (**Figure 12**). While turning
the pushrod, slowly tighten the nut until all lash is just removed. Then tighten the nut an additional 3/4 turn on
MX6.2 models or one full turn on all other models.
6. Rotate the crankshaft clockwise exactly one turn and
align the notch in the harmonic balancer with the 0 mark
on the timing tab (**Figure 13**).

*CAUTION*
*Do not rotate the balancer counterclock-*
*wise or the water pump will be damaged.*

7. Repeat Step 5 and adjust the following valves:
   a.  No. 2 cylinder exhaust.
   b.  No. 3 cylinder intake.
   c.  No. 4 cylinder intake.
   d.  No. 5 cylinder exhaust.
   e.  No. 6 cylinder intake.
   f.  No. 6 cylinder exhaust.
   g.  No. 7 cylinder exhaust.
   h.  No. 8 cylinder intake.
8. Install the rocker arm covers. Tighten the cover fasteners in a crossing pattern to the specification in **Table 1**.
9. Install the spark plugs.

### PLACING THE NO. 1 PISTON AT TDC

**Intake Manifold or Lifter Cover Installed**

1. Disconnect the battery cables. Remove the spark
plugs.
2. Place a thumb over the No. 1 cylinder spark plug opening.
   a.  On 3.0L models, the No. 1 cylinder is closest to the
       front of the engine (see **Figure 8**).
   b.  On all other models, the No. 1 cylinder is on the port
       side closest to the front of the engine (see **Figure 11**).
3. Observe the timing marks (**Figure 13**) and turn the
harmonic balancer clockwise until air pressure forms in
the No. 1 cylinder. This indicates the cylinder is on its
compression stroke.
4. Continue rotating the balancer until the timing mark
aligns with the 0 mark (TDC).

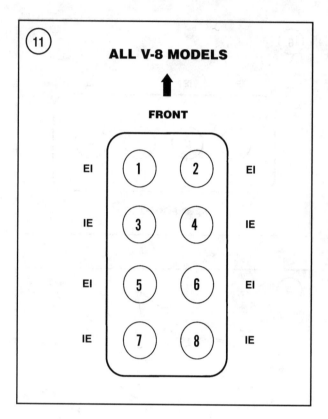

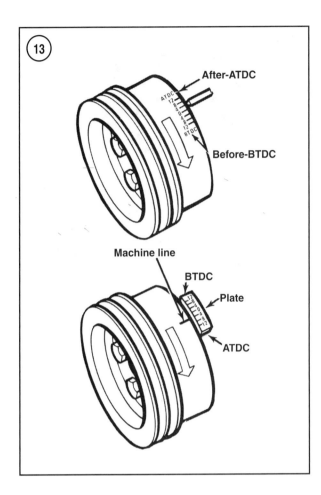

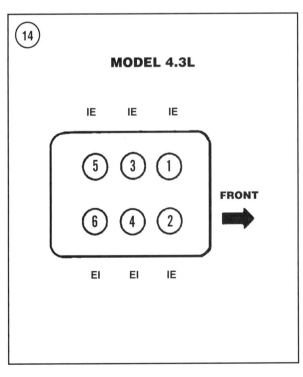

**MODEL 4.3L**

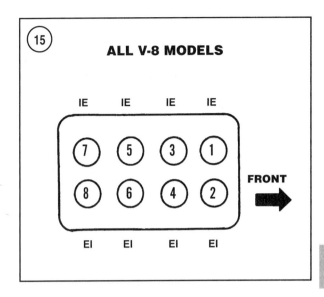

**ALL V-8 MODELS**

7

**Intake Manifold or Lifter Cover Removed**

1. On 3.0L models, remove the rocker arm cover as described in this chapter.

2. To identify the valve components for the No. 1 cylinder, refer to **Figure 8** (3.0L), **Figure 11** (5.0L, 5.7L, 350 Mag and MX6.2), **Figure 14** (4.3L) and **Figure 15** (all other models).

3. Engage a large breaker bar and socket to the harmonic balancer attaching bolt. If a bolt is not used in this location, rotate the engine by engaging a large pry bar to the pulley mounting bolts.

4. Observe the No. 1 intake rocker arm or lifter while rotating the harmonic balancer clockwise. Stop when the No. 1 intake lifter starts moving downward.

5. Observe the timing marks (**Figure 13**) and turn the harmonic balancer clockwise until the timing mark aligns with the 0 mark.

### CAMSHAFT LOBE LIFT

This measurement checks for excessive camshaft wear. This procedure requires a dial indicator and a clamp for attaching the indicator to the cylinder block or head. Attach the dial indicator before removing the cylinder head. Mark the original location of all valve train components before removing them. *All* parts must be reinstalled in their original locations.

**3.0L Models**

1. Disconnect the battery cables and remove the spark plugs.

2. Remove the fasteners and lift the rocker arm cover (**Figure 7**) from the cylinder head. Clean the rocker arm cover with solvent and dry with compressed air. Inspect the cover gasket for damage and replace if necessary.

3. Remove the lifter cover from the starboard side of the cylinder block. Remove and discard the cover gasket. Clean the cover with solvent and dry with compressed air.

4. Remove the nut and ball (**Figure 7**) from each rocker arm. Mark the original location and remove the rocker arms and pushrods from the cylinder head. Inspect all parts for discoloration, wear or damage and replace if necessary. Roll the pushrods across a flat surface to check for bending. Replace bent pushrods.

5. Attach a large breaker bar and socket to the harmonic balancer bolt. If a bolt is not used, rotate the engine with a large pry bar between the pulley mounting bolts.

6. Observe the No. 1 exhaust valve lifter (see **Figure 8**) while rotating the engine clockwise. Stop when the lifter drops in the bore and the base of the cam lobe aligns with the bottom of the lifter (**Figure 16**).

7. Insert the pushrod into the slot (**Figure 7**). Fit the pushrod into the recess in the lifter.

8. Attach the dial indicator to the cylinder head with a clamp or adapter (**Figure 17**). Align the plunger of the dial indicator with the tip of the pushrod. Rotate the face of the dial indictor to align the needle with the 0 mark.

9. Observe the dial indicator while rotating the harmonic balancer exactly one revolution clockwise. The amount of needle movement equals the camshaft lobe lift. Record the lobe lift measurement.

10. Repeat Steps 6–9 for the remaining camshaft lobes. Record each measurement.

11. Compare the lobe lift measurements with the specification in **Table 4**. Replace the camshaft if any of measurements are less than the minimum specification.

12. Install the pushrods, rocker arms, balls and nuts as described in this chapter.

13. Adjust the valves as described in this chapter.

14. Install the rocker arm cover. Tighten the cover fasteners in several stages, following a crisscross pattern. Torque to the specification in **Table 1**.

15. Install a new gasket onto the lifter cover. Install the cover onto the cylinder block. Torque the bolts to the specification in **Table 1**. Install the spark plugs and leads. Connect the battery cables.

### 5.0L, 5.7L, 350 Mag and MX 6.2 Models

1. Disconnect the battery cables and remove the spark plugs.

2. Remove the fasteners and lift the rocker arm cover (**Figure 7**) from the cylinder head. Clean the rocker arm

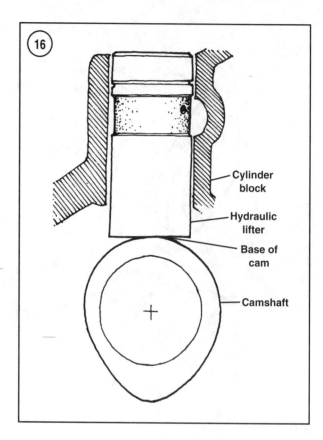

(16)

Cylinder block

Hydraulic lifter

Base of cam

Camshaft

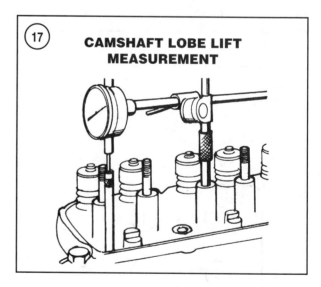

(17) **CAMSHAFT LOBE LIFT MEASUREMENT**

cover with solvent and dry with compressed air. Inspect the cover gasket for damage and replace if necessary.

3. Remove intake manifold as described in Chapter Eight.

4. Remove the nut and ball (**Figure 7**) from each rocker arm. Mark the original locations and remove the rocker arms and pushrods from the cylinder head.

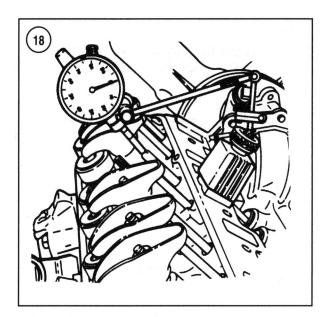

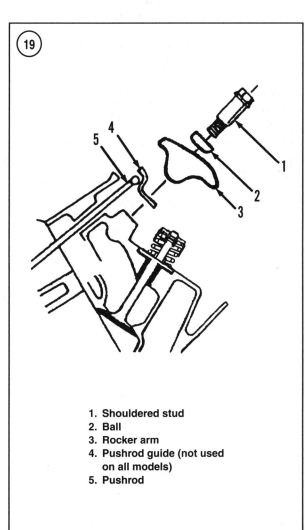

1. **Shouldered stud**
2. **Ball**
3. **Rocker arm**
4. **Pushrod guide (not used on all models)**
5. **Pushrod**

5. Attach a breaker bar and socket to the harmonic balancer bolt. If a bolt is not used, rotate the engine with a large pry bar between the pulley mounting bolts.

6. Observe the No. 1 exhaust valve lifter (see **Figure 11**) while rotating the harmonic balancer clockwise. Stop when the lifter drops in the bore and the base of the cam lobe aligns with the bottom of the lifter.

7. Insert the pushrod into the slot (**Figure 7**). Fit the pushrod into the recess in the lifter.

8. Attach the dial indicator to the cylinder head using a suitable clamp or adapter (**Figure 18**). Align the plunger of the dial indicator with the tip of the pushrod. Rotate the face of the dial indictor to align the needle with the 0 mark.

9. Observe the dial indicator while turning the harmonic balancer exactly one revolution clockwise. The amount of needle movement equals the camshaft lobe lift. Record the lobe lift measurement.

10. Repeat Steps 6-9 for the remaining camshaft lobes. Record each measurement.

11. Compare the lobe lift measurements with the specification in **Table 4**. Replace the camshaft if any measurements are less than the minimum specification.

12. Install the pushrods, rocker arms, balls and nuts as described in this chapter.

13. Adjust the valves as described in this chapter.

14. Install the intake manifold as described in Chapter Eight.

15. Install new gaskets and the rocker arm covers. Tighten the cover fasteners in several passes, following a crisscross pattern. Torque to the specification in **Table 1**.

### All Other Models

1. Disconnect the battery cables and remove the spark plugs.

2. Remove the fasteners and lift the rocker arm covers (**Figure 7**) from the cylinder head. Clean the rocker arm cover with solvent and dry with compressed air. Inspect the cover gasket for damage. Replace the gasket as needed.

3. Remove intake manifold as described in Chapter Eight.

4A. *2001 4.3L models*—Loosen the nuts and lift the roller rocker arms from the cylinder heads. Mark the original locations and remove the pushrods from the cylinder heads.

4B. *Other models*—Remove the nut from the shouldered stud (1, **Figure 19**) and ball (2, **Figure 19**) from each rocker arm. Mark the original locations and remove the rocker arms and pushrods from the cylinder heads. Remove the pushrod guide (4, **Figure 19**) if so equipped.

**7**

5. Attach a breaker bar and socket to the harmonic balancer attaching bolt. If a bolt is not used, rotate the engine with a pry bar between the pulley mounting bolts.

6. Watch the No. 1 exhaust valve lifter (see **Figure 14** or **Figure 15**) while turning the harmonic balancer clockwise. Stop when the lifter drops in the bore and the base of the cam lobe aligns with the lifter roller (**Figure 16**).

7. Insert the pushrod into the slot (**Figure 7**). Fit the pushrod into the recess in the lifter.

8. Attach the dial indicator onto the cylinder head using a suitable clamp or adapter (**Figure 18**). Align the plunger of the dial indicator with the tip of the pushrod. Rotate the face of the dial indictor to align the needle with the 0 mark.

9. Watch the dial indicator while turning the harmonic balancer exactly one revolution clockwise. The amount of needle movement equals the camshaft lobe lift. Record the lobe lift measurement.

10. Repeat Steps 6-9 for the remaining camshaft lobes. Record each measurement.

11. Compare the lobe lift measurements with the specification in **Table 4**. Replace the camshaft if any measurements are less than the minimum specification.

12. Install the pushrods, guides, rocker arms and shoulder bolts as described under *Cylinder Head* in this chapter.

13. Install the intake manifold as described in Chapter Eight.

14. Install the rocker arm covers. Tighten the cover fasteners in a crossing pattern to the specification in **Table 1**.

## CYLINDER HEAD

The cylinder head(s) can be removed and installed without removing the engine.

Take photographs or make sketches of bracket orientation, hose and wire routing before removing the cylinder head. This step saves a great deal of time during assembly and helps prevent incorrect installation.

Mark the mounting location and orientation of the pushrods, rocker arm and mounting hardware prior to removing them.

The cylinder head uses different length bolts. Label the bolts or make a diagram to show the location of each bolt as it is removed from the cylinder head.

With a wire brush, remove all sealant from the cylinder head bolts. Use a thread chaser to clean any sealant or corrosion from the bolt openings in the cylinder block. Apply a light coating of Perfect Seal (Mercury part No. 92-34227-1) onto the bolt threads before installing them.

Replace the head gasket each time the bolts are loosened. Apply a light coat of Perfect Seal to both sides of stainless steel ribbed gaskets. Do not apply sealant to composition type gaskets.

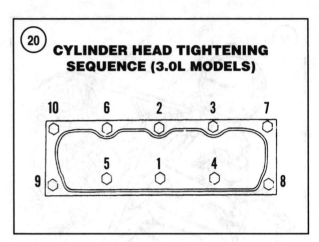

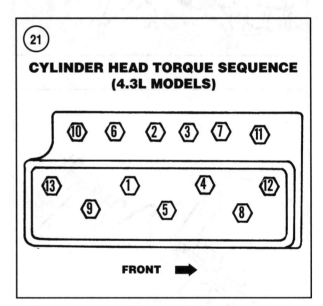

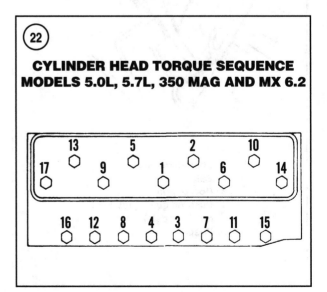

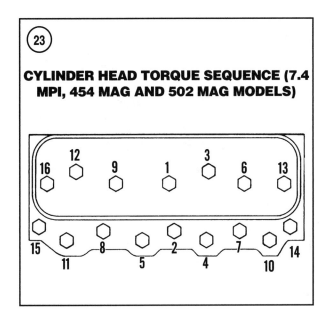

**(23)**

**CYLINDER HEAD TORQUE SEQUENCE (7.4 MPI, 454 MAG AND 502 MAG MODELS)**

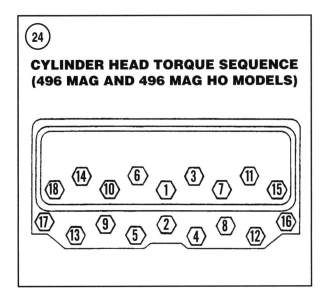

**(24)**

**CYLINDER HEAD TORQUE SEQUENCE (496 MAG AND 496 MAG HO MODELS)**

Follow the specified head bolt tightening sequence and procedure. Many engines use a torque-and-turn tightening procedure. The bolts are tightened in sequence to a specified torque, then turned an additional amount. Use an angle torque gauge and tighten the bolts the specified degrees of additional rotation. Purchase the torque angle gauge from a tool supplier or automotive part store.

**Cylinder Head Removal (All Models)**

1A. *Seawater cooled*—Drain water from the cylinder block and manifolds as described in Chapter Five.

1B. *Closed cooling system*—Drain water from the manifold and heat exchanger as described in Chapter Five. Drain coolant from the system as described in Chapter Four.

2A. *3.0L models*—Remove the exhaust manifold as described in Chapter Nine.

2B. *Other models*—Remove the intake manifold as described in Chapter Eight. Remove the exhaust manifolds as described in Chapter Nine.

3. Remove the rocker arm cover, rocker arms, pushrods and related fasteners as described in this chapter.

4. Relocate or remove any bracket, hoses, lines or other components that will interfere with cylinder head removal. Remove the spark plugs.

5. Refer to the appropriate diagram (**Figures 20-24**) and loosen the cylinder head bolts in the reverse order of the tightening sequence.

6. Remove the head bolts. Note each bolt length reference during installation. Carefully pry the cylinder head(s) from the cylinder block.

7. Remove the gasket from the cylinder block or head. Carefully scrape all gasket material from the mating surfaces. Do not scratch or gouge the mating surfaces. Clean the surfaces with a quick drying solvent.

8. Inspect the piston crowns for physical damage or excessive carbon deposits. Remove carbon deposits with a blunt scraper. Replace damaged pistons as described in this chapter.

**Cylinder Head Inspection**

1. Scrape all carbon deposits from the combustion chamber using a blunt scraper. Do not nick or gouge the cylinder head.

2. Use solvent and thoroughly clean the cylinder head.

3. Inspect the cylinder head for surface cracks, especially near the valve seats and spark plug openings.

4. Inspect the valves for damage and chipped or burned edges. Have the cylinder head repaired if these or other defects are present.

5. Check for valve recession. If the valve is recessed into the valve seat, the valve is recessed. Compare the valves to each other and suspect valve recession if any appear to be lower in the seat than the others.

6. Check for cylinder head warp by placing a straightedge at various positions across the cylinder head mating surface (**Figure 25**). Hold the straightedge firmly against the head and check the gap at various points along the straightedge using a feeler gauge. Compare the thickness of the feeler gauge that can be passed under the straightedge with the warp limit in **Table 2**. Have the cylinder head resurfaced if it is excessively warped.

**7**

7. Check for cylinder block warp by placing a straight-edge at various points on the cylinder head mating surface (**Figure 26**). Hold the straightedge firmly against the head and check the gap at various points along the straightedge using a feeler gauge. Compare the thickness of the feeler gauge that can be passed under the straightedge with the warp limit in **Table 2**. Have the cylinder block resurfaced if excessive warp or other surface damage occurs.

8. Position the cylinder head so the ports are higher than the valves. Pour light solvent into the ports (**Figure 27**). Check for solvent leaking between the valves and seats. Have the cylinder head repaired if solvent leaks from the valves.

9. Inspect the dowel pins in the cylinder block. They must fit tight in the opening. Replace damaged or loose fitting pins.

**Cylinder Head Installation**

1. Use a quick-drying solvent and thoroughly clean the cylinder head and cylinder block mating surfaces. Any residual debris may allow water, coolant or exhaust to leak.

2A. *Stainless steel ribbed head gasket*—Apply a light coat of Perfect Seal (Mercury part No. 92-34227-1) to both sides of the new gasket(s).

2B. *Composition type gasket*—Do not apply sealant to the gasket or mating surfaces.

3. Align the cylinder bore and dowel pin openings and place the gasket(s) on the cylinder block.

4. Align the openings with the dowel pins and install the head onto the cylinder block.

5. Apply a light coat of Perfect Seal (Mercury part No. 92-34227-1) to the threads of the head bolts. Install and hand-thread the bolts.

6A. *3.0L models*—Tighten the head bolts as follows:
   a. Tighten the head bolts in sequence (**Figure 20**) to 30 ft.-lb. (41 Nm).
   b. Tighten the head bolts in sequence to 60 ft.-lb (81 Nm).
   c. Tighten the head bolts in sequence to the specification in **Table 1**.

6B. *4.3L, 5.0L, 5.7L and 350 Mag models*—Tighten the head bolts as follows:
   a. Tighten the head bolts in sequence (**Figure 21** or **Figure 22**) to the specification in **Table 1**.
   b. Use an angle torque gauge and tighten the bolts in sequence a final time. Tighten the shorter bolts an additional 55°. Tighten medium length bolts an additional 65°. Tighten the longest bolt an additional 75°.

6C. *MX 6.2, 7.4 MPI, 454 Mag and 502 Mag models*—Tighten the head bolts as follows:

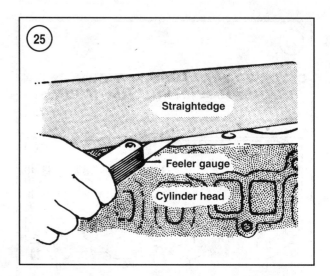
**25**
Straightedge
Feeler gauge
Cylinder head

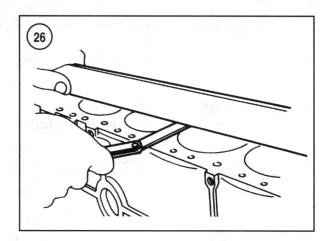
**26**

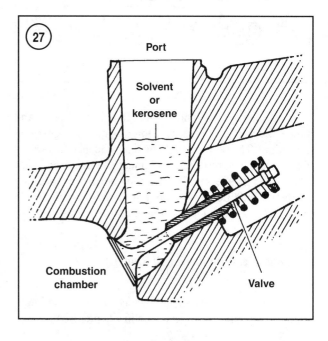
**27**
Port
Solvent or kerosene
Combustion chamber
Valve

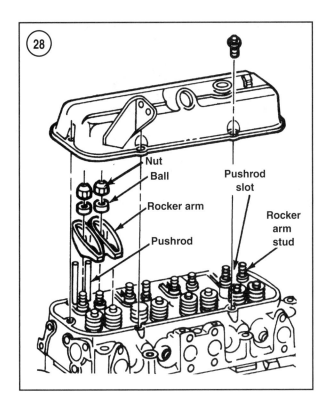

28

Nut
Ball
Rocker arm
Pushrod

Pushrod
slot

Rocker
arm
stud

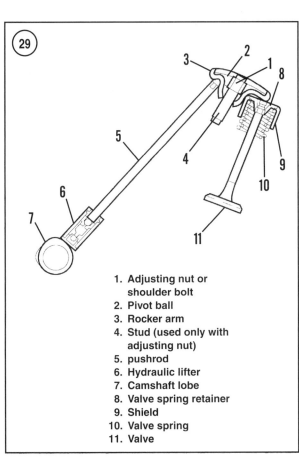

29

3
2
1
8
5
4
9
6
10
7
11

1. Adjusting nut or
   shoulder bolt
2. Pivot ball
3. Rocker arm
4. Stud (used only with
   adjusting nut)
5. pushrod
6. Hydraulic lifter
7. Camshaft lobe
8. Valve spring retainer
9. Shield
10. Valve spring
11. Valve

a. Tighten the head bolts in sequence (**Figure 22** or **Figure 23**) to the first step specification in **Table 1**.

b. Tighten the head bolts in sequence to the second step specification in **Table 1**.

c. Tighten the head bolts in sequence to the final step specification in **Table 1**.

6D. *496 Mag and 496 Mag HO models*—Tighten the head bolts as follows:

a. Tighten the head bolts in sequence (**Figure 24**) to the specification in **Table 1**.

b. Use an angle torque gauge and tighten the bolts in sequence an additional 120°.

c. Tighten the bolts in sequence a final time. Tighten the shorter bolts an additional 30°. Tighten medium length and the longest bolts an additional 60°.

7. Fill the cooling system (closed system) as described in Chapter Four.

8. Install all brackets, hoses, lines and wire harnesses.

9. Install the pushrods, rocker arms and covers as described in this chapter. Adjust the valves.

10A. *3.0L models*—Install the exhaust manifold as described in Chapter Nine.

10B. *All other models*—Install the intake manifold as described in Chapter Eight.

## PUSHROD, ROCKER ARM AND ROCKER ARM COVER

1. On 3.0L models, remove the pushrod and lifter cover from the starboard side of the cylinder block. Remove and discard the cover gasket. Clean the cover with solvent and dry with compressed air.

2. Position the No. 1 piston at TDC as described in this chapter.

3. Insert the pushrods through the slots in the cylinder head(s) (**Figure 28**). Insert the pushrod (5, **Figure 29**) into the lifter (6). Seat the lifter against the camshaft lobe (7, **Figure 29**).

4A. *2001 4.3L models*—Fit the rocker arm onto the cylinder head as follows:

a. Align the opening in the roller rocker shaft with the stud.

b. Fit the pushrod into the recess on the rocker arm tip while fitting the rocker arm over the stud. The other end of the rocker arm must seat against the valve spring retainer (8, **Figure 29**).

c. Thread the nut onto the stud. Do not tighten the nut at this time.

4B. *All other models*—Fit the rocker arm onto the cylinder head as follows:

a. Align the rocker arm (3, **Figure 29**) with the stud.

7

b. Fit the pushrod into the recess on the rocker arm.

c. Fit the other end of the rocker arm against the valve spring retainer as shown in **Figure 29**.

d. Fit the ball (**Figure 28**) over the stud with the rounded side facing the rocker arm.

e. Seat the ball against the rocker arm.

f. Thread the nut onto the stud. Do not tighten the nut at this time.

5. Tighten the rocker arm nuts as described in this chapter.

6. Coat the rocker arm and pushrod surfaces with engine oil.

7A. *3.0L models*—Install a new gasket onto the lifter cover. Install the cover onto the cylinder block. Tighten the bolts to the specification in **Table 1**. Install the rocker arm cover as described in this chapter (see Valve Adjustment).

7B. *V6 and V8 engines*—Place a new gasket on the rocker arm covers. Install the covers onto the cylinder heads. Tighten the fasteners in a crossing pattern to the specification in **Table 1**.

### Tightening the Rocker Arm Nuts

The rocker arm nuts must be tightened in a specified sequence. Otherwise the nut may not be adequately tightened or the valve may contact the piston as the crankshaft rotates.

### *3.0L models*

1. Position the No. 1 piston at TDC as described in this chapter.

2. Tighten the adjusting nuts on the following valves (**Figure 8**):

a. No. 1 cylinder intake.

b. No. 1 cylinder exhaust.

c. No. 2 cylinder intake.

d. No. 3 cylinder exhaust.

e. No. 4 cylinder intake.

3. Tighten the adjusting nuts until a slight amount of lash exists between the rocker arm and pushrod (**Figure 30**). Do not remove all of the lash.

4. Turn the crankshaft one full turn clockwise and align the mark on the harmonic balancer with the 0 mark on the timing tab (**Figure 10**).

5. Next, tighten the adjusting nuts on the following valves (**Figure 8**):

a. No. 2 cylinder exhaust.

b. No. 3 cylinder intake.

c. No. 4 cylinder exhaust.

6. Tighten the adjusting nuts until a slight amount of lash exists between the rocker arm and pushrod. Do not remove all of the lash.

7. Adjust the valves as described in this chapter.

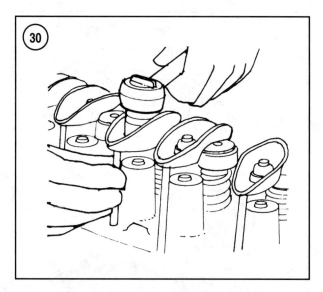

### *4.3L models*

1. Place the No. 1 piston at TDC as described in this chapter.

2. Tighten the rocker arm nuts on the following valves (**Figure 14**):

a. No. 1 cylinder intake.

b. No. 1 cylinder exhaust.

c. No. 2 cylinder intake.

d. No. 3 cylinder intake.

e. No. 5 cylinder exhaust.

f. No. 6 cylinder exhaust.

3. Tighten the rocker arm nuts to the specifications in **Table 1**.

4. Turn the crankshaft clockwise one full turn and align the timing mark on the harmonic balancer with the 0 mark on the timing tab (**Figure 13**).

5. Tighten the rocker arm nuts for the following valves (**Figure 14**):

a. No. 2 cylinder exhaust.

b. No. 3 cylinder exhaust.

c. No. 4 cylinder intake.

d. No. 4 cylinder exhaust.

e. No. 5 cylinder intake.

f. No. 6 cylinder intake.

6. Tighten the rocker arm nuts to the specification in **Table 1**.

### *5.0L, 5.7L, 350 Mag and MX 5.2 models*

1. Position the No. 1 piston at TDC as described in this chapter.

2. Tighten the adjusting nuts on the following valves (**Figure 11**):
    a. No. 1 cylinder intake.
    b. No. 1 cylinder exhaust.
    c. No. 2 cylinder intake.
    d. No. 3 cylinder exhaust.
    e. No. 4 cylinder exhaust.
    f. No. 5 cylinder intake.
    g. No. 7 cylinder intake.
    h. No. 8 cylinder exhaust.

3. Tighten the adjusting nuts until a slight amount of lash exists between the rocker arm and pushrod. Do not remove all of the lash.

4. Turn the crankshaft one full turn clockwise and align the timing mark on the harmonic balancer with the 0 mark on the timing tab (**Figure 13**).

5. Tighten the adjusting nuts on the following valves (**Figure 12**):
    a. No. 2 cylinder exhaust.
    b. No. 3 cylinder intake.
    c. No. 4 cylinder intake.
    d. No. 5 cylinder exhaust.
    e. No. 6 cylinder intake.
    f. No. 6 cylinder exhaust.
    g. No. 7 cylinder exhaust.
    h. No. 8 cylinder intake.

6. Tighten the adjusting nuts until a slight amount of lash exists between the rocker arm and pushrod. Do not remove all of the lash.

7. Adjust the valves as described in this chapter.

### 7.4 MPI, 454 Mag and 502 Mag models

1. Position the No. 1 piston at TDC as described in this chapter.

2. Tighten the following rocker arm nuts (**Figure 15**):
    a. No. 1 cylinder intake.
    b. No. 1 cylinder exhaust.
    c. No. 2 cylinder intake.
    d. No. 3 cylinder exhaust.
    e. No. 4 cylinder exhaust.
    f. No. 5 cylinder intake.
    g. No. 7 cylinder intake.
    h. No. 8 cylinder exhaust.

3. Torque the rocker arm nuts to the specification in **Table 1**.

4. Turn the crankshaft one full turn clockwise and align the timing mark on the harmonic balancer with the 0 mark on the timing tab (**Figure 13**).

5. Tighten the rocker arm nuts on the following valves (**Figure 15**):
    a. No. 2 cylinder exhaust.

    b. No. 3 cylinder intake.
    c. No. 4 cylinder intake.
    d. No. 5 cylinder exhaust.
    e. No. 6 cylinder intake.
    f. No. 6 cylinder exhaust.
    g. No. 7 cylinder exhaust.
    h. No. 8 cylinder intake.

6. Tighten the rocker arm nuts to the specification in **Table 1**.

### 496 Mag and 496 Mag HO models

1. Position the No. 1 piston at TDC as described in this chapter.

2. Inspect the lifters and camshaft lobes of the No. 1 cylinder for proper alignment. The roller on the lifters must align with the base of the camshaft lobes (**Figure 16**). Otherwise the components for the wrong cylinder are installed.

3. Tighten the rocker arm nuts to the specification in **Table 1**.

4. Refer to **Table 11** to determine the engine firing order.

5. Rotate the harmonic balancer *exactly* 90° clockwise. Do not rotate the balancer counterclockwise or the water pump will be damaged.

6. Refer to **Figure 15** to locate the valve train components for the next cylinder in the firing order.

7. Inspect the lifters and camshaft lobes for proper alignment. The roller on the lifters must align with the base of the cam (**Figure 16**). Otherwise the components for the wrong cylinder are installed.

8. Tighten the rocker arm nuts to the specification in **Table 1**.

9. Repeat Steps 5-9 until all rocker arm nuts are tightened.

### ENGINE REMOVAL AND INSTALLATION

Some service procedures can be performed with the engine in the boat; others require engine removal. The boat design and the service procedure determine whether the engine must be removed.

The drive unit must be removed in order to disengage the universal joint shaft from the engine coupler.

The engine is heavy, awkward to handle and has sharp edges. It may unexpectedly shift or drop during removal. To prevent serious injury, always observe the following precautions.

1. Never place any part of the body where it could be trapped, cut or crushed by a falling or shifting engine.

**7**

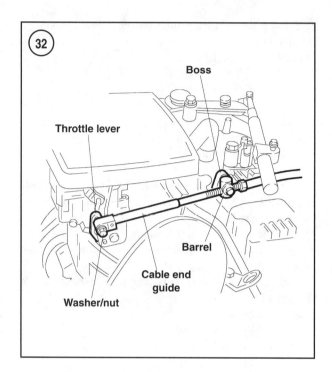

2. If the engine must be pushed during removal or installation, use a board or similar tool. Keep hands and feet out of danger.

3. Be sure the hoist is designed to lift engines and has enough load capacity for the engine. The engine may weigh 1000 lb. (453 kg) or more.

4. Be sure the hoist is securely attached to the lifting eyes on the engine.

5. The engine should not be difficult to lift with a proper hoist. If it is, stop lifting and lower the engine back to its mounts. Check for mounts, cables or hoses that have not been separated from the engine.

**Engine Removal**

*CAUTION*
*The bracket attached to the thermostat housing is not for lifting the engine, but may be used to lift the front of the engine only during engine alignment. Use the lifting brackets attached to the intake manifold (V6 and V8 models) or exhaust manifold and cylinder head (3.0L models) to lift the entire engine.*

1. Remove the drive unit as described in Chapter Eleven.

2. Remove the engine cover and any other part of the boat that will interfere with engine removal.

3. Remove the battery from the boat.

4. Unplug the instrument wire harness from the engine harness plug (**Figure 31**).

5. Disconnect the fuel tank hose from the water-separating fuel filter or fuel pump (3.0L models). Plug the hose to prevent fuel leakage.

6. Remove the flame arrestor cover or plastic engine cover.

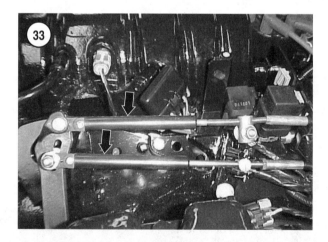

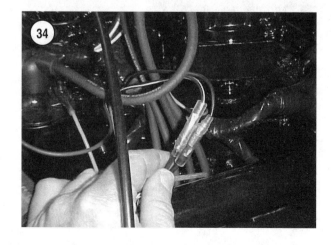

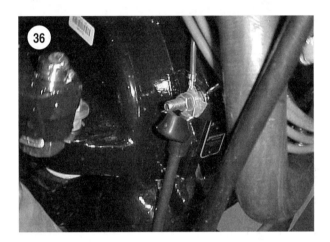

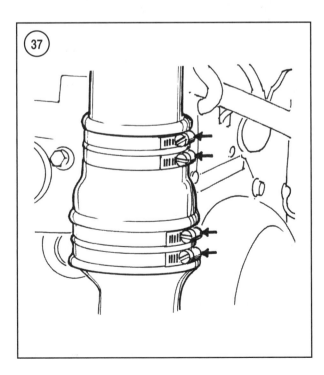

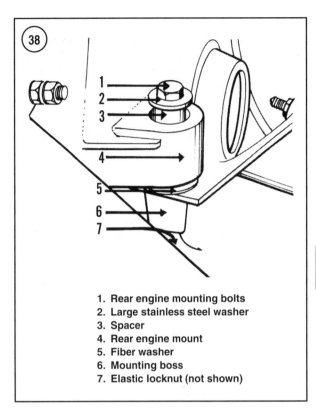

1. Rear engine mounting bolts
2. Large stainless steel washer
3. Spacer
4. Rear engine mount
5. Fiber washer
6. Mounting boss
7. Elastic locknut (not shown)

7. Disconnect the throttle cable from the carburetor (**Figure 32**) or throttle body (EFI models).

8. Disconnect both shift cables (**Figure 33**) from the shift plate assembly.

9. Disconnect the trim position sender wires (**Figure 34**) from the engine wire harness.

10. On power steering models, disconnect the hoses from the power steering actuator (**Figure 35**). Plug the hose fittings and actuator openings to prevent leakage and contamination.

11. Disconnect the cooling water hose from the transom fitting.

12. Drain all water from the engine as described in Chapter Five.

13. Disconnect all ground wires from the flywheel housing studs (**Figure 36**).

14. Fully loosen the hose clamps (**Figure 37**) on the exhaust tube(s).

15. Attach a suitable hoist to the engine lifting brackets. The hoist must have a minimum lift capacity of 1500 lb. (680 kg). Raise the hoist enough to just eliminate slack in the chain.

16. Remove the rear engine mounting bolts (1, **Figure 38**) from the flywheel housing.

17A. *3.0L models*—Remove the bolts (**Figure 39**) securing the front engine mount bracket to the boat structure.

17B. *V6 and V8 models*—Remove the bolts that secure the side engine mounts to the boat structure (**Figure 40**).

18. Carefully lift the engine from the boat. Guide the engine away from any boat structure that may contact any engine component(s). Move the boat to allow lowering of the engine.

19. Carefully lower the engine onto a stable surface. Place sturdy blocks under the engine mounts and flywheel housing to prevent the engine from resting on the oil pan.

### Engine Installation

1. While the engine is removed, tighten transom assembly fasteners, the exhaust tube, and all accessible fittings and hoses. Refer to the appropriate chapter for torque specifications.

2. Inspect the exhaust pipe for holes, cracks or damage. Replace the pipe if defective. Otherwise the pipe may allow water leakage into the boat.

3. Place the elastic locknuts (7, **Figure 38**) into the mounting bosses (6).

4. Glue the fiber washers and special split washers (**Figure 41**) onto the engine mount bosses. The washer openings must align with the bolt openings in the engine mounts.

5. To ease installation, apply a soap and water solution to the exhaust pipe and exhaust tube mating surfaces. Route all hoses, cables and wires to a location that prevents them from being trapped between the engine mounts.

6. Attach a suitable hoist to the engine lifting brackets.

7. Lift the engine enough to clear the boat structure. Move the boat into position directly under the engine.

8. Guide the exhaust tube onto the exhaust pipe and align the rear engine mount openings while lowering the engine. Stop when the rear engine mounts (4, **Figure 38**) are approximately 1/2 in. (13 mm) above the mounting bosses (6). Do not dislodge the special split washers or fiber washers (**Figure 41**). Insert the rear engine mounting bolts (1, **Figure 38**) through the washers and rear mounts. Thread the bolts into the elastic locknuts.

9. Guide the front or side mounts while lowering the engine onto the boat structure. Push the engine as needed to align the mounting bolt holes. Thread the mounting bolts (**Figure 39** or **Figure 40**) into the boat structure. Tighten the rear and side or front engine mounting bolts to the specification in **Table 1**.

10. Tighten the exhaust tube hose clamps (**Figure 37**) as described in Chapter Nine.

11. Connect all ground wires onto the flywheel housing stud (**Figure 36**). Securely tighten the nut.

12. Connect the cooling water hose onto the transom assembly fitting. Securely tighten the hose clamp.

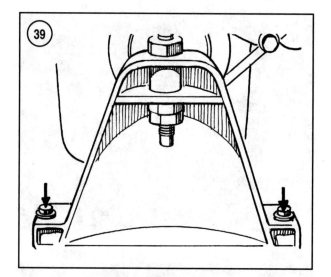

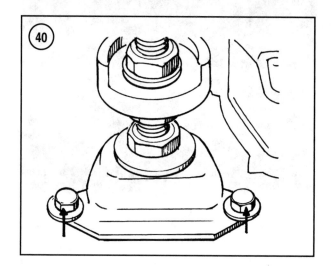

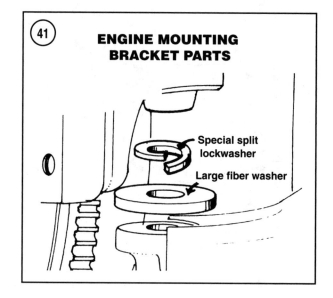

**ENGINE MOUNTING BRACKET PARTS**

Special split lockwasher

Large fiber washer

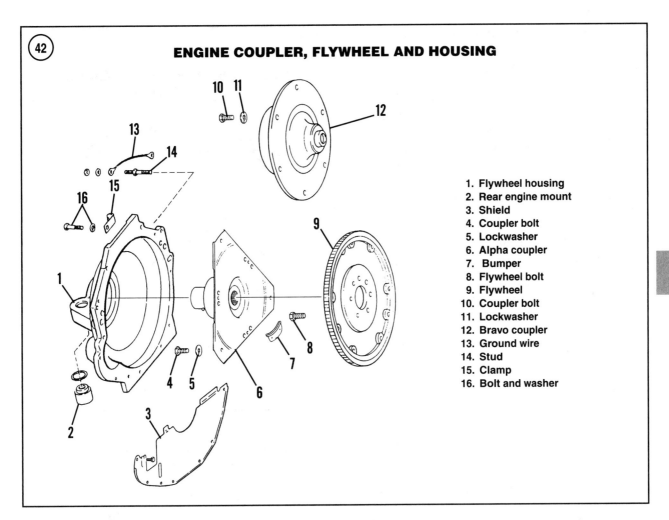

**42** **ENGINE COUPLER, FLYWHEEL AND HOUSING**

10 11
13
14
16 15
12
9
1
8
7
2 4 5 6
3

1. Flywheel housing
2. Rear engine mount
3. Shield
4. Coupler bolt
5. Lockwasher
6. Alpha coupler
7. Bumper
8. Flywheel bolt
9. Flywheel
10. Coupler bolt
11. Lockwasher
12. Bravo coupler
13. Ground wire
14. Stud
15. Clamp
16. Bolt and washer

7

13. On power steering models, connect hoses onto the power steering actuator (**Figure 35**) as described in Chapter Fourteen. Fill and bleed the power steering system as described in Chapter Fourteen.

14. Connect the trim position sender wires (**Figure 34**) to the engine wire harness.

15. Connect the shift cables (**Figure 33**) to the shift plate assembly.

16. Connect the throttle cable to the carburetor (**Figure 32**) or throttle body (EFI models). Adjust the throttle cable as described in Chapter Six.

17. Install the flame arrestor or plastic engine cover.

18. Connect the fuel tank hose to the water-separating fuel filter or fuel pump (on 3.0L models). Securely tighten the hose clamps.

19. Connect the instrument harness plug to the engine harness plug (**Figure 31**). Secure the connection with a hose clamp. Do not over-tighten the hose clamp.

20. Install the battery. Connect the cables to the battery.

21. Check for any hoses, cables, wires or other components that may contact moving parts. Secure them with clamps as needed.

22. Align the engine as described in this chapter.

23. Install any components that were removed for engine removal.

24. Install the drive unit as described in Chapter Eleven. Adjust the shift cables as described in Chapter Six.

**Engine Coupler, Flywheel and Housing Removal and Installation**

1. Lift the engine to allow removal of the flywheel housing (1, **Figure 42**).

2. Remove the starter motor as described in Chapter Ten.

3. Remove the screws and pull the shield (3, **Figure 42**) from the flywheel housing.

4. Remove the coupler bolts and lockwashers (**Figure 42**).

5. Pull the coupler from the flywheel.

6. Measure the flywheel runout as described in this chapter.

7. Remove the flywheel bolts and lockwashers (**Figure 42**). Clean Loctite from the bolt threads. Tap the flywheel with a rubber mallet to free it from the crankshaft flange.

8. Thoroughly clean the flywheel, engine coupler and crankshaft flange mating surfaces. The mating surfaces must be free of dirt, corrosion or paint overspray. Use sandpaper to remove burrs and other surface imperfections.

9. Inspect the flywheel for worn or damaged teeth and surface cracks. Replace the flywheel if these or other defects are visible.

10. Inspect the flywheel and engine coupler mounting bolts for damaged or corroded threads. Replace the bolts if these or other defects occur.

11. Inspect the engine coupler for worn or damaged splines, melted rubber material, missing or damaged bumpers (7, **Figure 42**), or other visual defects. Replace the coupler if defective. Replace missing or damaged bumpers.

12. Use a thread chaser to clean the flywheel and crankshaft threaded openings.

13. Apply Loctite 271 to bolt openings in the crankshaft flange.

14. Fit the flywheel onto the crankshaft flange. The locating dowel must fit into the hole in the flywheel. Install the flywheel bolts (8, **Figure 42**).

15. Torque the flywheel bolts in several passes, following a crisscross pattern, to the specification in **Table 1**.

16. Apply Loctite 271 to the coupler bolt openings in the flywheel.

17. Fit the engine coupler onto the flywheel. Install the coupler bolts and lockwashers (**Figure 42**).

18. Torque the coupler bolts in several passes, following a crisscross pattern, to the specification in **Table 1**.

19. Fit the flywheel housing over the alignment dowels. Seat the housing on the cylinder block. Install the bolts, nuts, wires and clamps (**Figure 42**). Tighten the bolts and nuts to the specification in **Table 1**.

20. Replace the gasket and install the shield (3, **Figure 42**) on the flywheel housing (1). Tighten the screws to the specification in **Table 1**.

21. Install the starter motor as described in Chapter Ten.

## Flywheel Runout

1. Remove the spark plugs. Remove the flywheel housing as described in this chapter.

2. Mount a dial indicator onto the cylinder block. Align the indicator with the back surface of the flywheel and as

**OIL PAN AND ONE PIECE GASKET (TYPICAL)**

Spacer

One-piece silicone rubber gasket

close as possible to the ring teeth. Push forward on the flywheel and zero the indicator needle.

3. Maintain forward pressure on the flywheel. Observe the dial indicator while slowly rotating the flywheel. The needle movement on the dial indicates the flywheel runout.

4. Compare the runout with the specification in **Table 7**. If the runout exceeds the specification, check for loose flywheel bolts or debris on the flywheel mating surfaces. If all the flywheel bolts are properly tightened and the mating surfaces are clean, the flywheel is warped and must be replaced.

## OIL PAN

### Removal and Installation (All Models)

All models covered in the manual use a one piece oil pan gasket (**Figure 43**). This type of gasket has molded-in metal spacers at the fastener openings, which prevents excessive gasket crushing and resulting oil leakage. Although the gasket is designed for re-use, it is a good practice to replace the gasket anytime the oil pan is removed. Small tears may not be easy to see, but will still allow oil to leak into the bilge. Unless the boat design provides good access to the oil pan fasteners, and clearance to remove the pan, remove the engine for oil pan removal.

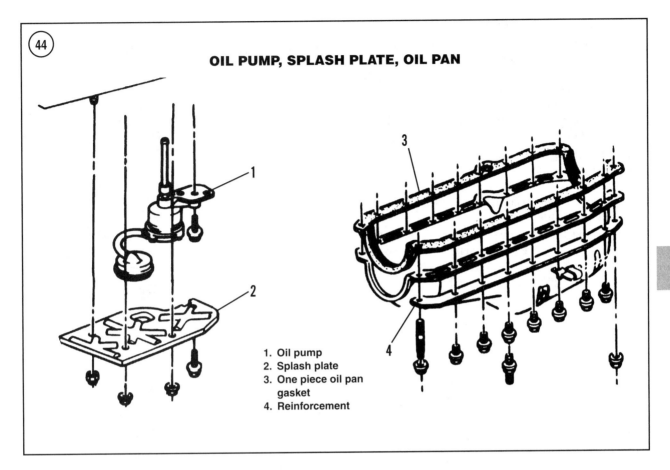

**OIL PUMP, SPLASH PLATE, OIL PAN**

1. Oil pump
2. Splash plate
3. One piece oil pan gasket
4. Reinforcement

7

1. Remove the engine as described in this chapter. Drain the oil from the engine.

2. Remove the starter motor as described in Chapter Ten.

3. Support the oil pan and remove the fasteners. Remove the reinforcement (4, **Figure 44**) if one is present. Carefully pull the oil pan from the cylinder block. If necessary, use a dull scraper and pry the pan from the cylinder block. Do not damage the gasket or mating surfaces.

4. Thoroughly clean the oil pan with solvent and dry with compressed air. Inspect the oil pan for cracks, dents, or corrosion and replace if necessary.

5. Clean gasket sealant from the mating surfaces.

6A. Apply a bead of Quicksilver RTV Sealer onto the corners where the oil pan gasket surface joins the front cover and rear main seal carrier. Apply just enough sealant to fill in the gap. Place the new gasket on the cylinder block. Align the metal spacers with the fastener openings. Align the front of the gasket with the groove in the front cover. Align the rear of the gasket with the groove in the rear main seal carrier.

6B. On 3.0 L models, insert the protrusions on the gasket into the small opening at the bottom of the front cover.

7. Seat the oil pan onto the cylinder block. The front and rear surfaces must fit in the groove in the gasket.

8. Install the fasteners. If so equipped, install the reinforcement (4, **Figure 44**). Tighten the oil pan fasteners, from the center outward, to the specification in **Table 1**.

9. Install the starter motor as described in Chapter Ten.

10. Install the oil drain plug and tighten to the specification in **Table 1**.

11. Install the engine as described in this chapter. Fill the engine with fresh oil as described in Chapter Four.

12. Start the engine and immediately check for oil leakage. Correct oil leakage before operating the engine.

### OIL PUMP

**Removal and Installation**

1. Remove the oil pan as described in this chapter.

2. On V8 models, remove the splash plate (2, **Figure 44** Typical).

3. Remove the mounting bolt and carefully pull the oil pump from the cylinder block.

4. On V6 and V8 engines (except 496 Mag and 496 Mag HO models), pull the pump drive shaft from the cylinder block.

5. Inspect the oil pump as described in this chapter.

6. On V6 and V8 engines (except Model 496 Mag and 496 Mag HO), insert the pumpdrive shaft into its opening in the cylinder block. If the distributor is installed, rotate the shaft and align the slot with the distributor shaft.

7. Install the distributor into the cylinder block. Rotate the oil pump body and align the pump with the shaft, distributor or oil pump drive (Model 496 Mag and 496 Mag HO). The oil pump will seat against the cylinder block as the shafts align.

8. Rotate the oil pump on the mount and align the mount bolt opening. Install the mount bolt and tighten to the specification in **Table 1**.

9. On V8 models, install the splash plate (2, **Figure 44**, typical). Evenly tighten the mounting bolts to the specification in **Table 1**.

10. Install the oil pan as described in this chapter.

### Disassembly, Inspection and Assembly

Internal oil pump components are not available separately. Refer to **Figures 45-47** during this procedure.

Use a pickup tube installer (Kent-Moore part No. J21882) and install the pickup and screen assembly into the pump cover. Otherwise the tube may fit improperly, causing low oil pressure and engine damage.

1. Remove the screws and carefully pull the cover from the pump body. Discard the gasket, if so equipped.

2. Make match marks on the drive gear and idler gear teeth. If reused, the teeth on one gear must align with the corresponding teeth on the other gear, or the gears will wear excessively or fail.

3. Pull the drive gear and idle gear from the pump body.

4. Remove the pin or retainer and remove the regulator valve and spring from the body.

5. Clean all components in solvent and dry with compressed air. Inspect the components as follows:

   a. Inspect the gears for wear, roughness, excessive polishing or discoloration.

   b. Inspect the cover and pump body for wear, grooves, discoloration or roughness.

   c. Inspect the regulator valve and spring for damage or corrosion.

   d. Replace the oil pump if these or other defects are visible.

6A. *Models 7.4 MPI, 454 Mag, 502 Mag, 496 Mag and 496 Mag HO*—Inspect the pickup and screen for damage. Replace the oil pump if either is defective. The tube is welded to the pump body.

6B. *All other models*—Inspect the pickup and screen for damage to the tube or screen. If either the pickup or tube is defective, replace both as follows:

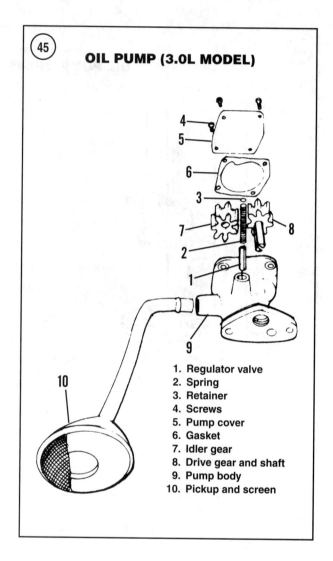

**OIL PUMP (3.0L MODEL)**

1. Regulator valve
2. Spring
3. Retainer
4. Screws
5. Pump cover
6. Gasket
7. Idler gear
8. Drive gear and shaft
9. Pump body
10. Pickup and screen

a. Make match marks on the pickup tube and oil pump cover.

b. Clamp the cover in a vise with protective jaws.

c. Carefully twist the tube from the cover.

d. Transfer the match marks to the replacement tube.

e. Fit the pickup and screen into the cover opening.

f. Drive the pickup tube into the cover until the bead on the tube contacts the cover. Use Kent-Moore tool part No. J21882 to install the tube. See **Figure 48**.

7. Align the match marks and install the drive and idle gears into the pump body. The gears must spin freely in the body. If not, replace the oil pump.

8. Install the regulator valve and spring into the pump body. Secure the spring with the pin or retainer.

9. Apply engine oil to the gears. Install a new gasket onto the oil pump body, if so equipped. Install the cover onto the pump body. Install the screws and tighten them in a crossing pattern to the specification in **Table 1**.

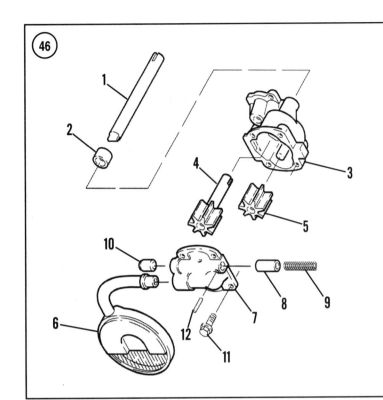

**OIL PUMP (4.3L, 5.0L, 5.7L, 350 MAG AND MX 6.2 MODELS)**

1. Drive shaft
2. Coupling
3. Pump body
4. Drive gear and shaft
5. Idle gear
6. Pickup and screen
7. Pump cover
8. Regulator valve
9. Spring
10. Plug
11. Screws
12. Pin

**7**

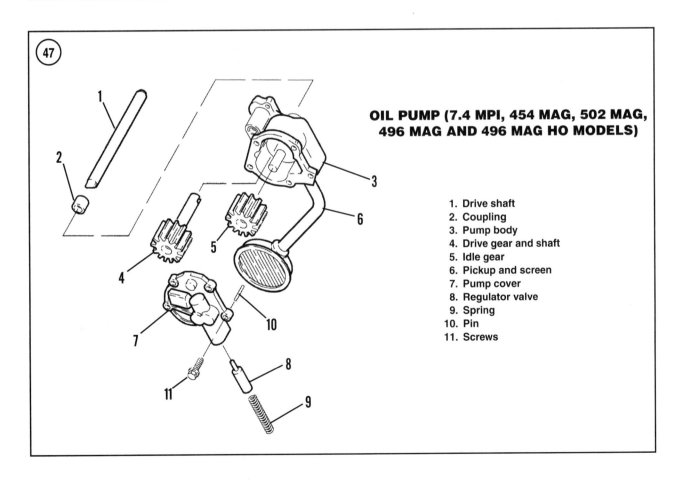

**OIL PUMP (7.4 MPI, 454 MAG, 502 MAG, 496 MAG AND 496 MAG HO MODELS)**

1. Drive shaft
2. Coupling
3. Pump body
4. Drive gear and shaft
5. Idle gear
6. Pickup and screen
7. Pump cover
8. Regulator valve
9. Spring
10. Pin
11. Screws

## HARMONIC BALANCER

Use a balancer removal and installation tool such as Kent-Moore part No. J-23523-E for this operation. Do not use makeshift tools, which can damage the balancer or other engine components.

The balancer can be replaced without removing the engine. If boat structure prevents access to the balancer, remove the engine as described in this chapter.

1. Disconnect the battery cables. Loosen the tension and remove the drive belt as described in Chapter Eight. Remove the drive belt pulley from the balancer.

2. Remove the retaining bolt and washer from the center of the balancer.

3. Attach the removal tool to the balancer. Thread the appropriate bolts from the removal tool into the balancer. Securely tighten the bolts. Thread the puller bolt into the removal tool until it contacts the crankshaft. Use the bolt with a tip that matches the crankshaft. Some crankshafts are tapered at the bolt opening.

4. Turn the puller bolt (**Figure 49**) and remove the balancer. Remove the tool from the balancer. Use solvent to clean the balancer and the exposed end of the crankshaft.

5. Inspect the drive key in the crankshaft for corrosion or damage and replace as needed.

6. Inspect the balancer at the seal contact surface. Replace the balancer if deeply grooved or pitted at this surface.

7. Inspect the balancer for protruding rubber material, cracks or other defects. Replace the balancer if necessary.

*NOTE*
*If the balancer is replaced, the seal in the timing gear cover must also be replaced.*

8. Inspect the seal in the timing gear cover for wear or damage. Replace the seal if defective or if replacing the balancer.

9. Apply a bead of Quicksilver RTV Sealant to the balancer key slot. Apply engine oil to the seal lip and the exposed end of the crankshaft.

10. Align the balancer key slot with the crankshaft drive key. Fit the balancer onto the crankshaft.

11. Thread the bolt from the installation tool fully into the crankshaft threads. Thread the puller hub onto the bolt until it contacts the balancer (**Figure 50**).

12. Turn the hub (**Figure 50**) until the balancer fully seats against the crankshaft. Remove the installation tool.

13. Install the balancer retaining bolt and washer. Tighten the bolt to the specification in **Table 1**.

14. Install the crankshaft pulley. Tighten the pulley retaining bolts to the specification in **Table 1**.

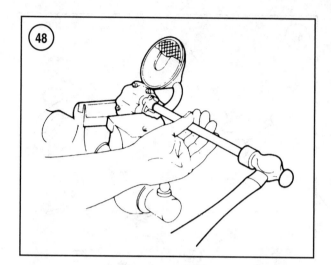

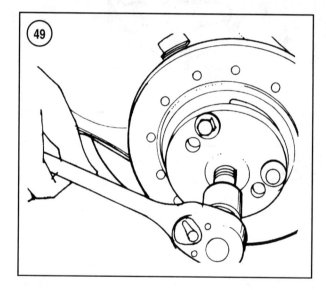

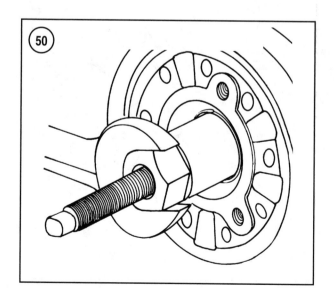

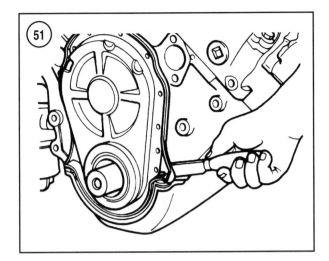

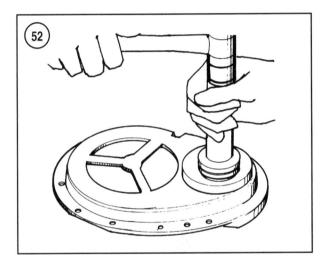

4. On 496 Mag, 496 Mag and 2002-2004 V-6 and V-8 models, remove the camshaft or crankshaft position sensor from the cover as described in Chapter Eight or Chapter Sixteen.

5. Remove the bolts from the timing gear cover. Use a blunt scraper and carefully pry the cover from the cylinder block (**Figure 51**).

6. Carefully scrape gasket material from the cover mating surfaces.

7A. *4.3L, 5.0L, 5.7L, 350 Mag and MX 6.2 models*—Discard the cover.

7B. *All other models*—Replace the seal as follows.

    a. Thoroughly clean the cover with solvent.

    b. Carefully pry the seal from the cover. Clean the bore using a quick drying solvent.

    c. Apply a light coat of Loctite 271 to the seal bore and the outer diameter of the seal.

    d. Place the cover on a suitable work surface with the inner side facing downward. Place a block of wood under the seal bore for support.

    e. Set the new seal into the bore with the lip side facing downward. Drive the seal fully into the bore (**Figure 52**).

    f. Wipe excess Loctite from the seal bore.

8. Apply Perfect Seal (Mercury part No. 92-34227-1) to both sides of the cover gasket. Fit the cover gasket onto the cover.

9. Fit the cover and gasket onto the cylinder block. The cover must fit over the alignment pins.

10. Install the bolts. Tighten them in stages, following a crisscross pattern, to the specification in **Table 1**.

11. On 496 Mag, 496 Mag and 2002-2004 V-6 and V-8 models, install the camshaft or crankshaft position sensor from the cover as described in Chapter Eight or Chapter Sixteen.

12. Install the circulating pump as described in Chapter Nine.

13. Install the harmonic balancer as described in this chapter.

14. Install the oil pan as described in this chapter.

15. Install the drive belt(s) as described under *Alternator* in Chapter Eight. Connect the battery cables.

## TIMING GEAR COVER

Remove the cover for seal replacement or as necessary to access the timing sprockets and chain. On 4.3L, 5.0L, 5.7L, 350 Mag and MX 6.2 models, the timing chain cover is manufactured from a composite material. It must be replaced if removed, or the cover may leak oil. On all other models, the cover is manufactured from metal and can be reinstalled.

1. Remove the oil pan as described in this chapter.

2. Remove the harmonic balancer as described in this chapter.

3. Remove the circulating pump as described in Chapter Nine.

## TIMING CHAIN AND SPROCKET

A timing chain is used on all V6 and V8 engines. Four-cylinder models are equipped with timing gears in place of a chain and sprockets.

1. Disconnect the battery cables. Position the No. 1 piston at TDC as described in this chapter.

2. To prevent possible interference between the pistons and valves, remove the rocker arms and pushrods as described in this chapter.

3. Remove the timing chain cover as described in this chapter.

4. Measure the timing chain deflection as follows:

**7**

a. Rotate the crankshaft counterclockwise to tighten the chain on the starboard side.

b. Scribe a reference mark on the cylinder block that aligns with the tight side of the chain.

c. Rotate the crankshaft clockwise to tighten the chain on the port side.

d. Pull the loose side of the chain (starboard side) toward the starboard side. Scribe a reference mark on the cylinder block that aligns with the chain.

e. Measure the distance between the two reference marks to determine the timing chain deflection. Compare the measured deflection with the specification in **Table 5**.

f. Replace the timing chain and both sprockets if the deflection exceeds the specification.

5. Rotate the crankshaft to align the marks on the crankshaft and camshaft sprockets (**Figure 53**).

6. Remove the bolts. Carefully pull the camshaft sprocket and timing chain from the engine.

7. Use a two jaw puller to remove the crankshaft sprocket. Inspect the drive key in the crankshaft for corrosion or damage and replace as needed.

8. Clean the chain and sprockets with solvent and dry with compressed air.

9. Inspect the timing chain and both sprockets for wear, cracks or damage. Replace all three components if any defects are visible.

10. Install the crankshaft sprocket as follows:

a. Align the key slot in the crankshaft sprocket with the crankshaft key.

b. Using a suitable driver, tap the crankshaft sprocket onto the crankshaft until seated against the shoulder on the crankshaft.

11. Align the locating pin and install the camshaft sprocket, without the chain, onto the camshaft. Do not install the bolts at this time. Rotate the camshaft and crankshaft as needed to align the timing marks (**Figure 53**). Remove the camshaft sprocket.

12. Fit the timing chain onto the camshaft sprocket and crankshaft sprocket while installing the camshaft sprocket onto the camshaft. The timing marks must align as shown in **Figure 53**. Do not drive the camshaft sprocket onto the camshaft, which can dislodge a plug on the rear of the motor.

13. Install the three camshaft sprocket bolts. Tighten them to the specification in **Table 1**.

14. Lubricate the timing chain and sprockets with engine oil.

15. Install the timing chain cover as described in this chapter.

16. Install the rocker arm and pushrods as described in this chapter.

17. Tighten the rocker arm nuts and adjust the valves as described in this chapter.

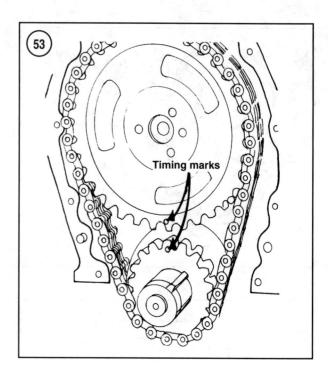

Timing marks

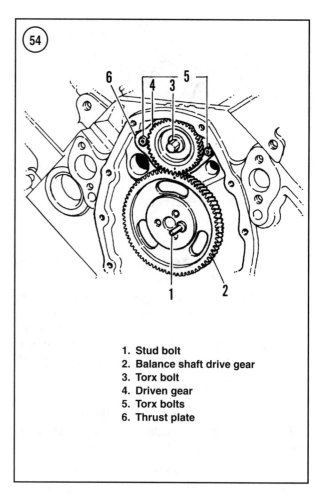

1. Stud bolt
2. Balance shaft drive gear
3. Torx bolt
4. Driven gear
5. Torx bolts
6. Thrust plate

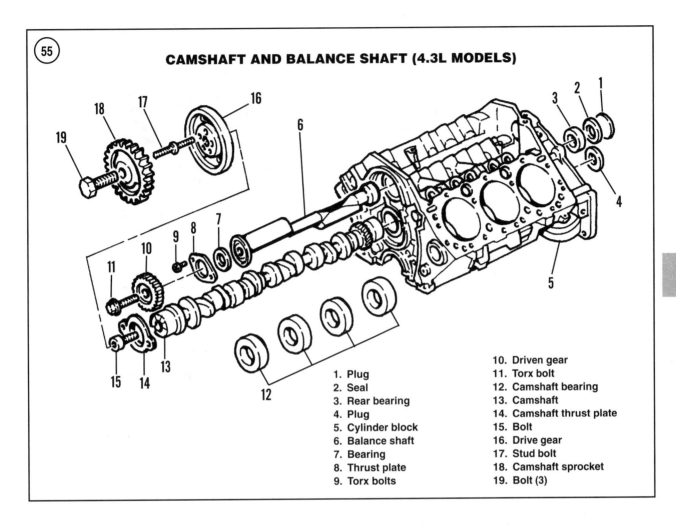

**55**

## CAMSHAFT AND BALANCE SHAFT (4.3L MODELS)

1. Plug
2. Seal
3. Rear bearing
4. Plug
5. Cylinder block
6. Balance shaft
7. Bearing
8. Thrust plate
9. Torx bolts
10. Driven gear
11. Torx bolt
12. Camshaft bearing
13. Camshaft
14. Camshaft thrust plate
15. Bolt
16. Drive gear
17. Stud bolt
18. Camshaft sprocket
19. Bolt (3)

**7**

## BALANCE SHAFT

### (4.3L Models)

A balance shaft is used on 4.3L models. The balance shaft can be replaced without complete disassembly of the engine.

1. Remove the timing chain and sprockets as described in this chapter.

2. Remove the intake manifold as described in Chapter Eight.

3. Wedge a piece of wood between the drive gear (2, **Figure 54**) and the driven gear (4). Remove the Torx bolt (3, **Figure 54**) from the driven gear. Pull the driven gear from the balance shaft.

4. Remove the stud bolts (2, **Figure 54**) from the drive gear. Remove the drive gear.

5. Remove the Torx bolts (9, **Figure 55**). Remove the thrust plate (8, **Figure 55**).

6. Insert a pry bar between the cylinder block and a solid section of the balance shaft (6, **Figure 55**). Carefully pry the shaft forward and remove it from the cylinder block.

7. Inspect the balance shaft bearings (3 and 7, **Figure 55**) for excessive wear, discoloration or roughness. If any defects are visible, have a reputable machine shop replace the bearings.

8. Clean the balance shaft with solvent. Inspect the rear bearing surface of the balance shaft for wear, discoloration or roughness. If any defects are visible, replace the balance shaft. Inspect the gears for missing or damaged teeth, excessive wear and discoloration. Replace both gears if these or other defects are present.

9. Lubricate the balance shaft and bearings with engine oil. Align the rear of the balance shaft with the bearing while guiding the balance shaft into the bore. With a rubber mallet, carefully drive the shaft into the cylinder block until the front bearing (7, **Figure 55**) seats in the bore.

10. Install the balance shaft thrust plate (8, **Figure 55**). Install the Torx screws (9, **Figure 55**) and tighten them to the specification in **Table 1**.

11. Install the driven gear (10, **Figure 55**) onto the balance shaft. Apply Loctite 271 onto the threads and install

the Torx bolt (11, **Figure 55**). Do not tighten the bolt at this time.

12. Install the drive gear (16, **Figure 55**) onto the camshaft. The timing marks on the gears must align as shown in **Figure 56**. Remove the drive gear and rotate the camshaft or balance shaft to achieve proper alignment.

13. Install the stud bolts (1, **Figure 54**) into the drive gear and camshaft. Wedge a piece of wood between the drive and driven gears and tighten the stud bolts to the specification in **Table 1**.

14. Tighten the balance shaft Torx bolt (3, **Figure 54**) to the initial torque specification in **Table 1**. Use an angle torque gauge to tighten the bolt an additional 35°.

15. Remove the wooden wedge. Clear any wood chips from the gear teeth with compressed air. Lubricate the gear teeth with engine oil.

16. Install the timing chain, sprockets, timing chain cover and oil pan as described in this chapter.

17. Install the intake manifold as described in Chapter Eight.

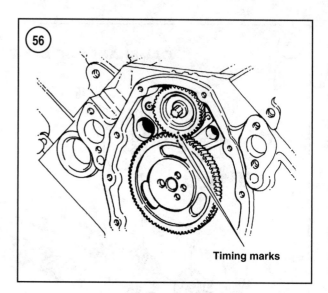

Timing marks

## CAMSHAFT AND LIFTER

Always replace the lifters if replacing the camshaft. Operating the engine with used lifters will damage a new camshaft. If reusing lifters, always install them in the original locations. Otherwise the camshaft and lifters will wear excessively and fail.

Apply General Motors Cam and Lifter Prelube onto the camshaft lobes and lifters prior to installation.

Repair of defective camshaft bearings should only be attempted by a mechanic with the proper equipment and experience. The bearings or cylinder block are easily damaged without the proper equipment, and the installation equipment is more expensive than having the bearings professionally replaced. Improper bearing installation can also result in camshaft failure.

### 3.0L Models

1. Remove the oil pan and timing gear cover as described in this chapter. Remove the distributor as described in Chapter Ten.

2. Remove the lifter cover, pushrods and rocker arms as described under *Measuring Camshaft Lobe Lift* in this chapter.

3. Remove the fuel pump as described in Chapter Eight.

4. Measure the timing gear runout as follows:

   a. Clamp a dial indicator onto the cylinder block.
   b. Position the plunger perpendicular to the front surface of the timing gear (**Figure 57**). The plunger

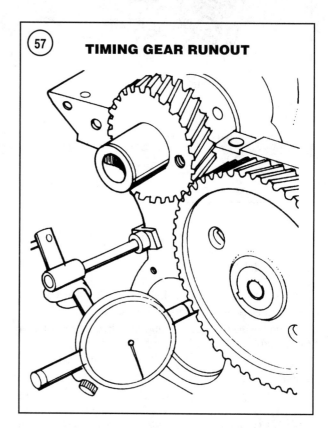

**TIMING GEAR RUNOUT**

must touch the gear as close to the teeth as possible. Zero the dial indicator.

   c. Observe the dial indicator while rotating the crankshaft. The needle movement indicates the timing gear runout. Replace the timing gear if the runout exceeds the specification in **Table 5**.

5. Measure the timing gear backlash as follows:

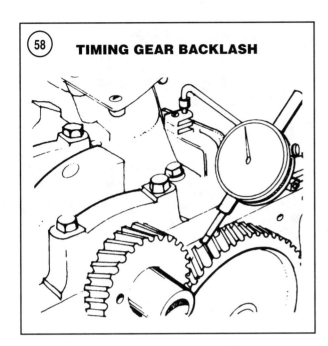

**TIMING GEAR BACKLASH**

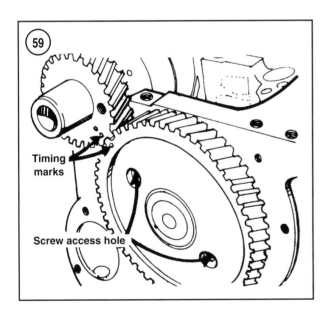

Timing marks

Screw access hole

a. Clamp a dial indicator onto the cylinder block.

b. Position the plunger in contact with one of the timing gear teeth (see **Figure 58**). Zero the dial indicator.

c. Observe the dial indicator while gently rotating the camshaft gear clockwise and counterclockwise. Do not drive the crankshaft gear. The needle movement indicates the timing gear backlash.

d. Replace the timing gear and crankshaft gear if the backlash exceeds the specification in **Table 5**.

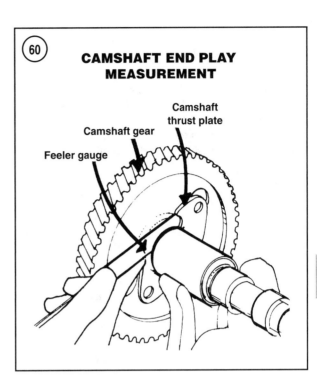

**CAMSHAFT END PLAY MEASUREMENT**

Camshaft thrust plate

Camshaft gear

Feeler gauge

7

6. Remove the lifters from the cylinder block, noting their original locations in the cylinder block. Used lifters must be installed in the original locations or the lifters and camshaft lobes wear rapidly and fail.

7. Rotate the crankshaft gear until the timing marks align as shown in **Figure 59**. Remove the thrust plate bolts through the access holes in the timing gear (**Figure 59**).

8. Carefully remove the camshaft and sprocket assembly from the cylinder block. Support the camshaft during removal. Otherwise the camshaft bearings may be damaged.

9. Use feeler gauges and measure the gap between the thrust plate and the camshaft surface (see **Figure 60**). The gap allows camshaft end play. Replace the timing gear and thrust plate if the end play exceeds the specification in **Table 4**.

10. Inspect the timing gear for wear or damage. Inspect the gear teeth for missing sections or uneven wear. Replace the timing gear and thrust plate if any defects are visible. Replacement instructions follow:

a. Place the camshaft on a press with the gear resting on the table and the camshaft in the table opening.

b. Support the camshaft. Press the camshaft from the gear.

c. Place the new gear on the table of the press with the timing mark facing downward.

d. Align the new thrust plate with the camshaft bore of the gear. Align the key slot in the gear with the key in the camshaft. Apply engine oil to the gear bore. Insert the camshaft into the gear opening.

e. Press the camshaft into the gear until fully seated.

11. Inspect the camshaft bearings for roughness, uneven wear or discoloration. Have the bearings replaced if these or other defects are noted.

12. Inspect the lifters for wear on lobe contact surfaces, scuffing on the sides, or other defects. Replace all of the lifters if any of them are defective.

13. Inspect the camshaft lobes for wear or rounded surfaces (**Figure 61**). Replace the camshaft, lifters and bearings if any of the lobes are worn or damaged.

14. Measure a camshaft bearing journal at several locations around its diameter (**Figure 62**). Record all measurements. The difference between the largest measurement and the smallest measurement is the amount the journal is out of round. Measure the diameter and out-of-round for each journal. Compare the measurements with the specifications in **Table 4**. If any of the journal diameters measure less than the minimum diameter or are excessively out of round, replace the camshaft, bearings and lifters.

15. Support the camshaft on V-blocks as shown in **Figure 63**. Set the plunger of a dial indicator so it touches one of the middle camshaft journals.

16. Observe the dial indicator while rotating the camshaft. The needle movement indicates the amount of camshaft runout. Replace the camshaft, lifters and bearings if the runout exceeds the specification in **Table 4**.

17. Apply engine oil to the camshaft bearings. Apply General Motors Cam and Lifter Prelube on the camshaft lobes and the bottom of the lifters.

18. Carefully guide the camshaft into the cylinder block and bearings. Support the camshaft to prevent damaged bearings. Align the timing marks (**Figure 59**) and gear teeth. Seat the camshaft into the cylinder block.

19. Align the thrust plate with the access holes (**Figure 59**). Install the thrust plate bolts and tighten them to the specification in **Table 1**.

20. Install the lifters into the cylinder block. Seat the lifters against the camshaft lobes.

21. Install the pushrods and rocker arms as described in this chapter. Install the distributor as described in Chapter Ten. Adjust the valves as described in this chapter.

22. Install a new gasket onto the lifter cover. Install the cover onto the cylinder block. Tighten the bolts to the specification in **Table 1**. Install the spark plugs and leads.

23. Install the fuel pump as described in Chapter Eight.

24. Install the timing gear cover, oil pan and harmonic balancer as described in this chapter.

25. Connect the battery cables. Adjust the ignition timing as described in Chapter Six.

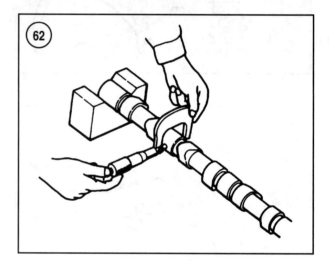

### V6 and V8 Models

1. Remove the oil pan and timing gear cover as described in this chapter. Remove the intake manifold as described in Chapter Eight.

2. Remove the pushrods and rocker arms as described under *Measuring Camshaft Lobe Lift* in this chapter.

3. Remove the timing chain and sprockets as described in this chapter.

4. On 496 Mag and 496 Mag HO models, remove the bolt and lift the oil pump drive (**Figure 64**) from the cylinder block. The gear must rotate freely. Otherwise replace the driver. Remove the oil pump as described in this chapter.

5. On V6 models, remove the balance shaft as described in this chapter.

6. Scribe match mars on the roller lifters guides and retainer (**Figure 65**) to make sure the roller turns the original direction after installation.

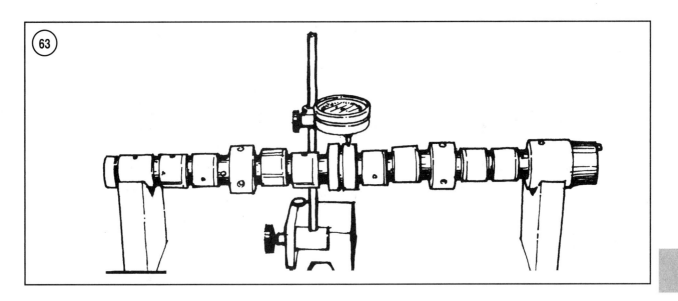

**7**

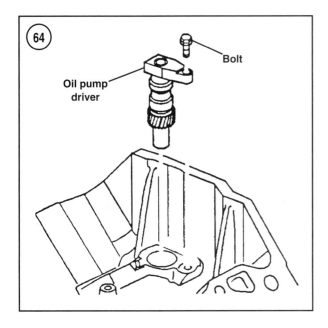

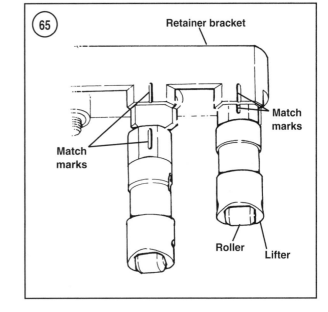

7. Remove the bolts and remove the lifter guides and re-tainer from the cylinder block. Keep all components arranged in a manner consistent with their original mounting location.

8. Remove the lifters from the cylinder block. Note the lifters' original placement in the cylinder block. Used lifters must be reinstalled in the original locations, or the lifter and camshaft lobe wear rapidly and fail.

9. On 4.3L, 496 Mag and 496 Mag HO models, remove the bolts and the camshaft thrust plate (14 and 15, **Figure 55**, typical).

10. Thread two 5/16 × 18 bolts into the camshaft bolt openings. Carefully pull on the bolts and remove the cam-

shaft from the cylinder block. Support the camshaft during removal to prevent damage to the camshaft bearing surfaces.

11. Inspect the thrust plate and camshaft surface for uneven wear, roughness or discoloration. Replace the thrust plate and/or camshaft and lifters if necessary.

12. Inspect the camshaft bearings for roughness, uneven wear or discoloration. Have the bearings replaced if necessary.

13. Inspect the lifters for discoloration, loose fitting rollers, scuffing on the sides, or other defects. Replace all of the lifters if any of them are defective.

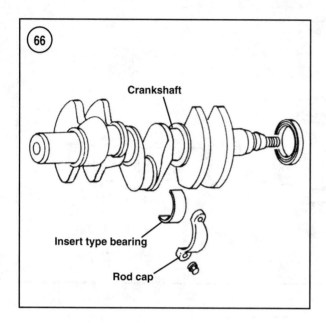

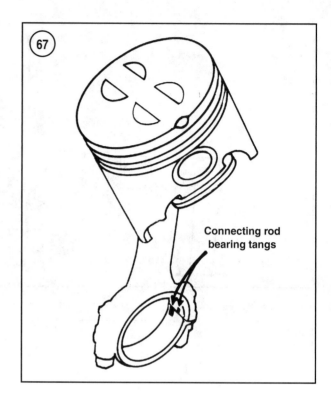

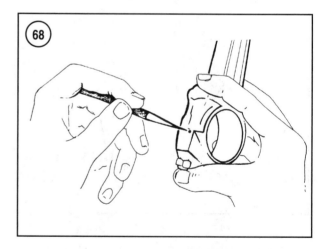

14. Inspect the camshaft lobes for wear, roughness or rounded surfaces (**Figure 61**). Replace the camshaft, lifters and bearings if any of the lobes are worn or damaged.

15. Inspect the lifter guides and retainers for wear or damage. Replace defective components.

16. Measure a camshaft bearing journal at several locations around the diameter (**Figure 62**). Record all measurements. The difference between the largest diameter measurement and the smallest measurement is the amount the journal is out of round. Determine the out-of-round for each journal. Compare the measurements with the specifications in **Table 4**. If any journal measures less than the minimum diameter or is excessively out of round, replace the camshaft, bearings and lifters.

17. Support the camshaft on V-blocks as shown in **Figure 63**. Set the plunger of a dial indicator so it touches one of the middle camshaft journals.

18. Observe the dial indicator while rotating the camshaft. The needle movement indicates the amount of camshaft runout. Replace the camshaft, lifters and bearings if the runout exceeds the specification in **Table 4**.

19. Apply engine oil to the camshaft bearings. Apply General Motors Cam and Lifter Prelube on the camshaft lobes and the lifter rollers.

20. Carefully guide the camshaft into the bearings. Support the camshaft to prevent damaged bearings.

21. On 4.3L, 496 Mag and 496 Mag HO models, install the camshaft thrust plate (14 and 15, **Figure 55** typical) and bolts. Tighten the bolts to the specification in **Table 1**.

22. Install the lifters into their respective openings in the cylinder block. Seat the lifter rollers against the camshaft lobes. Align the match markings and install the guides and

retainer. Tighten the retainer and guide bolts to the specification in **Table 1**.

23. On 4.3L models, install the balance shaft and gears as described in this chapter.

24. On 496 Mag and 496 Mag HO models, lubricate the oil pump driver (**Figure 64**) and install it into the cylinder block. Rotate the camshaft as needed to align the gear teeth. Tighten the mounting bolt to the specification in **Table 1**. Install the oil pump as described in this chapter.

25. Install the timing chain and sprockets as described in this chapter.

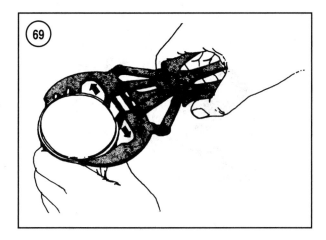

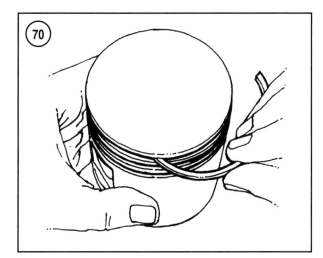

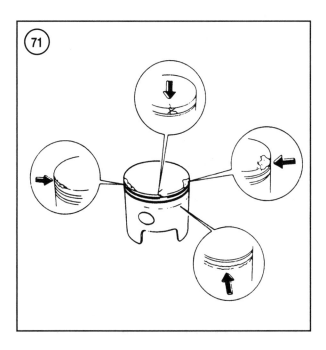

26. Install the pushrods and rocker arms as described in this chapter.

27. Install the timing chain cover, oil pan and harmonic balancer as described in this chapter.

28. Tighten the rocker arm nuts or adjust the valves as described in this chapter. Install the intake manifold as described in Chapter Eight.

29. Connect the battery cables. Adjust the ignition timing as described in Chapter Six.

## PISTON AND CONNECTING ROD

### Removal and Inspection

1. Remove the cylinder head(s), oil pan, and oil pump as described in this chapter.

2. Rotate the crankshaft until one of the pistons is at the bottom of its stroke.

3. Evenly loosen and remove the connecting rod nuts. Tap on the bottom of the cap until it falls free of the connecting rod (**Figure 66**). Reinstall the bearing if it dislodges from the rod cap.

4. Using a wooden dowel, carefully push the piston and rod from the cylinder block. Install the rod cap onto the rod and secure it with the nuts. The bearing tangs must align as shown in **Figure 67**. Mark the cylinder number on the side of the connecting rod and cap (**Figure 68**).

5. Mark the cylinder number on the inner surface of the piston. Do not scratch the top or side of the piston. Remove and mark all pistons and rods as described.

6. Remove the crankshaft as described in this chapter. Remove any remaining fittings, brackets or other components from the cylinder block. Thoroughly clean the cylinder block with pressurized soapy water. Direct the spray through all oil passages and into any crevices. Rinse the block with clean water and dry with compressed air. Direct air through all passages to remove residual water or debris. To prevent corrosion, promptly coat all unpainted surfaces with engine oil.

7. Use a piston ring expander (**Figure 69**) and remove the rings from the pistons. Use a broken ring to scrape carbon from the ring grooves (**Figure 70**). Do not remove aluminum material from the ring groove.

8. Clean the pistons and rods with solvent. Use a plastic bristle brush to remove carbon from the piston surfaces. Never use a wire brush, because small pieces of wire may become imbedded in the piston dome and cause pre-ignition or detonation damage.

9. Inspect the edge of the piston crowns for cracks, erosion or missing sections (**Figure 71**). Inspect the sides of the piston for scuffing (**Figure 72**) deep scratches or other damage. Rock each piston on the connecting rod while

**7**

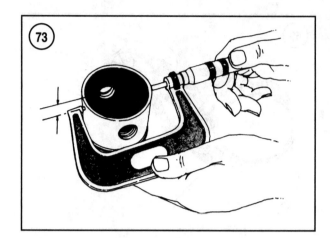

checking for binding or a loose fit of the piston pin and piston. Replace the piston and pin if necessary.

10. Using an outside micrometer, measure the piston diameter at two points: aligned with the piston pin, and at 90° to the pin (**Figure 73**). Record the measurements for each piston. Replace the piston as described in this chapter if the diameter is below the minimum specification.

11. Temporarily install new rings onto the pistons. Use feeler gauges and measure the clearance between the side of the ring and the ring groove (**Figure 74**). Compare the clearance with the side clearance specifications in **Table 6**. Replace the piston if the clearance exceeds the specification.

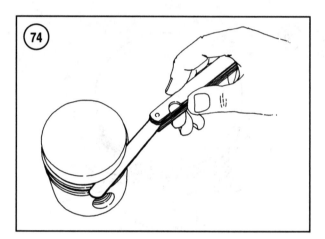

12. Use a cylinder bore gauge (**Figure 75**) to measure the cylinder bore diameter. Take the measurements at three or more evenly spaced depths in the bore, then again at 90° to the first measurements (**Figure 76**). Take the top measurement at a point even with the upper travel of the rings. Measure each cylinder and record all measurements.

13. Subtract the smallest diameter at the bottom of the bore from the largest diameter at the top of the bore. This number indicates the amount of cylinder bore taper. Record the taper for each cylinder.

14. Subtract the smallest diameter from the largest diameter measurement at each depth in the cylinder bore. This calculation indicates the amount the cylinder is out of round. Record the out-of-round amount for each cylinder.

15. Subtract the piston diameter (Step 10) from the smallest cylinder diameter to determine the minimum piston skirt clearance for the cylinder. Subtract the piston diameter from the largest cylinder clearance to determine the maximum skirt clearance for the cylinder.

16. Compare the cylinder diameter measurements, cylinder taper and out-of-round to the specifications in **Table 3**. Compare the skirt clearance calculations with the specifications in **Table 6**. If any of the measurements exceed the specification, have a reputable machine shop bore the cylinder to accept an oversize piston. It is not necessary to bore all of the cylinders as the oversize pistons weigh the

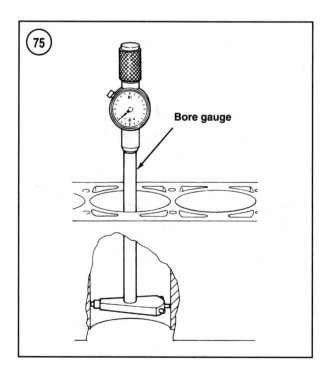

Bore gauge

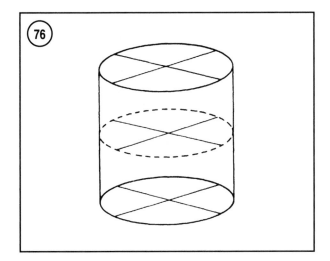

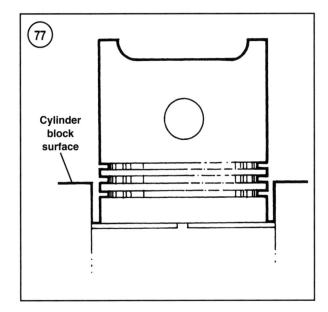

Cylinder
block
surface

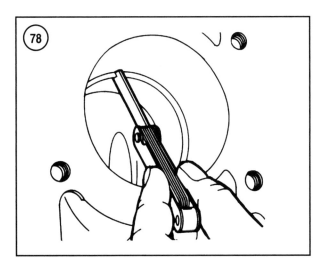

same as the standard pistons. Oversize piston availability varies by model. Always buy the oversize piston and supply it to the machinist before boring the cylinder. This allows the machinist to precisely fit the piston to the cylinder bore.

17. Inspect the cylinder bore for cracking, deep scratches, transferred piston material or corrosion pitting. Replace the cylinder block if cracks are visible. Have the cylinder bored if it is deeply scratched or pitted. Remove transferred piston material with a blunt scraper.

18. Hone the cylinders to achieve a 45-60° crosshatch before installing the pistons. Have a reputable machine shop hone the cylinders if you are unfamiliar with the honing operation or lack the proper equipment.

19. Remove the bearings from the connecting rods. Inspect the rod surfaces for discoloration, corrosion pitting, roughness and other damage. Remove the piston and replace the connecting rod if defective. Inspect the crankshaft for defects if discoloration, scratches, corrosion pitting or transferred material is found on the bearings.

20. Inspect the rod bolts and nuts for stretched or damaged threads. Replace the rod bolts and nut unless they are in excellent condition.

21. Thoroughly clean the cylinders with warm soapy water after the honing operation. Wipe a clean white shop towel through the bore to check for residual material. Any residual abrasive from the honing process will result in rapid wear and improper seating of the piston rings. To prevent corrosion, coat the cylinder walls and other unpainted surfaces with engine oil.

**Installation**

1. Install the crankshaft and seal carrier as described in this chapter.
2. Measure the ring end gap as follows:
    a. Insert one of the new compression (upper) rings into one of the cylinder bores. Use a piston without rings to push the ring into the bore, to a depth near the lowest point of ring travel (**Figure 77**).
    b. Measure the ring end gap (**Figure 78**) with a feeling gauge. Compare the end gap with the specification in **Table 6**.
    c. If the gap is incorrect, remove the ring and try a different ring. Continue until a ring with the correct gap is located for the cylinder. Measure and select the second compression and both oil ring rails as described.
    d. If unable to find rings with the correct gap, check the cylinder bore diameter.
    e. Attach a tag with the cylinder number to the selected rings.
    f. Select rings for each cylinder.

**7**

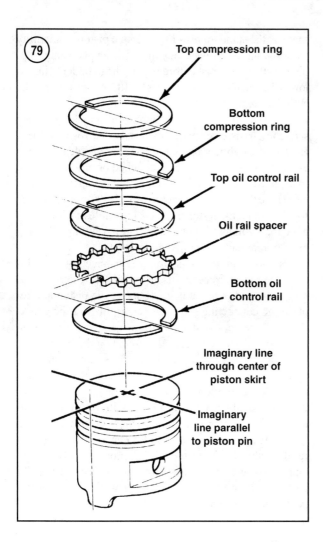

Top compression ring

Bottom compression ring

Top oil control rail

Oil rail spacer

Bottom oil control rail

Imaginary line through center of piston skirt

Imaginary line parallel to piston pin

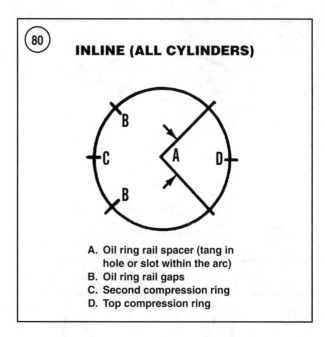

**INLINE (ALL CYLINDERS)**

A. Oil ring rail spacer (tang in hole or slot within the arc)
B. Oil ring rail gaps
C. Second compression ring
D. Top compression ring

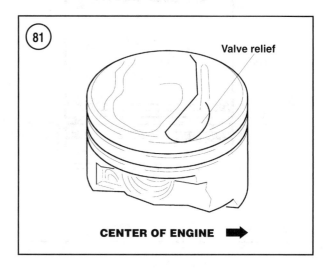

Valve relief

**CENTER OF ENGINE**

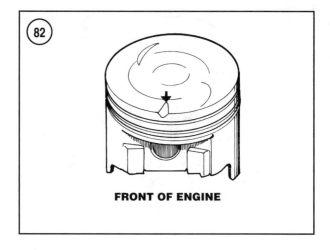

**FRONT OF ENGINE**

3. Coat the cylinder bores with engine oil. Use a ring expander (**Figure 69**) to install the rings onto the piston as shown in **Figure 79**. The marks on the compression rings must face the top of the piston.

4. Align the piston ring gaps as shown in **Figure 80**. The ring gaps must be aligned correctly for proper engine operation.

5. Make sure the piston is correctly attached to the connecting rod. If not, remove and reassemble the piston and connecting rod.

   a. On 3.0L models, the connecting rod bearing tangs (**Figure 67**) must face the port side of the engine with the piston installed.

   b. On V6 and V8 models, the connecting rod bearing tangs (**Figure 67**) must face the port side on odd-numbered cylinders and the starboard side on even-numbered cylinders.

6. Remove the rod cap and bearings. Wipe all oil or debris from the connecting rod. To prevent the rod bolts

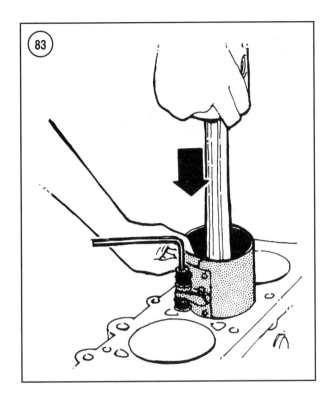

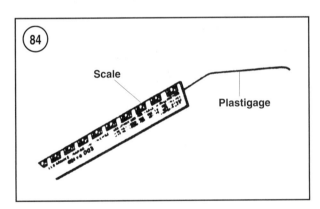

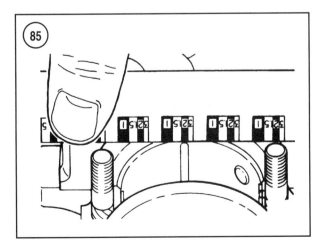

from damaging the crankshaft, fit short pieces of rubber tubing over the rod bolts.

7. Fit a ring compressor over the piston. Tighten the compressor until the rings fully compress into the grooves. Do not over tighten the compressor. The piston must slide from the compressor during installation.

8. Carefully guide the rod and piston skirt into the cylinder block. Rotate the piston and position the piston notch or mark toward the front of the engine.

    a. On 454 Mag and 502 Mag models, the machined valve relief notch (**Figure 81**) must face the center of the cylinder block with the piston installed. The notch must face the rear of the engine on odd numbered cylinders and the front of the engine on even numbered cylinders.

    b. On all other models, the notch in the piston crown (**Figure 82**) must face the front of the engine with the piston installed.

    c. On models without a notch, the valve relief notch (**Figure 81**) must be positioned toward the center of the block.

9. Hold the ring compressor tightly against the cylinder head mating surface (**Figure 83**). Use a wooden dowel and soft mallet to carefully tap the piston into the bore. Do not use excessive force. Check for insufficient ring compression if the piston will not enter the bore with light tapping.

10. Carefully guide the connecting rod toward the crankshaft while pushing the piston down in the bore. Fit the new bearing into the connecting rod. The bearing tang must fit into the notch in the rod. Seat the rod and bearing against the crankpin journal.

11. Place a section of Plastigage (**Figure 84**) on the crankpin journal. The Plastigage must be as long as the width of the bearing and aligned with the bottom of the journal (**Figure 85**).

12. Fit the bearing in the connecting rod cap. The bearing tang must fit into the notch in the cap. Install the rod cap onto the connecting rod. The bearing tangs must align on the same side of the rod. Carefully seat the cap onto the rod. Drag a pencil tip along the side of the cap and rod (**Figure 68**). The pencil should not catch on the split line. If the cap and rod do not align, make sure the correct cap is installed. The connecting rod cap may also be distorted. Replace the connecting rod if necessary.

13. Tighten the connecting rod fasteners as follows:

    a. On 4.3L models, evenly tighten the connecting rod nuts to the initial torque specification in **Table 1**. Check for proper rod cap alignment as described. Use an angle torque gauge and tighten the connecting rod nut an additional 70°.

**7**

b. On 5.0L, 5.7L and 350 Mag models, evenly tighten the connecting rod nuts to the initial torque specification listed in **Table 1**. Check for proper rod cap alignment as described. Use an angle torque gauge and tighten the connecting rod nut an additional 55°.

c. On MX 6.2 models, evenly tighten the connecting rod nuts to the first step specification in **Table 1**. Check for proper rod cap alignment as described. Tighten the rod nuts to the final step specification in **Table 1**.

d. On 496 Mag and 496 Mag HO models, evenly tighten the connecting rod nuts to the initial torque specification listed in **Table 1**. Check for proper rod cam alignment as described. Use an angle torque gauge and tighten the connecting rod nut an additional 90°.

e. On all other models, evenly tighten the connecting rod nuts to approximately one-half of the tightening specification in **Table 1**. Check for proper rod cap alignment as described. Tighten the nuts to the specification in **Table 1**.

14. Evenly loosen the nuts and remove the rod cap. Gauge the connecting rod bearing clearance by comparing the width of the flattened Plastigage with the scale on the envelope (**Figure 85**). Compare the clearance with the specification in **Table 7**.

a. If the clearance exceeds the specification, measure the crankshaft as described in this chapter. If using the original or a new crankshaft, install either 0.001 or 0.002 in. undersize bearings to correct the clearance. Never install bearings with an undersize amount that exceeds the out-of-round measurement of the journal. Otherwise inadequate clearance could occur at the wider journal diameter.

b. If the clearance is less than the specification, measure the crankshaft as described in this chapter. Check for improper rod cap or bearing installation and debris or an oil film between the rod or cap and the bearings.

c. If the clearance is correct, use a fingernail to scrape the Plastigage from the journal and bearing. Apply engine oil to the crankshaft and bearing surfaces. Install the rod cap and tighten the nuts as described in Step 13.

15. Rotate the crankshaft several revolutions. If the crankshaft binds or turns roughly, check for improper piston or rod installation.

16. Repeat Steps 3–15 for the remaining pistons and rods.

17. Measure the connecting rod side clearance as follows:

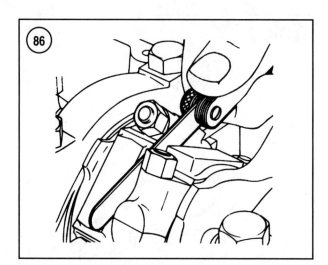

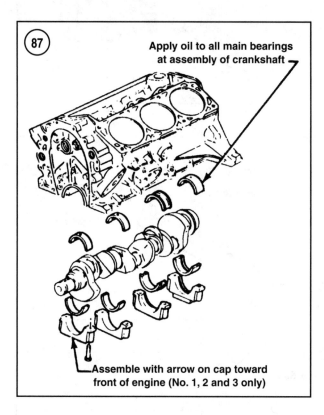

Apply oil to all main bearings at assembly of crankshaft

Assemble with arrow on cap toward front of engine (No. 1, 2 and 3 only)

a. On 3.0L models, move the connecting rod toward one side of the journal. Insert a feeler gauge between the side of the connecting rod and the crankshaft rod journal. Select the feeler gage that passes through the gap with a slight drag.

b. On all other models, push each connecting rod toward the crankshaft contact surface. Insert a feeler gauge between two connecting rods (**Figure 86**). Select the gage that passes between the gap with a slight drag.

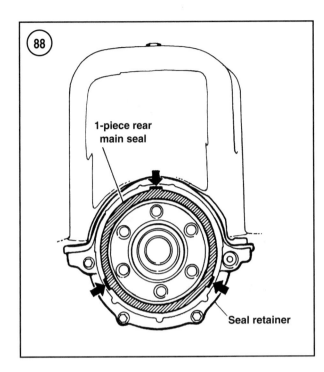

88

1-piece rear
main seal

Seal retainer

c. Repeat the measurement for all connecting rods. Compare the side clearance with the specification in **Table 7**.
d. If the clearance exceeds the specification, check for excessive wear on the connecting rod and crankshaft. Replace the connecting rod and recheck the clearance. If this does not correct the excessive clearance, replace the crankshaft.
e. If clearance is less than specified, check for faulty installation of the connecting rod, cap or piston.

18. Install the oil pump, timing chain cover, oil pan and cylinder head(s) as described in this chapter.

### Piston Pin Replacement

The piston pins are an interference fit in the connecting rod and hand-fitted into the piston. Removal requires a press and a special support stand. The cost of the support stand usually exceeds the cost of having the service performed. Have the replacement piston installed onto the rod at a machine shop.

## CRANKSHAFT AND REAR MAIN SEAL

Replace the main bearings (**Figure 87**) each time the crankshaft is removed. The main bearing caps (**Figure 87**) are machined to match the cylinder block. The caps must be installed in the proper location and with the arrows facing forward. Otherwise the crankshaft will bind in the cyl-

inder block and fail. The cap from one cylinder block cannot be installed on a different cylinder block.

To compensate for manufacturing variations, some engines are equipped with 0.009 in. undersized bearing inserts. On such engines, the cylinder block is stamped with a 9 mark on the front port side of the oil pan gasket, and the crankshaft is stamped with a 009 mark on the middle forward crankshaft flyweight. However, because 0.009 in. undersize bearings are not available separately, replace the bearings with 0.010 in. undersize main bearing inserts and check the main bearing clearance during assembly. On an engine with very low operating hours, the crankshaft may require machining to accept the 0.010 in. undersize bearings.

To fit precise factory tolerances, some engines are equipped with a 0.001 in. undersize and a standard size bearing insert on the same journal. Use standard size or 0.001 in. undersize bearings for service replacement.

### Rear Main Seal Replacement

The seal can be replaced without removing the oil pan or seal carrier.

1. Remove the engine coupler and flywheel as described in this chapter.

2. Insert a pry bar into one of the three seal retainer slots (**Figure 88**). Carefully pry the seal from the carrier. Discard the seal.

3. Use a quick drying solvent to clean the seal carrier.

4. Apply a light coating of Perfect Seal (Mercury part No. 92-34227-1) to the seal bore and the outer diameter of the seal. Apply a light coat of engine oil onto the seal lip.

5. Fit the seal into the carrier bore with the lip side facing inward. The seal retainers must align with the slots in the carrier (**Figure 88**). Use the seal installation tool (Kent-Moore part No. J-26817-A) and drive the seal fully into the bore.

6. Install the flywheel, engine coupler and housing as described in this chapter.

### Rear Main Seal and Carrier Replacement

1. Remove the engine coupler and flywheel as described in this chapter.

2. Remove the oil pan as described in this chapter. Remove the seal from the carrier as described in this chapter.

3. Remove the fasteners and carefully pry the carrier from the rear main bearing. Remove and discard the gasket.

**7**

4. Clean sealant and gasket material from the mating surfaces of the rear main bearing and the seal carrier. Fit a new gasket onto the seal carrier.

5. Align the locating pin and studs, then fit the carrier on the rear main bearing.

6. Apply a light coat of Loctite Pipe Sealant with Teflon onto the threads of the carrier fasteners. Install the fasteners and tighten them to the specification in **Table 1**.

7. Apply a light coat of engine oil to the seal lip. Install the seal into the carrier as described in this chapter.

8. Install the flywheel, engine coupler and oil pan as described in this chapter.

### Crankshaft Removal and Inspection

1. Remove the oil pan, oil pump, timing chain and cylinder heads as described in this chapter.

2. Remove the pistons and rods as described in this chapter. Remove the balance shaft (V6 models), camshaft and lifters as described in this chapter.

3. Position the crankshaft facing upward. Number the main bearing caps to indicate their locations on the cylinder block. Note the cast-in arrows or triangle marks on the bearing caps. The arrows or triangles must face the front of the engine.

4. Remove the rear main seal carrier as described in this chapter.

5. Remove the main bearing caps one at a time. Note the original mounting locations of each cap. Remove the lower bearing inserts (**Figure 87**) from the main bearing caps.

6. Carefully lift the crankshaft from the cylinder block. Place the crankshaft on a sturdy work surface with good lighting. Remove the upper main bearing inserts (**Figure 87**) from the cylinder block and inspect them. If the bearing inserts are discolored, scratched, corroded, pitted or have transferred material, inspect the crankshaft for defects.

7. Inspect the crankshaft journals and crankpins for cracks, discoloration, corrosion pitting, scratches and transferred material. Have the crankshaft machined to accept undersize bearings if any defects are present. Contact a MerCruiser dealership for undersize bearing availability before machining the crankshaft.

8. Use an outside micrometer to measure the diameter of the main and rod bearing journals (**Figure 89**). Take measurements at several points along the length of the journals and at several points around the circumference of the journals. Record all measurements for each journal.

   a. Subtract the smallest diameter at one end of the journal from the largest diameter at the other end of

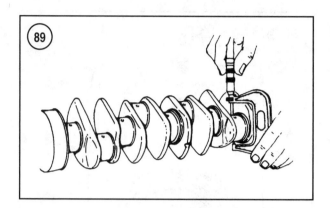

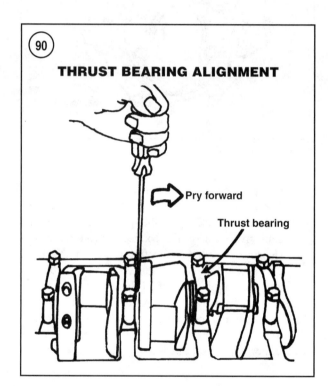

**THRUST BEARING ALIGNMENT**

Pry forward

Thrust bearing

the journal to determine the amount of bearing journal taper.

   b. Subtract the smallest diameter at one point along the length of the journal from the largest diameter taken around the circumference of the journal (and at the same point along the length) to determine the amount the journal is out of round.

   c. Have the crankshaft machined to accept the next undersize bearing inserts if any journal measurement exceeds the specification in **Table 7**.

9. Support the crankshaft with a V-block under the front and rear main bearing journals. Mount a dial indicator so the plunger touches one of the center main bearing journals. Zero the dial indicator. Observe the needle move-

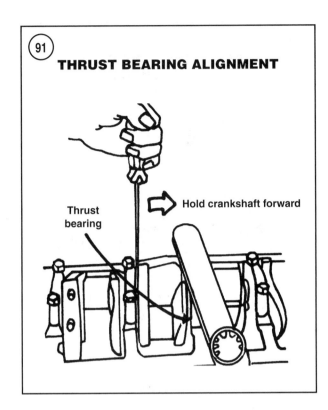

**THRUST BEARING ALIGNMENT**

Thrust bearing

Hold crankshaft forward →

ment while slowly rotating the crankshaft. The needle movement indicates the amount of crankshaft runout.

10. On 3.0L models, inspect the timing gear for worn, damaged or missing teeth.

If necessary, pull the gear from the crankshaft using a harmonic balancer puller or a suitable equivalent. Inspect the drive key and key slot in the crankshaft for excessive wear or damage. Tap a new gear onto the crankshaft using a suitable driver Make sure the gear seats fully on the shoulder on the crankshaft.

*Crankshaft installation*

1. Install the new main bearing inserts. The inserts with the grooves fit into the cylinder block. The inserts without grooves fit into the main bearing caps. Do not lubricate the inserts at this time.

2. Carefully lower the crankshaft into the cylinder block. Seat the crankshaft against the main bearings. Do not rotate the crankshaft.

3. Place sections of Plastigage (**Figure 85**) on the main bearing journals. The Plastigage must span the length of the journal and align with the bottom of the journal (**Figure 85**).

4. Fit the bearing into the main bearing cap. The bearing tang must fit into the notch in the cap. Install the main bearing cap onto the cylinder block. The arrow or triangle

marks must point toward the front of the engine. Install the main bearing bolts. Do not rotate the crankshaft.

5. Tighten the main bearing bolts as follows:

   a. On MX 6.2 models, evenly tighten all of the bolts to the first step specification in **Table 1**. Check for proper rod cam alignment as described. Tighten all of the bolts to the second step specification in **Table 1**. Tighten all of the bolts to the final step specification in **Table 1**.

   b. On 496 Mag and 496 Mag HO models, tighten the main bearing caps to the specification in **Table 1**. Use an angle torque gauge to tighten the inner bolts an additional 90°, then tighten the outer studs an additional 80°.

   c. On all other models, tighten the main bearing bolts evenly to the specification in **Table 1**.

6. Evenly loosen the bolts and studs. Remove the main bearing caps. Determine the connecting rod bearing clearance by comparing the width of the flattened Plastigage (**Figure 85**) with the marks on the envelope. Compare the clearance to the specification in **Table 7**.

   a. If the clearance exceeds the specification, measure the crankshaft as described in this chapter. Install either 0.001 or 0.002 in. undersize bearings to correct the clearance. Never install bearings with an undersize amount that exceeds the out-of-round measurement of the journal. Otherwise inadequate clearance could occur at the wider journal diameter.

   b. If the clearance is less than the specification, measure the crankshaft as described in this chapter. Check for improper bearing cap or bearing installation, debris, or an oil film between the cap or cylinder block and the bearings.

   c. If clearance is correct, use a fingernail to scrape the Plastigage from the journal and bearing. Apply engine oil to the crankshaft and bearing surfaces. Install the main bearing caps. Do not tighten the bolts at this time.

7. Tighten all except the rear main bearing bolts as described in Step 5.

8. Align the thrust bearing surfaces as follows:

   a. Insert a pry bar between one of the center main bearing caps and a crankshaft flyweight (**Figure 90**). Carefully pry the crankshaft toward the rear of the cylinder block.

   b. Move the pry bar to the gap on the other side of the main bearing cap. Carefully pry the crankshaft toward the front of the cylinder block (**Figure 91**).

   c. Maintain moderate pressure on the pry bar and tighten the rear main bearing cap as described in Step 5.

9. Measure the crankshaft end play as follows:

**7**

a. Gently pry the crankshaft toward the front of the cylinder block (**Figure 92**).

b. Maintain moderate pressure on the pry bar. Use a feeler gauge to measure the clearance between the rear main bearing and the thrust surface on the crankshaft. The crankshaft end play equals the thickness of the feeler gauge that passes through the gap with a slight drag.

c. Compare the end play with the specification in Table 7.

d. If the clearance exceeds the specification, check for wear on the rear main bearing and the crankshaft. Replace the rear main bearing and remeasure the end play. Replace the crankshaft if the excess end play persists.

e. If the clearance is less than the specification, loosen the rear main bearing cap and align the thrust bearing surfaces as described in Step 8. Tighten the main bearing bolts as described in Step 5.

10. Rotate the crankshaft several revolutions. Check for improper main bearing installation or inadequate clearance if binding or roughness occurs.

11. Install the rear main seal carrier and seal as described in this chapter.

12. Install the pistons and connecting rods as described in this chapter. Install the camshaft, lifters and balance shaft as described in this chapter.

13. Install the timing chain or gear, oil pump, oil pan and gear or chain cover as described in this chapter.

14. Install the cylinder head as described in this chapter. Install the harmonic balancer as described in this chapter.

15. Install the flywheel, engine coupler and housing as described in this chapter.

### BREAK-IN PROCEDURE

Perform the break-in procedure any time internal components of the engine are replaced. During the first few hours of running, many of the engine components must avoid full load until fully seated. Failure to properly break in the engine

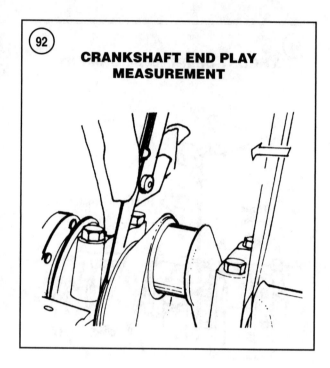

**92**

**CRANKSHAFT END PLAY MEASUREMENT**

can result in engine failure, decreased performance, short engine life and increased oil consumption.

An engine needs approximately 20 hours of running time to be fully broken in. Increased oil consumption can be expected during the this period. Check the oil frequently during break-in. Refer to Chapter Four. Check the tightness of all external fasteners during the break-in period.

1. During the first five hours of the break-in period, do not exceed 3500 rpm or half throttle. Do not run on any given throttle setting for more than a few minutes.

2. During the second five hours of operation, advance the engine to full throttle for two minutes or less. Otherwise run the engine at 3/4 throttle (3500 rpm) or less during the second five hours.

3. During the final ten hours, operate the engine at full throttle for a maximum of two minutes at a time. Otherwise run the engine at any throttle settings below full throttle.

## Table 1 TORQUE SPECIFICATIONS

| Fastener | ft.-lb. | in.-lb. | N•m |
|---|---|---|---|
| Cylinder head bolts | | | |
| 3.0L | 90 | – | 122 |
| 4.3L, 5.0L, 5.7L, 350 Mag | 22* | – | 30* |
| MX 6.2 | | | |
| First step | 26 | – | 35 |
| Second step | 44 | – | 60 |
| Final step | 70 | – | 95 |
| 7.4 MPI, 454 Mag, 502 Mag | | | |
| First step | 30 | – | 41 |
| Second step | 59 | – | 80 |
| Final step | | | |
| Short bolts | 89 | – | 120 |
| Long bolts | 92 | – | 125 |
| 496 Mag, 496 Mag HO | 22* | – | 30* |
| Rocker arm nuts | | | |
| 4.3L | 22 | – | 30 |
| 7.4L MPI, 454 Mag, 502 Mag | 40 | – | 54 |
| 496 Mag, 496 Mag HO | 19 | – | 26 |
| Rocker arm cover | | | |
| 3.0L | – | 44 | 5 |
| 4.3L, 5.0L, 5.7L, 350 Mag, MX 6.2 | – | 106 | 12 |
| 7.4 MPI, 454 Mag and 502 Mag | – | 71 | 8 |
| 496 Mag, 496 Mag HO | – | 106 | 12 |
| Intake manifold | | | |
| 4.3L | 11 | 133 | 15 |
| 5.0L, 5.7L, 350 Mag, MX 6.2 | 18 | – | 24 |
| 7.4 MPI | 30 | – | 41 |
| 454 Mag, 502 Mag | 35 | – | 47 |
| 496 Mag and 496 Mag HO | – | 106 | 12 |
| Lifter guide and retainer bolts | | | |
| 4.3L | 12 | 142 | 16 |
| 5.0L, 5.7L, 350 Mag, MX 6.2 | 18 | – | 24 |
| 7.4 MPI, 454 Mag, 502 Mag | 19 | – | 26 |
| 496 Mag and 496 Mag HO | 19 | – | 26 |
| Lifter/pushrod cover | | | |
| 3.0L | – | 44 | 5 |
| Camshaft thrust plate | | | |
| 3.0L | – | 80 | 9 |
| 4.3L | – | 106 | 12 |
| 496 Mag and 496 Mag HO | – | 106 | 12 |
| Camshaft sprocket bolts | | | |
| 4.3L | 20 | – | 27 |
| 5.0L, 5.7L, 350 Mag | 18 | – | 24 |
| All other models | 22 | – | 30 |
| Balance shaft thrust plate | | | |
| 4.3L | – | 124 | 14 |
| Balance shaft bolt | | | |
| 4.3L | 15* | – | 20* |
| Balance shaft drive gear stud bolt | 20 | – | 27 |
| Rear main seal carrier | | | |
| 3.0L, 4.3L | – | 133 | 15 |
| All other models | – | 106 | 12 |
| Main bearing caps | | | |
| 3.0L, 4.3L | 75 | – | 102 |
| 5.0L, 5.7L, 350 Mag | 77 | – | 105 |
| MX 6.2 | | | |
| First step | 15 | – | 20 |
| Second step | 50 | – | 68 |
| Final step | 75 | – | 102 |

(continued)

**Table 1 TORQUE SPECIFICATIONS (continued)**

| Fastener | ft.-lb. | in.-lb. | N•m |
|---|---|---|---|
| 7.4L MPI | 102 | – | 138 |
| 454 Mag, 502 Mag | 110 | – | 149 |
| 496 Mag and 496 Mag HO | | | |
| Bolt and stud | 22* | – | 30* |
| Rod caps | | | |
| 3.0L | 45 | – | 61 |
| 4.3L, 5.0L, 5.7L, 350 Mag | 20* | – | 27* |
| MX 6.2 | | | |
| First step | 20 | – | 27 |
| Final step | 45 | – | 61 |
| 7.4 MPI, 454 Mag, 502 Mag | | | |
| 3/8-24 nuts | 47 | – | 64 |
| 7/16-20 nuts | 73 | – | 99 |
| 496 Mag and 496 Mag HO | 22* | – | 30* |
| Oil pan | | | |
| 3.0L | | | |
| 1/4-20 fasteners | – | 80 | 9 |
| 5/16-18 fasteners | – | 168 | 19 |
| To timing gear cover | – | 44 | 5 |
| To rear main seal carrier | – | 15 | 1.7 |
| 4.3L | | | |
| 1/4-20 screws | – | 80 | 9 |
| 5/16-20 nuts | – | 165 | 19 |
| 5.0L, 5.7L, 350 Mag, MX 6.2 | | | |
| Corner nut (4) | 18 | – | 24 |
| 5/16-18 | – | 106 | 12 |
| 7.4 MPI, 454 Mag, 502 Mag | 18 | – | 25 |
| 496 Mag, 396 Mag HO | 19 | – | 26 |
| Oil pan drain plug | | | |
| 4.3L, 5.0L, 5.7L, 350 Mag | 15 | – | 20 |
| MX 6.2 | 18 | – | 25 |
| 7.4 MPI, 454 Mag, 502 Mag | 20 | – | 27 |
| 496 Mag, 396 Mag HO | 21 | – | 28 |
| Oil filter adapter | 20 | – | 27 |
| Oil by-pass valve | 20 | – | 27 |
| Oil splash plate | | | |
| All models | 25 | – | 34 |
| Flywheel bolts | | | |
| 3.0L | 75 | – | 102 |
| 4.3L, 50L, 5.7L, 350 Mag | 75 | – | 102 |
| MX 6.2 | 70 | – | 95 |
| 7.4 MPI, 454 Mag, 502 Mag | 65 | – | 88 |
| 496 Mag, 396 Mag HO | 74 | – | 100 |
| Coupler bolts (All models) | 35 | – | 47 |
| Flywheel housing bolts and studs (All models) | 30 | – | 41 |
| Flywheel housing shield | | | |
| All models | – | 80 | 9 |
| Timing chain/gear cover | | | |
| 3.0L | – | 97 | 11 |
| 4.3L | – | 124 | 14 |
| 5.0L, 5.7L, 350 Mag, MX 6.2 | – | 106 | 12 |
| 7.4L MPI, 454 Mag, 502 Mag | – | 89 | 10 |
| 496 Mag, 496 Mag HO | – | 106 | 12 |
| Oil pump mounting bolt | | | |
| 496 Mag, 496 Mag HO | 56 | – | 76 |
| All other models | 65 | – | 88 |
| Oil pump cover | | | |
| 3.0L | – | 80 | 9 |

(continued)

## Table 1 TORQUE SPECIFICATIONS (continued)

| Fastener | ft.-lb. | in.-lb. | N•m |
|---|---|---|---|
| 4.3L | – | 106 | 12 |
| 5.0L, 5.7L, 350 Mag | – | 80 | 9 |
| MX 6.2 | – | 106 | 12 |
| 7.4L MPI, 454 Mag, 502 Mag | – | 106 | 12 |
| 496 Mag, 496 Mag HO | – | 106 | 12 |
| Oil pump driver | | | |
| 496 Mag, 496 Mag HO | 19 | – | 26 |
| Oil pickup tube | – | 62 | 7 |
| Crankshaft pulley | | | |
| 3.0L | 35 | – | 47 |
| 4.3L | | | |
|   Steel | 35 | – | 47 |
|   Aluminum | 40 | – | 54 |
| 5.0L, 5.7L, 350 Mag | 35 | – | 48 |
| MX 6.2 | 43 | – | 58 |
| 7.4 MPI, 454 Mag, 502 Mag | 35 | – | 47 |
| Harmonic balancer bolt | | | |
| 3.0L | 70 | – | 95 |
| 4.3L, 5.0L, 5.7L, 350 Mag, MX 6.2 | 60 | – | 81 |
| 7.4 MPI, 454 Mag, 502 Mag | 110 | – | 149 |
| 496 Mag, 496 Mag HO | 189 | – | 256 |
| Remote oil filter adapter | | | |
|   adapter to engine | 20 | – | 27 |
|   1/2 x 13 connector | 25 | – | 34 |
| Oil line fittings | 20 | – | 27 |
| Rear engine mounts | 35-40 | – | 47-54 |
| Front or side engine mounts | | | |
| 3.0L | 21 | – | 28 |
| All other models | 30 | – | 41 |

*This value represents the first tightening sequence only. Perform the final torque using a torque angle gauge as described in Chapter Seven.

**7**

## Table 2 WARP LIMITS

| Surface | Maximum gap |
|---|---|
| Cylinder block (all models) | |
| 6 in. (152 mm) span | 0.003 in. (0.076 mm) |
| Overall length | 0.007 in. (0.177 mm) |
| Cylinder head | |
| 3.0L | |
| 6 in. (152 mm) span | 0.008 in. (0.203 mm) |
| Overall length | 0.007 in. (0.177mm) |
| 4.3L | 0.10 in. (0.254 mm) |
| 5.0L, 5.7L, 350 Mag, MX 6.2 | |
|   Cylinder block mating surface | 0.004 in. (0.101 mm) |
|   Exhaust manifold mating surface | 0.002 in. (0.050 mm) |
|   Intake manifold mating surface | 0.004 in. (0.101 mm) |
| 7.4L MPI | |
| 6 in. (152 mm) span | 0.003 in. (0.076 mm) |
| Overall length | 0.004 in. (0.101 mm) |
| 454 Mag, 502 Mag, | |
| 496 Mag, 496 Mag HO | |
| 6 in. (152 mm) span | 0.003 in. (0.076 mm) |
| Overall length | 0.007 in. (0.177 mm) |

**Table 3 CYLINDER BLOCK SPECIFICATIONS**

| Measurement | Specification |
|---|---|
| Cylinder bore diameter | |
| 3.0L | 3.9995-4.0025 in. (101.588-101.663 mm) |
| 4.3L | 4.0007-4.0017 in. (101.6178-101.6431 mm) |
| 5.0L | 3.7350-3.7384 in. (94.869-94.955 mm) |
| 5.7L, 350 Mag | 4.0000-4.0010 in. (101.600-101.625 mm) |
| MX 6.2 | 4.0007-4.0027 in. (101.618-101.669 mm) |
| 7.4L MPI | 4.2500-4.2507 in. (107.950-107.968 mm) |
| 454 Mag | 4.2451-4.2525 in. (107.826-108.013 mm) |
| 502 Mag | 4.4655-4.4662 in. (113.423-113.441 mm) |
| 496 Mag, 496 Mag HO | 4.2500-4.2507 in. (107.950-107.968 mm) |
| Maximum cylinder bore taper | |
| All models | 0.001 in. 0.0254 mm) |
| Maximum cylinder bore out of round | |
| All models | 0.002 in. (0.050 mm) |
| Balance shaft bearing bore | |
| 4.3L | 1.873-1.874 in. (47.574-47.599 mm) |

**Table 4 CAMSHAFT SPECIFICATIONS**

| Measurement | Specification |
|---|---|
| Lobe lift | |
| 3.0L | |
| Intake | 0.2529 in. (6.424 mm) |
| Exhaust | 0.2529 in. (6.424 mm) |
| 4.3L | |
| Intake | 0.286-0.290 in. (7.264-7.366 mm) |
| Exhaust | 0.292-0.296 in. (7.417-7.518 mm) |
| 5.0L, 5.7L, 350 Mag | |
| Intake | 0.2744-0.2783 in. (6.969-7.068 mm) |
| Exhaust | 0.2834-0.2874 in. (7.198-7.299 mm) |
| MX 6.2 | |
| Intake | N/A |
| Exhaust | N/A |
| 7.4L MPI | |
| Intake | 0.280-0.284 in. (7.112-7.213 mm) |
| Exhaust | 0.282-0.286 in. (7.163-7.264 mm) |
| 454 Mag, 502 Mag | |
| Intake | 0.299-0.303 in. (7.595-7.696 mm) |
| Exhaust | 0.299-0.303 in. (7.595-7.696 mm) |
| 496 Mag | |
| Intake | 0.280-0.284 in. (7.112-7.213 mm) |
| Exhaust | 0.282-0.286 in. (7.163-7.264 mm) |
| 496 Mag HO | |
| Intake | 0.298-0.302 in. (7.569-7.671 mm) |
| Exhaust | 0.298-0.302 in. (7.569-7.671 mm) |
| Journal diameter | |
| 3.0L | 1.8677-1.8697 in. (47.440-47.490 mm) |
| 4.3L, 5.0L, 5.7L, 350 Mag, MX 6.2 | 1.8682-1.8692 in. (47.452-47.478 mm) |
| 7.4L MPI, 454 Mag, 502 Mag | 1.9482-1.9492 in. (49.485-49.509 mm) |
| 496 Mag, 496 Mag HO | 1.9477-1.9479 in. (49.472-49.477 mm) |
| Maximum journal out of round | |
| All models | 0.001 in. 0.0254 mm) |
| Maximum camshaft runout | |
| All models | 0.002 in. (0.058 mm) |
| Camshaft end play | |
| 3.0L | 0.001-0.005 in. (0.024-0.127 mm) |

N/A—Not available.

**Table 5 TIMING CHAIN AND GEAR SPECIFICATIONS**

| Measurement | Specification |
| --- | --- |
| **Maximum timing gear runout** | |
| 3.0L | 0.004 in. (0.101 mm) |
| **Timing gear backlash** | |
| 3.0L | 0.004-0.006 in. (0.101-0.152 mm) |
| **Maximum timing chain deflection** | |
| 5.0L, 5.7L, 350 Mag | 0.43 in. (10.9 mm) |
| All other models | 0.375 in. (9.5 mm) |

**Table 6 PISTON SPECIFICATIONS**

| Measurement | Specification |
| --- | --- |
| **Piston skirt clearance** | |
| 3.0L | 0.0025-0.0035 in. (0.064-0.088 mm) |
| 4.3L | 0.0007-0.0020 in. (0.018-0.050 mm) |
| 5.0L, 5.7L, 350 Mag | 0.0007-0.0026 in. (0.018-0.066 mm) |
| MX 6.2 | 0.002-0.004 in. (0.051-0.102 mm) |
| 7.4L MPI | 0.0018-0.0030 in. (0.046-0.076 mm) |
| 454 Mag | 0.0025-0.0075 in. (0.064-0.190 mm) |
| 502 Mag | 0.0040-0.0065 in. (0.102-0.165 mm) |
| 496 Mag, 496 Mag HO | – |
| **Compression ring side clearance** | |
| 3.0L Top and second ring | 0.0012-0.0030 in. (0.030-0.076 mm) |
| 4.3L Top and second ring | 0.0020-0.0040 in. (0.051-0.101 mm) |
| 5.0L, 5.7L, 350 Mag | |
|   Top ring | 0.0012-0.0035 in. (0.030-0.088 mm) |
|   Second ring | 0.0015-0.0040 in. (0.038-0.101 mm) |
| MX 6.2 | |
|   Top and second ring | 0.0012-0.0042 in. (0.003-0.107 mm) |
| 7.4L MPI | |
|   Top and second ring | 0.0012-0.0039 in. (0.030-0.099 mm) |
| 454 Mag, 502 Mag | |
|   Top and second ring | 0.0017-0.0042 in. (0.043-0.107 mm) |
| 496 Mag, 496 Mag HO | |
|   Top and second ring | 0.0012-0.0039 in. (0.030-0.099 mm) |
| **Oil ring side clearance** | |
| 3.0L | 0.001-0.007 in. (0.025-0.177 mm) |
| 4.3L | 0.002-0.008 in. (0.051-0.203 mm) |
| 5.0L | 0.002-0.008 in. (0.051-0.203 mm) |
| 5.7L, 350 Mag | 0.002-0.0076 in. (0.051-0.193 mm) |
| MX 6.2 | 0.002-0.008 in. (0.051-0.203 mm) |
| 7.4L MPI, 454 Mag, 502 Mag | 0.0050-0.0075 in. (0.127-0.190 mm) |
| 496 Mag, 496 Mag HO | – |
| **Compression ring gap** | |
| 3.0L | |
|   Top and second ring | 0.010-0.035 in. (0.254-0.889 mm) |
| 4.3L | |
|   Top ring | 0.010-0.035 in. (0.254-0.889 mm) |
|   Second ring | 0.018-0.035 in. (0.457-0.889 mm) |
| 5.0L, 5.7L, 350 Mag | |
|   Top ring | 0.009-0.025 in. (0.228-0.635 mm) |
|   Second ring | 0.010-0.035 in. (0.254-0.889 mm) |
| MX 6.2 | |
|   Top and second ring | 0.016-0.036 in. (0.406-0.914 mm) |
| 7.4L MPI, 454 Mag | |
|   Top ring | 0.010-0.028 in. (0.254-0.722 mm) |
|   Second ring | 0.016-0.034 in. (0.406-0.863 mm) |
| | *(continued)* |

7

### Table 6 PISTON SPECIFICATIONS (continued)

| Measurement | Specification |
|---|---|
| 502 Mag | |
|   Top ring | 0.011-0.031 in. (0.279-0.787 mm) |
|   Second ring | 0.016-0.036 in. (0.406-0.914 mm) |
| 496 Mag, 496 Mag HO | |
|   Top ring | 0.0098-0.0161 in. (0.248-0.409 mm) |
|   Second ring | 0.0177-0.0256 in. (0.450-0.650 mm) |
| Oil ring gap | |
|   3.0L | 0.010-0.040 in. (0.254-1.016 mm) |
|   4.3L | 0.009-0.065 in. (0.229-1.651 mm) |
|   5.0L | 0.009-0.035 in. (0.229-0.889 mm) |
|   5.7L, 350 Mag | 0.009-0.030 in. (0.229-0.762 mm) |
|   MX 6.2 | 0.010-0.060 in. (0.254-1.52 mm) |
|   7.4L MPI | 0.010-0.031 in. (0.254-0.787 mm) |
|   454 Mag | 0.020-0.045 in. (0.508-1.143 mm) |
|   502 Mag | 0.010-0.035 in. (0.254-0.889 mm) |
|   496 Mag, 496 Mag HO | 0.0098-0.0099 in. (0.248-0.251 mm) |
| Piston pin diameter | |
|   3.0L | 0.9270-0.9271 in. (23.546-23.548 mm) |
|   4.3L | 0.9267-0.9271 in. (23.538-23.548 mm) |
|   5.0L, 5.7L, 350 Mag | 0.9269-0.9270 in. (23.543-23.546 mm) |
|   MX 6.2 | 0.9270-0.9271 in. (23.546-23.548 mm) |
|   7.4L MPI | 0.9895-0.9897 in. (25.133-25.138 mm) |
|   454 Mag, 502 Mag | 0.9995-0.9898 in. (25.133-25.140 mm) |
|   496 Mag, 496 Mag HO | 1.0400-1.0401 in. (26.416-26.418 mm) |
| Piston pin to pin bore clearance | |
|   3.0L | 0.0003-0.001 in. (0.0076-0.0254 mm) |
|   4.3L | 0.0002-0.001 in. (0.0051-0.0254 mm) |
|   5.0L, 5.7L, 350 Mag | 0.0005-0.001 in. (0.0127-0.0254 mm) |
|   6.2 MX | 0.0004-0.001 in. (0.010-0.0254 mm) |
|   7.4L MPI, 454 Mag, 502 Mag | 0.0002-0.001 in. (0.0051-0.0254 mm) |
|   496 Mag, 496 Mag HO | 0.00039-0.00066 in. (0.0099-0.0168 mm) |
| Piston pin to rod (interference) | |
|   3.0L | 0.0008-0.0019 in. (0.002-0.048 mm) |
|   4.3L, 5.0L, 5.7L, 350 Mag | 0.0008-0.0016 in. (0.020-0.041 mm) |
|   MX 6.2 | 0.0015-0.0020 in. (0.038-0.051 mm) |
|   7.4L MPI | 0.0021-0.0031in. (0.0533-0.0787) |
|   454 Mag, 502 Mag | 0.0008-0.0016 in. (0.020-0.041 mm) |
|   496 Mag, 496 Mag HO | 0.00019-0.0007 in. (0.0048-0.0178 mm) |

### Table 7 CRANKSHAFT AND CONNECTING ROD SPECIFICATIONS

| Measurement | Specification |
|---|---|
| Main journal diameter | |
|   3.0L | 2.2979-2.2994 in. (58.367-58.404 mm) |
|   4.3L | |
|     No. 1 journal | 2.4488-2.4495 in. (62.197-62.217 mm) |
|     No. 2 and 3 journal | 2.4485-2.4494 in. (62.192-62.215 mm) |
|     No. 4 journal | 2.4479-2.4489 in. (62.177-62.202 mm) |
|   5.0L, 5.7L, 350 Mag | |
|     No. 1 journal | 2.4483-2.4492 in. (62.187-62.209 mm) |
|     No. 2-4 journal | 2.4480-2.4490 in. (62.179-62.204 mm) |
|     No. 5 journal | 2.4479-2.4490 in. (62.177-62.204 mm) |
|   MX 6.2 | 2.4480-2.4485 in. (62.178-62.192 mm) |
|   7.4L MPI, 454 Mag, 502 Mag | 2.7482-2.7489 in. (69.8043-69.8220 mm) |
|   496 Mag, 496 Mag HO | 2.7482-2.7489 in. (69.8043-69.8220 mm) |
| (continued) | |

**Table 7 CRANKSHAFT AND CONNECTING ROD SPECIFICATIONS (continued)**

| Measurement | Specification |
|---|---|
| Maximum main journal out of round (All models) | 0.001 in. (0.0254 mm) |
| Maximum main journal taper (All models) | 0.001 in. (0.0254 mm) |
| Maximum crankshaft gear runout | |
| 3.0L | 0.003 in. (0.076 mm) |
| Main bearing oil clearance | |
| 3.0L | |
| No. 1-4 journal | 0.001-0.0025 in. (0.0254-0.0635 mm) |
| No. 5 journal | 0.002-0.0035 in. (0.0510-0.0889 mm) |
| 4.3L (All journals) | 0.001-0.002 in. (0.0254-0.0510 mm) |
| 5.0L, 5.7L, 350 Mag | |
| No. 1 journal | 0.0007-0.002 in. (0.018-0.0510 mm) |
| No. 2-4 journal | 0.0009-0.0025 in. (0.023-0.0635 mm) |
| No. 5 journal | 0.001-0.0029 in. (0.0254-0.0736 mm) |
| MX 6.2 | |
| No. 1-4 journal | 0.0015-0.0030 in. (0.0381-0.0.0762 mm) |
| No. 5 journal | 0.0025-0.0035 in. (0.0635-0.0889 mm) |
| 7.4L MPI, 454 Mag | |
| No. 1-4 journal | 0.001-0.0030 in. (0.0254-0.0762 mm) |
| No. 5 journal | 0.0025-0.0040 in. (0.0635-0.1016 mm) |
| 502 Mag | |
| No. 1 journal | 0.0010-0.0015 in. (0.0254-0.0381 mm) |
| No. 2-4 journal | 0.0010-0.0025 in. (0.0254-0.0635 mm) |
| No. 5 journal | 0.0025-0040 in. (0.0635-0.1016 mm) |
| 496 Mag, 496 Mag HO | |
| No. 1-4 journal | 0.0011-0.0024 in. (0.0279-0.0609 mm) |
| No. 5 journal | 0.0025-0.0038 in. (0.0635-0.0965 mm) |
| Rod journal diameter | |
| 3.0L | 2.0980-2.0995 in. (53.2892-53.3273 mm) |
| 4.3L | 2.2487-2.2497 in. (57.1170-57.1424 mm) |
| 5.0L, 5.7L, 350 Mag | 2.0977-2.0997 in. (53.2816-53.3323 mm) |
| MX 6.2 | 2.0990-2.0995 in. (53.3146-53.3273 mm) |
| 7.4L MPI, 454 Mag, 502 Mag | 2.1990-2.1996 in. (55.8546-55.8698 mm) |
| 496 Mag, 496 Mag HO | – |
| Maximum rod journal out of round (All models) | 0.001 in. (0.0254 mm) |
| Maximum rod journal taper (All models) | 0.001 in. (0.0254 mm) |
| Connecting rod bearing oil clearance | |
| 3.0L | 0.0017-0.0027 in. (0.043-0.068 mm) |
| 4.3L | 0.001-0.003 in. (0.025-0.0.076 mm) |
| 5.0L, 5.7L, 350 Mag | 0.0013-0.00029 in. (0.033-0.073 mm) |
| MX 6.2 | 0.0015-0.003 in. (0.038-0.076 mm) |
| 7.4L MPI | 0.0011-0.0029 in. (0.028-0.073 mm) |
| 454 Mag, 502 Mag | 0.0011-0.003 in. (0.028-0.076 mm) |
| 496 Mag, 496 Mag HO | 0.0011-0.0029 in. (0.028-0.073 mm) |
| Connecting rod side clearance | |
| 3.0L | 0.006-0.014 in. (0.152-0.355 mm) |
| 4.3L | 0.006-0.017 in. (0.152-0.431 mm) |
| 5.0L, 5.7L, 350 Mag | 0.006-0.024 in. (0.152-0.609 mm) |
| MX 6.2 | 0.008-0.017 in. (0.203-0.431 mm) |
| 7.4L MPI, 454 Mag, 502 Mag | 0.013-0.023 in. (0.330-0.584 mm) |
| 496 Mag, 496 Mag HO | 0.015-0.027 in. (0.381-0.685 mm) |
| Crankshaft end play | |
| 3.0L | 0.002-0.006 in. (0.05-0.152 mm) |
| 4.3L | 0.002-0.008 in. (0.05-0.202 mm) |
| 5.0L, 5.7L, 350 Mag | 0.0019-0.0078 in. (0.048-0.198 mm) |
| MX 6.2 | 0.002-0.008 in. (0.05-0.202 mm) |
| 7.4L MPI | 0.005-0.011 in. (0.127-0.279 mm) |
| 454 Mag, 502 Mag | 0.001-0.006 in. (0.025-0.152 mm) |
| 496 Mag, 496 Mag HO | 0.005-0.011 in. (0.127-0.279 mm) |

(continued)

**7**

**Table 7 CRANKSHAFT AND CONNECTING ROD SPECIFICATIONS (continued)**

| Measurement | Specification |
| --- | --- |
| Maximum crankshaft runout | |
| 4.3L | 0.001 in. (0.0254 mm) |
| 5.0L, 5.7L, 350 Mag | 0.0019 in. (0.0482 mm) |
| MX 6.2 | 0.0015 in. (0.0381 mm) |
| 7.4 MPI | – |
| 454 Mag | 0.0015 in. (0.0381 mm) |
| 502 Mag | 0.0035 in. (0.0889 mm) |
| 496 Mag, 496 Mag HO | – |
| Maximum flywheel runout (All models) | 0.008 in. (0.203 mm) |

**Table 8 BALANCE SHAFT SPECIFICATIONS**

| Measurement | Specification |
| --- | --- |
| Front bearing journal | 2.1648-2.1654 in. (54.986-55.001 mm) |
| Rear bearing journal | 1.499-1.500 in. (38.084-38.100 mm) |
| Rear bearing outer diameter | 1.875-1.876 in. (47.625-47.650 mm) |
| Rear bearing inside diameter | 1.501-1.503 in. (38.125-38.176 mm) |
| Rear bearing journal clearance | 0.001-0.036 in. (0.025-0.091 mm) |

**Table 9 VALVE AND SEAT SPECIFICATIONS**

| Measurement | Specification |
| --- | --- |
| Rocker arm ratio | |
| 3.0L | 1.75 to 1 |
| 4.3L, 5.0L, 5.7L, 350 Mag, MX 6.2 | 1.50 to 1 |
| 7.4L MPI, 454 Mag, 502 Mag | 1.70 to 1 |
| 496 Mag, 496 Mag HO | 1.70 to 1 |
| Valve face angle (All models) | 45° |
| Minimum valve margin (All models) | 0.031 in. (0.794 mm) |
| Valve seat angle (All models) | 46° |
| Valve seat width | |
| 3.0L | |
|   Intake | 0.0625 in. (1.58 mm) |
|   Exhaust | 0.0625-0.078 in. (1.58-1.98 mm) |
| 4.3L | |
|   Intake | 0.035-0.060 in. (0.89-1.52 mm) |
|   Exhaust | 0.062-0.093 in. (1.57-2.36 mm) |
| 5.0L | |
|   Intake | 0.035-0.070 in. (0.89-1.77 mm) |
|   Exhaust | 0.065-0.098 in. (1.65-2.48 mm) |
| 5.7L, 350 Mag | |
|   Intake | 0.040-0.065 in. (1.02-1.65 mm) |
|   Exhaust | 0.060-0.100 in. (1.52-2.54 mm) |
| MX 6.2 | |
|   Intake | 0.040-0.065 in. (1.02-1.65 mm) |
|   Exhaust | 0.065-0.098 in. (1.65-2.48 mm) |
| 7.4L MPI | |
|   Intake | 0.030-0.060 in. (0.76-1.52 mm) |
|   Exhaust | 0.060-0.095 in. (1.52-3.41 mm) |
| 454 Mag, 502 Mag | |
|   Intake | 0.031-0.062 in. (0.79-1.57 mm) |
|   Exhaust | 0.063-0.094 in. (1.60-2.38 mm) |
| | (continued) |

**Table 9 VALVE AND SEAT SPECIFICATIONS (continued)**

| Measurement | Specification |
|---|---|
| **496 Mag, 496 Mag HO** | |
| Intake | 0.030-0.060 in. (0.76-1.52 mm) |
| Exhaust | 0.060-0.095 in. (1.52-3.41 mm) |
| **Valve stem diameter** | |
| 3.0L, 4.3L, 5.0L, 5.7L, 350 Mag, MX 6.2 | |
| Standard | 0.341 in. (8.661 mm) |
| Oversize | 0.356 in. (9.042 mm) |
| 7.4L MPI, 454 Mag, 502 Mag | |
| Standard | 0.372 in. (9.449 mm) |
| Oversize | 0.387 in. (9.829 mm) |
| 496 Mag, 496 Mag HO | |
| Intake | 0.3715-0.3722 in. (9.436-9.454 mm) |
| Exhaust | 0.3713-0.3720 in. (9.431-9.449 mm) |
| **Valve stem clearance** | |
| 3.0L | |
| Intake | 0.001-0.003 in. (0.025-0.076 mm) |
| Exhaust | 0.0007-0.004 in. (0.018-0.101 mm) |
| 4.3L | |
| Intake and exhaust | 0.0011-0.0027 in. (0.028-0.068 mm) |
| 5.0L | |
| Intake and exhaust | 0.001-0.0037 in. (0.025-0.093 mm) |
| 5.7L, 350 Mag, MX 6.2 | |
| Intake | 0.001-0.0037 in. (0.025-0.093 mm) |
| Exhaust | 0.001-0.0076 in. (0.025-0.193 mm) |
| 7.4L MPI, 502 Mag | |
| Intake | 0.0010-0.0037 in. (0.0254-0.0939 mm) |
| Exhaust | 0.0012-0.0049 in. (0.0305-0.1244 mm) |
| 454 Mag | |
| Intake | 0.001-0.003 in. (0.025-0.076 mm) |
| Exhaust | 0.0012-0.004 in. (0.030-0.101 mm) |
| 496 Mag, 496 Mag HO | |
| Intake | 0.001-0.0029 in. (0.025-0.074 mm) |
| Exhaust | 0.0012-0.0031 in. (0.030-0.0079 mm) |
| Maximum valve seat runout (All models) | 0.002 in. (0.05 mm) |

**7**

**Table 10 VALVE SPRING SPECIFICATIONS**

| Measurement | Specification |
|---|---|
| **Free length** | |
| 3.0L | 2.06 (52.3 mm) |
| 4.3L | 2.03 in. (51.6 mm) |
| 5.0L, 5.7L, 350 Mag, MX 6.2 | 2.019 in. (51.2 mm) |
| 7.4L MPI | 2.12 in. (53.8 mm) |
| 454 Mag, 502 Mag | |
| Outer spring | 2.15 in. (54.6 mm) |
| Inner spring | 1.86 in. (47.2 mm) |
| 496 Mag, 496 Mag HO | 2.1929 in. (55.7 mm) |
| **Spring height (installed)** | |
| 3.0L | |
| Intake and exhaust | 1.63-1.68 in. (41.4-42.6 mm) |
| 4.3L | |
| Intake | 1.78 in. (45.2 mm) |
| Exhaust | 1.69-1.71 in. (42.9-43.4 mm) |
| 5.0L, 5.7L, 350 Mag, MX 6.2 | |
| Intake and exhaust | 1.68-1.70 in. (42.7-43.1 mm) |
| 7.4L MPI | |
| Intake and exhaust | 1.76-1.91 in. (44.7-48.51 mm) |
| | (continued) |

**TABLE 10 VALVE SPRING SPECIFICATIONS (continued)**

| Measurement | Specification |
|---|---|
| Spring height (installed) | |
|   454 Mag, 502 Mag | |
|     Intake and exhaust | 1.88 in. (47.7 mm) |
|   496 Mag, 496 Mag HO | |
|     Intake and exhaust | 1.838-1.869 in. (46.7-47.5 mm) |
| Valves spring pressure | |
|   3.0L | |
|     Closed 1.59 in. (40.3 mm) | 100-110 lb. (445-489 N) |
|     Open 1.22 in. (30.9 mm) | 208-220 lb. (925-978 N) |
|   4.3L, 5.0L, 5.7L, 350 Mag, MX 6.2 | |
|     Closed 1.70 in. (43.2 mm) | 76-84 lb. (338-374 N) |
|     Open 1.27 in. (32.3 mm) | 187-203 lb. (832-903 N) |
|   7.4L MPI | |
|     Closed 1.838 in. (46.7 mm) | 71-79 lb. (316-351 N) |
|     Open 1.347 in. (34.2 mm) | 238-262 lb. (1059-1165 N) |
|   454 Mag, 502 Mag | |
|     Closed 1.88 in. (47.8 mm) | 110 lb. (489 N) |
|     Open 1.34 in. (34 mm) | 316 lb. (1406 N) |
|   496 Mag, 496 Mag HO | |
|     Closed 1.838 in. (46.7 mm) | 58-64 lb. (267-293 N) |
|     Open 1.34 in. (34 mm) | 189-207 lb. (840-921 N) |

**Table 11 ENGINE FIRING ORDER**

| | |
|---|---|
| 3.0L models | 1-3-4-2 |
| 4.3L models | 1-6-5-4-3-2 |
| 5.0L, 5.7L, 350 Mag, MX 6.2 | 1-8-4-3-6-5-7-2 |
| MX 6.2 | 1-8-4-3-6-5-7-2 |
| 7.4L MPI, 454 Mag, 502 Mag | 1-8-4-3-6-5-7-2 |
| 496 Mag, 496 Mag HO | 1-8-7-2-6-5-4-3 |

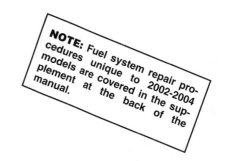

NOTE: Fuel system repair procedures unique to 2002-2004 models are covered in the supplement at the back of the manual.

# Chapter Eight

# Fuel System

8

This chapter describes replacement and repair procedures for all fuel system components.

Torque specifications are provided in **Table 1**. Carburetor specifications are provided in **Table 2**. **Tables 1** and **2** are located at the end of this chapter.

> *WARNING*
> *Use caution when working with the fuel system. Never smoke around fuel or fuel vapor. Make sure no flame or source of ignition is present in the work area. Flame or sparks can ignite fuel or vapor resulting in fire or explosion.*

Always use gloves and eye protection when working with the fuel system. Take all necessary precautions to prevent fire and explosion. Always disconnect the battery cables *before* servicing the engine. Drain fuel from disconnected hoses or fittings into a small container or clean shop towel. A clear container is best, because it allows a visual inspection of the fuel. Clean the fuel tank and all other fuel delivery components if the fuel is contaminated by debris, water or other fluids.

Inspect all hoses for leaks or deterioration. Damaged fuel hoses pose a safety hazard. Also, pieces of deteriorated or damaged hoses can break free and block fuel passages in the system.

## GASKETS, SEALS AND O-RINGS

To prevent fuel or air leakage, replace all seals and O-rings every time a fuel system component is removed from the engine. To minimize down time and the potential for contamination, have the required gasket or repair kit on hand before disassembling the system.

To ensure a safe and reliable repair use only factory recommended replacement parts. Some commonly available seals or O-rings are not suitable for contact with fuel.

### Cleaning the Fuel System and Other Components

The most important step in carburetor or fuel pump repair is the cleaning process. Use only solvents suitable for use on carburetors. Some cleaning agents can damage fuel system components. Spray-type carburetor cleaners are available at most auto parts stores. They effectively remove most stubborn deposits. Avoid any solvents not suitable for aluminum.

Remove all plastic or rubber components from the fuel pump, carburetor or filter before cleaning them with solvent. Gently scrape away gasket material. Use a stiff brush and solvent to remove deposits from the carburetor bowl. Never use a wire brush, which may damage the sealing surfaces. Clear all passages with compressed air (**Figure 1**). A piece of straw from a broom works well to

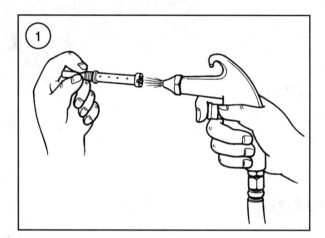

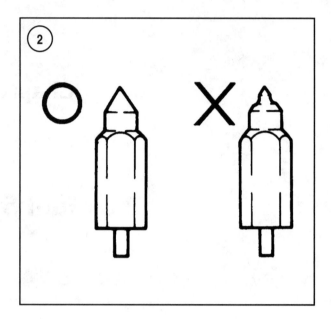

clean small passages. Never use stiff wire for this purpose as the wire may enlarge the size of the passage, possibly altering the carburetor calibration. Soak components in solvent for several hours if the deposits are particularly difficult to remove.

Use care and patience when removing fuel jets and other threaded or pressed-in components. Clean the passage without removing the jet if it cannot be removed without causing damage. Carburetor fuel jets are easily damaged.

One small particle left in the carburetor can cause poor performance. Continue cleaning until *all* deposits and debris are removed.

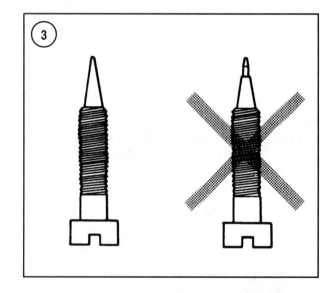

## CARBURETOR INSPECTION

Place all components on a clean surface as they are removed from the carburetor and cleaned.

Inspect the inlet needle for wear or deterioration (**Figure 2**). The tip should be perfectly cone-shaped. Inspect the inlet needle seat for grooves or damage. Carburetor flooding is likely if a worn or faulty inlet needle or seat is used.

Inspect the tip of the idle mixture screw for wear or damage (**Figure 3**). Damage to the tip usually occurs from improper seating of the screw during adjustment. In many instances the seat for the tip is also damaged. Damage to the screw or seat will cause rough idle and poor off-idle engine operation. Replace the screw or carburetor if either are damaged.

Inspect the float (**Figure 4**, typical) for wear or damage. Push a thumbnail gently against the body of the float. If fuel appears at the thumbnail contact area, the float is probably saturated and must be replaced. Inspect the float arm for elongation of the pivot pin bore. Replace the float if leakage or elongation of the pivot pin bore is noted.

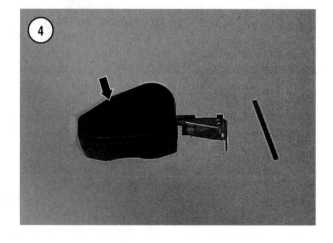

Adjust the float level settings (**Figure 5**) before assembling the carburetor. Use an accurate ruler or a caliper with depth-reading capability. Set the float *exactly* as specified. Specific instructions are provided in the carburetor disassembly and assembly procedure. Float level specifications are listed in **Table 2**.

## Fuel Jets

The fuel jets (**Figure 6**) and power valve (**Figure 7**) control the air/fuel mixture to the engine. Fuel jets nor-

mally have a number stamped on the side or end. Note the fuel jet number and location in the carburetor prior to removal. Reinstall the fuel jets and other carburetor components into their original locations.

Purchase replacement jets at a MerCruiser dealership or a carburetor specialty shop. For proper engine operation, replacement jets must have the same size and shape of opening as the original fuel jets. Using the wrong fuel jets can cause poor engine operation, increased exhaust emissions and potentially serious engine damage.

Operating the engine at elevations above 5000 ft. (1524 m) may require alternative fuel jets to achieve optimal engine operation. If necessary, contact a MerCruiser dealership in an area with a similar elevation for recommended jet changes.

Never install a damaged jet in the carburetor. The fuel or air flow characteristics may be altered, resulting in engine malfunction or serious engine damage.

### Flame Arrestor Removal and Installation (Carburetor and TBI Fuel Injection)

Refer to **Figure 8**.

1. Remove the nut and sealing washer (1 and 2, **Figure 8**). Lift the cover from the flame arrestor.

2. Pull the breather tube(s) from the flame arrestor fittings. Lift the flame arrestor from the carburetor. On models without clamps and fittings, lift the aluminum brace over the flame arrestor cover.

3. Wipe debris from the cover with a wet shop towel.

4. Clean the flame arrestor with nonflammable solvent and dry with compressed air.

5. Inspect the flame arrestor for bent or damaged surfaces. Replace the arrestor if damaged. Operating the engine with a dirty, missing or damaged arrestor poses a safety hazard.

6. Install by reversing the above steps, and note the following:

   a. Attach the breather tube(s) onto the flame arrestor fittings.

   b. Install the sealing washer (2, **Figure 8**) with the rubber side facing the flame arrestor.

   c. Do not over-tighten the nut, or the cover will crack.

## CARBURETOR

### Removal and Installation

1. Remove the flame arrestor as described in this chapter.

2. On 3.0L models, pull the sight hose (**Figure 9**) from the air horn fitting.

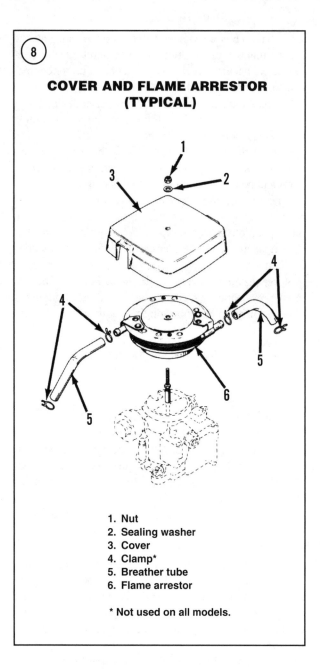

**COVER AND FLAME ARRESTOR
(TYPICAL)**

1. Nut
2. Sealing washer
3. Cover
4. Clamp*
5. Breather tube
6. Flame arrestor

* Not used on all models.

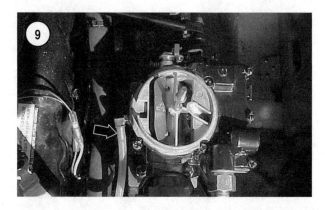

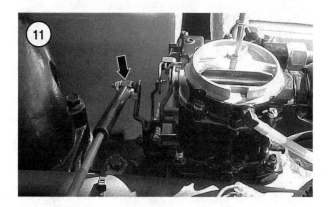

3. Carefully disconnect the choke heater wire (A, **Figure 10**). Disconnect the PVC hose (if so equipped) from the fitting on the back of the carburetor.

4. Remove the screw and pull the ground wire terminal (B, **Figure 10**) from the choke housing.

5. Remove the fasteners and the cable end (**Figure 11**, typical) from the throttle linkage.

6. Place a suitable container or shop towel under the fuel line fitting to catch spilled fuel.

7. Hold the fuel inlet fitting (A, **Figure 12**, typical) with a wrench and loosen the fuel line fitting (B). Pull the fuel line from the inlet fitting.

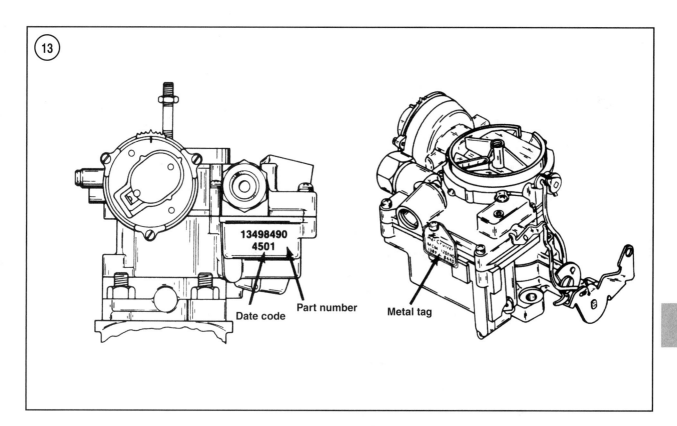

**13**

13498490
4501

Date code    Part number    Metal tag

**8**

8. Remove the mounting fasteners (C, **Figure 12**, typical). Pull the carburetor from the manifold.

9. Carefully scrape all gasket material from the manifold and carburetor base. Be careful not to damage the mating surfaces. Cover the intake openings with a shop towel or a piece of cardboard to keep debris out of the manifold.

10. Remove the cover from the intake manifold. Install a new gasket onto the manifold.

11. Set the carburetor on the manifold. Install the mounting bolts or nuts and tighten them to the specification in **Table 1**.

12. Thread the fuel line fitting into the fuel inlet fitting. Hold the fuel inlet fitting to prevent rotation. Tighten the fuel line fitting to the specification in **Table 1**.

13. Connect the choke heater wire to the choke heater. Secure the choke ground wire to the choke housing with the cover screw. Connect the PVC hose to its carburetor fitting (if so equipped).

14. Fit the cable end onto the throttle linkage. Install the washer and nut. Securely tighten the nut. The cable end must pivot freely on the throttle linkage.

15. Install the flame arrestor cover as described in this chapter.

16. Start the engine and immediately check for fuel leakage. Immediately stop the engine if leakage occurs. Correct the source of leakage before proceeding.

17. Adjust the idle mixture and idle speed as described in Chapter Six.

**Two-Barrel Carburetor**

Locate the carburetor part number and date code on the metal tag or the carburetor casting (**Figure 13**). This information may be required when ordering replacement parts.

*WARNING*
*Use caution when working with the fuel system. Never smoke around fuel or fuel vapor. Make sure no flame or source of ignition is present in the work area. Flame or sparks can ignite fuel or vapor, causing fire or explosion.*

*Disassembly*

Refer to **Figure 14**.

1. Remove the clip from the accelerator pump linkage (A, **Figure 15**). Separate the linkage from the throttle linkage. Remove the screw (B, **Figure 15**).

2. Position the linkage and cam as shown in **Figure 16**. Separate the linkage from the choke valve lever. Separate the cam from the linkage.

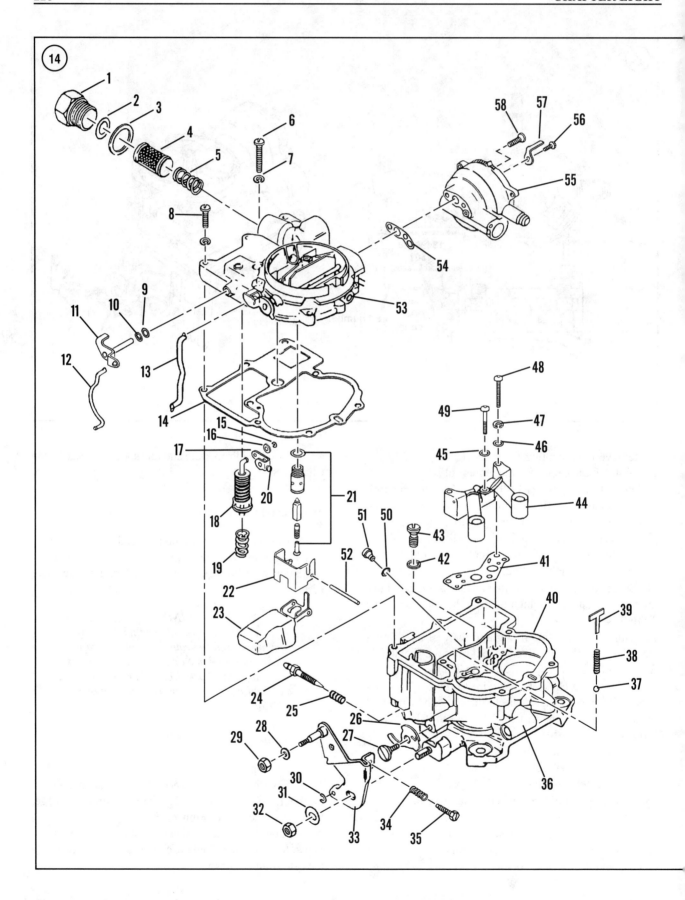

## TWO-BARREL CARBURETOR

1. Fuel inlet fitting
2. Gasket
3. Sealing ring
4. Fuel filter
5. Spring
6. Longer screw (1)
7. Lockwasher
8. Shorter screw (7)
9. Inner washer
10. Outer washer
11. Accelerator pump arm
12. Accelerator pump linkage
13. Choke linkage
14. Cover gasket
15. E-clip
16. Washer
17. Lever
18. Accelerator pump
19. Spring
20. Screw
21. Needle and seat
22. Deflector
23. Float
24. Idle mixture screw
25. Spring
26. Choke cam
27. Shouldered screw
28. Washer
29. Elastic lock nut
30. E-clip
31. Washer
32. Nut
33. Throttle linkage
34. Spring
35. Idle speed screw
36. PVC fitting
37. Check ball
38. Spring
39. Retainer
40. Carburetor body
41. Gasket
42. Sealing washer
43. Power valve
44. Venturi cluster
45. Gasket
46. Washer
47. Lockwasher
48. Screw
49. Screw
50. Sealing washer
51. Main fuel jet
52. Float pin
53. Air horn
54. Gasket
55. Choke
56. Screw
57. Ground tab
58. Screw

**8**

3. Remove the fuel inlet fitting, spring and filter (**Figure 17**). Remove the gasket from the fuel inlet fitting (**Figure 18**). Discard the gasket and filter. Remove and discard the sealing washer (3, **Figure 14**).

4. Loosen the screws (**Figure 19**) and carefully lift the cover assembly (**Figure 20**) from the carburetor.

5. Remove the float pin, float (**Figure 21**), inlet needle and spring (**Figure 22**). Use a large screwdriver to loosen the seat. Remove the seat and gasket (**Figure 23**).

6. Lift the gasket from the cover (**Figure 24**). Discard the gasket.

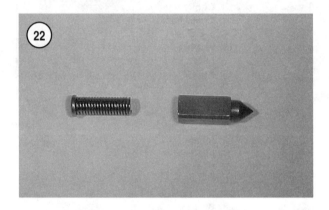

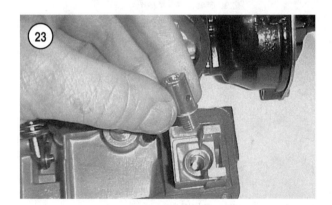

7. Loosen the screw (**Figure 25**) and pull the accelerator pump lever from the carburetor (**Figure 26**). Remove the accelerator pump (**Figure 27**). Remove the E-clip (15, **Figure 14**). Separate the lever (20, **Figure 14**) from the accelerator pump (18).

8. Remove the screws (**Figure 28**) and lift the venturi cluster from the carburetor (**Figure 29**). Remove and discard the gasket (41, **Figure 14**). Remove and discard the gasket from the middle screw.

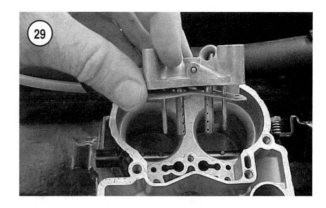

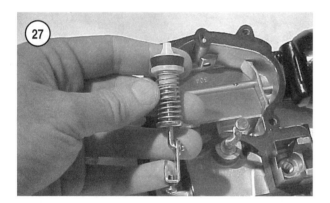

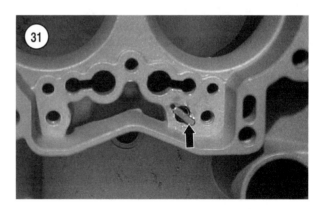

9. Remove the idle mixture screw (24, **Figure 14**) and spring (25). On 2003-2004 models, refer to Chapter Sixteen.

10. Lift the accelerator pump spring from the pump bore (**Figure 30**).

11. Grip the top of the retainer (**Figure 31**) with needlenose pliers. Pull the retainer, spring and check ball (**Figure 32**) from the bore.

12. Carefully pull the deflector from the cover (**Figure 33**).

13. Remove the power valve from the float bowl (**Figure 34**). Remove and discard the gasket (42, **Figure 14**). Re-

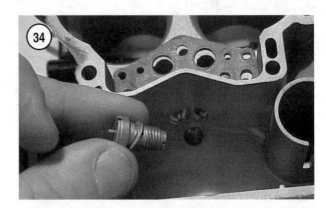

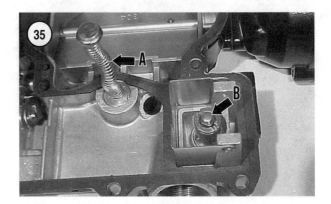

place the power valve if dirty or corroded. Do not disassemble the valve.

14. Remove the main fuel jets (51, **Figure 14**) and gaskets (50). Discard the gaskets.

15. Inspect the power valve piston and spring (A, **Figure 35**) for corrosion or binding. Remove the piston and clean the bore if binding occurs. Re-install the piston and stake the retainer into the housing. Replace the carburetor if binding persists or if the parts are corroded. The power valve piston is not available separately.

16. Remove and disassemble the electric choke as described in this chapter.

17. Clean and inspect the carburetor as described in this chapter.

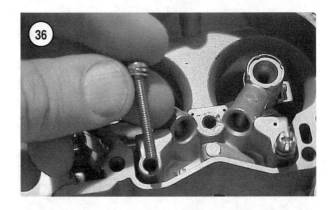

### *Assembly*

Refer to **Figure 14**.

1. Assemble and install the electric choke as described in this chapter.

2. Place new gaskets (50, **Figure 14**) on the main fuel jets (51). Install the jets into their openings in the float bowl. Do not over-tighten the jets.

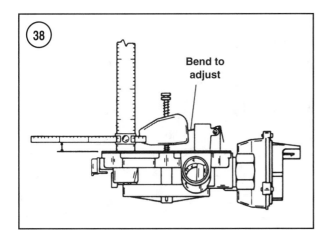

Bend to
adjust

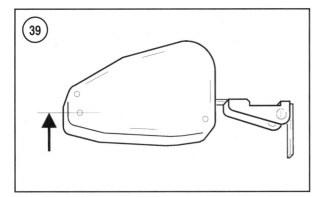

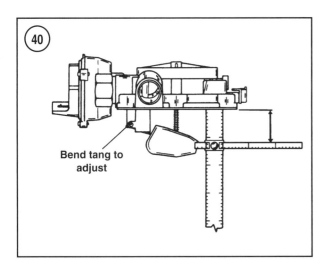

Bend tang to
adjust

3. Place a new gasket on the power valve. Install the power valve into the carburetor bowl. Do not over-tighten the valve.

4. Install the check ball, spring and retainer (**Figure 32**) into the carburetor body. Lightly stake the area around the opening (**Figure 31**) to secure the retainer.

5. Install a new gasket onto the venturi cluster. Install the venturi onto the carburetor body (**Figure 29**).

6. Install the two venturi screws that are threaded along their entire length into the outer openings of the cluster (**Figure 36**).

7. Install a new gasket (45, **Figure 14**) onto the narrow shouldered screw (49). Install the screw, washer and gasket into the middle opening (**Figure 37**). Evenly tighten the screws (**Figure 28**).

8. Install the spring (25, **Figure 14**) onto the idle mixture screw (24). Thread the screw and spring into the carburetor body until lightly seated. Back the screw out the number of turns specified in **Table 2**. On 2003-2004 models, refer to Chapter Sixteen.

9. Insert the accelerator pump spring into the bore (**Figure 30**).

10. Install the accelerator pump (18, **Figure 14**) onto the lever (20). Install the washer (16, **Figure 14**) and E-clip (15).

11. Place the accelerator pump and lever into the cover (**Figure 27**). Fit the outer washer (10, **Figure 14**) onto the shaft of the pump arm (11). Insert the pump arm into the cover (**Figure 26**) enough to place the inner washer (9, **Figure 14**) over the shaft.

12. Align the flat shaft surface with the lever opening. Slide the lever over the shaft. Seat the lever against the inner washer. Securely tighten the screw (**Figure 25**). Check for binding of the lever in the cover bore. Reposition the lever on the shaft to correct binding.

13. Place a gasket washer onto the needle seat. Install the seat into the cover (**Figure 23**). Securely tighten the seat. Do not damage the screw slot.

14. Install the deflector onto the cover. The slot in the deflector must align with the float arm. Seat the flange of the deflector into the recess in the cover.

15. Insert the guide into the spring. Insert the guide and spring (**Figure 22**) into the inlet needle. Place the inlet needle into the seat (B, **Figure 35**).

16. Place a new gasket onto the cover (**Figure 24**). Install the float on the cover (**Figure 21**) and insert the float pin (52, **Figure 14**) through the float arm and cover.

17. Adjust the float level as follows:
   a. Hold the carburetor cover with the float side facing upward (**Figure 38**).
   b. Measure the distance from the raised spot on the float (**Figure 39**) to the cover gasket (**Figure 38**).
   c. Compare the measurement with the float level specification in **Table 2**.
   d. Bend the float arm at the point shown in **Figure 38** to the specified float height.

18. Adjust the float drop as follows:
   a. Position the carburetor cover with the float facing downward (**Figure 40**).

8

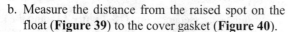

  b. Measure the distance from the raised spot on the
     float (**Figure 39**) to the cover gasket (**Figure 40**).
  c. Compare the measurement with the float drop spec-
     ification in **Table 2**.
  d. Bend the tang on the float arm to achieve the correct
     float drop measurement.
19.  Align the accelerator pump with the pump bore and
carefully install the cover onto the carburetor body. Align
the screw openings and install the longer screw and
lockwasher into its opening (**Figure 41**). Install the seven
shorter screws. Securely tighten the screws (**Figure 19**),
starting in the middle and working outward.
20.  Set a new gasket into the fuel inlet fitting (**Figure 18**).
Insert the new filter into the fitting. The open side of the
filter must face the gasket. Insert the spring into the carburetor. Place a new gasket (3, **Figure 14**) onto the fitting.
Thread the fitting into the opening and tighten to the specification in **Table 1**.
21.  Install the tang end of the linkage into the choke shaft
lever as shown in **Figure 16**. Attach the cam (26, **Figure
14**) to the linkage. Swing the linkage down and align the
cam with the opening for the shoulder screw (A, **Figure
42**). Insert the screw into the cam and thread it into the carburetor. The cam opening must fit over the shoulder of the
screw. Securely tighten the screw.
22.  Insert the tang end of the accelerator pump linkage
(12, **Figure 14**) into the middle opening on the pump arm
(B, **Figure 42**). Insert the other end of the linkage into the
throttle lever opening (C, **Figure 42**). Install the clip (30,
**Figure 14**) onto the groove in the linkage.

**Four-Barrel Carburetor**

   Locate the carburetor identification number on the carburetor casting (A, **Figure 43**). The identification number
may be required when ordering replacement parts.

*WARNING*
*Use caution when working with the fuel sys-*
*tem. Never smoke around fuel or fuel vapor.*
*Make sure no flame or source of ignition is*
*present in the work area. Flame or sparks*
*can ignite fuel or vapor resulting in fire or*
*explosion.*

*Disassembly*

   Refer to **Figure 44**.
1.  Use locking pliers to remove the flame arrestor mounting stud from the cover (B, **Figure 43**).
2.  Remove the screw (A, **Figure 45**). Remove the
S-shaped linkage (B, **Figure 45**) from the pump shaft.
Separate the pump arm and linkage (8 and 9, **Figure 44**)
from the cover (6).
3.  Remove the screws and lift the covers from the metering rod pistons (**Figure 46**). Lift the metering rods and
springs (**Figure 47**) from the carburetor. The metering
rods bend easily; handle with care.

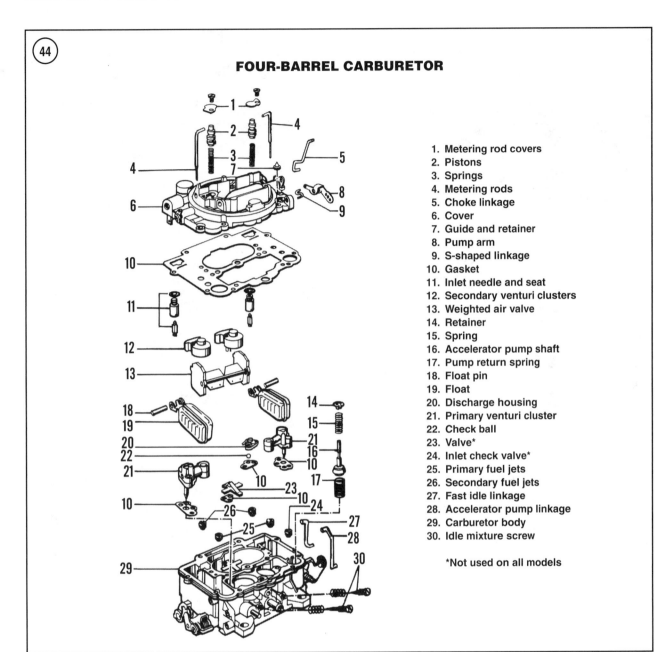

**FOUR-BARREL CARBURETOR**

1. Metering rod covers
2. Pistons
3. Springs
4. Metering rods
5. Choke linkage
6. Cover
7. Guide and retainer
8. Pump arm
9. S-shaped linkage
10. Gasket
11. Inlet needle and seat
12. Secondary venturi clusters
13. Weighted air valve
14. Retainer
15. Spring
16. Accelerator pump shaft
17. Pump return spring
18. Float pin
19. Float
20. Discharge housing
21. Primary venturi cluster
22. Check ball
23. Valve*
24. Inlet check valve*
25. Primary fuel jets
26. Secondary fuel jets
27. Fast idle linkage
28. Accelerator pump linkage
29. Carburetor body
30. Idle mixture screw

*Not used on all models

8

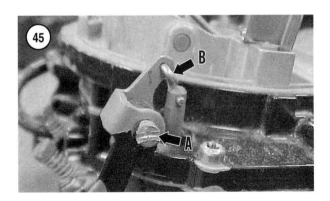

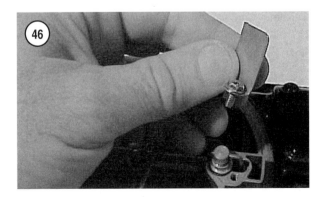

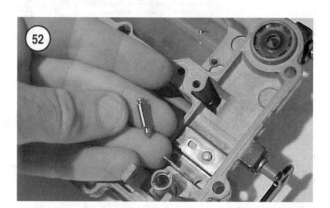

4. Remove the screws from the carburetor body (**Figure 48**). Carefully remove the cover (**Figure 49**). Retrieve the accelerator pump plunger from the port side float bowl (**Figure 49**). Lift the spring (17, **Figure 44**) from the accelerator pump bore.

5. Remove the pins (**Figure 50**) and lift the floats from the cover (**Figure 51**). Pull the inlet needles from the seats (**Figure 52**).

6. Unthread the seats from the cover (**Figure 53**). Separate the gasket, filter and seat (**Figure 54**). Discard the sealing washer.

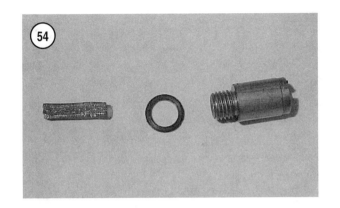

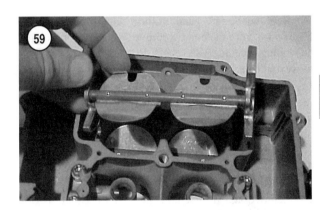

8

7. Carefully pry the retainer tabs out of the groove in the recess (**Figure 55**). Remove and discard the retainer. Lift the guide from the cover (**Figure 56**).

8. Remove the screws and lift the secondary venturi clusters (**Figure 57**) from the carburetor body. Mark the side in which they were installed for reference during assembly.

9. Remove and discard the gaskets from the venturi cover or carburetor body (**Figure 58**). Remove the weighted air valve (**Figure 59**) and pull the deflectors from the float bowls (**Figure 60**).

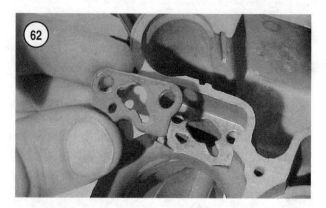

10. Remove the screw and lift the discharge housing (20, **Figure 44**) from the body. Remove the spring (or weight, depending on model) and check ball (22, **Figure 44**). Remove and discard the gasket from the housing.

11. Remove the screws and lift the primary venturi clusters (**Figure 61**) from the carburetor body. Mark the side in which they were installed for reference during assembly. Remove and discard the venturi gaskets (**Figure 62**).

12. Remove the idle mixture screws and springs (**Figure 63**). Mark the mounting locations, then remove the primary and secondary fuel jets (A and B, **Figure 64**).

13. Remove and disassemble the electric choke as described in this chapter.

14. Clean and inspect the carburetor as described in this chapter.

*Assembly*

Refer to **Figure 44**.

1. Assemble and install the electric choke as described in this chapter.

2. Install the primary (A, **Figure 64**) and secondary jets (B) into the float bowl. Do not overtighten the jets.

3. Insert the deflectors into the float bowls (**Figure 60**). Install the check ball (22, **Figure 44**) then the spring or weight into the accelerator pump passage (**Figure 65**). The tapered end of the spring must face downward. Install the gasket onto the carburetor body as shown in **Figure 65**. Fit the discharge housing (20, **Figure 44**) onto the gasket and secure it with the screws.

4. Place the weighted air valve into the carburetor body as shown in **Figure 59**. Install new secondary venturi cluster gaskets onto the carburetor casting. Orient the tabs on the gasket as shown in **Figure 66**. Install the secondary venturi clusters (**Figure 57**), making sure to install them on the correct side. Installing the clusters on the wrong side will damage them. Securely tighten the cluster mounting screws.

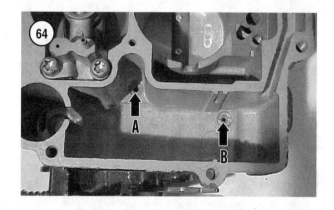

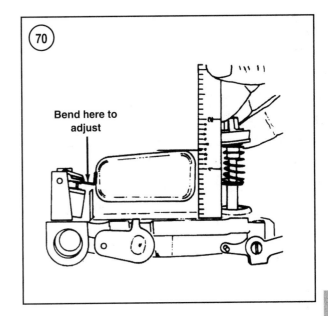

Bend here to adjust

**8**

5. Install new primary venturi cluster gaskets onto the carburetor casting (**Figure 62**). Align the notch on the cluster (**Figure 67**) with the boss on the carburetor body (**Figure 68**) and install the primary venturi cluster. If the notch and boss will not align, install the cluster onto the opposite side of the carburetor. Securely tighten the cluster mounting screws.

6. Place the guide into the recess (**Figure 56**). Place a new retainer into the recess with the tabs facing away from the guide (**Figure 69**). Use an appropriately sized socket and push the retainer into the recess. The tabs must engage the groove in the recess (**Figure 55**).

7. Insert the open ends of the filters into the threaded ends of the inlet seats. Place a new gasket over the threaded end of each seat (see **Figure 54**).

8. Thread the inlet seats into the caburetor cover (**Figure 53**). Tighten the seats. Do not over-tighten the seats. Insert the inlet needle into each seat (**Figure 52**).

9. Place a new gasket (10, **Figure 44**) onto the cover. Install the floats onto the inlet needles (**Figure 51**) with the tang facing the cover, then install the float pins (**Figure 50**).

10. Adjust the float level as follows:
   a. Hold the carburetor cover with the float facing up (**Figure 70**).
   b. Measure the distance from the bottom surface of the float to the cover gasket (**Figure 70**).
   c. Compare the measurement with the float level specification in **Table 2**.
   d. Bend the float arm at the point shown in **Figure 70** to adjust the float level.
   e. Repeat this step for the other float.

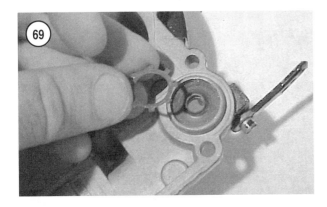

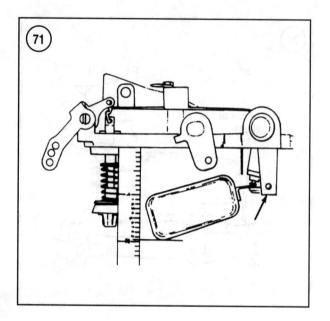

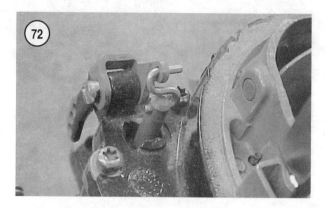

11. Adjust the float drop as follows:

   a. Position the cover with the float facing down (**Figure 71**).

   b. Measure the distance from the toe of the float (**Figure 71**) to the cover (not the gasket).

   c. Compare the measurement with the float drop specification in **Table 2**.

   d. Bend the tang on the float arm to adjust the float drop.

   e. Measure the float level as described in step 10. Correct as needed.

   f. Repeat this step for the other float.

12. Install the springs onto the idle mixture screws. Thread the screws and springs (**Figure 63**) into the carburetor body until lightly seated. Back the screws out the number of turns specified in **Table 2** under idle mixture adjustment.

13. Insert the accelerator pump spring (17, **Figure 44**) then the pump plunger into the bore.

14. Align the accelerator pump shaft with the guide opening and carefully install the cover onto the carburetor body (**Figure 49**). Install the cover screws (**Figure 48**). Securely tighten the screws from the center and working outward.

15. Apply Loctite 271 onto the coarser threaded end of the flame arrestor stud. Thread the flame arrestor stud into its opening (B, **Figure 43**). Securely tighten the stud. Connect the S-shaped linkage onto the pump shaft and arm (**Figure 72**). Align the pump arm openings with the screw openings. Install and securely tighten the screw.

16. If removed, fit the accelerator pump linkage (28, **Figure 44**) into the middle hole in the pump arm (8).

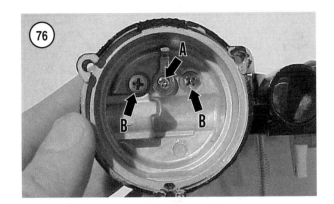

17. Insert the metering rod, pistons and springs. The metering rod tip must enter the primary fuel jets. Do not force the rods into the bore; the tips bend easily. Align the covers with metering rods and pistons. Carefully push down on cover to collapse the spring. Install and securely tighten the cover screws (**Figure 73**).

**Electric Choke Removal and Installation**

1. Make match marks on the choke heater and choke housing (**Figure 74**). Remove the screws and the retainer. Pull the choke heater away from the choke housing (**Figure 75**).
2. Remove the screw (A, **Figure 76**) and lift the choke lever from the shaft (**Figure 77**).
3. Remove the screws (B, **Figure 76**). Pull the choke housing from the carburetor (**Figure 78**). Remove and discard the gasket from the carburetor cover or choke housing.
4. Thoroughly clean and inspect all choke components. Replace damaged, worn or corroded components.
5. Install a new gasket onto the choke mating surface of the carburetor cover.
6. Fit the choke housing onto the carburetor cover. Install and securely tighten the screws (B, **Figure 76**).
7. Place the lever onto the choke shaft (**Figure 79**). Install and securely tighten the screw (A, **Figure 76**).
8. Engage the hooked end of the coil (A, **Figure 80**) onto the choke lever (B) while installing the choke heater onto the housing.
9A. If reusing the original choke heater, rotate the heater counterclockwise until the match marks align (**Figure 74**). Install the retainer and screws. Securely tighten the screws.
9B. If using a new choke heater, adjust the heater as follows:
    a. Rotate the choke heater counterclockwise to align the raised section on the heater (A, **Figure 81**) with

**8**

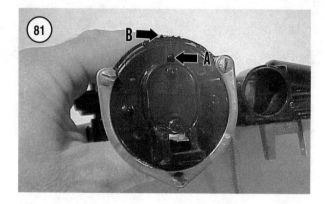

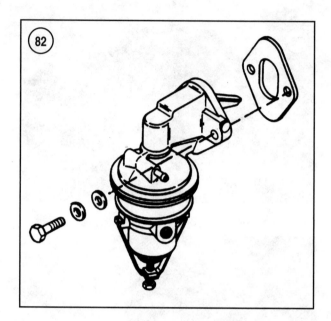

the middle index mark on the choke housing (B, **Figure 81**).

b. Align the heater mark with the index mark specified in **Table 2**. Tabs to the right of the middle mark (B, **Figure 81**) are for richer settings. Marks to the left are for leaner settings.

c. Install the retainer and securely tighten the screws.

## Mechanical Fuel Pump Removal and Installation (3.0L Models)

1. Wrap a shop towel around the fuel line fittings to catch spilled fuel. Disconnect the fuel lines and sight tube from the fuel pump.

2. Remove the mounting bolts (**Figure 82**) and fuel pump.

3. Remove and discard the thick spacer gasket from the fuel pump or cylinder block.

4. Apply a light coat of Perfect Seal (Mercury part No. 92-34227-1) to both sides of the new spacer gasket.

5. Insert the pump arm into the cylinder block opening. The top of the pump arm must contact the camshaft lobe.

6. Seat the fuel pump on the cylinder block. Install the mounting bolts and washers. Tighten them to the specification in **Table 1**.

7. Reconnect the fuel lines. Securely tighten the fittings.

8. Connect the sight tube to the barb fitting on the fuel pump.

9. Start the engine and immediately check for fuel leakage at the pump fittings. If fuel leakage occurs, immediately stop the engine. Correct the fuel leakage before operating the engine.

## Electric Fuel Pump Removal and Installation (Carbureted Models)

A low pressure electric fuel pump is used on all V6 and V8 engines equipped with a carburetor. Although similar in appearance, this pump is not interchangeable with the higher pressure pump used on EFI equipped engines. A bracket secures the pump to the starboard side cylinder head.

> **WARNING**
> *Use caution when working with the fuel system. Never smoke around fuel or fuel vapor. Make sure no flame or source of ignition is present in the work area. Flame or sparks can ignite fuel or vapor resulting in fire or explosion.*

1. Disconnect the battery cables. Trace the fuel pump wire harness (2, **Figure 83**) to the engine wire harness connection. Pull up on the tab and disconnect the fuel pump.

2. Wrap a shop towel around the fuel line fittings to catch spilled fuel. Hold fuel inlet and outlet fittings (3 and 4, **Figure 83**) with a wrench and loosen the fuel lines.

3. Disconnect the fuel lines. Pull the fuel pump assembly (1, **Figure 83**) from the mounting bracket (5). Drain the pump into a suitable container.

4. Attach a wrench to the flat surfaces next to the outlet fitting (**Figure 84**). Remove the outlet fitting and small grommet (**Figure 84**). Remove the O-ring from the outlet fitting. Discard the O-ring.

5. Remove the large grommet (**Figure 84**). Remove the inlet fitting. Remove and discard the O-ring from the inlet fitting.

6. Inspect the grommets for splitting or deterioration and replace as needed. Inspect the fuel fittings for cracking, damaged threads or other defects. Replace as needed.

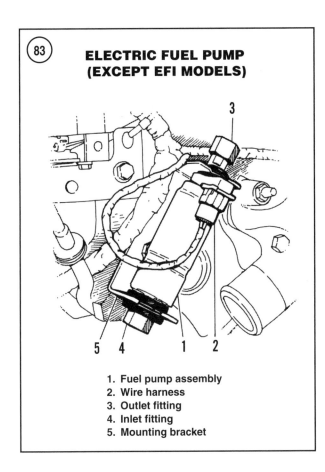

**ELECTRIC FUEL PUMP
(EXCEPT EFI MODELS)**

1. Fuel pump assembly
2. Wire harness
3. Outlet fitting
4. Inlet fitting
5. Mounting bracket

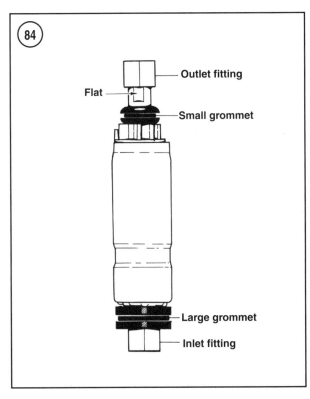

7. Lubricate the small grommet with soapy water and slide it onto the outlet end of the fuel pump (nearest the wire harness connection). Seat the grommet on the pump.

8. Lubricate a new O-ring with engine oil and install it on the outlet fitting. Thread the inlet fitting onto the fuel pump. Tighten the pump outlet fitting to the specification in **Table 1**. Lubricate the large grommet with soapy water and slide it over the inlet fitting (**Figure 84**). Seat the grommet on the pump.

9. Lubricate a new O-ring with engine oil and install it onto the inlet fitting. Thread the inlet fitting into the fuel pump. Tighten the pump inlet fitting to the specification in **Table 1**.

10. If the mounting bracket was removed, install it onto the starboard cylinder head. Position the larger grommet opening onto the lower side. Tighten the mounting bracket bolts to the specification in **Table 1**.

11. Align the grooves in the grommets with the slots in the mounting bracket. Push the pump fully onto the bracket.

12. Thread the fuel lines into the inlet and outlet fittings. Hold the inlet and outlet fittings with a wrench to prevent rotation, and tighten the fuel lines to the specification in **Table 1**.

13. Attach the pump harness to the enging harness. Tug on the connectors to make sure the connection is secure. Secure the wire harness with tie straps to prevent entanglement in moving components.

14. Connect the battery. Start the engine and immediately check for fuel leakage at the pump fittings. If fuel leakage occurs, immediately stop the engine. Correct the fuel leakage before operating the engine.

### Oil Pressure Switch Removal and Installation (Carbureted V6 and V8 Models)

The oil pressure switch supplies battery voltage to operate the electric fuel pump. The switch attaches to a fitting on the rear port side of the cylinder block.

1. Disconnect the battery. Disconnect the purple and purple/yellow wire (A, **Figure 85**).

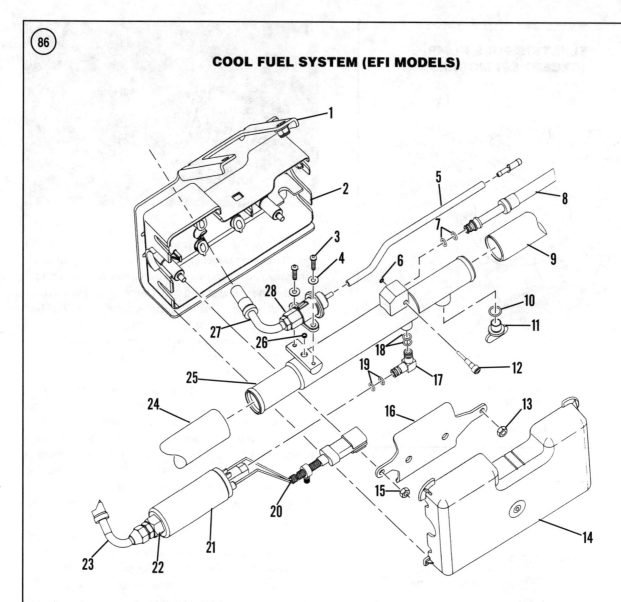

**COOL FUEL SYSTEM (EFI MODELS)**

1. Mounting bracket
2. Housing
3. Screws
4. Washers
5. Hose to intake manifold
6. Retainer
7. O-rings
8. Outlet fuel line
   (to TBI unit or fuel rail)
9. Cooling water hose (to seawater
   pump)
10. O-ring
11. Water drain plug (blue)
12. Step shouldered screw
13. Nut
14. Heat shield

15. Nut
16. Retainer
17. Fitting
18. O-rings
19. O-rings
20. Electric pump harness
21. High pressure electric pump
22. Inlet fitting
23. Inlet fuel line (from spin on filter)
24. Cooling water hose
   (to thermostat housing)
25. Fuel cooler
26. Filter
27. Regulator fuel line
   (to spin on fuel filter)
28. Fuel pressure regulator

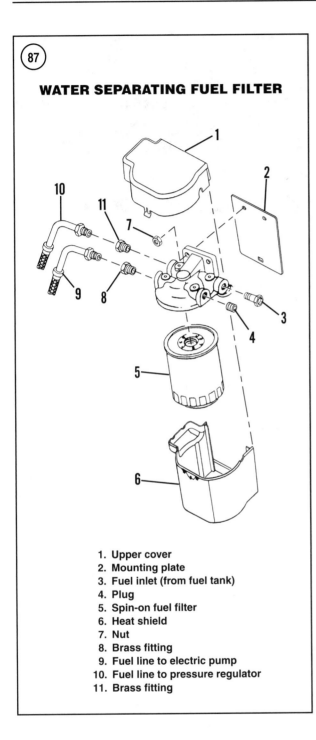

**WATER SEPARATING FUEL FILTER**

1. Upper cover
2. Mounting plate
3. Fuel inlet (from fuel tank)
4. Plug
5. Spin-on fuel filter
6. Heat shield
7. Nut
8. Brass fitting
9. Fuel line to electric pump
10. Fuel line to pressure regulator
11. Brass fitting

2. Hold the fitting with a wrench to prevent rotation and remove the switch (B, **Figure 85**). Clean sealant from the switch and fitting threads.

3. Apply a light coat of Loctite 592 Pipe Sealant with Teflon to the switch threads. Keep sealant away from the switch opening. Thread the switch into the fitting. Hold the fitting with a wrench to prevent rotation and securely tighten the switch.

4. Connect the purple and purple/yellow wires to the switch. The wires can be connected to either switch terminal.

5. Start the engine and check for oil leakage. Correct oil leakage before operating the engine.

**COOL FUEL SYSTEM**

The cool fuel system (**Figure 86**) is installed on all later MerCruiser EFI engines. The system incorporates the high-pressure electric fuel pump, fuel pressure regulator and fuel cooler into a single assembly.

The system is located between the port engine mount and the oil pan. Due to limited accessibility, the system must be removed to inspect or replace any components.

*WARNING*
*Use caution when working with the fuel system. Never smoke around fuel or fuel vapor. Make sure no flame or source of ignition is present in the work area. Flame or sparks can ignite fuel or vapor resulting in fire or explosion.*

**Removal and Installation**

1. Disconnect the battery cables.

2. Pull the heat shield (14, **Figure 86**) from the housing. Disconnect the pump harness.

3. Disconnect the outlet fuel line (8, **Figure 86**) from the fuel rail or TBI unit. Wrap a shop towel around the fitting to absorb spilled fuel. Slowly loosen the fitting to relieve pressure. Plug the fuel line and TBI or rail opening to prevent contamination.

4. Pull up on the tab of the upper cover (1, **Figure 87**). Lift the cover from the bracket (2, **Figure 87**). Pull the heat shield (6, **Figure 87**) downward and remove it from the bracket.

5. Disconnect the fuel pump, (9, **Figure 87**) and pressure regulator lines (10) from the fuel filter. Drain all fuel from the lines. Plug the fitting and filter openings to prevent contamination.

6. Disconnect the cooling water hoses (9 and 24, **Figure 86**) from the cooler. If the boat is moored in water, plug the hose ends and secure them above the water line.

7. Disconnect the vacuum hose (5, **Figure 86**) from the fitting on the TBI unit or intake manifold. Disconnect the hose. Plug the hose and fitting to prevent contamination.

8. Remove the nuts that attach the bracket (1, **Figure 86**) to the engine mount studs. Pull the system away from the engine.

9. To install, reverse the removal steps and note the following:

   a. Route cooling water hoses and fuel lines away from moving components.

b. Connect the fuel pump and pressure regulator lines onto the correct fittings on the filter housing (see **Figure 87**). The arrow cast into the housing faces toward the fuel pump line. The arrow on the housing faces away from the pressure regulator line.

c. Tighten the bracket mounting nuts to the specification in **Table 1**.

d. Tighten fuel line fittings to the specification in **Table 1**.

e. Securely tighten the clamps on the cooling water hoses.

10. Connect the battery cables. Turn the ignition switch to the ON position and immediately check for fuel leakage. If leakage occurs, immediately turn the key switch OFF. Correct leakage before operating the engine.

11. Snap the heat shield (14, **Figure 86**) onto the cool fuel system. Align the slot in the filter heat shield (6, **Figure 87**) with the bracket (2). Slide the shield over the filter. Align the upper cover (1, **Figure 87**) with the shield. Snap the tab of the cover over the boss on the shield.

### Disassembly

1. Disconnect the wire harness clamp from the housing. Place the entire system over a container to catch any spilled fuel.

2. Remove the nuts (13 and 15, **Figure 86**). Lift the retainer from the pump and cooler. Carefully remove the cooler and fuel pump as an assembly from the housing (2, **Figure 86**). Wipe the thermal conductive grease from the fuel cooler (25, **Figure 86**), pump (21) and retainer (16).

3. Remove the electric fuel pump (21, **Figure 86**) as follows:

a. Pull the electric pump forward until free from the fitting (17, **Figure 86**).

b. Pull the fitting out of the fuel cooler. Remove the O-rings (18 and 19, **Figure 86**) from the fittings. Discard the O-rings.

c. Disconnect the inlet line (22, **Figure 86**) from the inlet fitting.

d. Remove the inlet fitting from the fuel pump. Remove the O-ring from the fitting. Discard the O-ring.

4. Remove the fuel pressure regulator as follows:

a. Disconnect the fuel line from the regulator.

b. Pull the vacuum hose (5, **Figure 86**) from the regulator fitting.

c. Remove the screws (3 **Figure 86**) and lift the regulator from the cooler.

d. Remove the filter (26, **Figure 86**) from the cooler or regulator surface. Discard the filter.

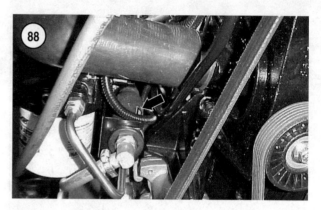

5. Loosen the shoulder screw (12, **Figure 86**) just enough to free the outlet fuel line (8) from the cooler. Do not remove the screw or the retainer (6, **Figure 86**) will be damaged.

6. Remove the O-rings (7, **Figure 86**) from the outlet line (8). Discard the O-rings.

7. Clean all components with solvent and dry with compressed air. Work only in a clean area and take all precautions to prevent contamination.

### Assembly

Apply liquid dishwashing soap to all O-rings prior to installing them. Thermal conductive grease (Mercury part No. 92-806701-1) must be applied to the fuel cooler- and fuel pump-to-retainer mating surfaces. This causes heat to dissipate properly, and helps prevent vapor lock.

1. Install the fuel pressure regulator (28, **Figure 86**) as follows:

a. Install the filter (26, **Figure 86**) into the fuel cooler (25). The open side of the filter must face toward the regulator.

b. Install the regulator onto the cooler. Install the screws and tighten them evenly to the specification in **Table 1**.

c. Thread the fuel line fitting onto the regulator fitting. Position the fuel line as shown in **Figure 86**. Hold the hose in place while tightening the fuel line fitting to the specification in **Table 1**.

d. Fit the vacuum hose fully onto the pressure regulator fitting.

2. Install the electric fuel pump as follows:

a. Install a new O-ring onto the fuel inlet fitting (22, **Figure 86**). Thread the fitting into the fuel pump. Tighten the fitting to the specification in **Table 1**.

b. Thread the fuel inlet line (23, **Figure 86**) onto the fuel inlet fitting (22). Position the fuel line as shown in **Figure 86**. Hold the line in place and tighten the fitting to the specification in **Table 1**.

c. Install new O-rings (18 and 19, **Figure 86**) into the grooves in the fitting (17).

d. Carefully insert the fitting into the outlet opening of the fuel pump.

e. Keep the fuel pump parallel with the fuel cooler and carefully insert the fitting into the fuel cooler.

3. Attach the outlet fuel line to the cooler as follows:

a. Install new O-rings (7, **Figure 86**) onto the grooves on the outlet fuel line (8) fitting.

b. Guide the fitting into the cooler. Push in on the fitting while hand-tightening the shoulder screw (12, **Figure 86**).

c. Tighten the shoulder screw to the specification in **Table 1**.

4. Keep the fuel pump parallel to the cooler while lowering the assembly into the housing (2, **Figure 86**). Guide the fuel line fittings into the notches provided in the housing. Proper installation prevents the fuel pump from separating from the cooler. Remove the assembly and reinstall as needed.

5. Route the fuel pump harness (20, **Figure 86**) so it will not be pinched between other components.

6. Apply thermal conductive grease to the fuel pump and cooler mating surfaces of the retainer (16, **Figure 86**). Install the retainer over the mounting studs with the curved sides facing the cooler and fuel pump. The short side of the retainer covers the fuel pump.

7. Make sure the fuel line fittings engage completely to the housing notches. Make sure the fuel pump harness is not pinched between other components. Install the nuts (13 and 15, **Figure 86**) and tighten them to the specification in **Table 1**.

8. Install the cool fuel system as described in this chapter.

## BOOST PUMP REMOVAL AND INSTALLATION (496 MAG AND 496 MAG HO)

The boost pump (**Figure 88**) is located on the starboard side of the engine and near the water separating fuel filter. Except for the mounting location, the replacement procedure is similar to that for the electric pump used on carbureted V6 and V8 engines. Refer to *Electric Fuel Pump Removal and Installation* in this chapter.

## THROTTLE BODY (TBI)

A TBI (throttle body injection) unit is used on fuel injected models 4.3L, 5.0L and 5.7L. The unit houses the fuel injectors, idle air control motor, throttle position sensor, pressure regulator chamber and throttle valve.

*WARNING*
*Use caution when working with the fuel system. Never smoke around fuel or fuel vapor. Make sure no flame or source of ignition is present in the work area. Flame or sparks can ignite fuel or vapor resulting in fire or explosion.*

*CAUTION*
*Do not use solvents containing methyl ethyl ketone to clean the throttle body and related components. Use only mild solvents designed to clean fuel system components. Harsh solvents can damage the throttle body and other components.*

### Removal and Installation

1. Remove the flame arrestor as described in this chapter.

2. Wrap a shop towel around the fuel line fitting (12, **Figure 89**). Slowly loosen the fuel line fitting to relieve the fuel pressure. Disconnect the fuel line and clean up any spilled fuel. Plug the fuel line and TBI fitting to keep out water and debris.

3. Disconnect the wire harness from the idle air control motor (15, **Figure 89**) and throttle position sensor (17). Squeeze the plastic tabs and pull the connectors from the fuel injectors. Pull the harness grommet from the slot in the throttle body.

4. Disconnect the throttle cable from the throttle lever on the TBI unit.

5. On 2000 models, disconnect the wire harness from the fuel pressure sensor.

6. Remove the mounting fasteners and lift the TBI unit from the manifold adapter. Remove and discard the gasket from the adapter or TBI unit. Thoroughly clean the adapter and TBI unit mating surfaces.

7. Install a new TBI gasket onto the adapter. Install the TBI unit onto the adapter. Install the mounting fasteners and tighten them to the specification in **Table 1**.

8. Connect the wire harness to the idle air control motor and the throttle position sensor.

9. On 2000 models, connect the wire harness to the fuel pressure sensor.

10. Attach the fuel line to the TBI unit fitting (12, **Figure 89**). Tighten the fuel line fitting to the specification in **Table 1**. Fit the harness grommet into the slot in the throttle body. Squeeze the tabs and attach the harness connectors to the fuel injectors.

11. Connect the throttle cable to the throttle lever. Adjust the throttle cable as described in Chapter Six.

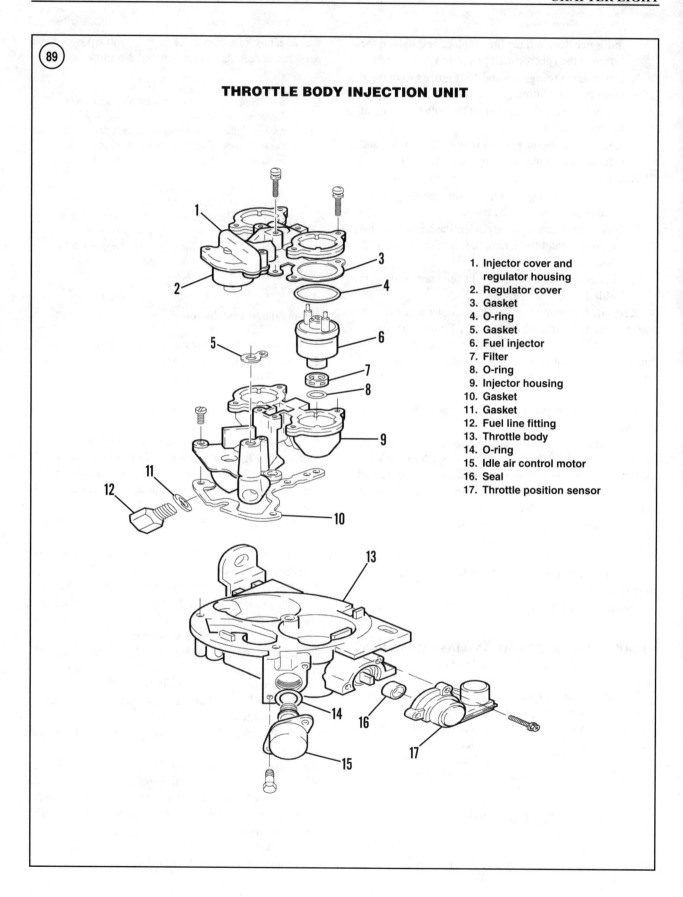

**89**

## THROTTLE BODY INJECTION UNIT

1. Injector cover and regulator housing
2. Regulator cover
3. Gasket
4. O-ring
5. Gasket
6. Fuel injector
7. Filter
8. O-ring
9. Injector housing
10. Gasket
11. Gasket
12. Fuel line fitting
13. Throttle body
14. O-ring
15. Idle air control motor
16. Seal
17. Throttle position sensor

12. Install the flame arrestor as described in this chapter.

13. Reset the idle air control motor as follows:

  a. Connect the battery cables.

  b. Turn the ignition switch to the ON position for 10 seconds. Do not start the engine.

  c. Turn the ignition switch OFF.

14. Turn the key switch ON and immediately check for fuel leakage. If leakage occurs, immediately turn the ignition switch OFF. Correct the leakage before operating the engine.

**Disassembly**

Refer to **Figure 89**.

1. Remove the idle air control motor, throttle position sensor and fuel pressure sensor, if so equipped as described in this chapter.

2. Remove the fuel line fitting (12, **Figure 89**) and gasket (11). Discard the gasket.

3. Remove the screws and lift the injector cover and regulator housing (1, **Figure 89**) from the injector housing (9). Remove and discard the gasket (3, **Figure 89**).

4. Remove and discard the gasket (5, **Figure 89**) from the cover or injector housing.

5. Slowly remove the screws and lift the regulator cover (2, **Figure 89**). Remove the diaphragm and spring from the housing. Inspect the diaphragm for holes or excessive wear and replace if necessary.

6. Carefully pull each fuel injector (6, **Figure 89**) from the housing (9). Remove the filter (7, **Figure 89**) from each injector. Remove and discard the O-rings (4 and 8, **Figure 89**) from the injector housing.

7. Inspect the filter for blockage, tears or damage. Replace the filter if defective.

8. Remove the screws and lift the injector housing (9, **Figure 89**) and gasket (10). Discard the gasket.

9. Clean all components, except the fuel injectors and the diaphragm with solvent and dry with compressed air.

**Assembly**

Apply liquid dishwashing soap to all O-rings before installing them. Refer to **Figure 89**.

1. Install a new gasket (10, **Figure 89**) and the injector housing (9) onto the throttle body. Install and securely tighten the mounting screws.

2. Install a new gasket (5, **Figure 89**) onto the injector housing. Slide a filter (8, **Figure 89**) over each injector. Seat the filters against the body of the injectors.

3. Fit the O-rings (4 and 8, **Figure 89**) into the grooves in the injector housing. Slide the injectors into the housing, taking care not to dislodge the O-rings. Rotate the injec-

tors to align the injector terminals with the throttle valve shaft. Seat the injectors in the housing.

4. Install the spring into the regulator cover (2, **Figure 89**). Install the diaphragm onto the cover, the install the cover, spring and diaphragm into the injector cover and regulator housing (1, **Figure 89**). Install and securely tighten the screws.

5. Place a new gasket (3, **Figure 89**) onto the injector housing. Fit the injector cover and regulator housing into the injector housing. Do not dislodge the gasket (5, **Figure 89**). Install the screws and tighten them evenly.

6. Place a new gasket (11, **Figure 89**) on the fuel fitting (12). Thread the fitting into the injector housing. Securely tighten the fitting.

7. Install the idle air control motor, throttle position sensor and fuel pressure sensor (if so equipped) as described in this chapter.

**Throttle Body and Manifold Adapter Removal and Installation (MPI models)**

The throttle body contains the throttle valve, throttle position sensor and idle air control motor (except models 496 Mag and 496 Mag HO). Replace all gaskets, O-rings and seals if disturbed.

*CAUTION*
*Do not use solvents containing methyl ethyl ketone to clean the throttle body and related components. Use only mild solvents designed to clean fuel system components. Harsh solvents can damage the throttle body and other components.*

*350 Mag MPI and MX 6.2 models*

Refer to **Figure 90**.

1. Disconnect the battery cables. Disconnect the throttle cable from the throttle lever.

2. Remove the nut (1, **Figure 90**) and lift the cover from the flame arrestor. Remove the washer and flame arrestor (5, **Figure 90**). Clean and inspect the flame arrestor. Replace the flame arrestor if damaged. Operating the engine with a dirty, missing or damaged flame arrestor poses a fire and explosion hazard.

3. Disconnect the wire harness from the idle air control motor and throttle position sensor.

4. Remove the screws (7, **Figure 90**) and lift the throttle body (8) from the manifold adapter (12). Remove and discard the gasket (9, **Figure 90**) from the throttle body or adapter.

5. Disconnect the vacuum hose from the fuel pressure regulator and the PVC hose (if so equipped).

**8**

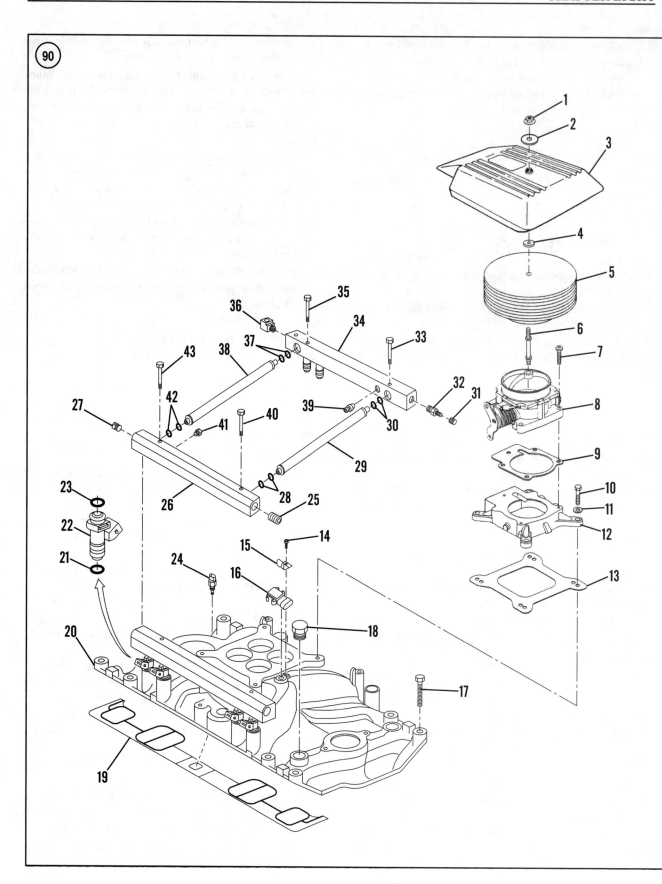

## THROTTLE BODY AND FUEL RAIL (350 MAG MPI AND MX6.2 MODELS)

1. Nut
2. Washer
3. Cover
4. Washer
5. Flame arrestor
6. Stud
7. Screw
8. Throttle body
9. Gasket
10. Bolt
11. Washer
12. Adapter
13. Gasket
14. Screw
15. Retainer
16. Air pressure sensor
17. Bolt
18. Plug
19. Gasket
20. Intake manifold
21. Seal
22. Fuel injector
23. Seal
24. Air temperature sensor
25. Plug
26. Starboard fuel rail
27. Fitting
28. O-rings
29. Tube
30. O-rings
31. Cover
32. Schrader valve
33. Bolt
34. Port fuel rail
35. Bolt
36. Fitting
37. O-rings
38. Tube
39. Fuel pressure sensor
40. Bolt
41. Plug
42. O-rings
43. Bolt

6. Remove the bolts (10, **Figure 90**) and carefully pry the adapter from the manifold. Do not use excessive force or the adapter will break.

7. Remove and discard the gasket (13, **Figure 90**) from the adapter or intake manifold. Remove the idle air control motor and throttle position sensor as described in this chapter.

8. Use a quick drying solvent to clean the throttle body and adapter. Inspect the throttle plate and shaft for binding or excessive wear and replace if necessary.

9. Place a new gasket (13, **Figure 90**) onto the intake manifold. Install the adapter (12, **Figure 90**) with the gasket (13) and install the bolts and washer. Securely tighten the bolts. Install the idle air control motor and throttle position sensor as described in this chapter.

10. Connect the vacuum hose and PVC hose (if so equipped) to the adapter.

11. Place a new gasket (9, **Figure 90**) onto the adapter (12) and install the throttle body (8, **Figure 90**) with the gasket (9). Install the screws (7, **Figure 90**). Evenly tighten the screws to the specification in **Table 1**.

12. Connect the wire harness to the idle air control motor and the throttle position sensor.

13. Connect the throttle cable to the throttle lever. Adjust the throttle cable as described in Chapter Six.

14. Install the flame arrestor, cover, washer and nut. The rubber side of the washer must face the cover. Do not over tighten the nut, or the cover may crack.

15. Connect the battery cables. Check for proper throttle operation before starting the engine. The idle and full throttle positions must correspond to the remote control positions. Correct improper operation before starting the engine.

16. Reset the idle air control motor as follows:

   a. Turn the ignition switch to the ON position for 10 seconds. Do not start the engine.

   b. Turn the ignition switch OFF.

### *7.4 MPI models*

Refer to **Figure 91**.

1. Disconnect the battery cables. Remove the Torx screw (1, **Figure 91**). Remove the starboard cover (2, **Figure 91**). Disconnect the throttle cable from the throttle lever and pivot point.

2. Loosen the clamp (31, **Figure 91**) and pull the flame arrestor (19) from the throttle body (30). Clean and inspect the flame arrestor. Replace the flame arrestor if damaged. Operating the engine with a dirty, missing or damaged flame arrestor creates a fire and explosion hazard.

**8**

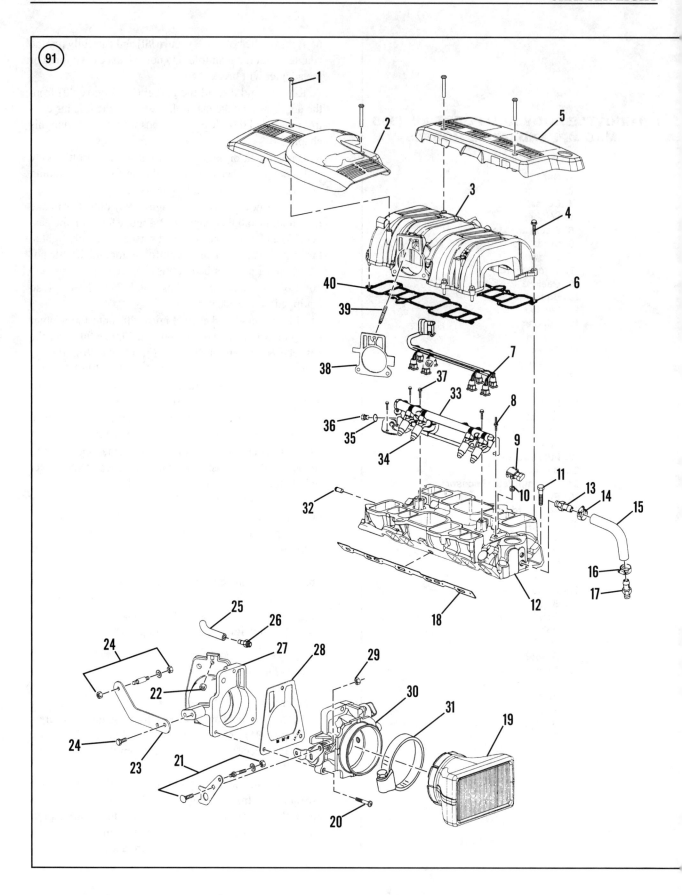

## THROTTLE BODY AND FUEL RAIL
## (7.4 MPI MODEL)

1. Torx screw
2. Starboard cover
3. Plenum
4. Bolt
5. Port cover
6. Plenum gasket
7. Injector harness
8. Stud
9. Air pressure sensor
10. Seal
11. Bolt
12. Intake manifold
13. Fitting
14. Clamp
15. Bypass hose
16. Clamp
17. Fitting
18. Intake gasket
19. Flame arrestor
20. Screw
21. Throttle lever hardware
22. Nut
23. Bracket
24. Cable pivot
25. PCV hose
26. Fitting
27. Adapter
28. Gasket
29. Nut
30. Throttle body
31. Clamp
32. Vacuum hose fitting
    (pressure regulator hose)
33. Fuel rail assembly
34. Fuel injector
35. O-ring
36. Plug
37. Screw
38. Gasket
39. Stud
40. Plenum gasket

3. Disconnect the wire harness from the idle air control motor and throttle position sensor.

4. Remove the screws (20, **Figure 91**) and lift the throttle body (30) and gasket (28) from the adapter. Discard the gasket. Disconnect the PCV hose (25, **Figure 91**) from the fitting (26).

5. Remove the idle air control motor and throttle position sensor as described in this chapter.

6. Remove the nuts (22, **Figure 91**) and pull the adapter (27, **Figure 91**) from the plenum (3). Discard the gasket.

7. Use a quick drying solvent to clean the throttle body and adapter. Inspect the throttle plate and shaft for binding or excessive wear. Replace the throttle body if necessary.

8. Place a new gasket (38, **Figure 91**) over the studs (38) on the plenum. Fit the adapter over the studs and seat it on the plenum. Install the mounting nuts. Tighten the nuts to the specification in **Table 1**.

9. Install the idle air control motor and throttle position sensor as described in this chapter.

10. Place a new gasket (28, **Figure 91**) onto the adapter. Align the openings and install the mounting screws (20, **Figure 91**). Securely tighten the screws.

11. Connect the wire harness to the idle air control motor and throttle position sensor.

12. Connect the throttle cable to the throttle lever and pivot point. Adjust the throttle cable as described in Chapter Six.

13. Slide the flame arrestor (19, **Figure 91**) onto the throttle body flange. Securely tighten the clamp (31, **Figure 91**). Attach the PVC hose (25, **Figure 91**) to the fitting (26).

14. Connect the battery cables. Check for proper throttle operation before starting the engine. The idle and full throttle position must coordinate with the remote control position. Correct improper operation before starting the engine.

15. Reset the idle air control motor as follows:
    a. Connect the battery cables.
    b. Turn the ignition switch to the ON position for 10 seconds. Do not start the engine.
    c. Turn the ignition switch OFF.

16. Install the port and starboard covers (2 and 5, **Figure 91**) and secure it with the torx screws (1). Do not over tighten the screws.

*454 Mag and 502 Mag models*

Refer to **Figure 92**.

1. Disconnect the battery cables. Remove the screw (9, **Figure 92**) and lift the flame arrestor (8) from the throttle body (5). Clean and inspect the flame arrestor. Replace the flame arrestor if damaged. Operating the engine with a

**8**

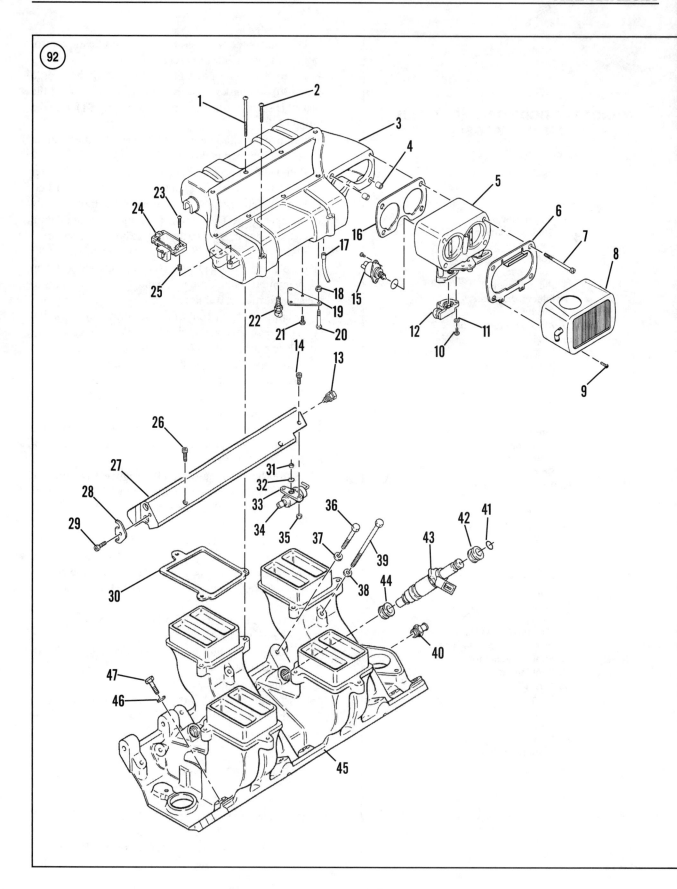

## THROTTLE BODY AND FUEL RAIL (454 MAG AND 502 MAG MODELS)

1. Long bolt
2. Short bolt
3. Plenum
4. Alignment dowels
5. Throttle body
6. Bracket
7. Allen bolt
8. Flame arrestor
9. Screw
10. Screw
11. Washer
12. Throttle position sensor
13. Schrader valve
14. Screw
15. Idle air control motor
16. Gasket
17. Sight tube*
18. Nut
19. Cable bracket
20. Cable stud
21. Screw
22. Air temperature sensor
23. Screw
24. Air pressure sensor
25. Seal
26. Screw
27. Fuel rail
28. Retainer
29. Screw
30. Gasket
31. Filter
32. O-ring
33. Fuel pressure dampner
34. Plug
35. Nut
36. Bolt
37. Washer
38. Washer
39. Bolt
40. Fitting
41. O-ring
42. Grommet
43. Fuel injector
44. Sealing grommet
45. Intake manifold
46. Washer
47. Bolt

* Not used on all models

dirty, missing or damaged flame arrestor creates a fire and explosion hazard.

2. Disconnect the wire harness from the idle air control motor (15, **Figure 92**) and throttle position sensor (12).

3. Remove the Allen bolts (7, **Figure 92**). Pull the bracket and throttle body from the plenum. Remove and discard the gasket (16, **Figure 92**).

4. Remove the idle air control motor and throttle position sensor as described in this chapter.

5. Use a quick drying solvent to clean the throttle body and bracket. Inspect the throttle plate and shaft for binding or excessive wear. Replace the throttle body if necessary.

6. Place a new gasket (16, **Figure 92**) over the alignment dowels (4).

7. Install the idle air control motor and throttle position sensor as described in this chapter.

8. Connect the wire harness to the idle air control motor and throttle position sensor. Install the throttle body onto the plenum. Install the bracket and Allen bolts. Securely tighten the Allen bolts.

9. Connect the throttle cable to the throttle lever and pivot point. Adjust the throttle cable as described in Chapter Six.

10. Fit the flame arrestor (8, **Figure 92**) onto the bracket (6). Secure the flame arrestor with the screws (9, **Figure 92**).

11. Connect the battery cables. Check for proper throttle operation before starting the engine. The idle and full throttle positions must correspond with the remote control position. Correct improper operation before starting the engine.

12. Reset the idle air control motor as follows:
    a. Turn the ignition switch to the ON position for 10 seconds. Do not start the engine.
    b. Turn the ignition switch OFF.

### *496 Mag and 496 Mag HO models*

Refer to **Figure 93**.

1. Disconnect the battery cables. Loosen the hose clamp and lift the flame arrestor from the throttle body (2, **Figure 93**). Clean and inspect the flame arrestor. Replace the flame arrestor if damaged. Operating the engine with a dirty, missing or damaged flame arrestor creates a fire and explosion hazard.

2. Disconnect the wire harness from the throttle position sensor. The sensor is mounted on the port side of the throttle body.

3. Disconnect the idle control motor hose from the throttle body fitting.

**8**

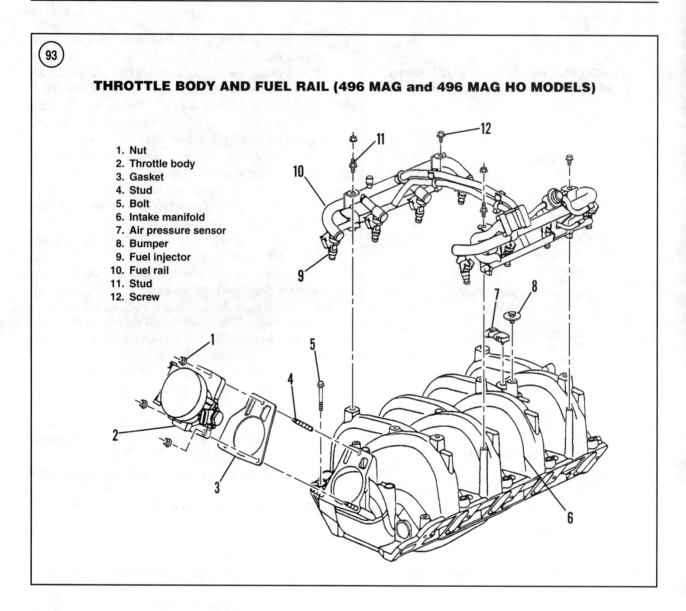

**THROTTLE BODY AND FUEL RAIL (496 MAG and 496 MAG HO MODELS)**

1. Nut
2. Throttle body
3. Gasket
4. Stud
5. Bolt
6. Intake manifold
7. Air pressure sensor
8. Bumper
9. Fuel injector
10. Fuel rail
11. Stud
12. Screw

4. Remove the nuts (1, **Figure 93**) and lift the throttle body (2) from the intake manifold. Remove and discard the gasket (3, **Figure 93**).

5. Remove the throttle position sensor as described in this chapter.

6. Use a quick drying solvent and thoroughly clean the throttle body. Inspect the throttle plate and shaft for binding or excessive wear. Replace the throttle body if necessary.

7. Place a new gasket (3, **Figure 93**) over the studs (4). Install the throttle position sensor as described in this chapter.

8. Install the throttle body over the studs and seat it against the gasket. Install and securely tighten the nuts (1, **Figure 93**). Connect the idle control motor hose to the throttle body fitting.

9. Connect the wire harness to the throttle position sensor. Connect the throttle cable to the throttle lever and pivot point. Adjust the throttle cable as described in Chapter Six.

10. Install the flame arrestor onto the throttle body flange. Securely tighten the clamp.

11. Connect the battery cables. Check for proper throttle operation before starting the engine. The idle and full throttle positions must correspond with the remote control positions. Correct improper operation before starting the engine.

12. Reset the idle air control motor as follows:

  a. Turn the ignition switch to the ON position for 10 seconds. Do not start the engine.

  b. Turn the ignition switch OFF.

## FUEL RAIL AND INJECTORS

### Disassembly and Assembly (MPI Models)

Perform this procedure only in a clean environment. Take all precaution to prevent contamination. Use only clean solvent and lint free shop towels when cleaning components. Dry components with compressed air and promptly cover them. Replace all gaskets, O-rings and seals if disturbed. Apply liquid dishwashing soap to all O-rings before installing them.

*WARNING*
*Use caution when working with the fuel system. Never smoke around fuel or fuel vapor. Make sure no flame or source of ignition is present in the work area. Flame or sparks can ignite fuel or vapor resulting in a fire and explosion.*

*CAUTION*
*Do not use solvents containing methyl ethyl ketone to clean the fuel rail and related components. Use only mild solvents designed to clean fuel system components. Harsh solvents can damage the fuel rail and other components.*

### 350 Mag MPI and MX 6.2

Refer to **Figure 90**.
1. Disconnect the battery cables. Remove the flame arrestor and throttle body as described in this chapter.
2. The fuel line connects to the fitting (36, **Figure 90**) on the aft end of the port fuel rail (34). Wrap a shop towel around the fitting and slowly loosen the fuel line to bleed pressure from the line. Disconnect the fuel line. Plug the line and rail fitting to prevent contamination.
3. Disconnect the wire harness from the eight fuel injectors (22, **Figure 90**). Disconnect the wire harness from the fuel pressure sensor (39, **Figure 90**).
4. Remove the bolts (33, 35, 40, and 43, **Figure 90**). Lift the fuel rail and injectors as an assembly from the intake manifold. Cover the injector openings to prevent contamination.
5. Carefully pull the fuel injectors from the fuel rail. Remove and discard the O-rings from each fuel injector.
6. Carefully pull the port and starboard fuel rails from the tubes. Remove and discard the O-rings (28, 30, 37 and 42, **Figure 90**).
7. Remove the fuel pressure sensor as described in this chapter. Thoroughly clean the fuel rail, external surfaces of the fuel injectors and the tubes. Clean the injector open-

ings in the intake manifold (20, **Figure 90**). Keep debris and loose objects out of the openings.
8. Install new O-rings onto the tubes. Carefully insert the tubes into the port and starboard fuel rails. Work carefully to avoid pinching or cutting the O-rings.
9. Install new O-rings onto the top of each fuel injector. Carefully insert each injector into the fuel rail.
10. Install new O-rings onto the bottom of each fuel injector. Carefully guide the injectors into the manifold and install the fuel rail assembly. Be careful not to damage the O-rings.
11. Rotate the injector until the connectors face the exhaust manifolds. Install the fuel rail mounting bolts. Evenly tighten the bolts to the specification in **Table 1**.
12. Install the fuel pressure sensor as described in this chapter. Connect the wire harness to each injector.
13. Thread the fuel line into the fitting on the port fuel rail. Tighten the fuel line to the specification in **Table 1**.
14. Install the throttle body and flame arrestor as described in this chapter.
15. Connect the battery cables. Turn the ignition switch to the ON position and immediately check for fuel leakage. If leakage occurs, immediately turn the ignition switch OFF. Correct the leakage before operating the engine.

### 7.4 MPI models

Refer to **Figure 91**.
1. Disconnect the battery cables. Remove the oil fill cap, starboard cover (2, **Figure 91**) and port cover (5). Remove the flame arrestor and throttle body as described in this chapter.
2. Disconnect the wire harness from the air temperature sensor. The air temperature sensor mounts to the port side of the plenum (3, **Figure 91**). Disconnect the breather tube from the fitting next to the air temperature sensor.
3. Remove the bolts (4, **Figure 91**) and lift the plenum (3) from the intake manifold (12). Remove and discard the gaskets (6 and 40, **Figure 91**).
4. Wrap a shop towel around the fitting and slowly loosen the fuel line fitting. The fuel line connects to the fitting on the aft end of the port fuel rail. Plug the line and rail fitting to prevent contamination.
5. Disconnect the fuel injector harness (7, **Figure 91**) from the engine wire harness.
6. Remove the studs and bolts (8 and 37, **Figure 91**). Remove the fuel rail and injectors as an assembly from the intake manifold. Cover the injector openings to prevent contamination.
7. Disconnect the wire harness from the fuel injectors (34, **Figure 91**). Remove the retaining clip and carefully

**8**

pull the fuel injectors from the fuel rail. Remove and discard the O-rings (21 and 23, **Figure 90**) from each fuel injector.

8. Thoroughly clean the fuel rail, plenum and external surfaces of the fuel injectors. Clean the injector opening in the intake manifold. Keep debris out of the openings.

9. Install new O-rings onto the top of each fuel injector. Carefully insert each injector into the fuel rail. Fit the retaining clip onto each fuel injector and the bosses on the fuel rail. Connect the injector harness onto each fuel injector.

10. Install new O-rings on the bottom of each fuel injector. Carefully guide the injectors into the manifold openings and install the fuel rail assembly. Work carefully to avoid damaging the O-rings.

11. Install the bolts and studs (8 and 37, **Figure 91**). Tighten them to the specification in **Table 1**.

12. Connect the engine wire harness to the injector harness (7, **Figure 91**).

13. Attach the fuel line to the port fuel rail. Tighten the fuel line to the specification in **Table 1**.

14. Install new gaskets (6 and 40, **Figure 91**) onto the intake manifold. Install the plenum (3, **Figure 91**) onto the manifold. Install the bolts (4, **Figure 91**). Tighten the bolts in a crossing pattern to the specification in **Table 1**.

15. Connect the wire harness to the air temperature sensor. Connect the breather tube to its fitting on the port side of the plenum.

16. Install the throttle body and flame arrestor as described in this chapter.

17. Connect the battery cables. Turn the ignition switch to the ON position and immediately check for fuel leakage. If leakage occurs, immediately turn the ignition switch OFF. Correct the leakage before operating the engine.

18. Install the starboard cover, port cover and oil fill cap. Do not over tighten the screws or the covers will break.

### 454 Mag and 502 Mag models

Refer to **Figure 92**.

1. Disconnect the battery cables. Remove the flame arrestor and throttle body as described in this chapter.

2. Disconnect the wire harness from the air temperature sensor (22, **Figure 92**) and air pressure sensor (24).

3. Remove the bolts (1 and 2, **Figure 92**). Lift the plenum (3, **Figure 92**) from the intake manifold (45). Remove and discard the gasket (30, **Figure 92**). Remove the air temperature sensor and air pressure sensor as described in this chapter.

4. Wrap a shop towel around the fitting and slowly loosen the fitting retainer bolt (29, **Figure 92**) to bleed residual

pressure from the line. Remove and discard the O-ring from the fuel line fitting. Plug the line and rail fitting to prevent contamination.

5. Disconnect the wire harness from each fuel injector (40, **Figure 92**). Remove the four screws (26, **Figure 92**) and gently rock the fuel rail (27, **Figure 92**) to free the injectors. Remove the fuel rail. Remove the injectors from the fuel rail or intake manifold openings. Cover the injector openings to keep out water and debris.

6. Remove and discard the O-rings and grommets from the fuel injectors.

7. Remove the screws and nuts (14 and 35, **Figure 92**). Separate the fuel pressure damper (33, **Figure 92**) from the rail. Remove the O-ring and filter (31, **Figure 92**). Discard the O-ring and filter.

8. Install a new filter into the fuel rail. Place a new O-ring onto the damper. Fit the damper onto the fuel rail. Apply Loctite 8831 to the screw threads (14, **Figure 92**). Install the screws and nuts and tighten them to the specification in **Table 1**.

9. Thoroughly clean the fuel rail, plenum and external surfaces of the fuel injectors. Clean the injector openings in the intake manifold. Keep debris or loose objects out of the openings.

10. Install new grommets and O-rings on the top of each fuel injector. Carefully insert four of the fuel injectors into the port side of the fuel rail. Install new sealing grommets (44, **Figure 92**) onto the bottom of the fuel injectors.

11. Install the fuel rail, guiding the four injectors into the manifold. Rock the fuel rail toward the port side.

12. Install new sealing grommets (44, **Figure 92**) onto the bottom side of the remaining four fuel injectors. Insert the injectors into the intake manifold.

13. Install new grommets and O-rings (42 and 43, **Figure 92**) onto the top of the four fuel injectors. Align the injectors with the opening in the fuel rail and rock the rail toward the starboard side. Work carefully to avoid dislodging the injectors or damaging the O-rings.

14. Gently rock the rail and push down until the rail seats into the manifold. Install the screws (26, **Figure 92**) and tighten them to the specification in **Table 1**.

15. Connect the engine wire harness to each fuel injector. Install a new O-ring on the fitting on the high pressure fuel line. Install the fitting into the upper opening in the fuel rail. Install the retainer (28, **Figure 92**) over the ridge on the fitting. Secure the retainer using the short bolt (29, **Figure 92**). Tug on the line to verify a secure connection.

16. Install new gaskets (30, **Figure 92**) onto the intake manifold (45). Install the air temperature sensor and air pressure sensor as described in this chapter.

17. Install the plenum (3, **Figure 92**) onto the manifold and install the bolts (1 and 2, **Figure 92**). Tighten the bolts in a crossing pattern to the specification in **Table 1**.

18. Attach the wire harness connections to the air temperature sensor and air pressure sensor.

19. Install the throttle body and flame arrestor as described in this chapter.

20. Connect the battery cables. Turn the ignition switch to the ON position and immediately check for fuel leakage. If leakage occurs, immediately turn the ignition switch OFF. Correct the leakage before operating the engine.

## 496 Mag and 496 Mag HO Models

Refer to **Figure 93**.

1. Disconnect the battery cables. Remove the cover from the engine.

2. Wrap a shop towel around the fitting and slowly loosen the fuel line fitting to bleed residual pressure from the line. Disconnect the fuel line. Plug the line and rail fitting to prevent contamination.

3. Disconnect the fuel injector harness from the engine wire harness. Remove the studs (11, **Figure 93**) and bolts (12). Remove the fuel rail and injectors as an assembly from the intake manifold. Cover the injector openings to prevent contamination.

4. Disconnect the injector harness from each injector. Carefully pull the fuel injectors from the fuel rail.

5. Remove and discard the O-rings (21 and 23, **Figure 90**) from each fuel injector.

6. Thoroughly clean the fuel rail, plenum and external surfaces of the fuel injectors. Clean the injector opening in the intake manifold. Keep debris or loose objects out of the openings.

7. Install new O-rings onto the top of each fuel injector. Carefully insert each injector into the fuel rail. Connect the injector harness to each fuel injector.

8. Install new O-rings onto the bottom of each fuel injector. Carefully guide the injectors into the manifold openings and install the fuel rail assembly. Work carefully to avoid damaging the O-rings.

9. Install the bolts and studs. Tighten them to the specification in **Table 1**.

10. Connect the engine wire harness onto the injector harness. Attach the fuel line to the port fuel rail and tighten the fuel line to the specification in **Table 1**.

11. Connect the battery cables. Turn the ignition switch to the ON position and immediately check for fuel leakage. If leakage occurs, immediately turn the ignition switch OFF. Correct the leakage before operating the engine. Install the cover.

## AIR PRESSURE SENSOR

### Removal and Installation

1. Remove the flame arrestor cover or fuel injection component cover(s).

2. Refer to the following information to locate the air pressure sensor.

    a. On TBI models 4.3L, 5.0L and 5.7L, the sensor (**Figure 94**) is located on the manifold adapter between the TBI unit and the thermostat housing.

    b. On 350 Mag and MX 6.2 models, a screw and retainer (14, **Figure 90**) secure the sensor (16) to the intake manifold.

    c. On 7.4 MPI models, a screw and retainer secure the sensor (9, **Figure 91**) to the intake manifold, directly behind the thermostat housing.

    d. On 454 Mag and 502 Mag models, screws (23, **Figure 92**) secure the sensor (24) to the rear of the plenum.

    e. On 496 Mag and 496 Mag HO models, a screw and retainer secure the sensor (7, **Figure 93**) to the intake manifold (6).

3. Carefully pull on the tab and disconnect the wire harness from the sensor.

4A. *454 Mag and 502 Mag models*—Remove the screws (23, **Figure 92**). Lift the sensor from the plenum.

4B. *All other models*—Remove the screw (14, **Figure 90**) and retainer (15, typical) and remove the sensor from the intake manifold.

5. Remove and discard the seal (10, **Figure 91**, typical) from the sensor. Clean the sensor mounting surfaces and the manifold opening.

6. Apply a light coat of liquid dishwashing soap to the seal. Slide the seal over the fitting on the bottom of the sensor.

7. Insert the fitting into the opening and seat the sensor onto the manifold or plenum.

**8**

8A. *454 Mag and 502 Mag models*—Install the screws (23, **Figure 92**). Tighten the screws to the specification in **Table 1**.

8B. *All other models*—Fit the retainer (15, **Figure 90**, typical) onto the body of the sensor and install the mounting screw. Tighten the screw to the specification in **Table 1**.

9. Align the tab on the harness connector with the boss on the sensor. Connect the harness to the sensor. Tug on the harness to verify a secure fit. Route the wire harness away from moving components.

10. Connect the battery cables. Install the flame arrestor cover or fuel injection component cover(s).

## ENGINE TEMPERATURE SENSOR

### Removal and Installation (All EFI Models and 1999-On V6 And V8 Carbureted Models)

*NOTE*
*The overheat switch and engine temperature sender are similar in appearance and mount in the same area on the engine. Refer to the wire diagrams at the end of the manual and identify the component by the connecting wire color.*

1. Remove the flame arrestor cover or fuel injection component cover(s).

2A. *Standard cooling system*—Drain water from the cylinder block as described in Chapter Five.

2B. *Closed cooling system*—Drain the engine coolant as described in Chapter Four.

3. Refer to the following information to locate the engine temperature sensor.

   a. On 4.3L, 5.0L, 5.7L and 6.2L models, the sensor (**Figure 95**) is located on the port side of the thermostat housing.

   b. On 7.4 MPI models, the sensor is located at the front of the intake manifold, directly below the thermostat housing.

   c. On 454 Mag and 502 Mag models, the sensor is located on the port side of the thermostat housing.

   d. On 496 Mag and 496 Mag HO models, the sensor is located on the front starboard side of the crossover/thermostat housing. The crossover/thermostat housing mounts onto the front of each cylinder head.

4. Pull on the tab and carefully disconnect the wire harness from the sensor. Clean corrosion from the contacts in the harness connector and the sensor.

5. Using a deep socket, remove the sensor. Clean all sealant from the threaded opening and the sensor threads.

6. Apply a very light coat of Loctite Pipe Sealant with Teflon to the threads of the sensor.

7. Install and tighten the sensor to the specification in **Table 1**.

8. Align the tab on the wire harness connector with the boss on the sensor. Carefully attach the wire harness to the connector. Route the wire harness away from moving parts.

9. On models equipped with a closed cooling system, fill the cooling system with coolant as described in Chapter Five.

10. Install the flame arrestor or fuel injection component cover(s). Start the engine and check for water or coolant leakage. Remove the sensor and clean the threads if leakage occurs.

## AIR TEMPERATURE SENSOR

1. Disconnect the battery cables. Remove the flame arrestor or fuel injection component cover(s).

2. Refer to the following information to locate the air temperature sensor.

   a. On TBI models 4.3L, 5.0L and 5.7L, the sensor (**Figure 96**) mounts on the flame arrestor.

   b. On 350 Mag and MX 6.2 models, the sensor (24, **Figure 90**) is located in the intake manifold directly behind the throttle body.

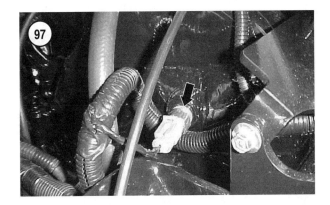

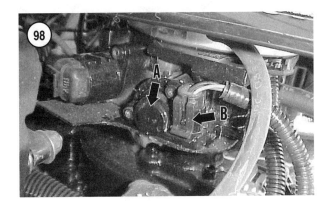

c. On model 7.4 MPI, the sensor threads into an opening on the port side of the plenum (3, **Figure 91**).

d. On 454 Mag and 502 Mag models, the sensor (22, **Figure 92**) threads into an opening on the bottom starboard side of the plenum (3),

e. On 496 Mag and 496 Mag HO models, the sensor (**Figure 97**) threads into an opening on the rear starboard side of the intake manifold.

3. Carefully pull on the tab and disconnect the wire harness from the sensor. Use a deep socket to remove the sensor.

4. Clean all sealant from the threads.

5. Apply a very light coat of Loctite Pipe Sealant with Teflon to the threads of the sensor.

6. Thread the sensor into the opening and tighten it securely.

7. Connect the wire harness to the sensor. Route the wire harness away from moving parts.

8. Connect the battery cables. Install the flame arrestor or fuel injection component cover(s).

## FUEL PRESSURE SENSOR

A fuel pressure sensor is used only on an engine with a MEFI 3 ECU engine control unit. Refer to *Fuel Injection* in Chapter Three to identify the ECU.

1. Disconnect the fuel pump harness from the engine harness as described in this chapter. Start the engine and allow it to run out of fuel. (This step is necessary to relieve fuel pressure.) Reconnect the fuel pump harness. Remove the flame arrestor or fuel injection component cover(s).

2. Disconnect the battery.

a. On 4.3L, 5.0L and 5.7L models with TBI, the sensor threads into the rear and starboard side of the throttle body injection unit.

b. On all other models with MPI, the sensor (39, **Figure 90**, typical) threads directly into the fuel rail.

3. Pull on the tab and carefully pull the connector from the sensor.

4. Wrap the sensor with clean shop towels to capture spilled fuel. Slowly loosen the sensor. Remove the sensor and promptly clean up spilled fuel.

5. Apply a very light coat of Loctite Pipe Sealant with Teflon to the last four or five threads closest to the sensor body. Do not apply sealant into the threaded opening or the hole in the sensor, because the sealant may foul the fuel injectors or the sensor.

6. Install the sensor and tighten securely. Attach the connector and tug on the harness to verify a secure connection.

7. Connect the battery cables. Turn the ignition switch ON and immediately check for fuel leakage. If leakage occurs, immediately turn the ignition switch OFF. Correct the leakage before operating the engine. Install the cover.

## THROTTLE POSITION SENSOR

Two screws secure the throttle position sensor (A, **Figure 98**) to the side of the throttle body.

1. Disconnect the battery cables. Remove the flame arrestor or fuel injection component cover(s).

2. Pull on the tab (B, **Figure 98**) and carefully disconnect the wire harness.

3. Remove the mounting screws and the sensor. Retrieve the seal from the throttle or sensor shaft.

4. Place the seal onto the sensor. Align the flat surfaces of the throttle shaft with the opening in the sensor and seat the sensor onto the throttle body.

5. Rotate the sensor to align the mounting screw openings. Apply Loctite 242 to the threads of the mounting screws. Install the screws and tighten them to the specification in **Table 1**.

6. Connect the wire harness to the sensor.

7. Install the flame arrestor or fuel injection component cover(s). Connect the battery cables.

**8**

## KNOCK SENSOR MODULE

A knock sensor module is used on early EFI models equipped with a MEFI 1 or 2 type ECU (engine control unit). Replace the module as described in Chapter Ten.

## IDLE AIR CONTROL MOTOR

1. Disconnect the battery cables. Remove the flame arrestor or fuel injection component cover(s).

2. Pull on the tab and unplug the harness connector from the idle air motor.

3A. On 496 Mag and Mag HO models, loosen the clamp and disconnect the hose (B, **Figure 99**) from the idle air motor. Remove the two screws and remove the idle air motor (A, **Figure 99**) from the throttle body. Remove and discard the motor O-ring.

3B. On all other models remove the two screws (A, **Figure 100**) and remove the idle air motor (B). Remove and discard the motor O-ring.

> *CAUTION*
> *Do not push or pull on the pintle valve. or the motor may be damaged.*

4. Thoroughly clean the mounting surfaces for the motor. Use carburetor cleaner to remove oil or carbon deposits.

5. Fit a new O-ring onto the motor. Guide the pintle into the opening and seat the motor onto the throttle body or manifold. Rotate the motor to align the screw openings.

6. Install the screws and tighten them to the specification in **Table 1**.

7. Attach the wire harness to the sensor.

8. On 496 Mag and 496 Mag HO models, slide the hose (B, **Figure 99**) onto the motor fitting. Securely tighten the hose clamp.

9. Install the flame arrestor or fuel injection component cover(s).

10. Reset the idle air control motor as follows:
   a. Turn the ignition switch to the ON position for 10 seconds. Do not start the engine.
   b. Turn the ignition switch to the OFF position.

## MANIFOLD TEMPERATURE SENSOR (496 MAG AND MAG HO)

1. Disconnect the battery cables. Disconnect the sensor wire terminal from the engine wire harness.

2. Remove the sensor from the exhaust manifold (**Figure 101**). Thoroughly clean the threads in the manifold and on the sensor.

3. Apply a very light coat of Loctite Pipe Sealant with Teflon to the threads of the sensor.

4. Thread the sensor into the manifold and tighten. Connect the sensor wire to the engine wire harness and connect the battery cables.

## CAMSHAFT POSITION SENSOR (496 MAG AND MAG HO)

1. Disconnect the battery cables. Pull the tab and disconnect the wire harness from the sensor.

2. Remove the screw (**Figure 102**) and pull the sensor from the cover. Remove the O-ring from the sensor. Discard the O-ring.

3. Clean the sensor and mounting surface on the cover. Apply engine oil to a new O-ring and install it in the groove on the sensor.

4. Carefully insert the sensor into the cover. Install and tighten the screws evenly. Route the wire harness away from moving parts.

5. Connect the battery cables. Start the engine and check for oil leakage. Correct oil leakage before operating the engine.

## CRANKSHAFT POSITION SENSOR
## (496 MAG AND MAG HO)

A screw secures the crankshaft position sensor to the rear of the cylinder block, just forward of the flywheel housing mating surface.

1. Disconnect the battery cables. Disconnect the wire harness from the sensor.

2. Remove the screw and pull the sensor from the cylinder block bore. Use a mild solvent and clean the sensor.

3. Insert the sensor into the cylinder block bore and install the retaining screw. Securely tighten the screw.

4. Connect the engine wire harness to the crankshaft position sensor. Connect the battery cables.

## SYSTEM RELAY AND FUEL PUMP RELAY

The system and fuel pump relays (A and B, **Figure 103**) are identical. Refer to the wire diagrams at the end of the manual to identify the wires for each relay.

1. Disconnect the battery cables. Pull the relay from the mounting boss. Push in on the tab (C, **Figure 103**) and pull the relay from the connector.

2. Clean the terminals in the harness connector and on the relay.

3. Align the tab on the relay with the latch on the harness connector. Carefully push the relay into the connector until the tab engages the latch. Tug on the relay to verify a secure connection.

4. Align the slot in the relay with the mounting boss, and slide it onto the mounting boss. Connect the battery cables.

## ENGINE CONTROL UNIT

1. Disconnect the battery cables.

2. Refer to **Figure 91** and **Figures 104-107** as needed during this procedure.

3. Push in on the tabs and remove the connectors from the control unit. Remove the mounting bolts. Disconnect any ground wires and remove the control unit.

4. Wipe the mounting surfaces clean. Inspect the pins and harness connections for corroded, bent or damaged terminals. Straighten slightly bent pins or terminals. Replace the control unit or engine harness if the terminals cannot be fully straightened or if they are excessively corroded.

5. Install the control unit and mounting hardware. Connect the ground wire, if so equipped. Securely tighten the mounting fasteners.

6. Before connecting the wire harness to the unit, carefully inspect the harness connectors and opening in the control unit. Some terminals differ only slightly from others. The connectors must be connected to the proper terminals to prevent damage to the control unit.

7. Push in on the tabs and carefully push each connector into the control unit. Do not force the connector. Release the tabs and tug on the connector to verify secure connections.

8. Connect the battery cables.

**8**

## INTAKE MANIFOLD

Remove the intake manifold (**Figure 108**, typical) if leaking or as necessary to replace the camshaft, lifters or pushrods. Replace the manifold gaskets each time the manifold is removed. Gasket failure can lead to water, air or exhaust leakage and serious engine damage. Never use automotive gaskets on the intake manifold. Purchase the gaskets only from a MerCruiser dealership. Quicksilver RTV Sealer (Mercury part No. 92-809826) is also required for this operation.

> *WARNING*
> *Use caution when working with the fuel system. Never smoke around fuel or fuel vapor. Make sure no flame or source of ignition is present in the work area. Flame or sparks can ignite fuel or vapor resulting in fire or explosion.*

### 3.0L Models

The intake manifold is integrated into the exhaust manifold on this model. Refer to Chapter Nine for the replacement procedure.

### 4.3L, 5.0L, 5.7L, 350 Mag MPI and MX 6.2 Models

1. Disconnect the battery cables.

2A. *Standard cooling system*—Drain water from the block as described in Chapter Five.

2B. *Closed cooling system*—Drain the coolant as described in Chapter Four.

3A. On 4.3L, 5.0L and 5.7L models, remove the carburetor or TBI unit as described in this chapter.

3B. On 350 Mag MPI and MX 6.2 models, remove the throttle body, fuel rails and injectors (**Figure 90**) as described in this chapter.

4. Remove the thermostat housing as described in Chapter Nine.

5. Loosen the fittings and remove the metal tube from the starboard side exhaust manifold and intake manifold.

6. Remove the distributor as described in Chapter Ten. Remove any remaining brackets or other components from the manifold.

7. Remove the manifold attaching bolts. Fit a pry bar into the gap at the front of the manifold and carefully pry the manifold from the cylinder heads and block.

8. Cover the openings and carefully scrape gasket material from the manifold and cylinder heads.

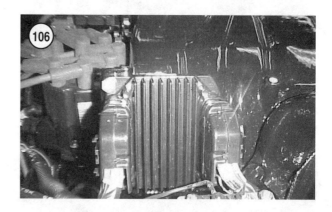

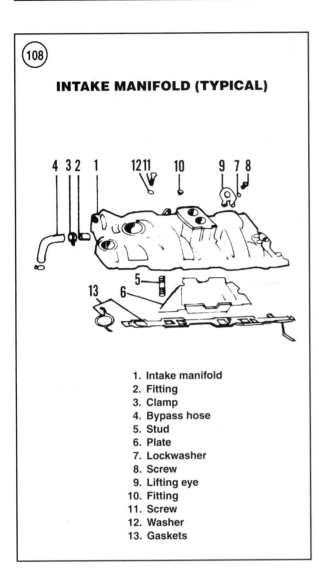

**INTAKE MANIFOLD (TYPICAL)**

1. Intake manifold
2. Fitting
3. Clamp
4. Bypass hose
5. Stud
6. Plate
7. Lockwasher
8. Screw
9. Lifting eye
10. Fitting
11. Screw
12. Washer
13. Gaskets

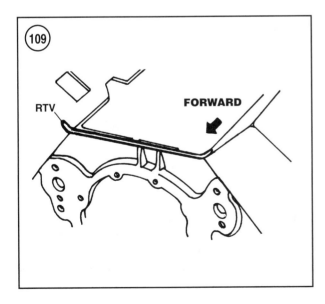

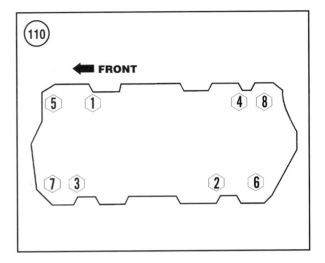

9. Inspect the mating surfaces for deep corrosion pits, cracks or gouges. Defective mating surfaces will allow water, coolant, air or exhaust leakage.

10. Apply a light coat of Perfect Seal (Mercury part No. 92-34227-1) to both sides of the new manifold gaskets and around the cooling passages on the cylinder heads. Install the gaskets onto each cylinder head. The marks on the gaskets must face up.

11. Apply a 3/16 in. (4.8 mm) diameter bead of RTV onto the front and rear manifold mating surfaces (**Figure 109**). Extend the bead approximately 1/2 in. (12.7 mm) up onto the manifold gaskets.

12. Carefully lower the manifold into position on the cylinder heads. Align the bolt holes in the manifold, gaskets and cylinder heads. Do not remove the manifold or the RTV sealant must be re-applied.

13. Apply a light coat of Perfect Seal to the manifold bolt threads. Thread the bolts into the manifold and cylinder head.

14. Tighten the bolts in sequence (**Figure 110**) to the specification in **Table 1**.

15. Install the distributor as described in Chapter Ten. Install the thermostat housing as described in Chapter Nine.

16. Connect the metal tube to the fittings on the intake manifold and the starboard exhaust manifold. Securely tighten the fittings. Install any brackets or other components.

17A. On 4.3L, 5.0L and 5.7L models, install the carburetor or TBI unit as described in this chapter.

17B. On 350 Mag MPI and MX 6.2 models, install the throttle body, fuel rails and injectors (**Figure 90**) as described in this chapter.

18. On models equipped with a closed cooling system, refill the engine with coolant as described in Chapter Four.

19. Perform all applicable adjustments as described in Chapter Six.

20. Connect the battery cables. Start the engine and immediately check for fluid or exhaust leakage. Correct fluid leakage before operating the engine.

### 7.4 MPI Models

Refer to **Figure 91**.

1. Disconnect the battery cables.

2A. *Standard cooling system*—Drain water from the block as described in Chapter Five.

2B. *Closed cooling system*—Drain the coolant as described in Chapter Four.

3. Remove the plenum (3, **Figure 91**) and fuel rail assembly (33) as described in this chapter.

4. Remove the air pressure sensor and engine temperature sensor as described in this chapter.

5. Remove the thermostat housing as described in Chapter Nine. Disconnect the bypass hose (15, **Figure 91**) from the fittings on the intake manifold (13) and circulation pump (17).

6. Remove the distributor as described in Chapter Ten. Remove any remaining brackets or other components from the manifold.

7. Remove the manifold attaching bolts (11, **Figure 91**). Fit a pry bar into the gap at the front of the manifold and carefully pry the manifold from the cylinder heads and block.

8. Cover the openings and carefully scrape gasket material from the manifold and cylinder heads.

9. Inspect the mating surfaces for deep corrosion pits, cracks or gouges. Replace damaged components

10. Apply a light coat of Perfect Seal (Mercury part No. 92-34227-1) to both sides of the new manifold gaskets (18, **Figure 91**) and around cooling passages on the cylinder heads. Align the port openings and install the gaskets onto each cylinder head. The marks on the gaskets must face up.

11. Apply a light coat of Bellows Adhesive (Mercury part No. 92-86166Q1) to the front and rear manifold mating surfaces of the cylinder block. Install the neoprene gasket on the front and rear of the cylinder block. Hold the gaskets in position until the adhesive dries.

12. Apply a 3/16 in. (4.8 mm) diameter bead of RTV onto the ends of the neoprene gaskets. Extend the bead approximately 1/2 in. (12.7 mm) up onto the manifold gaskets.

13. Carefully lower the manifold into position on the cylinder heads. Move the manifold and gaskets slightly to align the bolt holes in the manifold, gaskets and cylinder heads. Do not remove the manifold, or the RTV sealant must be re-applied.

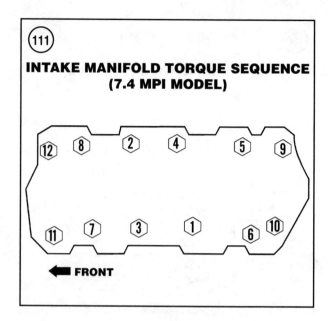

**INTAKE MANIFOLD TORQUE SEQUENCE (7.4 MPI MODEL)**

14. Apply a light coat of Perfect Seal to the manifold bolt threads. Thread the bolts into the manifold and cylinder head. Tighten the bolts in sequence (**Figure 111**) to the specification in **Table 1**.

15. Install the distributor as described in Chapter Ten. Install the thermostat housing as described in Chapter Nine.

16. Install the plenum (3, **Figure 91**) and fuel rail assembly (33) as described in this chapter.

17. Install the air pressure sensor and engine temperature sensor as described in this chapter. Install the thermostat housing as described in Chapter Nine. Connect the bypass hose (15, **Figure 91**) to the fittings on the manifold (13) and circulation pump (17). Securely tighten the hose clamps.

18. On models equipped with a closed cooling system, refill the engine with coolant as described in Chapter Four.

19. Perform all applicable adjustments as described in Chapter Six.

20. Connect the battery cables. Start the engine and immediately check for fluid or exhaust leakage. Correct fluid leakage before operating the engine.

### 454 Mag and 502 Mag Models

Refer to **Figure 92**.

1. Disconnect the battery cables.

2A. *Standard cooling system*—Drain water from the block as described in Chapter Five.

2B. *Closed cooling system*—Drain the coolant as described in Chapter Four.

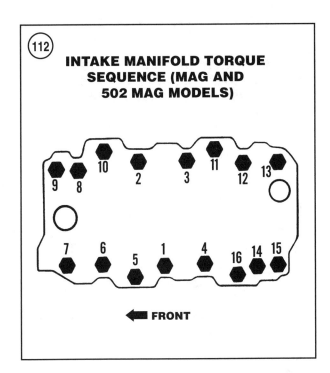

8. Inspect the mating surfaces for deep corrosion pits, cracks or gouges. Defective surfaces will allow water, coolant, air or exhaust leaks.

9. Apply a light coat of Perfect Seal (Mercury part No. 92-34227-1) to both sides of the new manifold gaskets and around the cooling passages on the cylinder heads. Align the port openings and install the gaskets onto each cylinder head. The marks on the gaskets must face upward.

10. Apply a light coat of Bellows Adhesive (Mercury part No. 92-86166Q1) to the front and rear manifold mating surfaces of the cylinder block. Install the neoprene gaskets on the front and rear of the cylinder block. Hold them in position until the adhesive dries.

11. Apply a 3/16 in. (4.8 mm) diameter bead of RTV to the ends of the neoprene gaskets. Extend the bead approximately 1/2 in. (12.7 mm) up onto the manifold gaskets.

12. Carefully lower the manifold into position on the cylinder heads. Move the manifold and gaskets slightly to align the bolt holes in the manifold, gaskets and cylinder heads. Do not remove the manifold. Otherwise RTV sealant must be re-applied.

13. Apply a light coating of Perfect Seal to the manifold bolt threads. Thread the bolts into the manifold and cylinder head. Tighten the bolt in sequence (**Figure 112**) to the specification in **Table 1**.

14. Install the distributor as described in Chapter Ten. Install the thermostat housing as described in Chapter Nine. Connect the bypass hose onto the fittings on the intake manifold and circulation pump. Securely tighten the hose clamps.

15. Install the plenum and fuel rail assembly as described in this chapter. Install the thermostat housing as described in Chapter Nine.

16. On models equipped with a closed cooling system, refill the engine with coolant as described in Chapter Four.

17. Perform all applicable adjustments as described in Chapter Six.

18. Connect the battery cables. Start the engine and immediately check for fluid or exhaust leakage. Correct fluid leakage before operating the engine.

### 496 Mag and 496 Mag HO Models

Refer to **Figure 93**.

1. Disconnect the battery cables.

2. Drain the coolant as described in Chapter Four.

3. Remove the throttle body (2, **Figure 93**) and fuel rail assembly (10) as described in this chapter.

4. Remove the bracket (**Figure 113**) supporting the automatic drain system and gearcase lubricant monitor.

3. Remove the plenum (3, **Figure 92**) and fuel rail assembly (27) as described in this chapter.

4. Remove the thermostat housing as described in Chapter Nine. Disconnect the bypass hose from the fittings on the intake manifold and circulation pump.

5. Remove the distributor as described in Chapter Ten. Remove any remaining brackets or other components from the manifold. Reposition the wire harness and hoses to allow free access to the manifold.

6. Remove all of the manifold attaching bolts and washers (**Figure 92**). Fit a pry bar into the gap at the front of the manifold and carefully pry the manifold from the cylinder heads and block.

7. Cover the openings and carefully scrape gasket material from the manifold and cylinder heads.

5. Remove any remaining brackets or other components from the manifold. Reposition wire harness and hoses to allow free access to the manifold.

6. Remove the manifold attaching bolts (5, **Figure 93**). Fit a pry bar into the gap at the front of the manifold and carefully pry the manifold from the cylinder heads and block.

7. Cover the openings and carefully scrape gasket material from the manifold and cylinder heads.

8. Inspect the mating surfaces for deep corrosion pits, cracks or gouges. Replace damaged components.

9. Apply a light coat of Perfect Seal (Mercury part No. 92-34227-1) to both sides of the new manifold gaskets (18, **Figure 91**) and around cooling passages on the cylinder heads. Align the port openings and install the gaskets onto each cylinder head. The marks on the gaskets must face upward.

10. Apply a light coat of Bellows Adhesive (Mercury part No. 92-86166Q1) to the front and rear manifold mating surfaces of the cylinder block. Install the neoprene gasket on the front and rear of the cylinder block. Hold them in position until the adhesive dries.

11. Apply a 3/16 in. (4.8 mm) diameter bead of RTV to the ends of the neoprene gaskets. Extend the bead approximately 1/2 in. (12.7 mm) up onto the manifold gaskets.

12. Carefully lower the manifold into position on the cylinder heads. Align the bolt holes in the manifold, gaskets and cylinder heads. Do not remove the manifold, or the RTV sealant must be re-applied.

13. Apply a light coat of Perfect Seal to the manifold bolt threads. Thread the bolts into the manifold and cylinder

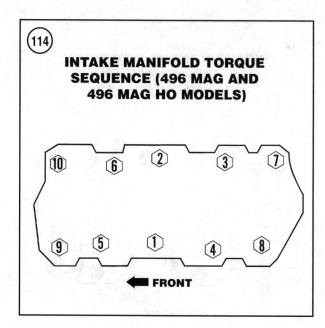

(114)

**INTAKE MANIFOLD TORQUE SEQUENCE (496 MAG AND 496 MAG HO MODELS)**

⑩  ⑥  ②  ③  ⑦

⑨  ⑤  ①  ④  ⑧

◄ **FRONT**

head. Tighten the bolts in sequence (**Figure 114**) to the specification in **Table 1**.

14. Install the bracket (**Figure 113**) that supports the automatic drain system and gearcase lubricant monitor.

15. Install the throttle body and fuel rail assembly as described in this chapter.

16. Refill the engine coolant as described in Chapter Four. Perform all applicable adjustments as described in Chapter Six.

17. Connect the battery cables. Start the engine and immediately check for fluid or exhaust leakage. Correct fluid leakage before operating the engine.

## Table 1 TORQUE SPECIFICATIONS

| Fastener | ft.-lb. | in.-lb. | N•m |
|---|---|---|---|
| Carburetor | | | |
| Mounting bolts/nuts | | | |
| Two -barrel carburetor | 20 | – | 27 |
| Four-barrel carburetor | – | 132 | 15 |
| Fuel line to fuel fitting | 18 | – | 24 |
| Fuel inlet fitting | 18 | – | 24 |
| Plenum to intake | | | |
| 7.4L MPI | 30 | – | 41 |
| 454 Mag, 502 Mag | – | 150 | 17 |
| Mechanical fuel pump (3.0L) | 20 | – | 27 |
| Electric fuel pump (carburetor models) | | | |
| Pump bracket to cylinder head | 25 | – | 34 |
| Outlet (smaller) fitting | – | 84 | 9 |
| Inlet (larger) fitting | – | 96 | 11 |
| Fuel line fittings | 18 | – | 24 |
| Water separating filter mounting bracket | 25 | – | 34 |
| Cool fuel system | | | |
| Mounting nuts | 18 | – | 24 |
| Fuel pump/cooler retainer | – | 50 | 6 |
| Fuel line fitting | 18 | – | 24 |
| Stepped shouldered screw | – | 81 | 9 |
| Fuel pressure regulator | – | 53 | 6 |
| EFI sensors and actuators | | | |
| Engine temperature sensor | 20 | – | 27 |
| Throttle position sensor | – | 20 | 2 |
| Air pressure sensor | – | 44.-62 | 5-7 |
| Idle air control motor | – | 20 | 2 |
| Throttle body assembly | | | |
| Throttle body to adapter | | | |
| TBI unit | 15 | – | 20 |
| 350 Mag MPI | – | 89 | 10 |
| 496 Mag and 496 Mag HO | – | 89 | 10 |
| Adapter to plenum | | | |
| 7.4 MPI | – | 75 | 8.5 |
| Fuel rail fasteners | – | 105 | 12 |
| Injector retainer | | | |
| 7.4 MPI | – | 28 | 3 |
| Fuel pressure dampner | – | 88-124 | 10-14 |
| Intake manifold | | | |
| 4.3L | 11 | 132 | 15 |
| 5.0L, 5.7L, 350 Mag, MX 6.2 | 18 | – | 24 |
| 7.4 MPI | 30 | – | 41 |
| 454 Mag, 502 Mag | 35 | – | 47 |
| 496 Mag and 496 Mag HO | – | 106 | 12 |

## Table 2 CARBURETOR SPECIFICATIONS

| Model | Specifications |
|---|---|
| 3.0L | |
| Carburetor part No. | 3310-807504 |
| Idle mixture adjustment | 1 1/4 turn out |
| Float level | |
| Spring loaded needle | 9/16 in. (14 mm)* |
| Two-piece (solid) needle | 3/8 in. (9.5 mm)* |
| Float drop | 1 3/32 in. (28 mm)* |
| Maximum float weight | 9 grams |
| | (continued) |

8

**Table 2 CARBURETOR SPECIFICATIONS (continued)**

| Model | Specifications |
|---|---|
| 3.0L (continued) | |
|   Choke setting | Two marks lean (to the right of the index mark) |
|   Choke unloader | 0.080 in. (2 mm) |
|   Main jet size | 1.55 mm |
|   Power valve size | 0.65 mm |
| 4.3L (two-barrel carburetor) | |
|   Carburetor part No. | 3310-807764 |
|   Idle mixture adjustment | 1 1/4 turn out |
|   Float level | |
|     Spring loaded needle | 9/16 in. (14 mm)* |
|     Two-piece (solid) needle | 0.375 in. (9.5 mm)* |
|   Float drop | 1 3/32 in. (28 mm)* |
|   Maximum float weight | 9 grams |
|   Choke setting | Two marks lean (to the right of the index mark) |
|   Choke unloader | 0.080 in. (2 mm) |
|   Main jet size | 1.55 mm |
|   Power valve size | 0.74 mm |
| 4.3L (four-barrel carburetor) | |
|   Carburetor identification No. | 3310-807826 |
|   Idle mixture adjustment | 1 1/4 turns out |
|   Float level | 1 9/32 in. (33 mm) |
|   Float drop | 2 in. (51 mm) |
|   Primary jet size | 0.092 in. |
|   Secondary jet size | 0.089 in. |
|   Primary metering rod No. | 16-686457 |
|   Metering rod spring color | Green |
|   Accelerator pump height | 7/16 in. (11 mm) |
| 5.0L (two-barrel carburetor) | |
|   Carburetor part No. | 3310-861448 |
|   Idle mixture adjustment | 1 1/2 turns out |
|   Float level | 11/32 in. (8.7 mm) |
|   Float drop | 15/16 in. (23.8 mm) |
|   Maximum float weight | 9 grams |
|   Choke unloader | 5/64 (2 mm) |
|   Main jet size | 1.65 mm |
|   Power valve size | 0.90 mm |
| 5.7L (two-barrel carburetor) | |
|   Carburetor part No. | 3310-861245 |
|   Idle mixture adjustment | 1 1/2 turns out |
|   Float level | 11/32 in. (8.7 mm) |
|   Float drop | 15/16 in. (23.8 mm) |
|   Maximum float weight | 9 grams |
|   Choke unloader | 5/64 (2 mm) |
|   Main jet size | 1.65 mm |
|   Power valve size | 0.90 mm |

*Measured from the gasket surface to the protrusion on the float.

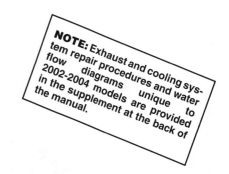
**NOTE:** Exhaust and cooling system repair procedures and water flow diagrams unique to 2002-2004 models are provided in the supplement at the back of the manual.

# Chapter Nine

# Exhaust and Cooling System

This chapter describes replacement and repair of the exhaust, standard cooling and closed cooling systems (**Figure 1**). Closed cooling is standard on 496 Mag and 496 Mag HO models. Closed cooling is a factory or dealer installed option on all other models.

**Table 1** lists torque specifications for exhaust and cooling system fasteners. **Table 2** lists closed cooling system test specifications. Tables 1 and 2 are located at the end of this chapter.

> *NOTE*
> *Most Mercruiser engines use a standard exhaust system that vents exhaust through the propeller. Some V6 and V8 engines use a through-the-transom exhaust system. This chapter describes repair procedures for the standard exhaust system.*

## EXHAUST ELBOW

### Removal and Installation

Replace all gaskets and O-rings anytime the exhaust elbow is removed. Unless otherwise specified, apply Loctite 510 Sealant to the elbow mating surfaces. Allow three hours curing time before starting the engine.

Inspect the elbow mating surfaces for cracks, pits or other damage. Pay particular attention to the surface which contacts the gasket sealing bead. Damage to this surface allows water into the engine, causing serious engine damage.

Lay a straightedge across the manifold and elbow mating surfaces. Pass a feeler gauge under the straightedge to check for warp. The maximum allowable warp is 0.003 in. (0.07 mm) along the entire length of the surface and 0.001 (0.02 mm) within a 1 in. (25.4 mm) span.

Have the surfaces machined to correct surface warp or pitting. Replace the manifold or elbow if the surfaces cannot be repaired without removing more than 0.010 in (0.25 mm) of material.

Inspect the water and exhaust passages for corrosion or mineral deposits. To remove deposits, soak the elbow in a cleaner suitable for iron, stainless steel and aluminum, available from a marine dealership or marine supply store.

> *CAUTION*
> *Do not remove more than 0.010 in. (0.25 mm) from the manifold or elbow mating surfaces. The fasteners may touch the bottom of their bores and not provide adequate clamping force.*

> *CAUTION*
> *Use an appropriate sealant and replace the exhaust manifold gasket(s) every time the elbow fasteners are loosened. Gasket failure allows water into the engine, resulting in serious engine damage.*

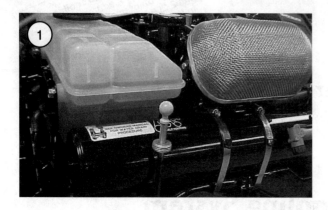

### 3.0L Models

1. Disconnect the battery cables. Drain the exhaust manifold as described in Chapter Five.

2. Loosen the exhaust tube clamps (**Figure 2**).

3. Remove the mounting bolts and lift the elbow from the manifold.

4. Remove the gasket from the elbow or manifold. Discard the gasket.

5. Inspect the flapper valve (**Figure 2**) for wear, burns or missing sections. If defective, replace the flapper valve as described in this chapter.

6. Verify proper installation of the exhaust tube on the exhaust pipe. The raised ridge in the inner diameter of the tube must just contact the end of the pipe. Loosen the clamps and reposition the tube as needed.

7. Thoroughly clean the elbow and manifold mating surfaces. Inspect the mating surface and correct defects as described in this chapter.

8. Install a new gasket on the exhaust manifold. Sealant is not required on the gasket.

9. Seat the exhaust elbow on the manifold, aligning the elbow with the exhaust tube (**Figure 2**).

10. Apply a light coat of Perfect Seal to the bolts and thread them into the elbow and manifold. Tighten the bolts to the specification in **Table 1**.

11. Tighten the exhaust tube clamps to the specification in **Table 1**. Connect the battery cables. Start the engine and check for water or exhaust leakage. Correct as needed.

### V6 and V8 Models
### (Except 496 Mag and 496 Mag HO)

Refer to **Figure 3**.

1. Disconnect the battery cables. Drain the exhaust manifold as described in Chapter Five.

2. Loosen the exhaust tube clamps (**Figure 4**).

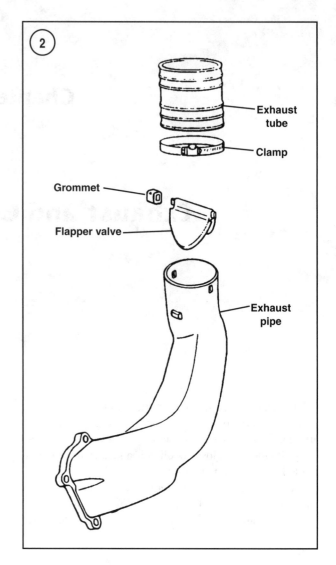

3. Remove the nuts and washers (1, **Figure 3**) and lift the elbow (2) from the manifold studs. Pull the elbow from the exhaust tube.

4A. *Without risers or muffler spacers*—Remove the gasket (3, **Figure 3**) from the elbow or manifold. Discard the gasket.

4B. *With risers and/or muffler spacer*—Lift the muffler spacer, risers and gaskets (4-7, **Figure 3**) from the manifold studs. Discard the gaskets.

5. Inspect the flapper valve (**Figure 2**) for wear, burns or missing sections. If defective, replace the flapper valve as described in this chapter.

6. Make sure the exhaust tube is properly attached to the exhaust pipe (**Figure 2**). The raised ridge in the inner diameter of the tube must just contact the end of the pipe. Loosen the clamps and reposition the tube as needed.

**③**

## EXHAUST ELBOW AND MANIFOLD V-6 AND V-8 MODELS (EXCEPT 496 MAG, 496 MAG HO AND V-6 WITH ONE-PIECE MANIFOLD)

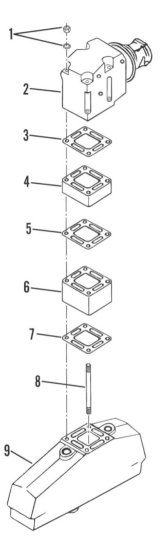

1. Nut and washer
2. Exhaust elbow
3. Gasket
4. Spacer (used with muffler only)
5. Gasket (used with muffler or riser kit only)
6. Riser (optional)
7. Gasket (used with riser kit only)
8. Stud
9. Manifold

**④**

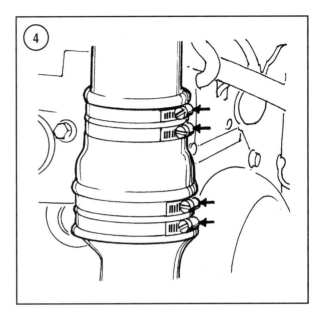

9

7. Thoroughly clean the elbow and manifold mating surfaces. Inspect the mating surface and correct defects as described in this chapter.

8. Apply a continuous bead of Loctite 510 to both sides of the new gasket (3, **Figure 3**). The bead must surround the water, exhaust and stud openings on the gasket. Place the gasket onto the exhaust manifold. Avoid shifting the gasket on the mating surface.

9. Install the riser, spacer (if so equipped) and gaskets over the studs as shown in **Figure 3**.

10. Slide the aft end of the elbow into the exhaust tube. Do not tighten the clamps (**Figure 4**) at this time. Seat the elbow on the manifold.

11. Install the washers and nuts (1, **Figure 3**). Tighten the nuts in a crossing pattern to the specification in **Table 1**.

12. Tighten the exhaust tube clamps to the specification in **Table 1**. Connect the battery cables. Start the engine and check for water or exhaust leakage. Correct as needed.

### *496 Mag and 496 Mag HO Models*

Refer to **Figure 5**.

1. Disconnect the battery cables. Drain the exhaust manifold as described in Chapter Five.

2. Loosen the hose clamps (A, **Figure 6**) and pull the water hoses (B) from the elbow.

3. Loosen the exhaust tube clamps (**Figure 4**). Remove the shift plate bracket, ignition module bracket or ECM, fuse and relay bracket from the elbow.

4. Disconnect the hoses from the sides of the riser (3, **Figure 5**), if so equipped.

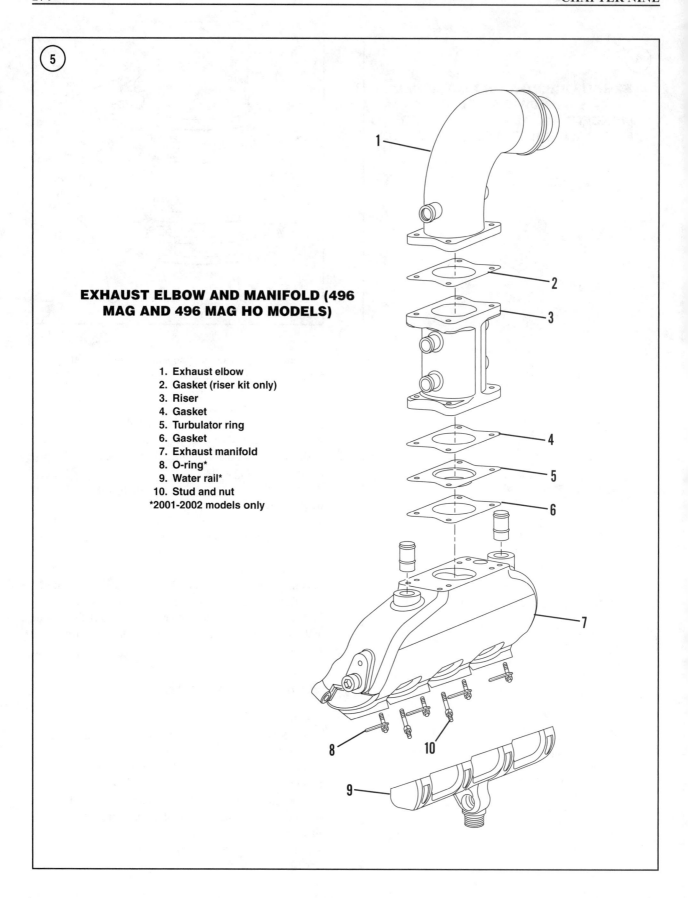

⑤

**EXHAUST ELBOW AND MANIFOLD (496 MAG AND 496 MAG HO MODELS)**

1. Exhaust elbow
2. Gasket (riser kit only)
3. Riser
4. Gasket
5. Turbulator ring
6. Gasket
7. Exhaust manifold
8. O-ring*
9. Water rail*
10. Stud and nut
*2001-2002 models only

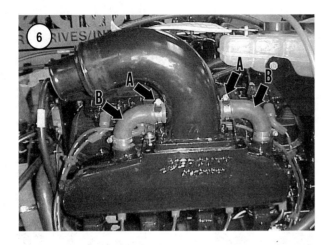

5. Remove the mounting fasteners and lift the elbow (1, **Figure 5**) from the manifold (7) or riser (3). Pull the elbow from the exhaust tube.

6. If equipped with exhaust risers, lift the riser (3, **Figure 5**) from the manifold.

7. Lift the turbulator ring and gaskets (4-6, **Figure 5**) from the manifold. Remove and discard all gaskets.

8. Thoroughly clean the elbow and manifold mating surfaces. Inspect the mating surface and correct defects as described in this chapter.

9. Inspect the turbulator ring for pits or damage. Replace as needed.

10. Set the gaskets and turbulator ring (4-6, **Figure 5**) on the exhaust manifold. The lip on the turbulator ring must face downward.

11. If equipped with exhaust risers, set the riser and gasket onto the manifold.

12. Slide the aft end of the elbow into the exhaust tube. Do not tighten the clamps (**Figure 4**) at this time.

13. Seat the elbow on the manifold or riser.

14A. *Without exhaust risers*—Apply Loctite 271 to the threads of the mounting bolts.

14B. *With exhaust risers*—Apply Loctite 242 to the nut end of the studs.

15. Install the bolt or nuts. Tighten them in a crossing pattern to the specification in **Table 1**.

16. Attach the water hoses to their fittings on the elbow and riser. Securely tighten all hose clamps.

17. Install the shift plate bracket, ignition module, or ECM, fuse and relay bracket to the elbow.

18. Tighten the exhaust tube clamps to the specification in **Table 1**. Connect the battery cables. Start the engine and check for water or exhaust leakage. Correct as needed.

## EXHAUST FLAPPER VALVE

1. Remove the exhaust elbow as described in this chapter.

2. Loosen the hose clamps (**Figure 2**) and pull the exhaust tube from the exhaust pipe.

3. Hold the flapper valve open and pull the grommets (**Figure 2**) from the pipe.

4. Lift the flapper valve from the pipe. Gently scrape carbon deposits from the exhaust pipe opening, taking care not to remove aluminum material from the pipe.

5. Insert the flapper valve into the exhaust pipe. The flaps must face down as shown in **Figure 2**.

6. Carefully fit the opening in the grommets over each end of the flapper valve bar. Seat the grommets into the square opening of the pipe.

7. Apply soapy water to the inner diameter of the exhaust tube. Without dislodging the grommets, fit the tube over the exhaust pipe. The ridge on the inner diameter of the tube must contact the end of the pipe. If the tube does not have a ridge, the bottom of the tube must contact the external stop on the pipe.

8. Install the clamps on the tube, but do not tighten them at this time.

9. Install the exhaust elbow as described in this chapter. Tighten the exhaust tube clamps to the specification in **Table 1**.

## EXHAUST MANIFOLD

Apply Perfect Seal (Mercury part No. 92-34227-1) to the threads of the studs before installing them into the manifold. Use a stud tool to remove and install the studs. Makeshift tools usually weaken the stud or damage the threads.

Inspect the water and exhaust passages for corrosion or mineral deposits. To remove deposits, soak the manifold in a cleaner designed for iron, stainless steel and aluminum materials, available from a marine dealership or marine supply facility.

Drain water from the exhaust manifold as described in Chapter Five before beginning this procedure.

> *CAUTION*
> *The manifold used on models 496 Mag and 496 Mag HO is made of aluminum. Use only a cleaner suitable for aluminum materials to clean deposits from the manifold. Never use muriatic acid on aluminum parts. Muriatic acid and some cleaners will react chemically with aluminum, causing severe damage to these surfaces. Always read and follow the manufacturer's instructions.*

9

## 3.0L Models

1. Drain the water from the manifold as described in Chapter Five.

2. Remove the carburetor as described in Chapter Eight.

3. Remove the exhaust elbow as described in this chapter.

4. Loosen the clamp and remove the water hose from the fitting at the front of the manifold.

5. On 2000-on models, remove the bolts and lift the drain tube bracket (**Figure 7**) from the manifold.

6. Remove the gear lubricant monitor bracket from the manifold.

7. Remove the mounting bolts, nuts and washers. Pull the manifold from the studs. Remove the gasket from the manifold and cylinder head mating surfaces.

8. Thoroughly clean and inspect the cylinder head and manifold mating surfaces. Replace the components if the surface is deeply pitted, cracked or damaged.

9. Slide a new manifold gasket onto the mounting studs. Slide the manifold over the mounting studs.

10. Install the mounting fasteners. Tighten the fasteners from the center out to the specification in **Table 1**.

11. Install the drain tube bracket, if so equipped, and gear lubricant monitor bracket.

12. Install the carburetor as described in this Chapter Eight. Install the exhaust elbow as described in this chapter.

## V6 and V8 Models
## (Except 496 Mag and 496 Mag HO)

1. Drain the water from the manifold as described in Chapter Five.

2. Remove the exhaust elbow as described in this chapter.

3. As required, remove the alternator, seawater pickup pump and power steering pump brackets from the manifolds.

4. Loosen the clamp (**Figure 8**) and pull the water hose from the bottom of the manifold.

5. Support the manifold while removing the manifold bolts. If allowed to drop, the spark plug or other components may be damaged. Pull the manifold from the cylinder head. Remove the gasket from the manifold and cylinder head mating surfaces.

6. Thoroughly clean and inspect the cylinder head and manifold mating surfaces. Replace the components if the surface is deeply pitted, cracked or damaged.

7. Inspect the water hose fitting for cracks, melting or other damage. To replace the fitting, unscrew it from the manifold. If the fitting breaks off in the manifold, heat the remaining fitting using a torch and remove the softened material from the threads using tweezers or needlenose

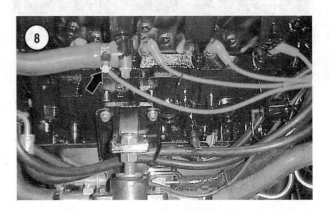

pliers. Apply Perfect Seal to the threads of the new fitting and tighten it in the manifold securely.

8. Place appropriately sized studs into the manifold bolt holes. The studs must be longer than the mounting bolts and be strong enough to support the manifold. Slide a new gasket onto the studs.

9. Guide the manifold over the studs. Remove the studs one at a time and replace with the mounting bolts. Tighten the fasteners from the center out to the specification in **Table 1**.

10. Install the alternator, seawater pickup pump and power steering pump brackets on the manifold.

11. Install the water hose over the fitting. Securely tighten the clamp (**Figure 8**).

12. Install the exhaust elbow as described in this chapter.

## 496 Mag and 496 Mag HO Models

1. Drain the water from the manifold as described in Chapter Five. Remove the manifold temperature sensor as described in Chapter Eight.

2. Remove the exhaust elbow as described in this chapter.

3. As required, remove the alternator, seawater pickup pump and power steering pump brackets from the manifolds.

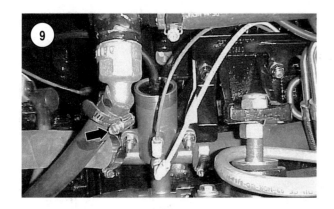

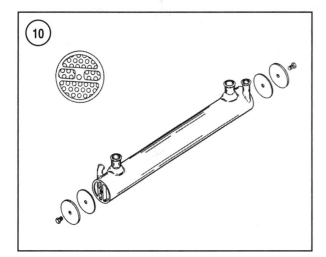

4. Loosen the clamps (**Figure 9**) and pull the water drain and cooling water hoses from the water rail.

5. Support the manifold while removing the manifold bolts. If allowed to drop, the spark plugs or other components could be damaged. Pull the manifold from the cylinder head. Remove the gasket material from the manifold and cylinder head mating surfaces.

6. Thoroughly clean and inspect the cylinder head and manifold mating surfaces. Replace the affected components if the surface is deeply pitted, cracked or damaged.

7. On 2001 and 2002 models, if replacing the manifold, remove the water rail (9, **Figure 5**) as described in this chapter. Install the water rail onto the replacement manifold.

8. Insert appropriately sized studs into the manifold bolt holes. The studs must be longer than the mounting bolts and be strong enough to support the manifold. Slide a new gasket onto the studs.

9. Guide the manifold over the studs. Remove the studs one at a time, replacing them with the mounting bolts. Tighten the fasteners from the center out to the specification in **Table 1**.

10. As required, attach the alternator, seawater pickup pump and power steering pump brackets on the manifold.

11. Attach the water drain and cooling water hoses to the water rail fittings. Securely tighten the clamps (**Figure 9**).

12. Install the exhaust elbow as described in this chapter. Install the manifold temperature sensor as described in Chapter Eight.

## WATER RAIL (2001-2002 MODELS)

Refer to **Figure 5**.

1. Drain water from the manifold as described in Chapter Five.

2. Remove the water rail mounting nuts (10, **Figure 5**). Remove the nuts from the studs as needed.

3. Pull the water rail from the manifold (7, **Figure 5**). Remove and discard the O-rings.

4. Use an appropriate tool to remove the studs (10, **Figure 5**) from the manifold. Replace corroded or damaged studs.

5. Thoroughly clean the mating surfaces and water passages. Inspect the rail and manifold mating surfaces for deep pits, cracks or other defects. Replace the component if necessary.

6. Apply Loctite 271 to the manifold end of the stud. Use an appropriate tool and install the studs. Apply Loctite 242 to the nut end of the stud.

7. Install new O-rings in the mating surface recesses. Seat the rail in the manifold, aligning the water passages and stud openings.

8. Install the nuts and tighten them, from the center out, to the specification in **Table 1**.

9. Start the engine and check for water leakage. Correct leakage as needed.

## HEAT EXCHANGER

### Removal and Installation

On 3.0L models, the heat exchanger (**Figure 10**) is mounted on the port side of the engine. It is mounted to the front of the engine on all other models.

Note all hose connections before disconnecting them. Refer to **Figures 11-14** for correct hose routing and connections.

Use automotive cooling system cleaner to remove corrosion, mineral deposits or other contaminants from the heat exchanger. Always follow the manufacturer's instructions when using these cleaners.

If the exchanger is leaking or has heavy deposits, have it cleaned and repaired at a radiator shop.

Refer to **Figures 11-14**.

1. Drain the coolant as described in Chapter Four.

**9**

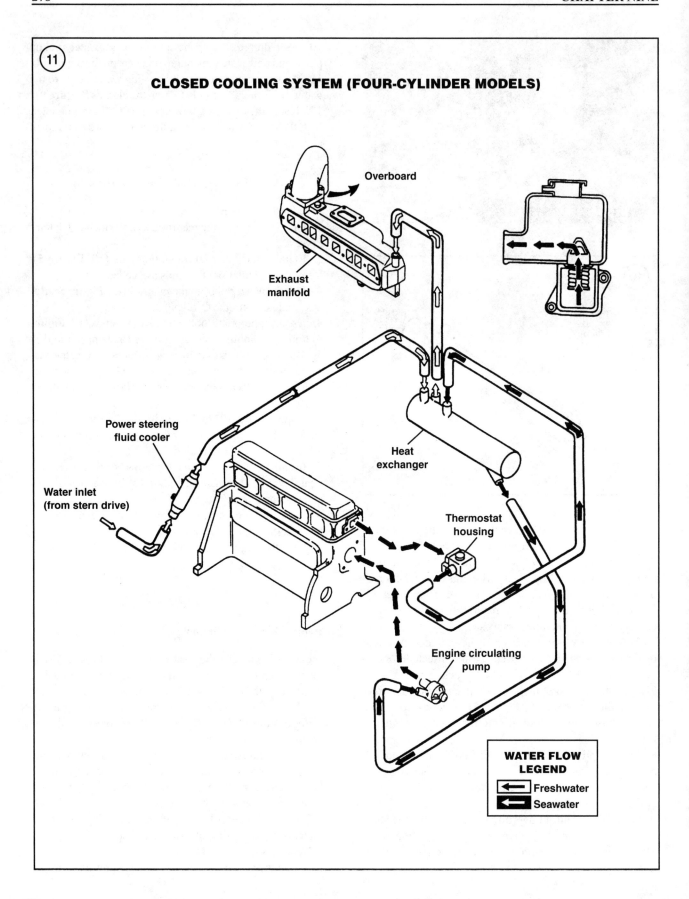

⑪

**CLOSED COOLING SYSTEM (FOUR-CYLINDER MODELS)**

Overboard

Exhaust
manifold

Power steering
fluid cooler

Water inlet
(from stern drive)

Heat
exchanger

Thermostat
housing

Engine circulating
pump

**WATER FLOW
LEGEND**

⬅ Freshwater
⬅ Seawater

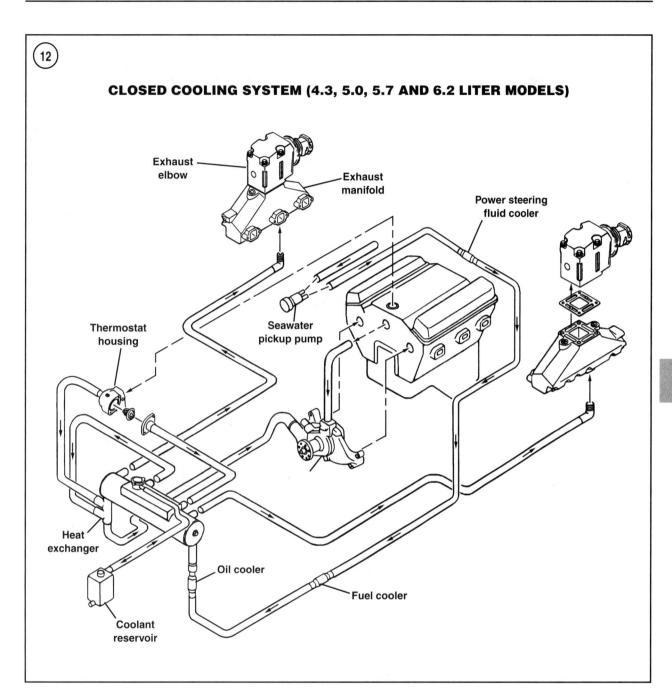

**12**

**CLOSED COOLING SYSTEM (4.3, 5.0, 5.7 AND 6.2 LITER MODELS)**

Exhaust
elbow

Exhaust
manifold

Power steering
fluid cooler

Thermostat
housing

Seawater
pickup pump

Heat
exchanger

Oil cooler

Fuel cooler

Coolant
reservoir

**9**

2. Disconnect each hose from the heat exchanger. Drain coolant or water from the hoses.

3. Fully loosen the clamps and pull the exchanger from the bracket. Inspect the rubber cushions on the bracket for wear or damage. Replace the bumpers as needed.

4. Place the bracket onto the mounting bracket.

5A. On 496 Mag and 496 Mag HO models, rotate the exchanger to position the hose fittings as shown in **Figure 14**).

5B. On 3.L models, rotate the exchanger to position the hose fittings as shown in **Figure 11**.

5C. On all other models, rotate the exchanger until the pressure cap fitting is on top.

6. Attach the hoses to the heat exchanger fittings. Refer to **Figures 11-14** to verify proper routing.

7. Fill the system with coolant as described in Chapter Four. Connect the battery cables. Start the engine and check for coolant or water leakage. Correct as needed.

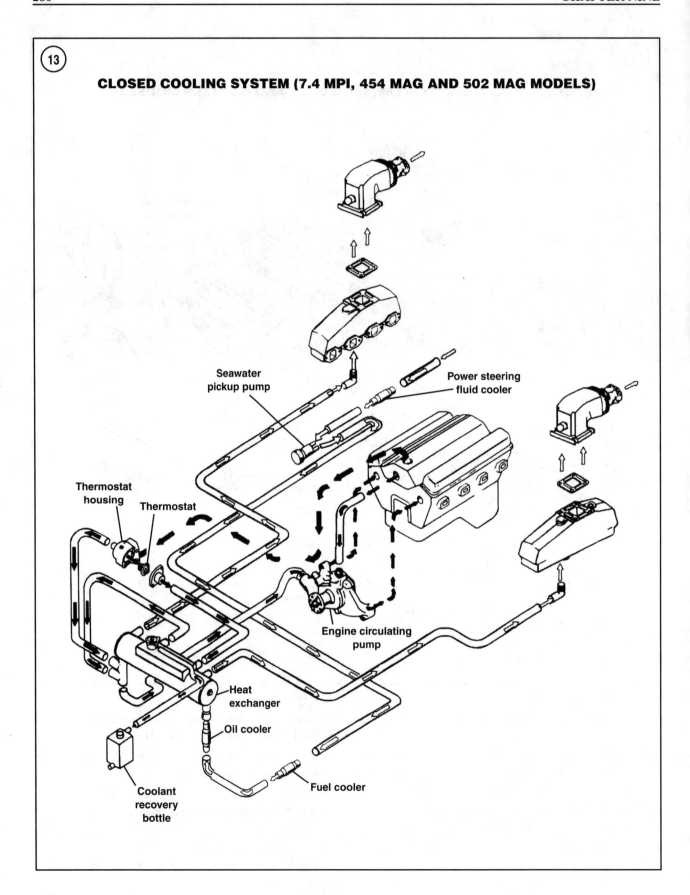

(13)

**CLOSED COOLING SYSTEM (7.4 MPI, 454 MAG AND 502 MAG MODELS)**

Seawater
pickup pump

Power steering
fluid cooler

Thermostat
housing

Thermostat

Engine circulating
pump

Heat
exchanger

Oil cooler

Fuel cooler

Coolant
recovery
bottle

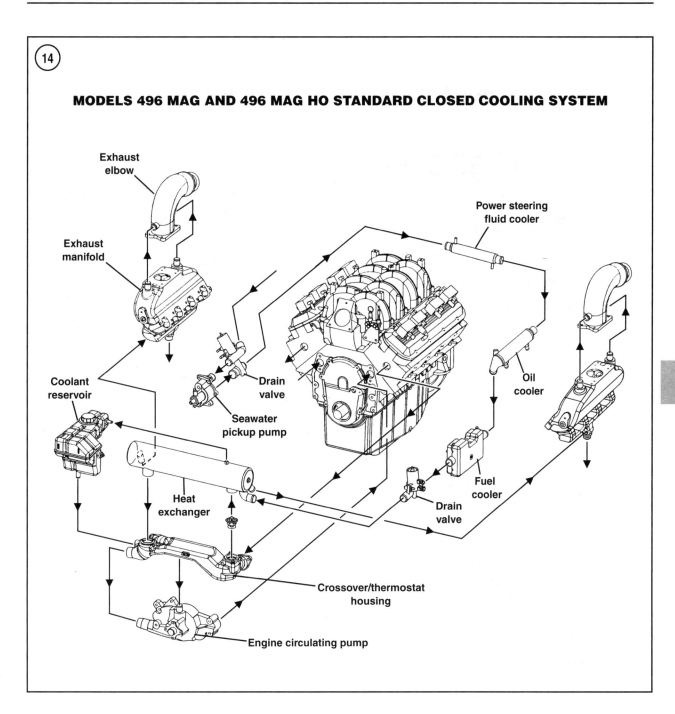

**14**

## MODELS 496 MAG AND 496 MAG HO STANDARD CLOSED COOLING SYSTEM

Exhaust elbow

Exhaust manifold

Power steering fluid cooler

Coolant reservoir

Drain valve

Seawater pickup pump

Oil cooler

Heat exchanger

Fuel cooler

Drain valve

Crossover/thermostat housing

Engine circulating pump

**9**

### Cleaning

1. Remove the heat exchanger as described in this chapter.

2. Remove the bolts, plate and rubber gasket from each end of the heat exchanger.

3. Soak the exchanger in the cleaning solution until deposits soften. Pass a radiator tube brush through each tube of the exchanger until clean.

4. Flush freshwater through the exchanger until the exiting water is clear. Check the exchanger for leakage as described in this chapter.

5. Apply a very light coat of Perfect Seal to one side of the new rubber gasket. Place the gaskets onto the ends of the heat exchanger with the sealant side facing inward. Apply a light coat of Perfect Seal to the bolt threads. Install the plate and bolt on each side of the exchanger. Tighten the bolt to the specification in **Table 1**.

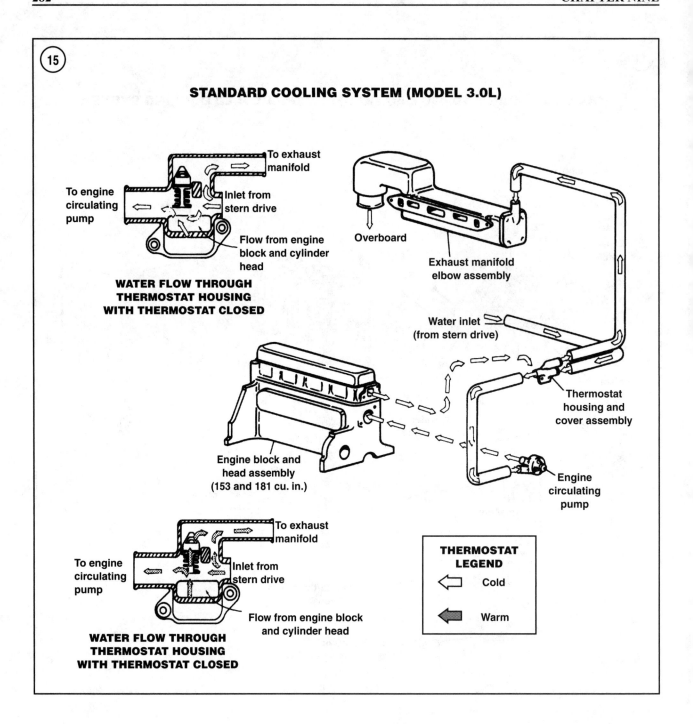

⑮

**STANDARD COOLING SYSTEM (MODEL 3.0L)**

To exhaust manifold

To engine circulating pump

Inlet from stern drive

Flow from engine block and cylinder head

**WATER FLOW THROUGH THERMOSTAT HOUSING WITH THERMOSTAT CLOSED**

Overboard

Exhaust manifold elbow assembly

Water inlet (from stern drive)

Engine block and head assembly (153 and 181 cu. in.)

Thermostat housing and cover assembly

Engine circulating pump

To exhaust manifold

To engine circulating pump

Inlet from stern drive

Flow from engine block and cylinder head

**WATER FLOW THROUGH THERMOSTAT HOUSING WITH THERMOSTAT CLOSED**

**THERMOSTAT LEGEND**

⇦ Cold

⬅ Warm

## Pressure Test

Pressure testing requires a pressure cap tester with filler neck adapter, appropriately sized hose clamps and rubber plugs that fit the coolant hose fittings. Rubber plugs are available from most plumbing supply businesses.

1. Clean the exchanger and remove the end plates as described in this chapter.

2. Position one of the coolant hose fittings face upward. Use rubber plugs to block the remaining coolant hose fitting.

3. Fill the coolant hose fitting with clear water. Look through each end of the exchanger to see if any of the tubes are leaking. Repair or replace the exchanger if leakage occurs.

4. Add water into the fitting until it reaches the top of the opening. Install a rubber plug and clamp onto the fitting.

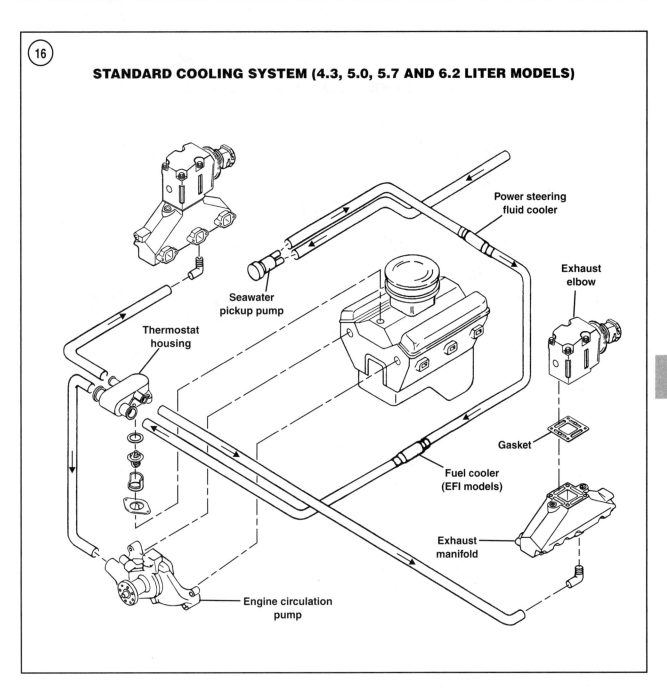

**STANDARD COOLING SYSTEM (4.3, 5.0, 5.7 AND 6.2 LITER MODELS)**

(16)

Power steering
fluid cooler

Seawater
pickup pump

Thermostat
housing

Exhaust
elbow

Gasket

Fuel cooler
(EFI models)

Exhaust
manifold

Engine circulation
pump

5A. *3.0L, 496 Mag and 496 Mag HO models*—Attach the pressure tester to one of the coolant hose fittings or the drain fitting on the exchanger.

5B. *All other models*—Attach the pressure cap tester and adapter to the filler neck of the heat exchanger.

6. Refer to **Table 2** to determine the system test pressure. Pump the cap tester until the pressure just reaches the specification. Wait a few minutes, then look through the end of the exchanger. Repair or replace the exchanger if water appears in any of the tubes.

7. Remove the pressure tester and plugs.

### ENGINE CIRCULATING PUMP

Refer to **Figures 11-17**.

1. Disconnect the battery cables.

2A. *Standard cooling system*—Drain the water from the cylinder block as described in Chapter Five.

2B. *Closed cooling system*—Drain the coolant from the system as described in Chapter Four.

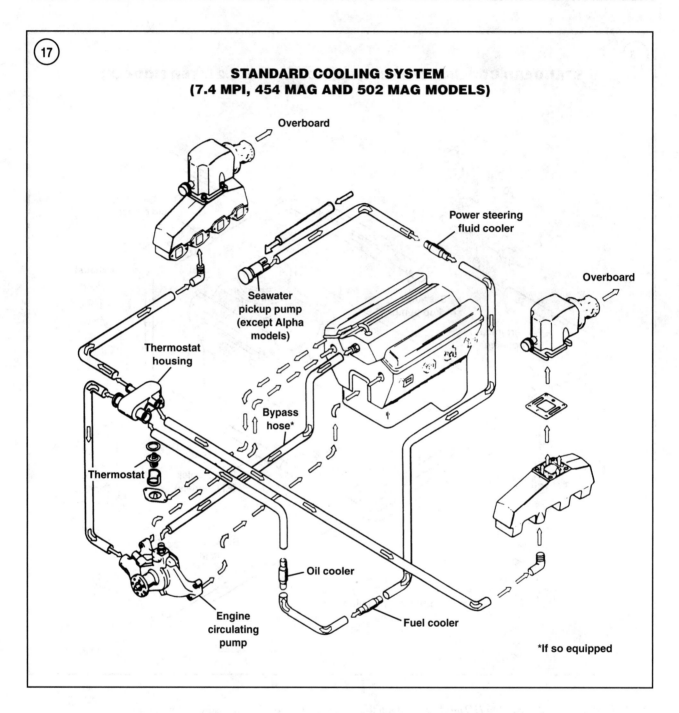

**STANDARD COOLING SYSTEM**
**(7.4 MPI, 454 MAG AND 502 MAG MODELS)**

Overboard

Power steering
fluid cooler

Overboard

Seawater
pickup pump
(except Alpha
models)

Thermostat
housing

Bypass
hose*

Thermostat

Oil cooler

Engine
circulating
pump

Fuel cooler

*If so equipped

3. Detach all hoses from the circulation pump.

4. Loosen but do not remove the pulley bolts (**Figure 18**). Loosen the belt tension and remove the belt as described in Chapter Ten.

5. Remove the bolts (**Figure 18**) and pulley from the circulating pump. Remove any nuts and brackets from the water pump stud bolts.

6. Support the pump and remove the mounting fasteners. Tap on the pump body with a soft-faced hammer to free it from the engine. Do not pry against the timing chain or gear cover.

7. Carefully scrape the gasket material from the pump and cylinder block mating surfaces.

8. Apply a light coat of Perfect Seal (Mercury part No. 92-34227-1) to each side of the new gaskets. Stick the gaskets to the pump mating surfaces.

9. Install the circulating pump on the engine. Apply a light coat of Perfect Seal to the bolt threads. Make sure the

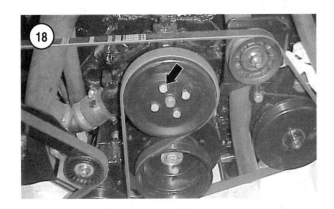

gasket is aligned properly and install the bolts. Tighten them to the specification in **Table 1**.

10. Place the pulley onto the hub of the pump. Install and securely tighten the bolts. Transfer fittings or plugs to the replacement pump.

11. Attach all hoses to the circulating pump. Refer to **Figures 11-17**.

12. Install the drive belt as described in Chapter Ten.

13. On a closed cooling system, refill the engine with coolant as described in Chapter Four.

14. Connect the battery cables. Start the engine and check for water or coolant leakage. Correct as needed.

## THERMOSTAT AND HOUSING

1A. *Standard cooling system*—Drain the water from the cylinder block as described in Chapter Five.

1B. *Closed cooling system*—Drain the coolant from the system as described in Chapter Four.

2. Remove the engine temperature sender, overheat switch and engine temperature sensor as described in Chapter Ten.

3. Remove the bolts and thermostat housing from the engine. Pull the spacer, thermostat and gaskets from the housing. Discard the gaskets.

4. Use automotive cooling system cleaner to remove corrosion or mineral deposits from the thermostat housing. Inspect the thermostat housing for cracks, deteriorated gasket and thermostat contact surfaces or other damage. Replace the housing if necessary.

5. Test the thermostat as described in Chapter Three.

6. Install the thermostat spacers and new gaskets onto the thermostat housing. Refer to **Figures 11-17** as needed. The brass end of the thermostat must face the engine.

7. Apply a light coat of Perfect Seat (Mercury part No. 92-34227-1) to the threads of the mounting bolts. Install the bolts and tighten them to the specification in **Table 1**.

8. Install the engine temperature sender, overheat switch and engine temperature sensor as described in Chapter Ten.

9. On a closed cooling system, refill the engine with coolant as described in Chapter Four.

10. Start the engine and check for water or coolant leakage. Correct as needed.

11. If the engine overheats or fails to reach normal operating temperature, check for improper spacer or thermostat installation.

9

## SEAWATER PUMP

1. Drain water from the seawater pump as described in Chapter Five.

2. Loosen the hose clamps and pull the inlet (A, **Figure 19**) and outlet hoses (C) from the seawater pump fittings.

3. On 496 Mag and 496 Mag HO models, remove the water pressure sensor (B, **Figure 19**) as described in Chapter Ten.

4. Loosen the belt tension and remove the drive belt as described in Chapter Ten.

5. Remove the mounting bolts and pull the pump from the engine.

6. To install, reverse the above steps and note the following:

    a. Tighten the pump mounting bolts to the specification in **Table 1**.

    b. Install the drive belt as described under *Alternator Replacement* in Chapter Ten.

    c. Connect the inlet water hose from the drive unit to the fitting marked RH OUT.

    d. Connect the outlet water hose leading to the engine onto the fitting marked LH OUT.

7. On 496 Mag and 496 Mag HO models, install the water pressure sensor (C, **Figure 19**) as described in Chapter Ten.

8. Start the engine and check for water leakage or overheating.

**Impeller Replacement
(All Models except 496 Mag and Mag HO)**

Refer to **Figure 20**.

1. Remove the seawater pump as described in this chapter.

2. Make alignment marks on the pump mounting bracket, bearing and shaft housing (8, **Figure 20**) and pump body (3).

3. Mark the location of each bolt, washer and nut on the pump before removing them. Remove the bolts and separate shaft and bearing housing from the mounting bracket.

4. Pull the pump body (3, **Figure 20**) from the shaft and bearing housing. Remove the impeller (5, **Figure 20**) from the pump housing or pump shaft. Discard the impeller.

5. Remove and discard the O-ring (4, **Figure 20**) from the pump housing.

6. Remove the wear plate (6, **Figure 20**) from the shaft and bearing housing. Remove and discard the quad ring seal from the recess in the pump housing.

7. Rotate the shaft and check for side play. Disassemble the housing and replace defective components if roughness or play is present.

8. Inspect the inner bore of the pump housing for excessive wear and replace as needed. Transfer the match marks to the replacement housing.

9. Inspect the wear plate (6, **Figure 20**) for discoloration, wear grooves or warpage and replace as needed.

10. Install a new quad ring seal into the recess in the shaft and bearing housing. Apply water-resistant grease to the seal.

11. Slide the wear plate over the pump shaft. Seat the plate against the housing.

12. Apply grease to the pump shaft. Align the flat surfaces and slide the impeller over the shaft.

13. Install a new O-ring (4, **Figure 20**) into the groove in the pump housing (3). Apply a light coat of grease to the inner bore of the pump housing.

14. Rotate the water pump pulley clockwise while pushing the pump housing over the impeller. Continue until the impeller fully enters the housing.

15. Rotate the pump body (counterclockwise) to align the match marks. Align the bolt opening in the wear plate with openings in the pump body and housing.

16. Match the alignment marks on the pump body and housing with the marks on the pump mounting bracket.

17. Install the mounting bolts, washers and nuts. Securely tighten the bolts in a crossing pattern.

18. Install the pump as described in this chapter.

**Pump Shaft, Bearings and Seals**

1. Remove the water pump body, impeller and wear plate as described in this chapter.

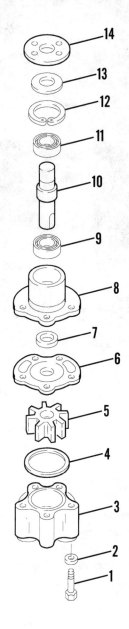

**20**

**SEAWATER PICKUP PUMP
(EXCEPT 496 MAG AND 496 MAG HO)**

1. Bolt
2. Washer
3. Water pump body
4. O-ring
5. Impeller
6. Wear plate
7. Seal
8. Bearing and seal housing
9. Bearing
10. Pump shaft
11. Bearing
12. Snap ring
13. Outer seal
14. Pulley hub

2. Remove the bolts and lift the pulley from the pulley hub (14, **Figure 20**).

3. Remove the pulley boss as follows:

   a. Place the edge of a bearing separator against the pulley boss.

   b. Place the pump housing on a press with the boss facing upward.

   c. Use a suitable driver to press the shaft from the boss.

4. Use an awl to punch a small hole in the outer seal (13, **Figure 20**). Pry the seal from the housing. Discard the seal.

5. Remove the snap ring (12, **Figure 20**). Tap on the impeller end of the shaft to remove the shaft from the housing.

6. Remove the bearings (9 and 11, **Figure 20**) only if they must be replaced. The removal process damages the bearings. To remove the bearings:

   a. Place the edge of a bearing separator against one of the bearings.

   b. Place the shaft on a press with the bearing facing upward.

   c. Use a suitable driver to press the shaft from the bearing.

   d. Repeat this procedure for the remaining bearing.

7. Carefully push the seals (7, **Figure 20**) from the shaft bore. Discard the seals.

8. Inspect the pump shaft for discoloration and wear or pitting at the seal surface. Replace the shaft if these or other defects exist.

9. Install the impeller end seals as follows:

   a. Thoroughly clean the seal bore. Apply Loctite 271 to the seal bore and the outer diameter of the seals.

   b. Place the first seal into the bore with the seal lip facing outward. Use an appropriately sized driver to seat the seal in the bore.

   c. Install the second seal into the bore with the lip side facing outward. Press the seal into the bore until it contacts the first seal.

   d. Apply a bead of water-resistant grease to the seal lips.

10. Install new bearings onto the pump shaft as follows:

   a. Place the shaft on a press.

   b. Press the bearing onto each end of the shaft.

   c. Press the bearings onto the shaft until they seat against the shoulders.

11. Pack the area between the bearings with Shell Alvania No. 2 grease or its equivalent.

12. Insert the shaft and bearings into the housing. Push in on the shaft until the snap ring is exposed.

13. Install the snap ring into the groove.

14. Thoroughly clean the seal bore. Apply Loctite 271 to the seal bore and the outer diameter of the seal. Apply Shell Alvania No. 2 onto the seal lips. Place the seal into the bore with the seal lip facing inward. Use a suitable driver to press the seal fully into the bore.

15. Install the pulley hub onto the shaft as follows:

   a. Place the housing on a press with the hub end facing upward.

   b. Press the hub onto the shaft, using a suitable driver. Stop when the shaft protrudes 0.260 in. (6.6 mm) from the hub.

16. Install the pulley onto the shaft. Install the lockwashers and bolts. Securely tighten the bolts.

17. Install the impeller, pump body and mounting bracket as described in this chapter.

## COOLANT RESERVOIR

Refer to **Figures 12-14**.

1A. On 496 Mag and 496 Mag HO models, drain coolant from the system as described in Chapter Four. Disconnect the reservoir hoses from the thermostat housing and the fitting on the top of the heat exchanger.

1B. On all other models, disconnect the lower reservoir hose from the filler neck fitting.

2. Direct the hose into a suitable container and drain the reservoir.

3. Remove the mounting bolts (**Figure 21**, typical) and lift the reservoir from the engine.

4. Remove the reservoir cap. Flush the reservoir with clean water.

5. To install, reverse the above steps and note the following:

   a. Securely tighten the reservoir mounting bolts.

   b. Attach all hoses as shown in **Figures 12-14**.

   c. Refill the reservoir as described in Chapter Four.

**9**

**Table 1 TORQUE SPECIFICATIONS**

| Fastener | ft.-lb. | in.-lb. | N•m |
|---|---|---|---|
| Exhaust elbow | | | |
| 3.0 liter models | 20-25 | – | 27-34 |
| 4.3L | | | |
|   1998-2001 | 25 | – | 34 |
|   2002-2004 | | | |
|     First step | – | 84 | 9.5 |
|     Final step | 45 | – | 61 |
| 5.0L, 5.7L, 350 Mag, MX 6.2 | | | |
|   1998-2001 | 33 | – | 45 |
|   2002-2004 | | | |
|     First step | – | 84 | 9.5 |
|     Final step | 45 | – | 61 |
| 7.4 MPI, 454 Mag, 502 Mag | 30 | – | 41 |
| 496 Mag and 496 Mag HO | | | |
|   Nuts | 12 | 144 | 16 |
|   Studs | 15 | 180 | 20 |
| Exhaust manifold | | | |
| 3.0L | | | |
|   Center bolts/nuts | 20-25 | – | 27-34 |
|   Outer bolts/nuts | 15-20 | – | 20-27 |
| 4.3L | 20 | – | 27 |
| 5.0L, 5.7L, 350 Mag | 25 | – | 34 |
| 7.4 MPI, 454 Mag, 502 Mag | 30 | – | 41 |
| 496 Mag and 496 Mag HO | 26 | – | 35 |
| Water rail | | | |
| 496 Mag and 496 Mag HO | | | |
|   Studs | – | 84 | 10 |
|   Nuts | – | 72 | 8 |
|   Cap screws | – | 85 | 10 |
| Exhaust pipe | 23 | – | 31 |
| Exhaust block off plate | 23 | – | 31 |
| Exhaust tube clamps | – | 30-40 | 3-5 |
| Heat exchanger end cap | | | |
| 3.0L | 16 | 192 | 22 |
| 4.3L, 5.0L and 5.7L | – | 36-72 | 4-8 |
| Thermostat cover | | | |
| 3.0L | | | |
|   Standard cooling | 30 | – | 41 |
|   Closed cooling | 20 | – | 27 |
| 4.3L, 5.0L, 5.7L, 350 Mag | 30 | – | 41 |
| Thermostat housing | 30 | – | 41 |
| Seawater pump brace to block* | 30 | – | 41 |
| Brace to seawater pump | 15 | 180 | 20 |
| Seawater pump mount* | | | |
| 4.3L, 5.0L, 5.7L, 350 Mag | 30 | – | 41 |
| 7.4LMPI, 454 Mag, 502 Mag | 45 | – | 61 |
| Hull mounted water pickup | 35 | – | 47 |
| Circulation pump | | | |
| 3.0L | 15 | 180 | 20 |
| 4.3L | 30 | – | 41 |
| 5.0L, 5.7L, 350 Mag | 33 | – | 45 |
| 7.4L MPI, 454 Mag, 502 Mag | 30 | – | 41 |
| Coolant reservoir | 30 | – | 41 |

*Bravo drives only

### Table 2 CLOSED COOLING SYSTEM TEST SPECIFICATIONS

| Model | Pressure |
|---|---|
| 3.0L | |
| Pressure cap | |
| Relief pressure | 14 psi (97 kPa) |
| Minimum holding pressure | 11 psi (76 kPa) |
| System test specification | 17 psi (117 kPa) |
| 496 Mag and 496 Mag HO | |
| Pressure cap rating | 14 psi (103 kPa) |
| System test specification | 19 psi (131 kPa) |
| All other models | |
| Pressure cap | |
| Relief pressure | 16 psi (110 kPa) |
| Minimum holding pressure | 11 psi (76 kPa) |
| System test specification | 20 psi (138 kPa) |

9

**NOTE:** Electrical and ignition system repair procedures unique to 2002-2004 models are covered in the supplement at the back of the manual.

# Chapter Ten

# Electrical and Ignition Systems

This chapter describes battery maintenance, as well as testing and repair procedures for engine electrical components. **Table 1** list tightening torque specifications. **Tables 2-9** list battery, starter and alternator specifications.

*WARNING*
*Incorrect or improperly installed electrical parts can disable the flash protection features of the electrical system, causing fire or explosion. Never install automotive electrical parts onto a marine engine.*

## BATTERY

Batteries used in marine applications are subjected to far more vibration and pounding than automotive applications. Always use a battery designated for marine applications (**Figure 1**). These batteries are constructed with thicker cases and plates than typical automotive batteries. This allows them to better withstand the marine environment.

Choose a battery that meets or exceeds the cold cranking amperage requirements of the engine. Cold cranking amperage requirements are listed in **Table 2**.

Deep cycle batteries are designed to allow repeated discharge and charge cycles. These batteries are excellent for powering accessories such as trolling motors. Always charge deep cycle batteries at a low amperage rate. They are not generally designed to be charged or discharged at a rapid rate. Rapid charging rates can significantly reduce the life of a deep cycle battery.

**Table 4** lists the hour capacity for both 80 and 105 amp-hour batteries. Approximate recharge times are listed in **Table 6**. Deep cycle batteries can be used as the starting battery if they meet the cold cranking amperage requirement for the engine.

Loose or corroded cable connections frequently cause problems in marine applications. Use cable connectors securely crimped or molded onto the cable. Do not use temporary or emergency clamps for everyday operation. Emergency clamps are prone to corrosion and do not meet the Coast Guard requirements for terminal connections.

Use good quality battery cables that meet or exceed the diameter requirements (**Table 3**). Longer cable lengths require a larger cable diameter. If possible, use cables with a diameter larger than the minimum requirement. The specifications in **Table 3** apply to both the positive and negative cables.

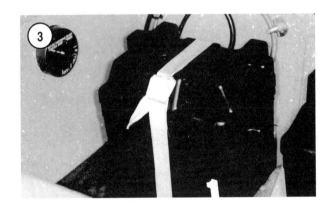

Use a cover on the positive terminal post. They are available at marine dealerships.

Make sure the battery is securely mounted in the boat to avoid acid spills or electrical arcing which can cause a fire. The most common methods of battery mounting use a bracket mounted to the floor of the boat, with a support across the top of the battery (**Figure 2**). Another type of battery mounting uses the battery case and cover to enclose the battery and secure it to the boat structure (**Figure 3**). When properly installed either of these methods provide secure mounting and protection for the terminals.

Mount the battery in a location that allows easy access for maintenance. Make sure the battery terminals can not contact any component in the mounting area. Rigorous marine usage can cause the battery to shift during use.

*WARNING*
*When mounting a battery in an aluminum boat, make sure the battery is securely mounted and can not contact any metal components. Electricity can arc from the battery terminals to the aluminum body of the boat, possibly causing a fire or an explosion. Batteries produce explosive gas that can ignite when arcing is present.*

*WARNING*
*Always wear gloves and eye protection when working with batteries. Batteries contain a corrosive and dangerous acid solution. Never smoke or allow any source of ignition near a battery. Batteries produce gas that can ignite and result in an explosion if a source of ignition is present.*

**Battery Inspection**

Any time the battery is removed for charging, inspect the battery case for cracks, leakage, abrasions or other damage. Replace the battery if any questionable condition exists. During normal usage a corrosive deposit forms on the top of the battery. These deposits may allow the battery to discharge at a rapid rate as current can travel from one post to the other.

Make sure the battery caps are properly installed. Remove the battery from the boat and carefully wash loose material from the top of the battery with clean water. Use a solution of warm water and baking soda and a soft-bristle brush to clean deposits from the battery (**Figure 4**). Wash the battery again with clean water to remove all of the baking soda solution from the battery case.

*CAUTION*
*Never allow the water and baking soda solution to enter the battery cells. The baking soda will react chemically with the battery acid and neutralize it, permanently disabling the battery.*

Check the electrolyte level on a regular basis. Heavy usage or usage in warm climates increases the frequency for adding water to the battery. Carefully remove the vent caps (**Figure 5**) and inspect the electrolyte level in each cell. The electrolyte level should be 3/16 in. (4.8 mm) above the plates yet below the bottom of the vent well

**10**

(**Figure 5**). Use distilled water to fill the cells to the proper level. Never use battery acid to correct the electrolyte level. The acidic solution will be too strong and damage the plates.

*CAUTION*
*Never overfill the battery. Heat generated during charging may cause the electrolyte to expand and overflow from the battery.*

Clean the battery terminals at regular intervals and every time a terminal is removed. Use a battery cleaning tool available at most automotive part stores to remove corrosion and deposits. Remove the terminal and clean the post (**Figure 6**). Avoid removing too much material from the post or the terminal may not attach securely to the post.

Use the other end of the tool to clean the cable end terminal. Clean flat spade type connectors and the attaching nuts with the wire brush end of the tool (**Figure 7**).

Apply a coat of petroleum gel or other corrosion preventative to the battery posts and cable terminals. Tighten the fasteners securely. Avoid using excessive force when tightening these terminals. The battery and terminals can sustain considerable damage if excessive force is applied.

**Battery Testing**

Two methods are commonly used to test batteries. A load tester (**Figure 8**) measures the battery voltage as it applies a load across the terminals. If a load tester is not available, perform a *Cranking Voltage Test* as described in this chapter.

Use a hydrometer to check the specific gravity of the battery electrolyte. This gives an accurate indication of the charge level of the battery. Hydrometers are available at most automotive part stores.

*NOTE*
*Checking the specific gravity immediately after adding water to the battery will give an inaccurate reading. To ensure accuracy, charge the battery at a high rate for 15-20 minutes.*

To use the hydrometer, insert the tip into a single cell and use the bulb to draw out some of the electrolyte (**Figure 9**). Read the specific gravity of all cells. When using a temperature compensating hydrometer, take several readings in each cell to allow the hydrometer to adjust to the electrolyte temperature.

*NOTE*
*If the hydrometer used is not a temperature compensating model, add 0.004 to the reading for every 10° above 80° F (25° C). Subtract 0.004 from the reading for every 10° below 80° F (25° C).*

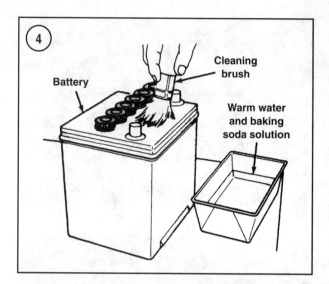

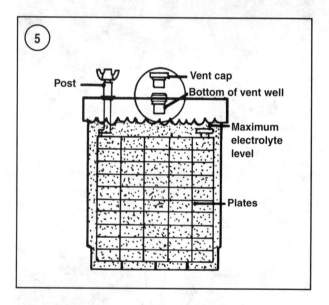

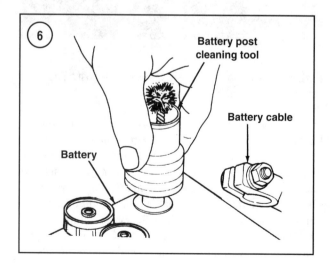

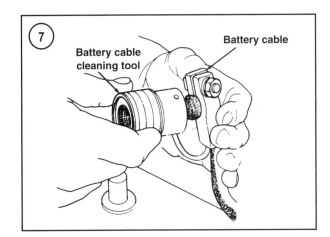

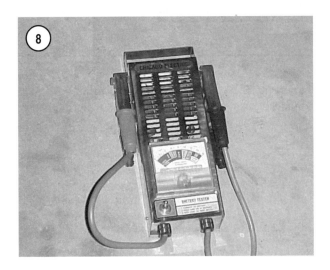

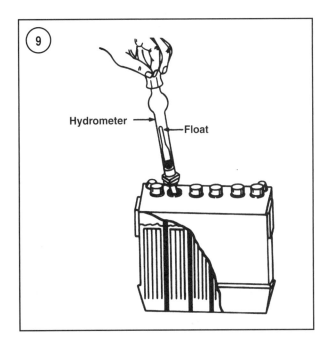

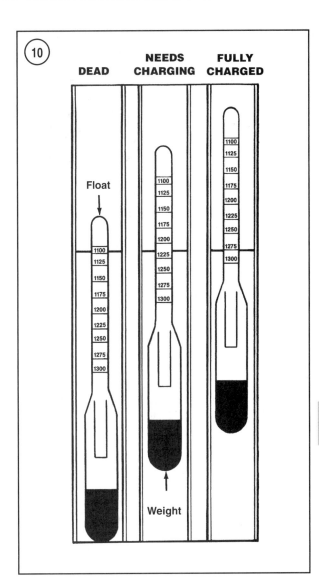

Always return the electrolyte to the cell from which it was drawn. With the hydrometer in a vertical position, determine the specific gravity by reading the level of the float (**Figure 10**). A specific gravity reading of 1.260 or higher indicates a fully charged battery. Compare the hydrometer readings with the information in **Table 5** to determine the state of charge. Always charge the battery if the specific gravity varies more than 0.050 from one cell to another.

### Cranking Voltage Test

To check the battery condition, measure the battery voltage while cranking the engine.

1. Connect the positive meter lead to the positive battery terminal. Connect the negative meter test lead to a suitable engine ground.

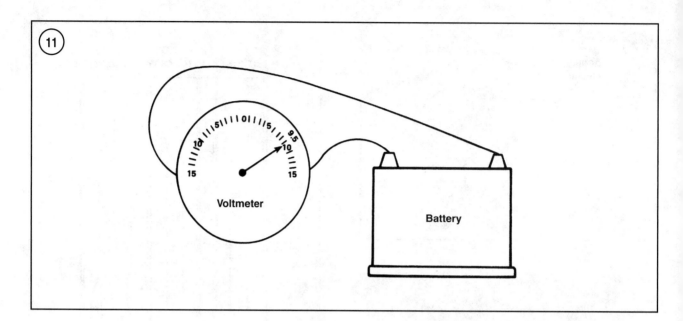

2. Measure the voltage while cranking the engine (**Figure 11**).
3. Fully charge the battery if the voltage drops below 9.6 volts while cranking. Repeat the cranking voltage test.
4. Replace the battery if it does notsustain at least 9.6 volts under a cranking load.

### Battery Storage

Batteries lose some power during storage. To minimize the loss of voltage, store the battery in a cool, dry location. Check the specific gravity every 30 days and charge the battery as needed. Maintain the battery case and terminals as described in this chapter. Refer to *Battery Charging* in this chapter for battery charging times.

### Battery Charging

*WARNING*
*Batteries produce explosive hydrogen gas. Charge the battery only in a well-ventilated area. Wear eye protection and gloves when working around batteries. Never smoke or allow any source of ignition in the area where batteries are stored or charged. Never allow any uninsulated components to contact the battery terminals as arcing can occur and ignite the hydrogen gas.*

Always remove the battery from the boat to charge it. Batteries produce explosive hydrogen gas while charging. This explosive gas can remain in the area long after the charging process is complete. In addition to the explosion

hazard, the gas causes accelerated corrosion in the area around the battery compartment. Removing the battery also allows easier inspection and cleaning.

*WARNING*
*Use extreme caution when connecting any wires to the battery terminals. Avoid making the last connection at the battery terminal. Explosive hydrogen gas in and around the battery can ignite and explode.*

Connect the battery charger to the battery *before* plugging in the charger or switching the charger on. This important step can help prevent dangerous arcing at the terminals. Connect the battery charger cables to the proper terminals on the battery. Plug the charger into its power supply and select the 12-volt setting.

Charging the battery at a slow rate (lower amperage) results in a more efficient charge and helps prolong the life of the battery. With an extremely discharged battery it may be necessary to charge the battery at a higher amperage rate for a few minutes before starting the lower rate charge. A severely discharged battery may not allow the charging to begin without first boost charging at a high rate.

Battery charging time varies by the battery capacity and the state of charge. Typical battery charging times are provided in **Table 6**. Check the specific gravity often and stop charging when the battery is at full charge. Severely discharged batteries may take eight hours or longer to recharge. Monitor the temperature of the electrolyte during the charging process. Stop charging if the electrolyte temperature exceeds 125° F (53° C).

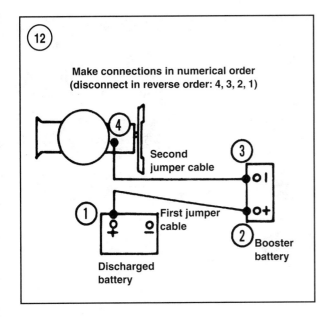

Make connections in numerical order
(disconnect in reverse order: 4, 3, 2, 1)

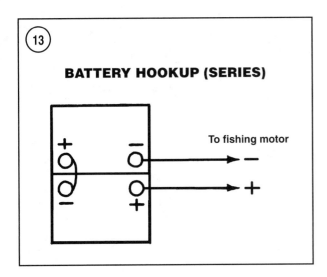

**BATTERY HOOKUP (SERIES)**

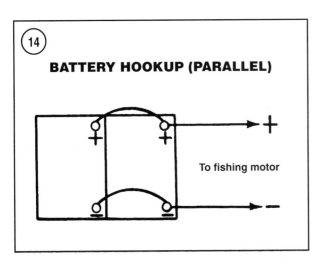

**BATTERY HOOKUP (PARALLEL)**

## Jump Starting

Jump starting is an operation to start an engine with a severely discharged battery, by connecting it to a fully charged one. Jump starting can be dangerous if not performed correctly. Never attempt to jump start a frozen battery. Always check and correct the electrolyte level in each battery before making any connection. An explosion is likely if the electrolyte level is at or below the top of the plates. Always use a good pair of jumper cables with clean clamps. Keep all clamps totally separated from any metallic or conductive material. Never allow the clamps to contact other clamps.

1. Connect the jumper cable clamp onto the positive terminal of the discharged battery (1, **Figure 12**).

2. Connect the same jumper cable clamp onto the positive terminal of the fully charged battery (2, **Figure 12**).

3. Connect the second jumper cable onto the negative terminal of the fully charged battery (3, **Figure 12**).

4. Connect the second jumper cable remaining clamp onto a good engine ground, such as the starter ground cable (4, **Figure 12**).

5. Make sure the cables and clamps are positioned so they will not touch or interfere with moving components.

6. Start the engine, then remove the cables in the exact reverse of the connection order (Steps 1-4).

**10**

## 12 and 24 Volt Electric Trolling Motors

Many fishing boats are provided with an electric trolling motor requiring 24 volts to operate. Two or more batteries are necessary for this application. A series battery connection (**Figure 13**) provides 24 volts for the trolling motor.

A series connection provides the approximate total of the two batteries (24 volts). The amperage provided is the approximate average of the two batteries.

Connect the trolling motor batteries in a parallel arrangement (**Figure 14**) if the trolling motor requires 12 volts to operate.

The voltage provided is the approximate average of the two batteries (12 volt). The amperage provided is the approximate total of the two batteries.

### STARTING SYSTEM

This section describes replacement instructions for the starter motor, slave solenoid and starter solenoid. Starter motor repair instructions are included in this section.

*WARNING*
*Incorrect or improperly installed electrical parts can disable the flash protection features of the electrical system, resulting in*

*possible fire or explosion. Never install auto-
motive electrical parts onto a marine engine.*

### Slave Solenoid Removal and Installation

On carbureted models, the solenoid is located on a
bracket behind or near the carburetor. On EFI models, the
solenoid is located near the engine control module.

Open the electrical component box or remove the plastic engine covers to access the solenoid on EFI models.
Refer to the wiring diagrams at the end of this manual to
identify the wires. To prevent corrosion, apply a light coat
of liquid neoprene onto exposed terminals of the slave solenoid. Liquid neoprene is available from most automotive parts stores.

1. Disconnect the battery cables.
2. Remove the terminal protector from the solenoid (**Figure 15**).
3. Pull the small terminals from the solenoid (A, **Figure
16**). Disconnect the yellow/red and red/purple wires (B,
**Figure 16**).
4. Remove both mounting screws (C, **Figure 16**) and lift
the solenoid from the bracket or block.
5. To install, reverse the above steps and note the following:
    a. Securely tighten the mounting screws.
    b. Clean all terminals.
    c. Apply a coat of liquid neoprene onto the terminal
       nuts after tightening.
    d. Route all wires away from moving parts.
    e. Snap the terminal connector onto the solenoid (**Fig-
       ure 15**).
6. Connect the battery cables.

### Starter Motor Removal and Installation

In some instances, engine removal is necessary to access the starter motor mounting bolts. Engine removal and
installation are described in Chapter Seven.

> ### CAUTION
> *Some engines use a shim between the starter
> housing and the cylinder block. If so
> equipped, the shim must be re-installed to
> provide adequate pinion gear-to-flywheel
> clearance. Inadequate clearance can cause
> rapid wear and eventual failure of the fly-
> wheel teeth, as well as failure of the starter.*

1. Disconnect the battery cables.
2. Disconnect all wires (**Figure 17**) from the starter solenoid.

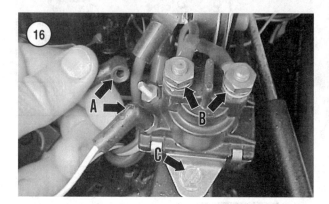

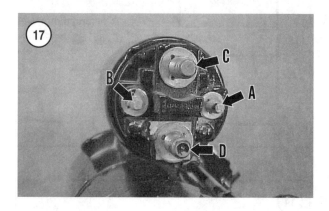

3. On 3.0L models, remove the nut, spacer and washer
from the through bolt. Loosen the bolt then swing the
starter brace away from the starter.
4. Support the starter while removing both mounting
bolts. Back the nose of the starter out of the flywheel
housing. Pull the starter away from the block. Retrieve the
shim (if so equipped) from the starter or cylinder block
mating surface.
5. Clean the starter mating surfaces. Use a thread chaser
to clean and dress the mounting bolt holes.
6. Guide the nose of the starter into the flywheel housing.
Align the starter with the cylinder block mounting holes.

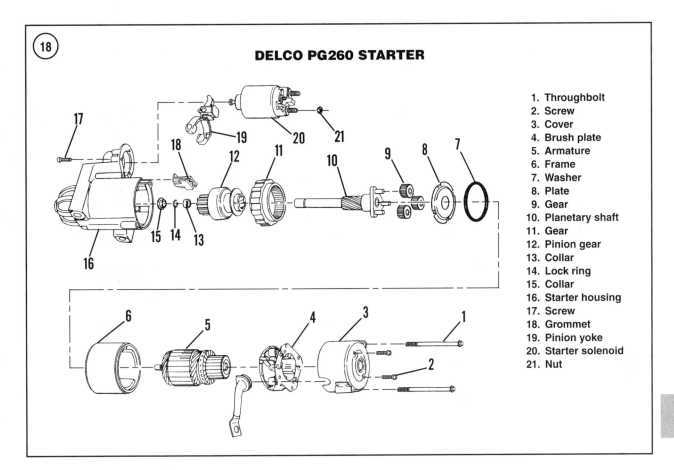

**DELCO PG260 STARTER**

1. Throughbolt
2. Screw
3. Cover
4. Brush plate
5. Armature
6. Frame
7. Washer
8. Plate
9. Gear
10. Planetary shaft
11. Gear
12. Pinion gear
13. Collar
14. Lock ring
15. Collar
16. Starter housing
17. Screw
18. Grommet
19. Pinion yoke
20. Starter solenoid
21. Nut

Insert the shim (if so equipped) between the starter and the cylinder block. Align the holes in the shim with the mounting bolt holes.

7. Install the mounting bolts into the cylinder block. Do not tighten the bolts at this time.

8. On 3.0L models, position the brace over the starter throughbolt. Install the spacer washer and nut.

9. Tighten the starter mounting bolts to the specification in **Table 1**.

10. On 3.0L models, securely tighten the starter brace bolt and nut.

11. Connect the wires and cables onto the starter solenoid as follows:

   a. Connect the yellow/red wire to the S terminal (A, **Figure 17**).

   b. Connect the purple/yellow wire to the R terminal (B, **Figure 17**). The terminal is used only on V6V6 and V8V8 models equipped with a carburetor. On other models, thread the insulator cover onto the terminal.

   c. Fit the fuse terminal onto the upper terminal (C, **Figure 17**).

   d. Connect the battery cable, red lead and orange lead onto the upper terminal. Do not overtighten the terminal nut or the starter solenoid housing may crack.

*NOTE*
*Some 2000 7.4 MPI, 454 Mag and 502 Mag models are equipped with a Mando starter motor. If the starter is faulty, replace the entire unit with a Delco starter. The manufacturer does not offer replacement parts or repair instructions for the Mando starter. Identify the Mando starter by the label on the starter housing.*

**Starter Identification**

The engine may be equipped with a Delco PG260, Delco PG260 F1 or a Mando starter motor. The Delco starters are very similar in appearance. The PG260 starter uses a recessed cover (3, **Figure 18**) on the end of the frame assembly (6). On the PG260 FT, the cover on the end of the frame is not recessed (3, **Figure 19**). Identify the Mando starter by the blue label on the starter housing. The manufacturer does not offer replacement parts for the Mando starter.

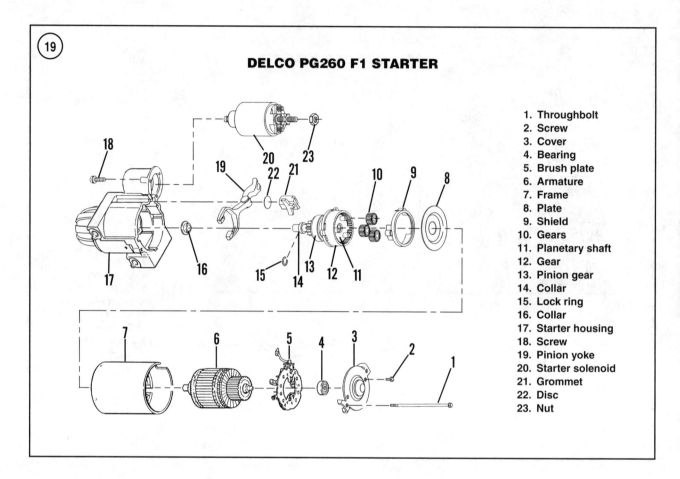

**DELCO PG260 F1 STARTER**

1. Throughbolt
2. Screw
3. Cover
4. Bearing
5. Brush plate
6. Armature
7. Frame
8. Plate
9. Shield
10. Gears
11. Planetary shaft
12. Gear
13. Pinion gear
14. Collar
15. Lock ring
16. Collar
17. Starter housing
18. Screw
19. Pinion yoke
20. Starter solenoid
21. Grommet
22. Disc
23. Nut

## Starter Solenoid Removal and Installation

Refer to **Figure 18** or **Figure 19** as needed.

1. Remove the starter motor as described in this chapter.

2. Remove the nut and wire (D, **Figure 17**) from the solenoid.

3. Remove the three external Torx screws (**Figure 18** or **Figure 19**) to free the solenoid from the starter housing.

4. Carefully remove the solenoid plunger from the notch in the yoke (**Figure 18** or **Figure 19**). Remove the solenoid.

5. Clean the solenoid mating surfaces.

6. Attach the plunger of the solenoid to the notch in the yoke. Seat the body of the solenoid on the starter housing.

7. Rotate the solenoid to position the R terminal (B, **Figure 17**) toward the starboard side (with the starter installed onto the engine).

8. Install and securely tighten the three screws.

9. Attach the brush plate lead and terminal nut onto the bottom terminal (D, **Figure 17**) of the solenoid. Securely tighten the nut, but do not overtighten or the solenoid housing may crack.

10. Install the starter motor as described in this chapter.

## *Disassembly (Delco starter)*

Refer to **Figure 18** or **Figure 19** as needed.

1. Remove the starter solenoid as described in this chapter.

2. Make alignment marks (**Figure 20**) on the cover, frame and starter housing.

3. Remove the throughbolts and pull the cover from the armature and frame.

4. Remove the screws (2, **Figure 18** or **Figure 19**) and lift the brush plate (4, **Figure 18** or 5, **Figure 19**) from the cover.

5. Pull the armature and frame from the starter housing. Pull the armature from the frame. Magnets hold the armature in the frame.

6A. *Delco PG260 starter*—Pull the washer (7, **Figure 18**) and plate (8) from the starter housing. Remove the grommet (18, **Figure 18**). Pull the planetary shaft and related components (10-14, **Figure 18**) from the housing.

6B. *Delco PG260 F1starter*—Remove the plate (8, **Figure 19**) and shield (9) from the starter housing. Pull the grommet (21, **Figure 19**) and disc (22). Pull the planetary

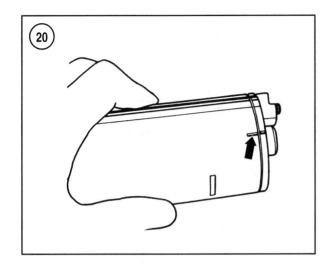

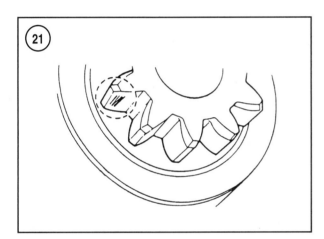

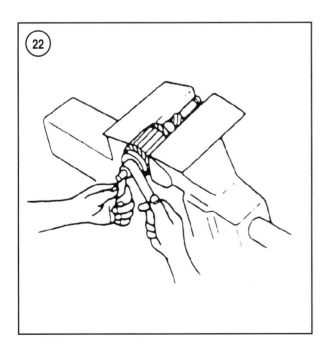

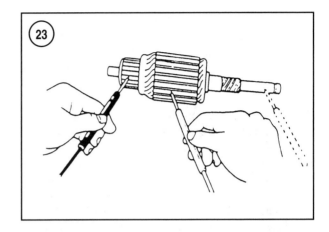

shaft and related components (10-15, **Figure 19**) from the housing.

7. Lift the pinion yoke (19, **Figure 18** or 19, **Figure 19**) from the housing. Remove the stepped washer (15, **Figure 18** or 16, **Figure 19**) from the housing.

8. Using a punch, drive the collar (13, **Figure 18** or 14, **Figure 19**) toward the pinion gear until the lock ring is exposed. Carefully pry the lock ring from the groove in the planetary shaft (10).

9. Separate the planetary shaft, gears and pinion gear.

10. Clean all components in a mild solvent. Do not use solvents that are damaging to plastic or rubber.

### Inspection (Delco starter)

1. Inspect the pinion gear for chipped, cracked or worn teeth (**Figure 21**). Inspect the helical splines at the pinion end of the planetary shaft. Replace the armature if corroded, damaged or excessively worn.

2. Repeatedly thread the pinion drive onto the armature shaft. Replace the pinion drive or armature if the pinion drive does not turn smoothly on the shaft.

3. Secure the armature in a vise with protective jaws (**Figure 22**). Carefully polish the commutator using 600 grit carburundum cloth. Avoid removing too much material. Rotate the armature often to polish the surfaces evenly.

4. Calibrate an ohmmeter to the R × 1 scale.

    a. Connect the ohmmeter between any commutator segment and the armature lamination (**Figure 23**). The meter should indicate no continuity. If continuity is present, the armature is shorted and must be replaced.

    b. Connect the ohmmeter between any commutator segment and the armature shaft (**Figure 23**). The meter should indicate no continuity.

**10**

c.  Connect the ohmmeter between commutator seg-
    ments (**Figure 24**). Continuity must be present be-
    tween any two segments. Repeat this test with the
    meter connected to each commutator segment. If
    any segment does not have continuity, the armature
    must be replaced.

5.  Remove the mica particles from the undercut between
the commutator segments using a small file (**Figure 25**).

6.  Inspect the brushes for grooves, discoloration or corrosion. Inspect the brush springs for corrosion or lost spring
tension. Replace the brush plate assembly if necessary.

7.  Measure the brush length (**Figure 26**). Compare the
brush length with the specification in **Table 7**. Replace the
brush plate assembly if any of the brushes measure less
than the specification. Replace the brush plate if corroded,
contaminated, chipped or broken. Inspect the brush
springs for corrosion damage or weak spring tension. Replace the springs if defective.

8.  Inspect the bearing surfaces on the armature and planetary shaft for excessive or uneven wear. Inspect the planetary gears for worn, cracked or missing teeth. Inspect the
needle bearing in the starter housing for wear, corrosion or
discoloration. Replace all worn or damaged components.

### Assembly (Delco starter)

Apply a light coat of Quicksilver 2-4-C Marine Lubricant (Mercury part No. 92-825407A12) to the needle
bearings, bushings, planetary shaft and gear teeth during
assembly. Do not apply grease or other lubricants to the
brushes or commutator. Refer to **Figure 18** or **Figure 19**
for this procedure.

1.  Collapse the brush springs and fit the brush plate over
the commutator. Release the brush springs. The brush surfaces must contact the commutator (**Figure 27**).

2A. *Delco PG260 starter*—Assemble the cover, armature
and brush plate as follows:

    a.  Align the brush lead grommet with the notch while
    inserting the brush plate and armature into the cover
    (3, **Figure 18**).

    b.  Install and securely tighten the screws (2, **Figure
    18**).

    c.  Hold the armature firmly into the brush plate and
    cover. Slide the frame (6, **Figure 18**) over the arma-
    ture (5).

    d.  Align the antirotation structures (**Figure 28**) while
    seating the frame against the cover.

2B. *Delco PG260 F1 starter*—Assemble the cover, armature and brush plate as follows:

    a.  Hold the armature firmly against the brush plate.
    Align the brush lead grommet with the notch while
    sliding the frame over the armature.

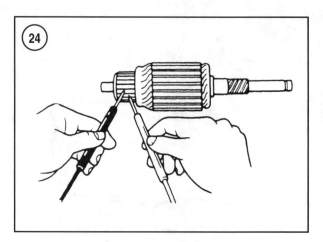

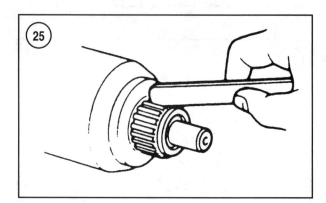

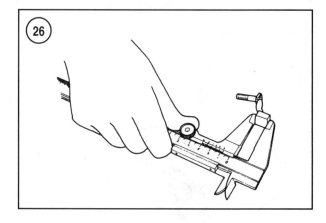

    b.  Guide the bearing (4, **Figure 19**) into the opening
    while installing the cover (3).

    c.  Install the screws (2). Securely tighten the screws.

3.  Align the pivot with the notch while sliding the pinion
yoke into the housing.

4.  Insert the planetary shaft into the larger planetary gear.
Apply 2-4-C Marine Lubricant to the smaller planetary
gears. Align the gear teeth and install the smaller gears
into the larger gear.

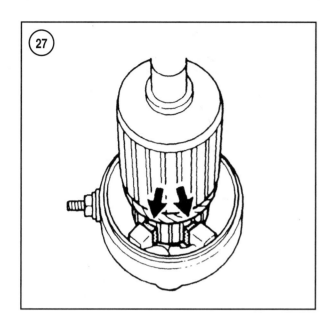

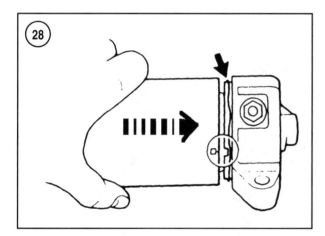

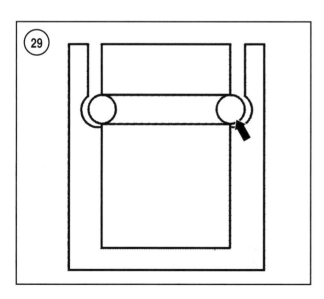

5. Apply a light coat of 2-4-C Marine Lubricant to the planetary shaft. Thread the pinion gear onto the shaft. Slide the collar over the shaft with the open end facing away from the pinion gear.

6. Carefully drive the lock ring onto the end of the shaft. Work the ring down the shaft and into the groove. Use two pliers to squeeze the collar over the lock ring. The ring must fully seat into the collar (**Figure 29**).

7. Place the stepped washer (15, **Figure 18** or 16, **Figure 19**) over the end of the planetary shaft. Align the arms of the yoke with the spool of the pinion gear. Insert the shaft into the starter housing. Align the end of the shaft with the needle bearing in the housing. Seat the planetary assembly into the housing.

8A. *Delco PG260*—Slip the grommet (18, **Figure 18**) into the starter housing opening. Seat the offset end of the grommet in the recess in the starter housing.

8B. *Delco PG260 F1*—Align the disc (22, **Figure 19**) with the opening then seat it against the pinion yoke (19). Align the grommet (21, **Figure 19**) with the disc. Fit the grommet over the notch while seating it into the starter housing opening.

9A. *Delco PG260*—Align the notches in the plate (8, **Figure 18**) with the alignment bosses in the housing. The concave side of the plate must face outward. Seat the washer (7, **Figure 18**) against the plate.

9B. *Delco PG260 F1*—Align the tabs on the shield with the notches in the starter housing. Seat the shield into the starter housing. Seat the plate (8, **Figure 19**) against the shield. The concave side of the plate must face outward.

10. Align the gear teeth on the armature shaft with the planetary gear teeth while inserting the armature into the starter housing. Rotate the armature and frame assembly to align the match marks (**Figure 20**).

11. Insert the throughbolts through the cover and frame assembly. Insert the studded throughbolt into the opening closest to the starter solenoid. Hand-tighten the throughbolts.

12. Make sure the antirotation structures (**Figure 28**) are correctly aligned. Make sure the housing and cover are seated onto the frame.

13. Securely tighten the throughbolts. The starter housing and cover must fully seat onto the frame.

14. Install the starter solenoid as described in this chapter.

**Checking Pinion Clearance**

> *WARNING*
> *Batteries produce explosive hydrogen gas. Charge the battery only in a well-ventilated area. Wear eye protection and gloves when working around batteries. Never smoke or*

**10**

*allow any source of ignition in the area where batteries are stored or charged. Never allow any non-insulated components to contact the terminals as arcing can occur and ignite the hydrogen gas.*

1. Carefully clamp the starter into a vise with protective jaws. Disconnect the brush lead from the lower terminal (D, **Figure 17**) on the starter solenoid. Wrap the disconnected terminal and lead with electrical tape to prevent arcing.

2. Use a jumper lead to connect the positive battery terminal to the S terminal on the starter solenoid (A, **Figure 17**).

3. Connect a second jumper lead to the negative battery terminal. Connect the other end of this lead onto the starter housing. The relay must activate and move the starter pinion. If not, check for an improperly installed relay, improperly installed pinion yoke or poor jumper lead connections.

4. Push the pinion gear toward the planetary as shown in **Figure 30**. Use a feeler gauge to measure the clearance between the pinion gear and the lock ring collar.

5. Compare the clearance with the specification in **Table 7**. If incorrect, disassemble the starter and check for excessively worn or improperly installed components.

6. Disconnect the jumper lead. Remove the electrical tape and reconnect the brush lead onto the solenoid terminal (D, **Figure 17**).

## IGNITION SYSTEM

This section describes removal and installation of ignition system components. Refer to Chapter Three to troubleshoot, test and identify the components.

> *WARNING*
> *Incorrect or improperly installed electrical parts can disable the flash protection features of the electrical system, resulting in possible fire or explosion. Never install automotive electrical parts onto a marine engine.*

### Ignition Coil Removal and Installation (EST Ignition)

A Delco EST ignition coil (**Figure 31**) is used on 3.0L, 7.4 MPI, 454 Mag, and 502 Mag models. It is also used on 1998-prior 4.3, 5.0 and 5.7 liter EFI engines with a MEFI 2 ECM (engine control module). Refer to *Fuel Injection* in Chapter Three to properly identify the ECM.

1. Disconnect the battery cables. Push in the latches and pull the black and gray wires from the coil. Remove both

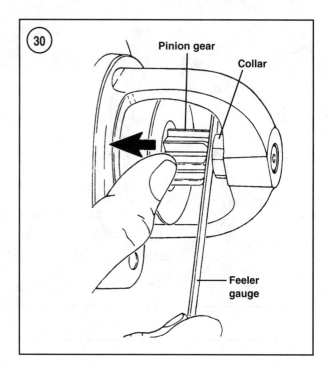

connectors as an assembly. The gray terminal fits onto the black connector.

2. Pull the high tension lead from the coil tower. Clean corrosion or oily deposits from the wire and ignition coil terminals.

3. Remove the mounting bolts. Lift the coil from the cylinder block or intake manifold.

4. Install the coil on the cylinder block or intake manifold. Install and thoroughly tighten the mounting bolts.

5. Attach the black and gray primary wires to the coil.

6. Apply a bead of silicone dielectric compound (Mercury part No. 92-802882A1) to the inner diameter of the high tension wire boot. Do not apply compound to the terminal. Push the terminal into the coil tower. Slide the boot over the terminal.

## Ignition Coil Removal and Installation (Thunderbolt V Ignition)

A Thunderbolt V ignition coil (**Figure 32**) is used on all carbureted V6 and V8 models, and on 1999-2001 4.3, 5.0 and 5.7 liter EFI engines with a MEFI 3 ECM. Refer to *Fuel Injection* in Chapter Three to properly identify the ECM. The coil is secured to a bracket on the rear port side of the engine.

1. Disconnect the battery cables.

2. Remove the nuts and disconnect the wires from the positive and negative coil terminals.

3. Carefully pull the high tension wire from the coil tower.

4. Loosen the mounting bracket clamp screw and pull the coil from the bracket.

5. Slide the coil fully into the bracket. Securely tighten the clamp screw in the bracket.

6. Connect the purple or red wire terminal to the positive coil terminal. Connect the gray or white wire terminal to the negative coil terminal. Securely tighten the nuts.

7. Apply a bead of silicone dielectric compound (Mercury part No. 92-802882A1) to the inner diameter of the high tension wire boot. Do not apply compound to the ter-

minal. Carefully push the terminal into the coil tower. Slide the boot over the terminal connection.

8. Connect the battery cables.

## Ignition Coil Removal and Installation (496 Mag and Mag HO)

Eight individual ignition coils (**Figure 33**) are used on 496 Mag and 496 Mag HO. Four coils mount to the top of each rocker arm cover.

1. Disconnect the battery cables. Carefully disconnect the high tension wire and wire harness from the coil.

2. Remove the mounting screws and lift the coil from the rocker arm cover.

3. Install the coil onto the rocker arm cover. Insert the mounting screws and securely tighten them.

4. Connect the wire harness connector and high tension wire to the coil terminals. Connect the battery cables.

## Distributor Cap and Rotor Removal and Installation

Refer to *Ignition System* in Chapter Three to identify the type of distributor used. Replace both the cap and rotor if either is worn or defective.

On four-cylinder models, the cylinders are numbered from front to rear, with the front cylinder being No. 1.

On V6 and V8 models, the cylinders are numbered front to rear, with the front port cylinder being No. 1. The odd numbered cylinders are on the port side and the even numbered cylinders are on the starboard side.

### *Delco EST distributor*

Refer to **Figure 34**.

1. Mark the cylinder numbers on the spark plug wires and the distributor cap. Disconnect the wires from the cap.

2. Loosen the screws and lift the cap (1, **Figure 34**) from the distributor.

3. Use compressed air to blow loose material from the distributor. Pull the rotor (2, **Figure 34**) from the distributor.

4. Inspect the rotor for worn or burnt contacts. Inspect the cap (**Figure 35**) for cracks, carbon tracking and worn, corroded or burnt contacts. Replace the cap and rotor if these or other defects are visible.

5. Align the raised boss in the bore of the rotor (2, **Figure 34**) with the notch in the top of the shaft (3). Slide the rotor onto the shaft. Push straight down until the rotor fully seats onto the shaft.

6. Install the cap, aligning the distributor cap screws with the holes in the housing. The notches in the cap must fit

**10**

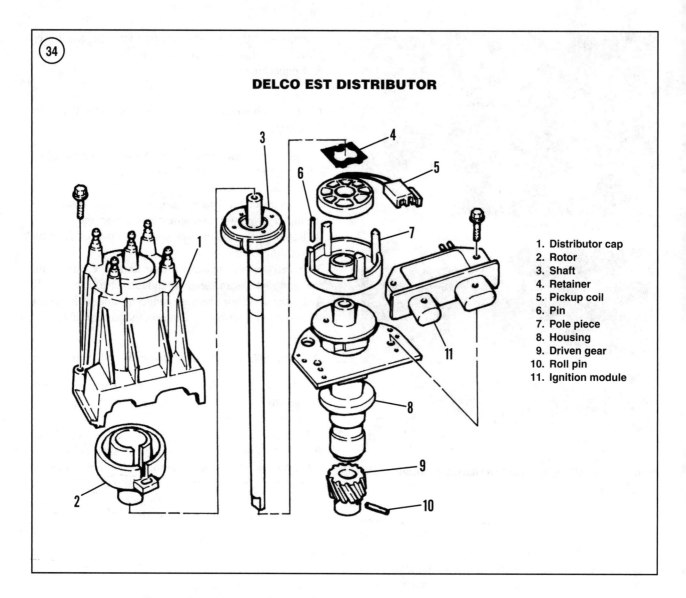

**DELCO EST DISTRIBUTOR**

1. Distributor cap
2. Rotor
3. Shaft
4. Retainer
5. Pickup coil
6. Pin
7. Pole piece
8. Housing
9. Driven gear
10. Roll pin
11. Ignition module

over the ignition module (11, **Figure 34**) connections, and the raised ridge on the module must fit into the slot in the cap. Securely tighten the distributor cap screws.

7. Apply a bead of silicone dielectric compound (Mercury part No. 92-802882A1) onto the inner diameter of the spark plug wire boots. Do not apply compound to the terminal. Carefully push the wires into the terminals.

### Thunderbolt V distributor

Refer to **Figure 36**. Install a new gasket (2, **Figure 36**) each time the cap is removed.

*NOTE*
*Apply heat to the rotor to ease rotor removal from the distributor shaft. Use a heat lamp*

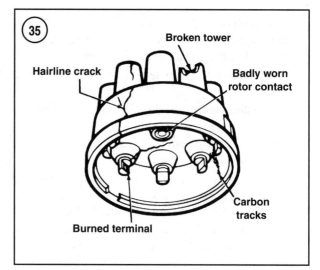

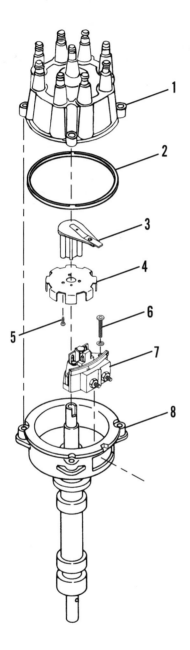

**THUNDERBOLT V DISTRIBUTOR**

1. Distributor cap
2. Gasket
3. Rotor
4. Sensor wheel
5. Screw
6. Screw and washer
7. Sensor
8. Distributor body

*or hair dryer to heat the rotor. Do not use an open flame.*

1. Mark the cylinder numbers on the spark plug wires and the distributor cap. Disconnect the wires from the cap.

2. Loosen the screws and lift the cap (1, **Figure 36**) from the distributor. Remove the gasket (2, **Figure 36**) from the cap. Discard the gasket.

3. Use compressed air to dislodge loose material from the distributor.

4. Remove the rotor and sensor wheel as follows:

   a. Insert a 6 in. long, 1/4 in. socket extension into the slot and position the tip against the screw (5, **Figure 36**).

   b. Rest the other end of the extension against the mating surface of the distributor. Place a folded shop towel between the extension and distributor to protect the surfaces.

   c. Press down on the free end of the extension and pry the wheel (4, **Figure 36**) and rotor (3) from the distributor shaft.

5. Remove the three screws (5, **Figure 36**) and separate the sensor wheel and rotor.

6. Inspect the rotor for worn or burnt contacts. Inspect the cap (**Figure 35**) for cracks, carbon tracking and worn, corroded or burned contacts. Replace the cap and rotor if these or other defects are visible.

7. Inspect the sensor wheel for corrosion and bent or damaged tabs. Replace the sensor wheel if these or other defects occur. Do not attempt to straighten the sensor wheel. If bent, the wheel can contact the sensor (7, **Figure 36**) and cause an ignition system malfunction.

8. Align the raised pin on the rotor with the corresponding opening in the sensor wheel. Insert the three screws (5, **Figure 36**). Securely tighten the screws.

9. Apply two drops of Loctite 271 to the slot at the top of the distributor shaft and the boss in the bore of the rotor.

10. Align the raised boss in the bore of the rotor (3, **Figure 36**) with the notch in the top of the distributor shaft. Slide the rotor onto the shaft. Push straight down until the rotor fully seats onto the shaft.

11. Install a new gasket in the cap.

12. Align the square locating boss of the distributor cap with the square notch in the distributor housing and seat the cap onto the distributor. Securely tighten the distributor cap screws.

13. Apply a bead of silicone dielectric compound (Mercury part No. 92-802882A1) to the inner diameter of the high tension wire boots. Do not apply compound to the terminal. Carefully push the wires into the coil terminals.

**10**

### Distributor Removal and Installation

Do not rotate the crankshaft with the distributor re-moved, or the crankshaft and camshaft will have to be timed to the No. 1 cylinder firing position (Chapter Seven) before installing the distributor.

> *NOTE*
> *A replacement distributor driven gear must drilled to accommodate the roll pin. If the gear must be replaced, have the new gear installed by a reputable machine shop. Improper drilling will damage the distributor shaft and cause the roll pin to loosen.*

1. Disconnect the battery cables. Remove the distributor cap as described in this chapter. Do not remove the rotor.

2. Scribe a mark on the distributor housing that aligns with the rotor contact (**Figure 37**). Scribe a similar mark on the cylinder block or intake manifold that aligns with the distributor marks.

3. Disconnect all wires from the distributor. Use a distributor wrench to loosen the bolt on the hold down clamp (**Figure 38**). Slide the clamp away from the distributor base. Lift the distributor from the engine.

4. Remove and discard the gasket from the distributor base. Inspect the driven gear (9, **Figure 34**) for broken or excessively worn gear teeth. Have a machine shop replace the gear if it is defective. Move the distributor shaft from side to side to check for excessive side play. A slight amount of side play is acceptable. Replace the distributor if the shaft fits loosely in the bore.

5. Place a new gasket onto the lower side of the distributor base. Temporarily tape the gasket in place.

6A. *Crankshaft was not rotated*—Perform the following steps if installing the original distributor with the original driven gear.

    a. Rotate the distributor shaft to align the rotor contact with the distributor mark (**Figure 37**).

    b. Align the distributor marking with the cylinder block or intake manifold mark. Insert the distributor.

    c. Rotate the distributor shaft a few degrees to align the gear teeth and oil pump shaft. When properly aligned, the distributor will seat against the cylinder block or intake manifold.

    d. Rotate the distributor body and align the marks as described in step 2. Place the hold-down clamp over the distributor base and securely tighten the bolt (**Figure 38**).

6B. *Crankshaft was rotated*—Install the distributor as follows:

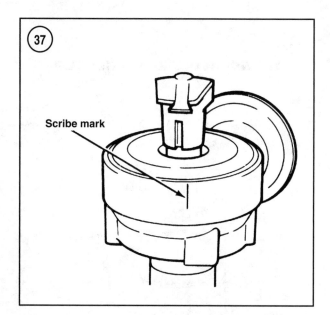

**37**

Scribe mark

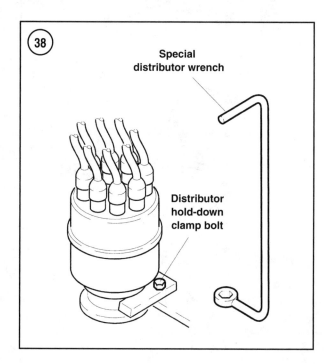

**38**

Special distributor wrench

Distributor hold-down clamp bolt

    a. Place the engine at TDC for the No. 1 cylinder as described in Chapter Seven.

    b. Temporarily install the cap onto the distributor. Scribe a mark on the distributor body that aligns with the terminal for the No. 1 spark plug lead. Remove the cap.

    c. Rotate the distributor shaft to align the rotor contact with the distributor body mark (**Figure 37**).

    d. Carefully insert the distributor into the engine. Rotate the distributor shaft a few degrees to align the

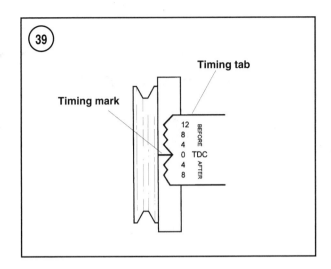

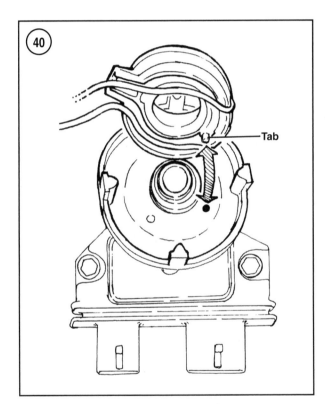

gear teeth. The distributor will drop down when the gear teeth mesh.

e. Push down on the distributor and have an assistant rotate the crankshaft clockwise. As the distributor shaft aligns with the oil pump shaft, the distributor will seat against the cylinder block or intake manifold. Rotate the crankshaft until the rotor contact aligns with the distributor mark and the harmonic balancer timing mark aligns with the TDC mark

(**Figure 39**). If the marks do not align, repeat step 6B.

f. Rotate the distributor body to align the mark on the distributor with the rotor contact (**Figure 37**). Place the hold down clamp over the distributor base and securely tighten the bolt (**Figure 38**).

7. Install the distributor cap as described in this chapter. Reconnect the wires to the distributor. Connect the battery cables. Adjust the ignition timing as described in Chapter Six.

### Pickup Coil Removal and Installation (Delco EST Ignition)

The pickup coil is located in the distributor housing.

1. Disconnect the battery cables. Remove the distributor cap and rotor as described in this chapter.
2. Unplug the pickup coil (5, **Figure 34**) leads from the ignition module (11).
3. Grip two opposing corners of the retainer (4, **Figure 34**) with needlenose pliers. Pull upward on the corners until the retainer slips from the distributor bushing. Discard the retainer.
4. On V6 and V8 models, lift the copper shield from the distributor.
5. Lift the pickup coil (5, **Figure 34**) from the pole piece. Use compressed air to remove loose material from the distributor.
6. Insert the tab on the pickup coil into the opening (**Figure 40**) and seat the coil onto the pole piece.
7. On V6V6 and V8V8 models, align the notch over the pickup coil wires and seat the copper shield onto the pickup coil.
8. Fit a new retainer (4, **Figure 34**) over the distributor bushing with the teeth side facing outward. Place the opening of a 5/8 in. socket over the bushing and seat it against the retainer. Tap on the socket until the teeth of the retainer fit into the groove in the bushing. The retainer must hold the shield, coil and pole piece firmly.
9. Plug the pickup coil leads onto the ignition module. The lock on the connector must engage the tab on the module.
10. Install the rotor and distributor cap as described in this chapter. Connect the battery cables. Adjust the ignition timing as described in Chapter Six.

### Ignition Module Removal and Installation (Delco EST Ignition)

The ignition module is located in the distributor housing. Heat transfer compound must be applied to the bot-

**10**

tom of the ignition module before installation to prevent overheating and failure. A small tube of compound is supplied with the replacement module.

1. Disconnect the battery cables. Remove the distributor cap as described in this chapter.

2. Pull up on the locking tab and disconnect wires and wire connectors from the module.

3. Carefully unplug the pickup coil (5, **Figure 34**) leads from the ignition module (11).

4. Remove the two screws and lift the ignition module from the distributor. Wipe the heat transfer compound from the distributor and the bottom of the module.

5. Apply an even film of Heat Transfer Compound to the metal plate on the bottom of the ignition module.

6. Align the tab on the bottom of the module with the corresponding opening in distributor body. Firmly seat the module on the distributor to spread the compound.

7. Install and tighten the module mounting screws.

8. Plug the pickup coil leads onto the ignition module. The lock on the connector must engage the tab on the module.

9. Reconnect the wires to the module. The locking tab must fit over the locking lugs on the module.

10. Install the distributor cap as described in this chapter. Connect the battery cables. Adjust the ignition timing as described in Chapter Six.

### Sensor Removal and Installation (Thunderbolt V Ignition)

The sensor is located in the distributor housing.

1. Disconnect the battery cables. Remove the distributor cap and rotor as described in this chapter.

2. Disconnect the white/red and white/green sensor wires from the engine wire harness.

3. Remove the mounting screws (**Figure 41**) and lift the sensor from the distributor. Wipe the opening and sensor mounting surfaces clean.

4. Guide the sensor wires through the opening. Fit the sensor into the opening while seating the sensor onto the distributor. Install and tighten the mounting screws.

5. Connect the white/red and white/green wires to the wire harness.

6. Install the rotor and distributor cap as described in this chapter. Connect the battery cables. Adjust the ignition timing as described in Chapter Six.

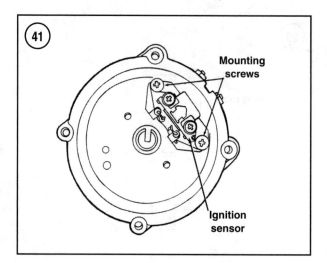

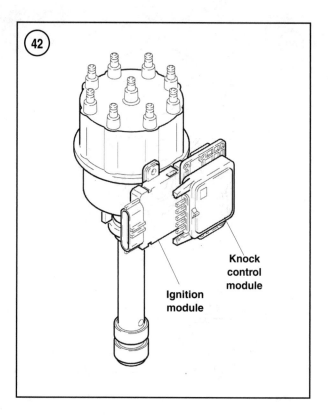

### Knock Control Module Removal and Installation (Thunderbolt V Ignition)

On early 1998 carbureted models, the ignition and knock control modules are mounted to a bracket on the rear of the distributor (**Figure 42**). On late 1998 and 1999-on engines, the module (A, **Figure 43**) is mounted on a bracket affixed to the port side exhaust elbow.

On EFI models, the module is mounted to a bracket on the port side exhaust elbow. A knock control module is not

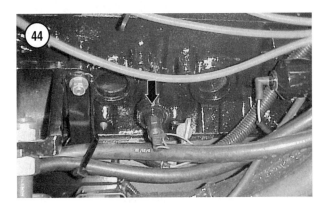

used on EFI models with a MEFI 3 ECU (engine control unit).

1. Disconnect the battery cables. Pull up on the connector tab and disconnect the wire harness from the module.

2. Remove the mounting screws and lift the module from the bracket. Wipe the mounting bracket clean.

3. Install the module with the metal side facing the mounting bracket. Connect the eyelet of the grounding wire (if so equipped) onto one of the mounting screws. Install and securely tighten the mounting screws.

4. Attach the wire harness connector to the module. The locking tab must engage the locking lug.

5. Connect the battery cables.

### Ignition Module Removal and Installation (Thunderbolt V Ignition)

On early 1998 models, the ignition and knock control modules are mounted to the rear side of the distributor (**Figure 42**). On late 1998 and all 1999-on engines, the modules are mounted to the side of the port exhaust elbow. The knock control module (A, **Figure 43**) must be removed to access the ignition module (B) mounting screws. The distributor module uses a single wire harness

connector. The elbow-mounted module uses two wire harness connectors.

1. Disconnect the battery cables. Remove the knock control module as described in this chapter.

2A. *Distributor-mounted module*—Pull out on the tab and disconnect the wire harness from the module.

2B. *Elbow-mounted module*—Push in on the locking tabs and pull both wire connectors from the module.

3. Remove the mounting screws and lift the module from the bracket. Wipe debris from the mounting bracket.

4. Install the module with the metal side facing the mounting bracket. Connect the eyelet of the grounding wire (if so equipped) onto one of the mounting screws. Install and securely tighten the mounting screws.

5A. *Distributor-mounted module*—Attach the wire harness to the module. The locking tab must engage the locking lug

5B. *Elbow mounted module*—Attach the wire harness to the module.

6. Connect the battery cables. Adjust the ignition timing as described in Chapter Six.

### Knock sensor Removal and Installation

On all models except 7.4 MPI, 496 Mag and 496 Mag HO, the knock sensor (**Figure 44**) threads into a brass fitting on the starboard side of the cylinder block.

On model 7.4 MPI, a sensor threads directly into both sides of the cylinder block. A brass fitting is not used on this model.

On models 496 Mag and 496 Mag HO, a nut retains the sensor to a stud on the starboard side of the cylinder block.

Handle the knock sensor with care. The sensor is easily damaged if dropped or handled roughly.

1. Disconnect the battery cables.

2A. *Standard cooling system*—Drain water from the cylinder block as described in Chapter Five.

2B. *Closed cooling system*—Drain the engine coolant as described in Chapter Four (see Changing the Coolant).

3. Pinch the sides of the connector and pull it from the knock sensor. Clean the wire terminal in the connector. Engage a wrench to the brass fitting (if so equipped) to prevent it from rotating.

4A. *496 Mag and 496 Mag HO models*—Remove the nut and pull the sensor from the mounting stud.

4B. *All other models*—Unthread the sensor from the fitting or cylinder block. Thoroughly clean the threads in the brass fitting or cylinder block.

5A. *496 Mag and 496 Mag HO models*—Slip the sensor over the mounting stud. Install and tighten the nut to the specification in **Table 1**. Do not over-tighten the nut or sensor will be damaged.

**10**

5B. *All other models*—Hand-thread the sensor into the fitting. Do not apply sealant to the sensor or brass fitting threads. Tighten the sensor to the specification in **Table 1**. Over-tightening will damage the sensor.

6. Pinch the sides of the connector and fit it over the knock sensor terminal. Release the connector. Tug on the wire to verify a secure connection.

7. On a closed cooling system, fill the system with the correct coolant as described in Chapter Five.

8. Connect the battery cables. Start the engine and check for water or coolant leaks. Remove and re-install the sensor if leakage occurs.

### Shift Interrupt Switch Removal and Installation (Alpha Models)

A shift interrupt switch (A, **Figure 45**) is installed on all models equipped with an Alpha drive unit. Two screws (B, **Figure 45**) secure the switch to the shift plate assembly. Although they appear identical, the switch used on carbureted models operates differently than the switch used for earlier EFI models. Poor performance, difficult shifting, or no spark at the coil will occur if the wrong switch is installed.

1. Disconnect the battery cables. Disconnect both interrupt switch leads from the engine wire harness.

2. Remove both screws (B, **Figure 45**). Guide the switch leads and connectors through the opening in the shift plate (C, **Figure 45**) and remove the switch. Clean the switch mating surface. Do not use flammable solvent.

3. Guide the switch leads and connectors through the opening in the shift plate and install the switch onto the plate. Install the mounting screws, but do not tighten.

4. Insert a 0.031 mm (0.8 mm) feeler gauge between the plunger of the switch and the V-block (D, **Figure 45**). Move the switch in or out until the plunger just touches the feeler gauge. Securely tighten the mounting screws (B, **Figure 45**). Recheck the clearance and adjust accordingly.

5. Connect both interrupt switch leads to the wire harness connectors. Connect the battery cables.

### WARNING SYSTEM

Warning system components vary by the model and the type of fuel system used. Refer to Chapter Three (see *Warning System*) to identify, test and troubleshoot the components.

### OIL PRESSURE SENDER

An oil pressure sender (**Figure 46**) is used on all models.

On 3.0L models, the sender is mounted on the starboard side of the cylinder block.

On 4.3 L models, the sender is mounted on the rear port side of the cylinder block.

On other models, the sender is mounted on the rear port side of the cylinder block, directly above the flywheel housing.

The boat builder may have relocated the sender to accommodate aftermarket equipment. If the sender is not found in the specified location, refer to the wire diagrams at the end of the manual. Trace the indicated wire color to the sender. The sender is constructed of soft material, and the hex portion of the sender rounds over easily, making removal difficult. If the hex is rounded, grip it with locking pliers.

1. Pull the wire connector from the sender terminal.

2. Attach a wrench to the brass fitting to prevent rotation. Place a shop towel under the sender to capture spilled oil.

3. Remove the sender. Do not remove the fitting. Clean all sealant from the sender and fitting threads.

4. Apply a very light coat of Loctite Pipe Sealant with Teflon to the sender threads. Do not allow sealant to enter the small opening in the sender. Excessive amounts of sealant may electrically insulate the sender and prevent the gauge from operating.

5. Install the sender into the fitting. Hold the fitting with a wrench to prevent rotation and securely tighten the sender.

6. Connect the wire connector to the sender.

7. Start the engine and immediately check for oil leakage. Correct oil leakage before operating the engine. Make sure the oil pressure gauge operates correctly.

### OIL PRESSURE SWITCH

An oil pressure switch is used on all V6 and V8 engines. The switch is also used on 3.0L models equipped with the optional audio warning system.

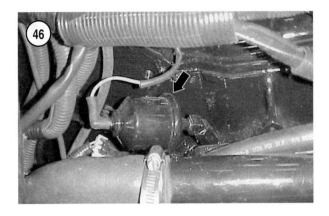

On 3.0L models, the switch is located on the starboard side of the cylinder block. The switch mounts to the same fitting as the oil pressure sender.

On all other models, the switch is located on the rear port side of the cylinder block.

The switch is constructed of soft material, and the hex portion of the sender rounds over easily, making removal difficult. If the hex is rounded off, grip it with locking pliers to remove. Replace the sender as follows:

1. Pull the wire connector from the sender terminal.

2. Attach a wrench to the brass fitting to prevent rotation. Place a shop towel under the sender to capture spilled oil.

3. Remove the switch from the fitting. Clean the sender and fitting threads.

4. Do not apply sealant to the sender or fitting threads. Sealant may electrically insulate the switch and prevent the switch from operating.

5. Install the switch into the fitting. Hold the fitting with a wrench to prevent rotation and securely tighten the sender.

6. Push the wire connector onto the sender terminal.

7. Start the engine and immediately check for oil leakage. Correct oil leakage before operating the engine. Make sure the oil pressure gauge operates correctly.

## OVERHEAT SWITCH

An overheat switch is used on 1999-prior V6 and V6 engines equipped with a carburetor. This switch is also used on 3.0L models equipped with the optional audio warning system.

*3.0L models*—The switch mounts on the front and starboard side of the thermostat housing.

*V6 and V8 models*—The switch mounts on the port side of the thermostat housing. Install the switch into the fitting closest to the thermostat.

*NOTE*
*The overheat switch and engine temperature sender are very similar in appearance and mount to the same general area of the engine. Refer to the wire diagrams at the end of the manual to identify the wires for the switch.*

1A. *Standard cooling system*—Drain water from the cylinder block as described in Chapter Five.

1B. *Closed cooling system*—Drain the engine coolant as described in Chapter Four under *Changing the Coolant*.

2. Disconnect the tan/blue wire from the switch. Remove the switch from the housing.

3. Thoroughly clean the threads on the switch and in the thermostat housing.

4. Apply a light coat of Loctite Pipe Sealant with Teflon to the threads of the switch. Install the switch into the housing. Securely tighten the switch.

5. Connect the tan/blue wire to the switch.

6. *Closed cooling system*—Fill the cooling system with the proper coolant as described in Chapter Five.

7. Start the engine and check for water or coolant leakage. If leakage is present, remove the switch and clean the threads. Reinstall the switch.

## ENGINE TEMPERATURE SENSOR

An engine temperature sensor is used on all 1999-on V6 and V8 engines equipped with a carburetor. A yellow wire connects the sender to the ignition module. The switch is similar in appearance and installs in the same location as the temperature sensor used on EFI models. Replace the sensor as described in Chapter Eight under *Engine Temperature Sensor*.

## ENGINE TEMPERATURE SENDER

On 3.0L models, the sender is located on the front port side of the thermostat housing.

On model 7.4 MPI, the sender is mounted to the intake manifold, directly below the thermostat.

On all remaining models, the sender is located on the port side of the thermostat housing. Install the switch into the fitting closest to the thermostat.

*NOTE*
*The overheat switch and engine temperature sender are very similar in appearance and mount to the same area on the engine. Refer to the wire diagrams at the end of the manual to identify the wires for the sender.*

**10**

1A. *Standard cooling system*—Drain water from the cylinder block as described in Chapter Five.

1B. *Closed cooling system*—Drain the engine coolant as described in Chapter Four (see Changing the Coolant).

2. Disconnect the tan wire from the sender. Remove the sender from the housing.

3. Thoroughly clean the threads on the sender and in the thermostat housing.

4. Apply a light coat of Loctite Pipe Sealant with Teflon to the threads of the sender. Install the sender into the housing. Securely tighten the sender.

5. Connect the tan wire to the switch.

6. *Closed cooling system*—Fill the cooling system as described in Chapter Five.

7. Start the engine and check for water or coolant leakage. Remove and reinstall the sender if leakage occurs.

## GEARCASE LUBRICANT MONITOR

A gearcase lubricant monitor (**Figure 47**) is used on all stern drive models.

1. Drain the gearcase lubricant as described in Chapter Four.

2. Loosen the clamp and carefully pull the hose from the fitting. Do not use excessive force.

3. Disconnect the monitor leads from the engine wire harness. On 3.0L models, the leads are only connected if the engine is equipped with the optional audio warning system.

4. Remove the rubber retaining strap and lift the monitor from the bracket. Wipe oily debris from the bracket.

5. Use solvent to clean residual lubricant from the monitor. Dry the monitor with compressed air. Inspect the monitor for cracks or other damage and replace as needed.

6. Push the lubricant hose fully over the monitor fitting. Install and tighten the hose clamp.

7. Fit the raised boss into the recess in the bracket and install the monitor. Install the rubber retaining strap.

8. Connect the monitor leads to the engine wire harness.

9. Refill the gearcase with lubricant as described in Chapter Four. Check for lubricant leakage and correct as needed.

## WATER PRESSURE SENSOR

A water pressure sensor (**Figure 48**) is used on 496 Mag, 496 Mag HO and 2002-2004 MPI models. The sensor threads into the fitting on the seawater pump or power steering fluid cooler.

1. Drain water from the seawater pump as described in Chapter Four.

2. Pull up the locking latch and disconnect the wire harness from the sensor.

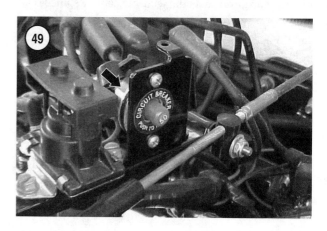

3. Remove the sensor from the pump fitting. Clean residual sealant from the sensor and fitting threads.

4. Apply a light coat of Loctite Pipe Sealant with Teflon to the threads of the sensor. 5. Install the sensor into the fitting. Securely tighten the sensor.

5. Snap the wire connector onto the sensor. Tug on the wire to verify a secure connection. Route the wire away from moving components.

6. Start the engine and check for water leakage. Correct leakage as necessary.

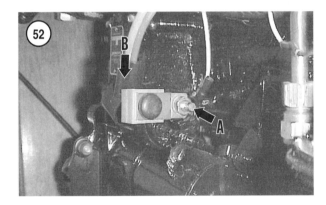

## CHARGING SYSTEM

This section describes removal and installation of the fuse, circuit breaker and alternator. Refer to Chapter Three to identify and test the charging system.

If testing indicates a faulty alternator, replace it with a new or rebuilt unit. Make sure the new or rebuilt alternator is the exact replacement for the original alternator. Consider having the alternator rebuilt at an alternator repair shop. The cost of a repair is usually less than the cost of new or rebuilt alternator.

Alternator repair should be performed only by a qualified technician. The alternator uses soldered connections for all internal components. These connections must be de-soldered for testing or replacement. A special soldering technique must be used. Otherwise new or good used components may be damaged.

Always inform the repair shop that the alternator is used on an inboard marine engine. Special parts or repair procedures are required to maintain the flash protection features of the alternator. Never install automotive components on a marine inboard engine.

*WARNING*
*Incorrect or improperly installed electrical parts can disable the flash protection features of the electrical system, which may result in fire or explosion. Never install automotive electrical parts on a marine engine.*

### Circuit Breaker Removal and Installation

A circuit breaker (**Figure 49**) is used on all EFI engines and 5.7L (carbureted) models. It is mounted in the electrical component box (**Figure 50**), beneath the fuel injection system cover (**Figure 51**) or onto a bracket located behind the throttle body.

1. Disconnect the battery cables. Disconnect the red and red/purple wires from the circuit breaker.
2. Remove the fasteners and lift the circuit breaker from the engine.
3. Secure the circuit breaker to the mount and securely tighten the fasteners.
4. Connect the red and red/purple wires to the circuit breaker. Arrange the terminals to prevent contact with one another and securely tighten the screws.
5. Connect the battery cables.

### Fuse Removal and Installation

1. Disconnect the cables from the battery. Disconnect the positive battery cable from the starter solenoid (A, **Figure 52**).
2. Remove the second nut from the terminal and pull the fuse from the terminal.
3. Remove the nut on the back side of the fuse (B, **Figure 52**). Pull the fuse from the wire harness.
4. Connect the wire harness to the terminal on the back of the fuse. Orient the wire harness as shown in **Figure 52** and tighten the nut.
5. Place the fuse onto the starter solenoid terminal as shown in **Figure 52**. Install and securely tighten the nut.

**10**

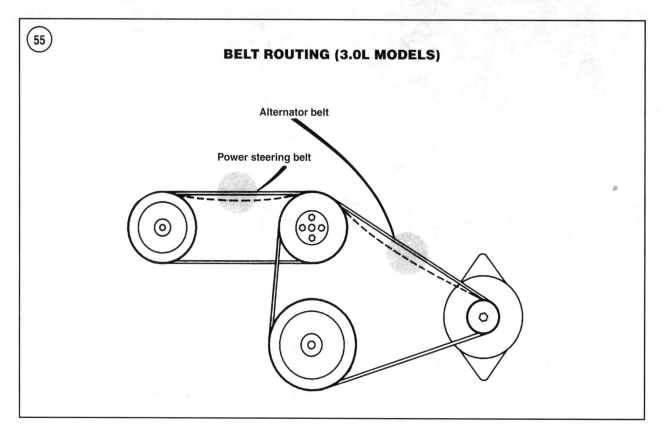

**BELT ROUTING (3.0L MODELS)**

Alternator belt

Power steering belt

6. Connect the positive battery cable onto the starter sole-noid terminal. Connect the cables to the battery.

**Alternator Removal and Installation**

Make a sketch of the wire connections if the alternator requires repair. Marks on a rebuilt alternator may be illegible.

1. Disconnect the battery cables. Mark a directional arrow on the flat side of the belt. If reused, the belt must be oriented to turn in the original direction.
2. Disconnect all wires from the alternator.
3A. *3.0L models*—Loosen the alternator pivot bolt, but do not remove it at this time. Loosen the bolt located in the adjustment slot.
3B. *496 Mag and 496 Mag HO models*—Loosen the nut (A, **Figure 53**) on the adjustment mechanism. Turn the bolt (B, **Figure 53**) until the belt loosens.

**(56)**

# BELT ROUTING V6 AND V8 ENGINES
## (EXCEPT MODELS 496 MAG AND 496 MAG HO) (SERIAL NO. 0L618999-PRIOR)

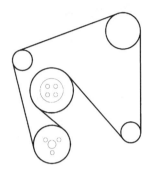

**Alpha with power steering**

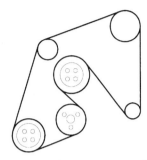

**Bravo with power steering**

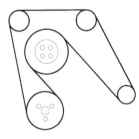

**Alpha with closed cooling
without power steering**

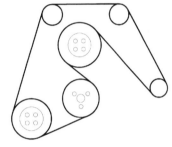

**Bravo without power steering**

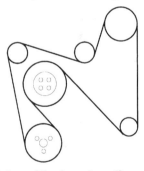

**Alpha with closed cooling
and power steering**

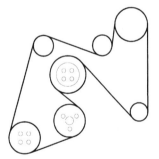

**Bravo with closed cooling and
power steering**

**10**

3C. *All other models*—Hold the stud (A, **Figure 54**) on the tensioner pulley with a 5/16 in. end wrench. Use a 5/8 in. end wrench to loosen the lock nut (B, **Figure 54**).

4. Remove the drive belt from the pulleys. Support the alternator while removing the mounting bolts. Lift the alternator from the engine.

5. Inspect the mounting brackets for cracks or damage. Replace all damaged brackets. Tighten the bracket mounting bolts to the specification in **Table 1**.

6. Fit the alternator onto the mounting brackets. Install the alternator mounting bolts. Do not tighten the bolts at this time.

7. Install the belt over the pulleys. Refer to **Figures 55-58** for belt routing. If reusing the original belt, install it with the arrow facing in the original direction of rotation.

8. Connect the wires to the alternator. Adjust the belt tension as described in Chapter Six.

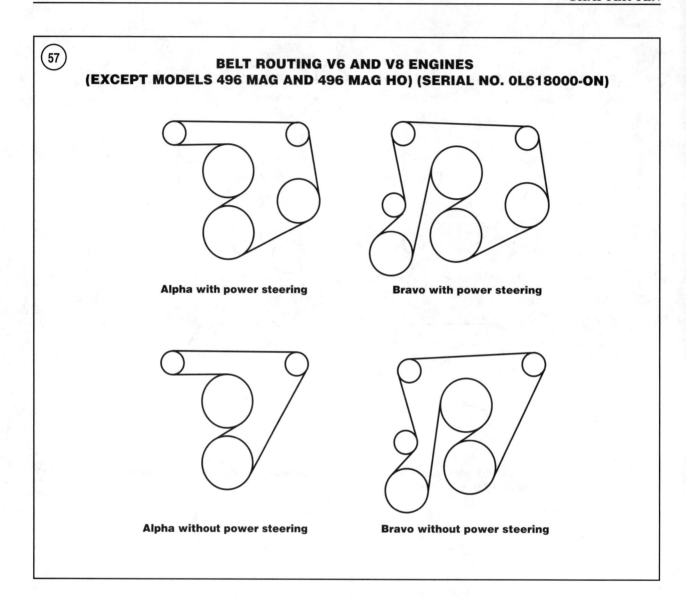

**(57)**

**BELT ROUTING V6 AND V8 ENGINES**
**(EXCEPT MODELS 496 MAG AND 496 MAG HO) (SERIAL NO. 0L618000-ON)**

Alpha with power steering          Bravo with power steering

Alpha without power steering          Bravo without power steering

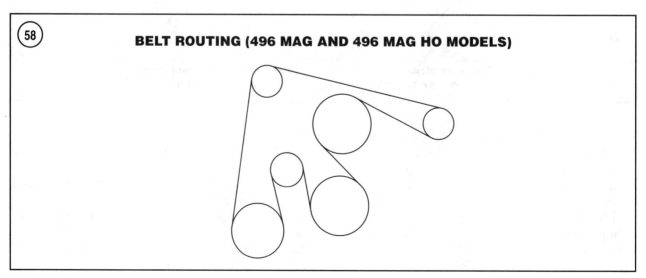

**(58)**

**BELT ROUTING (496 MAG AND 496 MAG HO MODELS)**

**Table 1 TORQUE SPECIFICATIONS**

| Fastener | ft.-lb. | in.-lb. | N•m |
|---|---|---|---|
| Starter motor mounting bolts | | | |
| 3.0L | 37 | – | 50 |
| All other models | 50 | – | 68 |
| Mando alternator | | | |
| Brace to alternator | 20 | – | 27 |
| Brace to cylinder block | 30 | – | 41 |
| Alternator to bracket | | | |
| Pivot bolt | 35 | – | 47 |
| Anchor bolt | 20 | – | 27 |
| Bracket to cylinder block | | | |
| 3.0L, 4.3L, 5.0L, 5.7L | 30 | – | 41 |
| 350 Mag | | | |
| 7.4 MPI, 454 Mag, 502 Mag | 40 | – | 54 |
| Pulley nut | 42 | – | 57 |
| Ground terminal nut | – | 25 | 3 |
| Regulator terminal nuts | – | 25 | 3 |
| Regulator mounting screws | – | 43 | 5 |
| Brush retaining screws | – | 18 | 2 |
| End frame screws | – | 55 | 6 |
| Delco alternator | | | |
| Pulley nut | 70 | – | 95 |
| Ground terminal nut | – | 55 | 6 |
| Bracket to cylinder block | 30 | – | 41 |
| Alternator to bracket | 35 | – | 47 |
| Regulator terminal nuts | – | 25 | 3 |
| Regulator mounting screws | – | 42 | 5 |
| Brush retaining screws | – | 18 | 2 |
| End frame screws | – | 55 | 6 |
| Coolant temperature sender | | | |
| 4.3L, 5.0L, 5.7L, 350 Mag | 20 | – | 27 |
| Knock sensor | | | |
| 496 Mag and 496 Mag HO | 14 | 168 | 19 |
| All other models | 12-16 | 144-192 | 16-22 |
| Camshaft position sensor | – | 106 | 12 |

**10**

**Table 2 BATTERY REQUIREMENTS**

| Model | CCA rating | MCA rating | Ah rating |
|---|---|---|---|
| 3.0L | 375 | 475 | 90 |
| 4.3L, 5.0L and 5.7L | | | |
| Carburetor models | 375 | 475 | 90 |
| EFI models | 750 | 950 | 180 |
| MX 6.2, 7.4 MPI, 454 Mag, 502 Mag | 750 | 950 | 180 |
| 496 Mag, 496 Mag HO | 750 | 950 | 180 |

**Table 3 BATTERY CABLE REQUIREMENTS**

| Cable length | Minimum cable gauge |
|---|---|
| 0-3.5 ft. (0-1.06 m) | 4 |
| 3.6-6 ft. (1.10-1.83 m) | 2 |
| 6.1-7.5 ft. (1.86-2.29 m) | 1 |
| 7.6-9.5 ft. (2.32-2.90 m) | 0 |
| 9.6-12 ft. (2.93-3.66 m) | 00 |
| 12.1-15 ft. (3.69-4.57 m) | 000 |
| 15.1-19 ft. (4.60-5.80 m) | 0000 |

### Table 4 BATTERY CAPACITY (HOURS OF USE)

| Amperage draw | Hours of usage |
|---|---|
| With 80 amp-hour battery | |
|   5 amps | 13.5 hours |
|   15 amps | 3.5 |
|   25 amps | 1.8 |
| With 110 amp-hour battery | |
|   5 amps | 15.8 hours |
|   15 amps | 4.2 |
|   25 amps | 2.4 |

### Table 5 BATTERY STATE OF CHARGE

| Specific gravity reading | Percentage of charge remaining |
|---|---|
| 1.120-1.140 | 0 |
| 1.135-1.155 | 10 |
| 1.150-1.170 | 20 |
| 1.160-1.180 | 30 |
| 1.175-1.195 | 40 |
| 1.190-1.210 | 50 |
| 1.205-1.225 | 60 |
| 1.215-1.235 | 70 |
| 1.230-1.250 | 80 |
| 1.245-1.265 | 90 |
| 1.260-1.280 | 100 |

### Table 6 BATTERY CHARGING SPECIFICATIONS

| Charging rate | Recharge time (approximate) |
|---|---|
| 5 amps | 16 hours |
| 15 amps | 13 hours |
| 25 amps | 12 hours |

### Table 7 STARTER SPECIFICATIONS

| | |
|---|---|
| Pinion clearance | |
|   Delco PG260 | 0.010-0.160 in. (0.25-4.06 mm) |
|   Delco PG260 F1 | 0.009-0.160 in. (0.23-4.06 mm) |
|   Mando  M59601 | 0.010-0.160 in. (0.25-4.06 mm) |
| Brush length | |
|   Delco PG260 | N/A |
|   Delco PG260 F1 | 0.18-0.42 in. (4.57-10.66 mm) |
|   Mando M59601 | N/A |
| N/A- Not available | |

### Table 8 ALTERNATOR SPECIFICATIONS

| Alternator type | Specification |
|---|---|
| Rotor resistance | |
|   Mando 55A | 4.3-5.5 ohms |
| Minimum brush length | |
|   Mando 55A | 0.25 in. (6.3 mm) |
| | (continued) |

**Table 8 ALTERNATOR SPECIFICATIONS (continued)**

| Alternator type | Specification |
|---|---|
| Maximum slip ring out of round | |
| Mando 55A | 0.002 in. (0.051 mm) |
| Condenser capacity | |
| Mando 55A | 4 mfd. |
| Minimum brush length | |
| Delco 65 A | 0.25 in. (6.3 mm) |

**Table 9 ENGINE FIRING ORDER**

| 3.0L models | 1-3-4-2 |
|---|---|
| 4.3L models | 1-6-5-4-3-2 |
| 5.0L, 5.7L, 350 Mag | 1-8-4-3-6-5-7-2 |
| MX 6.2 | 1-8-4-3-6-5-7-2 |
| 7.4L MPI, 454 Mag, 502 Mag | 1-8-4-3-6-5-7-2 |
| 496 Mag, 496 Mag HO | 1-8-7-2-6-5-4-3 |

**10**

# Chapter Eleven

# Drive Unit and Propeller

This chapter describes removal, disassembly, assembly and adjustment of the drive unit (**Figure 1**). Propeller removal and installation instructions are also included. **Tables 1-4** list torque specifications, drive unit identification and bearing preload specifications. **Tables 1-4** are located at the end of this chapter.

All drive unit rotation is described based on the direction the propeller rotates in forward gear as viewed from the rear (**Figure 2**) facing forward. Some drive units are designed to rotate the propeller shaft in one direction only while in forward gear. They are commonly referred to as uni-rotational. Other types of drive units are designed to rotate the propeller shaft in either direction for forward gear. They are commonly referred to a bi-rotational.

Although the Alpha and Bravo type drive units are similar in appearance, the internal components are very different. Refer to the following information for a general overview of the drive units.

Most single engine boats use a standard rotation drive unit. To balance propeller torque, most dual engine boats use both a standard and counter-rotation drive unit. Generally, dual engine applications perform best with the standard rotation drive unit and propeller mounted on the starboard side and the counter-rotation drive unit and propeller on the port side (**Figure 3**). This is commonly referred to as having outboard-turning propellers. Some dual engine boats perform better with the drives and pro-

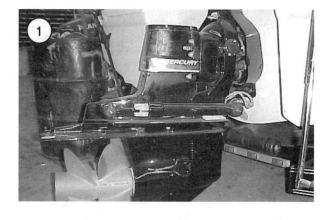

pellers installed in the opposite positions, referred to as inboard-turning propellers (**Figure 4**). Contact the boat manufacturer for recommendations on propeller rotation.

## ALPHA DRIVE

The Alpha drive unit is used on 3.0- 5.7 Liter models. This drive is available in numerous drive unit ratios and in standard or counter-rotation versions. The upper part of the drive unit is referred to as the drive shaft housing and the lower portion is the gearcase. Five different gear ratios are available for the drive shaft housing and two different

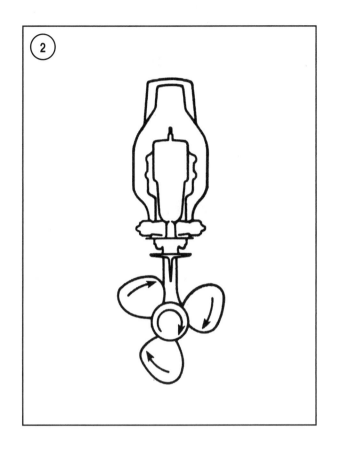

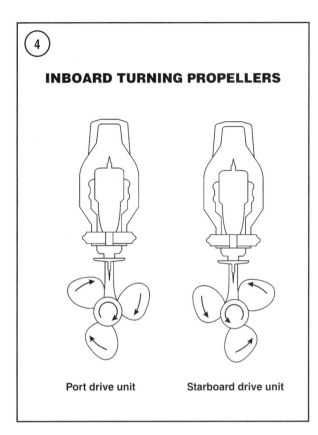

**INBOARD TURNING PROPELLERS**

Port drive unit        Starboard drive unit

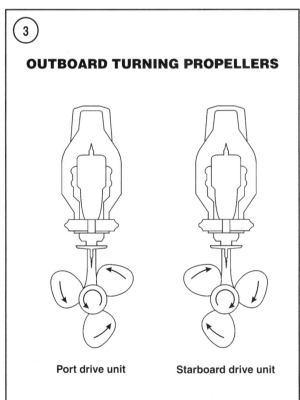

**OUTBOARD TURNING PROPELLERS**

Port drive unit        Starboard drive unit

11

ratios are available for the gearcase. The various combinations provide ten different drive unit ratios.

On Alpha models, the seawater pump (**Figure 5**) mounts in and is driven by the gearcaseAlpha. This type of pump is a floppy vane design that provides a long life and trouble free operation. Under normal operating conditions this pump can last for years. Service procedures for the Alpha seawater pump are included in the gearcase section in this chapter.

Alpha drive units are uni-rotational. Right hand drives are referred to as standard rotation units. Left-hand drives

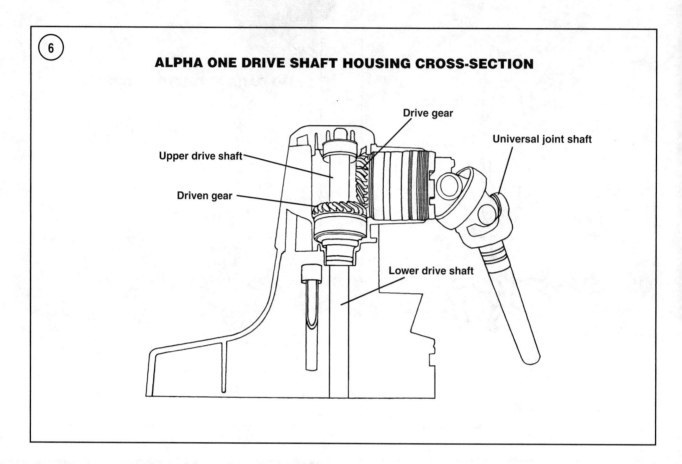

**⑥**

# ALPHA ONE DRIVE SHAFT HOUSING CROSS-SECTION

Drive gear

Universal joint shaft

Upper drive shaft

Driven gear

Lower drive shaft

are referred to as counter-rotation units. Each rotation uses different internal gearcase components. The drive shaft housing assembly and the basic gearcase housing is identical for either rotation.

The drive shaft housing contains the universal joint shaft and the drive and driven gears (**Figure 6**). These components transfer the horizontal drive shaft rotation to the vertical drive shafts. Universal joints in the horizontal shaft allow steering or tilting of the drive unit.

The gearcase contains the lower drive shaft along with the pinion, forward and reverse gears (**Figure 7**), the shifting mechanism and propeller shaft. The gearcase transfers the rotation of the vertical drive shaft (**Figure 7**) to the horizontal propeller shaft. The forward and reverse gear along with the sliding clutch (**Figure 7**) transfer the rotational force to the propeller shaft. The shift selector and linkage move the clutch.

The pinion and both driven gears (**Figure 7**) rotate at all times when the engine is running. A sliding clutch (**Figure 7**) engages the propeller shaft with either the front or rear mounted gear.

When neutral is selected (**Figure 7**) the propeller shaft remains stationary as the gears rotate. No propeller thrust is delivered.

When forward gear is selected (**Figure 7**), the shift mechanism moves the sliding clutch to engage the forward gear on standard rotation drives or the rear gear on counter-rotation drives.

When reverse gear is selected (**Figure 7**), the shift shafts and linkage move the sliding clutch toward the rear gear on standard rotation drives or the front mounted gear on counter-rotation drives.

## Identifying drive unit rotation

Never rely solely on the propeller rotation to identify the drive rotation. The easiest way to identify a counter rotation drive is by the *counter rotation* decal or R stamped on the end of the propeller shaft. If neither of these marks are present, remove the propeller and inspect the bearing carrier (**Figure 8**). Counter-rotation models have a raised area in the exhaust passage area (**Figure 8**) and a surface texture (**Figure 9**) that resembles Styrofoam. This texture forms during the casting process. The bearing carrier on standard rotation models has neither of these characteristics.

⑦

## GEARCASE OPERATION

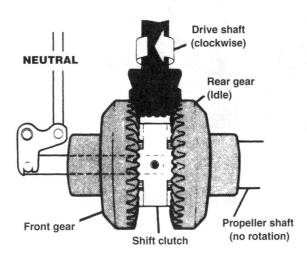

**NEUTRAL**

Drive shaft
(clockwise)

Rear gear
(Idle)

Front gear

Shift clutch

Propeller shaft
(no rotation)

**FORWARD
(Standard rotation)**

**REVERSE
(Counter rotation)**

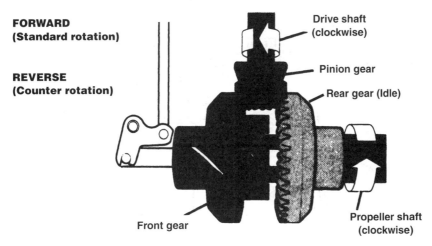

Drive shaft
(clockwise)

Pinion gear

Rear gear (Idle)

Front gear

Propeller shaft
(clockwise)

**REVERSE
(Standard rotation)**

**FORWARD
(Counter rotation)**

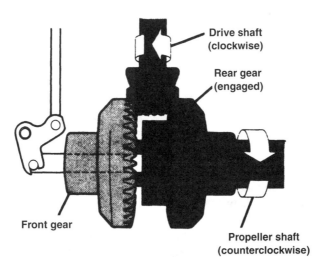

Drive shaft
(clockwise)

Rear gear
(engaged)

Front gear

Propeller shaft
(counterclockwise)

**11**

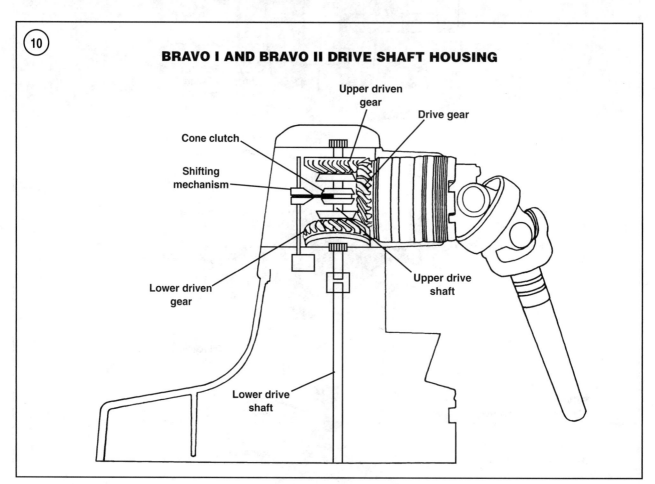

**BRAVO I AND BRAVO II DRIVE SHAFT HOUSING**

Upper driven gear

Drive gear

Cone clutch

Shifting mechanism

Lower driven gear

Upper drive shaft

Lower drive shaft

## Bravo Drive

Bravo drives are available in numerous drive ratios and with a single or twin propeller gearcases (**Figure 1**). Refer to **Table 2** to determine the available Bravo drive gear ratios. The upper part of the drive unit is referred to as the drive shaft housing and the lower portion is the gearcase. The basic design of the drive shaft housing is similar for all model variations. The drive shaft housing is available in five different gear ratios.

All Bravo I and Bravo II drive units are bi-rotational. Although the Bravo III drive unit (**Figure 1**) shares many characteristics of the bi-rotational Bravo I and Bravo II drive units, it is uni-rotational. The front propeller rotates counterclockwise and the rear propeller rotates clockwise for forward thrust. Even with dual engines, bi-rotational

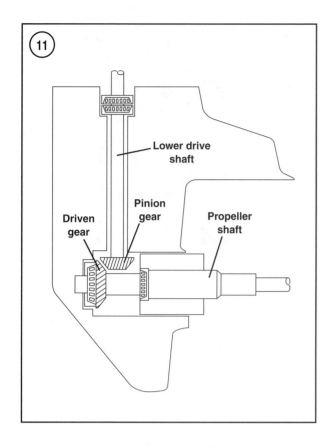

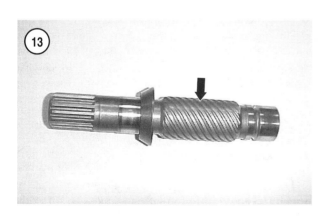

capability is not necessary; the twin counter-rotating propellers balance out propeller torque.

### *Operation (Bravo I and Bravo II)*

The drive shaft housing contains the universal joint shaft, drive gear, driven gears and shifting mechanism (**Figure 10**). These components transfer horizontal drive shaft rotation to the vertical drive shafts and allow shifting of the drive unit. Universal joints in the horizontal shaft allow steering or tilting of the drive unit.

The gearcase contains the lower drive shaft, pinion gear, driven gear and propeller shaft(s). The gearcase transfers the rotation of the vertical drive shaft (**Figure 11**) to the horizontal propeller shaft.

The drive and both driven gears in the drive shaft housing (**Figure 10**) rotate at all times when the engine is running. For forward or reverse gears, the cone clutch (**Figure 12**) engages the helical splined upper drive shaft (**Figure 13**) with the tapered opening (**Figure 14**) in either the upper or lower driven gear. A coupler connects the upper drive shaft to the lower drive shaft of the gearcase (**Figure 11**).

When in neutral, the clutch is positioned midway between, but does not contact, the upper or lower driven gears. Without clutch engagement, the upper drive shaft, lower shaft and propeller shaft remain stationary. No propeller thrust is delivered.

When clockwise propeller shaft rotation is selected, the shift mechanism moves the cone clutch into the tapered opening in the lower driven gear. The clutch engages and rotates in the direction of the gear. As the clutch rotates, it drives against the helical splines of the upper drive shaft, engaging it and the upper drive shaft to the gear. This results in clockwise rotation of the upper and lower drive shafts. Clockwise rotation of the lower drive shaft and

**11**

pinion gear (**Figure 11**) drives the driven gear and propeller shaft clockwise.

When counterclockwise propeller shaft rotation is selected, the shift mechanism moves the cone clutch into the tapered opening in the upper driven gear. The clutch engages with and rotates in thesame direction as the gear. As the clutch rotates, it drives against the helical splines of the upper drive shaft, engaging it and the upper drive shaft to the gear. This results in counterclockwise rotation of the upper and lower drive shafts. Counterclockwise rotation of the lower drive shaft and pinion gear (**Figure 11**) drives the driven gear and propeller shaft counter-clockwise.

Shifting the remote control to the neutral position moves the various linkage and levers connected to the shift shaft. This makes the shift shaft rotate, causing the ramp on shift cam and yoke assembly (**Figure 15**) to drive against the driven gear. This action pushes the clutch away from the driven gear. Clutch and drive shaft rotation ceases as the clutch breaks contact with the gear.

### Operation (Bravo III)

The drive shaft housing contains the universal joint shaft, drive gear, driven gears and shifting mechanism (**Figure 10**). These components transfer horizontal drive shaft rotation to the vertical drive shafts and shifting of the drive unit. Universal joints in the horizontal shaft allow steering or tilting of the drive unit.

The gearcase contains the lower drive shaft, pinion gear, front driven gear, rear drive gear inner and outer propeller shaft(s). The gearcase transfers the rotation of the lower drive shaft (**Figure 11**) to both horizontal propeller shafts.

The front driven gear connects by splines to the inner propeller shaft. The rear mounted propeller mounts to the inner propeller shaft. The rear driven gear is connected by splines to the outer propeller shaft. The front (left-hand) propeller mounts onto the outer propeller shaft.

The drive and both driven gears in the drive shaft housing (**Figure 10**) rotate at all times when the engine is running. For forward or reverse gear, the cone clutch (**Figure 12**) engages the helical splined upper drive (**Figure 13**) shaft with the tapered opening in either the upper or lower driven gear. A coupler (**Figure 14**) connects the upper drive shaft to the lower drive shaft of the gearcase (**Figure 11**).

When neutral is selected, the clutch is positioned midway between, but does not contact, the upper or lower driven gears. Without clutch engagement, the upper drive shaft, lower shaft and propeller shaft remains stationary. No propeller thrust is delivered.

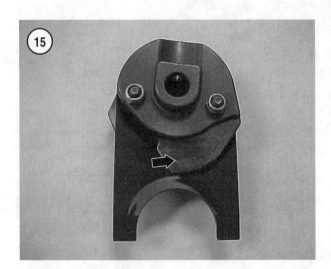

When forward propeller thrust is selected, the shift mechanism moves the cone clutch into the tapered opening in the lower driven gear. The clutch egages with and rotates in the direction of the gear. As the clutch rotates, it drives against the helical splines of the upper drive shaft, clamping it and the upper drive shaft to the gear. This results in clockwise rotation of the upper and lower drive shafts. Clockwise rotation of the lower drive shaft and pinion gear (**Figure 16**) drives the front gear and inner propeller shaft clockwise. Likewise, the rear gear and outer propeller shaft rotate counterclockwise. This rotates each propeller in the direction necessary for forward thrust.

When reverse propeller thrust is selected, the shift mechanism moves the cone clutch into the tapered opening in the upper driven gear. The clutch engages and rotates in the same direction as the gear. As the clutch rotates, it drives against the helical splines of the upper drive shaft, clamping it and the upper drive shaft onto the gear. This results in counterclockwise rotation of the upper and lower drive shafts. Counterclockwise rotation of the lower drive shaft and pinion gear (**Figure 16**) drives the front gear and inner propeller shaft *counterclockwise*, and the rear gear and outer propeller *clockwise*. This rotates each propeller in the direction necessary for reverse thrust.

Shifting the remote control to the neutral position moves various linkages and levers that push the shift cam and yoke assembly (**Figure 15**) against the driven gear. This action pushes the clutch away from the driven gear. Clutch and drive shaft rotation ceases as the clutch breaks contact with the gear.

### Drive Ratio Identification

The drive unit ratio describes the number of rotations which the universal joint shaft must make to rotate the

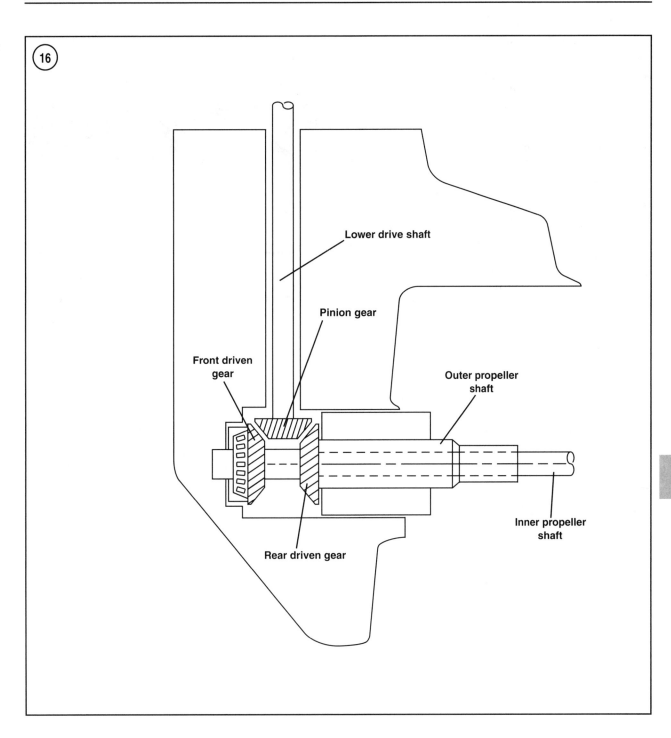

(16)

Lower drive shaft

Pinion gear

Front driven gear

Outer propeller shaft

Rear driven gear

Inner propeller shaft

11

propeller shaft(s) exactly one revolution. It is absolutely essential to identify the drive unit ratio before ordering replacement parts or beginning the repair. Aside from using different internal parts, some repair procedures vary by the drive unit ratio. Usually, the ratio is stamped into the decal on the port side of the drive shaft housing,but the decal may be missing or unreadable. Fortunately, other methods can be used to accurately identify the ratio.

**Drive Yoke**

All late model and most early Mercruiser drive units have a ratio code letter stamped on the yoke portion of the universal joint shaft. Replacement yokes or universal joint shaft assemblies do not have this letter stamp.

1. Remove the drive unit as described in this chapter.
2. Use solvent to clean grease and metal filings from the yoke.

3. Compare the letter stamped into the yoke portion of the universal joint shaft (**Figure 17**) to the key in **Table 3**.

4. If the letter is missing, identify the drive unit by counting the gear teeth as described in this chapter.

5. Install the drive unit as described in this chapter.

### Counting the gear teeth

The drive shaft housing and gearcase must be partially disassembled to count the gear teeth. This method is only practical if the drive ratio must be identified, and all external marks are missing, or the drive needs major repairs.

In many instances, the tooth count of the drive shaft housing gears provides a clear indication of the drive unit gear ratio. Count the teeth on the gearcase gears only if another drive unit ratio shares the same tooth count for the drive shaft housing gears. A tooth count-to-gear ratio comparison is listed in **Table 3**.

1. Drain the gearcase lubricant as described in Chapter Four.

2A. *Alpha drive unit*—Remove the upper cover from the drive shaft housing as described in this chapter under *Drive Shaft Housing*. Count the number of teeth on the drive and driven gear (see **Figure 6**). Install the upper cover as described in this chapter.

2B. *Bravo drive unit*—Remove the upper cover and rear cover as described in this chapter under *Drive Shaft Housing*. Count the number of teeth on the drive and driven gear(s) (**Figure 10**). Install the upper cover and rear cover as described in this chapter.

3A. *Alpha drive unit*—Perform this procedure only if a count of the drive shaft housing gear teeth fails to positively identify the drive unit ratio.

   a. Remove the bearing carrier as described in this chapter under *Gearcase*.

   b. Count the teeth on the rear gear and pinion gear (**Figure 7**). It is not necessary to count the front gear.

   c. Compare the tooth count from the gearcase and drive shaft housing gears with the information listed in **Table 3**.

   d. Install the bearing carrier as described in this chapter.

3B. *Bravo I drive unit*—Gearcase disassembly is not required to identify the drive unit ratio. All Bravo I drive units use the same gear tooth count in the gearcase. Refer to **Table 3**.

3C. *Bravo II drive unit*—Perform this operation only if counting the drive shaft housing gear teeth fails to positively identify the drive unit ratio.

   a. Separate the gearcase from the drive shaft housing as described in this chapter. Remove the bearing

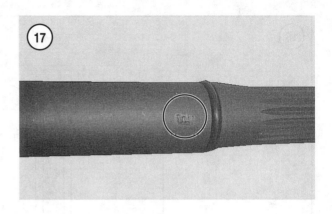

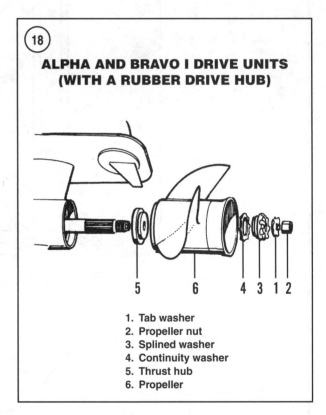

## ALPHA AND BRAVO I DRIVE UNITS (WITH A RUBBER DRIVE HUB)

  5      6      4 3 1 2

1. Tab washer
2. Propeller nut
3. Splined washer
4. Continuity washer
5. Thrust hub
6. Propeller

carrier and propeller shaft as described in this chapter under *Gearcase*.

b. Count the teeth on the pinion and driven gear (**Figure 11**).

c. Compare the tooth count from the gearcase and drive shaft housing gears with the information listed in **Table 3**.

d. Measure the lower drive shaft preload then install the bearing carrier as described under *Gearcase* in this chapter.

e. Reassemble the gearcase onto the drive shaft housing as described in this chapter.

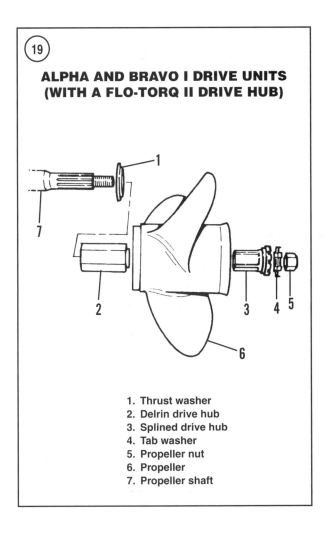

**ALPHA AND BRAVO I DRIVE UNITS (WITH A FLO-TORQ II DRIVE HUB)**

1. Thrust washer
2. Delrin drive hub
3. Splined drive hub
4. Tab washer
5. Propeller nut
6. Propeller
7. Propeller shaft

3D. *Bravo III drive unit*—Perform this operation only if counting the drive shaft housing gear teeth fails to positively identify the drive unit ratio.

   a. Remove the bearing carrier, bearing retainer, propeller shafts and rear driven gear as described under *Gearcase* in this chapter. Insert the smaller diameter side of the Delrin drive hub (2, **Figure 19**) into the opening on the forward side of the propeller. Align the hub with the propeller bore then press it into the propeller by hand.

   b. Count the teeth on the pinion and rear mounted gear.

   c. Compare the tooth count from gearcase and drive shaft housing gears with the information listed in **Table 3**.

   d. Install the rear driven gear, propeller shafts, bearing retainer and bearing carrier as described in this chapter.

4. Fill the drive unit with lubricant as described in Chapter Four.

## PROPELLER

Quicksilver propellers use either a rubber drive hub, Flo-torq II drive hub or solid hub design. Most after market propellers use the rubber drive hub, a sleeve similar to the Flo-torq drive hub or a solid hub design. Both the rubber and Flo-torq II type drive hubs are designed to flex or break if the propeller strikes an underwater object. This feature helps minimize, but not totally prevent, damage to internal drive unit components.

This section discribes propeller removal and installation for Quicksilver propellers, which are the most common brand used. If using an after market propeller, follow its manufacturer's instructions and use their attaching hardware.

Most Alpha drive units use either a rubber drive hub (**Figure 18**) or Flo-torq II (**Figure 19**) design propeller. Do not use a solid hub propeller on an Alpha drive unit.

Most Bravo I drive units use either a rubber drive hub or Flo-torq II design propeller. Use a solid hub propeller on high-performance boats with a Bravo I drive and a large displacement engine (7.4 Liter or larger) engine. Other types of propeller drive hubs may prematurely fail on these applications.

All Bravo II drive units use a rubber drive hub propeller (**Figure 20**). All Bravo III drive units use a solid hub propeller.

*NOTE*
*To add strength and durability, some Quicksilver propellers with the Flo-torq II drive hub have a tapered bushing installed in the bore of the drive hub. The tapered bushing is usually required only on V8 engines. Install this bushing into the hub bore if the drive hub fails but the propeller does not show impact damage.*

**Removal and Installation
(Alpha, Bravo I and Bravo II)**

Refer to **Figure 18-20**.

1. Disconnect the battery cables. Shift the engine into NEUTRAL.

2. Carefully bend the tabs of the locking tab washer away from the splined washer (**Figure 21**). Place a block of wood between the propeller blade and the antiventilation plate (**Figure 22**). Loosen the propeller nut by turning it counterclockwise.

3. Remove the propeller nut and tab washer.

4A. *Rubber or solid drive hub*—Pull the splined washer (3, **Figure 18** or 3, **Figure 20**) from the propeller. Remove the continuity washer (4, **Figure 18**) from the propeller or

11

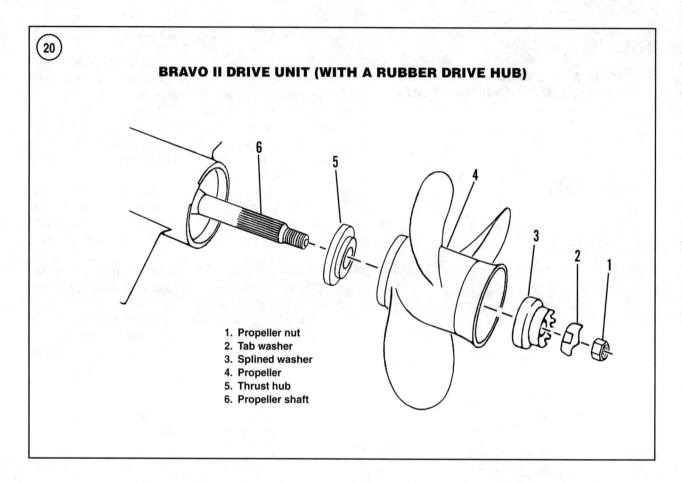

**BRAVO II DRIVE UNIT (WITH A RUBBER DRIVE HUB)**

1. Propeller nut
2. Tab washer
3. Splined washer
4. Propeller
5. Thrust hub
6. Propeller shaft

splined washer. A continuity washer is not used with solid hub propellers or on Bravo II type propellers.

4B. *Flo-torq II drive hub*—Carefully pull the splined drive hub (3, **Figure 19**) from the propeller shaft.

5. Pull the propeller from the propeller shaft.

6A. *Rubber drive hub*—Inspect the propeller for melted or protruding drive hub material. If defective, have the propeller repaired at a propeller repair shop.

6B. *Flo-torq II drive hub*—Remove and inspect the drive hub as follows:

    a. Push the tapered bushing from the bore of the drive hub (if so equipped).

    b. Use a brass drift and drive the Delrin drive hub (2, **Figure 19**) from the propeller.

    c. Scrape any remnants of the hub from the propeller bore.

    d. Inspect the drive hub and tapered bushing for cracks or softness and replace as needed.

7. Tap lightly on the thrust hub to free it from the propeller shaft. Pull the thrust hub from the propeller shaft. Remove grease and corrosion from the propeller shaft splines, propeller shaft threads, continuity washer, elastic

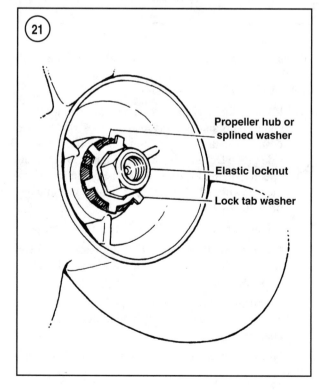

Propeller hub or splined washer

Elastic locknut

Lock tab washer

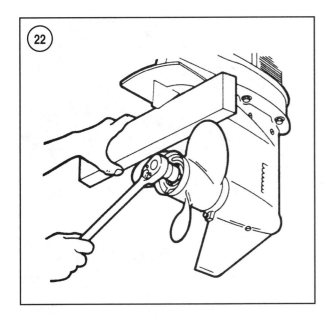

lock nut and the thrust washer. Inspect the thrust hub for wear or cracks and replace as needed.

8. Apply a coat of Quicksilver 2-4-C Marine Lubricant or water-resistant grease to the propeller shaft (except the threads). Slide the thrust hub over the propeller shaft with the tapered inner diameter facing the gearcase.

9A. *Rubber drive hub*—Slide the propeller fully onto the propeller shaft. Seat the propeller against the thrust washer.

9B. *Solid drive hub*—Slide the propeller fully onto the propeller shaft. Align the thrust hub with its recess while seating it in the propeller.

9C. *Flo-torq II drive hub*—Install the drive hub and propeller as follows:

  a. Insert the smaller diameter side of the Delrin drive hub (2, **Figure 19**) into the opening on the forward side of the propeller. Press the hub firmly into the propeller.

  b. Slide the bushing (if so equipped) into the drive hub bore with the tapered side facing inward.

  c. Slide the propeller over the propeller shaft. Seat the four raised tabs on the Delrin drive hub (2, **Figure 8**) against the thrust washer (1).

10A. *Rubber or solid drive hub*—Install the propeller attaching hardware as follows:

  a. If so equipped, install the continuity washer (4, **Figure 18**) onto the propeller. Align the washer with the splined washer opening.

  b. Slide the splined washer (3, **Figure 18** or 3, **Figure 20**) onto the propeller shaft with the tab slots facing outward.

  c. Seat the splined washer against the propeller. Make sure the continuity washer (if so equipped) seats fully against the stepped portion of the splined washer.

  d. Place the locking tab washer (1, **Figure 18**) or (2, **Figure 20**) over the propeller shaft with the open end facing outward. Seat the locking tab washer against the splined washer.

10B. *Flo-torq II drive hub*—Install the propeller attaching hardware as follows:

  a. Align the splines of the drive hub (3, **Figure 19**) with the splines of the propeller shaft.

  b. Slide the drive hub (3, **Figure 19**) onto the propeller shaft.

  c. Rotate the propeller until the four slots in the Delrin drive hub align with the four raised ridges of the splined drive hub. Seat the drive hub against the propeller.

11. Place the locking tab washer (**Figure 21**) over the propeller shaft with the open end facing outward. Seat the locking tab washer against the splined washer or drive hub.

12. Thread the elastic locknut onto the propeller shaft with the rounded side facing outward. Align the nut with the hexagon shaped opening in the locking tab washer as the nut seats against the washer.

13. Place a block of wood between the propeller blade and the antiventilation plate (**Figure 22**). Tighten the propeller nut to the specification in **Table 1**.

14. Inspect the alignment of the locking tabs and tab slots in the splined drive hub (**Figure 21**). Tighten the nut an additional amount if necessary to align two of the tabs with the washer. Carefully bend the tabs into the slots into the tab slots.

15. Verify adequate clearance between the trim tab (if so equipped) and the propeller as described in Chapter Fifteen. Connect the battery cables.

**Removal and Installation (Bravo III)**

1. Disconnect the battery cables. Shift the engine into NEUTRAL.

2. Place a block of wood between the rear propeller blade and the antiventilation plate (**Figure 22**). Remove the rear propeller nut (**Figure 23**) by turning it counterclockwise. Pull the rear propeller from the inner propeller shaft.

3. Tap lightly on the thrust hub to free it from the propeller shaft. Pull the thrust hub from the propeller shaft (**Figure 24**).

4. Place a block of wood between the rear propeller blade and the antiventilation plate (**Figure 22**). Use the propeller nut tool (Mercury part No. 91-805457) to remove

**11**

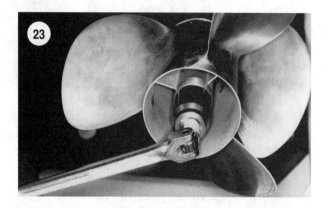

(counterclockwise) the front propeller nut (see **Figure 25**). Pull the front propeller from the outer propeller shaft.

5. Clean grease or corrosion from the propeller shaft splines, propeller shaft threads, elastic locknut and thrust hubs. Inspect the thrust hub for wear or cracks and replace as needed.

6. Apply a coat of Quicksilver 2-4-C Marine Lubricant (Mercury part No. 92-825407A12) or other water-resistant grease to the propeller shaft, excluding the threads.

7. With the shorter tapered side facing the gearcase, slide the larger diameter thrust hub over the outer propeller shaft (**Figure 26**). The longer tapered side must contact the propeller. Slide the front propeller onto the outer propeller shaft and seat it against the thrust hub.

8. Thread the larger propeller nut onto the outer propeller shaft with the tapered side facing the gearcase. Place a block of wood between the front propeller blade and the antiventilation plate (**Figure 22**). Use the propeller nut tool (Mercury part No. 91-805457) to tighten the front propeller nut to the specification in **Table 1**.

9. With the shorter tapered side facing the gearcase, slide the smaller diameter thrust hub over the inner propeller shaft. The longer tapered side must contact the rear propeller.

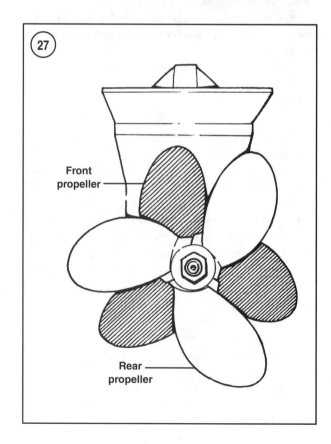

Front propeller

Rear propeller

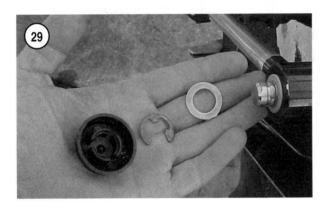

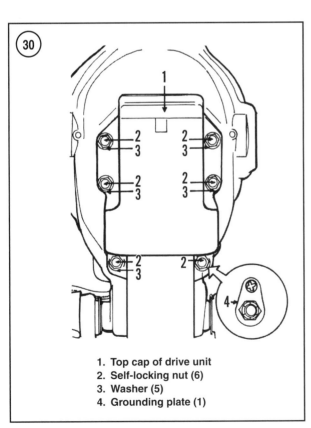

1. Top cap of drive unit
2. Self-locking nut (6)
3. Washer (5)
4. Grounding plate (1)

10. Position the front propeller with one blade facing straight UP (**Figure 27**). Slide the rear propeller onto the outer propeller shaft with one blade facing straight DOWN (**Figure 27**) and seat it against the thrust hub.

11. Thread the smaller propeller nut onto the inner propeller shaft with the tapered side facing the propeller. Place a block of wood between the front propeller blade and the antiventilation plate (**Figure 22**). Tighten the front propeller nut (**Figure 25**) to the specification in **Table 1**.

12. Rotate the propellers, noting any binding or roughness. If binding or roughness occurs, remove the propellers and check for a bent propeller shaft or improperly installed propellers. Connect the battery cables.

## DRIVE UNIT REMOVAL AND INSTALLATION

To prevent possible water leakage, replace all applicable gaskets, seal rings and O-rings anytime the drive is removed. Have the necessary gaskets, seals, lubricants, adhesives and equipment on hand before beginning this procedure

### Removal (Alpha Models)

*WARNING*
*Do not attempt to remove the stern drive from the boat without the aid of a suitable hoist. The drive unit is heavy and may slip, causing damage to the drive and possibly injury.*

Determine the drive unit rotation before removing or installing the drive unit.

1. Tilt the drive unit to the fully up position. Push the tab (**Figure 28**) inward and disconnect the speedometer connector from the gearcase. Lower the drive unit to the fully down position and remove the propeller as described in this chapter.

2. Remove the hardware (**Figure 29**) and the aft anchor pin as described under *Hydraulic Cylinder and Anchor Pins* in Chapter Thirteen.

3A. *Standard rotation drive*—Shift the remote control into forward gear.

3B. *Counter-rotation drive*—Shift the remote control into reverse gear.

4. Attach an overhead hoist to the opening at the rear of the upper cover (1, **Figure 30**). Apply just enough lift to support the drive.

5. Remove the six locking nuts (2, **Figure 30**) and five washers (3). Place a wooden block between the upper cover and the gimbal ring bolts as shown in **Figure 31**.

**11**

6. Manually tilt the drive up to wedge the drive unit away from the bell housing. When free, pull the drive straight back and away from the bell housing.

7. Carefully lay the drive on its side on a clean work surface. The drive may slip if resting on the skeg.

8. Remove and discard the bell housing gasket (**Figure 32**). Remove all gasket material from the drive unit. Thoroughly clean the drive unit surfaces that contact the rubber seal ring.

9. Remove the rubber seal ring (2, **Figure 33**) and O-ring (3) from the bell housing (1). Discard the seal ring and O-ring. Carefully scrape all corrosion and old grease from the shift lever (4, **Figure 33**), slide (5) and surrounding areas. seal

10. Support the trim cylinders if the drive is going to be off the bell housing for any length of time. Wire the cylinders to the bell housing studs or attach a block of wood to the studs as shown in **Figure 34**.

11. Inspect both thrust pads (**Figure 35**) for wear or damage. Replace both pads if either one is defective:

   a. Working through the opening (**Figure 36**), push the aft end of the pad away from the housing.

   b. Guide the pad from the groove and pull it from the drive shaft housing (**Figure 37**).

   c. Clean all dirt, grease or corrosion from the pad mating surfaces. Match the replacement pad to the removed one. Differently shaped pads are used on each side. The pad must match the contour of the mating surface.

   d. Guide the forward boss of the pad into the groove in the housing. Slide the pad toward the rear until the tabs align with the opening (**Figure 36**). Press on the pad to seat the tabs into the opening. The pad must seat against the housing.

12. Clean and inspect the universal joint shaft as follows:

   a. Wipe all grease, corrosion or other residue from the universal joint shaft and the drive shaft housing

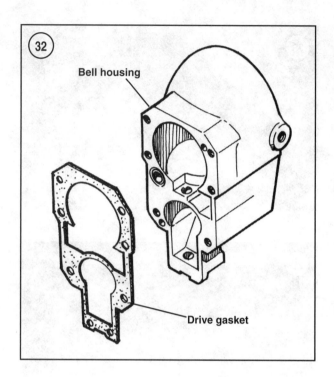

Bell housing

Drive gasket

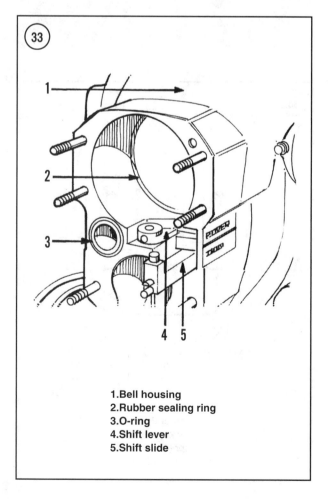

1. Bell housing
2. Rubber sealing ring
3. O-ring
4. Shift lever
5. Shift slide

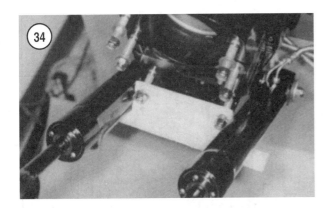

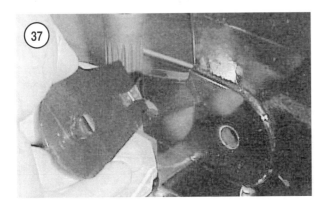

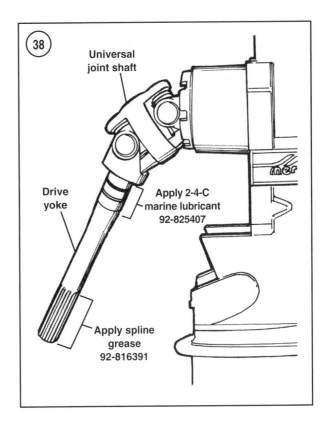

(**Figure 38**). Remove and discard the three O-rings from the drive shaft yoke (**Figure 38**).

b. Manipulate the universal joint shaft (**Figure 38**) in all directions while checking for binding or looseness of the universal joints.

c. Inspect the shaft for corrosion, cracks or damage.

d. Carefully scrape all grease and other material from the splined end of the drive yoke (**Figure 38**). Use a quick drying solvent, such as carburetor cleaner, to remove residual material from the splines.

e. Inspect the splines for excessive wear or sharp edges. If worn splines, sharp edges, binding or loose universal joints or other damage is present, replace the faulty components as described under *Drive Shaft Housing* in this chapter.

13. Inspect the inside of the universal joint bellows for water, gearcase lubricant or physical damage. Wipe all grease and debris from the bellows.

14. If water is present, check for a faulty drive gasket, rubber seal ring or universal joint bellows. Also check for water marks, indicating a high water level in the bilge. A high water level in the bilge allows water to enter the bellows. Small holes in the bellows are very difficult to locate. Replace the bellows as described in Chapter Twelve if a thorough inspection of other components fails to locate the leak.

**11**

15. If gearcase lubricant is found in the bellows, replace the universal joint shaft seals and O-rings as described under *Drive Shaft Housing* in this chapter.

16. Check the engine alignment and lubricate the engine coupler as described in Chapter Seven.

17. Inspect the gimbal bearing for wear or defects as described in Chapter Twelve.

### Installation (Alpha Models)

1. Install new O-rings over the splined end of the yoke (**Figure 38**). Position an O-ring into each groove at the upper end of the yoke. Slide the slightly larger diameter O-ring over the yoke and position it into the groove nearest the splines.

2. Apply 2-4-C Marine Lubricant (Mercury part No. 92-825407) to the housing and universal joint surfaces indicated in **Figure 38**. Apply spline grease (Mercury part No. 92-816391) to the yoke splines (**Figure 38**).

3. Use a quick drying solvent to remove residual grease or adhesive from the seal ring, gasket and O-ring mating surfaces. Apply a light coat of bellows adhesive (Mercury part No. 92-86166) onto the seal ring surfaces in the bell housing (2, **Figure 33**). Insert the new seal ring and seat it against the step in the opening. Wipe away excess adhesive. Do not install the drive until the adhesive dries.

4. Apply a light coat of bellows adhesive to the gasket mating surfaces of the bell housing. Install the new gasket onto the bell housing (**Figure 32**) with the silicone seal bead facing the starboard side. Hold the gasket in position until the adhesive dries.

5. Apply a light coat of bellows adhesive to the O-ring groove (3, **Figure 33**) in the bell housing. Place the new O-ring into the groove and hold it in position until the adhesive dries.

6. Position the roller on the bottom of the shift lever (4, **Figure 33**) into the slots on the top of the shift slide (5).

7. Carefully push or pull on the shift slide (1, **Figure 39**) until the slot at the bottom of the shift shaft (2) faces straight ahead. Move the remote control lever if the slot alignment cannot be corrected by pushing or pulling the shift slide.

8. Rotate the lower shift shaft until the offset end (**Figure 40**) faces straight forward. Remove the supports from the hydraulic cylinders.

9. Attach an overhead hoist to the opening at the rear of the upper cover (1, **Figure 30**). Lift the drive and align it with the bell housing.

10. While an assistant supports the trim cylinders, guide the drive yoke (**Figure 38**) through the universal joint bellows and into the gimbal bearing.

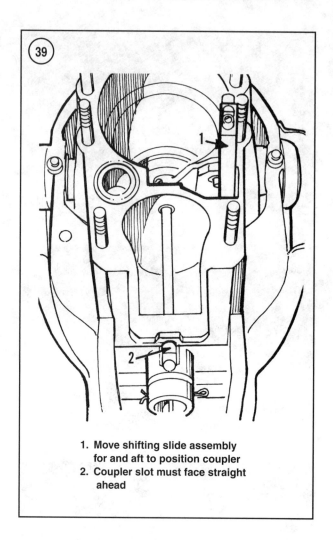

1. Move shifting slide assembly for and aft to position coupler
2. Coupler slot must face straight ahead

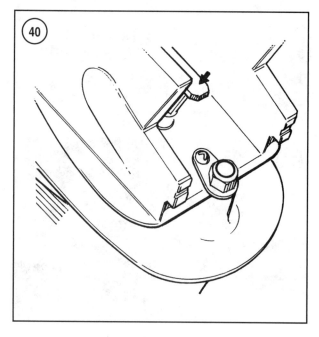

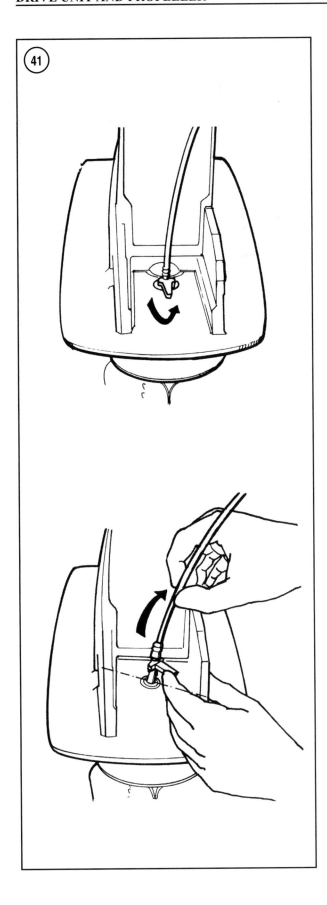

11. Verify proper alignment of the shift slide and shift shaft as described in Step 6 and Step 7. Guide the thrust pads (**Figure 35**) between the flanges on the gimbal ring and push the drive straight toward the bell housing. Guide the studs into the drive shaft housing.

12. Maintain pressure on the drive and rotate the propeller shaft counterclockwise to align the coupling splines. Do not rotate the propeller shaft clockwise. The drive will seat against the bell housing as the splines align. Check for improper engine alignment or misalignment of the shift shaft if the drive fails to seat. Do not force the drive against the bell housing. Minimal force is needed when all the components are aligned correctly.

13. Install the six locking nuts (2, **Figure 30**) and five washers (3). Tighten the nuts in a crossing pattern to the specification in **Table 1**.

14. Install the aft anchor pin and hardware (**Figure 29**) as described in Chapter Thirteen under *Hydraulic Cylinder and Anchor Pins*. Connect the battery cables.

15. Place the drive in the full up position. Release the tab (**Figure 28**) and push the speedometer connector over the gearcase fitting. Release the tab and pull on the connector to make sure it is secure. Place the drive in the down position. Disconnect the battery cables.

16. Install the propeller as described in this chapter. Adjust the shift cables as described in Chapter Six. Check the drive lubricant level as described in Chapter Four. Connect the battery cables.

**Removal (Bravo I, II and III)**

> *WARNING*
> *Do not attempt to remove the stern drive from the boat without the aid of a suitable hoist. The drive unit is heavy and may slip, causing damage to the drive or possibly injury.*

1. Place the drive in the fully up position. Rotate the yellow speedometer fitting in the direction shown in **Figure 41**. Pull the fitting from the gearcase. Place the drive in the down position Remove and propeller as described in this chapter.

2. Disconnect the battery cables. Remove the hardware (**Figure 42**) and the aft anchor pin as described under *Hydraulic cylinder and anchor pins* in Chapter Thirteen.

3. Place the remote control into neutral.

4. Attach an overhead hoist to the opening at the rear of the upper cover (4, **Figure 43**). Apply just enough lift from the hoist to support the drive.

5. Remove the six locking nuts (1, **Figure 43**) and five washers (3). Place an appropriately sized wooden block

**11**

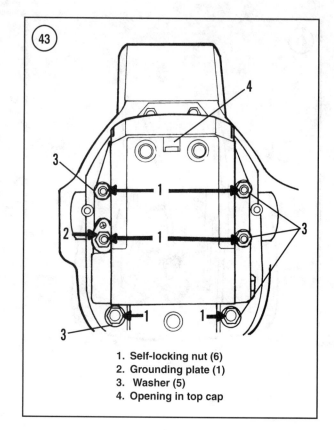

1. Self-locking nut (6)
2. Grounding plate (1)
3. Washer (5)
4. Opening in top cap

between the upper cover and the gimbal ring bolts as shown in **Figure 31**.

6. Manually tilt the drive up to wedge the drive unit away from the bell housing. When free, pull the drive straight back and away from the bell housing.

7. Lay the drive on its side, on a clean work surface. The drive may slip if resting on the skeg.

8. Remove the O-rings surrounding the water passage and shift linkage cavity (**Figure 44**). Discard the O-rings. Use a quick drying solvent to clean adhesive from the O-ring grooves. Thoroughly clean the surfaces of the drive shaft housing that contact the universal joint bellows.

9. Support the trim cylinders if the drive is going to be off the bell housing for any length of time. Wire them to the bell housing studs or attach a block of wood to the studs as shown in **Figure 34**.

10. Inspect both thrust pads (**Figure 35**) for wear or damage. Replace both pads if either one is defective.

    a. Working through the opening (**Figure 36**), push the aft end of the pad away from the housing.

    b. Guide the pad from the groove and pull it from the drive shaft housing (**Figure 37**).

    c. Clean all dirt, grease or corrosion from the pad mating surfaces. Match the replacement pad to the removed one. Differently shaped pads are used for each side. The pad must match the contour of the mating surface.

    d. Guide the forward boss of the pad into the groove in the housing. Slide the pad rearward until the tabs align with the opening (**Figure 36**). Press on the pad to seat the tabs into the opening. The pad must seat against the housing.

11. Clean grease or corrosion from the shift linkage on the drive unit. Clean the shift cable end on the bell housing (**Figure 45**). Inspect the cable for corrosion damage or

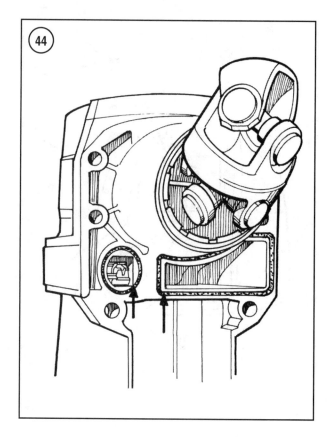

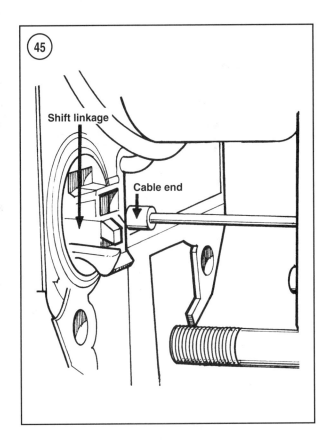

45

Shift linkage

Cable end

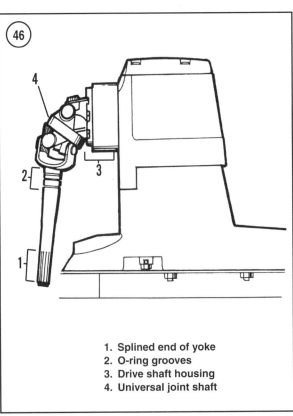

46

4

2

3

1

1. Splined end of yoke
2. O-ring grooves
3. Drive shaft housing
4. Universal joint shaft

bends in the core wire. Inspect the shift linkage for corrosion or other damage. Replace the shift linkage as described in this chapter if corroded or damaged as described under *Drive Shaft Housing Repair*. If water is in the shift linkage cavity, inspect the shift cable bellows for wear or damage. If the shift cable and/or bellows are defective, replaced as described in Chapter Twelve.

12. Clean and inspect the universal joint shaft as follows:

    a. Wipe all grease, corrosion or other residue from the universal joint shaft (4, **Figure 46**) and the drive shaft housing (3). Remove the O-rings from the drive shaft yoke (2, **Figure 46**).

    b. Manipulate the universal joint shaft (4, **Figure 46**) in all directions while checking for binding or looseness of the universal joints.

    c. Inspect the shaft for heavy corrosion, cracks or damage.

    d. Carefully scrape all grease and other material from the splined end of the drive yoke (1, **Figure 46**). Use a quick drying solvent to clean the splines.

    e. Inspect the splines for excessive wear or sharp edges. If worn or sharpened, replace the shaft as described in this chapter.

13. Inspect the inside of the universal joint bellows for water, gearcase lubricant or physical damage. Wipe all grease and debris from the bellows. Thoroughly clean the seal surfaces at the aft end of the bellows. The drive unit seals against this surface.

14. If water is present, check for worn or damaged seals at the aft of the universal joint bellows. Also check for water marks, indicating a high water level in the bilge. A high water level in the bilge can allow water into the bellows. Small holes in the bellows are very difficult to find. Replace the bellows (Chapter Twelve) if a thorough inspection of other components fails to locate the leak.

15. If gearcase lubricant is found in the bellows, replace the universal joint shaft seals and O-rings as described in this chapter.

16. Check the engine alignment and lubricate the engine coupler as described in Chapter Seven.

17. Inspect the gimbal bearing for wear or defects as described in Chapter Twelve.

## Installation (Bravo I, II and III Models)

1. Slide the new O-rings over the splined end of the yoke (1, **Figure 46**). Position a new O-ring into each groove at the upper end of the yoke (2, **Figure 46**).

2. Apply 2-4-C Marine Lubricant (Mercury part No. 92-825407) to the housing (3, **Figure 46**) and the O-ring surface (2) at the upper end of the yoke. Apply spline

11

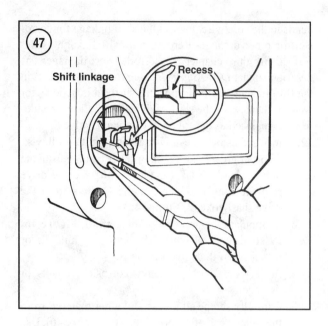

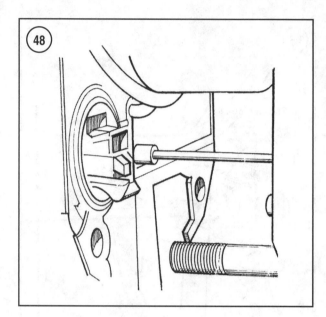

grease (Mercury part No. 92-816391) to the yoke splines (1, **Figure 46**).

3. Use a quick drying solvent to remove grease or adhesive from the O-ring grooves in the bell housing (**Figure 44**). Apply a light coat of Bellows Adhesive (Mercury part No. 92-86166) to the grooves and insert the O-rings. Hold the O-rings in position until the adhesive dries.

4. With a grease gun, pump Quicksilver Universal Joint and Gimbal Bearing Lubricant (Mercury part No. 92-828052A2) into the universal joint grease fittings until clean lubricant flows from the bearing cap seals.

5. Use needlenose pliers to pull the shift linkage out of the drive shaft housing until the cable end recess (**Figure 47**) is exposed. Have an assistant rotate the universal joint shaft clockwise to make linkage extraction easier.

6. Apply Special Lube 101 (Mercury part No. 92-13872A1) to the cable recess and exposed surfaces of the shift linkage. Remove the supports from the hydraulic cylinders.

7. Attach an overhead hoist to the opening at the rear of the upper cover (4, **Figure 43**). Lift the drive and align it with the bell housing.

8. While an assistant supports the trim cylinders, guide the drive yoke (1, **Figure 46**) through the universal joint bellows and into the gimbal bearing.

9. Align the cable end with the recess in the shift linkage (**Figure 48**) and guide the drive unit into the bell housing. Guide the thrust pads (**Figure 35**) between the flanges on the gimbal ring while pushing the drive straight toward the bell housing. Install the drive, guiding the studs into the drive shaft housing.

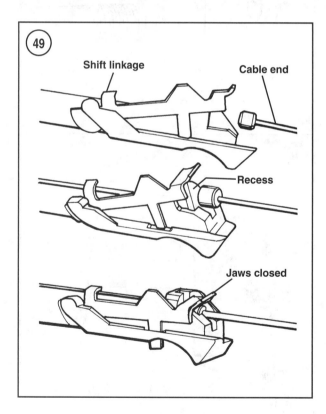

10. Maintain pressure on the drive and rotate the propeller shaft (inner propeller shaft on Bravo III drives) counterclockwise to align the coupling splines. Stop when the drive mating surface is approximately 2 in. (51 mm) from the bell housing.

11. Guide the cable end into the cable recess and close the jaws (**Figure 49**) while pushing the drive toward the bell

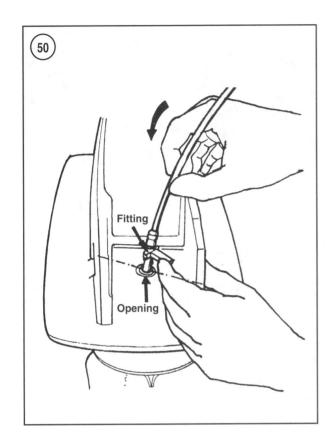

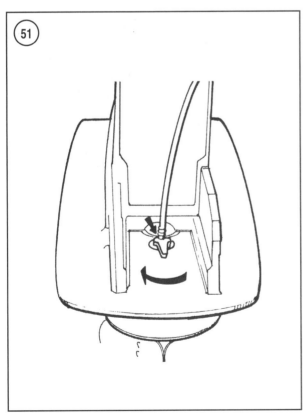

housing. If the drive fails to seat against the bell housing, check for improper engine alignment or improper alignment of the shift linkage with the cable. Do not force the drive against the bell housing. Only minimal force is needed if all the components are correctly aligned.

12. Install the six locking nuts (1, **Figure 43**) and five washers (3). Tighten the nuts in a crossing pattern to the specification in **Table 1**.

13. Install the aft anchor pin and hardware (**Figure 42**) as described in Chapter Thirteen.

14. Place the drive in the fully up position and connect the speedometer fitting (**Figure 50**) to the drive shaft housing. Rotate the arm of the fitting straight ahead (**Figure 51**) to secure the fitting. Place the drive in the full down position. Disconnect the battery cables.

15. Install the propeller as described in this chapter. Adjust the shift cables as described in Chapter Six. Check the lubricant level as described in Chapter Four. Connect the battery cables.

**Housing Separation (Alpha Models)**

1. Drain the gearcase as described in Chapter Four. Remove the propeller as described in this chapter.

2. If repairing the drive shaft housing, remove the drive unit as described in this chapter. Clamp the gearcase firmly in a vise with protective jaws.

3. Remove the anode plate or trim tab (**Figure 52**) from the area above the propeller shaft as described in Chapter Fifteen.

4. Remove the bolt (**Figure 53**) from the plate or tab cavity. Remove the self-locking nut or bolt from the lower front side of the drive shaft housing (**Figure 54**).

5A. *Gearcase removal only*—Separate the housings as follows:

a. Place the drive in the full up position. Disconnect the battery.

b. Support the gearcase while removing the self-locking nuts and bolts (**Figure 55**) from each side of the gearcase.

c. Pull the gearcase free from the drive shaft housing. If removal is difficult, support the gearcase and tap lightly with a plastic mallet on the flat surface at the rear of the gearcase (**Figure 56**). Do not pry the gearcase from the drive shaft housing. The pry bar may damage mating surfaces. Apply heat to the mating surfaces if the gearcase refuses to separate from the drive shaft housing.

d. When the housings separate, carefully lower the gearcase from the drive shaft housing. If dislodged, retrieve the water tube guide or water dam. Clamp the gearcase firmly in a vise with protective jaws.

5B. *With the drive removed*—Separate the housings as follow:

a. Support the drive shaft housing while removing the self-locking nuts and bolts (**Figure 55**) from each side of the gearcase.

b. Carefully rock the drive shaft housing side to side until free from the gearcase. If removal proves difficult, support the drive shaft housing and lightly tap the sides of the housing with a plastic mallet. Do not pry the drive shaft housing from the gearcase. The pry bar may damage mating surfaces. Apply heat to the mating surfaces if the housing refuses to separate from the gearcase.

c. When the housings separate, carefully lift the drive shaft housing over the lower drive shaft. If dislodged, retrieve the water tube guide or water dam.

6. Remove and discard the orange quad ring seal from the recess next to the seawater pump.

7. Clean all grease, corrosion or other material from the mating surfaces.

### Housing Separation (Bravo I, II and III Models)

1. Drain the gearcase lubricant as described in Chapter Four. Remove the propeller(s) as described in this chapter.

2. If the drive shaft housing requires service, remove the drive unit as described in this chapter. Clamp the gearcase in a vise with protective jaws.

3A. *Bravo I and III drive*—Remove the anode plate (**Figure 52**) from the area above the propeller shaft as described in Chapter Fifteen.

3B. *Bravo II drive*—Loosen the bolt on the top rear of the gearcase. Pull the anode plate from the cavity located just above the propeller shaft(s).

4A. *Bravo I and III drive*—Remove the bolt (**Figure 53**) from the anodic plate cavity.

4B. *Bravo II drive*—Remove the bolt from the opening located forward of the anode plate cavity, directly above the propeller shaft.

5A. *Gearcase removal only:*

a. Place the drive in the fully up position. Disconnect the battery.

b. Support the gearcase while removing the three self-locking nuts and washers (**Figure 57**) from each side of the gearcase.

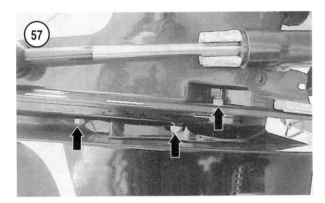

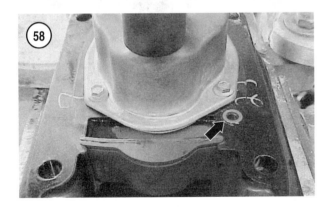

c. Carefully tug on the gearcase until free from the drive shaft housing. If removal is difficult, support the gearcase and use a soft-faced mallet to tap the flat surface at the rear of the gearcase (**Figure 56**). Do not pry the gearcase from the drive shaft housing. The pry bar may damage mating surfaces. Apply heat to the mating surfaces if the gearcase refuses to dislodge from the drive shaft housing.

d. When the housings separate, carefully lower the gearcase from the drive shaft housing. Clamp the gearcase firmly in a vise with protective jaws.

5B. *With the drive unit removed*—Separate the housings as follows:

    a. Support the drive shaft housing. Remove the three self-locking nuts and washers (**Figure 57**) from each side of the gearcase.

    b. Carefully rock the drive shaft housing side to side until free from the gearcase. If removal is difficult, support the drive shaft housing and lightly tap the sides of the housing with a plastic mallet. Do not pry the drive shaft housing from the gearcase. The pry bar may damage mating surfaces. Apply heat to the mating surfaces if the housing refuses to separate from the gearcase.

    c. When the housings separate, carefully lift the drive shaft housing over the lower drive shaft.

6. Remove the O-ring from the groove surrounding the water passage. Remove the orange quad ring seal from the recess between the water passage and the drive shaft. Pry the O-ring from the groove surrounding the drive shaft. Discard the O-rings and quad ring seal.

7. Remove the drive shaft coupler from the lower drive shaft. Clean all grease, corrosion or other material from the mating surfaces.

**Attaching the Gearcase to the Drive Shaft Housing (Alpha Models)**

The gearcase can be installed with the drive shaft housing removed or installed on the transom assembly.

1. Install the water tube guide as described in this chapter. Place the water dam into the slots in the drive shaft housing.

2. Apply a light coat of Perfect Seal (Mercury part No. 92-34227-1) to the quad ring seal, then install the seal into the recess next to the seawater pump (**Figure 58**).

3. Rotate the lower shift shaft to position the offset facing straight ahead (**Figure 40**).

4. Apply a light coat of Quicksilver 2-4-C Marine Lubricant (Mercury part No. 91-825407) to the grommet in the water tube guide, drive shaft splines, offset end of the shift shaft and the housing mating surfaces.

5. Make sure the water tube guide, water tube and water dam are correctly installed.

6. If the drive shaft housing is removed, install the drive shaft housing onto the gearcase as follows:

    a. Securely clamp the gearcase in a vise with protective jaws.

    b. Align the drive shaft with the upper drive shaft opening. Align the plastic water tube with the water tube guide. Lower the drive shaft housing onto the gearcase.

**11**

c. Align the gearcase locating pins with the openings in the drive shaft housing.

d. Rotate the universal joint shaft clockwise to align the upper and lower drive shaft splines. The drive shaft housing will drop and seat onto the gearcase as the splines align.

e. Hold the gearcase in position while installing the bolts and self locking nuts (**Figure 55**) on each side of the gearcase. Install the bolts with the bolt heads on top and the nuts on the bottom. Tighten the bolts and nuts to the specification in **Table 1**.

f. Install the drive unit as described in this chapter.

7. If the drive shaft housing is installed, install the gearcase as follows:

a. Align the plastic water tube with the water tube guide and insert the drive shaft and lower shift shaft into the drive shaft housing.

b. Align the gearcase locating pins with the openings in the drive shaft housing. Make sure the lower shift shaft is aligned with the slot in the upper shift shaft.

c. Lift up and rotate the propeller shaft clockwise to align the upper and lower drive shaft splines. The gearcase will seat against the drive shaft housing as the splines align. If the gearcase will not seat, remove it and check for misalignment of the water tube and guide, shift shafts or drive shaft.

d. Maintain upward pressure and install the bolts and self locking nuts (**Figure 55**) onto each side of the gearcase. Install the bolts with the bolt heads on top and the nuts on the bottom. Tighten the bolts and nuts to the specification in **Table 1**.

8. Apply a light coat of Perfect Seal (Mercury part No. 92-34227-1) to the threads and install the bolt and lockwasher (**Figure 53**) into the anode or trim tab cavity. Tighten the bolt to the specification in **Table 1**.

9. Install the anode plate or trim tab (**Figure 52**) as described in Chapter Fifteen. Install the self-locking nut or bolt into the lower front side of the drive shaft housing (**Figure 54**). Tighten the nut or bolt to the specification in **Table 1**.

10. Fill the drive unit with lubricant as described in Chapter Four. Install the propeller as described in this chapter. Adjust the shift cables as described in Chapter Six.

11. Check for proper shifting and cooling system operation before putting the engine into service.

### Attaching the Gearcase to the Drive Shaft Housing (Bravo I, II and III Models)

1. Slide the drive shaft coupler onto the splines of the lower drive shaft (**Figure 59**). The coupler can be installed in either direction.

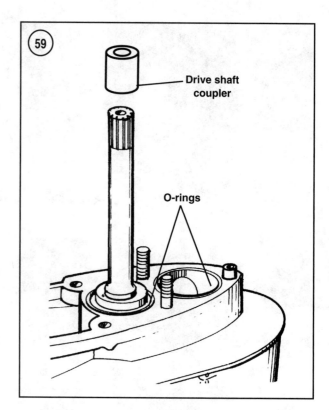

Drive shaft coupler

O-rings

2. Apply a light coat of Quicksilver 2-4-C Marine Lubricant (Mercury part No. 91-825407) to new O-rings and install them into the grooves surrounding the water passage and the drive shaft (**Figure 59**).

3. Apply a light coat of Perfect Seal (Mercury part No. 92-34227-1) to the quad ring seal and install it into the recess between the water passage and the drive shaft.

4. If the drive shaft housing is removed, install the drive shaft housing onto the gearcase as follows:

a. Securely clamp the gearcase in a vise with protective jaws.

b. Insert the drive shaft and coupler into the drive shaft bore in the drive shaft housing while lowering the

drive shaft housing onto the gearcase. Do not insert the drive shaft into the water passage.

c. Align the studs with the openings in the drive shaft housing.

d. Rotate the propeller shaft in either direction to align the coupler splines with the upper drive shaft. The drive shaft housing will drop and seat against the gearcase as the splines align.

e. Thread the self-locking nuts and washers (**Figure 57**) onto the studs on each side of the gearcase. Tighten the nuts to the specification in **Table 1**.

f. Install the drive unit as described in this chapter.

5. If the drive shaft housing is installed, install the gearcase as follows:

a. Align the drive shaft and coupler with the drive shaft bore in the drive shaft housing. Move the gearcase up toward the drive shaft housing.

b. Align the studs with the openings in the drive shaft housing. Verify proper alignment of the lower shift shaft with the slot in the upper shift shaft.

c. Maintain upward pressure and rotate the propeller shaft clockwise to align the upper and lower drive shaft splines. The gearcase will seat against the gearcase as the splines align. If the gearcase will not seat, remove the gearcase and check for improper alignment of the water tube and guide, shift shafts and drive shaft.

d. Hold the gearcase in position while installing the three self-locking nuts and washers onto the studs on each side of the gearcase. Tighten the nuts to the specification in **Table 1**.

6A. *Bravo I and III drive*—Apply a light coat of Perfect Seal to the threads, then install the bolt and lockwasher (**Figure 53**) into the opening in the anode plate cavity. Tighten the bolt to the specification in **Table 1**.

6B. *Bravo II drive*—Install the bolts into the opening located forward of the anode plate cavity directly above the propeller shaft. Tighten the bolts to the specification in **Table 1**.

7A. *Bravo I and III drive*—Install the anode plate (**Figure 52**) as described in Chapter Fifteen.

7B. *Bravo II drive*—Install the anode bolt into the opening on the top rear of the gearcase. Install the anode plate as described in Chapter Fifteen. Tighten the bolt to secure the anode.

8. Fill the drive unit with lubricant as described in Chapter Four. Install the propeller(s) as described in this chapter. Adjust the shift cables as described in Chapter Six.

9. Check for proper shifting and cooling system operation before putting the engine into service.

## WATER PUMP

### Disassembly and Inspection (Alpha Models)

1. Remove the gearcase as described in this chapter.

2. Remove the water tube guide (**Figure 60**) and adapter (**Figure 61**) from the seawater pump. Inspect the tube guide and adapter for melted or cracked surfaces and replace if necessary. Inspect the plastic water tube in the drive shaft housing if either of these components are damaged. In most instances the water tube is damaged as well.

3. Slide the seal from the drive shaft (**Figure 62**). Inspect the seal for cracks or other defects and replace as needed.

4. Remove the four screws (**Figure 63**) and lift the water pump body (A, **Figure 64**) and impeller (B) from the drive shaft. Use a chisel to break the hub of the impeller if it is seized to the drive shaft. Work carefully to avoid damaging the drive shaft.

**11**

5. Remove the drive key from the flat surface of the drive shaft (**Figure 65**).

6. Use a brass brush to remove mineral deposits from the outer surfaces of the water pump body. Inspect the inner bore for wear grooves or pitting. Scrape a fingernail across any surface imperfections. Replace the water pump body if the defect is deep enough to detect with a fingernail.

7. Inspect the water pump impeller for burns, wear or grooves surfaces on the vane tips and the areas near the drive shaft bore. Replace the impeller if any of these defects are present.

8. Check for excessive vane set (bending) 20 minutes or more after the impeller is removed. Replace the impeller if the vanes remain curled or bent 20 minutes after removal.

9. Remove the wear plate and gaskets (**Figure 66**). Use compressed air to blow all loose material from the water pump mounting area. Scrape the gaskets from both sides of the wear plate. Never reuse these gaskets.

10. Lift the filler block from the gearcase (**Figure 67**). Replace the filler block if burned. Clean all corrosion, mineral deposits or carbon from the exposed surfaces of the drive shaft. The impeller must slide freely along the length of the drive shaft.

11. Carefully scrape all gasket material, corrosion and loose paint from the wear plate mating surface of the gearcase. Carefully wipe sand, corrosion, mineral deposits or other debris from the water inlets and the area below the wear plate. Inspect the plastic drive shaft seal carrier for melted surfaces or other damage. If defective, replace the seal carrier as described in this chapter.

**Assembly (Alpha Models)**

1. Apply a bead of Special Lube 101 (Mercury part No. 92-13872A1) to the drive shaft seal carrier and gearcase mating surfaces. Wipe the lubricant into the gap at the mating surface.

2. Align the protrusions with the notches while installing the filler block (**Figure 67**)

3. Apply a light coat of Perfect Seal (Mercury part No. 92-34227-1) to the gasket and the wear plate mating surfaces on the gearcase. This step reduces corrosion of the housing at this surface and improves seal of the pump.

4. Install the lower gasket on the bottom of the wear plate. The small drain opening in the wear plate must align with the small opening in the lower gasket. Carefully slide the lower gasket and wear plate over the drive shaft. Seat the gasket and plate onto the gearcase.

5. Apply a light coat of Special Lube 101 to the bore of the water pump body and the drive key. Place the drive

key on the flat surface of the drive shaft as shown in **Figure 65**. Wipe a light coat of Special Lube 101 on the impeller mating surface area of the drive shaft.

6. Slide the impeller over the drive shaft. If reusing the impeller the vanes must curl in a counterclockwise direction as viewed from the top (**Figure 68**). Otherwise remove and invert the impeller.

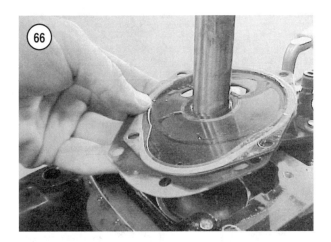

7. Align the slot in the impeller hub with the raised ridge of the drive key (**Figure 65**) while seating the impeller against the wear plate.

8. Install the upper wear plate gasket onto the water pump body. The silicone bead on the gasket must face the body.

9. Place the water pump body over the drive shaft and rest it on top of the impeller. Do not force the impeller into the body at this time.

10. Hold the body in position and apply light downward pressure. Rotate the drive shaft clockwise until the impellerenters the bore and the body seats against the wear plate.

11. Apply a light coat of Perfect Seal to the threads of the four bolts and install them (**Figure 63**). Do not tighten the bolts at this time.

12. Hold the water pump body in position and tighten the bolts to the specification in **Table 1**.

13. Apply a bead of Special Lube 101 to the area where the drive shaft protrudes from the water pump body. Slide the seal over the end of the shaft with the skirt facing down (**Figure 62**). Do not seat the seal against the body at this time.

14. Position the seal installation tool over the drive shaft with the open end facing downward. The tool is included with a replacement seal. Rest the tool on the seal.

15. Push down lightly on the drive shaft. Push down on the seal installation tool until it contacts the water pump body. Remove the tool from the drive shaft (**Figure 69**). Do not pull on the seal.

16. Install new O-rings into the grooves in the adapter. Apply a light coat of Special Lube 101 to the O-rings. Push the adapter onto the water pump outlet with the larger opening facing upward (**Figure 61**). Rotate the adapter to position the drain notch to the rear. Insert the water tube guide into the adapter (**Figure 60**).

**11**

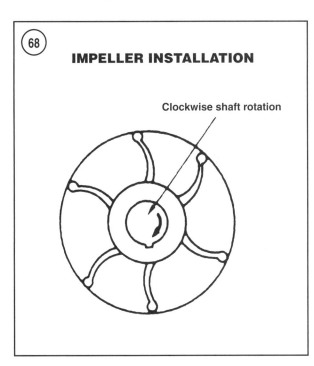

## IMPELLER INSTALLATION

Clockwise shaft rotation

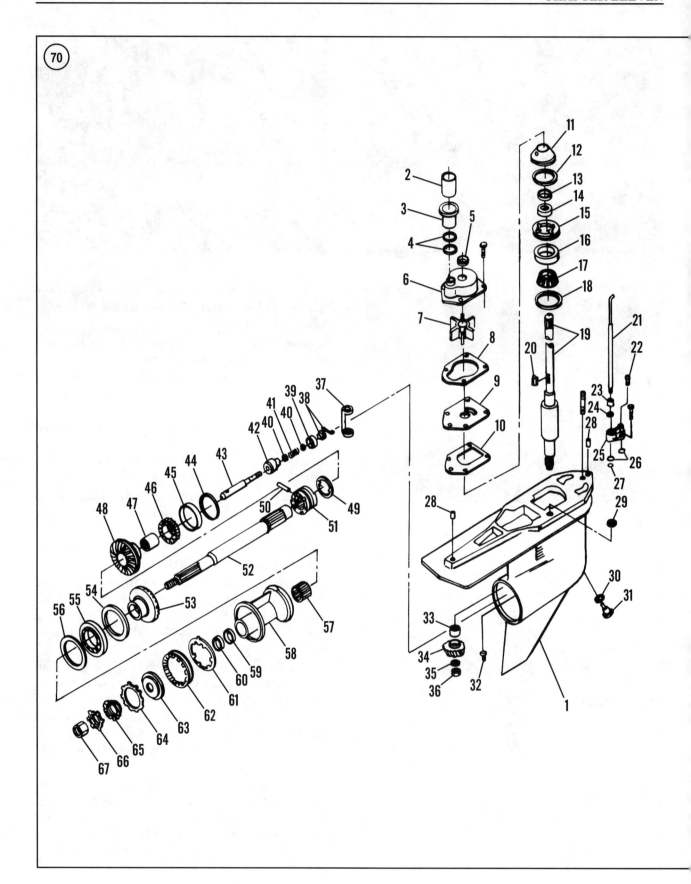

## ALPHA STANDARD ROTATION GEARCASE

1. Gearcase housing
2. Tube guide
3. Adapter
4. O-rings
5. Seal
6. Pump body
7. Impeller
8. Upper gasket
9. Wear plate
10. Lower gasket
11. Plastic seal carrier
12. O-ring
13. Seal
14. Seal
15. Drive shaft retainer
16. Bearing race
17. Tapered roller bearing
18. Shims (pinion gear height)
19. Lower drive shaft
20. Drive key
21. Lower shift shaft
22. Speedometer fitting
23. Rubber sleeve
24. Shift shaft seal
25. Shift shaft bushing
26. O-rings (orange)
27. E-clip
28. Locating pin
29. Quad ring seal (orange)
30. Sealing washer
31. Drain/fill plug
32. Shift crank pin
33. Lower drive shaft bearing
34. Pinion gear
35. Washer
36. Pinion nut
37. Shift crank
38. Cotter pin and castle nut
39. Threaded retainer
40. Washer
41. Spring
42. Shift spool
43. Shift actuator shaft
44. Shims (forward gear)
45. Bearing race
46. Tapered roller bearing
47. Needle bearing
48. Forward gear
49. Spring
50. Cross pin
51. Shift clutch
52. Propeller shaft
53. Reverse gear
54. Thrust spacer
55. Ball bearing
56. O-ring
57. Needle bearing (propeller shaft)
58. Bearing carrier
59. Inner seal
60. Outer seal
61. Tab washer
62. Cover nut
63. Thrust hub
64. Continuity washer
65. Splined washer
66. Tab washer
67. Propeller nut

## GEARCASE

### Bearing Carrier Removal and Installation (Alpha Models)

Refer to **Figure 70** (standard rotation) or **Figure 71** (counter rotation) during this procedure.

1. Remove the gearcase from the drive shaft housing as described in this chapter.

2. Remove the carrier anode (**Figure 72**) as described in Chapter Fifteen.

3. Use a large screwdriver and push all tabs away from the slots in the cover nut (**Figure 73**).

4. Slide the cover nut tool (Mercury part No. 91-61069) over the propeller shaft (**Figure 74**). Engage the lugs into the slots in the cover nut.

5. Use a large breaker bar and socket or impact wrench to remove, the cover nut (**Figure 75**).

6. Pull the bottom edge of the tab washer away from the bearing carrier. Pull the tab from the opening in the gearcase then pull the tab washer from the gearcase (**Figure 76**).

7. Attach a two jaw puller (Mercury part No. 91-46086 A1) and puller bolt (Mercury part No. 91-85716) to the bearing carrier and propeller shaft as shown in **Figure 77**). Remove the carrier from the propeller shaft (**Figure 78**).

8. Remove the O-ring from the carrier. Discard the O-ring.

9. Clean the carrier with solvent. If the bearing race (36, **Figure 71**) was dislodged, install it in the carrier. Apply a light coat of Special Lube 101 (Mercury part No. 92-113872A1) to the race to hold it in position.

10. If necessary, disassemble and assemble the bearing carrier as described in this chapter.

11. Use a shop towel soaked in quick-drying solvent to clean the carrier bore in the gearcase housing. Avoid contaminating other gearcase components.

12. Install a new O-ring onto the bearing carrier. Apply a light coat of Perfect Seal (Mercury part No. 92-34227-1) to the surfaces of the bearing carrier that contact the housing. Do not contaminate bearings or gears with Perfect Seal. Apply a bead of Special Lube 101 (Mercury part No. 92-13872A1) to the lips of the propeller shaft seals.

13. Slide the carrier over the propeller shaft (**Figure 78**). To prevent damage to the gears, rotate the lower drive shaft clockwise during carrier installation. Align the V-notch (**Figure 79**) with the top side while seating the carrier in the housing.

14. Slide the tab washer over the propeller shaft (**Figure 76**). Place the external tab (2, **Figure 79**) of the tab washer into the opening in the gearcase (3).

11

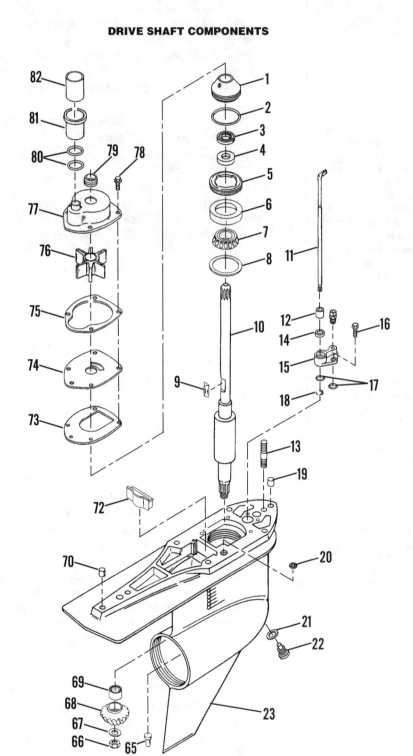

**ALPHA COUNTER ROTATION GEARCASE**

**DRIVE SHAFT COMPONENTS**

1. Plastic seal carrier
2. O-ring
3. Upper seal
4. Lower seal
5. Retainer
6. Bearing race
7. Tapered roller bearing
8. Shims (pinion gear height)
9. Drive key
10. Lower drive shaft
11. Lower shift shaft
12. Rubber sleeve
13. Stud or bolt
14. Shift shaft seal
15. Shift shaft bushing
16. Screws (2)
17. O-rings (orange)
18. E-clip
19. Locating pin
20. Quad ring seal (orange)
21. Sealing washer
22. Fill/drain plug
23. Gearcase housing
24. Shift crank
25. Shift spool and actuator
26. Shims (reverse gear)
27. Bearing carrier (reverse gear)
28. Roller bearing
29. Bearing race
30. Thrust bearing
31. Needle bearing
32. Reverse gear
33. Spring
34. Clutch
35. Cross pin
36. Bearing race
37. Thrust bearing
38. Collar
39. Keepers
40. Collar
41. Thrust bearing
42. Bearing race
43. Bearing carrier (Forward gear)
44. Roller bearing
45. Thrust bearing
46. Shim
47. Forward gear
48. Propeller shaft
49. O-ring
50. Needle bearing (propeller shaft)

## ALPHA COUNTER ROTATION GEARCASE (continued)

**PROPELLER SHAFT COMPONENTS**

51. Bearing carrier
52. Anode screws
53. Inner seal
54. Outer seal
55. Tab washer
56. Cover nut
57. Thrust hub
58. Continuity washer
59. Splined washer
60. Tab washer
61. Propeller nut
62. Anodic plate
63. Lockwasher
64. Bolt
65. Shift crank pin
66. Pinion nut
67. Washer
68. Pinion gear
69. Lower drive shaft bearing
70. Locating pin
71. Bolt
72. Filler block
73. Lower gasket
74. Wear plate
75. Upper gasket
76. Impeller
77. Pump body
78. Bolts
79. Seal
80. O-rings
81. Adapter
82. Tube guide

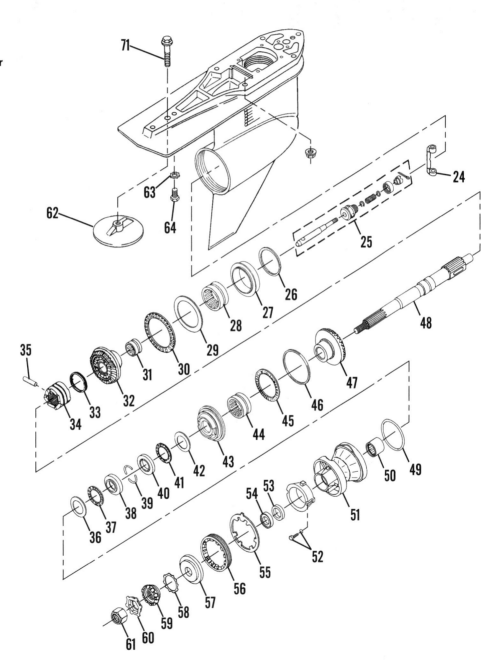

11

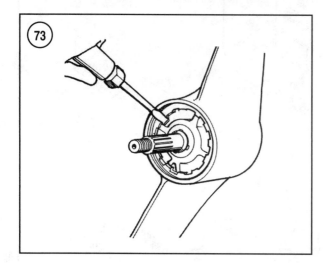

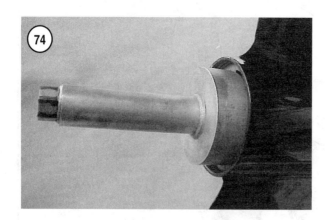

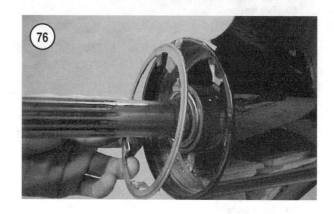

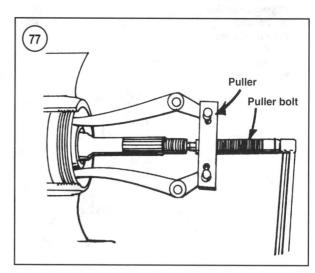

Puller

Puller bolt

15. Rotate the bearing carrier to align the V-notch in the carrier (1, **Figure 79**) with the V-tab of the tab washer. Seat the tab washer against the carrier.

16. Apply Special Lube 101 (Mercury part No. 92-13872A1) to the threads of the cover nut. Thread the cover nut (**Figure 75**) into the gearcase. The directional marks must face outward.

17. Slide the cover nut tool (Mercury part No. 91-61069) over the propeller shaft (**Figure 74**). Engage the lugs into slots in the cover nut. Tighten the cover nut to the specification in **Table 1**.

18. Use slip joint pliers to bend one of the tabs into a slot in the cover nut (**Figure 80**). Tighten the cover nut as needed to align the tab with the slot. Never loosen the nut to align the tab.

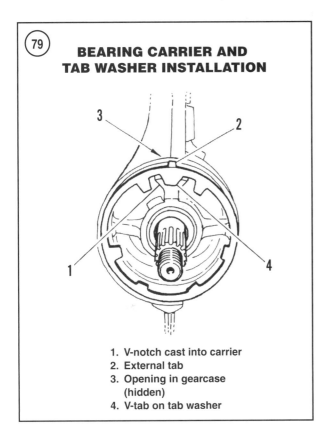

**BEARING CARRIER AND
TAB WASHER INSTALLATION**

1. V-notch cast into carrier
2. External tab
3. Opening in gearcase
   (hidden)
4. V-tab on tab washer

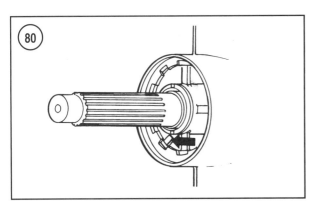

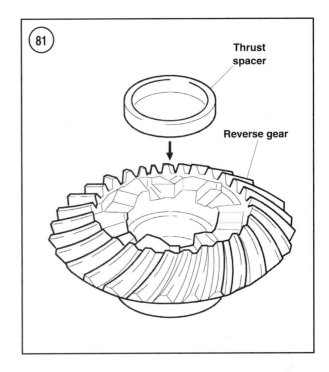

Thrust
spacer

Reverse gear

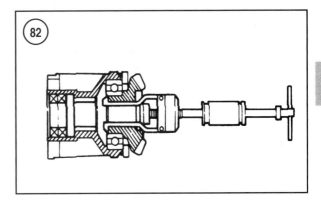

19. Install the carrier anode (**Figure 72**) as described in Chapter Fifteen.

20. Install the gearcase as described in this chapter.

**Reverse Gear Removal and Installation (Alpha Models–Standard Rotation)**

Remove the reverse gear or reverse gear ball bearing only if replacement is necessary. Refer to *Inspection* in this chapter to determine the need for replacement.

1. Remove the thrust spacer (**Figure 81**) from the recess in the reverse gear or the propeller shaft. Clamp the carrier in a vise with protective jaws.

2. Attach a slide hammer to the reverse gear (**Figure 82**).

11

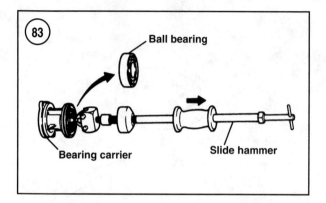

(83)

Ball bearing

Bearing carrier

Slide hammer

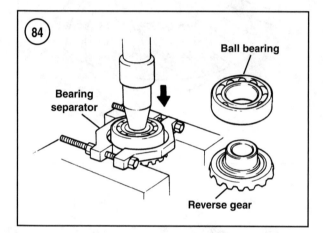

(84)

Ball bearing

Bearing separator

Reverse gear

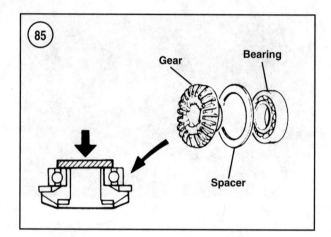

(85)

Gear

Bearing

Spacer

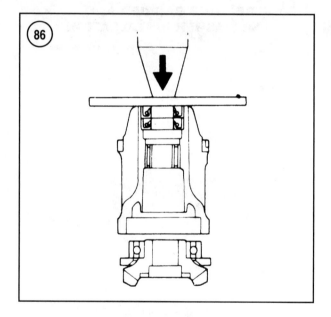

(86)

3. Use short hammer strokes to remove the gear or gear and bearing from the carrier.

4. If the bearing remains in the carrier, remove it using the slide hammer (**Figure 83**). Discard the bearing if removed.

5. If the bearing remains on the gear, separate the gear, bearing and thrust spacer as follows:

   a. Install a bearing separator between the gear and thrust spacer (**Figure 84**).

   b. Place the gear and bearing separator on a press with the gear facing downward. Press the gear from the bearing using a suitable driver.

6. Inspect the gear for wear or damageas described under *Inspection* in this chapter.

7. Install the bearing and thrust spacer onto the gear as follows:

   a. Place the gear on the table of a press with the tooth side facing downward. Lubricate the hub of the gear and the new bearing with gearcase lubricant.

   b. Place the thrust spacer (**Figure 85**) over the hub of the gear. Center the spacer with the gear.

   c. Use a suitable mandrel, large diameter socket or section of tubing as a bearing installation tool. The tool must contact only the inner bearing race.

   d. Place the bearing onto the hub of the gear with the numbers facing away from the gear.

   e. Press the bearing into the hub of the gear unit it seats against the shoulder.

8. Install the gear and bearing into the carrier as follows:

   a. Lubricate the outer bearing race and carrier bore with gearcase lubricant.

   b. Place the reverse gear and bearing assembly on the table of a press with the tooth side facing downward.

   c. Place the carrier onto the bearing as shown in **Figure 86**.

   d. Place a flat piece of metal or other sturdy material against the seal side of the carrier.

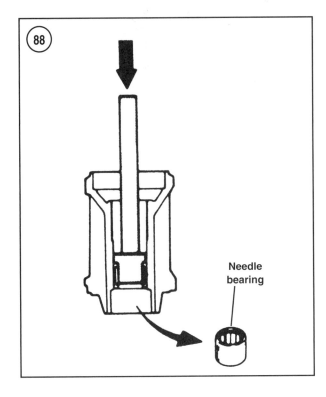

Needle
bearing

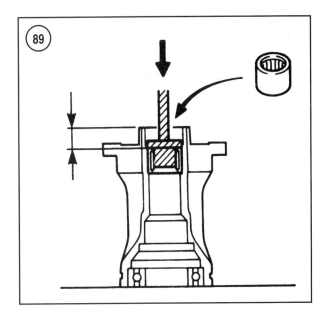

1. Clamp the carrier in a vise with protective jaws.

2. Pry the propeller shaft seals from the carrier (**Figure 87**). Be careful not to damage the bore. Discard the seals.

3. Remove the propeller shaft needle bearing only if it must be replaced. The removal process damages the bearing.

    a. Use a section of tubing as a bearing removal tool. The tool diameter must be slightly larger than the inner diameter of the bearing but not contact the bore of the carrier.

    b. Place the carrier on a press with the seal side facing downward. Insert the removal tool into the gear side bore of the carrier (**Figure 88**). The tool must contact the lip of the bearing cage.

    c. Press the needle bearing out of the carrier. Discard the bearing.

4. Thoroughly clean the bearing carrier. Replace the carrier if deeply pitted from corrosion, cracked or is damaged in the bearing or seal bore.

5. Install the needle bearing as follows.

    a. Lubricate the bearing and carrier bore with gearcase lubricant.

    b. Insert the new needle bearing into the seal end of the bore with the numbered side facing outward (**Figure 89**).

    c. Insert the installation tool (part No. 91-15755) into the bore with the larger diameter side facing outward. The smaller diameter side must squarely contact the numbered side of the bearing.

    d. Place the carrier on a press with tool side facing upward.

    e. Align the ram of the press with center of the seal bore. The alignment must be perfect or the bearing may bind during installation and possibly damage the carrier.

    f. Press the carrier onto the gear and bearing assembly until seated.

### *Propeller shaft seals and needle bearing removal and installation (Alpha models)*

Use a special mandrel (Mercury part No. 91-15755) to install the bearing at the proper depth in the bore. Use a seal installation tool (Mercury part No. 91-31108) to position the seals at the proper depth.

**11**

e. Press the bearing into the carrier (**Figure 89**) until the large diameter of the tool seats against the bearing carrier.

6. Install the propeller shaft seals as follows:

   a. Clean all lubricant from the seal bore with a quick drying solvent.

   b. Apply a light coat of Loctite 271 (Mercury part No. 92-32609-1) onto the seal bore and the outer diameter of the new seals.

   c. Insert the seal and taller side of the tool into the aft end of the carrier (**Figure 90**). The lip side of the inner seal must face the needle bearing.

   d. Place the carrier on a press with the seal bore facing upward. Press in the seal until the tool seats against the carrier.

   e. Place the second seal onto the shorter side of the seal installation tool. The lip side of the seal must face toward the shoulder.

   f. Insert the seal and shorter shouldered side of the tool into the aft end of the carrier. The lip side of the seal must face away from the needle bearing.

   g. Place the carrier on a press with the seal bore facing upward. Carefully press in the seal until the tool seats against the carrier.

7. Wipe excess Loctite from the seal bore. Apply a bead of Special Lube 101 (Mercury part No. 92-13872A1) onto the seal lips.

### Forward Gear Removal and Installation (Alpha Counter-Rotation Models)

Refer to **Figure 71**.

1. Pull the thrust bearing (37, **Figure 71**) and outer collar (38) from the propeller shaft.

2. Pull out slightly on the propeller shaft and remove the keepers (39, **Figure 71**).

3. Pull the inner thrust bearing and collar from the propeller shaft.

4. Bend a piece of stiff wire into a hook. Hook the wire into one of the holes in the side of the bearing carrier (43, **Figure 71**). Pull the wire to remove the carrier. Pull the spacer from the carrier.

5. Pull the shim spacer (46, **Figure 71**) from the shoulder in the housing. Pull the bearing race (42, **Figure 71**) from the carrier. Pull the thrust bearing and forward gear from the housing.

6. Remove the roller bearing (28, **Figure 71**) from the carrier only if it must be replaced.

   a. Clamp the carrier into carrier into a vise with protective jaws. Attach a slide hammer to the back side of the bearing. Use short hammer strokes to remove the bearing. Discard the bearing.

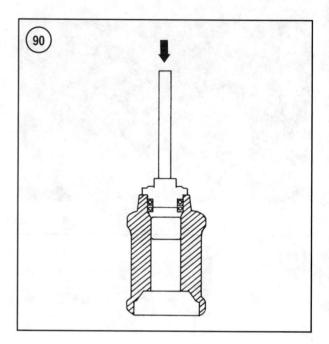

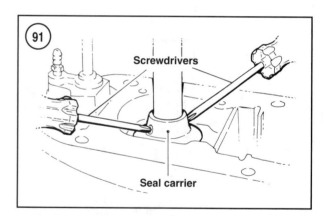

   b. Apply gearcase lubricant to the bearing bore.

   c. Place the carrier on the table of a press with the open side of the bearing facing upward. Use a piece of tubing to install the bearing. The tool must contact near the outer edge of the bearing but not the bearing bore during installation.

   d. Press the bearing into the carrier until seated.

7. Place the spacer onto the carrier. The smaller-diameter side must contact the carrier. Lubricate the thrust bearing (45, **Figure 71**) with gearcase lubricant and place in onto the carrier.

8. Slide the hub of the forward gear into the roller bearing. Seat the gear against the thrust bearing. Place the shim spacer (46, **Figure 71**) onto the carrier.

9. Position the propeller shaft pointing downward. Slide the forward gear and carrier assembly over the propeller

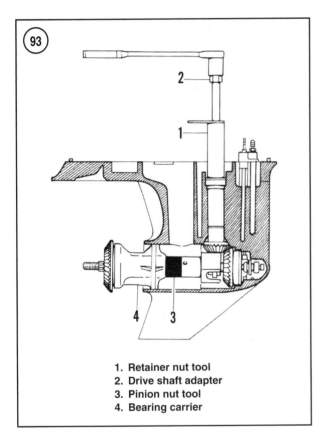

1. Retainer nut tool
2. Drive shaft adapter
3. Pinion nut tool
4. Bearing carrier

shaft. While an assistant rotates the lower drive shaft, push the assembly into the housing. When the assembly is seated against the step, rotate the gearcase until the propeller shaft points upward.

10. Lubricate the bearing race (42, **Figure 71**) with gearcase lubricant and slide it over the propeller shaft. Seat the race onto the bearing carrier.

11. Slide the inner bearing (black side out) over the propeller shaft and set it against the race. Slide the inner collar (40, **Figure 71**) over the propeller shaft with the shouldered side facing the bearing.

12. Pull up on the propeller shaft until the keeper groove is exposed. Place both keepers (39, **Figure 71**) in the groove so they seat against the recess in the inner collar. Lower the propeller shaft.

13. Slide the outer collar (38, **Figure 71**) over the propeller shaft with the shouldered side facing outward. Seat the recess in the collar over the exposed sides of the keepers.

14. Slide the outer bearing (black side out) over the propeller shaft and seat it against the collar.

### Drive Shaft Seal Carrier and Seals Removal and Installation (Alpha Models)

Have a new carrier assembly on hand before beginning this procedure. The removal process usually damages the seal carrier.

1. Clean all loose material from around the seal carrier.

2. Insert two Phillips screwdrivers (with the tip ground flat) into the openings in the carrier (**Figure 91**). Use shop towels as pads to protect the housing. Pry up on the the housing from opposite sides. If removal is difficult, chisel the carrier from the housing, taking care not to damage the housing or drive shaft.

3. Remove and discard the O-ring from the seal carrier. Turn the gearcase so the drive shaft faces downward. Clean any debris and corrosion from the drive shaft bore.

4. Replace the drive shaft seals as follows:
   a. Clamp the carrier into a vise with protective jaws.
   b. Carefully pry the seals from the carrier. Do not damage the seal bore.
   c. Clean the seal bore.
   d. Use a socket or piece of tubing to install the replacement seal. Apply Perfect Seal (Mercury part No. 92-34227-1) onto the seal bore.
   e. Insert the upper seal into the bore with the lip facing toward the smaller diameter side of the carrier. Push the seal into the bore until fully seated.
   f. Insert the lower seal into the bore with the lip facing outward. Push the seal into the bore until fully seated.

5. Install a new O-ring onto the seal carrier. Apply a bead of Special Lube 101 (Mercury part No. 92-13872A1) to the seal lips and the O-ring.

6. Slide the seal carrier over the drive shaft (**Figure 92**) and into the bore. Push down on the carrier until fully seated in the bore.

### Pinion Gear and Lower Drive Shaft Removal

This operation requires a drive shaft adapter, retainer nut tool and pinion nut tool (Mercury part No. 91-56775, 91-43506 and 91-61067A2).

1. Slide the retainer nut tool (1, **Figure 93**) over the lower drive shaft. Engage the lugs of the tool with the notches in

**11**

the retainer. Loosen the retainer nut approximately three turns. Do not remove the nut at this time.

2. Install the drive shaft adapter (2, **Figure 93**) onto the lower drive shaft splines.

3. Slide the pinion nut tool (3, **Figure 93**) over the propeller shaft. Rotate the drive shaft enough to engage the slot stamped MR onto the pinion nut.

4. Slide the bearing carrier (4, **Figure 93**) over the propeller shaft with the gear side facing outward. Push the carrier into the bore until it contacts the pinion nut tool.

5. Turn the lower drive shaft counterclockwise to loosen the pinion nut. Do not unscrew the nut at this time.

6. Remove the retainer nut (**Figure 94**). Turn the drive shaft counter-clockwise to unscrew the pinion nut. Pull the drive shaft from the gearcase (**Figure 95**). Remove the shims from the drive shaft bore (**Figure 96**). Measure and record the shim thickness.

7. Remove the bearing carrier and pinion nut tool.

8. Pull the pinion gear from the housing, manipulating the propeller shaft if necessary to free the gear. Retrieve the rollers from the lower drive shaft bearing if dislodged. Remove the washer from the pinion gear (**Figure 97**). Pull the bearing race from the drive shaft (**Figure 98**).

9. Remove the tapered roller bearing from the drive shaft bearing only if it or the shaft must be replaced. Refer to *Inspection* in this chapter.

   a. Slide the drive shaft into a bearing separator with the pinion gear side facing down (**Figure 99**). The separator must contact the large diameter side of the tapered bearing.

   b. Place the drive shaft and separator onto the table of a press.

   c. Support the drive shaft and press the shaft from the bearing. Discard the bearing.

   d. Lubricate the inner diameter of the replacement bearing with gearcase lubricant. Slide the bearing over the upper end of the shaft with the large diameter side facing the shoulder on the shaft. Slide the

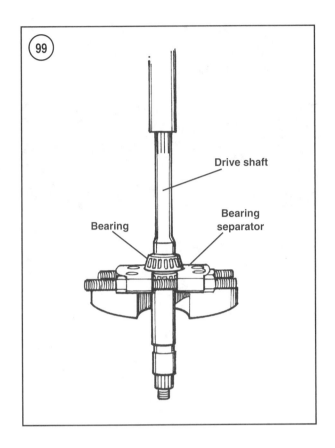

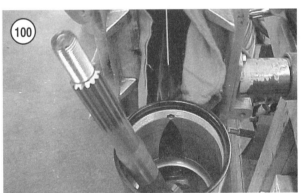

shaft into the bearing separator. Adjust the separator until the opening contacts only the inner race of the bearing. Insert the shaft and separator into the press with the pinion gear end facing upward. Thread the used pinion nut onto the drive shaft to protect the threads.

e. Press on the pinion nut until the bearing seats against the shoulder on the shaft. Remove the pinion nut.

**Propeller Shaft Removal**

1A. *Standard rotation*—Position the gearcase with the propeller shaft pointing up.

1B. *Counter rotation*—Position the gearcase with the propeller shaft pointing down.

2. Move the aft end of the propeller shaft to the port side of the opening (**Figure 100**). Rotate the shift shaft slightly to free the shift spool from the shift crank. Pull the propeller shaft assembly from the housing (**Figure 101**).

3. On counter-rotation gearcases, pull the thrust bearing (30, **Figure 71**) and bearing race (29) from the gearcase.

*Propeller shaft disassembly and assembly*

1. Slip a small screwdriver under the clutch spring (**Figure 102**). Carefully unwind the spring from the clutch. Pull the spring from the aft end of the propeller shaft. Replace the spring if it is damaged or has lost tension.

2. Pull the cross pin from the clutch (**Figure 103**). Pull the shift spool and actuator from the propeller shaft (**Figure 104**). Spin and pull on the spool (42, **Figure 70**). The spool must spin freely without excessive (0.010 in. [0.25 mm] or greater) end play. Otherwise replace the shift spool and actuator assembly. Individual replacement parts are not available.

**11**

3. Pull the front gear and bearing from the shaft (**Figure 105**). Slide the clutch from the propeller shaft (**Figure 106**).

4. Thoroughly clean and inspect all components for wear or damage as described in this chapter.

5. Align the numbered side of the clutch with the propeller side of the propeller shaft. Align the cross pin hole in the clutch with the slot in the propeller shaft and slide the clutch onto the propeller shaft (**Figure 106**).

6. Slide the front gear onto the propeller shaft (**Figure 105**). The gear teeth must face toward the clutch. Slide the shift spool and actuator into the bore of the propeller shaft (**Figure 104**). Rotate the shaft to align the cross pin hole in the actuator shaft with the hole in the clutch. Insert the cross pin through the holes in the clutch pin and actuator (**Figure 103**).

7. Carefully wind the spring onto the clutch. The spring loops must not cross one another and three of them must span each end of the cross pin. Reposition the spring if necessary.

### Lower Drive Shaft Bearing Removal and Installation

Remove the lower drive shaft bearing only if it must be replaced. The removal process damages the bearing. Refer to *Inspection* in this chapter. Bearing removal requires a special mandrel, pilot and driver rod (Mercury part No. 91-36569, 91-36571 and 91-37323). Bearing installation requires a puller bolt and nut, pilot, plate and puller head (Mercury part no. 91-31229, 91-36571, 91-29310 and 91-38628).

1. Insert the bearing rollers into the bearing (**Figure 107**). Slide the pilot over the driver rod. Thread the large diameter side of the mandrel onto the driver rod. Insert the mandrel, pilot and driver rod into the gearcase as shown in **Figure 108**.

2. Hold the mandrel in firm contact with the rollers. Tap on the end of the rod until the bearing drops from the bore.

Do not use excessive force, which can break the bearing housing.

3. Discard the bearing.

4. Install the puller bolt, plate and pilot into the drive shaft bore as shown in **Figure 109**. Place the new bearing onto the puller head. The numbered side must face away from the shouldered side of the puller head. Do not remove the cardboard sleeve at this time.

5. Thread the puller head completely onto the puller bolt. Rest the plate against the housing. Hold the puller bolt with a wrench while tightening the large nut. Continue un-

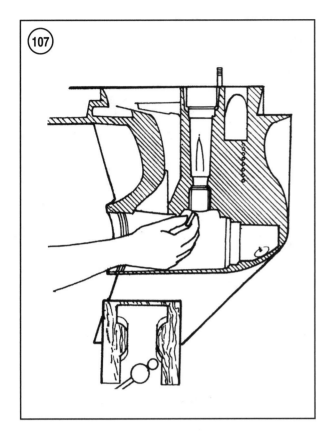

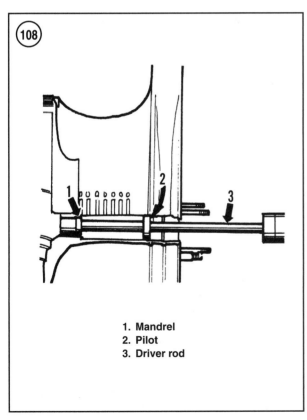

1. Mandrel
2. Pilot
3. Driver rod

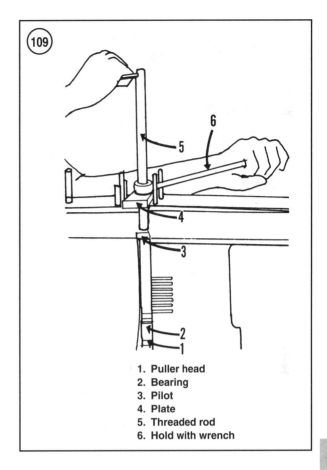

1. Puller head
2. Bearing
3. Pilot
4. Plate
5. Threaded rod
6. Hold with wrench

til the bearing seats against the shoulder in the drive shaft bore. Remove the installation tools.

**Tapered Roller Bearing Removal and Installation (Standard Rotation)**

Remove the tapered roller bearing only if it must be replaced. Do not remove the bearing if the forward gear requires replacement. A replacement gear set includes a new tapered bearing.
1. Use a hack saw or chisel to remove the cage and rollers from the bearing.
2. Install a bearing separator around the remaining inner race of the bearing.
3. Place the separator and gear on the table of a press. Block the separator as needed to allow space for gear travel.
4. Use a suitable driver to press the gear from the bearing. The tool must be slightly smaller in diameter than the hub of the gear. Save the inner bearing race for use as a bearing installation tool. Press the gear from the bearing.
5. Place the gear onto the table of a press with the teeth facing downward. Place the new tapered bearing onto the

**11**

hub of the gear. The large diameter side must face toward the gear.

6. Place the used inner bearing race or other suitable tool against the inner race of the bearing.

7. Press the bearing onto the gear until fully seated (**Figure 110**).

### Front Gear Needle Bearing Removal and Installation

Remove the needle bearing from the front gear only if it must be replaced. The removal process damages the bearing. Do not remove the bearing if the gear must be replaced. The replacement gear includes a new needle bearing.

1. Place the forward gear (teeth side up) onto a vise with open jaws. Place a towel under the gear to protect the roller bearing.

2. Use a small chisel and hammer to drive the needle bearing from the gear. Work carefully to avoid damaging the gear.

3. Place the forward gear, tooth side facing downward, on the table of a press. Use a suitable driver to press the bearing into the gear. The tool must be large enough to contact the outer cage of the bearing but not contact the bearing bore in the gear.

4. Place the new bearing into the bore with the numbered side facing away from the gear. Press the bearing into the gear until it just contacts the seat. Do not use excessive force, which can damage the new bearing.

### Forward Bearing Race Removal and Installation (Standard Rotation)

Use a bearing driver and installation tool (Mercury part No. 91-31106 and 91-18605A1) to install the bearing race.

1. Attach a slide hammer to the slots behind the race (**Figure 111**).

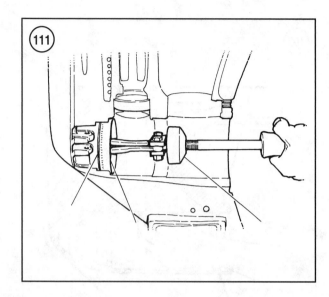

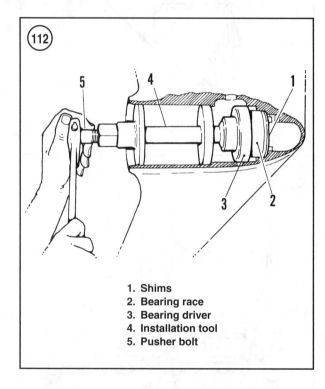

1. Shims
2. Bearing race
3. Bearing driver
4. Installation tool
5. Pusher bolt

2. Use short hammer strokes to pull the race and shims from the housing. Measure and record the thickness of each shim. Replace bent or corroded shims with the same thickness as the original ones.

3. Place the shims (1, **Figure 112**) into the housing and seat them against the shoulder. Lubricate the race (2, **Figure 12**) with gearcase lubricant and install it into the housing. The tapered side must face outward.

4. Place the bearing driver (3, **Figure 112**) onto the bearing race. Align the shaft of the installation tool with the

housing in the area near the bearing race. Keep the flame moving to avoid damaging the finish.

2. Use short hammer strokes to remove the carrier and shims from the housing. Measure and record the thickness of each shim. Replace bent or corroded shims with new shims of the same thickness.

3. Remove the bearing (28, **Figure 71**) only if it must be replaced. Replace as follows:

    a. Place the carrier onto the table of a press.

    b. Press the bearing from the carrier using a suitable driver. Discard the bearing.

    c. Place the carrier onto the table of a press with the stepped side facing upward. Place the new bearing into the carrier with the numbered side facing upward.

    d. Press the bearing into the carrier until flush with the carrier.

4. Place the shims (1, **Figure 112**) into the housing and seat them against the shoulder. Lubricate the carrier with gearcase lubricant and install it into the housing.

5. Place the reverse gear (32, **Figure 71**) into the carrier with the tooth side facing outward. Do not install the thrust bearing (30, **Figure 71**) or race (29). Align the shaft of the installation tool with the opening in the gear and thread the tool into the cover nut threads.

6. Thread the large bolt into the installation tool. Tighten the bolt until resistance is felt. Remove the installation tools and reverse gear. Make sure the race is fully seated.

### Lower Shift Shaft and Crank
### Removal and Installation

1. Remove the screws and lift the shift crank and bushing assembly from the housing (**Figure 113**).

2. Remove the shift crank (**Figure 114**).

3. Remove the E-clip (**Figure 115**) and pull the shift shaft from the bushing.

4. Remove and discard the orange O-rings from the shift shaft bushing (**Figure 116**).

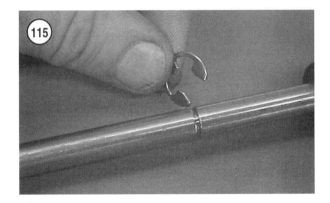

opening in the driver and thread the tool into the cover nut threads.

5. Thread the large bolt into the installation tool. Tighten the bolt until resistance is felt. Remove the installation tools and verify proper seating of the race.

### Reverse Gear Bearing Carrier
### Removal and Installation (Counter-Rotation)

1. Attach the jaws of a slide hammer to the slots behind the race. Use a heat lamp or propane torch to heat the

**11**

5. Carefully pry the seal from the shift shaft bushing (**Figure 117**). Discard the seal.

6. Use a quick drying solvent to clean the shift shaft bushing.

7. Apply Loctite 271 to the outer diameter of the new seal and to its bore in the bushing.

8. Position the seal in the bore with the lip side facing out. Use an appropriate size socket to push the seal fully into the bore. The seal must fit snugly in the bore. If it fits loosely, replace the shift shaft bushing.

9. Lubricate the seal lip with Special Lube 101 then slide the shift shaft through the bushing. Install the E-clip into the groove of the shift shaft.

10. Slide the shift crank onto its pin at the front of the gearcase. Position the offset side of the crank toward the port side of the gearcase (**Figure 118**).

11. Lubricate new orange O-rings with Special Lube 101 and install them onto the shift shaft bushing. One fits onto the hub of the bushing and the other fits into the groove in the bushing.

12. Insert the bushing and shaft into the shift shaft bore. Orient the offset end of the lower shift shaft toward the forward side while inserting the shaft into the shift crank.

13. Seat the bushing onto the gearcase.

14. Apply Perfect Seal (Mercury part No. 92-34227-1) to the threads of the two screws. Install and tighten the screws to the specification in **Table 1**.

**Propeller Shaft Installation**

1. Position the gearcase with the carrier opening facing upward.

2. Position the shift crank as shown in **Figure 118**.

3. Insert the propeller shaft into the gearcase while holding the aft end toward the port side of the gearcase (**Figure 100**).

4. Rotate the shift shaft slightly to align the shift crank with its slot in the shift spool. When properly aligned the

propeller shaft will drop into place. Rotate the shift shaft. If everything is properly installed, only the shift clutch will move. Remove and reinstall the shaft if necessary. Several attempts may be required.

**Pinion Gear and Lower Drive Shaft Installation**

This procedure requires a drive shaft adapter, retainer nut tool and pinion nut tool (Mercury part No. 91-56775, 91-43506 and 91-61067A2).

1A. *Original lower drive shaft bearing*—If dislodged, apply Needle Bearing Grease (Mercury part No. 92-42649A1) to the rollers and install them into the bearing cage (**Figure 107**). Do not use other types of grease, as it may not dissipate and cause the rollers to slide instead of roll. The bearing will fail if the rollers slide.

1B. *New lower drive shaft bearing*—Remove the cardboard sleeve from the replacement bearing.

2. Place the pinion gear in the housing. Align the pinion gear with the drive shaft bore. The pinion gear teeth must mesh with the teeth on the front gear.

3. Apply Loctite 271 to the threads of the drive shaft and the new pinion nut.

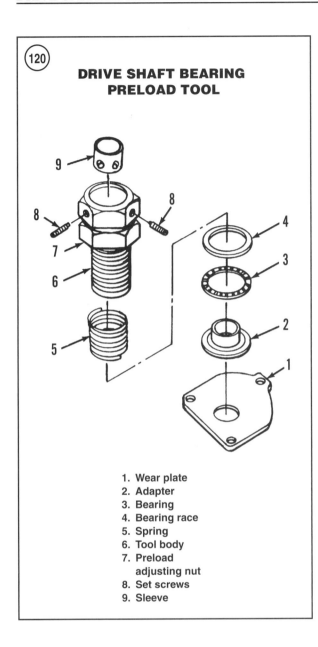

**DRIVE SHAFT BEARING PRELOAD TOOL**

1. Wear plate
2. Adapter
3. Bearing
4. Bearing race
5. Spring
6. Tool body
7. Preload adjusting nut
8. Set screws
9. Sleeve

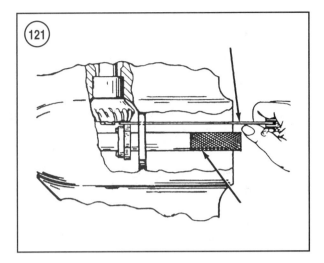

7. Slide the retainer nut over the drive shaft (**Figure 94**) with the directional mark facing upward. Slide the retainer nut tool (1, **Figure 93**) over the lower drive shaft. Hand tighten the retainer nut.

8. Install the drive shaft adapter (2, **Figure 93**) on the drive shaft splines. Slide the pinion nut tool (3, **Figure 93**) over the propeller shaft. Rotate the drive shaft enough to engage the slot stamped MR with the pinion nut.

9. Slide the bearing carrier (4, **Figure 93**) over the propeller shaft with the gear side facing outward. Push the carrier into the bore until it contacts the pinion nut tool.

10. Rotate the drive shaft clockwise and tighten the pinion nut to the specification in **Table 1**. Remove the pinion nut tool and bearing carrier.

11. Attach a torque wrench to the square opening in the retainer nut tool. Tighten the retainer to the specification in **Table 1**.

**Pinion Gear Height**

The pinion height must be adjusted if any gears, bearings, the housing or the drive shaft have been replaced. Piston gear height adjustment requires a pinion gear locating tool and preload tool (Mercury part No. 91-56048 and 91-14311A2).

1. Slide the water pump wear plate (9, **Figure 70**) over the drive shaft and rest it against the housing.

2. Install the preload tool onto the drive shaft as shown in **Figure 120**. Rest the main body of the tool on the spring, bearings and adapter. Tighten both set screws.

3. Rotate the lower nut to achieve a gap of approximately 1 in. (25.4 mm) between the upper and lower nuts. Rotate the drive shaft to seat the bearings.

4. Slide the pinion gear locating tool over the propeller shaft (**Figure 121**). Align one opening in the tool with the

4. Without dislodging the rollers in the lower drive shaft bearing, insert the drive shaft through the lower bearing and into the pinion gear splines. Rotate the drive shaft as needed to align the splines.

5. Use long needlenose pliers to install the washer and pinion nut onto the drive shaft. The recess in the pinion nut (**Figure 119**) must face the pinion gear. Hand-tighten the pinion nut.

6. Slide the shims over the drive shaft (**Figure 96**) and position them on the shoulder in the drive shaft bore. Slide the tapered bearing race over the drive shaft (**Figure 98**). The tapered end must face downward. Seat the race against the shims.

**11**

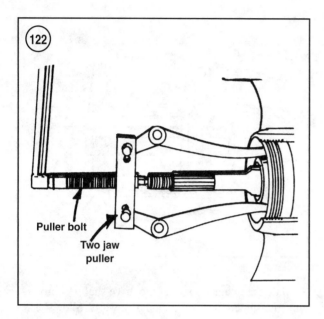

Puller bolt

Two jaw
puller

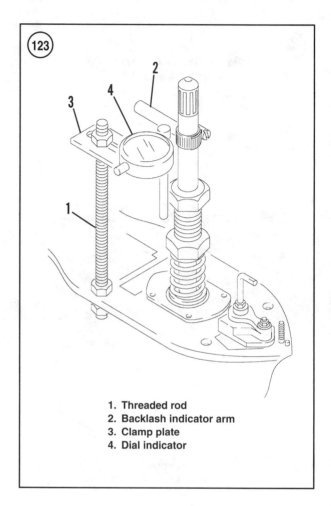

1. Threaded rod
2. Backlash indicator arm
3. Clamp plate
4. Dial indicator

pinion gear. Seat the tool against the shoulder in the housing.

5. Use long feeler gauges to measure the gap between the rounded surface of the locating tool and the pinion gear teeth. Rotate the drive shaft approximately 120° and measure the clearance again. Rotate the shaft again (120°), take a third measurement, and determine the average of the three measurements. The pinion gear height equals the thickness of the feeler gauge that passes between the locating tool and the pinion gear teeth with a slight drag.

6. If necessary, install thicker or thinner shims beneath the tapered bearing until the average pinion height equals 0.025 in. 7. Remove the pinion gear locating and preload tools.

**Gear Lash**

Check the gear backlash if replacing gears, bearings, the housing or the drive shaft. This procedure requires a preload tool (Mercury part No. 91-14311A2), backlash indicator arm (Mercury part No. 91-53459), two jaw puller (Mercury part No. 91-46086A1), puller bolt, (Mercury part No. 91-85716) and a dial indicator with mount.

1A. *Standard rotation*—Install the bearing carrier as described in this chapter.

1B. *Counter-rotation*—Remove the propeller shaft thrust bearings, collars and keepers (37-42, **Figure 71**) from the propeller shaft as described in this chapter under *Forward Gear (Counter Rotation)*. Install the bearing carrier as described in this chapter.

2. Measure the backlash between the pinion and front gear as follows:

a. Attach the two jaw puller and puller bolt to the bearing carrier and propeller shaft (**Figure 122**). Tighten the puller bolt to 45 in.-lb. (5 N•m). Rotate the drive shaft clockwise a few turns to seat the bearings then retighten the puller bolt.

b. Clamp the backlash indicator arm to the drive shaft as shown in **Figure 123**. Use a threaded rod and mount or other suitable method to clamp a dial indicator to the gearcase (**Figure 123**). Align the tip of the indicator with the I mark on the backlash indicator arm, at a 90° angle to the arm (**Figure 124**).

c. Record the dial indicator reading while gently rotating the drive shaft in both directions. Loosen the backlash indicator tool then rotate the drive shaft 90°. Reattach the dial indicator and backlash indicator tool, then repeat the measurement. Repeat this step until four measurements are taken. Record the average of the measurements.

d. Correct backlash is 0.017-0.028 in. (0.43-0.71 mm) for standard rotation and 0.040-0.050 (1.02-1.27 mm) for counter-rotation models.

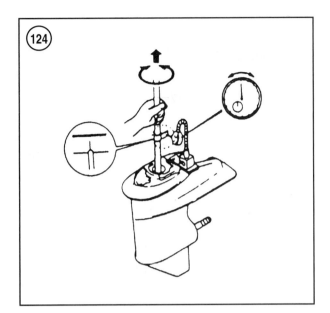

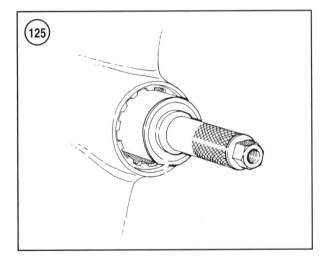

driver into the opening on the side of the tool. Tighten the propeller nut to 45 in.-lb. (5 N•m).

b. Clamp the backlash indicator arm to the drive shaft as shown in **Figure 123**. Attach a dial indicator onto the gearcase. Align the tip of the indicator with the I mark on the backlash indicator arm. The tip must meet the arm at a 90° angle (**Figure 124**).

c. Record the dial indicator reading while gently rotating the drive shaft in both directions. Loosen the backlash indicator tool then rotate the drive shaft 90°. Reattach the dial indicator and backlash indicator tool, then repeat the measurement. Repeat this step until four measurements are taken. Record the average of the measurements. Remove the backlash indicator arm, dial indicator and preload tool.

d. Correct backlash is 0.028-0.052 in. (0.71-1.32 mm) for standard rotation and 0.017-0.028 in. (0.43-0.71 mm) for counter rotation models.

5A. *Standard rotation*—Check for improper bearing carrier seating if the backlash measurement is greater than 0.052 in. (1.32 mm). Check for improper reverse gear or ball bearing installation if the measurement is below 0.028 in. (0.71 mm). Remove the bearing carrier and correct the condition before operating the gearcase.

5B. *Counter-rotation*—Correct improper gear backlash as follows:

a. Remove the bearing carrier and forward gear as described in this chapter.

b. If the backlash is too low, install a thinner shim spacer (26, **Figure 71**).

c. If the backlash is too high, install a thicker shim spacer (26, **Figure 71**).

d. Reinstall the forward gear and bearing carrier without the thrust bearings and collars.

e. Measure the backlash. Several measurements and shim changes may be required.

6. *Counter-rotation*—Remove the bearing carrier. Install the thrust bearing and collars. Reinstall the bearing carrier.

7. Bend the tab of the tab washer into the cover nut as described in this chapter (see Bearing Carrier).

3. If the backlash is incorrect, correct it as follows:

a. Disassemble the gearcase enough to access the shims beneath the forward bearing race (45, **Figure 70**) or the reverse bearing carrier (27, **Figure 71**).

b. Install thinner or fewer shims to increase the gear backlash. Install thicker or additional shims to decrease the gear backlash.

c. A 0.005 in. change in shim thickness changes the backlash reading by approximately 0.004 in. Several changes may be required.

4. Measure the backlash between the pinion and rear gear as follows:

a. Slide the pinion nut tool over the propeller shaft (**Figure 125**). Install a suitable washer, then the propeller nut. To prevent shaft rotation, insert a screw-

## BRAVO I AND II MODELS

Disassemby and assembly procedures for the Bravo I and Bravo II gearcases are very similar. Except for the drive shaft, Bravo II components are considerably larger than Bravo I components. Also, the Bravo II gearcase uses additional components in the bearing carrier. For component identification and orientation, refer to **Figure 126** (Bravo I) and **Figure 127** (Bravo II).

**11**

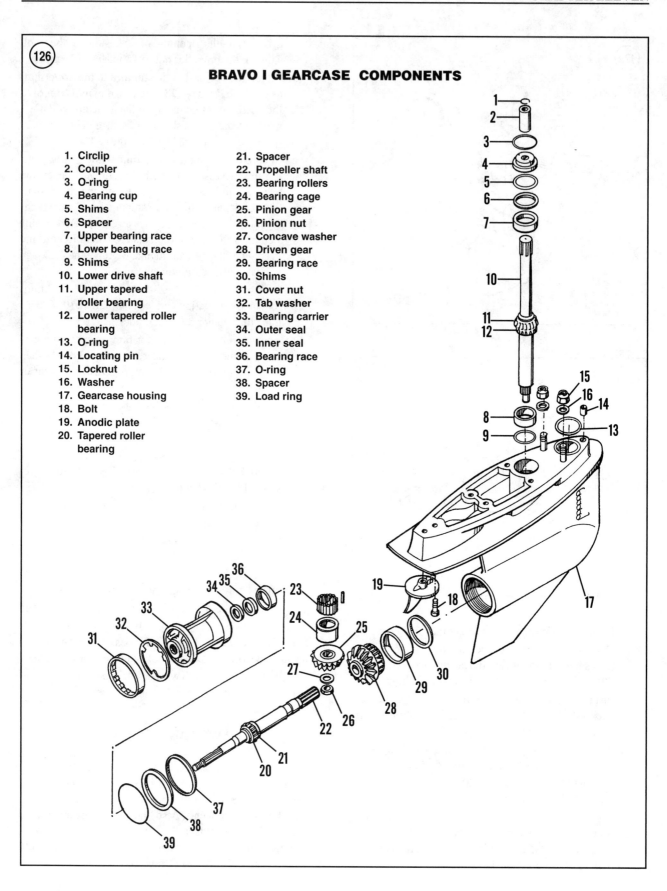

**BRAVO I GEARCASE COMPONENTS**

1. Circlip
2. Coupler
3. O-ring
4. Bearing cup
5. Shims
6. Spacer
7. Upper bearing race
8. Lower bearing race
9. Shims
10. Lower drive shaft
11. Upper tapered roller bearing
12. Lower tapered roller bearing
13. O-ring
14. Locating pin
15. Locknut
16. Washer
17. Gearcase housing
18. Bolt
19. Anodic plate
20. Tapered roller bearing
21. Spacer
22. Propeller shaft
23. Bearing rollers
24. Bearing cage
25. Pinion gear
26. Pinion nut
27. Concave washer
28. Driven gear
29. Bearing race
30. Shims
31. Cover nut
32. Tab washer
33. Bearing carrier
34. Outer seal
35. Inner seal
36. Bearing race
37. O-ring
38. Spacer
39. Load ring

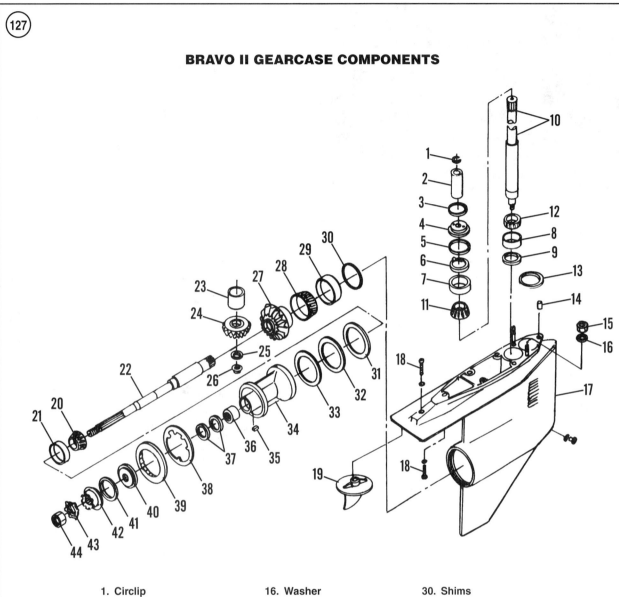

**BRAVO II GEARCASE COMPONENTS**

1. Circlip
2. Coupler
3. O-ring
4. Bearing cup
5. Shims
6. Spacer
7. Upper bearing race
8. Lower bearing race
9. Shims
10. Lower drive shaft
11. Upper tapered roller bearing
12. Lower tapered roller bearing
13. O-ring
14. Locating pin
15. Locknut
16. Washer
17. Gearcase housing
18. Bolt and washer
19. Trim tab
20. Tapered roller bearing
21. Bearing race
22. Propeller shaft
23. Lower drive shaft bearing
24. Pinion gear
25. Concave washer
26. Pinion nut
27. Driven gear
28. Tapered roller bearing
29. Bearing race
30. Shims
31. Load ring
32. Spacer
33. O-ring
34. Bearing carrier
35. Key
36. Needle bearing
37. Seals
38. Tab washer
39. Cover nut
40. Thrust hub
41. Washer
42. Splined washer
43. Tab washer
44. Propeller nut

11

## Propeller Shaft Side Play and Run-Out

This measurement requires a dial indicator and clamp to attach the indicator to the gearcase. Perform this measurement before disassembling the gearcase.

1. Clamp the dial indicator to the gearcase so that the indicator tip touches the propeller shaft. The dial indicator tip must be perpendicular (90°) to the length of the propeller shaft and touch just behind the propeller shaft taper.

2. Move the propeller shaft toward the opposite side of the dial indicator.

3. Rotate the dial indicator face to position the 0 mark over the needle.

4. Move the propeller shaft toward the dial indicator. Hold the propeller shaft in this position while reading the amount of needle movement.

5. If the side play exceeds 0.007 in. (0.178 mm), check for worn bearings or insufficient preload on the propeller shaft bearings. Replace the bearings or correct the preload.

6. Observe the dial indicator while rotating the propeller shaft. If the runout exceeds 0.005 in. (0.127 mm), the propeller shaft is bent and must be replaced.

## Bearing Carrier and Propeller Shaft Removal

Removing the bearing carrier requires a cover nut tool and a two jaw puller. Use Mercury part No. 91-61069 for Bravo I gearcases and Mercury part No. 91-17257 for Bravo II gearcases.

1. Separate the gearcase from the drive shaft housing as described in this chapter.

2. Remove the carrier anode (**Figure 128**) as described in Chapter Fifteen.

3. Use a large screwdriver to push all tabs from the slots in the cover nut (**Figure 129**).

4. Slide the cover nut tool over the propeller shaft (**Figure 130**).

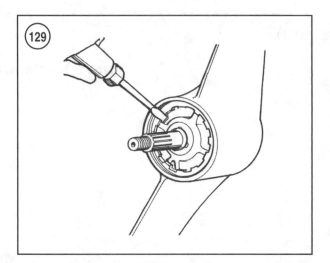

5. Use a large breaker bar and socket or impact wrench to remove the cover nut (**Figure 131**).

6. Pull the bottom edge of the tab washer away from the bearing carrier. Pull the tab from the gearcase (**Figure 132**).

7. Attach a two jaw puller (Mercury part No. 91-46086 A1) and puller bolt (Mercury part No. 91-85716) to the bearing carrier and propeller shaft as shown in **Figure**

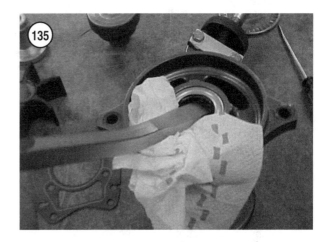

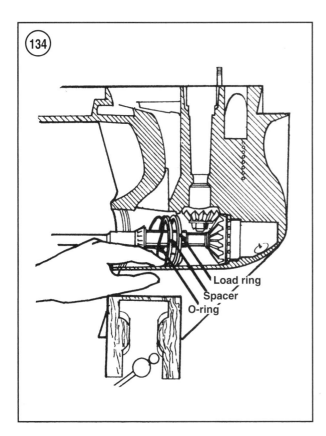

**122**. Turn the puller bolt to remove the carrier from the gearcase. (**Figure 133**).

8. *Bravo II*—Pull the key (35, **Figure 127**) from the groove in the bottom of the bearing carrier or the gearcase opening.

9. Pull the propeller shaft from the gearcase housing. Remove the O-ring, spacer and load ring (**Figure 134**).

10. Clean all sealant, metal filings and other debris from the carrier.

**Propeller Shaft Seal Replacement**

Use the seal installation tool to install the seals to the proper depth in the carrier. Use Mercury part No. 91-89865 for Bravo I gearcases and Mercury part No. 91-55916 for Bravo II gearcases.

1. Clamp the carrier in a vise with protective jaws.

2A. *Bravo I*—Working through the slots in the propeller shaft bore, drive both seals from the carrier. Do not allow the driver to contact the seal bore. Discard the seals.

2B. *Bravo II*—Pry the propeller shaft seals from the carrier (**Figure 135**), taking care not to damage the bore. Discard the seals.

3. Clean the seal bore with quick drying solvent. The bore must be clean and dry.

4. Apply a light coat of Loctite 271 to the seal bore and the outer diameter of the new seals.

5. *Bravo I*—Install the seals as follows:

    a. Place the bearing carrier on the table of a press with the open side facing upward.

    b. Place one of the seals onto the small diameter side of the seal installation tool. The lip side must face away from the shoulder.

    c. Insert the seal and tool into the bore from the open end of the carrier. The lip side of the inner seal must

**11**

face toward the propeller side of the carrier. Press the seal into the bore until seated.

   d. Place the second seal onto the small diameter side of the seal installation tool. The lip side of the seal must face toward the shoulder.

   e. Insert the seal and tool into the bore from the open end of the carrier. The lip side of the seal must face toward the gear side of the carrier. Press the seal into the bore until it seats against the first seal.

6. *Bravo II*—Install the seals as follows:

   a. Place the bearing carrier on the table of a press with the open side facing downward.

   b. Insert the seal and tall side of the tool into the aft end of the carrier (**Figure 136**). The lip side of the inner seal must face the needle bearing.

   c. Press on the tool until the large diameter shoulder of the tool seats against the carrier.

   d. Place the second seal onto the short side of the seal installation tool. The lip side of the seal must face toward the shoulder.

   e. Insert the seal and shorter shouldered side of the tool into the aft end of the carrier. The lip side of the seal must face away from the needle bearing.

   f. Place the carrier on a press with the seal bore facing upward. Press on the tool until the large diameter shoulder of the tool seats against the carrier.

7. Wipe excess Loctite from the seal bore. Apply a bead of Special Lube 101 (Mercury part No. 92-13872A1) to the seal lips.

**Propeller Shaft Needle Bearing Removal and Installation (Bravo II)**

Remove the propeller shaft needle bearing only if it must be replaced, as the removal process damages the bearing. Use an installation tool (Mercury part No. 91-55918) to set the bearing to the proper depth in the bearing carrier.

1. Use an appropriately sized socket and extension or section of tubing as a bearing removal tool.

2. Place the carrier on a press with the seal side facing downward. Insert the removal tool into gear side of the carrier (**Figure 137**). The tool must contact only the lip of the bearing cage.

3. Press the needle bearing out of the carrier. Discard the bearing.

4. Thoroughly clean the bearing carrier. Replace the carrier if deeply pitted from corrosion, cracked or has damage in the bearing or seal bore.

5. Lubricate the bearing and carrier bore with gearcase lubricant. Insert the new needle bearing into the seal end

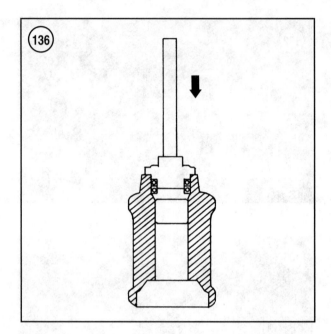

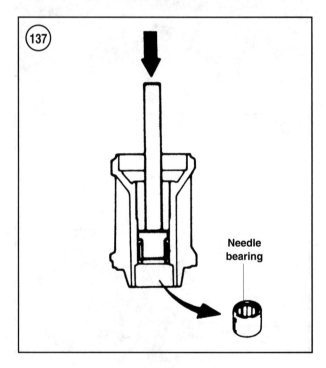

Needle bearing

of the bore with the numbered side facing outward (**Figure 138**).

6. Insert the installation tool (part No. 91-55918) into the bore with the large diameter side facing outward. The small diameter side must squarely contact the numbered side of the bearing.

7. Place the carrier on a press with tool side facing upward.

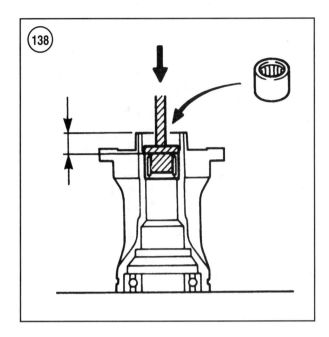

8. Press the bearing into the carrier (**Figure 138**) until it seats against the shoulder in the bore.

### Propeller Shaft Bearing Removal and Installation

Remove the propeller shaft bearing and race only if one of them is defective.

1. Slide the gear end of the propeller shaft into a bearing separator. Adjust the opening in the separator enough to just contact the spacer (21, **Figure 126**).

2. To prevent damage to the shaft, thread the propeller nut onto the propeller shaft.

3. Place the separator and shaft on the table of a press as shown in **Figure 139**. Center the ram of the press over the propeller nut.

4. Support the lower end of the shaft while pressing against the propeller nut. Remove the tapered bearing and spacer from the shaft. Discard the bearing. Retain the spacer. Remove the propeller nut.

5. Slide the spacer and bearing over the propeller end of the shaft. The tapered side of the bearing must face the threaded end of the shaft.

6. Use a section of tubing to install the bearing. The tubing must be large enough to slide over the aft end of the propeller shaft but contact the inner race of the bearing.

7. Use a bearing separator to support the installation tool. Place the tool, separator and shaft onto the table of a press.

8. Center the ram of the press over the forward end of the shaft. Press on the shaft until the bearing and spacer seat against the step on the propeller shaft.

9. Clamp the bearing carrier in a vise with protective jaws. Grind the jaws of a slide hammer to the size necessary to fit beneath the bearing race (36, **Figure 126**) or (21, **Figure 127**).

10. Use short hammer strokes to remove the race. Thoroughly clean the bore. Lubricate the bore and new bearing race with gearcase lubricant.

11. Place the carrier in a press with the open side facing upward. Use an appropriately sized socket, mandrel or section of tubing to install the race. The tool must be large enough to contact the outer edge of the race, but not contact the bore.

12. Place the race in the bore with the tapered side UP. Press the race into the bore until fully seated.

### Pinion Gear, Lower Drive Shaft and Driven Gear Removal

This operation requires a clamp plate (Mercury part No. 91-43559) and a drive shaft adapter (Mercury part No. 91-61077).

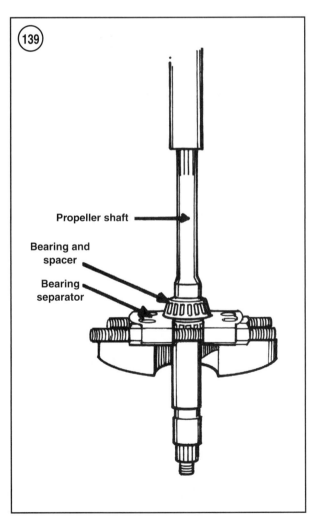

Propeller shaft

Bearing and spacer

Bearing separator

**11**

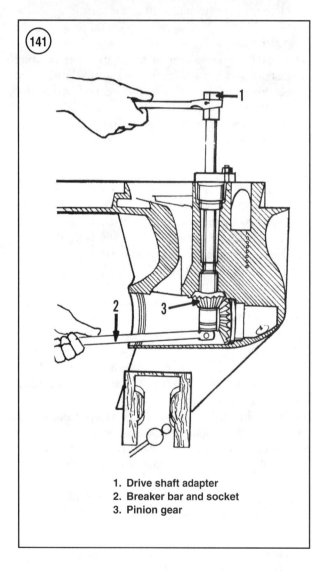

1. Drive shaft adapter
2. Breaker bar and socket
3. Pinion gear

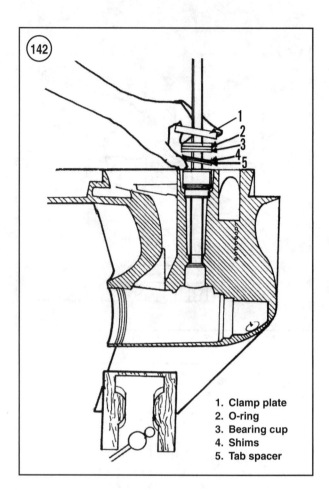

1. Clamp plate
2. O-ring
3. Bearing cup
4. Shims
5. Tab spacer

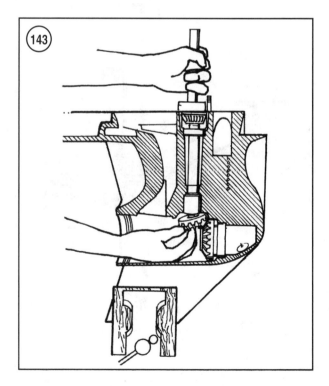

1. Place the clamp plate over the drive shaft mounting studs as shown in **Figure 140**. Place two washers over each stud and secure the plate with the gearcase mounting nuts.

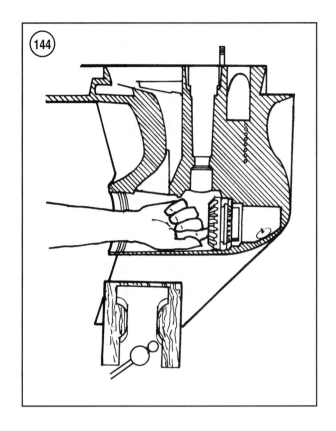

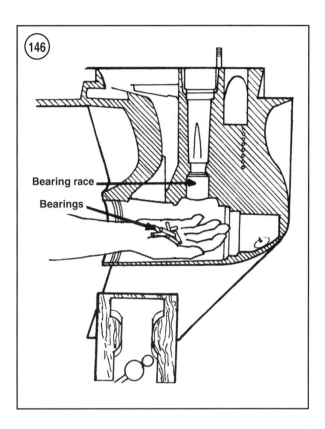

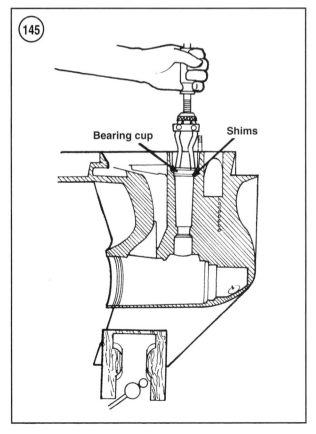

2. Place the drive shaft adapter onto the drive shaft as shown in **Figure 141**. Temporarily thread the cover nut into the gearcase to protect the threads.

3. Attach a breaker bar and socket to the pinion nut (**Figure 141**). Remove the pinion nut and washer.

4. Remove the clamp plate. Remove and discard the O-ring (2, **Figure 142**) from the bearing cup and housing. Lift the bearing cup (3, **Figure 142**) and shims (4) over the drive shaft. Pull up on the port side of the tab spacer (5, **Figure 142**) to free the tab from the drive shaft bore. Remove the tab spacer.

5. Reach into the housing to support the pinion gear while lifting the drive shaft from the gearcase (**Figure 143**). Remove the driven gear (**Figure 144**).

6. Remove the lower bearing race only if necessary to correct the pinion gear height or if replacing the lower tapered roller bearing. Remove the race as follows:

   a. Attach a slide hammer to the back side of the race (**Figure 145**). Use short hammer strokes to remove the race and shims.

   b. Retrieve the bearing rollers if dislodged (**Figure 146**). Record the thickness of each shim. Replace bent or corroded shims with the same thickness as the original ones.

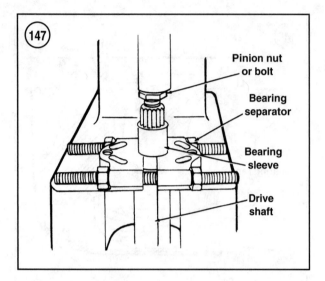

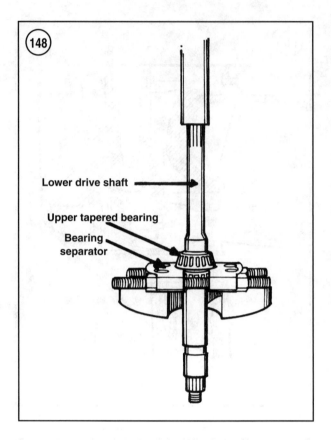

c. Insert the shims in the drive shaft bore. Use an appropriately sized socket and extension or section of tubing as a tool to install the bearing race.

d. Place the race into the bore with the tapered side facing upward. Drive the race into the bore until fully seated.

### *Lower drive shaft disassembly and assembly*

Disassemble the lower drive shaft only if the shaft or bearings must be replaced. The removal process damages the bearings.

1. Remove the bearing sleeve as follows:
   a. Thread the pinion nut onto the drive shaft (**Figure 147**).
   b. Adjust the bearing separator to the size needed to contact the upper edge of the sleeve.
   c. Place the separator and drive shaft onto the table of a press. Center the ram of the press over the pinion nut.
   d. Support the end of the drive shaft and press the shaft from the sleeve. Discard the sleeve.

2. Install the sleeve as follows:
   a. Use a section of strong tubing to install the sleeve. The inner diameter of the tubing must be large enough to contact the end of the sleeve and still slide over the lower end of the drive shaft.
   b. Slide the replacement sleeve over the pinion gear end of the shaft. Place the shaft on the table of a press. The sleeve must be on top.
   c. Place the installation tool against the sleeve. Center the ram of the press over the installation tool.
   d. Press on the tool until the sleeve seats against the shoulder of the shaft.

3. Remove the tapered roller bearings as follows:
   a. Align the edge of the bearing separator with the gap between the tapered roller bearings (**Figure 148**).
   b. Place the separator and shaft onto the table of a press. The pinion gear side of the shaft must face downward.
   c. Center the ram of the press over the upper end of the drive shaft (**Figure 148**). Support the lower end of the drive shaft while pressing the upper tapered bearing from the shaft.
   d. Align the edge of the bearing separator with the bottom of the lower tapered bearing. Press the bearing from the shaft.

4. Install the tapered roller bearings as follows:
   a. Use a section of tubing to press the bearing onto the shaft.
   b. Slide the short bearing over the upper end of the drive shaft. The tapered side of the bearing must face toward the threaded end of the drive shaft. Slide the tubing over the shaft.
   c. Support the tubing and drive shaft with a bearing separator as shown in **Figure 149**. Place these components on the table of a press. Thread the pinion nut onto the shaft.

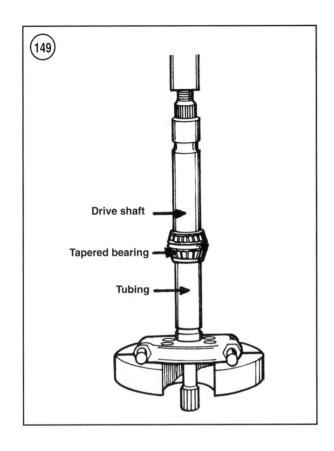

**Drive shaft**

**Tapered bearing**

**Tubing**

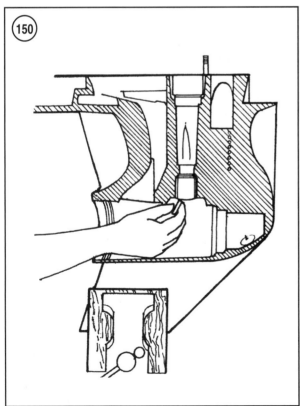

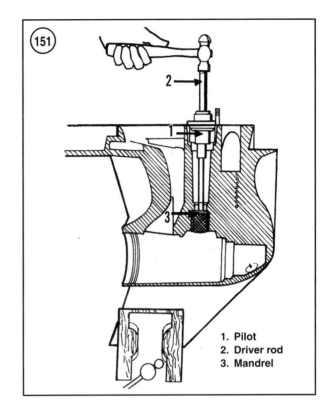

1. Pilot
2. Driver rod
3. Mandrel

d. Center the ram of the press over the pinion nut. Press on the nut until the lower bearing contacts the shoulder on the shaft. Remove the tubing.

e. Slide the tall bearing over the upper end of the drive shaft. The tapered side of the bearing must face toward the *unthreaded* end of the drive shaft. Slide the tubing over the shaft.

f. Press the tall bearing onto the drive shaft as described in this procedure.

**Lower Drive Shaft Bearing Removal and Installation**

Remove the lower drive shaft bearing from the housing only if it must be replaced. The removal process damages the bearing. Refer to *Inspection* in this chapter. Bearing removal requires a special mandrel (Mercury part No. 91-63638), pilot (Mercury part No. 91-813653) and driver rod (Mercury part No. 91-37323). Bearing installation requires a puller bolt and nut (Mercury part Nos. 91-31229 and 91-813653), pilot (Mercury part No. 91-29310) and puller head (Mercury part No. 91-89867T).

1. Insert the bearing rollers into the bearing (**Figure 150**). Slide the pilot over the driver rod. Thread the large diameter side of the mandrel onto the driver rod. Insert the mandrel, pilot and driver rod into the gearcase as shown in **Figure 151**.

**11**

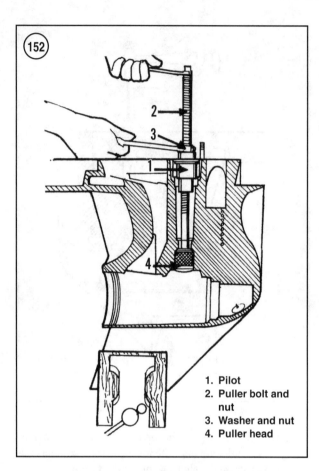

1. Pilot
2. Puller bolt and nut
3. Washer and nut
4. Puller head

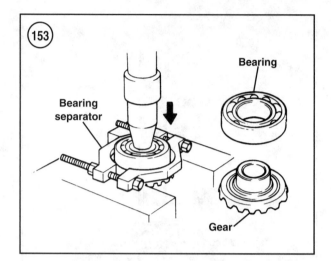

2. Hold the mandrel firmly against the rollers. Tap on the end of the rod until the bearing drops from the bore. Discard the bearing.

3. Install the puller bolt, washer, nut and pilot into the drive shaft bore as shown in **Figure 152**. Place the new bearing onto the puller head. The numbered side must face away from the stepped side of the puller head.

4. Thread the puller head fully onto the puller bolt. Hold the puller bolt with a wrench while tightening the large nut. Continue until the bearing seats in the drive shaft bore. Remove the installation tools.

### Driven Gear Bearing Removal and Installation

Remove the tapered bearing from the driven gear only if it must be replaced. The removal process damages the bearing.

1. Install a bearing separator into the gap between the bearing and the gear (**Figure 153**).

2. Place the separator and gear on the table of a press. Block the separator to allow room for gear travel.

3. Use a suitable driver to press the gear from the bearing. The tool must be slightly smaller in diameter than the hub of the gear. Press the gear from the bearing.

4. Place the gear, tooth-side down, on the table of a press. Place the new tapered bearing onto the hub of the gear. The large diameter side must face toward the gear.

5. Place the used inner bearing race or other suitable tool against the inner race of the bearing.

6. Press the bearing onto the gear until fully seated (**Figure 154**).

### Driven Gear Bearing Race Removal and Installation

Remove the driven gear bearing race when replacing its corresponding tapered roller bearing, or if necessary to correct gear backlash. A driver rod, such as a used propeller shaft or equivalent, is required to install the bearing race. Use Mercury part No. 91-31106 for Bravo I

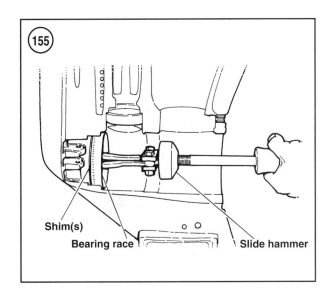

155

Shim(s)

Bearing race    Slide hammer

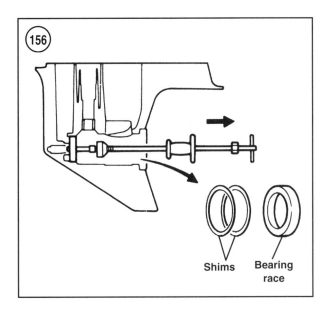

156

Shims    Bearing race

157

**Driven Gear, Pinion Gear and Lower Drive Shaft Installation**

This procedure requires a clamp plate (Mercury part No. 91-43559) and a drive shaft adapter (Mercury part No. 91-61077). A depth micrometer and outside micrometer are also required.

1. Lubricate the bearing with gearcase lubricant, then install the driven gear into the housing (**Figure 144**). Seat the tapered roller bearing against the race. Apply a light coat of gearcase lubricant to the bearings on the drive shaft.

2. If dislodged, apply Needle Bearing Grease (Mercury part No. 92-42649A1) onto the rollers and install them into the bearing cage (**Figure 150**). Do not use other types of grease, as it may cause the rollers to slide instead of roll. The bearing will fail if the rollers slide.

3. Place the pinion gear in the housing. Align the pinion gear with the drive shaft bore. The pinion gear teeth must mesh with the teeth on the front gear.

4. Apply Loctite 271 to the threads of the drive shaft and the new pinion nut.

5. Without dislodging the rollers from the lower drive shaft bearing, insert the drive shaft through the lower bearing and into the pinion gear splines. Rotate the drive shaft as needed to align the splines.

6. Install the washer (27, **Figure 126**) with the concave side facing the pinion gear. Thread a new pinion nut onto the drive shaft. Do not tighten the pinion nut at this time.

7. Slide the tapered bearing race over the drive shaft with the tapered end facing downward. Seat the race against the upper bearing.

8. Place the tab in the opening while installing the tab spacer (5, **Figure 142**). Seat the spacer against the race. Do not install the shims at this time.

9. Use a depth micrometer to measure the distance from the housing surface to the tab spacer (**Figure 157**). Take the measurement at several locations. Record the average depth.

**11**

gearcases. Use Mercury part No. 91-63626 for Bravo II gearcases.

1. Attach a slide hammer to the slots behind the race (**Figure 155**).

2. Use short hammer strokes to remove the race and shims from the housing. Record the thickness of each shim. Replace bent or corroded shims with the same thickness as the original ones.

3. Install the shims (**Figure 156**) in the housing. Lubricate the race with gearcase lubricant and install it into the housing with the tapered side facing out.

4. Set the tapered side of the bearing driver on the bearing race. Insert the driver rod. Keep the driver rod straight and drive the race fully into the bore.

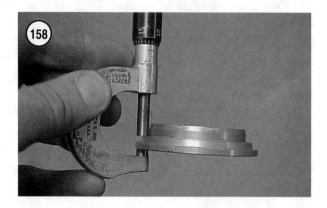

10. Use an outside micrometer to measure the thickness of the bearing cup at the location shown in **Figure 158**. Take the measurement at several locations. Record the average thickness.

11. Subtract the bearing cup thickness (Step 10) from the housing-to-tab spacer distance (Step 9), and then add 0.001 in. to the difference. This value should be approximately 0.051 in.

12. Place shims with a total thickness equal to the amount determined in step 11 onto the tab spacer.

13. Slide the bearing cup (3, **Figure 142**) over the drive shaft with the large diameter side facing the shims. Seat the cup against the shims. Lubricate an O-ring with gearcase lubricant and install it into the groove surrounding the bearing cup.

14. Place the clamp plate over the drive shaft and mounting studs as shown in **Figure 140**. Place two washers over each stud. Tighten the nuts to 35 ft.-lb. (47 N•m).

15. Place the drive shaft adapter onto the drive shaft as shown in **Figure 141**. Rotate the drive shaft several revolutions to seat the bearings.

16. Attach a dial type torque wrench to the drive shaft. Observe the torque reading while rotating the drive shaft. The torque reading indicates the drive shaft bearing preload. The drive shaft preload must be 3-5 in.-lb (0.4-6 N•m).

17. Correct the preload as follows:
   a. Remove the clamp plate (1, **Figure 142**), O-ring (2), bearing cup (3) and shims (4) as described in this chapter.
   b. If the preload is excessive, install a thinner shim pack.
   c. If the preload is insufficient, install a thicker shim pack.
   d. Install the shims, bearing cup, O-ring and clamp plate (**Figure 142**) as described in Steps 7-14.
   e. Measure the drive shaft preload and correct as needed. Several adjustments may be required.

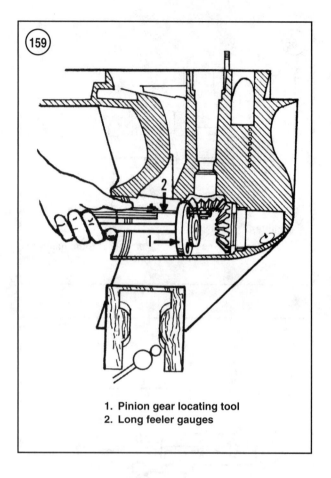

1. Pinion gear locating tool
2. Long feeler gauges

18. Record the drive shaft bearing preload for future reference. Temporarily thread the cover nut into the gearcase to protect the threads.

19. Attach a breaker bar and socket to the pinion nut (**Figure 141**). Tighten the pinion nut to the specification in **Table 1**. Do not remove the clamp plate at this time.

### Pinion Height Adjustment

Set the pinion height if replacing the drive shaft, gears, related bearings or gearcase housing. Long feeler gauges and a pinion gear locating tool are required for this procedure. Purchase or rent the locating tool from a marine dealership. Use Mercury part No. 91-42840 for Bravo I gearcases and Mercury part No. 91-96512 for Bravo II gearcases.

1. Count the number of teeth on the pinion and driven gear.

*NOTE*
*The pinion gear locating tool may have the tooth count stamped next to the openings in the tool. Use the tooth count marks to deter-*

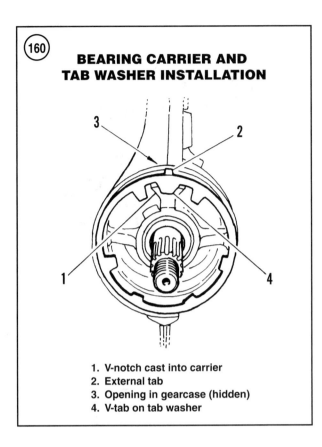

**BEARING CARRIER AND TAB WASHER INSTALLATION**

1. V-notch cast into carrier
2. External tab
3. Opening in gearcase (hidden)
4. V-tab on tab washer

*mine which opening to use while checking pinion gear height. If tooth count marks are not present, use either opening.*

2. Use long feeler gauges to measure the gap between the rounded surface of the locating tool and the teeth or machined surface of the pinion gear (**Figure 159**). Rotate the drive shaft approximately 120° and measure the clearance again. Rotate the shaft another 120° turn and take a third measurement. The pinion gear height equals the thickness of the feeler gauge that passes between the locating tool and the pinion gear teeth with a slight drag. The average pinion gear height must be 0.025 in. (0.64 mm).

3. If the pinion height requires adjustment, determine the necessary shim changes as follows:

   a. If the pinion gear height is below the specification, subtract the measured clearance from 0.025 in. Increase the total shim thickness beneath the lower tapered bearing race by this amount. Decrease the total shim thickness above the upper bearing race by the same amount.

   b. If the pinion gear height exceeds the specification, subtract 0.025 in. from the measured clearance. Decrease the total shim thickness beneath the lower tapered bearing race by this amount. Increase the total

shim thickness above the upper bearing race by the same amount.

4. If a shim change is required, remove the components necessary to access the shims. Reinstall the drive shaft and related components according to the directions in this chapter. Correct the drive shaft preload and measure the pinion height again. Several shim changes may be required. Always install a new pinion nut during assembly.

**Propeller Shaft and Bearing Carrier Installation**

Use a dial type in.-lb. torque wrench to measure the propeller shaft bearing preload. Tighten the cover nut using a cover nut tool. Use Mercury part No. 91-61069 for Bravo I gearcases and Mercury part No. 91-17257 for Bravo II gearcases. The clamp plate (**Figure 140**) must remain in position during this operation.

*NOTE*
*Preload specifications for new bearings may differ from those for used bearings. Bearings are used if spun one revolution under power.*

1. Place the new load ring, spacer and O-ring into the gearcase as shown in **Figure 134**. The tapered side of the spacer must face the O-ring.

2. Apply a light coat of Perfect Seal (Mercury part No. 92-34227-1) to the surfaces of the bearing carrier that contact the housing. Apply a bead of Special Lube 101 (Mercury part No. 92-13872A1) to the lips of the propeller shaft seals.

3. Slide the carrier over the propeller shaft (**Figure 133**). Align the V-notch in the carrier casting (**Figure 160**) with the top side.

4. *Bravo II*—Align the locating key slot in the carrier with the key slot in the housing. Insert the key (35, **Figure 127**) into the slots.

5. Slide the tab washer over the propeller shaft (**Figure 132**). Place the external tab (2, **Figure 160**) of the tab washer into the opening in the gearcase (3).

6. Rotate the bearing carrier to align the V-notch in the carrier (1, **Figure 160**) with the V-tab of the tab washer. Seat the tab washer against the carrier.

7. Apply Special Lube 101 (Mercury part No. 92-13872A1) to the threads of the cover nut (**Figure 131**). Install the cover nut into the gearcase. The directional marks must face outward.

8. Position the gearcase with the propeller shaft facing upward. Thread the nut onto the propeller shaft. Use a

**11**

socket to attach an in.-lb. torque wrench to the propeller shaft (**Figure 161**).

9. Observe the reading on the torque wrench while rotating the propeller shaft. Subtract the drive shaft preload (recorded during drive shaft installation) from the reading to determine the actual propeller shaft preload.

10. Slide the cover nut tool (Mercury part No. 91-61069) over the propeller shaft (**Figure 130**). Tighten the cover nut until the propeller shaft can be moved in and out approximately 1/8 in (3.2 mm). Do not eliminate all propeller shaft play at this time.

11. Measure the propeller shaft preload as described in step 9. Tighten the cover nut approximately 1/16 turn and measure the preload again. Continue this sequence until the propeller shaft preload reaches the specification in **Table 4**. Do not exceed the preload specification. If exceeded, remove the bearing carrier and replace the load ring.

12. Use large slip joint pliers and bend one of the tabs into a slot in the cover nut (**Figure 162**). Tighten the cover nut to align the tab with the slot. Monitor the bearing preload while tightening the nut. Do not exceed the preload specification. Never loosen the nut to align the tab.

### Gear Lash

This operation requires a dial indicator and, backlash indicator arm (Mercury part No. 91-53459). The clamp plate (**Figure 140**) must remain in position for this operation.

1. Position the gearcase with the lower drive shaft facing upward.

2. Clamp the backlash indicator arm onto the drive shaft as shown in **Figure 163**. Use a clamp or one of the clamp plate studs to attach the dial indicator to the gearcase (**Figure 163**). Position the tip of the indicator at a 90° angle to the arm (**Figure 164**) and aligned with the proper mark.

   a. *Bravo I*—Align the pointer tip with the *I* mark.

   b. *Bravo II*—Align the pointer tip with the *II* mark.

3. Record the dial indicator reading while gently rotating the drive shaft in both directions. Loosen the backlash indicator tool and rotate the drive shaft 90°. Reposition the dial indicator and backlash indicator tool and repeat the measurement. Repeat this step until four measurements are taken. Record the average of the measurements.

4. Correct backlash is 0.012-0.015 in. (0.30-0.38 mm) for Bravo I gearcases and 0.009-0.015 in. (0.23-0.38 mm) for Bravo II gearcases. If the backlash is incorrect, perform the following:

   a. Disassemble the gearcase to access the shims beneath the driven gear bearing race (30, **Figure 126** or 30, **Figure 127**).

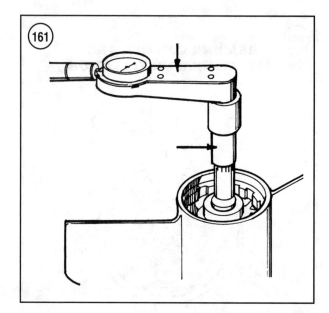

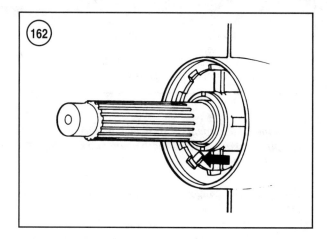

   b. Install thinner or fewer shims to increase the gear backlash. Install thicker or additional shims to decrease the gear backlash.

   c. A 0.001 in. change in shim thickness changes the backlash reading by approximately 0.001 in. Several changes may be required to correct the backlash.

5. Install the carrier anode (**Figure 128**) as described in Chapter Fifteen.

6. Remove the clamp plate (**Figure 140**), backlash indicator arm and dial indicator. Attach the gearcase to the drive shaft housing as described in this chapter.

### BRAVO III DRIVE

The drive shaft, pinion gear and front driven gear used on the Bravo III gearcase are very similar to those used on

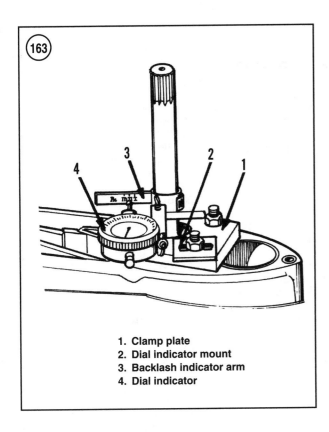

1. Clamp plate
2. Dial indicator mount
3. Backlash indicator arm
4. Dial indicator

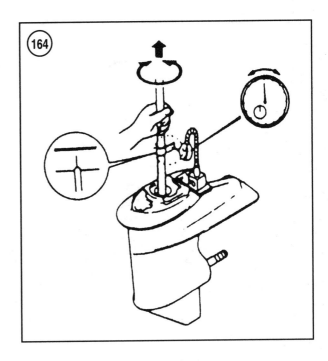

Bravo I and II gearcases. The propeller shaft, bearing carrier and related components are different.

For component identification and orientation, refer to **Figure 165**.

### Propeller Shaft Runout

Runout measurement requires a dial indicator and a clamp to attach the indicator to the gearcase. Perform this measurement before disassembling the gearcase.

1. Clamp the dial indicator to the gearcase so that the dial indicator tip touches the inner propeller shaft (**Figure 166**). The dial indicator tip must be at a 90° angle to the length of the propeller shaft, touching midway between the splines and the tapered section of the shaft.
2. Observe the dial indicator while rotating the inner propeller shaft. A reading above 0.005 in. (0.127 mm) indicates excessive propeller shaft runout. Replace the inner propeller shaft.
3. Clamp the dial indicator to the gearcase so that the dial indicator tip touches the outer propeller shaft (**Figure 167**). The dial indicator tip must be at a 90° angle to the length of the propeller shaft, touching midway between the splines and the tapered section of the shaft..
4. Observe the dial indicator while rotating the outer propeller shaft. A reading above 0.005 in. (0.127 mm) indi-

cates excessive propeller shaft runout. Replace the outer propeller shaft.

### Bearing Carrier and Propeller Shaft Removal

Use a bearing carrier tool (Mercury part No. 91-805374-1) to loosen the bearing carrier. Use a bearing retainer tool (Mercury part No. 91-905382) and the bearing carrier tool to loosen the bearing retainer.

*NOTE*
*The bearing carrier and the bearing retainer have left-hand threads. Rotate the bearing carrier and bearing retainer clockwise to loosen and counterclockwise to tighten.*

1. Position the gearcase with the drive shaft facing upward.
2. Slide the bearing carrier tool over the carrier.
3. Attach a 1/2 in. breaker bar to the bearing carrier tool (**Figure 168**). Turn the carrier clockwise until fully loosened. Pull the carrier from the housing. Remove the O-ring from the carrier. Discard the O-ring.
4. Slide the retainer tool over the propeller shaft (**Figure 169**). Engage the lugs of the tool with the notches in the bearing retainer (41, **Figure 165**).
5. Align the flat surfaces and slide the adapter over the retainer tool (**Figure 170**).
6. Attach a 1/2 in. breaker bar to the adapter. Turn the retainer tool clockwise until fully loosened.

**11**

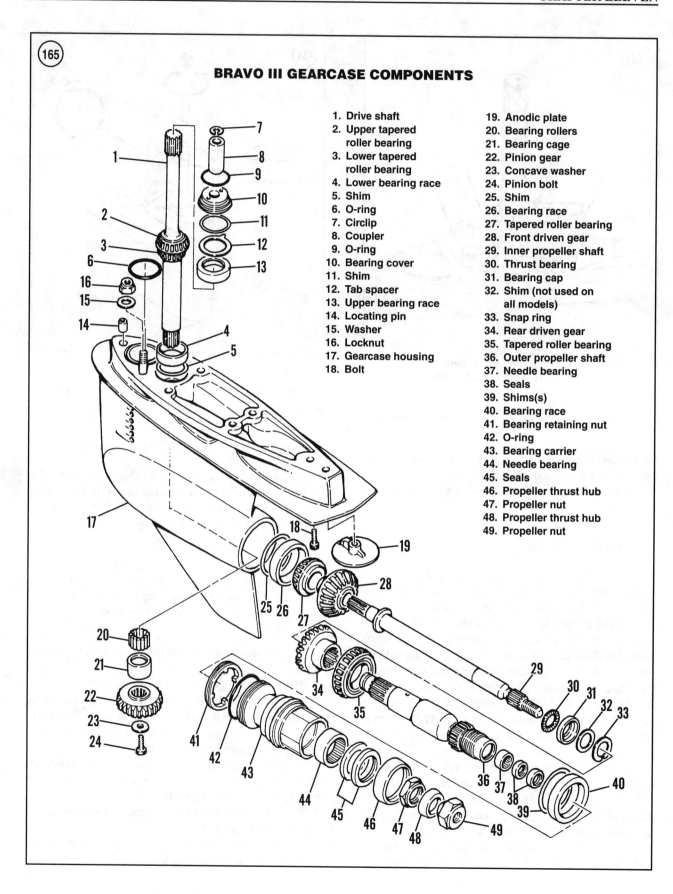

**BRAVO III GEARCASE COMPONENTS**

1. Drive shaft
2. Upper tapered roller bearing
3. Lower tapered roller bearing
4. Lower bearing race
5. Shim
6. O-ring
7. Circlip
8. Coupler
9. O-ring
10. Bearing cover
11. Shim
12. Tab spacer
13. Upper bearing race
14. Locating pin
15. Washer
16. Locknut
17. Gearcase housing
18. Bolt
19. Anodic plate
20. Bearing rollers
21. Bearing cage
22. Pinion gear
23. Concave washer
24. Pinion bolt
25. Shim
26. Bearing race
27. Tapered roller bearing
28. Front driven gear
29. Inner propeller shaft
30. Thrust bearing
31. Bearing cap
32. Shim (not used on all models)
33. Snap ring
34. Rear driven gear
35. Tapered roller bearing
36. Outer propeller shaft
37. Needle bearing
38. Seals
39. Shims(s)
40. Bearing race
41. Bearing retaining nut
42. O-ring
43. Bearing carrier
44. Needle bearing
45. Seals
46. Propeller thrust hub
47. Propeller nut
48. Propeller thrust hub
49. Propeller nut

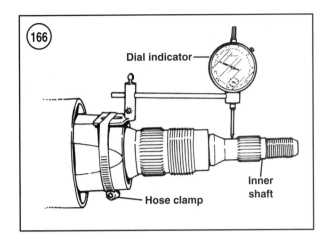

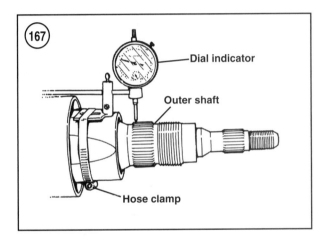

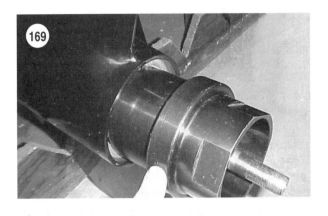

7. Position the gearcase with the propeller shaft facing upward. Grasp the inner propeller shaft (29, **Figure 165**) and pull the propeller shaft assembly from the gearcase.

8. Pull the bearing race (40, **Figure 165**) from the rear tapered roller bearing (35). Remove the shims (39, **Figure 165**) from the housing.

**Bearing Carrier Propeller Shaft Seals
Removal and Installation**

**11**

Remove the propeller shaft seals only if leaking, worn or damaged. The removal process damages the seals. Use an installation tool (Mercury part No. 91-805372) to seat the seals to the proper depth in the carrier.

1. Clamp the carrier in a vise with protective jaws.

2. Pry the propeller shaft seals from the carrier (**Figure 135**), taking care not to damage the bore. Discard the seals.

3. If the needle bearing (44, **Figure 165**) needs replacement, do so before installing the propeller shaft seals.

4. Clean all lubricant from the seal bore with a quick drying solvent.

5. Apply a light coat of Loctite 271 to the seal bore and the outer diameter of the new assembly. The replacement seal assembly incorporates both seals into a single casing.

6. Place the bearing carrier on the table of a press with the threaded side down. Place the seal assembly into the bore with the white plastic side facing up.

7. Insert the seal installation tool through the seal bore. Press the tool until it seats against the carrier (**Figure 136**).

8. Wipe excess Loctite from the seal bore. Apply a bead of Special Lube 101 (Mercury part No. 92-13872A1) to the seal lips.

### Bearing Carrier Needle Bearing Removal and Installation

Remove the needle bearing only if it must be replaced. The removal process damages the bearing. Use the installation tool (Mercury part No. 91-805356) to seat the bearing at the proper depth in the bore.

1. Use an appropriately sized socket and extension or section of tubing as a bearing removal tool.

2. Place the carrier on a press with the threaded side face up. Block the carrier to allow bearing clearance beneath the carrier. Insert the removal tool into the gear side bore of the carrier (**Figure 137**). The tool must contact the lip of the bearing cage.

3. Press the needle bearing out of the carrier. Discard the bearing.

4. Thoroughly clean the bearing carrier. Replace the carrier if it is pitted from corrosion, cracked or has damage in the bearing or seal bore.

5. Lubricate the bearing and carrier bore with gearcase lubricant. Insert the new needle bearing into the seal end of the bore with the numbered side facing outward (**Figure 138**).

6. Insert the installation tool (part No. 91-805356) into the bore with the large diameter side facing outward. The small diameter side must squarely contact the numbered side of the bearing.

7. Place the carrier on a press with the threaded side facing downward.

8. Press the bearing into the bore (**Figure 138**) until the installation tool seats against the carrier.

### Propeller Shaft Disassembly

Refer to **Figure 165**.

1. Pull the inner propeller shaft from the outer propeller shaft.

2. Remove the thrust bearing (30, **Figure 165**) from the inner propeller shaft.

3. Use a brass drift to drive the bearing cap (31, **Figure 165**) from the outer propeller shaft. Position the drift between the cap and the snap ring. Tap gently while working the drift around the circumference of the cap. Retrieve the shim(s) (32, **Figure 165**) from the bearing cap. Later production drives do not use shims.

4. Remove the snap ring (33, **Figure 165**) from the outer propeller shaft. Pull the rear driven gear and bearing assembly from the shaft.

5. Thoroughly clean the propeller shaft components. Inspect the components for wear or damage as described in this chapter.

### *Propeller shaft seals removal and installation (outer propeller shaft)*

Remove the seals (38, **Figure 165**) from the outer propeller shaft only if leaking, worn or damaged. The removal process damages the seals. Use an installation tool (Mercury part No. 91-805358T) to seat the seals at the proper depth in the carrier.

1. Clamp the outer propeller shaft in a vise with protective jaws.

2. Attach a slide hammer puller against the back of the inner seal casing. Use short hammer strokes to remove the seals from the shaft. Discard the seals.

3. If the needle bearing (37, **Figure 165**) needs to be replaced, do so before installing the propeller shaft seals.

4. Clean the seal bore with a quick drying solvent.

5. Apply a light coat of Loctite 271 to the seal bore and the outer diameter of the new seal assembly. The replacement seal assembly incorporates both seals into a single casing.

6. Support the outer propeller shaft on the table of a press with the seal bore facing upward. Place the seal assembly into the bore with the white plastic side facing upward.

7. Insert the seal installation tool through the seal bore. Press on the tool until it seats against the propeller shaft.

8. Wipe excess Loctite from the seal bore. Apply a bead of Special Lube 101 (Mercury part No. 92-13872A1) to the seal lips.

### *Needle bearing removal and installation (outer propeller shaft)*

Remove the needle bearing (37, **Figure 165**) from the outer propeller shaft only if it must be replaced. The removal process damages the bearing. Use a bearing installation tool (Mercury part No. 91-805352T) to install the bearing at the proper depth.

1. Clamp the outer propeller shaft in a vise with protective jaws.

2. Attach a slide hammer puller to the back of the bearing cage. Use short hammer strokes to pull the bearing from the shaft.

3. Thoroughly clean the propeller shaft bore. Replace the propeller shaft if the bore is rough, discolored or pitted.

4. Lubricate the replacement bearing and propeller shaft bore with gearcase lubricant. Insert the new needle bearing into propeller shaft bore with the numbered side facing outward.

5. Support the propeller shaft on the table of a press.

6. Insert the installation tool (part No. 91-805352T) into the bearing bore with the larger diameter side facing outward. The smaller diameter side must squarely contact the numbered side of the bearing.

7. Press the bearing into the bore (**Figure 138**) until the installation tool seats against the propeller shaft.

## Pinion Gear, Lower Drive Shaft and Driven Gear Removal

This operation requires a clamp plate (Mercury part No. 91-43559) and a drive shaft adapter (Mercury part No. 91-61077).

1. Place the clamp plate over the drive shaft and mounting studs as shown in **Figure 140**. Place two washers over each stud and secure the plate using the gearcase mounting nuts.

2. Place the drive shaft adapter onto the drive shaft as shown in **Figure 141**. Temporarily thread the cover nut into the gearcase to protect the threads.

3. Attach a breaker bar and socket to the pinion bolt (**Figure 141**). Remove the pinion bolt and washer.

4. Remove the clamp plate. Carefully pry the O-ring (2, **Figure 142**) from the bearing cup and housing. Discard the O-ring. Lift the bearing cup (3, **Figure 142**) and shims (4) over the drive shaft. Pull up on the port side of the tab spacer (5, **Figure 142**) to free the tab from the opening in the drive shaft bore. Remove the tab spacer.

5. Support the pinion gear while lifting the drive shaft from the gearcase (**Figure 143**). Remove the driven gear (**Figure 144**).

6. Remove the lower bearing race only if necessary to correct the pinion gear height, or if replacing the lower tapered roller bearing. Remove the race as follows:

   a. Attach a slide hammer puller to the back side of the race (**Figure 145**). Use short hammer strokes to remove the race and shims.

   b. Retrieve the bearing rollers if dislodged (**Figure 146**). Record the thickness of each shim. Replace bent or corroded shims with the same thickness as the original ones.

   c. Position the shims in the drive shaft bore. Use an appropriately sized socket and extension or section of tubing to install the bearing race. The tool must be large enough to contact the outer diameter of the race, but not contact the housing.

   d. Place the race into the bore with the tapered side facing upward. Drive the race into the bore until fully seated.

## Lower Drive Shaft Disassembly and Assembly

Disassemble the lower drive shaft only if the shaft or bearings must be replaced.

1. Remove the bearing sleeve as follows:

   a. Thread the pinion bolt into the drive shaft (**Figure 147**).

   b. Adjust the bearing separator to the size needed to contact the upper edge of the sleeve.

   c. Place the separator and drive shaft onto the table of a press. Center the ram of the press over the pinion bolt.

   d. Support the end of the drive shaft and press the shaft from the sleeve. Discard the sleeve.

2. Install the sleeve as follows:

   a. Use a section of strong tubing to install the sleeve. The inner diameter of the tubing must be large enough to contact the end of the sleeve but still slide over the lower end of the drive shaft.

   b. Slide the new sleeve over the pinion gear end of the shaft. Place the shaft on the table of a press with the sleeve on top.

   c. Place the installation tool against the sleeve. Center the ram of the press over the installation tool.

   d. Press on the tool until the sleeve seats against the shoulder on the shaft.

3. Remove the tapered roller bearings as follows:

   a. Position the edge of a bearing separator into the gap between the tapered roller bearings (**Figure 148**).

   b. Place the separator and shaft onto the table of a press. The pinion gear side of the shaft must face downward.

   c. Center the ram of the press over the upper end of the drive shaft (**Figure 148**). Support the lower end of the drive shaft while pressing the upper tapered bearing from the shaft.

   d. Align the edge of the bearing separator with the bottom of the lower tapered bearing. Press the remaining bearing from the shaft as described in this procedure.

4. Install the tapered roller bearings as follows:

   a. Use a section of tubing to press the bearing onto the shaft.

   b. Slide the short bearing over the upper end of the drive shaft. The tapered side of the bearing must face toward the threaded end of the drive shaft. Slide the tubing over the shaft.

**11**

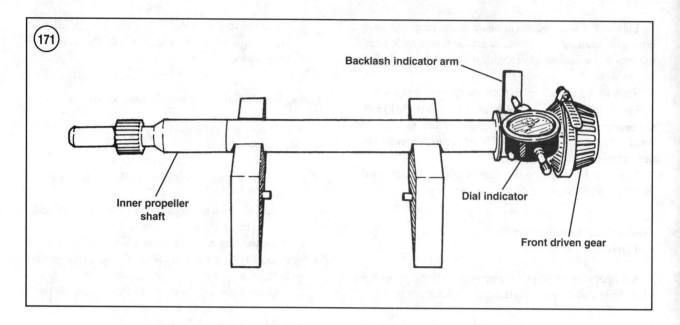

c. Support the tubing and drive shaft with a bearing separator as shown in **Figure 149**. Place these parts on the table of a press. Thread the used pinion bolt into the shaft.

d. Press on the bolt until the lower bearing contacts the shoulder on the shaft. Remove the tubing.

e. Slide the tall bearing over the upper end of the drive shaft. The tapered side of the bearing must face the *unthreaded* end of the drive shaft. Slide the tubing over the shaft.

f. Press the tall bearing onto the drive shaft as described in this procedure.

## Lower Drive Shaft Bearing Removal and Installation

Remove the lower drive shaft bearing only if it must be replaced. The removal process damages the bearing. Bearing removal requires a special mandrel (Mercury part No. 91-63638), pilot (Mercury part No. 91-813653) and driver rod (Mercury part No. 91-37323). Bearing installation requires a puller bolt and nut (Mercury part Nos. 91-31229 and 91-813653), pilot (Mercury part No. 91-29310) and puller head (Mercury part No. 91-89867T).

1. Insert the bearing rollers into the bearing (**Figure 150**). Slide the pilot over the driver rod. Thread the larger diameter side of the mandrel onto the driver rod. Insert the mandrel, pilot and driver rod into the gearcase as shown in **Figure 151**.

2. Hold the mandrel tightly against the rollers. Tap on the end of the rod until the bearing drops from the bore. Do not use excessive force which can break the bearing cage.

3. Discard the bearing.

4. Install the puller bolt, washer, nut and pilot into the drive shaft bore as shown in **Figure 152**. Place the new bearing onto the puller head. The numbered side must face away from the stepped side of the puller head.

5. Thread the puller head onto the puller bolt. Hold the puller bolt with a wrench while tightening the large nut. Continue until the bearing seats in the drive shaft bore. Remove the installation tools.

## Driven Gear Bearing Removal and Installation

Remove the tapered bearing from the driven gears (28 and 34, **Figure 165**) only if defective. The removal process damages the bearing.

1. Position the edge of a bearing separator into the gap between the bearing and the gear (**Figure 153**).

2. Place the separator and gear on the table of a press.

3. Use a socket or section of tubing to press the gear from the bearing.

4. Press the gear from the bearing.

5. Place the gear, teeth facing down, on the table of a press. Place the new tapered bearing onto the hub of the gear. The large diameter side must face the gear.

6. Place the used inner bearing race or other suitable tool against the inner race of the bearing. Press the bearing onto the gear until fully seated (**Figure 154**).

### *Gear spline play measurement*

Measure the gear spline wear if replacing the gears and related bearings. This procedure requires a dial indicator,

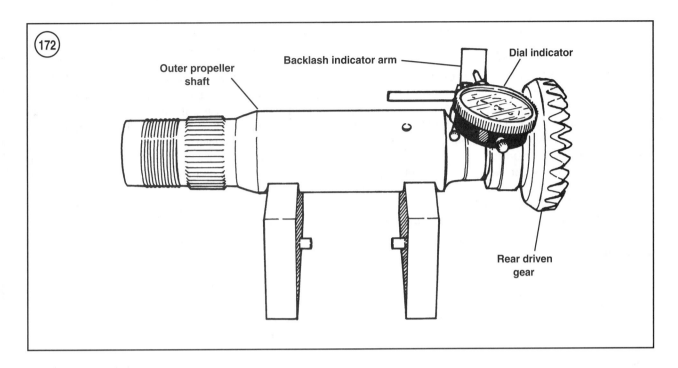

backlash indicator arm (Mercury part No. (91-806192) and an appropriate size hose clamp.

1. Support the inner propeller shaft on V-blocks (**Figure 171**).

2. Slip the backlash indicator arm over the front of the propeller shaft. Tighten the clamp screw. Slide the front driven gear onto the propeller shaft splines as shown in **Figure 171**.

3. Use a hose clamp to attach the dial indicator to the driven gear. Align the tip of the dial indicator with the mark on the backlash indicator arm. Position the tip at a 90° angle to the arm (**Figure 171**).

4. Observe the dial indicator movement while gently rotating the gear on the shaft. Record the dial indicator reading as front gear spline play.

5. Support the outer propeller shaft on V-blocks (**Figure 172**).

6. Slip the backlash indicator arm over the front of the propeller shaft. Tighten the clamp screw. Slide the front driven gear onto the propeller shaft splines as shown in **Figure 172**.

7. Use a hose clamp to attach the dial indicator to the driven gear. Align the tip of the dial indicator with the mark on the backlash indicator arm. Position the tip at a 90° angle to the arm (**Figure 172**).

8. Observe the dial indicator movement while gently rotating the gear on the shaft. Record the dial indicator reading as rear gear spline play.

**Front Bearing Race**
**Removal and Installation**

Remove the front bearing race (26, **Figure 165**) if replacing its corresponding tapered roller bearing, or if necessary to correct gear backlash. Use a bearing driver (Mercury part No. 91-805454) and a used propeller shaft or other suitable rod to install the bearing race.

1. Attach a slide hammer puller to the slots behind the race (**Figure 155**).

2. Use short hammer strokes to pull the race and shims from the housing. Record the thickness of each shim. Replace bent or corroded shims.

3. Place the shims (**Figure 156**) into the housing. Lubricate the bearing race with gearcase lubricant and install it into the housing. The tapered side must face outward.

4. Set the tapered side of the bearing driver onto the bearing race (**Figure 156**). Insert the driver rod. Keep the driver rod straight and drive the race fully into the bore.

**Driven Gear, Pinion Gear and Lower Drive Shaft**
**Removal and Installation**

This procedure requires a clamp plate (Mercury part No. 91-43559) and a drive shaft adapter (Mercury part No. 91-61077). A depth micrometer and outside micrometer are also required.

*NOTE*
*Preload specifications for new bearings may differ from those for used bearings.*

**11**

*Bearings are used if spun one revolution under power.*

1. Lubricate the bearing with gearcase lubricant, then place the driven gear into the housing (**Figure 144**). Seat the tapered roller bearing against the race. Apply a light coat of gearcase lubricant to the bearings on the drive shaft.

2. If dislodged, apply Needle Bearing Grease (Mercury part No. 92-42649A1) onto the rollers and install them into the bearing cage (**Figure 150**). Do not use other types of grease, which can cause the rollers to slide instead of roll. The bearing will fail if the rollers slide.

3. Place the pinion gear in the housing. Align the pinion gear with the drive shaft bore. The pinion gear teeth must mesh with the teeth on the front mounted gear.

4. Apply Loctite 271 to the threads of the drive shaft and the new pinion bolt.

5. Without dislodging the rollers from the lower drive shaft bearing, insert the drive shaft through the lower bearing and into the pinion gear splines. Rotate the drive shaft as needed to align the splines.

6. Install the washer (23, **Figure 165**) with the concave side facing the pinion gear. Thread a new pinion bolt into the drive shaft. Do not tighten the pinion bolt at this time.

7. Slide the tapered bearing race over the drive shaft with the tapered end facing downward. Seat the race against the upper bearing.

8. Place the tab in the opening while installing the tab spacer (5, **Figure 142**). Seat the spacer against the race. Do not install the shims at this time.

9. Use a depth micrometer to measure the distance from the housing surface to the tab spacer (**Figure 157**). Take the measurement at several locations. Record the average depth.

10. Use an outside micrometer to measure the thickness of the bearing cup at the location shown in **Figure 158**. Take the measurement at several locations. Record the average thickness.

11. Subtract the housing surface-to-tab spacer distance (Step 9) from the bearing cup thickness (Step 10), then add 0.001 in. to the difference. This value should be approximately 0.051 in.).

12. Place shims with a total thickness equal to the amount determined in step 11 onto the tab spacer.

13. Slide the bearing cup (3, **Figure 142**) over the drive shaft with the large diameter side toward the shims. Seat the cup against the shims. Lubricate an O-ring with gearcase lubricant, then install it into the groove around the bearing cup.

14. Place the clamp plate over the drive shaft and mounting studs as shown in **Figure 140**. Place two washers over each stud. Tighten the nuts to 35 ft.-lb. (47 N•m).

15. Install the drive shaft adapter onto the drive shaft as shown in **Figure 141**. Rotate the drive shaft several revolutions to seat the bearings.

16. Attach a dial type torque wrench to the drive shaft. Observe the torque reading while rotating the drive shaft. The torque reading indicates the drive shaft bearing preload. The bearing preload must be 3-5 in.-lb. (4-6 N•m).

17. Correct the preload as follows:

   a. Remove the clamp plate (1, **Figure 142**), O-ring (2), bearing cup (3) and shims (4) as described in this chapter.

   b. If the preload exceeds the specification, install shims with less total thickness.

   c. If the preload is below the specification, install shims with greater total thickness.

   d. Install the shims, bearing cup, O-ring and clamp plate (**Figure 142**).

   e. Measure the drive shaft preload and correct as needed. Several adjustments may be required.

18. Temporarily thread the cover nut into the gearcase to protect the threads.

19. Using a breaker bar and socket (**Figure 141**), tighten the pinion bolt to the specification in **Table 1**. Do not remove the clamp plate at this time.

## Pinion Gear Height Adjustment

The pinion gear height must be set if the pinion gear, drive shaft, driven gears or any bearing is replaced. This procedure requires long feeler gauges and a pinion gear locating tool (Mercury part No. 91-806462T). Purchase or rent the locating tool from a marine dealership.

1. Count the number of teeth on the pinion and driven gear.

*NOTE*
*The pinion gear locating tool may have the tooth count stamped next to the openings in the tool. Use the tooth count marks to determine which opening to use while checking pinion gear height. If tooth count marks are not present, use either opening.*

2. Slide the pinion gear locating tool into the gearcase (**Figure 159**). Position the opening in the tool that has the correct tooth count under the pinion gear. Seat the tool against the shoulder in the housing.

3. Use long feeler gauges to measure the gap between the rounded surface of the locating tool and the teeth or machined surface of the pinion gear. Rotate the drive shaft approximately 120° and measure the clearance again. Rotate the shaft (120°) and take a third measurement. The pinion gear height equals the thickness of the feeler gauge

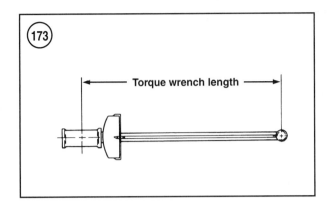

that passes between the locating tool and the pinion gear teeth with a slight drag. The average pinion gear height must be 0.025 in. (0.64 mm).

4. If the pinion height is incorrect, determine the necessary shim changes as follows:

    a. If the pinion height below the specification, subtract the measured clearance from 0.025 in. Increase the total shim thickness beneath the lower tapered bearing race by the difference. Decrease the total shim thickness above the upper bearing race by the same amount.

    b. If the pinion height exceeds the specification, subtract 0.025 in. from the measured clearance. Decrease the total shim thickness beneath the lower tapered bearing race by the difference. Increase the total shim thickness above the upper bearing race by the same amount.

5. Remove the drive shaft components to access the shims. Reinstall the drive shaft and related components as described in this chapter. Correct the drive shaft preload and remeasure the pinion height again. Several shim changes may be required. Always install a new pinion bolt during assembly.

**Propeller Shaft Assembly**

Refer to **Figure 165**.

1. Align the splines while sliding the rear driven gear (34, **Figure 165**) onto the outer propeller shaft (36). The gear teeth must face away from the propeller end of the shaft. Do not apply lubricant to the shaft splines. Install the snap ring (33, **Figure 165**) into the groove next to the gear.

2. Support the outer propeller shaft on the table of a press with the gear side facing upward. Apply a light coat of Loctite 242 to the mating surface then place the shims (32, **Figure 165**) on the top of the shaft. Place the open end of the bearing cap (31, **Figure 165**) over the shims and the

end of the shaft. Center the cap and shaft under the press ram. Press the cap fully onto the shaft.

3. Slide the thrust bearing (30, **Figure 165**) over the propeller end of the inner propeller shaft (29). Seat the bearing against the step near the front of the shaft.

4. Without dislodging the thrust bearing, slide the splined end through the outer propeller shaft bore. Seat the inner propeller shaft and thrust bearing against the thrust cap on the outer propeller shaft.

**Propeller Shaft and Bearing Carrier Installation**

Use a bearing carrier tool (Mercury part No. 91-805374-1) to tighten the bearing carrier. Use a bearing retainer tool (Mercury part No. 91-905382) and the bearing carrier tool to tighten the bearing retainer.

*NOTE*
*The bearing carrier and the bearing retainer have left-hand threads. Rotate the bearing carrier and bearing retainer clockwise to loosen and counterclockwise to tighten.*

1. Turn the gearcase so the bearing carrier opening faces up. Install the shims (39, **Figure 165**) into the gear housing.

2. Grasp the propeller end of the inner propeller shaft. Carefully lower the propeller shaft assembly into the housing. Guide the splined end of the inner propeller shaft into the front driven gear. Rotate the outer propeller shaft to mesh the gear teeth and seat the propeller shaft against the front gear.

3. Lubricate the bearing race (40, **Figure 165**) with gearcase lubricant and install it in the housing. The tapered side must face inward. Seat the race against the tapered roller bearing (35, **Figure 165**) of the rear driven gear.

4. Lubricate the threads of the bearing retainer (41, **Figure 165**) with gearcase lubricant. Thread the retainer onto the gearcase threads. The directional marks on the retainer must face outward.

5. Slide the retainer tool over the propeller shaft (**Figure 169**). Engage the lugs of the tool with the notches in the bearing retainer (41, **Figure 165**).

6. Slide the adapter over the retainer nut tool (**Figure 170**), aligning the flat surfaces.

7. Measure the torque wrench length from the center of the handle with the center of the square socket connector (**Figure 173**). Record the measurement.

8. Connect the torque wrench to the adapter. Torque the retainer (counter-clockwise) to the specification in **Table 1**.

9. Lubricate a new O-ring with Special Lube 101 (Mercury part No. 92-13872A1) then slide it (42, **Figure 165**)

**11**

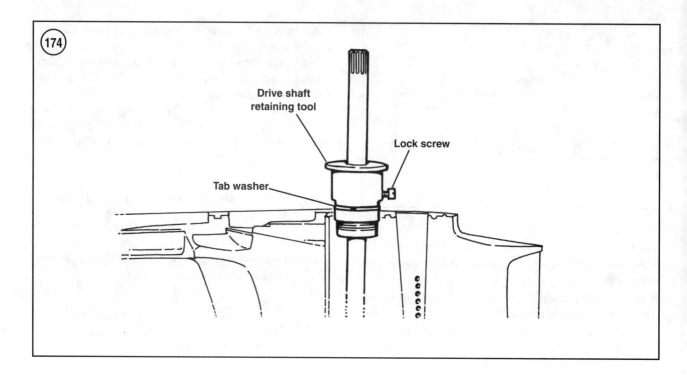

Drive shaft retaining tool

Lock screw

Tab washer

into in the carrier (43). Apply a light coat of Special Lube 101 to the bearing carrier.

10. Slide the bearing carrier over the propeller shafts. Thread the carrier into the housing. Slide the bearing carrier tool over the body of the carrier (**Figure 168**), aligning the lugs into the slots.

11. Torque the carrier (counterclockwise) to the specification in **Table 1**.

### Gear Lash

Check the gear backlash if replacing gears, shafts, bearings or the housing. This procedure requires a dial indicator, inner shaft backlash indicator arm (Mercury part No. 91-805481), outer shaft backlash indicator arm (Mercury part No. 91-805482), and a drive shaft retainer (Mercury part No. 91-805381).

1. Remove the clamp plate (1, **Figure 142**), O-ring (2), bearing cup (3) and shims (4) from the drive shaft. Do not remove the tab spacer or bearing race.

2. Slide the drive shaft retainer over the drive shaft as shown in **Figure 174**. Position the gearcase so the propeller shafts face upward. Rotate the drive shaft while pushing the retainer against the tab spacer. Hold the retainer in position and securely tighten the lock screw (**Figure 174**).

3. Attach the backlash indicator arm (Mercury part No. 91-805481) to the inner propeller shaft as shown in **Figure 175**. Attach a dial indicator to the bearing carrier using hose clamps.

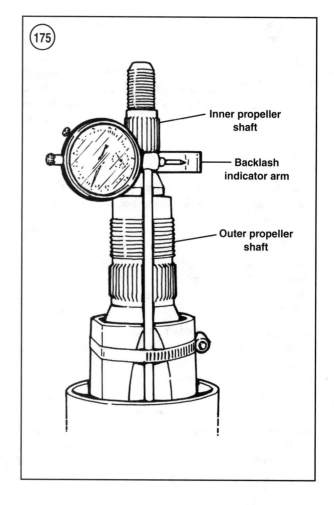

Inner propeller shaft

Backlash indicator arm

Outer propeller shaft

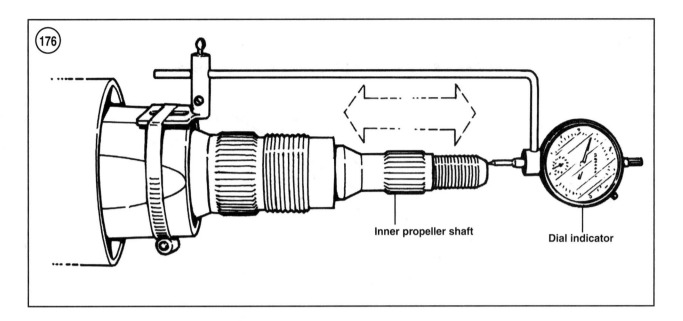

Inner propeller shaft

Dial indicator

4. Position the dial indicator tip at a 90° angle to the indicator arm and align the indicator tip with the mark on the arm.

5. Record the dial indicator reading while gently rotating the inner propeller shaft in both directions. Subtract the recorded *front gear spline play* (see *Measuring Gear Spline Play Measurement*) from the dial indicator reading to determine the actual gear backlash. The gear backlash for the front gear must be 0.012-0.016 in. (0.3-0.4 mm).

6. Correct the front gear backlash as follows:

   a. Disassemble the gearcase enough to access the shims beneath the driven gear bearing race (25. **Figure 165**).

   b. If the backlash measurement is too low, install thinner or fewer shims beneath the race.

   c. If the backlash measurement is excessive, install thicker or additional shims beneath the race.

   d. A 0.001 in. change in shim thickness changes the backlash measurement by approximately 0.001 in.

   e. Reassemble the gearcase as described in this chapter.

7. Install the drive shaft retainer as described in step 1 and step 2.

8. Position the gearcase with the propeller shaft facing downward. Attach the backlash indicator arm (Mercury part No. 91-805482) to the outer propeller shaft. Position the dial indicator as described in Step 3 and Step 4.

9. Record the dial indicator reading while gently rotating the outer propeller shaft in both directions. Subtract the recorded *rear gear spline play* (*Gear Spline Play Measurement*) from the dial indicator reading to determine the

actual gear backlash. The gear backlash for the rear gear must be 0.012-0.016 in. (0.3-0.4 mm).

10. Correct the front gear backlash as follows:

   a. Disassemble the gearcase to access the shims beneath the driven gear bearing race (39, **Figure 165**).

   b. If the backlash measurement is low, install thicker or additional shims beneath the race.

   c. If the backlash measurement is excessive, install thinner or fewer shims beneath the race.

   d. A 0.001 in. change in shim thickness changes the backlash measurement by approximately 0.001 in.

   e. Assemble the gearcase as described in this chapter.

   f. Measure the backlash again. Several shim changes may be required.

**Propeller Shaft End Play**

This procedure requires a dial indicator, a 20 in. (51 cm) section of stiff metal rod and a clamp to mount the dial indicator on the rod. Bend the rod as shown in **Figure 176**.

1. Position the gearcase with the propeller shafts facing upward.

2. Use a hose clamp to attach the metal rod to the bearing carrier (**Figure 176**).

3. Align the dial indicator in with the flat surface at the end of the inner propeller shaft.

4. Push down on the inner propeller shaft. Rotate the face of the dial indicator to align the pointer with the 0 mark.

5. Observe the dial indicator while pulling up and pushing down on the inner propeller shaft. Do not move the outer propeller shaft. The end play must be 0.001-0.050 in. (0.025-1.27 mm). Adjust the end play as follows:

**11**

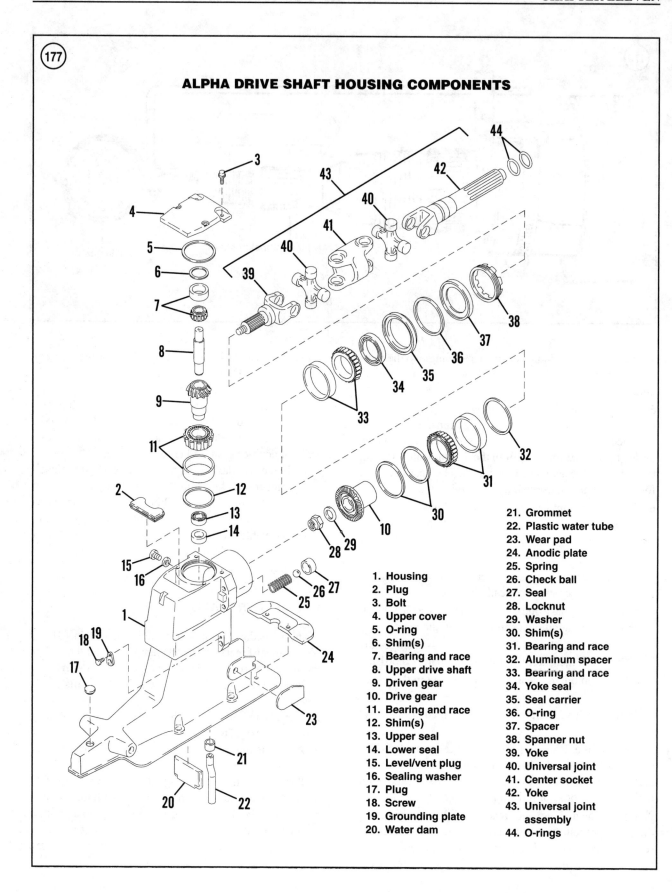

(177)

# ALPHA DRIVE SHAFT HOUSING COMPONENTS

1. Housing
2. Plug
3. Bolt
4. Upper cover
5. O-ring
6. Shim(s)
7. Bearing and race
8. Upper drive shaft
9. Driven gear
10. Drive gear
11. Bearing and race
12. Shim(s)
13. Upper seal
14. Lower seal
15. Level/vent plug
16. Sealing washer
17. Plug
18. Screw
19. Grounding plate
20. Water dam

21. Grommet
22. Plastic water tube
23. Wear pad
24. Anodic plate
25. Spring
26. Check ball
27. Seal
28. Locknut
29. Washer
30. Shim(s)
31. Bearing and race
32. Aluminum spacer
33. Bearing and race
34. Yoke seal
35. Seal carrier
36. O-ring
37. Spacer
38. Spanner nut
39. Yoke
40. Universal joint
41. Center socket
42. Yoke
43. Universal joint
    assembly
44. O-rings

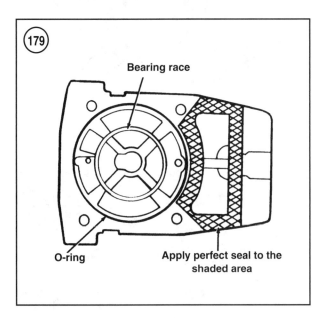

Bearing race

O-ring

Apply perfect seal to the shaded area

a. Remove the bearing carrier and propeller shaft as described in this chapter.

b. Remove the bearing cap (31, **Figure 165**) as described in this chapter.

c. If the end play measurement is below specification, install thinner or fewer shims beneath the bearing cap.

d. If the end play measurement exceeds the specification, install thicker or additional shims beneath the bearing cap.

e. A 0.001 in. change in shim thickness changes the end play by 0.001 in.

f. If there are no shims beneath the cap, check for an improperly installed propeller shaft component or bearing carrier.

6. Remove the drive shaft retainer (**Figure 174**). Install the O-ring (2, **Figure 142**), bearing cup (3) and shims (4) as described in this chapter. Do not install the clamp plate.

## DRIVE SHAFT HOUSING

Mark the location and orientation of each component before removing it. Arrange components in an orderly fashion as they are removed, or make diagrams showing the locations of parts. This simple step can save time and helps ensure correct assembly.

### Alpha Drive

For component identification and orientation, refer to **Figure 177**.

### Upper Cover Removal and Installation

1. Drain the lubricant as described in Chapter Four.

2. Remove the four bolts (3, **Figure 177**). Tap the side of the upper cover (4, **Figure 177**) until the cover moves. Insert a pry bar into the opening at the back of the housing (**Figure 178**) and pry the cover from the housing.

3. Remove the O-ring (5, **Figure 177**) from the upper cover or drive shaft housing. Discard the O-ring.

4. Use a quick drying solvent and clean sealant from the mating surfaces of the upper cover and drive shaft housing.

5. Apply a light coat of Perfect Seal (Mercury part No. 92-34227-1) to the surfaces indicated in **Figure 179**.

6. Install a new O-ring (**Figure 179**) over the boss on the upper cover. Lubricate the upper bearing race (**Figure 179**) with gearcase lubricant.

7. Install the cover onto the housing. Rotate the cover to align the bolt holes then firmly seat the cover.

8. Install the four bolts (3, **Figure 177**). Tighten the bolts, following a crisscross pattern, to the specification in **Table 1**.

9. Refill the lubricant as described in Chapter Four.

### Upper Bearing Race
### Removal and Installation

Remove the upper bearing race only if it must be replaced, or if necessary to access the shims beneath the race (7, **Figure 177**). Refer to *Inspection* in this chapter. This procedure requires a slide hammer, press, and a suitable race installation tool.

1. Clamp the upper cover in a vise with protective jaws. Attach a slide hammer puller to the back side of the race. Use short hammer strokes and remove the race and shims.

2. Thoroughly clean the upper cover. Replace the upper cover if the race bore is cracked or rough. Replace cor-

**11**

roded or damaged shims with the same thickness as the original ones.

3. Support the upper cover on a press with the race bore facing upward. Insert the shims into the bottom of the race bore.

4. Place the bearing race in the bore with the tapered side facing upward. Place the tool against the race.

5. Center the tool and race under the press ram and press the race fully into the bore.

### Universal Joint Shaft Removal and Installation

Remove the universal joint shaft only to replace gears, bearings, universal joints or related seals, or to access the drive gear shims. Count the teeth on the drive (9, **Figure 177**) and driven gears (10) before removing the universal joint shaft. Some housings use gears with the same tooth count. In such cases, a given tooth on the drive gear drives only against a given tooth on the driven gear. With use, the gear teeth develop a matching wear pattern that must be maintained. Before removing the universal joint shaft, make timing marks on the gears (**Figure 180**) with a metal scribe or permanent marker. Timing marks are not required on gears with an unequal tooth count. If reusing timed gears, align the timing marks during installation to prevent rapid wear or failure.

This procedure requires a spanner wrench (Mercury part No. 91-17256) and a 1/2 in. drive torque wrench.

1. Clamp the drive shaft housing firmly in a large vise with protective jaws. Remove the upper cover as described in this chapter.

2. Attach a spanner wrench to the spanner nut (**Figure 181**). Fully loosen the spanner nut. If the nut is hard to break loose, tap the spanner wrench with a rubber mallet.

3. Slowly and steadily, pull the universal joint shaft and drive gear assembly from the housing. Excessive effort or jerking on the shaft may damage the housing or other components.

4. Retrieve the shim(s) (30, **Figure 177**) from the housing. Replace corroded or damaged shims. Remove and discard the O-ring from the drive gear bearings.

5. Use a solvent to clean residue from the housing bore, drive gear, bearing and spanner nut.

6. Insert the shims into the bore. If a split ring type shim is used, place the thinner shims against the housing and the split ring shim against the thinner shims.

7. Apply a coat of gearcase lubricant to the bore of the housing. Without dislodging the shims, slide the universal joint assembly into the housing. Install a new O-ring on the drive gear bearings.

8. If the gears have timing marks, rotate the shafts to align the marks as shown in **Figure 180**.

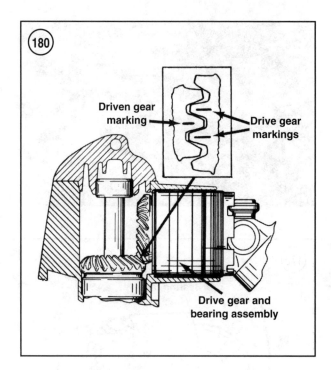

Driven gear marking

Drive gear markings

Drive gear and bearing assembly

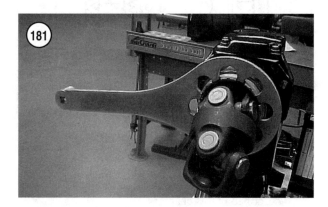

9. Mesh the gear teeth while seating the universal joint in the bore. Thread the spanner nut (38, **Figure 177**) into the housing. Do not tighten the nut at this time.

10. Measure the torque wrench length from the center of the handle to the center of the socket connector (**Figure 182**). Refer to the information in **Table 2** to determine the spanner nut torque for the torque wrench length.

11. Tighten the spanner nut to the specification in **Table 3**. Install the upper cover as described in this chapter.

### Universal Joint Shaft Disassembly

1. Slide a flat metal bar through the shaft and clamp it in a vise (**Figure 183**).

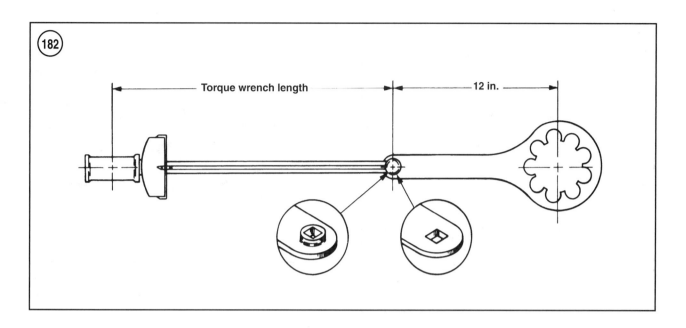

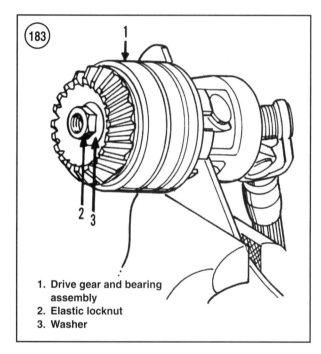

1. **Drive gear and bearing assembly**
2. **Elastic locknut**
3. **Washer**

2. Support the gear and bearing assembly (1, **Figure 183**) while removing the nut (2) and washer (3). Discard the nut. Carefully pull the gear and bearing assembly from the shaft.

3. Pull the seal carrier (35, **Figure 177**), O-ring (36), spacer (37) and spanner nut (38) from the shaft.

4. Inspect the drive gear yoke (39, **Figure 177**) for wear or pitting on the seal contact surface. Replace the yoke and seal if the surface is defective, or lubricant may leak into the bellows.

*Yoke seal replacement*

Replace the yoke seal (34, **Figure 177**) if worn or leaking, or if replacing the drive gear yoke (39).

1. Place the seal carrier on a vise or other suitable work surface with the open side down.

2. Use a blunt punch to drive the seal from the carrier (**Figure 184**). Take care not to damage the aluminum carrier. Discard the seal.

3. Use a quick drying solvent to clean all material from the seal carrier. Replace the seal carrier if damaged or corroded.

4. Place the seal carrier on a press with the open side facing downward. Apply a light coat of Loctite 271 to the outer diameter of the new seal. Place the seal into the carrier bore opening with the seal lip facing downward.

5. Place a suitable mandrel or flat piece of steel on the seal. The mandrel or steel must be larger than the diameter of the seal.

6. Center the seal and carrier under the press ram and press the seal into the bore until flush with the carrier.

**Drive Gear and Bearings Removal and Installation**

Remove the drive gear bearings (31 and 33, **Figure 177**) only if defective or if replacing the gears. Removing the bearings will damage them.

1. Use a socket or section of tubing to press the gear from the bearings.

2. Engage the edge of a bearing separator with the gear side of the aluminum spacer (32, **Figure 177**). Place the separator and gear on the table of a press.

**11**

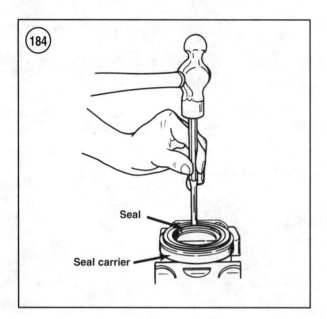

Seal

Seal carrier

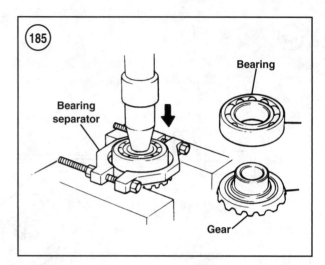

Bearing

Bearing
separator

Gear

3. Center the removal tool and gear under the press ram and press the small diameter race and gear from the spacer, large diameter race and bearing.

4. Clamp the aluminum spacer in a vise with protective jaws. Remove the bearing race from the spacer using a slide hammer puller.

5. Install a bearing separator into the gap between the small diameter bearing and the gear (**Figure 185**). Place the separator and gear on the table of a press. Press the smaller diameter bearing from the gear.

6. Use a section of steel pipe to install the bearings. The tubing surface must contact only the flat surface of the inner bearing races during installation or the new bearings will be damaged.

7. Place the drive gear on the table of a press with the teeth facing downward. Place the small diameter bearing onto the gear hub with the tapered side facing upward. Apply gearcase lubricant to the drive gear and tapered roller bearings.

8. Press the bearing over the hub until seated against the gear. Place the smaller diameter bearing race over the gear hub with the tapered end facing downward. Seat the race against the bearing.

9. Place the aluminum spacer on the table of a press with the open side facing upward. Place the large diameter bearing race into the opening with the tapered side facing upward. Use a suitable mandrel or piece of flat steel and fully press the race into the aluminum spacer.

10. Place the drive gear, teeth down, on the table of a press. Place the aluminum spacer over the drive gear hub with the bearing race side facing upward.

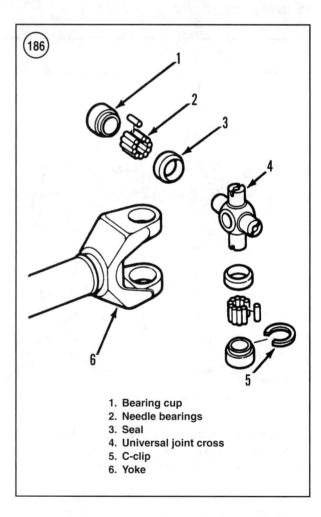

1. Bearing cup
2. Needle bearings
3. Seal
4. Universal joint cross
5. C-clip
6. Yoke

11. Monitor the aluminum spacer for movement while pressing the bearing onto the gear. Press the bearing onto the hub until only a slight amount of movement is present. Do not eliminate all movement.

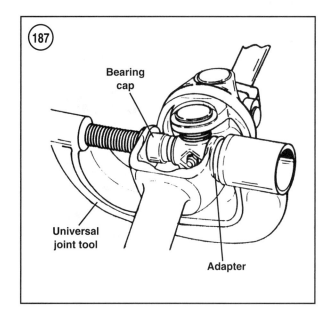

(187)

Bearing
cap

Universal
joint tool

Adapter

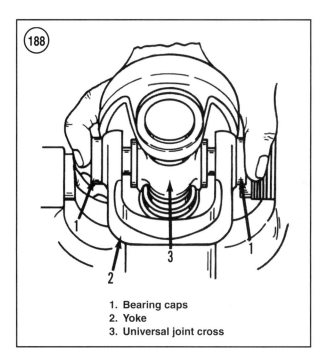

(188)

1. Bearing caps
2. Yoke
3. Universal joint cross

### Universal Joint, Socket and Yokes
### Disassembly and Assembly

Disassemble the universal joint assembly only if replacing the drive gear (10, **Figure 177**) or engine coupling yoke (42). The universal joint which connects to the defective component must also be replaced. All late model Alpha drive units use a non-serviceable universal joint. The non-serviceable joint is not designed for reuse if removed.

These joints can be identified by the absence of the grease fittings and the orange seals on the bearing caps.

If both yokes, the socket (41, **Figure 177**) or both universal joints are defective, replace the universal joint shaft assembly. The cost of the individual components usually exceeds the cost of the assembly. An automotive-type universal joint tool and adapter (Mercury part No. 38758) are required for this procedure. Refer to **Figure 186**.

> *CAUTION*
> *Improperly installed, damaged or worn universal joints can unexpectedly fail, causing severe damage to the drive shaft housing, transom assembly or even the structure of the boat. Universal joint repair should only be performed by an experienced mechanic with access to the proper tools.*

1. Clamp the socket part of the universal joint assembly in a vise with protective jaws. Use a punch and hammer to remove the C-clips (5, **Figure 186**) from the universal joint. Discard the C-clips.

2. Clamp a universal joint tool in a vise. Place the adapter into the open end of the tool with the larger opening facing the bolt. Remove the caps from the universal joint cross as follows:

    a. Insert the exposed end of one of the bearing caps into the adapter while mounting the shaft in the tool (**Figure 187**).

    b. Turn the bolt until the flat end just contacts the opposite bearing cap. Center the flat end of the bolt over the bearing cap. Turn the bolt to push the bearing cap into the adapter. Remove the cap from the adapter.

    c. Loosen the bolt. Rotate the universal joint shaft 180° and center the remaining cap in the adapter opening.

    d. Turn the bolt until the flat end just contacts the shaft of the universal joint cross. Turn the bolt to push the opposite cap into the adapter.

    e. Remove the cap from the adapter. Repeat these steps for the remaining two bearing caps.

    f. Slip the universal joint cross from the yoke and socket.

3. Install the caps onto the universal joint cross as follows:

    a. Slip the universal joint cross into the opening in the yoke or socket.

    b. Align the bearing surface of the cross with the caps while inserting both caps into the openings (**Figure 188**).

**11**

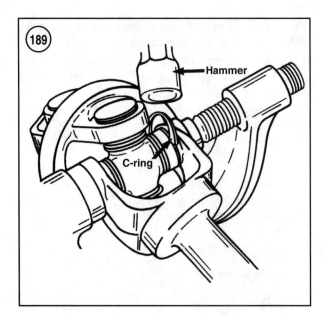

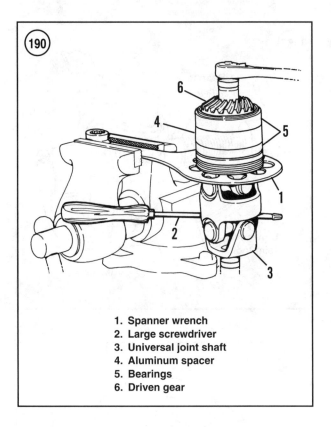

1. Spanner wrench
2. Large screwdriver
3. Universal joint shaft
4. Aluminum spacer
5. Bearings
6. Driven gear

c. Insert the exposed end of one of the caps into the adapter while mounting the shaft in the tool (**Figure 187**).

d. Turn the bolt until the flat end just contacts the opposite bearing cap.

e. Turn the bolt to push the cap through the opening. Stop when the C-clip groove is exposed. Install the new C-clip into the groove. Use a hammer to tap the clip completely into the groove (**Figure 189**).

f. Loosen the bolt. Rotate the universal joint shaft 180° and insert the fully installed cap into the adapter.

g. Turn the bolt until the flat end just contacts the opposite bearing cap. Turn the bolt to push the opposite cap into the adapter. Stop when the C-clip groove is exposed. Install the new C-clip into the groove. Use a hammer to tap the clip into the groove (**Figure 189**). If the clip will not seat fully into the groove, inspect the cap to make sure it is properly installed.

h. Repeat these steps for the remaining two bearing caps.

i. Thread the plug into the replacement universal joint cross. Tighten the plug until the hex end breaks away from the plug.

### Universal Joint Shaft Assembly

*NOTE*
*Preload specifications for new bearings may differ from those for used bearings.*

*Bearings are used if they have spun one revolution under power.*

1. Slide a flat metal bar through the universal joint shaft and clamp it in a vise (**Figure 183**).

2. Place the spanner nut over the gear end of the shaft and seat it against the metal bar. Slide the spacer (37, **Figure 177**) over the shaft with the open side facing away from the spanner nut.

3. Lubricate the seal lip with gearcase lubricant. Slide the seal carrier (35, **Figure 177**) over the shaft. The lip side of the seal must face away from the spanner nut. Fit the shoulder on the carrier into the opening in the spacer.

4. Align the splines and slide the drive gear and bearing assembly onto the universal joint assembly.

5. Support the gear while placing the washer (29, **Figure 177**) over the shaft. The NUT mark on the washer must face outward. Thread the new elastic locknut (28, **Figure 177**) onto the shaft. Do not tighten the nut at this time. Remove the metal bar.

6. Clamp the spanner wrench into a vise as shown in **Figure 190**. Slide the universal joint through the wrench. Align the lugs of the wrench with the notches in the spanner nut and rest the shaft on the wrench.

7. Slide a large screwdriver through the universal joint shaft. Rest the screwdriver against the vise as shown in

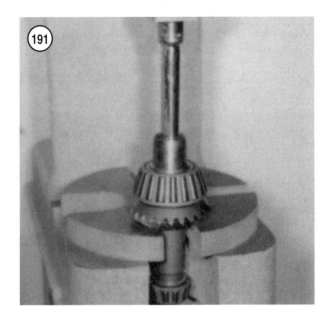

Figure 190. Apply gearcase lubricant to the bearing rollers.

8. Tighten the nut (28, **Figure 177**) until the washer is just captured between the nut and the gear, and very little end play is present between the gear and shaft. Do not overtighten the nut.

9. Remove the screwdriver. Attach a dial type in.-lb. torque wrench to the nut. Rotate the shaft a few revolutions to seat the bearings.

10. Hold the bearings (4, **Figure 190**) and aluminum spacer (4) to prevent rotation. Observe the torque reading while turning the shaft. The torque reading indicates the bearing preload for the universal joint shaft bearings.

11. Compare the preload with the specification in **Table 4**. If the preload is below the specification, tighten the nut approximately 1/16 of a turn (do not use the torque wrench) and measure the preload again.

12. Continue until the preload reaches the specification. If the bearings are used, tighten the nut enough to reach the upper end of the used bearing specification.

**Upper Drive Shaft and Driven Gear Disassembly and Assembly**

Disassemble the upper drive shaft only if the gear or bearing(s) must be replaced. Refer to **Figure 177**.

1. Pull the upper drive shaft assembly from the housing.
2. Remove the upper bearing as follows:
    a. Position the flat edge of a bearing separator against the lower side of the inner bearing race.
    b. Place the separator on the table of a press with the bearing facing upward.
    c. Use a suitable socket to press the upper drive shaft from the gear.
    d. Support the driven gear and press the shaft from the bearing.

3. Remove the driven gear and bearing from the shaft as follows:
    a. Place the separator on the table of a press with the bearing and gear facing up (**Figure 191**).
    b. Insert a suitable tool into the splined end of the lower gear.
    c. Support the driven gear and press the shaft from the bearing.

4. Remove the bearing from the driven gear only if it is defective. The removal process damages the bearing. To remove the bearing:
    a. Position the edges of a bearing separator between the bearing and the driven gear. Tighten the separator bolts to secure the gear.
    b. Place the bearing separator on the table of a press with the bearing side facing upward.
    c. Use a suitable driver to press the bearing from the gear.
    d. Support the gear and press the bearing from the gear. Discard the bearing.

5. Install the bearing on the driven gear as follows:
    a. Use a section of steel tubing as a bearing installation tool. The tubing must be of sufficient length and have an inner diameter slightly larger than the inner diameter of the bearings.
    b. Place the gear on the table of a press with the splined end facing upward. Lubricate the inner bore with gearcase lubricant and place the bearing onto the gear hub.
    c. Press the bearing onto the gear until fully seated.

6. Install the upper drive shaft as follows:
    a. Place the driven gear and bearing assembly on the table of a press with the splined opening facing down.
    b. Apply gearcase lubricant to the driven gear bore. Align the larger diameter end of the upper drive shaft with the gear bore.
    c. Press the shaft into the driven gear until fully seated.

7. Install the upper bearing as follows:
    a. Use a short section of steel tubing for use as a bearing installation tool.
    b. Place the upper drive shaft on the table of a press with the gear side face down. Apply gearcase lubricant onto the inner diameter of the bearing.
    c. Place the upper bearing onto the upper end of the shaft with the taper face up.
    d. Press the bearing onto the shaft until fully seated.

**11**

### Driven Gear Bearing Race
### Removal and Installation

Remove the driven gear bearing race if replacing the driven gear bearing, or if necessary to access the shims (12, **Figure 177**) beneath the race. Use a bearing driver (Mercury part No. 91-33493) and a suitable driver rod to install the race.

1. Attach a slide hammer puller to the back edge of the race. Use short hammer strokes to remove the race.
2. Retrieve the shims (12, **Figure 177**). Replace corroded or damaged shims.
3. Thoroughly clean the race bore. Turn the housing so the cover faces up. Insert the shims and seat them against the step in the bore.
4. Apply gearcase lubricant to the outer diameter then place the bearing race into the bore. The tapered side must face outward.
5. Seat the bearing driver against the race. Insert the drive rod into the driver. Drive the race into the bore until fully seated.

### Drive Shaft Seals Replacement

1. Position the housing with the upper cover opening face down.
2. Insert a screwdriver into the slot in the lower drive shaft opening.
3. Drive both seals (13 and 14, **Figure 177**) from the drive shaft.
4. Turn the housing so the upper cover opening is face up.
5. Use a quick drying solvent to clean the seal bore.
6. Use a suitable driver to install the seals.
7. Apply a coat of Loctite 271 to the seal bore and the outer diameter of the seals. Place the small diameter seal in the bore with the lip facing down. Seat the seal in the bore.
8. Place the large diameter seal into the larger diameter bore with the seal lip facing up. Seat the seal in the bore.
9. Wipe the excess Loctite from the seals. Apply a bead of Special Lube 101 (Mercury part No. 92-13872A1) to the seal lips.

### Water Dam and Water Tube
### Removal and Installation

1. Pull the water dam (20, **Figure 177**) from the exhaust passage in the drive shaft housing.
2. Pull the water tube (22, **Figure 177**) from the grommet (21). Wipe any contaminants from the grommet in the housing.
3. Apply a light coat of grease to the grommet. Align the protrusion on the grommet with the opening in the bore. Press the grommet into the bore.

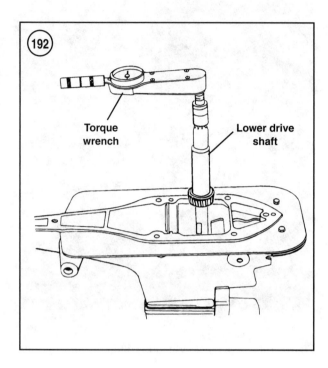

Torque wrench — Lower drive shaft

4. Insert the shorter offset end of the water tube into the bore. Turn the lower offset toward the rear of the housing.
5. Insert the water dam into the slots in the exhaust passage with the tapered side in and the X mark toward the water tube.

### Lubricant Check Valve
### Removal and Installation

1. Carefully pry the brown seal (27, **Figure 177**) from the housing. Discard the seal if torn or damaged.
2. Pull the spring (25, **Figure 177**) and check ball (26) from the bore. Flush the bore with solvent. Replace the spring or check ball if corroded or damaged.
3. Slip the spring, then the check ball into the bore. Apply a very light coat of Perfect Seal (Mercury part No. 92-34227-1) onto the outer diameter of the new seal. Press the new seal into the bore with the open side facing the check ball.

### Upper Drive Shaft Preload

Set the upper drive shaft preload if replacing the gears, upper drive shaft related bearings or the housing. This procedure requires a dial type in.-lb. torque wrench, a used lower drive shaft and a pinion gear nut.

*NOTE*
*Preload specifications for new bearings may differ from those for used bearings.*

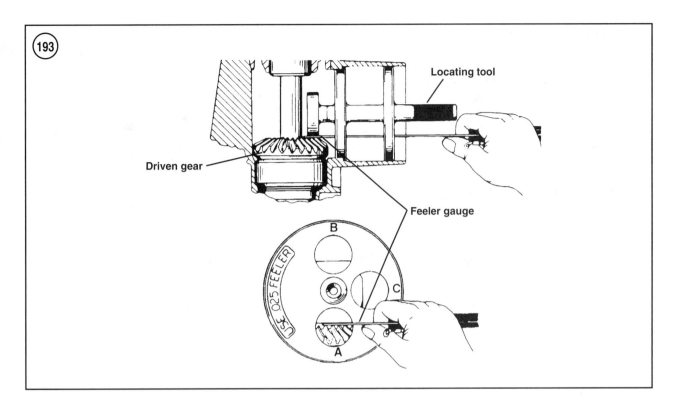

*Bearings are used if spun one revolution under power.*

1. Apply a coat of gearcase lubricant to the tapered roller bearing, then install the upper drive shaft assembly into the housing. Seat the lower bearing against the race.
2. Install the upper cover as described in this chapter. Position the housing so the upper cover faces down. Do not install the O-ring or apply sealant to the cover at this time.
3. Thread the pinion nut onto the lower drive shaft. Mesh the splines while inserting the lower drive shaft into the housing. Rotate the drive shaft several revolutions to seat the bearings.
4. Attach a torque wrench to the pinion nut (**Figure 192**). Observe the dial while slowly turning the drive shaft. The torque reading indicates the upper drive shaft bearing preload.
5. Compare the preload measurement with the specification in **Table 4**. Correct the preload as follows:
   a. Remove the upper cover and upper bearing race as described in this section.
   b. If the preload is less than the specification, install more or thicker shims under the upper bearing race.
   c. If the preload exceeds the specification, install fewer or thinner shims under the upper bearing race.
   d. A 0.001 in. change in shim thickness changes the preload approximately 1-2 in.-lb. Repeat Step 4 and Step 5 until the preload is correct.

6. Remove the used drive shaft. Position the housing so the upper cover faces up. Do not remove the upper cover.

**Driven Gear Height**

This procedure requires a driven gear locating tool (Mercury part No. 91-854377) and long feeler gauges. Identify the drive unit ratio, as described in this chapter, before beginning.

1. Insert the driven gear locating tool into the drive gear bore (**Figure 193**), aligning the correct opening (A, B or C) with the driven gear teeth.
   a. On 1.81-, 1.94-, and 2.41:1 drive ratio, use the slot next to the B mark.
   b. On 2.0- and 1.62:1 drive ratio, use the slot next to the A mark.
   c. On 1.47 and 1.32:1 drive ratio, use the slot next to the C mark.
2. Seat the tool in the bore. Use feeler gauges to measure the clearance between the gear teeth and the gauging surface. Rotate the tool in the bore to achieve parallel gauging surfaces. The driven gear height equals the thickness of the feeler gauge that passes between these surfaces with a slight drag. The gear height must be 0.025 in. (0.635 mm).
3. Correct the driven gear height as follows:
   a. Remove the upper cover and upper bearing race as described in this chapter.

**11**

b. Remove the upper drive shaft and driven gear bearing race as described in this chapter.

c. If the gear height exceeds the specification, subtract 0.025 in. from the measured clearance. Increase the total thickness of the shims below the driven gear bearing race by this amount. Decrease the total thickness of the shims above the upper bearing race by the same amount.

d. If the gear height is below the specification, subtract the measured clearance from 0.025 in. Decrease the total thickness of the shims below the driven gear bearing race by this amount. Increase the total thickness of the shims above the upper bearing race by the same amount.

e. Install the driven gear bearing race, upper drive shaft, upper bearing race and upper cover as described in this chapter.

f. Set the upper drive shaft bearing preload as described in this chapter. Check the driven gear height as described in step 2. Continue until both the upper drive shaft preload and driven gear height are correct.

### Drive Gear Depth

This procedure requires a drive gear locating tool (Mercury part No. 91-60523) and feeler gauges. Identify the drive unit ratio before beginning. Refer to *Drive Ratio Identification*.

1. Remove the upper cover as described in this chapter. Do not remove the upper drive shaft.

2. Install the universal joint shaft as described in this chapter.

3. Align the correct opening (X, Y or Z) with the driven gear teeth while placing the tool over the upper bearing (**Figure 194**).

   a. On 1.81:1, 1.94:1, and 2.41:1 drive ratio, use the slot next to the Y mark.

   b. On 2.0:1, and 1.62:1 drive ratio, use the slot next to the X mark.

   c. On 1.47:1 and 1.32:1 drive ratio, use the slot next to the Z mark.

4. Seat the tool in the bore. Use feeler gauges to measure the gap between the gear teeth and the gauging surface. Rotate the tool in the bore to achieve parallel gauging surfaces. The driven gear depth equals the thickness of the feeler gauge that passes between these surfaces with a slight drag. The gear depth must be 0.025 in. (0.635 mm).

5. Correct the drive gear depth as follows:

   a. Remove the universal joint shaft as described in this section.

   b. If the gear depth is below the specification, subtract the measured clearance from 0.025 in. Increase the

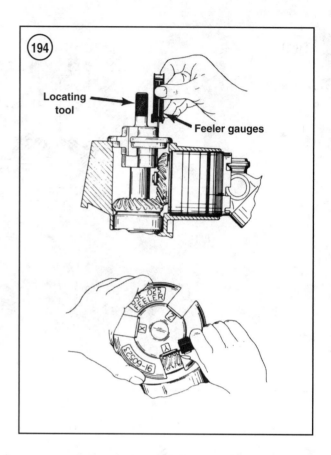

total thickness of the shims in the shaft bore (30, **Figure 177**) by this amount.

   c. If the gear depth exceeds the specification, subtract 0.025 in. from the measured clearance. Decrease the total thickness of the shims in the shaft bore (30, **Figure 177**) by this amount.

   d. Install the universal joint shaft as described in this section. Re-measure the drive gear depth and correct as needed. Several shim changes may be required.

6. Install the upper cover as described in this chapter. Apply sealant and install a new O-ring on the final installation.

7. Install the gearcase onto the drive shaft housing as described in this chapter.

### Bravo Drive

For component identification and orientation, refer to **Figure 195**.

### Upper Cover Removal and Installation

Drive unit removal is not required to remove the upper cover. Replace all O-rings during cover installation. Apply gearcase lubricant to all bearings and O-rings.

(195)

## BRAVO DRIVE SHAFT HOUSING COMPONENTS

1. Upper cover
2. Bolt
3. Washer
4. O-ring
5. Inner bearing race
6. Needle bearing
7. Thrust bearing race
8. Thrust bearing
9. Upper drive shaft assembly
10. Thrust bearing
11. Thrust bearing race
12. Needle bearing
13. Inner bearing race
14. O-ring
15. O-ring*
16. O-ring
17. Shift shaft bushing*
18. Shift shaft bushing
19. Shift shaft bushing
20. Seal
21. Sealing washer
22. Level/vent screw
23. O-ring
24. Universal joint shaft and
    drive gear assembly
25. Housing
26. Studs
27. Washers
28. Locknuts
29. Plug
30. Shift cam and linkage assembly
31. O-ring
32. Detent plunger
33. Rear cover
34. Washer
35. Bolt

*Not used on all models

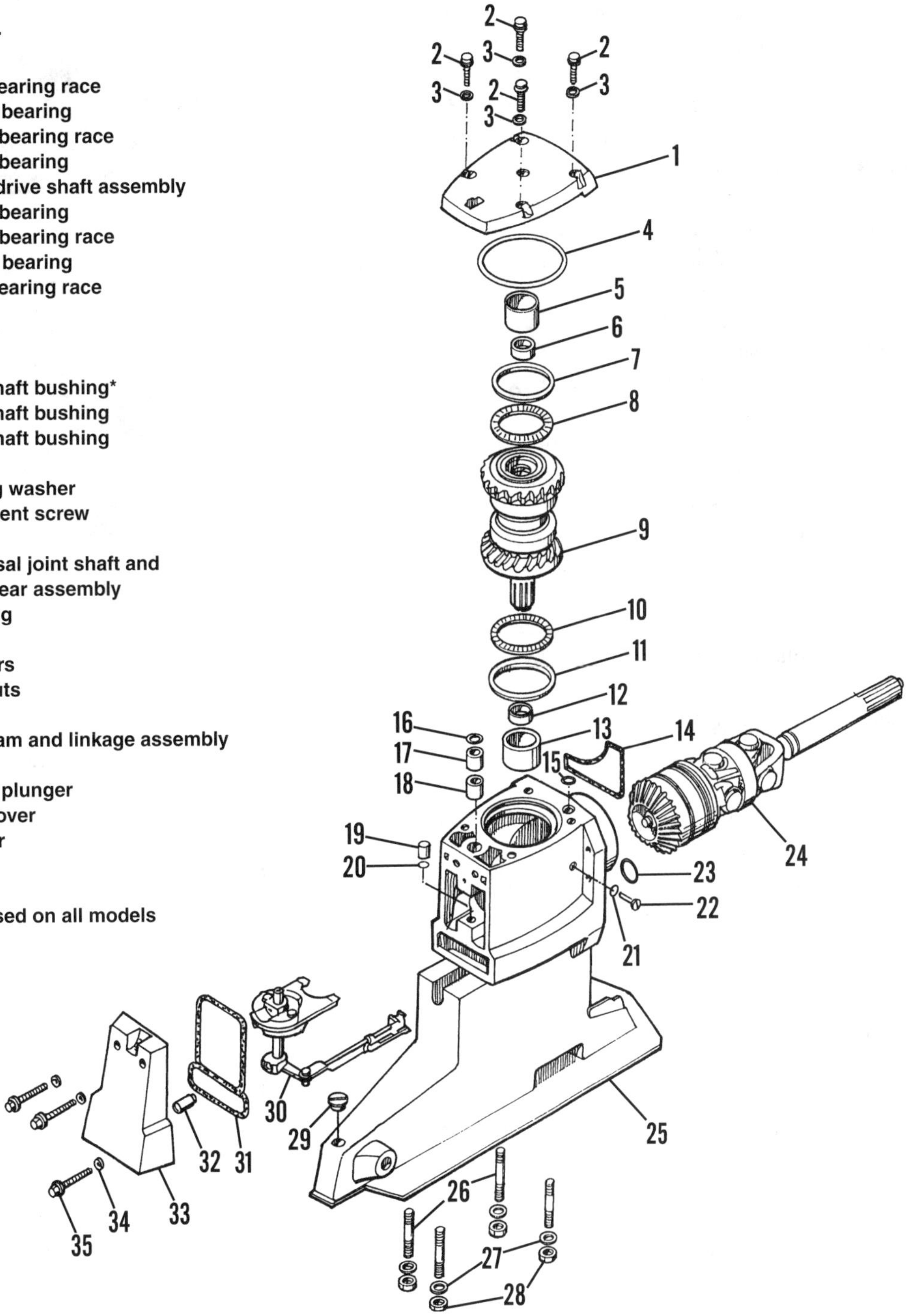

11

1. Drain the lubricant as described in Chapter Four.

2. Remove the four bolts (2 and 3, **Figure 195**). Tap the side of the upper cover (1, **Figure 195**) until the cover moves. Insert a pry bar into the opening at the back of the housing (**Figure 178**) and pry the cover from the housing.

3. Remove the O-ring (4, **Figure 195**) from the upper cover or drive shaft housing. Remove the O-ring (16, **Figure 195**) from the shift shaft bore. Discard the O-rings.

4. Remove the upper thrust bearing race (4, **Figure 195**) from the upper cover. Install the race onto the upper thrust bearing (8, **Figure 195**) on the upper drive shaft assembly (9).

5. Use a quick drying solvent and clean the mating surfaces of the upper cover and drive shaft housing.

6. Install a new O-ring (4, **Figure 195**) over the boss on the upper cover (1). Place a new O-ring (16, **Figure 195**) on the step in the shift shaft bore. Apply gearcase lubricant to the upper bearing race (5, **Figure 195**), needle bearing (6) and thrust bearing (8).

7. Align the upper bearing race with the bearing opening in the upper driven gear and install the cover. Rotate the cover to align the bolt holes, then firmly seat the cover. Apply a light coat of Perfect Seal (Mercury part No. 92-34227-1) to the threads of the cover bolts (2, **Figure 195**).

8. Install the four bolts and washers (2 and 3, **Figure 195**). Tighten the bolts in a crossing pattern to the specification in **Table 1**.

9. Refill the housing with lubricant as described in Chapter Four.

### Rear Cover Removal and Installation

Replace the rear cover O-ring (31, **Figure 195**) during cover installation. Refer to **Figure 195**.

1. Drain the gearcase lubricant as described in Chapter Four.

2. Push in on the shift linkage to shift the drive shaft housing into neutral. The end of the linkage should be flush with the bore when in neutral.

3. Evenly loosen and remove the three bolts (34, **Figure 195**). Carefully pull the rear cover (33, **Figure 195**) from the housing.

4. Pull the detent plunger (32, **Figure 195**) and spring from the bore in the rear cover. Remove the O-ring from the rear cover. Clean all lubricant, corrosion and O-ring adhesive from the rear cover and detent plunger.

5. Inspect the detent plunger and spring for corrosion pitting or excessive wear. Replace as needed.

6. Apply a light coat of bellows adhesive (Mercury part No. 92-86166) to the O-ring groove in the rear cover. In-

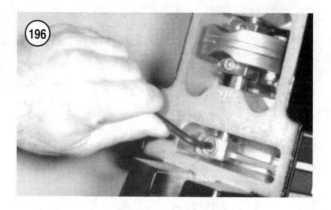

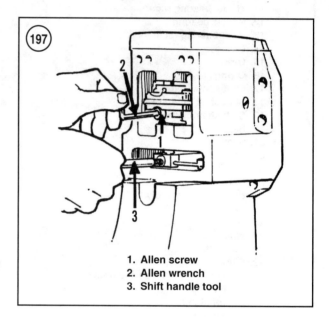

1. **Allen screw**
2. **Allen wrench**
3. **Shift handle tool**

stall the O-ring into the groove. Do not install the cover until the adhesive dries.

7. Apply a light coat of Special Lube 101 (Mercury part No. 92-13872A1) to the detent plunger and spring. Do not fill the plunger bore with lubricant.

8. Insert the spring, then the plunger into the rear cover bore. The ball side of the plunger must face outward. Shift the drive shaft housing into neutral as described in step 2.

9. Apply a light coat of Perfect Seal (Mercury part No. 91-34227-1) to the threads of the cover bolts.

10. Align the detent plunger with the recess in the shift linkage while seating the cover onto the housing.

11. Thread the longer bolt and washer into the lower opening and the two shorter bolts and washers into the upper openings. Evenly tighten the bolts to the specification in **Table 1**.

12. Refill the gearcase with lubricant as described in Chapter Four.

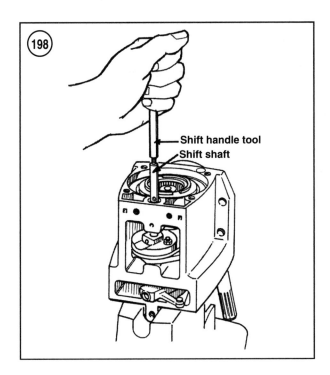

Shift handle tool
Shift shaft

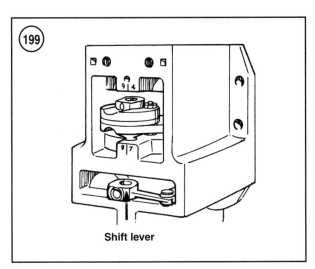

**Shift lever**

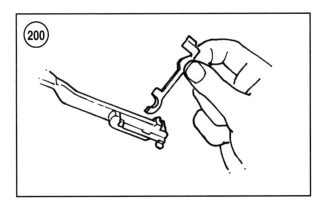

## Shift Shaft and Linkage
## Removal and Installation

This procedure requires a shift handle tool (Mercury part No. 91-17302) or a suitable bolt. The threads of the bolt must match the threads in the shift shaft bore.

1. Remove the drive unit as described in this chapter.

2. Remove the Allen screw from the shift shaft and shift linkage (**Figure 196**).

3. Thread the shift handle tool (3, **Figure 197**) into the shift shaft and linkage. Remove the Allen screw (1, **Figure 197**) from the shift shaft and cam/yoke assembly.

4. Thread the shift handle tool (**Figure 198**) into the upper end of the shift shaft. Pull the shift shaft from the housing.

5. Swing the lever of the shift linkage (**Figure 199**) out of the housing. Rotate the shift linkage 90° clockwise. The detent ball recess in the linkage must face downward. Carefully pull the linkage from the housing.

6. Inspect the shift shaft bushings (17 and 18, **Figure 195**) and seal (16) for wear or damage.

7. Remove the latch from the linkage (**Figure 200**). Remove the cotter pin (13, **Figure 201**) and washer (12). Separate the lever from the link bar. Discard the cotter pin. Remove the pivot pin (11, **Figure 201**). Late models do not use a detachable pivot pin.

8. Inspect all components for wear or damage and replace as needed.

9. Insert the pivot pin (11, **Figure 201**) into the shift link bar. Install the washer (12, **Figure 201**) and a new cotter pin (13) onto the pivot pin. Bend the ends of the cotter pin.

10. Slip the latch into the slot of the linkage as shown in **Figure 200**. Extend the lever (10, **Figure 201**) until it aligns with the link bar. Slide the linkage into the housing. The detent ball side of the lever must face downward.

11. Rotate the shift linkage 90° counterclockwise. Swing the lever into position under the shift shaft bore. The detent ball side of the linkage must face outward.

12. Lubricate the shift shaft and related bushings with Special Lube 101 (Mercury part No. 92-13872A1). Thread the shift handle tool (**Figure 198**) into the upper end of the shift shaft.

13. Carefully insert the shift shaft through the bores in the bushings, shift cam/yoke assembly and shift linkage.

14. Thread the shift handle tool (3, **Figure 197**) into the shift shaft and linkage.

15. Apply Loctite only to the first three threads of both Allen screws. Thread the longer screw into the shaft. Tighten the screw to the specification in **Table 1**.

16. Remove the shift handle tool (3, **Figure 197**). Thread the shorter screw into the shift shaft. Tighten the screw (**Figure 196**) to the specification in **Table 1**.

**11**

**Shift Cam and Yoke Disassembly and Assembly**

Refer to **Figure 201**.

1. Pull the shift cam and yoke assembly from the housing (**Figure 202**).
2. Disassemble the shift cam and yoke only if replacing worn or damaged components.
    a. Remove the bolts and nuts (3 and 7, **Figure 201**).
    b. Lift the upper cam (4, **Figure 201**) from the assembly.
    c. Remove the spacers (6, **Figure 201**) then lift the yoke (5) from the lower cam (4).
3. Inspect the components for wear, discoloration or damage and replace as needed. Reassemble the shift cam and yoke as follows:
    a. Insert the bolts (3, **Figure 201**) into the upper cam (4). Place the cam on a work surface with the flat side facing upward.
    b. Place the yoke on the cam (**Figure 203**), aligning the bolts with the slots in the yoke. Orient the cam and yoke as shown in **Figure 204**.
    c. Place the spacers over the bolts and position them in the slots as shown in **Figure 203**.
    d. Align the bolt holes while seating the flat side of the lower cam onto the yoke. Orient the cam and yoke as shown in **Figure 204**. Thread the nuts (7, **Figure 201**) onto the bolts (3). Do not tighten them at this time.
    e. Temporarily slide the shift shaft (2, **Figure 201**) through the bores in the shift cams and the yoke.
    f. Tighten the bolts and nut to the specification in **Table 1**. Remove the shift shaft.
4. Orient the bolt heads to the top side while sliding the assembly into the housing (**Figure 202**). Align the yoke opening with the slot in the clutch. Pivot the cam (horizontally) to align the shift shaft bores with the bushings.

**Shift Shaft Bushing and Seal Removal and Installation**

Remove the bushings and seal only if the bushings are worn or the seal is leaking. Seal leakage allows gearcase lubricant to enter the shift linkage cavity.

Use the bushing driver (Mercury part No. 91-17273), or a suitable driver to remove the bushings.

Use the seal and bushing installation tool (Mercury part No. 91-17275A 1) along with the removal tool to install the bushings and seals. This tool automatically installs the bushings and seal at the proper depth in the bore.

1. Working from the top of the housing, drive the upper bushing(s) (17 and 18, **Figure 195**) into the shift cam and yoke opening.

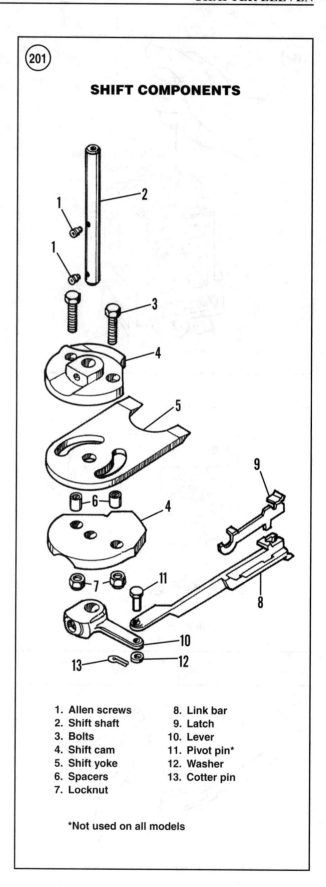

**(201)**

**SHIFT COMPONENTS**

1. Allen screws
2. Shift shaft
3. Bolts
4. Shift cam
5. Shift yoke
6. Spacers
7. Locknut
8. Link bar
9. Latch
10. Lever
11. Pivot pin*
12. Washer
13. Cotter pin

*Not used on all models

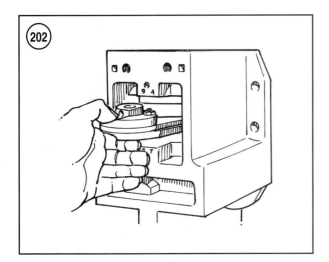

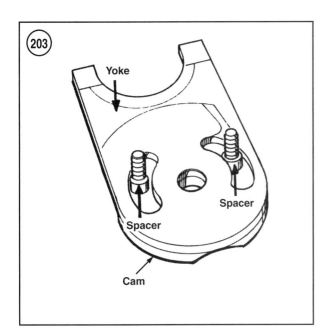

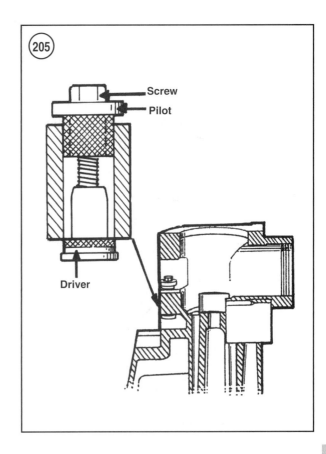

**11**

2. Drive the lower bushing (19, **Figure 195**) and seal (20) into the shift linkage cavity. Discard the seal.

3. Clean the bushings, seal bore and seal recess in the housing. Inspect the bushings for wear or damage and replace if necessary.

4. Drive the lower bushing into the bore until the top edge protrudes approximately 1/8 in. (3.2 mm) from the top of the bore. Use a quick drying solvent and thoroughly clean the outer diameter of the seal and the seal recess in the housing.

5. Apply Loctite 271 onto the outer diameter of the new seal and the housing. Place the seal on the driver part of the installation tool. The seal lip must face away from the shoulder on the tool.

6. Insert the screw and pilot into the bushing in the upper end of the bore as shown in **Figure 205**. Insert the driver and seal into the lower end of the bore. Thread the screw into the driver. Tighten the screw until the pilot and driver seat against the housing.

7. Drive the bushing (18, **Figure 195**) into the bore until it protrudes from the lower end of the bore (**Figure 206**).

8. Drive the upper bushing (17, **Figure 195**) into the bore until the upper end is approximately 1/8 in. (3.2 mm) above the housing surface (**Figure 207**).

9. Insert the screw and pilot into the upper bushing (**Figure 208**). Insert the driver into the second bushing. Thread

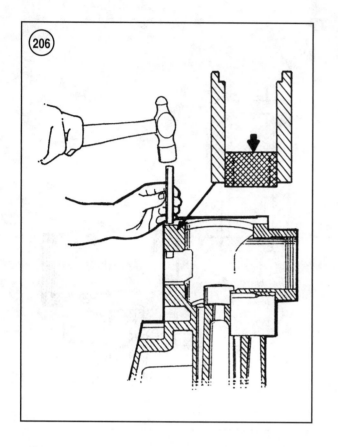

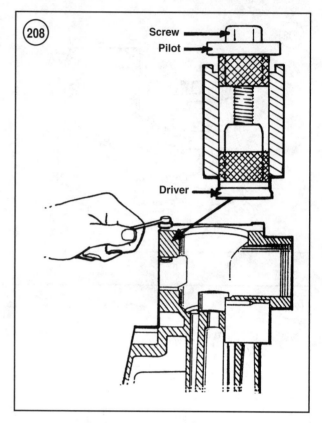

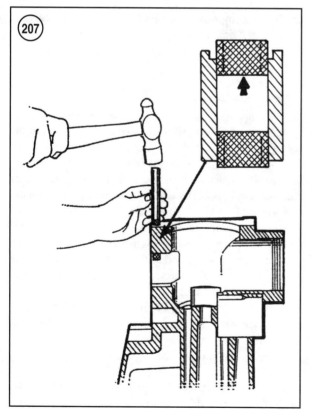

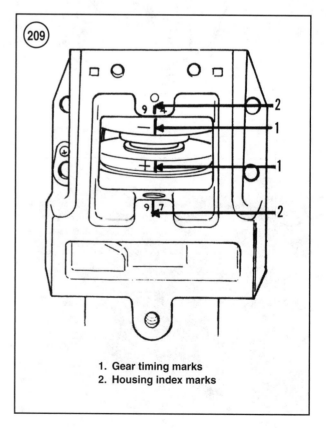

1. Gear timing marks
2. Housing index marks

**UPPER DRIVE SHAFT ASSEMBLY**

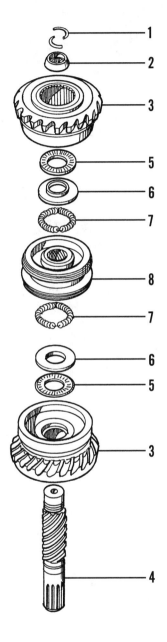

1. Keepers
2. Collar
3. Driven gear
4. Upper drive shaft
5. Thrust bearing
6. Race
7. Garter spring
8. Clutch

the screw into the driver. Tighten the screw until the pilot and drive seat against the housing. Remove the tool.

### Universal Joint Shaft Removal and Installation

Universal joint shaft removal and installation requires a spanner wrench (Mercury part No. 91-17256) and a 1/2 in. drive torque wrench.

1. Clamp the drive shaft housing firmly in a large vise with protective jaws. Remove the upper and rear covers, shift linkage, and shift cam/yoke assembly as described in this chapter.

2. Attach the spanner wrench to the slots in the spanner nut (**Figure 181**). Fully loosen the spanner nut. Tap on the spanner wrench with a rubber mallet if necessary.

3. Pull the universal joint shaft and drive gear assembly from the housing. Use patience while removing the assembly. Excessive effort or jerking on the shaft may damage the housing or other components.

4. Use a suitable solvent and clean residual sealant, oil or corrosion from the bore of the housing, drive gear, bearing and spanner nut. Remove the O-ring from the drive gear bearings. Discard the O-ring.

5. Rotate the gears relative to the upper drive shaft to align the index marks as follows:

   a. The mark next to the - on the upper gears must align with the upper mark on the housing (**Figure 209**).

   b. The mark next to the + on the lower gear must align with the lower mark on the housing (**Figure 209**).

6. Apply a coat of gearcase lubricant to the bore of the housing. Place a new O-ring onto the drive gear bearings. Carefully guide the drive gear and universal joint assembly into the housing. Align the gear teeth and seat the assembly in the bore.

7. Check the alignment of the timing marks as described in Step 5. If improperly aligned, pull the universal joint shaft out enough to disengage the gear teeth. Realign the mark and reinstall the shaft. Several attempts may be necessary.

8. Thread the spanner nut into the housing. Do not tighten the nut at this time.

9. Measure the torque wrench length from the center of the handle to the center of the socket connector (**Figure 182**).

10. Tighten the spanner nut to the specification in **Table 1**.

### Upper Drive Shaft Removal and Disassembly

Refer to **Figure 210**.

1. Remove the universal joint shaft as described in this chapter. Remove the level vent plug (22, **Figure 195**). Lift

**11**

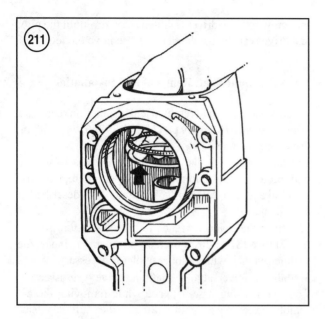

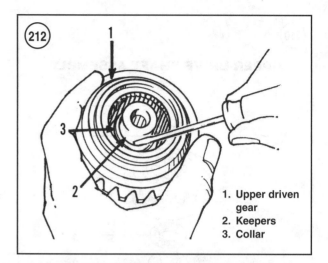

1. Upper driven
   gear
2. Keepers
3. Collar

the race (11, **Figure 195**) and thrust bearing (10) from the upper drive shaft assembly (9).

2. Lift the upper drive shaft from the housing. Clamp the lower end of the shaft (4, **Figure 210**) in a vise with protective jaws. Remove the lower thrust bearing and race (**Figure 211**).

3. Inspect the bearing races (5 and 13, **Figure 195**) for wear, discoloration or damage. Replace the race(s) if defective or it replacing the driven gear(s). See *Driven Gear Bearing Race* in this chapter.

4. Inspect the drive shaft needle bearings (6 and 12, **Figure 195**) for wear, discoloration or damage. Replace the bearings if defective or if replacing the upper drive shaft. See *Drive Shaft Needle Bearing* in this chapter.

5. Rotate clockwise while pushing down on the upper driven gear. Push down on the collar (**Figure 212**) and remove the keepers from the drive shaft groove.

6. Pull the collar from the shaft (**Figure 213**). Lift the upper driven gear from the shaft (**Figure 214**).

7. Lift the upper thrust bearing and race from the clutch (**Figure 215**). Pull the garter spring from the clutch (**Figure 216**).

8. Rotate the clutch counterclockwise to remove it from the shaft (**Figure 217**). Pull the lower garter spring from the shaft (**Figure 218**).

9. Lift the race, thrust bearing (**Figure 219**), and lower driven gear from the shaft. Inspect the components for wear, damage or discoloration as described in this chapter. Replace faulty components. Replace the driven gear(s) if the roller bearing is defective. The bearing is not available separately.

## Upper Drive Shaft Assembly and Installation

1. Clamp the splined end of the shaft in a vise with protective jaws. Slide the lower driven gear over the upper end of the shaft (**Figure 220**). Apply gearcase lubricant to the thrust bearings (5, **Figure 210**).

2. Place the thrust bearing and race onto the lower gear (**Figure 219**). The lip of the race must face the lower

**11**

driven gear. Slide the lower garter spring over the shaft and seat it against the thrust bearing race (**Figure 221**).

3. Thread the clutch onto the upper drive shaft. Slide the upper garter spring over the shaft and seat it against the clutch (**Figure 222**).

4. Place the upper thrust bearing race and bearing onto the garter spring (**Figure 215**). The lip of the race must face away from the clutch. Place the upper driven gear over the shaft (**Figure 214**).

5. Push down on the upper driven gear, turning it clockwise. Hold the gear in position and slip the collar over the

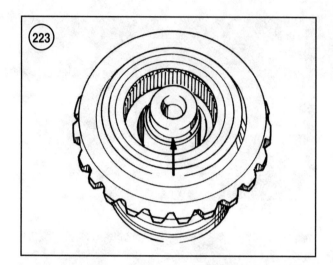

drive shaft (**Figure 213**) with the tapered side facing up-ward. Seat the collar onto the gear. Install the keepers into the groove in the upper drive shaft. Slowly release the gear while fitting the keepers into the recess in the collar (**Figure 223**).

6. Mix an equal volume of gearcase lubricant and Special Lube 101 (Mercury part No. 92-13872A1). Apply the lu-bricant to the roller bearings in the driven gears (3, **Figure 210**) and the thrust bearings (8 and 10, **Figure 195**).

7. The numbers cast into the rear of the housing (**Figure 224**) indicate the thickness and mounting locations for the thrust bearing races (7 and 11, **Figure 195**). The upper number indicates the race thickness code for the upper bearing race (7, **Figure 195**). The lower number indicates the code for the lower race.

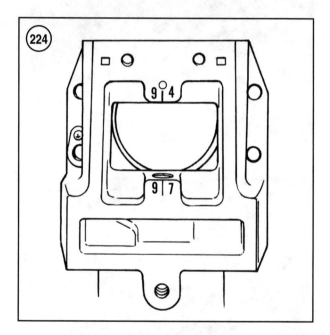

8. Use an outside micrometer to measure the thickness of the races. A race of the correct thickness must be installed in each location or the gears in the housing may operate noisily, wear rapidly or fail.

    a. If the casting number is 91, use a 0.091 in. thick race.

    b. If the casting number is 94, use a 0.094 in. thick race.

    c. If the casting number is 97, use a 0.097 in. thick race.

9. Install the correct race into the housing. Install the lower thrust bearing on the lower driven gear (**Figure 225**).

10. Guide the lower thrust bearing onto the lower bearing race while installing the upper drive shaft. Spin the upper drive shaft. If the shaft binds or spins roughly, remove the drive shaft and check for an incorrectly installed bearing or race.

11. Place the upper thrust bearing onto the upper driven gear. Install the correct race onto the upper thrust bearing.

12. Install the universal joint assembly as described in this chapter.

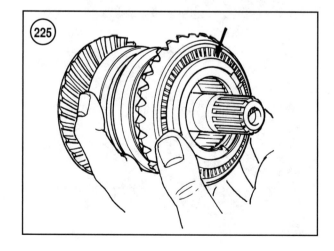

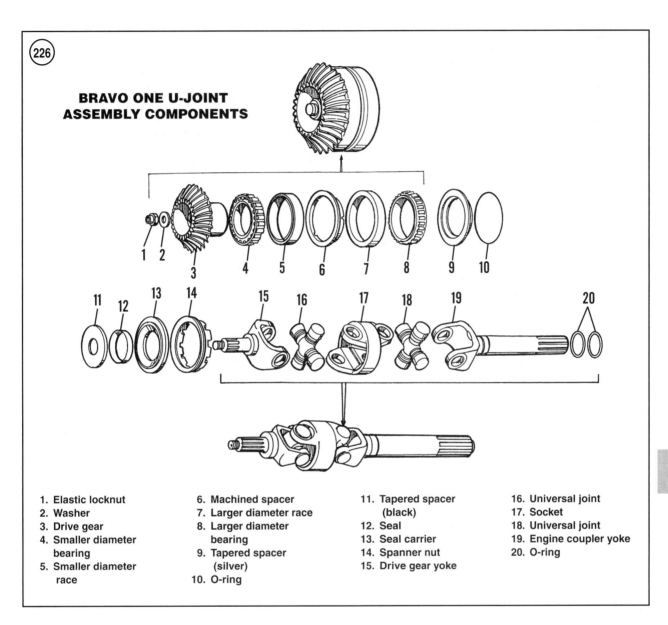

**BRAVO ONE U-JOINT ASSEMBLY COMPONENTS**

1. Elastic locknut
2. Washer
3. Drive gear
4. Smaller diameter bearing
5. Smaller diameter race
6. Machined spacer
7. Larger diameter race
8. Larger diameter bearing
9. Tapered spacer (silver)
10. O-ring
11. Tapered spacer (black)
12. Seal
13. Seal carrier
14. Spanner nut
15. Drive gear yoke
16. Universal joint
17. Socket
18. Universal joint
19. Engine coupler yoke
20. O-ring

**11**

**Universal Joint Shaft Dissassembly**

Refer to **Figure 226**.

Remove the universal joint shaft only if gears, bearings, universal joints or related seals must be replaced.

1. Slide a flat metal bar through the shaft and clamp it in a vise (**Figure 183**).

2. Support the gear and bearing assembly (1, **Figure 183**) while removing the nut (2) and washer (3). Discard the nut. Carefully pull the gear and bearing assembly from the shaft.

3. Remove the spacers, O-ring, seal carrier and the cover nut.

4. Inspect the drive gear yoke (15, **Figure 226**) for wear or pitting on the seal contact surface. Replace the yoke and seal if the surface is defective.

*Yoke seal replacement*

Replace the yoke seal (12, **Figure 226**) if worn or leaking, or if replacing the drive gear yoke (15).

1. Place the seal carrier on a vise or other suitable work surface with the open side facing downward.

2. Use a blunt punch and carefully drive the seal from the carrier (**Figure 184**). Work carefully to avoid damaging the aluminum carrier. Discard the seal.

3. Use a quick drying solvent and clean all material from the seal carrier. Replace the seal carrier if damaged or corroded.

4. Place the seal carrier on the table of a press with the open side facing down. Apply a light coat of Loctite 271

to the outer diameter of the new seal. Install the seal into the carrier bore opening with the seal lip side facing downward.

5. Place a suitable mandrel or flat piece of steel on the seal. The mandrel or piece of steel must be larger than the diameter of the seal.

6. Press the seal into the bore until flush with the carrier.

### Drive bear and bearings removal and installation

Remove the drive gear bearings (31 and 33, **Figure 177**) only if defective or if replacing the gear. The removal process will damage the bearings.

1. Use an appropriately sized socket or section of tubing to press the gear from the bearings. The tool must be slightly smaller in diameter than the hub of the gear.

2. Wedge a bearing separator into the gap between the drive gear (3, **Figure 226**) and the smaller bearing (4). Place the separator and gear on the table of a press.

3. Press the gear from the bearings.

4. Use a section of tubing to install the bearings. The tubing must be of sufficient length and have an inner diameter slightly larger than the hub of the gear. The tubing surface must contact only the flat surface of the inner bearing races to avoid damaging the races during installation.

5. Place the drive gear on the table of a press with the teeth facing downward. Place the smaller diameter bearing onto the gear hub with the tapered side facing upward. Apply gearcase lubricant to the drive gear and tapered roller bearings.

6. Press the bearing over the hub until it seats against the gear. Place the smaller diameter bearing face over the gear hub with the tapered end facing down. Seat the race against the bearing.

7. Place the spacer onto the smaller diameter bearing race. The larger diameter side of the spacer must contact the smaller diameter bearing race.

8. Place the larger diameter race (7, **Figure 226**) over the drive gear hub with the tapered opening facing up.

9. Place the large diameter bearing (8, **Figure 226**) onto the hub of the gear with the tapered side facing down.

10. Monitor the spacer (6, **Figure 226**) for movement while pressing the bearing onto the gear hub. Press the bearing onto the hub until only a slight amount of movement is present. Do not eliminate all movement.

11. Apply gearcase lubricant to the bearings.

### Universal joint, socket and yokes removal and installation

Remove the universal joint only if it must be replaced. Use an automotive-type universal joint tool and adapter (Mercury part No. 38758) to remove and install the universal joints. Refer to **Figure 186**.

> *CAUTION*
> *Improperly installed, damaged or worn universal joints can unexpectedly fail, damaging the drive shaft housing, the transom assembly and even the boat structure. Repair of the universal joints should only be performed by an experienced mechanic with access to the appropriate tools.*

1. Clamp the socket of the universal joint assembly in a vise with protective jaws. Use a punch and hammer to remove the C-rings (5, **Figure 186**) from the universal joint. Discard the C-rings.

2. Clamp the universal joint tool in a vise. Place the adapter into the open end of the tool with the larger opening facing the bolt. Remove the caps from the universal joint cross as follows:

   a. Insert the exposed end of one of the bearing caps into the adapter while mounting the shaft into the tool (**Figure 187**).

   b. Turn the bolt until the flat end just contacts the opposite bearing cap. Turn the bolt to push the bearing cap into the adapter. Remove the cap from the adapter.

   c. Loosen the bolt. Rotate the universal joint shaft 180° and center the remaining cap in the adapter opening.

   d. Turn the bolt until the flat end just contacts the shaft of the universal joint cross. Turn the bolt to push the opposite cap into the adapter.

   e. Remove the cap from the adapter. Repeat this process for the remaining two bearing caps.

   f. Slip the universal joint cross from the yoke and socket.

3. Install the caps onto the universal joint cross as follows:

   a. Slip the universal joint cross into the opening in the yoke or socket. The grease fitting must face toward the engine coupling yoke.

   b. Align the bearing surface of the cross with the caps and insert both caps into the openings (**Figure 188**).

   c. Insert the exposed end of one of the caps into the adapter and mount the shaft into the tool (**Figure 187**).

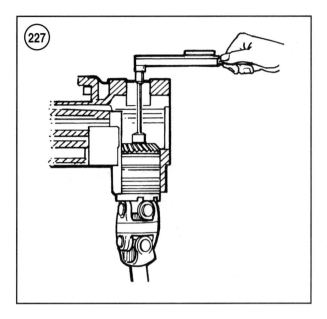

d. Turn the bolt until the flat end just contacts the opposite bearing cap. Turn the bolt and push the cap through the opening. Stop when the C-clip groove is exposed. Align the ends of the new C-clip with the groove in the cap. Use a hammer to tap the clip into the groove. The clip must seat fully in the groove.

e. Loosen the bolt. Rotate the universal joint shaft 180° and insert the fully installed cap into the adapter.

f. Turn the bolt until the flat end just contacts the opposite bearing cap. Turn the bolt and push the opposite cap into the adapter. Stop when the C-clip groove is exposed. Align the ends of the new C-clip with the groove in the cap. Use a hammer and tap the clip into the groove. The clip must seat fully in the groove. If not, check for proper cap installation.

g. Repeat this process for the remaining two bearing caps. Thread the plug into the replacement universal joint cross. Pump grease into the universal joints as described in this chapter.

**Universal Joint Shaft Assembly**

Refer to **Figure 226**. Remove the upper drive shaft from the housing for this operation.

*NOTE*
*Preload specifications for new bearings may differ from those for used bearings. Bearings are used if spun one revolution under power.*

1. Slide a flat metal bar through the universal joint shaft and clamp it in a vise (**Figure 183**).
2. Place the spanner nut (14, **Figure 226**) over the drive gear yoke (15) and seat it against the metal bar.
3. Apply gearcase lubricant to the seal lip. Slide the seal carrier (13, **Figure 226**) over the yoke with the seal lip facing away from the spanner nut. Seat the carrier against the spanner nut.
4. Slide the black spacer (11, **Figure 226**) onto the shaft with the tapered side facing the spanner nut. Fit the spacer into the recess in the seal carrier.
5. Slide the larger diameter spacer (9, **Figure 226**) over the shaft with the tapered side facing the spanner nut.
6. Slide the drive gear and bearing assembly onto the universal joint assembly.
7. Slide the washer (2, **Figure 226**) over the shaft. The concave side of the washer must contact the gear. Thread the new elastic locknut (1, **Figure 226**) onto the shaft. Do not tighten the nut at this time. Remove the metal bar.
8. Slide the universal joint assembly into the bore. Hand-tighten the spanner nut. Position the gearcase so the universal joint hangs down. The drive gear and universal joint assembly must spin freely. If if the joint spins roughly or binds, disassemble the shaft and check for damaged or improperly installed components.
9. Connect a dial-type in.-lb. torque wrench to the drive gear nut (**Figure 227**). Observe the torque reading while turning the shaft. The torque reading indicates the bearing preload for the universal joint shaft bearings.
10. Compare the measured preload with the specification in **Table 4**. Correct the preload as follows:
   a. If the preload is below the specification, tighten the nut approximately 1/16 turn (do not use the torque wrench) and the preload again. Repeat this step until the preload reaches the specification.
   b. If the preload exceeds the specification, disassemble the universal joint assembly. Press the outer bearing only from the drive gear. Do not use excessive force, which may damage the bearing. Reinstall the bearing as described in this chapter.
11. Remove the universal joint shaft. Handle the shaft with care to prevent the spacers from falling out of alignment, which will make reassembly of the housing difficult.
12. Install the upper drive shaft assembly and the universal joint assembly as described in this chapter.

**Driven Gear Bearing Race Removal and Installation**

Remove the bearing race(s) (5 and 13, **Figure 195**) only if defective, or to replace the corresponding driven gear. Use a bearing removal tool (Mercury part No.

**11**

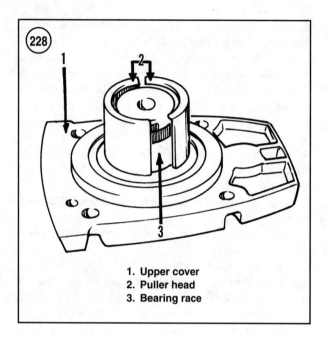

1. Upper cover
2. Puller head
3. Bearing race

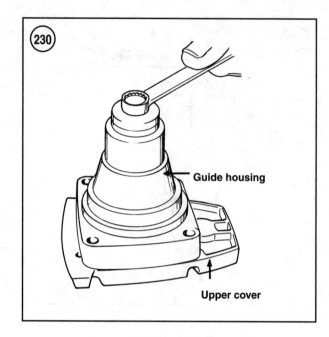

Guide housing

Upper cover

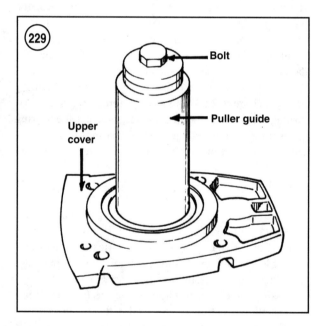

Bolt

Puller guide

Upper
cover

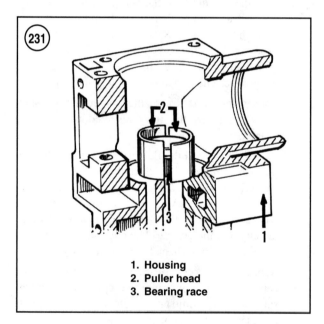

1. Housing
2. Puller head
3. Bearing race

91-90774A1) and driver (Mercury part No. 91-862530) for this procedure.

1. Remove the bearing race from the upper cover as follows:

   a. Attach both halves of the puller head to the race as shown in **Figure 228**.

   b. Slip the puller guide over the puller head as shown in **Figure 229**. Insert the bolt (**Figure 229**) through the guide. Thread the bolt into the puller head. Do not tighten the bolt.

   c. Slip the guide housing over the puller guide as shown in **Figure 230**. Seat the housing against the cover.

   d. Tighten the bolt until the race pulls from the cover. Remove the bolt, puller head and race.

2. Remove the bearing race from the housing as follows:

   a. Attach both halves of the puller head to the race as shown in **Figure 231**.

   b. Slip the puller guide over the puller head as shown in **Figure 232**. Insert the bolt (**Figure 232**) through

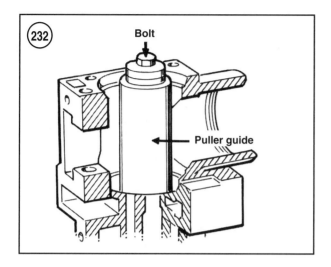

232

**Bolt**

**Puller guide**

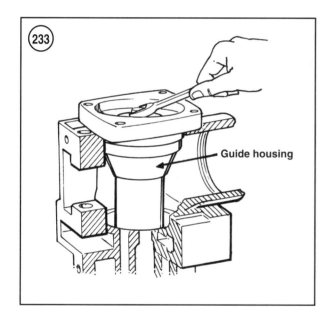

233

**Guide housing**

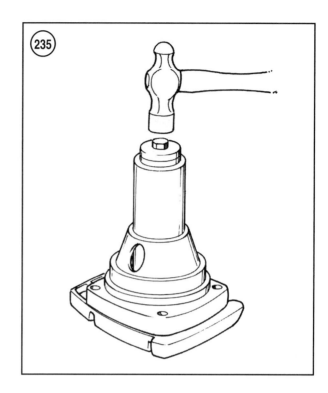

235

the guide. Thread the bolt into the puller head. Do not tighten the bolt.

c. Slip the guide housing over the puller guide and into the housing as shown in **Figure 233**.

d. Tighten the bolt until the race pulls from the housing. Remove the bolt, puller head and race.

3. Inspect the race mounting bosses. Minor surface imperfections are acceptable. Apply gearcase lubricant to the mounting bosses before installing the race.

4. Install the bearing race into the upper cover as follows:

a. Place the driver (**Figure 234**) onto the open end of the puller guide. The open end of the driver must face outward. Slide the bolt (**Figure 234**) into the guide and thread it into the driver. Place the bearing race (**Figure 234**) into the driver.

b. Place the guide housing on the upper cover as shown in **Figure 235**. Insert the puller guide through the housing.

c. Drive against the bolt until the driver just seats against the boss. The race must be flush with the boss.

5. Install the bearing race onto the drive shaft housing as follows:

a. Position the driver (**Figure 234**) at the open end of the puller guide. The open end of the driver must face out. Slide the bolt (**Figure 234**) into the guide and thread it into the driver. Place the bearing race (**Figure 234**) into the driver.

**11**

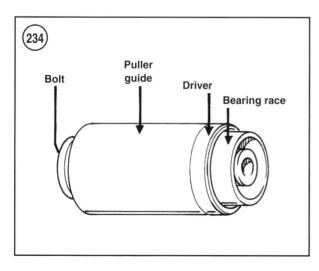

234

**Bolt** **Puller guide** **Driver** **Bearing race**

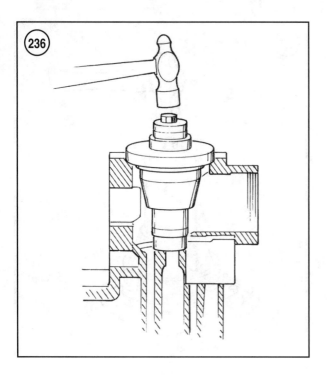

b. Place the guide housing into the drive shaft housing as shown in **Figure 236**. Carefully guide the puller guide through the puller housing. Align the bearing race with the boss on the housing.

c. Drive against the bolt until the driver just seats against the boss. The race must be flush with the boss.

### Drive Shaft Needle Bearing Removal and Installation

Remove the drive shaft needle bearing(s) (6 and 12, **Figure 195**) only if defective, or to replace the upper drive shaft. The removal process damages the bearing. A slide hammer, bearing removal tool (Mercury part No. 91-90774A1) and driver (Mercury part No. 91-862530) are required for this procedure.

1. Position the housing with the upper cover opening face up.

2. Use a suitable socket and extension or section of tubing for a bearing removal tool. Hold the tool tightly against the bearing and drive the bearing from the bore (**Figure 237**). Discard the bearing.

3. Clamp the upper cover in a vise with protective jaws (**Figure 238**). Attach the slide hammer jaws to the back of the bearing. Use short hammer strokes to remove the bearing. Discard the bearing.

4. Install the bearing into the upper cover as follows:

   a. Set the driver (**Figure 234**) on the open end of the puller guide. The open end of the driver must face

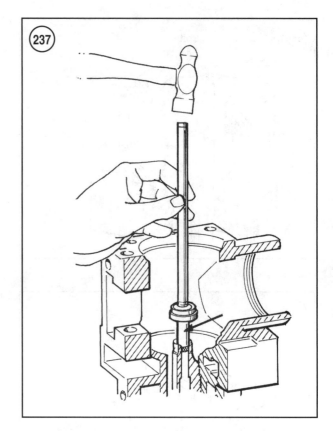

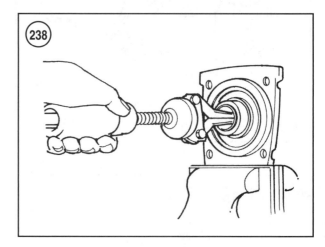

outward. Slide the bolt into the guide and thread it into the driver. Place the needle bearing over the end of the driver. The numbered side of the bearing must contact the driver.

b. Apply gearcase lubricant to the needle bearing. Position the puller guide on the upper cover. Guide the needle bearing into the bore, fitting the driver over the race. Place the guide housing over the puller guide as shown in **Figure 235**.

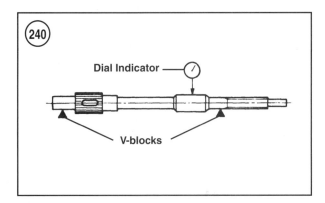

c. Tap the bolt until the driver just seats against the boss and the bearing race.

5. Install the bearing race onto the drive shaft housing as follows:

a. Set the driver (**Figure 234**) on the open end of the puller guide. The open end of the driver must face out. Slide the bolt (**Figure 234**) into the guide and thread it into the driver. Place the needle bearing over the end of the driver. The numbered side of the bearing must contact the driver.

b. Place the guide housing in the drive shaft housing as shown in **Figure 236**. Slide the puller guide through the puller housing. Align the needle bearing with the bore, fitting the driver over the bearing race.

c. Tap the bolt until the driver just seats against the boss and the bearing race.

## DRIVE SHAFT UNIT INSPECTION

Thoroughly clean all components using clean solvent. Note component orientation before cleaning. Use compressed air to dry all components then arrange them in an orderly fashion on a clean work surface. Never allow bearings to spin while using compressed air to dry them.

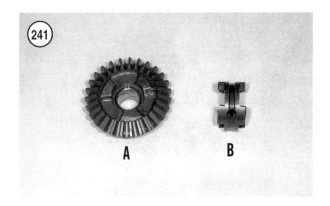

Make sure all components are removed, then use pressurized water to clean the gearcase housing. Inspect all passages and crevices for debris or contaminants. Use compressed air to thoroughly dry the gearcase.

*WARNING*
*Never allow bearings to spin when using compressed air to dry them. The bearing may fly apart or explode and cause injury.*

### Propeller Shaft

1. Inspect the propeller shaft for visibly wear, roughness or damage (**Figure 239**).

2. Position the propeller shaft on V blocks. Rotate the shaft and note any deflection or wobble. Replace the propeller shaft if deflection or wobble is visible.

3. Inspect the propeller shaft at the seal contact areas. Replace the propeller shaft if deep grooves are evident.

4. Support the propeller shaft on V-blocks as shown in **Figure 240**. Mount a dial indicator at the rear bearing support area. Rotate the propeller shaft and note the runout. Replace the propeller shaft if runout exceeds 0.006 in. (0.15 mm).

### Gear and Clutch

1A. *Alpha drive*—Inspect the clutch (B, **Figure 241**) and gears for chips, damage, wear or rounded surfaces. Replace the clutch and gears if any of these conditions is found on either component.

1B. *Bravo drive*—Inspect the clutch for irregularities, highly polished surfaces, damaged helical splines or obvious damage in the clutch grooves. Minor surface polishing (**Figure 242**) is acceptable. Replace the clutch if it is highly polished, damaged or excessively worn.

2. Inspect the gears (A, **Figure 241**) for worn, broken or damaged teeth, pits, roughness or excessive wear. Re-

**11**

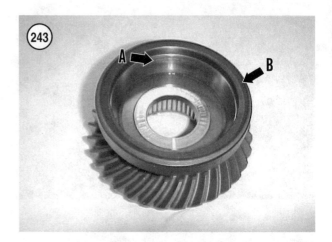

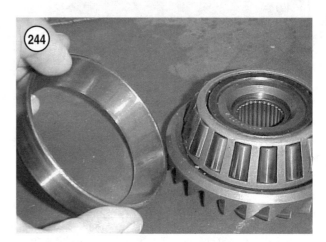

place all of the gears if any of these conditions are found, especially on engines with high operating hours.

3. *Bravo drive*—Inspect the clutch contact surfaces of the driven gear (A, **Figure 243**). Replace the gear if it is discolored, deeply grooved or rough. Minor surface polishing is acceptable. Inspect the torrodial ring surfaces (B, **Figure 243**) for deep grooves, highly polished surfaces or a loose fit to the gear. Replace the gear if these or other defects are visible.

*NOTE*
*Replace all gears if any of the gears require replacement. A wear pattern forms on the gears in a few hours of use. The wear patterns will be disturbed if a new gear is installed with a used gear.*

### Bearing, Shaft and Yoke

1. Clean all bearings thoroughly in solvent and air dry them. Replace bearings if the gear lubricant drained from the gearcase is heavily contaminated with metal particles. These particles tend to collect inside the bearings.
2. Inspect the roller bearings and bearing races (**Figure 244**) for pitting, rusting, discoloration or roughness. Inspect the bearing race for unevenly wear surfaces. Replace the bearing assembly if any of these defects are noted.
3. Rotate ball bearings and note any rough operation. Move the bearing in the directions shown in **Figure 245**. Replace the bearing if rough operation or looseness is noted.
4. Inspect the needle bearings for flattened rollers, discoloration, rusting, roughness or pitting.
5. Inspect the propeller shaft and drive shaft at the bearing contact area (C, **Figure 246**). Replace the drive shaft and propeller shaft along with the needle bearing if discoloration, pitting, transferred bearing material or roughness is present.

6. Inspect the drive shaft splines (A, **Figure 246**) for twisting or excessive wear. Replace the shaft if necessary.
7. *Bravo drive*—Inspect the helical splines (B, **Figure 246**) for wear or damage. Thread the clutch onto the shaft. Replace the shaft if the clutch binds or threads roughly onto the shaft.
8. Inspect all needle or roller bearings for highly polished, excessively worn or damaged surfaces. Replace the shaft if these or other visible defects are noted. Lightly polished surfaces are acceptable.
9. Inspect all seal contact surfaces for deep grooves or pitting. Polish minor surface imperfections with 320 grit carburundum. Do not remove an excessive amount of material. Replace the shaft if these or other defects occur.

### Shift Cam and Yoke Inspection (Bravo Models)

1. Inspect the ramps of the shift cam (A, **Figure 247**) for discoloration or transferred material.
2. Inspect the yoke for discolored or worn areas at the clutch contact surfaces.

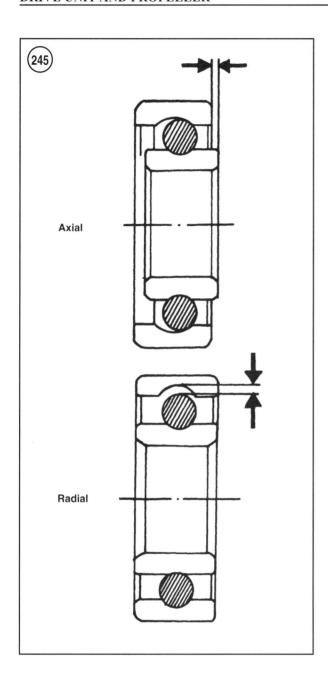

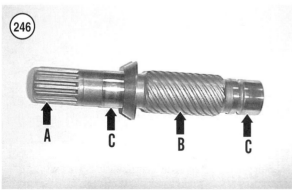

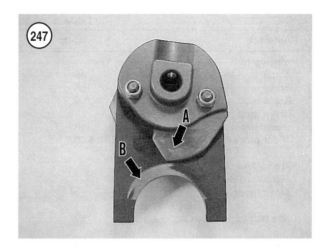

3. Disassemble the cam/yoke assembly if these or other visible defects are evident. Replace the defective components.

### Shims, Spacers, Fasteners and Washers Inspection

1. Inspect all shims for bending, rusting or damage. Replace any shim in less than new condition.
2. Spacers are used in various locations within the drive unit. Replace them if they are worn, bent, corroded or damaged. Be sure to replace them with the correct part. In most cases they are a specific size and material.
3. Replace any locknut unless it is in excellent condition. Always replace the pinion nut during final assembly.

### Seals and O-rings

Replace all seals unless the seal and contacting component has very few operating hours and the seal appears new. Never reuse a seal that has been removed from its bore.

Never reuse an O-ring. Used O-rings generally are flattened or deformed. Flattened or deformed O-rings generally do not provide a reliable seal.

### Universal Joints

1. Move the universal joint shaft in all direction while checking for looseness, binding or roughness. Replace both universal joints if any of these conditions occur. Defects are rarely confined to only one of the joints.

2. Surface irregularities in the needle bearing surfaces may not be detected by feel alone. Inspect or replace the universal joints if knocking or unusual noises occur when the drive is turned and other causes are ruled out.

**11**

### Table 1 TORQUE SPECIFICATIONS

| Fastener | ft.-lb. | in.-lb. | N•m |
|---|---|---|---|
| **Propeller nut** | | | |
| Alpha | 55 | – | 75 |
| Bravo one | 55 | – | 75 |
| Bravo two | 60 | – | 81 |
| Bravo three | | | |
| Front propeller | 100 | – | 136 |
| Rear propeller | 60 | – | 81 |
| | | | |
| **Fill and vent plugs** | | | |
| Alpha models | – | 30-50 | 3.4-5.6 |
| Bravo models | – | 40 | 4.5 |
| | | | |
| **Drive unit to bell housing** | 50 | – | 68 |
| | | | |
| **Upper cover bolts** | 20 | – | 27 |
| | | | |
| **Rear cover (bravo)** | 20 | – | 27 |
| | | | |
| **U-joint shaft spanner nut** | 200* | – | 271* |
| | | | |
| **Drive shaft housing to gearcase** | | | |
| Alpha models | | | |
| Bolts and nuts (side) | 35 | – | 47 |
| Bolts and nuts (front or rear) | 28 | – | 38 |
| Bravo models | 35 | – | 47 |
| | | | |
| **Bravo shift shaft** | | | |
| Linkage to shift shaft | – | 110 | 12 |
| Shift cam to shift shaft | – | 110 | 12 |
| | | | |
| **Bravo shift cam locknuts** | – | 80 | 9 |
| | | | |
| **Trim tab bolt** | 23 | – | 31 |
| | | | |
| **Anodic plate bolts** | 23 | – | 31 |
| | | | |
| **Pinion nut or bolt** | | | |
| Alpha | 70 | – | 95 |
| Bravo one | | | |
| Bolt | 45 | – | 61 |
| Nut | 100 | – | 136 |
| Bravo two | 100 | – | 136 |
| Bravo three | 45 | – | 61 |
| | | | |
| **Cover nut** | | | |
| Alpha, Bravo I and Bravo II | 210* | – | 285* |
| | | | |
| **Bearing retainer** | | | |
| Bravo III | 200* | – | 271* |
| | | | |
| **Bearing carrier** | | | |
| Bravo III | 150* | – | 203 |
| | | | |
| **Water pump screws (alpha)** | – | 60 | 7 |
| | | | |
| **Shift shaft bushing (alpha)** | – | 60 | 7 |
| | | | |
| **Drive shaft retainer (alpha)** | 100 | – | 136 |

\* Applied torque is relative to the length of the torque wrench and adapter. Refer to the repair instructions in the text.

## Table 2 CALCULATING TORQUE WRENCH EFFECTIVE LENGTH

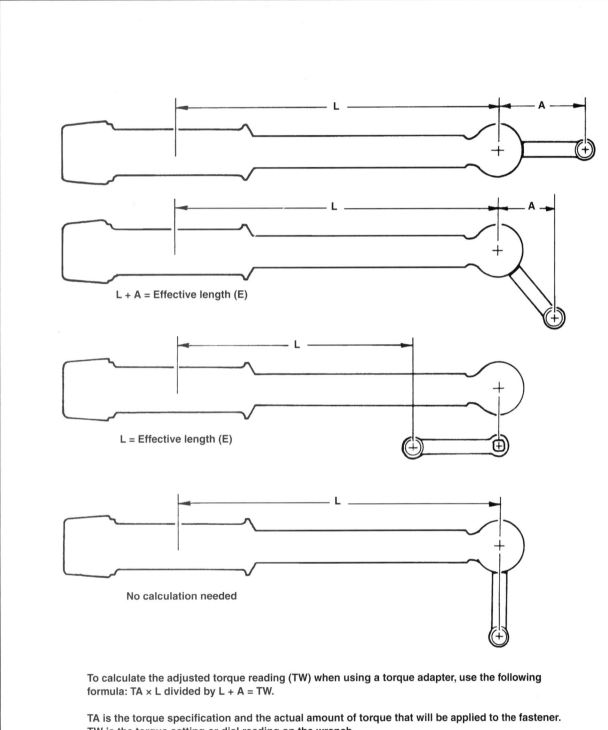

L + A = Effective length (E)

L = Effective length (E)

No calculation needed

**11**

To calculate the adjusted torque reading (TW) when using a torque adapter, use the following formula: TA × L divided by L + A = TW.

TA is the torque specification and the actual amount of torque that will be applied to the fastener.
TW is the torque setting or dial reading on the wrench.
L is the torque wrench length.
A is the adapter length.

**Table 3 DRIVE RATIO IDENTIFICATION**

| Overall ratio | Yoke marking | Upper unit gear tooth count | Lower unit gear tooth count |
|---|---|---|---|
| **Alpha drive** | | | |
| 2.4 to 1 | K | 20/24 | 14/28 |
| 2.0 to 1 | * | 24/24 | 14/28 |
| 1.98 to 1 | B | 20/24 | 17/28 |
| 1.84 to 1 | D | 17/19 | 17/28 |
| 1.81 to 1 | * | 17/19 | 13/21 |
| 1.65 to 1 | C | 24/24 | 17/28 |
| 1.62 to 1 | * | 24/24 | 13/21 |
| 1.50 to 1 | F | 22/20 | 17/28 |
| 1.47 to 1 | * | 22/20 | 13/21 |
| 1.32 to 1 | H | 20/16 | 17/28 |
| | | | |
| **Bravo I drive** | | | |
| 1.65 to 1 | C | 23/30 | 15/19 |
| 1.50 to 1 | F | 27/32 | 15/19 |
| 1.36 to 1 | H | 27/29 | 15/19 |
| | | | |
| **Bravo II drive** | | | |
| 2.20 to 1 | C | 23/30 | 16/27 |
| 2.00 to 1 | F | 27/32 | 16/27 |
| 1.81 to 1 | H | 27/21 | 16/27 |
| 1.65 to 1 | T | 27/32 | 18/25 |
| 1.50 to 1 | * | 27/29 | 18/25 |
| | | | |
| **Bravo III drive** | | | |
| 2.43 to 1 | N | 23/30 | 13/24 |
| 2.20 to 1 | K | 23/30 | 16/27 |
| 2.00 to 1 | B | 23/32 | 16/27 |
| 1.81 to 1 | G | 27/29 | 16/27 |
| 1.65 to 1 | C | 27/32 | 18/25 |
| 1.50 to 1 | F | 27/32 | 15/19 |
| 1.36 to 1 | P | 27/29 | 15/19 |
| | | | |
| **Bravo ZX** | | | |
| 1.50 to 1 | Z | 27/32 | 15/19 |
| 1.36 to 1 | T | 27/29 | 15/19 |
| | | | |
| **Bravo ZR** | | | |
| 1.50 to 1 | R | 16/19 | |

*Code for this ratio was not available at the time of printing.

**Table 4 BEARING PRELOAD SPECIFICATIONS**

| | in.-lb. | N•m. |
|---|---|---|
| **Lower drive shaft** | | |
| **All bravo drives** | | |
| New bearings | 3-5 | 0.3-0.6 |
| Used bearings | 3-5 | 0.3-0.6 |
| | | |
| **Propeller shaft** | | |
| **Bravo I and II drives** | | |
| New bearings | 8-12 | 0.9-1.4 |
| Used bearings | 5-8 | 0.6-0.9 |
| (continued) | | |

**Table 4 BEARING PRELOAD SPECIFICATIONS (continued)**

|  | in.-lb. | N•m. |
|---|---|---|
| **Upper drive shaft** | | |
| **All alpha drives** | | |
| New bearings | 6-10 | 0.7-1.1 |
| Used bearings | 3-7.5 | 0.3-0.8 |
| | | |
| **Universal joint shaft** | | |
| **All alpha drives** | | |
| New bearings | 6-10 | 0.7-1.1 |
| Used bearings | 3-7.5 | 0.3-0.8 |
| All bravo drives | 6-10 | 0.7-1.1 |

**11**

# Chapter Twelve

# Transom Assembly

Transom assembly components are constantly exposed to the elements, plus the normal wear and tear of steering, tilting and shifting the drive unit. Even with frequent maintenance, some components eventually fail. This chapter describes repair procedures for all components of the transom assembly.

## GIMBAL BEARING

Alpha and Bravo drive units (except XR and XZ models) use the same gimbal bearing. The replacement procedures are identical for either type of drive unit.

Failure of the gimbal bearing (**Figure 1**) is almost always due to water entering the universal joint bellows. Water displaces the lubricant in the gimbal bearing and promotes corrosion. Before replacing the gimbal bearing, correct the source of water intrusion. Typical causes include a hole in the universal joint bellows, a damaged or out of position seal ring, a high water level in the bilge compartment and loose drive attaching nuts.

Gimbal bearing failure can also occur from inadequate lubrication or using the wrong type of lubricant. Although a replacement gimbal bearing is filled with grease to prevent corrosion during storage and shipping, this grease does not provide adequate lubrication for use. Improper installation can make lubrication of the gimbal bearing extremely difficult. Make sure the gimbal bearing is properly lubricated before installing the drive unit.

### Inspection

1. Remove the drive unit as described in Chapter Eleven.
2. Reach into the universal joint bellows and rotate the inner race of the gimbal bearing. The race must rotate without binding or roughness.
3. Push and pull the inner race of the bearing while checking for radial or axial play (**Figure 2**). Replace the gimbal bearing if worn or defective.
4. Check the engine alignment as described in Chapter Seven. Correct the alignment if necessary.
5. Lubricate the gimbal bearing (Chapter Four) until fresh lubricant flows from the bearing (**Figure 3**).
6. Install the drive unit as described in Chapter Eleven.

### Replacement

Remove the gimbal bearing only if worn or defective. The removal process damages the bearing. The tolerance

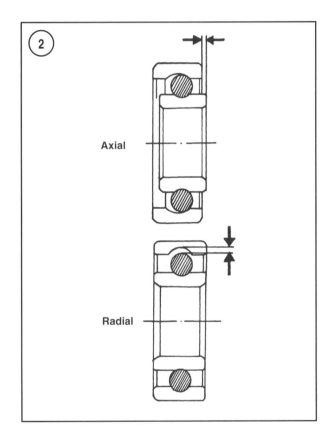

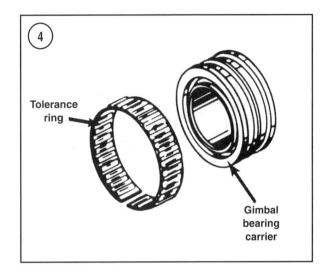

ring (**Figure 4**) in the housing retains the gimbal bearing carrier by compressing and conforming with the bearing bore during installation. The replacement gimbal bearing includes a new tolerance ring.

Always correct the engine alignment as described in Chapter Seven before removing the gimbal bearing. It is very difficult and time consuming to realign both the engine coupler and the gimbal bearing.

Gimbal bearing replacement requires a heavy duty slide hammer with expanding jaws, a bearing tool kit (Mercury part No. 91-31229A 7) and an alignment bar (Mercury part No. 91-805475A 1). Have the bearing replaced by a professional if the required tools are unavailable. Improper installation can result in irreparable damage to the bearing. This procedure includes two methods for removing the gimbal bearing. Removal with a slide hammer and jaw type puller is the most commonly used method. Use the threaded rod method if unable to remove a seized bearing using a slide hammer.

1. Remove the drive unit as described in Chapter Eleven.

2. Check and correct the engine alignment as described in Chapter Seven.

3A. *Slide hammer method*—Remove the bearing as follows:

    a. Insert the slide hammer into the gimbal bearing. Expand the jaws enough to securely grasp the back side of the inner bearing race.

    b. Pull and maintain constant pressure on the free end of the slide hammer. Use short hammer strokes to pull the bearing from the transom housing.

3B. *Threaded rod method*—Remove the bearing as follows:

    a. Thread the expanding jaws (5, **Figure 5**) fully onto the threaded rod. Expand the jaws enough to se-

**12**

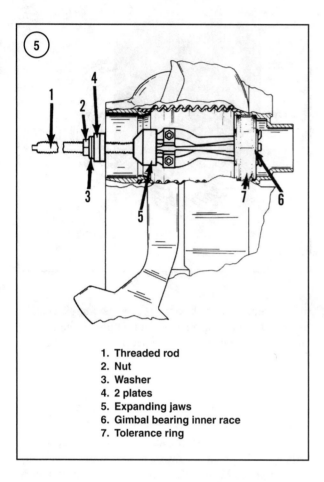

1. Threaded rod
2. Nut
3. Washer
4. 2 plates
5. Expanding jaws
6. Gimbal bearing inner race
7. Tolerance ring

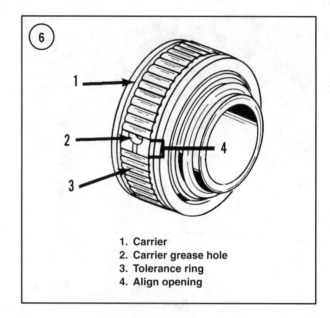

1. Carrier
2. Carrier grease hole
3. Tolerance ring
4. Align opening

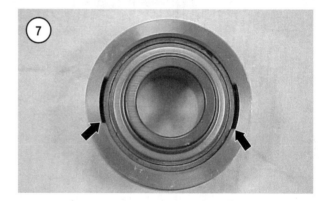

curely grasp the back side of the inner bearing race (6, **Figure 5**).

b. Slide both plates (4, **Figure 5**) and the washer (3) over the threaded rod (1).

c. Arrange the plates to span the opening then seat them against the aft end of the bell housing.

d. Thread the nut (2, **Figure 5**) onto the threaded rod until seated against the washer. Engage an end wrench onto the flats on the end of threaded rod to prevent rotation.

e. Tighten the nut and pull the bearing from the bore. Tap the exposed end of the rod with a plastic hammer if the nut is exceedingly hard to turn or the bearing refuses to budge. Continue tightening the nut and tapping the rod to remove a stubborn bearing from the bore.

4. Wipe all grease and other contaminants from the bearing bore. Inspect the seal in the bore for damage and replace if necessary. Remove the seal using a slide hammer. Use a large socket or section of tubing to fully seat the new seal into the bore. Apply a light coat of grease to the gimbal bearing bore.

5. Install the gimbal bearing as follows:

a. Rotate the tolerance ring until the gap aligns with the carrier grease hole (**Figure 6**).

b. Locate the notches (**Figure 7**) on the bearing carrier and the lubrication passage boss (**Figure 8**) on the transom housing. The grease fitting (3, **Figure 9**) on

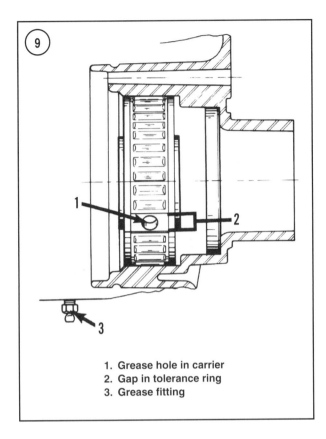

1. Grease hole in carrier
2. Gap in tolerance ring
3. Grease fitting

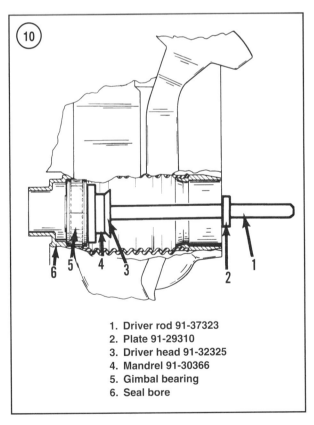

1. Driver rod 91-37323
2. Plate 91-29310
3. Driver head 91-32325
4. Mandrel 91-30366
5. Gimbal bearing
6. Seal bore

the lower starboard side of the transom housing must align with this boss.

c. Align the gap with the grease passage in the carrier.

d. Position the gimbal bearing into its bore in the transom housing. The notches must face toward the engine and the tolerance ring gap must align with the lubrication passage boss.

e. Thread the driver rod (1, **Figure 10**) into the driver head (3). Fit the mandrel (4, **Figure 10**) over the driver head (3). Fit the plate over the unthreaded end of the rod.

f. Insert the end of the driver head into the shaft bore of the gimbal bearing. Seat the rod, driver and mandrel against the gimbal bearing as shown in **Figure 10**.

g. Hold the drivers in firm contact with the bearing while driving the bearing fully into the bore. Proper seating occurs when the pitch changes as the hammer strikes the rod.

h. The chamfered approach for the bearing bore (**Figure 11**) must be fully exposed or the bearing is not fully seated in the bore. Correct improper seating before installing the drive unit.

6. Insert the unthreaded end of the alignment bar into the bearing. Manipulate the bar until it slips into the engine coupler (**Figure 12**). Push the bar into the coupler until fully seated.

7. Tap the exposed end in four locations (**Figure 13**) with a plastic or hard rubber mallet to fully align the bearing) with the engine coupler If correctly aligned, the bar will slide freely into and out of the engine coupler.

8. Lubricate the gimbal bearing (Chapter Four) until fresh lubricant flows from the bearing (**Figure 3**).

9. Install the drive unit as described in Chapter 11.

**12**

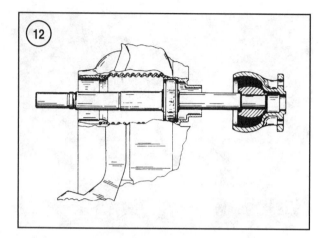

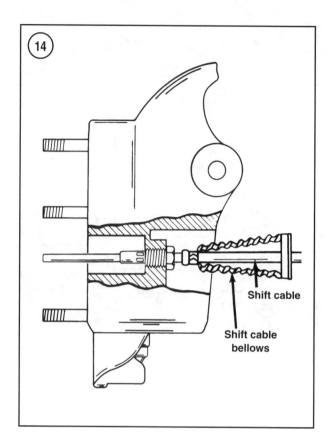

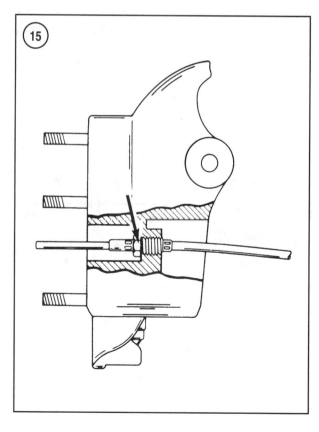

## SHIFT CABLE REPLACEMENT

It is good practice to replace the shift cable bellows (**Figure 14**) when replacing the shift cable. Failure of the shift cable bellows will allow significant water leakage into the boat. An old, brittle or worn bellows usually tears during shift cable replacement.

On Alpha models, a brass nut and tapered threaded section of the cable (**Figure 15**) threads into a non-tapered threaded bore in the bell housing. The tight fit of the tapered threads provide a water tight and secure attachment for the cable.

On Bravo models, a nut (**Figure 16**) secures the shift cable to the bell housing. A sealing washer (**Figure 16**) prevents water leakage between the shift cable and the bell housing.

Shift cable replacement on Alpha models requires a shift cable socket (Mercury part No. 91-12037) and a 1/4-18 NPSF pipe tap (or Mercury part No. 91-95639). Do not use a standard or tapered pipe tap. Using the wrong tap will result in cable loosening and water leakage between the threads.

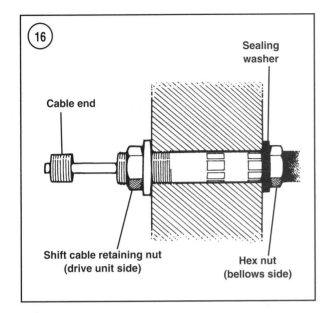

Figure labels: Sealing washer, Cable end, Shift cable retaining nut (drive unit side), Hex nut (bellows side)

16

17

18

19

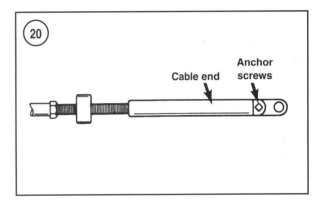

20

Figure labels: Anchor screws, Cable end

Shift cable replacement on Bravo models requires a cable barrel adjusting tools (Mercury part No. 91-17262 and 91-17263). Have the cable barrel adjustments performed by a qualified professional if these tools are unavailable.

On Alpha drives, the replacement shift cable includes a short section of stainless steel safety wire. If reusing the original shift cable, purchase safety wire (0.030-0.032 in. diameter) from a tool supplier or aircraft maintenance facility.

**Shift Cable Removal**

1. Remove the drive unit as described in Chapter Eleven.

2A. *4.3L, 5.0L, 5.7L, 350 Mag and MX 6.2 models*—Remove the nut (**Figure 17**) and lift the flame arrestor cover from the engine.

2B. *7.4L MPI, 496 Mag and 496 Mag HO models*—Remove the Torx screws and oil fill cap (**Figure 18**). Lift the EFI components covers from the engine.

3. Remove the cotter pin, washers and nuts (**Figure 19**) and free the cables from the shift plate.

4. Loosen the anchor screws (**Figure 20**) and pull the cable end from the drive shift cable. Do not remove the cable end from the remote control shift cable.

5. Grip the brass part of the shift cable with locking pliers. Loosen the jam nut (**Figure 21**) then unthread the stainless steel tube from the shift cable. Remove the locking pliers.

12

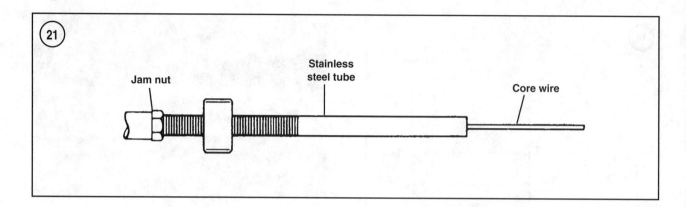

6. Use a block of wood to block the bell housing in the full tilt position as indicated in **Figure 22**.

7. Carefully pry open and remove the crimp clamp (1, **Figure 23**) from the aft end of the shift cable bellows (2). Discard the clamp.

8. Working from inside the boat, remove the protective spiral wrap (**Figure 24**) from the shift cable. Free the cable from any clamps or retainers that could interfere with cable removal.

9A. *Alpha models*—Grasp the shift slide (3, **Figure 25**) and carefully pull the slide and core wire from the shift cable. Cut the safety wire (1, **Figure 25**), then remove the set screw (2) and core wire from the shift slide.

9B. *Bravo drive models*—Grasp the cable end (**Figure 16**) and carefully pull the core wire from the shift cable.

10A. *Alpha drive models*—Remove the cable as follows:

    a. Make a large loop while pulling the shift cable (3, **Figure 23**) through the shift cable bellows (2). Straighten the cable and direct it under the boat. The cable must be free to allow rotation during removal.

    b. Slide the shift cable socket (part No. 91-12037) over the shift slide end of the cable and engage it with the shift cable nut (**Figure 15**).

    c. Engage a 3/4 in. socket onto the hex end of the socket. Loosen the nut until the cable is free from the bell housing.

10B. *Bravo drive models*—Remove the cable as follows.

    a. Attach a wrench to the hex nut (**Figure 16**) on the bellows side of the shift cable attachment. Install a socket wrench onto the drive side nut.

    b. Hold the bellows side nut stationary while removing the drive side nut.

    c. Use a blunt rod and push the shift cable out of its bell housing bore. Remove the seal washer (**Figure 16**) from the shift cable. Discard the washer.

    d. Pull the shift cable through the aft end of the shift cable bellows.

11. Insert the core wire into the shift cable. Push in and pull on the core wire while checking for binding or rough-

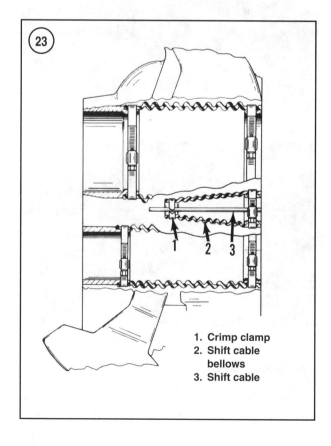

1. Crimp clamp
2. Shift cable bellows
3. Shift cable

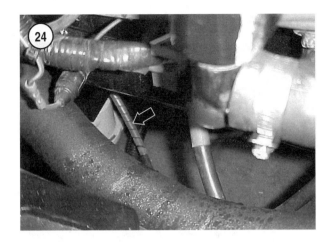

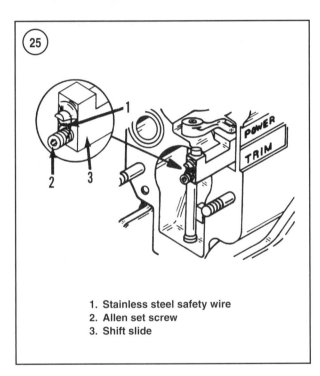

1. **Stainless steel safety wire**
2. **Allen set screw**
3. **Shift slide**

ness in the cable. The core wire must move freely. If not, replace the shift cable assembly.

12. Inspect the cable jacket for burned, abraded, worn or damaged surfaces. Replace if necessary.

13. Manipulate the cable to check for excessive stiffness or a broken inner jacket. Replace the cable if any of these imperfections are noted.

14A. *Alpha models*—Thread the special tap (Mercury part No. 91-95639) into the shift cable bore of the bell housing. This step is necessary to remove old sealant and corrosion from the threads.

14B. *Bravo drive models*—Clean corrosion from the cable bore, and seal washer contact surface of the bell hous-

ing. Replace the bell housing if the washer seal surface is in questionable condition.

### Shift Cable Installation

*CAUTION*
*Do not apply any lubricant to the shift cable core wire. The material in the shift cable jacket provides lubrication for the core wire. The chemicals in some lubricants may damage the shift cable causing shifting difficulty or shift cable failure.*

1. Use a block of wood to block the bell housing in the full tilt position as shown in **Figure 22**.

2. If the shift cable bellows was removed, install it as described in this chapter.

3. On Alpha models, attach the shift cable to the bell housing as follows:
   a. Apply a light coat of perfect seal (Mercury part No. 92-34227-1) to the threaded section of the shift cable.
   b. Slide the engine end of the shift cable through the shift cable bore from the drive side of the bell housing. Direct the end of the shift cable under the boat. This allows cable rotation while securing the cable to the bell housing.
   c. Slide the shift cable socket (part No. 91-12037) over the shift slide end of the cable and engage it with the shift cable nut (**Figure 15**).
   d. Using the shift cable socket, thread the cable into the bell housing. Do not cross thread the cable in the bell housing threads.
   e. Attach a 3/4 in. socket wrench to the socket. Tighten the cable until the brass nut is within two thread widths of contacting the bell housing surface. The cable usually fits very tightly in the bell housing. Remove the cable and clean the threads if the cable is exceedingly tight or cannot be threaded into the bell housing.

4. Route the shift cable as follows:
   a. Lubricate the outer jacket of the cable with soapy water. Cover the threaded opening in the engine end of the shift cable with tape to prevent contamination during installation.
   b. Carefully insert the engine end of the cable into the aft opening of the shift cable bellows.
   c. While an assistant (working from inside the boat) guides the shift cable above the starboard side exhaust pipe, push the cable through the shift cable bellows. Avoid making any sharp bends to the ca-

**12**

ble. Do not allow the cable to enter the flywheel and engine coupler housings.

   d. Route the cable across the starboard exhaust pipe then back toward the boat transom.

   e. Route the cable behind the steering actuator or cable, then toward the shift plate assembly.

5. Install the protective spiral wrap onto the cable jacket. Slide the wrap down the area on the cable where it contacts the exhaust pipe. Remove the protective tape from the shift cable.

6. On Bravo models, attach the shift cable to the bell housing as follows:

   a. Place a new seal washer over the end of the shift cable (**Figure 16**). Seat the washer against the hex nut on the shift cable.

   b. Guide the shift cable into its opening from the bellows side of the bell housing. Seat the hex nut and seal washer against the bell housing. Apply a light coat of perfect seal (Mercury part No. 92-342271-) to the threads of the shift cable.

   c. Thread the shift cable retaining nut onto the shift cable. Attach a wrench to the hex nut on the bellows side of the shift cable.

   d. Hold the bellows side nut stationary and tighten the shift cable retaining nut to the specification in **Table 1**.

7. Install a new crimp type clamp over the aft end of the shift cable bellows. Remove the blocks and position the bell housing to the full down position. Use 1/2 in. diameter crimping pliers and secure the clamp onto the bellows.

8. Measure the diameter of the hose clamp at several locations. The clamp must have a consistent diameter of 1/2 in. (13 mm). If not, crimp the clamp again.

9. Turn the bell housing to full port. Observe the bellows while tilting the bell housing to the full up position. Carefully slide the aft end of the bellows away from the bell housing to correct excessive stretching or distorting of the bellows.

10A. *Alpha models*—Install the shift slide and core wire as follows:

   a. Straighten the plastic end of the cable if bent during installation. Slide the shift slide (3, **Figure 25**) over the plastic end of the shift cable. The threaded opening must face away from the transom housing.

   b. Slide the core wire through the threaded shift slide and into the shift cable.

   c. Thread the set screw (2, **Figure 25**) into the shift slide with the safety wire hole side facing out.

   d. Tighten the set screw until it just contacts the core wire end. Back the screw out just enough to allow the shift slide to rotate on the shift cable. Do not back the screw out more than needed for slide rota-

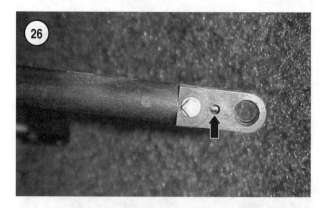

tion. The shift slide must rotate without detectable end play.

   e. Secure the set screw by passing a section of safety wire through the set screw and around the boss on the shift slide as shown in **Figure 25**. Securely twist the wire and cut off any excess length. The wire must not protrude beyond the sides of the shift slide or shifting difficulty may occur.

10B. *Bravo models*—Slide the core wire into the shift cable until the cable end (**Figure 16**) is approximately 2 in. (51 mm) from the cable retaining nut.

11. Working from inside the boat, thread the stainless steel tube (**Figure 21**) with the brass adjusting barrel onto the shift cable. Grip the brass section of the shift cable with locking pliers and securely tighten the jam nut (**Figure 21**).

12. Slide the stainless steel cable anchor into the plastic cable end. Align the core wire opening in the cable anchor with the wire opening in the cable end.

13. Rotate the cable end and anchor while sliding them over the core wire (**Figure 21**) and stainless steel tube. Continue rotating until the core wire passes through the cable anchor and appears in the small hole in the cable end (**Figure 26**).

14. Thread the anchor screws (**Figure 20**) into the anchor until they just contact the core wire. Tighten the screws evenly to the specification listed in **Table 1**.

15A. *Alpha models*—Adjust the shift cable after adjusting the drive unit (Chapter Six).

15B. *Bravo models*—Adjust the shift cable with the drive unit removed as follows:

  a. Insert the bell housing end of the core wire through the slot in the adjustment plate (Mercury part No. 91-17263) as shown in **Figure 27**. Pull lightly on

the cable end (inside the boat) to seat the cable end against the adjusting plate.

  b. Slide the stud on the cable adjusting tool (Mercury part No. 91-17262) through the large opening in the plastic cable end. Pull lightly on the tool to remove any slack.

  c. Rotate the brass barrel until it aligns with and enters the opening in the cable adjusting tool. Remove both adjusting tools. Apply tape to the threads to prevent the barrel from rotating before final adjustment.

16. Install the drive unit as described in Chapter Eleven.

17. Install the shift cables onto the shift plate and perform final adjustments as described in Chapter Six.

### Shift Cable Bellows Replacement

Replace the bellows if torn, cracked, or has developed a set. Small tears in the crease of the bellows are particularly difficult to spot. It is a good practice to replace the bellows if water leakage is detected and other causes are ruled out. Bellows adhesive (Mercury part No. 92-86166-1) is required for this operation. Replace the bellows as follows.

1. Remove the shift cable as described in this chapter.

2. Loosen the hose clamp (**Figure 28**) and carefully pry the bellows from the transom housing.

3. Use a wire brush to remove the bellows adhesive from the bellows mounting boss.

4. Look into the boss and inspect the shift cable bushing (A, **Figure 29**). Carefully pry the bushing from the housing and replace it if broken or worn. Do not remove the bushing unless defective. The bushing usually breaks during removal.

5. If removed, carefully push a new bushing into the shift cable bore until it snaps into place. The large diameter side must face out.

6. Use carburetor and choke cleaner to clean the mounting surface of the bellows (**Figure 30**) and the mounting boss on the transom assembly (B, **Figure 29**). Apply a light coat of bellows adhesive to these surfaces.

7. Quickly push the shift cable bellows fully onto the boss. Install the clamp onto the bellows with the clamp screw positioned as indicated in **Figure 28**. Hold the clamp in position while tightening the clamp screw to the specification listed in **Table 1**. Wait a few minutes for the bellows material to compress and retighten the clamp.

8. Install the shift cable as described in this chapter.

**12**

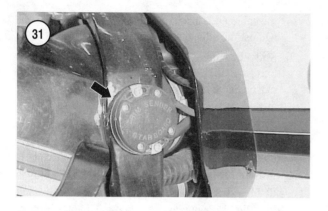

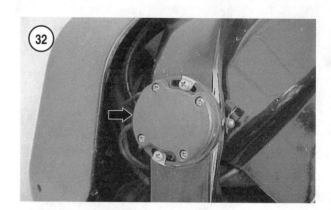

## TRIM LIMIT SWITCH AND TRIM SENDER

The trim sender (**Figure 31**) attaches to the starboard side of the gimbal ring; the trim limit switch (**Figure 32**) attaches to the port side of the ring. Water leaking through cracked wire insulation is the most common cause of failure for both these components. If one component fails, it is usually a good idea to replace both parts at the same time, since both are exposed to the same conditions. Also, a combination trim limit and sender kit, available from a Mercruiser dealership, is less expensive than buying the two parts separately. Replacement of the switch and sender requires a hinge pin tool (Mercury part No. 91-78310).

### Removal

1. Remove the drive unit as described in Chapter Eleven.

2. Turn the steering slightly to port to access the sender mounting screws. Remove both screws and pull or pry the sender from the gimbal ring (**Figure 33**). Tape the sender to the transom housing to prevent it from becoming trapped between the housing and ring.

3. Turn the steering slightly to the starboard side to access the limit switch mounting screws. Remove both screws and carefully pull or pry the switch from the gimbal ring. Tape the twitch to the transom housing.

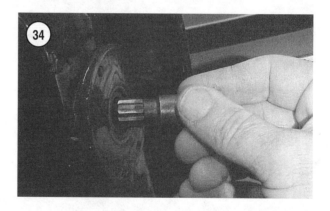

4. Turn the steering wheel to allow access to the starboard side hinge pin. Position the bell housing in the full down position. Insert the hinge pin tool (Mercury part No. 91-78310) into the starboard side hinge pin (**Figure 34**). Use a 1/2 in. heavy duty socket and breaker bar to remove the starboard side hinge pin (**Figure 35**).

5. Turn the steering wheel to allow access to the port side hinge pin. Position the bell housing in the full up position. Remove the port side hinge pin (**Figure 36**) using the same tools described in Step 4.

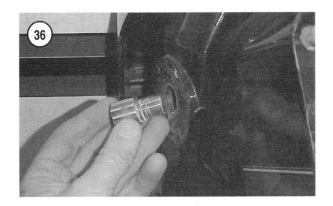

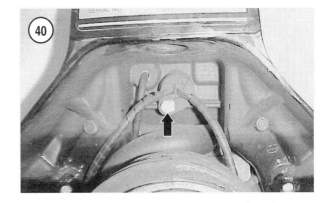

6. On Bravo models, pull out on the bell housing and remove the thrust washer (**Figure 37**) from the port and starboard sides of the gimbal ring.

7. Use a tap and die to clean the gimbal ring and hinge pin threads.

8. Working from inside the boat, disconnect the trim limit switch wires from the trim pump harness (**Figure 38**). Disconnect the trim sender wires from the engine wire harness (**Figure 39**). Remove all clamps from the wires.

9. Push down on the bell housing to access the wire retainer bolt (**Figure 40**). Use a 1/4 in. drive universal adapter and 7/16 in. socket to remove the bolt. If the bolt is inaccessible, remove the bell housing as described in this chapter.

10. Pry the retainer away from the housing. Pull the wires and retainer from the opening. Pull wires from the slot in the retainer.

11. Pull the plastic clamp (**Figure 41**) from the limit switch and water hose.

**Installation**

1. Feed the limit and sender wires through the wire opening and into the engine compartment.

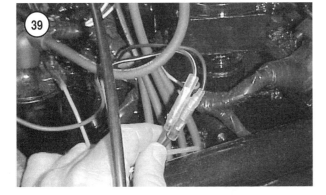

**12**

2. Align the two plastic pieces as shown in **Figure 42**. Apply electrical tape to the engine side of the wires as shown in **Figure 43**. This step prevents the wires from becoming pinched by the retainer.

3. Insert both wires through the slot in the retainer. Install the retainer with the stamped number facing away from the transom housing. Direct both plastic pieces into the opening of the retainer.

4. Guide the retainer and plastic pieces into the transom housing opening while as assistant pulls up the slack on both wires. Align the bolt openings, then insert the bolt. Tighten the bolt to the specification listed in **Table 1**.

5. Pass the trim sender and its wires between the gimbal ring and the starbord side of the transom housing. Tape the sender to the side of the gimbal housing.

6. Pass the trim limit switch and its wires between the gimbal ring and the port side of the transom housing. Tape the sender to the side of the gimbal housing.

7. On Bravo models, place the thrust washer (**Figure 37**) into the recess on each side of the bell housing.

8. Align the openings in the bell housing with the hinge pin opening in the gimbal ring. Apply Locquic Primer T (Mercury part No. 92-59327-1) to the gimbal ring and hinge pin threads. After the primer dries, apply Loctite 8831 (Mercury part No. 92-823089-1) to the bell housing and hinge pin threads.

9. Hand-thread both hinge pins into the bell housing. Evenly tighten the hinge pins to the specification listed in **Table 1**. Place the bell housing in the full down position.

10. Time the sender by aligning the raised mark on the sender rotor (A, **Figure 44**) with the raised mark on the sender (B, **Figure 44**). Position the steering wheel so the hinge pin is accessible. Without disturbing the sender timing, insert the rotor portion of the trim sender into the starboard side hinge pin. Install and lightly tighten both screws, washers and retainers.

11. Time and install the limit switch following the same procedure as the trim sender (Step 11).

12. Install the plastic clamp on to the limit switch wire and water hose (**Figure 41**).

13. Connect the trim limit switch to the trim pump harness (**Figure 38**). The trim limit wires use two male bullet connectors. Connect the trim sender wires to the engine wire harness (**Figure 39**). Secure the wires with plastic clamps to keep them away from moving components.

14. Install the drive unit as described in Chapter Eleven. Adjust the trim sender and trim limit switch as described in Chapter Six.

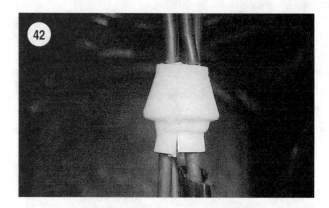

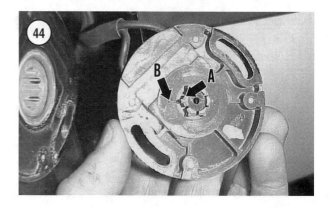

## WATER HOSE REPLACEMENT

### Alpha Models

1. Remove the drive unit as described in Chapter Eleven.

2. The water supply hose connects to the transom housing above the universal joint shaft. Loosen the clamp (2, **Figure 45**) and pull the water supply hose (3) from the water tube fitting (1).

3. Remove both bolts (1, **Figure 46**) and pull the retainer (3) from the transom housing. Pry the grommet from the water tube fitting and transom assembly.

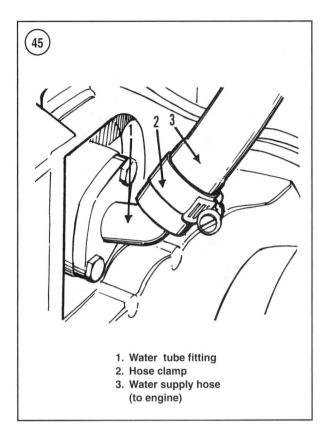

45

1. Water tube fitting
2. Hose clamp
3. Water supply hose
   (to engine)

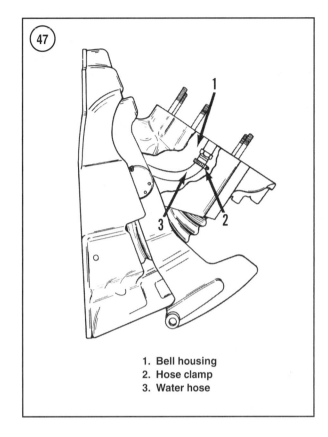

47

1. Bell housing
2. Hose clamp
3. Water hose

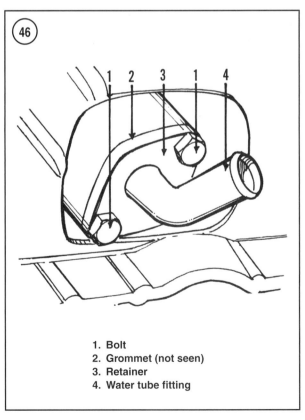

46

1. Bolt
2. Grommet (not seen)
3. Retainer
4. Water tube fitting

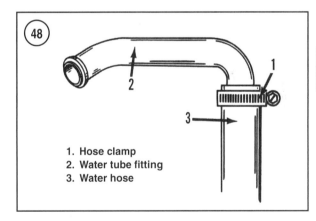

48

1. Hose clamp
2. Water tube fitting
3. Water hose

**12**

4. Push the water tube fitting into the opening and free the fitting and water hose from the transom housing. Pull the plastic hose clamp (**Figure 41**) from the trim limit switch wires and water hose.

5. Place the bell housing in the full up position as shown in **Figure 47**. Loosen the hose clamp (2, **Figure 47**) and pull the water hose (3) from the fitting. If replacing the hose, slit the hose at the fitting for easier removal. Remove the bell housing as described in this chapter.

6. Pull the water hose and fitting from the transom housing. Loosen the hose clamp (1, **Figure 48**) then pull the

water tube fitting (2) from the water hose (3). If replacing the hose, slit the hose at the fitting for easier removal.

7. Inspect the water tube for cracks or distortion. Inspect the water hose for wear, weathering or leaks. Replace if necessary.

8. Apply a soap and water solution to the hose openings to ease installation onto the water tube or fitting. Install the hose over the water tube fitting until it just reaches the bend in the fitting. Install the hose clamp (1, **Figure 48**) on the hose as shown in **Figure 48**. Do not tighten the clamp at this time.

9. Insert the water tube through the transom housing. Direct the engine end of the tube slightly up toward the engine. Direct the water hose toward the port side of the transom housing. Rotate the hose clamp until the screw is on top of the hose, facing outward. Securely tighten the clamp.

10. Lubricate the water tube grommet with soapy water, then slide the smaller diameter end of the grommet over the tube (4, **Figure 46**). Seat the grommet in the transom housing. Place the retainer (3, **Figure 46**) over the tube. Install and securely tighten the bolts (1, **Figure 46**).

11. Slide the water supply hose (3, **Figure 45**) over the water tube until it reaches the bend in the tube. Install and securely tighten the hose clamp (2, **Figure 45**).

12. Place the hose clamp (2, **Figure 47**) over the water hose. Position the screw on top of the hose, facing the port side. Install the bell housing as described in this chapter.

13. Lubricate the drive end of the water hose (3, **Figure 47**) with soapy water and slide the hose fully over the bell housing fitting. Position the hose clamp (2, **Figure 47**) with the screw facing down, on the opposite side of the hose from the bellows. Securely tighten the hose clamp.

14. Install the plastic clamp onto the limit switch wire (**Figure 41**) and water hose as described in this chapter under *Trim Limit Switch and Trim Sender*.

15. Install the drive unit as described in Chapter Eleven.

### Bravo Models

Water hose replacement requires a special water hose insert tool (Mercury part No. 91-43579). Attempting to remove the inserts without the tool will damage the inserts.

1. Remove the drive unit as described in Chapter Eleven.

2. Remove the bell housing as described in this chapter.

3. Loosen the clamp (A, **Figure 49**) and pull the water hose from the hose fitting (B). Remove the bolts (C, **Figure 49**). Carefully pry the fitting from the transom assembly. Scrape gasket material and corrosion from the transom surface and hose fitting.

4. Slide the insert tool (Mercury part No. 91-43579) into the water hose insert (**Figure 50**). Use a 3/8 in. extension to unthread the insert from the hose (**Figure 51**). Inspect

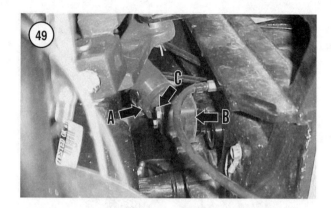

the insert for a collapsed opening or other damage and replace as required.

5. Use a blunt object to push the hose from the transom opening. Clean all corrosion from the transom opening.

6. Inspect the water hose for wear, weathering or leaks. Pay particular attention to the surfaces that contact the transom and bell housing hose opening, which are often damaged by corrosion deposits. Replace the hose if its condition is questionable.

7. Apply a light coat of water resistant grease to the hose opening in the transom assembly. Use needlenose pliers to

grip the hose from the engine side of the opening. Twist the pliers and collapse the hose as shown in **Figure 52**. Pull the hose into the opening until approximately 1/8 in. (3.2 mm) below the fitting surface (**Figure 53**).

8. Rotate the hose until the bend extends down and toward the port side as shown in **Figure 54**. Place the threaded insert into the hose with the tapered side facing in. Use the insert tool and 3/8 in. extension to thread the insert into the hose. Stop when the insert is flush with the water hose. The hose and insert must not protrude beyond the water hose fitting surface. Remove the fitting and reposition the hose as required.

9. Install a new gasket and the water tube fitting (C, **Figure 49**) onto the transom assembly. The hose end must face up toward the starboard side. Install the bolts (B, **Figure 49**) and tighten them to the specification in **Table 1**.

10. Install the bell housing as described in this chapter. Install the drive unit as described in Chapter Eleven.

## BELL HOUSING

A slide hammer with two expandable jaws, a hinge pin tool (Mercury part No. 91-78310) and a bellows installation driver (Mercury part No. 91-818162) are required to remove and install the bell housing. Bravo drive units also require an insert tool (Mercury part No. 91-43579)

> *WARNING*
> *Use extreme caution when cleaning with lacquer thinner or other flammable solvents. Flammable liquids and vapors can ignite, causing a fire or explosion. Never smoke or allow sparks or open flame in the work area. Never use gasoline as a cleaning solvent.*

### Removal

1. Remove the drive unit as described in Chapter Eleven. If the model is equipped with an exhaust bellows, disconnect it from the bell housing as described in this chapter.

2A. *Alpha models*—Remove the shift cable as described in this chapter.

2B. *Bravo models*—Disconnect the shift cable from the bell housing as described in this chapter. Do not remove the cable from the shift cable bellows or transom assembly.

3. Slide the insert tool (Mercury part No. 91-43579) into the water tube insert (**Figure 55**). Use a 3/8 in. extension to unthread the insert from the hose (**Figure 56**). Inspect the insert for a collapsed opening or other damage and replace if necessary. Use a blunt object to push the hose

**12**

from the transom opening. Clean all corrosion from the hose opening.

4.  On Alpha models, place the bell housing in the full up position as shown in **Figure 47**. Loosen the hose clamp (2, **Figure 47**) and pull the water hose (3) from the fitting. If replacing the hose, slit the hose at the fitting for easier removal.

5.  Attach a slide hammer to the rear edges of the bellows retaining ring (**Figure 57**). Use short hammer strokes to remove the retainer from the bellows (**Figure 58**). Discard the retainer.

6.  With a blunt screwdriver, pry up the lower edge of the bellows (**Figure 59**). Pry only against the thicker part near the back edge of the bellows, taking care not to puncture the bellows.. Carefully roll the bellows from the bell housing lip.

7.  Disconnect the ground wire (**Figure 60**) from the bell housing.

8.  Pinch the aft end of the clip (**Figure 61**) and pull the speedometer hose retainer from the bell housing.

9.  Turn the steering slightly toward the port side to access the sender mounting screws. Remove both screws and carefully pull or pry the sender from the gimbal ring (**Figure 33**). Tape the sender to the transom housing so it will not fall or become pinched.

10.  Turn the steering slightly toward the starboard side to access the limit switch mounting screws. Remove both screws and pull or pry the switch from the gimbal ring. Tape the switch to the transom housing.

11.  Turn the steering wheel so to the starboard side hinge pin is accessible. Position the bell housing in the full down position. Insert the hinge pin tool (Mercury part No. 91-78310) into the starboard hinge pin (**Figure 34**). Use a 1/2 in. heavy duty socket and breaker bar to remove the starboard side hinge pin (**Figure 35**).

12.  Turn the steering wheel to allow access to the port hinge pin. Position the bell housing in the full up position. Remove the port side hinge pin (**Figure 36**).

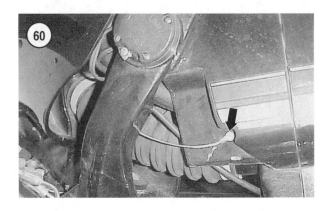

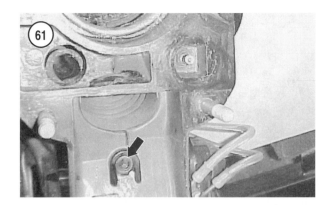

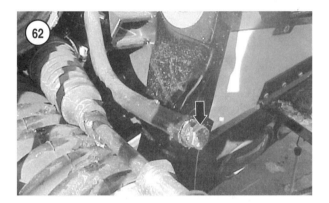

13. On Bravo models, pull out on the bell housing and remove the thrust washers (**Figure 37**) from the port and starboard sides of the gimbal ring.

*NOTE*
*Before performing step 14, have a suitable*
*plug on hand, to block the hose.*

14. Pull the bell housing away from the gimbal ring. Carefully remove the clamp from the aft end of the gearcase lubricant hose. Use a screwdriver to push the hose from the fitting on the bell housing. Quickly plug the hose (**Figure 62**).

15. Use the proper size tap and die and clean all corrosion and Loctite material from the gimbal ring and hinge pin threads.

16. Inspect the Synthane washers (**Figure 63**) on each side of the gimbal ring for wear or damage. Pry worn or damaged washers loose using a chisel. Take care not to damage the aluminum gimbal ring. Use lacquer thinner to remove the washer adhesive from the gimbal ring.

17. Removal usually damages the gearcase lubricant valve (**Figure 64**). Remove it only if replacing the valve, lubrication hose fitting or bell housing. Grip the exposed end of the valve with pliers and pull it from the bell housing with a rocking motion.

18. On Alpha models, remove the water hose fitting from the bell housing only if replacing the fitting or bell housing. Clamp the bell housing into a vise with soft jaws. Use a deep socket to remove the fitting. If necessary, apply moderate heat to the fitting and bell housing to ease removal.

19. On Alpha models, remove the upper shift shaft, seals and shift crank only if defective.

    a. Remove the screw (A, **Figure 65**) then lift the shift crank (B) from the bell housing.

    b. Remove the Teflon washer from the shaft.

    c. Pull the upper shift shaft from the bell housing (**Figure 66**).

**12**

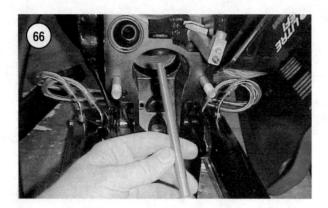

d. Carefully pry both seals (**Figure 67**) from the bell housing.

e. Inspect the roller on the shift crank (B, **Figure 65**) for wear or damage. Replace the shift crank as needed.

20. On Alpha models, inspect the bushings (**Figure 68**) in the bell housing for wear or damage. If any defects are visible, replace the bushings as follows:

a. Use a 1/4 in. socket extension or section of tubing to drive the bushings from the bell housing.

b. Apply a light coat of water resistant grease to the outer diameters of both bushings.

c. Use a 1/4 in. socket extension to drive the upper bushing into the bell housing. The bushing must be flush or slightly recessed below the upper bore.

d. Apply Loctite 8831 (Mercury part No. 92-823089-1) to the outer diameters of both seals. Use an socket and extension to push the seals (**Figure 67**) into the upper shift shaft bore. Install the seals with the lip facing in or toward the shift crank.

e. Drive the lower bushing into the bell housing until flush with the bottom of the bore.

21. Thoroughly clean grease and corrosion deposits from the bell housing surfaces.

**Installation**

1. Apply a light coat of Perfect Seal (Mercury part No. 92-34227-1) to the threads of the lubricant hose fitting. Thread the fitting into the bell housing by hand. Tighten the hose fitting to the specification in **Table 1**. Apply light oil to the O-rings on the gearcase lubricant valve (**Figure 64**). Push the valve into the bell housing until the stepped surface is flush or recessed in the bore.

2. On Alpha models, if the water hose fitting was removed, apply a light coat of perfect seal (Mercury part No. 92-34227-1) to the threads and install the fitting into the bell housing. Tighten securely.

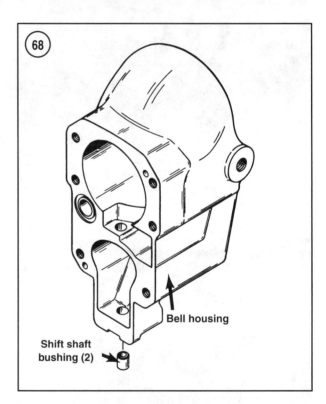

Bell housing

Shift shaft bushing (2)

3. Clean oil, grease or other contaminants from the Synthane washer mounting surface (**Figure 63**). Peel the backing from the replacement Synthane washers. Align the hinge pin openings and attach the washers to the gimbal ring with the adhesive sides toward the gimbal ring. Press firmly to adhere the washers to the gimbal ring.

4. Remove the plug from the gearcase lubricant hose and quickly slide hose fully onto its bell housing fitting. Secure the hose with the reusable plastic clamp. Pull on the hose to verify a tight fit.

5. On Bravo models, install the thrust washers (**Figure 37**) into the recesses on each side of the bell housing.

6. Apply Locquic Primer T (Mercury part No. 92-59327-1) to the gimbal ring and hinge pin threads. After

the primer dries, apply Loctite 8831 (Mercury part No. 92-823089-1) to the bell housing and hinge pin threads.

7. Hand-thread both hinge pins into the bell housing. Evenly tighten the hinge pins to the specification listed in **Table 1**. Place the bell housing in the full down position.

8. To time the sender, align the raised mark on the sender rotor (A, **Figure 44**) with the raised mark on the sender (B). Position the steering so the hinge pin is accessible. Without disturbing the sender timing, insert the rotor portion of the trim sender into the starboard side hinge pin. Install and seat both screws.

9. Time and install the limit switch, following the procedure for the trim sender (Step 8).

10. Attach the ground wire (**Figure 60**) to the bell housing.

11. Roll the end of the bellows back into position as shown in **Figure 69**. Position the bell housing to the full down position. Seat the groove of the bellows over the lip in the bell housing while unrolling the bellows. The groove in the bellows must rest over the lip to properly retain the bellows.

12. Install the bellows retainer as follows:
   a. Position the new bellows retainer on the bellows installation tool as shown in (**Figure 70**).
   b. Apply soapy water or glass cleaner to the exposed surfaces of the bellows retainer. Insert the retainer and installation tool into the bellows with the lip side facing out.
   c. Use a section of tubing to drive the retainer and tool into the bellows. Drive in the retainer until the lip contacts the bellows. Remove the installation tool.
   d. Make sure the retainer is properly seated to the bellows.

13. On Alpha models, attach the water hose to the bell housing as follows:
   a. Position the bell housing full up.
   b. Place the hose clamp (2, **Figure 47**) over the water hose with the screw at the top of the hose, facing the port side.
   c. Lubricate the end of the water hose (3, **Figure 47**) with soapy water and slide the hose fully over the bell housing fitting.
   d. Position the hose clamp (2, **Figure 47**) with the screw facing down and on the opposite side of the hose from the bellows. Securely tighten the hose clamp.

14. Install the plastic clamp onto the limit switch wire (**Figure 41**) and water hose as described in this chapter.

15. Insert the speedometer hose retainer into its bell housing opening (**Figure 61**). Attach the hose to the water tube with the plastic clamp (**Figure 71**). Do not over-tighten the clamp.

16. On Bravo models, attach the water hose to the bell housing as follows:
   a. Apply a light coat of water resistant grease to the hose opening in the bell housing.
   b. Use needlenose pliers to grip the hose from the drive side of the opening. Twist the pliers and collapse the hose as shown in **Figure 52**.
   c. Pull the hose into the opening until it extends approximately 1/8 in. (3.2 mm) beyond the bell housing surface (**Figure 72**). To prevent leakage the hose must be position in the opening as described.

**12**

d. Place the threaded insert into the hose with the tapered side in.

e. Use the insert tool (Mercury part No. 91-43579) and a 3/8 in. extension and thread the insert into the hose. Stop when the insert is flush with the water hose. Remove the insert tool.

17A. *Alpha models*—Install the shift cable as described in this chapter.

17B. *Bravo models*—Attach the shift cable to the bell housing as described in this chapter under *Shift Cable Installation*.

18. Install the plastic clamp onto the limit switch wire and water hose (**Figure 41**).

19. If equipped with an exhaust bellows, install it as described in this chapter.

20. On Alpha models, install the upper shift shaft and shift crank as follows:

a. Lubricate the bores of both bushings and seals with water resistant grease.

b. Slide the upper shift shaft through the lower and upper bushings. Position the offset slot of the shift shaft toward the transom.

c. Apply grease to the Teflon washer and slide it over the shift shaft. Rest the washer against the bell housing.

d. Slide the shift crank (B, **Figure 65**) onto the shift shaft with the roller side facing down. Rest the crank against the Teflon washer. Do not allow grease into the screw openings.

e. Rotate the shift crank to align the screw openings. Apply Loctite 8831 to the threads and install the screws (A, **Figure 65**). Securely tighten the screws.

21. Install the drive unit as described in Chapter Eleven.

22. Adjust the trim sender and limit switch as described in Chapter Six.

### GEARCASE LUBRICANT HOSE AND FITTING

Two different types of fittings connect the hose to the transom housing. Early models use a brass fitting retained to the housing with a washer and lock nut. A 90° tapered seat fitting (**Figure 73**) connects the gearcase lubricant monitor hose to this fitting.

Later models use a plastic material fitting retained into the housing with an E-clip (**Figure 74**). A 90° quick connect fitting attaches the gearcase lubricant monitor hose onto the transom fitting.

1. Drain the gearcase lubricant as described in Chapter Four.

2. Remove the bell housing as described in this chapter.

3A. *Brass fitting*—Remove the 90° hose fitting from the transom fitting (**Figure 73**). Remove the nut and washer from the fitting.

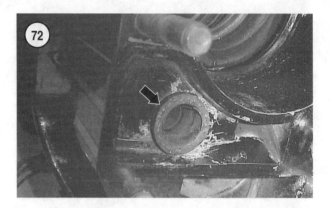

3B. *Plastic fitting* —Push in on the tab and release the hose from the transom fitting. Remove the E-clip from the fitting using needle nose pliers.

4. Carefully pull the fitting (A, **Figure 75**) from the drive side of the transom housing. Inspect the O-rings on the fitting for damage and replace as needed.

5. Loosen the clamp (B, **Figure 75**) and pull the lubricant hose from the fitting.

6. Inspect the hose for damage or abrasion. Replace the fitting if its condition is questionable.

7. Cut the replacement hose to a length of 10 in. (25.4 cm). Slide the gearcase lubricant hose fully onto the fit-

ting. Secure the hose with the reusable plastic clamp. Align the clamp relative to the fitting as shown in **Figure 75**. Pull on the hose to verify a tight fit.

8. Clean all corrosion and debris from the opening and seating surfaces of the fitting. Debris can prevent seating of the O-rings and allow water leakage.

9. Install the O-rings onto the fitting as follows:
   a. Lubricate the O-ring(s) with gearcase lubricant before installation.
   b. On a brass fitting, install the single O-ring over the threaded end of the fitting and seat it against the hex shaped lug.
   c. On a plastic fitting, install both O-rings into the grooves in the fitting.

10. Guide the fitting into the opening. Seat the fitting in the transom housing as shown in **Figure 75**.

11A. *Brass fitting*—Install the washer and locknut. Tighten the nut to the specification in **Table 1**. Install the 90° hose fitting onto the transom fitting. Tighten the fitting to the specification in **Table 1**.

11B. *Plastic fitting*—Install the E-clip (**Figure 74**) into its groove on the fitting. Press in on the tab and push the quick connect fitting fully onto the transom fitting. Release the tab. Pull on the hose to make sure it is securely connected.

12. Install the bell housing as described in this chapter. Fill the gearcase and lubricant reservoir as described in Chapter Four. Check for and correct lubricant leakage before operating the engine.

## EXHAUST BELLOWS

All Alpha models and most Bravo models use an exhaust bellows (**Figure 76**) to direct exhaust gasses from the transom housing toward the drive unit. Hose clamps attach the bellows to fittings on the transom housing and the bell housing. Bellows installation requires a bellows expander tool (Mercury part No. 91-45497A1).

1. Remove the drive unit as described in this chapter.

2. Block the bell housing in the full up position. Fully loosen the clamp screw (**Figure 76**). If replacing the bellows, slit the end to allow easy removal from the bell housing. Otherwise use a blunt screwdriver to pry the exhaust bellows from the bell housing. Be careful not to puncture other components.

3. Insert a 1/4 in. extension through the access opening (**Figure 77**) in the port side of the transom housing. Attach a 5/16 in. socket and universal adapter onto the end of the extension.

4. Fully loosen the clamp screw (**Figure 78**). If replacing the bellows, slit the end to allow easy removal from the transom housing. Otherwise use a blunt screwdriver to

**12**

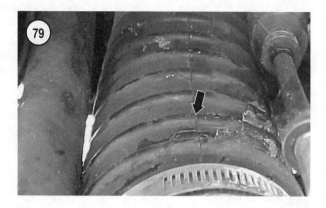

pry the exhaust bellows from the transom housing. Be careful not to puncture other components.

5. Use solvent to thoroughly clean the bellows mount openings on the bell housing and transom housing. Clean the openings at each end of the bellows.

6. Apply bellows adhesive (Mercury part No. 92-86166-Q1) to the bellows mount opening on the transom housing.

7. Place the hose clamp over one end of the bellows. Refer to the mold split line (**Figure 79**) to determine the top and bottom sides of the bellows. The clamp screw must align with the split line on top of the bellows and must face the access hole (**Figure 77**).

8. Slide the ground clip (**Figure 80**) onto the lower edge of the bellows.

9. Push the bellows fully onto the mount opening.

10. Use the tools described in Step 3 to tighten the hose clamp to the specification in **Table 1**. Pull on the bellows to verify a secure attachment.

11. Remove the upper shift shaft, shift crank and Teflon washer as described in this chapter.

12. Apply bellows adhesive (Mercury part No. 92-86166-Q1) to the bellows mount opening (5, **Figure 81**) on the bell housing. Install the clamp on the aft end of the bellows as shown in **Figure 81**. Fit the ground clip under the clamp.

13. Slide the bellows expander tool (3, **Figure 81**) through the bellows (5) on the bell housing. Align the U-shaped plates with the third fold (4, **Figure 81**) of the bellows (1).

14. Squeeze the handle of the tool (1, **Figure 82**) to expand the bellows. Pull the handle to slide the bellows onto the mount opening (5, **Figure 81**). Stop pulling when the small retaining pin holes (3, **Figure 82**) align with the bell housing surface.

15. Slide the retaining pin through both holes until it protrudes equally from both sides of the handle. Insert the clip (2, **Figure 82**) though the small holes at each end of

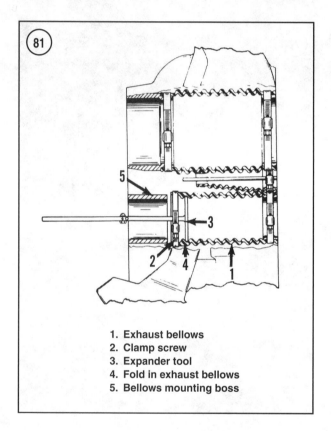

1. Exhaust bellows
2. Clamp screw
3. Expander tool
4. Fold in exhaust bellows
5. Bellows mounting boss

the handle. Slowly release the handle and rest the pin against the bell housing as shown in **Figure 83**.

16. Position the clamp screw (2, **Figure 81**) as shown in **Figure 81**. The screw must face down on the opposite side of the bellows from the water hose. Tighten the clamp to the specification in **Table 1**.

17. Remove the bellows expander tool from the bell housing.

18. Install the upper shift shaft, shift crank and Teflon washer as described in this chapter. Allow the bellows adhesive to dry for at least an hour.

19. Install the drive unit as described in Chapter Eleven.

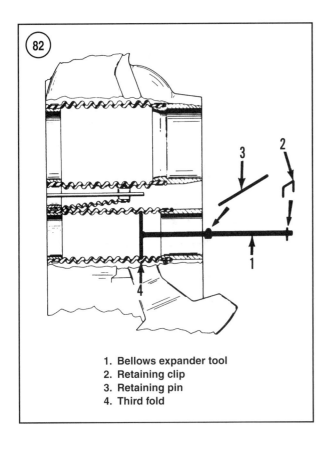

1. Bellows expander tool
2. Retaining clip
3. Retaining pin
4. Third fold

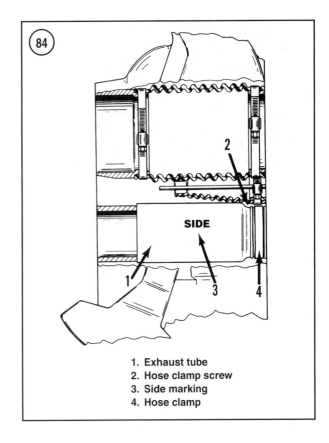

1. Exhaust tube
2. Hose clamp screw
3. Side marking
4. Hose clamp

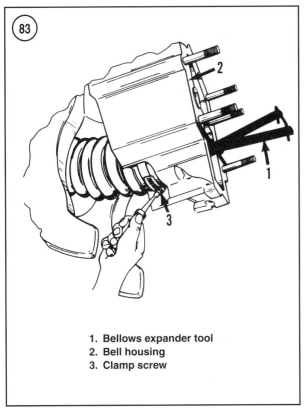

1. Bellows expander tool
2. Bell housing
3. Clamp screw

## EXHAUST TUBE

An exhaust tube (1, **Figure 84**) is used on all big block engines and some small block engines equipped with a Bravo III drive unit. The exhaust tube attaches to an opening on the transom housing and is open at the aft end. With the drive unit trimmed down, the aft end slips over a fitting on the bell housing. Most of the exhaust gas is directed through the drive unit and propeller. With the drive unit trimmed out, the aft end pulls away from the fitting, allowing exhaust gas to bypass the drive unit and propeller. Although the exhaust noise is greater, this arrangement reduces exhaust back pressure and improves performance on some models.

Use of an exhaust tube is not recommended on models using an Alpha drive unit or with small block engines. Performance improvement is negligible, and under some conditions, an exhaust tube can allow water to enter the engine through the exhaust system.

1. Tilt the drive unit to the full up position. Install support clips onto the trim cylinders (**Figure 85**) to prevent the drive unit from dropping. Disconnect the cables from the battery.

2. Insert a 1/4 in. extension through the access opening (**Figure 77**) in the port side of the transom housing. At-

**12**

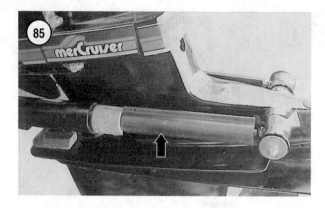

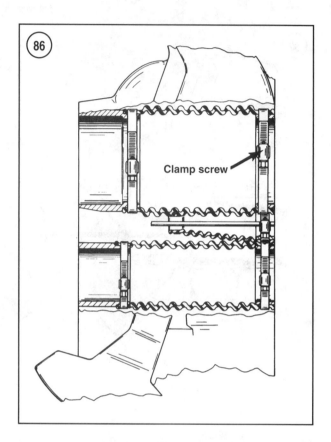

tach a 5/16 in. socket and universal adapter onto the end of the extension.

3.  Fully loosen the clamp screw (**Figure 78**). If replacing the tube, slit the end to ease removal from the transom housing. If the tube will be reused, pry the tube from the transom housing with a screwdriver. Take care not to puncture other components.

4.  Use solvent to thoroughly clean adhesive from the tube mount on the transom housing. Clean the mold release compound from the forward opening of the tube.

5.  Apply bellows adhesive (Mercury part No. 92-86166-Q1) to the tube mount opening on the transom housing.

6.  Place the hose clamp over the forward end of the tube. Align the clamp screw relative to the SIDE mark (3, **Figure 84**). The clamp screw (2, **Figure 84**) must align with the top of the tube, facing the access hole (**Figure 77**) in the transom housing.

7.  Slide the ground clip (**Figure 80**) onto the edge of the tube and position it directly below the clamp screw.

8.  Align the SIDE mark as shown in **Figure 84**. Push the tube onto the mount until the step in the opening contacts the housing.

9.  Tighten the hose clamp to the specification in **Table 1**. Pull on the tube to verify a secure attachment.

10.  Remove the support clips from the trim cylinders (**Figure 85**). Connect the cables and the battery.

## UNIVERSAL JOINT BELLOWS

Failure of the universal joint bellows occurs from age, wear, exposure to direct sunlight and/or improper storage. Always store the engine with the drive unit fully down. If stored with the drive up, the bellows can develop a set in as little as two weeks. If distorted enough, the universal joints will contact the bellows and wear a hole in them. Water will leak through the hole, eventually causing failure of the universal joints and gimbal bearing.

Consider replacing all rubber components of the transom assembly at the same time as the universal joint bellows.

1.  Remove the bell housing as described in this chapter.

2.  Loosen the hose clamp (**Figure 86**). If replacing the bellows, slit the end to allow easy removal from the bell housing. If the bellows will be reused, insert a blunt screwdriver through the aft opening of the bellows and carefully pry it from the transom housing. Take care not to puncture other components.

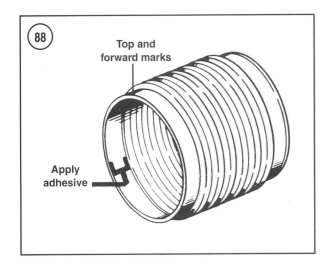

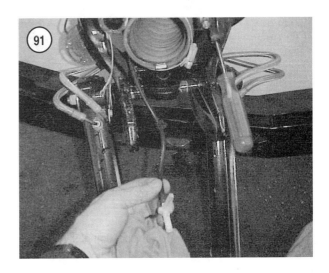

3. Use solvent to clean the bellows mounting boss on the transom housing. Remove the mold release compound from each end of the bellows.

4. Carefully sand corrosion and adhesive from the mounting boss. Thoroughly clean the grooved section of the boss. The mounting surfaces must be completely clean for a water tight connection.

5. Apply bellows adhesive (Mercury part No. 92-86166-Q1) to the bellows mounting boss on the transom housing.

6. Place the hose clamp over one end of the bellows. Refer to the TOP mark (**Figure 87**) for proper bellows and clamp screw orientation. The top mark also faces forward, toward the boat transom. The clamp screw must be on the starboard side, facing down as shown in **Figure 86**.

7. Slide the ground clip (**Figure 80**) onto the top edge of the bellows. Position the hose clamp over the grounding clip.

8. Apply bellows adhesive (Mercury part No. 82-86166Q1) to the forward opening of the bellows (**Figure 88**).

9. Align the top with the forward side while sliding the bellows onto the mounting boss of the transom assembly. The ridge in the forward opening must fit into the groove and the bellows must contact both stops (**Figure 89**).

10. Align the clamp screw as shown in **Figure 86**. Fit the clamp onto the bellows. Hold the clamp in position while tightening the clamp to the specification in **Table 1**. Pull on the bellows to verify a secure connection.

11. Install the bell housing as described in this chapter.

### SPEEDOMETER HOSE AND FITTING

A quick connector (**Figure 90**) attaches the hose to the drive shaft housing on Alpha models. A plastic fitting (**Figure 91**) connects the hose to the housing on Bravo models. A brass fitting connects the hose to the transom housing on both Alpha and Bravo models.

1. Remove the drive unit as described in Chapter Eleven.

2. Pinch the aft end of the clip (**Figure 61**) and pull the speedometer hose retainer from the bell housing.

**12**

3. Cut the plastic clamp from the speedometer hose and connector (B, **Figure 90**). Pull the connector from the hose.

4. Remove the plastic clamp (**Figure 71**) and speedometer hose from the water hose. Pull the retainer (**Figure 61**) from the hose.

5. Cut the clamp from the speedometer hose (inner transom plate side). Remove the hose from the brass fitting (**Figure 92**). Remove the fitting from the transom housing. Pull the fitting and speedometer hose from the transom housing.

6. Inspect the speedometer hose for wear or damage. Remove the hose from the fitting only if defective. Cut the clamp and pull the speedometer hose from the brass fitting. Trim the replacement hose to the same length as the original.

7. Clean corrosion and old sealant from the threads. Heat the end of the hose with a blow dryer or heat gun until the material softens. Quickly push the hose onto the barb end of the brass fitting. Secure the hose with a plastic clamp of the same size as the original.

8. Guide the hose through the speedometer fitting in the transom housing. Apply a light coat of perfect seal (Mercury part No. 92-34227-1) to the fitting threads. Thread the fitting into the transom housing and tighten to the specification in **Table 1**.

9. Attach the engine side speedometer hose as described in Step 7. Route the engine side hose to prevent interference with moving components. Secure the hose with clamps as needed.

10. Guide the speedometer hose to the port side of the universal joint bellows. Install the retainer (**Figure 61**) over the speedometer hose.

11. Attach the speedometer hose to the connector (**Figure 90** or **Figure 91**) as described in Step 7.

12. Attach the hose to the water tube with a plastic clamp as shown in **Figure 71**. Do not over-tighten the clamp.

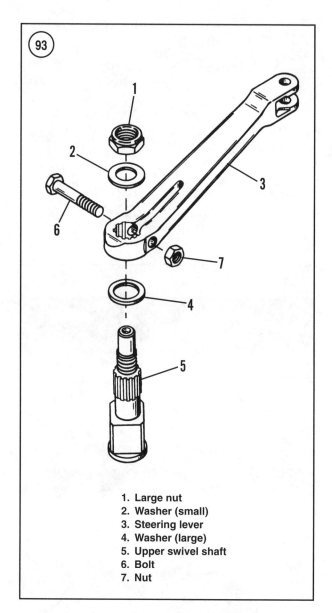

1. Large nut
2. Washer (small)
3. Steering lever
4. Washer (large)
5. Upper swivel shaft
6. Bolt
7. Nut

13. Insert the speedometer hose retainer into the bell housing (**Figure 61**).

14. Install the drive unit as described in Chapter Eleven.

## GIMBAL RING, SWIVEL SHAFT AND STEERING LEVER

To remove the upper swivel shaft, the steering lever and upper swivel shaft fasteners (**Figure 93**) must be accessible. Two methods may be used to gain access to the fasteners.

The first is to remove the engine and transom assembly. This method is the most time efficient if the construction of the boat and access to the mounting fasteners allows easy engine removal.

The second method is to loosen or remove the fasteners through precisely placed access holes in the transom housing (**Figure 94**). A hole saw, access plug kit (Mercury part No. 22-88847A1) and special tap are required for this method.

### Lower Swivel Shaft Removal And Installation

1. Remove the bell housing and exhaust bellows as described in this chapter.

2. Disconnect the ground wire from the bottom of the gimbal ring (**Figure 95**).

3. Turn the steering toward the full starboard direction. Straighten the cotter pin (**Figure 96**). Use locking pliers to bend the pin into an arc while pulling it from the gimbal ring. Discard the cotter pin.

4. Use a section of tubing or a socket and extension to push the lower swivel shaft (**Figure 97**) from the gimbal ring and transom housing. Apply moderate heat to the shaft, gimbal ring and transom housing if necessary to ease removal. Do not use excessive heat. Excessive heat will damage the plastic bushing in the gimbal ring.

5. Remove the thin washer from the gimbal ring or transom housing. Inspect the lower swivel shaft for wear or deep pits. Replace the shaft if defective.

6. Lightly coat the lower swivel shaft, gimbal ring bushing and transom housing bores with water resistant grease. Slide the lower swivel shaft into the bottom of the bore with the slot (**Figure 98**) facing down and aligned in the fore and aft directions.

7. Slide the thin washer (3, **Figure 99**) between the gimbal ring and transom housing boss (4).

8. Push the shaft up until the bottom of the shaft is flush with the gimbal housing boss. Bend the replacement cotter pin into a slight arc.

9. Starting from the port side, feed the cotter pin into its opening in the lower transom housing boss. Use small

**12**

locking pliers to push the pin through the bosses and lower swivel shaft. Bend the ends over on the starboard side and secure the cotter pin. Check the gimbal ring end play as described in this chapter under *Gimbal Ring Installation*.

10. Attach the ground wire onto the bottom of the gimbal ring (**Figure 95**). Install the exhaust bellows and bell housing as described in this chapter.

## Gimbal Ring Removal

1. Remove the bell housing, universal joint bellows and lower swivel shaft as described in this chapter. Remove the forward anchor pin as described in Chapter 13.

2A. *Without access holes*—Remove the engine as described in Chapter Seven. Remove the transom assembly as described in this chapter.

2B. *With access holes*—Drill an access holes as described in this chapter.

3A. *Alpha models*—Loosen the gimbal ring through-bolts as follows:

    a. Turn the steering to the full port position.

    b. Attach a 9/16 in. wrench to the port side bolt head (**Figure 100**).

    c. Loosen the nut (**Figure 100**) until the bolt spins freely.

    d. Turn the steering to the full starboard position. Hold the starboard side bolt head and fully loosen the nut.

3B. *Bravo models*—Loosen both nuts (A, **Figure 101**) until the plate (B) separates from the gimbal ring.

4A. *Without access holes*—Place the steering lever in the straight ahead position. Use two wrenches to fully loosen the nut (3, **Figure 102**).

4B. *With access holes*—Loosen the steering lever nut (3, **Figure 102**) as follows:

    a. Turn the steering toward the starboard direction until the bolt head aligns with the port side access hole.

    b. Attach a box-end wrench to the nut (3, **Figure 102**) through the starboard side access hole.

    c. Attach a socket to the lever bolt (2, **Figure 102**). Do not remove the nut from the bolt.

5A. *Without access holes*—Remove the upper swivel shaft and steering lever as follows:

    a. Support the upper swivel shaft (5, **Figure 93**) while loosening the large elastic locknut (1).

    b. Pull the upper swivel shaft (5, **Figure 93**) from the transom housing.

    c. Pull the steering lever, nut and both washers (**Figure 93**) from the housing.

5B. *With access holes*—Remove the upper swivel shaft as follows:

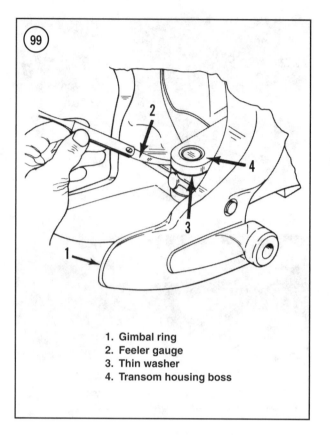

1. Gimbal ring
2. Feeler gauge
3. Thin washer
4. Transom housing boss

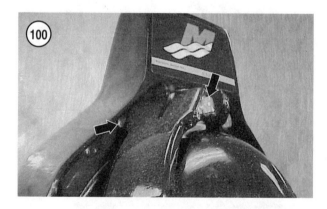

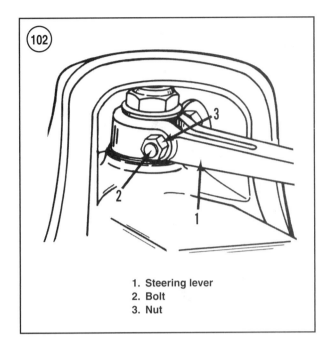

1. Steering lever
2. Bolt
3. Nut

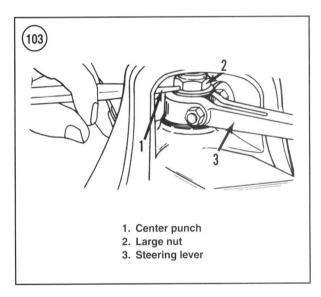

1. Center punch
2. Large nut
3. Steering lever

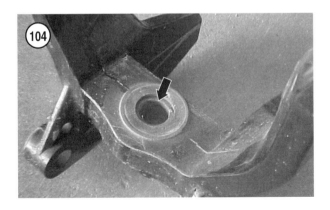

a. Insert a center punch through the access plug opening.

b. Drive the punch against the corners of the nut (2, **Figure 103**) until fully loosened.

c. Pull the upper swivel shaft (5, **Figure 93**) straight down and out of the transom housing. If necessary, pry the shaft from the gimbal ring.

d. Use a piece of stiff wire to pull the nut (1, **Figure 93**) and small washer (2) from the access plug opening.

e. Do not turn the steering wheel. Otherwise the steering lever and large washer (3 and 4, **Figure 93**) will move out of position.

6. Pull the gimbal ring away from the transom housing. Temporarily slide the upper swivel shaft into the gimbal ring. Check for looseness at the square connection. Inspect the square opening for wear and cracks. Replace the gimbal ring if necessary.

7. Inspect the bushing (**Figure 104**) at the lower swivel shaft for melting, wear or damage. If these or other defects are visible, replace the bushing as follows:

a. Use a punch to drive the bushing from the bore.

b. Use a quick drying solvent to clean the bushing bore.

c. Apply Resiweld sealer (Mercury part No. 92-65150-1) to the outer diameter of the new bushing.

d. Use a socket or section of tubing to install the bushings. The tool must be slightly smaller in diameter than the bushing.

e. Slowly drive the bushing into the bore until flush with the upper surface.

8. On Alpha models, inspect the hinge pin bores on both sides of the gimbal ring for wear or damage. Slide the hinge pin into the opening and check for a loose fit or elongated bores. Replace the gimbal ring if the bores are worn, damaged or elongated.

9. *Bravo drive*—Inspect both hinge pin bushings (**Figure 105**) for melted, worn or damaged surfaces. If these or other defects are visible, replace the bushings as follows:

**12**

a. Use a punch to drive the bushings from the bores.

b. Use a quick drying solvent to clean the bushing bores.

c. Apply Resiweld sealer (Mercury part No. 92-65150-1) to the outer diameter of the new bushings.

d. Use a socket or section of tubing to install the bushings. The tool must be slightly smaller in diameter than the bushings.

e. Slowly drive the bushing into the bore until flush with the recessed surface.

10. Inspect the upper swivel shaft (**Figure 106**) for wear or corrosion. Replace the shaft if defective. Pitting at the seal surfaces allows water leakage into the boat.

11. Inspect the seal and bushing (**Figure 107**) for wear or damage. Inspect the upper end of the swivel shaft to determine the condition of the upper bushing (**Figure 108**). Replace both bushings if either is defective or the swivel shaft is worn at the contact surfaces. Replace the seal if damaged, or if replacing the upper swivel shaft or bushings.

12. Remove the swivel shaft bushings as follows:

a. Position the jaws of a slide hammer against the inner edge of the bushing (1, **Figure 107**). Use short hammer strokes to pull the lower bushing (1, **Figure 107**) and seal (2) from the housing.

b. Insert a blind bushing removal tool or (Snap-On part No. CG40CB) into the upper bushing (**Figure 108**). Turn the collet to expand the tool and engage the bushing.

c. Thread the slide hammer onto the tool. Use short hammer strokes to remove the upper bushing.

d. Clean all corrosion and grease residue from the bushing bores with quick drying solvent.

13. Install the replacement bushings and seal as follows:

a. Install the upper bushing (**Figure 108**) onto the upper end of the swivel shaft. Use the shaft to push the bushing into the bore. With a socket and extension,

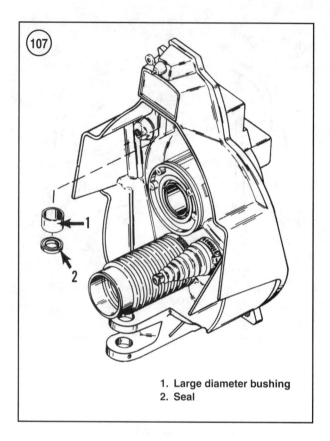

1. **Large diameter bushing**
2. **Seal**

push the bushing into the bore until flush with the bore opening.

b. With a socket and extension, drive the lower bushing into the bore until slightly recessed in the bore opening.

c. Apply Loctite 271 to the outer diameter of the seal. Set the seal in the opening with the seal lip facing in. Use the bushing to drive the seal and bushing into the bore. Stop when the seal surface is slightly recessed in the bore opening.

14. Replace the shaft seal (2, **Figure 107**) as follows:

a. Pry the seal from the bore, taking care not to damage the aluminum bore.

b. Clean the seal bore with a quick drying solvent.

c. Use a socket to install the seal. The socket must be slightly smaller in diameter than the seal.

d. Apply Loctite 271 to the outer diameter of the seal. Place the seal into the opening with the seal lip facing in.

e. Using the installation tool, drive the seal into the bore until it contacts the bushing. The seal surface must be slightly recessed in the bore opening.

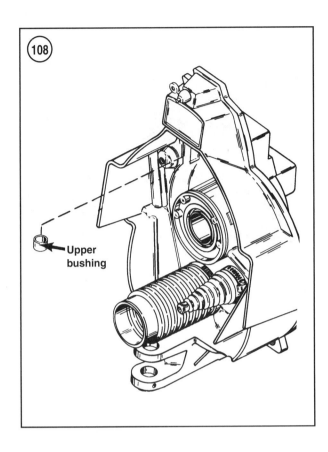

Upper bushing

**Gimbal Ring Installation**

1. Position the gimbal ring in the transom housing so the thrust flanges face outward (**Figure 99**).

2. Apply a light coat of water resistant grease to the swivel shaft bushings and seal lips.

3. Rotate the gimbal ring and align its square opening with the opening in the steering lever.

4A. *Without access plugs*—Install the upper swivel shaft and steering lever as follows:

   a. Place the steering lever, washers and large nut as shown in **Figure 93**.

   b. Slide the upper swivel shaft through the gimbal ring and into the steering lever (3, **Figure 93**). Make sure the shaft passes through both washers and into the large nut.

   c. Move the steering lever back and forth while tightening the large nut (1, **Figure 93**). Stop tightening the nut when the steering just begins to stiffen.

4B. *With access plugs*—Install the upper swivel shaft, washer and nut as follows:

   a. Guide the upper swivel shaft through the gimbal ring and into the upper swivel shaft. Make sure the shaft passes through the large washer (4, **Figure 93**)

beneath the steering lever (3). Rotate the shaft to align the square bores.

   b. Lower the shaft just enough to allow installation of the washer (2, **Figure 93**) and the special notched nut included with the access plug kit.

   c. Slide the washer and nut through the access openings. Use a piece of stiff wire and to the washer and nut into position.

   d. Push up on the swivel shaft and capture the washer and nut. Make sure the shaft passes through the openings in both components.

   e. Use a screwdriver to rotate the nut until it threads onto the shaft.

   f. Insert a center punch through the access plug opening. Drive the punch against the notches of the nut to tighten it. Adjust the steering direction as needed to access the corners of the nut. Continue until all up and down gimbal ring play is eliminated and the steering effort increases.

*NOTE*
*Do not over-tighten the nut. The gimbal ring, transom housing and other components can break if over-tightened. Do not tighten the steering lever nut (7, **Figure 93**) at this time.*

5A. *Alpha models*—Tighten the gimbal ring throughbolts as follows:

   a. Turn the steering toward the full port direction.

   b. Attach a 9/16 in. wrench to the port side bolt head (**Figure 100**).

   c. Tighten the nut (**Figure 100**) to the specification in **Table 1**.

   d. Turn the steering to the full starboard position. Hold the starboard side bolt head and tighten the nut to the specification in **Table 1**.

5B. *Bravo drive*—Tighten both nuts (A, **Figure 101**) evenly to the specification in **Table 1**.

6. Check the gimbal ring end play as follows:

   a. Loosen the large nut approximately 1/8 turn.

   b. With a soft-faced mallet, tap the gimbal ring flange (1, **Figure 99**) one time to seat the upper components.

   c. Use feeler gauges to measure the clearance between the thin washer and the gimbal ring as shown in **Figure 99**.

   d. Repeat these steps until a clearance of 0.005-0.010 in. (0.13-0.25 mm) is attained. Tighten the large nut (1, **Figure 93**) to reduce the clearance.

7A. *Without access holes*—Place the steering lever in the straight-ahead position. Use a wrench and socket and tighten the nut (3, **Figure 102**) to the specification in **Table 1**.

7B. *With access holes*—Tighten the steering lever nut (3, **Figure 102**) as follows:

    a. Turn the steering toward the starboard direction until the bolt head aligns with the port side access hole.

    b. Hold the nut (3, **Figure 102**) with a box-end wrench through the starboard side access hole.

    c. Engage a socket and torque wrench to the bolt head through the port side access hole.

    d. Tighten the steering lever bolt (2, **Figure 102**) to the specification in **Table 1**.

8. Check the gimbal ring end play as described in step 6. Loosen the steering lever bolts and nut and correct the end play as needed. Tighten the bolt after the correction. Cycle the steering to the full port and starboard directions. If binding occurs, check for incorrect gimbal ring end play or improperly installed components.

9A. *Without access holes*—Install the engine as described in Chapter Seven. Install the transom assembly as described in this chapter.

9B. *With access holes*—Install the access plugs as described in this chapter.

10. Install the bell housing, universal joint bellows and lower swivel shaft as described in this chapter. Install the forward anchor pin as described in Chapter 13.

### Drilling Access Holes

This procedure requires a 1 in. hole saw suitable for cutting aluminum, a 1/4 in. pilot rod for the hole saw, 3/8 in. or larger drill motor and clear access to the sides of the transom housing. If any of these requirements are not available, use the alternate method of accessing the steering lever fasteners. Use the template supplied with the access plug kit (Mercury part No. 22-88847A1) to locate the *exact* location to drill the holes. A hole drilled as little as 1/8 in. (3.2 mm) out of position will be useless.

1. Cut out the template provided with the access plug kit. Bend the template along the dotted lines. Align the mark on the template (A, **Figure 109**) with the dimple beneath the decal (B). Tape the template in position.

2. Center punch the transom housing at the port and starboard locations (C, **Figure 109**) indicated by the template.

3. Make sure the template and center punch marks are correctly positioned. Remove the template.

4. Drill 1/4 in. diameter pilot holes through the transom housing. The holes must be centered over the center punch marks and perpendicular to the transom housing.

5. Adjust the pilot rod depth (**Figure 110**) to 1/8-1/4 in. (3.2-6.3 mm). Insert the pilot rod into one of the pilot

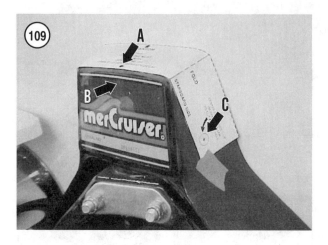

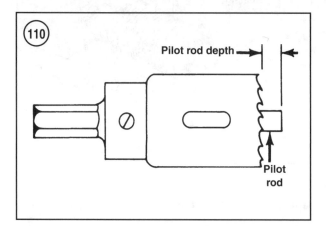

holes. Keep the saw teeth parallel with the transom housing while drilling. Drill until the saw just enters the steering lever cavity. Remove the aluminum plug from the hole saw. Use the same procedure to drill the remaining hole.

6. Use a round file to remove any burrs or sharp edges from the holes. Use compressed air to blow aluminum filings from the openings.

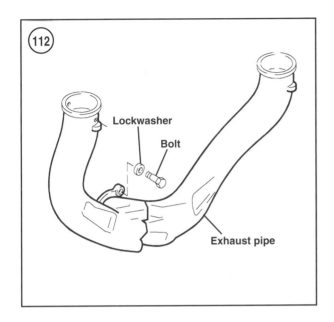

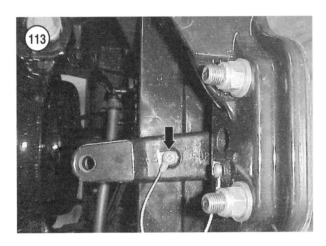

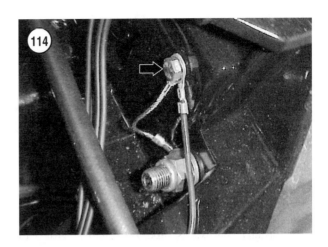

### Access Plug Installation

This procedure requires a 1 in. #180 pipe tap and a 5/8 in. Allen wrench. Perform this operation *after* installing the gimbal ring and steering lever. Keep the access plugs in a cool location for a few hours before installing them. This prevents heat from softening the material and causing distortion during installation.

1. Apply a coat of grease to the flutes of the tap to capture aluminum cuttings.
2. Wrap a rubber band or piece of tape around the tap, approximately 1-1/8 in. (28.6 mm) from the end of the tap.
3. Turn the steering to the full starboard postition. Insert the tap into the starboard access hole. Maintain inward pressure while cutting the threads. Keep the tap perpendicular to the transom housing. Turn the tap 1/4 turn clockwise, then 1/8 turn counterclockwise until the tape

or rubber band is flush with the transom housing surfaces. Remove the tap.
4. Clean the cuttings from the tap. Apply grease to the flutes.
5. Turn the steering to the full port position. Cut threads in the port access hole.
6. Use compressed air to blow all cuttings from the openings and steering lever cavity.
7. Apply perfect seal to the access plug threads. Hand-thread the plugs into the openings. Insert the 5/8 in Allen wrench into the access plug opening. Tighten the plugs until flush with the transom housing.
8. Touch-up any unpainted areas near the access plugs.

### INNER TRANSOM PLATE

**Removal and Installation**

1. Remove the engine as described in Chapter Seven.
2. Remove the power steering actuator and other transom plate steering components as described in Chapter Fourteen.
3. Disconnect the trim hoses and trim limit switch wires from the trim pump (**Figure 111**).
4. Remove the four bolts (**Figure 112**) and pull the exhaust pipe from the transom plate.
5. Remove the screw and ground wire (**Figure 113**) from the steering lever
6. On Bravo models, remove the bolts and the water hose fitting as described in this chapter.
7. Remove the bolt and ground wires (**Figure 114**) from the inner transom plate.
8. Disconnect the engine side speedometer hose as described in this chapter.
9. Disconnect the gearcase lubricant hose from the transom housing as described in this chapter.

**12**

10. Loosen evenly and remove the eight locknuts and washers (**Figure 115**) that retain the transom plate to the boat transom.

11. Tap lightly on the inner transom plate with a plastic mallet and free it from the boat transom. Check for overlooked fasteners if the plate will not come free. Pry the plate from the transom only after removing all fasteners.

12. Remove the O-ring from the exhaust pipe and transom housing mating surface. Discard the O-ring.

13. To install, reverse the removal steps and note the following:

    a. Thoroughly clean the inner transom plate and the exhaust pipe mating surfaces.

    b. Install a new exhaust pipe O-ring into the groove of the transom housing.

    c. To prevent pinched wires, cables and hoses, guide them through their openings while installing the plate onto the boat transom. Tighten the exhaust pipe mounting screws evenly to the specification in **Table 1**.

    d. Tighten the transom plate mounting nuts to the specification in **Table 1**, following the sequence shown in **Figure 115**.

    e. Reconnect the speedometer, water and gearcase lubricant hoses as described in this chapter.

    f. Connect all ground wires as described in Chapter Fifteen.

    g. Connect the trim hoses and trim limit switch wires to the trim pump as described in Chapter Thirteen.

    h. Attach the steering actuator and other transom plate steering components as described in Chapter Fourteen.

14. Install the engine as described in Chapter Seven.

### TRANSOM ASSEMBLY

Always replace the transom assembly O-ring when installing the transom assembly. Failure of this O-ring allows water leakage into the boat.

1. Remove the engine as described in Chapter Seven.

2. Remove the inner transom plate as described in this chapter.

3. Push the assembly away from the boat transom, using the help of an assistant if necessary.

4. Pull the large diameter O-ring from the transom assembly. Clean all remaining O-ring material and adhesive from the O-ring groove.

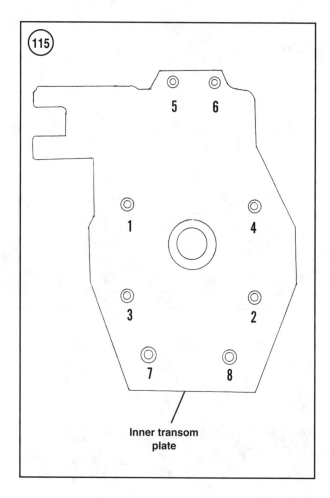

**Inner transom plate**

5. Inspect the cutout in the boat transom for rotted, cracked or water-saturated wood. Have the transom repaired at a fiberglass repair shop if either of these conditions exist. Water leakage and failure of other engine components will occur if the transom is weak.

6. Apply a light coat of bellows adhesive (Mercury part No. 92-86166Q1) to the O-ring groove in the transom assembly.

7. Quickly install the O-ring into the groove. Hold the O-ring in place until the adhesive starts to dry.

8. Install the assembly, guiding the shift cable, trim switch wires and hydraulic hoses through the transom cutout.

9. Have an assistant support the assembly. Install the inner transom plate as described in this chapter.

10. Install the engine as described in Chapter Seven.

## Table 1 TORQUE SPECIFICATIONS

| Fastener | ft.-lb. | in.-lb. | N•m |
|---|---|---|---|
| Gimbal ring bolts | | | |
| Alpha | 55 | – | 75 |
| Gimbal ring U-bolt | 53 | – | 72 |
| Bravo models | | | |
| Steering lever bolt/nut | | | |
| Alpha drive | 60 | – | 81 |
| Bravo models | 50 | – | 68 |
| Hinge pins | | | |
| Alpha models | 102 | – | 138 |
| Bravo models | 150 | – | 203 |
| Bellows hose clamps | – | 35 | 4 |
| Sender/switch wire retainer | | | |
| Alpha | – | 90 | 10 |
| Lubricant hose 90° fitting | | | |
| Alpha | – | 70-90 | 8-10 |
| Lubricant fitting nut | | | |
| Alpha | 10-14 | 120-168 | 14-19 |
| Lubricant hose fitting | | | |
| Bell housing | – | 84-108 | 9-12 |
| Lubricant hose clamp | | | |
| Bravo | – | 45 | 5 |
| Water tube grommet cover | – | 90-100 | 10-11 |
| (Alpha models) | | | |
| Water hose fitting | – | 45 | 5 |
| (Bravo models) | | | |
| Inner transom plate nuts | 23 | – | 31 |
| Core wire anchor screws | – | 20 | 2 |
| Shift cable nut (Bravo) | – | 65 | 7 |
| Anode block to terminal block | – | 80-120 | 9-14 |
| Speedometer hose fitting | – | 50-70 | 6-8 |
| Exhaust pipe bolts | 20-25 | – | 27-34 |

**12**

# Chapter Thirteen

# Trim and Tilt System

The hydraulic system must operate with clean fluid. Always perform the service in a clean environment. Dirt or other material can block valves and passages, resulting in system malfunction. Install plugs or fitting covers, available from most hardware and parts stores, in place of all disconnected hoses or fittings. Use only lint free shop towels. Dry all components with compressed air and promptly cover all openings with clean shop towels.

Unless otherwise specified, place the drive unit in the down position before disconnecting or disassembling any of the trim system components. If the trim system is not operational, refer to *Relieving System Pressure* in this chapter to lower the drive. After assembly, fill and bleed the system as described in this chapter.

## RELIEVING SYSTEM PRESSURE

Relieve the system pressure before disconnecting any trim hoses or disassembling any trim system components. Hold the brass trim pump fittings with a wrench to prevent them from loosening while loosening or tightening the trim hose fittings (A and B, **Figure 1**).

1. Place shop towels under the hose fittings (C, **Figure 1**). Remove all obstructions from under the drive unit.

2. Wrap the gray DOWN hose fitting (B, **Figure 1**) with a shop towel to prevent fluid spray. *Slowly* loosen the down hose fitting (B, **Figure 1**). Do not disconnect the hose.

3. Wrap the black coloed UP hose fitting (A, **Figure 1**) with a shop towel to prevent fluid spray. *Slowly* loosen the up hose fitting (A, **Figure 1**). Do not disconnect the hose.

4. Tighten both hose fittings (A and B, **Figure 1**) after fluid stops flowing and the drive reaches the fully down position.

5. Fill and bleed the system as described in this chapter.

## TRIM PUMP

*WARNING*
*The hydraulic system contains fluid under very high pressure. Wear safety glasses and protective clothing when working with the hydraulic system.*

1. Place the drive unit in the fully down position. Relieve the system pressure as described in this chapter.

2. Disconnect the positive and negative trim pump leads from the battery.

3. Loosen the clamp and unplug the wire harness connector (C, **Figure 1**) from the trim pump.

4. Place shop towels under the fittings (A and B, **Figure 1**) to capture spilled fluid.

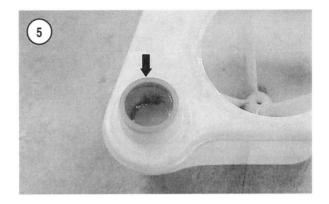

5. Loosen the fittings and remove both hoses from the trim pump fittings. Plug all disconnected fittings to prevent contamination.

6. Remove the four lag bolts (D, **Figure 1**). Keep the trim pump in a vertical during removal.

7. To install, reverse the removal steps and note the following:

    a. Refer to the marks on the pump adapter (**Figure 2**) to identify hose connections. Connect the black hose to the UP mark. Connect the gray hose to the DN mark.

    b. Direct the bend in the hose fitting down and toward the left while tightening the hose fitting. Do not bind the hoses against any boat structure or the hoses may loosen.

    c. Hold the brass trim pump fittings with a wrench to prevent them from turning, and tighten the hose fittings to the specification in **Table 1**.

8. Connect the positive and negative pump leads to the battery. Fill and bleed the system as described in this chapter.

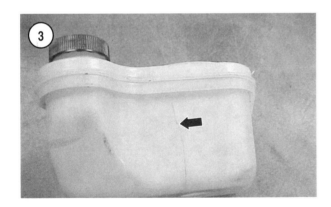

**13**

**FLUID RESERVOIR**

Damage to the reservoir (**Figure 3**) is usually caused by the reservoir striking the boat structure or other objects during operation in rough water. The reservoir fluid level fluctuates during normal operation. As the fluid level rises, slots in the fill cap threads (**Figure 4**) vent air to relieve pressure in the reservoir. Remove and discard the shipping plug (**Figure 5**) if found in the fill cap. Do not install the unvented cap used on earlier production trim pumps. Failure to remove the shipping plug or using an unvented fill cap will allow pressure to build in the reservoir and eventually make it crack.

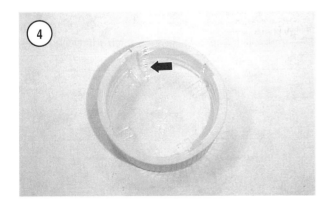

1. Remove the trim pump as described in this chapter.

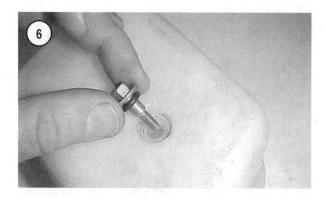

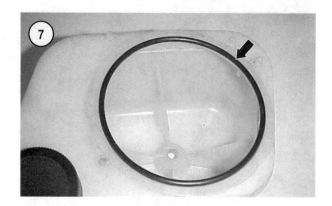

2. Open the fill cap and pour the fluid from the reservoir. The neck in the fill opening prevents all of the fluid from pouring from the reservoir.

3. Turn the pump on its side with the fill cap side facing downward. Remove the shoulder screw and O-ring (**Figure 6**) from the reservoir. Discard the O-ring.

4. Pull the reservoir from the pump adapter. Pull the large O-ring from the pump adapter or fluid reservoir. Discard the O-ring.

5. Pour all remaining fluid from the reservoir. Use lint free shop towels to wipe fluid or contaminants from the pump adapter.

6. Clean the fluid reservoir with warm soapy water. Do not use lacquer thinner, carburetor cleaner or gasoline. Dry the reservoir with compressed air. Inspect the fluid reservoir for cracks or damage. Pay particular attention to the area near the support ribs. Replace the reservoir if any cracks are present, no matter how small.

7. Lubricate a new large O-ring with engine oil and install it onto the reservoir (**Figure 7**). Align the fill cap opening with the hose fittings (**Figure 8**) and place the reservoir onto the pump adapter.

8. Align the antirotation structures on the pump adapter and reservoir as shown in **Figure 9**.

9. Install a new O-ring onto the shoulder screw (**Figure 6**). Apply engine oil to the O-ring. Insert the screw through the reservoir and into the threaded boss. Make sure the reservoir and pump are aligned, then securely tighten the screw.

10. Install the trim pump as described in this chapter.

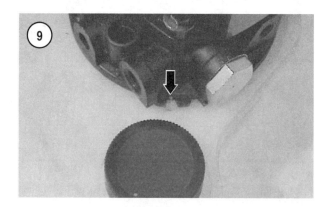

## TRIM MOTOR

1. Remove the trim pump as described in this chapter.

2. Disconnect the blue, green and black trim motor wires as described under *Solenoid Replacement* in this chapter.

3. Use a 5/16 in. wrench to remove both bolts (**Figure 10**) from the motor and pump adapter.

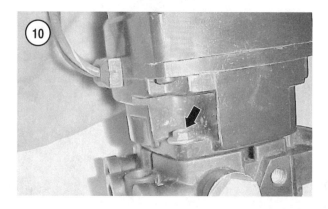

4. Lift the trim motor from the adapter. Remove and discard the O-ring (**Figure 11**) from the adapter or trim motor.

5. Pull the shaft coupling (**Figure 12**) from the pump or motor shaft.

6. Wipe all oil and debris from the pump and pump adapter mating surfaces.

7. Apply a light coat of water resistant grease to the coupling. Install the shaft coupling into the pump shaft (**Figure 13**). Fit the pump shaft into the slot in the coupling.

8. Apply oil to a *new* O-ring and install it onto the pump adapter (**Figure 11**).

9. Install the motor onto the pump adapter, aligning the motor shaft with the slot in the shaft coupling. Rotate the motor until the wire grommet aligns with the hose fittings (**Figure 14**).

10. Insert both bolts (**Figure 10**). Tighten the bolts to the specification in **Table 1**.

11. Connect the blue, green and black trim motor wires as described under *Solenoid Replacement* in this chapter.

12. Install the trim pump as described in this chapter.

**Trim Solenoid Removal and Installation**

Make a diagram showing the trim solenoid wires and routing before removing the solenoids.

1. Disconnect the positive and negative trim pump leads from the battery.

2. Remove the screw from the terminal cover (**Figure 15**). Remove the cover.

3. Mark the connection points of the large blue and green wires, then detach them from the solenoids.

4. Remove the nuts and lift the terminal plate (**Figure 16**) from the solenoid post.

5. Remove the nuts from the small terminal post of the solenoids. Lift the small blue, green and black wires from the solenoids.

**13**

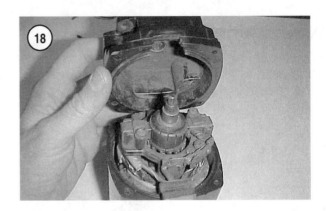

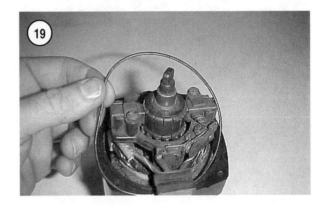

6. Remove the mounting bolts and washers, then lift the solenoids from the pump bracket. Clean all corrosion or contaminants from the pump bracket. Remove the bolt, lockwasher and nut. Remove the black wire from the pump bracket.

7. To install, reverse the removal steps and note the following:

    a. The blue wires connect to the upper solenoid and the green wires connect to the lower solenoid.

    b. Attach the terminal plate (**Figure 16**) to the large terminal post on each solenoid.

    c. Attach the black trim motor and solenoid wires to the ground bolt on the pump bracket.

**Trim Motor Disassembly**

1. Remove the four Phillips screws (**Figure 17**), then remove the lower cover from the motor housing (**Figure 18**). Pull the washer from the lower cover or armature shaft.

2. Remove the O-ring from the cover or housing (**Figure 19**). Loosen both retainer arm screws (**Figure 20**), but do not remove them.

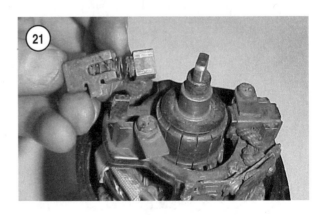

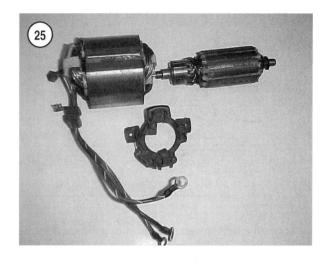

trim motor wires. Remove the frame, brush mounting bracket and armature (**Figure 24**).

6. Pull the armature and brush mounting bracket from the frame assembly (**Figure 25**).

**Trim Motor Testing and Inspection**

1. Clean oil, grease or corrosion from all components with electrical contact cleaner. Inspect the bushing (**Figure 26**) in the lower cover and motor housing for wear, loose fit or discoloration. Replace the motor housing if the bushing is defective.

2. Secure the armature in a vise with protective jaws (**Figure 27**). Gently polish the commutator with 00 grit garnet sandpaper (**Figure 27**), being careful not to remove too much material. Rotate the armature often while polishing. Inspect the commutator for deep pitting or grooves. Replace the armature if defective.

3. Pull straight up on the brass brush retainers. Remove the retainers and springs from the brush mounting bracket (**Figure 21**).

4. Unplug the black wire from the thermal switch terminal. Remove the screw and lift the thermal switch from the brush mounting bracket (**Figure 22**).

5. Remove the long screws (**Figure 23**) from the bracket, frame and housing. The second screw is located under the

13

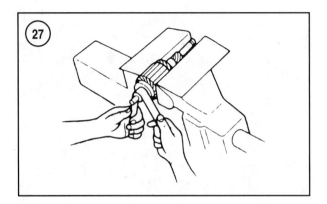

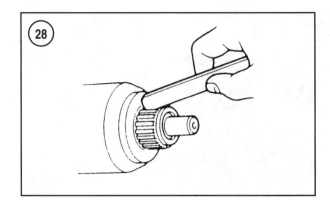

3. Use a small file to remove any mica particles from the undercut between the commutator segments (**Figure 28**).
4. Test the armature as follows:
   a. Calibrate an ohmmeter on the R × 1 scale.
   b. Connect the ohmmeter between one of the commutator segments and the armature lamination (**Figure 29**). The meter should indicate no continuity. If the meter shows continuity, the armature is shorted and must be replaced.
   c. Connect the ohmmeter between any commutator segment and the armature shaft (**Figure 29**). The meter should indicate no continuity. If the meter shows continuity, the armature is shorted and must be replaced.
   d. Connect the ohmmeter between two commutator segments (**Figure 30**). Continuity must be present between any two segments. Repeat this test with the meter connected to each commutator segment. No continuity between two of the segments indicates an open winding. Replace the armature if this condition occurs.
5. Test the frame winding as follows:
   a. Calibrate an ohmmeter on the R × 1 scale.
   b. Connect the ohmmeter to the brush lead (A, **Figure 31**) and the blue white wire (B) of the frame assembly. Continuity must be present. If not, replace the frame assembly.
   c. Connect the ohmmeter to the brush lead (A, **Figure 31**) and the green white wire (C) of the frame assembly. Continuity must be present. If not replace the frame assembly.
   d. Connect the ohmmeter to the brush lead (A, **Figure 31**) and the frame laminations (D). The meter should indicate no continuity. If not, the frame is shorted and must be replaced.
6. Test the thermal switch as follows:
   a. Calibrate and ohmmeter on the R ×1 scale.
   b. Connect the ohmmeter to the terminal (A, **Figure 32**) and the brush (B). Continuity must be present, or the switch is open and must be replaced.

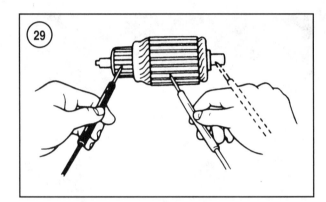

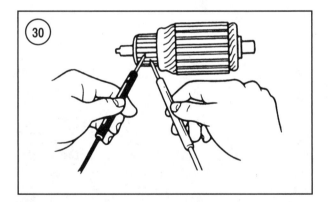

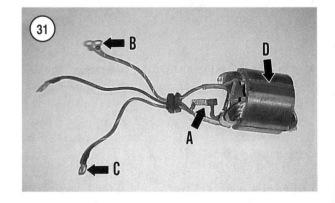

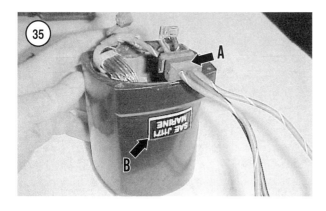

c. Slip a piece of paper or cardboard between the switch contacts (**Figure 33**). Connect the ohmmeter to the terminal (A, **Figure 33**) and the brush (B). The meter must indicate no continuity, or the switch is shorted and must be replaced. Remove the paper or cardboard.

7. Inspect the brushes (**Figure 34**) for pits, corrosion, wear or discoloration surfaces.

   a. Replace the thermal switch if its connected brush is defective.

   b. If the brush attached to the frame winding is defective, cut the brush lead as close as possible to the brush. Connect the replacement brush to the frame winding lead with the supplied crimp connector.

**Trim Motor Assembly**

1. Place a new O-ring into the groove in the motor housing (**Figure 19**). Use a cotton-tipped swab to apply a light coat of water resistant grease to the bore of the bushings (**Figure 26**).

2. Slide the frame assembly into the motor housing. Align the wire grommet (A, **Figure 35**) with the SAE sticker on the side of the motor housing (B).

3. Slide the washer over the lower armature shaft (**Figure 36**). Guide the armature into the motor housing. Insert the armature shaft into the bushing.

4. Install the brush holder. Install the screws (**Figure 23**) and evenly tighten them.

5. Slide the spring into each brush holder. Push the brush holder over the brushes and collapse the springs (**Figure 21**). Drop the legs at the bottom of the brush holder into the slots in the bracket.

6. Swing the retaining arms over the brush holders. Securely tighten the screws (**Figure 20**).

7. Align the wire grommet with the opening and install the lower cover onto the motor housing.

8. Apply Loctite 271 to the threads of the four Phillips screws (**Figure 17**). Install and securely tighten.

**13**

## HYDRAULIC PUMP AND PUMP ADAPTER

### Removal and Installation

*CAUTION*
*Do not disassemble the hydraulic pump.*
*Without special equipment, it is almost im-*
*possible to properly realign the pump hous-*
*ing. Improper alignment causes rapid wear*
*and eventual failure of the pump. Remove*
*only the pump mounting screws to prevent*
*inadvertent loosening of the pump housings.*

1. Remove the fluid reservoir and trim motor as described in this chapter.
2. Remove the pump mounting screws (A, **Figure 37**).
Do not loosen or remove the pump housing screws (B,
**Figure 37**). Lift the hydraulic pump from the pump
adapter (**Figure 38**). Remove the two small O-rings from
the pump or adapter.
3. Pry the seal from the pump adapter (**Figure 39**). Discard the seal.
4. Clean all components with solvent. Dry the pump and
adapter with compressed air. Cover them to prevent contamination.
5. Place the new seal into the pump shaft opening with
the lip side out. Push the seal into the bore.
6. Lubricate the two small O-rings with engine oil. Install
them into the grooves in the hydraulic pump. Place the
pump on the adapter, aligning the reservoir mounting boss
(**Figure 40**) with the screw opening in the reservoir. Install the pump mounting screws (A, **Figure 37**) and
tighten them to the specification in **Table 1**.
7. Install the fluid reservoir and trim motor as described
in this chapter.

### Pump Adapter
### Disassembly and Assembly

Always replace the O-rings, seals and pilot valves when
assembling the pump adapter. Purchase the repair kit from
a Mercruiser dealership. Work in a clean environment to
avoid contamination.

Identify the replacement pressure relief valve by color.
The UP pressure relief valve is blue. The DOWN pressure
relief valve is green. The thermal relief valve is gold.

*CAUTION*
*Remove the UP pressure, DOWN pressure*
*and thermal relief valves only if defective.*
*Removing the original valves disturbs the*
*factory adjusted pressure settings. Replace-*
*ment valves are of a different design with a*
*pre-adjusted pressure setting.*

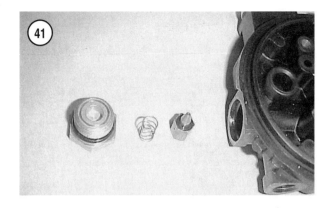

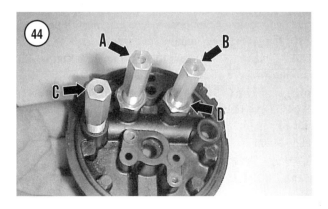

1. Remove the pump adapter from the pump and the hydraulic pump as described in this chapter under *Hydraulic Pump and Pump Adapter*. Remove both covers, springs and valves from adapter (**Figure 41**). Remove the O-rings from the pilot valve covers (plugs). Discard the O-rings.

2. Insert a small screwdriver into the opening in one of the pilot valve seats (**Figure 42**). Push on the shuttle piston and push the piston and seat from the opposite side of the adapter (**Figure 43**).

3. Working from the end without a seat, push the valve seat from the adapter. Be careful not to damage the piston bore.

4. Remove the thermal relief valve (C, **Figure 44**), UP pressure valve (A), or DOWN pressure valve (B) only if they are defective.

    a. Loosen the jam nut (D, **Figure 44**) and unthread the valve from the pump adapter.

    b. Remove the spring, ball and seat from the valve opening in the pump adapter.

    c. Discard the valve, spring, ball and seat.

5. Use a suitable solvent to clean the pump adapter. Inspect the piston bore for scratches or roughness. Install the piston into the bore. The piston must move freely through the bore. Replace the pump adapter if the bore is damaged or if the piston binds in the bore.

6. Install the replacement pressure and/or thermal relief valves as follows:

    a. Lubricate a new O-ring and install it onto the threaded end of the valve.

    b. Hand-thread the valve into the pump adapter. The thermal relief valve (C, **Figure 44**) must be on the same side of the adapter as the UP pressure relief valve (A) and aligned with the UP hose fitting. The UP pressure relief valve must be on the same side of the adapter as the UP hose fitting. The DOWN pressure relief valve (B, **Figure 44**) must be on the same side of the adapter as the DOWN hose fitting.

    c. Tighten the valve to the specification in **Table 1** using only the hex portion nearest the pump adapter, or the pressure setting will be changed and the valve must be replaced.

7. Lubricate the piston bore with engine oil. Slide the piston into the bore.

8. Lubricate the O-rings with engine oil then slide them into the grooves on the pilot valve seat.

9. Insert one of the pilot valve seats into the bore. The open end must face outward. Push the seat fully into the bore. Make sure the piston remains in the bore. Install the pilot valve seat into the bore on the opposite side of the pump adapter.

10. Install the pilot valve, spring and covers (**Figure 41**).

**13**

a. Lubricate the new O-rings with engine oil and install them into the pilot valve covers.

b. Insert a pilot check valve into the seat with the rubber seal side facing the seat.

c. Place the spring into the recess in the cover (**Figure 45**).

d. Thread the cover into the pump adapter, aligning the spring with the back side of the pilot valve.

e. Tighten the pilot valve cover to the specification in **Table 1**. Repeat this step for the remaining valve.

11. Install the hydraulic pump into the pump adapter as described in this chapter. Install the trim motor and reservoir as described in this chapter.

## HYDRAULIC TRIM CYLINDER AND ANCHOR PINS

### Removal and Installation

1. Place the drive unit in the full down position. Relieve the system pressure as described in this chapter.

2A. *Alpha drive*—Remove the plastic covers, E-clips and washers (**Figure 46**) from forward and aft anchor pins.

2B. *Bravo drive*—Remove the plastic covers from the threaded ends of the anchor pins. Remove the locknut, outer washer and bushing (3-5, **Figure 47**) from the forward and aft anchor pins.

3. Remove the anode block or lower the Mercathode electrode from the transom assembly as described in Chapter Fifteen.

4. Place a container under the trim hose connections at the transom assembly. Slowly loosen the fittings then disconnect the hoses from the terminal block (**Figure 48**). Disconnect the hydraulic cylinder ground wires from the bottom of the gimbal housing as described in Chapter Fifteen.

5. Pry the cylinder from the anchor pins. Repeat Steps 1-5 for the other cylinder.

6A. *Alpha drive*—Pull the forward anchor pin from the gimbal ring. Pull the aft anchor pin from the drive shaft housing.

6B. *Bravo drive*—Remove the anchor pins as follows:

a. Pull the aft anchor pin from the drive shaft housing.

b. Note the orientation then pull the spacer block (**Figure 49**) from the anchor pin bore.

c. Remove the snap ring (**Figure 50**) and slide the inner washer from the forward anchor pin. Pull the forward anchor pin from the bore on the opposite side of the gimbal ring. Slide the remaining inner washer and bushing from the forward anchor pin. Remove the snap ring only if replacing the anchor pin or gimbal ring.

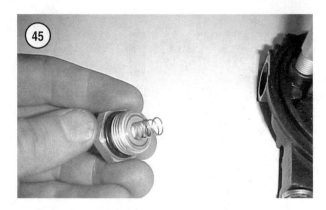

7. On Alpha models, remove the bushings (7, **Figure 46**) from the hydraulic cylinders. Inspect them for wear or cracks. Replace any defective bushings.

8. On Bravo models, install the rear spacer block into the rear anchor pin bore. Orient the spacer block as follows:

a. On Bravo I or Bravo II models, orient the spacer block with the opening closer to the rear of the drive shaft housing (**Figure 51**).

b. On Bravo III models, orient the spacer block with the opening closer to the front of the drive shaft housing (**Figure 52**).

9A. *Alpha drive*—Install the anchor pin(s) as follows:

a. Apply water resistant grease to the anchor pin.

b. Slide the short anchor pin through the drive shaft housing. Slide the long anchor pin through the gimbal ring.

9B. *Bravo drive*—Install the anchor pin(s) as follows:

a. Apply water resistant grease to the anchor pin.

b. Hold the spacer block in the bore and slide the short anchor pin through the drive shaft housing. Install a washer over each end of the anchor pin. Seat the washers against the drive shaft housing.

c. Slide the long anchor pin (1, **Figure 47**) through the gimbal ring. Install a washer over each end of the anchor pin. Seat them against the gimbal ring.

d. Using snap ring pliers, install a snap ring over each end of the anchor pin. The washer must fit between the gimbal ring and the snap ring.

10A. *Alpha drive*—Slip the four bushings (7, **Figure 46**) into the pin bore of each hydraulic cylinder.

10B. *Bravo drive*—Slide a rubber bushing (3, **Figure 47**) over the end of each anchor pin with the larger diameter side facing the washer.

11A. *Alpha drive*—Install the hydraulic cylinder(s) as follows:

a. The flat surface must face down and extend away from the drive shaft housing.

**46**

## ALPHA HYDRAULIC TRIM CYLINDER

1. Down pressure hose
2. Up pressure hose
3. Anchor pin
4. Screw
5. Ground wire
6. Hose retainer
7. Bushing
8. Washer
9. E-clip
10. Plastic cover
11. Hydraulic trim cylinder
12. Anode
13. Screw
14. Ground washer

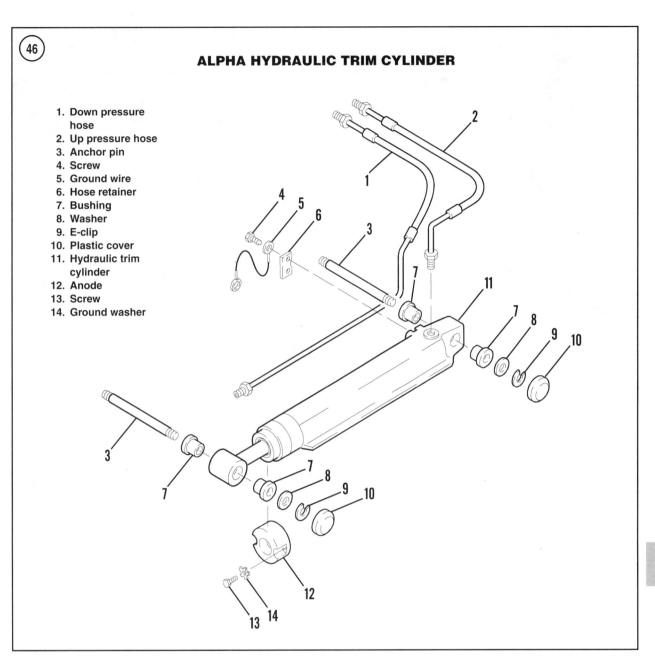

**47**

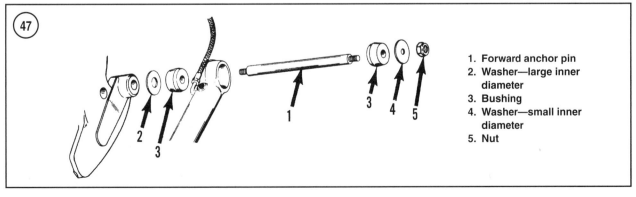

1. Forward anchor pin
2. Washer—large inner diameter
3. Bushing
4. Washer—small inner diameter
5. Nut

**13**

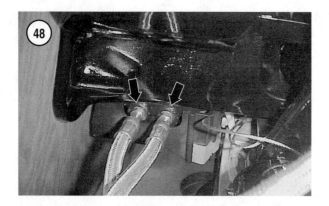

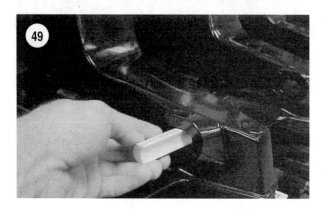

b. The hose retainer (6, **Figure 46**) must face the gimbal ring.

c. The long cylinder end of the ram must face the drive shaft housing (**Figure 53**). Rotate the ends as required.

d. Slide the cylinder over each anchor pin. Place a washer (8, **Figure 46**) over each end of the anchor pin and seat it against the bushing flange. Push the cylinder inward to expose the inner groove on the anchor pin (**Figure 54**).

e. Install the E-clip into the inner groove. The washer must fit between the bushing and E-clip.

f. Push the plastic cover (10, **Figure 46**) onto the anchor pin until it locks into the outer groove of the pin. Repeat this step for the remaining cylinder.

11A. *Bravo drive*—Install the hydraulic cylinder(s) as follows:

a. The casting number (**Figure 55**) must face toward the drive shaft housing.

b. Position the threaded opening (**Figure 55**) toward the top forward side.

c. The offset angle at the end of the rams must align as shown in **Figure 56**. Rotate the end of the ram as required.

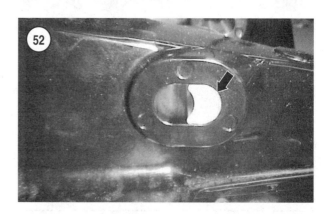

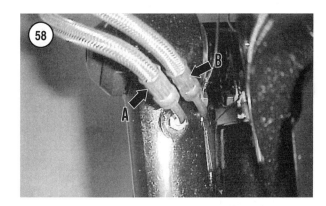

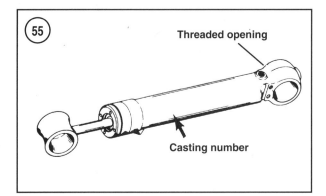

Threaded opening

Casting number

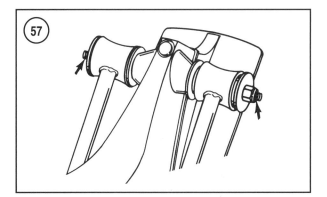

d. Slide the cylinder over each anchor pin. Slide a bushing (7, **Figure 47**) over each anchor pin end with the small diameter facing the cylinder. Push the bushings into the openings in the cylinder.

e. Slide a washer over each end of the anchor pins. Seat the washer against the bushing (7, **Figure 47**).

f. Thread a locknut (5, **Figure 47**) onto each anchor pin. Tighten each anchor pin nut (**Figure 57**) until seated against the step.

g. Thread the plastic covers onto the anchor pins. Securely tighten the covers.

12. Attach the hydraulic hoses as follows.

a. Apply a light coat of Perfect Seal (Mercury part No. 92-34227-1) to the threads of each hose fitting. Do not apply Perfect Seal to the hose openings.

b. Attach the UP pressure hose (A, **Figure 58**) into the UP pressure port (A, **Figure 59**). The UP pressure hose connects to the front top of the cylinder. The other end of this hose connects to the UP pressure port on the terminal block. The UP pressure port on the terminal block is closest to the boat transom. Do not tighten the hose at this time.

c. Connect the DOWN pressure hose (B, **Figure 58**) fitting into the DOWN pressure port (B, **Figure 59**) on the terminal block. The down pressure hose con-

**13**

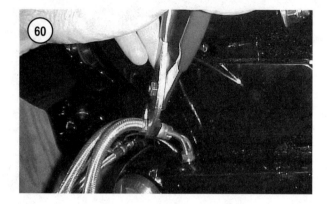

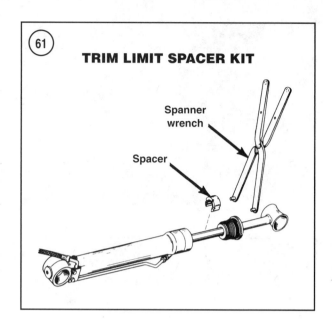

TRIM LIMIT SPACER KIT

Spanner wrench

Spacer

nects to a stainless line leading to the rear of the cylinder. The other end of this hose connects to the DOWN pressure port on the terminal block. The DOWN pressure port is located furthest from the boat transom.

  d. Grip the crimping flange (**Figure 60**) while tightening the hose to prevent twisting. Twisting will loosen the hose and reduce its service life. Securely tighten the hose fitting. Do not strip the terminal block threads.

13. Attach the hydraulic cylinder ground wires to the gimbal housing as described in Chapter Fifteen. Install the anode block or Mercathode electrode as described in Chapter Fifteen.

14. Fill and bleed the system as described in this chapter.

### Hydraulic Trim Cylinder Overhaul

Failure of the cylinder is usually caused by worn or damaged O-rings, scored or pitted cylinders, or corrosion damage to the end cap or hose fittings.

Hydraulic cylinder disassembly requires a spanner wrench (**Figure 61**) and experience in hydraulic system service. Have the repairs performed by a qualified technician if you are uncomfortable with the repair procedures.

Work in a clean environment and take all necessary precautions to keep contaminants out of the cylinders. Dirt or other contaminants can damage seal surfaces and block passages throughout the system.

Different cylinder castings and pressure hoses are used for the port and starboard sides. To prevent improper assembly or installation, mark the components prior to removal.

Refer to **Figure 62** (Alpha drives) or **Figure 63** (Bravo drives).

### External Component Removal

1. Clamp the forward end of the cylinder into a vise with protective jaws.

2. Direct the hydraulic hoses into a container to catch any fluid. Extend and retract the ram several times until all fluid is expelled from the cylinder.

3. Remove the anode (24, **Figure 62**) as described in Chapter Fifteen.

4. Remove the screws and hose retainer (**Figure 64**) from the cylinder. Remove the ground wire terminal from the lower screw.

5. Carefully loosen the fittings and remove trim hoses from the cylinder.

*NOTE*
*Some O-rings are the same outer diameter, but have a different shape and inner diameter. Note the location of each O-ring and compare the original and replacement O-rings before installation.*

### Cylinder Disassembly

1. Attach the spanner wrench to the end cap (**Figure 65**). Loosen the end cap. Tap the spanner wrench with a soft-faced mallet to loosen the cap. If the cap does not loosen, apply heat to it.

2. Pull the hydraulic ram (1, **Figure 66**) from the cylinder (3). Clamp the anchor pin end of the ram in a vise.

3. If the ram is quipped with trim limit spacers (**Figure 61**), remove them.

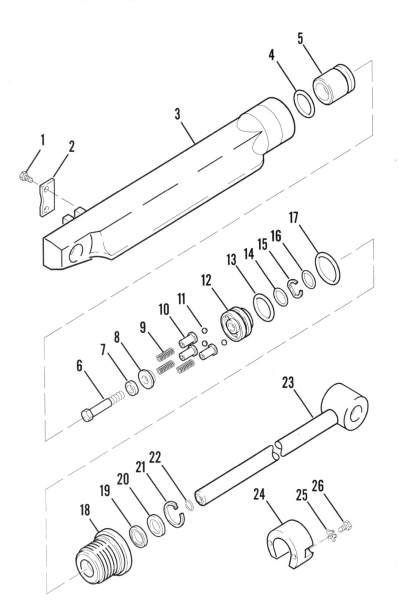

**HYDRAULIC TRIM CYLINDER (ALPHA DRIVES)**

62

**13**

1. Screw
2. Hose retainer
3. Hydraulic cylinder
4. O-ring
5. Floating piston
6. Shock piston bolt
7. Spacer (not used in all cylinders)
8. Stepped washer

9. Springs (3)
10. Spring guides (3)
11. Check balls (3)
12. Shock piston
13. Large O-ring
14. Small O-ring
15. Continuity clip
16. Small O-ring
17. Large O-ring

18. End cap
19. Scraper
20. Stainless steel washer
21. Retaining clip
22. Small O-ring
23. Cylinder ram
24. Anode
25. Ground washer
26. Screw

(63)

## HYDRAULIC TRIM CYLINDER (BRAVO DRIVES)

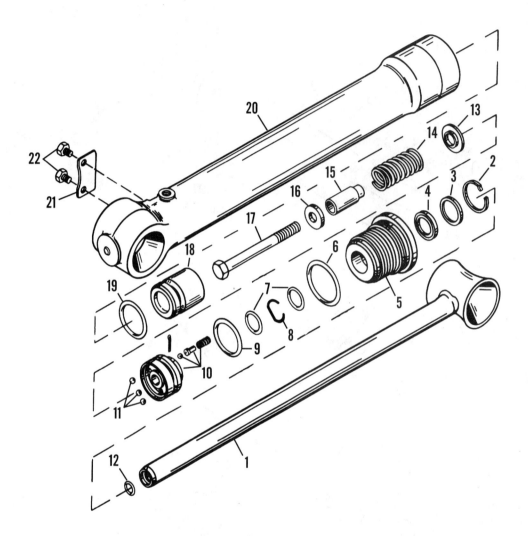

1. Cylinder ram
2. Retaining clip
3. Stainless steel washer
4. Scraper
5. End cap
6. Large O-ring
7. Small O-rings
8. Continuity clip
9. Large O-ring
10. Shock piston
11. Check balls
12. Small O-ring
13. Spring guide washer
14. Spring
15. Spring guide
16. Spring guide washer
17. Shock piston bolt
18. Floating piston
19. Large O-ring
20. Hydraulic cylinder
21. Hose retainer
22. Screws

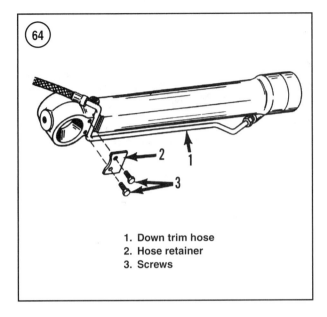

1. Down trim hose
2. Hose retainer
3. Screws

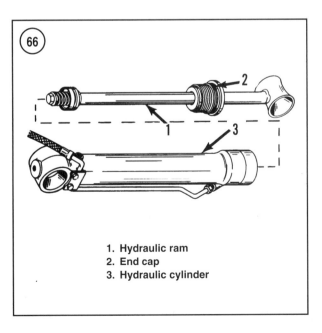

1. Hydraulic ram
2. End cap
3. Hydraulic cylinder

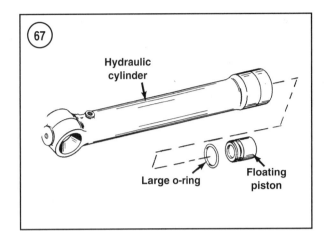

Hydraulic cylinder

Large o-ring

Floating piston

4. Tap the open end of the hydraulic cylinder against a block of wood to remove the floating piston. Remove the large O-ring from the floating piston (**Figure 67**).

5. Loosen, but do not remove the shock piston bolt (6, **Figure 62**) or (17, **Figure 63**).

6A. *Alpha drive*—Remove and disassemble the shock piston assembly as follows:

  a. Hold the shock piston (12, **Figure 62**) against the bolt (6) and unthread it from the cylinder ram (23). Place the shock piston, bolt side up, on a clean work surface.

  b. Remove the small O-ring (22, **Figure 62**) from the ram (23) or shock piston (12).

  c. Pull the bolt (6, **Figure 62**), spacer (7) and stepped washer (8) from the shock piston. Some cylinders do not use the spacer. Lift the springs (9, **Figure 62**), guides (10) and check balls (11) from the shock piston.

  d. Remove the large O-ring (13, **Figure 62**) from the shock piston.

6B. *Bravo drive*—Remove and disassemble the shock piston assembly as follows:

  a. Hold the shock piston (10, **Figure 63**) and spring (14) tightly against the bolt (17). Remove the shock piston. Place the shock piston, bolt side up, on a clean work surface.

  b. Remove the small O-ring (12, **Figure 63**) from the ram or shock piston (10).

  c. Remove the bolt (17, **Figure 63**), spring guide washer (16), spring (14) and spring guide (15) from the shock piston. Lift the spring washer and balls (13 and 11, **Figure 63**) from the shock piston.

  d. Remove the large O-ring (9, **Figure 63**) from the shock piston.

7. Slide the end cap (2, **Figure 66**) from the cylinder ram. Remove the large O-ring from the end cap.

**13**

8. Use a sharp pick or scribe to remove the retaining clip from its groove in the end cap. Be careful not to damage the groove. Remove the stainless steel washer and scraper from the cap.

9. Use a toothpick to remove the small O-ring and continuity clip.

10. Clean all components with solvent and dry them with compressed air.

11. Inspect the end cap for damage to the O-ring or retaining clip grooves and wear in the inner bore. Replace the end cap if these or other defects are present.

12. Inspect the cylinder ram (**Figure 68**) for pits or scratches. Replace the cylinder ram if any surface imperfection can be detected with a fingernail.

13. Inspect the floating piston and shock piston components for corrosion, pits or scratches. Replace any damaged or questionable components.

14. Shine a light into the hydraulic cylinder bore and inspect the internal surface. Replace the cylinder if the surface is pitted or scratched.

### Cylinder Assembly

1. Slide the new ground clip into the end cap. Fit the clip into the middle groove of the bore. Install a new O-ring into the grooves on either side of the ground clip.

2. Install the new scraper and stainless steel washer into the end cap. Fit the new retaining clip into its groove in the end cap.

3. Clamp the anchor pin end of the cylinder ram into a vise with protective jaws. Lubricate the inner bore of the end cap with engine oil and slide it onto the cylinder ram. The threaded section of the cap must face away from the anchor pin end of the ram. Install the large O-ring into the end cap.

4. Apply Loctite 8831 (Mercury part No. 92-823089-1) to the threaded opening in the cylinder ram. Place the small O-ring into the recess in the end of the ram.

5A. *Alpha drive*—Install the shock piston onto the cylinder ram as follows:

   a. Install a new O-ring (13, **Figure 62**) onto the shock piston (12). Place the shock piston, open side up, on a clean work surface.

   b. Place the check balls (11, **Figure 62**) into the pockets in the shock piston. Install a spring guide (10, **Figure 62**) onto each ball with the large diameter side facing the ball. Slide a spring (9, **Figure 62**) over each guide.

   c. Install the stepped washer (8, **Figure 62**) onto the springs with the stepped side facing downward. Install the spacer (7, **Figure 62**) onto the washer. Some cylinders do not use this spacer. Clean all oil,

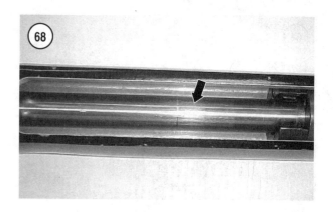

grease or other contaminants from the bolt threads with quick drying solvent. Slip the bolt (6, **Figure 62**) through the bore of the shock piston.

   d. Hold the shock piston tightly against the bolt while threading the bolt into the cylinder ram. Tighten the shock piston bolt to the specification in **Table 1**.

5B. *Bravo drive unit*—Install the shock piston onto the cylinder ram as follows:

   a. If installing a new shock piston, slide the spring guide and spring into the piston as shown in **Figure 63**. Use a small pick to collapse the spring, then slide the small roll pin into the bore. The spring must fit below the roll pin.

   b. Install a new O-ring (9, **Figure 63**) into its groove on the shock piston (10). Place the shock piston on a clean work surface with the open side facing upward.

   c. Install the check balls (11, **Figure 63**) into the pockets in the shock piston. Set the spring washer (13, **Figure 63**) on the check balls with the stepped side facing up.

   d. Install the spring (14, **Figure 63**) onto the washer. Slide the spring guide (15, **Figure 63**) into the spring with the shouldered side facing the shock piston. Install the spring guide washer (16, **Figure 63**) onto the spring with the stepped side facing the shock piston. Slip the bolt (17, **Figure 63**) through the bore of the spring and shock piston.

   e. Hold the piston tightly against the bolt while threading the bolt into the cylinder ram. Tighten the bolt to the specification in **Table 1**.

6. Lubricate the large O-ring with engine oil and install it onto the floating piston (**Figure 67**).

7. If so equipped, snap the spacer(s) onto the shaft of the cylinder ram. Position the spacer(s) between the shock piston and the end cap (**Figure 61**).

8. Apply oil to the bore of the hydraulic cylinder. Place the floating piston (**Figure 67**) onto the shock piston with the open end facing the shock piston bolt.

9. Apply oil to the O-rings on the shock piston and floating piston. Guide the floating piston and shock piston into the bore.

10. Clamp the forward end of the cylinder into a vise with protective jaws. Push the ram fully into the cylinder. Pour 10W-30 or 10W-40 engine oil into the open end of the cylinder until approximately 3 in. (7.6 cm) below the opening.

11. Apply water resistant grease to the threads and O-ring of the end cap. Thread the cap into the cylinder. Use a spanner wrench to tighten the end cap to the specification in **Table 1**.

### External Component Installation

1. Clamp the forward end of the cylinder in a vise with protective jaws.

2. Install the hydraulic cylinder anode (24, **Figure 62**) as described in Chapter Fifteen.

3. Attach the trim hoses to the cylinder. Do not tighten the hose fittings at this time.

4. Set the stainless steel tube into the recess near the front of the cylinder. Install the hose retainer and screws as shown in **Figure 64**. The curved edge of the retainer must face the forward anchor pin bore. Attach the ground wire to the lower screw.

5. Position and tighten the trim hoses as described under *External Hose Removal and Installation* in this chapter.

### Trim Limit Spacers Installation

Some cylinders are equipped with trim limit spacers (**Figure 61**) to prevent the drive unit from contacting the boat when in the fully up position. Some applications require two or more of these spacers. The same number of spacers must be installed in each cylinder. Using a different number of spacers causes uneven cylinder travel, resulting in serious damage to drive or transom assembly. A spanner wrench is required for this procedure.

1. Remove the hydraulic cylinders as described in this chapter. Thoroughly clean the end cap area to prevent contamination from entering the cylinders.

2. Clamp the forward end of the cylinders into a vise with protective jaws. Attach the spanner wrench to the end cap (**Figure 61**). Loosen the end cap. Tap the spanner wrench with a soft-faced mallet to loosen the cap. If necessary, apply heat to the end cap area of the cylinder to loosen the cap.

3. Without removing the cylinder ram, pull the end cap away from the cylinder. Snap the spacer(s) onto the shaft of the ram.

4. Apply water resistant grease to the threads and O-ring of the end cap. Thread the cap into the cylinder. Use a spanner wrench to tighten the end cap to the specification in **Table 1**.

5. Repeat Steps 2-4 for the remaining cylinder.

6. Install the hydraulic cylinders as described in this chapter.

### EXTERNAL HOSES

### Removal and Installation

If replacing the DOWN pressure hose, remove the hydraulic cylinder. Replace the UP pressure hoses without removing the hydraulic cylinder. While loosening or tightening the hoses, grip the crimping flange (**Figure 60**) to prevent twisting. Twisting promotes loosening and substantially reduces the service life of the hose.

> *WARNING*
> *The hydraulic system contains fluid under very high pressure. Wear safety glasses and protective clothing if working with the hydraulic system.*

### Up Pressure Hose

1. Place the drive in the fully down position. Relieve the system pressure as described in this chapter.

2. Remove the anode block or lower the Mercathode electrode as described in Chapter Fifteen.

3. Unthread the UP pressure hose from the port (A, **Figure 59**) on the terminal block. The UP port is on the side of the terminal block nearest the boat transom.

4. Unthread the UP pressure hose from the front of the cylinder (**Figure 69**).

5. Apply perfect seal (Mercury part No. 92-34227-1) to the fitting threads. Do not apply perfect seal to the hose openings.

6. Hand-thread the 90° fittings into the cylinder. Thread the straight fitting into the UP pressure port of the terminal block (A, **Figure 59**). Do not tighten the hose fittings at this time.

7. Position the 90° fitting at a 45° angle to the cylinder with the hose extending away from the drive shaft housing (**Figure 69**). Hold the crimped end and securely tighten the fitting.

8. Hand-thread the straight hose fitting into the UP pressure port (A, **Figure 59**) of the terminal block. Hold the crimped end and securely tighten the fitting.

**13**

9. Install the anode block or Mercathode electrode as described in Chapter Fifteen.

10. Fill and bleed the system as described in this chapter.

### Down Pressure Hose

1. Place the drive in the fully down position. Relieve the system pressure as described in this chapter.

2. Remove the anode block or lower the Mercathode electrode as described in Chapter Fifteen.

3. Remove the cylinder(s) as described in this chapter. Remove the DOWN pressure hose and hose retainer as described under *External component removal* in this chapter.

4. Hand-thread the 45° angle fitting into the DOWN pressure opening at the rear of the cylinder. Do not tighten the fitting at this time.

5. Attach the DOWN pressure hose and retainer to the cylinder as described in this chapter.

6. Install the cylinder(s) onto the anchor pin as described in this chapter. Hand-thread the straight fitting into the DOWN pressure port (B, **Figure 59**) of the terminal block. Hold the crimped end and securely tighten the fitting.

7. Securely tighten the hose fitting at the rear of the cylinder. Connect and tighten the UP pressure hose as described in this chapter.

8. Install the anode block or Mercathode electrode as described in Chapter Fifteen.

9. Fill and bleed the system as described in this chapter.

### TERMINAL BLOCK

#### Removal and Installation

1. Remove the anode block or lower the Mercathode electrode as described in Chapter Fifteen.

2. Disconnect the trim hoses from the terminal block as described under *Hydraulic Cylinder and Anchor Pins* in this chapter. Do not remove the cylinders.

3. Remove the locknuts and ground washers (**Figure 70**). Pull down on the terminal block to access the internal hose fittings (**Figure 71**). To prevent contamination, clean the top side of the terminal block and the hose fittings with a spray cleaner.

4. Mark the hose fitting closest to the boat transom (UP pressure). Loosen both fittings and remove the terminal block from the mounting studs. Remove and discard the gasket from the terminal block or transom housing. Clean corrosion, oily deposits or debris from the terminal block and gasket surfaces.

5. Install a new gasket onto the top side of the terminal block. Pull the marked hose (UP pressure) out until it extends approximately 2 in. (5.1 cm) from the opening. Thread the hose fitting into one of the upper threaded openings. Do not tighten the fitting at this time.

6. Turn the terminal block so the UP pressure hose fitting is closest to the boat transom and the 90° bend faces forward.

7. Pull the DOWN pressure hose out of the opening enough to thread its fitting into the terminal block. Orient its 90° fitting facing forward and above the UP pressure fitting. Do not tighten the fitting at this time.

8. Install the terminal block over the mounting studs, guiding the fittings into the opening. Seat the terminal block against the transom housing and align the hose fittings.

9. Lower the terminal block enough to access the fittings (**Figure 71**). Securely tighten the fittings.

10. Seat the terminal block. Secure the terminal block with the two ground washers and locknuts.

11. Attach the external trim hoses to the terminal block as described in this chapter.

12. Fill and bleed the system as described in this chapter. Install the anode block or Mercathode electrode as described in Chapter Fifteen.

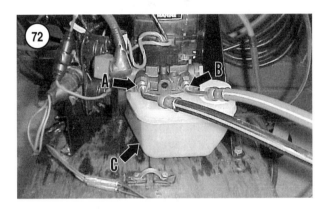

## INTERNAL HOSE

### Removal and Installation

Always replace both internal hoses if either is defective.

1.  Place the drive unit in the fully down position. Relieve the system pressure as described in this chapter.

2.  Disconnect the positive and negative trim pump leads from the battery.

3.  Place shop towels under the fittings (A and B, **Figure 72**) to catch spilled fluid.

4.  Loosen the fittings and remove both hoses. Remove any clamps connecting the hoses onto the boat or engine.

5.  If the model is equipped with a Mercathode electrode, remove it with its wiring as described in Chapter Fifteen. Remove the terminal block as described in this chapter.

6.  While an assistant guides the hoses from inside the engine compartment, pull the hoses from the terminal block opening. Inspect the hoses for melted surfaces, cracks or signs of leakage. Replace both hoses if either is defective.

7.  Install caps or tap over the hose openings to prevent contamination during installation.

8.  Have an assistant guide the hoses toward the trim pump during installation. The 90° fitting end of the hoses

connects to the terminal block. The 45° fitting connects to the trim pump.

9.  Guide the trim pump fitting end of the UP hose (black) through the terminal block and into the engine compartment. Leave approximately 6 in. (15.2 cm) of hose protruding from the opening. Mark the UP hose fitting to ensure a correct connection.

10.  Apply soapy water to the outer surface of the DOWN hose (gray). Feed the trim pump end of hose into the opening and above the up pressure hose. Push the hose into the opening until its 90° fitting aligns with the up hose fitting.

11.  Position the longer DOWN hose fitting toward the rear and extending above the UP hose fitting. Push both hoses into the opening. Do not push the fittings into the opening.

12.  Install the terminal block as described in this chapter.

## FILLING AND BLEEDING THE SYSTEM

Follow the procedure in this section after replacing or repairing any trim system components except the electrical components.

> *WARNING*
> *The hydraulic system contains fluid under very high pressure. Wear safety glasses and protective clothing when working with the hydraulic system.*

### Fluid Level

1.  Place the drive unit in the fully down position. If the trim system is inoperative, refer to *Relieving System Pressure* to lower the drive unit.

2.  Remove the yellow oil fill cap. Pour 10W-30 or 10W-40 engine oil into the reservoir (C, **Figure 72**) until the level just reaches the full mark. Do not overfill the reservoir. Reinstall the fill cap. Do not install the red shipping plug.

3.  Raise the trim. Stop immediately if the trim motor suddenly increases in speed. This indicates a low fluid level is ventilating the pump. Immediately lower the drive and correct the fluid level. Continue until the drive reaches the fully up and down positions without ventilating.

4.  Place the drive in the down position. Allow a few minutes for foam in the reservoir to dissipate. Correct the fluid level.

### Bleeding

1.  Place the drive unit in the full down position. If the trim system in inoperative, refer to *Relieving System Pressure* to lower the drive unit.

**13**

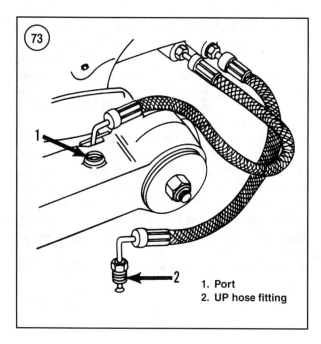

1. Port
2. UP hose fitting

1. Down hose fitting
2. Terminal block
3. Plug (Mercury part No. 22-38609)

2. Remove the anode block or lower the Mercathode electrode as described in Chapter Fifteen.

3. Remove the yellow oil fill cap. Pour 10W-30 or 10W-40 engine oil into the reservoir (C, **Figure 72**) until the level reaches the full mark on the translucent reservoir. Do not overfill the reservoir. Reinstall the fill cap. Do not install the red shipping plug.

4. Disconnect the UP pressure hose from the port at the front and top of both hydraulic cylinders (**Figure 73**). Direct the disconnected hoses into a container.

5. Have an assistant operate the pump in the UP direction until there are no air bubbles in the fluid stream exiting the hoses. Attach and align the UP hose as described in this chapter.

6. Correct the fluid level as described in this chapter. Disconnect both DOWN hoses (2, **Figure 74**) from the terminal block (2). The DOWN hoses connect to the terminal block opening furthest from the boat transom.

7. Install plugs (3, **Figure 74**) (Mercury part No. 22-38609 or equivalent) into both terminal block openings. Direct the disconnected hoses into a container.

8. Operate the trim pump in the UP direction until the drive is fully up. Stop immediately if the trim motor suddenly increases in speed. This indicates the pump is ventilating due to a low fluid level. Add a small amount of fluid to the reservoir. Continue until the drive reaches the fully up position.

9. Remove the plugs (3, **Figure 74**). Have an assistant operate the pump in the DOWN direction until no air bubbles are detected in the fluid stream exiting the openings.

10. Remove the plugs. Reconnect the down hoses as described in this chapter.

11. Install the anode block or Mercathode electrode as described in Chapter Fifteen. Correct the fluid level and purge remaining air from the system as described in this chapter.

## Table 1 TORQUE SPECIFICATIONS

| Fastener | ft.-lb. | in.-lb. | N•m |
|---|---|---|---|
| Hydraulic cylinder end cap | 40-50 | – | 54-68 |
| Shock piston bolt | 15-20 | 180-240 | 20-27 |
| Trim hoses to pump | – | 100-150 | 11-17 |
| Up pressure relief valve | – | 70 | 8 |
| Down pressure relief valve | – | 70 | 8 |
| Thermal relief valve | – | 70 | 8 |
| Hydraulic pump to adapter | – | 70 | 8 |
| Trim motor to pump adapter | – | 25 | 3 |
| Pilot valve cover | 38-50 | – | 52-68 |

# Chapter Fourteen

# Steering System

Mercruiser stern drives may be equipped with a manual or power steering system. Proper operation of the stern drive steering system is essential for safe boating. The steering system should be only be rigged and serviced by an experienced marine technician. This chapter covers steering safely precautions and steering system service. Tightening torque specifications are listed in **Table 1**, located at the end of this chapter.

## SAFETY PRECAUTIONS

The steering system connects the drive unit to the steering wheel (**Figure 1**). When making adjustments or repairs to the steering system, use only the fasteners supplied with the steering attachment kit or equivalent fasteners sold as replacement items by marine dealers. After performing any procedure that affects the steering system, make sure that:

1. Cable movement is not restricted. See **Figure 2**. The cable must make a smooth bend to the steering actuator and not bind against the boat structure or other components. Cable restrictions can cause the system to jam. On power steering models, a cable restriction can prevent the power steering from operating or cause the drive unit to unexpectedly go into a full turn without turning the wheel.

2. The boat structure or other components do not contact the power steering pump or pulley (**Figure 3**).

3. The power steering cable moves freely and operates the actuator (**Figure 4**) only then turning the steering wheel.

## MECHANICAL STEERING SYSTEM

A mechanical steering system is used only on 3.0L models. All other models are equipped with power steering. A mechanical system (**Figure 5**) consists of the helm and steering wheel assembly, the steering cable and hardware connecting the cable to the steering lever.

> *WARNING*
> *Failure of the steering system can cause a serious accident. Do not operate a boat with loose or binding steering.*

> *WARNING*
> *The steering cable must have a self locking coupler (**Figure 6**) or coupler locking mechanism (**Figure 7**) to prevent the cable from loosening. A loose cable will result in excessive steering play and eventual lack or steering control. Do not operate the boat if this important safety feature is lacking.*

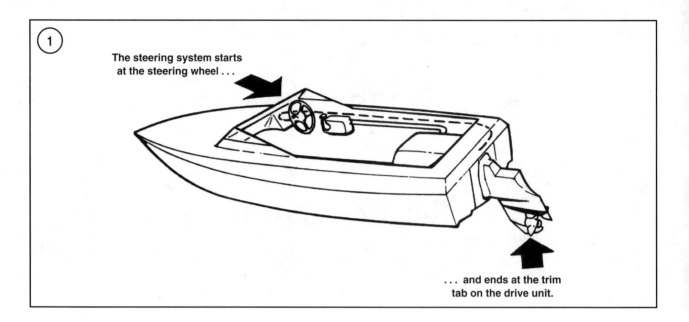

The steering system starts at the steering wheel . . .

. . . and ends at the trim tab on the drive unit.

### Steering Cable and Helm
### Removal and Installation

Replace the steering cable and helm as an assembly. Both components are subject to wear and the effects of corrosion, and failure of one usually proceeds the other. Purchase the helm and cable from a marine dealership or marine supply business. Follow the manufacture's instructions to install the helm onto the boat.

1. Remove the cotter pin and clevis pin that connects the cable end to the steering lever.

2A. *With a self locking cable coupler*—Loosen the cable coupler (**Figure 6**). Pull the cable from the guide tube and pivot block.

2B. *With a coupler locking mechanism*—Disconnect the cable (**Figure 7**) as follows:

    a. Turn the steering to the full port position.

    b. Remove the cotter pin (5, **Figure 7**). Slide the locking sleeve (6, **Figure 7**) from the nut.

    c. Fully loosen the coupler. Pull the cable from the guide tube and pivot block.

3. Remove the faulty steering cable and helm from the boat. Install the replacement cable and helm according to the manufacturer's instructions.

4. Clean all grease, corrosion or other contaminants from the bore of the tube guide. Inspect the tube for cracks, pits or damage. Replace the tube if damaged.

5. Apply a light coat of Special Lube 101 (Mercury part No. 92-113872A1) to the guide tube bore.

6. Rotate the steering wheel to the full starboard position. Guide the cable end through the guide tube. Align the clevis pin opening at the end of the cable with the pin

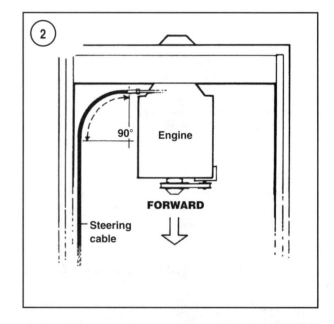

90°  Engine

**FORWARD**

Steering cable

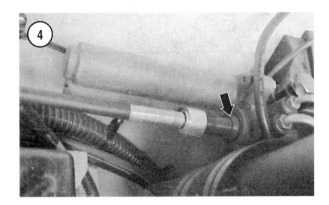

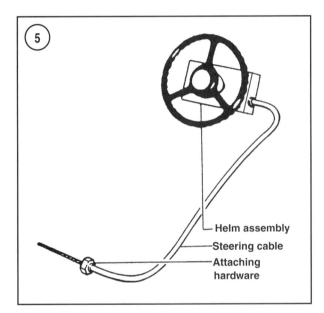

Helm assembly
Steering cable
Attaching hardware

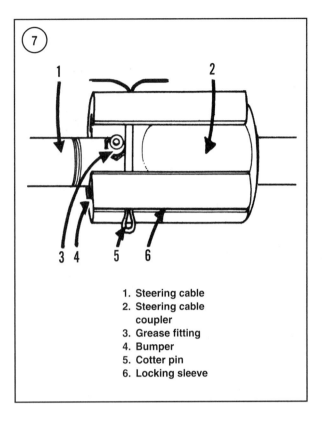

1. Steering cable
2. Steering cable coupler
3. Grease fitting
4. Bumper
5. Cotter pin
6. Locking sleeve

7. Guide the steering cable onto the pivot block. The cable must not make any sharp bends or bind against the engine, boat structure or other objects.

8. Rotate the steering wheel one full turn in the port direction. Thread the steering cable coupler (**Figure 6**) or (2, **Figure 7**) onto the tube guide.

9A. *With a self locking cable coupler*—Tighten the coupler to the specification in **Table 1**.

9B. *With a coupler locking mechanism*—Attach the cable as follows:

   a. Tighten the coupler (2, **Figure 7**) to the specification in **Table 1**.

   b. Slide the cable jacket into the slot of the coupler. Slide the sleeve over the coupler, aligning the slot in the coupler with the grease fitting (3, **Figure 7**). Align the sleeve, grease fitting and cable coupler.

   c. Insert the cotter pin as shown in **Figure 7**. Bend over the ends of the cotter pin.

10. Turn the steering wheel lock-to-lock. The drive unit must move smoothly in each direction. If it binds or turns roughly, inspect the guide tube dimension.

11. Rotate the steering wheel until the drive unit is centered. The steering must be centered. If not, check the guide tube dimension. If the dimension is correct but the steering will not center, the cable or steering wheel are probably installed incorrectly.

**14**

opening in the steering lever. Install the clevis pin through both openings. The shouldered side must rest against the top of the steering lever. Insert the cotter pin through the bottom of the clevis pin. Bend over the ends of the cotter pin.

## Guide Tube and Pivot Block
## Removal and Installation

1. Disconnect the steering cable from the pivot block as described in this chapter.

2. Bend the locking tabs (A, **Figure 8**) away from the pivot bolts. Remove both pivot bolts and tab washers. Pull the tube and block from the inner transom plate.

3. Remove the guide tube only if it must be replaced, as removal may damage the threads.

   a. Grip the unthreaded end of the tube with locking pliers. Apply heat to the sides of the pivot block to soften the threadlocking compound.

   b. Loosen and remove the cable guide nut.

   c. Unthread the pivot block from the tube.

4. Inspect the Teflon bushing in the pivot block for wear or damage. Remove and replace the bushing if defective.

5. Thread the pivot block onto the tube until the unthreaded end protrudes 2-1/2 in. (63.5 mm) from the side of the block (**Figure 9**). Thread the nut onto the guide tube until it touches the block. Mark the guide tube at the edge of the nut and the side of the pivot block.

6. Thread the nut and block away from the unthreaded end until the area between the marks is exposed.

7. Apply a thick coat of Loctite 8831 (Mercury part No. 92-826089-1) to the threads between the marks.

8. Thread the pivot block toward the unthreaded end protrudes 2 1/2 in. (63.5 mm) from the side of the block. Thread the nut toward the end until it just contacts the pivot block. Clamp the pivot block in a vise with protective jaws. Tighten the guide tube nut to the specification in **Table 1**.

9. Apply Special Lube 101 (Mercury part No. 92-113872A1) to the pivot bolts and bushing in the pivot block.

10. With the unthreaded end of the tube facing the steering lever, slide the guide tube and block between the transom plate bosses. Align the Teflon bushing with the holes for the pivot bolts.

11. Align the upper tab washer with the pivot bolt opening. Position the tangs of the washer over the ridge on the mounting boss (B, **Figure 8**). Insert the pivot bolt through the washer and into the opening. Hand-thread the bolt into the block. The bolt head must seat against the tab washer. If not, align the bolt with the bushing.

12. Install the lower tab washer and pivot bolt as described in step 11. Verify free movement of the pivot block then tighten both pivot bolts to the specification in **Table 1**.

13. Make sure the washer tangs align with the ridge (B, **Figure 8**). Correct if necessary before proceeding. Care-

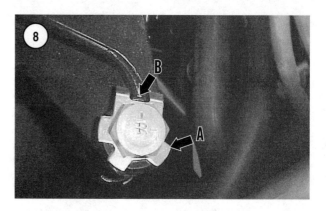

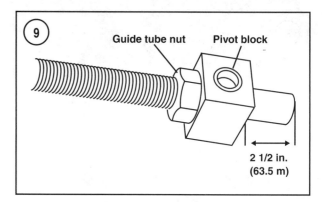

fully bend a tab of the washer (A, **Figure 8**) against a flat side of the pivot bolt.

14. Attach the steering cable onto the pivot block and steering lever as described in this chapter.

## POWER STEERING

Power steering is installed on all V6 and V8 models. The system consists of the belt driven power steering pump (**Figure 3**), power steering actuator (**Figure 4**), steering cable, fluid cooler and the hardware to connect the actuator to the steering lever. Refer to Chapter Three for a description of the system and troubleshooting procedure.

## Power Steering Actuator
## Removal and Installation

*CAUTION*
*Make sure the upper and lower pivot bolts are aligned with the pivot block or actuator bushing before tightening them. If not aligned, the mounting bosses on the inner transom plate will break as the bolts are tightened.*

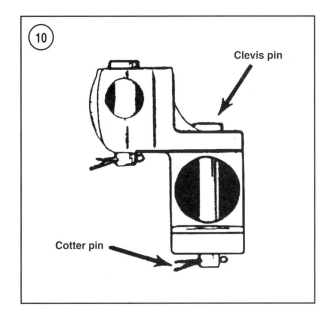

Clevis pin

Cotter pin

The power steering actuator (**Figure 4**) is secured to the inner transom plate with pivot bolts (A, **Figure 8**). This component is not serviceable. Replace the entire assembly if faulty.

1. Place the steering in the centered position. Remove the cotter pin and short clevis pin (**Figure 10**) to free the steering cable from the actuator arm. Remove the cotter pin and long clevis pin (**Figure 10**) to free the steering lever from the actuator.

2. Place shop towels or a suitable container under the actuator to catch spilled fluid. Disconnect the hose fittings (**Figure 11**). Inspect the O-ring on each fitting for cuts, flattening or damage and replace as needed. Tie the hose fittings to a location slightly higher than the power steering pump to reduce fluid leakage. Cover the fittings with a shop towel to prevent contamination.

3. Attach an open end wrench to the flat surfaces of the actuator (**Figure 12**).

4A. *With a self locking cable coupler*—Hold the end wrench to prevent valve rotation. Fully loosen the cable coupler (**Figure 6**). Remove the cable from the bore of the actuator.

4B. *With a coupler locking mechanism*—Disconnect the cable (**Figure 7**) as follows:

    a. Turn the steering to the full port position.

    b. Remove the cotter pin (5, **Figure 7**). Slide the locking sleeve (6, **Figure 7**) from the nut.

    c. Hold the wrench to prevent valve rotation. Fully loosen the cable coupler. Pull the cable from the bore of the actuator.

5. Bend the locking tabs (A, **Figure 8**) away from the pivot bolts. Remove both pivot bolts and tab washers. Detach the actuator from the inner transom plate.

6. Clean all grease, corrosion or other contaminants from the cable bore of the actuator. Inspect the bore for cracks, bending, pitting or other damage. Replace the actuator if damaged.

7. Inspect the Teflon pivot pin bushings for wear or damage. Remove and replace the bushing if defective.

8. Apply Special Lube 101 (Mercury part No. 92-13872A1) to the pivot bolts and bushings in the pivot block.

9. With the threaded end facing starboard, slide the actuator between the mounting bosses in the transom plate. Align the Teflon bushing with the hole for the pivot bolts.

10. Align the upper tab washer with the pivot bolt opening. Position the tangs of the washer over the ridge on the mounting boss (B, **Figure 8**). Insert the upper pivot bolt through the washer and into the opening. Hand-thread the bolt into the block. The bolt head must seat against the tab washer. If not, align the bolt with the bushing.

11. Install the lower tab washer and pivot bolt as described in Step 11. Make sure the actuator can move freely, then tighten both pivot bolts to the specification in **Table 1**. Make sure the washer tangs align with the ridge (B, **Figure 8**). Correct improper alignment before pro-

**14**

ceeding. Carefully bend a tab of the washer against a flat side of the pivot bolt (A, **Figure 8**).

12. Apply automatic transmission fluid to the O-rings on the hose fittings. Hand-thread both hose fittings into the actuator. Align the hose fittings as shown in **Figure 11** and tighten them to the specification in **Table 1**.

13. Apply Special Lube 101 (Mercury part No. 92-113872A1) to the cable bore of the actuator.

14. Rotate the steering wheel to the full starboard steering position. Guide the cable end through its bore in the actuator. Rotating the cable jacket if necessary, align the clevis pin opening at the end of the cable with the pin opening in the actuator. Install the clevis pin through both openings. The shouldered side of the pin must rest against the top side of the actuator arm. Insert the cotter pin through the clevis pin. Bend over the ends of the cotter pin.

15. Rotate the steering wheel in the port steering direction until the cable coupler contacts the threads of the actuator. Hand-thread the steering cable coupler (**Figure 6**) or (2, **Figure 7**) onto the tube guide.

16. Attach a wrench to the actuator (**Figure 12**). Rotate the valve until the flattened surfaces are parallel with the transom.

17A. *With a self locking cable coupler*—Tighten the coupler to the specification in **Table 1**.

17B. *With a coupler locking mechanism*—Tighten the coupler and attach the mechanism as follows:

    a. Tighten the coupler (2, **Figure 7**) to the specification in **Table 1**.

    b. Slide the cable jacket into the slot of the coupler. Slide the sleeve over the coupler and align the slot of the coupler with the grease fitting as shown in **Figure 7**. Rotate the cable jacket as required to align the sleeve, grease fitting and cable coupler.

    c. Insert the cotter pin as shown in **Figure 7**. Bend over the ends of the cotter pin.

18. Rotate the steering wheel until the clevis pin openings in the actuator arm perfectly align with the pin openings in the steering lever. Install the clevis pin through the four openings. The shouldered side of the pin must rest against the top side of the actuator arm. Insert the cotter pin through the clevis pin. Bend over the ends of the cotter pin.

19. Correct the fluid level and bleed air from the system as described in this chapter. Without starting the engine, turn the steering wheel lock-to-lock. The drive unit must move smoothly in each direction. If the steering binds or turns roughly, look for for an improperly installed clevis pin, binding steering lever or faulty steering cable or helm.

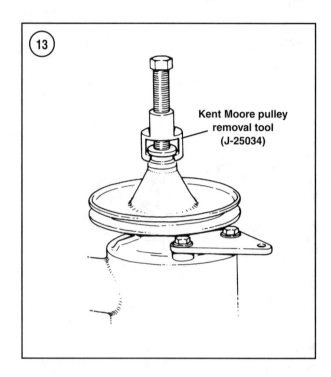

Kent Moore pulley removal tool (J-25034)

### Power Steering Pulley

Use a power steering pulley removal tool (**Figure 13**) to pull the pulley from the pump shaft. This tool may be purchased or rented from an automotive parts store. Use a pulley installation tool (Mercury part No. 91-93656A1) and a long straightedge to install the pulley. Install the pulley with the pump installed on the engine, to ensure alignment of the belts and pulleys. Improper alignment will cause noisy operation, increased wear on the pulley(s) and premature drive belt failure.

The pulley must fit tightly onto the pump shaft. If the fit is loose, the pulley or the pump shaft or both are excessively worn. If the replacement pulley fits loosely, replace the power steering pump. The pump shaft is not available separately.

> *CAUTION*
> *Make a sketch of the routing before removing the belt from the power steering pump pulley. Belt routing varies by model, model year, type of drive used and optional equipment. An improperly routed belt may contact and damage hoses, brackets or other components.*

### *Pulley removal*

1. Disconnect the battery cables.

2A. *3.0L models*—Loosen the power steering bolt mounting bolts, but do not remove them. Tilt the top of the pump

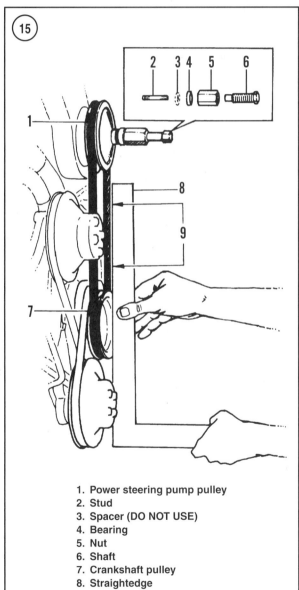

1. Power steering pump pulley
2. Stud
3. Spacer (DO NOT USE)
4. Bearing
5. Nut
6. Shaft
7. Crankshaft pulley
8. Straightedge
9. Parallel surfaces

toward the engine. Remove the power steering belt from the pump pulley.

2B. *V6 and V8 models*—Use a 5/8 in. end wrench to loosen the nut on the tensioner pulley (**Figure 14**). Loosen the nut just enough move the pulley. Remove the belt from the pulley.

3. Slide the pulley removal tool onto the hub of the pulley as shown in **Figure 13**. Hand-thread the puller bolt into the puller until it contacts the pump shaft. Hold the body of the tool with a wrench and tighten the bolt to remove the pulley.

4. Clean grease from the pulley with warm soapy water. Use carburundum paper to remove surface corrosion from steel pulleys. Thoroughly clean all abrasive material from the pulley. Paint the pulley to help prevent corrosion. Inspect the pulley and pump shaft for cracks or wear. Replace as needed.

*Pulley installation*

This procedure requires a pulley installation tool (Mercury part No. 91-93656A1). Refer to **Figure 15**.

1. Position the pulley on the pump shaft. Fit the drive belt around the pulleys. Do not adjust the belt tension at this time.

2. Thread the stud (2, **Figure 15**) from the pulley installation tool as far as possible into the pump shaft.

3. Position the bearing from the tool assembly over the stud. Do not use the spacer (3, **Figure 15**).

4. Thread the nut (5, **Figure 15**) onto the shaft (6). Thread the shaft and nut as far as possible into the stud.

5. Position the straightedge against the crankshaft and power steering pulleys as shown in **Figure 15**. Tighten the nut (5, **Figure 15**) until the drive belt surfaces are parallel to the straightedge.

6. Remove the straightedge and installation tool components.

7. Adjust the belt tension as described in Chapter Six. Connect the battery cables.

**Flow Control Valve**

On 3.0L models, service the flow control valve with the pump mounted on the engine. On other models, the pump may be removed if access to the valve is restricted. Replace all seals and O-rings if removed from the pump. Purchase a seal kit from a GM dealership (part No. 5688044). Lubricate all O-rings with DEXRON II automatic transmission fluid before installation.

1. Disconnect the battery cables.

**14**

2. *V6 and V8 models*—Remove the power steering pump as described in this chapter.

3A. *3.0L models*—Place a suitable container or shop towels under the pump.

3B. *Except 3.0L models*—Remove the fill cap. Pour the fluid from the reservoir.

4. Remove the fitting (1, **Figure 16**). Pull the control valve (3, **Figure 16**) and spring (4) from the pump. Remove and discard the O-rings (2, **Figure 16**). Clean the components and flush the pump's valve bore using a mild solvent.

5. Use crocus cloth to polish burrs from the control valve. The valve must slide freely in the pump bore. If the spring is corroded, replace the pump. The spring is not available separately.

6. Lubricate the the spring and control valve and install them.

7. Lubricate the O-rings with automatic transmission fluid. Place the O-rings (2, **Figure 16**) onto the fitting. Hand-thread the fitting into the pump, then tighten to the specification in **Table 1**.

8. *V6 and V8 models*—Install the power steering pump as described in this chapter.

9. Correct the fluid level and bleed air from the system as described in this chapter. Connect the battery cables.

### POWER STEERING PUMP

The power steering pump may be disassembled, but internal components (except for seals and O-rings) are not available separately. Replace the pump if any components are defective.

> *NOTE*
> *A newly designed power steering pump, using a remote reservoir, is used on 2001 8.1 liter models. On all other models, the reservoir is integrated into the pump. Service or repair procedures for this type of pump were not available at the time of printing. The pulley replacement, filling and air bleeding procedures are similar to the other type of pump. Any other repairs to the new design pump should be performed by a qualified technician.*

### Power Steering Pump Replacement

> *CAUTION*
> *Metric hose fittings and fasteners are used on all pumps. Use metric wrenches to prevent rounding of the fittings or fasteners.*

1. Disconnect the battery cables.

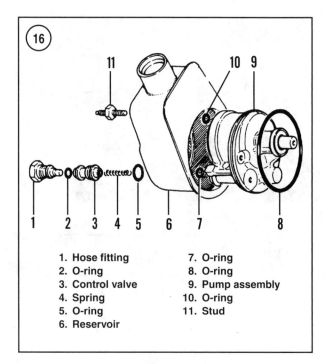

1. Hose fitting
2. O-ring
3. Control valve
4. Spring
5. O-ring
6. Reservoir
7. O-ring
8. O-ring
9. Pump assembly
10. O-ring
11. Stud

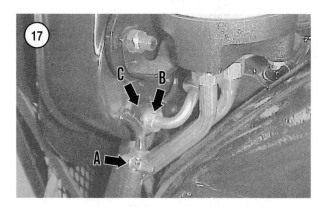

2. A hose clamp (A, **Figure 17**) connects the return hose to the trim pump. A flare fitting (B, **Figure 17**) connects the pressure hose onto the pump.

3. Place shop towels or a container under the fittings. Rotate the steering wheel in the port and starboard directions to relieve residual fluid pressure.

4. Hold the control valve fitting (B, **Figure 17**) and loosen the pressure hose fitting. Cap the hose fitting immediately to minimize fluid leakage and prevent contamination.

5. Loosen the clamp and pull the return hose from the pump. Discard the return hose clamp. Plug the hose with wooden dowel or other suitable object. To prevent fluid seepage, tie both hoses to the top of the engine.

6A. *3.0L models*—Loosen, but do not remove the power steering fasteners. Do not remove the bolts. Tilt the top of

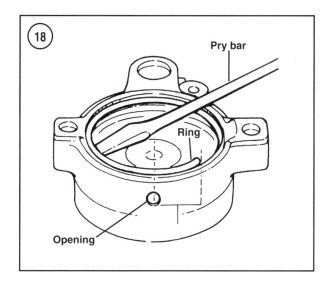

18

Pry bar

Ring

Opening

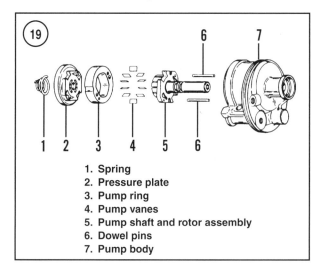

19

6    7

1   2   3   4   5   6

1. Spring
2. Pressure plate
3. Pump ring
4. Pump vanes
5. Pump shaft and rotor assembly
6. Dowel pins
7. Pump body

the pump toward the engine. Remove the power steering belt from the pump pulley.

6B. *V6 and V8 models*—Use a 5/8 in. wrench to loosen the nut on the tensioner pulley (**Figure 14**). Loosen the nut just enough to move the tensioner pulley. Remove the belt from the pulley.

7. Remove the pump mounting fasteners, then lift the pump from the mounting bracket. Remove the fill cap. Pour the fluid into a suitable container.

8. Place the pump into its mounting bracket. Install the mounting fasteners, but do not tighten them.

9. Hand-thread the pressure hose fitting into the control valve fitting. Securely tighten the hose fitting.

10. Fit a clamp over the return hose. Remove the plug and quickly install the return hose into its pump fitting. Securely tighten the hose clamp.

11. If the pump pulley was removed, install it as described in this chapter.

12. Fill the system with fluid and bleed air from the system as described in this chapter.

13. Adjust the belt tension as described in Chapter Six.

14. Connect the battery cables. Start the engine and immediately check for fluid leakage. While an assistant rotates the steering through several lock-to-lock cycles, check for fluid leakage or unusual noises. Correct fluid leakage before proceeding.

15. Correct the fluid level as described in this chapter. Refer to Chapter Three to determine the cause of any unusual noises.

### *Pump disassembly*

Replace all seals and O-rings if removed from the pump. Purchase a seal kit from a GM dealership (part No. 5688044). Lubricate all O-rings with DEXRON II automatic transmission fluid during assembly.

1. Remove the power steering pump as described in this chapter. Remove the pulley and flow control valve as described in this chapter.

2. Remove the stud(s) (10, **Figure 16**) from the reservoir and pump body. Carefully tap the reservoir (5, **Figure 16**) from the pump body (7). Remove and discard the O-rings (6, **Figure 16**).

3. Place the pump body, shaft side down, in a vise with open jaws. Do not clamp the body with the jaws.

4. Insert an awl into the opening on the side of the body (**Figure 18**) and push the ring from its groove, then pry the ring from the body. Lift the end plate and spring (1, **Figure 19**) from the pump.

5. Lift the pressure plate (2, **Figure 19**) and pump ring (3) from the pump. Press the exposed end of the pump shaft to remove the rotor and shaft assembly (5, **Figure 19**). Remove the two O-rings and dowel pins (6, **Figure 19**). Discard the O-rings.

6. Slide the pump vanes (4, **Figure 19**) from the rotor. Remove the retaining ring (1, **Figure 20**), then slide the rotor and thrust plate (2 and 3) from the pump shaft (4).

7. Remove the magnet from the pump body (**Figure 21**). Carefully pry the seal from the pump shaft bore, making sure not to damage the seal bore.

8. Clean all components using solvent and dry them with compressed air.

### *Pump inspection*

1. Inspect the pump body for cracks or damage.

**14**

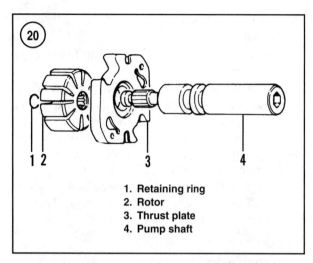

1. Retaining ring
2. Rotor
3. Thrust plate
4. Pump shaft

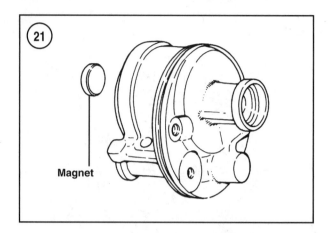

Magnet

2. Slide each vane, rounded side out, into the slots in the rotor. The vanes must slide freely into and out of the slots.

3. Inspect the pump shaft, pressure plates and rotor for wear, discoloration or roughness.

4. Replace the pump assembly if any components are worn, damaged or discolored, or if the vanes bind or stick in the rotor slots. Internal components are not available separately.

### *Pump assembly*

1. Install the pump shaft seal as follows:
   a. Clean the seal bore in the pump body with quick drying solvent.
   b. Place the pump body on the base of a press as shown in **Figure 22**. The body must be well supported to prevent it from distorting as the seal is installed.
   c. Place the seal, lip side down, into the bore opening. Use a 1 in. socket to press the seal fully into the bore.

2. Lubricate all metal components and the seal lip with DEXRON II automatic transmission fluid. Install a new pressure plate O-ring into the third groove of the housing. Install the two dowel pins (**Figure 23**).

3. Slide the thrust plate (3, **Figure 20**) and rotor (2) onto the pump shaft (4). Install the retaining ring into the shaft groove. Slide the rotor and shaft assembly into the pump body (**Figure 24**).

4. Fit the two smaller holes over the dowel pins while installing the pump ring into the body (**Figure 25**).

5. Insert the rotor vanes into the rotor slots with the rounded edges facing the ring (**Figure 26**).

6. Install the pressure plate (2, **Figure 19**) with its spring groove facing outward. Install a new end plate O-ring into the second groove in the pump body (**Figure 27**). Align

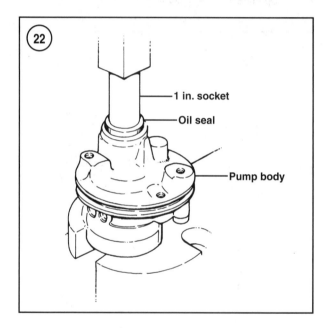

1 in. socket

Oil seal

Pump body

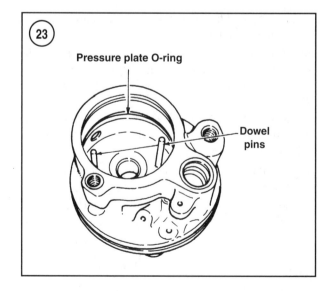

Pressure plate O-ring

Dowel pins

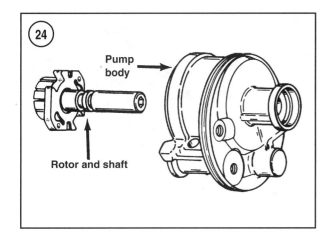

**24**

Pump body

Rotor and shaft

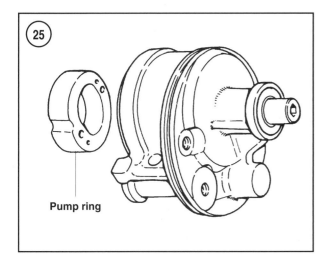

**25**

Pump ring

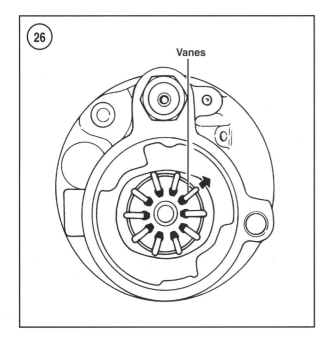

**26**

Vanes

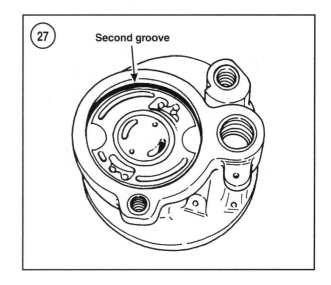

**27**

Second groove

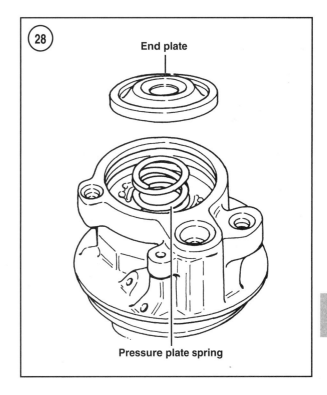

**28**

End plate

Pressure plate spring

the spring (1, **Figure 19**) with the groove in the pressure plate. Place the end plate onto the spring (**Figure 28**).

7. Press down on the end plate just enough to expose the groove for the ring (**Figure 18**). Carefully work the ring into the groove. Do not align the ring gap with the opening. The ring must fit into its groove around the entire perimeter of the body.

8. Install new O-rings onto the pump body (**Figure 29**). Slide the body into the reservoir. Insert the studs (10, **Fig-**

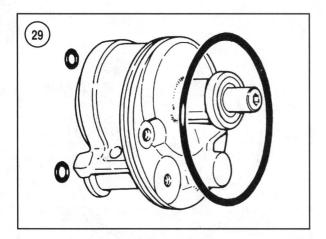

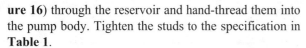

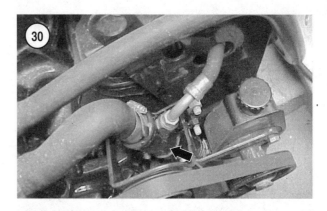

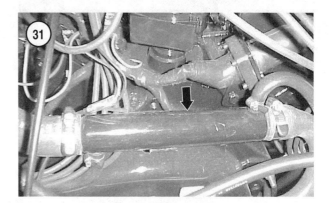

**ure 16**) through the reservoir and hand-thread them into the pump body. Tighten the studs to the specification in **Table 1**.

9. Install the flow control valve as described in this chapter. Install the pump onto the engine as described in this chapter.

### Power Steering Cooler
### Removal and Installation

Damage to the power steering cooler usually occurs because the engine was not properly winterized. Refer to Chapter Five for winterizing procedures. If water is contaminating the power steering fluid, have the cooler pressure tested and repaired at a reputable radiator shop. A radiator shop can also repair minor freeze damage.

On 7.4 and 8.2 Liter models, the power steering cooler (**Figure 30**) is mounted vertically on the front of the engine. On all other models, the cooler is mounted horizontally on the rear of the engine (**Figure 31**).

Note the orientation of the cooler fittings and hose connection before disconnecting any components.

1. Disconnect the battery cables. Place a shop towel or container under the cooler.

2. Loosen the large diameter hose clamps, then carefully push the water hoses from the cooler fittings. Do not bend the fittings.

3. Loosen the small diameter hose clamps then carefully push the power steering hoses from the cooler. Quickly plug the hoses to minimize fluid leakage. Raise the hose ends to a point higher than the trim pump and secure them. Remove and discard the hose clamps.

4. Remove the bracket fasteners or hose clamps and lift the cooler from the engine.

5. Use water to flush sediment, rocks or other material from water passages in the cooler. Inspect the seawater

pump for damage if pieces of rubber are found in the cooler.

6. Use solvent to flush metal debris or contaminants from the steering fluid passages in the cooler. Disassemble and inspect the power steering pump if metal is found in these passages.

7. Install the cooler with the fittings orientated in their original positions. Secure the cooler mounting bracket onto the engine.

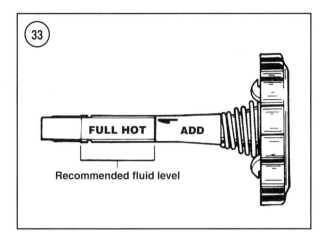

FULL HOT    ADD

Recommended fluid level

8. Install new clamps over the hoses. Remove the plugs and quickly install the water and steering fluid hoses onto the cooler. Securely tighten the hose clamps.

9. Correct the fluid level and bleed air from the system as described in this chapter.

**Filling and Bleeding Air From the System**

Perform this operation if the system was operated with a low fluid level, or after replacing any trim system component. Use only DEXRON II automatic transmission fluid or Quicksilver Power Trim and Steering Fluid (Mercury part No. 92-90100A1) to fill the power steering system.

*CAUTION*
*Never operate the power steering system with a low or high fluid level. Operating the system while low on steering fluid causes foaming of the fluid, increased steering effort and damage to the hydraulic pump com-*

*ponents. Operating the system with a high fluid causes fluid overflow.*

1. Place the drive unit in the straight ahead position. Disconnect the battery cables. Remove the fill cap (**Figure 32**).

2. Wipe the dipstick on the fill cap with a shop towel and install it into the pump reservoir.

3. Remove the cap and note the fluid level on the dipstick (**Figure 33**). Correct the fluid level as follows:
   a. *Warm engine*—Add fluid into the cap opening until the fluid level just reaches the upper end of the range (**Figure 33**).
   b. *Cold engine*—Add fluid into the cap opening until the fluid level just reaches the groove below the *add* mark.

4. Bleed air from the system as follows:
   a. Without starting the engine, rotate the steering wheel to the port and starboard directions while observing the fluid in the reservoir. Stop immediately and add fluid if the level drops below the tip of the dipstick.
   b. Continue until the wheel reaches a minimum of five turns lock-to-lock and bubbles stop appearing in the reservoir.
   c. Position the steering wheel in the straight ahead position. Correct the fluid level as described in Step 3. Connect the battery cables.

5. Start the engine and cycle the steering wheel through several complete turns. Stop immediately if foam appears in the reservoir. Allow a few minutes for the foam to dissipate then repeat Step 4. The air bleeding procedure is complete when neither bubbles nor foam appear in the reservoir.

6. Install the fill cap.

**14**

**Table 1 TORQUE SPECIFICATIONS**

| Fastener | ft.-lb. | in.-lb. | N•m |
|---|---|---|---|
| Steering system pivot bolt | 25 | – | 34 |
| Steering cable coupler | 35 | – | 47 |
| Coupler retaining plate | – | 60-72 | 7-8 |
| Guide tube nut | 40 | – | 54 |
| Power steering hose fitting (actuator) | | | |
|   Alpha models | | | |
|     Small fitting | – | 96-108 | 11-12 |
|     Large fitting | 20-25 | – | 27-34 |
|   Bravo models | 23 | – | 31 |
| Power steering pump bracket | 30 | – | 41 |
| Power steering pump brace | 30 | – | 41 |
| Circulating pump pulley | 20 | 240 | 27 |
| Flow control valve fitting | 35 | – | 47 |

# Chapter Fifteen

# Corrosion Control System

## ANODES

Anodes are made of a highly active zinc or aluminum alloy and take on a variety of forms. Anode mounting locations vary by the type of drive and optional equipment.

In addition to the drive system anodes, a special anticorrosion anode kit (Mercury part No. 71320A 3) is available. This waffle-style plate (**Figure 1**) attaches to the boat and grounds to the drive unit with stainless steel wire. It provides the additional protection needed if a stainless steel propeller or other exposed accessories, such as trim tabs, are added to the vessel.

### Trim Tab and Anodic Plate
### Removal and Installation

An aluminum/indium alloy trim tab type anode (**Figure 2**) is installed on all 3.0L models without power steering. Although not generally needed, a trim tab can be installed on models equipped with power steering. The trim tab mounts to the bottom of the antiventilation plate, above the propeller. A trim tab can be pivoted on its mounting pad. Proper adjustment of the tab compensates for normal steering torque. Trim tab adjustment is described in Chap-

ter Six. It is important to note that the trim tab looses steering surface area as it deteriorates. Inspect and/or replace the trim tab frequently to ensure maximum corrosion protection and reduced steering torque.

All other models have standard power steering and a trim tab is not used. On these models, an anodic plate (**Figure 3**) is installed in place of a trim tab type anode. The anodic plate is constructed of aluminum/indium and like the trim tab provides sacrificial protection. It is not absolutely necessary to remove the tab or plate for cleaning, but if this component requires removal for any reason, follow the directions below.

1. Remove the propeller as described in Chapter Eleven. Pry the plastic cover from the drive shaft housing (**Figure 4**).

2. Use tape or a colored marker to make alignment marks on the gearcase and trim tab (**Figure 5**). Do not scratch the gearcase.

3. Insert a 1/2 in. socket wrench and extension into the opening. Remove the bolt. Carefully tap the tab or plate loose from the gearcase.

4. Use a stiff bristle brush or scraper to remove all corrosion or organic material from the tab or anodic plate and the mounting surface on the gearcase. Sand the mounting

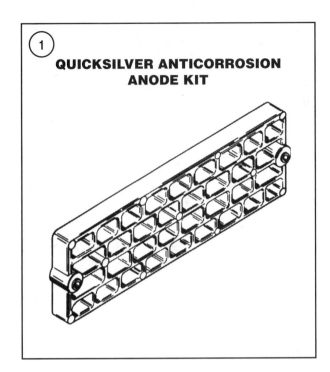

QUICKSILVER ANTICORROSION ANODE KIT

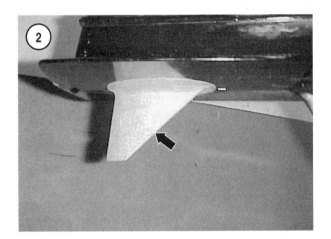

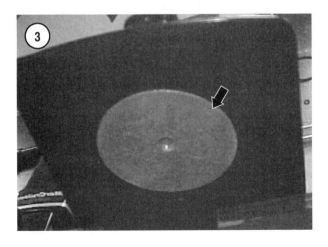

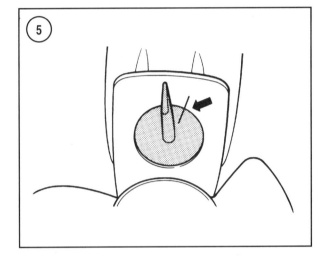

surfaces until bare aluminum is exposed. Do not apply paint, grease or other material to these surfaces.

5. Inspect the tab or plate for cracks, deep pitting or a significant loss of material (40 % or greater). Replace the tab or plate if these conditions occur or if a dark gray coating has formed on its surfaces. Duplicate the alignment marks (**Figure 5**) on the replacement tab or plate.

6. Push the bolt up and out of the drive shaft housing. Use a suitable solvent to rinse all loose material from the bolt hole. Use a wire brush to remove the salt and mineral deposits from the bolt. Avoid removing the patch lock material from the lower threads. Inspect the bolt for pitting or corrosion damage. Replace the bolt if it is defective, or if replacing the tab or plate.

7. Install the bolt into the drive shaft housing opening with the threaded side facing toward the propeller. Use a small screwdriver to align the bolt with the lower opening. The bolt must drop into the lower opening.

8. Set the tab or plate in position. Match the alignment marks (**Figure 5**) and hand-tighten the bolt. Hold the trim

**15**

tab in position with locking pliers and tighten the bolt to the specification in **Table 1**.

> *CAUTION*
> *Check for adequate clearance between the trim tab and propeller blades after replacing the trim tab or propeller. Some propellers have a greater amount of blade rake than others. Likewise a replacement trim tab may be larger than the original. Changing either of these components can reduce or eliminate the clearance between the trim tab and propeller. Inadequate clearance can cause interference between these components when shifted in reverse and during deceleration.*

9. Install the propeller as described in Chapter Eleven. Pull back and slowly rotate the propeller, checking the clearance between the trim tab and the propeller blades (**Figure 6**). If necessary, file material from the trim tab to achieve a minimum clearance of 0.100 in. (2.5 mm). Check for proper grounding of the anodes as described under *Mercathode System* in Chapter Three.

> *NOTE*
> *If the boat is moored or operated in saltwater or heavily polluted water, resulting corrosion may make it difficult to loosen the trim tab bolt. If the bolt cannot be loosened with a socket wrench, apply heat to the exposed surface of the tab or plate. With the surface heated, loosen the bolt with an air-driven impact wrench. If difficulty persists, carefully chisel the trim tab or anodic plate material away from the bolt.*

### Cylinder Anode Removal and Installation

Later models are equipped with anodes mounted on the hydraulic trim cylinders (A, **Figure 7**). These anodes frequently become coated with calcium or salt deposits and lose efficiency. Use a stiff bristle brush to clean deposits from the anode. Work carefully to avoid scratching the machined surface of the trim rams (B, **Figure 7**). Damage to this surface allows fluid leakage and eventual contamination of the trim fluid.

Inspect the anodes for deep pitting, significant material loss or a dark gray coating. Replace both anodes if any of these conditions occur. If the anodes are not deteriorating, but the cylinders show corrosion damage, inspect the hydraulic trim cylinder ground wires (**Figure 8**) on the bottom of the transom plate and on each hydraulic trim cylinder. If the wires are intact and making good contact,

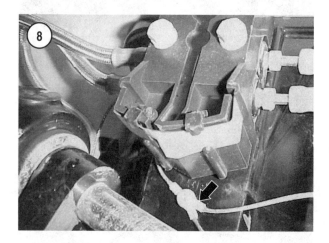

remove the anodes and clean the anode mounting surfaces. Remove and replace the hydraulic trim cylinder anodes as follows:

1. Place the drive in the full up position.

2. Remove the mounting screws and star washers (**Figure 9**) from the anode. Use a plastic mallet to tap the anode free from the cylinder.

3. Use a stiff bristle brush to clean salt and mineral deposits from the cylinder and anode mating surfaces. Clean all

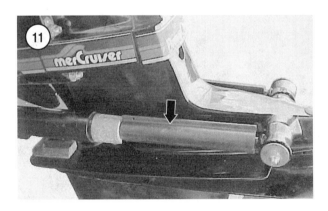

deposits from the anode screw openings with a thread chaser.

4. Inspect the anode for defects and replace if necessary. Sand or scrape the mounting screw surface of the anode until bare metal is exposed.

5. Install the anode, star washers and mounting screws. Align the anodes on the cylinder so they cannot touch the cylinder ram (B, **Figure 7**). Evenly tighten the screws to the specification listed in **Table 1**. Make sure the anode is properly grounded as described under *Mercathode System* in Chapter Three.

6. Operate the trim system to the full down and up position, making sure the anodes cannot touch the trim rams. Reposition the anodes if necessary.

**Transom Anode Removal and Installation**

An aluminum/indium anode block (**Figure 10**) is installed on all models except those equipped with a Mercathode system. This anode is mounted on the bottom side of the transom assembly and fits over the hydraulic hose terminal block. The finned design of the anode creates a great deal of surface area in a relatively small space, and can protect units with a stainless steel propeller under light and moderate corrosion conditions.

Remove corrosion, salt or mineral deposits from the anode using a stiff bristle brush or scraper. Although not absolutely necessary, the anode may be removed to clean the mounting surfaces and hidden crevices. Replace the transom mounted anode if heavy deposits, deep pitting, physical damage, significant material loss or a dark gray deposit occurs.

> *WARNING*
> *The drive can unexpectedly drop from a tilted position. Never work under the drive unit without support clips (**Figure 11**), sturdy support blocks or overhead support.*

1. Place the drive in the fully up position. Secure the cylinders in the up position with support clips (**Figure 11**).

2. Remove the two bolts and washers from the anode and terminal block. Use a plastic mallet to tap the anode loose from the terminal block (**Figure 12**). Remove and discard the gasket (**Figure 13**) from the anode or terminal block.

3. With a plastic brush, clean salt and mineral deposits from the terminal block and anode mating surfaces. Carefully scrape any gasket material from all surfaces. Remove all deposits from the bolt openings in the terminal block with a thread chaser. Replace the terminal block if the threads are so damaged that the anode cannot be se-

**15**

curely mounted. Terminal block replacement is described in Chapter Thirteen.

4. Inspect the anode for defects. Replace if necessary. Sand or scrape the mounting screw surface of the anode until bare metal is exposed.

5. Install the star washers and mounting bolts into the anode. Place a new anode gasket over the threaded end of the bolts and seat it against the anode. Apply Quicksilver perfect seal (Mercury part No. 92-34227 1) to the bolt threads.

6. Install the anode and the terminal block with the rounded end facing away from the boat transom (**Figure 10**). Make sure the gasket is aligned, then hand-thread the bolts into the terminal block. Make sure the anode is not contacting the hydraulic hoses before tightening the bolts. Evenly tighten the screws to the specification in **Table 1**. Make sure the anode is grounded as described in Chapter Three.

7. Remove the support clips, block or overhead support. Operate the trim system through several up and down cycles while checking for trim fluid leakage. If leakage occurs, tighten the hose fittings.

**Carrier Anode Removal and Installation**

An aluminum/indium material anode (A, **Figure 14**) is installed on the bearing carrier. Two screws and star washers (B, **Figure 14**) secure this anode to the bearing carrier. The propellor must be removed to access the anode.

Oily deposits often form on this anode, preventing full corrosion protection. Removing this anode makes cleaning easiler and allows access to the bearing carrier mating surfaces. Use a stiff bristle bush to remove corrosion, salt or mineral deposits from the anode. Use solvent to remove oily deposits.

Replace the anode if it is deeply pitted, has lost a significant amount of material or has formed a dark gray coating.

1. Remove the propeller and thrust washer as described in Chapter Eleven. Remove the screws and star washers (B, **Figure 14**). Use a plastic mallet to tap the anode loose. Pull the anode from the carrier (**Figure 15**).

2. With a stiff bristle brush, remove salt and mineral deposits from the cylinder-to-anode mating surfaces. Clean all deposits from the screw openings in the bearing carrier with a thread chaser.

3. Inspect the anode for defects and replace if necessary. Sand or scrape the mounting screw surface of the anode until bare metal is exposed.

4. Align the anode on the bearing carrier.

   a. *Alpha models*—The casting number must be visible and facing upward (**Figure 14**).

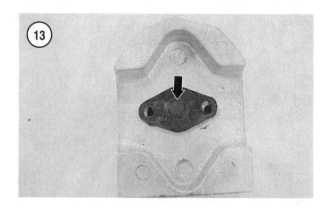

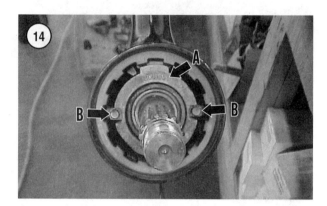

   b. *Bravo I models*—The screw bosses must contact the bearing carrier and the gap in the anode must align with the lubricant drain screw.

5. Hold the anode tightly against the bearing carrier while installing the star washers and mounting screws. Securely tighten the mounting screws.

6. Install the thrust washer and seat it against the propeller shaft taper. Push in and rotate the propeller shaft and check for contact of the thrust washer and anode. If contact occurs, check for an excessively worn thrust washer or improperly installed anode.

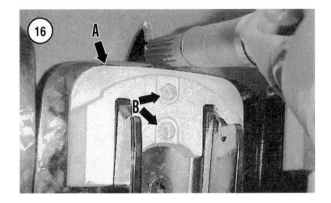

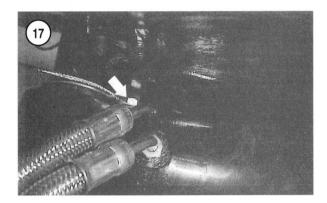

7. Install the thrust washer and propeller as described in Chapter Ten.

### Drive Shaft Housing Anode
### Removal and Installation

An aluminum/indium material anode (A, **Figure 16**) is installed on the drive shaft housing. This anode protects units with a stainless steel propeller under light and moderate corrosion conditions. An anode with a smooth exposed surface is used on Alpha models; a slightly larger anode with a finned surface is used on Bravo models.

Remove corrosion, salt or mineral deposits from the exposed surfaces with a stiff bristle brush or scraper. The anode may be removed for easier cleaning, and to clean the mounting surfaces. Replace the anode if heavy deposits, deep pitting, physical damage, significant material loss or a dark gray deposit occurs.

*WARNING*
*The drive can unexpectedly drop from a tilted position. Never work under the drive unit without support clips (**Figure 11**), sturdy support blocks or overhead support.*

1. Place the drive in the full up position. Secure the cylinders in the up position with support clips (**Figure 11**).
2. Remove the two bolts and star washers (B, **Figure 16**) from the anode and drive shaft housing. Carefully pry the anode free.
3. Use a plastic brush to remove salt and mineral deposits from the anode mating surfaces. Clean all deposits from the bolt holes in the drive shaft housing with a thread chaser.
4. Inspect the anode for defects and replace if necessary. Sand or scrape the mounting bolt surface of the anode until bare metal is exposed.
5. Place the anode in position on the drive shaft housing with the curved or finned side facing away from the housing. The slot in the plate must straddle the speedometer fitting.
6. Install the star washers and bolts. Tighten them evenly to the specification in **Table 1**.
7. Check for proper grounding of the anode as described in Chapter Three. Remove the support clips, block or overhead support.

### GROUND WIRES

Ground wires (**Figure 8**) provide a constant connection to ground for pivoting or insulated components and assemblies. If replacing the wires, use only those offered by the manufacturer. Using a wire that is too short can cause binding of the steering or tilt and eventual failure of the wire. Using a wire that is too long can allow the wire to snag and damage other components.

A single self tapping screw attaches the wires from each hydraulic trim cylinder (**Figure 17**) and the gimbal ring (**Figure 18**) to the bottom boss on the transom assembly (**Figure 8**). Stainless steel screws attach the trim line retainer and ground wires to the hydraulic trim cylinders.

A self tapping screw on the port side of the bell housing (**Figure 19**) and on the inside of the gimbal ring (**Figure 20**) attaches a single wire to each of these components.

**15**

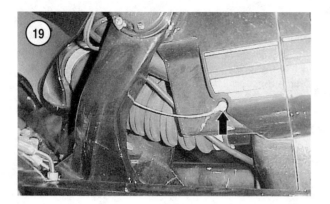

Access to the gimbal ring screw is somewhat limited; Drive unit removal is usually required to access this screw.

Inside the boat, a ground wire attaches to a transom mounting nut (A, **Figure 21**) and the stainless steel ground bolt (B). An insulated wire connects the ground bolt to a grounding stud on the flywheel housing (**Figure 22**). Screws attach a ground wire to the top side of the steering lever and the inner transom plate.

To gain access to the screws, tilt the drive unit to the full tilt position. Secure the drive unit with support clips (**Figure 11**), sturdy blocks or overhead support. Remove the drive unit if necessary to access hidden screws. Drive unit removal and installation is described in Chapter Eleven.

Replace any wire that is removed from the terminal. These wires tend to fray, are difficult to reinsert, and usually will not maintain a secure connection after recrimping.

The self-tapping screw holes will often enlarge due to corrosion or over-tightening. An enlarged opening makes the screw fit loosely and may not provide a solid ground. If the screw fits loosely, use a small center punch and lightly stake the surface at three or four locations around the outside the edge of the opening (**Figure 23**). Staking deforms the material toward the opening, tightening the fit of the screw. Touch up any damage to the finish before installing the screw.

After installation, observe the wires while an assistant operates the trim and steering systems to the maximum ranges. The wires must not bind or stretch at any time. Reposition wires and/or terminals as required.

## MERCATHODE ELECTRODE

The Mercathode electrode (A, **Figure 24**) is mounted on the terminal block at the bottom of the transom assembly, just forward of the hydraulic trim cylinder anchor pin.

Two bolts (B, **Figure 24**) secure the electrode to the terminal block. Replace the electrode assembly as follows:

1. Disconnect the cables from the battery. Disconnect the brown and orange wires (**Figure 25**) from the Mercathode controller. Remove any clamps from these wires.

2. Remove the two bolts (B, **Figure 24**) and pull the electrode assembly away from the terminal block (**Figure 26**).

3. Using several laps of electrical tape, attach both disconnected electrode wires to a section of flexible cable or heavy twine. Make sure the wire terminals are completely covered to prevent them from snagging other components during removal.

4. Guide the wires through the terminal block while an assistant slowly pulls the electrode and wires from the block. Continue until the cable or twine extends from the terminal. Do not jerk or pull hard on the wires.

5. Make sure the sealing grommet (or O-rings on early models) is properly positioned on the electrode. Using several laps of electrical tape, attach the brown and orange wires of the replacement electrode to the cable or twine extending from the terminal block. Make sure the wire terminals are completely covered to prevent them from snagging other components while installing the electrode.

6. While an assistant slowly pulls the cable or twine, guide the wires through the opening in the terminal block. Do not jerk or pull hard on the cable or twine.

7. Guide the wires into the terminal block until the electrode almost touches the terminal block. Align the finned and flat side of the electrode as shown in **Figure 24** and seat it against the terminal block. Do not pinch the orange and brown wires.

8. Hold the electrode in place and install the flat washers, lockwashers and bolts. Tighten the bolts evenly to the specification listed in **Table 1**.

9. Remove the electrical tape and cable or twine from the orange and brown wires then route them to the Mercathode controller. Route them in a path that prevents contact with any moving parts. Secure them with plastic clamps as needed.

10. Connect the orange and brown wires to the controller. Connect the cables onto the battery.

**15**

### Mercathode Controller Removal and Installation

On most models the controller (**Figure 25**) mounts to a bracket on the top or starboard side of the engine. On some earlier (1999-prior) EFI models, the controller mounts inside the electrical component box (**Figure 27**). On 7.4 L MPI, 496 Mag and 496 Mag HO models, the controller mounts under one of the EFI component covers (**Figure 28**). The controller is bright blue and easy to locate.

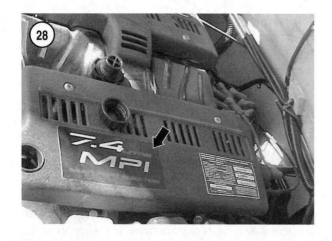

1. Disconnect the battery cables.

2. Pull the rubber boot away from the terminal, then disconnect the red wire from the controller. Disconnect the orange, brown and black wires from the controller.

3. Remove the mounting nuts and washers. Lift the controller from the mount.

4. Clean the mounting base. Inspect the connection for the black controller wire. This wire must have a solid connection to ground. Clean, tighten or repair the wire connector if necessary.

5. Install the controller onto the mounting base. Install and securely tighten the mounting washers and nuts.

6. Connect the red wire to the positive terminal on the controller. Slip the rubber boot over the terminal.

7. Connect the remaining wires as follows:

    a. Connect the black wire to the negative terminal of the controller.

    b. Connect the brown wire to the R terminal of the controller.

    c. Connect the orange wire to the A terminal of the controller.

8. Connect the battery cables. Test for proper operation of the Mercathode system as described in Chapter Three.

## Table 1 TORQUE SPECIFICATIONS

| Fastener | ft.-lb. | in.-lb. | N•m |
|---|---|---|---|
| Mercathode electrode | – | 20-30 | 2-3 |
| Trim tab bolt | 23 | – | 31 |
| Anodic plate (gearcase) | 23 | – | 31 |
| Drive shaft housing anode | 23 | – | 31 |
| Trim cylinder anode | – | 30 | 3 |
| Transom plate anode | – | 80-120 | 9-14 |

# SUPPLEMENT

# 2002-2004 MODEL SERVICE INFORMATION

This supplement provides test, maintenance, adjustment and repair procedures unique to the fuel, electrical, ignition, exhaust and cooling systems used on 2002-2004 Mercruiser gasoline stern drive engines.

Many of the service procedures on 2002-2004 models are identical to 1998-2001 models. If a specific procedure is not included in this supplement, refer to the procedure in the main body of the manual.

This supplement is divided into *sections* that correspond to the chapters in the main body of the manual. Specifications unique to 2002-2004 models are at the end of the applicable section (**Table 1** and **Table 2**). Applicable torque specifications are listed in **Table 3** at the end of this supplement.

16

# CHAPTER THREE

# TROUBLESHOOTING

This section describes the troubleshooting procedures for the ignition and fuel systems used on 2002-2004 4.3L, 5.0L, 350 Mag and MX6.2L models with multi-port electronic fuel injection (MPI). For all other engine models, refer to the troubleshooting procedures in Chapter Three of the main body of the manual.

## IGNITION SYSTEM

*NOTE*
*All 2002-2004 carburetor-equipped 3.0L, 4.3L, 5.0L and 5.7L models use the same Delco EST or Thunderbolt V type ignition system used on 1998-2001 models. Troubleshooting procedures for the Delco EST and Thunderbolt V type ignition system are described in Chapter Three of the main body of the manual.*

The Distributor Ignition (DI) type ignition system is used on 4.3L, 5.0L, 350 Mag and MX6.2L models with multi-port electronic fuel injection (MPI). This high output system uses the distributor and ignition coil shown in **Figure 1**.

The major components of the ignition system include the ignition coil, coil driver, crankshaft position sensor and engine control module (ECM). The epoxy coated ignition coil (17, **Figure 1**) and ignition module (14) mount along with the heat sink (15) onto a common bracket (16). Coil failure is rare and almost always caused by corroded or dirty terminals. The ignition coil and driver are serviced as an assembly and are not available separately. The crankshaft position sensor is located on the bottom of the timing chain cover (**Figure 2**). The engine control module (ECM) is located on the port side exhaust elbow (**Figure**

3). Platinum-tipped spark plugs must be used with the DI ignition system. Refer to *Lubrication, Maintenance and Tune-up* in this supplement.

### DI Ignition System Operation

Current to operate the ignition system is supplied by the EFI system relay (A, **Figure 4**) and the relay is controlled by the ECM (**Figure 3**). Battery voltage is continually supplied to the No. 30 and No. 86 terminals on the system relay. The terminal number is molded into the white relay base (**Figure 5**) next to each terminal. A purple/dark green wire connects the No. 85 relay terminal to the ECM. When the ignition is switched to ON or RUN, battery voltage is applied to the purple wire leading into the ECM. This causes the ECM to connect the purple/dark green to ground, using internal circuitry. The ECM completes the activation circuit and switches on the system relay. The relay then supplies battery current to the No. 87 terminal connecting to the red/black and pink/white fused wires, which provide current to the ignition coil and coil driver.

The crankshaft position sensor (**Figure 2**) creates electrical pulses as the protrusion on the crankshaft passes near the sensor tip. Three pulses are generated per crankshaft revolution on V-6 models and four pulses are generated per revolution on V-8 models. The pulses are directed to the ECM, where they are used to compute each piston's position relative to the top of its compression stroke.

A camshaft position sensor is located within the distributor housing. Although the sensor is not used or even connected to the engine wiring, it must remain in the distributor to maintain the U.S. Coast Guard ignition protection features required for all marine electrical compo-

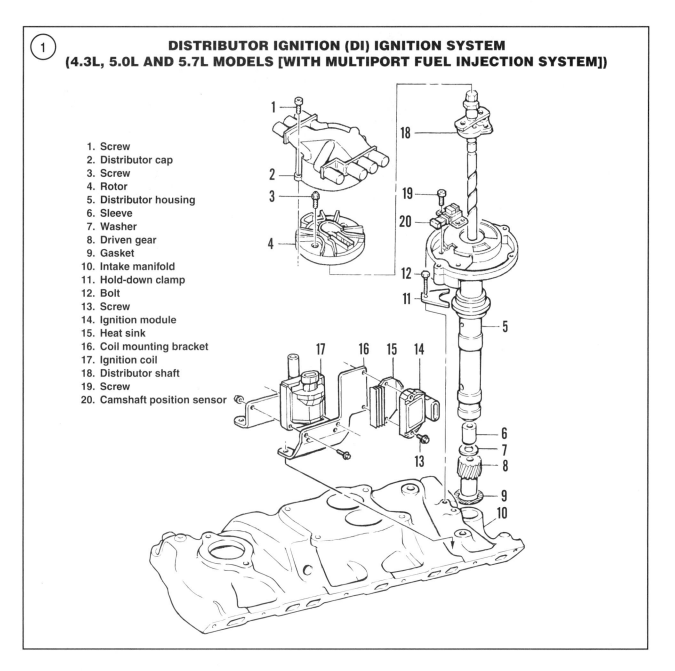

**DISTRIBUTOR IGNITION (DI) IGNITION SYSTEM
(4.3L, 5.0L AND 5.7L MODELS [WITH MULTIPORT FUEL INJECTION SYSTEM])**

1. Screw
2. Distributor cap
3. Screw
4. Rotor
5. Distributor housing
6. Sleeve
7. Washer
8. Driven gear
9. Gasket
10. Intake manifold
11. Hold-down clamp
12. Bolt
13. Screw
14. Ignition module
15. Heat sink
16. Coil mounting bracket
17. Ignition coil
18. Distributor shaft
19. Screw
20. Camshaft position sensor

**16**

nents. On this type of ignition system, the distributor functions only as a means to direct spark to the correct cylinder.

The coil driver controls current flow through the ignition coil primary by completing or opening the primary winding ground circuit. The coil driver is controlled by the ECM. At the predetermined time, the ECM switches on the driver, which in turn completes the primary winding ground circuit. This allows battery current to flow through the primary winding and creates a strong magnetic field. At the predetermined time, the ECM switches off the driver, which interrupts the ignition coil ground circuit, preventing battery current from flowing and causing the magnetic field to collapse. The collapsing field passes through the ignition coil secondary winding, inducing very high voltage current in this winding. The current flows from the coil tower (coil wire terminal) to the distributor rotor. The rotor directs the current to the distributor cap terminals for the individual spark plug. High tension wires connect the cap terminals to the spark plugs.

The air/fuel mixture in the cylinder must ignite and burn at a precise time to push the piston down on the power stroke. Since fuel burns at a relatively constant rate, spark must occur earlier with increased engine speed. Ideally, the pressure from the burning fuel should peak as the piston starts moving downward on the power stroke. This provides the maximum push on the piston and maximum power output. If the spark timing is not advanced, the pressure peaks well after the piston starts moving downward and power output decreases. The ECM computes the optimum ignition timing advance for the given operating conditions and adjusts the timing accordingly. The ignition system does not provide engine overspeed protection; however, the ECM limits engine speed by shutting off the fuel injectors at a pre-determined limit.

### DI Ignition System Troubleshooting

This section describes procedures to determine the cause of weak or no spark at the spark plugs. In some cases, scanning equipment (**Figure 6**) must be attached to the engine to troubleshoot the ignition system. The scanning equipment is expensive and requires specialized training to interpret the displayed information. If ignition operation is not restored after performing the following procedures, have the engine scanned by a Mercruiser dealership.

*WARNING*
*High voltage is present in the ignition system. Never touch any wires or electrical components while running the engine or*

*performing a test. Never perform ignition system tests in wet conditions.*

*WARNING*
*The engine may unexpectedly start during testing. Keep all persons, clothing, tools or loose objects away from the drive belts and other moving components on the engine.*

*CAUTION*
*Use a flush test device to supply the engine with cooling water if testing the ignition system with the boat out of the water. Operation of the starter motor results in operation of the seawater pump. The seawater pump is quickly damaged if operated without adequate cooling water.*

Test the DI ignition system as follows:
1. Check for blown fuses and/or a tripped circuit breaker. Refer to the wiring diagrams at the end of the manual to identify fuses, circuits breakers and connecting wiring.
2. Check for spark at the coil and spark plugs and check for distributor rotation as described in this section. Weak spark indicates a faulty coil or wiring. Even weak spark indicates the crankshaft position sensor and ECM ignition control circuits are operational.

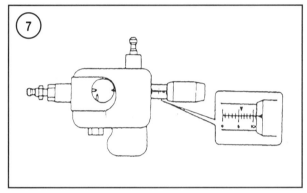

3. Turn the ignition key switch to the ON or RUN position. The warning horn should sound and the electric fuel pump(s) should operate for a few seconds, then cease. Test the EFI system relay as described in this chapter if the warning horn does not sound and the fuel pumps do not operate as specified.

*NOTE*
*If no spark is present at the coil, the tachometer does not indicate cranking speed and the fuel pumps do not operate while cranking, yet the horn sounds and the fuel pumps operate for a few seconds after turning the ignition on, the no spark condition is almost always caused by a faulty crankshaft position sensor. The sensor is relatively inexpensive and easy to replace. Replacing the sensor will likely restore spark at the coil.*

4. Attempt to start the engine while noting the tachometer reading and operation of the electric fuel pumps. Refer to the following:
   a. If the tachometer indicates 200 rpm or greater and the fuel pump(s) operate while cranking, the crankshaft position sensor and ignition control circuits in the ECM are operational. Check for faulty wiring

and corroded, dirty or loose terminals at the coil and coil driver. If no faults are found with the wiring, replace the ignition coil and driver assembly as described in the Chapter Ten section of this chapter. The ignition coil and driver are not available separately.

   b. If the tachometer does not indicate engine speed and the fuel pump(s) are not operating, check for faulty wiring and corroded, dirty or loose terminals at the engine wire harness-to-crankshaft position sensor. If no faults are found with the wiring, replace the crankshaft position sensor as described in this supplement. If spark is not restored with the replacement sensor, replace the ignition coil and driver assembly as described in this supplement.

5. If spark is not restored with the replacement sensor and coil, have a Mercruiser dealership connect scanning equipment (**Figure 6**) to the engine harness and check for engine speed input while cranking. Faulty wiring, connections, replacement coil and driver or ECM are indicated if engine speed input is displayed while cranking, yet no spark is present at the coil. Faulty wiring, connections, replacement crankshaft position sensor or ECM are indicated if no engine speed input is displayed while cranking.

*NOTE*
*Replace the ECM to restore ignition system operation only after ruling out failure of other ignition system components. Failure of the ECM is extremely rare and its replacement seldom corrects an ignition system malfunction.*

### Checking for spark at the plugs and coil

The most basic ignition system test is checking for spark at the plugs and ignition coil(s). If a strong blue spark is present at the plugs and coil, the voltage supply, ignition coil, and ignition module or engine control unit is operating the ignition system. A faulty spark plug wire or distributor rotor is indicated if good spark is present at the coil(s) but not at the plugs.

Check or test the fuel system if the engine will not start or runs improperly and good spark is present at the plugs. This test requires a spark gap tester (**Figure 7**). Purchase the spark gap tester from a tool supplier or an automotive part store.

*WARNING*
*High voltage is present in the ignition system. Never touch any wires or electrical components while running the engine or*

**16**

performing a test. Never perform ignition system tests in wet conditions.

*WARNING*
*The engine may unexpectedly start during testing. Keep all persons, clothing, tools or loose objects away from the drive belts and other moving components on the engine.*

*CAUTION*
*Use a flush test device to supply the engine with cooling water if testing the ignition system with the boat out of the water. Operation of the starter motor results in operation of the seawater pump. The seawater pump is quickly damaged if operated without adequate cooling water.*

*CAUTION*
*The system relay (A, **Figure 4**) and fuel pump relay (B) are identical and mount in the same general location. Refer to the wiring diagrams at the end of the manual to identify the wires connecting to the fuel pump relay.*

1. Shift the engine into neutral.
2. On electronic fuel injection models, lift up on the locking tab, then unplug the electric fuel pump relay (B, **Figure 4**) from the engine wire harness. This step prevents operation of the electric fuel pump(s) while cranking the engine.
3. Disconnect the coil wire from the ignition coil tower (high-tension lead terminal).
4. Connect the ground lead of the spark gap tester to a suitable engine ground.
5. Connect the spark gap tester to the coil tower. Adjust the gap to approximately 6 mm (1/4 in.).
6. Observe the spark gap tester while an assistant attempts to start the engine. The presence of a strong blue spark indicates the ignition system is producing output at the coil. If the spark is weak or absent, test the ignition system as described in this section.
7. Remove the spark gap tester and reconnect the spark plug wire to the coil tower.
8. Connect the ground lead of the spark gap tester to a suitable engine ground.
9. Connect one of the spark plug wires to the spark gap tester. Adjust the gap to approximately 6 mm (1/4 in.).
10. Observe the spark gap tester while an assistant attempts to start the engine. The presence of a strong blue spark at the tester indicates the ignition system is producing spark to that cylinder.
11. Remove the spark gap tester and reconnect the spark plug wire.

12. Repeat Steps 8-11 for the remaining cylinders.
13. Note the test results and refer to the following:
   a. If the spark is missing on all cylinders and the spark is good at the coil, the fault is with the distributor rotor or coil wire. Substitute a different wire and retest. Replace the distributor rotor if spark is not present with the substitute wire.
   b. If the spark is good on some cylinders, but the spark is weak or missing on others, the fault is with the spark plug wire(s) or distributor cap. Substitute a known good wire in place of a suspect wire and retest. Replace the distributor cap and rotor if spark is not present with the substitute wire.
14. Remove the spark gap tester and reconnect the spark plug lead.
15. On electronic fuel injection models, lift up on the locking tab then carefully plug the fuel pump relay (B, **Figure 4**) into the engine wire harness connector. Make sure the locking tab engages the tab on the relay. Tug on the connector to ensure a secure connection.

### *Checking for distributor rotation*

*WARNING*
*The engine may unexpectedly start during testing. Keep all persons, clothing, tools or loose objects away from the drive belts and other moving components on the engine.*

*WARNING*
*High voltage is present in the ignition system. Never touch any wires or electrical components while running the engine or performing a test. Never perform ignition system tests in wet conditions.*

*CAUTION*
*Use a flush test device to supply the engine with cooling water if testing the ignition system with the boat out of the water. Operation*

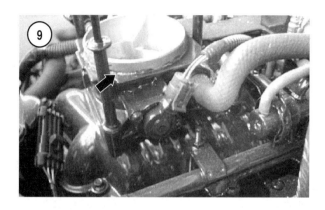

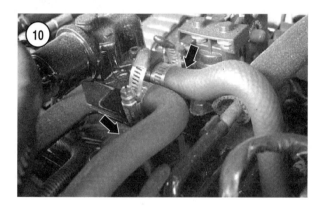

*of the starter motor results in operation of the seawater pump. The seawater pump is quickly damaged if operated without adequate cooling water.*

1. Disconnect the negative battery cable.

2. Remove the two screws (1, **Figure 1**), then lift the distributor cap (2) off the distributor body. It is not necessary to unplug the spark plug wires for this procedure.

3. Reconnect the battery cable. Position the distributor cap to prevent contact with the distributor or other moving components on the engine.

4. Pull the cord to *activate* the emergency stop (lanyard) switch (**Figure 8**). This prevents the ignition system from operating. The lanyard switch does not prevent starter motor operation. If the control does not incorporate an emergency stop (lanyard) switch, disconnect the coil wire from the distributor cap and connect to an engine ground to disable the ignition system.

5. Observe the distributor rotor (4, **Figure 1**) while an assistant attempts to start the engine. The rotor must rotate while cranking the engine. If it does not, the distributor gear is stripped and must be replaced as described in this supplement. If no fault is found with the distributor gear, the camshaft, timing gear or timing chain or related sprocket is faulty. Refer to Chapter Seven in the main

body of the manual for camshaft, timing gear, timing chain or sprocket removal inspection and installation procedures.

6. Disconnect the negative battery cable.

7. Align the screw openings, then carefully lower the distributor cap onto the distributor body. Install the two screws (1, **Figure 1**) and securely tighten.

8. Reconnect the battery cable and reattach the lanyard cord onto the emergency stop (lanyard) switch or reconnect the coil wire onto the distributor cap to allow engine starting.

## FUEL INJECTION SYSTEM

This section describes troubleshooting procedures for the multi-port fuel injection system used on 4.3L, 5.0L, 350 Mag and MX6.2L MPI models.

The major components of the fuel delivery system include the water separating fuel filter, Cool Fuel System, low-pressure boost pump, fuel rails and throttle body. The intake manifold mounted throttle body (**Figure 9**) contains the throttle position sensor, throttle valve and the idle air passage. The idle air control (IAC) motor mounts on the intake manifold and just to the rear of the throttle body. Hoses (**Figure 10**) connect the IAC to the positive crankcase ventilation valve and idle passage in the throttle body. The engine control module (ECM) sends electrical pulses that operate a plunger-type valve within the IAC. The frequency of pulses controls the duration of valve opening, which regulates the amount of air and crankcase gasses flowing to the throttle body idle air passage. A higher frequency results in a longer duration valve opening, causing increased air flow and a higher idle speed. Conversely, a lower frequency results in a shorter duration valve opening, causing decreased air flow and a lower idle speed. The frequency of pulses is often referred to as the duty cycle. A duty cycle value closer to 100 percent would indicate a higher frequency of pulses and greater air flow. A value closer to 0 percent would indicate a lower frequency and lesser air flow. Generally the ECM will allow greater air flow and a higher idle speed when the engine is cold and the air flow and idle speed will gradually decrease as the engine warms to normal operating temperature. The ECM also uses the IAC to compensate for additional load when the drive unit is shifted into gear. This allows for a consistent idle speed in or out of gear.

The fuel rail (18, **Figure 11**) secures the six or eight fuel injectors (25) in the intake manifold. The fuel injectors discharge directly into each cylinder's intake port. The fuel rail also supplies pressurized fuel to the injectors.

**16**

**INTAKE MANIFOLD, FUEL RAIL, INJECTORS AND THROTTLE BODY (4.3L, 5.0L, 5.7L AND MX 6.2L MODELS WITH MULTI-PORT FUEL INJECTION [MPI])**

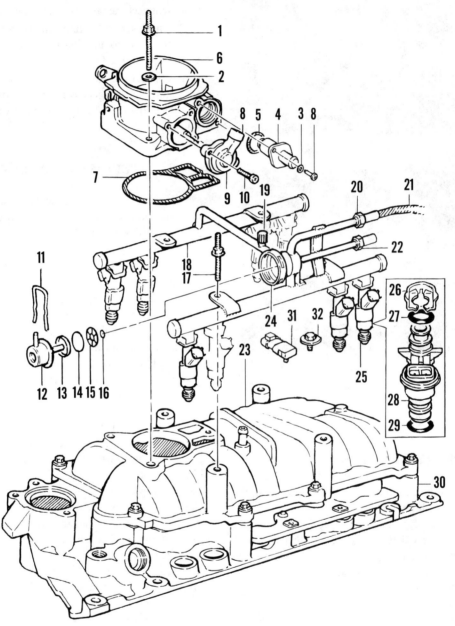

1. Stud bolt
2. Washer
3. Washer
4. Idle air passage hose fitting (leads to idle air control motor [IAC])
5. O-ring
6. Throttle body
7. Gasket
8. Screw

9. Throttle position sensor (TPS)
10. Screw
11. Retainer
12. Fuel pressure regulator
13. Spacer
14. O-ring
15. Filter
16. O-ring
17. Stud bolt

18. Fuel rail
19. High-pressure test port
20. Quick connector
21. Pressure line (from cool fuel system)
22. Cap fitting (quick connect type)
23. Upper intake manifold
24. Regulator housing
25. Fuel injector

26. Retaining clip
27. O-ring
28. Fuel injector
29. O-ring
30. Lower intake manifold
31. Manifold air pressure and temperature sensor (MAPT)
32. Retainer and screw

## FUEL DELIVERY SYSTEM MULTI-PORT INJECTION (MPI) SYSTEM

(12)

1. Fuel injectors
2. Fuel rail
3. Fuel line (pressure)
4. Fuel cooler
5. Water flow
6. Hose (regulator to intake manifold)
7. Fuel pressure regulator
8. Fuel return hose
9. Water separating fuel filter
10. Electric fuel pump
11. Fuel inlet hose (to fuel tank or boost pump [Bravo drive models])

(13)

### Fuel Delivery System Operation

The Cool Fuel System consists of the electric high pressure fuel pump (10, **Figure 12**), fuel cooler (4) and fuel pressure regulator (7). The Cool Fuel System mounts to the port side of the engine between the engine mount and oil pan.

The electric high pressure fuel pump draws fuel from the water separating fuel filter (9, **Figure 12**) and pumps it through the fuel cooler, where it is cooled by water flowing through the cooler. The fuel cooler effectively prevents fuel boiling and resultant vapor lock during hot weather operation. After the fuel cooler, the fuel flows through a line to the fuel rail and into the fuel injectors. The ECM controls fuel injector operation.

The fuel pump is capable of delivering more fuel than the engine can consume. Also, the fuel pressure must be consistent for proper engine operation at all speeds and loads. Therefore, a fuel pressure regulator (7, **Figure 12**) is used to control fuel pressure and to provide a return path back to the water-separating fuel filter for unused fuel. A regulator (12, **Figure 11**) is also incorporated into the fuel rail. The diaphragm within the regulator moves to absorb pressure pulses that occur from normal fuel injector operation. This feature helps ensure consistent fuel pressure under all conditions.

Models using a Bravo drive unit are also equipped with an electric low-pressure boost pump (A, **Figure 13**) to prevent fuel starvation that may occur on these models under certain operating conditions. Due to different load characteristics and cooling system operating, the low-pressure boost pump is not required on models using an Alpha drive unit. The low-pressure boost pump is located on the front and starboard side of the engine (near the water separating fuel filter). To prevent contaminants from entering the low-pressure boost pump, an in-line type fuel filter (**Figure 14**) is incorporated into the fuel hose connecting the low-pressure boost pump to the boat fuel tank. Brackets secure the pump to the boat structure

**16**

near the low-pressure boost pump. Current to operate the low-pressure boost pump is supplied by the fuel pump relay, causing the low-pressure boost pump to operate anytime the high-pressure electric fuel pump in the Cool Fuel System operates.

The air pressure in the intake manifold varies with engine load and throttle setting. For light loads or lower throttle settings, the air pressure is lower (higher vacuum). For higher loads or throttle settings, the air pressure is higher (lower vacuum). With an MPI system, the fuel pressure must be regulated to compensate for varying intake manifold pressure. A hose (6, **Figure 12**) connecting the regulator and intake manifold applies the actual intake manifold vacuum to the diaphragm inside the regulator. This causes the regulator to open at a lower pressure with higher vacuum, or higher pressure with lower vacuum. If the regulator develops an internal leak, fuel will flow through the hose and into the intake manifold.

### Electric Control System Operation

Battery voltage is continually supplied to the No. 30 and No. 86 terminals on the system relay. The terminal number is molded into the white relay base (**Figure 5**) next to each terminal. A purple/dark green wire connects the No. 85 terminal on the relay to the ECM. When the ignition key switch is turned to the ON or RUN position, battery voltage passes through the purple wire directly to the ECM. This switches on the ECM, causing it to connect the purple/dark green to ground, using internal circuitry. The ECM completes the activation circuit and switches the system relay to on or run. The relay then supplies battery current to the No. 87 terminal, which connects to the red/black, pink/white, pink and pink/light green fused wires leading to the ignition coil and coil driver, fuel pump relay and fuel injectors. At this time, the ECM uses internal circuitry to connect the dark green wire (leading to the fuel pump relay) to ground for approximately two seconds. This completes the circuit necessary to switch on the fuel pump relay, causing the electric fuel pump(s) to operate. The fuel pump(s) pressurize the fuel delivery system in preparation for starting the engine. When the ignition key is switched on, the ECM also grounds the brown/blue wire leading to the dash-mounted warning horn for approximately two seconds. This completes the circuit necessary to operate the horn. This feature tests the operation of the warning horn and indicates that the ECM is operational. After the two-second period, the ECM removes the ground circuits for the fuel pump relay and warning horn, causing the fuel pump(s) to stop and the horn to stop sounding.

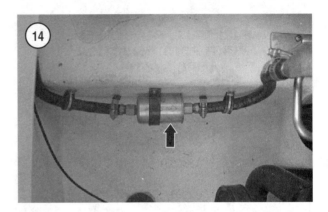

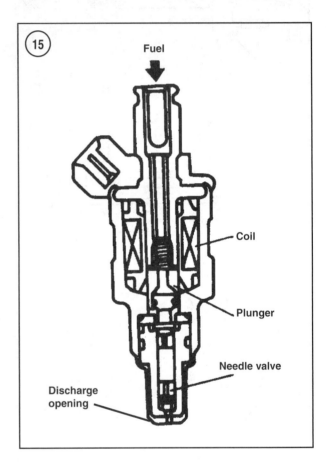

When the ignition key switch is turned to the *start* position, the crankshaft rotates and the ECM receives input from the crankshaft position sensor and switches on the fuel pump relay. The ECM will keep the relay activated as long as it receives input from the crankshaft position sensor.

The fuel injectors (**Figure 15**) are essentially solenoid activated fuel valves. When supplied with voltage, the injectors open and allow fuel to flow into the intake manifold air passages. Battery voltage is supplied to the

the shift plate assembly and activates only when the load associated with shifting out of forward or reverse gear exceeds the spring tension on the shift lever. When activated, the switch sends a signal to the ECM. The ECM then interrupts ignition operation just long enough to unload the clutch and allow disengagement. When the clutch disengages, the switch resets and signals the ECM to resume ignition system operation. When operating properly, the engine will appear to stumble for a split second but not stall when shifting out of gear. Stalling during shifting generally indicates improper shift cable adjustment, binding shift cable or fault with other shift system components.

Alpha and Bravo drive models are equipped with a shift anticipation switch (**Figure 17**). This switch mounts on the shift plate assembly and is operated by the shift arm. The switch sends a signal to the ECM indicating if the drive unit is in neutral gear or one of the driven gears (forward or reverse). This causes the ECM to detect shifting before the gears actually engage, allowing it to raise idle speed in anticipation of the load. This feature prevents stalling that may occur under certain conditions.

All EFI models are equipped with a knock sensor system that helps prevent engine damage from preignition or detonation. The detonation sensor (**Figure 18**) are mounted on the side of the cylinder block and extend into the cooling water. The sensors create electrical pulses when exposed to the noise produced by the engine and carried by the cooling water. These electrical pulses are directed to the ECM, where they are used to determine if preignition or detonation is occurring. Preignition and detonation produce an engine noise very different from that produced by normal combustion and this is reflected in the sensor pulses. The ECM delivers the normal spark timing advance and fuel delivery if the frequency from the sensor is within normal range. The ECM retards ignition timing and increases fuel delivery to stop detonation if abnormal pulse frequency is detected.

### Warning System Operation

The ECM continuously monitors input from several different sensors and activates the warning system in the event of overheating, low oil pressure, low gearcase lubricant level or excessive engine speed. The ECM uses input from the engine temperature sensor (**Figure 19**) to determine if the engine is overheating. All 2002-2004 MPI models are equipped with water pressure and oil pressure sensors. The water pressure sensor is located on the seawater pump or power steering fluid cooler. The oil pres-

injectors by the system relay. The ECM controls injector operation, making and breaking the injector ground circuit.

The ECM determines injector on-time based on input from the manifold air pressure and temperature sensor, engine temperature sensor and throttle position sensor.

Models using an Alpha Drive unit are equipped with a shift interrupt switch (**Figure 16**). Propeller load prevents easy disengagement of the clutch from the gears in the Alpha type drive unit. The shift interrupt switch is located on

**16**

sure sensor is located on the rear and port side of the cylinder block. The gearcase lubricant level sensor is integrated into the lubricant reservoir (**Figure 20**).

If overheating, low water pressure, low oil pressure or low gearcase lubricant level is detected, the ECM will sound the dash-mounted warning horn, then retard the timing and reduce engine power to minimize damage to the engine. The amount of power reduction is determined by the severity of the fault. For example, if the oil pressure is marginally low for the given engine speed, the amount of power reduced would be less than if the oil pressure was very low. Likewise, if the engine temperature is marginally too high or the water pressure is marginally low for the given engine speed, the power reduction would be less than if the engine temperature was much higher than normal or the water pressure was much lower than normal.

If the engine speed exceeds the predetermined limit, the ECM sounds the warning horn and reduces fuel delivery to reduce engine speed to a safe level. If the warning horn sounds during operation, check the gauges to help determine the fault, then stop the engine as soon as possible.

If the temperature gauge indicates overheating, disassemble and inspect the seawater pump as described in this supplement. If no fault is found with the seawater pump, check for debris blocking the water inlets in the drive unit. If the inlets are clear, test the thermostat as described in Chapter Three of the main body of the manual.

If the oil pressure gauge indicates low oil pressure, check the oil level as described in Chapter Four of the main body of the manual. If the oil level is correct, test the oil pressure as described in Chapter Three of the main body of the manual.

If the gauges indicate normal engine temperature and oil pressure, check the gearcase lubricant level in the reservoir. If necessary, add the recommended lubricant (Chapter Four) to the reservoir. Operate the engine to see if the fault is corrected.

If the engine temperature, oil pressure and gearcase lubricant level are within the normal range and the warning horn is sounding, have a Mercruiser dealership connect scanning equipment to the engine harness (**Figure 6**) to identify the fault. The ECM records the number of events and total time in which the fault is detected. Having the engine scanned is the only way to identify a faulty sensor. Although relatively rare, a faulty sensor or related wiring can falsely indicate a fault with the engine operating normally. For example, the scanning equipment may indicate that the ECM detects a low gearcase lubricant level, yet a visual inspection reveals a normal level. In such cases, inspect the related wiring for faults and replace the suspect sensor if no fault is found with the wiring.

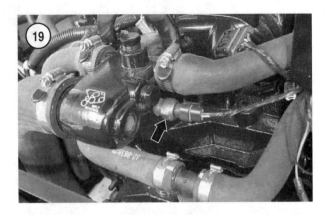

**Fuel Injection System Troubleshooting**

The most basic test for any fuel injection system is the fuel pressure test. Perform this test if the engine will not start or performs improperly. Check or test other components only after verifying that the fuel pressure is correct. If the fuel pressure is correct, perform all of the test provided in this section. If testing fails to identify the malfunction, have a Mercruiser dealership connect scanning equipment to the engine harness (**Figure 6**) and compare the sensor input values displayed on the scanner screen with actual conditions, such as the engine temperature on the dash-mounted gauge, ambient air temperature where testing, and manifold vacuum using a vacuum gauge attached to an intake manifold attached hose (fuel pressure regulator hose). Replace sensors with a value displayed on the scanning equipment that is significantly different from the gauge readings. Unlike many other fuel injection systems, this system does not store diagnostic trouble codes. However, if one of the sensor values exceeds a predetermined value, the ECM records the number of events and total time (in seconds). This information can be retrieved only with the scanning equipment. If a fault is detected, first check for faulty wiring or terminals in the suspect sensor. Replace the suspect sensor if no fault is found with the wiring.

> *NOTE*
> *Keep in mind that loose or dirty battery cable connections or a faulty battery can cause the fuel injection system to malfunction and develop very unusual symptoms, including sudden stalling, incorrect idle speed, false operation of the warning system and misfiring at any engine speed. Before beginning the troubleshooting procedures, clean and tighten the battery cable connections and test the battery as*

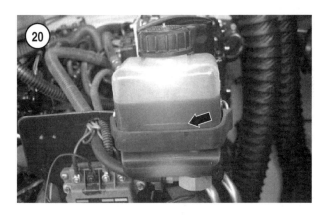

*described in Chapter Ten of the main body of the manual.*

The following guidelines recommend testing or items to check by symptom.

1. If the engine refuses to start, perform the following:
   a. Place the throttle in the idle position.
   b. Place the lanyard switch in the *RUN* position.
   c. Check for blown fuses. Refer to the wiring diagrams at the end of the manual to assist with locating the fuses.
   d. Check for spark at the coil as described in this supplement.
   e. Inspect the fuel for contaminants as described in Chapter Three of the main body of the manual.
   f. Test the system relay as described in this supplement.
   g. Test the fuel pressure as described in this supplement.
   h. Check for injector operation as described in this supplement.
   i. Have a Mercruiser dealership check for abnormal input from the sensors and related circuits.

2. If the engine stalls at idle speed, perform the following:
   a. Inspect the fuel for contaminants as described in Chapter Three of the main body of the manual.
   b. Test the fuel pressure as described in this supplement.
   c. Check the idle air control (IAC) motor as described in this supplement.
   d. Have a Mercruiser dealership check for abnormal input from the sensors and related circuits.

3. If the engine idles roughly, perform the following:
   a. Inspect the fuel for contaminants as described in Chapter Three of the main body of the manual.
   b. Inspect the spark plugs as described in Chapter Four of the main body of the manual.

c. Test the fuel pressure as described in this supplement.
   d. Check the idle air control (IAC) motor as described in this supplement.
   e. Have a Mercruiser dealership check for abnormal input from the sensors and related circuits.

4. If the engine stumbles during acceleration, perform the following:
   a. Inspect the fuel for contaminants as described in Chapter Three of the main body of the manual.
   b. Test the fuel pressure as described in this supplement.
   c. Have a Mercruiser dealership check for abnormal input from the sensors and related circuits.

5. If the engine misfires or runs rough at higher engine speeds, perform the following:
   a. Inspect the fuel for contaminants as described in Chapter Three of the main body of the manual.
   b. Test the fuel pressure as described in this supplement.
   c. Inspect the spark plugs as described in Chapter Four of the main body of the manual.
   d. Have a Mercruiser dealership check for abnormal input from the sensors and related circuits.

6. If the engine stalls during deceleration, perform the following:
   a. Check the idle air control (IAC) motor as described in this supplement.
   b. Test the fuel pressure as described in this supplement.
   c. Inspect the fuel for contaminants as described in Chapter Three of the main body of the manual.

*NOTE*
*High-power electrical equipment such as stereos and communication radios may interfere with the electronic fuel injection system. Switch off these devices if the engine malfunctions.*

**16**

**Basic Fuel System Troubleshooting**

Most fuel system malfunctions are caused by the fuel. Using the proper type of fresh, good quality fuel and storing it properly, together with regular maintenance of the fuel filters, will reduce fuel system problems. Fuel storage recommendations and filter maintenance are described in Chapter Four of the main body of the manual.

### Determining a rich or lean condition

A gasoline engine must receive fuel and air mixed in precise proportions to operate efficiently at various loads and engine speeds. Determining if a fuel system malfunction is causing a rich or lean condition can help determine the cause of the malfunction and identify the corrective action.

An engine that is receiving too much fuel for the amount of air flowing into the engine is operating *rich*. Symptoms of a rich condition include rough operation (particularly at idle speed), excessive exhaust smoke, soot deposits on the transom and drive unit surfaces near the exhaust outlet, hesitation during rapid acceleration, dark black fluffy deposits on the spark plugs and stalling during extended periods or idling (commonly called loading up). Operating an engine that is rich will result in increased fuel usage, increased exhaust emissions, premature fouling of the spark plugs, increased combustion chamber deposits and rapid blackening and dilution of the crankcase oil. To positively identify a rich condition, remove and inspect the spark plugs as described in this supplement.

A rich condition is usually caused by one or more of the following:

1. A dirty or damaged flame arrestor.
2. Leaking fuel injector.
3. Too high fuel pressure.
4. Malfunction of a fuel injection system sensor.
5. Inadequate ventilation of the engine compartment.

An engine that is receiving too little fuel for the amount of air flowing into the engine is operating *lean*. Symptoms of a lean mixture include hard starting, hesitation or backfiring during rapid acceleration, poor high speed performance, overheating (particularly at higher throttle settings) and overheating of the spark plug insulator tip. Operating an engine that is lean will result in poor performance and promotes preignition and detonation that damages the pistons and valves. To positively identify a lean condition, remove and inspect the spark plugs as described in this supplement.

A lean condition is usually caused by one or more of the following:

1. A restriction in the fuel supply line.
2. Air leaks in the fuel supply line.
3. Blockage or air leaks in the fuel filters.
4. Low fuel pressure.
5. Malfunction of a fuel injection system sensor.
6. Faulty or blocked fuel injector(s).

### System relay test

The system relay provides current to operate the fuel injectors, ignition system and fuel pump relay. A fault with the EFI system relay will prevent the engine from starting.

A test light is required for this procedure.

1. Make sure the lanyard switch is in RUN position.

2. Turn the ignition key switch to the ON or RUN position. The dash-mounted instruments must turn on and the warning horn must sound for two seconds. Turn the ignition key switch to the OFF or STOP position, then refer to the following:

   a. If the instrument did not turn on, check for a blown fuse, tripped circuit breaker or loose wire connection at the ignition key switch. Correct faulty wiring, replace the fuse or reset the circuit breaker to restore gauge operation. If this does not restore gauge operation, test the ignition switch as described in Chapter Three of the main body of the manual.

   b. If the instruments are on but the warning horn did not sound, proceed to Step 3.

   c. If the instruments are on and the warning horn did sound, the system relay and ECM are operational. Proceed to Step 13 to check the injector wire circuit.

3. Lift up on the locking tab, then carefully unplug the system relay (A, **Figure 4**) from the engine wire harness connector.

4. Refer to the terminal number molded into the white system relay base (**Figure 5**) to identify the corresponding terminal openings in the engine wire harness connector.

5. Connect the test light to a known good engine ground. Touch the test light probe to the No. 30 terminal in the engine wire harness connector. The light must illuminate. If not, proceed as follows:

   a. Touch the test light probe to the starter motor-mounted 90 amp fuse. The light must illumi-

nate. If not, replace the 90 amp fuse after inspecting the related wiring for a shorted circuit.

b. Touch the test light probe to the red wire terminal on the 50 amp circuit breaker (**Figure 21**). The light must illuminate. If not, repair the faulty wiring or terminal on the red wire connecting the circuit breaker to the starter motor-mounted 90 amp fuse.

c. Touch the test light probe to the red/purple wire terminal on the 50 amp circuit breaker (**Figure 21**). The light must illuminate. If not, reset the circuit breaker and repeat the test. Replace the circuit breaker if power cannot be restored to the red/purple wire terminal by resetting the breaker.

d. If the light illuminates when touched to the circuit breaker terminals and not when touched to the No. 30 system relay harness terminals, repair the faulty wiring or terminal on the red/purple wire connecting the circuit breaker to the No. 30 system relay harness connector.

6. Turn the ignition key switch to the OFF or STOP position. Connect a test light to a known good engine ground. Touch the test light probe to the No. 86 terminal in the engine wire harness connector. The light must illuminate. If not, repair the faulty wiring or terminal on the red/purple wire connecting the circuit breaker to the No. 86 system relay harness connector.

7. Connect the test light to a battery positive terminal. Touch the test light probe to a known good engine ground to verify the ground and battery positive circuits. Touch the test light probe to the No. 85 system relay harness connector. The light *must not illuminate*. If otherwise, unplug the engine harness connectors from the ECM (**Figure 3**) and repeat the test. If the light illuminates with the harnesses disconnected from the ECM, the purple/dark green wire connecting the ECM to the system relay harness connector is shorted to ground. Repair the wiring as needed.

8. If disconnected, carefully plug the engine wire harness connectors onto the ECM. Connect the test light cord to a battery positive terminal. Touch the test light probe to the No. 85 system relay harness connector. Observe the test light while an assistant turns the ignition key switch to the ON or RUN position. The test light must illuminate. Refer to the following:

a. If the light does illuminate, replace the system relay and repeat Step 1 and Step 2.

b. If the light does not illuminate, proceed to Step 9.

9. Turn the ignition key switch to the OFF or STOP position. Carefully unplug the engine harness connectors from the ECM (**Figure 3**). Trace the purple engine harness wire to the No. 18 terminal in the ECM engine harness connectors. Connect the test light to a known good engine ground. Touch the test light probe to the No. 18 (purple wire) terminal in the engine harness connector.

10. Observe the test light while an assistant turns the ignition key switch to the ON or RUN position. The light must illuminate. If not, proceed as follows:

a. Test the ignition key switch as described in Chapter Three in the main body of the manual.

b. Check for a fault with the lanyard (emergency stop switch) if no fault is found with the ignition key switch.

c. If no fault is found with the ignition key and lanyard (emergency stop) switch, check for a short to ground or open along the purple wire connecting the ignition key switch and lanyard (emergency stop) switch to the ECM.

11. A fault in the ECM power up circuit is indicated if the light did not illuminate in Step 8 and did illuminate in Step 10. Replace the ECM to restore operation of the system relay only after verifying that no faults are present on all connecting wiring and terminals. Failure of the ECM is extremely rare and replacement seldom corrects an engine malfunction. Most faults are caused by bent, corroded or otherwise damaged terminals.

12. Reconnect the engine wire harness connectors onto the ECM. Lift up on the locking tab and carefully plug the system relay onto the engine wire harness connector. Make sure the tab on the relay engages the slot in the locking tab.

13. Turn the ignition key switch to the OFF or STOP position. Disconnect the plug containing the pink/white wire from one of the fuel injectors (**Figure 22**). Connect the test light to the negative battery terminal. Touch the test light probe to the pink/white wire terminal in the connector. The test light *must not illuminate*. If the light illuminates, the relay is shorted internally or stuck in the energized position and must be replaced.

14. Connect the test light to the negative battery terminal. Touch the test light probe to the pink/white wire terminal in the injector connector. Observe the light while an assis-

**16**

tant turns the ignition key switch to the ON or RUN position. The light *must illuminate.* If not, the 20 amp injector fuse is blown, the relay has failed open or stuck in the de-energized position or the pink/white wire is faulty. Inspect the fuse and wiring. If no fault is found with the fuse or wiring, replace the relay and repeat the test.

15. Turn the ignition key switch to the OFF or STOP position. Carefully plug the engine harness connector onto the fuel injector.

### Fuel pressure test

The fuel pressure test verifies that fuel is being supplied to the fuel injectors at the required pressure.

Use a suitable pressure gauge with a bleed-off hose (Mercury part No. 91-881833A 2 or equivalent) for this procedure.

> *WARNING*
> *Safely performing on-water testing or adjustments requires two people. One person is needed to operate the boat, the other to monitor the gauges or test equipment and make necessary adjustments. All personnel must remain seated inside the boat at all times. Do not lean over the transom while the boat is moving. Use extensions to allow all gauges and test equipment to be located in normal seating areas.*

> *WARNING*
> *The engine may unexpectedly start during testing. Keep all persons, clothing, tools or loose objects away from the drive belts and other moving components on the engine.*

> *CAUTION*
> *Use a flush test device to supply the engine with cooling water if testing the engine with the boat out of the water. Operation of the starter motor results in operation of the seawater pump. The seawater pump is quickly damaged if operated without adequate cooling water.*

1. Inspect the fuel and check for a restriction in the fuel supply hose as described in this section.

2. Make sure the lanyard switch is in the RUN position.

3. Turn the ignition key to the ON or RUN position. The dash-mounted instruments must turn on, the warning horn must sound for two seconds and the fuel pump(s) must operate for two seconds, then cease. The low-pressure boost pump (A, **Figure 13**) is used only on Bravo drive models. Note if one pump or both pumps are operating. If so equipped, both pumps must operate simultaneously. The

fuel pump mounted in the Cool Fuel System generates considerably more noise than the low-pressure boost pump. If necessary, touch the tip of a mechanic's stethoscope to the body of the low-pressure boost pump to listen for operation. Refer to the following:

  a. If the instruments turn on, the warning horn sounds and the pumps operate, proceed to Step 4.

  b. If the instruments turn on, the warning horn does not sound, and the fuel pumps do not operate, test the system relay as described in this section.

  c. If the instruments turn on, the warning horn sounds and the fuel pump(s) do not operate, test the fuel pump relay as described in this section.

  d. If the instruments do not turn on, the warning horn does not sound, and the fuel pumps do not operate, check for a blown fuse, tripped circuit breaker or loose wire connection at the ignition key switch. Correct faulty wiring, replace the fuse or reset the circuit breaker to restore gauge operation. If this does not restore gauge operation, test the ignition switch as described in Chapter Three of the main body of the manual.

  e. On Bravo drive models, if only one fuel pump operates, the suspect fuel pump or connecting wiring is faulty. Replace the suspect fuel pump as described in this supplement if no fault is found with the wiring.

4. Turn the ignition key switch to the off position.

5. Unthread the retainer (**Figure 23**). Then remove the metal and rubber washer. Lift the plastic cover off the flame arrestor (**Figure 24**).

6. Locate the high pressure test port (19, **Figure 11**) and remove the cap.

7. Wrap a suitable shop towel around the test point to capture spilled fuel. Pull up on the locking lever, *quickly* push the connector of the fuel pressure gauge onto the test point, then release the locking lever.

8. Observe the pressure gauge while an assistant turns the ignition key switch to the ON or RUN position. Note the pressure reading, then have the assistant turn the ignition key switch to the OFF or STOP position. Wait approximately 30 seconds for the ECM to reset. Repeat this step several times to purge any air from system. The pressure gauge must indicate 40-46 psi (276-317 kPa). Refer to the following:

a. If the fuel pressure is within the specification, proceed to Step 9.

b. If the fuel pressure is less than 40 psi (275 kPa), replace the fuel pressure regulator in the Cool Fuel System. Repeat the fuel pressure test with the replacement regulator. Replace the high-pressure electric fuel pump in the Cool Fuel System if the fuel pressure is not corrected with the replacement regulator. Refer to *Cool Fuel System* in Chapter Eight of the main body of the manual for fuel pressure regulator and high-pressure electric fuel pump replacement instructions.

c. If the fuel pressure exceeds 46 psi (317 kPa), replace the fuel pressure regulator in the Cool Fuel System. Refer to *Cool Fuel System*. Repeat the fuel pressure test with the replacement regulator. The fuel return line connecting the regulator to the water-separating fuel filter is restricted if the fuel pressure is not corrected with the replacement regulator. Remove the blockage or replace the hose as needed to correct the fuel pressure.

9. Prepare the boat and engine for operating under actual running conditions. Do not disconnect the fuel pressure gauge at this time; however, route the gauge hose to prevent contact with drive belts, pulleys and other moving components. Secure the hose with clamps as needed.

10. Observe the gauge while an assistant operates the engine, under normal load, at the speeds from idle to wide-open throttle. The gauge must indicate 40-46 psi

(276-317 kPa) at all engine speeds. Refer to the following:

a. If the fuel pressure is correct at all engine speeds, the fuel delivery system is operating properly. Any engine malfunction is related to old or contaminated fuel, faulty spark plug or other ignition system components, fuel injection control system or mechanical problem with the engine. Check these items as described in the appropriate section of this chapter. Proceed to Step 11.

b. If the fuel pressure exceeds the maximum specification at any engine speed, replace the fuel pressure regulator in the Cool Fuel System as described in Chapter Eight of the main body of the manual. Refer to *Cool Fuel System*. Repeat the fuel pressure test with the replacement regulator. The fuel return line connecting the regulator to the water-separating fuel filter is restricted if the fuel pressure is not corrected with the replacement regulator. Remove the blockage or replace the hose as needed to correct the fuel pressure.

c. If the fuel pressure is less than the minimum specification at any engine speed, particularly at higher engine speed, check for a restriction in the fuel supply hose as described in this section.

11. Stop the engine. Lift up on the locking lever and *quickly* pull the connector off the test point. Clean up any spilled fuel and replace the cap. Open the valve and allow all fuel to drain from the bleed-off hose.

12. Install the plastic flame arrestor cover over the mounting stud. Place the rubber, then metal, washer onto the stud. Secure the cover and washers with the retainer. Do not overtighten the retainer. Overtightening will break the retainer.

### *Inspecting the fuel*

Fuel-related problems are common with most marine engines. Gasoline has a relatively short shelf life and becomes stale within a few weeks under some conditions. This gasoline works fine in an automobile because the fuel is consumed in a week or so. Because marine engines may sit idle for several weeks at a time, the gasoline often becomes stale.

As fuel evaporates, a gummy deposit usually forms in the carburetor or other fuel system components. These deposits may clog fuel filters, fuel lines, fuel pumps and small passages in the carburetor or fuel injection system.

Fuel stored in the fuel tank tends to absorb water vapor from the air. Over time, this water separates from the fuel, then settles to the bottom of the fuel tank. Water in the fuel tank can lead to the formation of rust and other contami-

**16**

nants in the fuel tank. These contaminants block fuel filters and other fuel system passages. Inspect the fuel when the engine refuses to start and the ignition system is not at fault. An unpleasant odor usually indicates the fuel has exceeded its shelf life and should be replaced.

*WARNING*
*Use extreme caution when working with the fuel system. Fuel is extremely flammable and, if ignited, can result in injury or death. Never smoke or allow sparks to occur around fuel or fuel vapor. Wipe up any spilled fuel at once with a shop towel and dispose of the shop towel in an appropriate manner. Check all fuel hoses, connections and fittings for leakage after any fuel system repair.*

All EFI models are equipped with a spin-on water-separating type fuel filter (**Figure 25**) mounted on the lower front and starboard side of the engine.

To inspect the fuel, place a suitable container under the filter. Wrap a shop towel around the filter to capture spilled fuel. Use a common oil filter wrench to loosen and unthread the filter. Carefully pour the contents into a suitable container. Inspect and carefully smell the fuel. An unusual odor, debris, cloudy appearance or the presence of water indicates a problem with the fuel. If any of these conditions are noted, dispose of all the fuel in an environmentally responsible manner. Contact a local marine dealership or automotive repair facility for information on the proper disposal of the fuel. Clean and inspect the entire fuel system if water or other contamination is in the fuel.

The fuel delivery system cannot develop the required pressure to start the engine unless any introduced air is first purged from the system. Any air in the system must exit at the fuel injectors and the fuel injectors only operate when the engine is starting or running. To prevent a no-start condition or starter damage from excess cranking, carefully fill the filter with fresh, clean fuel before installation. Apply a light coating of engine oil to the filter sealing ring (**Figure 26**), then carefully thread the filter onto the housing. Work carefully to avoid spilling fuel. Hand-tighten the filter 2/3 to 3/4 turns after the sealing ring contacts the housing. Wipe up any spilled fuel.

### Checking for a restriction in the fuel supply hose

*WARNING*
*Safely performing on-water testing or adjustments requires two people. One person is needed to operate the boat, the other to monitor the gauges or test equipment and*

*make necessary adjustments. All personnel must remain seated inside the boat at all times. Do not lean over the transom while the boat is moving. Use extensions to allow all gauges and test equipment to be located in normal seating areas.*

Perform this check if the engine will not start or has low fuel pressure symptoms at higher engine speeds.

1. Wrap a shop towel around the water-separating fuel filter (**Figure 25**) to capture spilled fuel. Use a common oil filter wrench to loosen and unthread the filter. Check for the presence of fuel. If no or very little fuel is found in the filter, perform the following:

   a. Check the fuel tank for fuel and check all hoses and connections for broken or loose clamps and loose or damaged fittings.

   b. Inspect the fuel line for cut, broken, cracked or weathered surfaces. If not found in excellent condition, replace the hose with a *new* U.S Coast Guard approved fuel hose.

   c. Inspect the fuel as described in this section. If the fuel is contaminated, debris may be present in the fuel tank pickup, fuel hose fittings and filters. Inspect these components as required.

   d. Locate the anti-siphon valve threaded into the fuel supply hose fitting on the boat fuel tank. Remove and inspect the anti-siphon valve for blockage, a loose fit to the fuel line fitting, cracking of the valve housing or damaged threads. Replace the valve with a *new* suitable replacement if any defects are evident.

   e. On Bravo drive models, test the low-pressure boost pump as described in this section.

2. Fill the filter with fresh, clean fuel before installation. Apply a light coating of engine oil to the filter sealing ring (**Figure 26**), then carefully thread the filter onto the housing. Work carefully to avoid spilling fuel. Hand-tighten

the filter 2/3 to 3/4 turns after the sealing ring contacts the housing. Wipe up any spilled fuel.

*WARNING*
*Never install a simple fitting in place of the anti-siphon valve, modify the anti-siphon valve or bypass the anti-siphon valve. The valve provides an important safety feature by preventing fuel in the tank from siphoning into the engine compartment if a fuel hose, fuel line or other fuel system component develops a leak.*

3A. On Alpha drive models, disconnect the fuel supply hose from the inlet fitting on the spin-on fuel filter housing (**Figure 27**).

3B. On Bravo drive models, disconnect the fuel supply hose (B, **Figure 13**) from the inlet fitting on the low-pressure boost pump.

4. Drain residual fuel from the hose into a suitable container. If not contaminated, pour the fuel back into the boat fuel tank. Clean up any spilled fuel.

5. Temporarily connect a common outboard fuel supply hose with primer bulb onto the fuel inlet fitting. The arrow on the primer bulb must face the hose end connecting to the fitting.

6. Connect the other end of the fuel supply hose to a compatible outboard portable fuel tank filled with fresh fuel. Make sure the hose and portable tank fittings have at least a 1/4 in. (6.1 mm) inside diameter. Open the vent on the portable fuel tank.

7. Pump the primer bulb to prime the system and check for leakage at the hose, hose fittings and the engine fuel lines and hoses. Correct any leaks before proceeding.

*WARNING*
*Safely performing on-water testing or adjustments requires two people. One person is needed to operate the boat, the other to monitor the gauges or test equipment and make necessary adjustments. All personnel must remain seated inside the boat at all times. Do not lean over the transom while the boat is moving. Use extensions to allow all gauges and test equipment to be located in normal seating areas.*

8. Operate the engine at the engine speed and under the conditions when the malfunction occurs. Refer to the following.

   a. If the engine performs properly using portable tank, the malfunction is caused by a blocked fuel tank pickup, damaged fittings, faulty anti-siphon valve, loose or leaking fuel tank pickup, improper fuel tank venting, air leakage at fittings or faulty fuel hose. Inspect and repair or replace these components to restore proper engine operation. Proceed to Step 10.

   b. If the malfunction is still present, proceed to Step 9.

9. Have an assistant operate the engine at the engine speed and under the conditions when the malfunction occurs. As soon as the symptoms occur, *vigorously* pump the primer bulb and note the reaction. Wait a few minutes for symptoms to reappear, then repeat the pumping action. Refer to the following.

   a. If the motor operates properly only after pumping the primer bulb, the fault is likely due to a faulty low-pressure boost pump (Bravo drive models) or air being drawn into the fuel system at some point. Inspect the water-separating fuel filter, filter housing, fuel lines and fittings connecting the water separating fuel filter to the Cool Fuel System while an assistant pumps the primer bulb. The pressurized fuel should leak from the point where air is drawn into the system. On Bravo drive models, replace the low-pressure boost pump, as described in the Chapter Eight section of this chapter, if no air leak is found and the engine operates properly only while pumping the primer bulb.

**16**

b. If the malfunction is still present, check the fuel pressure as described in this chapter. If the fuel pressure is correct, have a Mercruiser dealership connect scanning equipment to the engine harness (**Figure 6**) to identify the fault.

10. Stop the engine. Disconnect the portable tank hose from the inlet fittings. Drain residual fuel from the hose. Reconnect the boat fuel tank supply hose. Securely tighten the clamp(s). Clean up any spilled fuel.

11. Operate the engine at engine speed and under the conditions when the malfunction occurs to verify the fault. Often the fault is corrected by securely tightening the supply hose clamp.

### Checking the fuel tank vent

A fault with the fuel tank vent can cause a no-start condition or restrict fuel flow at any engine speed. Typically the symptom worsens the longer the engine operates. This occurs because as fuel is drawn from the tank, improper venting will cause a vacuum to form in the area above the fuel. The more fuel withdrawn, the stronger the vacuum. In time the vacuum will overcome the pumping ability of the fuel pump and fuel starvation occurs. To verify a venting problem, simply open the fuel fill cap when the symptoms occur. Improper venting is evident if the symptoms quickly improve. Improper venting is usually caused by insects, insect nest or webs or other debris in the vent fitting (on the boat) or in the vent hose connecting the vent fitting to the fuel tank.

### Low-pressure boost pump test

The low-pressure boost pump is used only on Bravo drive models.

1. Make sure the lanyard switch is in RUN position.

2. Turn the ignition key to the ON or RUN position. The dash-mounted instruments must turn on, the warning horn must sound for two seconds and both fuel pumps must operate for two seconds, then cease. Note if one pump or both pumps are operating. Both pumps must operate simultaneously. The high-pressure fuel pump mounted in the cool fuel system generates considerably more noise than the low-pressure boost pump. If necessary, touch the tip of a mechanic's stethoscope to the body of the low-pressure boost pump (A, **Figure 13**) to listen for operation. Refer to the following:

a. If the instruments turn on, the warning horn sounds and both pumps operate, proceed to Step 3.

b. If the instruments turn on, the warning horn does not sound and the fuel pumps do not operate, test the system relay as described in this section.

c. If the instruments turn on, the warning horn sounds and only one fuel pump operates, the suspect fuel pump or connecting wiring is faulty. Replace the suspect fuel pump as described in this supplement if no fault is found with the wiring.

3. After verifying that both fuel pumps are operational, check for a restriction in the fuel supply hose and operate the engine, using a portable fuel tank and outboard fuel supply hose with primer bulb as described in this section. Refer to *Checking for a restriction in the fuel supply hose* in this section. Replace the low-pressure boost pump, as described in the this supplement, if the engine operates properly only while pumping the primer bulb.

4. Stop the engine. Disconnect the portable tank hose from the inlet fittings. Drain residual fuel from the hose. Reconnect the boat fuel tank supply hose. Securely tighten the clamp(s). Clean up any spilled fuel.

### Fuel pump relay test

The fuel pump relay supplies battery current to operate the high-pressure electric fuel pump in the Cool Fuel System and the low-pressure boost pump used only on Bravo drive models. When activated by turning on the ignition key switch, the system relay supplies battery current to the pink wire leading to the No. 85 fuel pump relay terminal and the pink/light green wire leading to the No. 30 fuel pump relay terminal. At this time the ECM uses internal circuitry to connect the dark green fuel pump relay wire to ground for approximately two seconds. This completes the circuit necessary to switch on the fuel pump relay and deliver current on the No. 87 terminal and the pink/yellow wire leading to the fuel pump(s). The fuel pump(s) then operate to pressurize the fuel delivery system in preparation for starting the engine. After two seconds, the ECM removes the ground circuits for the fuel pump relay and warning horn, causing the fuel pump(s) to stop and the horn to stop sounding.

When the ignition key switch is turned to the START position, the crankshaft rotates and the ECM receives input from the crankshaft position sensor and switches on the fuel pump relay. The ECM will keep the fuel pump relay activated as long as it receives input from the crankshaft position sensor indicating cranking speed or higher.

An unpowered test light is required for this procedure.

*WARNING*
*The engine may unexpectedly start during testing. Keep all persons, clothing, tools or*

*loose objects away from the drive belts and other moving components on the engine.*

*WARNING*
*High voltage is present in the ignition system. Never touch any wires or electrical components while running the engine or performing a test. Never perform ignition system tests in wet conditions.*

*CAUTION*
*Use a flush test device to supply the engine with cooling water if testing the engine with the boat out of the water. Operation of the starter motor results in operation of the seawater pump. The seawater pump is quickly damaged if operated without adequate cooling water.*

1. Make sure the lanyard switch is in the RUN position.
2. Turn the ignition key switch to the ON or RUN position. The dash-mounted instruments must turn on and the warning horn must sound for two seconds. Turn the ignition key switch to the OFF or STOP position, then refer to the following:
   a. If the instrument did not turn on, check for a blown fuse, tripped circuit breaker or loose wire connection at the ignition key switch. Correct faulty wiring, replace the fuse or reset the circuit breaker to restore gauge operation. If this does not restore gauge operation, test the ignition switch as described in Chapter Three of the main body of the manual.
   b. If the instruments are on but the warning horn did not sound, test the system relay as described in this section.
   c. If the instruments are on and the warning horn did sound, the system relay and ECM are operational. Proceed to Step 3.
3. Lift up on the locking tab, then carefully unplug the fuel pump relay (B, **Figure 4**) from the engine wire harness connector.
4. Refer to the terminal number molded into the fuel pump relay base (**Figure 5**) to identify the corresponding terminal openings in the engine wire harness connector.
5. Connect a test light to a known good engine ground. Touch the test light probe to the No. 85 terminal in the engine wire harness connector. Observe the light while an assistant turns the ignition key switch to the ON or RUN position. The light must illuminate. If not, test the system relay as described in this section. If the system relay tests correctly, check the 20 amp fuse connecting to the pink and red/black wires leading into the fuse holder. If no fault is found with the fuse, check for an open circuit or short to

ground along the pink wire connecting the fuse to the fuel pump relay.

6. Turn the ignition key switch to the OFF or STOP position. Connect a test light to a known good engine ground. Touch the test light probe to the No. 30 terminal in the engine wire harness connector. Observe the light while an assistant turns the ignition key switch to the ON or RUN position. The light must illuminate. If not, test the system relay as described in this section. If the system relay tests correctly, check the 20 amp fuse connecting to the pink/light green and red/black wires leading into the fuse holder. If no fault is found with the fuse, check for an open circuit or short to ground along the pink/light green wire connecting the fuse to the fuel pump relay.

7. Turn the ignition key switch to the OFF or STOP position. Connect a test light to a battery positive terminal. Touch the test light probe to a known good engine ground to verify the ground and battery positive circuits. Touch the test light probe to the No. 86 fuel pump relay harness connector. The light *must not illuminate*. If otherwise, unplug the engine harness connectors from the ECM (**Figure 3**) and repeat the test. If the light illuminates with the harnesses disconnected from the ECM, the purple/dark green wire connecting the ECM to the system relay harness connector is shorted to ground. Repair the wiring as needed.

8. Turn the ignition key switch to the OFF or STOP position. If disconnected, carefully plug the engine wire harness connectors onto the ECM. Connect the test light cord to a battery positive terminal. Touch the test light probe to the No. 86 system relay harness connector. Observe the test light while an assistant turns the ignition key switch to the ON or RUN position. The test light must illuminate for two seconds then go out. Refer to the following:
   a. If the ight does not illuminate or does not go out after two seconds, the ECM power up circuit is faulty. Replace the ECM to restore fuel pump relay operation only after verifying that no faults are present on connecting wiring and terminals. Failure of the ECM is rare and replacement seldom corrects an engine malfunction. Most faults are caused by bent, corroded or otherwise damaged terminals.
   b. If the light illuminates as specified, proceed to Step 9.

9. Connect a test light to the battery positive terminal. Touch the test light probe to the No. 86 system relay harness connector. Have an assistant turn the ignition key switch to the ON or RUN position. Wait two seconds for the power up circuit to illuminate, then turn off the test light. Observe the test light while an assistant turns the ignition key switch to the START position for approximately five seconds. The test light must illuminate while

**16**

operating the starter motor and go out approximately two seconds after stopping the starter motor. Refer to the following:

　　a. If the light illuminates as specified, the ECM relay control circuit is operating properly. Proceed to Step 10.

　　b. If the light does not illuminate while operating the starter motor, test the ignition system as described in this chapter. If the ignition system is operating, the ECM relay control circuit is faulty. Replace the ECM to restore fuel pump relay operation only after verifying that no faults are present on connecting wiring and terminals. Failure of the ECM is rare and replacement seldom corrects an engine malfunction. Most faults are caused by bent, corroded or otherwise damaged terminals.

10.　Lift up on the locking tab, then carefully plug the fuel pump relay (B, **Figure 4**) onto the engine harness connector.

11.　Turn the ignition key switch to the OFF or STOP position. Unplug the engine wire harness connector from the high-pressure fuel pump harness leading into the Cool Fuel System, which is located on the port side of the engine between the engine mount and oil pan. On Bravo drive models, also disconnect the engine wire harness connector from the low-pressure boost pump harness. The harnesses contain a pink/yellow and black wire.

12.　Connect a test light to the battery positive terminal. Touch the test light probe to a known good engine ground to test the light and verify the engine ground connection to the battery.

13.　Touch the test light probe to the terminal connecting to the black wire in the disconnected engine harness connector for the high-pressure electric fuel pump, then low-pressure boost pump (Bravo drive models). The light must illuminate at each connection point. If not, the black wire or terminal leading to the engine ground stud is open. Repair or replace the wiring to restore operation of the high-pressure electric fuel pump or low-pressure boost pump.

14.　Connect a test light to a known good engine ground. Touch the test light probe to the terminal connecting to the pink/yellow wire in the engine harness connector for the high-pressure electric fuel pump. Observe the test light while an assistant turns the ignition key switch to the ON or RUN position. The light must illuminate for two seconds, then go out. Turn the ignition key switch to the OFF or STOP position, then refer to the following:

　　a. If the light does not illuminate, the fuel pump relay has failed open or is stuck in the de-energized position. Replace the relay and repeat the test. The pink/yellow wire connecting the relay to the

high-pressure fuel pump connector is open or shorted to ground if the light does not illuminate with the replacement relay. Repair the faulty wiring to restore fuel pump operation.

　　b. If the light illuminates as specified, the fuel pump relay and connecting wiring are operating properly. If the high-pressure electric fuel pump does not operate, replace it as described in Chapter Eight of the main body of the manual.

15.　On Bravo drive models, touch the test light probe to the terminal connecting to the pink/yellow wire in the engine harness connector for the low-pressure boost pump. Observe the test light while an assistant turns the ignition key switch to the ON or RUN position. The light must illuminate for two seconds, then go out. Turn the ignition key switch to the OFF or STOP position, then refer to the following:

　　a. If the light does not illuminate, the pink/yellow wire connecting the relay to the low-pressure fuel pump connector is open or shorted to ground. Repair the faulty wiring to restore fuel pump operation.

　　b. If the light illuminates as specified, the fuel pump relay and connecting wiring are operating properly. If the low-pressure boost pump does not operate, replace it as described in this supplement.

16.　Connect the engine harness connector to the high-pressure electric fuel pump harness connector. Route the wiring to prevent interference with moving components.

17.　On Bravo drive models, connect the engine harness connector to the low-pressure boost pump harness connector. Route the wiring to prevent interference with the drive belts or other moving components.

### *Checking the fuel injectors*

　　A faulty fuel injector can cause either a rich or lean condition in the cylinder in which it supplies fuel. Refer to *Basic Fuel System Troubleshooting* in this supplement.

　　The leaking fuel injector introduces fuel into the intake manifold in excess of the amount determined by the ECM and will cause symptoms consistent with a rich condition. The engine may perform properly at higher engine speeds as the engine is able to burn the excess fuel.

　　A fuel injector with a poor spray pattern due to debris or deposits in the valve will usually cause a poor idle quality as the poor spray pattern may prevent the fuel from atomizing before it reaches the combustion chamber. Poor idle quality occurs because the fuel droplets will not burn efficiently at lower engine speeds. The engine will usually operate properly at mid-range throttle settings as the higher velocity of the air entering the intake will promote better atomizing. A lean condition may occur at higher throttle settings as the condition causing the poor spray pattern usually restricts fuel flow to some degree.

Blockage in the fuel injector will cause a lean operating condition because the injector will not spray the proper amount of fuel for the given operating conditions. The engine may perform properly at lower engine speeds if the blockage is not overly restrictive. The resulting lean condition will worsen as the engine speed and fuel demand increases.

The design of the multi-port injection (MPI) system prevents visual inspection of the fuel injector spray pattern. An easy way to identify injector trouble is to remove and inspect the spark plugs as described in this supplement. All spark plugs should appear the same. A suspect injector is one that feeds a cylinder with a spark plug that appears markedly different from the others. Replace the suspect fuel injector and all spark plugs only after verifying that the injector is operating, as described in this section, and the ignition system is operating properly. Run the engine for several hours, then remove and inspect the spark plugs. An ignition system fault or mechanical problem affecting only the suspect cylinder is indicated if the spark plug for that cylinder still indicates a rich or lean condition.

### Checking for fuel injector operation

*WARNING*
*The engine may unexpectedly start during testing. Keep all persons, clothing, tools or loose objects away from the drive belts and other moving components on the engine.*

*CAUTION*
*Use a flush test device to supply the engine with cooling water if testing the engine with the boat out of the water. Operation of the starter motor results in operation of the seawater pump. The seawater pump is quickly damaged if operated without adequate cooling water.*

*CAUTION*
*Safely performing on-water testing or adjustments requires two people. One person is needed to operate the boat, the other to monitor the gauges or test equipment and make necessary adjustments. All personnel must remain seated inside the boat at all times. Do not lean over the transom while the boat is moving. Use extensions to allow all gauges and test equipment to be located in normal seating areas.*

Perform this procedure if the engine will not start or if failure of one or more of the injectors is suspected of causing the engine to run improperly. Use a mechanic's stethoscope for this procedure.

1. Unthread the retainer (**Figure 23**). Then, remove the metal and rubber washers from the stud. Lift the plastic cover off the flame arrestor (**Figure 24**) to access the fuel injectors.

2. Touch the tip of the stethoscope to the body of one of the fuel injectors (**Figure 22**). Listen for the distinct clicking noise as an assistant attempts to start or runs the engine. Touch the stethoscope to the body of each fuel injector on the engine and note the clicking noise. Stop the engine and refer to the following:

   a. If all injectors make the same clicking noise, the injectors are operating. Low fuel pressure, an ignition malfunction or mechanical problem in one or more cylinders is the likely cause of the engine malfunction.

   b. If none of the injectors are making a clicking noise, test the EFI system relay and check for voltage at the fuel injectors as described in this section. An ignition system fault, faulty injector wiring or faulty ECM is evident if no fault is found with the relay and voltage is present at the fuel injectors. Replace the ECM to restore fuel injector operation only if no fault is found with the system relay, fuses, ignition system, wiring or terminals. Failure of the ECM is rare and its replacement seldom corrects an engine malfunction.

   c. If one or more of the injectors sounds markedly different from the others, check for voltage at the fuel injectors as described in this section. If the injector voltage checks correctly, remove and inspect the spark plugs to check for a rich or lean condition as described in this section. Replace the suspect injector if the spark plug in which it delivers shows a rich or lean condition.

3. Install the plastic flame arrestor cover onto the stud. Install the rubber, then metal, washer onto the stud. Secure the cover and washers with the retainer (**Figure 23**). Do not overtighten the retainer. Overtightening will break the retainer.

### Checking for voltage at the injectors

*WARNING*
*The engine may unexpectedly start during testing. Keep all persons, clothing, tools or loose objects away from the drive belts and other moving components on the engine.*

*CAUTION*
*Use a flush test device to supply the engine with cooling water if testing the engine with*

**16**

*the boat out of the water. Operation of the starter motor results in operation of the sea-water pump. The seawater pump is quickly damaged if operated without adequate cooling water.*

*CAUTION*
*Do not use a high-capacity test light to check the injector voltage. A high-capacity light may draw excessive amperage and damage the injector driver circuits in the engine control unit (ECM).*

This procedure checks for voltage at the harness connectors to the injectors and checks for proper switching from the engine control unit (ECM)

Use a test light for this procedure. *Do not* use a high-capacity test light. The test light must consume less than .3 amp when connected to a 12-volt source. To determine the amperage draw, connect the negative terminal of a digital amp gauge (usually integrated into a digital multimeter) to the negative terminal of the battery. Touch the test light probe to the positive terminal of the battery. Connect the positive terminal of the amp gauge to the cord of the test light and read the amperage draw. For accurate test results, the light must draw 0.1-0.3 amp.

1. Unthread the retainer (**Figure 23**). Then, remove the metal and rubber washer from the stud. Lift the plastic cover off the flame arrestor (**Figure 24**) to access the fuel injectors.

2. Disconnect the high tension coil lead from the distributor cap (**Figure 28**). Connect the coil lead securely to an engine ground to prevent engine starting.

3. Note the wire routing and connection points, then disconnect the wire harness connector from each of the fuel injectors (**Figure 22**).

4. Connect the cord of the un-powered test light to the engine ground. Touch the test light probe to the positive battery cable to verify the test light and battery-to-engine ground connection.

5. With the ignition key switch in the OFF or STOP position, touch the test light probe to the pink/white wire terminal in each of the injector harness connectors. The light *must not* illuminate at any of the test points. If the light illuminates, the system relay or relay circuit is faulty. Test the relay as described in this section. If the relay and related circuits test correctly, the pink/white in the suspect connector is shorted to a battery power source. Inspect the wiring and correct the fault before proceeding.

6. Turn the ignition key switch to the ON or RUN position. Touch the test light probe to the pink/white wire terminal in each of the injector harness connectors. The light *must* illuminate at each of the test points. If not, the system

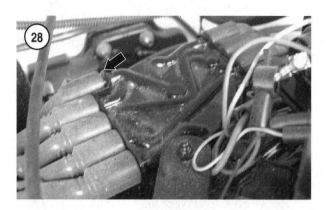

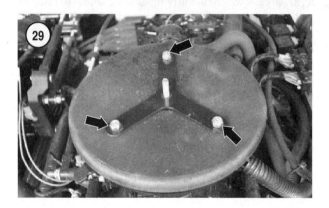

relay or relay circuit is faulty. Test the relay as described in this section. If the relay and related circuits test correctly, the pink/white in the suspect connector is open or shorted to engine ground. Inspect the wiring and correct the fault before proceeding.

7. Touch the test light probe to the other wire terminal (not the pink/white wire) in one of the injector harness connectors. Observe the test light while an assistant attempts to start the engine. The test light must flash repeatedly while cranking. Repeat this step for the remaining injector harness connector(s). Refer to the following:

   a. If the test light flashes at each connector, the injector voltage is correct and the ECM is switching on the injectors. Proceed to Step 8.

   b. If the test light does not flash at any of the connectors, test the ignition system as described in this chapter. If the ignition system tests correctly, the fault is due to faulty wiring between the ignition system and the ECM, faulty wiring between the ECM and the fuel injectors or the ECM is faulty. Check the wiring and terminals for faults and correct as needed. Replace the ECM to restore fuel injector operation only if all other components and wiring on the circuit test correctly. Failure of the

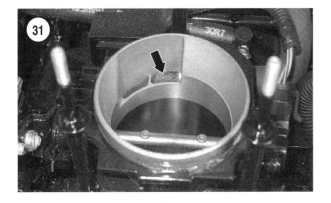

ECM is rare and its replacement seldom corrects an engine malfunction.

   c. If the light flashes at some connectors, but not at others, the wiring connecting the suspect injector connector to the ECM is open or shorted to ground, or the ECM is faulty. Check the wiring and terminals for faults and correct as needed. A failure of the injector driver circuit in the ECM will affect one-half or all of the fuel injectors. Otherwise the fault is with the wiring for individual fuel injector(s). Replace the ECM to restore fuel injector operation only if all other components and wiring on the circuit test correctly. Failure of the ECM is rare and its replacement seldom corrects an engine malfunction.

8. Turn the ignition key switch to the OFF or STOP position.

9. Reconnect each of the connectors onto the injectors. Route the wiring to prevent contact with moving or hot engine components. Reconnect the high tension lead to the distributor cap terminal (**Figure 28**).

10. Install the plastic flame arrestor cover onto the stud. Fit the rubber, then metal, washer onto the stud. Secure the cover and washers with the retainer (**Figure 23**). Do not overtighten the retainer. Overtightening will break the retainer.

### Idle air control motor test

   A faulty IAC motor can cause stalling at idle, excessive idle speed or stalling during deceleration. A faulty IAC motor will not cause operational problems at higher engine speeds. In almost all cases, a faulty IAC will cause the engine to stall at idle speed, particularly when shifted into gear. This symptom is especially prevalent when the engine is cold. During normal operation, the ECM will increase the duty cycle to allow more air flow, for a higher idle speed, when it detects a cold engine. As the engine warms to normal operating temperature, the ECM will decrease the duty cycle to lower air flow, for a lower idle speed. A fault with the engine temperature sensor or other EFI sensor can provide false information to the ECM that results in improper operation of the IAC. Perform this test if these symptoms are evident.

*WARNING*
*The engine may unexpectedly start during testing. Keep all persons, clothing, tools or loose objects away from the drive belts and other moving components on the engine.*

*CAUTION*
*Use a flush test device to supply the engine with cooling water if testing the engine with the boat out of the water. Operation of the starter motor results in operation of the seawater pump. The seawater pump is quickly damaged if operated without adequate cooling water.*

1. Unthread the retainer (**Figure 23**). Then, remove the metal and rubber washer. Lift the plastic cover off the flame arrestor (**Figure 24**) to access the fuel injectors.

2. Remove the three nuts and cover bracket (**Figure 29**) then lift the flame arrestor off the throttle body studs (**Figure 30**).

*NOTE*
*A dirty or damaged silencer/filter in the throttle body can restrict air flow and result in malfunction of the IAC motor. In such cases, cleaning or replacing the silencer/filter will restore normal IAC motor operation.*

3. Use needle nose pliers to pull the silencer/filter (**Figure 31**) out of the IAC passage in the throttle body. Use a soap and water solution to clean all material from the silencer/filter. Replace the silencer/filter if it is damaged or cannot be adequately cleaned.

4. Start the engine and operate at idle speed. Note if air is flowing into the IAC passage in the throttle body (**Figure 31**). Normal operation of the IAC causes air to flow into

 **16**

the passage and produces a loud hissing noise with the silencer/filter removed.

5. Monitor the noise level, the dash-mounted temperature gauge and the tachometer as the engine warms to the normal operating temperature of 160° F (71° C). The noise level and idle speed should gradually decrease as the engine temperature increases. Under certain conditions it may take as long as 20 minutes for the engine to reach normal operating temperature. Normal idle speed should be approximately 600 rpm in neutral gear. Stop the engine and refer to the following:

    a. If the engine reaches normal operating temperature and the idle speed drops to 600 rpm but the IAC does not decrease as specified, the IAC motor is operating properly under the present conditions. If stalling upon deceleration or other symptoms persist, have a Mercruiser dealership connect scanning equipment to the engine harness (**Figure 6**) and compare the displayed IAC duty cycle with the noise emanating from the passage. Suspect a faulty IAC if a high duty cycle is displayed without the corresponding loud noise level at the passage.

    b. If the engine does not reach normal operating temperature, test the thermostat as described in Chapter Three of the main body of the manual. Replace the thermostat as needed and repeat the test.

    c. If the engine reaches normal operating temperature and idle speed remains above 600 rpm, but the IAC noise does not decrease, replace the IAC motor as described in this supplement. Repeat the test. If the idle speed exceeds the specification and the intake air noise does not decrease as specified with the replacement IAC, have a Mercruiser dealership connect scanning equipment to the engine harness (**Figure 6**) and compare the sensor input values displayed on the scanner screen with actual conditions, such as the engine temperature on the dash-mounted gauge, ambient air temperature where testing, and manifold vacuum, using a vacuum gauge attached to an intake manifold attached hose (fuel pressure regulator hose). Replace sensors with a value displayed on the scanning equipment that is significantly different from the gauge readings.

    d. If the engine reaches normal operating temperature and the idle speed is below 600 rpm, but the IAC noise level is low, replace the IAC as described in this supplement. Repeat the test. If the idle speed does not reach 600 rpm and the intake air noise is not as specified with the replacement IAC, have a Mercruiser dealership connect scanning equipment to the engine harness (**Figure 6**) and compare the sensor input values displayed on the scanner screen with actual conditions, such as the engine temperature on the dash-mounted gauge, ambient air temperature where testing, and manifold vacuum using a vacuum gauge attached to an intake manifold attached hose (fuel pressure regulator hose). Replace sensors with a value displayed on the scanning equipment that is significantly different from the gauge readings.

6. Carefully push the silencer/filter (**Figure 31**) into the IAC passage in the throttle body. Do not compact the silencer/filter during installation. Compacting the silencer/filter may restrict air flow through the passage and cause the IAC to malfunction.

7. Guide the openings in the flame arrestor over the throttle body studs. The flame studs are not evenly spaced and the flame arrestor will fit in one direction only.

8. Fit the retainer over the studs and seat it against the flame arrestor. Install the three nuts (**Figure 29**) and tighten evenly to 108 in.-lb. (12.2 N·m.).

9. Install the plastic flame arrestor cover onto the stud. Fit the rubber, then metal, washer over the stud. Secure the cover and washers with the retainer (**Figure 23**). Do not overtighten the retainer. Overtightening will break the retainer.

## Table 1 FUEL SYSTEM SPECIFICATIONS

| Model | Speed (rpm) | Rev-limit activation | Fuel pressure |
|---|---|---|---|
| **4.3L models** | | | |
| 1998-2004 carb. models | 4400-4800 | 4850-4900 | 6-9 psi (41-62 kPa) |
| 1998-2004 FI models (TBI and MPI) | 4400-4800 | 4900 | 40-46 psi (276-317 kPa) |
| **5.0L and 5.7L models** | | | |
| 1998-2004 carb. models | 4400-4800 | 4850-4900 | 3-7 psi (21-48 kPa) |
| 2002-2004 MPI models | 4600-5000 | 5100 | 40-46 psi (276-317 kPa) |
| **350 Mag** | | | |
| 2002-2004 MPI models | 4600-5000 | 5100 | 40-46 psi (276-317 kPa) |

**CHAPTER FOUR**

# LUBRICATION, MAINTENANCE AND TUNE-UP

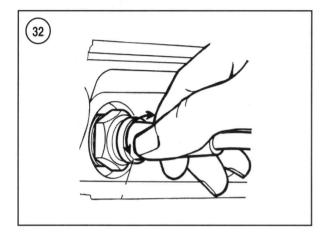

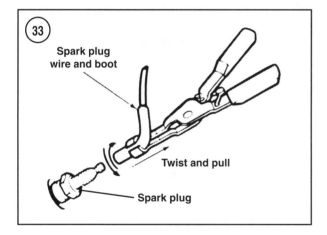

Spark plug wire and boot

Twist and pull

Spark plug

This section describes spark plug procedures unique to 2002-2004 4.3L, 5.0L, 350 Mag and MX6.2L (MPI) models.

### Spark Plug Inspection and Replacement (2002-2004 4.3L, 5.0L, 350 Mag and MX6.2L [MPI] Models)

All 2002-2004 4.3L, 5.0L, 350 Mag and MX6.2 multi-port fuel injection (MPI) models use platinum-tipped spark plugs (AC 41-932). The platinum-tipped spark plugs resist fouling, last longer and provide superior ignition system performance compared to the standard type spark plugs used on other models. This type of plug is not generally used on automobile applications and may not be available from automotive part stores. Purchase these spark plugs from a Mercruiser dealership if necessary.

### *Spark plug removal*

1. Mark the cylinder number on the spark plug leads before disconnecting them from the spark plug. The No. 1 cylinder is the front cylinder on the port side and the No. 2 cylinder is the front cylinder on the starboard side. Odd numbered cylinders are on the port side and even numbered cylinders are on the starboard side.
2. Disconnect the spark plug wires by twisting and pulling on the wire boot (**Figure 32**). If working on a hot engine and/or in cramped quarters, grip the boot with spark plug boot pliers. (**Figure 33**).
3. Use compressed air to blow debris from around the spark plug openings before removing them. If the spark plug threads are corroded, apply a penetrating oil and allow it to soak in.
4. Sometimes the threads in the cylinder head are damaged during spark plug removal. This condition can be repaired without removing the cylinder head by installing a special threaded insert. Have the repair performed by a professional if you are unfamiliar with the repair or do not have access to the equipment.
5. Clean the spark plug opening with a thread chaser (**Figure 34**). Thread the chaser by hand into each spark

**16**

# SPARK PLUG CONDITION

### NORMAL
- Identified by light tan or gray deposits on the firing tip.
- Can be cleaned.

### GAP BRIDGED
- Identified by deposit buildup closing gap between electrodes.

### OIL FOULED
- Identified by wet black deposits on the insulator shell bore and electrodes.
- Caused by excessive oil entering combustion chamber through worn rings and pistons, excessive clearance between valve guides and stems or worn or loose bearings. Can be cleaned. If engine is not repaired, use a hotter plug.

### CARBON FOULED
- Identified by black, dry fluffy carbon deposits on insulator tips, exposed shell surfaces and electrodes.
- Caused by too cold a plug, weak ignition, dirty air cleaner, too rich fuel mixture or excessive idling. Can be cleaned.

### LEAD FOULED
- Identified by dark gray, black, yellow or tan deposits or a fused glazed coating on the insulator tip.
- Caused by highly leaded gasoline. Can be cleaned.

### WORN
- Identified by severely eroded or worn electrodes.
- Caused by normal ear. Should be replaced.

### FUSED SPOT DEPOSIT
- Identified by melted or spotty deposits resembling bubbles or blisters.
- Caused by sudden acceleration. Can be cleaned.

### OVERHEATING
- Identified by a white or light gray insulator with small black or gray brown spots with bluish-burnt appearance of electrodes.
- Caused by engine overheating, wrong type of fuel, loose spark plugs, too hot a plug or incorrect ignition timing. Replace the plug.

### PREIGNITION
- Identified by melted electrodes and possibly blistered insulator. Metallic deposits on insulator indicate engine damage.
- Caused by wrong type of fuel, incorrect ignition timing or advance, too hot a plug, burned valves or engine overheating. Replace the plug.

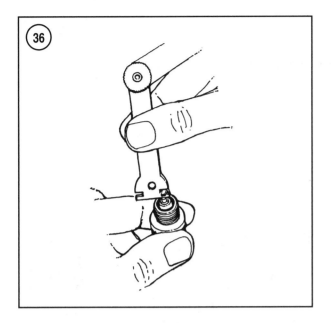

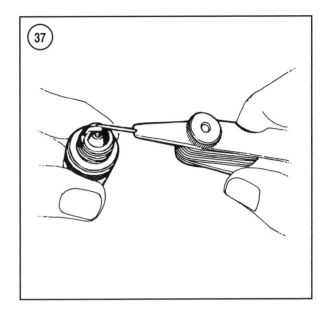

plug opening. Several passes may be required to remove all carbon or corrosion deposits from the threads. Flush all debris from the openings with compressed air.

### Spark plug inspection

Compare the spark plugs with those shown in **Figure 35**. Spark plugs can give a clear indication of problems in the engine sometimes before symptoms occur. Additional inspection and testing may be required if an abnormal condition is evident. Refer to the troubleshooting sections in this supplement or Chapter Three in the main body of the manual for troubleshooting instructions.

### Spark plug installation

Use only a gap adjusting tool (**Figure 36**) to adjust the spark plug gap. Gapping tools are available at most automotive parts stores.

1. Check the gap using a wire feeler gauge (**Figure 37**). The gauge should pass between the button on the side electrode and center electrode with a slight drag.

2. Open or close the gap as necessary. Work carefully to avoid bending the thin center electrode or dislodging the platinum button on the side electrode. Never tap the plug against a hard object to close the cap. The ceramic insulator can crack and break away.

3. Inspect the spark plug electrodes for parallel surfaces. Carefully bend the side electrode until the surfaces are parallel and the gap is correct.

4. Apply a very light coat of oil to the spark plug thread and thread them in by hand. Use a torque wrench to tighten the spark plugs to 18 ft.-lb. (24.4 N•m) if installing the spark plug into a *new* cylinder head and 132 in.-lb. (15 N•m) if installing the plugs into a *used* cylinder head.

5. Apply a light coat of silicone lubricant to the inner surface of the spark plug boots. Carefully slide the cap over the correct spark plug. Snap the connector in the boot fully onto the spark plug terminal.

**16**

### Table 2 SPARK PLUG SPECIFICATIONS

| Model | Spark plug No. | Gap specification |
|---|---|---|
| **4.3L, 5.0L, 5.7L, 350 Mag and MX6.2L** | | |
| **1998-2004 carburetor-equipped** | | |
|    **AC plug** | MR43LTS | |
|    **Champion plug** | RS12YC | |
|    **NGK plug** | BPR6EFS | |
|    **Plug gap** | – | 0.045 in. (1.1 mm) |
| **2002-2004 MPI** | | |
|    **AC plug** | 41-932 | 0.060 in. (1.5 mm) |

# CHAPTER FIVE

# LAY-UP, WINTERIZING AND FITTING OUT

This section describes changes to the lay-up, winterizing and fitting out procedures for 2002-2004 models. Refer to the instructions in Chapter Five in the main body of the manual to prepare the fuel, electrical and other engine systems for storage and fitting out.

## Draining Water From the Cooling System

### 3.0L models

All 2002-2004 3.0L models use the same water drain hoses (**Figure 38**) that are used on 2000 and 2001 models. Drain water from the cooling system as described in Chapter Five in the main body of the manual. See *Winterizing (3.0L Models)*.

## 4.3L, 5.0L, 5.7L, 350 Mag and MX6.2 Models

Almost all 2002-2004 4.3L, 5.0L, 5.7L, 350 Mag and MX6.2 models are equipped with a central point water drain system that provides a quick and easy means to drain water from the cooling system for short term storage. This feature can extend the boating season, as the cooling system can be easily drained in preparation for freezing temperatures and easily prepared for operation without the inconvenience of removing and reinstalling the numerous drain plugs and hoses required to drain earlier models. Keep in mind that the system drains only enough water to prevent freeze damage and some water will remain in the cooling system passages. To reduce corrosion damage during long term storage, remove the plugs and hoses and thoroughly drain the cooling system as described in this section.

Two different versions of the central point drain system are used on models with a standard (seawater) cooling system. On Alpha drive models, the water is drained from the engine by rotating the water drain knob (A, **Figure 39**) on the front port side of the engine, then removing the

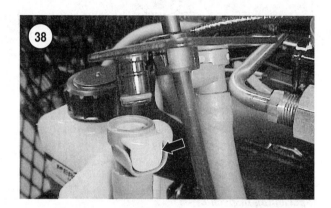

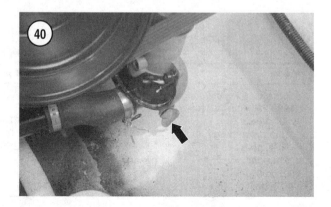

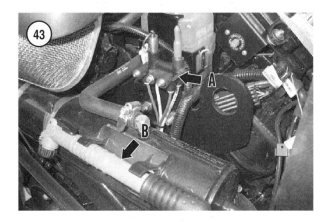

Alpha and Bravo drive models that are not equipped with a central point drain system must be drained manually for storage. On such models, drain water from the cooling system as described in Chapter Five in the main body of the manual. See *Winterizing (All V-6 and V-8 Models)*.

On 2002-2004 multi-port fuel injection (MPI) models, the drain plug for the fuel cooler (**Figure 42**) has been relocated from the rear to the front of the fuel cooler for easier access.

All 2002-2004 multi-port fuel injection (MPI) models that are factory-equipped with a closed-type cooling system are equipped with an air-activated water drain system. Air lines connect the drain control valve (A, **Figure 43**) to the central point drain housing on the lower front and port side of the engine. When activated, the system drains seawater from the seawater pump, heat exchanger, power steering fluid cooler and Cool Fuel System. Use the pump (B, **Figure 43**) to activate the system. If the pump is missing or damaged, a bicycle pump or other air source can be used to activate the system.

All 2002-2004 carburetor-equipped V-6 and V-8 models with a factory-installed closed-type cooling system must be manually drained.

### Draining the water (short term storage)

*CAUTION*
*Do not leave the boat in the water with the water drain system activated or with plug, hoses or other cooling system components removed. Otherwise water may continually flow through the water supply and/or exhaust passages and enter the bilge through the drain openings. If the boat must be left in the water, use an approved bilge heater or other means to prevent water in the cooling system from freezing.*

This section describes the procedures for using the central point drain system to drain water from the cooling system for short term storage. If the engine will not be operated for several weeks or more, thoroughly drain the cooling system for long term storage as described in the following section. For Alpha drive models without the central point drain system, drain water from the cooling system as described in Chapter Five in the main body of the manual.

1A. On Alpha drive models with a central point drain system (standard cooling system), rotate the blue knob (A, **Figure 39**) counterclockwise until red appears on the

**16**

plug from the side of the thermostat housing (B). A shaft connected to the knob rotates with the knob to open the central point drain housing on the lower front and port side of the engine. On Bravo drive models, water is drained from the engine by removing the blue drain plug from the central point drain housing (**Figure 40**) on the lower front and port side of the engine and the blue drain plug from the port side of the thermostat housing (**Figure 41**).

shaft (**Figure 44**) and water begins draining from the orange drain tube extending from the bottom of the drain housing (**Figure 40**). If water does not drain from the housing, drain the cooling system as described under *Draining the water (long term storage)* in the following section.

1B. On Bravo drive models with a standard cooling system, remove the blue drain plug from the drain housing (**Figure 40**) on the lower front and port side of the engine. Then remove the blue drain plug from the port side of the thermostat housing (**Figure 41**). If water does not drain from the fitting, insert a stiff piece of wire into the opening to clear sediment until all water drains from the fitting. If a water cannot be drained by this method, drain the cooling system as described under *Draining the water (long term storage)* in the following section.

1C. On Alpha and Bravo models without a central point drain system (standard cooling system), drain all water from the cooling system as described in Chapter Five in the main body of the manual. See *Winterizing (All V-6 and V-8 Models)*.

1D. On Alpha and Bravo drive (multi-port fuel injection [MPI]) models with a closed cooling system, activate the water drain system as follows:

    a. Remove the cover (**Figure 45**) to access the schrader valve opening.

    b. Attach the air pump (B, **Figure 43**) to the schrader valve fitting. Pump air into the fitting until the green indicators (**Figure 46**) extend from the water drain control valve.

    c. Verify that water is draining into the bilge and both indicators remain extended. Otherwise the system must be drained manually as described under *Draining the water (long term storage)* in the following section.

1E. On Alpha and Bravo drive (carburetor-equipped) models with a closed cooling system, drain water from the system as follows:

    a. On Bravo drive models, remove the drain plugs from the belt-driven seawater pump. If water does not drain from the fitting, insert a stiff piece of wire into the opening to clear sediment until all water drains from the fitting.

    b. Remove the blue drain plug from the plastic hose junction on the lower port side of the engine. The junction is located between the side engine mount and the oil pan. If water does not drain from the fitting, insert a stiff piece of wire into the opening to clear sediment until all water drains from the fitting.

2. On 4.3L and 5.0L models equipped with an inlet hose check valve, remove the blue plastic plug from the check valve. The check valve is located on the front of the en-

gine and just to the port side of the recirculation pump. Insert a stiff piece of wire into the plug opening to clear debris until all water drains from the check valve.

3. Prepare the drive unit for winter storage as described in Chapter Five of the main body of the manual.

### Draining the water (long term storage)

This section describes the procedures to thoroughly drain water from the cooling system for long term storage.

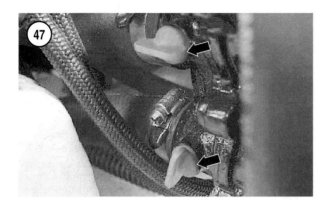

1A. On Alpha drive models with a central point drain system (standard cooling system), drain all water from the system as follows:

    a. Rotate the blue knob (A, **Figure 39**) counterclockwise until red appears on the shaft (**Figure 44**) and water begins draining from the orange drain tube extending from the bottom of the drain housing (**Figure 40**).

    b. Remove the blue drain plug from the drain housing (**Figure 40**) on the lower front and port side of the engine.

    c. Remove the blue drain plug from the port side of the thermostat housing (**Figure 41**). If water does not drain from the drain housing, insert a stiff piece of wire into the opening to clear sediment until all water drains from the fitting.

    d. Push in on the tab, then pull the quick connect fitting and drain hose from the fitting on each side of the cylinder block. If water does not drain from the fittings, insert a stiff piece of wire into the openings to clear sediment until all water drains from the fittings.

1B. On Bravo drive models with a standard cooling system, drain all water from the system as follows:

    a. Remove the blue drain plug from the drain housing (**Figure 40**) on the lower front and port side of the engine.

    b. Remove the blue drain plug from the port side of the thermostat housing (**Figure 41**). If water does not drain from the drain housing, insert a stiff piece of wire into the opening to clear sediment until all water drains from the fitting.

    c. Locate the seawater pump on the lower front and starboard side of the engine. Remove the drain plugs (**Figure 47**) from the seawater pump. If water does not drain from the fitting, insert a stiff piece of wire into the opening to clear sediment until all water drains from the fitting.

    d. Push in on the tab, then pull the quick connect fitting and drain hose from the fitting on each side of the cylinder block. If water does not drain from the fittings, insert a stiff piece of wire into the openings to clear sediment until all water drains from the fittings.

    e. Pull the lanyard cord from the lanyard switch to prevent the engine from starting. Turn the ignition key switch to the start position to activate the starter for approximately five seconds. This clears residual water from the seawater pump hoses.

1C. On Alpha and Bravo models without a central point drain system (standard cooling system), drain all water from the cooling system as described in Chapter Five in the main body of the manual. See *Winterizing (All V-6 and V-8 Models)*.

1D. On Alpha and Bravo models with a closed cooling system, drain water from the system as follows:

    a. On multi-port fuel injection (MPI) models, activate the water drain system as described in this section. See *Draining the water (short term storage)*.

    b. Remove the bolt (**Figure 48**), then carefully pull the end cap off the heat exchanger.

    c. On Bravo drive models, locate the seawater pump on the lower front and starboard side of the engine. Remove the drain plugs (**Figure 47**) from the seawater pump. If water does not drain from the fitting, insert a stiff piece of wire into the opening to clear sediment until all water drains from the fitting.

    d. On carburetor-equipped models, remove the blue drain plug from the plastic hose junction on the lower port side of the engine. The junction is located between the side engine mount and the oil pan. If water does not drain from the fitting, insert a stiff piece of wire into the opening to clear sediment until all water drains from the fitting.

    e. On multi-port fuel injection (MPI) models, remove the drain plug from the cool fuel system (**Figure**

**16**

42). If water does not drain from the fitting, insert a stiff piece of wire into the opening to clear sediment until all water drains from the fitting.

   f.  On Bravo drive models, pull the lanyard cord from the lanyard switch to prevent the engine from starting. Turn the ignition key switch to the start position to activate the starter for approximately five seconds. This clears residual water from the seawater pump hoses.

2. On 4.3L and 5.0L models equipped with an inlet hose check valve, remove the blue plastic plug from the check valve. The check valve is located on the front of the engine and just to the port side of the recirculation pump. Insert a stiff piece of wire into the plug opening to clear debris until all water drains from the check valve.

3. Prepare the drive unit for winter storage as described in Chapter Five of the main body of the manual.

**Fitting Out the Engine**

This section describes the procedures to prepare the cooling system for engine operation. Refer to Chapter Five in the main body of the manual for fitting out procedures for other engine system and components.

*3.0L models*

Reconnect the water drain hoses as described under *Fitting Out* in Chapter Five of the main body of the manual.

*4.3L, 5.0L, 5.7L, 350 Mag and MX6.2L models*

1A. On Alpha drive models with a central point drain system (standard cooling system), prepare the cooling system for operation as follows:

   a.  If removed, install the blue drain plug from the drain housing (**Figure 40**) on the lower front and port side of the engine.

   b.  If removed, install the blue drain plug from the port side of the thermostat housing (**Figure 41**). If water does not drain from the drain housing, insert a stiff piece of wire into the opening to clear sediment until all water drains from the fitting.

   c.  If disconnected, push in on the tab, then push the drain hose quick connectors fully onto the fittings on each side of the cylinder block. Release the tab, then tug on the hoses to verify a secure connection.

   d.  Rotate the blue knob (A, **Figure 39**) clockwise until fully seated and none of the red coloring on the shaft is visible (**Figure 49**).

1B. On Bravo drive models with a standard cooling system, prepare the cooling system for operation as follows:

   a.  Install the blue drain plug into the drain housing (**Figure 40**) opening on the lower front and port side of the engine.

   b.  Install the blue drain plug into the opening in the port side of the thermostat housing (**Figure 41**).

   c.  Install the drain plugs (**Figure 47**) into the openings in the seawater pump.

   d.  If disconnected, push in on the tab, then push the drain hose quick connectors fully onto the fittings on each side of the cylinder block. Release the tab, then tug on the hoses to verify a secure connection.

1C. On Alpha and Bravo models without a central point drain system (standard cooling system), prepare the cooling system for operation as described under *Fitting Out* in Chapter Five in the main body of the manual.

1D. On Alpha and Bravo models with a closed cooling system, prepare the cooling system for operation as follows:

   a.  On multi-port fuel injection (MPI) models, lift up on the relief valve ring (**Figure 50**) until the green indicators (**Figure 46**) fully retract into the water drain control valve.

b. If removed, fit the end cap onto the end of the heat exchanger. Align the opening, then thread the bolt (**Figure 48**) into the cap and heat exchanger boss. Tighten the bolt to 54 in.-lb. (6.1 N·m.).

c. On Bravo drive models, if removed, install the drain plugs (**Figure 47**) into the openings in the seawater pump.

d. On carburetor-equipped models, if removed, install the blue drain plug into the opening in the plastic hose junction on the lower port side of the engine. The junction is located between the side engine mount and the oil pan.

e. On multi-port fuel injection (MPI) models, if removed, install the drain plug into its opening in the Cool Fuel System (**Figure 42**).

2. On 4.3L and 5.0L models equipped with an inlet hose check valve, install the blue plastic plug into its opening in the check valve. The check valve is located on the front of the engine and just to the port side of the recirculation pump.

### *496 Mag and 496 Mag HO models*

De-activate the air operated water drain system and replace any removed hose, plug or seal as described under *Fitting Out* in Chapter Five of the main body of the manual.

# CHAPTER SIX

# ADJUSTMENTS

This section describes adjustment procedures unique to 2002-2004 models. Refer to the instructions in Chapter Six of the main body of the manual for adjustment procedures for other models and engine systems not covered in this section.

### Carburetor Adjustment

All carburetor-equipped Mercruiser engines produced after January 1, 2003 use a sealed idle mixture screw (**Figure 51**). These engines are factory certified to meet the California Air Resource Board (CARB) emission standards and the screw must not be adjusted to a setting outside the specification. If the seal is installed on the carburetor, adjust only the idle speed as described in Chapter Six of the main body of the manual.

If the idle mixture screw must be removed for carburetor repair, the tamper-proof screw components must be removed and reinstalled after the repair as described in this supplement.

### Ignition Timing Adjustment

All 2002-2004 4.3L, 5.0L, 350 Mag and MX6.2 models with multi-port electronic fuel injection use a Distributor Ignition (DI) ignition system. The ignition timing is controlled by the engine control module (ECM) and is non-adjustable. For all other models, adjust the ignition timing as described in Chapter Six of the main body of the manual.

**16**

# CHAPTER SEVEN

# ENGINE

Refer to Chapter Seven in the main body of the manual for engine repair on 2002-2004 models.

# CHAPTER EIGHT

# FUEL SYSTEM

This section describes changes to fuel system repair procedures for 2002-2004 models. Changes involve the installation of the sealed idle mixture screw on carburetor-equipped models, the use of composite material flame arrestor on all models except 496 Mag and 496 Mag HO and servicing the multi-port fuel injection system used on 4.3L, 5.0L, 350 Mag and MX6.2L multi-port fuel injection (MPI) models.

**Flame Arrestor Removal, Cleaning, Inspection and Installation**

All 2002-2004 models (except 496 Mag and 496 Mag HO) use a flame arrestor constructed of composite material instead of the metal material used on earlier models.

*CAUTION*
*Use only a soap and water solution to clean the composite material flame arrestor. Solvent may soften the material and compromise the flame arresting feature of the component.*

1. Disconnect the negative battery cable.
2A. On 3.0L, 4.3L, 5.0L and 5.7L carburetor-equipped models, remove the flame arrestor as follows:
   a. Carefully pull the breather tube (A, **Figure 51**) off the flame arrestor tab.
   b. Remove the locknut (B, **Figure 51**), then carefully lift the flame arrestor off the stud. Do not dislodge the washer from the opening in the decal.

2B. On 4.3L, 5.0L, 350 Mag and MX 6.2L (MPI) models, remove the flame arrestor as follows:
   a. Unthread the retainer (**Figure 52**). Then remove the metal and rubber washer from the stud. Lift the plastic cover off the flame arrestor (**Figure 53**).
   b. Carefully pull the breather tube (A, **Figure 51**) off the flame arrestor tab.
   c. Remove the three nuts and cover bracket (**Figure 54**), then lift the flame arrestor off the throttle body studs (**Figure 55**).

3. Use a soap and water solution to thoroughly clean the flame arrestor, then dry with compressed air.

4. Inspect the arrestor screen for torn or damaged surfaces. Replace the flame arrestor if any tear or other defects are evident. Operating the engine with a damaged flare arrestor presents a fire hazard.

5A. On 3.0L, 4.3L, 5.0L and 5.7L carburetor-equipped models, install the flame arrestor as follows:
   a. Make sure the washer is centered over the stud opening in the arrestor. The washer fits into the opening in the decal.
   b. Fit the flame arrestor over the stud. Install the locknut (B, **Figure 51**) and tighten it just enough to prevent the flame arrestor from rotating easily on the stud. Overtightening will damage the flame arrestor or break the stud boss in the carburetor.
   c. Slip the breather tube (A, **Figure 51**) onto the flame arrestor tab. Make sure the breather tube does not interfere with shift cables or linkages. Secure the tube with plastic locking clamps as needed.

5B. On 4.3L, 5.0L, 350 Mag and MX 6.2L (MPI) models, install the flame arrestor as follows:

  a. Guide the openings in the flame arrestor over the throttle body studs. The flame studs are not evenly spaced and the flame arrestor will fit in one direction only.

  b. Fit the retainer over the studs and seat it against the flame arrestor. Install the three nuts (**Figure 54**) and tighten evenly to 108 in.-lb. (12.2 N•m).

  c. Slip the breather tube (A, **Figure 51**) onto the flame arrestor tab. Make sure the breather tube does not interfere with shift cables or linkages. Secure the tube with plastic locking clamps as needed.

  d. Install the plastic flame arrestor cover over the stud. Fit the rubber, then metal, washer over the stud. Secure the cover and washers with the retainer (**Figure 52**). Do not overtighten the retainer. Overtightening will break the retainer.

## Carburetor Repair

All carburetor-equipped Mercruiser engines produced after January 1, 2003 use a sealed idle mixture screw. These engines are factory certified to meet the California Air Resource Board (CARB) emission standards. If the idle mixture screw must be removed for carburetor cleaning, the tamper-proof screw components must be removed and reinstalled during the repair as described in this section. Refer to the carburetor repair procedures in Chapter Eight of the main body of the manual to repair the carburetor. Order the replacement tamper-proof mixture screw kit from a Mercruiser dealership.

### *Removing the tamper-proof idle mixture screw*

Refer to **Figure 56**.

1. Remove the carburetor as described in Chapter Eight of the main body of the manual.

2. Use a small cut-off wheel mounted in a Dremel tool or other similar tool to cut slots in the side of the cup and cap (**Figure 56**). Work carefully to avoid cutting the screw.

3. Carefully pry the cup open at the slots, then pull the cap out of the cup.

4. Unthread the screw and spring. Discard the screw, spring, cap and cup.

5. Repair the carburetor as described in Chapter Eight of the main body of the manual.

**16**

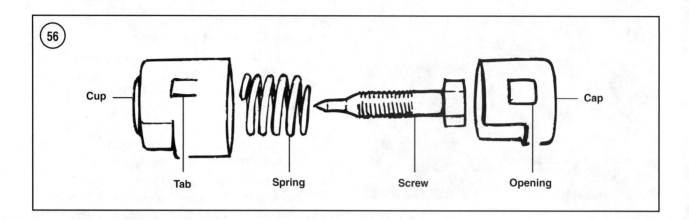

Cup — Tab — Spring — Screw — Opening — Cap

*Installing the tamper-proof idle mixture screw*

1. Fit the spring (**Figure 56**) over the screw. Insert the spring and screw into the open end of the cup. The screw tip must protrude through the small opening in the cup.

2. Thread the screw and spring with cup attached into the carburetor until lightly seated. Do not use excessive force. Otherwise the screw seat in the carburetor will be damaged and the carburetor must be replaced.

3A. On 3.0L and 4.3L models, back the screw out exactly 1 1/4 turns out from the lightly-seated position.

3B. On 5.0L and 5.7L models, back the screw out exactly 1 1/2 turns out from the lightly-seated position.

4. Align the opening in the cap with the tab on the cup (**Figure 56**), then carefully push the cap over the cup. The tab on the cup must snap into the opening in the cap. If not, pull the cap off the cup and repeat the installation.

5. Resume the carburetor repair and install the carburetor as described in Chapter Eight of the main body of the manual.

## Low-Pressure Boost Pump Replacement

The low-pressure boost pump (A, **Figure 57**) is used only on Bravo drive models. The pump mounts onto the lower starboard and front side of the engine.

1. Disconnect the negative battery cable.

2. Loosen the clamp, then carefully pull the fuel supply hose off the inlet fitting (B, **Figure 57**). Plug the disconnected hose to prevent fuel leakage.

3. Carefully unplug the engine wire harness connector from the boost pump harness.

4. Wrap a shop towel around the boost pump fittings to capture spilled fuel. Hold the pump outlet fitting (C, **Figure 57**) with a wrench to prevent pump rotation in the bracket, then fully loosen the outlet fuel line fitting. Clean up any spilled fuel.

5. Pull the outlet fuel line free from the pump fitting. Carefully pull the boost pump and grommets out of the mounting bracket. Work carefully to avoid damaging the grommets.

6. Align the slots in the grommets with the slots in the mounting bracket, then carefully push the pump and grommets into the bracket opening. If necessary, apply a coating of dishwashing soap on the grommets to ease installation.

7. Rotate the pump to position the fuel inlet fitting (B, **Figure 57**) facing downward.

8. Hand-thread the outlet fuel line fitting onto the fuel pump fitting. Hold the fuel pump fitting with a wrench to prevent pump rotation in the bracket, then tighten the outlet fuel line fitting to 15-21 ft.-lb. (20-28.5 N•m).

9. Apply the SAE J1171 MARINE decal to a visible side of the boost pump body.

10. Carefully plug the engine wire harness connector onto the pump harness connector. Route the wiring to prevent contact with moving components. If necessary, secure the wiring with plastic locking clamps.

> *CAUTION*
> *Use a flush test device to supply the engine with cooling water if testing the engine with the boat out of the water. Operation of the starter motor results in operation of the seawater pump. The seawater pump is quickly damaged if operated without adequate cooling water.*

11. Connect the battery cable. Start the engine and immediately check for fuel leaks. Correct any fuel leaks before putting the engine into service.

## Boost Pump Fuel Filter Replacement

The boost pump fuel filter (A, **Figure 58**) is used only on Bravo drive models with a low-pressure boost pump.

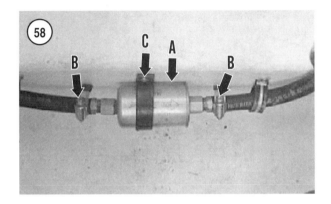

Screws secure the mounting bracket and filter to the boat structure. The fuel supply hose from the boat fuel tank connects to the inlet fitting on the filter. A second hose connect to the outlet fitting on the in-line filter and the inlet fitting on the water-separating fuel filter housing.

Replace the filter as follows:

1. Disconnect the negative battery cable.

2. Loosen the hose clamps (B, **Figure 58**), then carefully pull the fuel supply hoses off the filter fittings. Promptly clean up any spilled fuel.

3. Loosen the clamp screw (C, **Figure 58**), then slip the filter out of the clamp.

4. Engage a wrench onto the filter fitting, then unthread the male barb fittings from the filter inlet and outlet fittings.

5. Clean all thread sealing compound from the removed male barb fittings.

6. Apply a light coating of Loctite 565 PST sealing compound to the threaded section of the male barb fittings. Purchase the sealing compound from an automotive parts store. Do not allow the sealant to enter the fuel passage.

7. Hand-thread the male barb fittings into the fitting openings in the replacement filter.

8. Engage a wrench onto the filter fitting, then tighten the inlet and outlet barb fittings to 14-20 ft.-lb. (19-27 N•m).

9. Carefully guide the filter assembly into the mounting clamp. The ridge side of the filter must face toward the fuel supply hose leading to the engine.

10. Center the filter in the clamp, then tighten the clamp screw (C, **Figure 58**) to 108 in.-lb. (12.2 N•m).

11. Carefully push the fuel supply hoses onto the fuel filter fittings. Position the screw clamps (B, **Figure 58**) over the barb fittings, then tighten the clamps to 30-60 in.-lb. (3.4-6.8 N•m).

*CAUTION*
*Use a flush test device to supply the engine with cooling water if testing the engine with the boat out of the water. Operation of the starter motor results in operation of the seawater pump. The seawater pump is quickly damaged if operated without adequate cooling water.*

12. Connect the battery cable. Start the engine and immediately check for fuel leaks. Correct any fuel leaks before putting the engine into service.

## Throttle Body Removal
### (4.3L, 5.0L, 350 Mag and MX6.2L [MPI] Models)

Refer to **Figure 59**.

1. Disconnect the negative battery cable.

2. Remove the flame arrestor as follows:

   a. Unthread the retainer (**Figure 52**). Then remove the metal and rubber washer from the stud. Lift the plastic cover off the flame arrestor (**Figure 53**).

   b. Carefully pull the breather tube (A, **Figure 51**) off the flame arrestor tab.

   c. Remove the three nuts and cover bracket (**Figure 54**), then lift the flame arrestor off the throttle body studs (**Figure 55**).

3. Disconnect the throttle cable from the throttle arm on the starboard side of the throttle body (6, **Figure 59**).

4. Lift up on the locking tab, then disconnect the engine wire harness connectors from the throttle position sensor (A, **Figure 60**). Loosen the clamp (B, **Figure 60**), then pull the idle air control (IAC) motor hose (C) off the fitting.

5. Remove the three stud bolts (1, **Figure 59**) and washers (2), then lift the throttle body off the intake manifold.

6. Remove the gasket (7, **Figure 59**) from the intake manifold or throttle body. Discard the gasket. Carefully scrape residual gasket material from the mating surfaces. Do not damage the surfaces. Residual gasket material or damaged surfaces will allow air leakage and cause poor idle characteristics and a lean operating condition. Use

**16**

**59** **INTAKE MANIFOLD, FUEL RAIL, INJECTORS AND THROTTLE BODY (4.3L, 5.0L, 5.7L AND MX 6.2L MODELS WITH MULTI-PORT FUEL INJECTION [MPI])**

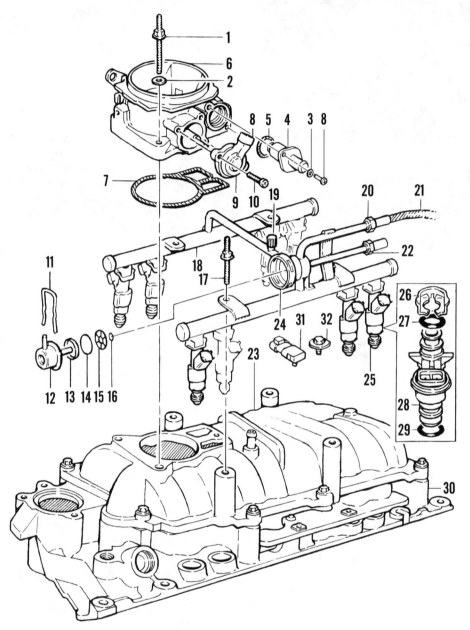

1. Stud bolt
2. Washer
3. Washer
4. Idle air passage hose fitting (leads to idle air control motor [IAC])
5. O-ring
6. Throttle body
7. Gasket
8. Screw

9. Throttle position sensor (TPS)
10. Screw
11. Retainer
12. Fuel pressure regulator
13. Spacer
14. O-ring
15. Filter
16. O-ring
17. Stud bolt

18. Fuel rail
19. High-pressure test port
20. Quick connector
21. Pressure line (from Cool Fuel System)
22. Cap fitting (quick connect type)
23. Upper intake manifold
24. Regulator housing
25. Fuel injector

26. Retaining clip
27. O-ring
28. Fuel injector
29. O-ring
30. Lower intake manifold
31. Manifold air pressure and temperature sensor (MAPT)
32. Retainer and screw

aerosol carburetor cleaner to remove oily deposits or other material from the mating surfaces.

7. Remove the throttle position sensor as described in this supplement.

8. Remove the screws and washers (3 and 8, **Figure 59**), then pull the fitting (4) off the throttle body. Remove the O-ring (5, **Figure 59**) from the fitting or opening in the throttle body. Discard the O-ring.

9. Soak the throttle body in a mild, cool solvent and blow dry with compressed air. Inspect the throttle body for cracked surfaces, looseness of the throttle shaft or plate or other defects. Replace the throttle body if these or other defects are evident.

### Throttle Body Installation
### (4.3L, 5.0L, 350 Mag and MX6.2L [MPI] Models)

Refer to **Figure 59**.

1. Install the throttle position sensor (9, **Figure 59**) as described in this supplement.

2. Install a *new* O-ring (5, **Figure 59**) onto the fitting (4). Guide the fitting into the throttle body opening. Rotate the fitting to align the screw openings, then thread the screws and washers (3 and 8, **Figure 59**) into the fitting and throttle body. Tighten the screws evenly to 24 in.-lb. (2.7 N•m).

3. Fit a *new* gasket (7, **Figure 59**) onto the intake manifold (30). Align the stud bolt and throttle bore openings, then install the throttle body (6, **Figure 59**) onto the intake manifold.

4. Apply a light coating of Loctite 242 (Mercury part No. 92-809821) to the threads of the throttle body mounting studs. Hand-thread the bolts into the throttle body and manifold openings. Tighten the studs evenly to 80 in.-lb. (9.0 N•m).

5. Lift up on the locking tab, then carefully plug the engine wire harness (A, **Figure 60**) onto the throttle position sensor.

6. Connect the idle air control (IAC) motor hose (C, **Figure 60**) onto the throttle body fittings. Securely tighten the hose clamp (B, **Figure 60**).

7. Connect the throttle cable to the throttle arm on the starboard side of the throttle body. Do not overtighten the cable anchor locknuts. The washer must spin freely on the lever and cable anchor studs.

8. Adjust the throttle cable as described in Chapter Five of the main body of the manual.

9. Install the flame arrestor as follows:
   a. Guide the openings in the flame arrestor over the throttle body studs. The flame studs are not evenly spaced and the flame arrestor will fit in one direction only.
   b. Fit the retainer over the studs and seat against the flame arrestor. Install the three nuts (**Figure 54**) and tighten evenly to 108 in.-lb. (12.2 N•m).
   c. Slip the breather tube (A, **Figure 51**) onto the flame arrestor tab. Make sure the breather tube does not interfere with shift cables or linkages. Secure the tube with plastic locking clamps as needed.
   d. Install the plastic flame arrestor cover over the stud. Fit the rubber, then metal, washer over the stud. Secure the cover and washers with the retainer (**Figure 52**). Do not overtighten the retainer. Overtightening will break the retainer.

10. Connect the negative battery cable.

### Fuel Rail and Injectors Removal
### (4.3L, 5.0L, 350 Mag and MX6.2L [MPI] Models)

A suitable pressure gauge with a bleed-off hose (Mercury part No. 91-881833A 2 or equivalent) is required to relieve the system fuel pressure for this procedure. An injector removal tool (Kent-Moore part No. J-43013) is required to remove the injector retainers. Purchase the injector removal tool from a tool supplier. A special separator tool is required to disconnect the push-lock quick connect fuel line from the fuel rail fitting. This type of connector is commonly used in automotive applications and is available from most automotive parts stores. If necessary, purchase the separator tool from a Volvo Penta dealership (Volvo Penta part No. 885384).

Refer to **Figure 59**.

1. Disconnect the negative battery cable.

2. Remove the throttle body as described in this chapter.

3. Remove the idle air control (IAC) motor as described in this chapter.

4. Relieve the fuel pressure as follows:
   a. Locate the fuel pressure test port (19, **Figure 59**) on the fuel rail and remove the cap.

**16**

b. Wrap a suitable shop towel around the test point to capture spilled fuel. Pull up on the locking lever, then *quickly* push the connector of the fuel pressure gauge onto the test point fitting. Release the locking lever to secure the connector.

c. Direct the bleed-off hose of the gauge into a container suitable for holding fuel. Open the valve on the gauge until the pressure is completely relieved. Allow all fuel to drain from the hose.

d. Lift up on the locking lever and pull the connector off the test point. Clean up any spilled fuel and replace the cap. Open the valve and allow all fuel to drain from the bleed-off hose.

e. Inspect the fuel for contamination. If not contaminated, empty the fuel into the boat fuel tank. Dispose of contaminated fuel in an environmentally responsible manner. Contact a marine dealership or local government official for information on the proper disposal of fuel.

5. Mark the cylinder number on each fuel injector harness connector (**Figure 61**). The fuel injectors are located above their respective cylinder. Odd-numbered cylinders are located on the port bank with the No. 1 cylinder at the front, followed by No. 3, 5, then 7 (V-8 models only). Even-numbered cylinders are located on the starboard bank with the No. 2 cylinders at the front, followed by 4, 6, then 8 (V-8 models only). Depress the locking clip, then unplug the connectors.

6. Use compressed air to blow all debris from the intake manifold, fuel rail and quick connector fittings (20, **Figure 59**).

7. Disconnect the pressure line (21, **Figure 59**) from the fuel rail as follows:

a. Place a shop towel under the fuel line fittings to capture spilled fuel.

b. Fit the separator tool over the fuel rail fitting (20, **Figure 59**).

c. Insert the projection on the separator tool into the opening in the female end of the fitting.

d. Push the tool toward the fitting to release the locking tab, then separate the fuel line from the fuel rail.

8. Remove the cap (22, **Figure 59**) from the fuel rail as described in Step 7.

9. Drain residual fuel from the fuel lines into a suitable container.

10. Remove the four nuts that retain the fuel rail (18, **Figure 59**) onto the stud bolts (17), then lift the fuel rail assembly off the intake manifold.

11. Remove the O-rings (29, **Figure 59**) from the injectors or corresponding openings in the intake manifold. Discard the O-rings.

12. Use aerosol solvent to thoroughly clean the intake manifold openings and dry with compressed air. Cover the openings to prevent contamination.

13. Remove the injectors from the fuel rail as follows:

a. Guide the slot in the injector removal tool (Kent-Moore part No. J-43013) between the fuel rail and the retaining clip (26, **Figure 59**). Purchase the removal tool from a tool supplier or automotive parts store.

b. Carefully pry the injector out of the fuel rail. Remove the retaining clip.

c. Remove the O-ring (21, **Figure 59**) from the injector or opening in the fuel rail. Discard the O-rings.

d. Repeat this step for the remaining injectors.

14. Remove the fuel pressure regulator from the rail as follows:

a. Push the regulator (12, **Figure 59**) toward the regulator housing (24), then pull the retainer (11) off the housing.

b. Pull the regulator, spacer, large O-ring, filter and small O-ring (12-16, **Figure 59**) out of the regulator housing. Separate the components. Discard the O-rings.

c. Soak the spacer and filter in mild solvent and dry in compressed air. *Do not* soak the regulator. Solvent may damage the regulator.

d. Inspect the filter for blockage or damaged surfaces. Replace the filter if damaged or if it cannot be completely cleaned with solvent.

e. Inspect the regulator housing for gummy deposits or other contaminants. If contaminated, clean the passages as described in Step 15.

15. Use mild solvent to flush the fuel rail and pressure regulator housing. Do not apply solvent to the injectors or fuel pressure regulator. Solvent may damage these components. Direct pressurized air into the passages to remove solvent and contaminants.

### Fuel Rail and Injectors Installation
### (4.3L, 5.0L, 350 Mag and MX6.2L [MPI] Models)

Refer to **Figure 59**.

1. Install the fuel pressure regulator into the fuel rail as follows:

   a. Fit the spacer (13, **Figure 59**) over the regulator (12) and seat it against the flange. Install a *new* large O-ring (14, **Figure 59**) over the regulator and rest it on the spacer.

   b. Fit the filter (15, **Figure 59**) over the tube on the regulator and rest it against the O-ring and spacer. Fit the *new* small O-ring (16, **Figure 59**) over the tube on the regulator and seat it against the filter.

   c. Apply a light coating of engine oil to the O-rings, regulator, filter and spacer.

   d. Insert the regulator and filter assembly into the housing. Guide the regulator tube into the opening at the rear of the housing, then seat the assembly into the housing.

   e. Push the regulator toward the regulator housing, then insert the retainer (11, **Figure 59**) into the slots in the regulator housing. Make sure the retainer passes through all four slots (two on each side). Release the regulator. Tug on the regulator to verify a secure connection.

2. Install the fuel injectors into the fuel rail as follows:

   a. Fit the retaining clip (26, **Figure 59**) onto the fuel injector with the bent-over edges facing away from the injector.

   b. Lubricate the surfaces with engine oil, then install the *new* O-rings onto the fuel injector. The upper O-ring (27, **Figure 59**) must fit into the groove near the fuel inlet end of the injector and the lower O-ring (29) must fit into the groove near the discharge pintle of the injector.

   c. Rotate the retainer to position the side without the bent-over end in line with the harness connection point on the injector.

   d. Without dislodging or pinching the upper O-ring, insert the injector into the fuel rail opening. *Slowly* rotate the injector to position the harness connector side of the injector facing away from the fuel rail, then seat the injector into the opening. The bent-over edges of the retainer must fit over the fuel rail pod.

   e. Repeat substeps a-d to install the remaining fuel injectors.

3. Remove the covering, then apply a light coating of oil into the injector openings in the intake manifold.

4. Carefully guide all of the injectors into their respective intake manifold openings while installing the fuel rail onto the intake manifold. Verify that all injectors have entered their openings, then guide the fuel rail openings over the stud bolts.

5. Thread the four nuts onto the stud bolt. Tighten the nuts in a crossing pattern to 27 in.-lb. (3.0 N•m).

6. Connect the pressure line (21, **Figure 59**) onto the fuel rail as follows:

   a. Apply a light coating of engine oil to the male end of the quick connect fitting (20, **Figure 59**).

   b. Guide the male end of the fitting into the fuel line fitting. Push the fittings together until they lock. Tug on the pressure line to verify a secure connection. Install the cap (22, **Figure 59**) onto the fuel rail fitting using the same method.

7. Depress the locking clip, then plug the injector harness connectors into their respective injector.

8. Thread the cap onto the fuel pressure test port (19, **Figure 59**).

9. Install the idle air control (IAC) motor as described in the Chapter Ten section of this chapter.

10. Install the throttle body as described in this chapter. Do not install the flame arrestor at this time.

11. Connect the negative battery cable.

> *CAUTION*
> *Use a flush test device to supply the engine with cooling water if testing the engine with the boat out of the water. Operation of the starter motor results in operation of the seawater pump. The seawater pump is quickly damaged if operated without adequate cooling water.*

12. Start the engine and immediately check for fuel leakage at the regulator housing, fuel rail, injectors and all fuel line and hose connections. Stop the engine and correct any leaks before operating the engine.

13. Stop the engine. Route the wiring to prevent interference with throttle linkages and other moving components. Secure the wiring with plastic locking clamps as needed.

14. Install the flame arrestor as follows:

   a. Guide the openings in the flame arrestor over the throttle body studs. The flame studs are not evenly spaced and the flame arrestor will fit in one direction only.

   b. Fit the retainer over the studs and seat it against the flame arrestor. Install the three nuts (**Figure 54**) and tighten them evenly to 108 in.-lb. (12.2 N•m).

   c. Slip the breather tube (A, **Figure 51**) onto the flame arrestor tab. Make sure the breather tube does not interfere with shift cables or linkages. Secure the tube with plastic locking clamps as needed.

**16**

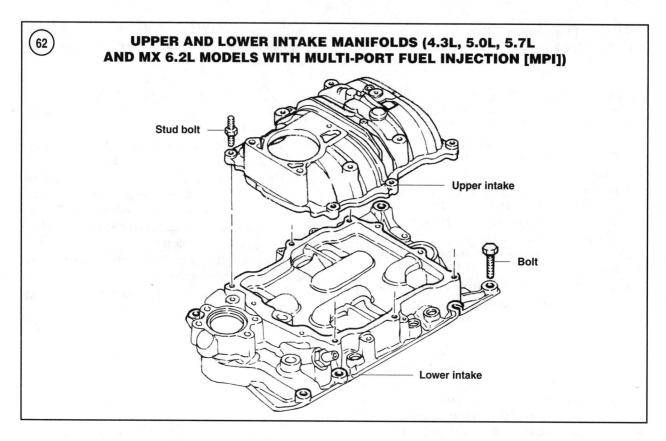

**UPPER AND LOWER INTAKE MANIFOLDS (4.3L, 5.0L, 5.7L AND MX 6.2L MODELS WITH MULTI-PORT FUEL INJECTION [MPI])**

Stud bolt

Upper intake

Bolt

Lower intake

---

d. Install the plastic flame arrestor cover over the stud. Fit the rubber, then metal, washer onto the stud. Secure the cover and washers with the retainer (**Figure 52**). Do not overtighten the retainer. Overtightening will break the retainer.

### Intake Manifold

This section describes removal and installation of the intake manifold used on 2002-2004 4.3L, 5.0L, 350 Mag and MX6.2L MPI (Multi-port fuel injection models). The upper intake manifold mounts onto the lower intake manifold. The lower intake manifold mounts onto the cylinder block and cylinder heads. The upper manifold can be removed without removing the lower manifold from the engine. The lower manifold can be removed from the engine without first removing the upper manifold.

#### Upper intake manifold removal

Refer to **Figure 62**.
1. Disconnect the negative battery cable.
2. Remove the throttle body as described in this chapter.
3. Remove the idle air control (IAC) motor and bracket as described in this supplement.

4. Remove the fuel rail and fuel injectors as described in this chapter.
5. Remove the manifold air pressure and air temperature (MAPT) sensor as described in this supplement.
6. Remove the stud bolts (**Figure 62**), then carefully lift the upper intake manifold off the lower intake manifold.
7. Cover the openings in the lower intake manifold to prevent contamination.
8. Remove the seal from the groove in the upper intake mating surface. Discard the seal.
9. Clean the upper intake manifold with solvent and dry with compressed air.

#### Upper intake manifold installation

Refer to **Figure 62**.
1. Remove the cover from the lower intake manifold. Use aerosol solvent to thoroughly clean the upper intake-to-lower intake mating surfaces.
2. Fit a *new* seal into the groove in the upper intake mating surface.
3. Align the stud bolt openings, then carefully lower the upper intake manifold onto the lower intake. Do not dislodge the seal.

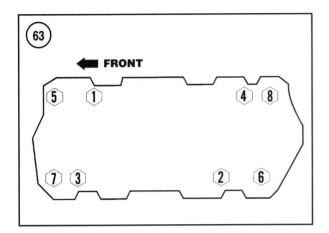

4. Apply a light coating of Loctite 242 (Mercury part No. 92-809821) to the threads of the upper intake manifold mounting studs. Hand-thread the stud bolds into the upper and lower intake manifold threaded openings.

5. Tighten the upper manifold mounting stud bolts in a crossing pattern to 44 in.-lb. (5.0 N•m).

6. Tighten the upper manifold mounting stud bolts in a crossing pattern a final time to 89 in.-lb. (10 N•m).

7. Install the manifold air pressure and air temperature (MAPT) sensor as described in this supplement.

8. Install the fuel rail and fuel injectors as described in this section.

9. Install the idle air control (IAC) motor and bracket as described in this supplement.

10. Install the throttle body as described in this section. Do not install the flame arrestor at this time.

11. Connect the negative battery cable.

*CAUTION*
*Use a flush test device to supply the engine with cooling water if testing the engine with the boat out of the water. Operation of the starter motor results in operation of the sea-water pump. The seawater pump is quickly damaged if operated without adequate cooling water.*

12. Start the engine and immediately check for fuel leak-age at the regulator housing, fuel rail, injectors and all fuel line and hose connections. Stop the engine and correct any leaks before operating the engine.

13. Stop the engine. Route the wiring to prevent interfer-ence with throttle linkages and other moving components. Secure the wiring with plastic locking clamps as needed.

14. Install the flame arrestor as follows:
   a. Guide the openings in the flame arrestor over the throttle body studs. The flame studs are not evenly

spaced and the flame arrestor will fit in one direc-tion only.
   b. Fit the retainer over the studs and seat it against the flame arrestor. Install the three nuts (**Figure 54**) and tighten them evenly to 108 in.-lb. (12.2 N•m).
   c. Slip the breather tube (A, **Figure 51**) onto the flame arrestor tab. Make sure the breather tube does not interfere with shift cables or linkages. Secure the tube with plastic locking clamps as needed.
   d. Install the plastic flame arrestor cover over the stud. Fit the rubber, then metal, washer over the stud. Se-cure the cover and washers with the retainer (**Fig-ure 52**). Do not overtighten the retainer. Overtightening will break the retainer.

*Lower intake manifold removal*

   Refer to **Figure 62**.
1. Disconnect the negative battery cable.
2. On models with a closed cooling system, drain all coolant from the cylinder block as described in Chapter Four of the main body of the manual.
3. Remove the rocker arm covers as described under *Push Rod, Rocker Arm and Rocker Arm Cover* in Chapter Seven in the main body of the manual.
4. Remove the throttle body as described in this chapter.
5. Remove the idle air control (IAC) motor and bracket as described in this supplement.
6. Remove the fuel rail and fuel injectors as described in this section.
7. Remove the manifold air pressure and air temperature (MAPT) sensor as described in this supplement.
8. Remove the ignition coil and coil driver assembly as described in this supplement.
9. Remove the distributor as described in this supplement.
10. Remove the thermostat housing as described in Chapter Nine of the main body of this manual.
11. Note the location of the throttle cable bracket mount-ing studs. The studs must be reinstalled in the correct loca-tion during manifold installation to allow proper positioning of the cable bracket.
12. Remove the nuts, then lift the throttle cable bracket off the manifold studs.
13. Remove any remaining brackets or components that may interfere with manifold removal. Route wiring away from the manifold.
14. Loosen the eight intake manifold bolts in the opposite of the tightening sequence shown in **Figure 63**.
15. Fit a pry bar into the gap at the front of the manifold and carefully pry the manifold from the cylinder heads and block. Remove and discard the gaskets.

 **16**

16. Cover the openings and carefully scrape gasket material and sealant from the mating surfaces.

17. If either manifold must be replaced or the seal is suspected of leaking, remove the upper intake manifold from the lower intake manifold as described in this section.

*CAUTION*
*Never apply muriatic (pool acid) to aluminum intake manifolds or other components that are constructed of aluminum. The acid will rapidly destroy exposed surfaces.*

18. Use clean solvent and a plastic bristle brush to remove carbon and oil residue from the intake manifold surfaces. Dry the manifold and bracket with compressed air. Direct the air into all passages to remove debris and contaminants.

19. Inspect the mating surfaces for deep corrosion pitting, cracks or gouges. Defective mating surfaces will allow water, coolant, air, oil or exhaust leakage.

20. Inspect the water or coolant passages in the manifold for corrosion or mineral deposits buildup. Have a machine shop soak the manifold in a special cleaning vat to remove the deposits. The manifolds used on multi-port injection (MPI) models are constructed of aluminum and some acids will damage the material.

### *Lower intake manifold installation*

Refer to **Figure 62**.

1. If removed, install the upper intake manifold onto the lower intake manifold as described in this section.

2. Apply a small bead of Loctite Ultra-Black RTV (Mercury part No. 92-809826) RTV into the front and rear corners where the cylinder head and cylinder block mate.

3. Apply a 5/32 in. (4 mm) bead of Loctite Ultra-Black RTV (Mercury part No. 92-809826) to the front and rear manifold-to-cylinder block mating surfaces. (**Figure 64**). Extend the bead up onto the intake gaskets approximately 1/2 in. (13 mm).

4. Fit the locating pins into the cylinder head openings while installing the *new* intake manifold gaskets onto the cylinder heads. The *TOP* markings on the gaskets must face up.

5. Use aerosol carburetor cleaner to remove all oily deposits from the manifold mating surfaces. Deposits may prevent the RTV sealant from bonding. Wipe the surfaces dry with a clean shop towel.

6. Carefully lower the manifold into position on the cylinder heads. Do not remove the manifold, or the RTV sealant must be re-applied.

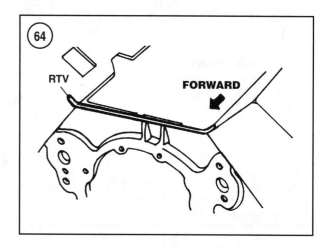

7. Apply a coating of Loctite 242 (Mercury part No. 92-809821) to the threads of the intake manifold mounting bolts and studs. Move the manifold *slightly* if necessary to align the openings, then hand-thread the bolts and studs into the manifold and cylinder head openings.

8. Tighten the intake manifold bolts in three steps as follows:

    a. Tighten the bolts in the sequence shown in **Figure 63** to 27 in.-lb. (3 N•m).

    b. Wait a few minutes, then tighten the bolts in sequence a second time to 106 in.-lb. (12 N•m).

    c. Wait a few minutes, then tighten the bolts in sequence a final time to 132 in.-lb. (15 N•m).

9. Install the throttle cable bracket onto the manifold studs. Tighten the throttle cable bracket nuts to 168 in.-lb. (19 N•m).

10. Install the thermostat housing as described in Chapter Nine of the main body of this manual.

11. Install the distributor as described in this supplement.

12. Install the ignition coil and coil driver assembly as described in this supplement.

13. Install the manifold air pressure and air temperature (MAPT) sensor as described in this supplement.

14. Install the fuel rail and fuel injectors as described in this chapter.

15. Install the idle air control (IAC) motor and bracket as described in this supplement.

16. Install the throttle body as described in this section. Do not install the flame arrestor at this time.

17. Install the rocker arm covers as described under *Push Rod, Rocker Arm and Rocker Arm Cover* in Chapter Seven in the main body of the manual.

18. On models with a closed cooling system, fill the cooling system with the recommended coolant as described in Chapter Four of the main body of the manual.

19. Connect the negative battery cable.

*CAUTION*
*Use a flush test device to supply the engine with cooling water if testing the engine with the boat out of the water. Operation of the starter motor results in operation of the sea-water pump. The seawater pump is quickly damaged if operated without adequate cooling water.*

20. Start the engine and immediately check for fuel, water or coolant leakage. Stop the engine and correct any leaks before operating the engine.

21. Stop the engine. Route the wiring to prevent interference with throttle linkages and other moving components. Secure the wiring with plastic locking clamps as needed.

22. Install the flame arrestor as follows:

a. Guide the openings in the flame arrestor over the throttle body studs. The flame studs are not evenly spaced and the flame arrestor will fit in one direction only.

b. Fit the retainer over the studs and seat it against the flame arrestor. Install the three nuts (**Figure 54**) and tighten them evenly to 108 in.-lb. (12.2 N•m).

c. Slip the breather tube (A, **Figure 51**) onto the flame arrestor tab. Make sure the breather tube does not interfere with shift cables or linkages. Secure the tube with plastic locking clamps as needed.

d. Install the plastic flame arrestor cover over the stud. Fit the rubber, then metal, washer over the stud. Secure the cover and washers with the retainer (**Figure 52**). Do not overtighten the retainer. Overtightening will break the retainer.

# CHAPTER NINE

# EXHAUST AND COOLING SYSTEM

This section describes repair procedures for exhaust and cooling system components unique to 2002-2004 models. Refer to Chapter Nine in the main body of the manual for service procedures for models and components not covered in this section.

Due to the introduction of the dry-joint exhaust system and central point water drain system, hose routing and connection points for 2002-2004 4.3L, 5.0L, 350 Mag and MX6.2L models are considerably different from 1998-2001 models. Refer to **Figures 65-76** to assist with hose routing and connection points when servicing the exhaust and cooling system.

## Dry Joint Exhaust Elbow

For improved durability, a dry joint exhaust elbow (**Figure 77**) to manifold sealing arrangement is used on all 2002-2004 V-6 and V-8 models. This system eliminates the common sealing surface separating the water and exhaust passages that is used on the earlier design. The dry joint elbow can be identified by the distinct water passage boss (**Figure 78**) that is visible at the front and rear of the elbow. Also, models using a dry-joint system use a thermostat housing with a T-fitting (**Figure 79**) to supply seawater or coolant (closed cooling models) to the passage.

Riser kits are available in both 3 in. (76 mm) and 6 in. (152 mm) heights to provide increased elbow-to-water line height when required.

The gaskets between the manifold and elbow or between the riser and manifold or elbow utilize a raised edge in the exhaust passage to help prevent reverse exhaust pressure waves that occur under some conditions from pulling cooling water back into the exhaust passages. The raised edge must face up or toward the exhaust elbow.

*CAUTION*
*The gaskets that fit between the exhaust manifold and elbow or rise and elbow or manifold are available with blocked-off cooling passages, restricted cooling passages and full open cooling passages. The gasket used in each location is determined by the type of cooling system on the engine, exhaust configuration (risers) and engine serial number. A multitude of combinations are used on 2002-2004 models. Always refer to the parts listing for the proper serial number, type of cooling system and exhaust configuration when ordering replacement gaskets. Using the wrong gasket or orienting the gasket improperly can adversely affect the cooling system and cause*

**16**

(65) **STANDARD COOLING SYSTEM WITHOUT RISERS (MANUAL DRAIN) (4.3L, 5.0L AND 5.7L CARBURETOR EQUIPPED MODELS [SERIAL NO. OM600000-ON])**

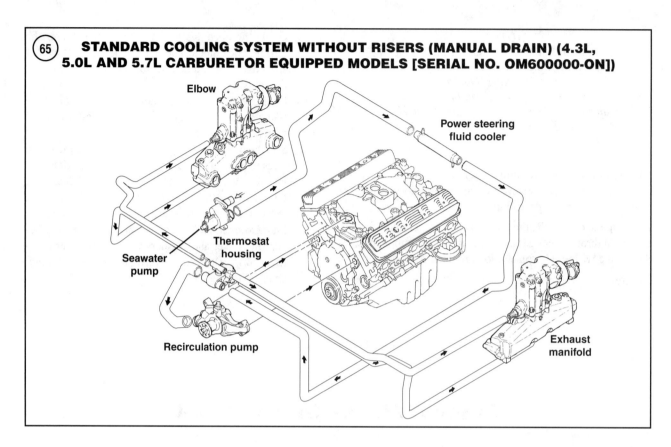

(66) **STANDARD COOLING SYSTEM WITH RISERS (MANUAL DRAIN) (4.3L, 5.0L AND 5.7L CARBURETOR EQUIPPED MODELS [SERIAL NO. OM600000-ON])**

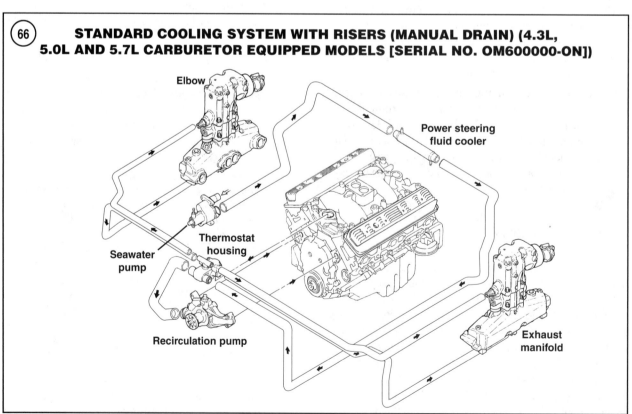

**STANDARD COOLING SYSTEM (ALPHA DRIVE MODELS WITH KNOB ACTIVATED CENTRAL POINT DRAIN SYSTEM) (4.3L, 5.0L AND 5.7L MPI (MULTI-PORT FUEL INJECTION) MODELS [SERIAL NO. OM300000-ON])**

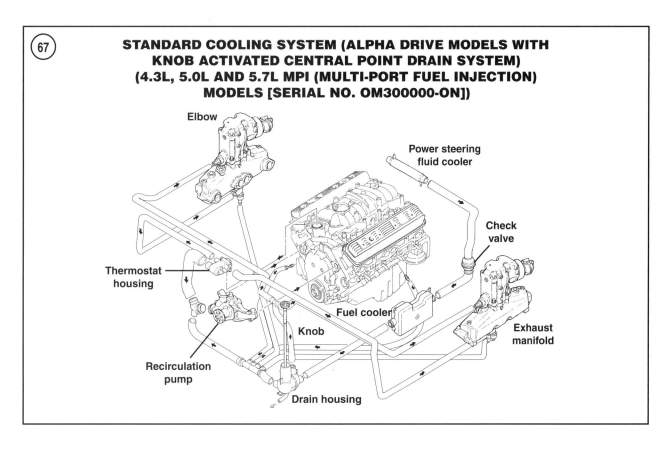

**STANDARD COOLING SYSTEM (ALPHA DRIVE MODELS WITHOUT A CENTRAL POINT DRAIN) (4.3L, 5.0L AND 5.7L MPI (MULTI-PORT FUEL INJECTION) MODELS [SERIAL NO. OM300000-ON])**

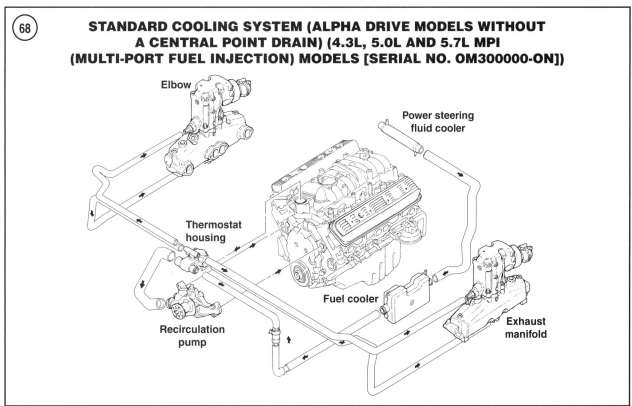

**16**

**69** STANDARD COOLING SYSTEM WITH EXHAUST RISERS
(WITH CENTRAL POINT DRAIN SYSTEM) (4.3L, 5.0L, 5.7L AND MX6.2 MPI
(MULTI-PORT FUEL INJECTION) MODELS [SERIAL NO. OM300000-OM614999])

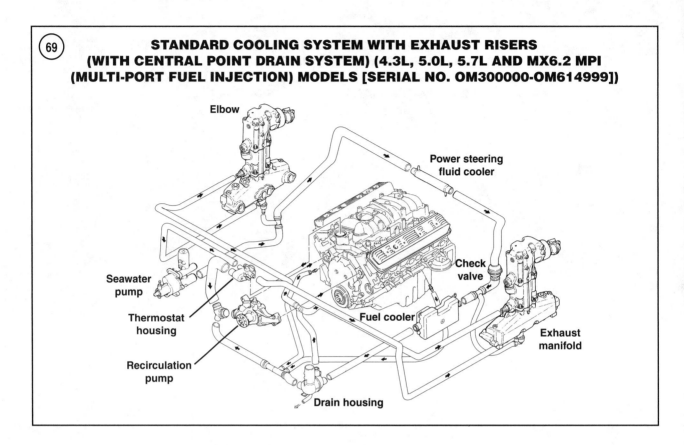

**70** STANDARD COOLING SYSTEM WITH EXHAUST RISERS
(WITH CENTRAL POINT DRAIN SYSTEM) (4.3L, 5.0L, 5.7L AND MX6.2 MPI
(MULTI-PORT FUEL INJECTION) MODELS [SERIAL NO. OM615000-ON])

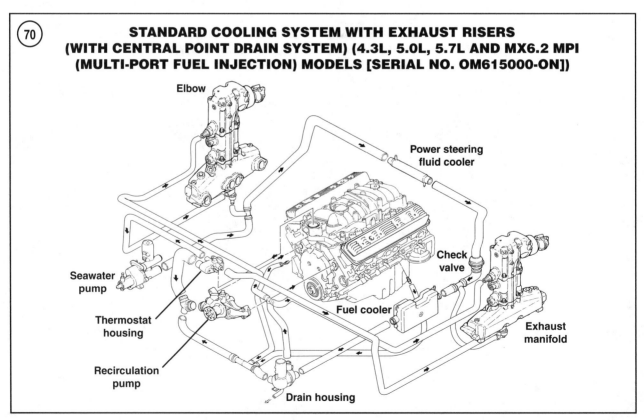

**71** CLOSED COOLING SYSTEM (4.3L, 5.0L AND 5.7L
CARBURETOR-EQUIPPED MODELS [SERIAL NO. OM300000- OM599999])

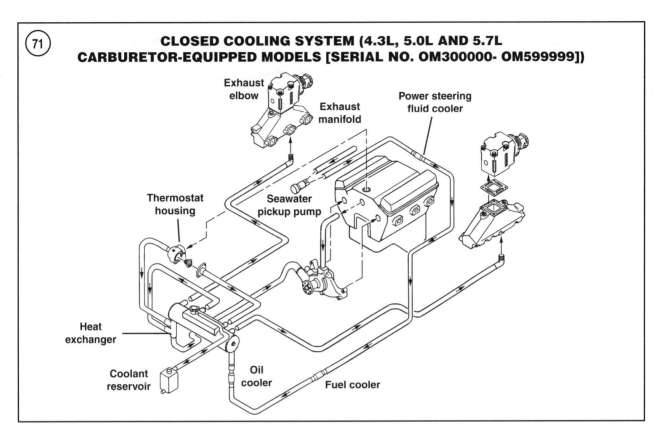

**72** CLOSED COOLING SYSTEM (4.3L, 5.0L AND 5.7L
CARBURETOR-EQUIPPED MODELS [SERIAL NO. OM600000-ON])

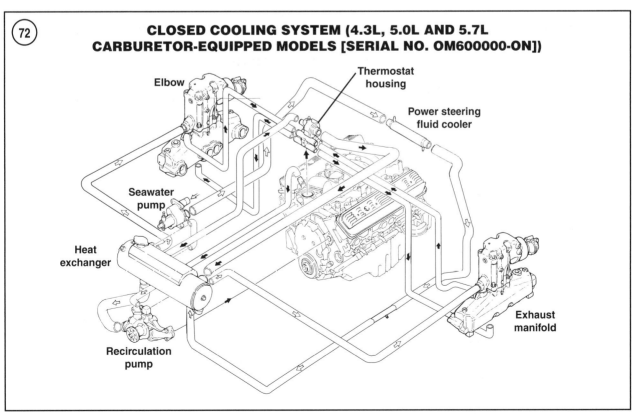

16

**73** **CLOSED COOLING SYSTEM WITHOUT EXHAUST RISERS (4.3L, 5.0L, 5.7L AND MX6.2 MPI (MULTI-PORT FUEL INJECTION) MODELS [SERIAL NO. OM300000-OM599999])**

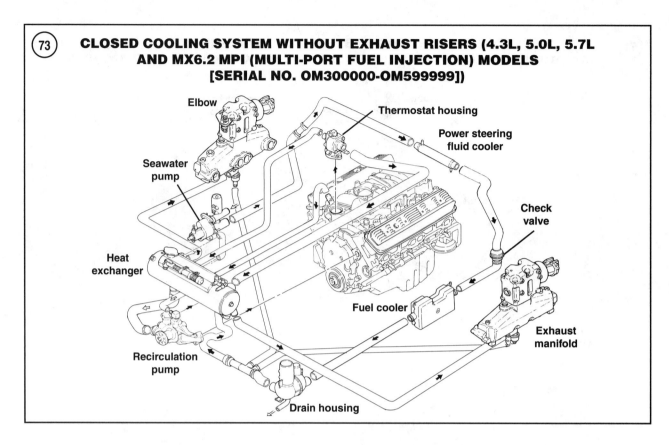

**74** **CLOSED COOLING SYSTEM WITHOUT EXHAUST RISERS (4.3L, 5.0L, 5.7L AND MX6.2 MPI (MULTI-PORT FUEL INJECTION) MODELS [SERIAL NO. OM600000-ON])**

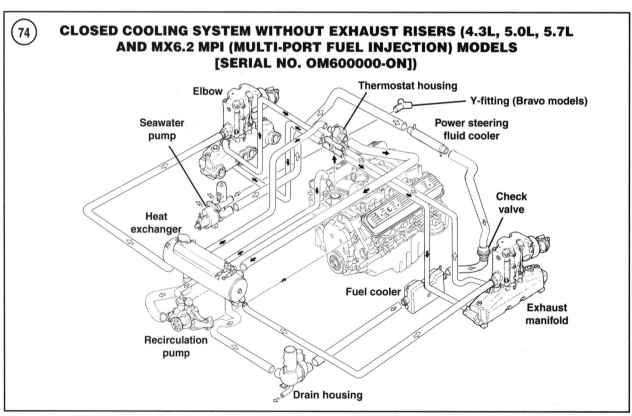

**75**

### CLOSED COOLING SYSTEM WITH EXHAUST RISERS (4.3L, 5.0L, 5.7L AND MX6.2 MPI (MULTI-PORT FUEL INJECTION) MODELS [SERIAL NO. OM600000-OM614999])

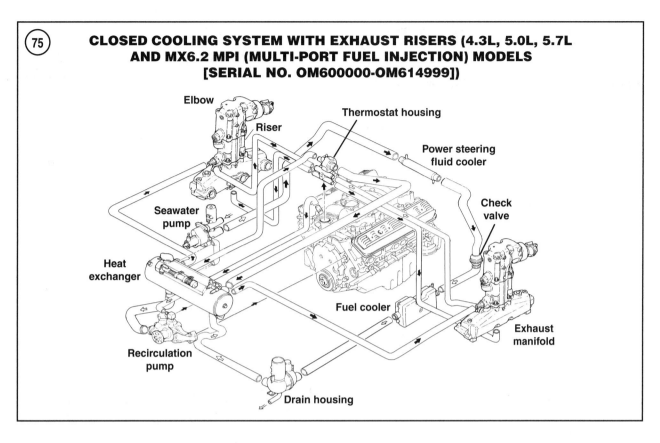

**76**

### CLOSED COOLING SYSTEM WITH EXHAUST RISERS (4.3L, 5.0L, 5.7L AND MX6.2 MPI (MULTI-PORT FUEL INJECTION) MODELS [SERIAL NO. OM615000-ON])

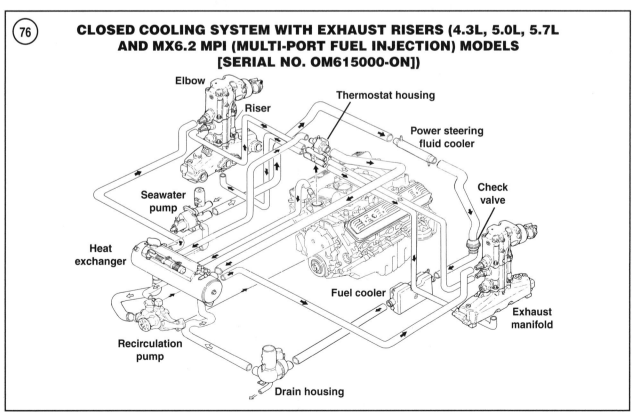

**16**

*overheating or overcooling that may damage the engine.*

## Exhaust Elbow, Riser and Manifold Disassembly

The exhaust elbow and risers can be removed and installed without removing the manifold from the engine. Refer to **Figures 65-76** to assist with hose routing and connection points.

1. Disconnect the negative battery cable.

2A. On models with a standard cooling system, drain all water from the cooling system as described in this supplement.

2B. On models with a closed cooling system, drain all coolant from the cylinder block as described in Chapter Four of the main body of the manual.

3. On the starboard side elbow, remove the shift plate assembly from the elbow. Do not remove the shift cables from the linkages for this procedure.

4A. On the port side elbow on carburetor-equipped models, remove the ignition module as described in Chapter Ten of the main body of the manual.

4B. On the port side elbow on multi-port fuel injection (MPI) models, remove the engine control module (ECM) as described in this supplement.

5. Loosen the four large hose clamps that connect the exhaust system to the exhaust elbow (3, **Figure 77**).

6. Loosen the clamp, then carefully pull the hose off the elbow or riser fitting.

7. Loosen the four long bolts (1, **Figure 77**), then pull the bolts and washers from the elbow. Make sure all washers are accounted for. If lost, they may fall into the exhaust passages during elbow or riser removal. Replacement and later models use washer-headed bolts that do not require a washer.

8. Carefully lift the elbow (3, **Figure 77**) off the manifold (7) or riser (11 or 13). Note the orientation of the gasket (5, **Figure 77**), then remove it from the elbow or riser. The gasket may have fully open, fully closed or restricted cooling water passages in the gasket. Many models use a fully open passage at one end and a restricted passage on the other. If so equipped, note the orientation of the restricted passage before removal. Remove the gasket from the elbow, manifold or riser surface. Tag the gasket, indicating its mounting location and forward orientation.

9. If equipped with exhaust risers, remove the riser from the manifold. Note the orientation of the gasket (9 or 15, **Figure 77**), then remove it from the manifold or riser. The gasket may have fully open, fully closed or restricted cooling water passages in the gasket. Many models use a fully open passage at one end and a restricted passage on the other. If so equipped, note the orientation of the re-

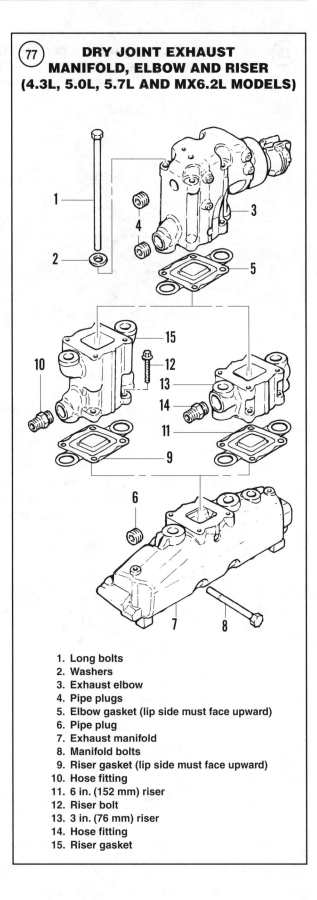

**(77) DRY JOINT EXHAUST MANIFOLD, ELBOW AND RISER (4.3L, 5.0L, 5.7L AND MX6.2L MODELS)**

1. Long bolts
2. Washers
3. Exhaust elbow
4. Pipe plugs
5. Elbow gasket (lip side must face upward)
6. Pipe plug
7. Exhaust manifold
8. Manifold bolts
9. Riser gasket (lip side must face upward)
10. Hose fitting
11. 6 in. (152 mm) riser
12. Riser bolt
13. 3 in. (76 mm) riser
14. Hose fitting
15. Riser gasket

stricted passage before removal. Remove the gasket from the manifold or riser surface. Tag the gasket, indicating its mounting location and forward orientation.

10. Thoroughly clean the elbow, riser (if so equipped) and exhaust manifold mating surfaces. Inspect the mating surfaces for defects as described in Chapter Nine of the main body of the manual.

## Exhaust Elbow, Riser and Manifold Assembly

Refer to **Figure 77**.

1. Apply a light coating of Perfect Seal (Mercury part No. 92-34227-1) to the exhaust riser or elbow mating surface on the exhaust manifold.

2. Align the bolt, water and exhaust openings, then install the *new* gasket onto the manifold. Make sure the proper gasket part number is used and the water passages are oriented as noted prior to removing the original gasket. The raised edge must face upward, or away from the exhaust manifold (**Figure 80**).

3. If equipped with exhaust risers, apply a light coating of Perfect Seal (Mercury part No. 92-34227-1) to the riser surface that mates with the exhaust manifold. Align the bolt, water and exhaust openings, then install the riser onto the gasket and manifold.

4. If equipped with risers, apply a light coating of Perfect Seal (Mercury part No. 92-34227-1) to the riser surface that mates with the exhaust elbow. Align the bolt, water and exhaust openings, then install the *new* gasket onto the riser. Make sure the proper gasket part number is used and the water passages are oriented as noted prior to removing the original gasket. The raised edge must face upward, or away from the exhaust manifold (**Figure 80**).

5. Apply a light coating of Perfect Seal (Mercury part No. 92-34227-1) to the exhaust elbow surface that mates to the exhaust manifold or riser.

6. Carefully slip the exhaust outlet end of the elbow into the exhaust system bellows or exhaust tube. Do not tighten the large hose clamps at this time. Work carefully to avoid dislodging or damaging the riser and/or gaskets.

7. Align the bolt, water and exhaust openings, then carefully lower the elbow onto the riser or manifold.

8. Apply a light coating of Perfect Seal (Mercury part No. 92-34227-1) to the threads of the bolts (1, **Figure 77**). Move the elbow and riser (if so equipped) as needed to align the bolt opening, then hand-thread the bolts into the elbow, riser and manifold.

9. Tighten the four bolts in a crossing pattern to 84 in.-lb. (9.5 N•m). Verify proper alignment of the elbow, riser (if so equipped) and manifold. Loosen the bolts as needed to realign the components. Tighten the bolts a final time in a crossing pattern to 45 ft.-lb. (61 N•m). The gaskets must be replaced each time the bolts are loosened after the final tightening sequence.

10. Install the hose onto the elbow and riser fitting. Position the screw clamp over the fitting, then securely tighten.

11. Position the four large screw hose clamps over their respective clamping locations on the exhaust elbow and connecting exhaust system components. Securely tighten the clamps.

12. On the starboard side elbow, install the shift plate assembly onto the elbow. Securely tighten the fasteners.

**16**

13A. On the port side elbow on carburetor-equipped models, install the ignition module as described in Chapter Ten of the main body of the manual.

13B. On the port side elbow on multi-port fuel injection (MPI) models, install the engine control module (ECM) as described in this supplement.

14. On models with a closed cooling system, fill the cooling system with the recommended coolant as described in Chapter Four of the main body of the manual.

15. Connect the negative battery cable.

*CAUTION*
*Use a flush test device to supply the engine with cooling water if testing the engine with the boat out of the water. Operation of the starter motor results in operation of the sea-water pump. The seawater pump is quickly damaged if operated without adequate cooling water.*

16. Start the engine and immediately check for exhaust, water or coolant leakage. Stop the engine and correct any leaks before operating the engine.

**Water Inlet Hose Check Valve**

The water inlet hose check valve (**Figure 81**) is used on 4.3L and 5.0L models. The valve mounts in the water hose connecting the seawater pump to the thermostat housing. The check valve prevents water in the cylinder block from draining back into the fuel cooler portion of the cool fuel system after stopping the engine. If heated water is allowed to drain back into the fuel cooler, it may heat the fuel and form vapor in the fuel injection system. Vapor in the system can cause hard starting or stalling under certain conditions. These symptoms typically occur after the engine reaches full operating temperature and is then stopped for 15-30 minutes.

Two different types of check valves are used. On earlier models, the check valve is blue and mounts onto the front of the engine, just to the port side of the recirculation pump. This type of check valve is equipped with a water drain plug that must be removed along with the other drain plugs before exposing the engine to freezing temperatures. Refer to Chapter Five in the main body to locate the other engine drain plugs. Later models use a black or gray check valve that is mounted on the rear and port side of the engine (**Figure 81**). This type of check valve is automatically drained by the central point drain system and does not contain a drain plug.

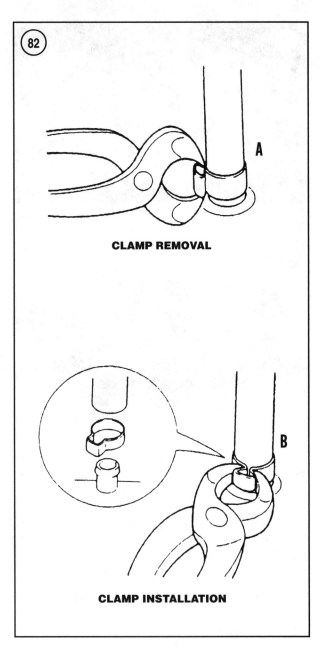

**CLAMP REMOVAL**

**CLAMP INSTALLATION**

### *Check valve replacement (early style blue valve)*

Refer to **Figures 65-76** to assist with cooling water hose routing and connection points.

1. Disconnect the negative battery cable.
2. Remove the blue plastic drain plug and allow all water to drain from the valve.
3. Loosen the hose clamps, then carefully pull the valve out of the water hoses.
4. Insert the fittings of the replacement valve into the water hoses. The drain plug end of the valve must face downward. Otherwise, the valve will not allow water flow into the engine, resulting in overheating and possible engine damage.
5. Twist the valve in the hoses to position the drain plug facing forward. Securely tighten the hose clamps.
6. Install the drain plug into the valve.
7. Connect the negative battery cable.

*CAUTION*
*Use a flush test device to supply the engine with cooling water if testing the engine with the boat out of the water. Operation of the starter motor results in operation of the seawater pump. The seawater pump is quickly damaged if operated without adequate cooling water.*

8. Start the engine and immediately check for water leakage. Stop the engine and correct any leaks before operating the engine.

### *Check valve replacement (later style gray valve)*

Refer to **Figures 65-76** to assist with cooling water hose routing and connection points.

1. Disconnect the negative battery cable.
2. Drain all water from the system as described in the Chapter Five section of this chapter.

3. Use sharp cutters to cut the clamps (**Figure 82**) that secure the hoses onto the valve. Pull the valve out of the hoses. Note that one of the hoses is a larger diameter than the other. Discard the clamps.
4. Note the diameter of the valve fittings and connecting water hoses before attempting to install the valve. One of the hoses and valve fitting is larger than the other hose and fitting.
5. Guide a *new* crimp clamp over the larger diameter hose. Insert the larger fitting end of the valve into the larger diameter hose.
6. Guide a *new* crimp clamp over the smaller diameter hose. Insert the smaller fitting end of the valve fully into the smaller diameter hose.
7. Position the clamps over the hose and fittings. Use cutters to squeeze the squared end of the clamp as shown in **Figure 82**. Do not use excessive force; otherwise, the hoses or fittings may become damaged. Tug on the hoses to verify a secure connection.
8. Connect the negative battery cable.

*CAUTION*
*Use a flush test device to supply the engine with cooling water if testing the engine with the boat out of the water. Operation of the starter motor results in operation of the seawater pump. The seawater pump is quickly damaged if operated without adequate cooling water.*

9. Start the engine and immediately check for water leakage. Stop the engine and correct any leaks before operating the engine.

### Water Drain Housing

The water drain housing (**Figure 83**) is located on the lower front and port side of the engine. Although numerous housing designs are used, replacement procedures are very similar.

Refer to **Figures 65-76** to assist with cooling water hose routing and connection points.

1. Disconnect the negative battery cable.
2. Drain all water from the system as described in the Chapter Five section of this chapter.
3. Note the connection point and routing of all hoses connecting onto the housing, then loosen the clamp and disconnect the hoses.
4. On models with a knob-activated drain system, remove the nut securing the upper knob shaft support bracket onto the cylinder block stud.
5. Remove the bolts securing the water drain housing onto the cylinder block, then remove the housing.

**16**

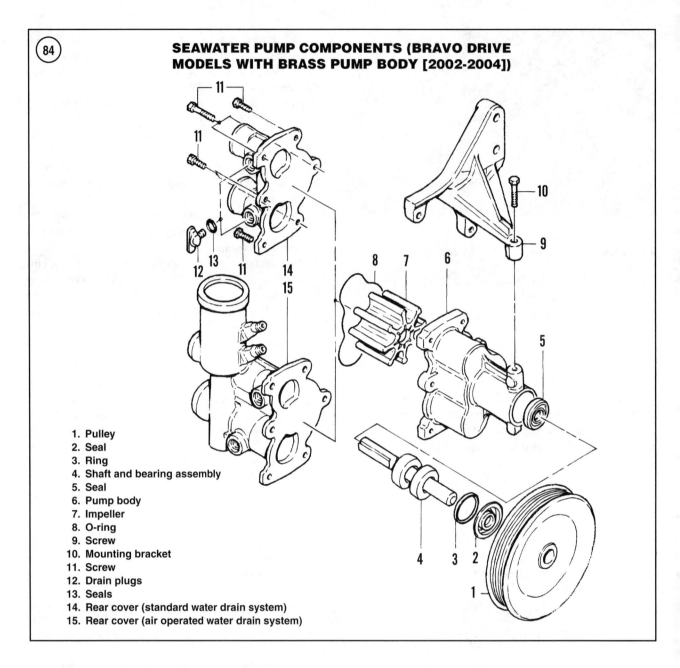

**84**

**SEAWATER PUMP COMPONENTS (BRAVO DRIVE MODELS WITH BRASS PUMP BODY [2002-2004])**

1. Pulley
2. Seal
3. Ring
4. Shaft and bearing assembly
5. Seal
6. Pump body
7. Impeller
8. O-ring
9. Screw
10. Mounting bracket
11. Screw
12. Drain plugs
13. Seals
14. Rear cover (standard water drain system)
15. Rear cover (air operated water drain system)

6. Remove the three screws, then pull the drain housing off the mounting bracket.

7. On models with a knob-activated drain system, rotate the knob fully counterclockwise, then pull the knob and shaft straight out of the water drain housing.

8. Fit the replacement water drain housing onto the mounting bracket. Thread the three screws into the housing and bracket. Tighten the screws evenly to 120 in.-lb. (13.6 N•m).

9. On models with a knob-activated drain system, insert the knob shaft straight into the replacement hous-

ing. Then rotate the knob and shaft clockwise until fully seated.

10. Fit the replacement water drain housing onto the cylinder block. Align the bolt openings, then thread the mounting bolts into the housing bracket and cylinder block. Do not tighten the bolts at this time.

11. On models with a knob-activated drain system, fit the upper knob shaft support bracket over the mounting stud. Then thread the nut onto the stud. Do not tighten the nut at this time.

12. Tighten the drain housing bracket-to-cylinder block bolt to 28 ft.-lb. (38 N•m).

13. On models with a knob-activated drain system, tighten the upper knob shaft support bracket nut to 28 ft.-lb. (38 N•m).

14. Connect all hoses to the water drain housing and secure with clamps. Route the hoses to prevent contact with belts, pulleys or other moving components. Secure the hoses with plastic locking clamps as needed.

15. Install any plug or hose removed for draining purposes.

16. Connect the negative battery cable.

*CAUTION*
*Use a flush test device to supply the engine with cooling water if testing the engine with the boat out of the water. Operation of the starter motor results in operation of the seawater pump. The seawater pump is quickly damaged if operated without adequate cooling water.*

17. Start the engine and immediately check for water leakage. Stop the engine and correct any leaks before operating the engine.

## Brass Seawater Pump Repair

All 2002-2004 Bravo drive models use a brass belt driven seawater pump in place of the plastic water pump used on earlier models. The seawater pump is located on the lower starboard and front of the engine.

Refer to **Figures 65-76** to assist with hose routing and connection points.

### *Seawater pump removal and installation*

Refer to **Figure 84**.
1. Disconnect the negative battery cable.
2. Drain water from the cooling system as described in the Chapter Five section of this chapter.
3. Loosen the hose clamps, then pull the inlet and outlet hoses off the rear cover (14 or 15, **Figure 84**).
4. On models with an air-activated water drain system, note the connection points, then disconnect the air hoses from the rear cover fittings.
5. Loosen the locknut on the belt tension adjusting pulley (**Figure 85**). Move the pulley downward to relieve the belt tension, then slip the belt off the water pump pulley.
6. Remove the bolt and nut that retain the pump assembly onto the cylinder block, then remove the pump.
7. If necessary, replace the impeller as described in this section.
8. Hold the pump in position on the cylinder block, then thread the fasteners into the block and onto the mounting stud. Tighten the bolt and nut to 30 ft.-lb. (40.7 N•m).
9. Locate the seawater inlet hose. The inlet hose leads to the transom assembly and drive unit. Connect the inlet hose onto the rear cover fitting marked LH OUT. Position the screw clamp over the hose and fitting. Securely tighten the clamp.
10. Locate the seawater outlet hose. The outlet hose leads to the thermostat housing (standard cooling system) or heat exchanger (closed cooling system). Connect the inlet hose onto the rear cover fitting marked RH OUT. Position the screw type clamp over the hose and fitting. Securely tighten the clamp.
11. On models with an air-activated water drain system, connect the air hoses to the rear cover fittings.
12. Replace any plug removed to drain water or deactivate the single point drain system.
13. Fit the belt around the pulleys. Engage a 5/16 in. wrench onto the center shaft of the belt tension adjusting pulley. Rotate the center shaft to raise the pulley until the belt tension allows the belt to deflect approximately 1/4-1/2 in. (6.5-13 mm) when pressed with a thumb at a point halfway between two pulleys (**Figure 86**). Hold the

**16**

center shaft in position while securely tightening the locknut (**Figure 85**).

14. Connect the negative battery cable.

*CAUTION*
*Use a flush test device to supply the engine with cooling water if testing the engine with the boat out of the water. Operation of the starter motor results in operation of the sea-water pump. The seawater pump is quickly damaged if operated without adequate cooling water.*

15. Start the engine and immediately check for water leakage and proper water flow from the exhaust system. Stop the engine and correct any leaks or cause of inadequate water flow before operating the engine.

*Seawater pump impeller replacement*

Refer to **Figure 84**.
1. Remove the seawater pump as described in this chapter. Place the pump on a clean work surface with the pulley side facing down.
2. Remove the six bolts (**Figure 87**) that secure the mounting bracket and rear cover onto the pump body.
3. Remove the single bolt (**Figure 88**) that secures the mounting bracket onto the side of the pump body, then lift the mounting bracket off the pump body (**Figure 89**).
4. Lift the rear cover off the pump body (**Figure 90**).
5. Remove the O-ring from the pump body groove (**Figure 91**). Inspect the O-ring for torn, deteriorated or flattened surfaces. Replace the O-ring if these or other defects are evident.
6. Remove the used impeller from the pump body. If necessary, carefully pry the impeller out. Do not exert force against the slotted water passages in the body. The pry tool may bend or break the passages. Discard the used impeller. Do not reuse the impeller unless a replacement is not available and the used impeller is found to be in excellent condition. Never use an impeller with worn, torn, brittle or distorted vanes.
7. Inspect the impeller contact surfaces in the pump body and on the rear cover. Replace the body or rear cover if deeply grooved or corrosion pitted.
8. Spin the pulley to check for binding or looseness. Have a Mercruiser dealership replace the bearings, seals and shaft if binding or looseness are evident. Special equipment is required to remove the pulley and other components. The cost of the equipment usually exceeds the cost of having a qualified technician perform the repair.

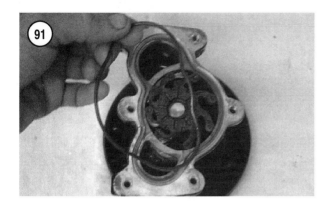

9. Apply a light coating of Quicksilver 2-4-C grease (Mercury part No. 92-802859A 1) to the impeller contact surfaces in the pump body and on the rear cover.

10. Place the *new* impeller onto the pump body (**Figure 92**) with the bore in the impeller aligned with the pump shaft.

11. Rotate the impeller counterclockwise, as viewed from the rear of the pump, while carefully pushing the impeller into the pump body. The counterclockwise rotation is necessary to curl the impeller vanes in the clockwise direction.

12. Continue rotating and pushing until the impeller enters the body and engages the pump shaft. Then rotate the pulley clockwise, as viewed from the pulley end, while pushing until the impeller is fully seated in the body.

13. Install the O-ring into the pump body groove (**Figure 91**). If necessary, use a light coating of grease to hold the O-ring in position.

14. Fit the rear cover onto the pump body (**Figure 90**). Move the cover slightly to align the cover screws. Do not dislodge the O-ring.

15. Fit the mounting bracket onto the pump body and rear cover (**Figure 89**). Align the bracket, cover and body screw openings.

16. Apply a light coating of Loctite 242 (Mercury part No. 92-809821) to the threads of the seven bracket and cover screws, then hand-thread the six screws into the mounting bracket, cover and body (**Figure 87**).

17. Align the opening, then hand-thread the single bolt into the mounting bracket and side of the pump body (**Figure 88**).

18. Tighten the seven bolts evenly to 88 in.-lb. (9.9 N•m).

19. Install the seawater pump as described in this section.

## CHAPTER TEN

# ELECTRICAL AND IGNITION SYSTEM

**16**

This section describes removal and repair of the electrical components used on 2002-2004 4.3L, 5.0L, 350 Mag and MX6.2L MPI (Multi-Port fuel Injection) models.

### Battery Requirements

All 4.3L, 5.0L and 350 Mag MPI models require a battery with a minimum of 750 CCA, 950 MCA and 180 Ah rating. This updated requirement also applies to earlier (1993-2001) models.

### Manifold Air Pressure and Air Temperature (MAPT) Sensor

This section describes removal and installation of the manifold air pressure and air temperature (MAPT) sensor.

Both sensors are incorporated into a single component. The MAPT is located on the top of the intake manifold and directly below the idle air control (IAC) motor.

Refer to **Figure 59**.

1. Disconnect the negative battery cable.
2. Remove the flame arrestor as follows:
   a. Unthread the retainer (**Figure 52**), then remove the metal and rubber washers from the stud. Lift the plastic cover off the flame arrestor (**Figure 53**).
   b. Carefully pull the breather tube (A, **Figure 51**) off the flame arrestor tab.
   c. Remove the three nuts and cover bracket (**Figure 54**), then lift the flame arrestor off the throttle body studs (**Figure 55**).
3. Use compressed air to remove any dust or loose debris from intake manifold surfaces.
4. Lift up on the locking tab, then carefully unplug the engine harness connector from the MAPT (31, **Figure 59**).
5. Remove the retainer and screw (32, **Figure 59**), then carefully lift the MAPT out of the intake manifold opening.
6. Carefully remove any debris from the sensor opening in the manifold. Clean the area with an aerosol solvent.
7. Remove the rubber seal from the nipple of the sensor. Discard the seal.
8. Install a *new* rubber seal over the nipple on the bottom of the replacement sensor. Apply a drop of engine oil to the seal to ease installation.
9. Guide the nipple of the sensor into the manifold opening. Make sure the seal is not dislodged or torn.
10. Seat the sensor onto the intake and rotate it slightly to align the harness connecting facing starboard.
11. Thread the retainer and screw into the manifold until it contacts the sensor. Tighten the screw to 53 in.-lb. (5.5 N•m).
12. Lift up on the locking tab, then carefully plug the engine wire harness connector onto the sensor. Release the tab, then tug on the harness to verify a secure connection.
13. Route the wiring to prevent interference with the throttle and shift linkages and other moving components. Secure the wiring with plastic locking clamps as needed.
14. Install the flame arrestor as follows:
   a. Guide the openings in the flame arrestor over the throttle body studs. The flame studs are not evenly spaced and the flame arrestor will fit in one direction only.
   b. Fit the retainer over the studs and seat it against the flame arrestor. Install the three nuts (**Figure 54**) and tighten them evenly to 108 in.-lb. (12.2 N•m).
   c. Slip the breather tube (A, **Figure 51**) onto the flame arrestor tab. Make sure the breather tube does not

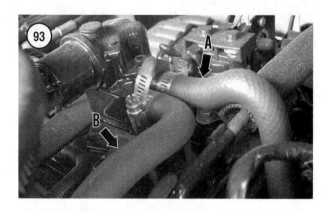

interfere with shift cables or linkages. Secure the tube with plastic locking clamps as needed.
   d. Install the plastic flame arrestor cover over the stud. Fit the rubber, then metal, washer over the stud. Secure the cover and washers with the retainer (**Figure 52**). Do not overtighten the retainer. Overtightening will break the retainer.
15. Connect the battery cable.

## Idle Air Control (IAC) Motor

The idle air control (IAC) motor is located on top of the intake manifold and just to the rear of the throttle body.

1. Disconnect the negative battery cable.
2. Remove the flame arrestor as follows:
   a. Unthread the retainer (**Figure 52**), then remove the metal and rubber washers from the stud. Lift the plastic cover off the flame arrestor (**Figure 53**).
   b. Carefully pull the breather tube (A, **Figure 51**) off the flame arrestor tab.
   c. Remove the three nuts and cover bracket (**Figure 54**), then lift the flame arrestor off the throttle body studs (**Figure 55**).
3. Loosen the clamps, then carefully pull the crankcase ventilation (A, **Figure 93**) and throttle body air hose (B) off the IAC.
4. Lift up on the locking tab, then carefully unplug the engine wire harness connector off the IAC.
5. Remove the two nuts that secure the IAC mounting bracket to the intake manifold stud bolts. Lift the IAC and bracket off the manifold.
6. Remove the two screws that secure the IAC to the mounting bracket. Wipe any oily debris or other contaminants from the bracket.
7. Fit the replacement IAC onto the bracket. The harness connector must face starboard when the bracket and IAC are installed onto the intake manifold. Thread the two

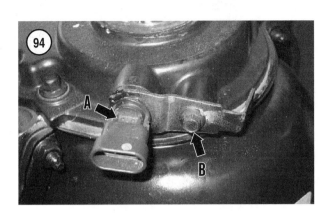

screws into the IAC and bracket opening. Tighten the screws evenly to 168 in.-lb. (19 N•m).

8. Install the IAC and bracket onto the intake manifold studs. Thread the nuts onto the studs and tighten them evenly to 132 in.-lb. (15 N•m).

9. Lift up on the locking tab, then carefully plug the engine wire harness connector onto the IAC. Release the locking tab, then tug on the harness to verify a secure connection.

10. Connect the crankcase ventilation hose (A, **Figure 93**) to the rear IAC fitting. Connect the throttle body air hose (B, **Figure 93**) to the front IAC fitting. Position the clamps over the hoses and fittings, then securely tighten the clamps.

11. Install the flame arrestor as follows:

    a. Guide the openings in the flame arrestor over the throttle body studs. The flame studs are not evenly spaced and the flame arrestor will fit in one direction only.

    b. Fit the retainer over the studs and seat it against the flame arrestor. Install the three nuts (**Figure 54**) and tighten them evenly to 108 in.-lb. (12.2 N•m).

    c. Slip the breather tube (A, **Figure 51**) onto the flame arrestor tab. Make sure the breather tube does not interfere with shift cables or linkages. Secure the tube with plastic locking clamps as needed.

    d. Install the plastic flame arrestor cover over the stud. Fit the rubber, then metal, washer over the stud. Secure the cover and washers with the retainer (**Figure 52**). Do not overtighten the retainer. Overtightening will break the retainer.

12. Connect the battery cable.

## Crankshaft Position Sensor

A single bolt secures the crankshaft position sensor (A, **Figure 94**) to the bottom of the timing chain cover.

*NOTE*
*On carburetor-equipped 4.3L, 5.0L and 5.7L models, a crankshaft position sensor is installed into the timing chain cover simply to prevent oil from leaking from the opening. The engine wire harness does not connect to the sensor, as it is not used by the electrical or ignition system. On carburetor-equipped models, remove the sensor only if replacing the timing chain cover or to correct an oil leak from the sensor.*

1. Disconnect the negative battery cable.

2. On multi-port fuel injection (MPI) models only, lift up on the locking tab, then carefully unplug the engine harness connector from the sensor.

3. Use compressed air to remove any dust or loose material from the timing chain cover surfaces.

4. Remove the bolt (B, **Figure 94**), then carefully pull the sensor out of the cover opening. Clean up any spilled oil.

5. Remove the O-ring from the sensor or opening in the cover. Discard the O-ring.

6. Wipe any oily deposits or other contaminants from the opening and sensor mounting surfaces.

7. Lubricate the surfaces with engine oil, then fit a *new* O-ring onto the replacement crankshaft position sensor.

8. Guide the tip of the sensor into the cover opening. Rotate the sensor to align the bolt opening, then seat the sensor in the cover. Hand-thread the bolt into the sensor and cover. Verify proper alignment and seating, then tighten the bolt to 80 in.-lb. (9 N•m).

9. On multi-port fuel injection (MPI) models only, lift up on the locking tab, then carefully plug the engine wire harness connector onto the sensor. Release the tab, then tug on the harness to verify a secure connection.

10. Route harness wiring to prevent interference with the drive belts and pulleys, then secure the wiring with the clamp provided on the lower starboard side of the cover.

11. Connect the battery cable.

*CAUTION*
*Use a flush test device to supply the engine with cooling water if testing the engine with the boat out of the water. Operation of the starter motor results in operation of the seawater pump. The seawater pump is quickly damaged if operated without adequate cooling water.*

12. Start the engine and immediately check for oil leakage. Stop the engine and correct any leaks before operating the engine.

**16**

**Throttle Position Sensor (TPS)**

Two screws secure the throttle position sensor (TPS) to the port side of the throttle body.

1. Disconnect the negative battery cable.
2. Remove the flame arrestor as follows:
   a. Unthread the retainer (**Figure 52**), then remove the metal and rubber washers from the stud. Lift the plastic cover off the flame arrestor (**Figure 53**).
   b. Carefully pull the breather tube (A, **Figure 51**) off the flame arrestor tab.
   c. Remove the three nuts and cover bracket (**Figure 54**), then lift the flame arrestor off the throttle body studs (**Figure 55**).
3. Use compressed air to remove any dust or loose material from the throttle body surfaces.
4. Make sure the throttle control is in the idle speed position.
5. Lift up on the locking tab, then carefully unplug the engine wire harness connector (A, **Figure 95**) from the sensor.
6. Remove the two screws (B, **Figure 95**) and washers, then carefully pull the TPS off the throttle body.
7. Remove the O-ring from the sensor or sensor opening in the throttle body. Discard the O-ring.
8. Wipe any debris or oily contaminants from the sensor opening in the throttle body.
9. Install the *new* O-ring onto the sensor and seat it against the sensor body.
10. Rotate the sensor to align the sensor shaft and throttle body shaft. The harness connector on the sensor must be facing upward. When aligned, guide the sensor into the throttle body opening. Rotate the sensor slightly to align the shaft, then carefully seat the sensor in the throttle body.
11. Apply a light coating of Loctite 242 (Mercury part No. 92-809821) to the threads, then thread the two mounting screws and washers into the sensor and throttle body openings. Tighten the screws (B, **Figure 95**) evenly to 20 in.-lb. (2.3 N•m).
12. Lift up on the locking tab, then carefully plug the engine harness connector onto the TPS. Release the locking tab, then tug on the harness to verify a secure connection.
13. Route the wiring to prevent interference with throttle linkages or other moving components. Secure the wiring with plastic locking clamps as needed.
14. Install the flame arrestor as follows:
   a. Guide the openings in the flame arrestor over the throttle body studs. The flame studs are not evenly spaced and the flame arrestor will fit in one direction only.

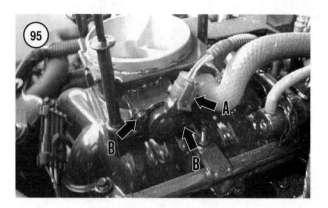

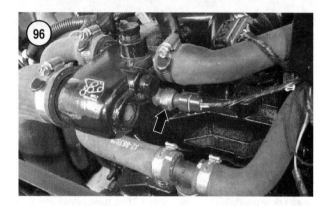

   b. Fit the retainer over the studs and seat it against the flame arrestor. Install the three nuts (**Figure 54**) and tighten them evenly to 108 in.-lb. (12.2 N•m).
   c. Slip the breather tube (A, **Figure 51**) onto the flame arrestor tab. Make sure the breather tube does not interfere with shift cables or linkages. Secure the tube with plastic locking clamps as needed.
   d. Install the plastic flame arrestor cover over the stud. Fit the rubber, then metal, washer over the stud. Secure the cover and washers with the retainer (**Figure 52**). Do not overtighten the retainer. Overtightening will break the retainer.
15. Connect the battery cable.

**Engine Temperature Sensor (ECT)**

The engine temperature sensor (ECT) threads into the port side of the thermostat housing (**Figure 96**) at the front of the engine. The sensor is used on carburetor equipped and multi-port fuel injection (MPI) 4.3L, 5.0L, 5.7L, 350 Mag and MX6.2L models.

1. Disconnect the negative battery cable.
2A. On models with a standard cooling system, drain all water from the cooling system as described in this

supplement. Replace plugs and reconnect any hoses after completely draining the water.

2B. On models with a closed cooling system, drain all coolant from the cylinder block as described in Chapter Four of the main body of the manual. Replace plugs and reconnect any hoses after completely draining the coolant

3. Lift up on the locking tab, then carefully unplug the engine harness connector from the sensor. If necessary, disconnect the seawater inlet hose (used on Alpha drive models) from the thermostat to allow easier access to the sensor.

4. Use a suitable deep-socket wrench to remove the sensor from the thermostat housing. Clean up any spilled water or coolant.

5. Remove any corrosion and old sealant from the sensor opening in the thermostat housing.

6. Apply a light coating of Loctite 565 PST sealant to the threads of the replacement sensor. Purchase the sealant from an automotive parts store.

7. Hand-thread the sensor into the thermostat housing, then use a deep socket to tighten the sensor to 180 in.-lb. (20 N•m).

8. Lift up on the locking tab, then carefully plug the engine harness connector onto the ECT. Release the locking tab, then tug on the harness to verify a secure connection.

9. Route the wiring to prevent interference with belts, pulleys or other moving components. Secure the wiring with plastic locking clamps as needed.

10. On models with a closed cooling system, fill the cooling system with the recommended coolant as described in Chapter Four of the main body of the manual.

11. Connect the battery cable.

*CAUTION*
*Use a flush test device to supply the engine with cooling water if testing the engine with the boat out of the water. Operation of the starter motor results in operation of the sea-water pump. The seawater pump is quickly*

*damaged if operated without adequate cooling water.*

12. Start the engine and immediately check for water or coolant leakage. Stop the engine and correct any leaks before operating the engine.

### Knock Sensor (KS)

The knock sensor(s) (KS) thread into the sides of the cylinder block (**Figure 97**).

1. Disconnect the negative battery cable.

2A. On models with a standard cooling system, drain all water from the cooling system as described in this supplement. Replace plugs and reconnect any hoses after completely draining the water.

2B. On models with a closed cooling system, drain all coolant from the cylinder block as described in Chapter Four of the main body of the manual. Replace plugs and reconnect any hoses after completely draining the coolant.

3. Lift up on the locking tab, then carefully unplug the engine wire harness connector from the sensor.

4. Use a suitable wrench to unthread the sensor from the cylinder block. Clean up any spilled water or coolant.

5. Remove any corrosion from the sensor opening in the cylinder block.

6. If necessary, remove the sensor from the other side of the cylinder block as described in Step 4 and Step 5.

7. Carefully thread the replacement sensor into the cylinder block opening. Do not apply sealant to the threads. Sealant may electrically insulate the sensor from the cylinder block and prevent proper sensor operation.

8. Tighten the sensor to 180 in.-lb. (20 N•m).

9. Lift up on the locking tab, then carefully plug the engine wire harness connector onto the sensor. Release the locking tab, then tug on the wire to verify a secure connection.

10. If removed, install the sensor into the opposite side of the cylinder block as described in Step 8 and Step 9.

11. Route the wiring to prevent close proximity to the spark plug wires. Operating the engine with the wires in close proximity can cause interference in the knock sensor circuitry that may adversely affect the ignition and fuel system. Secure the wiring with plastic locking clamps as needed.

12. On models with a closed cooling system, fill the cooling system with the recommended coolant as described in Chapter Four of the main body of the manual.

13. Connect the battery cable.

*CAUTION*
*Use a flush test device to supply the engine with cooling water if testing the engine with*

**16**

*the boat out of the water. Operation of the starter motor results in operation of the seawater pump. The seawater pump is quickly damaged if operated without adequate cooling water.*

14. Start the engine and immediately check for water or coolant leakage. Stop the engine and correct any leaks before operating the engine.

### Engine Control Module (ECM)

This section describes removal and installation of the engine control module (ECM).

1. Use compressed air to blow debris from the ECM and surrounding areas.
2. Disconnect the negative battery cable.
3. Make sure no fuel source is present, then touch a known good engine ground to dissipate any static discharge. Static discharge can easily damage the ECM internal circuitry.
4. Depress the locking tabs (A, **Figure 98**), then carefully unplug the two harness connectors from the ECM.
5. Remove the three bolts (B, **Figure 98**) and washers, then pull the ECM off the mounting plate. Pull the sleeves out of the mounting grommets, then pull the grommets out of the mounting slots.
6. Inspect the terminal pins in the ECM for bending, corrosion or looseness. Replace the ECM if the terminal pins are damaged.
7. Carefully wipe any contamination from the ECM and mounting plate mating surfaces.
8. Apply a soap and water solution to the surfaces, then carefully push the three rubber grommets into the ECM mounting slots.
9. Insert the sleeves into the grommet openings. Align the bolt openings, then fit the ECM onto the mounting plate. Thread the bolts and washer into the openings. Securely tighten the three bolts.
10. Align the terminal pin openings, then depress the locking tab on the rear engine harness connector. Plug the connector fully into the rear ECM opening, then release the locking tab. Tug lightly on the connector to verify a secure connection. Repeat the process for the other harness connector.
11. Connect the negative battery cable.

### Water Pressure Sensor

The water pressure sensor (**Figure 99**) threads into the power steering fluid cooler at the rear of the engine and directly above the flywheel.

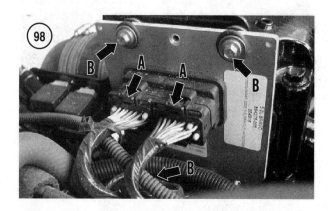

1. Disconnect the negative battery cable.
2. Lift up on the locking tab, then carefully unplug the engine wire harness connector from the sensor.
3. Use a suitable wrench to unthread the sensor from the cooler.
4. Remove any corrosion, old sealant or other contaminants from the sensor tip and opening in the cooler.
5. Apply a light coating of Loctite 565 PST sealant to the threads of the replacement sensor. Purchase the sealant from an automotive parts store.
6. Hand-thread the sensor into the cooler. Securely tighten the sensor.
7. Lift up on the locking tab, then carefully plug the engine wire harness connector onto the sensor. Release the locking tab, then tug on the harness to verify a secure connection.
8. Route the harness wiring to prevent contact with the steering linkages or other moving components. Secure the wiring with plastic locking clamps as needed.

*CAUTION*
*Use a flush test device to supply the engine with cooling water if testing the engine with the boat out of the water. Operation of the starter motor results in operation of the seawater pump. The seawater pump is quickly*

*damaged if operated without adequate cooling water.*

9. Connect the battery cable.

10. Start the engine and immediately check for water leakage. Stop the engine and correct any leaks before operating the engine.

## Oil Pressure Sensor

The oil pressure sensor (**Figure 100**) threads into a fitting on the rear and port side of the engine alongside the oil pressure sender (for dash gauge).

1. Disconnect the negative battery cable.

2. Lift up on the locking tab, then carefully unplug the engine wire harness connector from the sensor.

3. Use a suitable wrench to unthread the sensor from the fitting.

4. Remove any corrosion, old sealant or other contaminants from the sensor tip and opening in the fitting.

5. Apply a light coating of Loctite 565 PST sealant to the threads of the replacement sensor. Purchase the sealant from an automotive parts store.

6. Hand-thread the sensor into the fitting. Securely tighten the sensor.

7. Lift up on the locking tab, then carefully plug the engine wire harness connector onto the sensor. Release the locking tab, then tug on the harness to verify a secure connection.

8. Route the harness wiring to prevent contact with moving or hot components, such as the exhaust manifold and pipe. Secure the wiring with plastic locking clamps as needed.

*CAUTION*
*Use a flush test device to supply the engine with cooling water if testing the engine with the boat out of the water. Operation of the starter motor results in operation of the sea-*

*water pump. The seawater pump is quickly damaged if operated without adequate cooling water.*

9. Connect the battery cable.

10. Start the engine and immediately check for oil leakage. Stop the engine and correct any leaks before operating the engine.

## Distributor Cap and Rotor
## (4.3L, 5.0L, 350 Mag and MX 6.2L
## Multi-Port Fuel Injection [MPI] Models)

Refer to **Figure 101**.

1. Disconnect the negative battery cable.

2. Remove the flame arrestor as follows:

   a. Unthread the retainer (**Figure 52**), then remove the metal and rubber washers from the stud. Lift the plastic cover off the flame arrestor (**Figure 53**).

   b. Carefully pull the breather tube (A, **Figure 51**) off the flame arrestor tab.

   c. Remove the three nuts and cover bracket (**Figure 54**), then lift the flame arrestor off the throttle body studs (**Figure 55**).

3. Mark the cylinder numbers on the plug wire caps and next to the corresponding terminals on the distributor cap. Carefully disconnect the spark plug leads and ignition coil secondary lead from the cap.

4. Make match markings on the side of the cap and distributor housing to aid in installation. Use two side-by-side markings on each component to avoid confusion with other alignment markings.

5. Fully loosen the two screws (1, **Figure 101**), then lift the cap (2) off the distributor. Use compressed air to blow loose material from the distributor and cap.

6. Scribe a *single* marking on the distributor housing that aligns with the rotor tip (**Figure 102**).

7. Remove the two screws (3, **Figure 101**), then lift the rotor (4) off the distributor shaft.

8. Inspect the rotor for worn or burnt contacts. Inspect the cap (**Figure 103**) for hairline cracks, carbon tracking and worn, burned or corroded contacts. Replace the cap and rotor if these or other defects are evident. Transfer the marking made in Step 6 and the cylinder number markings onto the replacement cap.

9. Fit the rotor (4, **Figure 101**) onto the distributor shaft with the tip aligned with the *single* scribe marking. Do not confuse the scribe marking with the distributor cap and housing match markings made in Step 4.

10. Thread the two screws (3, **Figure 101**) into the rotor and distributor shaft and securely tighten.

**16**

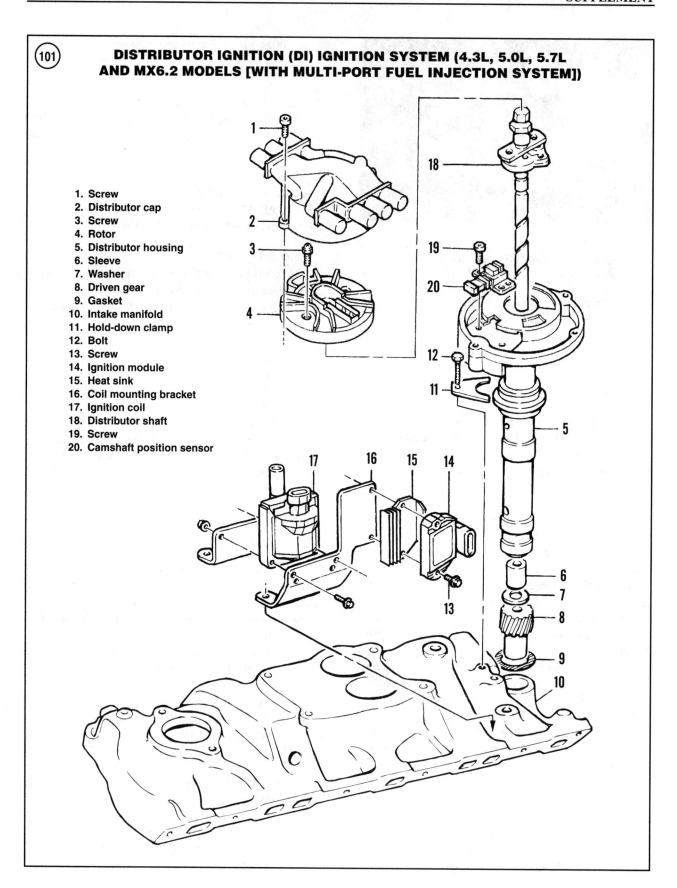

(101) **DISTRIBUTOR IGNITION (DI) IGNITION SYSTEM (4.3L, 5.0L, 5.7L AND MX6.2 MODELS [WITH MULTI-PORT FUEL INJECTION SYSTEM])**

1. Screw
2. Distributor cap
3. Screw
4. Rotor
5. Distributor housing
6. Sleeve
7. Washer
8. Driven gear
9. Gasket
10. Intake manifold
11. Hold-down clamp
12. Bolt
13. Screw
14. Ignition module
15. Heat sink
16. Coil mounting bracket
17. Ignition coil
18. Distributor shaft
19. Screw
20. Camshaft position sensor

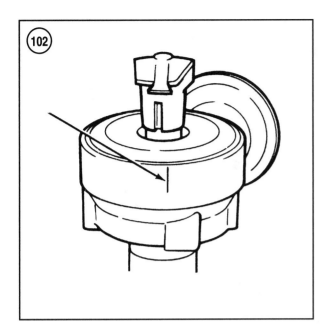

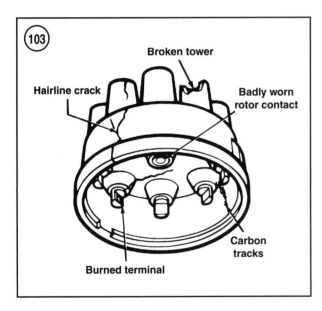

spaced and the flame arrestor will fit in one direction only.

b. Fit the retainer over the studs and seat it against the flame arrestor. Install the three nuts (**Figure 54**) and tighten them evenly to 108 in.-lb. (12.2 N•m).

c. Slip the breather tube (A, **Figure 51**) onto the flame arrestor tab. Make sure the breather tube does not interfere with shift cables or linkages. Secure the tube with plastic locking clamps as needed.

d. Install the plastic flame arrestor cover over the stud. Fit the rubber, then metal, washer over the stud. Secure the cover and washers with the retainer (**Figure 52**). Do not overtighten the retainer. Overtightening will break the retainer.

14. Connect the battery cable.

**Distributor Removal**
**(4.3L, 5.0L, 350 Mag and MX 6.2L**
**Multi-Port Fuel Injection [MPI] Models)**

Refer to **Figure 101**.
1. Disconnect the negative battery cable.
2. Remove the flame arrestor as follows:
   a. Unthread the retainer (**Figure 52**), then remove the metal and rubber washers from the stud. Lift the plastic cover off the flame arrestor (**Figure 53**).
   b. Carefully pull the breather tube (A, **Figure 51**) off the flame arrestor tab.
   c. Remove the three nuts and cover bracket (**Figure 54**), then lift the flame arrestor off the throttle body studs (**Figure 55**).
3. Remove the spark plugs.
4. Place the No. 1 piston at TDC as described in Chapter Seven in the main body of the manual.
5. Mark the cylinder numbers on the plug wire caps and next to the corresponding terminals on the distributor cap. Carefully disconnect the spark plug leads and ignition coil secondary lead from the cap.
6. Remove the distributor cap as described in this chapter. Do not remove the rotor or disconnect the spark plug leads from the cap. Verify that the tip of the rotor would align with the No. 1 cylinder wire terminal if the cap were installed onto the distributor. If it does not, refer to Step 4.
7. Scribe a *single* marking on the distributor housing that aligns with the rotor tip (**Figure 102**).
8. Note the wiring routing and connection points, then disconnect all wires from the distributor.
9. Scribe match markings on the intake manifold and the base of the distributor.

11. Align the match markings (Step 3) and fit the distributor cap (2, **Figure 101**) onto the distributor housing (5). The slot in the cap must fit over the camshaft position sensor body. Turn the cap slightly to align the screw openings. Thread the two screws (1, **Figure 101**) into the openings and securely tighten.

12. Starting with the No. 1 cylinder, plug the spark plug wire cap onto the corresponding cap terminals.

13. Install the flame arrestor as follows:
   a. Guide the openings in the flame arrestor over the throttle body studs. The flame studs are not evenly

**16**

10. Use a special distributor wrench (**Figure 104**) to loosen the bolt, then slide the hold-down clamp away from the base of the distributor. Lift the distributor out of the intake manifold.

11. Remove the gasket from the intake manifold, cylinder block or base of the distributor.

12. Inspect the driven gear teeth for excessive wear and cracked or missing teeth. Have a machine shop replace the driven gear if excessively worn or damaged. The replacement gear must be drilled to match the distributor shaft and requires special equipment and expertise. If gear teeth are missing, remove the oil pan and retrieve the remnants. Oil pan removal and installation is described in Chapter Seven of the main body of the manual. Look into the distributor opening and check for damage to the camshaft teeth. If the camshaft gear teeth are damaged, replace the camshaft and lifters as described in Chapter Seven of the main body of the manual.

### Distributor Installation
### (4.3L, 5.0L, 350 Mag and MX 6.2L
### Multi-Port Fuel Injection [MPI] Models)

Refer to **Figure 101**.

1. If the crankshaft was rotated with the distributor removed, place No. 1 piston at TDC as described in Chapter Seven of the main body of the manual.

2. If the distributor or intake manifold was replaced, transfer any markings made during the distributor removal procedures onto the replacement components.

3. Fit a *new* gasket over the driven gear and onto the distributor base.

4. Turn the driven gear until the rotor tip aligns with the *single* scribe marking (**Figure 102**) made in Step 7 of the *Distributor Removal* procedure.

5. Carefully guide the distributor into the intake manifold or cylinder block opening. Do not insert the distributor into the opening enough to engage the driven gear teeth onto the camshaft teeth at this time.

6. Rotate the distributor housing to align the distributor base-to-intake manifold match markings made in Step 9 of the *Distributor Removal* procedure.

7. Verify that the rotor is aligned with the *single* scribe marking as described in Step 4. Turn the rotor *counterclockwise* (as viewed from the top) approximately 45° (1/8 of a turn).

8. Carefully guide the driven gear into the camshaft gear while installing the distributor. The rotor will move toward alignment with the *single* scribe marking as the gear teeth mesh. The distributor base may not fully seat at this time, as the oil pump drive shaft may not be aligned with the slot in the driven gear. If the distributor is seated, pro-

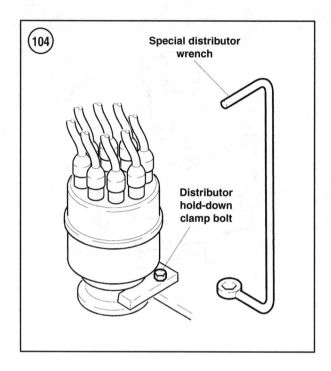

Special distributor wrench

Distributor hold-down clamp bolt

ceed to Step 10. If the distributor is not seated, proceed to Step 9.

9. Hold the distributor in position with the match markings aligned. Apply light downward pressure, while an assistant *slowly* rotates the harmonic balancer *clockwise* while counting the turns. The distributor base will drop onto the intake manifold or cylinder block when the oil pump drive shaft aligns with the slot in the gear. Have the assistant stop when the harmonic balancer has rotated *exactly* two revolutions and the timing mark aligns with the 0 TDC marking on the timing scale (**Figure 105**, typical). This should again place No. 1 piston at TDC (firing position) as described in Chapter Seven of the main body of the manual.

10. Turn the distributor to align the match markings as described in Step 6. The rotor tip should align with or be within a few degrees of the *single* scribe marking (**Figure 102**). Verify that the tip of the rotor would align with the No. 1 cylinder wire terminal if the cap were installed on the distributor. If not, remove the distributor and repeat the installation procedures.

11. Hold the distributor in position while placing the hold-down clamp over the distributor base. Tighten the distributor hold-down clamp bolt to 18 ft.-lb. (24.4 N•m).

12. Install the distributor cap as described in this section.

13. Apply a very light coat of oil to the spark plug threads and thread them into the cylinder heads by hand. Use a torque wrench to tighten the spark plugs to 18 ft.-lb. (24.4 N•m) if installing the spark plug into a *new* cylinder head

and 132 in.-lb. (15 N•m) if installing the plugs into a *used* cylinder head. Connect the spark plug leads to the spark plugs.

14. Install the flame arrestor as follows:

   a. Guide the openings in the flame arrestor over the throttle body studs. The flame studs are not evenly spaced and the flame arrestor will fit in one direction only.

   b. Fit the retainer over the studs and seat it against the flame arrestor. Install the three nuts (**Figure 54**) and tighten them evenly to 108 in.-lb. (12.2 N•m).

   c. Slip the breather tube (A, **Figure 51**) onto the flame arrestor tab. Make sure the breather tube does not interfere with shift cables or linkages. Secure the tube with plastic locking clamps as needed.

   d. Install the plastic flame arrestor cover over the stud. Fit the rubber, then metal, washer over the stud. Secure the cover and washers with the retainer (**Figure 52**). Do not overtighten the retainer. Overtightening will break the retainer.

15. Connect the battery cable.

### Ignition Coil and Coil Driver Assembly

Refer to **Figure 101**.

1. Disconnect the negative battery cable.

2. Lift up on the locking tabs, then disconnect the engine wire harness connectors from the ignition coil (17, **Figure 101**) and ignition module driver (14). Unplug the high-tension wire from the coil tower.

3. Remove the nuts, then lift the mounting bracket (16, **Figure 101**) along with the coil and driver, from the intake manifold studs. It is not necessary to remove the coil and driver from the mounting bracket, as the components are not available separately. Replace the coil and driver assembly if either of the components fail.

4. Guide the stud openings in the replacement coil and driver assembly over the manifold studs. Thread the two nuts onto the studs and securely tighten.

5. Apply a coating of Tite Seal Compound (Mercury part No. 92-41669—1) into the coil tower opening, then plug the high-tension wire into the opening. Make sure the wire does not work out due to the sealant creating a hydraulic pressure in the opening. Remove and reinstall the wire as needed.

6. Lift up on the locking tabs, then carefully plug the engine wire harness connectors onto the ignition coil and coil driver.

7. To avoid ignition and fuel system malfunction due to electrical interference, route the wiring to avoid close proximity to the spark plug and coil wires. Secure the engine wire harness with plastic locking clamps as needed.

8. Connect the battery cable.

| **Table 3 TORQUE SPECIFICATIONS (2002-2004 MODELS)** | | | |
|---|---|---|---|
| **Fastener location** | **in.-lb.** | **ft.-lb.** | **N•m** |
| Boost pump filter clamp | 108 | – | 12.2 |
| Boost pump filter fittings | – | 14-20 | 19-27 |
| Boost pump outlet fitting | – | 15-21 | 20-28.5 |
| Crankshaft position sensor | 80 | – | 9.0 |
| Distributor hold down clamp bolt | – | 18 | 24.4 |
| Engine temperature sensor (ECT) | 180 | – | 20 |
| Exhaust elbow/riser to manifold | | | |
|   First step | 84 | – | 9.5 |
|   Final step | – | 45 | 61 |
| Flame arrestor retainer/bracket | 108 | – | 12.2 |
| Fuel rail retaining nuts | 27 | – | 3.0 |
| Fuel supply hose clamps | | | |
|   Boost pump filter | 30-60 | – | 3.4-6.8 |
| (continued) | | | |

**16**

**Table 3 TORQUE SPECIFICATIONS (2002-2004 MODELS) (continued)**

| Fastener location | in.-lb. | ft.-lb. | N•m |
|---|---|---|---|
| Heat exchanger end cap bolt | 54 | – | 6.1 |
| Idle air control motor (IAC) | | | |
| Fitting on throttle body | 24 | – | 2.7 |
| IAC to mounting bracket | 168 | – | 19 |
| IAC bracket to intake manifold | 132 | – | 15 |
| Knock sensor (KS) | 180 | – | 20 |
| Lower intake manifold | | | |
| First step | 27 | – | 3.0 |
| Second step | 106 | – | 12 |
| Final step | 132 | – | 15 |
| Manifold air pressure and temperature (MAPT) sensor | | | |
| Retainer and screw | 53 | – | 5.5 |
| Spark plug | | | |
| New cylinder head | – | 18 | 24.4 |
| Used cylinder head | 132 | – | 15 |
| Seawater pump | | | |
| Mounting bolt and nut | – | 30 | 40.7 |
| Rear cover to pump body bolts | 88 | – | 9.9 |
| Throttle body studs | 80 | – | 9.0 |
| Throttle cable bracket nuts to | 168 | – | 19 |
| Throttle position sensor (TPS) | | | |
| Mounting screws | 20 | – | 2.3 |
| Upper intake manifold stud bolts | | | |
| First step | 44 | – | 5.0 |
| Final step | 89 | – | 10.0 |
| Water drain housing to bracket | 120 | – | 13.6 |
| Drain housing bracket to cylinder block | – | 28 | 38 |

# Index

**17**

# 3.0L MODEL

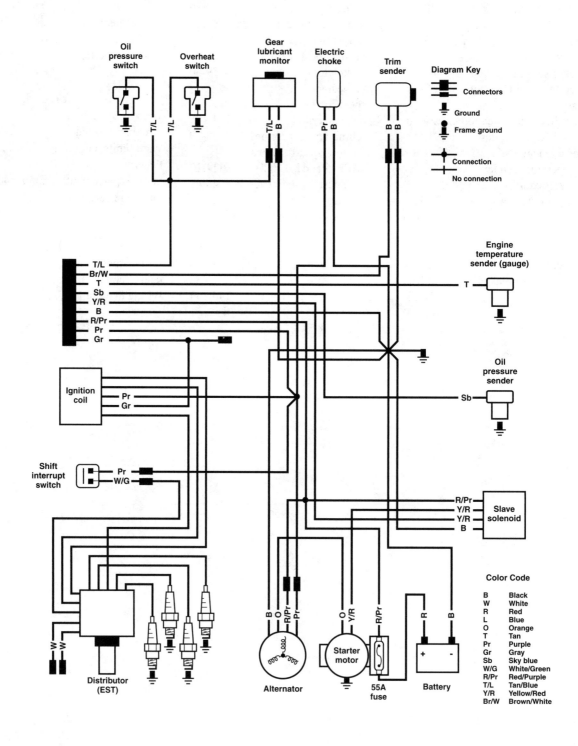

# 4.3L AND 5.0L MODELS (CARBURETOR-EQUIPPED)

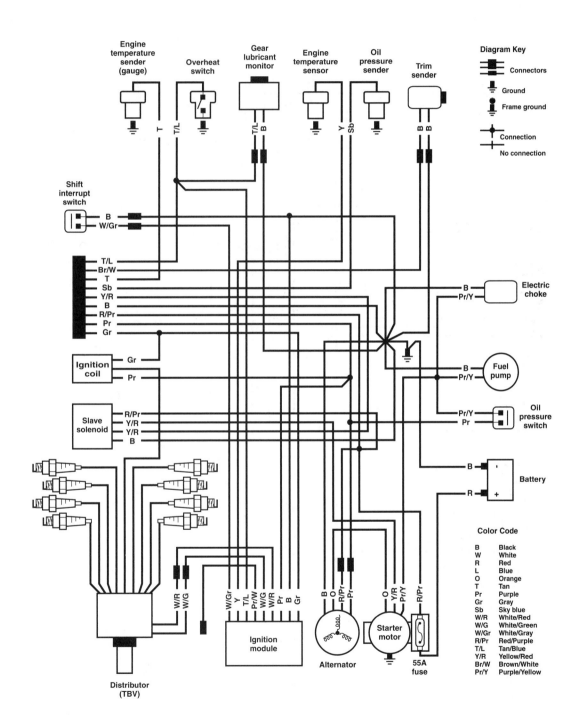

**Diagram Key**

Connectors
Ground
Frame ground
Connection
No connection

**Color Code**

| | |
|---|---|
| B | Black |
| W | White |
| R | Red |
| L | Blue |
| O | Orange |
| T | Tan |
| Pr | Purple |
| Gr | Gray |
| Sb | Sky blue |
| W/R | White/Red |
| W/G | White/Green |
| W/Gr | White/Gray |
| R/Pr | Red/Purple |
| T/L | Tan/Blue |
| Y/R | Yellow/Red |
| Br/W | Brown/White |
| Pr/Y | Purple/Yellow |

18

# 5.7L MODEL (CARBURETOR-EQUIPPED)

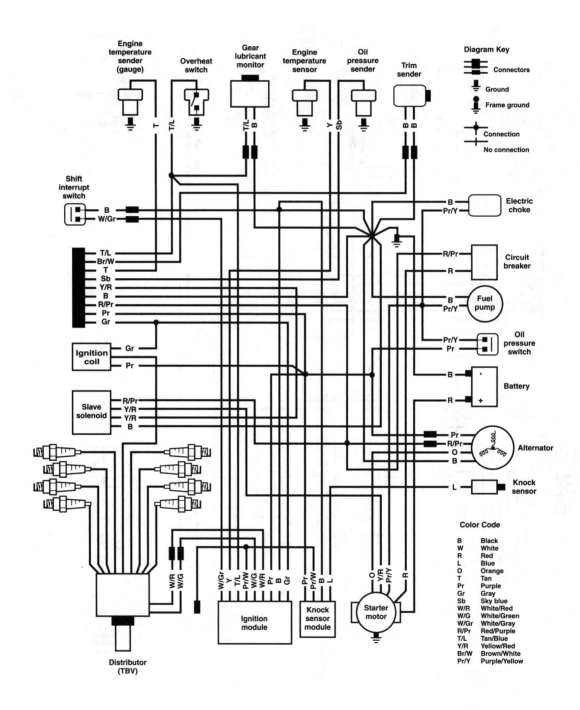

# ELECTRONIC FUEL INJECTION SYSTEM THROTTLE BODY INJECTION (MODELS 4.3L, 5.0L AND 5.7L WITH MEFI 2 TYPE ECM [EARLY 1998-PRIOR])

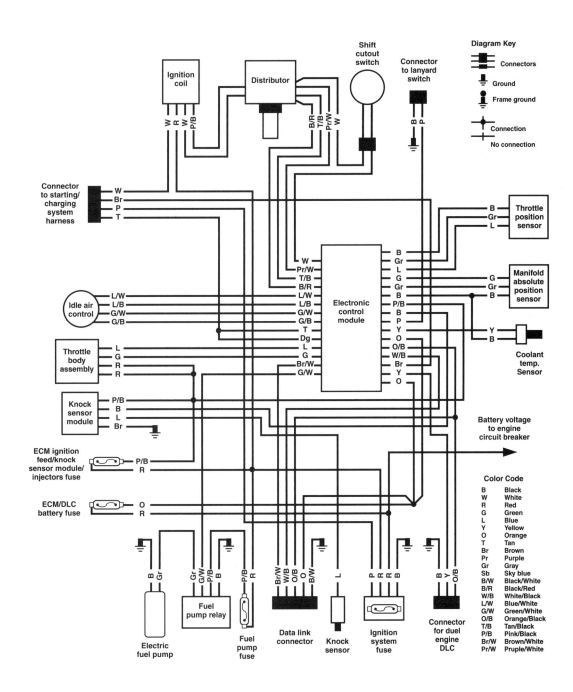

**18**

## ELECTRONIC FUEL INJECTION SYSTEM THROTTLE BODY INJECTION (MODELS 4.3L, 5.0L, AND 5.7L WITH MEFI 3 TYPE ECM [LATE 1998-2001])

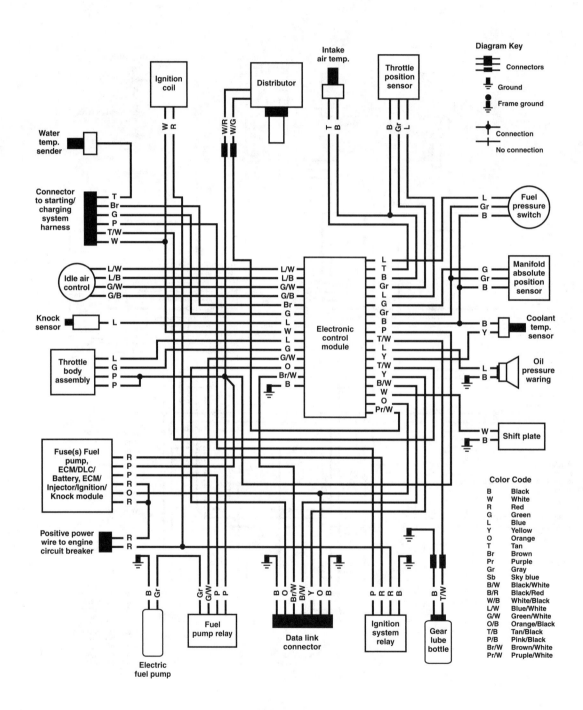

# ELECTRONIC FUEL INJECTION SYSTEM MULTI-PORT INJECTION (MODELS 350 MAG AND MX6.2 WITH MEFI 3 TYPE ECM [1998-2001])

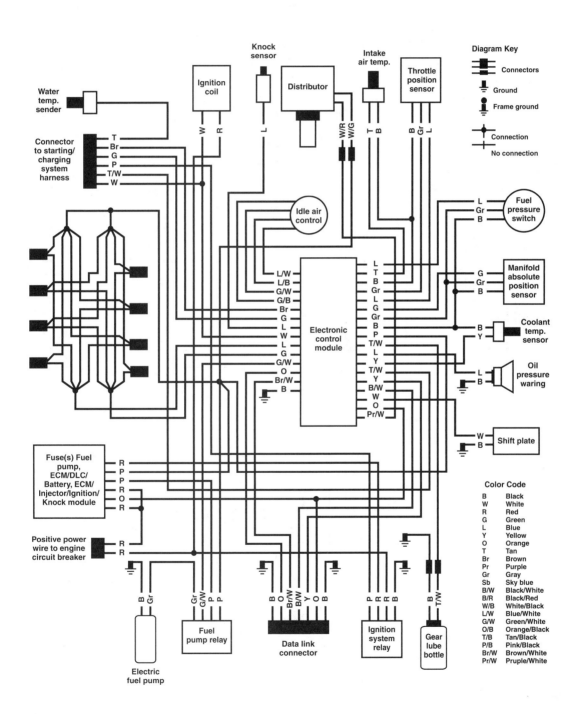

## ELECTRONIC FUEL INJECTION SYSTEM
## (MODEL 7.4L MPI WITH MEFI 2 TYPE ECM)

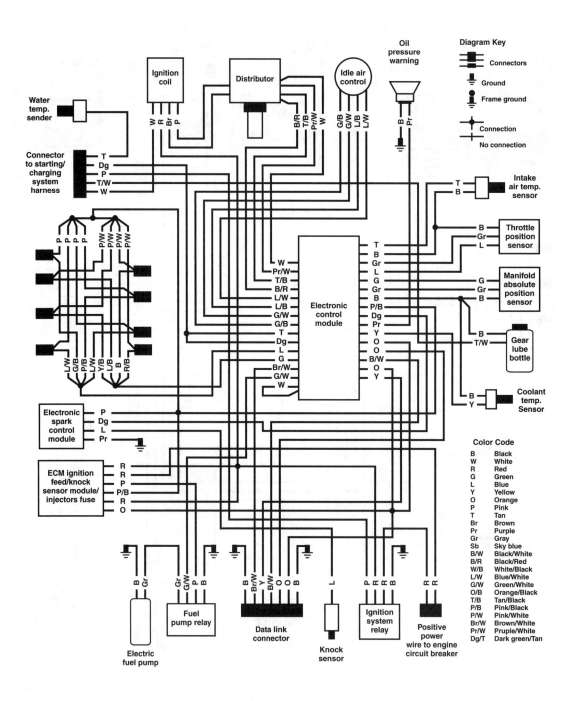

Color Code

| | |
|---|---|
| B | Black |
| W | White |
| R | Red |
| G | Green |
| L | Blue |
| Y | Yellow |
| O | Orange |
| P | Pink |
| T | Tan |
| Br | Brown |
| Pr | Purple |
| Gr | Gray |
| Sb | Sky blue |
| B/W | Black/White |
| B/R | Black/Red |
| W/B | White/Black |
| L/W | Blue/White |
| G/W | Green/White |
| O/B | Orange/Black |
| T/B | Tan/Black |
| P/B | Pink/Black |
| P/W | Pink/White |
| Br/W | Brown/White |
| Pr/W | Pruple/White |
| Dg/T | Dark green/Tan |

# ELECTRONIC FUEL INJECTION SYSTEM
## (MODEL 7.4L MPI WITH MEFI 3 TYPE ECM)

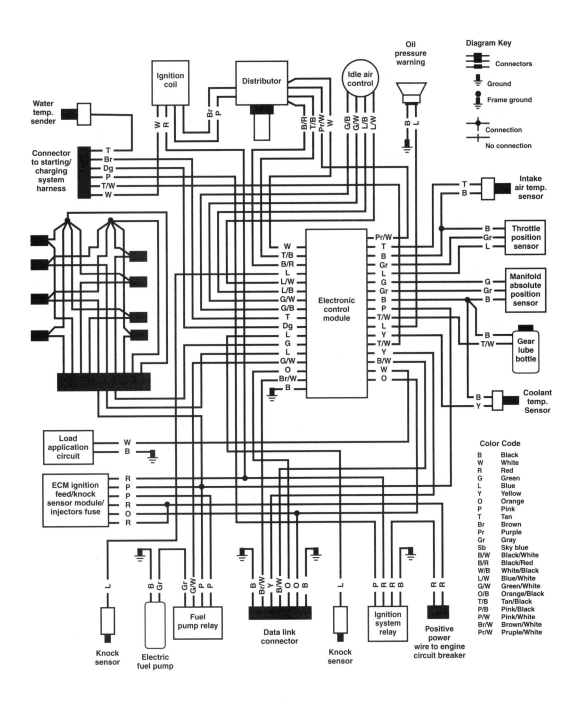

# ELECTRONIC FUEL INJECTION SYSTEM
## (MODELS 454 MAG AND 502 MAG WITH MEFI 2 TYPE ECM)

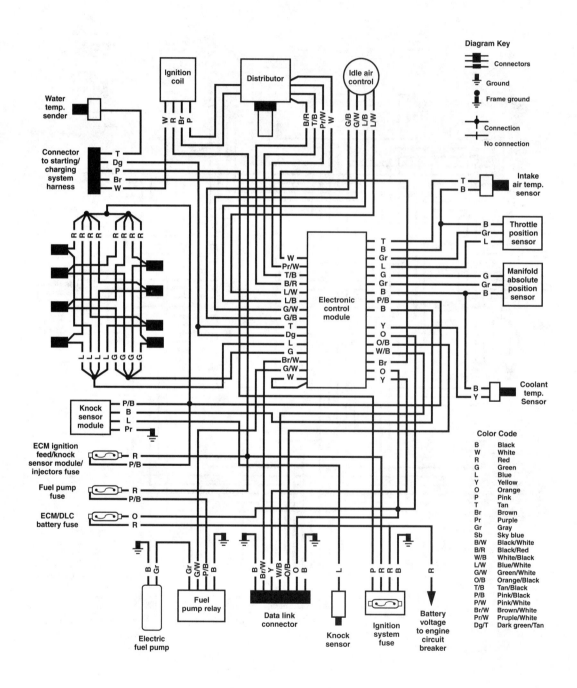

# ELECTRONIC FUEL INJECTION SYSTEM
# (MODELS 454 MAG AND 502 MAG WITH MEFI 3 TYPE ECM)

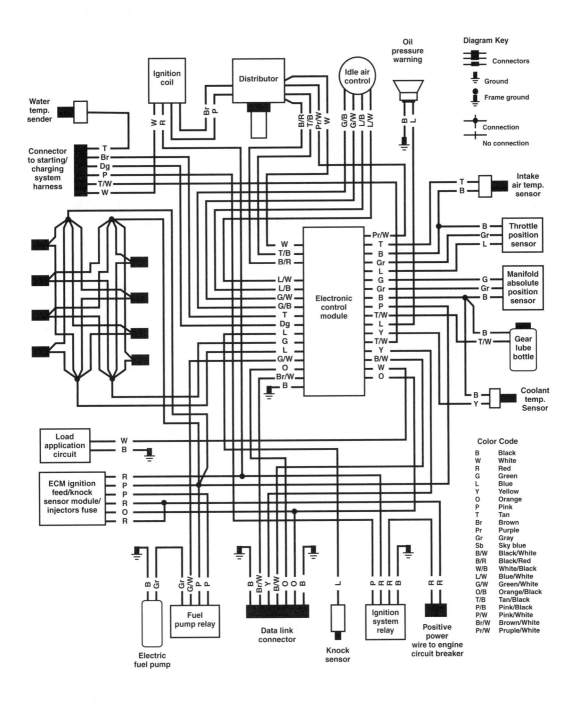

**Diagram Key**

- Connectors
- Ground
- Frame ground
- Connection
- No connection

**Color Code**

| | |
|---|---|
| B | Black |
| W | White |
| R | Red |
| G | Green |
| L | Blue |
| Y | Yellow |
| O | Orange |
| P | Pink |
| T | Tan |
| Br | Brown |
| Pr | Purple |
| Gr | Gray |
| Sb | Sky blue |
| B/W | Black/White |
| B/R | Black/Red |
| W/B | White/Black |
| L/W | Blue/White |
| G/W | Green/White |
| O/B | Orange/Black |
| T/B | Tan/Black |
| P/B | Pink/Black |
| P/W | Pink/White |
| Br/W | Brown/White |
| Pr/W | Pruple/White |

18

# ELECTRONIC FUEL INJECTION SYSTEM

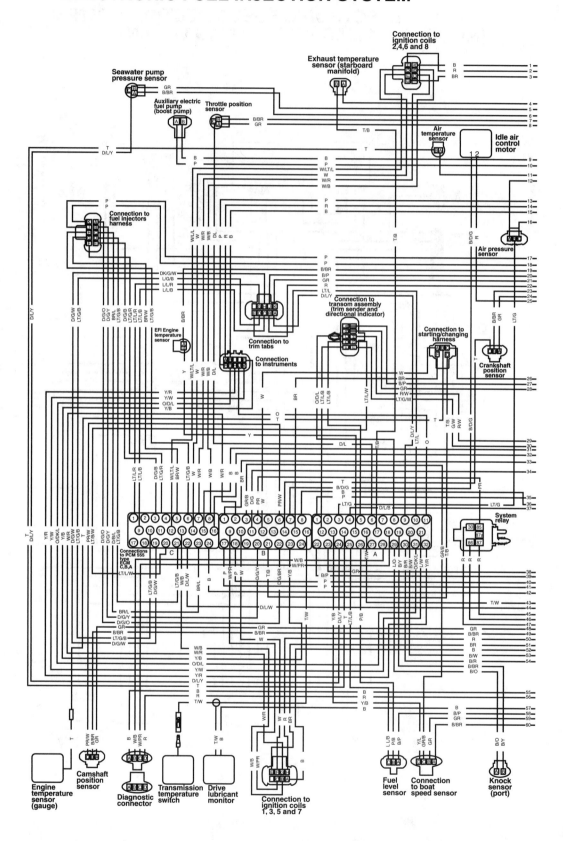

# MODEL 8.1L MPI AND 496 MAG

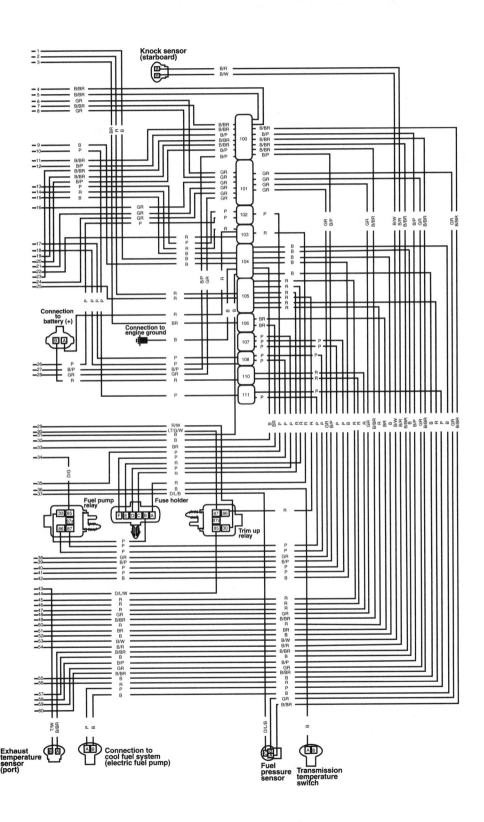

## STARTING/CHARGING SYSTEM
## (ALL V6 AND V8 EFI MODELS WITH MEFI 2 TYPE ECM [EARLY 1998])

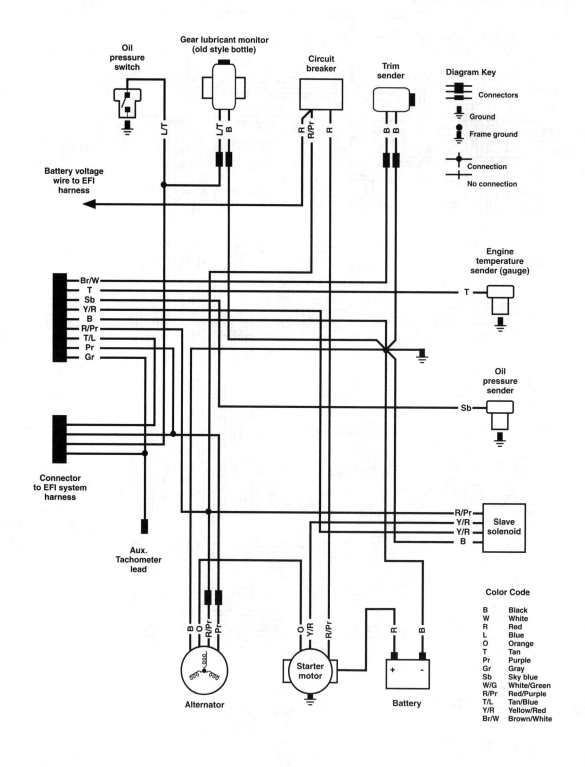

## STARTING/CHARGING SYSTEM
## (EFI MODELS 4.3L, 5.0L, 350 MAG, MX6.2
## WITH MEFI 3 TYPE ECM [LATE 1998-2001])

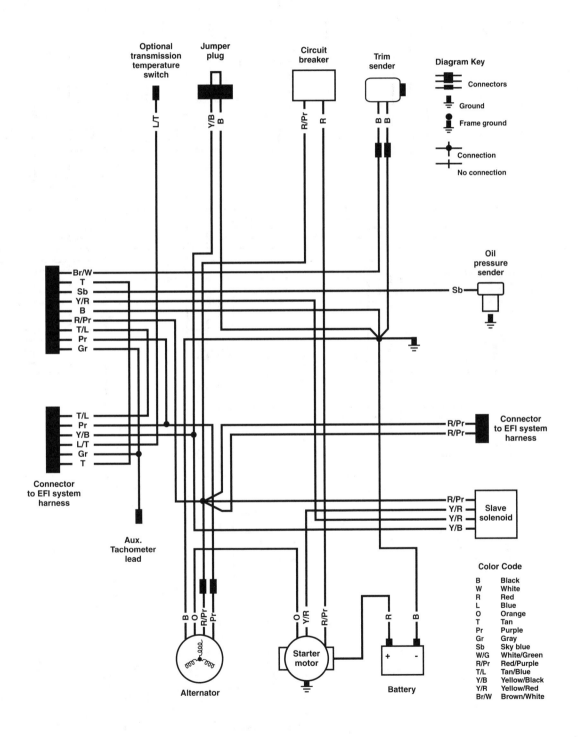

**18**

## 2002-2004 4.3L V6 MODELS WITH
## MULTI-PORT ELECTRONIC FUEL INJECTION (MPI)

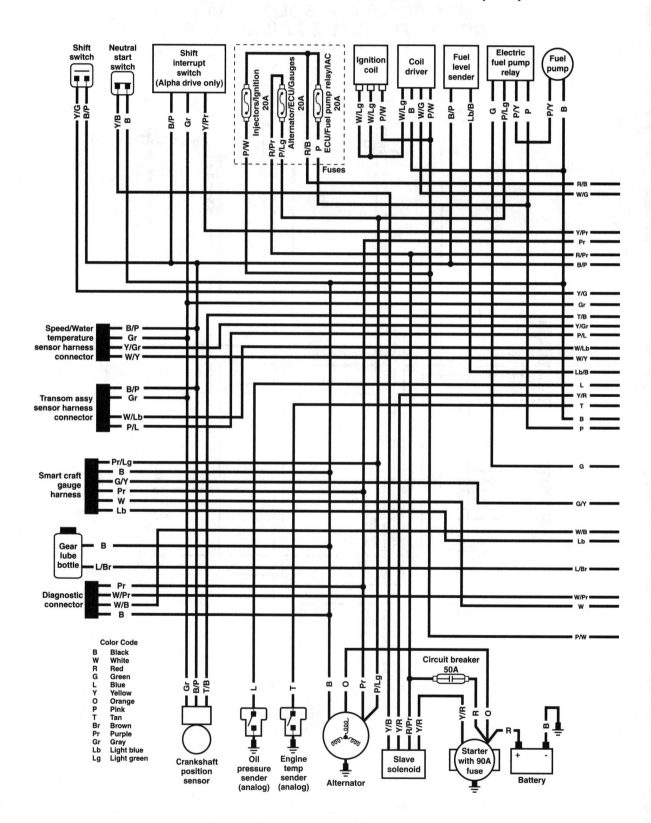

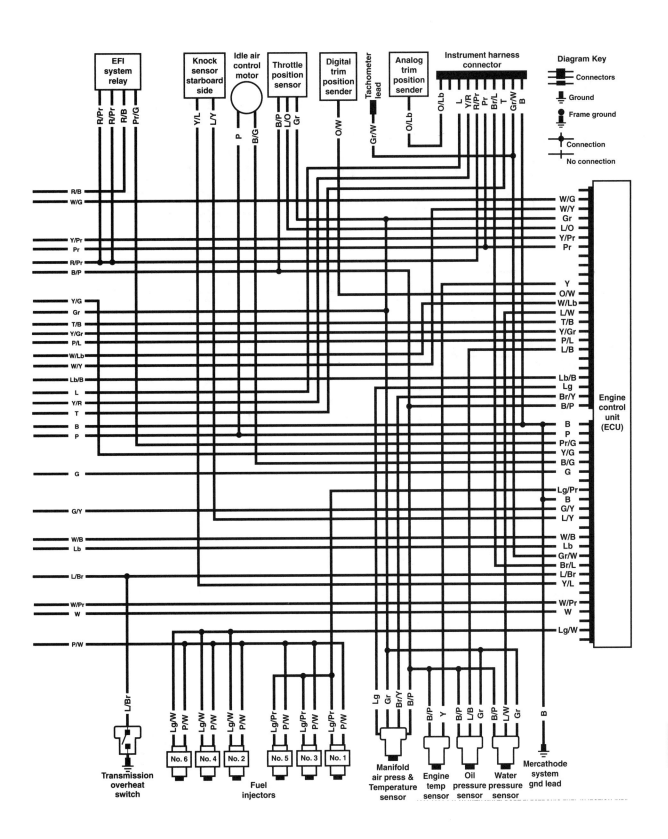

## 2002-2004 5.0, 5.7 AND MX6.2L MPI V8 MODELS

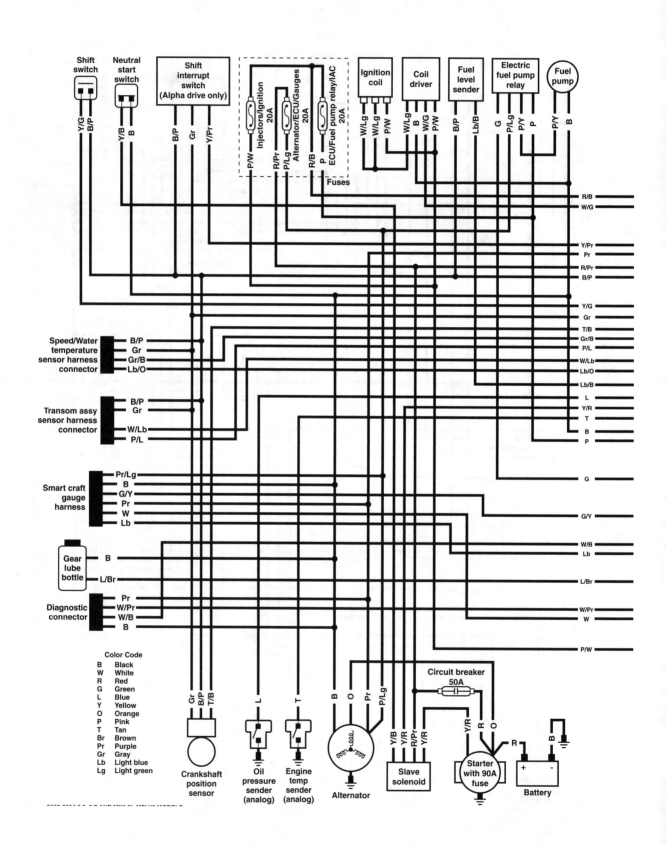

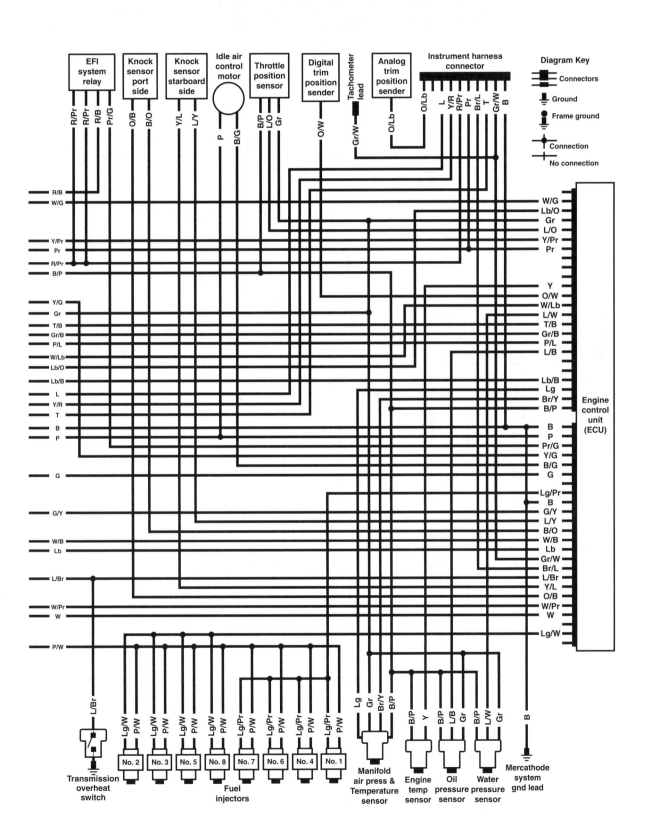

## STARTING/CHARGING SYSTEM
## (MODELS 7.4L MPI, 454 MAG AND 502 MAG WITH MEFI 3 TYPE ECM)

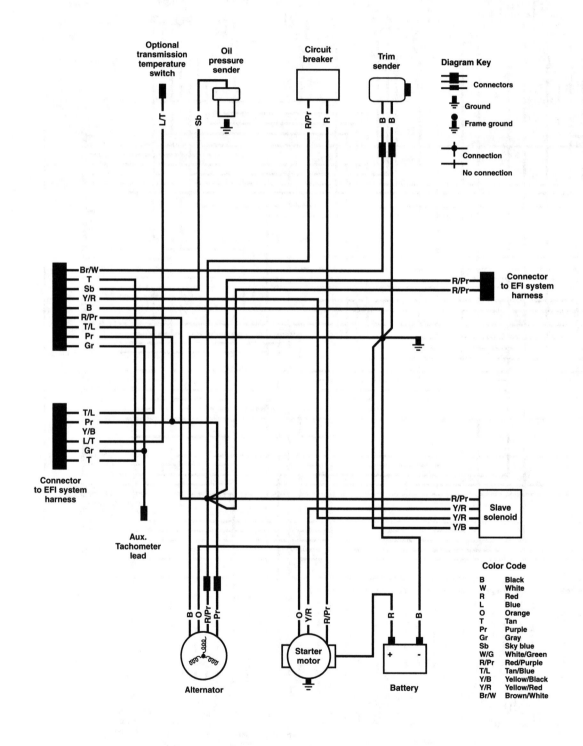

# NOTES

# NOTES

# NOTES

# NOTES

# NOTES

# MAINTENANCE LOG

| Date | Maintenance performed | Engine hours |
|------|----------------------|--------------|
|      |                      |              |
|      |                      |              |
|      |                      |              |
|      |                      |              |
|      |                      |              |
|      |                      |              |
|      |                      |              |
|      |                      |              |
|      |                      |              |
|      |                      |              |
|      |                      |              |
|      |                      |              |
|      |                      |              |
|      |                      |              |
|      |                      |              |
|      |                      |              |
|      |                      |              |
|      |                      |              |
|      |                      |              |
|      |                      |              |
|      |                      |              |
|      |                      |              |
|      |                      |              |
|      |                      |              |
|      |                      |              |